DUXBURY SERIES IN BUSINESS STATISTICS AND DECISION SCIENCES

Execustat 3.0 Mini-Guide
Albright

Linear Statistical Models: An Applied Approach, Second Edition
Bowerman and O'Connell

Forecasting and Time Series: An Applied Approach, Third Edition
Bowerman and O'Connell

An Introduction to Modern Business Statistics
Canavos and Miller

Making Hard Decisions: An Introduction to Decision Analysis
Clemen

Time Series Analysis
Cryer

Statistics for Business: Data Analysis and Modeling, Second Edition
Cryer and Miller

Applied Regression Analysis for Business and Economics
Dielman

Modern Statistical Quality Control and Improvement
Farnum

Quantitative Forecasting Methods
Farnum and Stanton

Statistical Thinking for Managers, Third Edition
Hildebrand and Ott

Statistics Laboratory Manual: Experiments Using Minitab
Keller

Essentials of Business Statistics, Second Edition
Keller and Warrack

Statistics for Management and Economics, Abbreviated Edition
Keller, Warrack, and Bartel

Statistics for Management and Economics, Third Edition
Keller, Warrack, and Bartel

Introductory Statistics for Management and Economics, Third Edition
Kenkel

A Course in Business Statistics, Third Edition
Mendenhall and Beaver

Statistics for Management and Economics, Seventh Edition
Mendenhall, Reinmuth, and Beaver

Data Analysis Using Microsoft Excel 5.0
Middleton

Minitab Handbook for Business and Economics
Miller

JMP IN®: Statistical Visualization Software for the Macintosh®, Student's Edition
SAS Institute Inc.

Introductory Business Statistics with Computer Applications, Second Edition
Shiffler and Adams

Student Edition of Execustat 3.0
Strategy Plus Inc.

Introduction to Mathematical Programming: Applications and Algorithms, Second Edition
Winston

Operations Research: Applications and Algorithms, Third Edition
Winston

Duxbury Press
An Imprint of Wadsworth Publishing Company
Belmont, California

SECOND EDITION

Statistics for Business

Data Analysis and Modeling

JONATHAN D. CRYER

University of Iowa

ROBERT B. MILLER

University of Wisconsin

Duxbury Press

An Imprint of Wadsworth Publishing Company
A division of Wadsworth, Inc.

Editor   *Curt Hinrichs*
Assistant Editor   *Jennifer Burger*
Managing Development Editor: *Alan Venable*
Editorial Assistant   *Michelle O'Donnell*
Production Editor   *Sandra Craig*
Cover and Text Designer   *Cloyce Wall*
Print Buyer   *Randy Hurst*
Art Editor   *Donna Kalal*
Permissions Editor   *Peggy Meehan*
Development Editor   *Susan Schwartz*
Copy Editor   *Elizabeth Judd*
Cover Photograph   *Pierre Goavec*
Technical Illustrator and Compositor   *Interactive Composition Corporation*
Printer   *The Maple-Vail Book Manufacturing Group*

This book is printed on acid-free recycled paper

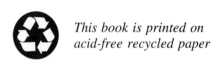

International Thomson Publishing
The trademark ITP is used under license.

Printed in the United States of America
1 2 3 4 5 6 7 8 9 10—98 97 96 95 94

Library of Congress Cataloging-in-Publication Data
Cryer, Jonathan D.
    Statistics for business : data analysis and modeling / Jonathan D. Cryer, Robert B. Miller. — 2nd ed.
        p. cm.
    Includes bibliographical references (p.   ) and index.
    ISBN 0-534-20388-4
    1. Management—Statistical methods.   2. Commercial statistics.
3. Business—Mathematical models.   I. Miller, Robert B. (Robert
Burnham), 1942–   . II. Title.
HD30.215.C79   1994
519.5—dc20   93-42360

Part 2   Elements of Modeling   175

7   Straight-Line Models   176

8   Multiple Regression Models   207

9   Normal Distributions   244

10   Control Charts for Continuous Variables   274

Part 3 Randomized Data Collection and Inference **347**

18 Completely Randomized Experimental Designs
and the Analysis of Variance 508

Part 5   Statistics in Organizations   773

In recent years business and industry have gained a new appreciation of statistical thinking because of intensified international competition in major items such as motor vehicles, cameras, copiers, and integrated circuits, and in services such as banking, word processing, and computer software. In the international arena the key competitive factors are quality, cost, and scheduling, and the improvement of all of these requires statistical approaches to design and control.

This text offers training in statistical thinking and statistical techniques for business students. Statistical thinking makes people better managers, accountants, financial analysts, manufacturers, health care providers, administrators, and so on. It is a formal framework for systematic clarification of ambiguous and uncertain processes, and it provides efficiencies of thought that result in improved designs and cost savings that have measurable impact in the marketplace. Statistics, despite its reputation as an abstract and difficult subject, is an eminently practical one. We hope to convey some of the practical flavor in this text.

Objectives

The reader who works through this text may expect to accomplish the following goals:

- To understand and apply basic statistical analysis techniques
- To use statistical techniques in the context of real data analysis
- To practice a scientific approach to problem formulation and solution
- To recognize and remedy defects in statistical analysis

We achieve these goals by sticking closely to the analysis of real data sets. We also stress the critical link between the procedure for collecting data and the conclusions that realistically can be drawn from them. In addition to the analysis techniques, we give considerable coverage to design and collection issues. This helps put analysis into proper context.

Changes to the Second Edition

Many readers, students, instructors, and editors made enormously helpful comments on the First Edition of the text. Our responses embodied in this Second Edition are highlighted below:

- All of the chapters have been edited for clarity and precision. Each chapter opens with a list of objectives, and most chapters close with a summary. Most sections in the text open with a statement of what is to be covered, and many end with a brief summary statement. We hope these improvements make the text more accessible to students.

- Chapter 6 covers only scatterplots, correlation, and autocorrelation using many new examples. The important autocorrelation material has been expanded and improved. Pearson's X^2 has been moved to Chapter 17.

- Chapters 7 and 8 are substantial revisions of the old Chapter 7 on descriptive regression. The new Chapter 7 concentrates solely on straight-line models, while the new Chapter 8 presents the descriptive aspects of multiple regression models. These changes make the level of presentation more accessible to beginning students.

- Chapter 17 is a substantial expansion of the significance testing material in Chapter 19 of the First Edition. It should be a very useful bridge to the two new design of experiments chapters and the regression inference chapters that follow it.

- Chapter 16 of the First Edition has become a brief sketch of sample survey designs, which now appears at the end of Chapter 15.

- Old Chapters 17 and 18 are scaled down and revised and now appear as Appendix 2 and Appendix 3.

- Finally, many new exercises and data sets appear in the Second Edition.

It is hard to imagine doing statistics today without access to a computer and easy-to-use statistical software. Throughout the text we presuppose such access, but we do not teach any particular combination of hardware and software because the number of such combinations grows and changes almost daily. Duxbury Press, however, now offers a *Minitab Handbook*, prepared by Jon Cryer, Darin Lovelace, and George Woodworth, which shows how easy it is to use Minitab for IBM PC and Macintosh computers to do the analyses in the text. In addition, a disk with more than 100 data sets accompanies the text. The data sets are available in a number of formats to ease interface with a variety of software packages, including spreadsheets.

Section 1.9 of the text provides an overview of the contents. A variety of course structures is possible. An instructor who wishes to stress quality improvement could cover Chapters 1–5, 25, 9–12, 17–19, followed by whatever else time allows. For a more traditional course, coverage could include Chapters 1–9, 11, 17, and 20, followed by additional material as time allows. See the *Instructor's Resource Guide and Solutions Manual* that accompanies the text for more suggestions.

Acknowledgments

We acknowledge with gratitude and respect the many people who have supported us as authors. Some, but not all, will be mentioned by name here. Our families have taken an interest in and have actively participated in the project. Alex Kugushev, Curt Hinrichs, and Sandra Craig and the production staff at Duxbury Press have been helpful and patient. Alan Venable and Susan Schwartz did a superb job of developmental editing, and Phyllis Barnidge checked content for accuracy. Our colleagues Sangit Chatterjee, Johannes Ledolter, and George Woodworth provided many helpful comments on the First Edition.

Reviewers for the Second Edition included: John S. Y. Chiu, University of Washington; Scott D. Grimshaw, University of Maryland, College Park; Donald L. Marx, University of Alaska, Anchorage; Dale McFarlane, Oregon State University; Michael R. Middleton, University of San Francisco; A. Narayanan, Procter & Gamble; Roy E. Welsch, Massachusetts Institute of Technology; Wayne L. Winston, Indiana University; and Douglas A. Zahn, Florida State University.

Finally, all the students in our own classes and many colleagues have provided feedback in one way or another. We thank them and hope that future readers will be as diligent in pointing out ways to improve the text.

Jonathan D. Cryer and Robert B. Miller
Iowa City, Iowa
Madison, Wisconsin
December 1993

1

Data Description

Data Analysis and Model Building: An Introduction

Chapter Objectives

After mastering this chapter, you will be able to:

- Explain the steps in scientific investigation

- Define *process*

- Explain the Deming wheel

- Distinguish among simple observation, surveys, and experiments

- Distinguish between designed and observational studies

1.1 Science and Its Methods

Science, with a capital *s*, and our modern scientific community are of relatively recent origin. The lineage of Galileo, Kepler, Newton, Laplace, Pasteur, Darwin, and Einstein dates only from the seventeenth century. The ancient world had sufficient "scientific" knowledge to construct pyramids, treat illnesses, and govern empires, and the methods of modern science are applications of mental activities common to all intellectual pursuits. But what distinguishes science now from other studies is the emphasis on the natural, rather than the spiritual, world and the requirement that theories be testable by repeated observation. These concepts are so common today that we have difficulty appreciating how revolutionary and controversial they once were.

The logical methods of science are techniques for reasoning from available evidence and are common to all scientific investigation. They are the core of the scientific method. While science may involve a wide variety of tools and approaches, many authorities summarize scientific investigation in the steps of *observation*, *hypothesis*, *deduction*, and *experimental verification*. Scientists may follow these steps more or less unconsciously because they are trained to do so, but it is important not to look on the steps as part of a mechanical procedure. Actual scientific investigations involve a great deal of trial and error, outright guesswork, backtracking, and starting over again. Yet when an investigation is completed, hindsight often reveals a progression that corresponds in some degree to these four steps.

E X A M P L E   **1.1A**

A passage from an encyclopedia article published in 1946 will help to illustrate the four steps.[†] The article describes the work of Frederick Winslow Taylor, who was employed as an engineer by the Midvale Steel Company in Pennsylvania and who is credited with founding scientific management.

No doubt, most of us when we first hear of such a thing as the science of shovelling by hand, are apt to be amused; shovelling is labour which anybody is supposed to be fitted for if he is sufficiently strong and phlegmatic. So far as is known, no one ever made a systematic study of shovelling, until Taylor, whose personal experience in manual work had been only as a machinist and pattern-maker, undertook to develop the science of shovelling in a large steel plant where many kinds of material were being handled, the heaviest being iron ore, the lightest, small size anthracite coal. Taylor selected a few of the better shovellers whom he placed under the instruction of trained observers; these men worked on various materials, using several sizes of shovels under differing conditions. Careful records were kept of every phase of the work; the effect of rest periods of different lengths and frequency was noted. It was finally determined that the best results were obtained when the shovel load was kept as close as possible to 21 lb., which was much less than the usual load for the heavier materials and much more than for the lighter ones, in other words, shovels had been regularly over-loaded for the heavy iron ore and much under-loaded for the lighter coal. Special shovels were then secured, each designed to hold 21 lbs. of the material for which it was to be used. Teaching and supervision were maintained, and when the new plan was in full operation, the average wages of the shovellers were 63% higher, though the cost of handling had decreased 54%. During the first year the total savings to the works in the cost of shovelling, including all increased overhead, amounted to $36,417.69.

Taylor's initial observation was to notice the shoveling operations. Somehow he formed the hypothesis that these operations were not as efficient as they could be.[‡] We are told that as he observed the workers shoveling, he deduced that their efficiency was influenced by a variety of conditions, including the frequency and length of rest periods and the

[†]From "Scientific Management," *Encyclopaedia Britannica*, 14th ed. (1946), vol. 20, p. 123.

[‡]The article does not mention how Taylor came to be concerned about shoveling or what raised the question of efficiency. We know from his writings that he was quite concerned with workers' welfare, and he believed it was in a firm's interest to create the best possible working conditions. This may have been his concern when he conceived the shoveling experiment.

weight of a shovel-load of material. The passage describes in some detail the process of experimental verification that Taylor used. The conclusions of his investigations were that the weight of the load was the critical factor in efficiency and that standardizing the shovel-loads at 21 pounds created a situation that was beneficial for both the steel company and the workers.   ■

SECTION

1.2 Science and Practical Affairs

The methods of science seek to discover order in natural phenomena. Strictly speaking, scientists seek *explanations*—that is, models—for how and why things work. Explanations need not have great predictive power to be valuable from a strictly scientific point of view, but people with practical concerns, such as managers, engineers, doctors, and farmers, tend to value explanations that can be put to use.

For example, psychologists have learned a great deal about human preferences by studying everything from overt behavior to brain waves. But all this knowledge helps very little in predicting what products people will purchase. Although the diligence of psychological researchers and the elegance of their theories may be impressive, the only way to find out if products will be purchased is to offer them in the marketplace. In the same vein, F. W. Taylor might have tried to discover the optimal weight of a shovel-load of coal by studying the literature on human physiology, but we have no doubt that the method he chose was preferable.

Phenomena of practical interest can be seen as systems of interrelated processes. The emphasis on relationships helps keep each process in perspective. The emphasis on process helps keep the focus on dynamic and evolutionary issues, which is critical because practical applications often need to be discussed in terms of predictions or expectations or "trends." Because the idea of a process is so fundamental, we will look at it in some detail.

SECTION

1.3 What Is a Process?

Definition of Process

process

In simplest terms, a **process** is a sequence of steps taken to achieve a goal. In industry, processes are sequences of steps taken to produce goods and services. In business, the process may be a series of negotiations that lead to a sale, merger, or plan for building a shopping center. In medicine, the process may be a treatment that should cure a patient. And in agriculture, the process may be the steps that lead to a bumper harvest of soybeans. Practical processes can be exceedingly complex, and studying and managing them can command considerable resources. In this chapter, we introduce some elementary processes to help you become familiar with this basic concept.

A relatively simple process is the sequence of steps you take to brew some coffee. An incredibly complex process is the sequence of steps taken to produce the output of the economy of the United States.[†]

Even a relatively simple process consists of subprocesses. Consider the following steps in brewing coffee:

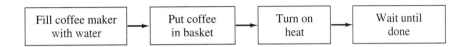

These steps presuppose the choice of coffee maker, type of water, brand of coffee, amount of coffee, and the strength setting on the coffee maker (if it has one), but each of these is a process as well.[‡] Once we purchase a coffee maker, we use it until it fails or someone gives us a new one. But we may experiment frequently with the type of water, the brand of coffee, the amount, and the strength setting. These processes can become elaborate or can be kept simple. Think about the process of choosing a brand of coffee. How elaborate can you make it?

In brewing coffee, we control all the steps in the process because we make the choices. In complex processes, no individual controls all the steps, so the behavior of such processes is the collective behavior of the people, machines, materials, and methods involved in it.

Processes Yield Results

Every process produces results, but we are seldom content simply to observe them; we are usually interested in their quality. After you make coffee, you pour a cup, drink it, and register your satisfaction or dissatisfaction with it. If you share your coffee with someone else, your satisfaction may be determined by your friend's comments.

It is likewise with GDP. When the U.S. Department of Commerce reports the quarterly GDP, we instinctively compare it to the GDP for the previous quarter and to the GDP for the same quarter a year ago. Only within such a context is a GDP figure meaningful. If GDP is substantially higher than it was in the previous quarter and in the same quarter a year ago, the productivity of the economy is applauded. If the growth in GDP is slight or negative, not only the poor showing but also the future of the economy are of concern.

[†]In the following discussion, gross domestic product—a measure of a country's economic production invented by economists—is referred to. GDP is the standard abbreviation for gross domestic product.

[‡]This example assumes that an automatic coffee maker that stops when the coffee is brewed is used. The brewing process is quite different if a "manual" pot is used.

Processes Yield Data

Data are measures of characteristics of a process. For example, Matt brews some coffee every morning. If each morning Matt records the date and the number of cups of coffee he makes, then Matt is collecting data on his coffee-brewing process. Other data Matt might record are the number of tablespoons of coffee used and the brand of coffee. Even though coffee brand is not naturally a numerical measure, coffee brands may be analyzed as data called *categorical data*; the coffee brands are treated as categories of coffee. If Matt faithfully records the data each day, he soon has a lengthy record of numerical and other measures that may be processed statistically to give insight into his coffee-making habits.

Matt may attempt to measure the quality of the coffee numerically. The simplest scheme is to record a 1 if he is satisfied and a 0 if he is not. This is a *binary coding* of the quality of the coffee he makes. Or he might use a more discriminating five-point scale:

0 = very unsatisfactory

1 = unsatisfactory

2 = neither unsatisfactory nor satisfactory

3 = satisfactory

4 = very satisfactory

However he elects to measure quality, he will be able to analyze it to obtain insights into the coffee-making process.

The GDP is the result of two processes: the economy that produces actual goods and services and the process that measures the dollar values of the goods and services and uses them to calculate the GDP. The production of goods and services is analogous to brewing the coffee, and the GDP is analogous to a measure of the quality of the coffee.

Many measures are needed to give insights into a complex process such as the economy. Most of them are reported monthly in the *Survey of Current Business*, published by the U.S. Department of Commerce.

Process Data Vary

Processes often involve creating and communicating information. As a simple illustration, consider some counts collected daily from a copy machine at the University of Wisconsin. Only weekdays are included in this study. The process is the sequence of steps taken to produce photocopies. One of the important characteristics of the process is the number of photocopies made each day. A reading of the counter on the machine is taken at 7:45 A.M. and at 4:30 P.M. each workday. The difference between the two readings is the number we require. Exhibit 1.3A reports 30 such numbers.

You can see that the number of copies varies from day to day. The largest number of copies, 1199, was made on November 16. The smallest number was 238, made on October 16. How might these data be displayed to get more insights into the process? We will find out in Chapter 2.

Date	Number of Copies	Date	Number of Copies
10/12	416	11/2	616
10/13	556	11/3	797
10/14	395	11/4	456
10/15	447	11/5	364
10/16	238	11/6	589
10/19	532	11/9	607
10/20	349	11/10	780
10/21	390	11/11	374
10/22	579	11/12	456
10/23	274	11/13	393
10/26	621	11/16	1199
10/27	362	11/17	362
10/28	447	11/18	547
10/29	440	11/19	530
10/30	505	11/20	741

Exhibit 1.3B lists quarterly U.S. GDP figures (in billions of current dollars) for the years 1989, 1990, and 1991. The figures are seasonally adjusted—that is, seasonal effects such as the Christmas-buying binge are removed. As you can see, the GDP figures vary from quarter to quarter.

EXHIBIT **1.3B**
Quarterly U.S. GDP,
1989–1991, Seasonally
Adjusted (in billions of current
dollars)

Quarter	Year		
	1989	1990	1991
I	5150.0	5445.2	5585.8
II	5229.5	5522.6	5657.6
III	5278.9	5559.6	5713.1
IV	5344.8	5561.3	5753.3

Source: Survey of Current Business. December 1992, p. 3.

SECTION

1.4   Statistics in Science

Statistical tools help with efficient acquisition, analysis, and presentation of data. They are valuable to science, because one of the hallmarks of science is the development and testing of theories based on data. Looking at the four steps of the methods of science—observation, hypothesis, deduction, and experimental verification—we see that statistics should be more prominent in the first and fourth steps than in the second and third. Much of modern statistical research and practice concentrates on the experimental-verification step, the step in which new explanations and predictions are tested. Significant findings in this step can lead to process improvements that lower costs, as they did in Taylor's shoveling experiments, or to new products, as they did when nylon was discovered at Du Pont. Since experimental verification is the "payoff step," it is only natural that efforts are devoted to improving statistical tools for this step.

We will often emphasize the diagnostic aspects of statistics, which put explanations and theories to the test. When we collect data from a process, we are always on the lookout for measurements that appear exceptional. Unusual measurements may hint at a point where the process went out of control, where the measuring instruments failed, or even where something unusually beneficial occurred.

One of the major risks in using scientific methods is that the data are subject to bias that can completely invalidate conclusions drawn from the data. Statisticians have contributed much to the methods of experimental design and to the design and execution of sample surveys. These tools help us collect data that are free of bias and hence help us draw proper conclusions.

To illustrate, a sampling scheme that consists of measuring the air temperature at noon each day for a year tells us nothing about the variations in temperature within a day. Using the range of the daily noon temperatures as an estimate of the range of temperatures within a day would lead to a vast overestimate for most locations. It is hard to imagine someone making this elementary error, but subtle errors of comparable magnitude are quite possible. For example, a marketing survey may select a cross-section panel of consumers and track their purchasing behavior over an extended time. A danger in this design is that the panel may, through attrition due to age or loss of panel members to follow-up, become atypical of consumers in the marketplace as a whole. If this occurs, a large number of observations on the panel can be as useless in estimating the range of variation in the market as noon temperatures are in estimating the range of temperatures in a day. For this reason, the constant updating of marketing panels is an established part of modern market-research practice.

1.5   Process Analysis and Process Control

Recall that a process is a sequence of steps taken to achieve a goal. At each step, something happens to the material, paper, or information that constitutes input to the step; the transformed material, paper, or information is output from the current step and becomes input for the next step.

Scientific study of a process seeks to model each step and the relationships among the steps. A successful model yields understanding of the fundamental causes of the variations in the process. Activities leading to such an understanding are called **process analysis**.

process analysis

Ideally, a model also yields accurate predictions of the future behavior of the process. If so, the model can be used as a basis for **process control**. Control may mean keeping the process outcomes near a predetermined "target" so the output from the process is dependable. This kind of control, which is also called *process regulation*, is typical in manufacturing, agriculture, and some management applications. Another

process control

kind of control seeks to change the steps in the process so that it operates more efficiently, produces superior output, or both. This kind of control is also called *process improvement* or *quality improvement*. It is applicable to processes found in all walks of life.

PDCA—The Deming Wheel

Walter A. Shewhart was a pioneer in the development of the concept of process improvement. He noted that process improvement is never a "one-shot" proposition but rather cycle after cycle of painstaking planning, experimenting, checking, setting new standards, looking for new ways to improve, and so on. W. Edwards Deming elaborated Shewhart's ideas and popularized them in Japan in the 1950s and more recently in the United States.

Exhibit 1.5A displays a diagram that Deming calls "Shewhart's cycle" but that is more widely known as *Deming's wheel*.[†] It is an outline of the application of the methods of science to process improvement. It involves repeated application of the steps of **PDCA**: planning (P), doing (D), checking (C), and acting (A). Notice the emphasis on prediction in step 4 of the cycle. This is typical of applications in which we wish to achieve objectives. Also note the suggestion that the cycle is repeated over and over again, as the wheel revolves—an illustration of the concept called "never-ending improvement."

PDCA

PDCA

E X H I B I T   **1.5A**
Deming's Wheel (PDCA)

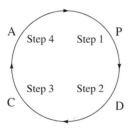

Step 1   What could be the most important accomplishments of this team? What changes might be desirable? What data are available? Are new observations needed? If yes, plan a change or test. Decide how to use the observations.
Step 2   Carry out the change or test decided on, preferably on a small scale.
Step 3   Observe the effects of the change or test.
Step 4   Study the results. What did we learn? What can we predict?
Step 5   Repeat step 1, with knowledge accumulated.
Step 6   Repeat step 2, and onward.

[†]Shewhart was an engineer employed by Bell Telephone Labs. His book *Economic Control of Quality of Manufactured Product* (New York: Van Nostrand, 1931) sets forth much of the scientific approach to quality control in use today. See W. Edwards Deming, *Out of the Crisis* (New York: Wiley, 1986) for commentary. Another useful reference is Masaaki Imai, *Kaizen* (New York: Random House, 1986).

Step 1 in Exhibit 1.5A is the planning step. Here the current situation is evaluated, goals are set, and a test, experiment, or survey is planned. Statistical experimental design or survey design can play a major role in this step. Step 2 is the doing step, in which the plan is carried out. If the experiment or survey is complicated, statistical methods may be used to audit work in progress to ensure adherence to the work plan. Step 3 is checking. Do the data suggest that substantial change has taken place? Statistical methods are usually needed to answer such a question. Step 4 is the action step. Here the implications of the experiment or survey are studied. In particular, we want to know if a significant change found in the experiment or survey may be projected into the future. This returns us to the planning step and repetition of the cycle.

Every process can be improved. Improvement comes about by eliminating unnecessary steps, using better equipment, developing better definitions of work required, involving workers in decision making, redesigning products and services to meet customer needs, and so on. The advantage of a scientific approach to improvement is that both efforts and achievements are documented through the collection and presentation of data. This tends to eliminate ambiguity and misunderstanding and to focus attention on those aspects of problems that are most difficult and most in

EXHIBIT 1.5B
Organization of Research and Development at AT&T

Source: Bruce F. Gundaker, David E. Martinich, and Michael J. Tortorella, "Quality Technology in Product Realization Systems," *AT&T Technical Journal*, 66(5) (1987), 7.

need of attention. In other words, using scientific methods *speeds up* the process of improvement.

Exhibit 1.5B is a diagram of the organization of research and development at AT&T. The core of this diagram is the PDCA wheel. The activities arranged around the wheel are the ones needed for the productive pursuit of research and development at AT&T.

In terms of our discussion about the methods of science, how do the steps of observation, hypothesis, deduction, and experimental verification fit into the PDCA wheel? The observation step may precede the PDCA cycle, as when one first notices a need for change. Observation may well take place during the planning step, as the process needing improvement is evaluated. Formulations of hypotheses and deduction also take place during the planning step. Experimental verification is the doing and checking steps, in which the hypotheses are put to the test. Although the action step may seem more germane to a decision-making setting, it also occurs in science, though it is not listed in the usual paradigm called scientific method. The steps of observation, hypothesis, deduction, and experimental verification are not ends in themselves but means for learning and gaining understanding. Thus even in science, the questions in step 4 of the Deming wheel come up: What have we learned? Where do we go next? In science these questions are answered on the basis of desire to explain natural phenomena better, whereas in practical affairs they are answered on the basis of the desire to achieve a commercial advantage, a new cure, a better crop, and so on.

SECTION

1.6 Statistics: Listening to Processes

To improve processes, we "listen" to them—that is, collect data and take appropriate actions on the information we receive. While it is obvious that the quality of decisions is affected by the quality of data, it may not be so obvious that collecting good-quality data is difficult in practice. We are so bombarded with data that we are in danger of accepting the fallacy that because data are abundant they must be right. Nothing could be further from the truth! Our society's ability to collect quantities of data is far ahead of its ability to collect trustworthy data.

Data vary in accuracy, reliability, quantity, and relevance. Thus to use data effectively, we must learn not only how to analyze data but also how to evaluate their worth.

Simple Observation

simple observation

The simplest scheme for collecting data is to record outcomes generated by the process as it evolves. These outcomes can be measured systematically at predetermined instants. This entire process is called **simple observation**.

EXAMPLE   **1.6A**   Data on business operations must be collected for accounting and other management reports. Records of sales, inventories, accounts receivable, expenses, and so on result in huge databases that are summarized and reported in a variety of ways.   ▪

EXAMPLE   **1.6B**   Dimensions of important parts in an assembly operation must be measured to make sure that the finished product meets design specifications. For critical assemblies, *every* part is measured for conformance to specifications.   ▪

EXAMPLE   **1.6C**   For each departure and arrival of an airplane at an airport, many pieces of data are recorded, including time, crew, weather, and so on.   ▪

It is not always necessary to collect every possible piece of data to monitor a process for decision making. To take an extreme example, when we go to a clinic for a checkup, we only need to give a small amount of blood for testing—fortunately the small sample tells about all the blood in our bodies. Many of the quantities studied in physics are like this. The laws of motion, thermodynamics, and atomic behavior are the same everywhere, so their discovery in the lab, wind tunnel, or cyclotron is as good as learning them anywhere else. Few characteristics of human behavior are so stable or predictable. On the other hand, it is wasteful to take more measurements than are needed to make the appropriate decisions.

EXAMPLE   **1.6D**   In a well-managed manufacturing operation, a typical sampling scheme is to take batches of product from a work location at five or six set times each workday, once every hour, or according to some other schedule. The sampled items are inspected and the resulting measurements put into a special sequence plot called a *control chart*. As long as the control chart signals that the process is operating normally, the process is allowed to continue. Only when the chart signals trouble, referred to as a *special cause of variation*, is corrective action taken. This procedure ensures the smooth functioning of the process, with minimal interruption, while simultaneously providing sufficient basis for detecting trouble in a timely fashion. Control charts, their application and interpretation, are the subject of Chapters 10 and 12.   ▪

Surveys

In practice, collecting data can be time consuming and expensive. Advanced methods of data collection are designed to gain the maximum information at minimum cost. The most commonly used advanced method is the sample **survey**, in which a sample of elements is selected for measurement from a universe of elements. The subject of surveying is covered in detail in Chapters 14–16, but some examples are given here as an introduction.

survey

universe

sample

In this discussion, **universe** refers to the collection of all elements of interest, such as customers who purchase a product during a given time period, inventory of items in stock, people in a country, and so on. A **sample** is a collection of elements drawn from the universe and studied by collecting data, such as answers to questions, observation of certain behaviors, and so forth.

E X A M P L E   **1.6E**

Opinion polls are surveys. A number of polling organizations, such as Gallup, Roper, ABC-*Washington Post*, and NBC-*New York Times*, take polls at regular intervals (many of them weekly). These polls are conducted by "random digit dialing" telephone survey techniques. Telephone numbers are drawn using probability methods in such a way that the information obtained from the people at these numbers (the sample) may be inferred, within limits, to be true about the universe of people who can be reached by telephone. Certain questions, such as those about the president's popularity, are asked each time a poll is conducted. In this way a pollster can track the evolution of public opinion on a particular question. The polls are analogous to a series of snapshots. Telephone surveying is relatively inexpensive, so the pollster can afford to survey frequently.

Market researchers also use telephone surveying extensively because it is relatively inexpensive and data can be collected rapidly. One serious difficulty with surveying by telephone is the ease with which a respondent can refuse to cooperate, simply by hanging up the phone. Even a fairly small number of refusals can seriously damage survey data, and the telephone surveyor has few options for correcting for this "nonresponse bias." ▪

E X A M P L E   **1.6F**

Another survey technique is the personal interview. Surveyors typically use housing units as elements in the universe. Interviewers visit the chosen units and interview specified occupants. The personal interview allows more extensive questioning than the telephone survey, but it is expensive. An example of a personal interview survey is the Current Population Survey, a monthly study of about 60,000 households done by the Census Bureau for the Bureau of Labor Statistics. It is the basis for monthly estimates of population, labor force, employment, and unemployment. ▪

Experiments

Observation and surveying are passive listening devices used mainly for discovering the characteristics of a process or a universe. Experiments, on the other hand, are active listening devices because with them we attempt to discern what *would be* true of a process or universe if it were changed. An **experiment** is the study of the effects of change in a limited environment that is, to some degree, under the control of the experimenter. Although experiments help explain the effects of changes, their results cannot always be immediately generalized to practical situations, because the control exercised in the experiment may not be replicated in the real world.

experiment

Much research effort goes into creating realistic settings that will increase the practical value of experiments. Experimenters distinguish between *laboratory experiments* in which they create the experimental environment and *field experiments* in real-world settings, such as supermarkets or actual production sites. Field experiments produce results more readily applicable to immediate problems, but they may be expensive to conduct and may not yield the level of control needed to isolate the effects of different experimental conditions. Designing a relevant and affordable experiment requires the experimenter's utmost ingenuity and intimate knowledge of the process under study.

In industrial experiments especially, there is a heavy emphasis on experimentation to help create products that work under a wide variety of conditions. Such products are called "robust." As an example, consider the task of an automobile maker who wants to sell automobiles in the United States. The automobiles must be capable of functioning in a bewildering variety of climates and under an incredible variety of driving and care practices of their owners. It is not sufficient to make an automobile that runs only in the laboratory or on the test track!

Many people think experimentation takes place only in a laboratory setting, as is characteristic of "pure" sciences such as physics and chemistry. On the contrary, experimentation is a staple of practical science.

SECTION

1.7   Designed and Observational Studies

In this section, we define two terms that are crucial for the proper interpretation of statistical analyses: *designed study* and *observational study*. The distinction between the two is whether randomization is used in collecting the data.

Randomization

randomization

Randomization means actions whose outcomes can be modeled by the mathematics of probability.

EXAMPLE   **1.7A**

The simplest randomization device is an ordinary coin. If we place the coin on our thumb, flip it in the air, and let it fall to a table or the floor, we find that the coin falls either heads up or tails up. Call this activity a *trial*. It is an example of a process. A sequence of trials constitutes the evolution of the process. We find that in a large number of trials the coin tends to yield about 50% heads and 50% tails. Even though the outcome of a *particular* trial cannot be predicted with certainty, a collection of trials exhibits predictable behavior.

Exhibit 1.7A is a plot of the cumulative proportion of heads for 50 flips. The trials are numbered 1, 2, . . . , 50. At the first trial we get a tail (T), and the proportion of heads to date is $0/1 = 0$. At the second trial we get another tail (T), and the proportion of heads to date is $0/2 = 0$. At the third trial we get

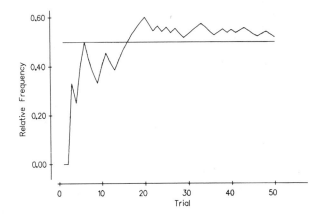

a head (H), and the proportion of heads to date is $1/3 = 0.3333$. Continuing this way, we obtain the sequence of fractions plotted in the exhibit. The solid horizontal line in the middle of the plot marks the value 0.5.[†] For 50 or fewer trials, the deviations of the cumulative proportions from 0.5 (which means 50% heads) can be quite large.

As the number of trials increases, the cumulative proportion of heads tends to stabilize in the neighborhood of 0.5 (or 50%). The proportions vary from trial to trial, but the amount of deviation from 0.5 tends to decrease as the number of trials increases. Exhibit 1.7B shows the results of 200 trials; the tendency to decrease in the deviations from 0.5 is evident.   ∎

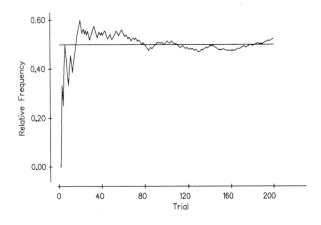

[†]The plot in Exhibit 1.7A is a sequence plot. Sequence plots, important statistical tools in the study **of** processes, are the topic of Chapter 2.

The variation exhibited by the coin in Example 1.7A is the type of variation that can be modeled by the mathematics of probability. When, as in Example 1.7A, the variation in a ratio tends to stabilize as the number of trials increases indefinitely, we say the ratio approaches a "limiting value." We call this value the **probability** of an event. In Example 1.7A, the event is getting a head. In general, an event is the outcome that is counted in the numerator of the ratio. In Example 1.7A, the limiting value is the value we expect the ratio to approach over many trials, as we count the number of heads that occur and divide it by the number of trials.

probability

E X A M P L E   **1.7B**

As another example of limiting values, consider a bowl containing 10 chips that are identical physically except that they are numbered 0, 1, . . . , 9. Let a trial be the thorough mixing of the chips and the random drawing of a chip. The outcome of the trial is the number on the chip. To perform a second trial, return the chip to the bowl, mix thoroughly, and draw a chip. Exhibit 1.7C is a table showing the outcomes of 1000 trials of this process. Analysis shows that each of the digits 0, 1, 2, . . . , 9, accounts for about 10% of the trials. We can say that the probability of getting a 0 from a trial is 1/10, the probability of getting a 1 is 1/10, and so on. Each digit has the same probability of being drawn in a trial.   ▪

table of random digits

A table of equally likely digits, such as the one in Exhibit 1.7C, is called a **table of random digits**. The digits can be grouped to form random numbers with any desired number of digits. To illustrate, group the numbers in groups of three. Reading across the first row, the first five three-digit numbers are 219, 463, 955, 717, and 244.

There are 1000 three-digit numbers: 000, 001, 002, . . . , 999. Were we to go through a very large table of random digits and form the three-digit numbers, as just illustrated for the small table, we would find that each of the 1000 possible numbers accounts for about 1/1000 of the outcomes—that is, each of the possible three-digit numbers has probability 1/1000 of being formed in a table of random digits. The same argument applies to two- and four-digit numbers—in fact, to numbers with any desired number of digits.

More information about probability models is presented in Chapters 9 and 11 and Appendices 2 and 3.

E X H I B I T **1.7C**   A Table of 1000 Random Digits

Row	1	2	3	4	5	6	7	8	9	10	11	12	13	14	15	16	17	18	19	20
1	2	1	9	4	6	3	9	5	5	7	1	7	2	4	4	6	7	1	7	8
2	9	5	5	6	6	0	3	0	7	3	5	5	7	0	8	4	2	8	9	6
3	2	5	2	3	2	0	0	4	5	3	1	4	8	1	3	7	7	6	4	0
4	3	9	4	4	3	8	5	4	3	9	0	2	8	4	6	4	9	7	7	6
5	6	4	0	9	4	6	8	0	5	5	7	6	1	1	9	8	1	5	4	1
6	1	3	7	3	8	1	9	9	8	7	5	8	0	3	7	0	1	4	2	1
7	0	3	0	9	9	6	9	1	2	1	4	7	4	7	5	5	2	3	1	9
8	9	7	8	2	2	1	1	6	7	6	0	9	7	8	0	1	2	5	2	1
9	9	9	3	6	1	3	3	9	7	6	8	5	9	1	2	4	9	7	0	1
10	7	5	0	3	6	8	9	5	4	9	9	4	6	5	0	4	9	7	4	9
11	7	8	5	7	1	7	9	3	7	1	1	7	1	9	1	5	7	8	1	1
12	4	2	6	8	1	1	8	7	6	0	5	6	7	1	2	1	9	8	3	4
13	0	0	7	5	9	4	1	8	6	4	4	0	6	6	8	4	0	9	7	8
14	0	4	6	0	5	3	8	7	9	0	7	1	0	2	4	7	4	7	5	7
15	0	4	0	1	8	0	6	8	8	7	5	5	1	2	1	5	8	7	7	4
16	5	4	8	5	3	4	1	9	1	5	0	1	9	5	3	0	3	3	9	1
17	0	5	4	8	7	9	0	4	9	9	0	0	5	0	8	8	1	4	0	3
18	6	2	4	8	9	9	0	2	2	5	0	1	6	0	8	7	7	6	4	0
19	0	1	8	4	2	2	3	5	9	2	5	7	8	0	6	1	9	4	9	0
20	8	9	8	2	4	1	0	0	9	6	8	9	5	4	3	9	1	4	9	6
21	4	9	8	1	1	9	0	6	0	6	9	9	7	3	7	0	4	2	7	2
22	2	9	4	1	8	2	9	9	3	3	8	2	8	3	5	0	3	5	4	3
23	5	3	4	1	0	3	2	0	4	1	2	5	3	5	3	5	5	8	5	2
24	9	6	4	5	4	4	6	0	9	7	9	8	5	5	2	5	2	6	1	4
25	3	4	1	5	1	3	0	2	1	3	3	1	2	9	4	8	9	8	2	8
26	7	7	2	9	6	2	4	6	3	2	1	3	6	7	3	9	4	1	6	7
27	5	3	9	2	7	8	2	6	7	6	6	9	1	5	9	2	5	4	4	3
28	6	7	7	8	7	7	8	1	0	4	1	7	0	6	4	3	6	8	0	6
29	6	4	6	0	6	0	2	3	3	0	6	7	3	5	0	7	3	9	8	7
30	0	7	2	6	5	9	1	7	4	2	2	7	9	2	9	5	2	9	5	0
31	1	3	7	8	4	5	2	4	2	6	7	3	2	9	9	3	5	1	6	4
32	1	8	5	6	6	3	7	7	0	0	1	9	2	6	1	4	2	1	0	9
33	0	7	6	5	0	3	8	2	6	0	1	0	4	4	0	1	1	4	9	7
34	7	1	7	3	2	6	6	4	5	0	6	2	6	6	9	3	6	8	8	4
35	1	0	5	9	9	6	7	7	6	3	5	1	3	3	7	4	4	0	6	1
36	9	9	6	7	7	2	8	3	9	8	8	0	1	8	8	8	0	2	1	2
37	5	3	4	9	7	9	2	9	2	9	9	1	1	1	5	3	5	0	6	5
38	0	4	6	6	8	5	2	9	3	5	2	9	2	0	0	7	3	1	3	6
39	6	9	8	4	0	3	4	2	8	2	8	0	9	1	7	3	0	8	9	6
40	3	0	3	0	5	0	7	8	0	9	1	3	0	7	8	6	8	6	0	8
41	9	5	1	2	8	1	8	2	6	3	9	9	0	1	0	7	7	2	3	3
42	5	3	2	2	2	4	0	0	3	9	6	8	9	1	7	4	2	7	6	8
43	2	1	6	1	3	3	1	6	5	7	7	3	5	1	7	4	5	7	3	8
44	5	7	1	4	4	7	1	2	9	1	8	5	9	9	7	7	9	8	7	9
45	9	0	0	5	4	6	3	6	1	5	0	0	4	8	3	5	9	5	3	2
46	0	5	0	0	0	2	1	9	2	3	0	1	0	2	8	6	6	3	6	7
47	0	2	4	1	1	5	0	2	5	5	7	7	8	2	2	9	0	4	0	9
48	4	0	1	7	9	7	7	3	0	2	0	7	0	0	1	2	3	2	2	6
49	1	6	0	8	0	7	8	6	6	6	6	5	2	7	1	1	8	2	1	7
50	5	9	9	5	0	7	4	7	1	1	5	4	6	3	5	9	7	5	6	4

Designed Studies

elements
designed study

probability survey

In statistical studies, the objects measured to produce data are called **elements**. A **designed study** is one in which the elements are chosen or assigned by a randomization device. The typical device is a table of random digits, such as the one in Exhibit 1.7C.

A **probability survey** is a designed study in which a sample of elements is chosen at random from the universe.

E X A M P L E   **1.7C**

A professor has a class of 279 students. It is necessary to select a random sample of 10 students. The professor plans to look up the cumulative grade-point average of the 10 students selected.

To illustrate a possible procedure, refer to row 5 of the table of random digits in Exhibit 1.7C. Form groups of three-digit numbers until 10 numbers that fall between 000 and 278 are obtained. These 10 numbers will pick corresponding entries from the class roster. The first student on the roster is numbered 000, the second 001, and so on. The last student is numbered 278. This procedure will draw the 10 entries from the class roster so that each entry has the same chance of being drawn, namely 1/279. Ignoring the numbers 279 through 999 does not affect the equal probability property of the numbers 000 through 278.

The first three-digit number in line 5 of the table is 640. Because this number is greater than 278, ignore it and go on to the next number, which is 946. This too is ignored. The first usable three-digit number occurs in columns 13, 14, and 15 of row 5. It is 119. It chooses the name on the class roster coded as 119.

Continuing to the end of row 5, we end with columns 19 and 20. We move down to row 6 and use the number in column 1 to complete the three-digit number 411, which must be ignored. The next usable number, 142, occurs in columns 17, 18, and 19 of row 6. We continue through the table, finding the usable numbers 103, 99 (which looks like 099 in the table), 214, 221, 107, 125, 219, and 133. The last number is in columns 5, 6, and 7 of row 9.

Using this procedure, it is possible for the table to yield the same three-digit number more than once. If this happens, the number is ignored the second and all subsequent times it comes up.

Now that the sample is drawn, the professor goes to the registrar's office and looks up the grade-point averages of the students whose names have been chosen. The preceding steps resulted in a random sample drawn from the universe of students. The set of grade-point averages of all the students in the universe is called the population of grade-point averages. The sample of 10 grade-point averages that the professor looks up is a random sample from the population. ▪

In an experiment, the goal is to compare the impact of different treatments on the elements. A treatment is a set of conditions set up by the experimenter and applied

designed experiment   to an element. A **designed experiment** is a designed study in which randomization is used to determine which of several treatments is applied to a given element.

E X A M P L E   **1.7D**   The simplest experiment uses two treatments. Here is an example. A computer manufacturer maintains a staff of telephone order takers and wishes to evaluate the effectiveness of a program of process improvement training designed for the staff by a consultant. The members of the staff are divided into two groups at random. One-third of the members are chosen at random to receive the program of training, which is to last six weeks. The rest of the staff are to continue their activities as usual. After the training period, the manufacturer will collect data on staff performance for three months. Several measures of productivity will be maintained, including speed with which telephone calls are answered, volume of sales, and customer satisfaction as determined by questionnaires filled out by the customers themselves. Data from the two groups will be compared for signs of substantial difference.

Because the two groups are chosen at random, the differences between them can be attributed to the training program. If instead staff are allowed to volunteer or are chosen by management for the training program, the differences could be attributed to factors other than the training program. For example, volunteers might be exceptionally ambitious employees and have superior performance at the outset. Staff chosen by management could be exceptionally good, or management might choose people who have poor records in hopes that the training would improve their performance. In the latter case, the benefits of the training program could be masked by the fact that more or less capable staff receive the training. The randomization eliminates these possibilities and allows objective evaluation of the training program.   ■

Observational Studies

observational studies   **Observational studies** are those in which randomization is not used to select elements for observation. Examples 1.6A through 1.6D all illustrated observational studies. In some observational studies, all available data are collected. In others, samples are collected but randomization is not used, as illustrated in Example 1.6D. In Example 1.7D, if the staff members had not been divided into groups at random, the study would have been observational.

In practice, studies often have both designed and observational aspects. An example is a sequence of weekly opinion polls. Each week a probability survey—a designed study—is conducted and an estimate of public opinion formed. But the study of the sequence of polls to discern trends is observational. The study of the evolution of a process is necessarily observational, even when measurements are taken from the process using randomization.

If a process evolves in a stable fashion, however, the measurements taken from the process over time may be treated *as if* they were random. When this is possible, the process is said to be in statistical control. This notion will be defined more precisely in Chapter 10. It forms the basis for a great deal of practical data analysis.

S E C T I O N

1.8 Exercises

1.8A   Explain the steps in scientific investigation.

1.8B   Define *process*.

1.8C   Distinguish among simple observation, surveys, and experiments.

1.8D   Distinguish between designed and observational studies.

1.8E   An auditor must audit a large number of accounts receivable. The auditor recommends the following sampling design: determine the top 5% of the accounts—that is, the 5% of the accounts with the largest value—and examine each one; select 200 accounts at random from the remaining accounts and examine them. From the resulting data, estimate the total amount of error in the whole set of accounts. Describe what you see as the advantages and disadvantages of this strategy compared to drawing the accounts to be audited at random from the whole set of accounts.

1.8F   Here are the names of 20 people in a department.

John	Norman
Bob M.	Jed
Kam	Zack
Bob W.	Gouri
Probal	Dave
George	Mary
Murray	Candy
Doug	Gloria
Wei-Yin	Mary Ann
Richard	Alice

A committee of five people is to be formed to discuss the adoption of rules for flexible work schedules. Use the table of random digits in Exhibit 1.7C to select a committee. The last five names in the list above are women. How many women are included in your sample? Is it possible to select a committee at random that has all women? Is it possible to select a committee at random that has all men? Mathematics can be used to show that it is possible to form 15,504 different committees. If a committee is formed at random, each possible committee has the same probability as any other of being chosen. What, therefore, is the probability of selecting a committee of five women?

1.8G   Reconsider the setup in Exercise 1.8F. Suppose it has been decided that the committee should consist of exactly 4 men and 1 woman. To accomplish this, 4 men will be selected at random from the group of 15 men, and 1 woman will be selected at random from the group of 5 women. Use the table of random digits in Exhibit 1.7C to select such a sample. In sampling work, this is called a *stratified sample*. The men form a stratum and the women form a stratum. A random sample is selected from each stratum. This guarantees that each stratum will contribute a predetermined number of elements to the sample. Mathematics can be used to show that there are 6825 possible stratified samples with 4 men and 1 woman. Stratification reduces the number of samples from the number possible in Exercise 1.8F. Identify at least two samples that are possible in Exercise 1.8F that are not possible in this exercise.

1.8H   The department studying flexible work hours in Exercise 1.8F is to be divided into two groups, one to receive a long questionnaire and the other to receive a short questionnaire. The long-form group is to contain 7 people, the short-form group 13.

> **a**   Why is this an experiment?
>
> **b**   What has to be done to make it a designed experiment?
>
> **c**   Use a table of random digits to select the two experimental groups.

1.8I   A professor wants to evaluate class performance on two different tests over the same material. He divides the class into two equal groups. The groups take the exams in different rooms.

> **a**   Why is this an experiment?
>
> **b**   What must be done to make it a designed experiment? Would it be sufficient for the professor to form the groups by taking the students with last names in the top half of the alphabet as one group? Why?

1.8J   Obtain an ordinary coin. Hold the coin on its edge on a table with the index finger of one hand. With the index finger of the other hand, flick the coin so it spins. Record whether the coin comes to rest heads up or tails up. Let one repetition of this process be a trial. Perform 60 trials, keeping track of whether the coin lands heads up or tails up on each trial. Prepare a sequence plot like the one in Exhibit 1.7A for the event "heads up." What probability would you assign to the event "heads up"? Do you feel that 1/2 is a reasonable probability? Do you feel you need more data to answer this question? How much more?

1.8K   Obtain an ordinary thumbtack. Toss the thumbtack in the air, let it fall to the table or floor, and determine whether it falls point up or point down. Let one repetition of this process be a trial. Perform 50 trials, keeping track of whether the tack falls point up or point down on each trial. Prepare a sequence plot like the one in Exhibit 1.7A for your data. What probability would you assign to the event "tack lands point up"? Do you feel you need more data to answer this question? How much more?

1.8L   Obtain an ordinary die. Roll the die and determine the number of spots on the up face. Let one repetition of this process be a trial. Perform 360 trials, keeping track of the outcome on each trial. Prepare a sequence plot like the one in Exhibit 1.7A for the event "one spot on the up face." What probability would you assign to this event? Do you feel you need more data to answer this question? Why?

1.8M   Obtain a record of the closing price of the Dow Jones 30 Industrials average for 61 consecutive days. The process of interest is the set of transactions that lead to the average. Define a trial as the determination of whether the average increased or decreased from one day to the next. Let the event of interest be "the average increased." The data you have collected allow you to perform 60 trials. Prepare a plot like the one in Exhibit 1.7A for your data. What probability would you assign to the event "the average increased"? Do you feel you need more data to answer this question? How much more?

> You are offered two lotteries. The first one pays $1 if an ordinary coin is tossed and lands heads up. The second one pays $1 if the Dow Jones 30 Industrials average increases tomorrow. Which lottery offers you a better chance of winning $1? Why?

1.8N   On Friday, September 25, 1987, the *Wisconsin State Journal* carried a story with the headline "People-Meters Add Perspective to Ratings" in section 4, page 6. Here are some excerpts from the article:

> The people-meter is a new, hand-held device that viewers punch in on when they watch TV. The device, according to Nielsen, will provide more accurate and more detailed information about the age and sex of viewers. Nielsen switched to the new people-meter device as of last week.
>
> CBS's "Wiseguy," a male-oriented crime drama, was 21st in the overall audience rankings, but it was a top-10 show, at seventh, among men [aged] 18–49.
>
> NBC's "St. Elsewhere" was a top-10 show among women [aged] 18–49, who placed it eighth. With overall audiences, it was 16th overall, and 21st with males [aged] 18–49.

Grouping TV watchers by age and gender is an example of stratification. Why was stratification useful in this application?

1.80 Look up and read Toshio Sugiman and Jyuji Misumi, "Development of a New Evacuation Method for Emergencies: Control of Collective Behavior by Emergent Small Groups," *Journal of Applied Psychology* 73(1)(1988):3–10. Explain the experimental plans used in the reported study. What treatments were applied? Discuss some of the limitations of the study. Explain the concept of an emergent small group. What additional studies would you like to see done to test the authors' conclusions?

SECTION

1.9 Overview of the Book

This book is divided into five major parts. The first describes the structure of data, both graphically and numerically. The second introduces the elements of modeling observational data. The third is on the analysis and modeling of data from a designed study. The fourth presents more advanced topics in modeling and inference, while the fifth deals with the organizational context of statistical practice.

SECTION

1.10 On Using Computers

By vastly increasing the speed with which enormous quantities of data can be stored and retrieved, the speed with which complicated computations can be performed, and the sophistication with which information can be displayed, computers have changed how we think and act. Not only does the computer increase our ability to communicate, it also places that ability in the hands of more people through the miracle of miniature chips. You can place on your desk a small, inexpensive computer that outperforms the large, expensive computers available just a few years ago. And you can fairly quickly learn to use an array of software packages that let you take advantage of the products of decades of painstaking research and development.

The impact of the computer revolution pervades the field of statistics, which is the study of the collection, analysis, and presentation of data. In view of this, we believe that today's textbooks on statistics must reflect the essential role of computers in statistical applications. We have chosen to do this by using statistical software throughout the text.

The exhibits we display can be made by many packages. To teach the mechanics of a particular package, however, is to limit access to the statistical material that is our primary subject. Thus we do not teach you how to use any particular software package.

Supplementary Exercises for Chapter 1

1A The process of interest is dealing a five-card hand from a well-shuffled standard deck of 52 cards. The event of interest is a hand with exactly one face card (jack, queen, or king of any suit). Repeat the process 100 times, keeping track of whether the hand does or does not contain exactly one face card. Use your data to construct a sequence plot like the one in Exhibit 1.7A. What probability would you assign to the event?

1B **a** Use a table of random digits to select a sample of 10 people from your class. How many of them are men? Measure the heights of the people in your sample and average the resulting numbers.

b Repeat part (a) four more times. On the basis of your data, what is your best guess at the average height of all the members of the class?

c Have all the members of the class report their heights. Average the numbers and compare the average with the guess you came up with in part (b).

1C **a** Divide your class into two groups: men and women. Use a table of random digits to draw a stratified sample consisting of five men and five women. Refer to Exercise 1.8G for the definition of stratified random sample. Average the five men's heights. Average the five women's heights. Average all 10 of the heights.

b Repeat part (a) four more times. On the basis of your data, what is your best guess at the average height of the men in your class? The average height of the women in your class? The average height of all the people in your class? Is the average of the 10 people in a stratified sample the best estimate of the average height of all the people in the class? If not, suggest a better estimate.

c Ask all the members of the class to report their height and their gender. Average the men's heights and the women's heights and compare them with the guesses you came up with in part (b). Average all the people's heights and compare the average you came up with in part (b).

Glossary for Chapter 1

designed experiment A designed study in which a randomization device is used to determine which treatment is applied to which elements.

designed study A study in which the elements are chosen or assigned by a randomization device.

element An object that is measured in a statistical study.

experiment The study of the effects of change in an environment that is, to some degree, under the control of the experimenter.

observational study A study in which randomization is not used to select elements for observation.

PDCA Plan. Do. Check. Act. The steps in Deming's wheel taken over and over again to bring about improvement in processes.

probability The hypothesized limiting value of the proportion of occurrences of an event in a large number of repetitions of a process that may yield the event.

probability survey A designed study in which a sample of elements is chosen at random from a larger collection of elements called a universe.

process A sequence of steps taken to achieve a goal or outcome.

process analysis Activities undertaken to understand and model the steps in a process and the relationships among the steps.

process control Activities undertaken to keep process outcomes as close as possible to a predetermined target or to effect an improvement in the performance of the process.

randomization   Actions whose outcomes can be modeled by the mathematics of probability.

sample   A collection of elements drawn from a universe.

simple observation   Observation of every outcome from a process or outcomes taken systematically at predetermined instants.

survey   A data-collection tool in which a sample of elements is selected from a universe of elements for measurement.

table of random digits   A table of the digits $0, 1, \ldots, 9$ constructed so that each of the digits has an equal chance of occurring in any location in the table.

universe   The collection of all elements that might be drawn into a sample for a survey.

Plotting Process Data

Chapter Objectives

After mastering this chapter, you will be able to:

- List the characteristics of a longitudinal study

- Prepare a sequence plot

- Identify seasonality in a sequence plot

- Calculate and plot changes and percentage changes of a sequence of observations

SECTION

2.1 Knowledge Through Data

We seldom have complete knowledge of a process, nor can we expect to exercise complete control over every step in a process. Fortunately, most processes can be managed by exercising control at just a few critical steps. A key ingredient in managing and improving business and industrial processes is to stay in touch with the critical steps by collecting relevant measurements. Such measurements are called *data*.

Ideally, data are collected systematically over a long period of time from the truly critical steps of the process. Studies of the evolution of a process over time are called **longitudinal studies**. More precisely, a longitudinal study consists of

longitudinal studies

- Collection of measurements from a process over time

- Comparison of measurements from different time periods

- Documentation of variation over time

- Evaluation of changes in behavior of the process

By thinking longitudinally, we focus on those aspects of the process most important for decision making. By limiting our attention to the points that make the most difference, we work at peak efficiency, avoiding wasted effort.

A basic tool in studying the longitudinal aspects of a process is the sequence plot.

2.2 Sequence Plots

Sequence plots are the basic tools for showing the evolution of a measured characteristic of a process. A **sequence plot** is a simple graph with time displayed on the horizontal axis and the corresponding quantity or quantities from the process displayed on the vertical axis.

sequence plot

EXAMPLE **2.2A**

Exhibit 2.2A shows a hand-drawn sequence plot of the photocopy counts that were given in Exhibit 1.3A. The vertical height of the dots represents the counts, and the horizontal positioning indicates time. The dots are joined by lines to reinforce the presentation of the passage of time. The letters M, T, W, R, and F code the days of the week. (R is the symbol for Thursday.)

The sequence plot displays a process with a great deal of variation. On two days, fewer than 300 copies were made; on two other days, almost 800 were made. Most of the numbers are between 300 and 650, but one day does not even fit on the graph. On this one day, November 16, an exception was made to allow students taking their master's degree oral examination to

EXHIBIT **2.2A**
Hand-Drawn Sequence Plot of
Photocopy Data

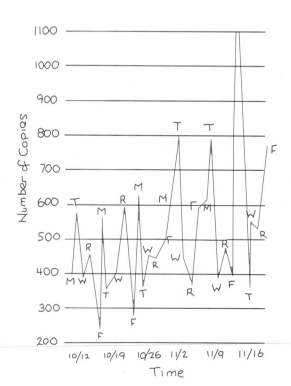

exceed the normal limit of 25 copies per job on the machine. This was done to accommodate the preparation of last-minute handouts for their exam.

Another exception to the 25-copy rule is the preparation of manuscripts to send to a central copy center for mass production. The office staff is authorized to exceed the limit in this case to minimize the time they must spend away from their workstations. Manuscripts are processed at irregular intervals, and this contributes to the variability and unpredictability in the photocopy process.

After looking at the sequence plot, we have a rough idea of how the process is likely to evolve. On most days, the number of copies will be between 300 and 650, but occasionally such unpredictable events as manuscript preparation and other special exceptions may cause the number to be substantially greater than 650. If the machine is down for repairs, if the office closes for part of a day, or if many department members are out of town to attend a conference, the number of copies can be below 300.   ■

Three Reasons for Collecting Data

The data presented in Example 2.2A are all that had been collected at the time of writing, but even they are useful for forming a tentative impression about the future of the process. Our impression of the process will be modified as we collect more data, but already we see one of the main functions of collecting data: *predicting future behavior*.

Making predictions allows us to look for changes in future behavior. Suppose, for example, that in the photocopy example, data collected for the first two weeks of December show that on most days the number of copies falls between 500 and 800. This would be a marked shift upward relative to the behavior observed in October and November. We would certainly look for reasons for the shift. The reason might be a sharp increase in the number of manuscripts being processed, or it might be that department members are reproducing their holiday letters on the machine, an unauthorized use! This illustrates another function of collecting data: *detecting changes in a process*.

A sequence plot such as the one in Exhibit 2.2A is posted above the copy machine, and it is updated every day. This allows the users of the machine to see the effects of their copying activity. If a major shift occurs, attention is called to it and reasons for the shift explained. The visual reporting of the data makes communication very easy. The data collected from the machine are also used as a basis for reporting department activity to the operations committee. We see yet another function of collecting data: *sharing information* (communication).

E X A M P L E   **2.2B**   Exhibit 2.2B is a hand-drawn sequence plot of the GDP data in Exhibit 1.3B. The symbols I, II, III, and IV denote the quarters of the year. GDP figures from many years are available, and the long historical record provides a proper context for studying the behavior of GDP. The short series of figures in Exhibit 2.2B is presented for illustrative purposes only.

An obvious feature in the plot is the upward trend. The years 1989–1991 are a period of growth in the GDP. Notice, however, that the amount by which GDP grows varies from quarter to quarter. The largest change occurs between quarter IV of 1989 and quarter I of 1990, an increase of $100.4 billion. The smallest change occurs between quarters III and IV of 1990, an increase of only $1.7 billion.

Exhibit 2.2C gives a table of the twelve quarterly GDP figures from Exhibit 1.3B and the eleven quarterly *changes* that may be computed from them. Exhibit 2.2D shows sequence plots of both the original GDP figures and the changes. The plot of the changes is on a different scale from the original figures, easing the comparison of magnitudes.

The sequence plot of the original GDP figures in Exhibit 2.2B tempts us to predict that GDP will rise in future quarters, as GDP has done historically. The sequence plot of the changes in GDP suggests that the amount of growth from quarter to quarter is quite variable. Eight of the eleven changes fall

E X H I B I T **2.2B**   Hand-Drawn Sequence Plot of GDP Data

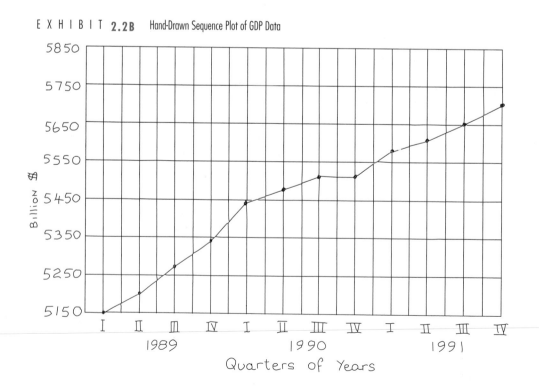

E X H I B I T **2.2C**

Quarterly U.S. GDP,
1989–1991, and the Quarterly
Changes (in billions of current
dollars)

Year	Quarter	GDP	Quarterly Change
1989	I	5150.0	†
1989	II	5229.5	79.5
1989	III	5278.9	49.4
1989	IV	5344.8	65.9
1990	I	5445.2	100.4
1990	II	5522.6	77.4
1990	III	5559.6	37.0
1990	IV	5561.3	1.7
1991	I	5585.8	24.5
1991	II	5657.6	71.8
1991	III	5713.1	55.5
1991	IV	5753.3	40.2

†This change cannot be computed without knowledge of
GDP in quarter IV of 1988.

E X H I B I T **2.2D**   Hand-Drawn Sequence Plot of GDP Data and Changes

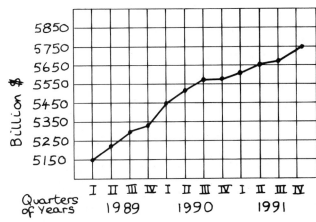

Quarterly U.S. G.D.P.
1989 - 1991, Current
dollar, seasonally
adjusted
(billions of dollars)

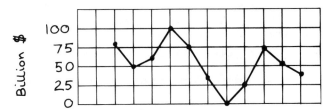

Quarterly changes in U.S.
G.D.P., 1989 - 1991, Current
dollar, seasonally
adjusted
(billions of dollars)

between \$35 billion and \$100 billion. The two smallest changes are \$1.7 billion and \$24.5 billion, and the largest change is \$100.4 billion. We feel uneasy about making predictions on the basis of so few observations. We would want to analyze a larger slice of the process before making predictions. (See Exercise 2.3G.) ∎

The sequence plot is an ideal tool for displaying process data. It emphasizes the time dimension and provides a basis for making useful predictions about the evolution of a process. It can be displayed in the workplace to promote communication, and it can also form the basis for higher-level reporting. The sequence plot is constructed from data collected regularly from an ongoing process and thus emphasizes the need to collect data carefully and faithfully. Despite its simplicity, the sequence plot is a fundamental statistical tool.

SECTION

2.3 Exercises

2.3A Describe a simple repetitive process that is part of your daily personal life. Examples are driving a car, getting a child ready for nursery school, preparing breakfast, shooting baskets, jogging, and so on. What quantities could be measured to help describe aspects of the process?

2.3B Describe a repetitive process that is part of your school or workplace life. What quantities could be measured to help describe aspects of that process?

2.3C Describe a process where the results have *no variability*! Would there be any interest in studying such a process?

2.3D Collect the most recent 50 to 100 consecutive balances from your checkbook. Make a table showing the balances and the balance-to-balance changes. Plot both sequences in a plot like Exhibit 2.2D. What predictions are you willing to make about the future of your checkbook balances? Can you explain some of the large changes? Can you anticipate some of the large changes that will occur? (If this exercise is to be handed in, you may wish to add a constant such as \$100 to all your data to protect the anonymity of your personal finances!)

An alternative data-collection scheme is to record the balance in the checkbook at the end of each day. Or the number of transactions made each day could be recorded. Try this scheme and made sequence plots of the end-of-day balances and the numbers of checks written. Compare these plots with the ones based on consecutive balances.

2.3E If you work in an office that keeps a log of photocopies, obtain a record of the number of copies for 200 to 300 consecutive jobs. Make a sequence plot of these figures. Can you give a reason for the highest and lowest figures? What predictions are you willing to make about the future of the process?

2.3F Collect a sequence of data from any process that interests you. Make a sequence plot and try to predict the future of the process. Collect new data from the process and compare them with your predictions.

2.3G Consult various issues of the *Survey of Current Business* and collect quarterly GDP figures for at least 10 years. Make a table showing the original GDP figures and the quarter-to-quarter changes. Plot both sequences in a plot like Exhibit 2.2D. What sorts of predictions are you willing to make about the future of the GDP process? As time passes, collect GDP data and compare them with the predictions you have made.

SECTION

2.4 Computer-Assisted Sequence Plots

Hand-drawn sequence or time series plots were introduced in Section 2.2 as one means of displaying process data in a meaningful way. However, especially with large data sets, the plots are tedious to produce and manipulate. A computer data analysis system allows us to do the plotting and to look at different aspects of process data with ease. Exhibits 2.4A and 2.4B display computer-produced plots corresponding to the hand-drawn Exhibits 2.2A and 2.2B.

EXHIBIT **2.4A**
Computer Sequence Plot of
Photocopy Process Data

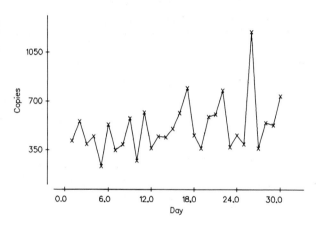

EXHIBIT **2.4B**
Computer Sequence Plot of
Quarterly GDP

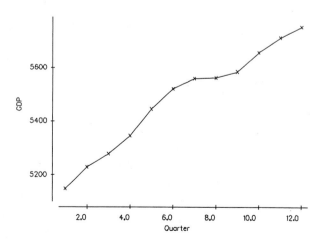

period

Time series or process data often have an associated **period**—that is, a time span at which a sequence *may* tend to repeat its general behavior.

E X A M P L E   **2.4A**

The photocopy data are collected for weekdays, so the same day of the week repeats with a period of five days. The GDP series is measured quarterly and so has an associated period of four measurements per year. If the same plotting symbol is used for the same day of the week, same quarter of the year, same month, and so on, process values that may be of interest can be easily compared. Do Monday counts tend to behave differently than Wednesday or Friday counts? Do fourth-quarter GDP values look any different from GDP values for other quarters? Exhibits 2.4C and 2.4D display the sequence plots corresponding to Exhibits 2.4A and 2.4B but with the period properly specified. In Exhibit 2.4C, all Mondays are plotted as A's, Tuesdays as B's,

E X H I B I T **2.4C**
Sequence Plot of Photocopy
Data with Period 5

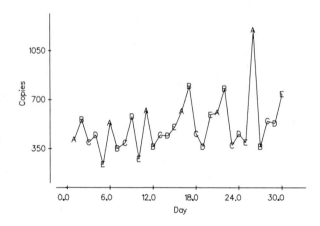

E X H I B I T **2.4D**
GDP Sequence Plot with Period 4

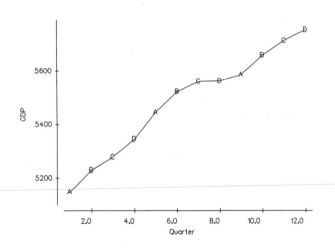

and so forth. With monthly data, the plotting symbols used are A, B, C, D, E, F, G, H, I, J, K, and L.

No particular day-of-the-week effect is evident in Exhibit 2.4C. Similarly, Exhibit 2.4D shows no particular patterns associated with the quarter of the year. For longer series, computer plotting is indispensable. ∎

E X A M P L E   **2.4B**

The top part of Exhibit 2.4E shows 120 consecutive balances recorded in a checkbook, and Exhibit 2.4F is a sequence plot of the balances. The high balances occur at the beginnings of months, when a paycheck is deposited. Then the balances rapidly decrease because a large number of bills are paid. Then follows a period of routine daily transactions, which may result in negative balances toward the end of the month. Small deposits may result to try to eliminate the negative balances. The sequence plot in Exhibit 2.4F shows two such cycles and the beginning of a third. Here we see a rather predictable pattern that recurs monthly.

Many transactions may take place on a single day, so the transaction, not calendar time, is the unit on the horizontal axis. If you wanted to use days as the time units, you could record, for example, the number of transactions in

E X H I B I T **2.4E**
Checkbook Balances (top) and
Balance-to-Balance Changes
(bottom)

```
(Read across, row by row)
Balances
4847 4304 4029 3629 3191 3097 3076 2876 2845 2641
2627 2572 2290  760  650  630  599  561  477  454
 409  373  338  331 -594 -597 -618 -705 -715 -738
 635  617  609  604  590  534  529  432  426  421
 289  261  241  323  225  214  122  120  116  401
 376  382  356  345  343  318  198  183   75   63
4315 3772 3472 3035 2634 2570 2536 2497 2475 1923
1643 1588 1557 1519 1512 1494 1466 1066 1026  942
 832  872  831  810  790  774  773  699  677  669
 667  566  496  646  412  404  356  252  253  248
 246  235  226  212  159  148   19   -3   -7  -14
-104 -111 -120   19 4262 3719 3688 3388 2951 2550
```

```
Changes
   * -543 -275  -400 -438  -94  -21 -200  -31 -204
 -14  -55 -282 -1530 -110  -20  -31  -38  -84  -23
 -45  -36  -35    -7 -925   -3  -21  -87  -10  -23
1373  -18   -8    -5  -14  -56   -5  -97   -6   -5
-132  -28  -20    82  -98  -11  -92   -2   -4  285
 -25    6  -26   -11   -2  -25 -120  -15 -108  -12
4252 -543 -300  -437 -401  -64  -34  -39  -22 -552
-280  -55  -31   -38   -7  -18  -28 -400  -40  -84
-110   40  -41   -21  -20  -16   -1  -74  -22   -8
  -2 -101  -70   150 -234   -8  -48 -104    1   -5
  -2  -11   -9   -14  -53  -11 -129  -22   -4   -7
 -90   -7   -9   139 4243 -543  -31 -300 -437 -401
```

Source: Confidential.

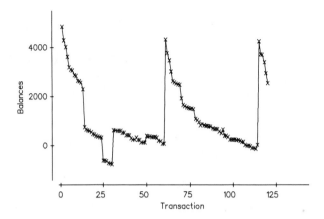

a day and the balance in the checkbook after the last transaction of the day. This would be analogous to recording trading volume and closing price for a stock on a stock exchange. The sequence lot of such data would present quite a different appearance from the one in Exhibit 2.4F.

The bottom part of Exhibit 2.4E shows the balance-to-balance changes, which are the amounts of the transactions recorded in the checkbook. A deposit yields a positive change, and writing a check yields a negative change. Exhibit 2.4G shows the sequence plot of the changes. The major changes occur at the beginnings of months.　■

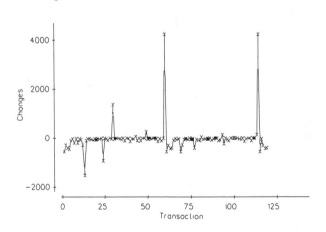

levels

first differences

In the analysis of financial data, you will often encounter the types of sequence plots shown in Exhibits 2.2D, 2.4F, and 2.4G. The balances are called **levels** of the measured variable, which are the actual values of a sequence where the first differences or changes may be of primary interest. The changes from one data value to the next are called **first differences**. Plots of levels and first differences often yield useful insights into such processes.

SECTION

2.5 Exercises

2.5A   The data below give 82 consecutive values for the amount of deviation (in 0.000025-inch units) from a specified target value that an industrial machining process at Deere & Co. produced under certain specified operating conditions. In these data, 0 means that the value was right on target and −3 means that the part produced measured 0.000075 inches below the target value. Plot the second line of values (beginning with −2 and ending with 2) by hand in a sequence plot. Repeat the sequence plot using all the values and a computer software package. Describe both the plots in words. Are there any unusual values that seem to be out of line with the rest of the values?

```
filename: DEERE1.DAT
Deere & Co. machining data, n=82
(Source: Jerri Matchinsky, M.S. thesis,
University of Iowa, 1988.)
Coded in 0.000025 inch deviations from target
(Read across, row by row)
  3  0 -1 -4  7  3  7  3  3 -1 -1  5 -4  1 -3  2 -3  1 -2 -3 -4
 -2  3  3  3  3 30  2  7 -7  3  2  3  0  3  0  3 -1  3  3  3  2
  3  3 -1  3  3  2  3  2  3  8  0 -1  0  0  1  2  2  0  8  0  1
 -2 -3  4  0  4 -1 -1  1 -7  3  1  3  1  0 -1 -4 -1 -1  3
```

2.5B   The data file below gives the average hourly wage ($\times 100$) for U.S. workers in the manufacturing industries by month over the period from July 1981 to June 1987. Create a sequence plot of the data over the six-year period. Describe the plot. Form the month-to-month difference sequence. Plot the differences in a sequence plot. Are there any striking features of this plot?

```
filename: MANWAGES.DAT
Average hourly earnings per worker (X100)
Manufacturing excluding overtime
(Source: Survey of Current Business, September issues, 1981-1987)
July 1981 through June 1987
Jul Aug Sep Oct Nov Dec Jan Feb Mar Apr May Jun
775 774 787 789 794 800 817 810 813 819 822 825
831 826 833 831 836 842 846 850 847 848 849 849
853 844 852 854 861 867 872 870 873 875 876 877
883 878 885 887 893 900 907 907 909 913 913 913
919 912 916 917 923 931 931 933 933 933 934 932
935 927 931 932 937 942 944 944 944 948 945 944
```

2.5C   The data file below gives the average hourly wage ($\times 100$) for workers in the apparel and other textile products industries. The data are given by month over the period from July 1981 to June 1987. Create a sequence plot of the data over the six-year period. Describe the plot. Form the month-to-month difference sequence. Plot the differences in a sequence plot. Are there any striking features of this plot?

```
filename: APAWAGES.DAT
Hourly wages (X100), apparel and other textile products
(Source: Survey of Current Business, September issues, 1981-1987)
July 1981 through June 1987
Jul Aug Sep Oct Nov Dec Jan Feb Mar Apr May Jun
492 496 504 505 504 504 518 513 515 518 516 518
519 520 523 521 524 528 533 533 533 535 533 536
535 535 539 540 543 544 550 546 548 549 548 550
553 555 563 561 561 568 573 570 573 574 569 570
570 569 575 574 575 580 582 579 580 581 578 579
579 583 591 587 587 590 594 593 593 594 589 591
```

SECTION

2.6   Monthly Sales Data and Seasonality

Exhibit 2.6A lists a set of sales data obtained from Deere & Co., a major worldwide manufacturer of John Deere tractors, other farm and construction machinery, and consumer products such as garden tractors and snowblowers. The data give monthly sales of a particular low-cost (approximately $10 in 1987) replacement oil filter from the manufacturer to John Deere dealers.[†] The series covers 48 months beginning in July 1983 and ending in June 1987. Exhibit 2.6B gives the sequence plot of these data. Notice that the plotting symbols have been selected to indicate the month of each observation. Since the first observation was taken in July, the first observation is plotted with a G. This makes it easy to keep track of actual monthly values and consider their patterns, if any. From the plot, we see that higher sales tend to occur in January and February, months A and B, and lower sales occur in July through December, months G through L. Peak sales of 5862 units occurred in January of 1984, and December 1987 produced the lowest number of sales—1586 units. The

seasonality

oil-filter data exhibit **seasonality**—that is, there is a pattern that tends to repeat itself according to the period of the series. Another way to look at the sales data to see the seasonality is to plot sales versus month of the year—that is, plot all January values above the same horizontal position, all February values above a second horizontal position, and so forth. Exhibit 2.6C gives such a display. Here on the horizontal axis January = 1, February = 2, and so on.

E X H I B I T   2.6A

Wholesale Oil-Filter Sales, Deere & Company, Inc.

```
filename: OILFILT.DAT
Deere & Co. oil filter sales to dealers ($10 part)
(Source: William Fullkerson, Deere & Co.,
Technical Center, Moline, Illinois.)
July 1983 through June 1987, n=48
Jul  Aug  Sep  Oct  Nov  Dec  Jan  Feb  Mar  Apr  May  Jun
2385 3302 3958 3302 2441 3107 5862 4536 4625 4492 4486 4005
3744 2546 1954 2285 1778 3222 5472 5310 1965 3791 3622 3726
3370 2535 1572 2146 2249 1721 5357 5811 2436 4608 2871 3349
2909 2324 1603 2148 2245 1586 5332 5787 2886 5475 3843 2537
```

[†]Data courtesy of William F. Fulkerson, Deere & Co. Technical Center, Moline, Illinois.

E X H I B I T 2.6B
Sequence Plot of Oil-Filter Sales
to Dealers

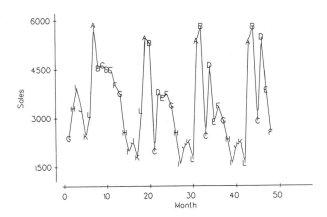

E X H I B I T 2.6C
Plot of Sales Versus Month

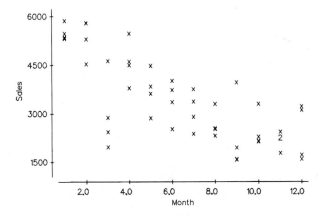

From this plot, we again see that sales are nearly always higher in January and February than later in the year. We also see an unusual drop in sales in March relative to the other months for three of the four years. September and March sales show substantial variability relative to other months. Note, however, that Exhibit 2.6C does not provide information concerning which years produced which values. Exhibit 2.6D displays the same sales information but by year rather than by month. Note that the first and last year contain only 6 observations each, whereas the other years contain a full 12 observations. In this plot, the information as to which month the values pertain to has been lost.

EXHIBIT **2.6D**
Plot of Sales Versus Year

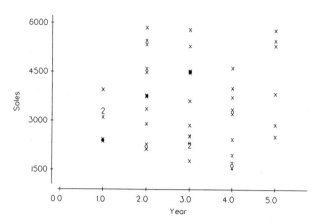

2.7   Exercises

2.7A   The data set below gives the monthly sales of a large part ($250 each) from the manufacturer, Deere & Co., to its John Deere distributors from July 1983 through June of 1987. Using these sales data, produce a sequence plot as in Exhibit 2.6B. Comment on any seasonal patterns that might be present. Are there any other distinctive features of the series that are apparent from the plot?

```
filename: STRAW.DAT
Deere & Co., straw walker sales to dealers ($250 item)
(Source: William Fullkerson, Deere & Co.,
Technical Center, Moline. Illinois.)
July 1983 through June 1987, n=48
Jul Aug Sep Oct Nov Dec Jan Feb Mar Apr May Jun
392 251 264 535 127  33 114  72 165 132 112 240
285 275 294 517 379 124  94 147 131 180 152 253
363 290 270 591 381  93  60  65 131 329 113 226
339 374 276 592 381  93  60  65 134  34 168 746
```

2.7B   Using the data of Exercise 2.7A, produce plots of sales versus month and sales versus year as in Exhibits 2.6C and 2.6D. Comment on the displays. Any patterns, any unusual values, and so on? (Filename: STRAW.DAT.)

2.8   Some Assembly-Line Data and Transformations

Amana Refrigeration, Inc., is a major U.S. manufacturer of home appliances including freezers, refrigerators, air-conditioning units, furnaces, and microwave ovens. Some assembly-line data from the manufacture of microwave ovens are presented here.[†] Some models of Amana microwave ovens use a stainless steel oven cavity wrapper—

[†]Data courtesy of Robert W. Cech, Director of Quality Assurance, Amana Refrigeration, Amana, Iowa.

the box in which the food is actually cooked. Hidden inside the oven is another steel box, called the waveguide, which literally guides the microwaves created by an electronic device into the oven cavity where the cooking takes place. The waveguide must be physically attached to the top of the oven cavity wrapper by spot welding. The positioning of the waveguide is important to the proper operation of the oven. The microwaves must be properly guided into the oven cavity, and the other electronic equipment must fit near the waveguide. Exhibit 2.8A shows a simplified top view of the basic setup. Design specifications state that for proper assembly the distances labeled "Left" and "Right" in the figure should be 6.056 inches with a tolerance of plus or minus 0.045 inch. However, the two distances interact in the sense that it is also important that the waveguide be parallel to the oven cavity wrapper. If the Left distance is a little long, it is preferable that the Right distance also be a little long so that the waveguide is still parallel to the oven cavity wrapper. As a check on the quality of the assembly process, for every 200–300 oven cavities coming down the assembly line, one oven cavity is selected and the Left and Right distances are measured and recorded. With a typical assembly line and production schedule, this process produces about two pairs of Left and Right measurements per day. A partial

E X H I B I T **2.8A**
Waveguide Positioning on the
Microwave Oven Cavity Wrapper

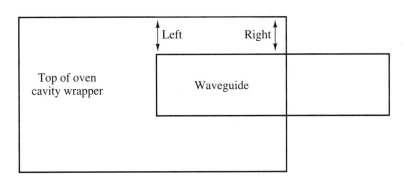

E X H I B I T **2.8B**
Data Sheet for Waveguide
Location

Waveguide Location on Oven Cavity Wrapper
Front edge of waveguide to front flange of oven cavity
wrapper is 6.056″ ± 0.045″

Date	Time	Card#	Left	Right
6-2-86	7:15	743	6.056	6.054
6-2-86	9:42	743	6.070	6.058
6-3-86	7:54	743	6.071	6.074
6-3-86	11:24	743	6.058	6.050

Card # refers to the timecard number of the employee taking the measurements.

data sheet is shown in Exhibit 2.8B, and the full data set is given in Appendix 4 and in data file AMANA.DAT.

The Left and Right measurements are typically of the form 6.050″, 6.073″, and so on. Usually they differ only in the hundredths and thousandths places. For entering the observations in a computer, it is easier to enter only the last two digits as an integer—that is, effectively 6 inches are subtracted from each measurement and then each value is multiplied by 1000. Thus 6.050 becomes 50 and 6.073 becomes 73. We say that we have coded the data. The data set used contains 120 pairs of coded Left and Right measurements recorded from June 2, 1986, to December 19, 1986. Exhibits 2.8C and 2.8D give separate sequence plots of the Left and Right values. Notice that the values obtained vary considerably over time. There are time periods with little variation of values and other time periods with considerable variation.

E X H I B I T **2.8C**
Sequence Plot of the Left
Measurement

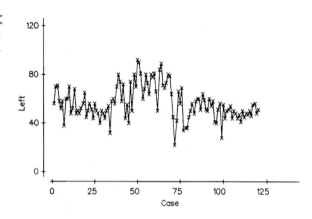

E X H I B I T **2.8D**
Sequence Plot of the Right
Measurement

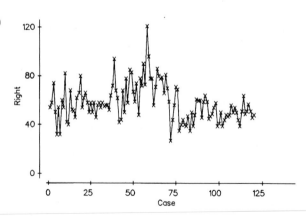

To compare the variation in the sequences with the tolerances that the product designers have specified for the process, it is useful to overlay on the sequence plots horizontal lines at the specification value and tolerance limits. With our coded data, the specification or target value of 6.056 inches is coded as 56, and the upper and lower tolerances are then $56 + 45 = 101$ and $56 - 45 = 11$, respectively. Exhibits 2.8E and 2.8F display the results. Exhibit 2.8F clearly shows that the Right measurement at "time" 58 is above the upper specification limit. Looking back through the data sheets, we see that this measurement was made on September 3, 1986. If we had been creating these plots immediately as the data came off the assembly line, we would be alerted to investigate the cause of the problem and correct it before possibly several hundred ovens were poorly assembled. The sequence plot also shows that whatever the difficulty was, it did not persist as a long-term production problem. Chapters 10 and 12 on control charts will deal extensively with such problems.

E X H I B I T **2.8E**
Sequence Plot of Left with
Specification Limits

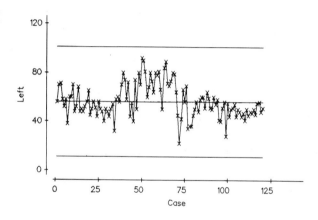

E X H I B I T **2.8F**
Sequence Plot of Right with
Specification Limits

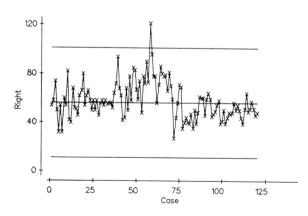

Transformations

As stated earlier, the Left and Right dimensions interact—they are required to be similar so that the waveguide can be parallel to the oven cavity. This suggests that it might be better to investigate some different sequences that are computed from the given Left and Right measurements. In particular, the Left and Right measurements could be averaged to get a value representing the distance from the waveguide to the outer edge of the oven cavity halfway between the left and right positions. Call that distance Midvalue. We also let the difference of the Left and Right values be a measure of the parallelism of the waveguide—the closer the difference is to zero the better. Let Diff denote the variable Left − Right. The time series plots with specification limits for the sequences of Midvalue and Diff values are given in Exhibits 2.8G and 2.8H. The unusually high Midvalue value at time 58 is still noticeable. The sequence of Diff values varies around zero quite closely, indicating no problems with lack of parallelism in the waveguide. The specification limits of 6.056″ ± 0.045″ translate into limits of ±90 for the differences of the coded measurements.

EXHIBIT **2.8G**
Sequence Plot of Midvalue with
Specification Limits

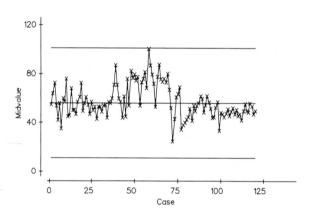

EXHIBIT **2.8H**
Sequence Plot of Diff with
Specification Limits

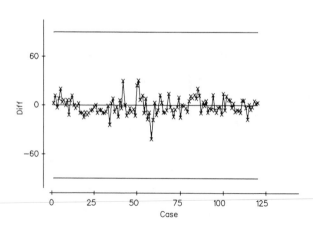

2.9 Exercise

2.9A The data file below gives some accounts receivable data for the Winegard Company of Burlington, Iowa—a worldwide manufacturer of electronic equipment. The data are the number of days for a particular independent retail electronics distributor, called XYZ Company to protect its anonymity, to pay its bills to Winegard. The terms of the account were 1% − 10 days and net −30 days—that is, if the bill is paid within 10 days a 1% discount can be taken, but, in any case, the full bill is due within 30 days. The data cover January 1986 through December 1986 with about 10 bills coming due each month.

Construct a sequence plot of the data. Are there any isolated points that seem out of line with the rest of the values? Compare the first half of the values with the last half. Are there important differences? Do you think Winegard should be concerned about the pattern of bill paying that seems to be emerging near the end of the series?

```
filename: XYZ1.DAT
Number of days to pay account: XYZ Company
Winegard, Inc. accounts receivable data
(Source: Mark Sellergren, Winegard, Inc.
Burlington, Iowa.)
January 1986 through December 1986
Terms: 10 days-1%, 30 days-net.  n=110
(Read across, row by row)
29 25 22 21 34 29 27 45 22 22 41 32 32 30 30
30 30 22 17 15 25 28 22 22 22 20 20 18 32 31
30 77 22 18 18 25 25 24 21 17 17 28 42 38 30
30 30 30 27 21 68 31 23 23 23  1 20 29 31 31
43 33 38 42 36 48 48 52 49 44 51 49 54 50 50
50 50 50 49 62 62 62 61 60 55 61 59 54 54 62
57 55 62 62 62 62 62 62 57 57 57 57 55 50 50
44 44 43 43 41
```

2.10 Some Regional Economic Data and Analysis of Changes

The data for an index of monthly flour prices in Buffalo, New York, for the period August 1972 through November 1980 are listed in Exhibit 2.10A. Exhibit 2.10B is a sequence plot that displays the movement of this flour price index during that time. The series exhibits no apparent seasonality or other discernible pattern. The

EXHIBIT 2.10A
Flour Price Index for Buffalo, New York

```
filename: BUFLOUR.DAT
Flour price index (X10) at Buffalo, New York,
August 1972 through November 1980.
(Source: G.C.Tiao and R.S.Tsay, Technical Report 61,
Graduate School of Business, University of Chicago.)
(Read across, row by row)
Aug  Sep  Oct  Nov  Dec  Jan  Feb  Mar  Apr  May  Jun  Jul
1071 1135 1127 1147 1234 1236 1163 1185 1198 1203 1274 1251
1276 1290 1246 1341 1465 1712 1786 1722 1715 1636 1856 1988
1957 1903 2079 2128 1999 1853 1830 1735 1722 1653 1599 1703
1722 1845 1850 1777 1691 1747 1694 1778 1701 1671 1714 1723
1526 1441 1435 1356 1354 1345 1361 1356 1228 1190 1085 1133
1148 1209 1237 1278 1254 1315 1277 1312 1452 1419 1393 1411
1359 1365 1372 1438 1387 1339 1377 1438 1408 1534 1575 1795
1775 1780 1768 1798 1742 1711 1759 1722 1647 1757 1774 1875
1907 1904 1924 1929
```

E X H I B I T **2.10B**

Sequence Plot of Flour Price
Index for Buffalo, New York

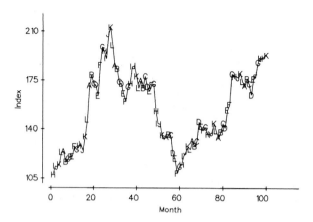

meandering series

series might best be described as meandering. A **meandering series** is one in which observations that are close in time are also close in value but observations that are far apart in time may be very different in value. Short-term variation is small but long-term variation may be quite large. The index grows for certain fairly long periods but then drops over other long periods, only to begin another upward path later on. The peak price over this time span occurred in October 1974, and the lowest price appears at the beginning of the series, August 1972, which is nearly equaled by the June 1977 value. By the end of this time period, November 1980, the index was nearly back up to its peak level.

E X H I B I T **2.10C**

Sequence Plot of Changes in
Flour Price Index, Buffalo, New
York

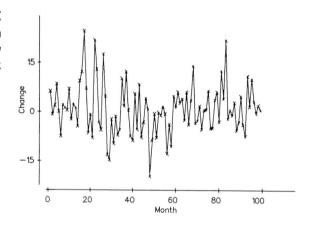

Differences

For many series that meander, especially economic series, it is the month-to-month (or quarter-to-quarter or year-to-year) changes, or first differences, that are most easily described, modeled, and predicted. Changes in the GDP series were plotted in Exhibits 2.2C and 2.2D. Any computer data analysis system will allow easy calculation of the required differences. The sequence of changes or month-to-month differences of the flour price index is plotted in Exhibit 2.10C. Note that changes vary quite "randomly" from low values of about −20 to high values of about 25.

Percentage Changes

percentage changes

Series that tend to meander frequently also have the property that the variation in the changes associated with large values of the series is greater than the variation in the changes associated with small values of the series. In such situations, it is most productive to investigate the **percentage changes** in the series—the relative changes from one data value to the next data value on a percentage basis and relative to the previous data value. The percentage change is 100 times the change divided by the previous value of the process. The following small table shows some illustrative calculations:

Time	Series Value	Change	Percentage Change
1	126	*	*
2	132	6	$100(6)/126 = 4.76$
3	128	−4	$100(-4)/132 = -3.03$
4	141	3	$100(3)/128 = 2.34$

Exhibit 2.10D gives the sequence plot of the percentage changes for the flour price index series. No patterns or seasonalities are apparent in the plot. The percentage changes vary quite "randomly" between about −15% on the low end to about 15% on the high side.

EXHIBIT **2.10D**
Sequence Plot of Percentage Changes in Flour Price Index, Buffalo, New York

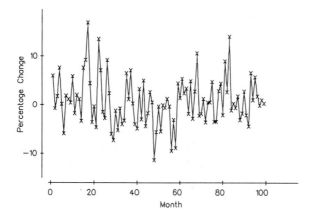

S E C T I O N

2.11 Exercises

2.11A   The data below are the monthly flour price index ($\times 10$) in the Kansas City area for August 1972 through November 1980. Display a sequence plot for the 100 data points and compare it with the corresponding plot in Exhibit 2.10B. Compute the month-to-month changes in the index and plot them in a sequence plot. Compare them with Exhibit 2.10C. Finally, compute the percentage changes of the index and plot their sequence plot. Comment on the similarities and dissimilarities with Exhibit 2.10D.

```
filename: KCFLOUR.DAT
Kansas City monthly flour price index (X10)
August 1972 through November 1980
(Source: G.C.Tiao and R.S.Tsay, Technical Report 61,
 Graduate School of Business, University of Chicago.)
(Read across, row by row)
Aug  Sep  Oct  Nov  Dec  Jan  Feb  Mar  Apr  May  Jun  Jul
1109 1146 1155 1170 1350 1328 1226 1238 1289 1267 1393 1357
1356 1460 1407 1470 1639 1943 2008 1934 1903 1880 1961 2150
2016 2034 2221 2287 2161 2002 1896 1733 1697 1610 1517 1671
1744 1897 1874 1784 1658 1649 1718 1754 1659 1573 1614 1592
1428 1385 1342 1261 1242 1227 1235 1183 1123 1057 0977 1058
1069 1100 1143 1188 1172 1261 1205 1256 1320 1346 1303 1370
1366 1370 1384 1429 1404 1360 1401 1482 1464 1585 1635 1871
1817 1815 1819 1909 1869 1801 1848 1748 1690 1784 1753 1782
1820 1886 1908 1922
```

2.11B   Yoichi Kuwabara collected the data listed below for a class project. His goal was to find variables that help to explain the level of Japanese direct investment in the United States. Each series of data and its definition and source is:

Japanese Direct Investment into U.S. (US$ million): *Bank of Japan*

Toshyo (Japan) Stock Price Average (yen): *Japan Economic Newspaper*

Japanese Real Deposits Outstanding (yen): *Bank of Japan*

Yen-to-dollar exchange rate (yen/dollar): *Toyo Keizai Inc.*

Dow Jones 30 Industrials Average (US$): *Statistics Journal (Toyo Keizai Inc.)*

U.S. Bond Yields (%): *Statistics Journal (Toyo Keizai Inc.)*

a   Make sequence plots of the six series and comment on their behavior.

b   Compute the month-to-month changes for each series and make the sequence plots. Comment on the behavior of the changes. Are there any anomalous values that seem to need investigation? (Filename: JAPANINV.DAT)

Month	Japanese Direct Investment in U.S. (US$ million)	Japanese Stock Price Average (yen)	Japanese Real Deposits Outstanding (yen)	Yen-to-Dollar Exchange Rate	Dow Jones 30 Industrials Average (US$)	Bond Yields (New Issues, High Grade Corporate)
5/90	1851.5	31826	3922795	153.52	2794	9.97
6/90	1889.5	32364	3977546	153.77	2895	9.69
7/90	2283.0	32170	3970928	149.28	2934	9.72
8/90	1439.0	26908	3972347	147.42	2682	10.01
9/90	1813.5	23975	4092396	138.99	2551	10.17
10/90	1428.0	23816	3985999	129.75	2461	10.09
11/90	1794.5	23468	4043181	129.08	2519	9.79
12/90	1910.5	23740	4090101	133.68	2611	9.55
1/91	1209.5	23321	3963681	133.90	2588	9.60
2/91	867.5	25219	3958391	130.48	2863	9.14
3/91	2867.0	32305	3903596	153.08	2700	9.79
4/91	1317.0	26469	4023382	137.10	2925	9.07
5/91	1611.0	25848	4053812	136.06	2928	9.13
6/91	1169.0	24533	4086630	139.82	2968	9.37
7/91	1063.0	23226	4051513	138.89	3006	8.88
8/91	1013.0	22730	4073256	138.01	2978	9.38
9/91	772.0	23038	4129287	134.58	3010	8.79
10/91	1115.5	24631	4040332	130.72	3019	8.81
11/91	1125.0	23795	4083159	129.68	2986	8.72
12/91	811.0	22304	4101681	128.06	2958	8.55
1/92	479.5	21857	4002872	125.03	3227	8.36
2/92	549.5	21412	4035327	127.50	3257	8.63
3/92	983.0	20350	4119461	132.70	3247	8.62
4/92	708.0	17593	4034436	133.57	3294	8.59
5/92	127.0	18335	4047356	130.57	3376	8.57
6/92	773.0	16948	4049274	126.81	3337	8.45
7/92	541.0	16278	4014796	125.65	3329	8.19

2.11C   If the price of a stock is $85 in January 1994, and its price is $96 in March 1994, compute the rate of return on the stock. Interpret as a percentage change.

2.11D   Use the data in Exercise 2.11C. Compute *log*(96/85), where *log* stands for natural logarithm. Compare this value with the rate of return computed in Exercise 2.11C. Explain why they are so close.

2.11E   I invest a dollar for a year, and it gains 10% in value. I invest the the $1.10 for another year, and it loses 10% in value. Thus, at the end of the two-year period I am back where I started, with $1. Comment.

SECTION

2.12   Some U.S. Macroeconomic Data and Seasonality

The U.S. Bureau of the Census regularly collects and reports many quantities of interest to the business community relating to the economic health of the nation. The *Survey of Current Business* gives monthly values broken down into categories such as manufacturing, construction, mining, and so on. Exhibit 2.12A shows the average weekly hours per worker on private, nonagricultural manufacturing payrolls by month for the time period July 1982 through June 1987. The sequence plot of data is shown in Exhibit 2.12B. By plotting the series with period 12, the seasonal nature of the series becomes readily apparent. High weekly hours occur most frequently in December (plotting symbol L), with low hours generally falling in July (symbol G). We also readily see the low weekly hours at the beginning of the series corresponding to the 1982 recession and the economic recovery during 1983. Models for seasonal sequences will be studied in Chapter 24.

EXHIBIT **2.12A**

Average Hours Worked per
Week in Manufacturing

```
filename: MANHOURS.DAT
Average hours worked per week per worker (X10)
Manufacturing (not seasonally adjusted)
(Source: Survey of Current Business, September issues, 1982-1987.)
July 1982 through June 1987
Jul Aug Sep Oct Nov Dec Jan Feb Mar Apr May Jun
389 390 389 390 393 397 392 388 396 398 399 403
400 402 408 407 408 412 406 407 407 409 406 408
403 404 407 405 407 412 403 397 404 401 403 406
401 405 408 408 409 417 407 403 407 405 406 408
402 407 410 407 410 415 408 408 409 404 409 411
```

EXHIBIT **2.12B**

Sequence Plot of Average Hours
Worked per Week in
Manufacturing

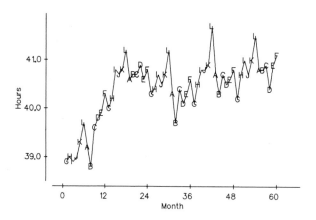

Chapter Summary

In this chapter, we have defined and given examples of processes. We have argued that processes yield results but that process results also vary. To describe and interpret this variation, we have shown how to construct sequence plots of various kinds to display different aspects of process data. Sequence plots help us predict future behavior, detect changes in a process, and share information. Always look for seasonality in monthly, quarterly, weekly, or daily data. Sometimes simple transformations of the data series, especially differences, changes, or percentage changes, will be much easier to analyze, understand, and predict than the original values.

. . . .

Supplementary Exercises for Chapter 2

2A **a** Construct a sequence plot of the following weekly sales data (in thousands of dollars): 100, 105, 110, 115, 115, 120, 125, 125, 130, 135.

   b Describe the sequence plot in part (a) using the terms *trend*, *random*, *seasonal*, and *meandering*.

   c Repeat parts (a) and (b) for the sequence 110, 100, 105, 100, 115, 110, 115, 105, 110, 105.

   d Repeat parts (a) and (b) for the sequence 100, 110, 115, 120, 115, 125, 120, 115, 110, 110.

2B Sequence data from an industrial process at Deere & Co. are listed below. (We will return to these data in the Supplementary Exercises for Chapter 23.)

   a Construct a sequence plot of these data.

   b Do values that are close in time tend to be close in value? That is, do the data meander?

```
filename: DEERE2.DAT
Deere & Co. machine data, n=102
(Source: Jerri Matchinsky, M.S. thesis,
University of Iowa, 1988.)
Deviations from target in 0.00000125ths of an inch
(Read across, row by row)
-18 -24 -17 -27 -37 -34  -8  14  18   7   4  17  10  13  -1
  3  -4  -3  -3  -5  -8   0  -9  -4  -3   4   7  14   9  -2
  0   2   7   5 -18   8   3   1 -10   4   5  11   3  11   5
  6   6  -8  -8  -9  -7   0  -6  15  10  15 -14  -3  -5 -13
-14  -3   0   7  10   4  -5   5   6  15   6  -5  -3  -8  -9
-16 -10 -10  -6  -4  -6  -7   0  -5   2   5   6   2   8  17
 11  21   9  11   9   9   7   4  14  12  12  10
```

2C The data file below gives the monthly total of U.S. retail sales (in billions of dollars) for 1983 through 1987. (We will return to these data in the Supplementary Exercises for Chapter 24.)

   a Construct a sequence plot of these data without using any special plotting symbols. Describe any features of the plot.

   b Now construct a sequence plot using monthly plotting symbols. Are there any patterns evident in this plot? Do the special plotting symbols help bring out the patterns?

```
filename: RETAIL.DAT
Monthly U.S. retail sales, 1983-1987
(Source: Survey of Current Business,
Washington, D.C., U.S. Government Printing Office, 1987.)
in billions of dollars
(Read across, row by row)
 Jan    Feb    Mar    Apr    May    Jun    Jul    Aug    Sep    Oct    Nov    Dec
 81.3   78.9   93.8   94.0   97.8  100.6   99.6  100.2   98.0  100.7  103.9  125.7
 93.1   93.7  104.3  104.3  111.3  112.0  106.6  110.7  103.9  109.2  113.3  131.8
 98.8   95.6  110.2  113.1  120.3  115.0  115.5  121.1  114.2  116.1  118.6  139.5
105.6   99.7  114.2  115.7  125.4  120.4  120.7  124.1  124.6  123.1  120.8  151.3
106.4  105.8  120.4  125.4  129.1  129.0  129.0  131.0  123.8  127.2  125.4  154.8
```

Glossary for Chapter 2

first differences   The sequence of changes from one data value to the next.

levels   The actual values of a sequence where the first differences or changes may be of primary interest.

longitudinal study   A study of the evolution of a process over time.

meandering series   A series whose observations close in time are also close in value but whose observations far apart in time may be quite different.

percentage changes   The relative changes from one data value to the next data value on a percentage basis and relative to the previous data value.

period   Time span at which a sequence *may* tend to repeat its general behavior—12 for monthly data, 4 for quarterly data, and so on.

seasonality   The tendency of a sequence to repeat its general behavior at regular time periods.

sequence plot   A graph with time displayed on the horizontal axis and values of the variable of interest on the vertical axis.

Plotting Distributions

Chapter Objectives

After mastering this chapter, you will be able to prepare, interpret, and explain the advantages and disadvantages of:

- Dotplots

- Stem-and-leaf displays

- Histograms

3.1 Introduction

To be analyzed statistically, data must be numerical or coded numerically. Even things that are not strictly "measurable" must be reduced to cold figures. We are all familiar with this reality, having had our performance in the classroom converted to a grade point average and ultimately to a class rank! Yet measurements give us a concrete handle on problems that no amount of speculation can replace. We strive to be realistic enough about data to know they are not truth, but we need to be able to draw from data the valuable information they contain. We want to be skeptical but not cynical.

continuous data
categorical data

We are accustomed to obtaining numerical measurements on quantities like length, weight, temperature, and so on. This type of data is called **continuous data**. Other somewhat different data, called **categorical data**, such as gender (1 = female, 0 = male), will be considered in Chapter 5.

When a collection of data values becomes available for analysis, it is important to gain an understanding of some basic characteristics of the collection. The sequence plots of Chapter 2 displayed the longitudinal aspects of a data set collected over time. In this chapter we ignore the time dimension, if any, of a data set. Instead we ask, What is a "typical" value? How far are the extreme values from the typical values? Are there gaps within the range of values where no data were observed? How spread out is the set of values? What proportion of the values is greater than the value for

cross-sectional

our own firm? When the time dimension is either absent or ignored, we say that we are considering the **cross-sectional** aspects of the data.

Most people cannot discern how the data are distributed over their range of values from a mere listing of the data. Summaries and, especially, graphic displays of the distribution of the data are needed to help us derive information.

In this chapter and the next, we show how to describe data collected on a single continuous variable. We begin with a basic graphic display—the dotplot—and go on to stem-and-leaf displays and various types of histograms. All these tools play an important role in statistical analysis. Generally speaking, dotplots are useful for small sets of data, stem-and-leaf displays for moderate-sized data sets, and histograms for large sets of data. The chapter concludes by highlighting the difference between the information shown in a distribution display (a cross-sectional display) and a time sequence plot (a longitudinal display).

SECTION

3.2 Dotplots

dotplot

A **dotplot** consists of a horizontal scale on which dots are placed to show the numerical values of the data points. If a data value repeats, the dots are piled up at that location, one dot for each repetition.

EXAMPLE   3.2A

Exhibit 3.2A shows the photocopy data from Exhibit 1.3A. The extreme values—those less than 300 and greater than 650—are shown in parentheses.

EXHIBIT 3.2A
Number of Photocopies by Date
(Exhibit 1.3A repeated with
extreme values in parentheses)

Date	Number of Copies	Date	Number of Copies
10/12	416	11/2	616
10/13	556	11/3	(797)
10/14	395	11/4	456
10/15	447	11/5	364
10/16	(238)	11/6	589
10/19	532	11/9	607
10/20	349	11/10	(780)
10/21	390	11/11	374
10/22	579	11/12	456
10/23	(274)	11/13	393
10/26	621	11/16	(1199)
10/27	362	11/17	362
10/28	447	11/18	547
10/29	440	11/19	530
10/30	505	11/20	(741)

EXHIBIT 3.2B
Hand-Drawn Dotplot of
Photocopy Data (extremes
excluded)

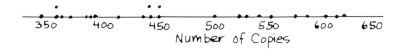

Exhibit 3.2B shows a hand-drawn dotplot of the data, excluding extreme values.

Statistical packages can also produce dotplots, as shown in Exhibit 3.2C. Since a computer display, unlike the real number line, contains only a limited number of unique positions, observations that are nearly equal but actually different may have to be plotted at the same plotting position. To conserve space, a colon (:) is plotted if two observations need to be plotted in the same position. Thus the display in Exhibit 3.2C is not identical to the corresponding portion of the hand-drawn plot, but its general interpretation is the same. The main impression left by the plot is the chaotic behavior of the observations between 300 and 650, which gives little basis for predicting any particular value or range of values over others within these limits. As more data become available, we may be able to detect tendencies for the data to cluster about some value or within a subinterval of [300, 650], but on the basis of the data in Exhibit 3.2C, we would not be surprised by any number between 300 and 650 in the future. ■

Statisticians say that a dotplot displays the *distribution* of the data. The dotplot is especially useful when the distribution behavior of a relatively small set of numbers needs to be displayed. It shows the position of the data points on a number line and displays the frequencies, but for large sets of data (say 100 or more observations) it is tedious to construct by hand. Furthermore, with larger data sets more useful distribution displays are available.

To see the detail of the dotplot display in the middle range of data more clearly, the dotplot can be redone with the extremes excluded. Exhibit 3.2D shows an example with the photocopy data but looking only at the values between 300 and 650.

Dotplots may also be used to make easy visual comparisons among variables that have been categorized by another variable.

EXHIBIT 3.2C
Computer-Drawn Dotplot of
Photocopy Data (extremes
included)

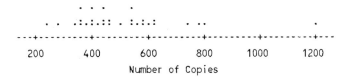

EXHIBIT **3.2D**
Computer-Drawn Dotplot of
Photocopy Data (extreme values
excluded)

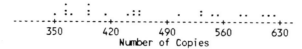

EXHIBIT **3.2E**
Dotplots of Sales Stratified by
Month

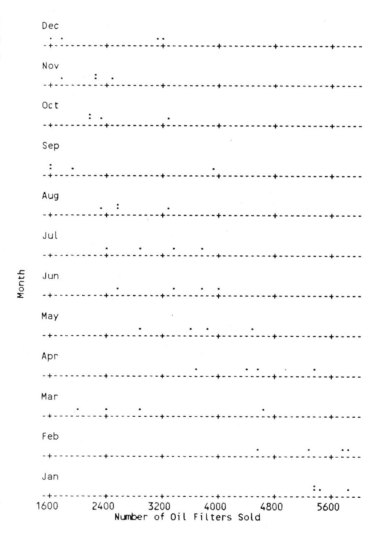

EXAMPLE **3.2B**

Exhibit 3.2E shows a sequence of dotplots of the oil-filter sales data by
month. Again we see the monthly effects that we saw earlier in sequence
plots. ▪

S E C T I O N

3.3 Exercises

3.3A Indicate whether each of the data sets described below is longitudinal or cross-sectional:

a Monthly sales data for Deere & Company for January 1993 through December 1994.

b Entry-level salaries for a variety of job classifications at Deere & Company on January 1, 1994.

c Daily closing stock price values of Deere & Company for the first quarter of 1994.

3.3B Indicate whether each of the data sets described below is longitudinal or cross-sectional:

a The ages of all Pella Windows, Inc., accountants on February 1, 1994.

b The number of hours worked during the week of March 1, 1994, for Pella Windows, Inc., engineers.

c The average number of hours worked per week for Pella Windows, Inc., engineers for the 52 weeks of 1994.

3.3C Display a dotplot for the following 20 exam scores: 87, 78, 96, 91, 89, 74, 59, 88, 67, 82, 93, 72, 79, 84, 65, 81, 95, 85, 89, 91. (Filename: SCORES.DAT.)

3.3D Form a dotplot for the following weights (in grams): 243, 267, 253, 244, 246, 235, 239, 249, 251, 244, 238, 262, 248, 234, 253, 260, 247, 238, 251, 244, 244, 240, 253, 262, 233. (Filename: WEIGHTS.DAT.)

3.3E Prepare a dotplot of the 82 data values from the Deere & Co. machining process given in Exercise 2.5A. Describe the appearance of the distribution displayed in the dotplot. Does it appear symmetric? Are there gaps in the distribution? What values occur most frequently? Least frequently? (Filename: DEERE1.DAT.)

3.3F Compute the month-to-month differences for the wage data in Exercise 2.5B. Describe the appearance of the distribution displayed in the dotplot. Does it appear symmetric? Are there gaps in the distribution? What values occur most frequently? Least frequently? Do the differences associated with certain months tend to be located together in the dotplot? (Filename: MANWAGES.DAT.)

3.3G Prepare a dotplot of the Winegard accounting data in Exercise 2.9A. Compare the dotplot with the sequence plot of the data. What information does the dotplot convey? What information does the sequence plot convey? (Filename: XYZ1.DAT.)

3.3H Compute the percentage changes for the Kansas City flour price index data in Exercise 2.11A. Prepare a dotplot of the percentage changes and compare the information the dotplot provides to the information in the sequence plot. (Filename: KCFLOUR.DAT.)

3.3I For each of the series in Exercise 2.11B, compute the percentage changes and prepare a dotplot. Compare the distributions of the percentage changes. (Filename: JAPANINV.DAT.)

SECTION

3.4 Stem-and-Leaf Displays

With a moderate-to-large data set on a variable that may take on a large number of different values, the distribution is best displayed by grouping together data values that are reasonably close together and displaying the frequencies of the groups. Stem-and-leaf displays were invented by John Tukey to speed the hand construction of such grouped frequency plots. The emphasis is on simplicity, so that even a fairly large set of data (say 100 observations) can be processed and displayed reasonably quickly by hand. (Another more complicated display, the histogram, is discussed in the next section.) The stem-and-leaf technique is presented using the data in Exhibit 3.2A. The **stem-and-leaf display** is a combination table and graphic display, since it retains (essentially) the numerical values of the individual data points while at the same time producing a profile that graphically displays the frequencies of the grouped data values. The basic idea is to let the digits in the data values do the work of grouping the data while also displaying the frequencies.

stem-and-leaf display

Usually only the two leading digits in the data values will actually be used, so the first step is to reduce all the numbers to two digits by chopping off the digits after the first two. If the data had consisted of four-digit numbers, two digits would have been chopped, keeping only two significant digits. The second step is to mentally separate each of the resulting two-digit numbers into a *stem* digit (the left-hand digit) and a *leaf* digit (the right-hand digit).

EXAMPLE **3.4A**

Because in our example the original numbers were restricted to be between 300 and 650, let us make a stem-and-leaf display whose stem digits are 3, 4, 5, and 6.

The stems are placed in numerical order on a vertical line. Frequently, a vertical bar is used to separate the stems from the leaves.

$$
\begin{array}{c|}
3 & \\
4 & \\
5 & \\
6 & \\
\end{array}
$$

The next step is to go through the data values one by one and place the leaf digit directly to the right of the corresponding stem digit. The first data value, 416, is then considered to be divided as

```
4  |  1      |  6
↑      ↑         ↑
Stem   Leaf    Ignored
```

Stem = leading digit; Leaf = trailing digit; Ignored = digit chopped

It is plotted as

```
3 |
4 | 1
5 |
6 |
```

The next data value, 556, is then chopped to 55 and the leaf of 5 is placed next to the stem of 5, as in

```
3 |
4 | 1
5 | 5
6 |
```

Proceeding in this way the entire data set is gone through, building up the stem-and-leaf display:

```
3 | 94966796
4 | 144455
5 | 5370843
6 | 210
```

Since the widths of the leaves are intended to reflect the frequencies of the various stem groupings, it is important, when hand drawing a stem-and-leaf display, *to use the same horizontal space for all digits*. A "thin" 1 must use the same space as a "thick" 8, for example. After the basic stem-and-leaf display is constructed, most authors recommend ordering the leaves in increasing numerical order to make the final display:

Leaf unit = 10

```
                              23, 27   (← low extreme values)
3 | 46667999
4 | 144455
5 | 0334578
6 | 012
              74, 78, 79, 119   (← high extreme values)   ∎
```

In our illustration, the grouping of the data into just four groups may mask some of the detail in the distribution.

E X A M P L E   3.4B

To see more detail, divide the leaf digits into two equal-sized groups:

Group 1:   0, 1, 2, 3, 4 (code = *)

Group 2:   5, 6, 7, 8, 9 (code = .)

To display these two groups for each stem digit, write down each stem digit and attach the appropriate group code:

```
3 *
3 .
4 *
4 .
5 *
5 .
6 *
6 .
```

Now again move through the data in Exhibit 3.2A and record the leaf digits at the appropriate spots on the corresponding stems. The first data value is 416, which is chopped to 41. The leaf digit is in group 1, so it goes next to the 4* in the stem. The second data value is 556, which is chopped to 55. The leaf digit is in group 2, so it goes next to the 5. in the stem. These two values appear in the more detailed diagram as:

```
3 *
3 .
4 * | 1
4 .
5 *
5 . | 5
6 *
6 .
```

Continue through the data in this fashion until the whole display is created again:

Leaf unit = 10

```
                                      23, 27   (← low extreme values)
        3 * | 4
        3 . | 9966796
        4 * | 1444
        4 . | 55
        5 * | 3043
        5 . | 578
        6 * | 210
                    74, 78, 79, 119   (← high extreme values)
```

The extreme values have been included in the display with their ones digits chopped off. A final cleaning up of the display usually consists of ordering the leaves on each stem from smallest to largest.

Leaf unit = 10

23, 27   (← low extreme values)

```
3 * | 4
3 . | 6667999
4 * | 1444
4 . | 55
5 * | 0334
5 . | 578
6 * | 012
```

74, 78, 79, 119   (← high extreme values)

In this fashion, a compact display of the complete set of data has been provided, with more detail than in the previous display. Because of the chopping and grouping of digits, the scale on which the data are displayed is still more compressed than it is in the dotplot. This is desirable when a large amount of data needs to be displayed. Within the limitations of the scale, the stem-and-leaf display presents the data in order, and since it displays frequencies, it is a frequency plot. ∎

Exhibits 3.4A and 3.4B show computer-drawn stem-and-leaf displays. The first column in the exhibits shows the cumulative count of observations on that line or on lines toward the nearer extreme. The line containing the middle of the ordered values has its own count, which is shown in parentheses. Otherwise, the displays are the same as the hand-constructed displays.

EXHIBIT **3.4A**
Computer-Drawn Stem-and-Leaf
Display

```
Stem-and-leaf of Copies    N=30
Leaf unit=10

     2     2 37
    10     3 46667999
   (6)     4 144455
    14     5 0334578
     7     6 012
     4     7 489
     1     8
     1     9
     1    10
     1    11 9
```

EXHIBIT **3.4B**
Computer-Drawn Stem-and-Leaf
with Extreme Value Shown
Separately

```
Stem-and-leaf of Copies     N=30
Leaf unit=10
         1      2 3
         2      2 7
         3      3 4
        10      3 6667999
        14      4 1444
        (2)     4 55
        14      5 0334
        10      5 578
         7      6 012
         4      6
         4      7 4
         3      7 89

        HI   119
```

Back-to-Back Stem-and-Leaf Displays

We often want to compare two distributions. This can be readily accomplished by constructing a back-to-back stem-and-leaf display using common stems for the two distributions. Here is an example.

EXAMPLE   **3.4C**

Thirty-nine students took first and second exams in a statistics course taught by one of the authors. Their exam scores are shown in Exhibit 3.4C. Using stems of 2 through 9, a back-to-back stem-and-leaf display is constructed and shown in Exhibit 3.4D. The display clearly demonstrates the similarity of the two distributions.   ∎

EXHIBIT **3.4C**
First and Second Exam Scores
for 39 Students

```
filename: EXAMS2.DAT
First and second exam scores for a statistics course
Fall 1989, 39 students
```

Exam1	Exam2	Exam1	Exam2
22	68	71	70
27	44	73	80
30	55	73	89
44	46	74	93
46	35	74	89
52	23	78	85
54	61	81	74
57	53	81	85
57	53	85	68
59	63	86	42
59	35	88	63
59	76	93	93
61	85	95	98
64	95	96	93
64	53	96	78
64	78	96	91
68	70	98	78
68	42	98	93
68	72	98	95
69	68		

EXHIBIT **3.4D**
Back-to-Back Stem-and-Leaf
Diagram for Exam Scores

```
Back-to-back Stem-and-leaf of Exam 1 and Exam 2
      Leaf Unit = 1.0  N=39


      Exam 1    Exam 2
         72 2  3
          0 3  55
         64 4  2246
    9997742 5  3335
   98884441 6  133888
     844331 7  00246888
      86511 8  055599
   88866653 9  13333558
```

The construction of an effective stem-and-leaf display depends on the choice of the stem digits. In the photocopy example, the hundreds digit was retained for the stem. Other choices will be indicated for other data sets. For example, if the observations consist of five-digit numbers of the form *abcde*, we may wish to retain the *ab* digits for the stem and use the *c* digits for the leaves. This means chopping the *de* digits. (See Exercise 3.7B for a numerical illustration.) There is no hard-and-fast rule for creating stems and leaves. The important thing is to get a good representation of the distribution without doing an excessive amount of work.

SECTION

3.5 Exercises

3.5A   Display a stem-and-leaf diagram for the following 20 exam scores: 87, 78, 96, 91, 89, 74, 59, 88, 67, 82, 93, 72, 79, 84, 65, 81, 95, 85, 89, 91. Compare this display to the dotplot in Exercise 3.3C. (Filename: SCORES.DAT.)

3.5B   Form a stem-and-leaf diagram for the following weights (in grams): 243, 267, 253, 244, 246, 235, 239, 249, 251, 244, 238, 262, 248, 234, 253, 260, 247, 238, 251, 244, 244, 240, 253, 262, 233. Compare the stem-and-leaf diagram to the dotplot constructed in Exercise 3.3D. (Filename: WEIGHTS.DAT.)

3.5C   Prepare a stem-and-leaf display of the Deere & Co. machining data in Exercise 2.5A. Compare the information conveyed by the stem-and-leaf display and the dotplot of Exercise 3.3E. (Filename: DEERE1.DAT.)

3.5D   Display a stem-and-leaf display of the month-to-month differences in the wage data given in Exercise 2.5B. Compare the information conveyed by the stem-and-leaf display and the dotplot of Exercise 3.3F. (Filename: MANWAGES.DAT.)

3.5E   Make a stem-and-leaf display of the Winegard accounting data in Exercise 2.9A. Compare the information conveyed by the stem-and-leaf display and the dotplot of Exercise 3.3G. (Filename: XYZ1.DAT.)

3.5F   Prepare a stem-and-leaf display of the percentage changes of the Kansas City flour price index data listed in Exercise 2.11A. Compare the information conveyed by the stem-and-leaf display and the dotplot of Exercise 3.3H. (Filename: KCFLOUR.DAT.)

3.5G   For each of the series in Exercise 2.11B, compute the percentage changes and prepare a stem-and-leaf display. Compare the stem-and-leaf displays with the dotplots you prepared in Exercise 3.3I. (Filename: JAPANINV.DAT.)

SECTION

3.6 Histograms

Histograms are graphic tools for displaying distributions of large sets of data. Histograms group the data into a relatively small number of classes and show the frequencies of the classes. In the statistical literature, several somewhat different displays are called histograms. We distinguish among three types: frequency histograms, relative frequency histograms, and density histograms.

Frequency Histograms

frequency histograms

Frequency histograms, the most basic histograms, are graphic displays of frequency distributions. All they require is grouping the data into *classes*, counting the number of observations in each class, and making a plot.

EXAMPLE   3.6A

class frequency

Exhibit 3.6A shows a computer-generated histogram for a variable called Outlook, which will be covered more completely in Chapter 5. This variable is part of a large data set obtained in a survey of Wisconsin restaurant owners and assumes one of the values 1, 2, 3, . . . , 6 according to the business outlook perceived by the owners. (See especially Exhibit 5.4A.) In Exhibit 3.6A, asterisks (∗) have been placed according to the count or **class frequency** of observations at each of the possible values 1 through 6. The frequencies are then easily seen and compared from the display. Sometimes the sizes of the frequencies are portrayed using *rectangles* instead of asterisks, as in Exhibit 3.6B. These displays are often turned on their side with the frequencies displayed vertically, as in Exhibit 3.6J. The information conveyed is the same in all these types of displays.   ▪

EXHIBIT 3.6A
Computer-Generated Histogram
of Business Outlook

```
Histogram of Outlook    N=278
Each * represents two observations

Midpoint    Count
       1       37   ******************
       2       40   ********************
       3       66   *********************************
       4       73   ************************************
       5       49   *************************
       6       13   *******
```

EXHIBIT 3.6B
Histogram of Business Outlook
(alternative form)

Outlook   N = 278

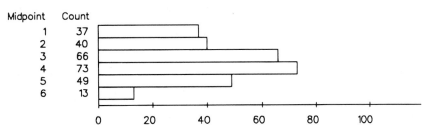

With continuous data that may assume a large number of possible values, the data must be grouped into **class intervals** to construct a histogram.

class intervals

EXAMPLE   3.6B

Let us divide the photocopy data in Exhibit 3.2A (extremes excluded) into five class intervals of equal length. The data range from a low value of 349 to a high value of 621, a difference of 272, so the class intervals need to be about $272/5 = 54.4$ in length. The determination of class intervals is somewhat arbitrary. A common approach is to pick a starting value that has more decimal places than any data value. Then none of the data values will coincide with an interval endpoint. This avoids having to decide which interval such a data value belongs to. If we decide to use a fractional starting value, we can use an integral interval length, which simplifies the addition.

We choose to start our system of intervals at 348.5 and to use an interval length of 55. The resulting five intervals are [348.5, 403.5), [403.5, 458.5), [458.5, 513.5), [513.5, 568.5), and [568.5, 623.5).[†] They cover all the values between 348.5 and 623.5 and do not overlap. Now we determine the class frequencies by counting the number of data values that fall in each of the intervals. The simplest way to do this is to move sequentially through the data and to place a tally mark by the interval that contains a data value. The first data value in Exhibit 3.2A is 416, and this puts a tally mark by the second interval because 416 falls between 403.5 and 458.5. The second data value in Exhibit 3.2A is 556, which falls in the fourth interval. The scheme below shows the results of tallying all the data values in Exhibit 3.2A.

[†]The notation [means the adjacent number is included in the interval; the) means the adjacent number is not included in the interval.

Interval	Tally	Count	Histogram Display
[348.5, 403.5)	||||| |||	8	********
[403.5, 458.5)	|||||		6	******
[458.5, 513.5)			1	*
[513.5, 568.5)	||||	4	****
[568.5, 623.5)	|||||	5	*****
Total		24	

The count is also called the *frequency* of the interval. Also shown is a simple histogram display. This is all there is to a frequency histogram. ▪

Compare the above frequency histogram with the stem-and-leaf displays in Section 3.4 and with the dotplots in Exhibits 3.2B and 3.2D. Each statistical tool displays the same data in a slightly different way. Remember that the histogram replaces the data with a system of intervals and their corresponding frequencies. It thus can reduce a sizable set of data to a small number of quantities that display the distribution of the data graphically.

Computer-Generated Histograms

Statistical computer packages can produce histograms at the touch of a few keys. Exhibit 3.6C shows such a histogram of the full photocopy data set. The software chose the class width of 100 and chose to use 11 class intervals to cover the complete data set. Exhibit 3.6D shows the corresponding histogram when values less than 300 and greater than 650 are excluded. Here the software chose to use 8 intervals each of width 40.

EXHIBIT 3.6C
Computer-Generated Histogram
of Photocopy Data (extremes
included)

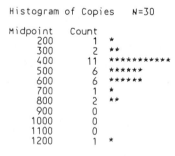

```
Histogram of Copies    N=30

Midpoint    Count
   200        1    *
   300        2    **
   400       11    ***********
   500        6    ******
   600        6    ******
   700        1    *
   800        2    **
   900        0
  1000        0
  1100        0
  1200        1    *
```

E X H I B I T **3.6D**
Computer-Generated Histogram
of Photocopy Data (extremes
excluded)

```
Histogram of Copies   N=30
Two observations below the first class
Four observations above the last class

Midpoint   Count
     350      4    ****
     390      4    ****
     430      4    ****
     470      2    **
     510      1    *
     550      4    ****
     590      3    ***
     630      2    **
```

Comparing Distributions

Histograms (and dotplots) are useful for comparing distributions.

E X A M P L E   **3.6C**

Winegard Company, based in Burlington, Iowa, is a worldwide manufacturer of television-reception products, antennas, satellite dishes, and so forth. One of their many manufacturing processes involves a punching operation to produce end caps for a particular satellite-dish antenna system. The punching operation is intended to produce an end cap with a certain specified dimension (width outside, bend-to-bend). However, as always, variation is present in the dimension actually obtained. Using the present punch method, 50 end caps were produced and measured, resulting in the data set[†] given in Exhibit 3.6E.

Exhibit 3.6F gives a histogram of these data. Most of the values are in the range from 1.798 to 1.800, with a few values below and a few above. Design specifications require that the measured dimension lie in the range $1.772 \pm .022$ inch. As the histogram clearly shows, none of the 50 parts meet those requirements. To reduce the dimension to more acceptable levels, a die change was introduced into the punch operation. Exhibit 3.6G lists the 50 data points observed after the change. The histogram of these data, given in Exhibit 3.6H, shows that the die change was indeed effective. The pair of histograms for both the before and after data in Exhibit 3.6I are done on the same scale to display the change even more dramatically.   ■

[†]Data courtesy of Mark R. Sellergren, former Vice President–Finance, Winegard Company.

E X H I B I T **3.6E**
Punch Data Before Die Change

```
filename: PUNCH_B.DAT
Winegard punch data before die change
(Source: Mark Sellergren, Winegard, Inc.,
Burlington, Iowa)
January 13, 1988. Width outside (in inches), bend-to-bend
1.799  1.799  1.800  1.798  1.798  1.798  1.798  1.798  1.799  1.798
1.799  1.797  1.800  1.800  1.800  1.800  1.797  1.798  1.799  1.798
1.798  1.801  1.799  1.799  1.797  1.798  1.802  1.800  1.798  1.797
1.798  1.798  1.798  1.800  1.799  1.799  1.799  1.799  1.798  1.799
1.798  1.798  1.798  1.798  1.798  1.799  1.798  1.798  1.802  1.799
```

E X H I B I T **3.6F**
Histogram of Punch Data Before
Die Change

```
Histogram of Before    N=50

Midpoint    Count
 1.79700      4    ****
 1.79800     22    **********************
 1.79900     14    **************
 1.80000      7    *******
 1.80100      1    *
 1.80200      2    **
```

E X H I B I T **3.6G**
Punch Data After Die Change

```
filename: PUNCH_A.DAT
Winegard punch data after die change
(Source: Mark Sellergren, Winegard, Inc.,
Burlington, Iowa)
January 13, 1988. Width outside (in inches), bend to bend
1.780  1.778  1.779  1.779  1.779  1.779  1.779  1.778  1.780  1.779
1.779  1.777  1.778  1.779  1.777  1.779  1.780  1.779  1.779  1.779
1.779  1.777  1.778  1.779  1.779  1.778  1.780  1.779  1.779  1.778
1.779  1.778  1.777  1.778  1.780  1.779  1.778  1.777  1.778  1.776
1.778  1.778  1.778  1.777  1.778  1.779  1.779  1.779  1.780  1.779
```

E X H I B I T **3.6H**
Histogram of Punch Data After
Die Change

```
Histogram of After    N=50

Midpoint    Count
 1.77600      1    *
 1.77700      6    ******
 1.77800     14    **************
 1.77900     23    ***********************
 1.78000      6    ******
```

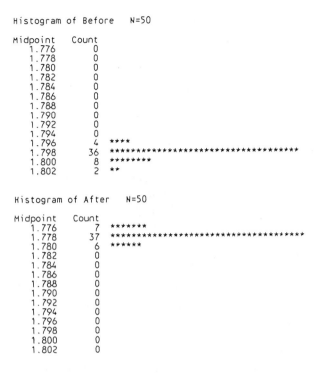

```
Histogram of Before   N=50

Midpoint    Count
   1.776        0
   1.778        0
   1.780        0
   1.782        0
   1.784        0
   1.786        0
   1.788        0
   1.790        0
   1.792        0
   1.794        0
   1.796        4   ****
   1.798       36   ***********************************
   1.800        8   ********
   1.802        2   **


Histogram of After   N=50

Midpoint    Count
   1.776        7   *******
   1.778       37   *************************************
   1.780        6   ******
   1.782        0
   1.784        0
   1.786        0
   1.788        0
   1.790        0
   1.792        0
   1.794        0
   1.796        0
   1.798        0
   1.800        0
   1.802        0
```

Relative Frequency Histograms

Relative frequency histograms are used to compare the distributions of two sets of data for which the numbers of observations in the two data sets are different. To take a hypothetical case, suppose the counts for two sets of data are as follows:

	Counts	
Interval	**Data Set A**	**Data Set B**
I1	40	80
I2	59	118
I3	102	204
I4	69	138
I5	37	74
Total	307	614

For each interval, the count in data set B is twice as large as the count in data set A, so the frequency histogram of data set B has piles of asterisks that are twice as high as the corresponding ones from data set A. Yet the two distributions are identical in terms of the proportions of observations allocated to the intervals. The proportions of observations allocated to the intervals are called *relative frequencies*. A histogram display in which the lengths of the piles of asterisks are equal to the relative frequencies of the intervals is called **relative frequency histogram**. When two distributions allocate observations to the same intervals, the relative frequency

**relative frequency
histogram**

histograms may be compared to discover similarities or differences between the two distributions.

Changing the number of intervals, the starting value, and the length of intervals changes the appearance of histograms for the same set of data, especially if the data set is small. Histograms are best used for data sets with at least 100 observations, at which size the appearance remains more constant.

EXAMPLE 3.6D

Exhibit 3.6J shows a histogram of the percentage changes in the Buffalo, New York, flour price index series introduced in Chapter 2. Here there are 99 data points. The histogram uses eight class intervals and is drawn by the software package Stata.[TM] For comparison purposes, Exhibit 3.6K shows histograms of the same data set based on 3, 5, 15, 25, and 50 class intervals, respectively. As more and more intervals are used, more detail in the distribution is displayed but at the expense of producing a more jagged graph, which may obscure the underlying smoothness of the distribution. On the other hand, too few intervals, say three, produces too much smoothing and nearly all of the details in the distribution are lost.

A reasonable guideline is to use about $\sqrt{n}$ intervals when dealing with n data points. In this case, we have a data set of 99 points, so about 10 intervals should be used. Statistical smoothing methods beyond the scope of this book can be used to yield smooth histogram-type displays. Exhibit 3.6L shows such a curve for the percentage changes of the flour price index. ■

EXHIBIT **3.6J**
Relative Frequency Histogram for Percentage Change in Flour Price Index

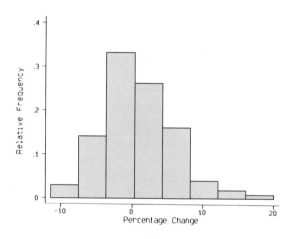

E X H I B I T **3.6K**   Relative Frequency Histograms for Percentage Change in Flour Price Index—Various Numbers of Intervals

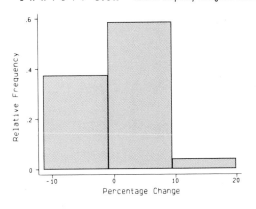

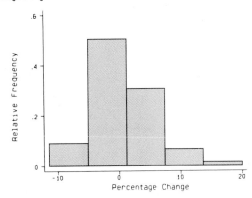

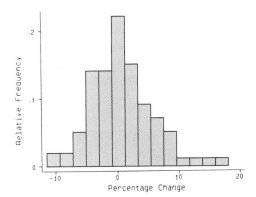

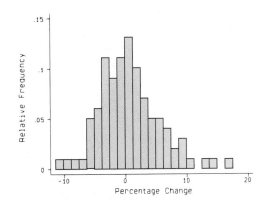

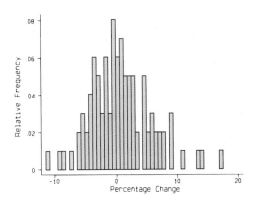

E X H I B I T   **3.6L**
Smooth Histogram for
Percentage Change in Flour Price
Index

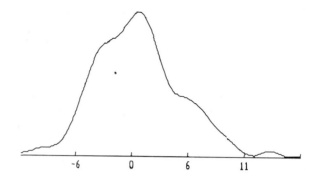

Density Histograms

When using data from published sources, we often find the data reported in class intervals of varying length, especially when the raw data set is large and when there are relatively few large observations. To display the distribution of the data summarized in this fashion without distortion, we must use histograms that use area to show relative frequency. They are called **density histograms** and are more complex than the histograms discussed above.

density histograms

E X A M P L E   **3.6E**

We will use the data in Exhibit 3.6M to illustrate the construction of a density histogram. The measured variable will be called revenue.
The steps in constructing a density histogram are as follows:

- Choose the intervals, as has been done in Exhibit 3.6M (column 1), or use the intervals reported in the published source.
- Determine the frequencies for each interval, or use the frequencies provided in the published source.
- Calculate the relative frequency (column 3) for each interval by dividing the frequency (column 2) by the total count (100).
- Calculate the length of each interval by subtracting the lower endpoint from the upper endpoint (column 4).

E X H I B I T   **3.6M**
Data for Construction of Density
Histogram

Interval	Frequency	Relative Frequency	Length of Interval	Density
[20, 40)	5	0.05	20	0.0025
[40, 60)	10	0.10	20	0.0050
[60, 120)	45	0.45	60	0.0075
[120, 180)	30	0.30	60	0.0050
[180, 500)	10	0.10	320	0.0003125
Totals	100	1.00	480	

- Calculate the density (column 5) for each interval by dividing the relative frequency by the corresponding interval length.
- Plot a bar over each interval whose height is the density for that interval.

Exhibit 3.6N shows the resulting graph.

Note that the areas of the rectangles are equal to the relative frequencies of the intervals. For example, the area of the bar over the interval whose endpoints are 120 and 180 is $60 \times 0.0050 = 0.30$, which is the relative frequency for that interval.

In more succinct form:

$$\text{Density} = \frac{\text{relative frequency}}{\text{length of interval}}$$

and

$$\text{Area} = \text{class interval length} \times \text{density} \quad \blacksquare$$

EXHIBIT **3.6N**
Density Histogram for Revenue
Data

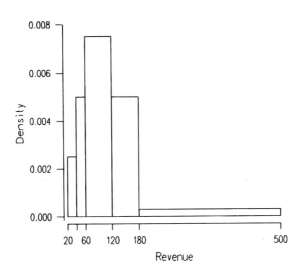

You see that density measures *the proportion of observations in the class interval per amount of interval length*. A wide interval with many observations may have the same density as a narrow interval with few observations. The intervals [40, 60) and [120, 180) in Exhibit 3.6N provide an example. Another important observation is that the total area of the rectangles in Exhibit 3.6N is 1. This is a property of density histograms by construction. The requirement that all density histograms have a total area of 1 makes comparison between histograms meaningful even when the histograms have intervals over varying lengths.

EXAMPLE 3.6F

Let us use density histograms to compare two real data sets related to family income, one for black Americans, the other for whites (Exhibit 3.6O). We are studying how many white families and black families fall within various income levels. The Census Bureau summarized the data in unequal intervals of income.

All the families with incomes over $50,000 are grouped into an open-ended category, one that has no upper limit. Because it is not possible to construct a density histogram with open-ended intervals we will omit this group and use only the first five categories. The subtotals given in Exhibit 3.6O are used to compute relative frequencies and densities. Exhibit 3.6P shows the computations.

EXHIBIT **3.6O**
Numbers of U.S. Families in Income Categories, by Race, 1982

Income Interval	Number of Families (in thousands)	
	White Population	Black Population
$0–$5,000	2,399	1,069
$5,000–$10,000	5,452	1,389
$10,000–$15,000	7,007	1,060
$15,000–$25,000	13,615	1,413
$25,000–$50,000	19,628	1,346
Subtotal	48, 101	6, 277
$50,000+	5,168	137
Grand total	53, 269	6, 414

Source: U.S. Bureau of the Census, *Statistical Abstract of the United States: 1984*,104th ed. (Washington, D.C.: U.S. Government Printing Office, 1983), Tables 37 and 38.

E X H I B I T **3.6P**
Computations for Density
Histograms for Data in
Exhibit 3.6O (incomes in
$1000 units)

White Population

Income Interval (in $1000 units)	Frequency	Relative Frequency	Interval Length	Density
0–5	2,399	0.0498742	5	0.0099748
5–10	5,452	0.1133448	5	0.0226690
10–15	7,007	0.1456727	5	0.0291345
15–25	13,615	0.2830502	10	0.0283050
25–50	19,628	0.4080581	25	0.0163223
Total	48, 101	1.0000000		

Black Population

Income Interval (in $1000 units)	Frequency	Relative Frequency	Interval Length	Density
0–5	1,069	0.1703043	5	0.0340609
5–10	1,389	0.2212841	5	0.0442568
10–15	1,060	0.1688705	5	0.0337741
15–25	1.413	0.2251075	10	0.0225108
25–50	1,346	0.2144336	25	0.0085773
Total	6, 277	1.0000000		

Exhibit 3.6Q shows the histograms for the white and black populations in a convenient back-to-back format. The exhibit shows that the black population is more dense in the three lower income intervals and less dense in the two higher income intervals than the white population. The black population has the greatest density in the interval [$5000, $10,000), whereas the white population has the greatest density in the interval [$10,000, $15,000). These conclusions would have been difficult to draw without the density histograms because intervals are not all the same length. The interval with the greatest frequency in the black population is [$15,000, $25,000), while the interval with greatest frequency in the white population is [$25,000, $50,000), but these intervals are not of equal length. The density histogram displays the correct relationship among the intervals. ▪

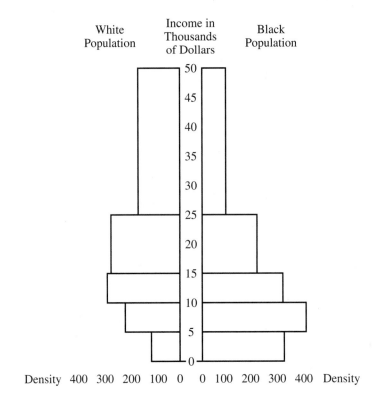

EXHIBIT **3.6Q**
Back-to-Back Density Histograms
for Comparison
(Density × 10,000)

SECTION

3.7 Exercises

3.7A   Explain the meaning of the term *distribution*.

3.7B   The following table shows median family incomes by state for the years 1969 and 1979. The incomes by state for a given year have no longitudinal component. Remember that statisticians call such data *cross-sectional*. If we try to compare the distributions of median incomes for the two years, then we encounter a longitudinal component.

Part I

In this part of the exercise we ask you to prepare frequency plots of the cross section of data from 1969.

a   Prepare a stem-and-leaf display. Use the ten-thousands and thousands digits for the stem and the hundreds digits for the leaves. In other words, chop off the ones and tens digits. You may wish to write the names of the states near the lines where their leaves are located. This will serve to order the states by median income.

b   Prepare a dotplot of the 1969 cross section. Compare the dotplot to the stem-and-leaf display in part (a). Do you gain insight from the additional detail in the dotplot?

State	Median Family Income		State	Median Family Income	
	1969	1979		1969	1979
Alabama	$ 7,263	$16,347	Montana	$ 8,509	$18,413
Alaska	12,441	28,395	Nebraska	8,562	19,122
Arizona	9,185	19,017	Nevada	10,687	21,311
Arkansas	6,271	14,641	New Hampshire	9,682	19,723
California	10,729	21,537	New Jersey	11,402	22,906
Colorado	9,552	21,279	New Mexico	7,845	16,928
Connecticut	11,808	23,149	New York	10,609	20,180
Delaware	10,209	20,817	North Carolina	7,770	16,792
D.C.	9,576	19,099	North Dakota	7,836	18,023
Florida	8,261	17,280	Ohio	10,309	20,909
Georgia	8,165	17,414	Oklahoma	7,720	17,668
Hawaii	11,552	22,750	Oregon	9,487	20,027
Idaho	8,380	17,492	Pennsylvania	9,554	19,995
Illinois	10,957	22,746	Rhode Island	9,733	19,448
Indiana	9,966	20,535	South Carolina	7,620	16,978
Iowa	9,016	20,052	South Dakota	7,490	15,993
Kansas	8,690	19,707	Tennessee	7,446	16,564
Kentucky	7,439	16,444	Texas	8,486	19,618
Louisiana	7,527	18,088	Utah	9,320	20,024
Maine	8,205	16,167	Vermont	8,928	17,205
Maryland	11,057	23,112	Virginia	9,044	20,018
Massachusetts	10,833	21,166	Washington	10,404	20,018
Michigan	11,029	22,107	West Virginia	7,414	17,308
Minnesota	9,928	21,185	Wisconsin	10,065	20,915
Missippi	6,068	14,591	Wyoming	8,944	22,430
Missouri	8,908	18,784			

c Prepare a density histogram of the 1969 cross section. Do you find it convenient to use intervals of equal length or do you prefer intervals of unequal length?

Part II

Repeat the items in Part I for the 1979 cross section. On the basis of the plots you have prepared, compare the 1969 to the 1979 cross section. If you ordered the states by median income, are the orderings the same in the two years? Do you feel the data provide a basis for predicting median family income in 1989? In 1980? Explain why or why not. (Filename: STATEINC.DAT.)

3.7C In Exercise 2.3G, you computed a series of quarter-to-quarter changes in GDP. Prepare an appropriate frequency plot of these changes. Describe the distribution of the changes.

3.7D Graph a histogram of the percentage changes for the Kansas City flour price index. The data appear in Exercise 2.11A. Compare and contrast this histogram with the corresponding one for the Buffalo, New York, flour price index shown in Exhibit 3.6J. (Filename: KCFLOUR.DAT.)

3.7E The following data show the number of research articles published in statistical theory during the period 1980 through 1986 in nine leading journals.

Number of Articles	Journal
796	*Annals of Statistics*
611	*Biometrika*
34	*Econometric Theory*
80	*International Statistical Review*
610	*Journal of the American Statistical Association*
146	*Journal of Multivariate Analysis*
129	*Journal of Time Series Analysis*
286	*Journal of the Royal Statistical Society* (Series B)
135	*Sankhya* (Series A)

Source: P. C. B. Phillips, I. Choi, and P. Z. Schochert, "Worldwide Institutional and Individual Rankings in Statistical Theory by Journal Publications Over the Period 1980–1986," *Econometric Theory*, 4 (1988), 1–34.

a Display these data in a bar chart ordering the journals from most to least articles.

b Would a density histogram be appropriate for these data?

3.7F In Exercise 2.3B, you collected a sequence of 50 to 100 checkbook balances and computed the balance-to-balance changes. Prepare appropriate histograms of the balances and the changes. For which sequence do you feel the histogram yields more useful insights, if any? Explain why.

3.7G Collect a set of cross-sectional data and make an appropriate histogram to display the distribution of the data. Describe the distribution. What predictive value do you feel the data have, if any? [*Suggestion:* Studying the price of a pound of coffee at the food outlets in your town or city makes for an interesting data set. You can study the variation across brands as well as across stores.]

3.7H Use the data in Exercise 2.11D. Compute the percentage changes in the Japanese stock price average and those in the Dow Jones 30 Industrials Average. Make back-to-back histograms of the percentage changes and compare the distributions. (Filename: JAPANINV.DAT.)

SECTION

3.8 Distribution Displays and Sequence Plots

Chapter 2 presented ways of looking at the longitudinal (time) aspects of a set of data. The current chapter has focused on histograms, which display a set of data without regard to the time dimension. Histograms and sequence plots are designed to show different features of data.

EXAMPLE 3.8A

Histograms of two sequences are given in Exhibit 3.8A. Notice that the histograms are identical! As batches of numbers, the distributions of the data sets are the same. (In fact, if we listed the data, you would see that the data values are identical.)

However, Exhibits 3.8B and 3.8C give the sequence plots for each of the series. What a difference! Series 1 seems quite random over time, while

EXHIBIT **3.8A**
Histograms for Series 1 and 2

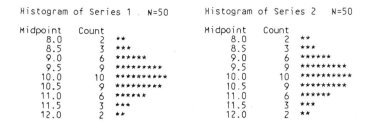

EXHIBIT **3.8B**
Sequence Plot for Series 1

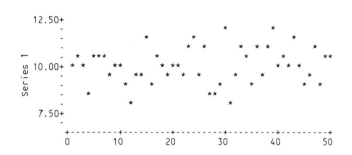

EXHIBIT **3.8C**
Sequence Plot for Series 2

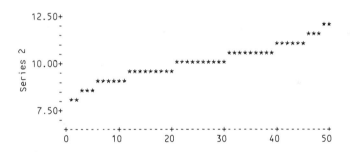

series 2 shows a steady upward pattern over its full extent. Histograms give *no information whatsoever* about the time aspects of the series.

If the sequence plots of Exhibits 3.8B and 3.8C are entered as documents into a word processor or editor and all the horizontal spaces between the plotted data points and the vertical column above 0 are deleted, the asterisks are pulled toward the vertical axis and the histogram display in Exhibit 3.8D is produced.[†] By doing this, the time aspect of the series has been removed. Compare these displays to each other and to the histograms in Exhibit 3.8A. Except for the fact that the larger numbers are at the top, the displays are identical!

Think about predicting the next value of series 1 and of series 2. If you were given only the histogram, you could make a good guess at the next value in series 1 because the sequence plot shows the series to be random. Your best guess is probably the middle value of the distribution, namely 10. For series 2, however, the histogram is not a good guide to the future. The information in the sequence plot is vital to making a good prediction. When you are confronted with having to make a prediction or asked to use a prediction made by someone else, you will find the longitudinal context of the prediction to be an important issue. Always ask these questions: What is the longitudinal context? (Is a sequence plot available?) Has the prediction properly taken this context into account? ■

EXHIBIT **3.8D**
Collapsed "Histograms" from
Sequence Plots

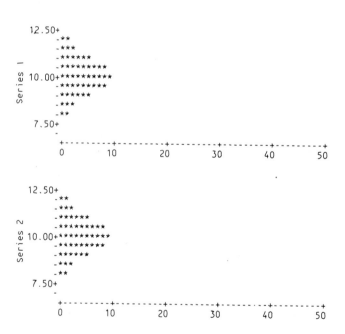

[†]Idea from Professor Harry V. Roberts, University of Chicago.

SECTION

3.9 Exercises

3.9A   Explain why frequency plots do not display the time dimension. Why is the time dimension important in decision making?

3.9B   Compare and contrast the information given in the sequence plot of the Deere & Co. machining data in Exercise 2.5A with the distribution given in the dotplot of Exercise 3.3E or the stem-and-leaf display of Exercise 3.5C. (Filename: DEERE1.DAT.)

3.9C   Prepare a histogram of the Buffalo, New York, flour price index data given in Exhibit 2.10A. Compare the information given in the histogram to the information given in the sequence plot in Exhibit 2.10B. Would the histogram help in guessing the next—that is, December 1980—value of the index? (Filename: BUFLOUR.DAT.)

3.9D   Compare and contrast the information given in the sequence plot of the percentage change in the Buffalo, New York, flour price index data in Exhibit 2.10D with the distribution given in Exhibit 3.6J. What is your guess for the next—that is, December 1980—percentage change in the series? What is your guess for the next value of the index? (Filename: BUFLOUR.DAT.)

Chapter Summary

Dotplots, stem-and-leaf displays, and histograms are tools for displaying the cross-sectional distribution of a data set. Dotplots are most useful for small-sized data sets, stem-and-leaf displays for medium-sized data sets, and histograms for large-sized data sets. All of them convey, in one way or another, the frequencies with which numerical outcomes occur in the data set. This information is useful in understanding the nature of a process. For processes that evolve more-or-less randomly over time, such information is the most useful in making predictions about the future evolution of the process. For processes that have trends, that meander, or have cycles, however, the information in the cross-sectional distribution is not sufficient for making good predictions and may not even be relevant. Thus the longitudinal context of a cross-sectional distribution must be understood in order to use it properly for decision making.

Supplementary Exercises for Chapter 3

3A   A data file showing the sizes of 84 football stadiums in the United States follows.

a   Display the stem-and-leaf diagram for these data. Divide the leaf digits into equal-sized groups as was done in Exhibit 3.4B.

b   Display the dotplot of these data.

c   Display a histogram of these data.

d   Compare the three plots obtained in parts (a), (b), and (c). Which of the three displays best portrays the distribution of these data? Are there features that can be seen in one but not another?

```
# filename: STADIUMS.DAT
# Size of U.S. university football stadiums (in 1000's)
# (Source: The World Almanac and Book of Facts, 1985)
   59   Alabama                    50   North Carolina
   70   Arizona State              30   Northern Illinois
   52   Arizona                    50   Northwestern
   42   Arkansas                   60   Notre Dame
   72   Auburn                     85   Ohio State
   48   Baylor                     51   Oklahoma State
   32   Boston College             75   Oklahoma
   30   Bowling Green State        41   Oregon State
   66   Brigham Young              41   Oregon
   77   California-Berkeley        84   Penn State
   73   Clemson                    61   Pennsylvania
   52   Colorado                   56   Pittsburgh
   34   Duke                       46   Princeton
   35   East Carolina              69   Purdue
   55   Florida State              70   Rice
   72   Florida                    72   South Carolina
   58   Georgia Tech               33   Southern Mississippi
   82   Georgia                    85   Stanford
   37   Harvard                    50   Syracuse
   50   Hawaii                     91   Tennessee
   71   Illinois                   72   Texas A & M
   52   Indiana                    46   Texas Christian
   50   Iowa State                 52   Texas, El Paso
   66   Iowa                       47   Texas Tech
   42   Kansas State               80   Texas
   52   Kansas                     40   Tulsa
   30   Kent State                 47   U.S. Air Force Academy
   58   Kentucky                   39   U.S. Military Academy
   76   Louisiana State            30   U.S. Naval Academy
   36   Louisville                 30   Utah State
   45   Maryland                   35   Utah
   50   Memphis State              41   Vanderbilt
   76   Michigan State             52   Virginia Tech
  102   Michigan                   42   Virginia
   32   Mississippi State          30   Wake Forest
   42   Mississippi                40   Washington State
   62   Missouri                   60   Washington
   74   Nebraska                   50   West Virginia
   32   Nevada-Las Vegas           52   Wichita State
   30   New Mexico State           77   Wisconsin
   31   New Mexico                 34   Wyoming
   46   North Carolina State       71   Yale
```

3B The data file below lists the county population sizes for the 99 counties of Iowa in 1980.

   a Display the stem-and-leaf display for these data. Divide the leaf digits into equal-sized groups as was done in Exhibit 3.4B.

   b Display the dotplot of these data.

   c Display a histogram of these data.

   d Compare the three plots obtained in parts (a), (b), and (c). Which of the three displays best portrays the distribution of these data? Are there features that can be seen in one but not another?

```
filename: COUNTIES.DAT
Population of Iowa counties - 1980 census (in 1000's)
(Source: The World Almanac and Book of Facts, 1985)
(in alphabetical order)
10 6 15 16 9 24 138 26 25 23 21 18 14 23 17 19 48 16 15 9 20 21 57 19
30 9 10 19 46 16 94 13 25 20 13 9 12 14 12 18 14 22 16 19 11 12 9 15
23 36 16 82 20 13 22 43 170 12 10 13 13 23 30 42 13 12 12 9 13 40 17
8 19 13 25 11 303 87 19 6 14 160 15 31 72 20 8 14 9 40 35 20 8 46 13
22 101 9 16
```

3C The data file that follows gives information on three variables—calories, sodium content, and percent edible—for eight brands of popcorn. In addition, these variables are reported for two different popping methods, hot-oil popped and hot-air popped, for each brand.

   a Display a dotplot of the calorie content of all 16 data points. Comment on the display.

b Display the dotplots of calorie content separately for hot-oil popped and hot-air popped. Comment on these dotplots.

c Repeat parts (a) and (b) for sodium content and percent edible. Do any clear differences show up between the two popping methods for these variables?

```
filename: POPCORN.DAT
Popcorn data
(Source: Consumer Reports, June 1989)
calories, sodium, percent edible
hot-oil popped=1, hot-air popped=0
182 1 87 1
133 1 98 1
152 2 93 1
141 1 93 1
131 1 97 1
135 1 97 1
127 2 98 1
138 1 96 1
 97 1 87 0
 81 1 92 0
 72 1 96 0
 71 1 97 0
 60 0 94 0
 79 2 91 0
 68 1 96 0
 79 1 95 0
```

3D The data file below shows the calories, sodium content, and percent saturated fat (all per tablespoon) for several brands of butter and margarine. There are 37 margarine brands and 9 butters.

```
filename: BUTTER.DAT
Butter and margarine data
(Source: Consumer Reports, September 1989)
calories, sodium, % saturated fat
per tablespoon
butter=1, margarine=0
100 115 64 1      100 115   9 0
 63  75 65 1      100  95  18 0
103  88 64 1      100   0  18 0
103   0 64 1       90  90  10 0
 99 110 64 1      100  95  18 0
 99   0 64 1      100  95  18 0
100   2 64 1      100   0  18 0
 96 115 66 1       60 100  14 0
 62   1 66 1       90 105  20 0
 90  95 20 0      100   0  18 0
100 115 18 0       60 110  19 0
100  95 18 0      100 100  18 0
 90  90 20 0       60 110  14 0
 60  75 14 0      100 120  18 0
100 115  9 0       60 110  14 0
100 100 18 0       80  70  25 0
100 115 18 0      100  95  18 0
 80 110 22 0      100  95  18 0
100 100 18 0       70 100  14 0
100  95 27 0       50   0  17 0
100  95 18 0      100 115  18 0
 90  90 20 0      100 110  18 0
100 100 19 0       50  50  17 0
```

a For the sodium content variable, construct histograms separately for butter and margarine. Since there are only 9 butters but 37 margarines, use relative frequency histograms so that the two may be compared.

b Repeat part (a) for the variables calories and percent saturated fat. Comment on the distributions.

3E The following table displays the frequencies of sales commissions at three levels in two sales regions.

Sales Commission	Region 1	Region 2
[0, $10,000)	20	10
[$10,000, $20,000)	40	20
[$20,000, $30,000)	40	20
Total	100	50

a   Graph the frequency histograms for each of the two regions.
b   Convert the frequencies to relative frequencies.
c   Graph the two relative frequency histograms.
d   Compare the distributions of sales in the two regions.
e   Construct a back-to-back relative frequency histogram for the two regions.

3F   The following table displays the frequencies of sales commissions at three levels in two sales regions.

Sales Commission	Region 1	Region 2
[0, $10,000)	10	10
[$10,000, $20,000)	20	20
[$20,000, $30,000)	70	20
Total	100	50

a   Graph the frequency histograms for each of the two regions.
b   Convert the frequencies to relative frequencies.
c   Graph the two relative frequency histograms.
d   Compare the distributions of sales in the two regions.
e   Construct a back-to-back relative frequency histogram for the two regions.

Glossary for Chapter 3

class frequencies   The frequencies or counts of data values within the class intervals.

class intervals   Intervals dividing up the values of a variable.

cross-sectional   Data where the time dimension is either absent or ignored.

density histogram   A graphic display of a distribution especially useful with unequal-width class intervals.

dotplot   The display of a distribution on a number line with no grouping.

frequency histogram	A graphic display of a frequency distribution.
relative frequency histogram	A graphic display of a relative frequency distribution especially useful for comparing distributions of different-sized data sets.
stem-and-leaf display	A display of a distribution using the digits of the data to form the groupings and graphic display of frequencies.

4

Summarizing Continuous Data

Chapter Objectives

After mastering this chapter, you will be able to:

- Summarize a distribution with its median, quartiles, and range

- Summarize a mound-shaped distribution with its mean and standard deviation

- Explain the meaning of degrees of freedom

- Calculate the effect of a linear transformation on the mean, median, interquartile range, range, and standard deviation

- Standardize a variable

4.1 Introduction

In the preceding chapters, we saw how to present continuous data in graphs. A time sequence plot reveals important time-related aspects of a data set—for example, seasonality or trend. A dotplot, stem-and-leaf display, or histogram shows how the observations are distributed. Sometimes, however, certain aspects of data must be summarized or described with just a few numbers.

In the first quarter of 1988, Nissan U.S.A. car sales were down 24% compared to the first quarter of the previous year—bad news for Nissan. Why had sales gone down? To address the problem and develop future marketing, planners at Nissan needed current data on who was (or was not) buying their cars and why. A profile giving income, education, occupation, marital status, and other information on current buyers would be useful. Based on extensive market-survey research,[†] Nissan found (among many other things) that the median age of buyers was 43 years, median family income was $54,000, and the average family size of buyers was 2.6 persons.

[†]Maritz and Rogers, 1988, "Early Model New Car Buyers' Study," as quoted in *PC Week*, June 28, 1988.

What aspects of the data do these single numbers describe? How can we interpret an average of 2.6 persons? What other numbers might help to characterize the data? This chapter investigates such numerical descriptors.

statistics

Numbers calculated from a data set are **statistics**. Statistics used to describe various features of a data set are typically called *descriptive statistics*.

4.2 Statistics Based on Ordered Values

Many useful statistics are calculated from the data values once they have been put into numerical order, say from the smallest to the largest. With a small data set, this is easily accomplished by hand. For larger sets, a statistical computer package is used. Exhibit 4.2A gives the ordered values for the photocopy data presented in Exhibit 1.3A. It often helps to know what values of a data set lie in the middle of the distribution. We may also want to know how widely the values range, how many values fall within specific intervals, and whether the values are arranged at all symmetrically around the middle of the distribution. Our first task is to define and discuss a statistic that measures the middle or center of a distribution.

EXHIBIT 4.2A
Photocopy Data, Ordered from
Smallest to Largest

238	274	349	362	362	364	374	390	393	395	416
440	447	447	456	456	505	530	532	547	556	579
589	607	616	621	741	780	797	1199			

Median

median

The middle value in an ordered list of numbers is called the **median**. In Exhibit 4.2A there are 30 observations and the 15th and 16th in order are both equal to 456. The median number of photocopies per day is thus 456 copies. In general, the specific value for the median depends on whether the data set contains an even or odd number of observations and, in the even case, whether or not the two middle values are the same or different. To find the median of a set of data,

1 Arrange the numbers in numerical order from smallest to largest.
2 If the number of data points, n, is odd, the median is the middle value in the ordered list. It is located by counting $(n + 1)/2$ positions from either end of the ordered list.
3 If n is even, the median is the average of the two middle data points. That is, it is the average of the data points at positions $n/2$ and $(n/2) + 1$.

For the ordered data set 3, 5, 5, 6, 7, 9, 9, the median is 6. For the data set 1, 4, 5, 7, the median is $(4 + 5)/2 = 4.5$. *The median value has the property that, as nearly as possible, half the data are below and half the data are above that value.*

The median may also be readily found from a stem-and-leaf display.

EXAMPLE **4.2A**

Exhibit 4.2B repeats Exhibit 3.4A—the computer-generated stem-and-leaf display for the full photocopy data. The display shows the number of data points, $n = 30$. In addition, the first column gives a cumulative count of the number of data on that line or on lines toward the nearer extreme. The line that contains the median shows a noncumulative count, in parentheses, of the values associated with that stem alone. Thus we need to look for the 15th and 16th observations, which are in the stem labeled 4. We see that the leaves for the 15th and 16th data points are both 5, corresponding to 50, so that, to the accuracy available due to the chopping of the tens digits, the median is 450. ∎

EXHIBIT **4.2B**
Stem-and-Leaf Display for
Photocopy Data (Exhibit 3.4A
repeated)

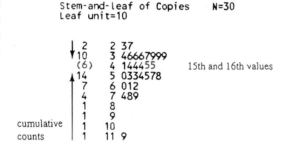

```
Stem-and-leaf of Copies     N=30
Leaf unit=10

     2     2 37
    10     3 46667999
    (6)    4 144455        15th and 16th values
    14     5 0334578
     7     6 012
     4     7 489
     1     8
     1     9
     1    10
     1    11 9
```

Influence of Extreme Values on the Median

Note that the median uses order information in the data but does not use the actual numbers to any large extent. The extremely large number of photocopies, 1199, that occurred on one day has essentially no effect on the median number of photocopies. If that 1199 had been any other number above 456—for example, 1999 or 524—the median would be unchanged. Similarly, small extreme values have no effect on the median. *The median is not influenced at all by the extreme observations in a data set.* For this reason, the median is often used as a typical or middle value for distributions that have many atypical extreme values, such as family income distributions as given in Exhibits 3.6O and 3.6Q, which contain a few very large values and a preponderance of smaller numbers.

Range

Another aspect of a data set is its *variability* around its middle. Exhibit 4.2C gives dotplots of two small data sets that have the same median but are grossly different in their amounts of variability around that middle value. If the median were used as a predictor of what might be observed in a future observation, we would surely be

E X H I B I T **4.2C**
Distributions with the Same
Median but Differing Variabilities

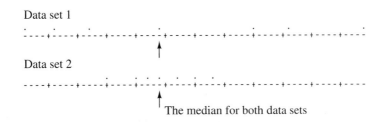

more confident in our prediction if data set 2 described the distribution than if data set 1 did.

range

The simplest measure of variability of a distribution is its **range**, which is the difference between the largest and smallest data value.

$$\text{Range} = \text{largest } y - \text{ smallest } y$$

The range for the photocopy data is $1199 - 238 = 961$ copies.

Although simple to compute, the range does have some rather undesirable features. By definition it is based on only the most extreme observations. Thus, it is highly sensitive to those extreme values and completely insensitive to the other observations and their variability. The distributions shown in Exhibit 4.2D have the same range (and same median for ease of comparison) but clearly have different patterns of variation. More sensible measures of variability are based on quartiles.

E X H I B I T **4.2D**
Distributions with the Same
Range but Differing Variabilities

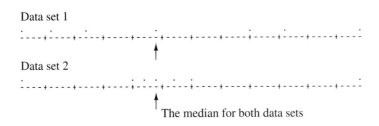

Quartiles and Interquartile Range

The median splits the ordered data set down the middle into two parts, each containing about half the observations. The first and third quartiles further divide these halves each in half. The **first quartile** is one-quarter up from the bottom of the ordered list; the **third quartile** is one-quarter down from the top of the ordered list. Thus the three descriptive statistics—the first quartile, the median, and the third quartile—divide the data set into quarters (thus the term *quartiles*). The first and third quartiles are computed as follows. To compute the first quartile,

first quartile, Q_1

1   Determine the lower half—that is, the ordered values less than the median.

2   The first quartile, denoted Q_1, is the median of the lower half.

To compute the third quartile,

third quartile, Q_3

1 Determine the upper half—that is, the ordered values greater than the median.

2 The third quartile, denoted Q_3, is the median of the upper half.

E X A M P L E   **4.2B**

To do an example by hand, suppose there are seven data points: 2.5, 2.1, 1.9, 3.6, 2.4, 1.2, 3.0. First arrange the data into numerical order: 1.2, 1.9, 2.1, 2.4, 2.5, 3.0, 3.6. The median is 2.4; the first quartile is $Q_1 = 1.9$; and the third quartile is $Q_3 = 3.0$. Exhibit 4.2E shows the corresponding dotplot with these statistics marked. ▪

E X H I B I T   **4.2E**
Quartiles and Median for a
Small Data Set

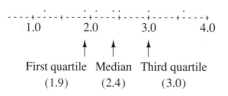

Several slightly different rules have been advocated for defining the quartiles.[†] It is important, however, not to get bogged down in specific computational details and lose the essence of the quartile idea: *the quartiles and median divide the ordered data set into quarters.* Notice that the quartiles are essentially unaffected by the actual values of the data that are below the first quartile or above the third quartile. Thus they are quite insensitive to extremely large or small values in the observations.

With the quartiles defined, our new measure of variability is simply the distance between the quartiles—the **interquartile range**:

interquartile range

$$\text{Interquartile range} = \text{third quartile} - \text{first quartile} = Q_3 - Q_1$$

From the discussion above, this measure is resistant to extreme observations. For the photocopy data, the interquartile range is equal to $598 - 382 = 216$ copies.

Exhibit 4.2F gives a display of the relationships among the median, quartiles, and interquartile range of a set of observations.

[†]Minitab uses a linear interpolation rule in its DESCRIBE command when computing quartiles. SAS has options for using any one of *five* slightly different definitions in its PROC UNIVARIATE.

E X H I B I T 4.2F
Interplay of Median, Quartiles,
and Interquartile Range

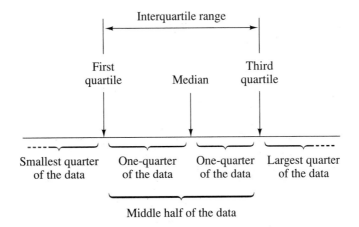

Symmetry and Skewness

symmetric distribution   Symmetry is a useful concept in data analysis. A distribution is **symmetric** if its left and right sides are mirror images of each other—every detail that appears on the left also appears on the right and at the same distance from the middle of the distribution. A substantial advantage of symmetric distributions is that the "middle" is unambiguously defined. When data are far from symmetrically distributed, analysts may very well disagree on a proper definition of the middle of the distribution. For a symmetric distribution the first quartile, Q_1, is the same distance below the median as the third quartile, Q_3, is above the median.

Many statistical procedures work best with (approximately) symmetrically distributed data. Exhibit 4.2G gives dotplots of three symmetric distributions. Notice that even though the third one is piled up at either end with very little data in the middle, it is still symmetric. Of course these artificial data sets are too good to be true. Exact symmetry will never be observed with real data. The histogram in Exhibit 3.6J shows that the distribution of percentage changes in the flour price index is approximately but not exactly symmetric.

E X H I B I T 4.2G
Dotplots of Symmetric
Distributions

```
Data Set 1
  .      .        .       .       . .       .        .         .    .
----+----+----+----+----+----+----+----+----+----
```

```
Data Set 2
         .        .        .      . .       .       .          .
----+----+----+----+----+----+----+----+----+----
```

```
Data Set 3
 . . ... . .     .        .           .       .       . . ... . .
----+----+----+----+----+----+----+----+----+----
```

Many real data sets are far from symmetric. The income distributions in Exhibit 3.6Q provide one example. Example 4.2C provides another.

E X A M P L E   **4.2C**

skewed distribution

Consider the data in Exhibit 4.2H and the frequency histogram in Exhibit 4.2I. The distribution of city sizes in Iowa is highly concentrated at the low end, with a few mid-sized cities and very few large cities. The median city size is computed as 8.5—that is, 8500 people. We say that the distribution is *skewed* toward the higher values. A **skewed distribution** is an asymmetric distribution with values stretched out on either the high or low end. The skewness in this example is also indicated by the quartiles, $Q_1 = 7000$ and $Q_3 = 25,000$, which are far from being equally spaced around the median of 8500.   ■

E X H I B I T   **4.2H**
Population of Iowa
Cities—1980 Census (in
thousands, only $\geq$ 5000
reported)

```
filename: CITIES.DAT
City populations of Iowa - 1980 census (in thousands, 5000 and over)
(Source: The World Almanac and Book of Facts, 1985)
(alphabetical order)
6 6 46 15 8 27 13 30 10 36 110 7 5 9 7 5 7 33 6 8 56 8 103 8 7 191 62
8 9 29 14 5 9 5 6 11 51 6 14 8 8 6 19 27 30 7 23 6 15 8 11 27 8 7
7 5 6 82 12 8 18 5 6 76 8 9 22 6
```

E X H I B I T   **4.2I**
Distribution of City Sizes in Iowa
(in thousands)

```
Histogram of Cities    N=68

Midpoint    Count
       0      38   ****************************************
      20      17   *****************
      40       5   *****
      60       3   ***
      80       2   **
     100       1   *
     120       1   *
     140       0
     160       0
     180       0
     200       1   *
```

S E C T I O N

4.3 Exercises

4.3A   Compute the median, quartiles, interquartile range, and range for each of the following data sets:

a   3, 5, 14, 9, 11, 6, 7   **b**   3, 5, 41, 9, 11, 6, 7   **c**   3, 4, 14, 9, 13, 6, 7

d   Comment on the differences among the statistics for the three data sets.

4.3B   A group of 50 employees has a median annual wage of $27,000. The highest-paid member of the group, Danforth, has an annual wage of $34,000. If Danforth gets a $4000 raise while all other wages increase by $1000, what now is the median annual wage for the employees?

4.3C   Suppose a group contains half men and half women. If we know the median salary for the men and the median salary for the women, can we calculate the median salary for everyone taken together? Why or why not?

4.3D   In the introduction to this chapter, we highlighted a study done for Nissan that showed that the median family income of Nissan buyers in 1988 was $54,000. Explain the meaning of this figure.

4.3E   An accountant at a car dealership keeps track of daily numbers of vehicles sold and the dollar value of the sales. Many of the days show no sales. When the accountant computes the median value of sales for a quarter, she does not include the no-sales days in her calculation—that is, she eliminates all zero values from her data before she computes the median.

   a   Construct a numerical example to show that an increase in the number of days on which sales occur could lead to a decrease in the median value of sales, using the accountant's approach.

   b   Write a brief memo explaining to management why the zero-sales days should be included in the calculation of median sales.

4.3F   The data file below gives exam scores for a class of 36 students.

   a   Prepare a dotplot of the scores.

   b   Use the rules outlined in this section to compute the range, median, quartiles, and interquartile range of the scores. Locate these statistics on the dotplot.

   c   Use statistical software to compute the quantities indicated in part (b). Compare them to the quantities you computed by hand. Determine the reason for any differences—that is, find out how the software algorithms differ from the algorithms given in the text.

   d   Comment on the skewness of the scores. (Filename: EXAMS1.DAT.)

```
filename: EXAMS1.DAT
First exam scores for an undergradute
business statistics course, 1989, n=36
54  62  69  69  72  72  74  75  76  76  76  76
77  77  78  81  82  82  82  82  82  82  82  84
84  86  86  87  89  90  90  92  92  92  94  96
```

4.3G   In Example 4.2C, the quartiles of the city sizes were computed by hand. Use statistical software to compute them and comment on any differences you find. Find out the algorithm used by the software and compare it to the algorithm given in the text. (Filename: CITIES.DAT.)

SECTION

4.4   Statistics Based on Averages

Some statistics are averages of a set of observations, their squares, their cubes, or higher powers. The most common of such statistics, the mean, is the arithmetic average. The mean is encountered every day with average miles per gallon of gasoline, average score on a midterm exam, average family size of Nissan car buyers, grade-point averages, and so on. In this section, it will be convenient to have some notation for data. Let n denote the number of observations in the data set, and let the individual observations be denoted $y_1, y_2, \ldots, y_n$.

Mean

mean

The **mean** of a set of data $y_1, y_2, \ldots, y_n$, denoted by $\bar{y}$, is given by the arithmetic average:

$$\bar{y} = \frac{y_1 + y_2 + \cdots + y_n}{n}$$

(Read the symbol $\bar{y}$ as "y bar.") As a simple example, the mean of the five numbers 3, 5, 2, 3, and 4 is $\bar{y} = (3 + 5 + 2 + 3 + 4)/5 = 17/5 = 3.4$. The median of these data is 3. In contrast to the median, the mean uses the actual value of each and every observation. Since the mean adds the actual data values, it generally makes sense only for continuous data.

An important exception occurs when we are dealing with binary variables. A *binary variable* assumes only the two values 0 and 1. For example, the variable might indicate gender with $1 = $ female, $0 = $ male. Here the total $y_1 + y_2 + \cdots + y_n$ is just the *number* of females in the data set. Thus the mean is the *proportion* or *rate* of females in the data. Even if we express the rate as a percentage, as we frequently do, we are still just working essentially with the mean of a special type of data.

The mean, when applied to continuous data, has a simple but enlightening physical interpretation as a measure of the middle. Consider a dotplot of the data set given above:

```
 .         :                 .            .
+----+----+----+----+----+----+----+----+
 2         3         4         5
```

Imagine the horizontal axis as a (weightless) stick with weights of equal size placed on the stick at the positions of each dot. Where will the stick balance? Arguments from elementary physics or mechanics show that the balance point will always be exactly at the mean:

```
 .         :                 .            .
+----+----+----+----+----+----+----+----+
 2         3   ↑     4         5
```

Balance point = mean = 3.4

If the observation (weight) at 5 were moved to the right, the mean (balance point) would also move to the right. Similarly, if the data point at 2 were to decrease to 1, the mean would also decrease. The mean and median measure the middle of a distribution in different ways. Notice that 60% of the observations lie below the mean in the case above and the dotplot does *not* balance at the median of 3.

For a perfectly symmetric distribution, the balance point is the same as the median, so the mean and median agree in that case. As an example of near symmetry, take the percentage changes in the flour price index in Exhibit 3.6L. Here the mean is 0.48% and the median is 0.28%, very little difference for a distribution that covers the interval from -12.9% to 14.4%.

E X A M P L E   4.4A

The city-size distribution given in Exhibit 4.2I gives an extreme example of how the mean and median may present quite different pictures of the middle. For that data set, the mean is 21,710 people compared with a median size of 8500 people. The few large cities have a large influence on the mean, since their actual numerical size is included in the numerator of the ratio used to find $\bar{y}$. As already noted, the median is resistant to the influence of extreme values. Which measure of the middle is correct? The answer depends on our purposes. As a typical value, the median is probably the best measure. However, if we are given only a measure of the middle and we wish to know the *total* population in the 68 cities, then 68 times the mean $(68 \times 21,710 = 1,476,280)$ will recover the total city population size. On the other hand, 68 times the median gives 578,000, a completely inappropriate total city population figure. ▪

If a data set contains extreme values that are erroneous for some reason, their strong influence on the mean is unfortunate. As a small example, suppose that the true data are 12, 15, 11, and 14 so that the mean is $(12 + 15 + 11 + 14)/4 = 13$. If when entering the data into a computer the 12 is mistakenly entered as 21, a typical error, then the mean changes to $(21 + 15 + 11 + 14)/4 = 15.25$, a substantial error. No statistic can protect against all errors in the data.

On several occasions, we have highlighted the effects of extreme observations. Statisticians call observations that are separated from the main body of the data **outliers**. Outliers may simply be the result of errors in measuring or recording the data. Alternatively, outliers may indicate changes in processes that can lead to new discoveries. Regardless of their origin, outliers must be detected and investigated.

outliers

The Standard Deviation

standard deviation

The most widely used measure of variability is the **standard deviation**, denoted by s. This statistic is the most complicated we have seen so far, so we need to spend some extra time understanding it. Fortunately we will compute s by hand only a few times for practice. In real applications, a computer or a statistical calculator will do the work.

The standard deviation measures variation around the mean, so we need to obtain the mean first. The standard deviation is then based on the squared deviations of the observations from their mean. The steps are as follows:

1 Compute the deviations $y_1 - \bar{y}, y_2 - \bar{y}, \ldots, y_n - \bar{y}$.

2 Square all the deviations and sum them.

3 Divide the sum by $n - 1$.

4 Finally, take the positive square root to get the standard deviation s.

Some of the deviations from the mean will be positive and some negative. However, since the deviations are squared, the farther an observation is from the mean in either direction, the larger that observation's contribution is to the standard deviation. The more spread out a distribution is around its mean, the larger its standard deviation. In one big formula, we have

$$ s = \sqrt{\frac{(y_1 - \overline{y})^2 + (y_2 - \overline{y})^2 + \cdots + (y_n - \overline{y})^2}{n - 1}} $$

E X A M P L E **4.4B**

A numerical example will help illustrate. We use the data set 3, 5, 2, 3, 4 with $n = 5$ for which we earlier found the mean to be 3.4. The calculations are best laid out in a table, as in Exhibit 4.4A. So for these data the standard deviation is $s = \sqrt{5.20/4} = \sqrt{1.3} \cong 1.140175425$, which we round off to $s = 1.14$. ▪

E X H I B I T **4.4A**
Calculations to Obtain the
Standard Deviation

Observation	Deviation	Squared Deviation
(y_i)	$(y_i - \overline{y})$	$(y_i - \overline{y})^2$
3	$3 - 3.4 = -0.4$	$(-0.4)^2 = 0.16$
5	$5 - 3.4 = 1.6$	$(1.6)^2 = 2.56$
2	$2 - 3.4 = -1.4$	$(-1.4)^2 = 1.96$
3	$3 - 3.4 = -0.4$	$(-0.4)^2 = 0.16$
4	$4 - 3.4 = 0.6$	$(0.6)^2 = 0.36$

Sum $\overline{17}$ $\overline{(0.0)}$ $\overline{5.20}$ ← sum of squared

(↑ Use to get $\overline{y}$)   deviations

Many calculators calculate the standard deviation almost automatically. Just enter the raw data and push the correct button to compute s. (The button may be labeled with the lowercase Greek letter sigma, σ.) Check yours with these data and see if you get the same answer. If not, your calculator may divide by n rather than $n - 1$.[†]

Notice also in Exhibit 4.4A that the sum of the deviations from the mean is zero. This is no coincidence. The following algebra shows that this is always the case:

$$ (y_1 - \overline{y}) + (y_2 - \overline{y}) + \cdots + (y_n - \overline{y}) = y_1 + y_2 + \cdots + y_n - n\overline{y} = n\overline{y} - n\overline{y} = 0 $$

To help interpret the standard deviation, observe the following facts:

1   The units for the standard deviation are the same as the units for the observations. That is, if y is measured in inches (or dollars), then s is also in inches (or dollars).

2   The standard deviation is never negative. It is zero if and only if all the data values are equal.

[†]There are theoretical arguments that support using $n - 1$ as the denominator in the definition of s. Other arguments support the choice of n as the denominator. For reasonably large n there is little difference in the final numerical result.

3 The standard deviation is strongly influenced by extreme observations and outliers.

EXAMPLE **4.4C**

As an example of the influence of outliers on s, suppose that the true data are 12, 15, 11, and 14, so that the mean is $\bar{y} = 13$. With these data, the standard deviation is

$$s = \sqrt{\frac{[(12-13)^2 + (15-13)^2 + (11-13)^2 + (14-13)^2]}{3}}$$

$$= \sqrt{\frac{10}{3}} = 1.826$$

If the 12 is mistakenly entered as 21, then, as we saw earlier, the mean changes to 15.25. In addition, the standard deviation changes to 4.193, more than double the correct value. ∎

Degrees of Freedom

You may wonder why in calculating the standard deviation we divide the sum of squared deviations by $n - 1$ instead of n, for division by n appears more consistent with the concept of averaging. The justification for division by $n - 1$ is that only $n - 1$ of the deviations from the mean are "free" bits of data. Recall that the deviations themselves sum to zero—that is, they satisfy a mathematical constraint. This means that if $n - 1$ deviations are given, we can solve for the nth one because it must be chosen to force the deviations to sum to zero. Mathematicians say that the deviations from the mean enjoy only $n - 1$ degrees of freedom.

In general, if n numbers must satisfy k mathematical constraints, they enjoy only $n - k$ degrees of freedom—that is, only $n - k$ of them may be chosen freely because the remaining k of them are determined by the constraints.

Deviations from the mean are constrained by only one equation, namely that they sum to zero. We will meet other sets of numbers in statistical practice that enjoy much less freedom than deviations from the mean. When we compute the standard deviation of such numbers, we will divide their sums of squared deviations by the number of degrees of freedom they enjoy and take the square root of this "average" sum of squared deviation. In other words, we average the number of free bits of data rather than the number of numbers.

Summarizing Mound-Shaped Distributions

For distributions with an approximate mound shape, the mean and standard deviation are especially useful for interpreting the variability of the observations. Consider once more the distribution of percentage changes in the flour price index. The histogram appears in Exhibit 3.6J. Because this distribution is approximately symmetric with a predominance of the data in the middle, the distribution has a mound-shaped appearance. For distributions of this kind, it may be argued theoretically (see Chapter 9) that *about 68% of the observations lie within one standard deviation of the mean.* For these 99 data points, the mean is 0.476% and the standard deviation is 4.818%, so about 68% of the distribution should lie in the interval from $0.476 - 4.818 = -4.342\%$ to $0.476 + 4.818 = 5.294\%$. If we count the number of data points within this interval, we find that 71 out of 99, or about 71%, are there. In addition, theory says that *about 95% lie within two standard deviations of the mean and nearly all of the data lie within three standard deviations of the mean.* For this set of data, the actual figures are 93 out of 99, or 94%, and 99 out of 99, or 100%, respectively. For mound-shaped frequency distributions, the mean and standard deviation are a compact summary of the complete distribution. Summarizing such distributions is one of the most common uses of the mean and standard deviation in statistical practice.

Simpson's Paradox (Optional)

For magazine publishers, the renewals of expiring subscriptions are essential to the survival of their business. The publisher of *American History Illustrated* noted in 1979 that the renewal rate increased from 51.2% in January to 64.1% in February.[†] However, it is also important to investigate the renewal rates among different categories of subscribers. The subscribers are categorized according to whether the previous subscription was a gift, a previous renewal, and so forth. To the publishers' surprise, they discovered that when broken down by these subscriber categories, the rates all *decreased* from January to February! How is this possible? The full data are given in Exhibit 4.4B.

E X H I B I T **4.4B**
Magazine Renewal Rates and
Simpson's Paradox

		Category				
Month	**Gift**	**Previous Renewal**	**Direct Mail**	**Subscription Service**	**Catalog Agent**	**Overall**
January						
Total	3,594	18,364	2,986	20,862	149	45,955
Renewals	2,918	14,488	1,783	4,343	13	23,455
Rate	81.2%	78.9%	59.7%	20.8%	8.7%	51.2%
February						
Total	884	5,140	2,224	864	45	9,157
Renewals	704	3,907	1,134	122	2	5,869
Rate	79.6%	76.0%	51.0%	14.1%	4.4%	64.1%

[†]Clifford H. Wagner, "Simpson's Paradox in Real Life," *American Statistician,* 36 (1982), 46–48.

The overall rate of renewals for January and for February can be written as

$$\text{January rate} = \frac{3,594}{45,955} \times \frac{2,918}{3,594} + \frac{18,364}{45,955} \times \frac{14,488}{18,364} + \frac{2,986}{45,955} \times \frac{1,783}{2,986}$$
$$+ \frac{20,862}{45,955} \times \frac{4,343}{20,862} + \frac{149}{45,955} \times \frac{13}{149}$$
$$= 0.08(0.81) + 0.40(0.79) + 0.06(0.60) + 0.45(0.21) + .00(0.09)$$
$$= 0.512$$

and

$$\text{February rate} = \frac{884}{9157} \times \frac{704}{884} + \frac{5140}{9157} \times \frac{3907}{5140} + \frac{2224}{9157} \times \frac{1134}{2224} + \frac{864}{9157} \times \frac{122}{864}$$
$$+ \frac{45}{9157} \times \frac{2}{45}$$
$$= 0.10(0.80) + 0.56(0.76) + 0.24(0.51) + 0.09(0.14) + 0.00(0.04)$$
$$= 0.641$$

Notice that in January a large percentage of the renewals were in the subscription service category ($20,862/45,955 = 45.4\%$), while in February only $864/9157 = 9.4\%$ were in that category. The overall renewal rate is a *weighted average* of the renewal rates for individual categories, with weights given by the percentages that the categories represent of the total renewals. Changes in the weights together with changes in the renewal rates of the individual categories affect the overall renewal rate.

The direction of an effect may often be reversed once data are broken down by another variable. In general, **Simpson's paradox** refers to this reversal when data are either combined or broken down by another variable.

Simpson's paradox

SECTION

4.5 Exercises

4.5A Compute the mean and standard deviation for each of the following data sets:

a 3, 5, 14, 9, 11, 6, 7   **b** 3, 5, 41, 9, 11, 6, 7   **c** 3, 4, 14, 9, 13, 6, 7

d Comment on the differences among the statistics for the three data sets.

4.5B A group of 50 employees has a mean annual wage of $27,000. The highest-paid member of the group, Danforth, has an annual wage of $34,000. If Danforth gets a $4000 raise while all other wages increase by $1000, what now is the mean annual wage for the employees?

4.5C Suppose a group contains half men and half women. If we know the mean salary for the men and the mean salary for the women, can we calculate the mean salary for everyone taken together? Why or why not?

4.5D Recently the *Des Moines Register* carried a story headlined "Des Moines lowest in survey of home prices." The story reported on a 62-city survey released by the National Association of Realtors. According to the survey the median price of an existing Des Moines home was $55,000 and had fallen 2.1% from the previous year. However, local real estate experts disputed these figures. According to the Greater Des Moines Board of Realtors, Mike Knapp of Iowa Realty claimed that the average sale price of an existing Des Moines home increased from

$61,012 a year earlier to $67,279 last month. "I guess it's a matter of how you keep your statistics," said Knapp.

a   Comment on the apparent discrepancy between the two measures of home prices.

b   What type of average must the Greater Des Moines Board of Realtors be using?

c   Which measure provides a prospective buyer with a better typical value?

d   Which measure would provide a tax assessor with a better typical value?

4.5E   When data are reported as frequencies within intervals, as in Exhibit 3.6P, means, medians, standard deviations, and so on may only be approximated. Can you think of a reasonable way to approximate the mean of the underlying, but unreported, data that led to Exhibit 3.6P? The median? The standard deviation?

4.5F   Suppose data are reported as in Exhibit 3.6O where an unbounded interval of the type $50,000+ occurs. Could we reasonably approximate the mean income in this situation? How about the median income?

4.5G   If a data set is (roughly) symmetrically distributed, argue that the mean and median will be nearly equal.

4.5H   Compute the mean and standard deviation of the number of photocopies made per day. The data are listed in Exhibit 4.2A. Recalculate the mean and standard deviation excluding the outlier at 1199. Do the values of the mean and standard deviation change much? (Filename: PHOTOCOP.DAT.)

4.5I   Ten accounts have a mean balance of $562. If an 11th account with balance $721 is added to the group, what is the new mean balance?

4.5J   Suppose 100 accounts have a mean balance of $562. If another account of size $721 is added to the group, what is the new mean balance? Compare with Exercise 4.5I.

SECTION

4.6   Linear Transformations and Standardization

The same variable can often be measured in different units—dollars or yen, miles or kilometers, pounds or kilograms, Fahrenheit or Celsius. If y_C is temperature measured in Celsius, then $y_F = 32 + \frac{9}{5}y_C$ is the corresponding temperature measured in Fahrenheit. For example, $20°$ Celsius corresponds to $32 + \frac{9}{5}(20) = 32 + 36 = 68°$ Fahrenheit. Similarly, if y is the number of photocopies made and each costs $0.05, then $0.05y$ is the cost of the copies. Other examples of linear transformations are data coding, conversion of currencies using exchange rates, and a computation called standardization, which is needed to study normal curves, as discussed in Chapter 9. In this section, we study the effect of linear transformations of data on the measures of center and variability we have introduced. We wish to measure center and variability consistently regardless of the units of measurement. The formulas in this section show how to do this when units are changed by a linear transformation.

Many similar transformations arise in practical applications. In general, the effect

linear transformations   of **linear transformations** is

$$y_* = a + by$$

where b is a positive number. Then the shape of the distribution of y_* is the same as the shape of the distribution of y; only the labeling of the values changes. Our discussion is limited to positive b values since nearly all practical examples satisfy this constraint.

E X A M P L E   **4.6A**   Exhibit 4.6A shows the histogram of photocopy costs at $0.05 per page. Compare this to the histogram of the photocopy counts shown in Exhibit 3.6C. The shapes are the same. Only the labeling of the values has changed. ▪

E X H I B I T **4.6A**
Histogram of Photocopy Costs

```
Histogram of Costs    N=30
Midpoint    Count
   10         1    *
   15         2    **
   20        11    ***********
   25         6    ******
   30         6    ******
   35         1    *
   40         2    **
   45         0
   50         0
   55         0
   60         1    *
```

Although the shape of a distribution remains unchanged by a linear transformation, the descriptive statistics for the distribution will change in a predictable way. It is easy to show that the mean of the transformed y_* value is given by

$$\overline{y}_* = a + b\overline{y}$$

Similarly, the median, first and third quartiles, and minimum and maximum for y and y_* are related as above. For example, the median of y_* is $a + b \times$ (median of y).

On the other hand, since measures of variability are all relative to the middle of a distribution, the standard deviation, range, and interquartile range are all multiplied by the coefficient b. For example, let s_y denote the standard deviation of y, and s_{y_*} denote the standard deviation of $y_* = a + by$. Then, in symbols, the relationship between the standard deviations is

$$s_{y_*} = bs_y$$

Notice that the value of a does not affect this relationship.

E X A M P L E   **4.6B**   Exhibit 4.6B shows the descriptive statistics for both the photocopy counts and costs. Here $y_{cost} = 0.05 y_{count}$, so $a = 0$ and $b = 0.05$. For example, the means are related by $25.60 = 0.05(512.1)$ and the standard deviations are related by $9.47 = 0.05(189.3)$ to the number of decimal places shown. ▪

	Mean	Median	Standard Deviation
Copies	512.1	456.0	189.3
Costs	25.60	22.80	9.47

	Minimum	Maximum	Q_1	Q_3
Copies	238.0	1199.0	382.0	598.0
Costs	11.90	59.95	19.1	29.9

Standardization

The particular linear transformation

$$z = \frac{y - \overline{y}}{s_y}$$

standardization

applied case by case is called **standardization** of the variable y. The variable z is called the standardized version of y.

Notice that the standardized version of y is a linear transformation, because we may write

$$z = \frac{y}{s_y} - \frac{\overline{y}}{s_y} = -\frac{\overline{y}}{s_y} + \frac{1}{s_y}(y) = a + by$$

where $a = -\overline{y}/s_y$ and $b = 1/s_y$. We can now show that any standardized variable has mean 0 and standard deviation 1. The mean of z is

$$\overline{z} = a + b\overline{y} = \frac{-\overline{y}}{s_y} + \frac{1}{s_y}\overline{y} = \frac{-\overline{y}}{s_y} + \frac{\overline{y}}{s_y} = 0$$

and the standard deviation of z is

$$s_z = bs_y = \frac{1}{s_y}s_y = 1$$

If y is measured in dollars, then $y - \overline{y}$ and s_y are also in dollars, so their ratio, which is the standardized variable, is *unitless*. This is true for any variable y regardless of the original units.

The standardized variable z measures the number of standard deviations, s_y, that y is away from its mean, $\overline{y}$. A z value of 1.6 means that y is 1.6 standard deviations above its mean, $\overline{y}$. In general, a positive value for z indicates that y is above its mean, and a negative value of z indicates that y is below its mean.

Our previous discussion of mound-shaped distributions may be cast in terms of standardized variables. If the distribution of y is mound shaped, the distribution of z is also mound shaped and approximately 68% of the standardized values lie within the interval from -1 to 1, 95% within $(-2, 2)$, and nearly all within $(-3, 3)$. Standardized values will be especially important when we deal with normal distributions, beginning in Chapter 9. The normal distribution is a theoretical model for mound-shaped distributions, and its applications rely heavily on the calculation of standardized values.

S E C T I O N

4.7 Exercises

4.7A   Consider the Deere & Co. machining data given in Exercise 2.5A. The data were coded in 0.000025-inch deviations from a target value.

    a   If y represents the coded value (as given), find the values of a and b so that $y_* = a + by$ represents the deviation from target *in inches*. [Answer: $a = 0$ and $b = 0.000025$.]

    b   Find the mean and standard deviation for the coded values and use $\overline{y}_* = a + b\overline{y}$ and $s_{y_*} = bs_y$ to obtain the mean and standard deviation in inches.

4.7B   The Amana microwave oven data of Section 2.8 were coded so that $6.050''$ is written as 50, $6.073''$ is 73, and so on.

    a   If y represents the coded value, find the values of a and b so that $y_* = a + by$ represents the actual measurement *in inches*. [Answer: $a = 6$ and $b = 0.001$.]

    b   If y represents the actual value and y_* the coded value, find the values of a and b so that $y_* = a + by$. [Answer: $a = -6000$ and $b = 1000$.]

4.7C   Suppose the rate of exchange for the Japanese yen was 112.12 per U.S. dollar. If on that day a data set is given in dollars and has a median value of $10,400 with an interquartile range of $2300, what were the corresponding median and interquartile range in yen on that date?

4.7D   Suppose a German mark is worth 1.57 U.S. dollars. If on that day a set of accounts payable had a mean of 640 marks and a standard deviation of 160 marks, what were the corresponding values in U.S. dollars?

4.7E   In Exercise 4.5H, you computed the mean and standard deviation of the number of photocopies made per day excluding the outlier at 1199. The data are in Exhibit 4.2A. Use that mean and standard deviation to obtain the standardized values for the photocopy data. Does the standardized value for the outlier seem out of line with the other standardized values? (*Hint*: Compare with what we expect for a mound-shaped distribution.) (Filename: PHOTOCOP.DAT.)

4.7F   One of the authors found seven pieces of U.S. paper currency in his pocket. The two leading digits of the serial numbers on these bills were: 01, 53, 46, 73, 04, 40, and 27.

    a   Prepare a dotplot of these numbers.

    b   Compute the mean and standard deviation of the numbers.

    c   Locate the mean, the mean minus one standard deviation, and the mean plus one standard deviation on the dotplot.

    d   Standardize the data.

    e   Compute the mean and standard deviation of the standardized data. Do they come out to be 0 and 1? Why?

    f   Prepare a dotplot of the standardized numbers and locate the mean, the mean minus one standard deviation, and the mean plus one standard deviation on the dotplot. Compare this dotplot to the one you prepared in parts (a) and (c).

4.7G   One of the authors found seven pieces of U.S. paper currency in his pocket. The last two digits of the serial numbers on these bills were: 03, 05, 62, 15, 48, 37, and 08.

    a   Prepare a dotplot of these numbers.

    b   Compute the mean and standard deviation of the numbers.

    c   Locate the mean, the mean minus one standard deviation, and the mean plus one standard deviation on the dotplot.

d   Standardize the data.

e   Compute the mean and standard deviation of the standardized data. Do they come out to be 0 and 1? Why?

f   Prepare a dotplot of the standardized numbers and locate the mean, the mean minus one standard deviation, and the mean plus one standard deviation on the dotplot. Compare this dotplot to the one you prepared in parts (a) and (c).

4.7H   Compare the two sets of numbers analyzed in Exercises 4.7F and 4.7G with regard to center, variability, and skewness.

4.7I   Use the 20 exam scores in Exercise 3.5A.

a   If you have not already done so, prepare a dotplot of these numbers.

b   Compute the mean and standard deviation of the numbers.

c   Locate the mean, the mean minus one standard deviation, and the mean plus one standard deviation on the dotplot.

d   Standardize the exam scores.

e   Compute the mean and standard deviation of the standardized scores. Do they come out to be 0 and 1? Why?

f   Prepare a dotplot of the standardized scores and locate the mean, the mean minus one standard deviation, and the mean plus one standard deviation on the dotplot. Compare this dotplot to the one you prepared in parts (a) and (c). (Filename: SCORES.DAT.)

4.7J   Repeat Exercise 4.7I for the weight data in Exercise 3.5B. (Filename: WEIGHTS.DAT.)

SECTION

4.8 Descriptive Statistics and the Computer

Statistical software packages include commands or menu selections to calculate the descriptive statistics we have discussed so far and many more.

Exhibit 4.8A displays the output obtained from the DESCRIBE command in the Minitab system applied to the city-size and flour price change variables we have been working with throughout the last few chapters. The data set count, together with the number of missing values, if any, is given for each variable "described." Three measures of the middle are reported: the mean, the median, and the trimmed mean (labeled TRMEAN). The trimmed mean is obtained by "trimming off" the 5% largest and 5% smallest observations and then calculating the arithmetic average of the middle 90% of the data. It can be considered as a compromise between the mean and median that attempts to maximize the advantages of each while minimizing the disadvantages. In addition, the standard deviation (STDEV) is given together with the standard error of the mean (SEMEAN), which is discussed in Chapters 9 and 15. Finally, the minimum, maximum, and quartiles are given. Similar output for StatGraphics and SPSS/PC+ is shown in Exhibits 4.8B and 4.8C. Although all are a little different, the overlap is considerable.

Few statistics based on ordered data are included in the SPSS/PC+ DESCRIP-TIVES command, but this system has other commands for obtaining quartiles. A large number of descriptive statistics are reported with the STATS command in Stat-Graphics, many of which we have not discussed.

EXHIBIT 4.8A
An Example of the DESCRIBE
Command in Minitab

	N	N*	MEAN	MEDIAN	TRMEAN	STDEV	SEMEAN
%Change	99	1	0.476	0.281	0.425	4.818	0.484

	MIN	MAX	Q1	Q3
%Change	-12.910	14.428	-2.976	3.205

	N	MEAN	MEDIAN	TRMEAN	STDEV	SEMEAN
Cities	68	21.71	8.50	17.05	30.82	3.74

	MIN	MAX	Q1	Q3
Cities	5.00	191.00	7.00	26.00

EXHIBIT 4.8B
Results from the STATS
Command in StatGraphics

Variable:	Copies	Percent
Sample size	30	99
Average	512.067	0.475974
Median	456	0.2809
Mode	362	0.2703
Geometric mean	484.138	
Variance	35849.2	23.2137
Standard deviation	189.339	4.81806
Standard error	34.5684	0.484233
Minimum	238	-12.9096
Maximum	1199	14.4276
Range	961	27.3372
Lower quartile	390	-2.9757
Upper quartile	589	3.2055
Interquartile range	199	6.1812
Skewness	1.76549	0.207597
Standardized skewness	3.94776	0.843265
Kurtosis	4.90642	0.590332
Standardized kurtosis	5.48554	1.19897

EXHIBIT 4.8C
Output from the DESCRIPTIVES
Command from SPSS/PC+

Page 19   SPSS/PC+   7/12/90

Number of Valid Observations (Listwise) =   99.00

Variable PERCENT

Mean	.476	S.E. Mean	.484
Std Dev	4.818	Variance	23.214
Kurtosis	.590	S.E. Kurt	.481
Skewness	.208	S.E. Skew	.243
Range	27.337	Minimum	-12.91
Maximum	14.43	Sum	47.122

Valid Observations - 99   Missing Observations -   1

SECTION

4.9   Exercises

4.9A   Preferably using a statistical package, compute the mean and median of the city sizes given in Exhibit 4.2H. Which gives a better measure of typical value? Which would be more useful if interest centers on the total population of the cities? (Filename: CITIES.DAT.)

4.9B   Compute the standard deviations of the "before" and "after" punch data given in Exhibits 3.6E and 3.6G. What are the units of measurement for these standard deviations? (Filenames: PUNCH_B.DAT. and PUNCH_A.DAT.)

4.9C   Refer to the monthly Deere & Co. oil-filter sales reported in Exhibit 2.6A.

   a   Find the means and standard deviations for each of the 12 months.

   b   Do these statistics agree with the graphic displays in Exhibit 2.6C? (Filename: OIL-FILT.DAT.)

4.9D   Refer to the Amana Refrigeration assembly data plotted in Exhibits 2.8C and 2.8D. The data are listed in Appendix 4 and are in file AMANA.DAT.

   a   Compute the means and standard deviations of both the Left and Right values.

   b   Do the means and standard deviations appear comparable?

4.9E   Find the mean, median, and standard deviation for the percentage changes in the Buffalo, New York, flour price index listed in Exhibit 2.10A. If the index stands at 172 this month, what would be a reasonable prediction for the index value for next month? Find standardized values for the percentage changes in the flour price index. Display a histogram for the standardized values and compare the shape of this histogram to that of the original values given in Exhibit 3.6J. (Filename: BUFLOUR.DAT.)

SECTION

4.10   A Case Study: Los Angeles Traffic

A retail firm is considering opening a store somewhere in metropolitan Los Angeles. Among other variables related to choosing a location, management estimates that the store will need to front a road whose weekday average traffic volume is at least 10,000 vehicles. Is it likely to find such a location? Where should it look?

Fortunately, some general traffic data from 1987 in that area are available— namely, traffic volumes measured as vehicles per weekday at 396 sites in the greater Los Angeles area.[†] The data set is listed in Appendix 4 and is available in data file TRAFFIC.DAT. The first report said that there was an average (mean) of 37,663 vehicles per weekday passing any given location on "typical" Los Angeles roads. This seems like an enormous number of vehicles even for Los Angeles! Surely a further look at the data is necessary to understand what this average means.

With 396 numbers, it is useless to look at the data directly, but the histogram in Exhibit 4.10A tells a great deal about the traffic volume distribution. The immediate reaction is to wonder about the extreme skewness of the distribution. Exhibit 4.10B gives the descriptive statistics for these data, and we see that the mean number of

---

[†]Data courtesy of Lee Cryer, Barton-Aschman Associates, Inc., Pasadena, California.

vehicles per weekday is indeed 37,663 while the median is only 15,268. Clearly, we need to dig deeper into this data set.

E X H I B I T **4.10A**
Weekday Traffic Volumes in Los Angeles

```
Histogram of Volume    N=396
Each * represents five observations

Midpoint    Count
      0        33   *******
  10000       158   **********************************
  20000        75   ***************
  30000         3   *
  40000         4   *
  50000         4   *
  60000        12   ***
  70000        14   ***
  80000        14   ***
  90000        21   *****
 100000        10   **
 110000        19   ****
 120000         8   **
 130000        15   ***
 140000         6   **
```

E X H I B I T **4.10B**
Descriptive Statistics for Los Angeles Traffic Volumes

	N	Mean	Median	Standard Deviation
Volume	396	37663	15268	41055

	Min	Max	Q_1	Q_3
Volume	954	137000	9095	70000

After going back to the data source, it was discovered that the traffic counts include data from sites at a number of different road types. Some of the sites are freeways, some major arterial roads, some minor arterial roads, and some 50 of them are along one major arterial road—Ventura Boulevard. The distribution portrayed in Exhibit 4.10A is really a mixture of volumes from some very different road types, not all of which pertain to the problem at hand—the retail store cannot be sited on a freeway!

Exhibits 4.10C–F show the histograms of the traffic volumes stratified according to road type: freeway, major arterial, minor arterial, and Ventura Boulevard. The dotplots in Exhibit 4.10G give a succinct display of the differences and similarities among the four distributions.

Notice that the dotplots for major arterial roads and for Ventura Boulevard are very similar. A little reflection and further investigation reveal that Ventura Boulevard is, in fact, a major arterial road. Exhibit 4.10H gives the descriptive statistics by road type. Here the similarities between major arterials and Ventura Boulevard may be examined more closely. The means are 13,789 and 15,802, respectively. The standard deviations are 4765 and 4838. Since both distributions are mound shaped, we would expect about 68% of traffic volumes to lie in the intervals 9024 to 18,554 and

EXHIBIT **4.10C**

Freeway Traffic Volume in Los
Angeles

```
Histogram of Freeway    N=127

Midpoint     Count
   40000         4    ****
   50000         4    ****
   60000        12    ************
   70000        14    **************
   80000        14    **************
   90000        21    *********************
  100000        10    **********
  110000        19    *******************
  120000         8    ********
  130000        15    ***************
  140000         6    ******
```

EXHIBIT **4.10D**

Major Arterial Traffic
Volume—Los Angeles

```
Histogram of Major      N=110

Midpoint     Count
    4000         4    ****
    6000         4    ****
    8000        12    ************
   10000         8    ********
   12000        17    *****************
   14000        19    *******************
   16000        21    *********************
   18000        16    ****************
   20000         4    ****
   22000         1    *
   24000         2    **
   26000         0
   28000         1    *
   30000         1    *
```

EXHIBIT **4.10E**

Minor Arterial Traffic
Volume—Los Angeles

```
Histogram of Minor      N=109

Midpoint     Count
       0         1    *
    2000        10    **********
    4000        17    *****************
    6000        21    *********************
    8000        26    **************************
   10000        17    *****************
   12000        10    **********
   14000         1    *
   16000         6    ******
```

EXHIBIT **4.10F**

Ventura Boulevard Traffic
Volume—Los Angeles

```
Histogram of Ventura    N=50

Midpoint     Count
    4000         2    **
    8000         2    **
   12000        11    ***********
   16000        21    *********************
   20000        11    ***********
   24000         2    **
   28000         1    *
```

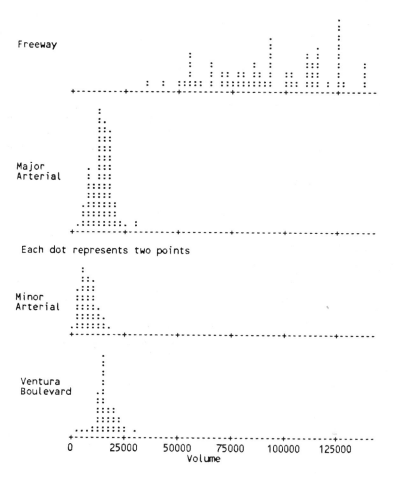

E X H I B I T **4.10G**
Dotplots of Traffic Volumes by
Road Type—Los Angeles

E X H I B I T **4.10H**
Descriptive Statistics for Different
Road Types— Los Angeles

	N	Mean	Median	Standard Deviation
Freeway	127	92,898	92,000	26,282
Major	110	13,789	13,860	4,765
Minor	109	7,427	7,236	3,626
Ventura	50	15,802	15,146	4,838

	Min	Max	Q_1	Q_3
Freeway	36,000	137,000	71,000	115,000
Major	3,522	29,230	10,671	16,658
Minor	954	16,555	4,870	9,499
Ventura	2,970	29,370	13,186	19,001

10,964 to 20,640, respectively. The interquartile ranges, $16,658 - 10,671 = 5987$
and $19,001 - 13,186 = 5815$, are close. In the absence of further information about

where the store is to be located, there is no compelling reason to keep the Ventura Boulevard data separate from the other major arterials data.

Exhibit 4.10I shows the distribution after combining the volumes from major arterials and Ventura Boulevard. A very symmetric distribution results. The descriptive statistics are given in Exhibit 4.10J. The mean and median are 14,418 and 14,748 with a standard deviation of 4863. The middle 50% lies in the interval from 11,737 to 17,047.5. We should be willing to take an even bet that the traffic volume will be in this range. Exhibit 4.10H shows that the volume on minor arterial streets averages 7427 vehicles per weekday with a standard deviation of 3626 vehicles per weekday.

Management desires a weekday average traffic volume of at least 10,000 vehicles. Locating the business on a major arterial road in Los Angeles would likely meet this criterion, but a minor arterial site probably would not.

E X H I B I T **4.10I**
Combined Major Arterial Road Volumes—Los Angeles

```
Histogram of Combined    N=160

Midpoint   Count
   2000       1    *
   4000       4    ****
   6000       6    ******
   8000      12    ************
  10000      10    **********
  12000      24    ************************
  14000      31    *******************************
  16000      32    ********************************
  18000      18    ******************
  20000       9    *********
  22000       6    ******
  24000       4    ****
  26000       0
  28000       1    *
  30000       2    **
```

E X H I B I T **4.10J**
Combined Major Arterial Descriptive Statistics—Los Angeles

	N	Mean	Median	Standard Deviation
Combined	160	14418	14748	4863

	Min	Max	Q_1	Q_3
Combined	2970	29370	11737	17047.5

Chapter Summary

This chapter introduced some numbers for describing various characteristics of distributions with many data points. The two most important characteristics are measures of the middle and the variability in a distribution. Statistics based on ordered data include the median, range, quartiles, and interquartile range. Other important statistics, the mean and standard deviation, measure middle and variability in another way. The chapter also discussed distribution shape in terms of symmetry or skewness.

Supplementary Exercises for Chapter 4

4A An article in the March 11, 1993, *Wall Street Journal* (page B2) lists ten major beer brands and their percent alcohol content. Here are the data:

Brand	Percent Alcohol
Budweiser	5.0
Miller High Life	4.7
Natural Light	4.7
Miller Genuine Draft	4.7
Busch	4.7
Old Milwaukee	4.5
Coors Light	4.4
Milwaukee's Best	4.3
Bud Light	4.2
Miller Lite	4.2

a Prepare a dotplot of the data.

b Compute the mean, median, and first and third quartiles of the data and locate these statistics on the dotplot.

c Compute the mean minus one standard deviation and the mean plus one standard deviation. Locate these numbers on the dotplot.

d Comment on the skewness of the data.

e Standardize the data and prepare a dotplot of the standardized data. Compute the median and the first and third quartiles of the standardized data and locate them on the dotplot.

4B A group of people contains 50 men and 50 women. The median salary for the men is $30,000, and the median salary for the women is $30,000. What can you say about the median salary for the group of 100 people?

4C A group of people contains 50 men and 50 women. The mean salary for the men is $30,000, and the mean salary for the women is $30,000. What can you say about the mean salary for the group of 100 people?

4D A group of people contains 25 men and 15 women. The mean salary for the men is $25,000, and the mean salary for the women is $30,000. What can you say about the mean salary for the group of 40 people?

4E During a December 1989 Hawkeye basketball game, a TV announcer commented that last year an average of $\frac{1}{3}$ of a player fouled out per game. His partner, the color commentator, remarked that he thought it was impossible for $\frac{1}{3}$ of a player to foul out. Assuming that average here means the mean, explain the color commentator's mistake.

4F Use the stadium-size data given in Supplementary Exercise 3A.

    a   Find the mean and median stadium sizes. Which is larger? Does this ordering agree with the shape of the distribution as given in either the stem-and-leaf display, dotplot, or histogram in Supplementary Exercise 3A?

    b   Find the first and third quartiles and the interquartile range for these data. Do the quartiles and median indicate that the distribution is symmetric or skewed? (Filename: STADI-UMS.DAT.)

4G   Use the Iowa county-size data given in Supplementary Exercise 3B.

    a   Find the mean and median county sizes. Which is larger? Does this ordering agree with the shape of the distribution as given in either the stem-and-leaf display, dotplot, or histogram in Exercise 3B?

    b   There are 99 counties in this data set. Is the mean or median more help in finding the total 1980 population of Iowa? Explain.

    c   Find the first and third quartiles and the interquartile range for these data. Do the quartiles and median indicate that the distribution is symmetric or skewed? (Filename: COUN-TIES.DAT.)

4H   In Supplementary Exercise 3C, several variables for eight brands of popcorn were considered. Use those data here.

    a   Calculate the mean calories of the 16 data points for the eight brands and two popping methods.

    b   Calculate the mean calories separately for the two popping methods. Compare these with the value obtained in part (a).

    c   Consider the percent edible variable. Compare the overall mean with the means calculated separately for the two popping methods. Comment on clear differences or lack thereof. (Filename: POPCORN.DAT.)

4I   In Supplementary Exercise 3D, butter and margarine were compared with respect to several variables. Using those data:

    a   Calculate the median and first and third quartiles for the calorie content of margarine.

    b   Using the numbers obtained in part (a), would you describe the distribution as symmetric or skewed? If skewed, is it skewed toward high values or low values?

    c   Do your conclusions in part (b) based on these descriptive statistics agree with the distribution plots obtained in Supplementary Exercise 3D?

    d   Repeat parts (a), (b), and (c) for percent saturated fat content of margarine. (Filename: BUTTER.DAT.)

Glossary for Chapter 4

first quartile	The data value one-quarter from the bottom of an ordered list.
interquartile range	The difference between the third quartile and the first quartile.
linear transformation	Replacing a variable y by $a + by$ for some choice of constants a and b.
mean	The arithmetic average of the data values.
median	The middle value for a data set ordered in magnitude.
outlier	An observation that is separated from the main body of the data.
range	The difference between the largest and smallest data value.
Simpson's paradox	A paradox in which an overall average changes in a way opposite to the changes in the averages for component parts.

skewed distribution   An asymmetric distribution with values stretched out on either the high or low end.

standard deviation   A measure of variability obtained as the square root of the number obtained from the sum of the squared deviations of the observations from their mean divided by $n - 1$.

standardization   Replacing a variable y by $(y - \bar{y})/s$, case by case.

statistics   Numbers calculated from a data set.

symmetric distribution   A distribution whose left and right sides are mirror images of one another.

third quartile   The data value one-quarter from the top of the ordered list.

Describing Categorical Variables

Chapter Objectives

After mastering this chapter, you will be able to:

- Explain categories and ordered categories

- Produce and interpret tallies for a categorical variable

- Produce and interpret two-way tables

- Collapse tables

- Display summary statistics and continuous or time series data within cells of a table

- Produce and interpret multiway tables

5.1 Introduction

Chapters 2 to 4 presented a number of tools for displaying and describing continuous data—numerical measurements of quantities such as length, temperature, or price. Another important type of data is **categorical data**—data that are arranged in classes, or categories.

categorical data

Counting is a basic data-collection technique. Whenever we count, we deal with categorical data. Counts are important statistics in practical applications. For example, we may wish to know how many firms belong to a certain Standard Industrial Classification (SIC) category, or the number of units sold in a given day or quarter, or how many firms from a certain geographic region responded to a questionnaire.

Another source of categorical data is the classification of elements into groups according to a common attribute. For example, we may group together firms with fewer than 100 employees and call them "small." Or we may group people according to their occupations or the brand of coffee they buy.

The tools presented in this chapter will help you analyze and report categorical data. You will move from an introduction to the idea of variables to tallies and then to the basic tool for analyzing categorical data—the multiway table.

SECTION

5.2 Variables

A variable is a characteristic of something you are studying. For example, people have different heights, weights, levels of education, incomes, and a host of other characteristics you could study. Each of these characteristics can take on different values and so is called a variable. This section discusses studying relationships among variables, forming new variables, and variables whose values form ordered categories.

Exhibit 5.2A displays a data set like many encountered in practice. The set is a small portion of one collected in the 1980 Wisconsin Restaurant Survey conducted by the University of Wisconsin Small Business Development Center.[†] Each of the seven columns of figures represents a characteristic of a restaurant—how restaurants answered one of seven questions on the survey. Each of the 10 data entries in each column corresponds to a restaurant that returned a questionnaire. A given restaurant's responses to the seven questions make up a row in the table. (A realistic data set would have many more rows because a large number of restaurants would be surveyed.)

variable

In a data set like this, each column of figures corresponds to a **variable**—that is, a characteristic of the elements under study, in this example, restaurants. The rows

EXHIBIT **5.2A**
Wisconsin Restaurant Survey: A
Small Data Set with 7 Columns
(Variables) and 10 Rows
(Cases)

Id No.	Business Outlook[†]	Sales $1000s	Wages % of sales	Advertising % of sales	Full-Time Employees	Part-Time Employees
1	2	480	25	2	8	30
2	4	507	20	5	6	25
3	5	210	24	3	0	17
4	5	246	30	1	2	13
5	2	148	35	1	*	*
6	3	135	30	10	2	*
7	2	72	10	5	0	5
8	3	99	25	1	1	8
9	4	160	*	*	2	10
10	4	243	15	2	2	19

[†] 1 = very unfavorable; 6 = very favorable.
* Asterisk in table denotes data not reported or reported incorrectly.

[†] An extensive analysis of the full data set may be found in R. B. Miller, *Minitab Handbook for Business and Economics* (Boston: PWS-KENT, 1988), chap. 4.

cases

in the data table are called **cases**. Each restaurant is a case of a variable—that is, it contributes an observation on the variable in question.

Although each variable can be studied separately by manipulating the figures in a single column, we can also study groups of variables, such as the relationship among sales, wages, and advertising.

Several of the entries in Exhibit 5.2A are asterisks (∗), which denote missing or inaccurate data. Sometimes respondents fail or refuse to answer some of the questions on a questionnaire, creating *partial nonresponse* because some of the questions are not answered. Sometimes the responses are unreadable or are clearly in error. If such responses cannot be corrected, they too must be coded as missing. The problem of missing data almost always creeps into survey work.

Creating New Variables

One of the most common statistical operations is the creation of new variables through arithmetic or functional operations on old variables. For example, in Chapter 2 the *averages* and the *differences* of the Left and Right measurements on microwave ovens were considered. Monthly differences of flour prices were also computed. Here are two more examples, using the data in Exhibit 5.2A.

E X A M P L E   **5.2A**

In Exhibit 5.2A a new variable, "full-time equivalent employees" (Fte), is defined by the rule Fte = Full + (0.5) × Part; that is, full-time equivalent is the number of full-time employees plus half the part-time employees. This definition understates the effort of part-time employees who work more than half-time and overstates the effort of part-time employees who work less than half-time. But it is a simple definition and probably does not represent a substantial error. For the restaurant business, which tends to be labor intensive, Fte might be used as a measure of the magnitude of the business operation.

The variable Fte may provide too fine a categorization for some analyses, and some grouping may be done to ease comparisons. To illustrate, let us also define a variable Size by the following rule:

If Fte is between 1 and 9.5, set Size = 1.

If Fte is between 10 and 20, set Size = 2.

If Fte is greater than 20, set Size = 3.

Here the value of Size depends on the value of Fte. For each case, Size assumes only one of the three values 1, 2, and 3, which might for practical purposes be interpreted as "small," "medium," and "large." Restaurants of different sizes can be grouped into a category such as "medium" when the truly important differences are between the categories rather than between individual restaurants. For some problems, grouping will be helpful. For other problems, grouping will mask important distinctions. The appropriateness of grouping must be decided in the context of the problems.

Exhibit 5.2B repeats Exhibit 5.2A with the variables Fte and Size added. Cases 5 and 6 have missing data for numbers of employees, so the values of the variables Fte and Size cannot be computed for these cases. Asterisks have been entered for these values. You see that missing data transmits itself to new variables.   ∎

E X H I B I T 5.2B
Wisconsin Restaurant Survey: A Small Data Set with 9 Columns (Variables) and 10 Rows (Cases)

Id No.	Business Outlook[†]	Sales $1000s	Wages, % of sales	Advertising % of sales	Full-Time Employees	Part-Time Employees	Fte[‡]	Rest. Size
1	2	480	25	2	8	30	23	3
2	4	507	20	5	6	25	18.5	2
3	5	210	24	3	0	17	8.5	1
4	5	246	30	1	2	13	8.5	1
5	2	148	35	1	*	*	*	*
6	3	135	30	10	2	*	*	*
7	2	72	10	5	0	5	2.5	1
8	3	99	25	1	1	8	5	1
9	4	160	*	*	2	10	7	1
10	4	243	15	2	2	19	11.5	2

1 = very unfavorable; 6 = very favorable.
‡ Fte = Full-time equivalent employees.
* Asterisk in table denotes data not reported or reported incorrectly.

Ordered Categories

ordered categories

If we agree to measure "size" of restaurant by number of employees, we can choose to use the variable Fte itself or we can use the Size variable we have defined. Since size divides the restaurants into three size categories, based on the numbers of employees, we can think of Size as a variable that allocates restaurants to ordered categories. **Ordered categories** are those categories that cannot be displayed in an arbitrary order without losing some information. For example, Male and Female or brands of automobiles could be reported in any order. But in Exhibit 5.2B, if the 1's and 2's in the Size column were interchanged, the order conveyed by the symbols would be destroyed.

S E C T I O N

5.3   Exercises

5.3A   Explain why the Restaurant Size variable in Exhibit 5.2B is an ordered-category variable. List the cases in each of the strata defined by Restaurant Size.

5.3B   Suppose you wanted to split up the cases in Exhibit 5.2B by Business Outlook *and* Restaurant Size. How many groups are defined in this way? List the cases in each of the groups.

5.3C   The data in the table below were collected as part of a study of real estate property valuation. They are part of a larger study that is presented in detail in Section 6.2. They are observations on 10 parcels that sold in a particular neighborhood in a particular year.

Sq.ft	Grade	Assessed	Market
521	−1	7.80	26.0
538	−1	28.20	19.4
544	0	23.20	25.2
577	−1	22.20	26.2
661	−1	23.80	31.0
662	0	19.60	34.6
677	0	22.80	36.4
691	−1	22.60	33.0
694	0	28.00	37.4
712	0	21.20	42.4

Sq.ft   = Square feet of living area
Grade   = Type of construction (-1 = low, 0 = medium, 1 = high)
Assessed = Most recent assessed value on city assessor's books (in thousands of dollars)
Market   = Selling price of parcel (in thousands of dollars)

a   Separate the parcels into two groups determined by their grades of construction. Find average Sq.ft, Assessed, and Market for each group. Does there appear to be a difference between the two groups?

b   Create a new variable by calculating for each case the ratio of Assessed to Market value. Such ratios are used extensively in property valuation work. Compute average ratios for the two groups formed in part (a). Is there a substantial difference in the averages?

5.4 Tallies

tally

A **tally** is a count of the number of cases in a category. This section discusses how to produce tallies and percents to report data in a useful way. We also touch on the effect on tallies of inevitable errors in the data.

Producing Tallies

Exhibit 5.4A shows a little more of the Wisconsin restaurant survey data introduced in Section 5.2. The full data set is listed in Appendix 4 and given in file RESTRNT.DAT.

In this data set, the variables Business Outlook (second column) and Size (last column) are ordered categorical variables. The variables Type (ninth column) and Owner (eleventh column) are categorical but not ordered. An asterisk (∗) indicates a missing measurement.

Exhibit 5.4B shows a tally of the variable Outlook produced by a statistical computer package. The last line in the tally, "∗ = 1," indicates that one restaurant

EXHIBIT **5.4A**
Excerpt of Restaurant Survey Data

```
Wisconsin Restaurant Survey Data for 1979
Variable:     Description
ID Number:
Business Outlook: categorized as
  1=very unfavorable,..., 6=very favorable
Sales: Gross 1979 sales in $1000's
New Capital: invested in 1979 ($1000's)
Value: Est. market value of business ($1000's)
Cost of goods sold: as % of sales
Wages: as % of sales
Advertising: as % of sales
Type: 1=fast food, 2=supper club, 3=other
Seats: number of dining seats
Owner: 1=sole proprietorship, 2=partnership, 3=corporation
Full Time: # of full time employees
Part Time: # of part time employees
Size: Size of restaurant categorized as
  1=1 to 9.5 full time equivalent employees
  2=10 to 20 full time equivalent employees
  3=more than 20 full time equivalent employees
  (Full time equivalent=full time+(1/2)part time)
```

ID	Outlook	Sales	New Capital	Value	Cost	Wages	Advert	Type	Seats	Owner	Full	Part	Size
1	2	480	0	600	35	25	2	2	200	3	8	30	3
2	4	507	22	375	59	20	5	2	150	1	6	25	2
3	5	210	25	275	40	24	3	1	46	1	0	17	1
4	5	246	*	80	43	30	1	1	28	3	2	13	1
5	2	148	*	85	45	35	1	3	44	1	*	*	*
6	3	50	*	135	40	30	10	2	50	3	2	*	*
7	2	72	0	125	85	10	5	2	50	.1	0	5	1
8	3	99	7	150	43	25	1	2	130	1	1	8	1
9	4	160	5	85	*	*	*	*	*	2	2	10	1
10	4	243	7	150	38	15	2	2	50	2	2	19	2
:	:	:	:	:	:	:	:	:	:	:	:	:	:
269	4	250	3	5	35	50	0	3	15	2	1	3	1
270	5	215	1	100	36	33	2	3	98	3	5	17	2
271	4	*	*	*	*	*	*	2	36	2	7	6	2
272	3	733	35	500	53	21	0	1	0	1	6	40	3
273	1	*	*	*	*	*	*	3	0	1	0	0	1
274	1	200	1	210	50	20	5	2	70	*	*	*	*
275	5	305	0	450	58	27	2	2	85	3	3	25	2
276	1	110	5	175	*	*	*	2	99	1	0	7	1
277	2	*	*	100	*	*	*	3	45	1	3	6	1
278	3	100	20	250	24	30	10	3	100	3	0	7	1
279	4	355	*	95	40	20	5	1	130	3	8	12	2

EXHIBIT **5.4B**
A Simple Tally

Outlook	Count
1	37
2	40
3	66
4	73
5	49
6	9
7	4
N =	278
* =	1

did not report a value for the variable Outlook. Outlook is a categorical variable taking values 1 to 6, meaning from very unfavorable to very favorable. However, the tally reveals four restaurants with Outlook value of 7. Clearly something is wrong. Welcome to the real world! Errors like this are quite common in data sets, especially in large, complex ones. If we do not discover errors and either correct them or temper our analysis in light of the errors, our conclusions will be affected.

In this case there are at least two ways of dealing with the errors. We could set the suspect values equal to the missing value code, *, and not use those values in any subsequent analysis. We took another approach here and replaced the 7's with 6's. Exercise 5.7A asks you to try the first approach and investigate the consequences.

Other errors remain in the data. In Exhibit 5.4A, zeros that do not make sense are found among the variables Sales, Value, Wages, Costgoods, and Seats. We set all the suspect 0's to the missing value code, *, before further analysis.

Exhibit 5.4C shows the tally of the corrected Outlook values converted to percentages. This exhibit shows that 13.31% of the 278 respondents viewed their business outlook as very unfavorable; only 4.68% thought their business outlook was very favorable. An Outlook value of 4 received the largest percent among the respondents, but a value of 3 was a close second. Exhibits 3.6A and 3.6B display this information graphically.

EXHIBIT 5.4C A Simple Percent Table	Business Outlook	Percent	Rounded Percent
	1	13.31	13
	2	14.39	14
	3	23.74	24
	4	26.26	26
	5	17.63	18
	6	4.68	5
	Total	100.00	100

Reporting Tallies

Statistical software and spreadsheet software packages prepare tallies quickly and easily, but their output is seldom in the best form for giving others information in a memorandum or a meeting. Typically the software packages print out too many decimal places in percentages, asking the reader to absorb figures that have no bearing on the message. As an illustration, compare the Percent and Rounded Percent columns in Exhibit 5.4C. Which conveys the important information quickly and easily? The Rounded Percent offers fewer figures for our eyes and brains to absorb. You quickly pick up that the middle two categories contain 50% of the responses.

The display in Exhibit 5.4C is still not as informative as it could be because the categories are coded numerically. Numerical coding is useful for computer processing, but for reporting, the categories should be named and the legend should explain where the data came from, along with other pertinent details that help the reader assess the relevance of the data.

Exhibit 5.4D is a fairly informative report. A Total row is not needed because the number of responses is given in the table footnote and the Percent column sums to 100 (unless the figures are wrong). For reporting, it is best to avoid redundant or extraneous symbols. Including them asks the reader to discount visible cues; leaving them out lets the important cues stand out. An even more compact report would give only the Percent column, leaving the reader to apply the percentages to the total.

Response	Number	Percent
Very unfavorable	37	13
Unfavorable	40	14
Mildly unfavorable	66	24
Mildly favorable	73	26
Favorable	49	18
Very favorable	13	5

Source: 1980 Wisconsin Restaurant Survey conducted by the University of Wisconsin Small Business Development Center. A mail survey of a random sample of 1000 restaurants in 19 Wisconsin counties yielded 278 usable responses to the question.

SECTION

5.5   Exercises

5.5A   Prepare a tally for the Restaurant Size variable in Exhibit 5.2B. Include both counts and percents. Create a presentation-quality table.

5.5B   Repeat Exercise 5.5A using the data on Restaurant Size reported in Exhibit 5.4A.

5.5C   Prepare a tally for the Grade variable in Exercise 5.3C. Include both counts and percents. Create a presentation-quality table.

SECTION

5.6   Two-Way Tables

two-way table

A table is data arranged in rows and columns. A **two-way table** shows the counts (or percentages) in each category formed by intersecting the categories of two variables. This section introduces the parts of a two-way table and shows ways to collapse tables to make their information more useful.

Exhibit 5.6A is a two-way table that shows the count of respondents in each Owner category broken down by each Outlook category. Recall that Owner $= 3$ corresponds to corporation-owned restaurants. We see that 14 corporation-owned restaurants indicated that the business outlook was very unfavorable (Outlook $= 1$). This entry is boxed in the exhibit.

Parts of a Table

cell

This boxed location, corresponding to Owner $= 3$ and Outlook $= 1$, is called a **cell**. A cell is defined by the intersection of a category of one variable with the category of another variable. Each location in a table is a cell.

ROWS: Owner	COLUMNS: Outlook						
	1	2	3	4	5	6	All
1	19	17	24	29	14	3	106
2	1	1	8	11	3	3	27
3	14	21	32	32	31	6	136
All	34	39	64	72	48	12	269

CELL CONTENTS—COUNT

body

The cells defined by all the combinations of categories of the variables in a table make up the **body** of the table. In Exhibit 5.6A, the body of the table consists of $3 \times 6 = 18$ cells.

For an arbitrary two-way table, r denotes the number of categories of the variable whose categories define the *rows* in the table, and c denotes the number of categories of the variable whose categories define the *columns* in the table. The table is said to be an $r \times c$ table. The table in Exhibit 5.6A is a 3×6 table.

The counts in the All row and the All column are called *marginal counts* because they occur in the margins of the table. We see that 106 of the restaurants were owned under a sole proprietorship arrangement. In the other margin, we see that 72 of the respondents viewed the business outlook at level 4.

The cell in the lower right-hand corner of the table shows the total number of responses reported in the table. Only 269 of the 279 questionnaires returned had complete data for both variables. Such incomplete returns are common.

Exhibit 5.6B presents the Owner-Outlook tabulation in another way. Instead of reporting counts, the table shows row percentages. The rows give the distribution of Outlook for each type of restaurant ownership. Column percents can be computed analogously.

ROWS: Owner	COLUMNS: Outlook						
	1	2	3	4	5	6	All
1	17.92	16.04	22.64	27.36	13.21	2.83	100.00
2	3.70	3.70	29.63	40.74	11.11	11.11	100.00
3	10.29	15.44	23.53	23.53	22.79	4.41	100.00
All	12.64	14.50	23.79	26.77	17.84	4.46	100.00

CELL CONTENTS—% OF ROW

The table in Exhibit 5.6B needs a lot of work to make it user-friendly. The "100.00" figures in the right-hand column repeat too many figures, and the numerical codes need to be interpreted. Exhibit 5.6C looks more pleasing and reports more information. The Outlook categories have been placed down the side of the table and the Ownership categories across the top. Therefore, as our eyes move across the table, we compare restaurants with different types of ownership. And as we read down the columns, we see the business outlooks of different types of ownership.

E X H I B I T **5.6C**
Percent Responding to Question
Concerning Economic Outlook
for the Coming Year, by Type of
Ownership; Percents in Columns
Sum to 100

Outlook	Sole Proprietorship	Partnership	Corporation
Very unfavorable	18	4	10
Unfavorable	16	4	15
Mildly unfavorable	23	29	24
Mildly favorable	27	41	24
Favorable	13	11	23
Very favorable	3	11	4

Source: 1980 Wisconsin Restaurant Survey conducted by the University of Wisconsin Small Business Development Center. A mail survey of a random sample of 1000 restaurants in 19 Wisconsin counties yielded 269 usable responses to the table.

Collapsing Tables

Exhibit 5.6A displays the distributions of Outlook responses for each of the three ownership categories: sole proprietorship (1), partnership (2), and corporation (3). The responses tend to cluster in the two middle Outlook responses, "mildly unfavorable" (3) and "mildly favorable" (4), with category 4 being the most frequent response. Looking at the group of restaurants as a whole, we see from Exhibit 5.6A that 137 out of the 269, approximately 51%, responded in one of the unfavorable categories.

collapsing   Working with the six-category Outlook variable is fairly complex. Perhaps we can gain insight by **collapsing** it—that is, combining categories to create a variable with fewer categories. A two-category variable with all the unfavorable categories coded as 0 and all the favorable categories coded as 1 yields Exhibit 5.6D. The new table makes it easier to explore the relationship between the variables Outlook and Owner.

E X H I B I T **5.6D**
Two-Way Table Showing the
Relationship Between Ownership
and Outlook

| Ownership | Outlook | | Total |
	Unfavorable No. (%)	Favorable No. (%)	No. (%)
Sole Proprietorship	60 (57%)	46 (43%)	106 (100%)
Partnership	10 (37%)	17 (63%)	27 (100%)
Corporation	67 (49%)	69 (51%)	136 (100%)
Total	137 (51%)	132 (49%)	269 (100%)

CELL CONTENTS—COUNT (row %)

Exhibit 5.6D shows that only 43% of the sole proprietorships, but 63% of partnerships and 51% of corporations, have a favorable outlook. Fewer than 50% of all respondents have a favorable outlook, but only *one* of the three ownership categories has fewer than 50% favorable responses. This example cautions us about applying conclusions about a group to its subgroups. (We saw this same message in the example of Simpson's paradox in Chapter 4.)

In Exhibit 5.6D, we could display percentages only. But it is redundant to report all the row percentages. We know that if 57% of the sole proprietorships responded unfavorably, then 43% responded favorably. In other words, we could report only the Ownership categories and the Favorable percentages and leave out the rest of the table.

When collecting categorical data, variables with many categories may be used. When analyzing and reporting data, however, we have the option of collapsing, or combining, some of the categories. If this operation does not significantly distort information, it is usually a good strategy, leading to both clarity and simplicity of analysis.

SECTION

5.7 Exercises

5.7A   For the restaurant data set, recode all the Outlook responses of 7 to the data code for "missing." Now redo all the calculations outlined in Sections 5.4 and 5.6. What difference does the different coding make?

5.7B   The data that follow are actual responses to a student survey done in a statistics class of about 250 students. For this exercise, the first 20 responses were chosen from the database. The rows correspond to students (cases); the columns correspond to questions on the questionnaire (variables). Responses are shown for five items.

```
filename: STUDENTS.DAT
Data from a survey of a statistics class
1. What is your gender? (0=male, 1=female)
2. I won't have much use for statistics beyond this course.
3. I am worried about how well I will do in this course.
4. I think statistics is a boring subject to learn.
5. Large lecture courses offer little opportunity for individual attention.
 For the last 4 questions: 1=strongly agree, 2=agree, 3=neutral,
 4=disagree, and 5=strongly disagree
 0 4 1 2 2
 1 3 4 2 2
 0 4 1 2 2
 1 2 2 1 1
 1 5 4 3 2
 0 5 4 3 3
 0 4 1 4 1
 0 3 4 1 1
 0 2 2 2 2
 0 4 5 4 4
 0 4 2 2 1
 0 4 4 2 3
 1 2 1 3 1
 0 3 2 1 3
 0 5 1 1 1
 0 4 5 1 3
 1 3 2 1 1
 0 4 5 4 3
 1 1 3 1 1
 0 3 1 1 1
```

a Prepare a 2 × 5 table of variables 1 and 2 (gender and future use). Compute the row percents. Do males and females seem to agree or disagree in their responses?

b Prepare a 5 × 5 table of variables 2 and 3 (future use and anxiety). Many of the cells have no data because there are only 20 cases. This illustrates the notion that a large number of cases are needed to study variables with many categories. When the number of cases is small, variables usually have to be collapsed into a small number of categories.

c Collapse the responses to variables 2 and 3 into two categories. Combine the original 1, 2, and 3 responses into a new category called "do not disagree." Combine the original 4 and 5 responses into a new category called "disagree." Prepare a 2 × 2 table using these new categories. How would you characterize the relationship between the two variables?

5.7C Use the data in Exercise 5.7B.

a Prepare a 2 × 5 table of variables 1 and 5 (gender and lecture size). Compute the row percents. Do males and females seem to agree or disagree in their responses?

b Prepare a 5 × 5 table of variables 2 and 5 (future use and lecture size). Many of the cells have no data because there are only 20 cases. This illustrates the notion that a large number of cases are needed to study variables with many categories. When the number of cases is small, variables usually have to be collapsed into a small number of categories.

c Collapse the responses to variables 2 and 5 into two categories. Combine the original 1, 2, and 3 responses into a new category called "do not disagree." Combine the original 4 and 5 responses into a new category called "disagree." Prepare a 2 × 2 table using these new categories. How would you characterize the relationship between the two variables? (Filename: STUDENTS.DAT.)

5.7D In the text, we suggest that Exhibit 5.6D could be greatly simplified by reporting only percentages. Prepare a table following the guidelines set forth in the text. Make it presentation quality. [*Hint*: In the legend of the table you need to report the number of responses on which the percentages are based. Why?]

5.7E Use only the data displayed in Exhibit 5.4A.

a Make a 5 × 3 table of the Outlook and Size variables. Compute row percents. Do the different Size categories tend to have different outlooks?

b Collapse the Outlook variable into the two categories used in the text and make the resulting 2 × 3 table of Outlook and Size. Do the different Size categories tend to have different outlooks?

5.7F Redo Exercise 5.7E using the same variables and all the cases in the restaurant data. Comment on the relationship between Outlook and Size. (Filename: RESTRNT.DAT.)

SECTION

5.8 Other Data Within Categories

The cells of a table may be used to report more than the basic counts and percents presented in Section 5.6. This section shows how the cells can be used to report data from other categories, continuous data, or time series.

Other Categorical Data

To show how table cells can report data from other variables, let us use both Ownership and Type of Restaurant to create categories, or cells. Because there are three ownership categories and three types of restaurant [Fast Food (1), Supper Club (2), and Other (3)], there are nine categories in the two-way classification. Exhibit 5.8A shows the counts of restaurants in each of the nine categories and also the percentage of those restaurants giving a favorable Outlook response. Because Outlook has been collapsed to only two categories, favorable and unfavorable, the information in the table in Exhibit 5.8A is reported economically. If a six-category classification of Outlook had been used, the table would have been much more complex.

Within each Ownership category, the responses by Type of Restaurant vary substantially. In the Sole Proprietorship category, 55% of the Fast Food restaurants responded favorably, but only 33% of the Supper Clubs and 38% of the Others did. Thus, although only 43% of all sole proprietorships had a favorable economic outlook, applying this 43% to the whole category would be misleading for Fast Food restaurants owned by sole proprietors. Similarly, the 62% favorable responses from the Partnerships overall is clearly inappropriate for the Fast Food Partnerships!

EXHIBIT **5.8A**
Business Outlook of Restaurants by Ownership and Type

| | Type of Restaurant | | | |
Ownership	Fast Food	Supper Club	Other	Total
Sole Proprietorship	42	30	32	104
	55%	33%	38%	43%
Partnership	8	9	7	24
	38%	78%	71%	62%
Corporation	59	35	37	131
	52%	46%	54%	51%
Total	109	74	76	259
	52%	45%	49%	49%

CELL CONTENTS { Number in category
{ Percent responding favorably on Outlook

Continuous Data

Tables may also be used to display quantities on a third, continuous, variable. In Exhibit 5.8B, the average sales (in $1000s) are broken down by the values of the Owner and Size categorical variables. For example, in the cell corresponding to Owner = 1 and Size = 1, sales for all the restaurants with these two characteristics were collected and averaged. Similar calculations were done for each cell. Notice that for each of the values of the nonordered variable Owner, the average sales increase as the value of the ordered categorical variable Size increases. Recall that Size is defined by number of employees. The table shows that increasing Size is associated with increasing Sales, at least on average.

The average sales of all sole proprietorships, regardless of size, which is 150.07, is displayed in the right margin of the table. The other marginal averages are computed similarly. None of these averages can be computed solely from the averages in the body of the table. The marginal averages provide additional information not obtainable from the averages in the body.

EXHIBIT **5.8B** Average Sales by Owner and Size	**ROWS: Owner**	**COLUMNS: Size**			
		1	**2**	**3**	**All**
	1	117.11	237.94	579.00	150.07
	2	88.12	321.25	695.00	228.12
	3	231.50	313.84	887.96	507.78
	All	147.45	291.57	861.74	340.41

CELL CONTENTS—Average Sales

To make the table in Exhibit 5.8B user-friendly, the categories need names, the averages could be reported with fewer figures, and the table needs a better legend. Exhibit 5.8C shows how Exhibit 5.8B might be improved. Reporting the averages only to two significant figures sacrifices a bit of detail, but the main message of the table comes through more clearly.

EXHIBIT **5.8C** Average Sales of Restaurants (in $10,000s) by Ownership and Size		**Size**			
	Ownership	**Small**	**Medium**	**Large**	**All**
	Sole Proprietorship	12	24	58	15
	Partnership	9	32	69	23
	Corporation	23	31	89	51
	All	15	29	86	34

Source: 1980 Wisconsin Restaurant Survey conducted by the University of Wisconsin Small Business Development Center. A mail survey of a random sample of 1000 restaurants in 19 Wisconsin counties yielded 261 usable responses to the table.

Time Series Data

Data collected in sequence, as considered in Chapter 2, are usefully tabled to display special features. Exhibit 5.8D shows how the Deere & Co. oil-filter sales data reported in Chapter 2 might originally appear, before analysis begins. Exhibit 5.8E shows the same information displayed in a more useful tabular format. Here the sales can be tracked over individual years and also across the same month for different years. Exhibit 5.8F adds additional information to the table by displaying the row (monthly) averages and the column (yearly) averages. The seasonality observed in Chapter 2 is readily apparent in the variation of the monthly averages in this display.

E X H I B I T **5.8D**
Deere & Co. Oil-Filter Sales:
Raw Data

Number Sold	Month	Year
2385	7	83
3302	8	83
3958	9	83
3302	10	83
2441	11	83
3107	12	83
5862	1	84
4536	2	84
4625	3	84
4492	4	84
⋮	⋮	⋮
5787	2	87
2886	3	87
5475	4	87
3843	5	87
2537	6	87

E X H I B I T **5.8E**
Deere & Co. Oil-Filter Sales:
Time Series in Month-by-Year
Layout

Month/Year	83	84	85	86	87
1	—	5862	5472	5357	5332
2	—	4536	5310	5811	5787
3	—	4625	1965	2436	2886
4	—	4492	3791	4608	5475
5	—	4486	3622	2871	3843
6	—	4005	3726	3349	2537
7	2385	3744	3370	2909	—
8	3302	2546	2535	2324	—
9	3958	1954	1572	1603	—
10	3302	2285	2146	2148	—
11	2441	1778	2249	2245	—
12	3107	3222	1721	1586	—

Month/Year	83	84	85	86	87	Average
1	—	5862	5472	5357	5332	5505
2	—	4536	5310	5811	5787	5361
3	—	4625	1965	2436	2886	2978
4	—	4492	3791	4608	5475	4591
5	—	4486	3622	2871	3843	3705
6	—	4005	3726	3349	2537	3404
7	2385	3744	3370	2909	—	3102
8	3302	2546	2535	2324	—	2676
9	3958	1954	1572	1603	—	2271
10	3302	2285	2146	2148	—	2470
11	2441	1778	2249	2245	—	2178
12	3107	3222	1721	1586	—	2409
Average	3082	3627	3123	3103	4310	3387

EXHIBIT **5.8F**
Deere & Co. Oil-Filter Sales:
Time Series in Month-by-Year
Layout with Averages

SECTION

5.9 Exercises

5.9A   Use Exhibit 5.9A to answer the following questions.

a   Rearrange the Establishments with Payrolls data into a two-way table showing number of establishments and sales by kind of business and by year.

b   Tidy up the figures in the table by displaying them to two significant digits only. Also arrange the kinds of business in decreasing order of 1977 sales.

c   Prepare another table with the same categories as in parts (a) and (b) but showing number of establishments as a percentage of total number of establishments within each year and showing sales as a percentage of total sales within each year. Examine this table for substantial changes in the percentages between 1972 and 1977. Are both sets of percentages in decreasing order within each year? Can you explain why?

d   Prepare another table with the same categories as in part (c) but showing the average sales per establishment. Examine this table for substantial changes in the averages. If you were to arrange the kinds of business in decreasing order of average sales in 1977, would the order be different from the one in your table? Can you explain why?

e   How would you go about obtaining more recent data so that the study begun in this exercise could be extended? What kinds of business would you most like to follow up on in an extended study?

5.9B   Consider Exhibit 5.9A.

a   Collapse the Kind of Business categories into two: Eating and Drinking Places and Other. Make a two-way table showing only the number of establishments with payroll by Kind of Business and Year.

b   Calculate the row percents for this table.

c   Prepare a table showing row percents that would be appropriate for presentation in a report or a meeting.

5.9C   Using the restaurant data, explain how you would construct a table showing the mean and standard deviation of sales in a Size by Type of Food classification. Do not carry out the calculations. Simply indicate the calculations needed. Design the table you would make to report the results in a meeting.

5.9D Redo the table in Exhibit 5.8F, reporting figures only to two significant figures. How does this change the information reported in the table?

EXHIBIT **5.9A** Numbers of Establishments and Total Retail Sales in 1972 and 1977 for Various Kinds of Business (establishments with payroll shown for 1972; establishments with payroll and all establishments shown for 1977)

| | 1972 | | 1977 | | | |
| | Establishments with Payrolls | | All Establishments | | Establishments with Payrolls | |
Kind of Business	Number (in 1000s)	Sales (in millions of dollars)	Number (in 1000s)	Sales (in millions of dollars)	Number (in 1000s)	Sales (in millions of dollars)
Building materials, hardware garden supply, and mobile home dealers	62.0	22,958	90.4	38,860	65.8	37,793
General merchandise group stores	44.4	64,669	48.9	93,948	38.4	93,455
Food stores	173.1	96,375	252.0	157,940	171.6	152,745
Automotive dealers	85.1	88,491	139.0	149,952	94.8	147,202
Gasoline service stations	183.4	31,440	176.5	56,468	146.5	53,749
Apparel and accessory stores	105.7	24,115	140.1	35,564	114.8	34,719
Furniture, home furnishings, and equipment stores	82.5	21,505	138.6	33,176	91.7	31,568
Eating and drinking places	287.36	35,048	368.1	63,276	308.6	61,307
Drug and proprietary stores	47.6	15,420	49.6	23,196	47.2	23,196
Miscellaneous retail stores	193.9	40,202	452.0	70,753	242.2	64,038
Retail trade, total	1,264.9	440,222	1,855.1	723,134	1,321.6	699,635

Source: Adapted from U.S. Bureau of the Census, "Establishments with Payroll, 1972, and Establishments, Sales and Employees, 1977, by Kind of Business," *Statistical Abstract of the United States: 1984,* 104th ed. (Washington, D.C.: U.S. Government Printing Office, 1983), Table 1434.

SECTION

5.10 Multiway Tables (Optional)

In a multiway table, the cells are defined by the categories of several categorical variables. In this section, we show how to display three-way tables and suggest how to deal with the complexity of such displays.

Exhibit 5.6D showed the relationship between the two categorical variables Ownership and Outlook, a two-way table. Exhibit 5.8A showed Outlook information for restaurants classified by Ownership and Type of Restaurant, another two-way classification. Another variable of interest in the survey is the restaurant's Size. Adding this variable to the analysis gives a three-way classification of the restaurants. The Size variable has three categories: Small (1), Medium (2), and Large (3), so the table will be $3 \times 3 \times 3$.

Exhibit 5.10A shows one way to display the distributions of the Outlook variable across restaurant sizes within each of the nine categories defined by ownership and type of restaurant. The entries in the body of the table are sets of three numbers showing the percentages of favorable responses for Small, Medium, and Large restaurants within the nine categories. The dashes (—) indicate no restaurants in the category. For example, there were no restaurants in the category Sole Proprietorship, Supper Club, and Large Size. Hence the corresponding cell contains a dash (—). Contrast this with the cell defined by Partnership, Fast Food, and Medium Size restaurant, which contains 0%. This means that some restaurants in this category responded to the survey, but none of them had a favorable business outlook. A 0% and a — mean different things. This example illustrates how we can "run out of data" in categories as more and more of them are created. While the figures in Exhibit 5.10A are interesting and suggestive, some of them are based on precious few cases, making us uneasy about the conclusions we draw from them.

EXHIBIT 5.10A
Business Outlook of Restaurants Categorized by Ownership, Type, and Size

| | Type of Restaurant | | | |
Ownership	Fast Food	Supper Club	Other	Total
Sole Proprietorship	50%	30%	35%	40%
	78%	43%	50%	61%
	0%	—	0%	0%
Partnership	50%	50%	60%	54%
	0%	100%	—	67%
	—	50%	100%	75%
Corporation	35%	44%	60%	44%
	68%	46%	56%	59%
	53%	45%	50%	50%
Total	45%	35%	44%	42%
	67%	54%	55%	60%
	50%	46%	52%	50%

CELL CONTENTS- { Percentage favorable of Small
Percentage favorable of Medium
Percentage favorable of Large

The table in Exhibit 5.10A shows Outlook responses at several levels of categorization. The entries in the margins show the distributions of Outlook responses by Size within the categories of Ownership (down the right margin) and Type of Restaurant (along the bottom). For example, at the bottom of the column labeled Fast Food, we see the numbers 45%, 67%, and 50%. This means that 45% of small fast food restaurants responded favorably on business outlook, while 67% of medium-sized fast food restaurants responded favorably, as did 50% of large fast food restaurants. These percentages apply to fast food restaurants without regard to style of ownership. The percentages in the lower right-hand corner of the table apply to the Size categories without regard to style of ownership or to type of restaurant.

Another table could be constructed using Size and Ownership as the marginal variables and Type of Restaurant as the variable displayed within the body of the table. Then the distribution in the lower right-hand corner would be the percentages that apply to Type of Restaurant alone.

We may also wish to study relationships among the three variables Ownership, Type of Restaurant, and Size. This can be accomplished by looking at counts or row or column percents within the cells of a $3 \times 3 \times 3$ classification. One possible format is shown in Exhibit 5.10B, which displays counts. Within each Type category, there is a 3×3 table for the variables Ownership and Size. Other formats are clearly possible. Exhibit 5.10C shows the row percents for the same classification.

EXHIBIT **5.10B**
Number of Restaurants by Size, Type, and Ownership

Fast Food

Ownership	Small	Medium	Large	All
Sole Proprietorship	32	9	1	42
Partnership	6	2	0	8
Corporation	20	19	19	58
All	58	30	20	108

Supper Clubs

	Small	Medium	Large	All
Sole Proprietorship	23	7	0	30
Partnership	2	4	2	8
Corporation	9	13	11	33
All	34	24	13	71

Other

	Small	Medium	Large	All
Sole Proprietorship	26	2	1	29
Partnership	5	0	2	7
Corporation	10	9	18	37
All	41	11	21	73

Using Three-Way Tables

Comparisons in a three-way table are somewhat complex. The marginal distributions are not usually much help in finding patterns in the body of the table. For example, look at the Fast Food section in Exhibit 5.10C. The marginal row percents are 54, 28, and 18%. Do these percents apply to the different types of restaurants in the table? Clearly not! Corporations are about evenly divided among Small, Medium, and Large firms, but there are practically no large sole proprietorships or partnerships. About 75% of both sole proprietorships and partnerships are small.

The marginal row percents for Supper Clubs are 48%, 34%, and 18%, not that different from the row percents for Fast Food. Again we find very different patterns within the body of the table.

Fast Food

Ownership	Small	Medium	Large
Sole Proprietorship	76	22	2
Partnership	75	25	—
Corporation	34	33	33
All	54	28	18

Supper Club

	Small	Medium	Large
Sole Proprietorship	77	23	—
Partnership	25	50	25
Corporation	27	40	33
All	48	34	18

Other

	Small	Medium	Large
Sole Proprietorship	90	7	3
Partnership	71	—	29
Corporation	27	24	49
All	56	15	29

When variables separate cases into categories, multi-way tables are the natural way to display relationships among the variables. As the number of variables grows, however, the size and complexity of the tables grow also, placing a premium on the efficient display of information. Two tools for doing this are (1) use only as many significant figures as the reader can absorb (two significant figures is recommended) and (2) display only the absolutely essential figures (eliminate redundant percentages, for example).[†]

[†] For further reading on the construction and use of multiway tables, see Ottar Hellevik, *Introduction to Causal Analysis: Exploring Survey Data by Crosstabulation* (London: Allen & Unwin, 1984) and A. S. C. Ehrenberg, *Primer in Data Reduction* (New York: Wiley, 1982).

S E C T I O N

5.11 Exercises

5.11A   The table below has the structure of Exhibit 5.10C except that column percents are displayed. Make as many comparisons as you can. How would you describe the relationships among the variables?

| | Fast Food | | | |
Ownership	Small	Medium	Large	All
Sole Proprietorship	55	30	5	39
Partnership	10	7	—	7
Corporation	35	63	95	54

| | Supper Club | | | |
	Small	Medium	Large	All
Sole Proprietorship	68	29	—	42
Partnership	6	17	15	12
Corporation	26	54	85	46

| | Other | | | |
	Small	Medium	Large	All
Sole Proprietorship	63	18	5	40
Partnership	12	—	9	9
Corporation	25	82	86	51

5.11B   Verify the row percents in Exhibit 5.10C—that is, carry out the necessary calculations in Exhibit 5.10B to obtain Exhibit 5.10C.

5.11C   The data below are part of a set collected from a business statistics class at the University of Wisconsin. Students were asked to write on a card their gender, age, and academic classification, among other items.

a   Make a 2 × 5 × 4 table for these three variables. Show counts.

b   From the table you made in part (a), make a table showing row percents.

c   From the table you made in part (a), make a table showing column percents.

d   Interpret the relationships among the variables.

```
filename: CLASS.DAT
Business statistics class data
Gender: 2=female, 1=male
Age coded as: 1=age less than 18, 2=ages 18 to 20, 3=ages 21 to 23
4=ages 24 to 25, and 5=ages greater than 25.
Academic classification coded as: 1=prebusiness, 2=business undergraduate,
3=business graduate, 4=nonbusiness student
variables: Gender, Age, Academic Classification
 1  5  4          1  2  1
 2  2  1          1  3  4
 2  2  1          1  2  1
 1  3  1          1  2  1
 2  2  1          2  2  1
 1  4  3          2  1  1
 2  2  1          1  2  1
 1  2  1          2  2  1
 1  2  1          2  1  1
 2  2  1          1  2  1
 2  3  1          2  2  1
 1  3  1          2  3  4
 2  2  1          2  4  4
 1  2  2          1  2  1
 1  2  1          1  4  1
 2  4  3          2  2  1
 1  2  2          2  3  2
 2  2  1          2  2  1
 1  3  2          2  2  1
 2  4  4          2  2  1
 2  2  1          2  2  1
 2  2  1          2  5  4
 1  2  1
```

5.11D Use the data in Exercise 5.11C. Collapse the age variable into two categories: age < 21 and age ≥ 21. Collapse the classification variable into two categories by combining the original 1 and 4 categories (call it "not in School of Business") and the original 2 and 3 categories (call it "in School of Business"). Now redo parts (a)–(d) in Exercise 5.11C.

Chapter Summary

Tables are tools for displaying and analyzing categorical data. Tables display counts, percentages, and descriptive statistics or data on other variables. Multiway classifications can be quite complex, so to make useful displays, we must learn to display data economically. Some techniques for economical display are collapsing, reducing the number of digits, and removing redundant material.

Supplementary Exercises for Chapter 5

5A The following data are taken from U.S. Bureau of the Census, *Statistical Abstract of the United States: 1989*, 109th ed. (Washington, D.C.: U.S. Government Printing Office, 1989), Table 850. Displayed are the Total Business Receipts (income from sales and operations) and Total Business Deductions for the years 1982–1986. All figures are in millions of dollars.

Year	Receipts	Deductions
1982	433,665	383,092
1983	465,169	404,809
1984	516,037	445,270
1985	540,045	461,273
1986	559,384	468,960

a   Net Income is the difference between Total Business Receipts and Total Business Deductions. Compute the values of this variable for the years 1982–1986.

b   Compute the ratio of Net Income to Total Business Receipts and express the ratio as a percentage.

c   Make a sequence plot of the ratio you computed in part (b). How has the ratio evolved over the years 1982–1986?

5B   The data below are taken from U.S. Bureau of the Census, *Statistical Abstract of the United States: 1989*, 109th ed. (Washington, D.C.: U.S. Government Printing Office, 1989), Table 857. Displayed are Current Assets and Current Liabilities for nonfinancial corporations in the United States for the years 1975–1985. All figures are in billions of dollars, as of December 31.

a   Working Capital is the difference between Current Assets and Current Liabilities. Compute the values of Working Capital for the years 1975–1985. Compute the annual percentage increases in the three variables Current Assets, Liabilities, and Working Capital for the years 1975–1985. Put the sequence plots of the three percentage increase series on the same set of axes, using different plotting symbols for the three series. Compare the behaviors of the three series.

b   The Current Ratio is Current Assets divided by Current Liabilities. Compute the Current Ratio for the years 1975–1985 and make a sequence plot of the resulting series. Describe the behavior of the series.

Year	Assets	Liabilities
1975	756.3	446.9
1976	823.1	487.5
1977	900.9	546.8
1978	1,028.1	661.9
1979	1,200.9	809.1
1980	1,281.6	877.2
1981	1,374.5	923.2
1982	1,425.4	977.8
1983	1,557.3	1,043.0
1984	1,703.0	1,163.6
1985	1,778.5	1,232.7

5C   The following data are taken from U.S. Bureau of the Census, *Statistical Abstract of the United States: 1989*, 109th ed. (Washington, D.C.: U.S. Government Printing Office, 1989), Table 859. Shown are numbers of establishments, numbers of employees, and annual payroll for selected industries and selected employment classes within industries, for the year 1986. To make the presentation of the table more compact, the following definitions are used:

E1 = Number of employees less than 20
E2 = Number of employees between 20 and 99
E3 = Number of employees between 100 and 499
E4 = Number of employees between 500 and 999
E5 = Number of employees 1000 or more
I1 = Agricultural services
I2 = Mining
I3 = Contract construction
I4 = Manufacturing
I5 = Transportation (and other public utilities)
I6 = Wholesale trade
I7 = Retail trade
I8 = Finance and insurance (including real estate)
I9 = Services
Counts in 1000s, payroll is presented in units of $1 billion.

Number of Establishments

Industry	E1	E2	E3	E4	E5	Total
I1	65	3	Z	Z	Z	68
I2	28	6	1	Z	Z	35
I3	445	42	5	Z	Z	492
I4	230	88	32	4	2	355
I5	170	32	7	1	Z	210
I6	374	59	6	Z	Z	440
I7	1237	184	19	1	Z	1441
I8	450	45	7	1	Z	504
I9	1639	139	29	3	2	1811
Total	5082	605	107	8	5	5807

Note: Z indicates that data remained confidential because fewer than 500 firms in the class were surveyed.

Number of Employees

Industry	E1	E2	E3	E4	E5	Total
I1	235	110	52	10	4	412
I2	141	240	278	103	85	847
I3	1877	1607	797	142	236	4659
I4	1420	3900	6525	2409	4888	19142
I5	823	1312	1352	418	980	4884
I6	2048	2231	1108	190	147	5725
I7	6418	7321	3230	346	235	17550
I8	1836	1807	1418	427	882	6371
I9	6746	5621	5499	1735	3277	22878
Total	22296	24311	20260	5780	10734	88380

Industry	Annual Payroll					Total
	E1	E2	E3	E4	E5	
I1	3.4	1.5	.7	Z	Z	5.8
I2	3.3	6.1	8.7	3.6	2.8	24.5
I3	37.0	37.3	20.3	3.7	6.2	104.5
I4	27.8	79.4	142.3	59.9	158.5	467.8
I5	16.3	30.1	35.8	13.0	32.4	127.7
I6	45.5	53.0	29.3	5.8	4.7	138.2
I7	68.0	76.4	38.4	5.6	5.0	193.0
I8	38.5	42.0	34.5	11.0	25.3	151.0
I9	121.8	86.8	80.7	29.5	62.6	381.4
Total	375	414	391	132	298	1609

Note: Z indicates that data remained confidential because fewer than 500 firms in the class were surveyed.

a   Collapse each table above into tables that report only three industry categories: Manufacturing, Services, and Other. Compare Manufacturing and Services with respect to Number of Establishments, Number of Employees, and Payroll. How are these quantities distributed within employment-size categories for Manufacturing and Services?

b   For each of the tables you constructed in part (a), collapse the Employment-Size categories into three: Under 100, Between 100 and 999, and 1000 or More. Compare the information displayed in these doubly collapsed tables with the information displayed in the original tables. Has the collapsing suppressed any significant information?

5D   Have each member of your class write the following information on an index card:

Gender
Classification
Age
Height
Mother's height
Amount of loose change in pocket or purse

Collapse Classification into three categories and Age into three categories (the choice of categories is up to you). Now make a $2 \times 3 \times 3$ table using Gender, Classification, and Age as the variables. Within each cell of the table place Height. Make another table that reports Mother's Height. Make a third table that reports Amount of Loose Change in pocket or purse. For each table, average the data in each cell. Does there appear to be a difference in the averages for males and females? Does there appear to be a difference in the averages for people of different Classifications? Different Ages?

. . . .

Glossary for Chapter 5

body   The cells defined by all the combinations of categories of the variables in a table.

cases   Rows in a data table.

categorical data   Data that are arranged in classes or categories.

cell	Location in a table defined by the intersection of a category of one variable with a category of another variable.
collapsing	Combining categories of a variable to create a variable with fewer categories.
multiway table	A table in which the cells are defined by the categories of several categorical variables.
ordered categories	Those categories that cannot be displayed in an arbitrary order without losing some information.
tally	A count of the number of cases in each category of a variable.
two-way table	A breakdown of the number of respondents (or counts) in each category that is formed by intersecting the categories of two variables.
variable	A characteristic of the elements under study.

6

Relating Continuous Variables

Chapter Objectives

After mastering this chapter, you will be able to:

- Prepare a scatterplot to show a relationship between variables

- Assess whether a relationship shown in a scatterplot is positive or negative, straight-line or curved

- Compute the correlation coefficient and interpret its value in light of the scatterplot

- Define and give an example of ecological correlation

- Explain how to document causation

- Explain the meaning of autocorrelation and assess common patterns of autocorrelation in data

SECTION

6.1 Introduction

Statistical analysis is used to compare variables and document relationships among them. Predictable relationships can be exploited commercially or used to eliminate waste from processes.

For example, marketers might study the impact of price changes on coffee purchases by measuring sales when prices are set at different levels over a period of time. In a process application, a manufacturer might document the relationship between the moisture content of a certain raw material and the yield of usable final product. This could result in determining acceptable standards on moisture content and working with suppliers to provide raw material that meets these standards.

This chapter presents two important tools for documenting relationships among variables: scatterplots and correlation.

6.2 Scatterplots

Scatterplots display statistical relationships between two variables. We begin this section by scatterplotting the data in Exhibit 6.2A, which were collected as part of a citywide study of real estate property valuation. They are observations on 60 parcels that sold in a particular calendar year and neighborhood. Data like those displayed in Exhibit 6.2A are available for each neighborhood of the city for a number of years. The present data are thus just a small part of a single cross section taken from a much larger data listing.

EXHIBIT **6.2A**
Data on 60 Residential Parcels
Sold in a Particular Year

Sq.ft = Square feet of living area
Grade = Type of construction(-1 = low, 0 = medium, 1 = high)
Assessed = Most recent assessed value on city assessor's books
Market = Selling price of parcel

Sq.ft	Grade	Assessed	Market	Sq.ft	Grade	Assessed	Market
521	−1	7.80	26.0	926	0	18.22	37.4
538	−1	28.20	19.4	931	0	24.60	38.0
544	0	23.20	25.2	965	0	14.60	37.2
577	−1	22.20	26.2	966	0	30.20	44.0
661	−1	23.80	31.0	967	0	26.00	44.2
662	0	19.60	34.6	1011	0	28.00	43.6
677	0	22.80	36.4	1011	0	26.00	38.4
691	−1	22.60	33.0	1024	0	27.00	42.2
694	0	28.00	37.4	1033	0	25.20	40.4
712	0	21.20	42.4	1040	0	22.40	40.4
721	0	21.60	32.8	1047	0	30.00	43.6
722	−1	7.40	25.6	1051	0	26.40	41.4
743	0	26.20	34.8	1052	0	20.20	39.6
760	0	26.60	35.8	1056	0	25.80	41.8
767	−1	22.20	33.6	1060	1	29.20	44.8
780	−1	22.60	31.0	1060	0	24.00	38.4
787	0	22.40	39.2	1070	0	22.80	43.6
802	0	25.40	36.0	1075	0	30.40	42.8
814	0	14.80	34.8	1079	0	24.20	40.6
815	0	14.40	34.4	1100	0	30.00	41.6
825	0	28.20	38.0	1106	0	31.60	42.8
834	−1	18.00	34.6	1138	0	25.60	39.0
838	0	25.60	35.6	1164	1	29.40	41.8
858	−1	22.40	35.8	1171	0	32.20	48.4
883	0	25.80	39.6	1237	0	17.00	39.8
890	0	20.20	35.0	1249	0	22.00	47.2
899	0	23.20	37.6	1298	1	23.60	45.2
918	0	32.20	41.2	1435	0	21.40	38.8
920	−1	20.80	31.2	1602	1	31.00	47.4
923	−1	4.60	30.0	1804	0	30.60	45.4

The purpose of our study is to find relationships among the listed variables. The purpose of the larger study is to document such relationships for all the neighborhoods in the city and also to document the stability or lack of stability of those relationships over time. Such a study is valuable to city and state governments, which must assess the value of each parcel of real estate each year for taxation. It is also valuable to the real estate industry as a basis for pricing parcels as they come on the market and for documenting market trends. This section focuses on basic cross-sectional analysis and does not go into longitudinal issues.

Exhibit 6.2B shows a table and a scatterplot of square footage and market data for the first five cases in Exhibit 6.2A. In the scatterplot, Market is plotted on the vertical axis and Sq.ft on the horizontal axis. Each **x** in the scatterplot marks the point of intersection for the Sq.ft and market data for a single case. Taking the first case as an example, we plot a point with 521 on the horizontal axis and 26 on the vertical axis.

scatterplot   A **scatterplot** is so-named because typically its points do not lie on a simple, smooth mathematical curve. Rather, it shows *variation* in the data. Scatterplots are used to try to discover a tendency for the variables to be related. Thus, the more the scatterplot reminds us of a mathematical curve, the more closely related we infer the variables are. Of course, with such a few points as in Exhibit 6.2B, we cannot be sure of any pattern that may suggest itself.

E X H I B I T **6.2B**
Scatterplot of Market Versus
Sq.ft for First Five Cases in
Exhibit 6.2A

Sq.ft	Market
521	26.0
538	19.4
544	25.2
577	26.2
661	31.0

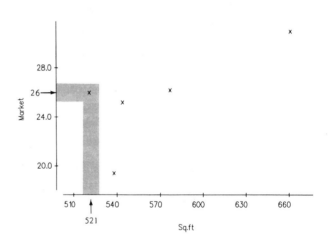

A relationship in which higher values of one variable tend to be associated with higher values of another variable is called a *positive* relationship. In a *negative* relationship, higher values of one variable are associated with lower values of another variable.

EXAMPLE   **6.2A**

Exhibit 6.2C shows the scatterplot of all 60 cases from Exhibit 6.2A. We see a distinct tendency for the higher values of Market to be associated with higher values of Sq.ft, and vice versa, despite the rather extensive amount of scatter in the plot. A positive relationship between the two variables is inferred. Not every case satisfies this condition, but the preponderance of cases do, so our eyes see the "trend." Exhibit 2.6C displays a negative relationship between oil-filter sales and month, indicating a tendency to have higher sales in the first part of the year, lower sales in the second part.   ▪

EXHIBIT **6.2C**
Scatterplot of Market versus Sq.ft for All 60 Cases in Exhibit 6.2A

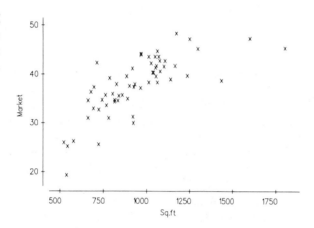

EXAMPLE   **6.2B**

Exhibit 6.2D repeats the scatterplot in Exhibit 6.2C and overlays it with a set of axes whose origin is the point whose first coordinate is the mean of the Sq.ft variable and whose second coordinate is the mean of the Market variable: the point (941.7, 37.8).

The four quadrants formed by this new axis system are labeled I, II, III, and IV. About equal numbers of points fall in quadrants I and III, a few points fall in quadrant II, and only one point falls in quadrant IV. This plot shows a limited tendency for the points to follow a straight line, but we also detect a slight "rainbow" shape in the scatterplot.   ▪

Example 6.2A displays a pair of variables that exhibit a positive relationship that is somewhat curved but also somewhat like a straight line. The next example displays a pair of variables whose relationship is negative and mostly straight-line, with some scatter about the line.

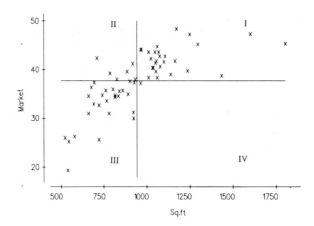

E X A M P L E   **6.2C**

An editorial in the *Wall Street Journal* reported on the relationship between government monetary policy and inflation rates. The author of the article asserted that a central bank under relatively more control of the government is pressured to respond to recession by increasing money supply, hence tending to fuel inflation, whereas a relatively independent central bank is able to stabilize money supply, hence tending to keep the lid on inflation. To support his argument, the author used data from different countries, as shown in Exhibit 6.2E and displayed in the scatterplot shown there. The author's independence rating gives low values to low degrees of central bank independence and high values to high degrees of central bank independence. The plotting symbol "3" in the plot shows France, Norway, and Sweden, all three of which have independence ratings of 2 and inflation rates of 6. Notice that four countries have an independence rating of 2.5 but that they all have different inflation rates. There is not a perfectly predictable relationship between the two variables. Nevertheless, the tendency for lower inflation to be associated with a higher independence rating is quite clear. The scatterplot displays the negative relationship. ▪

The next example shows two variables that display no relationship.

E X A M P L E   **6.2D**

In March 1992, *Consumer Reports* gave data on 24 compact disc players. One variable was a quality rating and the other was list price. Is there a relationship between rating and price? Exhibit 6.2F shows the data and a scatterplot.

No relationship between the variables is apparent. The visual impression is that prices could have been assigned to ratings at random. ▪

EXHIBIT **6.2E**
Data on Inflation Rate and
Central Bank Independence,
1955–1988, for 16 Countries

Country	Inflation Rate	Independence Index
New Zealand	7.8	1.00
Spain	8.5	1.50
Italy	7.2	1.75
United Kingdom	6.8	2.00
Australia	6.5	2.00
France	6.0	2.00
Norway	6.0	2.00
Sweden	6.0	2.00
Belgium	4.1	2.00
Denmark	6.5	2.50
Japan	4.9	2.50
Canada	4.5	2.50
The Netherlands	4.2	2.50
United States	4.2	3.50
Switzerland	3.3	4.00
Germany	2.9	4.00

Source: Robert J. Barro, "Keep Political Hands Off the Fed," *Wall Street Journal*, August 26, 1992, p. A6.

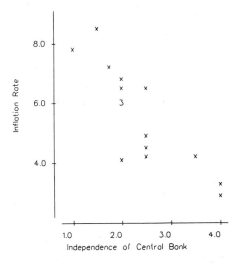

In this section, we have seen a variety of possible relationships between variables, as revealed in scatterplots. Variables may have positive or negative relationships, straight-line or curved relationships, or no relationship at all. In the next section, we introduce a statistic that helps capture some of these features numerically.

E X H I B I T **6.2F**
Quality Rating and List Price of
24 Compact Disc Players

Quality Rating	Price($)	Quality Rating	Price($)
88	185	90	400
85	150	89	370
85	150	87	335
85	150	85	300
85	145	84	330
83	135	83	330
79	135	82	425
79	130	82	560
79	160	81	265
75	120	81	510
74	120	78	470
74	130	77	330

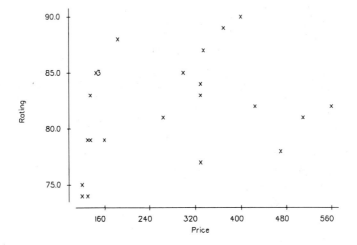

SECTION

6.3 Exercises

6.3A Here is a small set of pairs:

x	2	1	5	3	6	3	4	1
y	4	2	10	6	12	6	8	2

a Prepare a scatterplot of these data.
b Describe the relationship shown in the scatterplot.

6.3B Here is another small set of pairs:

x	2	1	5	3	6	3	4	1
y	6	4	12	8	14	10	8	4

a Prepare a scatterplot of these data.

b Describe the relationship shown in the scatterplot.

6.3C In March 1992, *Consumer Reports* gave data on 30 cassette tape decks. One variable was a quality rating and the other was list price. The players were also coded according to the number of decks: 0 if single deck, 1 if dual deck. Is there a relationship between rating and price, and is there a difference between single- and double-deck players? This exercise helps us answer the question.

Case	Rating	Price	Dual Deck	Case	Rating	Price	Dual Deck
1	94	350	0	16	88	410	1
2	91	280	0	17	83	285	1
3	88	285	0	18	82	460	1
4	88	260	0	19	80	280	1
5	87	360	0	20	80	380	1
6	86	360	0	21	80	280	1
7	86	375	0	22	79	375	1
8	85	200	0	23	78	520	1
9	83	395	0	24	78	210	1
10	82	300	0	25	77	370	1
11	82	240	0	26	77	250	1
12	80	350	0	27	76	330	1
13	80	275	0	28	74	270	1
14	79	400	0	29	71	250	1
15	79	379	0	30	71	300	1

a Make a scatterplot with rating on the vertical axis and price on the horizontal, with one plotting symbol for single-deck and another for dual-deck players.

b Comment on the relationship between the rating and price variables without regard to number of decks.

c Does there appear to be a different behavior for single- and dual-deck players?

d Prepare a dotplot of the rating variable.

e Prepare separate dotplots of the price variable of single- and dual-deck players on the same scale.

f Prepare a dotplot of the price variable.

g Prepare separate dotplots of the price variable of single- and dual-deck players on the same scale.

h Comment on your findings from the analysis of the data. (Filename: CASSETTE.DAT.)

6.3D An economic survey yields information on households. Among other variables, income and percentage of income spent on food are obtained. What relationship do you expect to see if a scatterplot of these variables is constructed?

6.3E How would you characterize the relationship between oil-filter sales and years in Exhibit 2.6D? What would the scatterplot look like if there had been a strong upward trend in sales over the years? A strong downward trend?

6.3F   Consider Exhibits 2.8C and 2.8D showing Amana manufacturing data. Suppose that for each case you plotted the Left reading on the horizontal axis and the Right reading on the vertical axis. Roughly what kind of relationship would be displayed? Suppose you plotted the Midvalue measurements in Exhibit 2.8G on the vertical axis instead of the Right reading. What kind of relationship would be displayed? What relationship would be displayed if you plotted the Diff measurements in Exhibit 2.8H on the vertical axis? Confirm your answers by preparing plots using the data reported in Appendix 4. (Filename: AMANA.DAT.)

6.3G   Using the data in Exhibit 6.2A, prepare a scatterplot of Market versus Assessed values. How would you characterize the relationship between the variables? (Filename: REALPROP.DAT.)

6.3H   The four data sets below were constructed by Frank Anscombe ["Graphs in Statistical Analysis," *American Statistician*, 27, (1973), 17–21]. Draw scatterplots of the four data sets, and verbally characterize the four relationships. Plot x on the horizontal axis and y on the vertical axis. (Filename: ANSCOMBE.DAT.)

Data Set 1		Data Set 2		Data Set 3		Data Set 4	
x	y	x	y	x	y	x	y
10	8.04	10	9.14	10	7.46	8	6.58
8	6.95	8	8.14	8	6.77	8	5.76
13	7.58	13	8.74	13	12.74	8	7.71
9	8.81	9	8.77	9	7.11	8	8.84
11	8.33	11	9.26	11	7.81	8	8.47
14	9.96	14	8.10	14	8.84	8	7.04
6	7.24	6	6.13	6	6.08	8	5.25
4	4.26	4	3.10	4	5.39	19	12.50
12	10.84	12	9.13	12	8.15	8	5.56
7	4.82	7	7.26	7	6.42	8	7.91
5	5.68	5	4.74	5	5.73	8	6.89

6.3I   Reproduce the scatterplot in Exhibit 2.6C. Describe the relationship in the plot. What factors cause the relationship? (Filename: OILFILT.DAT.)

6.3J   Formulate a practical problem in which it would be useful to document the relationship between two variables. Design and implement a scheme for collecting data on the variables. Prepare a scatterplot and interpret the information it conveys about the relationship. Carefully keep track of any problems you encounter in carrying out this exercise. Comment on how those problems may affect the information conveyed in the scatterplot. What further information would you like to have on the variables you studied? How would you go about getting that information?

SECTION

6.4 Correlation

The simplest relationship between two continuous variables is one whose scatterplot looks like a straight line except for scatter. The descriptive statistic most widely used to summarize a relationship between continuous variables is a measure of the degree to which the relationship follows a straight line. It is called the **correlation coefficient.**[†]

correlation coefficient

[†]The coefficient presented in the text is just one of many correlation coefficients defined in the literature, but it is by far the most widely used in statistical practice.

The correlation coefficient is denoted by the symbol r. Its computation is tedious, and although we demonstrate the computational algorithm, we recommend that for practical work you use a calculator or computer that has been preprogrammed. You should never have to do more than enter the data and run a routine that computes r.

In symbols, letting $(x_1, y_1), (x_2, y_2), \ldots, (x_n, y_n)$ denote the n pairs of observations on the x and y variables, the correlation coefficient is computed as

$$r = \left(\frac{1}{n-1}\right)\left[\left(\frac{x_1 - \bar{x}}{s_x}\right)\left(\frac{y_1 - \bar{y}}{s_y}\right) + \left(\frac{x_2 - \bar{x}}{s_x}\right)\left(\frac{y_2 - \bar{y}}{s_y}\right) + \cdots \right.$$
$$\left. + \left(\frac{x_n - \bar{x}}{s_x}\right)\left(\frac{y_n - \bar{y}}{s_y}\right)\right]$$

The correlation coefficient r for two variables is thus computed using these steps:

1   Compute the means and standard deviations for each variable.

2   Standardize each observation, case by case.

3   Multiply the standardized values of the observations together, case by case.

4   Add the resulting products and divide by *one less than the number of cases.*

EXAMPLE   6.4A

Exhibit 6.4A shows the calculations for the data in Exhibit 6.2B. As shown in Section 4.6, a value is standardized by subtracting the mean of the variable from the value and dividing the resulting difference by the standard deviation of the variable. So to standardize the first case of Sq.ft, compute $(521 - 568.2)/55.7109 = -0.8472$. To standardize the fifth case of Market, compute $(31 - 25.56)/4.1313 = 1.3168$, and so on.

Note in Exhibit 6.4A that the means of the standardized variables are zero and their standard deviations are 1. As explained in Section 4.6, standardized variables always have 0 mean and unit standard deviation. This means that

EXHIBIT 6.4A
Computation of Correlation
Coefficient for Data on Sq.ft and
Market in Exhibit 6.2

			Standardized		
Case	Sq.ft	Market	Sq.ft	Market	Product
i	x_i	y_i	$\dfrac{x_i - \bar{x}}{s_x}$	$\dfrac{y_i - \bar{y}}{s_y}$	$\left(\dfrac{x_i - \bar{x}}{s_x}\right)\left(\dfrac{y_i - \bar{y}}{s_y}\right)$
1	521	26.0	−0.8472	0.1065	−0.0902
2	538	19.4	−0.5421	−1.4910	0.8083
3	544	25.2	−0.4344	−0.0872	0.0378
4	577	26.2	0.1580	0.1549	0.0245
5	661	31.0	1.6657	1.3168	2.1934
Mean	568.2	25.56	0	0	—
Standard deviation	55.7109	4.1313	1	1	—

the standardized variables are *free of the units of measure* of the original variable.

The values in the product column of Exhibit 6.4A are the result of step 3—multiplying the standardized values for each case. Because both factors were standardized and free of units of measure, the product is also free of units.

Interestingly, when standardized variables are scatterplotted, the picture of their relationship is the same as the picture for the original variables. All that changes are the units of measure on the horizontal and vertical axes.

One less than the number of cases is $4 = 5 - 1$, so the computation of r is completed by dividing by 4:

$$r = \frac{-0.0902 + 0.8083 + 0.0378 + 0.0245 + 2.1934}{4} \simeq 0.74 \quad \blacksquare$$

The correlation coefficient is essentially the average of the products of the standardized variables. The divisor in the "average" is degrees of freedom, rather than the number of cases, as discussed in Chapter 4 regarding the standard deviation.

The correlation coefficient has many properties, the most important of which are:

1 Its numerical value lies between -1 and $+1$, inclusive.

2 If $r = 1$, the scatterplot shows that the data lie exactly on a straight line with a positive slope; if $r = -1$, the scatterplot shows that the data lie on a straight line with a negative slope.

3 An $r = 0$ indicates that there is no straight-line component in the relationship between the two variables.[†]

The more the scatterplot looks like a positively sloping straight line, the closer r is to $+1$, and the more the scatterplot looks like a negatively sloping straight line, the closer r is to -1.

EXAMPLE **6.4B**

We now consider the correlation coefficients of the data sets in Section 6.2.

Exhibit 6.2C shows a scatterplot of all 60 cases in the real estate data set. The correlation coefficient is $r = 0.75$. Although there is a trend in the plot, there is plenty of scatter, and the rainbow appearance suggests that some of the relationship between the variables is not of the straight-line variety.

Exhibit 6.2E shows a scatterplot of inflation rates and ratings of central bank independence for 16 countries. The correlation coefficient is $r = -0.843$. The negative relationship is reflected in the negative correlation coefficient. It is fairly close to -1, suggesting a substantial amount of straight-line behavior.

[†]If the points lie exactly on a vertical or horizontal line, r is not defined.

E X H I B I T **6.4B**   Scatterplots Showing Six Different Degrees of Correlation

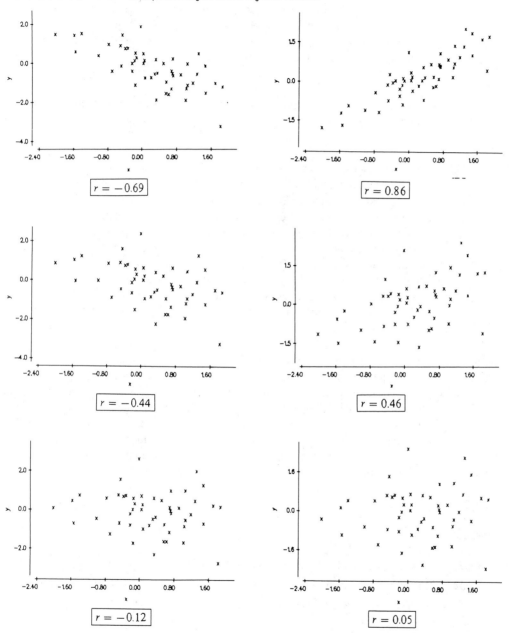

Exhibit 6.2F shows a scatterplot of quality ratings and prices of 24 compact disc players. The correlation coefficient is $r = 0.237$. This correlation is quite small and is consistent with the visual appearance of essentially no relationship between the variables. ▪

We see from these examples that the correlation coefficient responds to the direction and degree to which the relationship resembles a straight line.

EXAMPLE 6.4C   Exhibit 6.4B shows a set of scatterplots of data that display differing degrees of correlation. Pictures like these help interpret data collected from practical processes. For example, the tendency for the data to congregate along a line as the correlation coefficient approaches -1 or $+1$ is clear. On the other hand, it is useful to see that even for correlation coefficients near -1 and $+1$, there can be considerable scatter in the scatterplot. As a practical guideline, values of r larger than 0.5 in magnitude (that is, between -1.0 and -0.5 or between 0.5 and $+1$) indicate a straight-line relationship that is worthy of attention. Values of r less than 0.5 in magnitude signal a relatively weak straight-line relationship between variables. ▪

Summary   A relationship between a pair of variables is displayed in a scatterplot. The degree to which the relationship adheres to a straight line is measured numerically by the correlation coefficient, which is denoted by r. The data fall on a straight line with positive slope if and only if $r = +1$ and on a straight line with negative slope if and only if $r = -1$. Values of r between -1 and $+1$ occur when the relationship is only partially straight-line in nature. As a practical guideline, values of r between -1 and -0.5 and between $+0.5$ and $+1$ signal a substantial amount of straight-line relationship between variables.

SECTION

6.5 Exercises

6.5A   Compute the correlation coefficient r for the data given in Exercise 6.3A. Interpret its meaning.

6.5B   Compute the correlation coefficient r for the data given in Exercise 6.3B. Interpret its meaning.

6.5C   Use the cassette tape deck data given in Exercise 6.3C.

    a   Compute r for the whole data set.

    b   Compute r using only the single decks.

    c   Compute r using only the dual decks.

    d   Interpret the meaning of the correlation coefficients computed in parts (a), (b), and (c). (Filename: CASSETTE.DAT.)

6.5D   Use the last five cases in the property data set in Exhibit 6.2A as data. As in Exhibit 6.4A, lay out the steps and compute the correlation coefficients for the following pairs of variables:

a   Sq.ft and Market   **b**   Sq.ft and Assessed   **c**   Assessed and Market

6.5E   Examine the three scatterplots of the Amana data suggested in Exercise 6.3F.

    a   On the basis of your visual examination of the scatterplots, guess at the values of the correlation coefficients.

    b   Compute the correlation coefficients and compare them to your guesses. (Filename: AMANA.DAT.)

6.5F   **a**   For the real estate data set in Section 6.2, prepare scatterplots of market values versus assessed values and of assessed values versus square feet of living area. Compute the correlation coefficients corresponding to these two plots. To what extent do the correlation coefficients summarize the relationships displayed in the plots? What information should be conveyed in addition to that conveyed by the correlation coefficient?

    b   Both market and assessed values are correlated with square feet of living area, as is natural. What other factors besides square feet of living area would cause market and assessed values to be correlated? (Filename: REALPROP.DAT.)

6.5G   For each of the four Anscombe data sets in Exercise 6.3H, compute the means and standard deviations of the variables and compute the correlation coefficient r. Compare the values you have computed for the four data sets. What implications do these results have for someone attempting to summarize data using descriptive statistics? What information would you recommend reporting in addition to the descriptive statistics, on the basis of your experience with the data sets in this exercise? (Filename: ANSCOMBE.DAT.)

6.5H   Compute the correlation coefficient that corresponds to the scatterplot of oil-filter sales versus months in Exhibit 2.6C. To what extent does the coefficient summarize the relationship between the variables? What information should be conveyed in addition to that conveyed by the correlation coefficient? (Filename: OILFILT.DAT.)

6.5I   For the data you collected for Exercise 6.3J, compute the means and standard deviations of the variables and compute the correlation coefficient r. To what extent do the descriptive statistics summarize the information in the data? What important aspects of the data are not conveyed by the descriptive statistics?

6.5J   Look at the formula for r. Explain why the formula treats the variables x and y symmetrically. In other words, explain why you can interchange x and y without changing the values of r.

6.5K   Select any scatterplot you have constructed. Standardize the variables in the plot and scatterplot the standardized variables. Describe the differences and similarities in the two plots. Does standardization affect the relationship between the variables? What does standardization do?

6.5L   Write a one- or two-page essay explaining the meaning of the *correlation coefficient*. Include three examples, each using five cases, that illustrate negative, near zero, and positive correlation.

SECTION

6.6   Limitations of Correlation

Correlation helps convey information about relationships between continuous variables in a compact numerical form. It is useful for examining complex problems with many variables and helps us concentrate on patterns rather than detail. On the other hand, whenever summary measures are used, there is a risk of masking an important detail that hints at an important special feature of a relationship, as in Exercise 6.5G. One safeguard against errors in the use of descriptive statistics is to prepare plots that display relationships in detail. If descriptive statistics seem to summarize a scatterplot well, they may be used in place of it. If not, the unique features of the relationship as well as the descriptive statistics need to be reported.

The Effect of Outliers

Recall that an outlier is a value separated from the main body of the data. Section 4.4 discussed some popular statistics, such as means and standard deviations, that are sensitive to outliers; that is, their values can change substantially if an extreme value in the data set changes. The correlation coefficient is also sensitive to outliers, as you are asked to confirm in Exercise 6.7A. This means that changes in one or two data values may change the numerical value of r substantially. When you are confronted with outliers, you should attempt to determine their origin. They could be caused by mistyping data or by a mistake in collecting the data. Or they could be due to your mixing data from two groups that differ significantly. Always follow up on outliers. They often indicate problems or hint at a useful structure in a process (for example, the existence of a previously unsuspected subgroup).

Ecological Correlations

ecological correlations

Ecological correlations are correlations computed from data that are totals of smaller units of study.

E X A M P L E   **6.6A**

Exhibit 6.6A shows data on bank deposits and assets in 1982 by state for nine Midwestern states. The basic unit of study is the bank, but the data from all the banks in a given state are totaled, and only these totals are available in the data source. The scatterplot closely follows a straight line, which is reflected in the correlation coefficient of $r = 0.998$. Do not infer, however, that such a high degree of linearity would be present if the original data on the individual banks were plotted. In fact, a great deal more variation would be expected in the data on individual banks. The plot in Exhibit 6.6A displays the effect of a third variable, the population size of the state. In other words, totals for a large state, like Illinois, are naturally greater than totals for a small state, like

E X H I B I T **6.6A**
Data on Assets and Deposits in Banks by State for Nine States (All figures are in billions of current dollars)

State	Assets	Deposits
Nebraska	14.0	11.4
Kansas	19.6	16.5
Iowa	25.5	21.5
Wisconsin	30.0	24.3
Indiana	36.3	29.8
Minnesota	36.8	28.0
Michigan	56.6	46.0
Ohio	62.4	47.6
Illinois	130.2	91.8

Source: U.S. Bureau of the Census, *Statistical Abstract of the United States: 1984*, 104th ed. (Washington, D.C.: U.S. Government Printing Office, 1983), p.511.

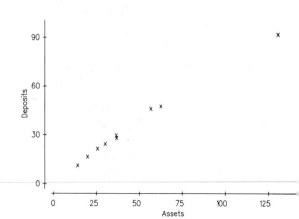

Iowa. The different sizes of the states and the totaling of all bank data to the state level induce the very high degree of correlation in Exhibit 6.6A.

There is nothing invalid about the correlation displayed in Exhibit 6.6A. The potential error is inferring from it that the same degree of correlation exists for individual banks. To solve a given problem, the ecological correlation may be just what is needed, whereas to solve a different problem, the correlation at the bank level may be needed.   ▪

EXAMPLE   6.6B

Consider a firm trying to assess the effect of a change in advertising expenditures on sales. The data may consist of advertising expenditures and total sales for a number of years (ideally adjusted for inflation, since inflation tends to make more recent dollar figures larger). Advertising expenditures and sales transactions are aggregated to an annual level in this example. A reasonably high degree of correlation between sales and advertising expenditures would support the use of advertising to boost sales.[†]

On the other hand, such data would be of little use to an advertising executive who is trying to learn *how* advertising affects individual buying behavior. He or she needs data on the effect of a certain type of ad on customers, data that are both difficult and expensive to obtain. Moreover, even an ad that only slightly increases customers' willingness to buy a product can be beneficial from an ecological point of view, for if out of a population of 100,000 potential customers, an additional 100 can be interested in buying, then an ad may be profitable. But it can be difficult to detect such a small yet commercially advantageous relationship between variables. This example underlines a problem that is pervasive in practice: the evaluation of actions that affect individuals in terms of measures that are highly aggregated. Drawing correct conclusions in such situations is not simple.   ▪

Curved Relationships

As illustrated in Exhibit 6.2D, relationships can, and often do, have curved as well as straight-lined features. Computing correlation coefficients may be of little value in such situations and can be misleading. For example, a correlation of $r = 0.7$ might be impressive until you learn that the data could be fitted almost perfectly with a nonlinear curve! As we have said before, there is no substitute for visual inspection of relationships. Only when descriptive statistics convey the important essentials of a relationship may they be substituted for graphs.

[†]The situation can be more complicated than suggested here. For example, an increase in advertising can be part of launching a new product or improving an existing one. The increase in sales could be attributed to the quality of the product rather than the advertising. As usual, the truth is probably somewhere in the middle. High sales are due to product quality, but advertising helps inform the public about the availability of the product.

Correlation and Cause

Correlation between two variables need not be the result of a causal link between them. Indeed, it is possible to find correlation between variables that in truth may have nothing to do with each other.

EXAMPLE   6.6C

Exhibit 6.6B shows death rates and divorce rates in 1985 for nine regions in the United States.[†] The rates are numbers of deaths and divorces per 1000 of population in the region. The negative correlation is clear in the scatterplot, with $r = -0.82$. Higher divorce rates are associated with lower death rates. Does divorce raise one's immunity to death? The proposition is difficult to accept, yet the correlation is strong. Almost surely the correlation points to an ignorable artifact. How might we argue for this conclusion?

According to Mosteller and Tukey[‡], to establish cause one must establish *consistency, responsiveness,* and *mechanism.* To establish consistency one must show that the relationship holds in a number of contexts. For example, would the relationship in Exhibit 6.6B hold if the study were conducted in countries in Europe, Asia, or Africa? If so, then there is consistency across countries. But consistency is not enough. Even if the correlation in Exhibit 6.6B fails to point to a real relationship between divorce and death rates, a similar correlation may occur in studies of other countries for the same reason it occurred in the United States.

To establish responsiveness, one must show that a change in x leads to a change in y. In our example, we would have to show that groups of couples, alike in every way except divorce rate, have different death rates. Such a study would require us to conduct an experiment in which groups of couples that are alike except for divorce rate are formed—a tall order, and one that would require a great deal of time and expense. Absence of such an experiment considerably weakens the support that Exhibit 6.6B lends to a cause-and-effect relationship between divorce and immunity to death.

To establish mechanism, one must construct a model that shows step by step how the presumed cause leads to the presumed effect. Moreover, one must show that the presumed effect does not lead step by step to the presumed cause! We invite you to invent a convincing model for how divorce leads to higher immunity to death. If you do, you will have added plausibility to the relationship in Exhibit 6.6B.

[†]This example comes from A.J. Jaffe and H.F. Spirer, *Misused Statistics: Straight Talk for Twisted Numbers* (New York: Dekker, 1987), p. 93. This book has a wealth of entertaining and instructive examples of statistical uses gone awry. We are indebted to Jaffe and Spirer for pointing out the discussion of cause by Mosteller and Tukey, cited in the footnote below, which is summarized in the text.

[‡]Frederick Mosteller and John W. Tukey, *Data Analysis and Regression* (Reading, Mass.: Addison-Wesley, 1977).

E X H I B I T **6.6B**
Death Rates Versus Divorce
Rates for Nine U.S.
Regions—1985

Region	Death Rate	Divorce Rate
Mountain	6.9	7.0
Pacific	7.7	5.4
West South Central	7.9	7.0
East North Central	8.9	4.6
South Atlantic	9.0	5.2
West North Central	9.2	4.2
East South Central	9.3	5.7
New England	9.3	3.9
Mid Atlantic	9.9	3.7

Mountain: Montana, Idaho, Wyoming, Colorado, New
    Mexico, Arizona, Utah, Nevada

Pacific: Washington, Oregon, California, Alaska, Hawaii

West South Central: Arkansas, Louisiana, Oklahoma, Texas

East North Central: Ohio, Indiana, Illinois, Michigan,
    Wisconsin

South Atlantic: Delaware, Maryland, District of Columbia,
    Virginia, West Virginia, North Carolina, South Carolina,
    Georgia, Florida

West North Central: Minnesota, Iowa, Missouri, North
    Dakota, South Dakota, Nebraska, Kansas

East South Central: Kentucky, Tennessee, Alabama,
    Mississippi

New England: Maine, New Hampshire, Vermont,
    Massachusetts, Rhode Island, Connecticut

Mid Atlantic: New York, New Jersey, Pennsylvania

Source: U.S. Bureau of the Census. *Statistical Abstract of the United States: 1989*,
109th ed. (Washington, D.C.: U.S. Government Printing Office, 1989), Tables 112
and 134.

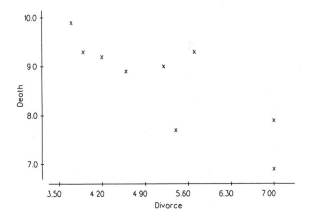

lurking variable

Another test of a presumed cause-and-effect relationship is to identify a third variable, called a **lurking variable**, that plausibly explains the relationship. For the relationship in Exhibit 6.6B, a plausible explanation is that age of couples leads to the observed correlation. The divorce rate in the United States used to be quite a bit lower than it is today. Thus, older couples in a study will tend to have lower divorce rates than younger couples. But they will also tend to have higher death rates than the younger couples.[†] It is therefore plausible to imagine that much, if not most, of the downward slope in Exhibit 6.6B is explained by a decrease in average age of couples as we move from left to right across the graph. This observation suggests that we try to find divorce rates and death rates grouped by age of couple and do the scatterplots of death rates versus divorce rates for different age groups.[‡] If there is still a negative correlation, we have observed a *consistency* that would help support a cause-and-effect relationship between divorce and immunity to death. If the negative correlation is not apparent in the age-dependent scatterplots, we have scotched the idea of cause and effect. See Exercise 6.7D. ∎

When changes in a variable x do directly influence changes in a variable y, correlation in a scatterplot of y versus x may be plausibly expected. Yet substantial correlation between observed x's and y's will appear only if there is a strong straight-line component in the causal relationship.

As you can see, cause can be studied with the help of correlation, but the study is subtle.[§]

[†] This analysis presumes that older people are more highly concentrated in some parts of the country than in others.

[‡] See Exercise 6.7D for a crude analysis in this direction.

[§] For a commonsense discussion see A. S. C. Ehrenberg, *A Primer in Data Reduction* (New York: Wiley, 1982), parts 4 and 6.

SECTION

6.7 Exercises

6.7A   Use the data set below.

Case	x	y	Case	x	y	Case	x	y
1	0	36	8	38	64	15	66	52
2	18	71	9	40	47	16	69	40
3	28	31	10	47	66	17	71	38
4	29	78	11	52	28	18	78	60
5	31	72	12	57	69	19	100	18
6	34	57	13	60	100			
7	36	29	14	64	34			

Construct a scatterplot of y versus x and compute the correlation coefficient. [Answer: $r = -0.205$.] Now add a 20th case in which $x = 150$ and $y = 150$. Add the point to your scatterplot and compute r. [Answer: $r = 0.410$.] The outlier makes a substantial difference! Experiment with the data set by making up a variety of 20th cases, constructing the scatterplot, and computing r. You may also wish to try adding several cases to the data set simultaneously and discovering the impact on r. For example, for some of the intermediate values of x, add some outlying y's. What would be the effect of doing this to the plot in Exhibit 6.6A? (Filename: EX6_7A.DAT.)

6.7B   The scatterplot below displays a relationship between a variable y and a variable x. The correlation coefficient has value $r = -0.008$. Does this value convey any useful information about the relationship? Draw a curve through the data. Describe the curve in words.

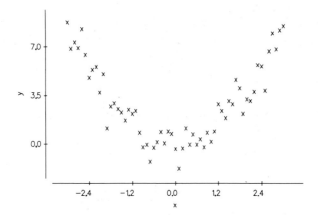

6.7C For the 50 cases below, the correlation coefficient between x and y is 0.095.

Case	x	y	Case	x	y	Case	x	y
1	−19	−4	18	−4	−1	35	3	12
2	−16	−15	19	−4	−14	36	3	−12
3	−13	−8	20	−3	15	37	4	10
4	−13	−4	21	−2	−1	38	4	−13
5	−11	3	22	−2	16	39	6	−9
6	−10	5	23	−2	28	40	6	5
7	−10	12	24	−2	1	41	7	8
8	−10	8	25	−2	2	42	12	11
9	−10	−7	26	−1	−2	43	12	1
10	−10	−3	27	−1	−7	44	13	0
11	−9	−3	28	−1	5	45	15	16
12	−8	0	29	0	4	46	17	−3
13	−8	11	30	0	−15	47	17	7
14	−6	8	31	0	−13	48	21	−19
15	−6	−19	32	1	−9	49	22	22
16	−4	6	33	2	0	50	23	−6
17	−4	23	34	2	−6			

a Make a scatterplot of y versus x and verify that $r = 0.095$.

b Form the cases into five subgroups: cases 1–10, cases 11–20, cases 21–30, cases 31–40, and cases 41–50. Find the averages of the x's and y's in each subgroup. Make a scatterplot with the x averages on the horizontal axis and the corresponding y averages on the vertical axis. Compute the correlation coefficient for this scatterplot. [Answer: $r = 0.341$.]

c Compare the two scatterplots and the two correlation coefficients you have made. How do they illustrate the concept of ecological correlation? (Filename: EX6_7C.DAT.)

6.7D This exercise is a continuation of Example 6.6C. Given below are the percent of population aged 65 or over in the nine regions given in Example 6.6C, and in the same order.

10.6   10.9   10.7   12.2   13.0   13.6   12.3   13.4   13.5

The source is Table 27 of the *Statistical Abstract* cited in Example 6.6C. These percentages are indexes of the age distributions in the regions; on average, a region with an older population has a higher percentage over the age of 65. Investigate this variable as a potential lurking variable. In other words, is it plausible to conclude that differing age distributions in the regions account for the relationship between death rates and divorce rates?

S E C T I O N

6.8 Autocorrelation

The previous sections of this chapter dealt with correlations between cross-sectional data—that is, data collected at one point in time. This section deals with longitudinal data analysis. Through analyzing data collected by making repeated observations on a process over time, we can examine past behavior for clues about future behavior.

Longitudinal data analysis often involves comparing data collected in a series of observations (for example, data collected during each month of 1995) with previous

autocorrelation

series collections (say, data collected during each month of 1994). Correlation of a series with its own past history is called **autocorrelation**.

Let's begin with the most common form of longitudinal data analysis, *time series analysis*. A **time series** is a sequence of observations collected from a process at fixed (and usually equally spaced) "moments" in time. The sequence plots in Chapter 2 are graphic displays of time series. How do we adapt scatterplots and correlation coefficients to the study of a series' dependence on its own past history?

time series

Lagging

lag

The first step is to associate observations made at different time periods. This process is called lagging the time series. A **lag** is an interval of time between observations in a time series. Lag length is the number of time periods back we reach to bring a past observation in line with a current observation. To illustrate this, consider the data on annual iron and steel exports from the United States, reported in Exhibit 6.8A.

E X H I B I T **6.8A**
Annual Exports from the United States of Iron and Steel (excluding scrap) in Million of Tons, 1937–1980.

Case (t)	Year	Exports (y_t)	Lag1 (y_{t-1})	Lag2 (y_{t-2})	Case (t)	Year	Exports (y_t)	Lag1 (y_{t-1})	Lag2 (y_{t-2})
1	1937	3.89	*	*	23	1959	2.13	3.46	6.95
2	1938	2.41	3.89	*	24	1960	3.47	2.13	3.46
3	1939	2.80	2.41	3.89	25	1961	2.79	3.47	2.13
4	1940	8.72	2.80	2.41	26	1962	2.52	2.79	3.47
5	1941	7.12	8.72	2.80	27	1963	2.80	2.52	2.79
6	1942	7.24	7.12	8.72	28	1964	4.04	2.80	2.52
7	1943	7.15	7.24	7.12	29	1965	3.08	4.04	2.80
8	1944	6.05	7.15	7.24	30	1966	2.26	3.08	4.04
9	1945	5.21	6.05	7.15	31	1967	2.17	2.26	3.08
10	1946	5.03	5.21	6.05	32	1968	2.78	2.17	2.26
11	1947	6.88	5.03	5.21	33	1969	5.94	2.78	2.17
12	1948	4.70	6.88	5.03	34	1970	8.14	5.94	2.78
13	1949	5.06	4.70	6.88	35	1971	3.55	8.14	5.94
14	1950	3.16	5.06	4.70	36	1972	3.61	3.55	8.14
15	1951	3.62	3.16	5.06	37	1973	5.06	3.61	3.55
16	1952	4.55	3.62	3.16	38	1974	7.13	5.06	3.61
17	1953	2.43	4.55	3.62	39	1975	4.15	7.13	5.06
18	1954	3.16	2.43	4.55	40	1976	3.86	4.15	7.13
19	1955	4.55	3.16	2.43	41	1977	3.22	3.86	4.15
20	1956	5.17	4.55	3.16	42	1978	3.50	3.22	3.86
21	1957	6.95	5.17	4.55	43	1979	3.76	3.50	3.22
22	1958	3.46	6.95	5.17	44	1980	5.11	3.76	3.50

Let t denote a year and y_t denote the amount of exports in that year. We arrange the data so that each year's observation y_t is associated with the previous year's observation y_{t-1}. Notice that the lagged value of exports in 1937—that is, the value of exports in 1936—is not available. We denote its "missing value" by placing a * in its location in the table. The sequence of values y_{t-1} is the first lag of the sequence y_t. The 43 values (y_t, y_{t-1}) are shown in the scatterplot in Exhibit 6.8B. The scatterplot suggests some degree of positive autocorrelation between observations in adjacent years.

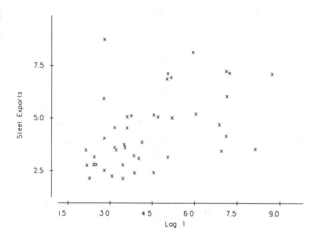

We may also study the second lag of a time series. For the iron and steel exports series, this entails associating the observation in 1939 with the observation in 1937, the observation in 1940 with the observation in 1938, and so on. See Exhibit 6.8A. The second lag is denoted by y_{t-2}. The second-lag values for 1937 and 1938 are not available, so there are only 42 available pairs (y_t, y_{t-2}) for scatterplotting. See Exhibit 6.8C for the scatterplot, which demonstrates negligible autocorrelation between observations in pairs of years that are two years apart.

E X H I B I T **6.8C**
Scatterplot of Iron and Steel
Exports and Second Lag of Iron
and Steel Exports

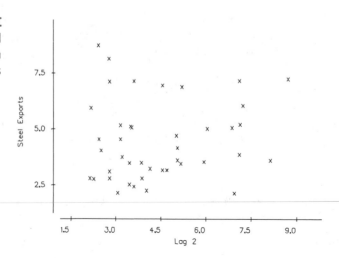

lag length

In general, the kth lag of a series y_t is denoted by y_{t-k}, and k is the **lag length**. The scatterplot of the available pairs (y_t, y_{t-k}) exhibits the autocorrelation at lag k. Autocorrelation is straight-line relationship between a series and its own past history, which is just the kind of information needed to search the past for clues about the future behavior of the process.

Autocorrelation Coefficients

Autocorrelation coefficients are numerical measures of the degree of autocorrelation in a time series. They are used to help describe the past behavior of a series and to help build models for its future behavior.

Let $y_1, y_2, \ldots, y_n$ denote a sequence of observation from a time series and let $\overline{y}$ and s denote the sample mean and sample standard deviation of the sequence. The kth-lag autocorrelation coefficient of the sequence is denoted by r_k and computed from the formula

kth-lag autocorrelation coefficient

$$r_k = \left(\frac{1}{n-1}\right)\left[\left(\frac{y_{k+1} - \overline{y}}{s}\right)\left(\frac{y_1 - \overline{y}}{s}\right) + \left(\frac{y_{k+2} - \overline{y}}{s}\right)\left(\frac{y_2 - \overline{y}}{s}\right)\right.$$
$$\left. + \cdots + \left(\frac{y_n - \overline{y}}{s}\right)\left(\frac{y_{n-k} - \overline{y}}{s}\right)\right]$$

Notice that this is essentially the formula for the correlation coefficient introduced in Section 6.4 for the pairs (y_t, y_{t-k}). The autocorrelation coefficient r_k is thus computed as follows:

1   Compute the mean and standard deviation of the sequence.
2   Standardize the sequence—that is, compute $(y_t - \overline{y})/s$, case by case.
3   Compute the kth lag of the standardized sequence.
4   Multiply the values in the standardized sequence and values in its kth lag together, case by case.
5   Add the resulting products and divide by one less than the number of cases.

Exhibit 6.8D demonstrates the computation of the lag 1 and lag 2 autocorrelation coefficients of the iron and steel export series in Exhibit 6.8A. The table in the exhibit shows the autocorrelation coefficients for lags 1 through 6. Only the lag 1 coefficient is close to 0.5. The other coefficients are negligible. We conclude that observations in adjacent years are substantially autocorrelated, while observations in years that are not adjacent are not substantially autocorrelated.

Informally, autocorrelation may be interpreted as a measure of the amount of "memory" a series has. For example, if observations in adjacent time periods, say t and $t-1$, have positive autocorrelation, we could say that the observation in period t "remembers" the observation in period $t-1$ and tries to be somewhat like it. The closer the autocorrelation coefficient is to $+1$, the more y_t tries to be like y_{t-1}. If the autocorrelation is negative, y_t tries to be unlike y_{t-1}. Similar interpretations can be given if y_t is autocorrelated with its kth lag y_{t-k}. The largest lag length that exhibits substantial autocorrelation then tells "how long" the memory of the series is. In the iron and steel export series, the memory was one year. If a sequence is made up of

$$r_1 = \left(\frac{1}{44-1}\right)\left[\left(\frac{2.41-4.418}{1.754}\right)\left(\frac{3.89-4.418}{1.754}\right)\right.$$
$$+ \left(\frac{2.80-4.418}{1.754}\right)\left(\frac{2.41-4.418}{1.754}\right)$$
$$\left. + \cdots + \left(\frac{5.11-4.418}{1.754}\right)\left(\frac{3.76-4.418}{1.754}\right)\right] \approx 0.5$$

$$r_2 = \left(\frac{1}{44-1}\right)\left[\left(\frac{2.80-4.418}{1.754}\right)\left(\frac{3.89-4.418}{1.754}\right)\right.$$
$$+ \left(\frac{8.72-4.418}{1.754}\right)\left(\frac{2.41-4.418}{1.754}\right)$$
$$\left. + \cdots + \left(\frac{5.11-4.418}{1.754}\right)\left(\frac{3.50-4.418}{1.754}\right)\right] \approx 0.1$$

k	1	2	3	4	5	6
r_k	0.472	0.105	0.045	0.103	0.099	0.008

purely random observations, the sequence should have no memory. *Thus a random sequence has autocorrelation coefficients essentially equal to 0 at all lags 1, 2, ...*
We now present examples that illustrate three different patterns of autocorrelation.

E X A M P L E **6.8A**

In Exhibit 2.8H, we presented a sequence plot of a measure called Diff, whose value indicated how parallel a waveguide was to a microwave oven wall. The closer Diff is to 0, the more parallel the waveguide. (The raw data are in the file AMANA.DAT.) Autocorrelation in this sequence signals a relationship between the measures of parallelism in ovens made at different times. Such a relationship would be disturbing because each oven is supposed to be the result of an independent sequence of steps. Memory in this process could be the result of machine wear, faulty batches of material, or failure to follow the steps in the manufacturing process. Exhibit 6.8E shows the sequence of Diff values, the scatterplot of Diff versus its first lag, and the autocorrelation coefficients for lags 1 through 5. The coefficients are practically negligible, indicating that the manufacturing process does not have substantial memory. The sequence evolves *as if* the parallelism measurements were purely random. ▪

EXHIBIT 6.8E Autocorrelation Analysis of Diff

Values of Diff (read across rows)

2	12	−3	8	20	4	6	0	6	−12	6	12	0
−4	−1	2	−10	−10	−15	−9	−12	−10	−7	−6	−2	0
−10	−6	−6	−10	−10	−8	−1	−24	2	8	−8	−2	−14
6	−4	30	0	−13	−10	−4	−8	−5	−13	25	31	7
12	−10	8	−17	−9	−41	−18	3	−12	−6	13	3	−9
−9	−6	14	−2	−6	−14	−5	−2	10	−15	0	−1	−4
−8	5	11	9	13	8	21	12	−10	4	−1	5	−9
−4	−5	13	−6	−9	−3	−2	−11	14	−6	11	7	6
−3	2	−8	−6	−7	−9	6	6	−3	−17	1	−5	−2
5	2	3										

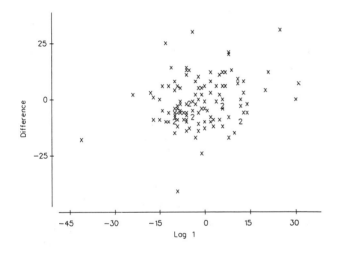

Autocorrelation Coefficients for Lags 1–5

0.24   0.16   0.03   0.09   −0.06

EXAMPLE 6.8B

Exhibit 2.10B is a sequence plot of monthly price indices of flour at Buffalo, New York (the data are in the file BUFLOUR.DAT). As noted in the discussion in Section 2.10, the series meanders. An autocorrelation analysis of these data illustrates the impact of meandering on the autocorrelation coefficients. Exhibit 6.8F shows a scatterplot of the flour price index versus its first lag. The plot indicates a large degree of autocorrelation.

The table in the exhibit shows the autocorrelation coefficients for the first 30 lags of the observed price index series. The first autocorrelation coefficient is 0.93, quite close to +1 and consistent with the scatterplot. Examination of the other autocorrelation coefficients reveals a gradual decline from 0.93 at lag 1 to a value of about 0 at lag 14, a value of −0.36 at lag 21, and −0.53 at

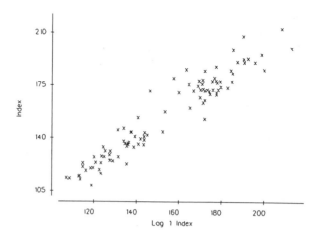

Autocorrelations of Buffalo Flour Index, Lags 1–30						
Lags 1–7	0.93	0.85	0.78	0.71	0.64	0.57	0.50
Lags 8–14	0.44	0.36	0.29	0.21	0.14	0.06	0.00
Lags 15–21	−0.06	−0.14	−0.21	−0.24	−0.27	−0.30	−0.35
Lags 22–28	−0.40	−0.43	−0.46	−0.48	−0.50	−0.51	−0.50
Lags 29–30	−0.51	−0.53					

lag 30. This is typical behavior of autocorrelation coefficients computed for meandering series. The behavior is complex and difficult to interpret.

A standard approach to analyzing a meandering series is to analyze the period-to-period changes in the observations. Often the changes behave more simply than the original observations. Exhibit 2.10G shows the sequence plot of the month-to-month changes in the Buffalo flour price index. An autocorrelation analysis of the changes is shown in Exhibit 6.8G. There we see that the autocorrelation coefficients of the change series are negligible, so the changes behave as if they were generated at random. Computation of the changes has produced a series that is easy to understand. ∎

random walk

The Buffalo flour price index exemplifies a type of time series behavior known as random walk. A **random walk** is a series whose changes behave as if they were random. See Appendix 3 for more details on random walks. Random walks play a surprisingly important role both in statistical theory and in statistical practice. Many time series exhibit random walk behavior or behavior that is only a slight variation on the random walk. This idea will be discussed further in Chapter 23.

E X H I B I T **6.8G**
Autocorrelation Analysis of
Changes in the Buffalo Flour
Price Index

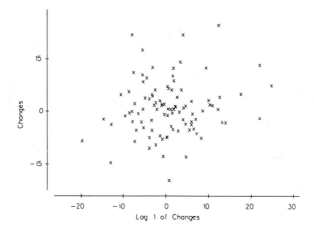

Autocorrelation Coefficients of First 5 Lags of Change Series
0.14   −0.00   −0.03   0.06   0.02

E X A M P L E   **6.8C**

Exercise 2C shows monthly retail sales in the United States (in billions of dollars) for the years 1983 through 1987 (data are in the file RETAIL.DAT). Exhibit 6.8H shows a sequence plot of the data. Months are coded by different letters, A for January, B for February, and so on. The months January (A), February (B) and December (L) consistently stand out from the others, which is characteristic of a *seasonal* time series. An upward drift in sales is also

E X H I B I T **6.8H**
Sequence Plot of Monthly Retail
Sales Data

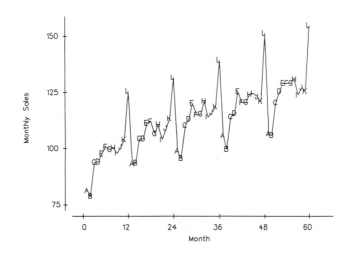

evident. How do these features affect the autocorrelation coefficients of the series? Exhibit 6.8I displays scatterplots of sales versus first lag of sales and sales versus twelfth lag of sales. Both exhibit high degrees of autocorrelation. The table in the exhibit shows the autocorrelation coefficients for lags 1 through 17. Those for lags 1 and 12 are greater than 0.5. A method for modeling this complex, trend-plus-seasonal behavior will be presented in Chapter 24. ▪

E X H I B I T **6.8I**
Autocorrelation Analysis of Retail
Sales Data

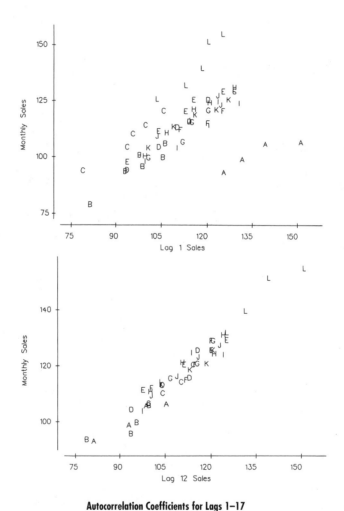

Autocorrelation Coefficients for Lags 1–17						
Lags 1–7	0.51	0.35	0.36	0.38	0.38	0.34	0.34
Lags 8–14	0.28	0.20	0.10	0.19	0.58	0.21	0.08
Lags 15–17	0.08	0.10	0.11				

Time series exhibit a variety of patterns of autocorrelation, and the computation of autocorrelation coefficients helps us identify the pattern in any series of interest. In this section, we exhibited examples of series with the following patterns: as if random (Diff measures for microwave ovens), memory at one lag only (iron and steel exports), meandering (Buffalo flour price index), and trend plus seasonal (retail sales). These are the most common patterns, but they can happen in various combinations in any given series. The analysis of such patterns is discussed in Chapters 23 and 24.

SECTION

6.9 Exercises

6.9A   You are given the following sequence of time series data: 3, 4, 2, 3, 4, 5, 6, 3, 2, 3, 2, 2, 2, 4, 3.
  a   Prepare a sequence plot of the data.
  b   Prepare a scatterplot of the sequence versus its first lag.

6.9B   You are given the following sequence of time series data: 9, 6, −6, −8, 6, 27, −13, 0, −1, 0, −4, −2, −11, −5.
  a   Prepare a sequence plot of the data.
  b   Prepare a scatterplot of the sequence versus its first lag.

6.9C   Use the data in Exercise 6.9A.
  a   Compute the lag 1 autocorrelation coefficient.
  b   Compute the lag 2 autocorrelation coefficient.
  c   Characterize the autocorrelation pattern.

6.9D   Use the data in Exercise 6.9B.
  a   Compute the lag 1 autocorrelation coefficient.
  b   Compute the lag 2 autocorrelation coefficient.
  c   Characterize the autocorrelation pattern.

6.9E   Use the photocopy data in Exhibit 1.3A. (Filename: PHOTOCOP.DAT.)
  a   Prepare a scatterplot of the sequence versus its first lag.
  b   Prepare a scatterplot of the sequence versus its second lag.
  c   Compute the lag 1 and lag 2 autocorrelation coefficients.
  d   Characterize the autocorrelation pattern of the sequence.

6.9F   Exercise 2.5A reports a sequence of measurements from a manufacturing process. (Filename: DEERE1.DAT.)
  a   Prepare a sequence plot of the data.
  b   Prepare a scatterplot of the sequence versus its first lag.
  c   Prepare a scatterplot of the sequence versus its second lag.
  d   Compute the autocorrelation coefficients for lags 1 through 6.
  e   Characterize the autocorrelation pattern of the sequence.

6.9G   Exercise 2B reports a sequence of measurements from a manufacturing process. (Filename: DEERE2.DAT.)
  a   Prepare a sequence plot of the data.
  b   Prepare a scatterplot of the sequence versus its first lag.
  c   Prepare a scatterplot of the sequence versus its second lag.
  d   Compute the autocorrelation coefficients for lags 1 through 12.

  e Characterize the autocorrelation pattern of the sequence.

6.9H Exercise 2B reports a sequence of measurements from a manufacturing process. (Filename: DEERE2.DAT.)

  a Compute the sequence of case-to-case changes.

  b Prepare a sequence plot of the changes.

  c Prepare a scatterplot of the sequence of changes versus its first lag.

  d Prepare a scatterplot of the sequence of changes versus its second lag.

  e Compute the autocorrelation coefficients for the sequence of changes for lags 1 through 6.

  f Characterize the autocorrelation pattern of the sequence of changes.

  g Contrast the results of analysis in this exercise with that of Exercise 6.9G.

6.9I Exercise 2.11A gives monthly values of a flour price index in Kansas City, Missouri. (Filename: KCFLOUR.DAT.)

  a Prepare a sequence plot of the data.

  b Prepare a scatterplot of the sequence versus its first lag.

  c Prepare a scatterplot of the sequence versus its second lag.

  d Compute the autocorrelation coefficients for lags 1 through 12.

  e Characterize the autocorrelation pattern of the sequence.

  f Compute the sequence of month-to-month changes.

  g Prepare a sequence plot of the changes.

  h Prepare a scatterplot of the sequence of changes versus its first lag.

  i Prepare a scatterplot of the sequence of changes versus its second lag.

  j Compute the autocorrelation coefficients for the sequence of changes for lags 1 through 6.

  k Characterize the autocorrelation pattern of the sequence of changes.

  l Contrast the results of analysis in this exercise with that of Exercise 6.9G.

6.9J Exhibit 2.6A gives monthly sales of oil filters, and Exhibit 2.6B shows a sequence plot of the data. (Filename: OILFILT.DAT.)

  a Prepare a scatterplot of the sequence versus its first lag.

  b Prepare a scatterplot of the sequence versus its second lag.

  c Prepare a scatterplot of the sequence versus its twelfth lag.

  d Compute the autocorrelation coefficients for lags 1 through 18. Which of the autocorrelations are larger than 0.5 in absolute value?

  e Characterize the autocorrelation pattern of the sequence.

6.9K Collect 40 quarterly GDP figures for the country of your choice. If possible, collect raw figures and seasonally adjusted figures.

  a Do a complete autocorrelation analysis of the seasonally adjusted figures. Characterize the behavior of the series. Is there any evidence of seasonality?

  b If you were able to collect raw figures, do a complete autocorrelation analysis of them. Characterize the behavior of the series.

Chapter Summary

Statistical analysis is used to compare variables and document relationships among them. Predictable relationships can be exploited commercially or used to eliminate waste from processes. Two of the most important tools for documenting relationships are the scatterplot and the correlation coefficient. Scatterplots display statistical relationships between two continuous variables. The correlation coefficient, denoted by r, measures the direction and the degree to which a relationship conforms to a straight line. If $r = +1$, the relationship is exactly a positively sloping straight line. If $r = -1$, the relationship is exactly a negatively sloping straight line. Values of r between -1 and $+1$ are associated with less than exact straight-line behavior. A purely random relationship yields a correlation coefficient equal to 0. In practice, values of r between -0.5 and 0.5 can usually be interpreted to mean that the degree of linear relationship is not substantial, whereas values of r between -1 and -0.5 or between 0.5 and $+1$ are worthy of attention.

Correlation coefficients are influenced by outliers, so their values cannot be interpreted without looking at the corresponding scatterplots. Grouping units and correlating their averages can produce very large correlation coefficients that are not characteristic of the relationship between the individual units. Applying the correlation based on grouping—ecological correlation—to individuals is a statistical fallacy. Correlation between variables need not be a sign of causal relationship. Often correlation is caused by a third, lurking, variable whose effect, when taken into account, reveals that no fundamental relationship between the original two variables exists. To establish cause-and-effect relationships, one must establish consistency, responsiveness, and mechanism.

Autocorrelation is correlation between the values of a time series and lagged values of the series. A variety of patterns arise in practice. Randomness implies no autocorrelation. Some series have memory at short lags, for example lag 1, and no autocorrelation at other lags. Meandering series have substantial autocorrelation at a large number of lags. Seasonal series have autocorrelations at periodic lags, as when a monthly series has autocorrelation at lag 12. Many series have both trend or meandering behavior and seasonal behavior. The modeling of such series is discussed further in Chapters 23 and 24.

Supplementary Exercises for Chapter 6

6A English statisticians investigated the smoking habits and lung cancer mortality rates for men in 25 occupational groups. Smoking habits were measured by forming a ratio of number of cigarettes smoked per day by men in the occupation group divided by the number smoked by all men of the same age. Mortality is a standardized ratio of lung cancer deaths. (Filename: CANCER.DAT.)

a Display the scatterplot of mortality (y) versus smoking (x).

b Describe the relationship shown in the scatterplot.

c Compute the correlation coefficient for these data.

d Explain why the correlation coefficient you computed in part (c) is probably not applicable to the relationship between smoking and mortality for an individual worker.

Occupational Group	Smoking	Mortality
Farmers, foresters, fishermen	77	84
Miners and quarrymen	137	116
Gas, coke, and chemical makers	117	123
Glass and ceramic makers	94	128
Furnace, forge, foundry, rolling mill workers	116	155
Electrical and electronic workers	102	101
Engineering and allied trades	111	118
Woodworkers	93	113
Leather workers	88	104
Textile workers	102	88
Clothing workers	91	104
Food, drink, and tobacco workers	104	129
Paper and printing workers	107	86
Makers of other products	112	96
Construction workers	113	144
Painters and decorators	110	139
Drivers of stationary engines, cranes, etc.	125	113
Laborers not included elsewhere	133	146
Transport and communications workers	115	128
Warehousemen, storekeepers, packers, and bottlers	105	115
Clerical workers	87	79
Sales workers	91	85
Service, sport, and recreation workers	100	120
Administrators and managers	76	60
Professional, technical workers, and artists	66	51

Source: Occupational Mortality: The Registrar General's Decennial Supplement for England and Wales, 1970–1972 (London: Her Majesty's Stationery Office, 1978).

6B   The data below are taken from James O. Ramsey, "Monotone Regression Splines in Action," *Statistical Science*, 3(4)(1988), 425–441.

The variables in the first five columns are:

Price ($100 U.S.)

Engine displacement (liters)

City gas consumption (liters/100 km)

Expressway gas consumption (liters/100 km)

Weight (100 kg)

Column 6 gives the make of automobile. Column 7 numbers the foreign makes, column 8 numbers all the makes, and column 9 numbers the domestic makes. This classification is a bit arbitrary because an automobile can be produced in a variety of countries!

56	1.6	13.3	6.8	10.0	Chevrolet Chevette		1	1
74	1.6	10.5	5.5	10.1	Chevrolet Nova		2	2
67	1.5	10.1	5.3	8.7	Chevrolet Spectrum		3	3
56	1.5	11.0	5.6	9.9	Dodge Colt		4	4
68	1.6	11.5	5.6	9.5	Dodge Omni		5	5
61	1.9	12.0	6.2	10.9	Ford Escort		6	6
56	1.5	11.5	6.5	9.2	Honda Civic	1	7	
75	2.0	12.0	6.3	10.9	Mitsubishi Tredia	2	8	
56	1.6	10.5	5.6	9.5	Nissan Sentra	3	9	
60	1.4	12.0	5.6	9.1	Renault Alliance	4	10	
80	1.8	12.0	5.6	10.4	Subaru	5	11	
73	1.6	11.0	5.3	10.3	Toyota Corolla	6	12	
56	1.5	11.0	5.5	9.7	Toyota Tercel	7	13	
74	1.8	12.0	6.3	10.1	Volkswagen Golf	8	14	
83	1.8	12.6	6.3	10.5	Volkswagen Jetta	9	15	
94	2.2	15.8	7.4	12.7	Chrysler Laser		16	7
73	1.5	9.4	5.6	9.0	Honda Civic CRX	10	17	
110	1.8	10.5	6.5	10.6	Honda Prelude	11	18	
109	1.9	14.9	6.8	12.4	Isuzu Impulse	12	19	
89	2.0	12.0	6.3	11.2	Mitsubishi Corida	13	20	
95	1.8	12.6	6.5	12.2	Nissan 200SX	14	21	
87	1.6	9.7	5.1	9.2	Nissan Pulsar NX	15	22	
89	2.5	12.6	6.7	11.5	Pontiac Fiero		23	8
142	2.2	14.1	8.2	10.7	Audi 4000S	16	24	
67	2.0	15.8	7.2	11.6	Chevrolet Cavalier		25	9
74	2.3	13.3	6.2	11.8	Ford Tempo		26	10
88	2.0	13.3	6.3	11.8	Honda Accord	17	27	
92	2.0	12.6	6.7	11.8	Mazda 626	18	28	
132	2.4	14.9	6.7	12.9	Mitsubishi Galant	19	29	
101	2.0	11.0	5.6	11.1	Nissan Stanza	20	30	
93	2.5	14.1	6.7	12.0	Oldsmobile Calais		31	11
126	2.0	14.1	7.9	12.9	Saab 900	21	32	
97	2.0	11.0	5.5	12.2	Toyota Camry	22	33	
144	2.3	14.1	7.9	13.3	Volvo	23	34	
101	2.5	16.9	6.5	12.6	Buick Century		35	12
149	5.2	23.0	9.7	16.2	Chrysler Fifth Avenue		36	13
100	2.2	13.3	7.9	11.7	Chrysler Le Baron		37	14
72	2.2	13.3	7.9	11.5	Dodge Aires		38	15
94	2.2	15.8	8.7	12.7	Dodge Lancer		39	16
114	3.8	15.8	8.7	14.1	Mercury Cougar		40	17
107	3.8	19.5	9.0	15.2	Oldsmobile Cutlass		41	18
95	2.8	16.9	8.7	12.6	Pontiac 6000		42	19
154	3.8	18.1	7.7	15.0	Buick Electra		43	20
106	5.0	18.1	8.2	16.5	Chevrolet Caprice		44	21

a Make scatterplots for each pair of variables and compute descriptive statistics and correlation coefficients. Which variables are most highly correlated?

b Repeat part (a), treating the foreign and domestic automobiles as two separate groups. Do the two groups differ in the behavior of the variables listed? (Filename: AUTOSPEC.DAT.)

6C The data below are annual U.S. GNP in trillions of dollars for the years 1978–1982. The current dollar figures are reported in dollars valued as of the reporting year. They do not take the effects of inflation into account. The constant dollar figures remove the effects of inflation by attributing to each dollar the value it would have had if it had been spent in 1972.

Year	Current Dollars	Constant Dollars
1978	2.13	1.40
1979	2.37	1.43
1980	2.63	1.48
1981	2.94	1.50
1982	3.06	1.48

a   Compute the correlation coefficient between the Current Dollars and Constant Dollars variables.

b   Define two new variables: $x = 5(\text{Current Dollars}) - 3$ and $y = 3(\text{Constant Dollars}) + 5$. Compute the values of these two new variables for each year and add them to the table above.

c   Compute the correlation coefficient between x and y. It should have the same value as the coefficient you computed in part (a). This illustrates a general property of the correlation coefficient: *its magnitude does not change if the variables are subject to linear transformations.*

d   Linear transformations of the variables do not change the magnitude of the correlation coefficient, but they can change the sign. Verify this by defining and computing the values of the variable $z = -3(\text{Constant Dollars}) + 5$ and then computing the correlation coefficient between z and the variable x defined in part (b).

e   Suppose you standardized two variables and computed the correlation coefficient between the standardized variables. How would this correlation coefficient relate to the correlation coefficient between the two original variables?

f   Suppose you standardized y and computed the correlation coefficient between x and the standardized version of y. How would this correlation coefficient relate to the correlation coefficient between x and y?

6D   Write a brief, one- to two-page, memo explaining the concept of ecological correlation. How does it arise in practice? What danger lurks in the interpretation of ecological correlations?

6E   Explain the relationship between correlation and causation.

6F   Write a short tutorial on autocorrelation and the patterns of autocorrelation found in practical data. Use examples of time series that you collect based on your interest and/or the types of data most useful in your work.

6G   Computer programs can simulate outcomes that behave as if they were random. Appendix 3 briefly discusses this idea. Most statistical packages have routines to generate random digits. This exercise asks you to check some output from such a routine for random behavior. Use a program at your computer installation or on your own computer to generate a sequence of 600 random digits—that is, the digits 0, 1, ... , 9 selected with equal probabilities of 0.1. Perform the following tests.

a   Prepare a sequence plot. Check the plot for trends and meandering behavior, both of which should be absent if the sequence behaves randomly. [Caution: To get usable sequence plots from some software packages, you may have to break the sequence into blocks of 200 observations.]

b   Do a tally of the numbers showing counts and percents. Check the percents to see how close they are to 10%, which is the probability of getting any one of the digits at random.

c   Scatterplot the sequence of digits versus its first lag, its second lag, and its third lag. Check for evidence of autocorrelation, which should be absent if the numbers behave randomly.

d   Calculate the autocorrelation coefficients for lags 1 through 6. Check to see if all of them are negligible.

Glossary for Chapter 6

autocorrelation   Correlation between values of a time series at a given lag.

correlation coefficient $r = \dfrac{1}{n-1}\left[\left(\dfrac{x_1 - \overline{x}}{s_x}\right)\left(\dfrac{y_1 - \overline{y}}{s_y}\right) + \left(\dfrac{x_2 - \overline{x}}{s_x}\right)\left(\dfrac{y_2 - \overline{y}}{s_y}\right) + \cdots \right.$
$$\left. + \left(\dfrac{x_n - \overline{x}}{s_x}\right)\left(\dfrac{y_n - \overline{y}}{s_y}\right)\right]$$

ecological correlation   Correlation computed from data that are aggregates of smaller units of study.

lag   An interval of time between observations in a time series.

lag length   The number of time periods skipped in associating a past value of a series with a current value.

lurking variable   A third variable whose influence plausibly explains the correlation between two other variables.

random walk   A series whose changes behave as if they were random.

scatterplot   An (x, y) plot that displays a statistical relationship between two variables.

time series   A sequence of observations collected from a process at fixed epochs of time.

2

Elements of Modeling

Straight-Line Models

Chapter Objectives

After mastering this chapter, you will be able to:

- Fit a straight line to a scatterplot

- Interpret fitted values and residuals

- Explain the method of least squares

- Interpret residual plots that result from fitting straight lines

7.1 Introduction

Chapter 6 discussed relationships between variables. Scatterplots and correlation coefficients help document those relationships, but neither scatterplots nor correlation coefficients provide models for *how* variables are related. Furthermore, correlation coefficients are limited to describing the strength of straight-line relationships. In this chapter, we introduce a statistical tool that overcomes some of these shortcomings: *regression analysis.*[†] A regression model consists of two parts:

- A mathematical curve that summarizes the general tendency of the relationship between the variables

- A measure of the amount of variation in the data around that mathematical curve

In general, any type of mathematical curve may be used to describe the relationship between two variables, making the regression tool much more powerful than correlation analysis. For simplicity and to introduce the ideas, we stick with straight-line

---

[†]The term *regression* is somewhat unfortunate but standard. It was introduced by Sir Francis Galton (1822–1911). Galton studied the relationship between fathers' and sons' heights and found that sons of tall fathers tended to be taller than average but not so tall as their fathers. This "regression toward the mean" terminology has persisted.

models in this chapter. Chapter 8 continues the discussion of regression and introduces more general curves. More advanced regression topics are covered in Chapters 20 to 24.

In regression analysis, the variables x and y are treated differently. The y variable is called the **response variable** (plotted on the vertical axis) and x is called the **predictor variable** (plotted on the horizontal axis). Other common names for x are *explanatory variable*, *independent variable*, or *regressor variable*. The y variable is sometimes called the *dependent variable* or the *outcome variable*. We will use the terminology of response and predictor, since these terms indicate the most common roles of the variables in business problems. That is, we usually want to use the predictor variable to predict the response variable.

response variable
predictor variable

S E C T I O N

7.2 Straight-Line Models

In this section, we discuss straight lines as well as fitted values and residuals.

Straight Lines

In correlation analysis, we measure the strength of straight-line relationships with the correlation coefficient. In regression analysis, we fit a straight line to the scatterplot to produce an equation to help describe the relationship. Recall that the equation for any straight line can be written in the form

$$y = b_0 + b_1 x$$

slope
y-intercept

constant term

where b_1 is the **slope** of the line and b_0 is the **y-intercept**—that is, the value of y when $x = 0$. Recall also that the slope parameter gives the amount of increase in y for a unit increase in x. In regression analysis, the parameter b_0 is also called the **constant term** in the equation.

For our beginning illustration, we take a sample of 10 cases from the real estate data of Exhibit 6.2A. To obtain the sample, we rolled a die; the result was three spots. Correspondingly, we chose the third case from Exhibit 6.2A and every sixth case thereafter for a total of 10 cases. We focus on the square feet of living area and market value variables, which are shown in Exhibit 7.2A. In this setting, the square feet of living area (Sq.ft) is the predictor variable (the x) and the corresponding market value (Market) is the response variable (the y).

Exhibit 7.2B shows the scatterplot of these data. Our eyes detect a marked straight-line trend in the plot. Before reading further, use a straightedge to draw a line that appears to you to be the best description of the trend. One simple analytic approach is to use the first and last cases to determine approximate values for the slope and intercept. Let (x_1, y_1) and (x_{10}, y_{10}) denote the coordinates of these two cases. The slope of the line through the first and last points is

$$\text{Slope} = \frac{y_{10} - y_1}{x_{10} - x_1} = \frac{45.2 - 25.2}{1298 - 544} = \frac{20.0}{754} = 0.026525$$

Square Feet (Sq.ft)	Market Value (Market)
544	25.2
694	37.4
767	33.6
825	38.0
899	37.6
965	37.2
1033	40.4
1060	44.8
1106	42.8
1298	45.2

EXHIBIT 7.2B
Scatterplot of Market Value
Versus Square Feet of Living
Area

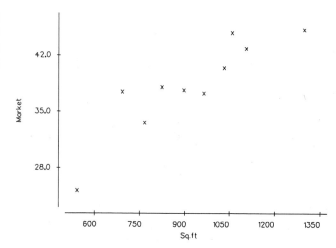

The y-intercept is

$$y\text{-intercept} = \frac{x_{10}y_1 - x_1 y_{10}}{x_{10} - x_1} = \frac{1298 \times 25.2 - 544 \times 45.2}{1298 - 544}$$

$$= \frac{32709.6 - 24588.8}{754} = \frac{8120.8}{754} = 10.77$$

Since this is just a trial line, we round off the slope to 0.03 and the y-intercept to 11 and consider the line with equation $y = 11 + 0.03x$ or

$$\text{Market} = 11 + 0.03\text{Sq.ft}$$

Exhibit 7.2C shows this trial line plotted on the scatterplot. For some cases, the line is above the actual data point, and for other cases, the line is below. You see that the actual data do not lie on this or any other line. The points scatter around the line.

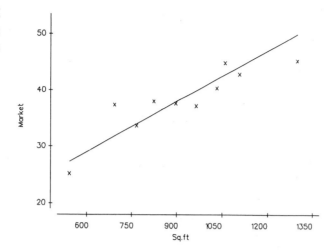

We would also like to take into account this scatter to give a range of plausible market values for a property of, say, 923 square feet of living area. A measure of the amount of scatter around the fitted line will help us assess this range of plausible values. Fortunately, regression analysis and statistical software allow us to systematically and routinely fit straight lines to scatterplots and to assess the degree of scatter around the fitted lines.

Fitted Values and Residuals

fitted value

To produce a well-fitting line, we need a measure of the closeness of fit for any given line. One way to measure closeness is to calculate the vertical distance from the observed y-value to the fitted line for each case. That is, we calculate the observed y-value minus the y-value on the line under consideration. For a particular x-value, the y-value on the line under consideration is called the **fitted value** and is denoted by $\hat{y}$. For a particular fitted line $\hat{y} = b_0 + b_1 x$, the fitted value is given by

$$\text{Fitted value} = \hat{y} = b_0 + b_1 x$$

residual

For a particular x-value, we next calculate the observed y-value minus the fitted value $\hat{y}$; the difference is called the **residual**. Thus,

$$\text{Residual} = (\text{observed } y) - (\text{fitted } y) = y - \hat{y} = y - b_0 - b_1 x$$

Exhibit 7.2D displays the trial fitted line $\hat{y} = 11 + 0.03x$, the scatterplot of the data, and the residuals for each case shown as vertical dashed lines from each observed y-value up or down to the fitted line. If the observed response is above the line, its residual is positive. If the observed response is below the line, its residual is negative. Some residuals are quite small, especially for cases 3 and 5. Some other residuals are

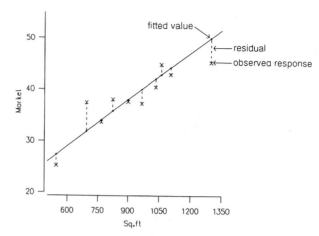

relatively large, especially cases 2 and 10. The residual for case 2 is positive, while the residual for case 10 is negative.

The numerical values of all the fitted values and residuals are listed in Exhibit 7.2E. For example, for case 1 where Sq.ft = 544 and Market = 25.2, the fitted value is

$$\text{Fitted value for case } 1 = 11 + 0.03(544) = 11 + 16.32 = 27.32$$

and the corresponding residual is

$$\text{Residual for case } 1 = 25.2 - 27.32 = -2.12$$

All the other fitted values and residuals are calculated similarly.

E X H I B I T **7.2E**
Fitted Values and Residuals for
the Trial Line

	The Data		Trial Line $y = 11 + 0.03x$		
Case	Sq.ft (x)	Market (y)	Fitted	Residual	Residual Squared
1	544	25.2	27.32	−2.12	4.4944
2	694	37.4	31.82	5.58	31.1364
3	767	33.6	34.01	−0.41	0.1681
4	825	38.0	35.75	2.25	5.0625
5	899	37.6	37.97	−0.37	0.1369
6	965	37.2	39.95	−2.75	7.5625
7	1033	40.4	41.99	−1.59	2.5281
8	1060	44.8	42.80	2.00	4.0000
9	1106	42.8	44.18	−1.38	1.9044
10	1298	45.2	49.94	−4.74	22.4676
			Totals	−3.53	79.4609

For any reasonable fitted line, some residuals will be large, some small, some positive, and some negative. How do we take all the residuals into account to obtain an overall measure of closeness between the data points and the line? The classical measure of the overall closeness of the fitted line to the data is the sum of the squared residuals. Exhibit 7.2E displays the sum of squared residuals for the trial line as 79.4609. Different lines produce different sums of squared residuals. *The smaller this sum of squared residuals, the better a particular line fits the overall scatterplot.* Fortunately, a method was discovered long ago that gives the line with the smallest possible sum of squared residuals—the method of least squares—which is the fundamental building block of most other fitting methods.

SECTION

7.3 Exercises

7.3A   Sketch the graph of the line with equation $y = 10 + 2x$ over the range of $0 < x < 15$.

7.3B   Each photocopy costs 6 cents. Sketch the graph relating number of copies made to the total price of the copies. Consider number of copies ranging from 1 to 100.

7.3C   A cellular phone company has two plans:

- The economy plan costs $20 per month and includes 20 minutes of free calls per month. Additional calls cost 20 cents per minute.

- The small business plan costs $50 per month and includes 100 free minutes of calls each month. Calls beyond the 100 minutes cost 24 cents per minute.

a   Sketch the graph relating total monthly costs to minutes of calls made for the economy plan. Consider call minutes ranging from 0 to 200 minutes per month.

b   On the same graph used in part (a), sketch the graph relating total monthly costs to minutes of calls made for the small business plan. Again consider call minutes ranging from 0 to 200 minutes.

c   Which plan provides the least cost for a user who makes 50 minutes of calls per month?

d   Which plan provides the least cost for a user who makes 150 minutes of calls per month?

e   At what number of minutes of calls do the two plans cost the same?

7.3D   Consider data from the sample of 10 real estate parcels displayed in Exhibit 7.2A. Use a trial line with equation Market $= 13 + 0.027$ Sq.ft.

a   Construct the scatterplot for the data and graph the trial line on the same plot.

b   Find the 10 fitted values for this trial line.

c   Find the 10 residuals for this trial line.

d   Calculate the sum of squared residuals for this line and compare to the sum of squared residuals for the trial line $y = 11 + 0.03x$ that was reported in Exhibit 7.2E.

7.3E   Consider the sample of 10 real estate parcels displayed in Exhibit 7.2A. Use a trial line with equation Market = Mean of Sq.ft—that is, a horizontal line at the height of the mean of Sq.ft.

a   Construct the scatterplot for the data and graph the trial line on the same plot.

b   Find the 10 fitted values for this trial line.

c   Find the 10 residuals for this trial line.

d   Calculate the sum of squared residuals for this line and compare to the sum of squared residuals for the trial line $y = 11 + 0.03x$ that was reported in Exhibit 7.2E

7.3F   Consider data from the sample of 10 real estate parcels displayed in Exhibit 7.2A. Use a trial line with equation Market $= 21 + 0.024$ Sq.ft.

a   Construct the scatterplot for the data and graph the trial line on the same plot.

b   Find the 10 fitted values for this trial line.

c   Find the 10 residuals for this trial line.

d   Calculate the sum of squared residuals for this line and compare to the sum of squared residuals for the trial line $y = 11 + 0.03x$ that was reported in Exhibit 7.2E.

SECTION

7.4 Least Squares

least-squares regression line

By definition, the **least-squares regression line** is the line that makes the sum of squared residuals as small as possible. Mathematical methods are available for finding the slope and intercept of the least-squares regression line, and we will give some relevant formulas shortly, but the computations are always done with statistical software, so we concentrate on interpretation. For the 10 cases from the real estate data, the equation of the least-squares regression line is $\hat{y} = 16.3 + 0.0239x$ or

$$\text{Market} = 16.3 + 0.0239 \text{ Sq.ft}$$

Exhibit 7.4A shows the fitted values, residuals, and squared residuals for both the trial line and the least-squares regression line. Notice that the sum of squared residuals for the least-squares line is 61.8004—a smaller value than the corresponding value of 79.4609 for the trial line. Note also that some of the individual residuals for the least-squares line are larger than the corresponding residuals for the trial line—in particular, for cases 1, 3, and 8. It is the nature of the method of least squares to consider the overall fit, increasing some residuals and decreasing others to obtain the line that has the smallest possible sum of squared residuals. Note further that the sum of the residuals for the least-squares line is zero. *It can be shown that the sum of the residuals is zero when fitting a general line by the method of least squares.*

Exhibit 7.4B shows a plot of the data and both the least-squares line (solid) and the trial line (dashed) superimposed. Notice that case 9 is below the trial line but above the least-squares line. This is reflected in its positive residual with respect to the least-squares line but negative residual for the trial line.

Equations for the Least-Squares Line

Numerous equations are available for finding and working with least-squares regression lines. We present only those that help with interpretation, since we assume the calculations will be carried out with statistical software.[†]

[†]Readers interested in more mathematical detail should consult the appendix to this chapter.

E X H I B I T **7.4A**
Fitted Values and Residuals for
the Trial Line and the
Least-Squares Line

	The Data		Trial Line $y = 11 + 0.03x$			Least-Squares Line: $y = 16.3 + 0.0239x$		
Case	Sq.ft (x)	Market (y)	Fitted	Residual	Residual Squared	Fitted	Residual	Residual Squared
1	544	25.2	27.32	−2.12	4.4944	29.27	−4.07	16.5649
2	694	37.4	31.82	5.58	31.1364	32.85	4.55	20.7025
3	767	33.6	34.01	−0.41	0.1681	34.59	−0.99	0.9801
4	825	38.0	35.75	2.25	5.0625	35.97	2.03	4.1209
5	899	37.6	37.97	−0.37	0.1369	37.74	−0.14	0.0196
6	965	37.2	39.95	−2.75	7.5625	39.32	−2.12	4.4944
7	1033	40.4	41.99	−1.59	2.5281	40.94	−0.54	0.2916
8	1060	44.8	42.80	2.00	4.0000	41.58	3.22	10.3684
9	1106	42.8	44.18	−1.38	1.9044	42.68	0.12	0.0144
10	1298	45.2	49.94	−4.74	22.4676	47.26	−2.06	4.2436
			Totals	−3.53	79.4609	Totals	0.00	61.8004

E X H I B I T **7.4B**
Scatterplot with Least-Squares
Regression Line (Solid) and Trial
Line (Dashed)

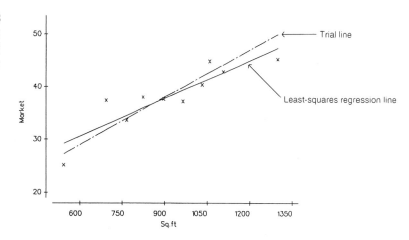

The most interpretable equations for least-squares regression lines are stated in terms of standardized variables. We standardize both y and x. Let y_* and x_* be the standardized variables—that is, let

$$y_* = \frac{y - \bar{y}}{s_y} \quad \text{and} \quad x_* = \frac{x - \bar{x}}{s_x}$$

and let r be the correlation coefficient between x and y. Then it may be shown that the least-squares regression line has the equation

**standardized
least-squares
regression line**

$$y_* = rx_*$$

In standardized terms, the least-squares regression line is the line through the origin (0,0) with slope r.

Exhibit 7.4C displays a scatterplot of standardized Market values versus standardized Sq.ft values with the regression line overlaid. This graph looks just like the plot in Exhibit 7.4B except that the scales of the two axes have been standardized (and the trial line is absent). The correlation coefficient between Market and Sq.ft is 0.895, so the equation of the regression line in standardized terms is $y_* = 0.895x_*$.

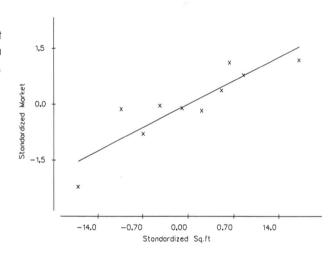

If we need the equation for the regression line in original terms, algebraic substitution and rearrangement give the expression

$$\hat{y} = \left(\bar{y} - r\frac{s_y}{s_x}\bar{x} \right) + \left(r\frac{s_y}{s_x} \right) x$$

so that the slope of the least-squares regression line is $b_1 = rs_y/s_x$ and the constant term or y-intercept is $b_0 = \bar{y} - r(s_y/s_x)\bar{x}$.

Another way to describe the regression line is that it passes through the point with coordinates $(\bar{x}, \bar{y})$ and has slope $b_1 = rs_y/s_x$.

E X A M P L E **7.4A**

In Example 6.2C, we introduced a data set showing the relationship between independence of central bank and inflation rates. The data listing and scatterplot appear in Exhibit 6.2E. The negative relationship shown was summarized by a correlation coefficient of $r = -0.843$, so that in standardized terms, the regression line is $y_* = -0.843x_*$. Further calculation establishes that $\bar{y} = 5.588$, $s_y = 1.629$, $\bar{x} = 2.359$, and $s_x = 0.837$. So, in original terms, the slope of the regression line is

$$\text{Slope} = -0.843 \times \frac{1.629}{0.837} = -1.640677419 \approx -1.64$$

The constant term is

$$\text{Constant term} = 5.588 - (-0.843) \times \left(\frac{1.629}{0.837}\right) \times 2.359$$
$$= 9.458358032 \approx 9.46$$

and the equation for the least-squares regression line is

$$\text{Inflation rate} = 9.46 - 1.64 \text{ Independence index}$$

A plot of the data with the regression line is shown in Exhibit 7.4D. ▪

E X H I B I T **7.4D**
Inflation Rate Versus
Independence of Central Bank
with Regression Line

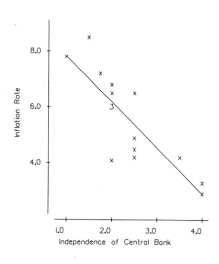

E X A M P L E   **7.4B**

Example 6.2D introduced data from *Consumer Reports* on 24 compact disc players. In a regression setting, we wonder if we can use a player's price to help predict the player's quality rating. The scatterplot was given in Exhibit 6.2F and the correlation coefficient was calculated as 0.237. In the exercises, you are asked to find the equation of the regression line. A scatterplot of quality rating versus price with the regression line overlaid is shown in Exhibit 7.4E. The graph clearly shows the futility of using price to predict quality. You do not always get what you pay for. ▪

E X H I B I T **7.4E**
Quality Rating Versus Price for
Compact Disc Players with
Regression Line

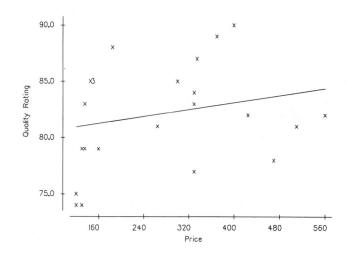

Using the Least-Squares Regression Line

prediction

The most important use of the regression line is to predict new values of the response y for specific values of the predictor variable x. The **prediction** is formed in the obvious way. Just substitute the value of x in the regression equation.

For example, to predict the market value of a property that has 1000 square feet of living space, we use the least-squares regression line Market = $16.3 + 0.0239$ Sq.ft to obtain the prediction

$$\text{Predicted market value } = 16.3 + 0.0239(1000) = 16.3 + 23.9 = 40.2$$

In the example of inflation rates and independence of central banks, the regression line is Inflation rate = $9.46 - 1.64$ Independence index. If we find a country whose index of independence is 1.5, we predict its inflation rate to be $9.46 - 1.64(1.5) = 9.46 - 2.46 = 7.00$.

Dangers of Extrapolation

extrapolate

Caution should be exercised in using regression lines for prediction. In particular, you should not substitute in an x-value that is far outside the range of x-values used to obtain the equation. To do so would be to **extrapolate** the line beyond the range of the data.

For example, it would be unwise to use the regression line for the real estate data for Sq.ft values outside of the range from about 500 to 1400 square feet. In the inflation rate example, the line should not be used for independence indices much outside the interval from 1 to 4. Outside the range of x-values observed, we have no information about the *shape* of the relationship. Does it continue to follow a straight line or does it curve?

SECTION

7.5 Exercises

7.5A   A set of 14 data pairs has summary statistics of $\bar{x} = 50$, $s_x = 2$, $\bar{y} = 20$, $s_y = 3$ and $r = 0.7$.

    a   Write down the equation of the least-squares regression line in standardized terms.

    b   Find the slope of the least-squares regression line in original terms.

    c   Find the y-intercept of the least-squares regression line in original terms.

    d   What is the value of $\hat{y}$ on the fitted line when $x = 48$?

7.5B   A set of 12 data pairs has summary statistics of $\bar{x} = 25$, $s_x = 4$, $\bar{y} = 30$, $s_y = 5$, and $r = -0.6$.

    a   Write down the equation of the least-squares regression line in standardized terms.

    b   Find the slope of the least-squares regression line in original terms.

    c   Find the y-intercept of the least-squares regression line in original terms.

    d   What is the value of $\hat{y}$ on the fitted line when $x = 30$?

7.5C   Consider data from the sample of 10 real estate parcels displayed in Exhibit 7.2A. Use a trial line with equation Market $= 15 + 0.03$ Sq.ft.

    a   Construct the scatterplot for the data and graph the trial line on the same plot.

    b   Find the 10 fitted values for this trial line.

    c   Find the 10 residuals for this trial line.

    d   Calculate the sum of squared residuals for this line and compare the sum to the sum of squared residuals for the least-squares line.

7.5D   Using the data from the 10 real estate parcels displayed in Exhibit 7.2A verify that the equation of the least-squares regression line is Market $= 16.3 + 0.0239$ Sq.ft. (Filename: SMALPROP.DAT.)

7.5E   Refer to the Anscombe data first shown in Exercise 6.3H.

    a   Find the least-squares regression lines for each of the four data sets.

    b   Plot the regression lines on each of the four scatterplots.

    c   Comment on the plots displayed in part (b). (Filename: ANSCOMBE.DAT.)

7.5F   Consider the data relating inflation rates and independence of central banks reported in Exhibit 6.2E. The scatterplot is shown in Exhibit 7.4D. (Filename: FREEBNK.DAT.)

    a   Find the equation for the least-squares line.

    b   If a country has an index of independence of 3, what is your prediction of its rate of inflation?

    c   If a country changed its laws so that its index of independence changed from a value of 2 to a value of 3, what is your prediction for the *change* in the inflation rate?

7.5G   Quality ratings and prices of 24 compact disc players were given in Example 7.4B. (Filename: CDPLAYER.DAT.)

    a   Calculate the least-squares regression line with the purpose of predicting quality rating from price.

    b   Verify the scatterplot and regression line shown in Exhibit 7.4E.

7.5H   Quality ratings and prices of 30 cassette tape decks were given in Exercise 6.3C. (Filename: CASSETTE.DAT.)

    a   Calculate the least-squares regression line with the purpose of predicting quality rating from price.

    b   Construct the scatterplot of quality rating versus price and graph the regression line on the plot.

c   Comment on the usefulness of using price to predict quality rating.

7.5I   Use data reported in Exhibit 6.2A on Market value and Assessed value.

a   Find the least-squares regression line for predicting Market value from Assessed value.

b   If a property has an Assessed value of 25.2, what is your prediction of its Market value? (Filename: REALPROP.DAT.)

7.5J   Use the full 60 data values for Market and Sq.ft shown in Exhibit 6.2A. The scatterplot is displayed in Exhibit 6.2C. (Filename: REALPROP.DAT.)

a   Find the equation of the least-squares line for these data.

b   Compare this line to the least-squares line we obtained using only the sample of 10 cases in Exhibit 7.4A.

7.5K   Fit the least-squares line to the bank data of Exhibit 6.6A. Use Deposits for the predictor variable and Assets for the response. (Filename: DEPOSITS.DAT.)

7.5L   Exhibit 3.4C gave the exam scores on two exams for 39 business statistics students. (Filename: EXAMS2.DAT.)

a   Find the least-squares regression line for predicting second exam scores from first exam scores.

b   What score would you predict for a student whose first exam score was 60?

7.5M   Suppose the roles of x and y are reversed so that x is plotted on the vertical axis and y is plotted on the horizontal axis. Argue that the equation of the least-squares regression line is

$$\hat{x} = \left(\bar{x} - r \frac{s_x}{s_y} \bar{y} \right) + \left(r \frac{s_x}{s_y} \right) y$$

S E C T I O N

7.6 Analysis of Residuals

Virtually all statistical modeling may be conveniently thought of within the framework of the equation

Observed Response = Fitted Value + Residual

The data-generating process yields the observed response, while the model produces the fitted value and residual. The fitted value attempts to show the general pattern, while the residual expresses how the observed response deviates from the general pattern. When the model does a good job of describing the general pattern in the observed responses, the residuals will look as if they were generated by a random process. Residuals containing nonrandom patterns, on the other hand, indicate that the model can be improved to capture those patterns.

residual plot   The most basic tool for looking for patterns in residuals is a **plot of residuals** versus the predictor variable—that is, the scatterplot of residual versus x. Our first example uses the market value and square feet living area data.

E X A M P L E   **7.6A**   We return to the real estate data and in particular to Exhibit 7.4A, where the least-squares residuals are displayed. We see that for case 1 the residual is -4.07. In the residual plot, a point is plotted with -4.07 on the vertical above the Sq.ft value of 544 for case 1. The rest of the residuals are plotted similarly against their corresponding Sq.ft values. The resulting graph is shown in Exhibit 7.6A.

This plot illustrates what is considered to be a fairly ideal residual plot with a random pattern. The residuals are spread around zero with some positive and some negative for all different sizes of Sq.ft—high, low, or middle sized. ■

E X H I B I T **7.6A**
Residuals Versus Sq.ft for
Least-Squares Regression Line

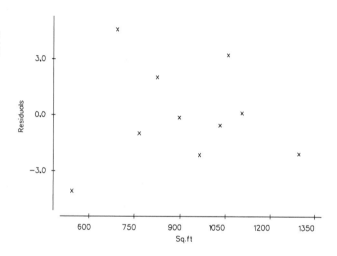

E X A M P L E   **7.6B**

Exhibit 7.6B shows the residual plot for the least-squares regression line fitted to the data on inflation rate and independence of central banks. The data appear in Exhibit 6.2E and the scatterplot and fitted line in Exhibit 7.4D. Again, the scatter in the residual plot seems random. The simple straight-line model seems to have captured most of the trend in the data. ■

Sometimes there is no relationship between variables, as in the quality ratings and price data shown in Exhibit 7.4E. Sometimes there is a relationship and straight-line models describe that relationship adequately. Other times, straight-line models do not work well. Some relationships are better modeled by more complicated, curved relationships, as illustrated in Example 7.6C.

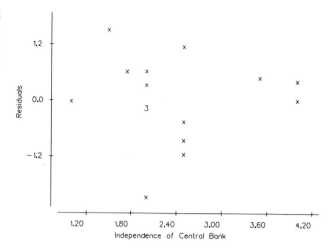

E X H I B I T **7.6C**
Concentration of Aluminum
Waste on the Forest Floor at
Various Distances from an
Aluminum Reduction Plant

Aluminum Concentration (mg/kg)	Distance to Plant (km)
6100	1.2
4400	1.4
2800	3.6
2700	4.4
2600	4.5
2800	8.8
2500	32.0
2700	33.0

Source: W. N. Beyer, W. J. Fleming, and D. Swineford, "Changes in Litter Near an Aluminum Reduction Plant," *Journal of Environmental Quality,*
16(3) (1987), 246–250.

E X A M P L E   **7.6C**

Toxic waste is a major problem for business today. Expensive processes are
necessary to control and dispose of this burdensome problem. Many wastes
from industrial processes can be carried through the air and deposited on the
earth's surface.

Exhibit 7.6C displays data on aluminum waste concentrations measured
at various distances from a particular aluminum reduction plant in Tennessee.
The least-squares regression line was fitted to the data to see if it helps
explain or predict the amount of aluminum waste found at certain distances
from the plant. The resulting residual plot is shown in Exhibit 7.6D. Here
we see a nonrandom pattern in the residuals. Both of the low distances have
positive residuals, the four middle-sized distances have negative residuals,
and the two large distances have positive residuals. The straight-line model

has systematically underfit, then overfit, and finally, underfit the data as distance ranges from low to high.

Exhibit 7.6E shows the scatterplot of the data with the fitted line overlaid. The problem could have been spotted from a careful look at the scatterplot of the data. A straight line simply is not an adequate model for these data. Aluminum concentration is not related to distance from the plant in a linear manner. The residual plot clearly shows the need for a more complex model. We will return to these data in Chapters 8 and 21 and attempt to improve the model. ■

E X H I B I T **7.6D**
Residuals from Straight-Line
Regression of Aluminum
Concentration Versus Distance

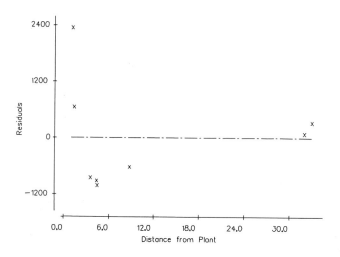

E X H I B I T **7.6E**
Scatterplot of Aluminum
Concentration Versus Distance
from Plant

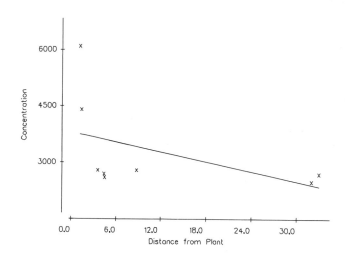

EXAMPLE 7.6D

Residual plots can easily detect lack of fit when a straight line is inadequate for a curved relationship. The residual plot shown in Exhibit 7.6F gives a further example. Again a nonrandom pattern emerges. Here all low values of the predictor variable have negative residuals. Large values of the predictor also have mostly negative residuals, but middle-sized predictor values all have positive residuals. In this example, the straight-line model has systematically overfit, underfit, and overfit.

Exhibit 7.6G shows the scatterplot of the original data. The curvature is not so apparent.

EXHIBIT 7.6F
Residual Plot for Curved
Relationship

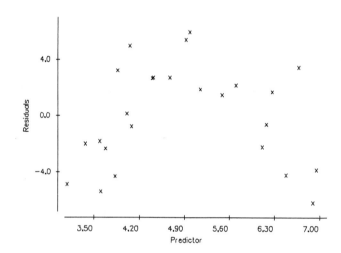

EXHIBIT 7.6G
Scatterplot of Original Data with
Curved Relationship

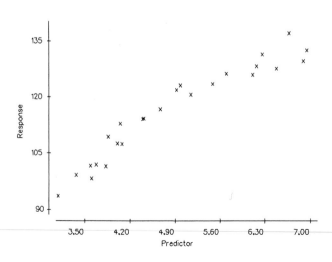

Exhibit 7.6H displays the scatterplot of the original data and the fitted line. *The subtle curvature in the scatterplot of y versus x is made quite dramatic in the residual plot.* This is an important feature of the residual plot and will be especially important when more complicated models are considered in Chapter 8.   ▪

EXHIBIT 7.6H
Scatterplot and Fitted Line for the Curved Relationship

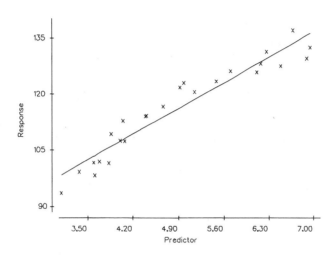

SECTION

7.7 Exercises

7.7A   Refer to the Anscombe data first shown in Exercise 6.3H. The least-squares lines were obtained in Exercise 7.5E.

   a   Plot the residual plots for each of the four data sets.

   b   Comment on the plots displayed in part (a).

   c   Which of the four data sets seem well-modeled by a straight line? (Filename: ANSCOMBE.DAT.)

7.7B   Use the bank data of Exhibit 6.6A with Deposits as the response variable and Assets as the predictor variable. (Filename: DEPOSITS.DAT.)

   a   Display the residual plot for the straight-line regression model.

   b   Comment on the adequacy of the straight-line model in the light of the residual plot obtained in part (a).

7.7C   Consider the Gross Domestic Product data introduced in Exhibit 1.3B. The sequence plot is shown in Exhibit 2.4B. (Filename: GDP.DAT.)

   a   Use least-squares to fit a straight line to the sequence plot. That is, use the time sequence 1, 2, 3, . . . , 12 as the predictor variable.

   b   Display the residual plot from the regression carried out in part (a).

c   Comment on the residual plot of part (b). Does it display a random scatter? Does it indicate that the straight line adequately describes the time trend in the data?

7.7D   The data below show the average height of girls at various ages from 1/2 year to 14.

Age (years)	Height (inches)	Age (years)	Height (inches)
0.5	26	8	50
1	29	9	52
2	33	10	54
3	36	11	56
4	39	12	58
5	41	13	60
6	44	14	62
7	47		

(Filename: AGEHGT_G.DAT.)

a   Fit a straight line to these tó predict height from age.

b   Display the residual plot for this regression.

c   Comment on the residual plot of part (b). In particular, does the residual plot show any model inadequacies?

7.7E   The data below show the average height for boys from ages from 1/2 year to 14 years.

Age (years)	Height (inches)	Age (years)	Height (inches)
0.5	26	8	50
1	29	9	52
2	33	10	54
3	36	11	56
4	39	12	58
5	42	13	60
6	45	14	62
7	47		

(Filename: AGEHGT_B.DAT.)

a   Fit a straight line to these to predict height from age.

b   Display the residual plot for this regression.

c   Comment on the residual plot of part (b). In particular, does the residual plot show any model inadequacies?

7.7F   Use the data reported in Exhibit 6.2A on Market value and Assessed value for 60 properties. (Filename: REALPROP.DAT.)

a   Produce the residual plot corresponding to the straight-line regression model.

b   Comment on the plot produced in part (a). In particular, does the straight-line model seem to adequately describe the relationship between Market value and Assessed value?

7.7G   Use the data reported in Exhibit 6.2A on Market value and Sq.ft for 60 properties. (Filename: REALPROP.DAT.)

a   Produce the residual plot corresponding to the straight-line regression model.

b   Comment on the plot produced in part (a). In particular, does there seem to be any suggestion of curvature in the relationship between Market value and Sq.ft value?

7.7H   Monthly data on average hourly wages in the apparel industry were used in Exercise 2.5C. (Filename: APAWAGES.DAT.)

a   Fit a straight line to the sequence plot of these data by using the time index, 1, 2, 3, . . ., 72 as the predictor variable.

b   Display the residual plot for the analysis done in part (a).

c   Does the residual plot indicate any model inadequacies? Do you see any evidence of curvature or other nonrandom patterns?

SECTION

7.8   Outliers in Regression Analysis

Recall that outliers were defined in Chapter 4 as observations that are separated from the main body of the data. We have noted that outliers can have a strong impact on statistics such as means, standard deviations, and correlations. Outliers also affect regression lines, as illustrated in the following example.

EXAMPLE   7.8A   Battery-powered portable computers have become immensely popular, and their sizes and weights are steadily decreasing. In August 1992, *PC Magazine* reported on their extensive tests of battery life for a large number of machines. Most portable computers have power-management systems that shut down various subsystems, such as the hard drive and screen display, when the keyboard or mouse pointing device are inactive for an extended time. Therefore, just turning on the computer and running down the battery without human intervention is not a realistic test of real-world battery life.

To obtain a more realistic figure, PC Magazine Labs created a mechanical device that pokes the keyboard to simulate real computer use. They called this test the ZDigit battery test. For comparison, they also tested battery life with the power-management software disabled, calling this the Rundown test. Sixty-five computers were tested in both ways, producing 65 pairs of ZDigit and Rundown hours. The data set is listed in Appendix 4.

The Rundown test is much easier to carry out. It would be helpful if we could predict real-world battery life (ZDigit) from the much simpler Rundown measurement. If a straight-line model works, all the better. Exhibit 7.8A shows the scatterplot of the data and indicates that a straight-line model is certainly worth considering. When least-squares is used to fit the line, we obtain the fitted line

$$\text{ZDigit} = 0.325 + 1.23 \text{ Rundown}$$

In other words, we predict a real-world battery life of about 23% more than the Rundown figure plus another third of an hour.

Exhibit 7.8B displays the residual plot for this regression analysis. We see one very large residual value of about 3.3. All other residuals are less than about 1.5 in magnitude. A review of the scatterplot in Exhibit 7.8C with the fitted regression line overlaid reveals one computer with an unusual

E X H I B I T **7.8A**
Scatterplot of ZDigit Battery Life
Versus Rundown Battery Life for
Portable Computers

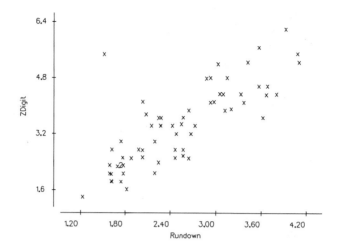

combination of large ZDigit value and small Rundown value. This data point is not that unusual in either variable separately, but it is an outlier within the framework of the two variables. Exhibit 7.8D depicts the original scatterplot with dotplot displays shown in the margins. The ZDigit value for the outlier is not the largest ZDigit value, nor is its Rundown value the smallest. The residual plot is thus the best tool to make the outlier stand out clearly. But what effect does the outlier have on the fitted regression equation?

E X H I B I T **7.8B**
Residual Plot for Battery Life
Data with Outlier

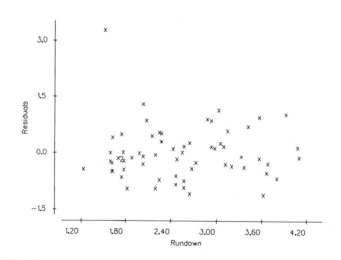

E X H I B I T **7.8C**
Scatterplot and Fitted
Regression Line of Battery Life
Data with Outlier

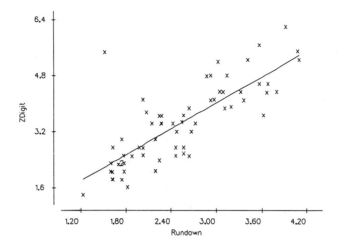

E X H I B I T **7.8D**
Scatterplot of Battery Life with
Dotplots of Each Variable in the
Margins

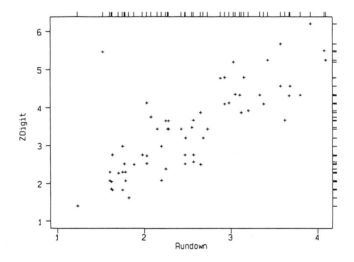

To see the effect of the outlier on the regression analysis, we remove that data point and redo the calculations. The equation for the fitted line then becomes

$$ZDigit = 0.026 + 1.33 \ Rundown$$

Now the relationship is quite simple. Real-world battery life is predicted to be about 33% greater than the Rundown value. (For all practical purposes, the intercept term of 0.026 hours can be ignored.)

Exhibit 7.8E shows the scatterplot and fitted regression line with the outlier removed. Exhibit 7.8F displays the corresponding residual plot. No unusual residuals or other nonrandom patterns are seen in this graphic, and the straight-line model seems to be an adequate description of the relationship between ZDigit battery life and Rundown battery life. More sophisticated methods for looking for outliers are covered in Chapter 21.   ▪

E X H I B I T **7.8E**
Scatterplot and Fitted
Regression Line of Battery Life
Data Without Outlier

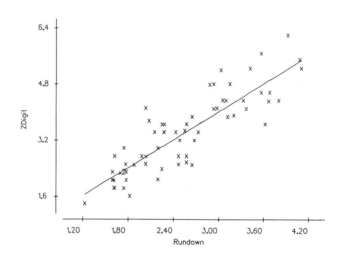

E X H I B I T **7.8F**
Residual Plot for Battery Life
Data Without Outlier

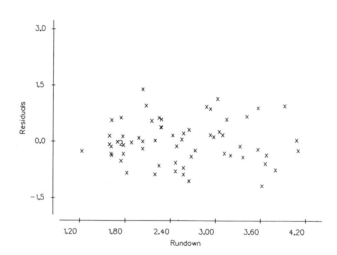

S E C T I O N

7.9 Exercises

7.9A   Consider the photocopy data from Exhibit 1.3A. From the sequence plot shown in Exhibit 2.4A, we saw that the sequence has considerable variation over time and has one unusually large value from November 16. (Filename: PHOTOCOP.DAT.)

a   Fit a line to the sequence plot by using time = 1, 2, ..., 30 as the predictor.

b   Plot the residual plot to look for outliers. Does the unusual data point stand out in this display?

c   Now remove the data point for November 16 and redo the regression and residual plot.

d   Comment on the change in the fitted line after removing the outlier.

e   Are there any unusual points after removing the November 16 data point?

7.9B   Consider the following data:

$$
\begin{array}{c|ccccccc}
x & 1 & 2 & 2 & 3 & 4 & 4 & 5 \\
y & 2 & 3 & 3 & 4 & 5 & 5 & 6
\end{array}
$$

a   Find the regression line for these data and plot the scatterplot and fitted line.

b   Construct the residual plot for the analysis in part (a).

c   Now alter the data in the following way:

$$
\begin{array}{c|ccccccc}
x & 1 & 2 & 2 & 3 & 4 & 4 & 5 \\
y & 2 & 2 & 4 & 4 & 4 & 6 & 6
\end{array}
$$

Find the least-squares regression line for these altered data. Compare your line to the one found in part (a).

d   Construct the scatterplot and fitted line for the altered data.

e   Construct the residual plot for the analysis of part (c).

f   Some of the altered data points might be considered outliers relative to the original data. What effect do these outliers have on the fitted line? What effect do these outliers have on the residual plots?

7.9C   Data on Japanese investment in the U.S. were presented in Exercise 2.11B. (Filename: JAPANINV.DAT.)

a   Use those data to calculate the regression line to predict Japanese investment in the U.S. in terms of Bond Yields (new issues, high grade corporate).

b   Plot the residual plot from the regression carried out in part (a).

c   Comment on any apparent outliers revealed in the residual plot of part (b).

d   Plot the scatterplot of Japanese investment versus Bond Yields and point out the observation that produced the outlier. Which time point (month and year) produced the outlier?

e   Remove the outlier from the data set and refit the regression line.

f   Construct the residual plot from the reduced data set and comment.

7.9D   Consider the data set presented in Exercise 6.7A. Repeat that exercise, computing least-squares regression lines instead of correlation coefficients. Note the effects of various kinds of outliers. (Filename: EX6_7A.DAT.)

Chapter Summary

Straight-line regression models summarize relationships between variables in many situations. When a straight-line model is adequate, it provides a convenient model for explaining that relationship or for predicting new response values. Least-squares is a reasonable method for fitting regression lines to data. It can be easily carried out with statistical software, leaving its interpretation to the analyst. The simplest equation for the regression line is in terms of standardized variables, $y_* = rx_*$.

The regression model is best described in terms of fitted values and residuals through the expression

Observed Response = Fitted Value + Residual

The least-squares method chooses values for the slope and intercept of the regression line to minimize the sum of squared residuals. The fitted values show the general trend in the observed responses, while the residuals display the deviation of the observations from the general pattern. When the model describes the general trend in the observations adequately, the residuals appear random. Residuals containing nonrandom patterns indicate that the model can be improved by incorporating those patterns into the model.

The user of regression models must always be aware of the influence that outliers can have on regression analysis. It is especially important to study both the scatterplot of the data and the residual plot to look for outliers that may dramatically alter the model.

Supplementary Exercises for Chapter 7

7A   Richard L. Schmoyer reports cost data for 26 construction projects at a large industrial facility. He reports actual costs and cost estimates made by engineers before the projects started. All cost figures are in millions of dollars. (Filename: ESTIMATE.DAT.)

   a   Display the scatterplot of Actual cost (y) versus Estimated cost (x).

   b   Use least-squares to fit a line to these data.

   c   We have just estimated a project at $3 million. What would we predict for the actual cost of this project when completed?

   d   Display the residual plot for the least-squares analysis carried out in part (b).

   e   Does the residual plot indicate any model inadequacies?

	Costs of Construction Projects			Costs of Construction Projects	
Project	**Actual Cost**	**Estimated Cost**	**Project**	**Actual Cost**	**Estimated Cost**
1	0.918	0.575	14	13.371	8.947
2	7.214	6.127	15	1.553	3.157
3	14.577	11.215	16	4.096	3.540
4	30.028	28.195	17	27.973	37.400
5	38.173	30.100	18	7.642	7.650
6	15.320	21.091	19	3.692	13.700
7	14.837	8.659	20	29.522	29.003
8	51.284	40.630	21	15.317	14.639
9	34.100	37.800	22	5.292	5.292
10	2.003	1.803	23	0.707	0.960
11	20.099	18.048	24	1.246	1.240
12	4.324	8.102	25	1.143	1.419
13	10.523	10.730	26	21.571	38.936

Source: Richard L. Schmoyer, "Asymptotically Valid Prediction Intervals for Linear Models," *Technometrics*, 34(4) (1992), 399–408.

7B Monthly data on average hourly earnings per worker in the manufacturing sector were given in Exercise 2.5B. (Filename: MANWAGES.DAT.)

   a Using least-squares, find the regression line that predicts wages in terms of the time variable = 1, 2, 3, . . . , 72.

   b Display the residual plot for the regression analysis of part (a).

   c Comment on any model inadequacies indicated from the residual plot.

   d Redo the residual plot done in part (b) using plotting symbols that indicate the corresponding month of the year. That is, plot all January residuals with an A, all Februaries with a B, and so on.

   e Are there any nonrandom patterns in the residual plot produced in part (d)?

7C Supplementary Exercise 2C gave monthly retail sales data for five years. (Filename: RETAIL.DAT.)

   a Find the least-squares regression line for the sequence plot of this series. That is, use time 1, 2, . . . , 60 as the predictor.

   b Display the residual plot for the regression analysis of part (a).

   c Comment on any model inadequacies indicated from the residual plot.

   d Construct a new residual plot using plotting symbols that correspond to month of the year. For example, plot all January residuals with an A, all Februaries with a B, and so on.

   e Comment on any nonrandom patterns in the residual plot produced in part (d).

   f Can you explain these patterns?

7D Revisit the data on Japanese investment in the U.S. introduced in Exercise 2.11B. Consider using the Japanese Stock Price Average to predict the Japanese Direct Investment in the U.S. (Filename: JAPANINV.DAT.)

   a Fit the regression line for this data.

   b Display the residual plot.

   c Does the residual plot show any nonrandom patterns?

7E Consider the data on quality ratings and price for cassette tape decks. The data appear in Exercise 6.3C. As noted there, some of these decks are single decks and some are dual decks. (Filename: CASSETTE.DAT.)

a Fit one regression line to the complete data disregarding whether the deck is single or dual.

b Now fit separate regression lines to the single and dual-deck data.

c Plot a scatterplot of the data using different plotting symbols for single and dual decks.

d Plot the regression line found in part (a) on the scatterplot of part (c).

e Now plot the separate regression line found in part (b) on the same scatterplot in part (c). Use different colors or line style (solid, dashed, dotted) to distinguish the lines.

f Would the regression lines in part (e) be best described as fairly similar or rather different?

7F In its October 29, 1990 issue, *Business Week* reported average salaries for men and women MBA graduates. Here are the data for some prestigious schools. (Filename: MBASALRY.DAT.)

Men's Salaries($)	Women's Salaries($)	Business School
54,322	52,934	Berkeley
65,009	54,817	Columbia
53,762	54,433	Cornell
57,393	54,643	Dartmouth
54,058	51,702	Michigan
78,539	58,500	MIT
46,521	40,367	Rochester
80,412	74,925	Stanford
62,785	51,147	UCLA
67,397	54,306	Virginia

a Using men's salaries as predictors, display the scatterplot.

b Find the correlation coefficient in the scatterplot.

c Now find the least-squares regression line.

d If some new school had an average starting salary for men of $55,000, what would you predict for the average starting salary of that school's women graduates?

e Construct the residual plot for the regression done in part (c).

f Does the residual plot show any nonrandom patterns?

7G The October 29, 1990 issue of *Business Week* also gave various rankings of MBA programs. *Business Week* gave its own ranking but also reported rankings by corporate executives and by graduates of the programs. The data are shown in the following table. (Filename: MBARANK.DAT.) Consider the *Business Week* ranking as the predictor variable.

a Prepare a scatterplot of Corporate Poll ranking versus *Business Week* ranking.

b Does the scatterplot in (a) indicate good agreement between the two rankings?

c Calculate the correlation coefficient between the Corporate Poll ranking versus *Business Week* ranking. (This is called the *Rank Correlation Coefficient*.)

d Find the regression line for the scatterplot of part (a).

e Display the residual plot for the regression of part (d).

f Does the residual plot show any outliers or curvature in the relationship?

g Repeat parts (a) through (f) for Graduates' rankings versus *Business Week* rankings.

Business Week Ranking	Corporate Poll Ranking	Graduates' Ranking	Business School
1	2	7	Northwestern
2	1	10	Pennsylvania
3	3	9	Harvard
4	5	1	Chicago
5	7	3	Stanford
6	8	5	Dartmouth
7	4	14	Michigan
8	6	11	Columbia
9	11	4	Carnegie-Mellon
10	16	2	UCLA
11	10	13	MIT
12	14	6	North Carolina
13	13	12	Duke
14	12	16	Virginia
15	9	23	Indiana
16	19	15	Cornell
17	20	18	NYU
18	28	8	Texas
19	23	19	Berkeley
20	27	17	Rochester

7H Statistical theory can be used to show that least-squares residuals and fitted values always have a correlation coefficient of zero. This is true regardless of the adequacy of the straight-line model.

  a Use several of the data sets we have presented to verify this fact empirically. That is, find the residuals and fitted values and compute the correlation between them.

  b Also verify that the residuals from least-squares always add to zero.

7I Perform the following experiment: Roll one die and record the number of spots showing. Call this x. Roll the die again and let the number of spots showing be the response y. Repeat the procedure 20 times to produce 20 pairs of x's and y's.

  a Prepare the scatterplot of y versus x.

  b Find the least-squares regression line.

  c Display the residual plot.

  d Does the residual plot show any nonrandom patterns? Would you expect it to?

7J For golfers: We want to investigate the relationship, if any, between the accuracy of your putting and the distance from the cup. The predictor variable x will be the distance from the cup and y will be the distance from the ball's final resting place and the center of the cup. We will putt from three distances—5 feet, 10 feet, and 15 feet—and try each of these putts five times for a total of 15 putts. Take 15 slips of paper and write 5 on 5 of them, 10 on 5 of them, and 15 on the remaining 5. To decide the order for performing the putts, mix the slips up in a box and draw them out randomly one at a time.

  a Carry out the experiment as described above.

  b Scatterplot the data.

  c Does a straight line seem like a reasonable summary of the trend in your data?

  d Find the correlation coefficient between x and y.

  e Calculate the regression line that we would use to predict putting accuracy from putting distance.

f   Would this regression be useful for predicting the accuracy of 40-foot putts?

g   Display the residual plot and comment on any patterns in the plot.

Glossary for Chapter 7

constant term   An alternative name for the y-intercept in the equation of a straight line.

extrapolation   Using a fitted line to predict responses with predictor values that are far outside the range of the predictor variable values used in fitting the relationship.

fitted value   The value on the fitted line corresponding to a particular predictor variable value.

least-squares regression line   The line with equation $y = b_0 + b_1 x$ where the regression coefficients b_0 and b_1 are selected to minimize the sum of squared vertical differences from the observed responses to the line.

prediction   Using the relationship to estimate the value of a response not observed.

predictor variable   The variable used to predict or explain the response variable.

residual   The observed response minus the fitted value.

residual plot   A plot of residuals versus corresponding values of the predictor variable.

response variable   The variable we wish to predict or explain through the regression model.

slope   The coefficient b_1 in the equation of a straight line $y = b_0 + b_1 x$.

standardized least-squares regression line   The equation $y_* = r x_*$, where y_* and x_* are standardized values of y and x.

y-intercept   The coefficient b_0 in the equation of a straight line $y = b_0 + b_1 x$.

APPENDIX

The Mathematics of Least Squares

The mechanics of least squares are sketched for the straight-line model. For a complete discussion, consult one of the many fine books on regression analysis.[†]

Let $\{(x_i, y_i): i = 1, 2, \ldots, n\} = \{(x_1, y_1), (x_2, y_2), \ldots, (x_n, y_n)\}$ denote the n data points formed by pairing the value of x and the value of y for each case. We wish to fit a straight-line model to these data points using the principle of ordinary least squares. To do this, we define a family of lines by the expression

$$y^*(\beta_0, \beta_1) = \beta_0 + \beta_1 x$$

[†] See N.R. Draper and H. Smith, *Applied Regression Analysis,* 2nd ed. (New York: Wiley, 1981); Raymond H. Myers, *Classical and Modern Regression Analysis,* 2nd ed. (Boston: PWS-KENT, 1990); and Sanford Weisberg, *Applied Linear Regression* (New York: Wiley, 1985).

where for each choice of β_0 and β_1 we obtain a linear function of x with y-intercept β_0 and slope β_1. We seek the choice $\beta_0 = b_0$ and $\beta_1 = b_1$ that best fits the data. To do this, we define the *sum-of-squares function*

$$S(\beta_0, \beta_1) = \sum_{i=1}^{n} [y_i - y_i^*(\beta_0, \beta_1)]^2$$

$$= \sum_{i=1}^{n} [y_i - \beta_0 - \beta_1 x_i]^2$$

which is nothing more than the squared Euclidean distance between the point with coordinates $(y_1, y_2, \ldots, y_n)$ and the point with coordinates $(\beta_0 + \beta_1 x_1, \beta_0 + \beta_1 x_2, \ldots, \beta_0 + \beta_1 x_n)$. The point $(y_1, y_2, \ldots, y_n)$ is the observed data point; the point $(\beta_0 + \beta_1 x_1, \beta_0 + \beta_1 x_2, \ldots, \beta_0 + \beta_1 x_n)$ is the fitted values point. We find b_0 and b_1 so that $S(b_0, b_1)$ is the minimum value of $S(\beta_0, \beta_1)$, and thus the observed data point and the point of fitted values are as close as possible in the Euclidean sense.[†]

To find b_0 and b_1 treat $S(\beta_0, \beta_1)$ as a function of the two variables β_0 and β_1 and minimize it by setting its partial derivatives equal to zero and solving the resulting equations for β_0 and β_1. The solutions of the equations are b_0 and b_1. It is a standard exercise in calculus to show that these values minimize rather than maximize the sum-of-squares function.

The partial derivatives are easiest to take if we first reexpress the sum-of-squares function as follows:

$$S(\beta_0, \beta_1) = \sum_{i=1}^{n} [y_i - \beta_0 - \beta_1 x_i]^2$$

$$= \sum_{i=1}^{n} [y_i^2 + \beta_0^2 + (\beta_1 x_i)^2 - 2\beta_0 y_i - 2\beta_1 x_i y_i + 2\beta_0 \beta_1 x_i]$$

$$= \sum_{i=1}^{n} y_i^2 + n\beta_0^2 + \sum_{i=1}^{n} x_i^2 \beta_1^2 - 2\sum_{i=1}^{n} y_i \beta_0 - 2\sum_{i=1}^{n} x_i y_i \beta_1 + 2\sum_{i=1}^{n} x_i \beta_0 \beta_1$$

The partial derivative of this expression with respect to β_0 is

$$2n\beta_0 - 2\sum_{i=1}^{n} y_i + 2\sum_{i=1}^{n} x_i \beta_1$$

The partial derivative of the sum-of-squares function with respect to β_1 is

$$2\sum_{i=1}^{n} x_i^2 \beta_1 - 2\sum_{i=1}^{n} x_i y_i + 2\sum_{i=1}^{n} x_i \beta_0$$

[†] Other fitting principles make these two points close in non-Euclidean senses. The basics of the theory are the same regardless of the fitting principle. What changes is the objective function. The sum-of-squares function is the objective function that yields least squares. Another possible objective function is $D(\beta_0, \beta_1) = \sum_{i=1}^{n} |y_i - y_i^*(\beta_0, \beta_1)|$. A very useful objective function is the weighted least-squares function $WS(\beta_0, \beta_1) = \sum_{i=1}^{n} w_i [y_i - y_i^*(\beta_0, \beta_1)]^2$, where $w_1, w_2, \ldots, w_n$ are weights that enhance the importance of some cases and diminish the importance of others. In this scheme, the fitted values tend to fit the cases with greater weights more closely than the cases with lesser weights.

Replace the β's with b's in these two expressions and set the expressions equal to zero. Solving the resulting two equations for the two unknowns b_0 and b_1 we get, after some algebra,

$$b_1 = r\frac{s_y}{s_x}$$

and

$$b_0 = \bar{y} - b_1\bar{x}$$

where r is the correlation coefficient between x and y, s_x and s_y are the standard deviations of x and y, and $\bar{x}$ and $\bar{y}$ are the means of x and y.

8

Multiple Regression Models

Chapter Objectives

After mastering this chapter, you will be able to :

- Understand and interpret quadratic regression models

- Understand and interpret models containing indicator variables

- Understand and interpret models containing several continuous variables

- Compare models using residual standard deviations

- Interpret residual plots for multiple regression models

SECTION

8.1 Introduction

The straight-line models of Chapter 7 are powerful tools for describing simple relationships, but we have seen some curved relationships for which the straight-line models are inadequate. In this chapter, we introduce multiple regression models that account for the influence of more than one predictor variable or account for curved relationships between the response and one or more predictors. In this setting, we use mathematical curves and surfaces to describe the general trend in the relationship between the variables. In general, these models permit many sources of variation to be considered.

Fortunately, the method of least squares can still be used to find the coefficients of the best-fitting curves and surfaces. We also continue to work within the framework of the equation

Observed Response = Fitted Value + Residual

Multiple regression simply means that the mathematical expressions used to obtain the fitted values are more complicated than in Chapter 7. Residuals continue to show

how individual observations differ from the general pattern expressed in the fitted values.[†]

8.2 Quadratic Regression

Sometimes curved relationships may be modeled by quadratic curves. A quadratic curve has an equation of the form

$$y = b_0 + b_1 x + b_2 x^2$$

constant term
linear term
quadratic term

The coefficient b_0 is called the **constant term** (or y-intercept), b_1 the coefficient of the **linear term**, and b_2 the coefficient of the **quadratic term**. The quadratic term allows the relationship to bend. However, the amount and place of the bend will depend on the specific numbers b_1 and b_2. Here are two examples.

E X A M P L E   **8.2A**

Exhibit 8.2A displays a plot of the quadratic curve $y = 20 + 30x - 2x^2$, as x ranges from 0 to 10. For values of x between 0 and 4, the curve is fairly straight, but beyond 4, the curve starts to bend, reaches its largest value, and then starts to go down. Every quadratic curve with a negative value for b_2 will look something like this one—rising and then falling.

On the other hand, Exhibit 8.2B shows a portion of the quadratic curve with equation $y = 20 + 3x + 2x^2$. On the range shown, 0 to 10, the curve rises at a slowly increasing rate. (If more of the curve were shown, we would

E X H I B I T **8.2A**
Plot of the Quadratic Curve
$y = 20 + 30x - 2x^2$

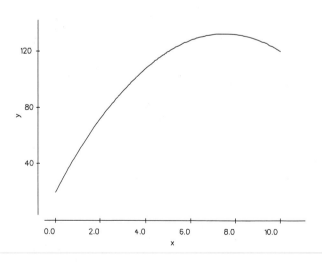

[†]There are no compact expressions for the least-squares coefficients in multiple regression analysis unless matrix algebra is used. The interested reader may consult the appendix to Chapter 20.

see a minimum value occurring at a negative value for x; the curve would also rise for large negative values of x.) ▪

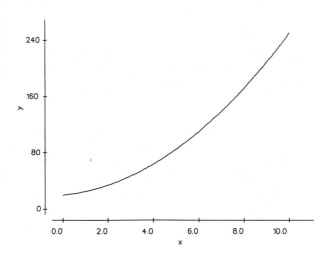

In regression modeling, we frequently use only a small portion of the whole quadratic curve to express a curved trend in a relationship. The values for the regression coefficients b_0, b_1, and b_2 are chosen by the method of least squares to make the sum of squared vertical differences between the observed response and the curve as small as possible. Fortunately, statistical software finds these coefficients routinely.

E X A M P L E   **8.2B**

The scatterplot of market values versus square feet of living space for 60 real estate parcels was shown in Exhibit 6.2C. We noted there that the shape of the relationship was somewhat curved. This "rainbow" effect is also noted in Exercise 7.7G, where the residual plot from fitting a straight line is analyzed. We consider fitting a general quadratic curve

$$\text{Market} = b_0 + b_1 \text{ Sq.ft} + b_2 \text{ (Sq.ft)}^2$$

using the method of least squares. Statistical software readily produces the fitted equation as

$$\text{Market} = 0.073 + 0.059729 \text{ Sq.ft} - 0.000019604 \text{ (Sq.ft)}^2$$

Even though the quadratic coefficient of -0.000019604 looks small, we must keep in mind that it is multiplied by $(\text{Sq.ft})^2$, which is large because Sq.ft ranges from about 500 to 1800. The quadratic effect is in fact dramatic when shown graphically. Exhibit 8.2C shows the quadratic curve on the scatterplot.

Another comparison is illustrated in Exhibit 8.2D, where the straight-line regression is shown with a dashed line and the quadratic is the solid curve. The curves are similar for Sq.ft values in the range of 750 to 1250 square feet. However, below 750 square feet and above 1250 square feet, the two diverge, with the quadratic following the general pattern in the data better.

Of course, the dangers in extrapolating beyond the range of observed predictor values are still with us. Notice that the quadratic curve starts to turn downward at about 1500 square feet. Is this really appropriate for the situation at hand? Should the market value of a house with 1800 square feet of living space tend to be less than the market value of a house with 1200 square feet of living space? For this data set, no observations are available for houses larger than 1804 square feet, but common sense tells that the market values do not decrease as the quadratic curve suggests. For the range of x-values in the observed data, the quadratic curve represents the situation reasonably well—the decrease over the range from $x = 1500$ to 1804 is small. Perhaps a more complicated curve would provide an even better representation of the relationship. ■

EXHIBIT **8.2C**
Market Value Versus Square
Feet of Living Space with
Least-Squares Quadratic Curve

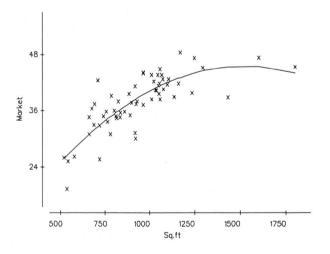

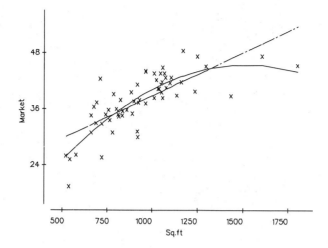

This example shows that common sense and knowledge of the particular problem at hand should always be used in problem solving. In particular, regression models must be used cautiously to predict y-values associated with x-values outside the range of x-values used to fit the model. Such predictions are risky because the model may not apply outside the observed range. Although this advice seems easy to follow, the situation is much more complicated when several x variables are incorporated into the fitted equations. Statisticians[†] say that all models are wrong, but some models are useful! Models are "wrong" because they do not apply to all situations and to every detail. Those that are useful yield insight in relevant situations. Models are not responsible for errors that result from applying them in inappropriate situations. Here is an example where the relationship is curved but a quadratic regression is not sensible.

E X A M P L E   **8.2C**

Example 7.6C presented data on the concentration of aluminum waste at various distances from an aluminum reduction plant in Tennessee. We saw there that the relationship was quite curved and could not be modeled well by a straight line. See especially Exhibit 7.6E. Let's fit a quadratic curve to

[†]G. E. P. Box, "Robustness in the Strategy of Scientific Model Building," in R. L. Lanner and G. N. Wilkerson, eds., *Robustness in Statistics* (New York: Academic Press, 1979), pp. 201–236.

this data and see if we can model the relationship better. Statistical software yields the fitted equation

$$\text{Concentration} = 5296.6 - 508.9\ \text{Distance} + 13.119\ (\text{Distance})^2$$

Exhibit 8.2E shows the fitted quadratic curve and the observed data. This curve fits the given data extremely well. However, it gives nonsensical results. It makes no sense for the concentration of aluminum waste to decrease and then increase at further distances from the plant. The quadratic regression equation does not explain this relationship much better than the straight line. We need to consider more complicated models before we reach a useful model for these data. We return to this problem in Chapter 21. ▪

EXHIBIT **8.2E**
Aluminum Concentration Versus
Distance from Plant with Fitted
Quadratic Regression

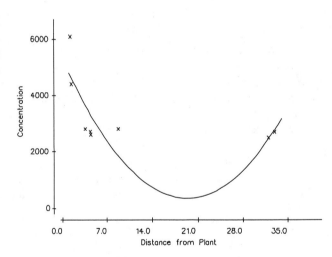

SECTION

8.3 Residual Standard Deviation

How do we measure the closeness of fit of a regression curve? The residuals give a good starting point, but we wish to summarize their variability in a single number. Their standard deviation is the measure usually chosen.

The Residual Standard Deviation

residual standard deviation

The **residual standard deviation**, s, is calculated according to the basic rules for standard deviations given in Chapter 4, namely,

- Find the residuals by subtracting the fitted value from the observed response for each case.
- Square the residuals and add them.
- Divide this sum of squares by the degrees of freedom for the residuals.
- Take the square root to obtain the residual standard deviation s.

degrees of freedom for residuals

The **degrees of freedom for residuals** is given by the number of observations minus the number of fitted coefficients in the regression model. For example, the degrees of freedom for residuals is $n - 2$ when fitting a straight line with an intercept and slope and is $n - 3$ when fitting a quadratic curve. Note that these degrees of freedom are consistent with our earlier definition of standard deviation for a set of numbers given in Section 4.4. There, there was just one coefficient, the sample mean, and the degrees of freedom were $n - 1$. Note also that we do not need to subtract the average of the residuals before squaring and summing. This is because the average residual is zero when fitting a model with an intercept by the method of least squares. As expected, statistical software provides the value of s along with the fitted regression equation. The appendix to this chapter displays regression output from a variety of statistical software packages. The residual standard deviation is identified by a number of different names in the various displays. Sometimes it is called Root MSE (root mean square error), sometimes SE (standard error), and sometimes Standard Error of Estimate.

E X A M P L E   **8.3A**

To demonstrate the calculation of the residual standard deviation, we return to the small sample of market and square feet values given in the 10 cases in Exhibit 7.2A. The residuals for the fitted regression line are given in Exhibit 7.4A. Their sum of squares is shown as 61.8004. When fitting a straight line with 10 cases, the degrees of freedom are $10 - 2 = 8$, so that the residual standard deviation is

$$s = \sqrt{\frac{61.8004}{10 - 2}} = \sqrt{7.72505} = 2.779 \cdots \approx 2.78$$

Since Market is in thousands of dollars, so also are fitted values, residuals, and the standard deviation of the residuals. Our measure of closeness of fit of the straight-line model is 2.78 thousand dollars. An important use of the residual standard deviation is to compare the closeness of fit of different models for the same data.   ▪

Comparison of Models

The smaller the value of the residual standard deviation, the better the regression curve fits the data. Thus, we can use the value of s to compare the fit of different regression models.

For example, both straight-line and quadratic regression curves are shown in Exhibit 8.2D for the 60 parcels of real estate. The residual standard deviation for the straight-line model is 3.981, while for the quadratic model it drops to 3.473. This reinforces our earlier claim that the quadratic model shows improvement over the straight-line model.

Example 7.6D presented data where the curvature was subtle but easily detected with the residual plot shown in Exhibit 7.6F. We ask you in the exercises to verify that the residual standard deviation for the straight-line model is 3.661, while it is only 2.560 for a quadratic curve model.

SECTION

8.4 Exercises

8.4A Exhibit 7.6A displays the residuals from the straight-line regression for the 10-case real estate sample. When a quadratic curve is fitted to these data, the fitted model has equation Market $= -1.5 + 0.0648$ Sq.ft $- 0.000022$ (Sq.ft)^2.

    a Find the fitted values for all 10 cases.

    b Find the residuals for all 10 cases.

    c Plot the scatterplot of the data and graph both the straight-line and quadratic regressions on the same plot.

    d Calculate the residual standard deviation for both the straight-line and quadratic regressions.

8.4B We began our study of the inflation rates of countries and the independence of their central banks with Example 6.2C. Exhibit 7.4D shows the least-squares regression line with equation $y = 9.46 - 1.64x$. (Filename: FREEBNK.DAT.)

    a Verify that the least-squares quadratic regression curve has equation $y = 11.4 - 3.26x + 0.302x^2$.

    b Display the scatterplot of the data and graph the least-squares regression straight line for the data and the least-squares quadratic regression curve on the same plot.

    c Calculate the residual standard deviations for both the straight-line and quadratic models.

    d In part (c), you should have found little difference in the two numbers. Does your plot in part (b) support this small difference?

8.4C The data presented in Example 7.6D showed subtle curvature in the scatterplot of the data. The curvature was much more dramatic when viewed through the residual plot. (Filename: EX8_4C.DAT.)

    a Verify that the equation of the least-squares regression line is $y = 68.1 + 9.81x$.

    b Verify that the equation of the least-squares quadratic regression curve is $y = 12.8 + 32.8x - 2.26x^2$.

    c Plot the scatterplot of the data and graph both the straight-line and quadratic curve on the plot.

    d Calculate the residual standard deviations for both the straight-line and quadratic regressions and verify that they are 3.661 and 2.560 as reported in the text.

   e   Does the plot in part (c) confirm this large difference in residual standard deviations?

8.4D Exercise 7.7D introduced data on the age and height of girls up to 14 years of age. In that exercise, the residual plot indicated that the relationship between Height and Age contained curvature. (Filename: AGEHGT_G.DAT.)

   a   Use a quadratic regression equation and least squares to predict Height from Age.

   b   What height would you predict for a 12-year-old girl?

   c   What height would you predict for a 20-year-old female?

   d   Find the residual standard deviations for both the straight-line and quadratic regression curves. Which is smaller?

8.4E Exercise 7.7E introduced data on the age and height of boys up to 14 years of age. In that exercise, the residual plot indicated that the relationship between Height and Age contained curvature. (Filename: AGEHGT_B.DAT.)

   a   Use a quadratic regression equation and least squares to predict Height from Age.

   b   What height do you predict for a 10-year-old boy?

   c   What height do you predict for a 25-year-old male?

   d   Find the residual standard deviations for both the straight-line and quadratic regression curves. Which is smaller?

SECTION

8.5   Several Straight Lines—Indicator Variables

So far, our discussion of regression models has been restricted to predictor variables that are continuous—for example, square feet of living space, distance from aluminum reduction plant, price, and so forth. But categorical variables are also useful predictors, especially when combined with continuous predictor variables. Categorical variables divide observations into categories or groups. To work with them numerically, it is convenient to introduce variables that *indicate* group membership.

Indicator Variables

indicator variable

An **indicator variable** is a binary variable that is equal to 1 for an observation that belongs to one particular category and is equal to zero for an observation that does not belong to that category. For example, an indicator variable for gender is defined to be 1 for females and 0 for males. Of course, the choice of 1 for females and 0 for males could be reversed without any loss of information. As we will see, either choice works equally well—all we need to know is which choice was made and stick with it throughout a given analysis.

Parallel-Lines Model

An important model combines one continuous variable and one indicator variable to obtain the **parallel-lines model**.

Let x represent the continuous variable and let z be the indicator variable that indicates membership in the first of two groups. Consider the regression model expressed in the equation

parallel-lines model

$$y = b_0 + b_1 x + b_2 z$$

where $z = 1$ if the observation belongs to the first group and $z = 0$ if the observation belongs to the second group. Consider what happens when we break the equation into two separate equations depending on which group the observation comes from. For any observation from group 1, we have

$$y = b_0 + b_1 x + b_2(1) = (b_0 + b_2) + b_1 x \quad \text{for group 1}$$

But this is just the equation of a straight line with slope b_1 and intercept $(b_0 + b_2)$.
For observations from group 2, we have

$$y = b_0 + b_1 x + b_2(0) = b_0 + b_1 x \quad \text{for group 2}$$

which is the equation for a straight line with slope b_1 and intercept b_0. These two lines have the same slope b_1 but different intercepts. This means they are parallel lines. The coefficient b_2 gives the vertical difference between the two lines.

With the help of statistical software, the method of least squares may be used to obtain the values for the regression coefficients b_0, b_1, and b_2. Here is an example.

E X A M P L E   8.5A

Supplementary Exercise 6B introduced data on gasoline consumption. Several variables were given, but we concentrate on gasoline consumption in city driving, the weight of the car, and whether the car is considered a foreign or domestic model. The data are given in Exhibit 8.5A. Gasoline consumption (CityGas) is measured in liters per 100 kilometers, weight (Weight) is given in 100 kilograms, and the categorical variable (Foreign) is described by an indicator variable that is 1 for foreign cars and 0 for domestic cars.

If we ignore the Foreign variable and fit a single straight line to the data, we obtain the regression equation CityGas$= -1.96 + 1.33$ Weight with residual standard deviation of $s = 1.354$.

Using the Foreign categorical variable in addition to Weight, we obtain the parallel-lines regression equation

$$\text{CityGas} = -0.24 + 1.23 \text{ Weight} - 1.05 \text{ Foreign}$$

and the (smaller) residual standard deviation is 1.273.
Breaking this down into the separate groups, we have

$$\text{CityGas} = -0.24 + 1.23 \text{ Weight} - 1.05(1)$$
$$= -1.29 + 1.23 \text{ Weight} \quad \text{for the foreign cars}$$

and

$$\text{CityGas} = -0.24 + 1.23 \text{ Weight} - 1.05(0)$$

EXHIBIT **8.5A**

Gasoline Consumption Versus Car Weight

City Gasoline Consumption (liters/100 km.)	Weight (100 kg)	Foreign (1 = yes) (0 = no)	Make and Model
13.3	10.0	0	Chevrolet Chevette
10.5	10.2	0	Chevrolet Nova
10.1	8.7	0	Chevrolet Spectrum
11.0	9.9	0	Dodge Colt
11.5	9.5	0	Dodge Omni
12.0	10.9	0	Ford Escort
11.5	9.2	1	Honda Civic
12.0	10.9	1	Mitsubishi Tredia
10.5	9.5	1	Nissan Sentra
12.0	9.1	1	Renault Alliance
12.0	10.4	1	Subaru
11.0	10.3	1	Toyota Corolla
11.0	9.7	1	Toyota Tercel
12.0	10.1	1	Volkswagen Golf
12.6	10.5	1	Volkswagen Jetta
15.8	12.7	0	Chrysler Laser
9.4	9.0	1	Honda Civic CRX
10.5	10.6	1	Honda Prelude
14.9	12.4	1	Isuzu Impulse
12.0	11.2	1	Mitsubishi Corida
12.6	12.2	1	Nissan 200SX
9.7	9.2	1	Nissan Pulsar NX
12.6	11.5	0	Pontiac Fiero
14.1	10.7	1	Audi 4000S
15.8	11.6	0	Chevrolet Cavalier
13.3	11.8	0	Ford Tempo
13.3	11.8	1	Honda Accord
12.6	11.8	1	Mazda 626
14.9	12.9	1	Mitsubishi Galant
11.0	11.1	1	Nissan Stanza
14.1	12.0	0	Oldsmobile Calais
14.1	12.9	1	Saab 900
11.0	12.2	1	Toyota Camry
14.1	13.3	1	Volvo
16.9	12.6	0	Buick Century
23.0	16.2	0	Chrysler Fifth Avenue
13.3	11.7	0	Chrysler Le Baron
13.3	11.5	0	Dodge Aries
15.8	12.7	0	Dodge Lancer
15.8	14.1	0	Mercury Cougar
19.5	15.2	0	Oldsmobile Cutlass
16.9	12.6	0	Pontiac 6000
18.1	15.0	0	Buick Electra
18.1	16.5	0	Chevrolet Caprice

$$= -0.24 + 1.23 \text{ Weight} \quad \text{for the domestic cars}$$

Exhibit 8.5B displays the scatterplot using plotting symbol F for the foreign cars and D for the domestics. The two parallel regression lines are also shown. By using the additional information contained in the categorical variable, the model explains more of the variation in gasoline consumption.

The equations may be used as before to predict gasoline consumption. For example, for a domestic car weighing 1200 kilograms, we predict gasoline consumption of

$$\text{Predicted gasoline consumption} = -0.24 + 1.23(12) - 1.05(0) = 14.52$$

or about 14.5 liters of gasoline per 100 kilometers of city driving. For a foreign car of the same weight, we predict gasoline consumption of $-0.24 + 1.23(12) - 1.05 = 14.52 - 1.05 = 13.47$ or about 13.5 liters of gasoline. These data suggest that the penalty in fuel efficiency for driving a domestic car is about one liter per 100 kilometers of city driving over the efficiency achieved by a foreign car of the same weight. ∎

EXHIBIT **8.5B**

Parallel Regression Lines for Foreign (solid) and Domestic (dashed) Gasoline Consumption Versus Car Weight (F = Foreign, D = Domestic)

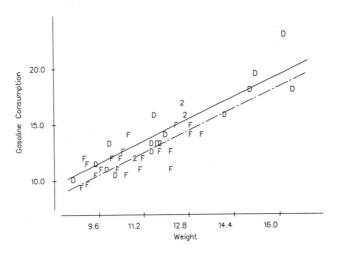

Categorical Variables with Several Categories

The real estate data displayed in Exhibit 6.2A contain several variables with potential for predicting market values. The Grade variable is a categorical variable with three numerical values $-1, 0,$ and $+1$. These values stand for low-, medium-, and high-grade construction—that is, the observations are in three groups according to construction grade. We present a regression model involving three parallel lines to incorporate the grade information, one line for each grade.

To indicate the three groups, we need two indicator variables, which we call Low and Medium. The third group is indicated by the lack of membership in the other two groups. Here is a small table of some cases from the full data set illustrating the indicator variables Low and Medium.

Case	Market	Sq.ft	Grade	Low	Medium
1	26.0	521	−1	1	0
2	19.4	538	−1	1	0
3	25.2	544	0	0	1
59	47.4	1602	1	0	0

Notice that the 59th case is of high-grade construction but that this is uniquely indicated by the values Low $= 0$ *and* Medium $= 0$. To obtain the model with three parallel lines, we define the regression model

$$\text{Market} = b_0 + b_1 \text{ Sq.ft} + b_2 \text{ Low} + b_3 \text{ Medium}$$

To see that this model gives three parallel lines, we break the equation into three equations—one for each construction grade. We have for Low grade

$$\text{Market} = b_0 + b_1 \text{ Sq.ft} + b_2(1) + b_3(0) = (b_0 + b_2) + b_1 \text{ Sq.ft} \qquad \text{for Low grade}$$

For Medium-grade construction

$$\text{Market} = b_0 + b_1 \text{ Sq.ft} + b_2(0) + b_3(1) = (b_0 + b_3) + b_1 \text{ Sq.ft} \quad \text{for Medium grade}$$

Finally, for High-grade construction we have

$$\text{Market} = b_0 + b_1 \text{ Sq.ft} + b_2(0) + b_3(0) = b_0 + b_1 \text{ Sq.ft} \qquad \text{for High grade}$$

These lines have different intercepts but a common slope of b_1. Thus we have a model that can be expressed as three parallel lines.

When this model is fitted with the full data on the 60 properties, we get the fitted model

$$\text{Market} = 27.9 + 0.0132 \text{ Sq.ft} - 7.79 \text{ Low} - 1.32 \text{ Medium}$$

with a residual standard deviation of 3.249.

The regression coefficients on the indicator variables are easy to interpret. The -7.79 coefficient shows that a Low-grade property has a predicted market value that is 7.79 thousand dollars *below* that of a similarly sized High-grade property. Similarly, a Medium-grade house is predicted to have a market value 1.32 thousand dollars below a High-grade house of the same size.

Parallel-lines models may be used to incorporate information from categorical variables into any regression model. If the categorical variable has k different values, we need $k - 1$ different indicator variables to account for the categorical variable in a parallel-lines regression model.

SECTION

8.6 Exercises

8.6A Using a large database created from company records for a certain year, a consultant derives the following model for salaried employees: $y = b_0 + b_1x_1 + b_2x_2$ where y denotes salary converted to an hourly rate, x_1 denotes years of employment with the company, and x_2 denotes gender of the employee ($x_2 = 1$ if male and 0 if female).

a Explain the meaning of each of the regression coefficients.

b Sketch a graph of y versus x_1, with x_2 indicated by distinct plotting symbols, showing that males and females seem to be treated somewhat equally.

c Sketch a graph of y versus x_1, with x_2 indicated by distinct plotting symbols, showing that males and females seem to be treated somewhat unequally.

8.6B Sales and advertising data are collected every quarter of the year at a certain company. Since sales are suspected of being seasonal, a model is needed that incorporates parallel lines, one for each quarter. Suppose data are available for two years.

a Set up a hypothetical data table with the seasonal indicator variables shown as appropriate.

b Write down the form of the regression model using your variables defined in part (a).

8.6C Data on the heights for boys and girls at various ages were introduced in Exercises 7.7D and 7.7E. Combine these data into one data set and define an indicator variable for gender. (Filenames: AGEHGT_B.DAT and AGEHGT_G.DAT.)

a Fit a parallel-lines regression model to the combined data.

b Compare the regression coefficients found in part (a) to the corresponding regression coefficients when the data are treated separately.

c Compare the residual standard deviation obtained for the model of part (a) with the residual standard deviations obtained when the data are treated separately.

d Now fit a parallel-quadratics model to the combined data. That is, use predictors Age, $(\text{Age})^2$, and the gender indicator variable.

e Calculate the residual standard deviation for the model fitted in part (d). Compare it to the one obtained for the parallel-lines models that you obtained in part (c).

8.6D Verify that when the parallel-lines model $\text{Market} = b_0 + b_1\text{Sq.ft} + b_2\,\text{Low} + b_3\text{Medium}$ is fit to the 60 cases of the real estate data, we obtain

$$\text{Market} = 27.9 + 0.0132\text{Sq.ft} - 7.79\text{Low} - 1.32\text{Medium}$$

with a residual standard deviation of 3.249. Here Low and Medium are indicator variables for Low- and Medium-Grade properties. (Filename: REALPROP.DAT.)

8.6E Consider the real estate data of Market, Sq.ft and Grade but use indicator variables for Medium- and High-Grade properties. (Filename: REALPROP.DAT.)

a Fit the model $\text{Market} = b_0 + b_1\,\text{Sq.ft} + b_2\,\text{Medium} + b_3\,\text{High}$ to all 60 cases.

b Show that the model obtained in part (a) is identical to the model obtained in the text (and in Exercise 8.6D) using $\text{Market} = b_0 + b_1\,\text{Sq.ft} + b_2\,\text{Low} + b_3\,\text{Medium}$.

8.7 Fitting Plane and Curved Surfaces

So far, the variables used to account for variation in the real estate market values are measures of physical characteristics that are more or less permanent, though square feet of living area and construction grade can change with improvements or deteriorations. These variables do not relate to economic factors in the marketplace, however. Regardless of the size of a house or the quality of the construction, the house may be located in a neighborhood that is gaining or losing popularity with buyers or it may be located in a city that is attracting or failing to attract new industry and business. Such factors are critical in assessing the market value of the parcel, and they are factors that are supposedly captured in the assessed values of the parcels.

Assessed values, even though they may be determined only once a year, attempt to account not only for the physical characteristics of the property but also for the dynamics of the housing market. No realistic model for market values can fail to include assessed values in addition to other variables.

Scatterplot Matrices

When modeling relationships among several variables, we look at scatterplots of the response versus each of the predictor variables. It is also interesting to look for relationships among the predictor variables. A scatterplot matrix facilitates the consideration of many scatterplots in a small amount of space.

scatterplot matrix

A **scatterplot matrix** displays scatterplots for pairs of variables in an array of rows and columns. Exhibit 8.7A shows such a display for the real estate data. The variable labels are given on the diagonal. For example, the bottom row shows Market versus each of the predictor variables in the various columns, with Market on the vertical axis. Market versus the three Grade levels, $-1, 0$, and $+1$, is shown in the lower left corner. Next to that plot is the plot of Market versus Assessed value. The third plot in the bottom row shows Market against Sq.ft. The other plots display relationships among predictor variables. For example, the top left plot shows how Assessed value tends to increase with increased value of Grade. A scatterplot matrix allows a large number of two-variable relationships to be investigated rapidly.

We temporarily ignore the Grade variable and consider a model that contains the two continuous variables Sq.ft and Assessed.

Regression Planes

In general, consider the equation

$$y = b_0 + b_1 x_1 + b_2 x_2$$

regression plane

In three-dimensional space, this equation determines a **regression plane**. Here x_1 and x_2 are continuous variables, and an observation consists of values for each of the three variables y, x_1, and x_2. For example, values for Market, Sq.ft, and Assessed are listed for the 60 parcels in Exhibit 6.2A. A three-dimensional scatterplot of these

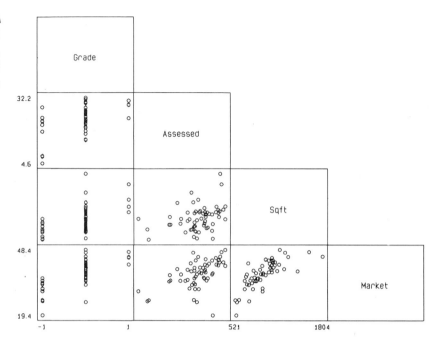

point cloud

60 points is shown in Exhibit 8.7B. Such a three-dimensional plot is called a **point cloud**.

Our least-squares regression problem can be described as fitting a plane through the point cloud in such a way as to minimize the sum of squared vertical differences from the plane to the points in the point cloud.

Exhibit 8.7B shows the three-dimensional point cloud with the size of the point proportional to the distance from the viewer. Dotted lines display the relative heights of the points—that is, value of Market. In this plot, Sq.ft values increase from the back corner toward the front right. Similarly, Assessed increases from the back corner toward the front left. In general, the smaller points are further from the viewer and get higher (larger values of Market) and larger in size (closer to the viewer) as either Sq.ft or Assessed increase.

A three-dimensional point cloud is difficult to interpret, since what we see depends on our viewpoint. Modern statistical software allows the point cloud and axes to be rotated and viewed from many different angles to look for interesting relationships. On the printed page, the three-dimensional scatterplot is of somewhat limited use.

Nevertheless, statistical software will again find the least-squares values for the regression coefficients that we require. For the real estate data, the fitted plane has equation

$$\text{Market} = 15.3 + 0.0156 \,\text{Sq.ft} + 0.332 \,\text{Assessed}$$

with residual standard deviation $s = 3.568$. A plot of this fitted least-squares regression plane is displayed in Exhibit 8.7C. Notice how the fitted plane increases as either Sq.ft or Assessed increases. Note also that orientation of the axes is different in Exhibits 8.7B and 8.7C.

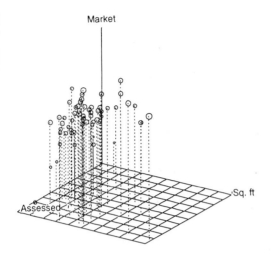

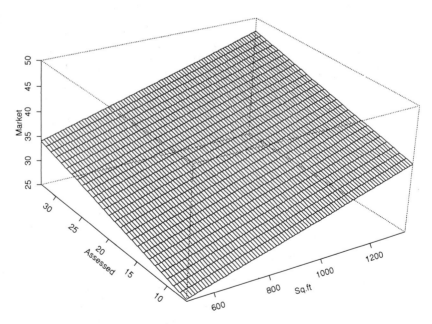

Regression Surfaces

In Example 8.2B, we saw that curvature in the relationship between Market and Sq.ft could be modeled by extending straight-line models to quadratics. We can also consider curved surfaces in two continuous variables. That is, we can introduce quadratic terms into the two-predictor model. For simplicity we introduce a square term in the Sq.ft variable only. The model is expressed through the equation

regression surface

$$\text{Market} = b_0 + b_1 \text{ Sq.ft} + b_2(\text{Sq.ft})^2 + b_3 \text{ Assessed}$$

For any given value of Assessed, this surface curves as Sq.ft increases, while for any given value of Sq.ft (and hence Sq.ft^2), the surface increases linearly with Assessed.

Statistical software finds the least-squares values for the regression coefficients, with the resulting equation

$$\text{Market} = -4.21 + 0.0556 \text{ Sq.ft} - 0.000019(\text{Sq.ft})^2 + 0.318 \text{ Assessed}$$

with residual standard deviation $s = 3.018$. Compare this value of s to the residual standard deviation of 3.568 when fitting the plane. The curved surface fits the data somewhat better. A plot of this regression surface is shown in Exhibit 8.7D. The curvature in the direction of increasing Sq.ft is evident in the plot.

E X H I B I T **8.7D**
Regression Surface for Market
Versus Sq.ft, (Sq.ft)^2, and
Assessed

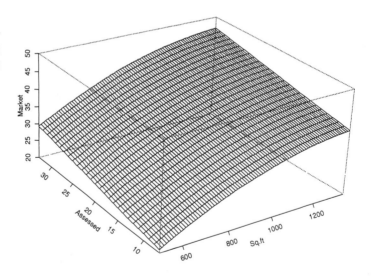

E X A M P L E **8.7A** Our final model for explaining Market value of the real estate data combines all of the ideas we have presented so far—several variables, quadratic terms, and indicator variables for categorical data. We have seen that the Sq.ft variable should enter with both a linear and quadratic term. Assessed can be just linear and Grade should be entered as two indicator variables. This time we use Medium and High for the Grade information. The model can then be expressed as

$$\text{Market} = b_0 + b_1 \text{ Sq.ft} + b_2(\text{Sq.ft})^2 + b_3 \text{ Medium} + b_4 \text{ High} + b_5 \text{ Assessed}$$

Statistical software finds the least-squares values for the five regression coefficients quickly. The fitted model is

$$\text{Market} = 1.111 + 0.044883 \text{ Sq.ft} - 0.000015064(\text{Sq.ft})^2$$
$$+ 4.150 \text{ Medium} + 5.216 \text{ High} + 0.22337 \text{ Assessed}$$

If we were to plot the fitted Market values versus Sq.ft and Assessed in three dimensions, as in Exhibit 8.7D, we would have three parallel curved surfaces corresponding to the three values for Grade.   ▪

When do we stop adding predictors to a model? This is an important problem in regression modeling, especially when many predictors are available. Chapters 20–22 explore this and other more advanced aspects of regression modeling.

As in Section 7.6, we look to residuals to check the adequacy of a fitted model.

SECTION

8.8 Residual Plots

residual plot

Recall that when the model does a good job of describing a relationship between the response and the predictor variables, the residuals appear to have come from a random process. When there are several predictor variables, the most basic **residual plot** is to graph residuals versus the corresponding fitted values. As before, residual plots containing nonrandom patterns indicate that the model can be improved. When several predictor variables are involved, the patterns may be subtle and the plots need to be carefully inspected and interpreted. Here are some examples.

E X A M P L E   8.8A

We return to the gasoline consumption data presented in Example 8.5A. First consider a simple straight-line model using Weight as the predictor. We ignore the indicator variable for Foreign and Domestic. A plot of the residuals versus the corresponding fitted values is displayed in Exhibit 8.8A. This plot looks reasonably random, and no nonrandom patterns are apparent. However, some of these residuals are associated with Foreign cars and some with Domestic cars. Perhaps if we could distinguish the cars in the plot, a nonrandom pattern would emerge.

Exhibit 8.8B shows the same residual plot but using plotting symbols to distinguish Foreign and Domestic vehicles. Although the pattern is somewhat subtle, you can see that a predominance of the negative residuals correspond to Foreign cars and Domestic cars seem to dominate the positive residuals.

E X H I B I T **8.8A**
Residual Plot Using a Single
Straight-Line Model for Gasoline
Consumption

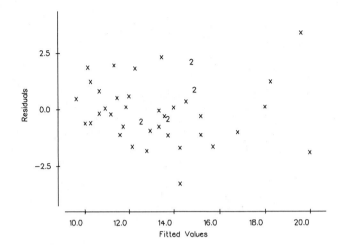

E X H I B I T **8.8A**
Residual Plot Using a Single
Straight-Line Model for Gasoline
Consumption

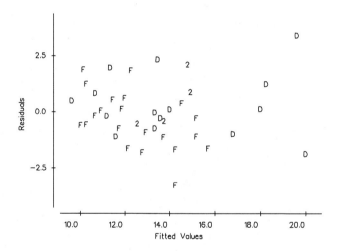

E X H I B I T **8.8B**
Residual Plot Using a Single
Straight-Line Model, F =
Foreign, D = Domestic

This plot suggests that a better model might treat Foreign and Domestic cars somewhat differently—just as we did with the parallel-lines model of Exhibit 8.5B.

Exhibit 8.8C shows the residual plot when the parallel-lines model is fit. Now the residuals corresponding to Foreign and Domestic cars are distributed quite randomly—some positive and some negative. The enhanced residual plot displayed in Exhibit 8.8B gives us clues to a better model.

EXHIBIT **8.8C**
Residual Plot Using the
Parallel-Lines Model, F =
Foreign, D = Domestic

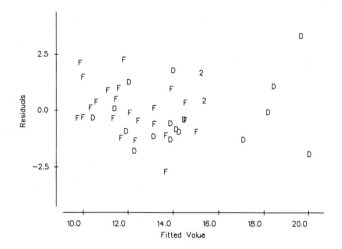

EXAMPLE **8.8B**

Let's look at residual plots for some of the models for Market value that we discussed in Section 8.7. Exhibit 8.8D shows the residual plot when we use the model

$$\text{Market} = b_0 + b_1 \text{Sq.ft} + b_2 \text{Assessed}$$

Again this plot looks reasonably random. However, recall that there is subtle curvature in the relationship of Market and Sq.ft. Careful inspection of the residual plot gives a hint of the curvature in that both low and high fitted values have negative residuals associated with them. Middle-sized fitted values have both positive and negative residuals. Furthermore, the magnitudes of the negative residuals are generally larger than the magnitudes

EXHIBIT **8.8D**
Residual Plot for Regression of
Market on Sq.ft and Assessed

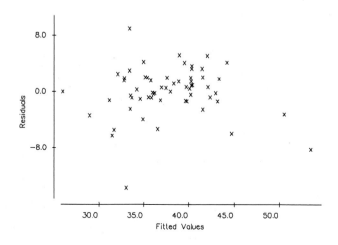

of the positive residuals. The plane regression surface is simply not fitting well at the extremes.

Our remedy for the curvature problem was to fit the model

$$\text{Market} = b_0 + b_1(\text{Sq.ft}) + b_2(\text{Sq.ft})^2 + b_3 \text{ Assessed}$$

The residuals and fitted values from this model are plotted in Exhibit 8.8E using the same vertical scale as in Exhibit 8.8D. First notice that the residuals, as a whole, are smaller. This confirms the reduction in residual standard deviation from 3.568 to 3.018 when going from the plane regression to the curved regression surface. Furthermore, the residuals are now more randomly distributed vertically around their mean of zero. This model seems to explain Market fairly well. Of course, the Grade information of the properties could be added to the model. ∎

EXHIBIT **8.8E**
Residual Plot for Regression of Market on Sq.ft, (Sq.ft)^2, and Assessed

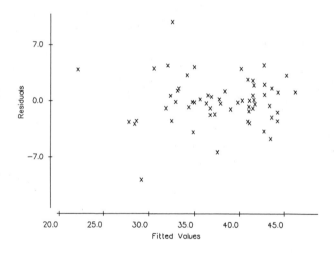

SECTION

8.9 Exercises

8.9A Consider two data sets:

Data Set 1		Data Set 2	
x	y	x	y
1	1	1	7
2	4	2	5
3	3	3	3
4	5	4	4
5	7	5	1

    a For each of the data sets, find the least-squares straight line.

    b Find the fitted values and residuals for each of the least-squares lines.

    c Plot the residuals versus the fitted values for each of the least-squares lines.

    d Plot the residuals versus x for the least-squares lines for each of the data sets.

    e Comment on the effect of plotting residuals versus x or residuals versus fitted values based on your plots in parts (c) and (d).

8.9B Using a large database from company records for a certain year, a consultant fits the following model for salaried employees: $y = b_0 + b_1x_1 + b_2x_2 + b_3x_3$, where y denotes salary converted to an hourly rate, x_1 denotes years of employment with the company, x_2 denotes the employee's age, and x_3 denotes the employee's gender ($x_3 = 1$ if male and 0 if female). Explain the implied behavior of this model. In particular, interpret the regression coefficients, paying special attention to b_3.

8.9C Refer to the restaurant survey data partially displayed in Exhibit 5.4A.

    a Write down the equation for a regression model that attempts to explain Sales as the response variable in terms of Wages, Advertising, and Type of food as predictor variables. (Be careful with your treatment of any categorical variables.) You need not fit the model, just express it.

    b Write down the equation for a regression model that attempts to explain Sales as the response variable in terms of new Capital, Wages, number of Fulltime employees, and type of Ownership as predictor variables. (Again be careful with any categorical variables.) You need not fit the model, just express it.

8.9D In Exercise 8.4C, we fit a quadratic curve to the data of Example 7.6D. (Filename: EX8_4C.DAT.)

    a Display the residual versus fitted plot for this regression.

    b Comment on the residual plot. Does the quadratic capture the trend in the relationship?

8.9E In Exercise 8.4D, we fit a quadratic curve to the data relating Height and Age of girls. Construct and interpret the residual plot for this regression. (Filename: AGEHGT_G.DAT.)

8.9F In Exercise 8.4E, we fit a quadratic curve to the data relating Height and Age of boys. Construct and interpret the residual plot for this regression. (Filename: AGEHGT_B.DAT.)

8.9G Exercise 8.6D fit the model Market $= b_0 + b_1$Sq.ft $+ b_2$Low $+ b_3$ Medium to the 60 cases of the real estate data. Construct and interpret the residual plot for this regression. (Filename: REALPROP.DAT.)

8.9H The data for this exercise came from a study conducted by a company that manufactures printed electronic circuit boards. The purpose of the study was to develop a technique for predicting completion time for assembly of the boards, to be used for incentive rate calculation and cost estimation. The variables are

x_1: Number of capacitors on the board

x_2: Number of integrated circuits on the board

x_3: Number of transistors on the board

x_4: Number of hand-soldered leads on the board

x_5: Total number of components on the board

x_6: Number of types of components on the board

x_7: Size of the board, where 1 indicates small and 4 indicates large (the area of the large board is 4 times the area of a small board)

y: the time to complete assembly of the board in hours. (Filename: BOARDS.DAT.)

x_1	x_2	x_3	x_4	x_5	x_6	x_7	y	x_1	x_2	x_3	x_4	x_5	x_6	x_7	y
87	9	5	0	320	75	4	2.62	0	3	0	0	88	0	1	0.79
36	16	0	0	132	28	4	0.84	0	0	0	0	132	2	1	0.64
43	0	0	0	171	32	4	0.98	0	0	0	0	67	2	1	0.51
43	0	0	0	155	32	4	0.86	16	8	0	0	55	12	1	0.33
39	12	0	0	176	60	4	1.10	14	0	0	0	59	14	1	0.35
72	0	0	0	318	35	4	1.98	0	0	0	0	6	4	1	0.10
72	0	0	0	318	35	4	1.89	22	0	0	0	100	14	1	0.52
75	4	8	0	280	68	4	1.72	8	0	0	0	73	20	1	0.47
70	6	0	0	297	42	4	1.70	14	1	4	0	79	30	1	0.55
37	16	1	0	156	41	4	0.89	12	1	0	0	26	11	1	0.25
53	2	0	0	229	46	4	1.37	27	2	8	0	90	31	1	0.81
57	8	1	0	246	55	4	1.54	2	0	2	0	41	13	1	0.26
76	4	9	0	280	68	4	2.08	10	0	0	0	61	13	1	0.38
0	0	0	10	14	4	1	0.08	2	0	1	0	19	12	1	0.34
0	0	0	12	17	4	1	0.11	14	5	0	0	49	19	1	0.35
9	0	0	73	97	13	1	0.25	12	16	0	0	25	11	1	0.32
0	0	0	24	36	2	1	0.10	10	19	0	0	73	25	1	0.48
0	0	0	14	23	4	1	0.12								

a Write down the equation of a regression plane that uses all of the x variables as predictors.

b Fit the regression plane described in part (a).

c Interpret each of the regression coefficients in the fitted plane.

d Find the residual standard deviation.

e Display a residual plot for the fitted regression model.

f Comment on the residual plot of part (e).

SECTION

8.10 The General Linear Model

This section introduces notation and terminology needed to discuss general linear models. The notation in this section gives a useful framework in which to develop the specific models needed in practice; it is a means to an end. For more complete information, see the appendix to Chapter 20.

The General Linear Model

general linear model (GLM)

The notation for the curve fitted by the **general linear model (GLM)** is

$$\hat{y} = b_0 + b_1 x_1 + b_2 x_2 + \cdots + b_k x_k$$

where the variable denoted by y is the *response* variable, and the variables denoted by $x_1, x_2, \ldots, x_k$ are the *predictor* variables. The model expresses a relationship between the response variable and the set of predictor variables. It is called the general linear model because it consists of a sum (or linear combination) of factors of the form bx, where x denotes a predictor variable and b denotes a *regression coefficient*.[†] In a particular model, x_2 might be $(x_1)^2$ and x_3 might be an indicator variable. Thus, the general linear model includes all of those models we have already discussed.

A regression coefficient may be thought of as a *partial slope* coefficient. For example, if the values of $x_2, \ldots x_k$ are held *fixed* and the value of x_1 is allowed to vary,[‡] b_1 is the slope of the resulting line. Some authors use the following language: b_1 measures the *effect* of x_1 on the fitted values, all other things being equal. This means holding all other variables in the model fixed, which is quite a bit less grandiose than holding all other things equal. Beware of grandiosity when interpreting regression models.

In some discussions, the cases in the data listing are referred to in the context of the GLM. The number of cases is denoted by n, and a general case is denoted by i. In other words, i can mean any of the cases $1, 2, \ldots, n$. The value of the response variable for the ith case is denoted by y_i. The value of the predictor variable x_j for the ith case is denoted by x_{ij}. A representation of the fitted value for the ith case is

$$\hat{y}_i = b_0 + b_1 x_{i1} + b_2 x_{i2} + \cdots + b_k x_{ik}$$

The equations displayed so far give fitted values. As seen in earlier sections, the fitted values do not equal the observed values of the response variable, and the differences between observed and fitted values are called residuals. The symbol $\hat{e}$ denotes the residual $y - \hat{y}$, so the residual for the ith case is

$$\hat{e}_i = y_i - \hat{y}_i$$

The residuals reflect the effect of variables not included in the model. We have seen that analysts frequently search various plots of the residuals for clues that point to ways the model can be improved.

As seen in earlier sections, the residuals are used to compute the standard deviation s, which is a measure of variation about the fitted values. For the GLM fitted by

---

[†]Technically, the model is linear in the coefficients $b_0, b_1, \ldots, b_k$. An example of a nonlinear model is $\hat{y} = b_0 + b_1 x_1^{b_3} + b_2 x_2^{b_4}$ because the model cannot be represented as a linear combination of the b's. These coefficients are scrambled in a nonlinear fashion. Nonlinear regression models are not discussed in this text.

[‡]This is impossible to do if any of the $x_2, \ldots, x_k$ is a function of x_1—for example, if $x_2 = x_1^2$.

the method of least squares, the number of degrees of freedom in the residuals is $n - k - 1$, and the residual standard deviation is

$$s = \sqrt{\frac{1}{n - k - 1}(\hat{e}_1^2 + \hat{e}_2^2 + \cdots + \hat{e}_n^2)}$$

because the mean of the residuals is zero.

The method of least squares is nothing more than a mathematical procedure for choosing the coefficients $b_0, b_1, \ldots, b_k$ so that the sum of the squared residuals is as small as it can be. Other criteria can be and are put forward for the choice of the b's, but none of them can yield a smaller sum of squared residuals than the least-squares coefficients. The sum of the squared residuals appears in the formula for s, so that in this sense the least-squares fitted values result in the smallest possible measure of variation and therefore the closest fit to the observed y values.

The computations of the appropriate quantities for a given GLM and a set of data are embodied in many statistical software packages, so the analyst does not need to be concerned with the technical details. The challenge in applications is to discover the appropriate GLM to describe the process of practical interest, and this may require a great deal of experimentation and analysis. Given the time-consuming nature of this kind of work, it is essential that an analyst be familiar with fruitful approaches to modeling and the capabilities of the software package but not necessarily with the mathematics or computer science aspects of the techniques. This chapter emphasizes the use of GLMs, especially in curve fitting.

Given a model and a set of data, b coefficients and the value of s can be computed. Then for any set of values for the predictor variables, $x_1, x_2, \ldots, x_k$, the model equation yields a "fitted value"

$$\hat{y} = b_0 + b_1 x_1 + b_2 x_2 + \cdots + b_k x_k$$

which in a predictive context is treated as a prediction of the observed value of y the process would yield if the predictor variables assumed the specified values. The chosen set of x values need not be one that corresponds to any case in the data set, which is why "fitted value" is in quotation marks above. Of course, we do not expect the prediction to be exactly equal to an observed y; process variability makes this impossible.

A Numerical Illustration of Computer-Assisted Regression Analysis

Each piece of statistical software prints out about the same information, but each arranges the output differently. Exhibit 8.10A shows a "generic" printout that includes the basic elements you would see using any software if you fitted the model in Section 8.7 to the 60 cases of real estate property data.

The coefficients reported in Exhibit 8.10A are the same as the coefficients of the model reported in Section 8.7, and the value of s is the same. You also see some unfamiliar items in Exhibit 8.10A: R-sq, R-sq(adj), and an analysis-of-variance table. It is easiest to start with the analysis-of-variance table. The first column, labeled Source, lists the sources of variation: Regression, Error, and Total. The second column, labeled SS for sum of squares, gives measures of variation for the three sources. The Total sum of squares, 2092.40, is simply the sum of the squared

E X H I B I T   8.10A
Essentials of Computer Output
for Fitting the Model in
Section 8.7

Predictor Variable		Coefficient	
Constant		1.111	$(= b_0)$
Sq.ft	$(= x_1)$	0.044883	$(= b_1)$
Sq.ft.sq	$(= x_1^2)$	-0.000015064	$(= b_2)$
Med	$(= x_2)$	4.150	$(= b_3)$
Hi	$(= x_3)$	5.216	$(= b_4)$
Assessed	$(= x_4)$	0.22337	$(= b_5)$

$s = 2.719$ $R\text{-sq} = 80.9\%$ $R\text{-sq(adj)} = 79.2\%$

Analysis of Variance

Source	SS	df	MS	F
Regression	1693.16	5	338.63	45.8
Error	399.24	54	7.39	
Total	2092.40	59		

residuals formed by using the average Market value as the fitted value for each parcel—that is

$$\text{Total } SS = (y_1 - \overline{y})^2 + (y_2 - \overline{y})^2 + \cdots + (y_n - \overline{y})^2$$

By dividing this quantity by $n - 1 = 60 - 1 = 59$ and then taking the square root, the standard deviation introduced in Chapter 4 is obtained. It is the residual standard deviation obtained if the information in the predictor variables is ignored and just the mean of the response variable is used as the fitted value for each case. This standard deviation is denoted by s_y.

The Error sum of squares, 399.24, is the residual sum of squares from the fitted model. In some computer printouts, it is called the residual sum of squares. By dividing this sum of squares by its degrees of freedom, $n - k - 1 = 60 - 5 - 1 = 54$, and taking the square root, the value of s is obtained. This is the measure of the variation left over after the fitted values are subtracted from the observed values of the response variable. The df column shows the degrees of freedom for each sum of squares. The MS column shows mean squares—that is, sums of squares divided by degrees of freedom. In the row labeled Error, $MS = SS/df = 399.24/54 = 7.39 = s^2$. The Error mean square is the square of the residual standard deviation.

In the analysis-of-variance table, you see that

$$\text{Total } SS = \text{Regression } SS + \text{Error } SS$$

or $2092.40 = 1693.16 + 399.24$, and Total $df = $ Regression $df + $ Error df. The Total sum of squares and the Total degrees of freedom decompose into two components, one associated with the fit (Regression) and one associated with the residual (Error). The relatively large value of the Regression sum of squares is interpreted to mean that the model accounts for a substantial amount of the variation in the response variable, leaving relatively little variation behind in the residuals. One index of the importance of the variation in the fitted values relative to the variation in the residuals is $F = $ Regression MS/Residual MS, where Regression $MS = $ Regression

SS/Regression df. The larger F is the greater the ability of the fitted values to mimic the observed values.

Another index that is widely used is the **multiple coefficient of determination**

multiple codefficient of determination

$$R^2 = 100 \left[1 - \frac{\text{Error } SS}{\text{Total } SS} \right] \%$$

which is close to 100% when the Error SS is small relative to the Total SS (that is, when the fitted values are close to the actual values), and is close to 0% when Error SS is large relative to Total SS (that is, when the fitted values are not close to the actual values, leaving a great deal of variation in the residuals). The value of R^2 for the model fitted in Exhibit 8.10A is 80.9%.

Although R^2 has some intuitive appeal, it is difficult to interpret predictively. It is also subject to misinterpretation because it can be made arbitrarily close to 100% by adding variables to the model, even extraneous ones. Ideally, useless variables would not be added to a model, but if a complex problem is not clearly understood, one may be "fishing" for useful predictor variables. Using R^2 as a guide to the usefulness of a variable or of a set of variables can actually lead to adopting complicated models that predict *worse* than less complicated ones. For this reason, we refrain from recommending R^2 as a useful index.

A more useful index is the R^2 adjusted for degrees of freedom, denoted by $R^2(\text{adj})$ in the computer output in Exhibit 8.10A. It is computed by the formula

adjusted multiple coefficient of determination

$$R^2(\text{adj}) = 100 \left[1 - \left(\frac{s^2}{s_y^2} \right) \right] \%$$

which is the formula for R^2 with sums of squares replaced by squared standard deviations. You can see that $R^2(\text{adj})$ is just a complicated way of using s^2 as an index, for s^2 is the only quantity in the formula that changes if the model is changed. If a coefficient of determination must be used, however, $R^2(\text{adj})$ is the one to use because it does not automatically increase when a variable is added to the model.

The items explained in this illustration are the basic ones in any regression program output. Many others are typically printed out; they will be explained in the later chapters on regression modeling. The appendix to this chapter displays output from four statistical software packages.

S E C T I O N

8.11 Exercises

8.11A   Consider the four Anscombe data sets of Exercise 6.3H. (Filename: ANSCOMBE.DAT.)

   a   For each of the four data sets, compute R^2, $R^2(\text{adj})$, and the analysis-of-variance table.

   b   Compare the items obtained in part (a) for the four data sets.

8.11B   Use the 60 cases of the real estate data in the following way. Split the data into five subsets of 12 cases each. To form the first subset, choose cases 1, 6, 11, 16, and so on to 56. To form the second subset, choose cases 2, 7, 12, 17, and so on to 57. Continue in this fashion to select the five subsets. (Filename: REALPROP.DAT.)

   a   Fit the model Market $= b_0 + b_1$Sq.ft $+ b_2$(Sq.ft)$^2 + b_3$Assessed separately to each of the five subsets of data.

    b   Compare values of s, R^2, and regression coefficients across the five subsets.

8.11C   You are given the following portion of an analysis-of-variance table from fitting a GLM to a set of data.

Source	SS	df	MS	F
Regression	510.90	3		
Error	127.33	6		
Total				

    a   Complete the analysis-of-variance table.
    b   Compute s_y.
    c   Compute s.
    d   Compute R^2.
    e   Compute $R^2(\text{adj})$.

8.11D   Suppose that in the analysis-of-variance table given in Exercise 8.11C, the Error $df = 12$ instead of 6.

    a   What effect does this have on the statistics computed in that exercise?
    b   Suppose now that Error $df = 24$. What will be the effect?

8.11E   You are given the following portion of an analysis-of-variance table from fitting a GLM to a set of data.

Source	SS	df	MS	F
Regression	8.584	2		
Error	126.879			
Total		223		

    a   Complete the analysis-of-variance table.
    b   Compute s_y.
    c   Compute s.
    d   Compute R^2.
    e   Compute $R^2(\text{adj})$.

SECTION

8.12 Internal and External Prediction

Decision making involves predictive thinking. From deciding whether to pack an umbrella to setting a budget for a department, every decision forces us to assess the likelihoods of a menu of outcomes and the consequences resulting from different courses of action. Regression modeling is used predictively when it is used to summarize information needed for making complex decisions. This section explores some of the subtleties of this predictive focus.

Internal Prediction

The sample of 60 parcels analyzed earlier in this chapter provides a concrete basis for discussion. The data are cross-sectional because they all come from a single year, and a model that proved to be internally consistent for that year was constructed. On the basis of this finding, we can be quite confident that the model could have predicted other market values that might have been generated by sales during the study year. This is internal predictiveness. But, of course, that year has passed, and we are more interested in knowing if the model might successfully predict market values in future years.

External Prediction

What evidence supports the model's ability to predict market values for years other than the study year—that is, its external predictiveness? One characteristic that shows promise is the presence of assessed value as a predictor variable. If assessed values are updated every year, as is common in many municipalities, this new information keeps the model updated to some extent. We still need to question the relevance of the coefficients in the model and the measure of variability s. As we noted, variation in the coefficients tends to have less impact than the process variation measured by s.

The most reliable way to assess the external predictiveness of a model is to compare its predictions to a truly external set of outcomes. This strategy could be implemented in the real estate study because the sales information is available over a series of years. Here are two tests that can be performed:

1   Let T denote the study year, and let $T + 1, T + 2, \ldots, T + L$ denote the L subsequent years for which data are available. For each of the subsequent years, feed the predictor variables associated with the sales data into the model derived from the data from year T, and compute two-standard-deviation prediction intervals for the market values. (See Chapter 20.) For each year, compute the percentage of actual market values contained in the associated prediction intervals. These are truly external predictions, and if they are successful—that is, if about 95% of the intervals contain the actual market values—we conclude that the real estate market is stable and the updating of the assessed values is sufficient to track the market. If the predictions fail, then we conclude that the market is too volatile to be captured in the model, and we look for other ways and means of making successful predictions.

2   For each of the subsequent years, build models based on the sales data for that year. Inspect the series of models for changes in form (that is, presence or absence of variables in different years), substantial differences in the values of the coefficients in different years, and, most important, substantial differences in the values of s over the different years. If large shifts in s are observed, we have documented a highly volatile market process for which accurate predictions may be only a dream. On the other hand, if fairly mild shifts in the models over the years are observed, we have documented a stable market process that can probably be successfully predicted.

The main point to remember from this discussion is that external predictiveness is impossible to document without comparing truly external cases. A model that performs internal predictions well may perform quite badly on external cases because the underlying process is volatile. Although the achievement of good internal predictive performance is important to model building, it does not guarantee good external predictive performance.

In practice, decision makers are frequently asked to make predictive analyses based on information from models built from a single cross section of data. In such situations, clues to the degree of volatility of the underlying process that generated the data should be sought. Lacking such clues, one should be cautious in interpreting predictions from the model. If the predictive analysis is to be made repeatedly, the decision maker should insist that data to test the external predictiveness of the model be collected and the tests performed. No amount of speculation can settle the question of external predictiveness.

SECTION

8.13 Practical Experiences

Two experiences from actual practice reinforce the usefulness of regression.

EXAMPLE   **8.13A**   This is an example of macroeconomic analysis using time series data.[†] Rogers discusses the impact of revisions on data supplied by government agencies. Because data are collected by nationwide surveys, they can be subject to revision over periods of many months. The revisions are necessary because not all the elements in the sample report on time. Several revisions may be needed before a final figure is reached. For example, in a June publication a figure for the previous March may be different from the one reported in the April issue. When collecting data, it is important to keep track of the revisions and to make sure that data in time series are reported on a consistent basis.

To illustrate this point, Rogers displays two regression equations, one based on data processed and made consistent by a professional data provider, the other based on data manually collected from a series of issues of the *Federal Reserve Bulletin* and not revised.

The two time series reported are quarterly percentage changes in U.S. gross national product, y, and percentage changes in U.S. indices of industrial production, x. The series contain data from the second quarter of 1980 to the fourth quarter of 1987, a total of $n = 31$ observations.

The regression equation based on the consistent data is

$$\hat{y}_i = 1.396 - 0.339 y_{i-1} + 0.046 x_i$$

[†]See R. Mark Rogers, "Tracking the Economy: Fundamentals for Understanding Data," *Economic Review*, Federal Reserve Bank of Atlanta, Mar./Apr. 1989, pp. 30–48. Read this article for useful advice on avoiding the pitfalls of using data supplied in government publications.

with $s = 2.224$ and $R^2(\text{adj}) = 75\%$. The symbol y_{i-1} implies that one of the predictor variables is the first lag value of the response variable, as introduced in Section 6.8. This sort of term arises often in regression analysis with time series data because of the presence of autocorrelation.

The regression equation based on the manually collected data is

$$\hat{y}_i = 2.285 - 0.449y_{i-1} + 0.035x_i$$

with $s = 3.919$ and $R^2(\text{adj}) = 41\%$. The value of s is substantially higher and the adjusted R^2 substantially lower for this model than for the one based on consistent data, and the coefficients of the two models also differ substantially. The differences are due entirely to the different ways in which the data were processed before being fitted to the models.

This discussion is not intended to disparage the data reported by the Federal Reserve. Revision is a fact of life in large surveys. The discussion warns us to pay attention to the revisions reported by the Federal Reserve. If we do not, we may derive models that lead us to different conclusions than we would have gotten if we had paid attention to the revisions. ▪

EXAMPLE 8.13B

This second example[†] is a prototype for many practical applications. The problem is the testing of a certain kind of telephone instrument for noise distortions—that is, disturbances that can be picked up by the human ear as a result of chance fluctuations in the electric current. The goal is to decide the extent to which distortion must be controlled, since controlling fluctuations that do not disturb the ear of the customer is not cost effective.

Shewhart notes that tests can be performed by having people listen to the instruments, but doing this for all manufactured instruments is too costly. The idea, therefore, is to come up with a machine measurement that is correlated with ear measurements. The machine measurements are much cheaper, and if they give sufficiently precise predictions of ear measurements, they can be used to judge the quality of the instruments.

Shewhart describes a study involving determinations of both ear and machine measurements for 942 instruments. He presents a scatterplot of the data but does not report the actual measurements. The straight-line model fitted to the data provides predictions that, according to Shewhart, justify the substitution of machine measurements for ear measurements. In this case, the model serves two purposes:

- It documents the usefulness of an appropriate machine measurement.

- It gives the curve needed to perform the predictions.

In many practical problems, the measurements that we would like to have are unavailable, either because they are too expensive or because we can

---

[†]The example is taken from Walter A. Shewhart, *Economic Control of Quality of Manufactured Product* (Princeton, N.J.: Van Nostrand, 1931), pp. 401–403.

measure only indirectly. As an illustration of the latter, consider customer loyalty or customer satisfaction. These are difficult things to measure directly, so we have to resort to eliciting responses to questionnaires or to observing behavior in relatively uncontrolled settings. For small samples of customers, we may be able to obtain direct indications of loyalty or satisfaction. Such data are precious because they allow us to calibrate our indirect measures with the direct ones. Often, however, the most important measures are literally impossible to get. In such cases, we base our decisions on indirect measurements that are palpably second-best. ∎

Chapter Summary

Multiple regression models provide powerful tools for describing relationships between a response and several predictor variables. Curved relationships can be accommodated through quadratic curves and categorical variables through indicator variables. Least-squares provides a general principle for obtaining the numerical values of the regression coefficients that make the sum of squared residuals as small as possible. The residual standard deviation provides a direct comparison of the fit of competing models—the smaller the better. Even models that fit a particular set of data well may fail to predict new cases because the underlying process is volatile. Thus, the study of external predictions is an important part of regression modeling.

Supplementary Exercises for Chapter 8

8A Suppose a regression analysis yields the following fitted equation: $\hat{y} = b_0 + b_1 x_1 + b_2 x_2$ where x_1 is a continuous variable and x_2 is an indicator variable. Sketch the graph of the fitted values versus x_1 for each choice of x_2 values.

8B A company tests three different safety programs by operating each program in 10 of its plants. The data available are y = number of accidents this year, x_1 = number of accidents last year,

$$x_2 = \begin{cases} 1 & \text{if safety plan 1 is in use} \\ 0 & \text{if safety plan 1 is not in use} \end{cases}$$

and

$$x_3 = \begin{cases} 1 & \text{if safety plan 2 is in use} \\ 0 & \text{if safety plan 2 is not in use} \end{cases}$$

Write a model that compares the safety plans, taking into account the ability of last year's accidents to predict this year's accidents.

8C We introduced ranking of business school MBA programs in Supplementary Exercise 7G. Use the ranking of corporations and graduates to predict the *Business Week* rankings. (Filename: MBARANK.DAT.)

    a Find the least-squares regression plane: BusWeek $= b_0 + b_1$ Corp $+ b_2$ Grad

    b Plot the residuals versus fitted values.

    c Comment on the shape of the residual plot obtained in part (b).

    d Find the least-squares regression surface of the form:
BusWeek $= b_0 + b_1$ Corp $+ b_2$ Grad $+ b_3$ (Corp) ^{2}

    e Plot the residuals versus fitted values for the model of part (d).

    f Comment on the shape of the residual plot displayed in part (e).

8D Use the data on quality ratings of cassette tape players given in Exercise 6.3C. Variables include quality rating, price, and whether the deck is a single or double deck. (Filename: CASSETTE.DAT.)

    a Fit a parallel-lines model to predict quality rating from price and an indicator showing whether the deck is a single deck or a double deck.

    b Interpret the regression coefficient associated with the indicator variable.

    c Interpret the regression coefficient associated with the price variable.

    d Interpret the constant term in the regression model.

    e Construct the plot of residuals versus fitted values and comment on any apparent patterns.

    f Now construct a plot of residuals versus fitted values using different plotting symbols for single and dual decks. Comment on any patterns now apparent.

8E Consider the gasoline consumption data reported in Supplementary Exercise 6B. Use the variables city gasoline consumption and weight. (Filename: AUTOSPEC.DAT.)

    a Treating the foreign and domestic cars as two separate groups of data, fit separate regression lines to each group.

    b Compare the slopes and intercepts found in part (a) with the slope and intercepts of the parallel lines displayed in Exhibit 8.5B.

8F Consider the gasoline consumption data reported in Supplementary Exercise 6B. However, use expressway gasoline consumption as the response variable and weight as the predictor variable. (Filename: AUTOSPEC.DAT.)

    a Fit a straight-line model using least squares.

    b Find the residual standard deviation based on the model of part (a).

    c Display the residual versus fitted plot for the model fitted in part (a) and comment on its shape.

    d Display the same residual plot as done in part (c) except use plotting symbols to denote the foreign and domestic cars. Do any patterns become apparent?

    e Now fit a parallel-lines model using an indicator variable for foreign and domestic cars.

    f Find the residual standard deviation for the model fit in part (e) and compare it to the one obtained in part (b).

    g Display the residual versus fitted plot for the model of part (f). Use appropriate plotting symbols and comment on the graph.

8G Suppose that a regression model uses the following equation:

$$y = b_0 + b_1 x_1 + b_2 x_2 + b_3 x_1 x_2$$

where x_1 is a continuous variable and x_2 is an indicator variable. Sketch a graph of the fitted values versus x_1 for each choice of x_2 values.

8H Suppose that a regression model uses the following equation:

$$y = b_0 + b_1 x_1 + b_2 x_2 + b_3 x_1 x_2$$

where x_1 and x_2 are both continuous variables.

a   Using three different values of x_2, sketch the graph of the fitted values versus x_1 on one graph.

b   Repeat part (a) when $b_3 = 0$ and comment on the difference in the plot.

8I   You are given the following portion of an analysis-of-variance table from fitting a GLM to a set of data.

Source	SS	df	MS	F
Regression	0.1379	5		
Error		21		
Total	0.2461			

a   Complete the analysis-of-variance table.

b   Compute s_y.

c   Compute s.

d   Compute R^2.

e   Compute $R^2(\text{adj})$.

8J   Construct a scatterplot of data to show how changing the position of a single outlier could change the slope of a regression line from positive to negative.

8K   Statistical theory says that the correlation coefficient between the residuals and each of the predictor variables is zero. This is true regardless of the adequacy of the multiple regression model as long as the model contains an intercept term.

a   Use several of the data sets and regression models presented in this chapter to verify this theory empirically. That is, fit the model, obtain the residuals, and show that the correlation coefficient between the residuals and each predictor is zero.

b   Theory also says that the residuals and fitted values have zero correlation. Verify this with several data sets and regression models.

c   Also verify that the residuals add to zero and, equivalently, that the average fitted value is the same as the average response.

8L   A coworker of yours likes to fit regression models but thinks that supplementing them with scatterplots is a waste of time. Write a memo to your coworker presenting an example that demonstrates the danger of that approach.

Glossary for Chapter 8

adjusted multiple coefficient of determination, $R^2(\text{adj})$	$100\left(1 - \dfrac{s^2}{s_y^2}\right)\%$
b_i	Regression coefficient associated with the ith predictor variable.
degrees of freedom for residuals	The number of observations minus the number of fitted coefficients in the regression model.
general linear model (GLM)	A regression model using fitted equation $y = b_0 + b_1 x_1 + b_2 x_2 + \cdots + b_k x_k$ with k predictor variables. It is linear in the regression coefficients $b_0, b_1, b_2, \ldots, b_k$.
indicator variable	A variable whose value is 1 when a case is in a specified category and is 0 otherwise.

multiple coefficient of determination, R^2	$100\left(1 - \dfrac{\text{Error } SS}{\text{Total } SS}\right)\%$
point cloud	A three-dimensional plot of the values of the response versus the values of two predictors.
regression plane	$y = b_0 + b_1 x_1 + b_2 x_2$ where x_1 and x_2 are continuous predictors.
residual plot	A scatterplot of residuals versus fitted values.
residual standard deviation, s	The square root of the sum of squared residuals divided by their degrees of freedom.
scatterplot matrix	Scatterplots for pairs of variables in an array of rows and columns.

A P P E N D I X

Computer Output

The regression analysis reported in Example 8.7B has been run through four statistical packages: Minitab, Stata, StatGraphics, and MYSTAT. Portions of the output from these packages are shown below. You will see all the basic quantities listed in Exhibit 8.10A plus others. Consult the reference manuals for the different packages to learn about the quantities not explained in the text.

Minitab Regression Results

```
The regression equation is
market = 1.11 + 0.0449 sq.ft - 0.000015 sq.ft.sq + 4.15 med
              + 5.22 hi + 0.223 assessed

Predictor          Coef         Stdev      t-ratio         p
Constant          1.111         4.242         0.26     0.794
sq_ft          0.044883      0.008073         5.56     0.000
sq_ft_sq     -0.00001506    0.00000366        -4.12     0.000
med               4.150         1.081         3.84     0.000
hi                5.216         1.926         2.71     0.009
assessed        0.22337       0.06940         3.22     0.002

s = 2.719         R-sq = 80.9%         R-sq(adj) = 79.2%

Analysis of Variance

SOURCE         DF          SS          MS          F         p
Regression      5     1693.16      338.63      45.80     0.000
Error          54      399.24        7.39
Total          59     2092.40
```

Stata Regression Results

```
. regr market sq_ft sq_ft_2 med hi assessed
(obs=60)
```

Source	SS	df	MS		
Model	1693.15672	5	338.631345	Number of obs =	60
Residual	399.243331	54	7.39339502	F(5, 54) =	45.80
				Prob > F =	0.0000
				R-square =	0.8092
Total	2092.40005	59	35.4644077	Adj R-square =	0.7915
				Root MSE =	2.7191

Variable	Coefficient	Std. Error	t	Prob > |t|	Mean
market					37.8
sq_ft	.044883	.008073	5.560	0.000	941.7333
sq_ft_2	-.0000151	3.66e-06	-4.117	0.000	944851
med	4.150356	1.080701	3.840	0.000	.7333333
hi	5.216019	1.926324	2.708	0.009	.0666667
assessed	.2233726	.0694006	3.219	0.002	23.56033
_cons	1.111179	4.241674	0.262	0.794	

StatGraphics Regression Results

```
                  Model fitting results for: market
```

Independent variable	coefficient	std. error	t-value	sig.level
CONSTANT	1.111177	4.241674	0.2620	0.7943
sq_ft	0.044883	0.008073	5.5597	0.0000
sq_ft_2	-0.000015	3.658916E-6	-4.1170	0.0001
med	4.150355	1.080701	3.8404	0.0003
hi	5.216018	1.926324	2.7078	0.0091
assessed	0.223373	0.069401	3.2186	0.0022

```
R-SQ. (ADJ.) = 0.7915   SE=  2.719080   MAE=       1.980337  DurbWat=  1.908
Previously:      0.0000        0.000000             0.000000           0.000
60 observations fitted
```

MYSTAT Regression Results

```
DEP VAR: MARKET   N: 60  MULTIPLE R: .900  SQUARED MULTIPLE R: .809
ADJUSTED SQUARED MULTIPLE R:  .792  STANDARD ERROR OF ESTIMATE: 2.719
```

VARIABLE	COEFFICIENT	STD ERROR	STD COEF	TOLERANCE	T	P(2 TAIL)
CONSTANT	1.111	4.242	0.000	.	0.262	0.794
SQ_FT	0.045	0.008	1.830	0.0326046	5.560	0.000
SQ_FT_2	-0.000	0.000	-1.321	0.0343082	-4.117	0.000
MED	4.150	1.081	0.311	0.5395250	3.840	0.000
HI	5.216	1.926	0.220	0.5336893	2.708	0.009
ASSESSED	0.223	0.069	0.218	0.7671128	3.219	0.002

```
                     ANALYSIS OF VARIANCE
```

SOURCE	SUM-OF-SQUARES	DF	MEAN-SQUARE	F-RATIO	P
REGRESSION	1693.157	5	338.631	45.802	0.000
RESIDUAL	399.243	54	7.393		

Normal Distributions

Chapter Objectives

After mastering this chapter, you will be able to:

- Use standardized values and the normal table to compute areas under a normal curve and percentiles of a normal distribution

- Explain the central limit effect for means and totals

- Check data for normality using histograms, normal counts, and normal probability plots

9.1 Introduction

As discussed in Chapters 2 to 4, many processes produce data whose distribution has a characteristic shape resembling a bell or a mound with tapered tails. In this chapter, that shape is further explored and related to indisputably the most important distribution in all of statistics—the *normal distribution*. You learn the mathematical characteristics of the normal curve and a few of its many uses. You see that even when data are not normally distributed, some aspects of samples of the data are useful because they are almost normally distributed. You learn several methods for checking whether a set of values is normally distributed. Finally, you learn to construct and assess cumulative distribution plots.

Exhibit 9.1A repeats a relative frequency histogram of the 99 percentage changes in the flour price index that you also saw in Exhibit 3.6J. This general histogram shape, with a predominance of data in the middle and less at both tails, is very common for values from processes (or transformations of these values) or from surveys or similar cross-sectional data. For example, the histogram of Los Angeles traffic volumes for major arterials, Exhibit 4.10I, also had this shape. Other distributions with this general shape include

- Heights of groups of adults of the same gender
- IQs of young adults
- Repeated measurements of a chosen dimension of a product

E X H I B I T **9.1A**
Histogram of Percent Changes in
Flour Price Index

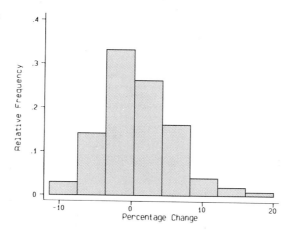

E X H I B I T **9.1A**
Histogram of Percent Changes in
Flour Price Index

However, the most important situations in which this shape occurs are the distributions of many statistics, such as the means obtained from individual values from a process or survey.

The Distribution of Means of Samples

Consider calculating the mean of five consecutive observations from a process that at each time period selects at random one of the integers $-5, -4, -3, -2, -1, 0, 1, 2, 3, 4$, or 5. For each nonoverlapping group of five observations, a new mean is obtained. If this is repeated enough times, a good picture of the distribution of the means will be obtained. It is possible to obtain a mean of -5, but this is rather unlikely since it will occur only if the process produces five -5's in a row in one group. Similarly, it is possible but unlikely to observe a mean of $+5$. However, many different groups of five will produce a mean of zero. For example, $-5, -4, 0, 5$ and $0, -5, 3, 0, 2$ both lead to a mean of zero. Thus, you expect a predominance of mean values near zero and very few around -5 or $+5$.

Simulation is a valuable technique for illustrating this important idea. (See Appendix 3 for a discussion of simulation methods.) Small simulations may be carried out by hand, but the task is tedious. The exercises in Section 9.2 ask you to do a simulation by hand, but once in a lifetime is sufficient. Computer simulations, on the other hand, are easy and allow many examples to be examined in a short time.

To illustrate these ideas, we used statistical software to simulate 5000 observations chosen randomly from the integers -5 to 5. We then used consecutive, nonoverlapping groups of five observations to produce a sequence of 1000 means. This seemingly large job is easy and quick with a computer.

Exhibit 9.1B shows the histogram of the full set of 5000 data points to illustrate the uniform distribution on the integers -5 to 5, the distribution of individual process values. Theoretically, each of the intervals should contain $1/11$ or about 455 of the 5000 observations.

E X H I B I T **9.1B**
Histogram of Individual Values
from Uniform Process

```
Histogram of Indiv. Values   N=5000
Each * represents 10 observations

Midpoint   Count
     -5     469     *************************************************
     -4     459     ************************************************
     -3     441     *********************************************
     -2     463     *************************************************
     -1     473     **************************************************
      0     443     *********************************************
      1     448     *********************************************
      2     439     *********************************************
      3     459     ************************************************
      4     437     ********************************************
      5     469     *************************************************
```

Exhibit 9.1C shows the distribution of the means of samples of five consecutive observations. The effect is dramatic. The mound-shaped distribution of the means is radically different from the rectangular shape of the distribution of individual values.

E X H I B I T **9.1C**
Histogram of Means of Five
from Uniform Distribution

```
Histogram of Means   N=1000
Each * represents 10 observations

Midpoint   Count
   -4.00      7     *
   -3.00     42     *****
   -2.00    117     ************
   -1.00    206     *********************
    0.00    258     **************************
    1.00    223     ***********************
    2.00    103     ***********
    3.00     39     ****
    4.00      5     *
```

Exhibit 9.1D gives various statistics for the two distributions. Notice that, to the accuracy displayed, the two means are equal and also close to zero. Notice also that the standard deviation for the distribution of means is 1.4760, which is much smaller than the standard deviation of the uniform distribution, 3.1756. Averaging five observations together pulls the means toward the middle, thus reducing the standard deviation. Section 9.5 specifies the particular way in which this reduction occurs.

E X H I B I T **9.1D**
Descriptive Statistics for
Individual and Mean
Distributions

	N	**Mean**	**Median**	**Standard Deviation**
Individual	5000	−0.0214	0.0000	3.1756
Means	1000	−0.0214	0.0000	1.4760

These observed distributions based on large data sets suggest that there may be a theoretical distribution that will conveniently describe many such situations and serve as a reference for comparison and calculation. This distribution is the normal distribution, or normal curve.[†]

SECTION

9.2 Exercises

9.2A Roll an ordinary six-sided die four times and record the total spots obtained in the four rolls. Repeat this experiment 50 times and produce a histogram of your 50 totals. Do your results produce a distribution that is mound shaped, as in Exhibits 9.1A and 9.1C?

9.2B Use a statistical software package to perform large-scale experiments similar to those reported in Exhibits 9.1B and 9.1C. Try different shapes for the distribution of individual values and different sample sizes—for example, 5, 10, and 30—to compute the means. Are your results similar to ours? Comment on the improvement, if any, in the mound-shapedness for larger sample sizes.

9.2C Repeat Exercise 9.2B but compute the standard deviation of each sample and display the distribution of the standard deviations. For $n = 5$, the distribution will not likely be very mound shaped. For $n = 30$ when sampling from a mound-shaped process distribution, the distribution of the standard deviation should itself be quite mound shaped.

9.2D Repeat Exercise 9.2B but compute the median of each sample and display the distribution of the medians.

9.2E Repeat Exercise 9.2B but compute the maximum value of each sample and display the distribution of the maximums. For neither $n = 5$ nor $n = 30$ will the distribution be very mound shaped.

SECTION

9.3 The Normal Curve

This section discusses the mathematical characteristics of normal curves. It explains how to use areas under normal curves to make valuable predictions about processes and sets of data. It also shows how all normal curves are easily related to the standard normal curve.

The normal curve has been used since the early 1700s. It began as a tool for analyzing games of chance but was eventually found to apply to numerous situations involving uncertainty. It describes the theoretical density histogram for an (infinite) collection of measurements along a continuous number line. In the real world, all measurements are discrete, being selected from a certain finite (but possibly very large) collection of possible values. For example, prices are usually no finer than cents, stock prices are measured in eighths of a dollar, and even measurements of weight, length, and time are limited by measuring instruments (scales, rulers, or clocks, respectively). The formula for the **normal curve** is

normal curve

$$f(y) = \frac{1}{\sqrt{2\pi}\sigma} e^{-\frac{1}{2}[(y-\mu)/\sigma]^2}$$

[†]In this context, the word *normal* is not used as the opposite of abnormal.

where e is the base of the natural logarithms (about 2.71828) and π is the well-known constant from geometry (about 3.14159). Here μ is the mean of the theoretical distribution and $\sigma > 0$ is the standard deviation. They measure center and variability, respectively, for a theoretical distribution in a fashion analogous to the mean and standard deviation for a set of data.

Exhibit 9.3A displays a graph of the normal curve for the case where $\mu = 0$ and $\sigma = 1$. This curve is called the **standard normal curve**. All calculations necessary for using any normal distribution can be related back to calculations for the standard normal curve.

standard normal curve

E X H I B I T **9.3A**
The Standard Normal Curve

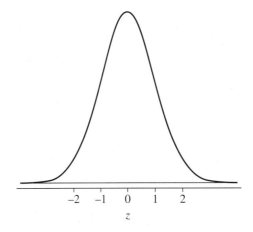

E X H I B I T **9.3A**
The Standard Normal Curve

Exhibit 9.3B shows the normal curve with mean 100 and standard deviation 16. Note that the shape is really the same. Only the center of the distribution and the

E X H I B I T **9.3B**
A Normal Curve with Mean 100
and Standard Deviation 16

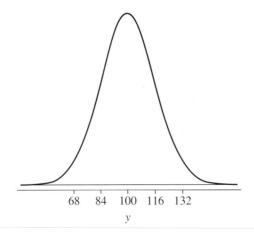

E X H I B I T **9.3C**   Normal Curves with Different Standard Deviations (drawn on same scale)

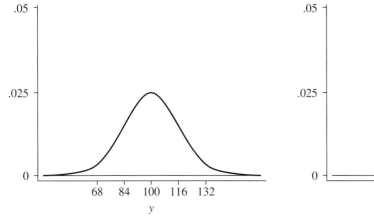
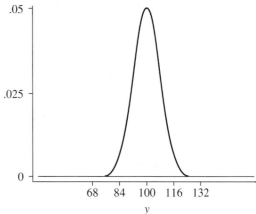

E X H I B I T **9.3D**   The Normal Curve in Words

```
                          THE
                        NORMAL
                    LAW OF ERROR
                 STANDS OUT IN THE
              EXPERIENCE OF MANKIND
             AS ONE OF THE BROADEST
          GENERALIZATIONS OF NATURAL
        PHILOSOPHY ★ IT SERVES AS THE
      GUIDING INSTRUMENT IN RESEARCHES
   IN THE PHYSICAL AND SOCIAL SCIENCES AND
     IN MEDICINE AGRICULTURE AND ENGINEERING ★
    IT IS AN INDISPENSABLE TOOL FOR THE ANALYSIS AND THE
INTERPRETATION OF THE BASIC DATA OBTAINED BY OBSERVATION AND EXPERIMENT
```

Source: W. J. Youden, in E. R. Tufte, *The Visual Display of Quantitive Information* (Cheshire, Conn.: Graphics Press, 1983).

scales on the axes have changed. If normal curves with different standard deviations are plotted on the same scale, they look different. Exhibit 9.3C gives an example.

Another unique way of picturing this curve is shown in Exhibit 9.3D.

The normal curve has two important features:

- The curve is symmetric about its mean μ

- The total area between the curve and the horizontal axis is 1, or 100%.

The first feature is apparent from the graphs in Exhibits 9.3A–C. The second one requires calculus applied to the normal curve formula. Another important characteristic of the normal curve is the proportion of values that fall within a given area under the curve. The area under a normal curve between two points on the axis a and b, as shown in Exhibit 9.3E, equals the proportion of values in the (theoretically infinite) collection of measurements that lie between a and b. For a standard normal curve ($\mu = 0$, $\sigma = 1$):

- About 68% of the distribution's area, or values, lie between -1 and $+1$, or within 1 standard deviation of the mean.

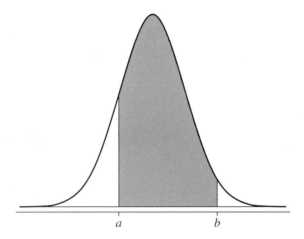

- About 95% of the distribution's values lie between −2 and +2, or within 2 standard deviations of the mean.
- About 99.7% of the distribution's values lie between −3 and +3, or within 3 standard deviations of the mean.

As can be seen in Exhibit 9.3F, the curve is very near zero outside of the interval from −3 to +3. Just beyond these limits, it appears to be at zero height, although in theory it never really gets to zero but only approaches zero as a limit.

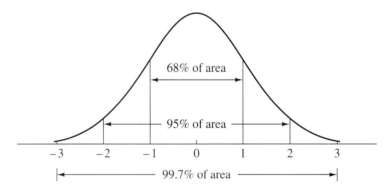

How are areas under a normal curve obtained? Unfortunately, not even calculus is helpful in finding such areas. Instead, tables such as the **normal distribution** **normal distribution table** **table** (see Exhibit 9.3G or Appendix 1) are frequently used. Normal curve areas may also be obtained from statistical calculators or directly in most statistical software packages. In addition, as the next subsection explains, by using standard units (or by standardizing), we really have to deal only with areas under the standard normal curve.

Standardized Units

Any area needed with respect to a normal variable can be reexpressed in terms of standardized units. The required area may then be found using the standard normal distribution table. If y has a normal distribution with mean μ and standard deviation σ, the new variable

$$z = \frac{y - \mu}{\sigma}$$

has a standard normal distribution—that is, a normal distribution with mean 0 and standard deviation 1.

standardized units

We also say that z is measured in **standardized units**. The variable z says how many standard deviations y is above (or below) the mean of y. This can be seen most easily by solving the above equation for y, obtaining

$$y = \mu + z\sigma$$

If z is positive, then y is above its mean, and if z is negative, then y is below its mean. The quantity z is called a **z-score** or **z-value**.

z-score
z-value

Since any normal distribution can be thus transformed into a standard normal curve, the proportions of values shown in Exhibit 9.3F apply to all normal curves. That is, about 68% of the values in a normal distribution lie within 1 standard deviation of the mean, about 95% lie within 2 standard deviations, and about 99.7%—or almost all—lie within 3 standard deviations.

As you will see in this and later chapters, the proportions of values that lie within areas of the normal curve are vital in many applications. The next chapter, for example, focuses on use of these proportions in monitoring and improving processes.

Using Standardized Units

An automatic machine is used to fill "one-pound" cans of coffee. In fact, there is inherent variability in the filling process. Suppose we know from past experience that the distribution of actual fill amounts can be described approximately as a normal distribution with standard deviation $\sigma = 1$ ounce. The machine has an adjustment that allows the mean fill amount, μ, to be set at any value desired. If the mean fill amount is set at 16 ounces, what fraction of the cans will be underfilled, that is, contain less than 16 ounces? Exhibit 9.3H illustrates the desired area and also shows the appropriate standardized units. An actual value of 16 corresponds to a z-value of $(16 - 16)/1 = 0$. The area to the left of 0 is, by symmetry, equal to 0.5. Thus if the mean fill amount is set at 16, half of the cans will be underfilled.

Suppose the mean fill amount is decreased to 15 ounces. What fraction will then be underfilled? Now the area below the standardized value of $(16 - 15)/1 = 1$ is needed. Exhibit 9.3I shows the required area. Using the normal distribution table, we see that the value below $z = 1.00$ is 0.8413. That is, about 84% will be underfilled.

Suppose the mean fill amount is increased to 17 ounces. What fraction will now be underfilled? The area below the standardized value of $(16 - 17)/1 = -1$ is

E X H I B I T **9.3G** Normal Distribution Table (Each entry is the total area under the standard normal curve to the left of z, which is specified to two decimal places by joining the row value to the column value. Values were obtained by rounding the results from Minitab's CDF command.)

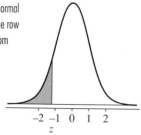

z	0.00	0.01	0.02	0.03	0.04	0.05	0.06	0.07	0.08	0.09
-3.9	0.0000	0.0000	0.0000	0.0000	0.0000	0.0000	0.0000	0.0000	0.0000	0.0000
-3.8	0.0001	0.0001	0.0001	0.0001	0.0001	0.0001	0.0001	0.0001	0.0001	0.0001
-3.7	0.0001	0.0001	0.0001	0.0001	0.0001	0.0001	0.0001	0.0001	0.0001	0.0001
-3.6	0.0002	0.0002	0.0001	0.0001	0.0001	0.0001	0.0001	0.0001	0.0001	0.0001
-3.5	0.0002	0.0002	0.0002	0.0002	0.0002	0.0002	0.0002	0.0002	0.0002	0.0002
-3.4	0.0003	0.0003	0.0003	0.0003	0.0003	0.0003	0.0003	0.0003	0.0003	0.0002
-3.3	0.0005	0.0005	0.0005	0.0004	0.0004	0.0004	0.0004	0.0004	0.0004	0.0003
-3.2	0.0007	0.0007	0.0006	0.0006	0.0006	0.0006	0.0006	0.0005	0.0005	0.0005
-3.1	0.0010	0.0009	0.0009	0.0009	0.0008	0.0008	0.0008	0.0008	0.0007	0.0007
-3.0	0.0013	0.0013	0.0013	0.0012	0.0012	0.0011	0.0011	0.0011	0.0010	0.0010
-2.9	0.0019	0.0018	0.0018	0.0017	0.0016	0.0016	0.0015	0.0015	0.0014	0.0014
-2.8	0.0026	0.0025	0.0024	0.0023	0.0023	0.0022	0.0021	0.0021	0.0020	0.0019
-2.7	0.0035	0.0034	0.0033	0.0032	0.0031	0.0030	0.0029	0.0028	0.0027	0.0026
-2.6	0.0047	0.0045	0.0044	0.0043	0.0041	0.0040	0.0039	0.0038	0.0037	0.0036
-2.5	0.0062	0.0060	0.0059	0.0057	0.0055	0.0054	0.0052	0.0051	0.0049	0.0048
-2.4	0.0082	0.0080	0.0078	0.0075	0.0073	0.0071	0.0069	0.0068	0.0066	0.0064
-2.3	0.0107	0.0104	0.0102	0.0099	0.0096	0.0094	0.0091	0.0089	0.0087	0.0084
-2.2	0.0139	0.0136	0.0132	0.0129	0.0125	0.0122	0.0119	0.0116	0.0113	0.0110
-2.1	0.0179	0.0174	0.0170	0.0166	0.0162	0.0128	0.0154	0.0150	0.0146	0.0143
-2.0	0.0228	0.0222	0.0217	0.0212	0.0207	0.0202	0.0197	0.0195	0.0188	0.0183
-1.9	0.0287	0.0281	0.0274	0.0268	0.0262	0.0256	0.0250	0.0244	0.0239	0.0233
-1.8	0.0359	0.0351	0.0344	0.0336	0.0329	0.0322	0.0314	0.0307	0.0301	0.0294
-1.7	0.0446	0.0436	0.0427	0.0418	0.0409	0.0401	0.0392	0.0384	0.0375	0.0367
-1.6	0.0548	0.0537	0.0526	0.0516	0.0505	0.0495	0.0485	0.0475	0.0465	0.0455
-1.5	0.0668	0.0655	0.0643	0.0630	0.0618	0.0606	0.0594	0.0582	0.0571	0.0559
-1.4	0.0808	0.0793	0.0778	0.0764	0.0749	0.0735	0.0721	0.0708	0.0694	0.0681
-1.3	0.0968	0.0951	0.0934	0.0918	0.0901	0.0885	0.0869	0.0853	0.0838	0.0823
-1.2	0.1151	0.1131	0.1112	0.1093	0.1075	0.1056	0.1038	0.1020	0.1003	0.0985
-1.1	0.1357	0.1335	0.1314	0.1292	0.1271	0.1251	0.1230	0.1210	0.1190	0.1170
-1.0	0.1587	0.1562	0.1539	0.1515	0.1492	0.1469	0.1446	0.1423	0.1401	0.1379
-0.9	0.1841	0.1814	0.1788	0.1762	0.1736	0.1711	0.1685	0.1660	0.1635	0.1611
-0.8	0.2119	0.2090	0.2061	0.2033	0.2005	0.1977	0.1979	0.1922	0.1894	0.1867
-0.7	0.2420	0.2389	0.2358	0.2327	0.2296	0.2266	0.2236	0.2206	0.2177	0.2148
-0.6	0.2743	0.2709	0.2676	0.2643	0.2611	0.2578	0.2546	0.2514	0.1483	0.2451
-0.5	0.3085	0.3050	0.3015	0.2981	0.2946	0.2912	0.2877	0.2843	0.2810	0.2776
-0.4	0.3446	0.3409	0.3372	0.3336	0.3300	0.3264	0.3228	0.3192	0.3156	0.3121
-0.3	0.3821	0.3783	0.3745	0.3707	0.3669	0.3632	0.3594	0.3557	0.3520	0.3483
-0.2	0.4207	0.4168	0.4129	0.4090	0.4052	0.4013	0.3974	0.3936	0.3897	0.3859
-0.1	0.4602	0.4562	0.4522	0.4483	0.4443	0.4404	0.4364	0.4325	0.4286	0.4247
-0.0	0.5000	0.4960	0.4920	0.4880	0.4840	0.4801	0.4761	0.4721	0.4681	0.4641

EXHIBIT **9.3G** (Continued) (Each entry is the total area under the standard normal curve to the left of z, which is specified to two decimal places by joining the row value to the column value. Values were obtained by rounding the results from Minitab's CDF command.)

z	0.00	0.01	0.02	0.03	0.04	0.05	0.06	0.07	0.08	0.09
0.0	0.5000	0.5040	0.5080	0.5120	0.5130	0.5199	0.5239	0.5279	0.5319	0.5359
0.1	0.5398	0.5438	0.5478	0.5517	0.5557	0.5596	0.5636	0.5675	0.5714	0.5753
0.2	0.5793	0.5832	0.5871	0.5910	0.5948	0.5987	0.6026	0.6064	0.6103	0.6141
0.3	0.6179	0.6217	0.6255	0.6293	0.6331	0.6368	0.6406	0.6443	0.6480	0.6517
0.4	0.6554	0.6591	0.6628	0.6664	0.6700	0.6736	0.6772	0.6808	0.6844	0.6879
0.5	0.6915	0.6950	0.6985	0.7019	0.7054	0.7088	0.7123	0.7157	0.7190	0.7224
0.6	0.7257	0.7291	0.7324	0.7357	0.7389	0.7422	0.7454	0.7486	0.7517	0.7549
0.7	0.7580	0.7611	0.7642	0.7673	0.7704	0.7734	0.7764	0.7794	0.7823	0.7852
0.8	0.7881	0.7910	0.7939	0.7967	0.7995	0.8023	0.8051	0.8078	0.8106	0.8133
0.9	0.8159	0.8186	0.8212	0.8238	0.8264	0.8289	0.8315	0.8340	0.8365	0.8389
1.0	0.8413	0.8438	0.8461	0.8485	0.8508	0.8531	0.8554	0.8577	0.8599	0.8621
1.1	0.8643	0.8665	0.8686	0.8708	0.8729	0.8749	0.8770	0.8790	0.8810	0.8830
1.2	0.8849	0.8869	0.8888	0.8907	0.8925	0.8944	0.8962	0.8980	0.8997	0.9015
1.3	0.9032	0.9049	0.9066	0.9082	0.9099	0.9155	0.9131	0.9147	0.9162	0.9177
1.4	0.9192	0.9207	0.9222	0.9236	0.9251	0.9265	0.9279	0.9292	0.9306	0.9319
1.5	0.9332	0.9345	0.9357	0.9370	0.9382	0.9394	0.9406	0.9418	0.9429	0.9441
1.6	0.9452	0.9463	0.9474	0.9484	0.9495	0.9505	0.9515	0.9525	0.9535	0.9545
1.7	0.9554	0.9564	0.9573	0.9582	0.9591	0.9599	0.9608	0.9616	0.9625	0.9633
1.8	0.9641	0.9649	0.9656	0.9664	0.9671	0.9678	0.9686	0.9693	0.9699	0.9706
1.9	0.9713	0.9719	0.9726	0.9732	0.9738	0.9744	0.9750	0.9756	0.9761	0.9767
2.0	0.9772	0.9778	0.9783	0.9788	0.9793	0.9798	0.9803	0.9808	0.9812	0.9817
2.1	0.9821	0.9826	0.9830	0.9834	0.9838	0.9842	0.9846	0.9850	0.9854	0.9857
2.2	0.9861	0.9864	0.9868	0.9871	0.9875	0.9878	0.9881	0.9884	0.9887	0.9890
2.3	0.9893	0.9896	0.9898	0.9901	0.9904	0.9906	0.9909	0.9911	0.9913	0.9916
2.4	0.9918	0.9920	0.9922	0.9925	0.9927	0.9929	0.9931	0.9932	0.9934	0.9936
2.5	0.9938	0.9940	0.9941	0.9943	0.9945	0.9946	0.9948	0.9949	0.9951	0.9952
2.6	0.9953	0.9955	0.9956	0.9957	0.9959	0.9960	0.9961	0.9962	0.9963	0.9964
2.7	0.9965	0.9966	0.9967	0.9968	0.9969	0.9970	0.9971	0.9972	0.9973	0.9974
2.8	0.9974	0.9975	0.9976	0.9877	0.9977	0.9978	0.9979	0.9979	0.9980	0.9981
2.9	0.9981	0.9982	0.9982	0.9983	0.9984	0.9984	0.9985	0.9985	0.9986	0.9986
3.0	0.9987	0.9987	0.9987	0.9988	0.9988	0.9989	0.9989	0.9989	0.9990	0.9990
3.1	0.9990	0.9991	0.9991	0.9991	0.9995	0.9992	0.9992	0.9992	0.9993	0.9993
3.2	0.9993	0.9993	0.9994	0.9994	0.9994	0.9994	0.9994	0.9995	0.9995	0.9995
3.3	0.9995	0.9995	0.9995	0.9996	0.9996	0.9996	0.9996	0.9996	0.9996	0.9997
3.4	0.9997	0.9997	0.9997	0.9997	0.9997	0.9997	0.9997	0.9997	0.9997	0.9998
3.5	0.9998	0.9998	0.9998	0.9998	0.9998	0.9998	0.9998	0.9998	0.9998	0.9998
3.6	0.9998	0.9998	0.9999	0.9999	0.9999	0.9999	0.9999	0.9999	0.9999	0.9999
3.7	0.9999	0.9999	0.9999	0.9999	0.9999	0.9999	0.9999	0.9999	0.9999	0.9999
3.8	0.9999	0.9999	0.9999	0.9999	0.9999	0.9999	0.9999	0.9999	0.9999	0.9999
3.9	1.0000	1.0000	1.0000	1.0000	1.0000	1.0000	1.0000	1.0000	1.0000	1.0000

EXHIBIT **9.3H**
Area Below 16 Under a Normal
Curve with Mean = 16 Ounces

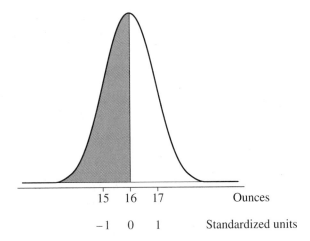

EXHIBIT **9.3I**
Area Below 16 Under a Normal
Curve with Mean = 15 Ounces

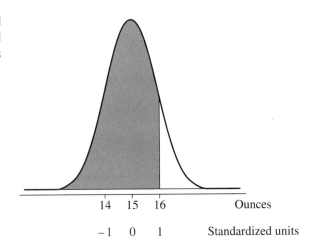

EXHIBIT **9.3J**
Area Below 16 Under a Normal
Curve with Mean = 17 Ounces

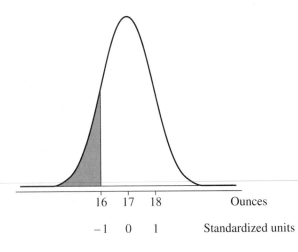

needed. Exhibit 9.3J displays the required area. From the normal distribution table, the required area is 0.1587, or about 16%.

What percent will be underfilled if the mean fill amount is 18.32 ounces? Here the standardized value is $(16 - 18.32)/1 = -2.32$. Again using the normal distribution table, the area is 0.0102; about 1% will be underfilled at this mean fill amount setting. Of course, cans that will hold more than 16 ounces of coffee must be used unless frequent spilling over is acceptable.

Suppose that the filling machine can be adjusted (or a better model purchased) so that the standard deviation of fill amount is reduced to 0.1 ounce. What percentage of cans then will be underfilled with a mean fill amount set at 16.3 ounces? In standardized units, 16 ounces corresponds to $(16 - 16.3)/0.1 = -3$, and the area below -3 on the standard normal curve is needed. This area is 0.0013; a little more than 1 in a thousand will be underfilled.

Thus, studying this process from a statistical point of view provides insights that translate into less waste, less cost, and fewer dissatisfied customers.

EXAMPLE   **9.3A**

A business that designs, manufactures, and sells women's coats needs information on the sizes of its customers. The heights of American women are normally distributed with mean 65 inches and standard deviation 2.5 inches. Assuming that the customers' heights follow a similar distribution, what fraction of the customers will be between 63 and 70 inches tall? Exhibit 9.3K shows the area required. In standardized terms, the area between $(63 - 65)/2.5 = -0.8$ and $(70 - 65)/2.5 = 2.0$ is needed. From the normal distribution table, the area below 2.0 is 0.9772 and that below -0.8 is 0.2119. The area required is thus $0.9772 - 0.2119 = 0.7653$; about 77% of the customers' heights will fall into the range from 63 inches to 70 inches.   ▪

EXHIBIT **9.3K**
Fraction of Women with Height
Between 63 and 70 Inches

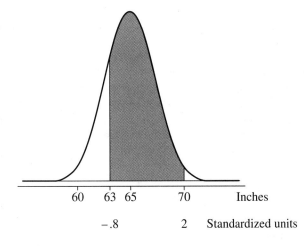

Statistical software has commands and procedures that allow the user to avoid referring to the normal distribution table.

Percentiles

percentile

The normal curve also must often be used "backward." That is, a fraction or area desired is given, and the z-value that produces that area must be found. A **percentile** is a number below which that percentage of a distribution's values lie. What is the 90th percentile of the standard normal distribution? Using a normal distribution table, we look through the body of the table to find an area as close as possible to 0.90. We find that 0.8997 corresponds to a z–value of 1.28, so the 90th percentile of the standard normal distribution is 1.28; 90 percent of the values lie below 1.28. Exhibit 9.3L displays the required area and z-value. If now the 90th percentile of a normal distribution with mean μ and standard deviation σ is needed, this is given by $\mu + 1.28\sigma$.

EXHIBIT **9.3L**
90th Percentile of the Standard Normal Curve

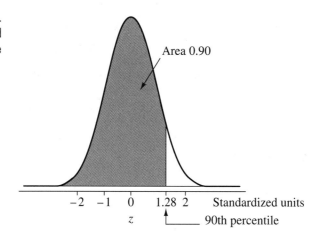

EXAMPLE **9.3B**

In the coffee-filling example, suppose that $\sigma = 0.1$ ounce and we want to set the mean fill adjustment so that in the long run only 1% of the cans are underfilled. Equivalently, we want 16 ounces to be the 1% point, or first percentile, of the distribution of fill amounts. We first find the point on a standard normal curve with 1% of the curve's area below it. From the normal distribution table, the closest value is -2.33. The 1% point of the fill amount distribution must satisfy

$$16 = \mu + (-2.33)0.1$$

Solving for μ, the required mean fill amount is

$$\mu = 16 - (-2.33)0.1 = 16.233 \text{ ounces}$$

Exhibit 9.3M displays these ideas graphically. ▪

E X H I B I T   **9.3M**
Finding the First Percentile of a
Normal Curve (mean μ,
standard deviation = 0.1)

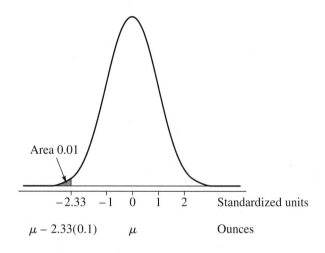

E X A M P L E   9.3C

In the distribution of women's heights in Example 9.3A, what height represents the 95th percentile of the distribution? Using the normal distribution table, we find areas of 0.9495 at $z = 1.64$ and 0.9505 at $z = 1.65$. In this case, a simple interpolation is easy, so we take 1.645 as the 95th percentile of the standard normal distribution. The 95th percentile of the original distribution of heights is then $65 + 1.645(2.5) = 69.1125$, which is rounded to 69.1 inches. ▪

Statistical software can usually find percentiles (for a variety of distributions).

S E C T I O N

9.4 Exercises

9.4A Find the following areas for the standard normal curve:
    a Below 1.00
    b Below 2.34
    c Above 0.5
    d Between 1.00 and 2.00
    e Below -1.00
    f Below -2.3

9.4B Find the following percentiles for a standard normal curve:
    a 50th
    b 99th
    c 97.5th
    d 84.13th

9.4C Find the following percentiles for a standard normal curve:
    a 1st
    b 5th
    c 25th
    d .1st

9.4D Consider a normal curve with $\mu = 100$ and $\sigma = 5$.
    a What is the z-score corresponding to $y = 107.5$?
    b What is the z-score corresponding to $y = 95$?
    c What is the standard unit corresponding to $y = 112$?

9.4E Consider a normal curve with $\mu = 23$ and $\sigma = 1.2$.
    a What is the y-value corresponding to a z-score of 2.1?
    b What is the y-value corresponding to a standard unit value of -1?

9.4F For a standard normal curve, what is the area
    a between 0 and 2?
    b between 1.1 and 3.23?
    c between -1 and 1?
    d between -2 and 1?
    e between -2.48 and -1.84?

9.4G Suppose that a distribution is normal with mean 10 and standard deviation 2. What is the area
    a between 11 and 13?
    b between 12 and 19?
    c above 11.2?
    d below 9.5?
    e between 9 and 10?
    f between 8.4 and 11.7?

9.4H For a normal distribution with mean 100 and standard deviation 16, what is
    a the 99th percentile?

    b   the 50th percentile (or median)?

    c   the 75th percentile (or third quartile)?

    d   the 25th percentile (or first quartile)?

9.4I   Recent experience indicates that monthly dollar sales of a certain nonseasonal product tend to follow a normal distribution with a mean of \$12,000 and standard deviation of \$1000. How would you react if sales next month turned out to be \$15,000? \$8000?

9.4J   A tire manufacturer claims that under normal driving conditions, the tread life of a certain tire follows a normal distribution with mean 50,000 miles and standard deviation 5000 miles.

    a   If *your* tires of this type wear out at 45,000 miles, would you consider this unusual?

    b   If the manufacturer sells 100,000 of these tires and warrants them to last *at least* 40,000 miles, about how many tires will wear out before their warranty expires?

SECTION

9.5 The Central Limit Effect

This section shows how means or totals of samples drawn from nonnormal distributions often are close to being normally distributed—the central limit effect. Because sampling is so important in statistical practice, the central limit effect provides a basis for many practical calculations.

Section 9.1 showed that the distribution of the means of samples of five consecutive process values looks normal even when the distribution of individual values is not normal. Exhibit 9.5A shows a similar result when the process selects values randomly from an asymmetric triangular distribution with most of its values on the low end. Here again, even though the distribution of individual process values is not normal, the distribution of the means of five consecutive process values resembles a normal distribution.

Both of these examples illustrate the **central limit effect for means**.

central limit effect for means

If $\bar{y}$ is the mean of n process values $y_1, y_2, \ldots, y_n$ drawn randomly from a distribution with mean μ and standard deviation σ, then the distribution of $\bar{y}$ is approximately a normal distribution with mean μ and standard deviation $\sigma/\sqrt{n}$. The larger the value of n, the better the approximation.

The practical meaning of this theoretical result is that the normal distribution allows predictions that are correct, within limits, for means of future process values from stable processes. This remarkable result was first established in a simpler setting by Abraham de Moivre in the early 1700s.[†] Note that the distribution of individual process values can have any shape. The standard deviation of the distribution of $\bar{y}$, namely, $\sigma/\sqrt{n}$, is usually called the *standard error of the mean*.

The accuracy of the approximating normal distribution depends in a complicated way on several factors. The following general statements can be made:

- The larger the sample size n, the better the approximation.

[†]A fascinating history of statistics before 1900 is given in Stephen M. Stigler, *The History of Statistics* (Cambridge, Mass.: Harvard University Press, 1986).

EXHIBIT 9.5A

Triangular Process and

Distribution of Mean of Five

Observations

```
Histogram of Triangle    N=5000
Each * represents 35 observations

Midpoint    Count
      -2     1722    ******************************************************************
      -1     1290    **************************************************
       0      983    ****************************************
       1      655    *******************
       2      350    **********


Histogram of Ybar    N=1000
Each * represents 5 observations

Midpoint    Count
  -2.000       4    *
  -1.800      16    ****
  -1.600      34    *******
  -1.400      72    ****************
  -1.200     111    **************************
  -1.000     120    ************************
  -0.800     144    *****************************
  -0.600     151    *******************************
  -0.400     111    ***********************
  -0.200      82    *****************
   0.000      67    **************
   0.200      43    *********
   0.400      16    ****
   0.600      19    ****
   0.800       4    *
   1.000       5    *
   1.200       0
   1.400       1    *
```

	N	Mean	Median	StDev
Triangle	5000	-0.6758	-1.0000	1.2610
Ybar	1000	-0.6758	-0.8000	0.5547

- The closer the distribution of the individual process values to a normal distribution, the better the approximation.

- The approximation is always better when applied to the middle portion of the distribution of $\bar{y}$ than to areas in the extremes.

In practice, we will operate as if $\bar{y}$ had a normal distribution with mean μ and standard deviation $\sigma/\sqrt{n}$, where n is the number of data points averaged and μ and σ are the mean and standard deviation of the distribution of individual process values. Notice how the standard deviation of $\bar{y}$, $\sigma/\sqrt{n}$, decreases as n increases but only at the rate of the square root of n. Notice also that the standard deviation of $\bar{y}$ is directly proportional to σ, the standard deviation of the process values.

Returning to Exhibit 9.1D, we can now see why certain descriptive statistics came out the way they did in our simulation. For the simple uniform process used there, it can be shown that the distribution of individual process values has $\mu = 0$ and $\sigma = \sqrt{10} \simeq 3.16$. Our simulated process of 5000 values had a mean of -0.0214 and standard deviation of 3.1756. For our simulated distribution of $\bar{y}$ we obtained a standard deviation of 1.4760, which agrees quite well with the value predicted by theory, $\sigma/\sqrt{n} = \sqrt{10}/\sqrt{5} = \sqrt{2} \simeq 1.41$.

Exhibit 9.5B gives a further example of the central limit effect. Here $n = 20$ data points from the triangular process distribution in Exhibit 9.5A have been averaged and the sampling has been repeated until 1000 such averages were obtained. The histogram of these 1000 means in Exhibit 9.5B strongly resembles a normal distribution. In addition, it may be shown that $\sigma \simeq 1.25$, so statistical theory predicts that the standard deviation of $\bar{y}$ should be $\sigma/\sqrt{n} \simeq 1.25/\sqrt{20} \simeq 0.28$. The descriptive statistics in Exhibit 9.5B show a standard deviation of 0.28016 for the 1000 means obtained.

E X H I B I T 9.5B
Distribution of $\bar{y}$ with $n = 20$ from the Triangular Process Distribution

```
Histogram of Ybar        N=1000
Each * represents 10 observations

Midpoint    Count
  -1.4         4    *
  -1.2        33    ****
  -1.0       121    *************
  -0.8       247    *************************
  -0.6       279    ****************************
  -0.4       188    *******************
  -0.2        92    **********
   0.0        28    ***
   0.2         6    *
   0.4         2    *


               N      Mean    Median    StDev
Ybar        1000  -0.64995  -0.65000  0.28016
```

Many practical applications of the central limit effect are given throughout the remainder of the book. Here are two examples.

E X A M P L E   9.5A

Return to the manufacturing of microwave ovens introduced in Section 2.8. The Left dimension of the waveguide positioning process has a historical mean of $\mu = 56.5$ and a standard deviation of $\sigma = 13.5$. If four ovens are to be sampled at random at 3:00 P.M. and if the process is operating as it has historically, what can we expect of the average of the four Left measurements? For example, what fraction of such averages are below 70? The standard error of the mean in this case is $\sigma/\sqrt{n} = 13.5/2 = 6.75$ and the corresponding z-value is $(70 - 56.5)/6.75 = 2.00$. From the normal distribution table in Exhibit 9.3G, we obtain an area below 2.00 of 0.9772, or about 98% of the averages are below 70. What fraction of such averages are above 50? Here the z-value is $(50 - 56.5)/6.75 = -0.96$ to the nearest hundredth. Using the symmetry of the normal curve, the area above -0.96 is the same as the area below $+0.96$, which, from the normal distribution table, is 0.8315. Thus about 83% of the averages of four Left measurements will exceed 50.   ∎

EXAMPLE   9.5B

As a second example, consider again the Winegard manufacturing process for producing a punched satellite-dish antenna part, first seen in Section 3.6. After the die change, the process appeared to be capable of producing parts well within the specifications the designers had agreed were acceptable for the part to function properly. The data set of 50 given in Exhibit 3.6G has a mean of 1.7785 and a standard deviation of 0.0009. This sample of 50 comes from a process that will produce many parts over a typical day, week, month, or longer period. For illustration, suppose that the values for the continuing process are $\mu = 1.78$ inches and $\sigma = 0.001$ inches. These values are quite consistent with the calculated values for the 50 observations. Now suppose that we consider sampling the process at 11:00 A.M. one day and measuring the required width on five of the parts chosen at random. We then average the five observations to produce $\bar{y}$. What should we expect concerning the "behavior" of $\bar{y}$ in this case? For example, what fraction of such means exceed 1.785 inches? The standard error of the mean for $n = 5$ is $\sigma/\sqrt{n} = 0.001/\sqrt{5} = 0.000447$. The z-value corresponding to 1.785 is then $(1.785 - 1.78)/0.000447 = 11.2$ to the nearest tenth. The number 1.785 is 11.2 standard deviations above the mean of $\mu = 1.78$ inches in the distribution of $\bar{y}$. This of course is out of the range of the normal distribution table, and such an occurrence is extremely unlikely: If the process continues to operate as it has historically, we can say that about 99.7% of the means of five of these dimensions are within $\mu \pm 3\sigma/\sqrt{n}$—that is, within

$$1.78 \pm (3 \times 0.000447) = 1.78 \pm 0.00134 = (1.779, 1.781)$$ ∎

The Central Limit Effect for Totals

Sometimes we are interested in totals rather than averages. For example, if account errors have a distribution with mean $25 and standard deviation $5, what can we say about the distribution of the total error for 20 accounts selected at random? We already know that the distribution of the average $\bar{y}$ is approximately normal with mean $\mu = \$25$ and standard deviation $\sigma/\sqrt{n} = \$5/\sqrt{20}$. But the total in the 20 accounts is just the multiple $20 \times \bar{y}$. Multiplying by 20 does not change the shape of the distribution, only its mean and standard deviation. Thus, the central limit effect also applies to totals. In particular, the mean of the total $n\bar{y}$ is $n\mu$ and the standard deviation is $n\sigma/\sqrt{n} = \sqrt{n}\sigma$.

central limit effect for totals

If $n\bar{y}$ is the total of n random values from a distribution with mean μ and standard deviation σ, then the distribution of the total $n\bar{y}$ is approximately a normal distribution with mean $n\mu$ and standard deviation $\sqrt{n}\sigma$.

E X A M P L E   **9.5C**   If samples of 20 accounts are randomly selected from a distribution of errors that has mean $25 and standard deviation $5, what can be said about the distribution of the total error in the samples of 20 accounts? It is approximately normal with mean $20 \times \$25 = \$500$ and standard deviation $\sqrt{20} \times \$5 = 4.472 \times \$5 = \$22.36$. Thus, the fraction of total errors exceeding $550 is approximately the area above the z-value $(550 - 500)/22.36 = 2.24$ or below -2.24, which is 0.0125, or about 1.25%. ∎

E X A M P L E   **9.5D**   A market study has suggested that shoppers at a particular large department store spend an average of $36 per shopping trip. The variability in the distribution of purchase amounts is measured by the standard deviation, $12. If during a particular morning 42 shoppers will make purchases at the store, what is the total purchase value expected for these shoppers? The central limit effect applied to totals says that total purchases will follow a normal distribution (approximately) with mean $42 \times \$36 = \$1512$ and standard deviation $\sqrt{42} \times \$12 = \$77.77$, which rounds to $78. About 95% of the time, the total purchase amount for 42 such customers falls in the range from $\$1512 - (2 \times \$78) = \$1356$ to $\$1512 + (2 \times \$78) = \$1668$. The fraction of such purchase totals below $1300 is approximately the area below $(1300 - 1512)/78 = -2.72$ in the standard normal curve. This fraction is 0.0033, or about 0.3% ∎

The most common mistake in calculations relating to the central limit effect is to use the wrong standard deviation for a mean or total. If the process mean and standard deviation are denoted as μ and σ and the mean or total is based on n observations, then keep in mind that for *means*

$$\mu_{\bar{y}} = \mu \quad \text{and} \quad \sigma_{\bar{y}} = \frac{\sigma}{\sqrt{n}}$$

But for *totals*,

$$\mu_{n\bar{y}} = n\mu \quad \text{and} \quad \sigma_{n\bar{y}} = \sqrt{n}\sigma$$

S E C T I O N

9.6 Exercises

9.6A   Suppose that in the long run, individual amounts spent at a grocery store have a distribution with mean $55 and standard deviation $5. If samples of nine amounts spent are randomly selected, what is the approximate distribution of the means of nine values? What fraction of the means of nine values exceed $60? What is the approximate distribution of the total of the nine amounts?

9.6B   A small airplane has 30 seats. Historically, the distribution of weights of individual passengers with their baggage has a mean of 175 pounds and a standard deviation of 25 pounds. On flights when the plane is full, what can be said about the distribution of total weight of the 30 passengers plus baggage? Discuss the implications with regard to safe carrying capacity of the plane.

9.6C   Historically, the number of days until a certain distributor pays its bills to a certain manufacturer has a distribution with mean 28.1 days and standard deviation 5.2 days. If samples of five paid bills are to be randomly selected, what fraction of the means of days until payment are less than 21 days?

9.6D   A tire manufacturer claims that under normal driving conditions, the tread life of a certain type of tire follows a normal distribution with mean 50,000 miles and standard deviation 5000 miles. A small company purchases 36 of these tires for a fleet of vehicles and carefully keeps track of the tire wear. After all the tires have worn out, the company calculates that the mean tire lifetime was only 45,000 miles. If the tire-manufacturing process is stable, what fraction of sets of 36 tires will produce a mean of 45,000 miles or less wear? On the basis of this calculation, what would you recommend to the company?

SECTION

9.7 Checking for Normality

Since the normal distribution is so useful in statistics, it is often important to find out whether a given set of data is normally distributed. This section explains several tools for making this determination. You will see uses for these tools in later chapters.

A first step in determining whether a distribution is normal is to look for obvious nonnormality in a dotplot or histogram of the data. Look for skewness and asymmetry. Look for gaps in the distribution—intervals with no observations. However, these visual checks do not always reveal observations that are extreme relative to what is expected from a normal distribution. Such extreme values are easier to spot if the data are first converted to standard units. The standardized value of the ith data point, y_i, is just the z-value based on the mean and standard deviation of the data. That is,

$$\frac{y_i - \bar{y}}{s}$$

With a computer package, the standardized data can be quickly obtained and their histogram plotted. Exhibit 9.7A gives the histogram of standardized values for the percent change in the Buffalo, New York, flour price index. Since we are now checking to see if a *standard* normal distribution fits the data, it is easier to relate to the scale of the numbers. For example, we know that values outside of ± 3 are quite unusual and about 95% of the values should lie within $(-2, +2)$. With 99 data points, we would expect about $0.05 \times 99 = 4.95$, or five, of the standardized points to be outside of ± 2, that is, farther than 2 standard deviations from the mean. This agrees quite well with the histogram shown in Exhibit 9.7A.

Exhibit 9.7B gives the histogram of the 1000 standardized $\bar{y}$-values with $n = 20$ from the triangular process. Again, normality is substantiated to a large degree.

E X H I B I T **9.7A**
Histogram of Standardized
Percent Changes in Flour Price
Index

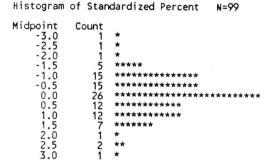

```
Histogram of Standardized Percent    N=99

Midpoint    Count
  -3.0        1    *
  -2.5        1    *
  -2.0        1    *
  -1.5        5    *****
  -1.0       15    ***************
  -0.5       15    ***************
   0.0       26    **************************
   0.5       12    ************
   1.0       12    ************
   1.5        7    *******
   2.0        1    *
   2.5        2    **
   3.0        1    *
```

E X H I B I T **9.7B**
Distribution of Standardized
Values of $\bar{y}$ with $n = 20$
from Triangular Process

```
Histogram of Standard    N=1000
Each * represents 5 observations

Midpoint    Count
  -2.5        8    **
  -2.0       29    ******
  -1.5       46    **********
  -1.0      136    ****************************
  -0.5      186    **************************************
   0.0      208    ******************************************
   0.5      181    ************************************
   1.0      120    ************************
   1.5       35    *******
   2.0       34    *******
   2.5       11    ***
   3.0        4    *
   3.5        2    *
```

Normal Counts

Another way to check for normality is to count the number of observations within 1, 2, and 3 standard deviations of the mean and compare the results with what is expected for a normal distribution. Once the observations are ordered from smallest to largest, these counts are easy to obtain. A computer package can do all the hard work.

For the percent change in flour price index, 70.7% are found to be within 1 standard deviation of the mean compared to 68.26% for a true normal distribution. Further counting shows that 93.9% lie within 2 standard deviations of the mean. This compares well with the normal value of 95.45%. Finally, *all* the data are within 3 standard deviations of the mean, while the figure is 99.73% for a normal distribution—again, good agreement.

The accompanying table gives the percentages of observations falling within 1, 2, and 3 standard deviations for the simulated data sets used in Exhibits 9.1C, 9.5A, and 9.5B. All these distributions agree well with the normal distribution.

Percent Within Interval	Data Set			Compare to Normal
	Uniform $n = 5$	Triangular $n = 5$	Triangular $n = 20$	
$\bar{y} \pm 1s$	68.7%	71.9%	67.6%	68.26%
$\bar{y} \pm 2s$	94.8%	95.1%	96.3%	95.45%
$\bar{y} \pm 3s$	100.0%	99.4%	99.6%	99.73%

Normal Scores

normal scores

For n random observations, it is mathematically possible to establish what the "ideal" values would be if they came from a standard normal distribution. Such numbers are called **normal scores**. There are minor differences in how various software packages define normal scores, but the basic idea is illustrated in Exhibit 9.7C for a sample size of five. In general, the normal scores for a sample of size n are n numbers along the horizontal axis that divide the total area under the standard normal curve into $n + 1$ equal areas. Thus for $n = 5$ the normal scores may be described as the standard normal percentiles corresponding to the fractions $\frac{1}{6}, \frac{2}{6}, \frac{3}{6}, \frac{4}{6},$ and $\frac{5}{6}$, or $-0.97, -0.43, 0, +0.43,$ and $+0.97$. Note that although the areas defined by the normal scores are equal, the scores themselves are not equally spaced. In fact, the normal scores are spread out like an ideal normal sample. Exhibit 9.7D gives a similar display for $n = 10$. The normal scores here are $-1.34, -0.91, -0.60, -0.35, -0.11, +0.11, +0.35, +0.60, +0.91,$ and $+1.34$.

EXHIBIT **9.7C**
Normal Scores for $n = 5$

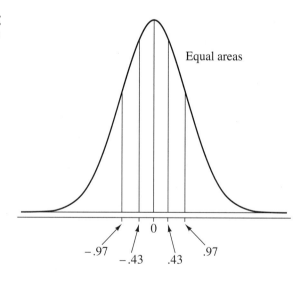

Equal areas

$-.97$ $-.43$ 0 $.43$ $.97$

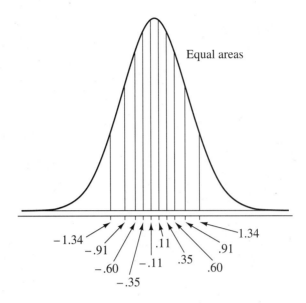

Equal areas

-1.34
$-.91$
$-.60$
$-.35$
$-.11$
$.11$
$.35$
$.60$
$.91$
1.34

Normal Probability Plots

Once you have normal scores, you can plot them with the observed values to tell whether the observed data is normally distributed. Such a plot is called a **normal probability plot**.

normal probability plot

To illustrate this, imagine standardizing the observed data and then associating pairs of values, the smallest normal score with the smallest observation, the next smallest normal score with the next smallest observation, and so on. If the observed data came from a normal distribution, the members of the pairs should be about equal. Plotting such pairs should give an approximately 45° straight line passing through the origin.

As we saw in the subsection on standardized units in Section 9.3, any normal variable is linearly related to a standardized normal variable through the equation $y = \mu + z\sigma$. Therefore, if the observations come from any normal distribution, plotting them against normal scores will give some straight line. If the sample comes from a nonnormal distribution, on the other hand, the plot will curve. The straighter the plot, the better the data fit a normal distribution.

For most of us, it is much easier to check whether such a plot follows a straight line than it is to see if a histogram matches a normal curve. To make a normal probability plot, put the normal scores on the vertical axis and the corresponding data values on the horizontal axis.

The normal probability plot of percentage changes in the Buffalo flour price index in Exhibit 9.7E gives a strong indication of normality. Exhibits 9.7F and 9.7G give similar output for the $\bar{y}$ distributions for samples of size five from uniform and triangular processes, respectively. These should be compared to the histograms in

EXHIBIT **9.7E**
Normal Probability Plot for
Percent Change in Flour Price
Index

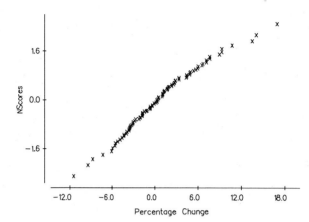

EXHIBIT **9.7F**
Normal Scores Plot for $\bar{y}$
Distribution from Uniform
Process

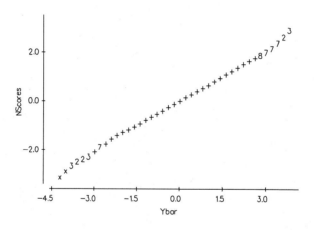

EXHIBIT **9.7G**
Normal Scores Plot for $\bar{y}$
Distribution with $n = 5$ from
Triangular Process

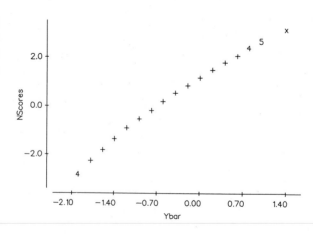

Exhibits 9.1C and 9.5A. In both cases, the assumption of a normal distribution seems warranted.

Not all distributions are normal. Exhibit 9.7H displays the normal probability plot for the city-size data in Exhibit 4.2H. Their distribution was displayed in Exhibit 4.2I. The normal probability plot in Exhibit 9.7H shows considerable curvature so normality is not supported. Operating as if this distribution were normal would mislead the decision maker.

E X H I B I T **9.7H**
Normal Scores Plot for the
City-Size Distribution—A
Nonnormal Distribution

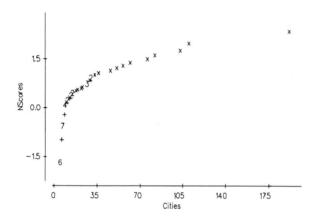

The histogram in Exhibit 9.7I is basically symmetric. However, the extreme values are somewhat far away from the rest of the data. This can be seen somewhat more easily in the histogram of standardized values given in Exhibit 9.7J The departure is more graphically shown in the normal scores plot in Exhibit 9.7K, which shows a distinctive S shape since both extremes are farther from the middle than in a normal distribution. Distributions like this are said to be *heavy tailed* compared to a normal distribution.

E X H I B I T **9.7I**
Histogram of Some Symmetric
but Nonnormal Data

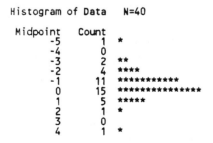

```
Histogram of Data    N=40

Midpoint    Count
       -5        1    *
       -4        0
       -3        2    **
       -2        4    ****
       -1       11    ***********
        0       15    ***************
        1        5    *****
        2        1    *
        3        0
        4        1    *
```

EXHIBIT **9.7J**
Histogram of Standardized Data
from Exhibit 9.7I

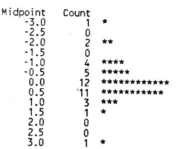

```
Histogram of Standardized Data    N=40
Midpoint    Count
   -3.0        1    *
   -2.5        0
   -2.0        2    **
   -1.5        0
   -1.0        4    ****
   -0.5        5    *****
    0.0       12    ************
    0.5       11    ***********
    1.0        3    ***
    1.5        1    *
    2.0        0
    2.5        0
    3.0        1    *
```

EXHIBIT **9.7K**
Normal Scores Plot for the Data
in Exhibit 9.7I—Another
Nonnormal Distribution

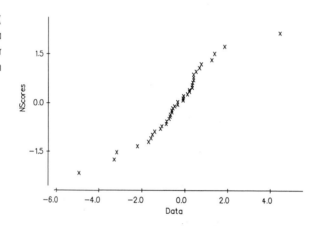

SECTION

9.8 Exercises

9.8A   Use the Exam 1 scores in Exercise 4.3F. Count the number of observations within each of the intervals: mean ± 1 standard deviation, mean ± 2 standard deviations, and mean ± 3 standard deviations. Compare your results to those expected with a normal distribution. (Filename: EXAMS1.DAT.)

9.8B   Use the percentage change in the Buffalo, New York, flour price data of Exhibit 2.10A. Count the number of observations within the interval mean ± 1 standard deviation. Compare your results to those expected with a normal distribution. (Filename: BUFLOUR.DAT.)

9.8C   Use the percentage change in the Kansas City flour price data of Exercise 2.11A. Count the number of observations within each of the intervals: mean ± 1 standard deviation, mean ± 2 standard deviations, and mean ± 3 standard deviations. Compare your results to those expected with a normal distribution. (Filename: KCFLOUR.DAT.)

9.8D   Use the normal distribution table in Exhibit 9.3G to find the normal scores for a sample of size $n = 4$. Use these scores to produce a plot similar to Exhibit 9.7C.

9.8E   Compute and plot a normal scores plot for the Exam 1 scores in Exercise 4.3F. Is this distribution a normal distribution? (Filename: EXAMS1.DAT.)

9.8F   Use the percentage change in the Kansas City flour price data of Exercise 2.11A. Display a normal scores plot for these data. Does normality seem appropriate? (Filename: KCFLOUR.DAT.)

9.8G   Compute and plot separate normal scores plots for the overall weekday Los Angeles traffic volume and for the minor arterial traffic volume whose histograms were displayed in Exhibits 4.10A and 4.10I, respectively. Which distribution seems better modeled as a normal distribution? Is your conclusion consistent with the histograms displayed earlier? The data are listed in Appendix 4 and are available in data file TRAFFIC.DAT.

Chapter Summary

A normal curve results from graphing $f(y) = \frac{1}{\sqrt{2\pi}\sigma} e^{-\frac{1}{2}\left[\frac{y-\mu}{\sigma}\right]^2}$ as a function of y for given values of μ and σ. This is a mathematical model for a distribution of data whose histogram has a shape resembling a bell or mound. The parameters μ and σ are the mean and standard deviation of the distribution, respectively. When $\mu = 0$ and $\sigma = 1$, the curve is called the standard normal curve.

Areas under a normal curve are interpreted as percentages of the distribution values in a given interval. About 68% of the distribution values lie in the interval $[\mu - \sigma, \mu + \sigma]$, about 95% in the interval $[\mu - 2\sigma, \mu + 2\sigma]$, and about 99.7% in the interval $[\mu - 3\sigma, \mu + 3\sigma]$.

A standardized unit, or z-value, is calculated with the formula $z = (y - \mu)/\sigma$. Standardized units are needed to use a table, to find areas under a normal curve, and to find percentiles of the distribution.

A normal distribution arises from averaging or summing items that are sampled randomly from a population or taken from a random process. This is called the central limit effect. If the population or process mean and standard deviation are denoted by μ and σ, respectively, and the sample mean or total is based on n items, the long-run theoretical mean and standard deviation of the sample mean are μ and $\sigma/\sqrt{n}$, respectively, and the long-run theoretical mean and standard deviation of the sample total are $n\mu$ and $\sqrt{n}\sigma$, respectively. The quantity $\sigma/\sqrt{n}$ is called the standard error of the sample mean.

Data can be checked for the tendency to follow a normal curve in a variety of ways. One is to inspect the histogram of the standardized observations, $(y_i - \bar{y})/s$, for a mound shape. Another is to compute the percentage of the standardized values that fall in the intervals $(-1, 1)$, $(-2, 2)$, and $(-3, 3)$, then to compare these percentages with the normal ones of 68%, 95%, and 99.7%. The most useful way is to prepare a normal probability plot. To do this, first compute the normal scores of the data—that is, the "ideal" values they would have if they were exactly normally distributed. The next step is to scatterplot the normal scores versus the corresponding data values. Finally, assess the degree to which the plot conforms to a straight line. Substantial deviation from a straight line signals that the data did not come from a normal distribution.

Supplementary Exercises for Chapter 9

9A The time necessary to complete a certain assembly-line task varies according to many factors: fatigue or freshness, worker skill, whether the required parts are available promptly, and so forth. Suppose that this variation may be adequately modeled using a normal distribution with mean 15 minutes and standard deviation 2 minutes.

    a Find the fraction of assembly times that are below 13 minutes.

    b Find the fraction of assembly times that are above 16 minutes.

    c Find the fraction of assembly times that are between 13 and 16 minutes.

    d What is the 95th percentile of the assembly-time distribution? Interpret its meaning in this context.

9B From past experience, a firm's marketing manager believes that a normal distribution with mean \$100,000 and standard deviation \$10,000 adequately describes the possible quarterly sales for a computer software product.

    a How likely are sales to be above \$115,000?

    b What fraction of sales will be between \$80,000 and \$120,000?

    c Would sales of \$135,000 be exceptional?

    d What level of sales represents the 95th percentile of the sales distribution?

9C Hawkeye Supply Company has randomly selected 100 steel bolts from a large shipment. Suppose that the bolt lengths in the shipment may be described by a normal distribution with mean 3 inches and standard deviation 0.1 inch.

    a What fraction of the 100 bolts would be expected to have lengths of between 2.7 and 3.3 inches?

    b What fraction of the 100 bolts would be expected to have lengths of between 2.9 and 3.1 inches?

    c Consider the average bolt length $\bar{y}$ for the sample of 100. If the sampling procedure were repeated many times, what fraction of the averages would be between 2.9 and 3.1 inches? Between 2.98 and 3.02?

9D A truck carries 40 standard-sized containers. The weight of the containers varies according to many factors but may be described by a distribution with mean 210 pounds and standard deviation 25 pounds. Over many loads, what fraction of loads will exceed the legal load limit of 10,000 pounds?

9E In Exercise 9.2C, the distribution of s from a normal process distribution was considered for $n = 5$ and $n = 30$. Display the normal scores plot for each of these distributions and comment on their shapes.

9F In Exercise 9.2E, the distribution of the maximum for $n = 5$ and $n = 30$ was investigated. Produce normal scores plots for these distributions and comment on their shapes.

9G Consider a standard normal distribution. Using the normal distribution table in Exhibit 9.3G,

    a What are the first and third quartiles?

    b What is the interquartile range?

    c For a general normal distribution, what is the relation between the interquartile range and the standard deviation?

· · · · · ■ ■ ■ ■ ■ ·

Glossary for Chapter 9

central limit effect	The distribution of a mean or total is approximately normal under many circumstances.
normal curve	The mathematical curve that describes the normal distribution.
normal distribution table	A table of areas under the standard normal curve.
normal probability plot	A plot of normal scores versus values used to support normality of a distribution and to detect lack of normality.
normal scores	A set of "ideal" values from a normal distribution.
percentile	A number below which a specified percent of a distribution's values lie.
standard normal curve	A normal curve with mean 0 and standard deviation 1.
standardized units	See z-values.
z-values (z-scores)	Standardized values or units: z-value $= (y - $ mean of $y)/$(standard deviation of y).

Control Charts for Continuous Variables

Chapter Objectives

After mastering this chapter, you will be able to:

- Define statistical control

- Construct mean and standard deviation control charts

- Define common and special causes of variation

- Use control charts for process analysis and for process control

SECTION

10.1 Introduction

In 1924, managers at a Chicago plant of Western Electric, then the manufacturing arm of the Bell Telephone System, had a production problem they could not solve: harmful variation in a product. They called on their research division, the Bell Telephone Laboratories in New Jersey, for help. There Dr. Walter A. Shewhart developed the ideas of statistical process control—statistical methods used to detect changes in processes. This chapter introduces these methods. Shewhart's ideas were later outlined in a book.[†] Unfortunately for the United States though, his approach was not widely adopted here but was exported to Japan after World War II and is credited with starting the quality revolution there.

Quality cannot be *inspected* into a product or service after it is made or provided, since this only differentiates between the good and the bad *after the fact*. This is very expensive as well as unreliable. Once a defective good or service is produced, the cost of correcting it may be more than 65% of the item's original cost. Resources are used more effectively if each of the critical processes involved in producing the good or service is individually monitored. If observations on any one production step deviate

[†]Walter A. Shewhart, *Economic Control of Quality of Manufactured Product* (Princeton, N.J.: Van Nostrand, 1931).

too much from what is expected under usual circumstances, production should be stopped and the problem should be found and fixed.

This chapter explains the usefulness of statistical control of processes. It explains two common ways of monitoring whether a process is in control: control charts of variation in means and standard deviations. It shows how those charts can be used to analyze both ongoing processes and new ones for which no base data exist. Finally it examines the use of control charts in several short case studies.

SECTION

10.2   What Is Statistical Control?

This section defines statistical control of processes. It introduces control charts, the most important tool used to monitor processes. It also explains the two kinds of causes of variation in processes and why it is important to distinguish between them.

Processes were introduced in Chapter 2. There we saw that process results vary in spite of the best efforts to produce the same thing every time. For example, in the assembly-line process for microwave ovens described in Section 2.8, ideally every oven assembled would be of the highest quality. In the real world, variation is inevitable. However, if the many processes involved in manufacturing can be "controlled" so that the values of various dimensions are within *acceptable limits*, reliable, high-quality products that meet customers' needs can be produced.

In 1944, W. Edwards Deming wrote

> There is no such thing as constancy in real life. There is, however, such a thing as a constant-cause system. The results produced by a constant-cause system vary, and in fact may vary over a wide band or a narrow band. They vary, but they exhibit an important feature called stability. Why apply the terms constant and stability to a cause system that produces results that vary? Because the same percentage of these varying results continues to fall between any given pair of limits hour after hour, day after day, so long as the constant-cause system continues to operate. It is the distribution of results that is constant or stable. When a manufacturing process behaves like a constant-cause system, producing inspection results that exhibit stability, it is said to be in statistical control. The control chart will tell you whether your process is in statistical control.[†]

statistical control

In other words, a process is in **statistical control** when its results fall within predictable limits.

control charts

Deming also mentions **control charts**. These plots of variation are key tools in analyzing processes. With control charts, past behavior of processes is analyzed and current and future behavior is monitored. Special problems and trends that lead to poor quality are detected. Control charts also show what a process is capable of and when a potential improvement in a process has been successful.

[†]W. Edwards Deming, "Some Principles of the Shewhart Methods of Quality Control," *Mechanical Engineering* 66 (1944), 173–177.

Common and Special Causes of Variation

Control charts make it possible to differentiate between two kinds of reasons why process results vary. In a constant-cause system, the variations in a measured variable are considered to be due to chance and to remain in the system unless the process itself is altered. Such causes are referred to as **common causes** or **(chance causes)**. The variation observed is considered to be the effect of the combination of many, individually small, unobserved influences. Shewhart likened this to the many forces that cause a coin to come up heads when tossed.

common causes
(chance causes)

Processes are also subject to the influence of **special** or **assignable causes**. Special causes are individually important and affect results only some of the time. They arise because of special circumstances. In a manufacturing setting, the introduction of a low-quality batch of raw materials into an otherwise stable process would be a special cause of variation. In the monitoring of overtime hours in a municipal police department, the fourth of July holiday would be a special (but easily predictable) cause of variation. In general, typical examples of special causes of variation include

special causes
(assignable causes)

- Differences among machines
- Differences among raw materials
- Differences among environmental variables such as temperature or humidity
- Differences among shifts
- Differences in worker training
- Differences among methods

A process is considered to be in control if only common causes are operating and no special causes are influencing the variability of process results. When a process is brought into control, process improvement is much easier because the normal operation of the process is not confused with special causes of variation.

Because of their underlying differences, dealing with two kinds of causes requires different techniques. Overreacting to common-cause variation usually leads to "tampering" with a process that may already be in control. This in turn leads to *increased* variation in the process results. On the other hand, failing to detect and deal with a special cause of variation means a lost opportunity to eliminate variation in the process or at least to understand and cope with the variation in the process.

SECTION

10.3 Mean Charts for Process Control

This section introduces the idea of taking regular samples to measure process control. It discusses one use of information from such sampling—examining the means of the samples to detect changes.

Special causes that affect the mean of a process can be detected by analyzing a **mean chart**, a statistical process control chart designed to detect changes in the mean of a process.

mean chart

To study the variation of process results over time, sequence plots of process data are needed. To assess both the mean level and the variability of the process over time, a group of data values taken reasonably closely in time is required. For instance, to control the thickness of processed meat products, such as bologna, it is common practice to cut and measure the thickness of five slices from one "log" of meat each hour. In some processes it is possible to measure the variable of interest on a sample of n items at regular times. Each of these samples is called a **subgroup**.[†] A subgroup may be selected all at one time from the product produced in an hour, shift, day, week, or other period. Or members of the subgroup may be taken at intervals spread out over the period.

subgroup

Making a Mean Chart

$\bar{y}_i$

In studying subgroups, $\bar{y}_i$ denotes the mean of the ith subgroup and k subgroups are assumed to be available. From the central limit effect explained in Chapter 9, we know that the distribution of $\bar{y}_i$ will be approximately normal when enough measurements from a stable process are averaged, even if the underlying variable is not exactly normally distributed. From Chapter 9, we also know that an n as small as five may lead to a workable approximation. If a constant-cause system is in effect, we know what to expect of $\bar{y}_i$, and unusual behavior of $\bar{y}_i$ should lead us to question whether a constant-cause system is really operating. A graphic display of the sequence plot of $\bar{y}_i$'s for $i = 1, 2, 3, \ldots, k$ helps point out unusual values.

s_i

We begin with the data in Exhibit 10.3A. Twenty-five samples of five measurements each are given in the shaded rows. The means, $\bar{y}_i$, and standard deviations, s_i, of each sample are also shown. Here $n = 5$ and $k = 25$. (The data and statistics in rows 26 through 30 are for later use.)

Control charts for means begin with a sequence plot of the means, as shown in Exhibit 10.3B. Variation in process results is expected. However, some guidance is needed concerning the amount of variability to be expected "under stable circumstances"—that is, when the process is in control. Exhibit 10.3C shows the same sequence plot of the means but with a horizontal line drawn in at the grand mean

$$\bar{\bar{y}} = \frac{1}{k}(\bar{y}_1 + \bar{y}_2 + \cdots + \bar{y}_k)$$ **(10.1)**

$\bar{\bar{y}}$

Note that is $\bar{\bar{y}}$ just the mean of *all* the $n \times k$ data points in all the subgroups put together. For the first 25 rows of data in Exhibit 10.3A, $\bar{\bar{y}} = 100.12$. If the process is in control, the sequence plot of $\bar{y}_i$ varies about that line.

How far might the $\bar{y}_i$'s vary and the process still be considered in control? We know that most of the values in a normal distribution lie in the interval with endpoints at the mean ± 3 standard deviations. In fact, for a true normal distribution, 99.7% of the data points lie in this range. When a process is in control, the averages

[†]The statistical quality control literature addresses the question of selecting rational subgroups to a much greater extent than in this brief introduction. One good reference is J. M. Juran and F. M. Gryna, eds., *Juran's Quality Control Handbook*, 4th ed. (New York: McGraw-Hill/ASQC Quality Press, 1988).

EXHIBIT **10.3A**
Control Chart Data: $n = 5$

Sample Number	Samples					Means	Standard Deviations
	1	2	3	4	5		
1	101.5	98.5	97.0	102.3	99.4	99.74	2.17
2	101.1	100.2	100.4	97.0	101.8	100.10	1.84
3	98.8	99.9	98.2	101.4	99.1	99.48	1.24
4	100.4	99.8	99.4	99.1	97.3	99.20	1.17
5	99.2	101.7	101.6	100.0	100.5	100.60	1.07
6	96.8	101.9	98.0	102.3	100.0	99.80	2.39
7	102.9	98.1	102.3	100.1	99.9	100.66	1.95
8	97.5	100.1	101.9	95.5	101.1	99.22	2.66
9	98.3	98.4	96.3	98.8	100.2	98.40	1.40
10	98.5	97.0	100.6	103.2	102.7	100.40	2.66
11	100.8	98.2	101.3	102.1	101.3	100.74	1.49
12	103.2	101.0	97.6	100.1	100.8	100.54	2.01
13	99.5	100.1	101.2	100.2	99.6	100.12	0.68
14	100.2	94.9	99.4	103.7	103.0	100.24	3.49
15	97.3	101.8	99.2	101.0	100.7	100.00	1.78
16	100.9	99.6	102.9	100.8	99.4	100.72	1.40
17	99.8	97.9	100.7	100.3	99.3	99.60	1.09
18	99.9	99.3	100.6	101.1	103.3	100.84	1.54
19	96.1	101.1	104.1	97.4	102.1	100.16	3.33
20	98.3	99.2	100.7	98.2	100.9	99.46	1.29
21	98.4	104.7	100.0	98.2	99.2	100.10	2.67
22	101.9	97.8	98.1	103.4	99.0	100.04	2.48
23	101.7	96.8	100.9	100.8	101.8	100.40	2.06
24	101.8	102.9	102.9	98.8	101.5	101.58	1.68
25	102.3	100.9	100.1	99.4	101.1	100.76	1.09
26	97.0	97.9	96.5	100.8	102.9	99.02	2.73
27	99.3	100.9	101.3	99.4	98.5	99.88	1.18
28	98.5	101.4	99.1	98.8	103.0	100.16	1.96
29	101.7	102.4	99.5	102.2	101.4	101.44	1.15
30	101.1	98.1	104.1	99.8	100.4	100.70	2.20

EXHIBIT **10.3B**
Sequence Plot of Means

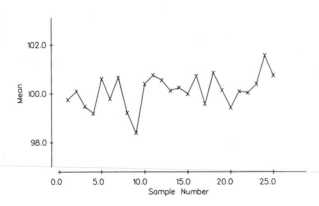

E X H I B I T **10.3C**

Sequence Plot of Means with
Grand Mean Displayed

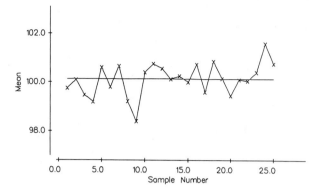

are approximately normally distributed with $\mu_{\bar{y}} = \mu$ and standard deviation $\sigma_{\bar{y}} = \sigma/\sqrt{n}$—that is, the $\bar{y}_i$'s should for the most part remain within the three-sigma limits $\mu_{\bar{y}} \pm 3\sigma_{\bar{y}} = \mu \pm 3\sigma/\sqrt{n}$. Since μ and σ are not known, in practice they are estimated from the available data. The grand mean $\bar{\bar{y}}$ is our guess at μ, and the average standard deviation, $\bar{s}$, over the k subgroups,

$\bar{s}$

$$\bar{s} = \frac{1}{k}(s_1 + s_2 + \cdots + s_k) \qquad \textbf{(10.2)}$$

is the estimate[†] of σ.

The factors given in Exhibit 10.3D may then be used to compute limits for the $\bar{y}_i$ sequence within which the subgroup means will almost surely fall *as long as the process remains in statistical control*. The limits are given as $\bar{\bar{y}} \pm a\bar{s}$ and are called **upper control limits (UCL)** and **lower control limits (LCL)**, respectively. The horizontal line at $\bar{\bar{y}}$ is called the **center line (CL)**. Control limits are *not* related to the process objectives or specification limits. That is, a process could be in control but out of specification. Or a process could meet objectives—get better—because of a change that put it out of control. Control limits tell you about consistency, not quality.

upper control limits (UCL)
lower control limits (LCL)
center line (CL)

[†]Some authors recommend alternative estimates of the standard deviation σ such as

$$\sqrt{\frac{\sum\limits_{i=1}^{k}(n_i - 1)s_i^2}{\left[\sum\limits_{i=1}^{k} n_i\right] - k}}$$

which arises in certain statistical theory. However, this estimate is more sensitive to extreme values of s_i than ours is.

E X H I B I T 10.3D

Factors for Computing Three-Sigma Control Limits[†] for Mean Charts: Subgroup Size n

Upper control limit $= UCL = \bar{\bar{y}} + a\bar{s}$
Lower control limit $= LCL = \bar{\bar{y}} - a\bar{s}$

n	a	n	a
2	2.66	14	0.82
3	1.95	15	0.79
4	1.63	16	0.76
5	1.43	17	0.74
6	1.29	18	0.72
7	1.18	19	0.70
8	1.10	20	0.68
9	1.03	21	0.66
10	0.98	22	0.65
11	0.93	23	0.63
12	0.89	24	0.62
13	0.85	25	0.61

[†]The factor a is slightly larger than $3/\sqrt{n}$ to adjust for the theoretical fact that, on the average, $\bar{s}$ underestimates σ, especially for small values of n. The amount of adjustment is less as n increases.

For the data in Exhibit 10.3A (first 25 rows), $\bar{\bar{y}} = 100.12$ and $\bar{s} = 1.86$. With $n = 5$, Exhibit 10.3D yields control limits of

$$UCL = 100.12 + (1.43 \times 1.86) = 100.12 + 2.66 = 102.78$$

and

$$LCL = 100.12 - (1.43 \times 1.86) = 100.12 - 2.66 = 97.46$$

Exhibit 10.3E gives the sequence plot of the means with horizontal lines at the mean $\bar{\bar{y}}$ and at the estimated "three-sigma" limits. As long as the sequence of subgroup means remains within the control limits, there is no evidence to suggest that special causes are influencing the variation seen in the process results. Exhibit 10.3E indicates that the means of the subgroups detect no special cause of variation in the process.

Suppose now that the process operates for five more time periods, producing the results in rows 26 through 30 of Exhibit 10.3A. Does the process remain in control? To check, plot the sequence of 30 subgroup means using the control limits already obtained from the first 25 means and standard deviations, where the process was deemed in control. Exhibit 10.3F shows the resulting graph. Since the sequence remains within the control limits, there is no reason to believe that the process is not still in control.

E X H I B I T   **10.3E**
Control Chart for Means

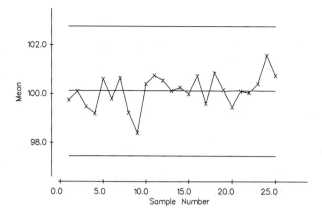

E X H I B I T   **10.3F**
Mean Chart for Process Control:
Limits Based on 25 Samples

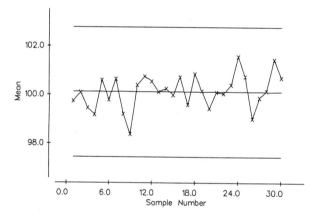

Changes in Level

Monitoring changes in mean level is the most important way of monitoring process control. Mean levels can go out of control in different ways. One of the most common ways is for the mean level to change in an isolated sample or subgroup. In particular, suppose that in the 26th sample a batch of raw materials from a new supplier was used. From the 27th sample on, the usual raw materials were used. Suppose that the effect of the new supplier is to *increase* typical process values. For this example, we increase the sample values in row 26 by four units each, to 101.0, 101.9, 100.5, 104.8, and 106.9, with a mean of 103.02. What will be the effect of such a change on the control chart? Exhibit 10.3G displays the results. Clearly something unusual has happened at sample 26. The mean level of the process has gone out of control at sample 26, and a search for the special cause should be initiated.

Another common out-of-control situation in our example would be to continue using the new supplier from sample 26 on. To simulate that case, the sample values for subgroups 26, 27, 28, 29, and 30 were all increased by four units, leading to a

E X H I B I T **10.3G**

Control Chart for
Means—Isolated Change in
Level at Sample 26

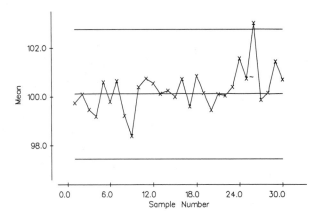

four-unit increase in all their means. (This alteration does not change the variability in the subgroups, only their mean.) The resulting control chart is shown in Exhibit 10.3H. Again the control limits are based on the first 25 samples known to be in control. The type of change induced is called a *step change*; Exhibit 10.3H shows its effects. Exhibits 10.3F and 10.3H are identical except that in 10.3H, the last five means have been increased by four units.

E X H I B I T **10.3H**

Control Chart for
Means—Change in Level from
Sample 26 on

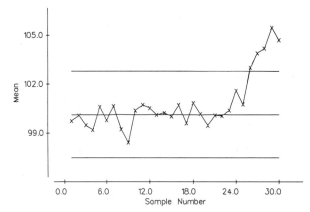

A third way in which the mean level of a process may go out of control is when the means increase (or decrease) over time. In this case, the process is said to have a *time trend* in its mean. An example is given in Exhibit 10.3I. Here the same basic data in Exhibit 10.3A have been used, but they have been altered by adding one unit to the members of sample 26, two units to sample 27, and so on, up to adding five units to sample 30. The effect will be to increase the means of those samples by the corresponding amount, with no change in their variability. With the aid of the plotted control limits, the time trend is clearly apparent in Exhibit 10.3I, and the chart would warrant searching for special causes of this aberrant behavior in the process.

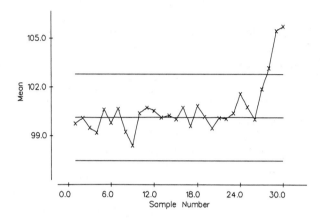

Change in Variability

Another common way to measure whether processes are in control is to measure changes in variability. A change in supplier of raw materials, for example, could easily change variability of the product without significantly changing the mean. As an example, return to Exhibit 10.3A. Carefully alter the data in sample 26 to keep the mean unchanged while doubling its standard deviation. (Can you think of how to do that?) The new values for sample 26 are 94.98, 96.78, 93.98, 102.58, and 106.78, with mean 99.02 (the same as before). The standard deviation is 5.47, twice as large as before. What effect will this have on the control chart for the mean? Since the means have not changed, the answer is *no change at all*. The same will be true for any kind of alteration of the variability in the samples that leaves the means unchanged. *A control chart for means does not detect changes in variability.* Control charts based on measures of variability are needed for that purpose.

SECTION

10.4 Exercises

10.4A If 25 samples of size 7 yield the statistics $\bar{\bar{y}} = 43.8$ and $\bar{s} = 3.6$, find the *UCL* and *LCL* for the corresponding mean chart.

10.4B Observation of 23 samples, each of size 4, on a certain process produced the following data: $n = 4, k = 23, \sum_{i=1}^{23} \bar{y}_i = 232.2$ inches, and $\sum_{i=1}^{23} s_i = 26.12$ inches.

  a   Find the *CL*, *UCL*, and *LCL* for the mean chart for the data.

  b   Using $\bar{\bar{y}}$ and $\bar{s}$ as estimates of μ and σ, respectively, and assuming that the process is in control, what fraction of the sample means would be expected to fall above 11 inches? Below 10 inches?

c As in part (b), and assuming that the individual y-values are approximately normally distributed, what fraction of individual y-values would be expected to lie above 12 inches? Below 9 inches?

SECTION

10.5 Standard Deviation Charts for Process Control

This section explains how standard deviations, as well as means, can be tracked to determine whether a process is in control.

Making a Standard Deviation Chart

A sequence plot of s_i, the standard deviations of subgroups, forms the basis of the chart used for controlling process variability. How should the control limits be determined for this chart? If there are large numbers of observations in each subgroup, the distribution of s_i will be *approximately* normally distributed with mean σ and standard deviation $\sigma/\sqrt{2(n-1)}$. But the effect does not hold well for subgroup sizes as small as four or five, which are typical. For such small groups, the distribution of s_i is likely to be quite asymmetric. However, statisticians have been able to work out the exact distribution of s_i for all sample sizes, provided the underlying process variable is normally distributed and the observations are independent.

standard deviation chart   To use these statistical findings, we apply the factors given in tables like the one in Exhibit 10.5A[†] to make a **standard deviation chart**, or s-chart, a statistical process control chart designed to detect changes in variability. In such a chart, CL or the center line is drawn at $\bar{s}$, the estimated standard deviation of the process. The LCL or lower control limit is obtained by multiplying $\bar{s}$ by the factor b from the table in Exhibit 10.5A. The UCL or upper control limit is obtained by multiplying $\bar{s}$ by the factor c. Some statistical software will calculate the limits and display the plots without your having to use external tables.

In our example $n = 5$, so that the required factors are $b = 0.160$ and $c = 2.286$. With an estimated process standard deviation of $\bar{s} = 1.86$, the control limits are drawn at $LCL = 0.160 \times 1.86 = 0.298$ and $UCL = 2.286 \times 1.86 = 4.25$. Exhibit 10.5B shows the standard deviations control chart for the data in the first 25 rows of Exhibit 10.3A. The process variability is clearly shown to be in control—the variation displayed within the subgroups is well within expectations for a constant-cause system.

[†]According to theory for a normal process with mean μ and standard deviation σ and subgroup size n, the factors b and c are determined so that $Pr(b\sigma < s_i < c\sigma) = 0.998$.

			LCL $= b\bar{s}$, **UCL** $= c\bar{s}$, **CL** $= \bar{s}$		
			n = **subgroup sample size**		
n	b	c	n	b	c
2	0.002	4.124	14	0.457	1.661
3	0.036	2.966	15	0.474	1.635
4	0.098	2.527	16	0.490	1.612
5	0.160	2.286	17	0.504	1.591
6	0.215	2.129	18	0.517	1.572
7	0.263	2.017	19	0.529	1.555
8	0.303	1.932	20	0.541	1.539
9	0.338	1.864	21	0.551	1.524
10	0.368	1.809	22	0.561	1.511
11	0.394	1.764	23	0.570	1.498
12	0.418	1.725	24	0.578	1.486
13	0.439	1.691	25	0.587	1.476

[†]Based on the χ^2 distribution of $(n-1)s^2/\sigma^2$ and equal tail probability limits of size 0.001.

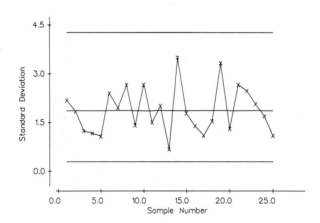

Change in Variability

What should we expect to see in a standard deviations control chart when variability changes? Suppose again that the observations in sample 26 of Exhibit 10.3A are altered so that the sample's standard deviation is doubled but its mean is kept intact. Exhibit 10.5C shows the resulting standard deviations control chart. As before, the limits are based on the statistics calculated from only the first 25 subgroups. The out-of-control variability in sample 26 is clearly evident. The company should begin a search for the special cause that produced the additional variability in sample 26.

Another possible way variability could go out of control is illustrated in Exhibit 10.5D. Here the standard deviations of samples 26 through 30 have been doubled in each case, while the original means of the subgroups have been retained. Again the change in variability is quite noticeable, although not every point so doubled leads

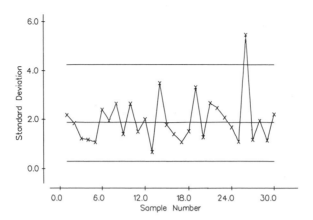

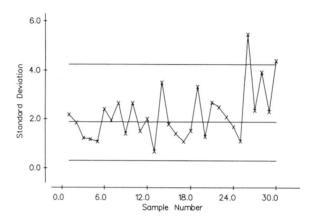

to a value above the *UCL* since several of the original standard deviations were quite small.

Mean and standard deviation control charts look similar, but they are interpreted quite differently. In a mean chart, variation up or down means a process is out of control. In a standard deviation chart, variation up indicates an increase in variability—almost always an out-of-control situation. Variation down, by contrast, indicates *decreased* variability—usually a desirable goal because it indicates the process is more consistent. Reduced variability means parts fit together better, uncertainty is lessened, or, in general, better control has been achieved. If a new method, technique, tool, and so on is thought to reduce variability, that effect must be documented. The standard deviation chart may be used for this purpose, but now the hope is that after the new method is put into effect the chart will track *below* the *LCL*. Exhibit 10.5E gives such an example. Here the basic process data have been modified so that the standard deviations of the samples from sample 26 on are one-fourth of their previous values (retaining their original means). Only two of the plotted standard deviations actually go below the *LCL*, but the trend is quite evident—the variability has been reduced from sample 26 on. Continued process monitoring (together with process analysis, discussed in Section 10.7) will allow us to narrow the control limits by basing them on the new reduced value of the process standard deviation. The process is now capable of better control, and monitoring should reflect the higher expectations in future production.

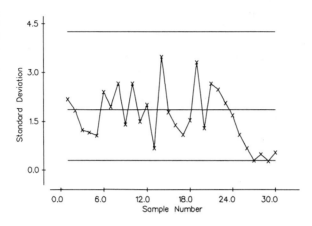

Change in Level

Control charts for variability are totally unaffected by changes in level as long as the variability around those new levels is unchanged. For example, standard deviation control charts based on the out-of-control data that produced the mean charts in Exhibits 10.3G–I will all be identical to the chart in Exhibit 10.5B, since variability is in control in all those cases. In general, it is important to monitor both the mean level and the variability in a process to ensure that both are under control.

SECTION

10.6 Exercises

10.6A   Using the information in Exercise 10.4A, find the *UCL* and *LCL* for an *s*-chart for this data set.

10.6B   (Continuation of Exercise 10.4B) Observation of 23 samples, each of size 4, on a certain process produced the following data: $n = 4, k = 23, \sum_{i=1}^{23} \bar{y}_i = 232.2$ inches, and $\sum_{i=1}^{23} s_i = 26.12$ inches.

   a   Find the *CL*, *UCL*, and *LCL* for the standard deviation chart for the data.

   b   If the standard deviation for the 10th sample is $s_{10} = 3.49$, would the process be considered in control with respect to variability at that point in time? Would the process be in control with respect to mean level at that point in time?

SECTION

10.7 Control Charts for Process Analysis

process analysis

In Sections 10.3 and 10.5, we worked under the assumption that the process was initially in control. When new processes are developed or old processes are first studied, however, such information is not available. When you do not yet have established control limits, you can produce meaningful control charts by **process analysis**. This section shows how, with process analysis, you can use observations from the past to investigate whether or not a process was in control and set appropriate limits for future control.

Standard Deviation Charts for Process Analysis

In process analysis, we start by studying control charts for variability. This is because lack of control of variability makes the control limits on the mean chart meaningless.

To make a standard deviation chart for process analysis, a sequence plot of the successive subgroup standard deviations is again created. The process is temporarily assumed to be in control with respect to variability, and an overall estimate of the process variability is computed by averaging the estimates for variability in the subgroups as before. Notice that since each s_i measures variability around its own subgroup mean, these standard deviations will not be influenced by changes of level in the process. Of course, $\bar{s}$ will be affected to some degree by subgroups that have unusually high or low variability. For that reason the control limits based on $\bar{s}$ are sometimes called *trial control limits*. Keeping this limitation in mind, control limits based on $\bar{s}$ are calculated.

To illustrate, the full 30 rows of data in Exhibit 10.3A are used. But now suppose no prior knowledge as to whether the process is in control or not. Interest thus centers on process analysis. We find that $\bar{s} = 1.86$, so the center line and control limits will be nearly the same as in Exhibit 10.5B. The new standard deviation chart is displayed in Exhibit 10.7A and supports the hypothesis of a constant-cause system *with respect to variability*. As already noted, since this chart depends only on the subgroup standard deviations, it will be totally unaffected by changes in subgroup means. For example, an isolated change in the mean of one sample (Exhibit 10.3G), a step change in the means for a sequence of samples (Exhibit 10.3H), or a trend in the means (Exhibit 10.3I) will all produce standard deviation charts exactly as in Exhibit 10.7A.

Our present concern is to detect lack of control in variability from a process analysis point of view. What will be the effect on the chart if the standard deviation of sample 26 is doubled? Notice that since our statistics are based on *all* the data, $\bar{s}$ will increase and the center line and both control limits will be affected by the abnormal variability in sample 26. In the new case, $\bar{s} = 1.95$, compared with 1.86 previously. Thus $LCL = 0.160 \times 1.95 = 0.31$ and $UCL = 2.286 \times 1.95 = 4.46$. The unusual variability in sample 26 inflates $\bar{s}$ somewhat, which in turn inflates the UCL. However, Exhibit 10.7B shows that the chart is still able to detect the out-of-control situation. (Compare it with Exhibit 10.5C.)

In process analysis, once an out-of-control situation is found and the special cause found and eliminated, sample 26 should be removed from further consideration and

E X H I B I T   **10.7A**
Standard Deviation Chart for
Process Analysis

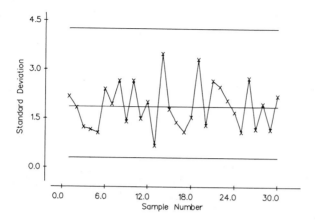

E X H I B I T   **10.7B**
Standard Deviation Control Chart
for Process Analysis—Increased
Variability in Sample 26

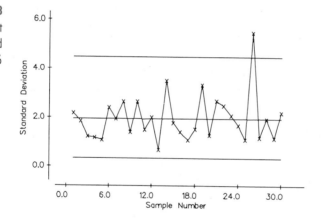

the control limits recalculated. With the special cause eliminated, a better estimate of the process standard deviation is possible. The revised chart will better indicate the characteristics of the process when it is in control, and the revised limits are appropriate for use in future process control. In this example, removing samples 26 leads to a new value of $\bar{s} = 1.83$ based on the remaining 29 subgroups. The new control chart is shown in Exhibit 10.7C. If the special cause either cannot be discovered or cannot be eliminated by suitable modification of the process, the aberrant samples should not be removed from consideration because they must be considered as common causes in future monitoring of the process.

An increase in variability of several subgroups will affect the process analysis standard deviation chart more substantially since $\bar{s}$ can be inflated considerably. Look again at the case in which samples 26 through 30 all have their standard deviations doubled but their old mean values retained. This causes the value of $\bar{s}$ to increase to 2.17 and the control limits to move to $UCL = 2.286 \times 2.17 = 4.96$ and $LCL = 0.160 \times 2.17 = 0.35$. The resulting control chart is shown in Exhibit 10.7D. Although only one point exceeds the upper control limit, the chart clearly signals

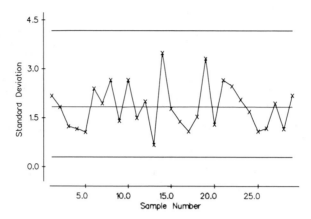

trouble that must be investigated. Notice also that many of the standard deviations for samples 1 through 25 are below the center line—another indication of the increased variability at the end of the series. If samples 26 through 30 are all omitted from consideration, then $\bar{s} = 1.86$, as in Exhibits 10.5B–D. The chart based on this value would be identical to the one in Exhibit 10.5D, where the increased variability is much easier to detect since the control limits are based on a proper measure of variability when a constant-cause system is operating.

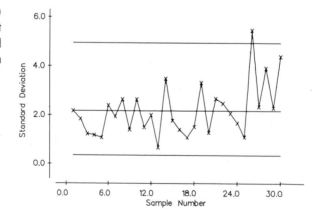

Process improvement indicated by reduced variability in results is illustrated in Exhibit 10.7E, where the standard deviations of samples 26 through 30 have been reduced to one fourth of their previous values. The trial control limits are affected by that reduction, with $\bar{s} = 1.63$ now compared with 1.86 before the reduction. The trend in the standard deviations at the end of the sequence is apparent. Having observed Exhibit 10.7E, we would suspect that a serendipitous special cause was reducing the variability, seek it out, and, if possible, arrange for it to continue in the future. If the reduced variability were due to a planned change in the process, the control limits would continue to be based on the old in-control process, as in process control, and not on the new one, as happens with process analysis.

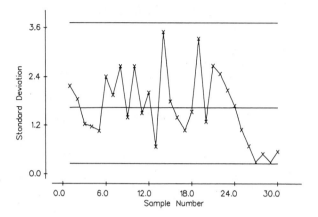

Mean Charts for Process Analysis

Although it is desirable to first show that process variability is in control, more often than not the stability of variability and the stability of mean values are looked at simultaneously.

As in process control, the standard method of constructing mean charts for process analysis is to use control limits based on the theoretical limits $\mu \pm 3\sigma_{\bar{y}} = \mu \pm 3\sigma/\sqrt{n}$ where μ and σ are estimated using the data at hand. We use $\bar{\bar{y}} \pm a\bar{s}$ for the trial control limits with $\bar{\bar{y}}$ and $\bar{s}$ computed from the full data set because we have no knowledge about the stability of the process. Again using the full data set in Exhibit 10.3A, the control chart displayed in Exhibit 10.7F is obtained. It shows that the process is in control with respect to the mean.

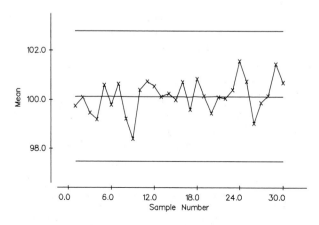

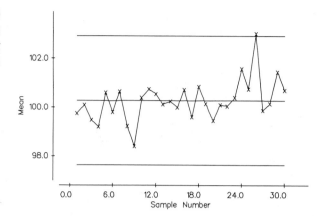

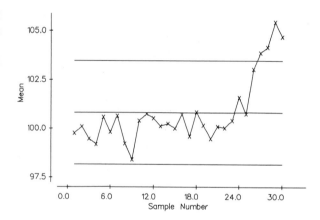

Now consider the same data set with an isolated change in level of four units at sample 26. Such a change will not affect the standard deviation of that sample and hence will not change $\bar{s}$. The change will increase $\bar{\bar{y}}$ from its original value of 100.14 to 100.27 so that the center line and control limits will all increase similarly. The resulting mean chart is shown in Exhibit 10.7G. The increased level in subgroup 26 is still evident. Compare this chart to Exhibit 10.3G, where the same data are used but the limits are based only on the first 25 data points that are deemed to be in control. If the control limits are based on the data with sample 26 excluded, a plot even more similar to Exhibit 10.3G results, reinforcing the anomalous nature of the 26th sample.

A similar analysis may be carried out on the data with the step change in the mean for the samples 26 through 30, as in Exhibit 10.3H. In this case $\bar{\bar{y}}$ changes a little more, from 100.14 to 100.80, which implies that the center line and control limits will increase, making it more difficult to detect mean changes. However, Exhibit 10.7H shows that the special cause is still reasonably clear although the mean of sample 26 does not exceed the trial *UCL*. This chart indicates that the limits should be redone based on the data with samples 27, 28, 29, and 30 excluded. With this change $\bar{\bar{y}}$ reverts to a value of 100.23, more in keeping with the mean of the earlier constant-cause data. The control chart in Exhibit 10.7I shows that with those four samples excluded from limit calculations, even sample 26 is out of control.

Finally, consider the data first analyzed in Exhibit 10.3I, whose means begin an upward trend at sample 26. Exhibit 10.7J displays the control chart, which shows that samples 29 and 30 are out of control with respect to the mean. However, we realize that the trending mean affects the trial control limits. Hence, the control limits are recomputed based only on samples 1 through 28, giving the chart in Exhibit 10.7K. We now see that sample 28 is also out of control. Using only the first 27 samples for the limits leads to Exhibit 10.7L, which does not indicate any other out-of-control points. This chart should be compared with Exhibit 10.3I, which is based on the data only through sample 25 and gives essentially the same conclusion.

EXHIBIT **10.7I**
Mean Chart for Process Analysis—Step Change in Level from Sample 26 on (control limits based on samples 1 through 26)

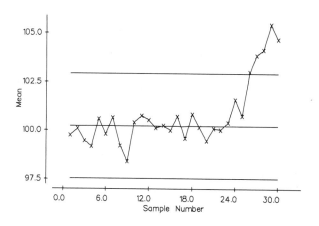

EXHIBIT **10.7J**
Mean Chart for Process Analysis—Trend in Means from Sample 26 on (control limits based on all data)

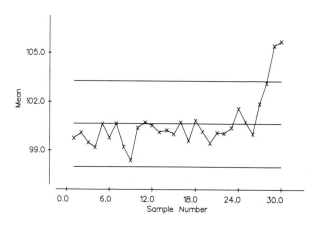

EXHIBIT 10.7K
Mean Chart for Process
Analysis—Trend in Means from
Sample 26 on (control limits
based on samples 1 through 28)

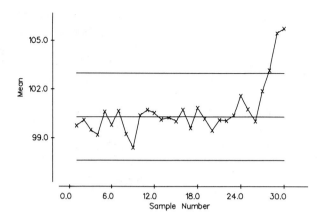

EXHIBIT 10.7L
Mean Chart for Process
Analysis—Trend in Means from
Sample 26 on (control limits
based on samples 1 through 27)

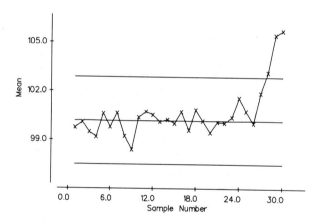

SECTION

10.8 Applications of Control Charts in Business

This section offers two case histories showing the use of process analysis and control in very different business situations.

Food Processing

The food processing industry must closely watch the process of filling containers to the proper amount. Underfilling raises the ire of customers (and may be illegal), and overfilling either raises the cost of the product or erodes company profits. Consider the filling of ice cream containers. The process was designed to produce actual fill amounts of between 196 and 204 ounces, with a target of 200 ounces. As a check on the fill process, four containers were taken from production at 10-minute intervals and their weights measured in ounces. Exhibit 10.8A lists the data for 24 such subgroups.[†] The grand mean of these $4 \times 24 = 96$ fills is 203.95 ounces, above the target value of 200 ounces. But of course there is variability to be considered.

```
filename: ICECREAM.DAT
Gross weight in ounces of ice cream fill
(Source: E.R.Ott, Process Quality Control
New York: McGraw-Hill, 1975)
25 samples of 4 in order of production at 10 minute intervals
Specifications were 200+-4 ounces
202 201 198 199
200 202 212 202
202 201 208 201
201 200 200 202
210 196 200 198
202 206 205 203
198 196 202 199
206 204 204 206
206 204 203 204
208 214 213 207
198 201 199 198
204 204 202 206
203 204 204 203
214 212 206 208
192 198 204 198
207 208 206 204
205 214 215 212
204 208 196 196
205 204 205 204
202 202 208 208
204 206 209 202
206 206 206 210
204 202 204 207
206 205 204 202
```

Since we are new to this process, process analysis is used to assess fill amount with respect to both variability and level over the historical data available. We will look for out-of-control situations and assess the capability of the process as it now stands. Instability of variability makes it difficult to make judgments about the mean of the process, so the standard deviation chart is done first. Calculation yields $\bar{s} = 2.72$. Exhibit 10.8B displays the standard deviation chart. Fortunately, the chart indicates no problems with respect to variability and we may reasonably proceed to the mean chart.

The lack of control in the mean is clear from Exhibit 10.8C. Three points are above the *UCL* and three points are below the *LCL*. Because such variation is extremely unusual for a constant cause system, we conclude that special causes must be operating in this process. The pattern of being below the *LCL*, then above the *UCL*, then below, and so on suggests the possibility that the process is being "overcontrolled"— that is, when the fill amount is too low, the filling equipment is readjusted to increase it. Then when the subsequent fill amount is too high, the equipment is readjusted downward,

[†]These data appear in Ellis R. Ott, *Process Quality Control* (New York: McGraw-Hill, 1975), p. 60, and are attributed to David Lipman, then a graduate student at Rutgers University.

E X H I B I T **10.8B**
Standard Deviation Control Chart
for Ice Cream Fill Amount

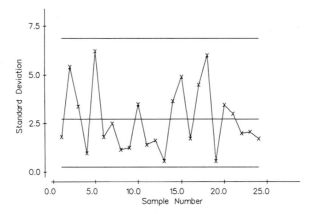

E X H I B I T **10.8C**
Mean Control Chart for Ice
Cream Fill Amount

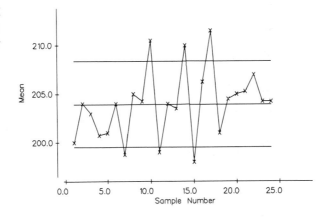

and so on. Such a hypothesis should be further investigated with the cooperation of the process supervisor and the workers directly associated with the process. As it stands, the process does not meet the criterion of producing containers with between 196 and 204 ounces of ice cream. The process needs to be modified to achieve the range of variation desired.

Accounting Processes

The Winegard Company of Burlington, Iowa, wants to understand the bill-paying behavior of the independent retail distributors of its television reception products. When Winegard receives payment on a bill, it records the number of days since the bill was issued. Suspecting that each distributor has a different paying pattern, Winegard decides to run separate process analyses for different distributors. Three distributors, referred to as ABC, DEF, and XYZ to protect their anonymity, are analyzed. For purposes of constructing control charts, the complete time history over several months is grouped into subgroups of five consecutive bills. For various periods throughout 1986, the three companies paid 260, 130, and 110 bills, respectively.

Company DEF's data are listed in Exhibit 10.8D. Since the complete time history is available, a sequence plot of the series is first done (see Exhibit 10.8E). Two or three suspect values that will likely have a large effect on any further analysis are obvious immediately. The standard deviation control chart for the subgrouped data is given in Exhibit 10.8F. The possible outliers do indeed show up as an out-of-control variability in samples 13 and 26. In addition, there is unusually little variability in subgroup 17 and rather little variability in subgroup 9. If the mean of a subgroup is at an acceptable level, the small variability is a desirable goal. Thus we will proceed with concern about the large variability but ignore the small variability.

E X H I B I T **10.8D**
Days to Pay Account: DEF
Company

```
filename: DEF.DAT
Accounts receivable data for DEF Company
Number of days to collection of account
(Source: Mark Sellergren, Winegard, Inc.,
Burlington, Iowa)
Terms: 1%-10 days, net 30 days
June 1987 through October 1987
(Read across, row by row)
39 39 41 26 28   Jun
28 25 26 24 38   Jun
35 38 38 25 38   Jun
24 38 25 40 38   Jun
38 25 25 35 35   Jun
35 32 41 33 31   Jun
21 21 26 26 28   Jul
28 28 28 28 20   Jul
27 25 27 25 28   Jul
20 28 22 26 34   Jul
21 21 33 33 21   Jul
33 22 17 22 20   Jul
27 20 55 39 26   Jul/Aug
26 26 39 25 22   Aug
33 33 19 32 32   Aug
42 27 37 27 27   Aug
27 26 26 26 25   Aug
25 35 35 35 35   Aug
20 30 25 25 27   Aug
27 25 25 25 34   Aug
28 28 21 22 21   Sep
49 35 28 28 27   Sep
20 27 27 26 26   Sep
26 22 22 22 34   Sep/Oct
26 19 28 19 27   Oct
16 27 20 63 25   Oct
```

Since the subgrouping was arbitrary, we do not want to ignore the "good" data that happen to have been arbitrarily grouped with the outliers. Thus for the next look at the data, the two outlying observations in samples 13 and 26 are treated as missing and the data are recharted, noting that two subgroups now contain only four observations. Exhibit 10.8G gives the resulting standard deviation chart. The small variability in sample 17 is still observed but otherwise the process variability appears to be in control, so we go on to the mean chart in Exhibit 10.8H. No points lie outside the control limits in this chart, so the process is accepted as being in control. The control limits in this chart are equal to $28.1 \pm (1.43)5.13 = 28.1 \pm 7.3$ or $LCL = 20.8$ days

E X H I B I T **10.8E**
Sequence Plot of Days Until
Payment: DEF Company

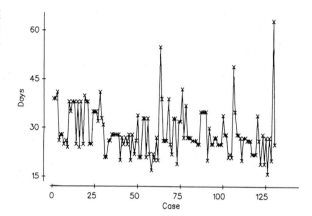

E X H I B I T **10.8F**
Standard Deviation Control
Chart: DEF Company

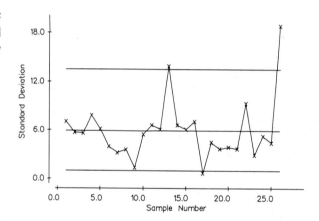

E X H I B I T **10.8G**
Standard Deviation Chart After
Outliers Removed: DEF Company

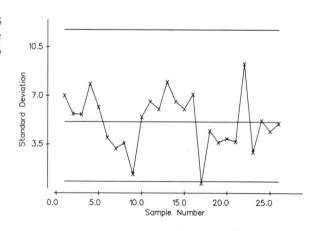

EXHIBIT **10.8H**
Mean Chart After Outliers
Removed: DEF Company

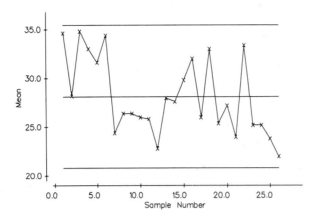

and $UCL = 35.4$ days. These limits will serve as control limits for future charts on the process mean and alert the Winegard accounts receivable department to potential difficulties with DEF Company if they arise.

The bill-paying behavior of XYZ Company is considered next. The data are listed in Exhibit 10.8I, and a sequence plot of the individual values is shown in Exhibit 10.8J. (These data first appeared in Exercise 2.9A.)

The sequence plot clearly shows two or three outliers that will greatly affect the subsequent charts, so we set the three values to the missing value code and proceed from that point. The standard deviation chart (with outliers removed) is shown in Exhibit 10.8K. Since we see no striking deviation from a stable system with respect to variability, we go on to consider the mean chart in Exhibit 10.8L. At this point in the analysis, we see the difficulty that was also somewhat apparent in the sequence plot of Exhibit 10.8J. They have become much slower in paying their bills. Thus, the mean level of the process has increased greatly from sample 14 onward, and the control limits based on the overall mean are essentially meaningless. Exhibit 10.8M shows the mean chart with control limits based only on samples 1 through 13. Clearly an important special cause must have occurred at about the time of the 13th sample. The control limits shown in Exhibit 10.8M have the potential for use in future monitoring. Unfortunately, in December 1986, XYZ Company filed for bankruptcy. Active charting of the accounting data as it became available to Winegard might have helped them foresee the difficulties that were to come.

Finally, accounts receivable data from ABC Company are examined. The sequence plot of the 260 observations listed in Exhibit 10.8N is given in Exhibit 10.8O. The sequence plot in Exhibit 10.8O shows immediately that the process variability is unusual and not due to a constant-cause system. Standard deviation and mean charts will not likely produce useful information on this process. However, a little data sleuthing does lead to a possible key to the observed behavior. Referring to the original data in Exhibit 10.8N reveals that the unusually large values—that is, the long

EXHIBIT **10.8I**

Days to Pay Account: XYZ

Company

```
filename: XYZ.DAT
Accounts receivable data for XYZ Company
Number of days to collection of account
(Source: Mark Sellergren, Winegard, Inc.,
Burlington, Iowa)
Terms: 1%-10 days, net 30 days
January 1986 through December 1986
(Read across, row by row)
29 25 22 21 34   Jan
29 27 45 22 22   Jan
41 32 32 30 30   Jan/Feb
30 30 22 17 15   Feb
25 28 22 22 22   Feb/Mar
20 20 18 32 31   Mar
30 77 22 18 18   Mar
25 25 24 21 17   Apr
17 28 42 38 30   Apr/May
30 30 30 27 21   May
68 31 23 23 23   May/Jun
 1 20 29 31 31   Jun/Jul
43 33 38 42 36   Jul/Aug
48 48 52 49 44   Aug
51 49 54 50 50   Sep
50 50 50 49 62   Sep
62 62 61 60 55   Sep
61 59 54 54 62   Oct
57 55 62 62 62   Oct/Nov
62 62 62 57 57   Nov
57 57 55 50 50   Nov
44 44 43 43 41   Dec
```

EXHIBIT **10.8J**

Sequence Plot of Days Until

Payment: XYZ Company

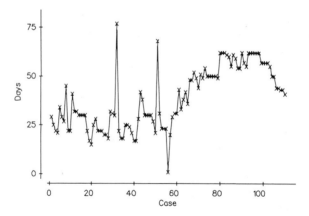

delays before paying—always occur at the end of the month and into the beginning of the next month. ABC Company is clearly paying their accounts to Winegard on a calendar month system. Perhaps some communication between the two companies can lead to a system that will smooth out the cash flow to the satisfaction of both parties.

EXHIBIT **10.8K**
Standard Deviation Control
Chart: XYZ Company

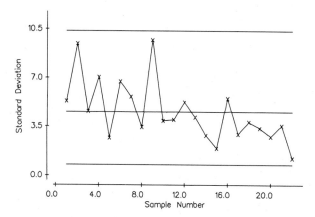

EXHIBIT **10.8L**
Mean Control Chart: XYZ
Company

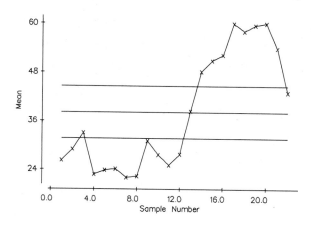

EXHIBIT **10.8M**
Mean Control Chart: XYZ
Company (limits based on
samples 1 through 13)

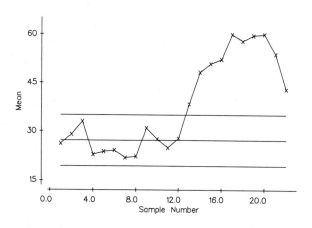

```
filename: ABC.DAT
Accounts receivable data for ABC Company
Number of days to collection of account
(Source: Mark Sellergren, Winegard, Inc.,
Burlington, Iowa.)
Terms: 1%-10 days, net 30 days
January 1987 through August 1987
(Read across, row by row)
53 53 48 47 47  Jan        47 44 42 42 36  May
47 46 42 41 40  Jan        34 34 34 33 33  May
40 36 35 33 33  Jan        33 33 33 33 33  May
33 32 29 29 29  Jan        33 29 28 26 49  May/Jun
29 29 29 29 29  Jan        47 47 47 47 46  Jun
29 29 29 29 29  Jan        45 42 41 40 40  Jun
29 28 49 49 49  Jan/Feb    40 39 39 38 35  Jun
47 46 46 45 41  Feb        35 34 33 32 28  Jun
41 39 38 35 32  Feb        28 28 28 28 28  Jun
32 32 32 32 32  Feb        28 28 28 27 27  Jun
32 28 28 28 28  Feb        26 25 25 25 53  Jun/Jul
28 28 28 28 28  Feb        53 52 52 51 51  Jul
27 27 25 46 45  Feb/Mar    51 46 45 45 44  Jul
43 38 37 37 36  Mar        43 42 39 38 38  Jul
28 28 28 28 28  Mar        37 36 36 36 36  Jul
28 28 28 28 28  Mar        32 32 32 32 32  Jul
28 28 25 25 24  Mar        32 32 32 32 32  Jul
24 24 24 24 24  Mar        31 31 31 29 28  Jul
22 49 42 41 35  Mar/Apr    28 25 25 25 24  Jul
34 33 32 29 29  Apr        24 48 43 38 35  Jul/Aug
29 29 29 29 29  Apr        34 34 31 31 31  Aug
29 29 29 29 29  Apr        31 31 31 31 31  Aug
29 29 29 29 29  Apr        31 29 29 29 29  Aug
29 28 27 26 26  Apr        29 29 29 28 28  Aug
26 25 25 25 25  Apr        28 27 27 27 24  Aug
22 21 54 50 48  Apr/May    23 23 21 21 20  Aug
```

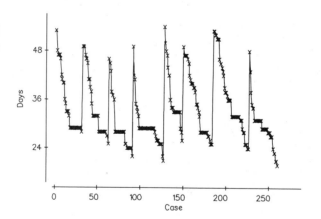

SECTION

10.9 Exercises

10.9A   Procter & Gamble (P&G) is a large worldwide producer of numerous consumer products including Crest toothpaste, Tide laundry detergent, and Prell shampoo. In 1986, a new production line was started in the Iowa City P&G plant to produce and package a hair conditioner. An automatic machine was used to put the caps on the conditioner containers. If the caps are not tight enough the package may leak, but if they are too tight the customer will not be able to open the container easily. A measure of cap tightness is the cap torque, which specifications said should lie in the range from 15 to 40 foot-pounds. Since many out-of-spec caps were found soon after starting the production line, a process analysis was instituted. Cap torques were measured on 18 subgroups, each of size 4. The data are shown below.

```
filename: P&G1.DAT
P&G data
(Source: Jeffrey Enck, Procter & Gamble,
Iowa City, Iowa)
Torque on hair conditioner caps
20 17 40 26
36 35 34 38
32 37 31 29
22 30 18 23
24 22 24 26
30 40 34 19
20 33 16 30
27 33 36 34
32 50 43 20
15 17 31 21
28 29 36 32
26 30 20 12
40 45 27 30
30 33 53 46
36 42 31 26
39 32 35 36
32 35 36 32
30 55 57 30
```

a   Show that $\bar{\bar{y}} = 31.194$ and $\bar{s} = 6.6942$.

b   Plot the s-chart for these data and show that variability of cap torque is in control.

c   Plot the mean chart for these data and see if the mean level of cap torque is in control.

d   Display a histogram of the individual measurements and comment on the appearance. Does a mound-shaped distribution appear to fit the histogram? [Based on part (c), should any subgroups be omitted before doing the histogram?]

e   Form a plot of the observations versus normal scores and compute the correlation in the plot. Does normality seem to be confirmed?

f   Using the values given in part (a), estimate the long-run fraction of caps that will *not* meet the specification limits of 15 to 40 foot-pounds. (This process is considered again in Section 11.6.)

10.9B   The data below are reported in Kaoru Ishikawa, *Guide to Quality Control*, 2nd ed. (White Plains, N.Y.: Kraus, 1986). They are measurements of the moisture content of a textile product taken five times a day for 25 consecutive days.

a   Using all the data, prepare standard deviation and mean control charts, with $n = 5$. Assuming you have been asked to do a process analysis, what conclusions about the state of statistical control would you draw from these charts?

b   Prepare a sequence plot of the data. Use the plotting symbol A or 1 for data collected at 6:00, the symbol B or 2 for data collected at 10:00, and so on. What predictable pattern emerges from the sequence plot? Speculate on possible reasons for this pattern. Does this pattern raise any doubts on your conclusions in part (a)? State why or why not.

c   Display separate dotplots on the same scale for each of the five times of day. Do these plots reinforce the conclusions drawn in part (b)? (Filename: MOISTURE.DAT.)

Day	Time				
Subgroup	6:00	10:00	14:00	18:00	22:00
1	14.0	12.6	13.2	13.1	12.1
2	13.2	13.3	12.7	13.4	12.1
3	13.5	12.8	13.0	12.8	12.4
4	13.9	12.4	13.3	13.1	13.2
5	13.0	13.0	12.1	12.2	13.3
6	13.7	12.0	12.5	12.4	12.4
7	13.9	12.1	12.7	13.4	13.0
8	13.4	13.6	13.0	12.4	13.5
9	14.4	12.4	12.2	12.4	12.5
10	13.3	12.4	12.6	12.9	12.8
11	13.3	12.8	13.0	13.0	13.1
12	13.6	12.5	13.3	13.5	12.8
13	13.4	13.3	12.0	13.0	13.1
14	13.9	13.1	13.5	12.6	12.8
15	14.2	12.7	12.9	12.9	12.5
16	13.6	12.6	12.4	12.5	12.2
17	14.0	13.2	12.4	13.0	13.0
18	13.1	12.9	13.5	12.3	12.8
19	14.6	13.7	13.4	12.2	12.5
20	13.9	13.0	13.0	13.2	12.6
21	13.3	12.7	12.6	12.8	12.7
22	13.9	12.4	12.7	12.4	12.8
23	13.2	12.3	12.6	13.1	12.7
24	13.2	12.8	12.8	12.3	12.6
25	13.1	12.8	12.0	12.3	12.2

Chapter Summary

Sequence plots of subgroup standard deviations and means, together with appropriate control limits, can help us identify and thus perhaps eliminate special causes of variation. The charts can also prevent unnecessary tampering with a process whose variability is due solely to common causes. Monitoring, adjusting, and improving the many individual processes that make up any business are effective ways of ensuring that quality goods and services are produced.

Supplementary Exercises for Chapter 10

10A   The Frito-Lay Company uses statistical process control in all of its food processing. In the manufacture of Ruffles, a ridged potato chip, the amount of salt added during the processing is very important. To control the salt levels, the company samples three batches of chips each 15 minutes, measures the salt content of the three batches, and plots the mean of the three batches on control charts. From long experience, it has established a known mean salt level of 1.6% as a desirable target value and a known process standard deviation of 0.28%. Any unusual deviation from these known values indicates that the process needs attention. Argue that in this situation, control limits for the mean chart should be of the form $1.6 \pm 3(0.28/\sqrt{3})$ rather than as given in this chapter, namely $\bar{\bar{y}} \pm a\bar{s}$.

10B   The data file below gives the thickness of paint-can "ears." Periodically, a sample of five ears is selected from a bin. Thirty samples are available for analysis.

```
filename: PAINTCAN.DAT
Thickness of paint can ears
(Source: R.D.Snee, Graphical Analysis of Process Variation Studies,
Journal of Quality Technology 15 (April 1983), 76-88)
Samples of five (rows) are selected periodically from
a bin of product produced by two different machines
29 36 39 34 34
29 29 28 32 31
34 34 39 38 37
35 37 33 38 41
30 29 31 38 29
34 31 37 39 36
30 35 33 40 36
28 28 31 34 30
32 36 38 38 35
35 30 37 35 31
35 30 35 38 35
38 34 35 35 31
34 35 33 30 34
40 35 34 33 35
34 35 38 35 30
35 30 35 29 37
40 31 38 35 31
35 36 30 33 32
35 34 35 30 36
35 35 31 38 36
32 36 36 32 36
36 37 32 34 34
29 34 33 37 35
36 36 35 37 37
36 30 35 33 31
35 30 29 38 35
35 36 30 34 36
35 30 36 29 35
38 36 35 31 31
30 34 40 28 30
```

a   Construct both s-charts and mean charts for these data.

b   Interpret the charts formed in part (a). Does the process appear to be in control with respect to both variability and mean level?

c   Now construct displays of the distribution of ear thickness based on all $5 \times 30 = 150$ data points. Use histograms, dotplots, and stem-and-leaf displays. Do all three displays confirm a special shape to the distribution?

d   The bin contains paint-can ears produced from two different machines. Could this explain the distribution shape?

e   In light of the results in parts (c) and (d), suggest a better way to collect and analyze data for this situation.

10C   Exhibit 10.8D contains accounting data for the DEF Company. In the earlier analysis of these data, outliers in samples 13 and 26 were converted to the missing value code before further analysis. There is also a suspicious data point in sample 22 (a value of 49). Change this value to "missing" also and repeat the analysis as in Exhibits 10.8G and 10.8H. Do the conclusions change? (Filename: DEF.DAT.)

Glossary for Chapter 10

center line (CL)	Center line in a control chart.
common causes (chance causes)	Causes of variation in a measured variable that are due to chance and remain in the system unless the process is fundamentally altered.
control limits	Limits within which the plotted characteristic (subgroup mean or standard deviation) is expected to vary when the process is in control.
lower control limit (LCL)	Lower control limit in a control chart.
mean chart	Statistical process control chart designed to detect changes in the mean of a process.
process analysis	Analysis of past process data to find appropriate limits for future control.
$\bar{s}$	The average of the subgroup standard deviations.
s_i	Standard deviation for the ith subgroup.
special causes (assignable causes)	Causes of variation in a measured variable that are individually important and affect process results only some of the time.
standard deviation chart	Statistical process control chart designed to detect changes in the variability of a process.
statistical control	Statistical methods used to detect changes in processes.
subgroups	Small samples of a process variable used to measure the current mean and standard deviation of a process variable.
upper control limit (UCL)	Upper control limit in a control chart.
$\bar{\bar{y}}$	The grand mean of all subgroups.
$\bar{y}_i$	The mean for the ith subgroup.

11

Binomial Distributions

Chapter Objectives

After mastering this chapter, you will be able to:

- Define a Bernoulli process

- Define the binomial distribution

- Explain how runs are used with control charts

- Compute the mean and standard deviation of a given binomial distribution

- Use the normal approximation to the binomial distribution

- Test hypotheses about the probability of success in a Bernoulli process

SECTION

11.1 Introduction

Many situations may be investigated by inspecting each item in a process for some one attribute, in a yes-no fashion. For example, a bank processes a large number of checks each day. Each check must be inspected and the check amount entered into the bank's computer system. It is important to know whether or not the amount was entered correctly. If the amount was entered correctly, the transaction is a success; otherwise it is a failure. In a manufacturing process, a particular item selected from the production line either conforms to the stated product specifications or does not. In screening loan applicants, the result is either accept or reject. In auditing, a check amount either agrees with the vendor's invoice amount or it does not. If a coin is tossed, it either comes up heads or it does not. Many situations fit into this either-or, yes-no, good-bad, or success-failure framework. For mathematical and computer convenience, success is usually indicated as a 1 and failure as a 0.

This chapter introduces ways to model such yes-no processes. You learn how the yes, or successful outcomes, in samples of such processes are likely to be distributed, and how to find the mean and standard deviation of such a distribution. You learn that with fairly large samples, you can use the normal distribution to approximate the likelihood of a given outcome. And you learn how to use knowledge about yes-no outcomes to test hypotheses.

11.2 Bernoulli Processes

This section defines a Bernoulli process, the kind of yes-no process studied with the methods covered in this chapter. Simulation is used to illustrate process outcomes.

Consider a process that at each observation produces either a 1 (a success) or a 0 (a failure). Each observation is called a *trial*. The following two conditions, or assumptions, are required for the process to be usefully studied with the methods covered in this chapter:

- The process is stable and generates a constant long-run proportion of successes, denoted by π.

- The trials are statistically independent of one another—that is, one trial does not influence another.[†]

Bernoulli process (Bernoulli trials)

Such success-failure trials are called a **Bernoulli process** or **Bernoulli trials** after James Bernoulli, a probabilist of the early 1700s. Exhibit 11.2A lists the results of a computer simulation[‡] of 60 Bernoulli trials with success rate $\pi = 1/2$. Descriptive statistics are also given. Notice that in the 60 trials there were 32 successes, with a mean or sample proportion of $32/60 = 0.5333$ successes per trial. For Bernoulli trials, the total number of successes is the statistic from which everything else of interest follows. For binary data, a simpler description is given by a tally of the number of successes and failures. Exhibit 11.2B shows the results of the tally for the data in Exhibit 11.2A.

E X H I B I T 11.2A
Sixty Success-Failure Trials with
Success Rate $\pi = 1/2$ and
Statistics

(Read across, row by row) (1=success, 0=failure)

0	0	1	0	1	0	0	1	0	1	1	0	0	0	0
1	1	1	1	1	1	0	1	1	1	0	0	1	1	1
1	0	1	0	0	0	0	1	1	1	1	1	0	1	1
1	1	0	0	0	1	0	1	0	1	0	0	0	0	1

Number	Mean	Standard Deviation
60	0.5333	0.5031

[†]See Appendix 2 for a technical definition.
[‡]See Appendix 3 for details on simulation.

EXHIBIT 11.2B
A Tally for Binary Data

	Count	Percent
0	28	47
1	32	53
$n = 60$		

It is also instructive to graph the sequence plot of Bernoulli process results to see how the successes and failures occur over time. Exhibit 11.2C displays the data of Exhibit 11.2A as a sequence plot.

EXHIBIT 11.2C
Sequence Plot—Bernoulli
Process with $\pi = 1/2$

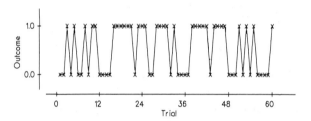

Exhibit 11.2D displays a simulated Bernoulli process with $\pi = 0.2$ along with the relevant statistics. In this case, the average number of successes is $13/60 = 0.2167$. Note also that the standard deviation is 0.4155, which is somewhat smaller than that given in Exhibit 11.2A for 32 successes out of 60 trials.

EXHIBIT 11.2D
Sequence Plot and
Statistics—Bernoulli Process
with $\pi = 0.2$

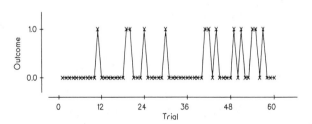

n	Mean	Standard Deviation
60	0.2167	0.4155

A third example simulates a Bernoulli process with $\pi = 0.9$. The results are reported in Exhibit 11.2E. For this particular sequence, 57 successes occurred, so the sample proportion of successes is $57/60 = 0.95$. Furthermore, the standard deviation for this data set is 0.2198, which is even smaller than in the previous two examples.

How theory supports these means and standard deviations is discussed in Section 11.7.

E X H I B I T **11.2E**
Sequence Plot and
Statistics—Bernoulli Process
with $\pi = 0.9$

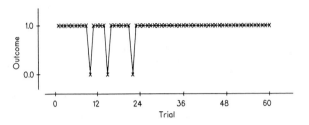

n	Mean	Standard Deviation
60	0.9500	0.2198

One concrete way of picturing a Bernoulli process is to consider a box that contains slips of paper, as in Exhibit 11.2F. A fraction π of the slips have a 1 on them, corresponding to success, and the remaining slips have a 0 on them. For the first trial, a slip is selected from the box at random—that is, all the slips have an equal chance of being selected. The trial is recorded either as a success or a failure and the slip is returned to the box and thoroughly remixed with the other slips. For the second, third, and subsequent trials, the process is repeated. Each time, the chosen slip is returned to the box and the slips are mixed thoroughly before the next selection is made. Repeating this procedure for n trials produces a process that satisfies the Bernoulli assumptions.

E X H I B I T **11.2F**
A Bernoulli Process Box

```
 0  1    1 0 1    0   1 1   00   1 0  0 1
01   1   00 0      0  0   1 10 1 0 1   01
 1  1 0  0     00   1 0 0 1    0 1 0 1 11
 0  1      1 0  01 0  01  0  01  0  0  0  1
   0 0 1 0 1    0   1 0    1   10 10   1 0
 1 10    0   1 0 1    1   1 1 0 1   01 0
01  0  0   1 0 1 0 11    0  1   0 1 01 01
 0  10 1 0     0 0   01  0 1   01  1 0 1 1
1110  01  0  11 01   01    0 01 0    0 0
 0 0  10   1 0 1 0 1    01 0 0   0 1 0  100
```

Whether the assumptions for a Bernoulli process are reasonable or not in real situations depends on the details of the particular situation. Suppose, for example, that households are being surveyed with regard to their television viewing habits. In particular, the survey is interested in whether household members are viewing NBC. If the survey is taken over the day from 8:00 A.M. to 11:00 P.M., it does not seem reasonable to assume a constant probability of success. The popularity of NBC's programs may very well vary over the day, and the success rate, π, could not be assumed to be constant.

As a second example, suppose that a manufacturing process is being observed and conforming and nonconforming product produced is being recorded. If every time a nonconforming item is found the machinery is readjusted, the trials are not independent. The fact that a nonconforming item had just been produced would affect the chance that a nonconforming item would be produced next.

SECTION

11.3 Exercises

11.3A Statistical software was used to produce Exhibit 11.2C.

a Produce a similar Bernoulli sequence. Compute the mean and standard deviation of the sequence and note the similarities and dissimilarities between our results and yours.

b Repeat part (a) and again note the similarities and dissimilarities.

c Repeat part (a) using other success rates, both low and high.

11.3B Simulate 30 Bernoulli trials by tossing a coin and recording the sequence of heads and tails obtained. How many heads did you obtain? What fraction of heads? How many heads did you expect to get?

SECTION

11.4 The Binomial Distribution

binomial distribution

This section introduces the **binomial distribution**, the theoretical distribution of the number of successes in repeated equal-sized samples of Bernoulli trials.

Suppose that a fixed number of trials n are under consideration. Let π denote the long-run proportion of successes and let p be the proportion of successes in a sample of n trials. Also let y denote the total number of successes recorded in a sample of n trials. Clearly both p and y will vary from sample to sample, and each of their distributions can be considered. Since $p = y/n$, it will be easy to relate facts about one variable to facts about the other one.

Consider $n = 12$ and $\pi = 0.83$. How many successes should be expected? With 12 trials it is possible to get a failure on each trial, giving 0 successes. It is also possible for all trials to produce a success, giving 12 successes. All totals from 0 through 12 are possible, but what is the probability that each of them occurs? Simulation can be used to answer this question. Exhibit 11.4A shows a portion of the data generated according to the rules for Bernoulli trials, with $\pi = 0.83$. Each row corresponds to 12 trials; row totals are also shown. This sequence of 12 trials was repeated 1000 times so that the distribution of totals could be considered. Exhibit 11.4B shows the histogram of the 1000 totals. Notice that although totals of 0, 1, 2, 3, and 4 are *possible*, they never occurred in 1000 repetitions of the simulation. Fortunately, not

Group of 12													Total Successes
1	1	1	1	1	1	1	1	0	1	0	1	0	9
2	1	0	1	1	0	1	1	1	1	1	0	1	9
3	1	1	0	1	1	1	1	1	1	1	1	0	10
4	1	1	1	1	1	1	1	1	1	1	1	1	12
5	1	1	1	1	1	1	1	0	1	0	1	1	10
6	1	0	1	0	1	0	1	1	1	1	1	1	9
7	1	1	0	1	0	1	1	1	1	1	1	1	10
8	1	0	1	1	0	1	1	1	1	1	1	1	10
9	1	1	1	0	1	1	1	1	1	0	0	1	9
10	1	1	1	1	1	1	1	1	1	1	1	1	12
11	1	1	1	0	1	1	1	0	1	1	0	1	9
12	1	0	1	1	1	1	1	1	1	1	0	1	10
13	1	1	1	1	0	1	1	1	1	1	1	1	11
14	1	1	1	0	1	1	1	1	1	0	1	1	10
⋮													⋮
994	1	0	1	1	1	1	0	1	1	0	0	1	8
995	1	1	1	1	1	1	1	0	1	1	1	1	11
996	1	1	1	1	0	0	1	1	1	1	0	1	9
997	1	1	1	1	1	1	1	1	0	1	0	1	10
998	1	0	1	1	1	0	0	0	1	0	0	1	6
999	1	1	1	1	1	1	1	0	1	1	1	1	11
1000	1	1	0	1	1	1	1	1	1	1	1	1	11

```
Histogram of Total, N=1000
Each * represents 10 observations

Midpoint   Count
    5         2   *
    6         4   *
    7        32   ****
    8        80   ********
    9       200   ********************
   10       305   *******************************
   11       276   ****************************
   12       101   ***********
```

every such situation must be simulated: there is a theoretical model that gives the required distribution in general.

The **binomial probability function** gives the probability that the total number of successes y will take on the value k. If k is an integer value between 0 and n, the probability of k successes is given by

binomial probability function

$$Pr(k \text{ successes}) = \frac{n!}{k!(n-k)!}\pi^k(1-\pi)^{n-k}$$

Recall that factorials are defined for any integer m by the following product:

$$m! = m(m-1)(m-2)\cdots(3)(2)(1)$$

For example, in dealing with $n = 12$ trials, suppose that we need to evaluate the chance of observing exactly 10 successes when $\pi = 0.83$ is the long-run fraction of successes. First work out the factorial part of the equation:

$$\frac{12!}{10!(12-10)!} = \frac{12 \times 11 \times 10 \times 9 \times 8 \times \cdots \times 2 \times 1}{10 \times 9 \times 8 \times \cdots \times 3 \times 2 \times 1 \times 2 \times 1} = \frac{12 \times 11}{2} = 66$$

This means that there are 66 different sequences of 12 trials, in which each sequence contains exactly 10 successes. The probability required is then given by

$$66(0.83)^{10}(1-0.83)^{12-10} = 66(0.83)^{10}(0.17)^2 = 66(0.155156)(0.0289) = 0.296$$

or approximately 30%. If 12 Bernoulli trials with $\pi = 0.83$ were repeated many times, in about 30% of the cases exactly 10 successes would be observed. In our simulation of 1000 trials, 305 totals of 10 successes were observed.

Most calculators and statistical software can compute any required binomial probability with ease. Exhibit 11.4C shows the results of certain Minitab calculations for both an individual binomial probability and for a whole table of probabilities. Comparing these probabilities with the simulation proportions observed in Exhibit 11.4B, we see that the theoretical model describes the overall situation very well.

EXHIBIT **11.4C**
Minitab Results with the
Binomial Probability Function
with $n = 12$ and
$\pi = 0.83$

k	$Pr(y = k)$	
10	0.2960	← **This also agrees with our hand calculation.**

k	$Pr(y = k)$	
0	0.000001	
1	0.000001	
2	0.000001	
3	0.000015	
4	0.000164	
5	0.001280	
6	0.007292	
7	0.030515	
8	0.093116	
9	0.202056	
10	0.295953	← **This also agrees with our hand calculation.**
11	0.262718	
12	0.106890	

k = theoretical number of successes
y = actual number of successes
Pr = probability

Exhibit 11.4D is a plot of the full binomial probability function when $n = 12$ and $\pi = 0.83$.

Now consider the distribution of the sample proportion p. For a given number of trials n, the collection of possible values for p is $0 = 0/n, 1/n, 2/n, \ldots,$

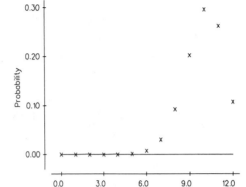

E X H I B I T **11.4D**

A Plot of the Binomial Probability
Function with $n = 12$ and
$\pi = 0.83$

$(n-1)/n, n/n = 1$. Furthermore, a sample proportion of y/n occurs only when the total number of successes is y. Thus the chance that a proportion y/n occurs is exactly the chance that y successes occur. The binomial probability function gives these probabilities.

For example, the chance that in 12 Bernoulli trials with $\pi = 0.83$ a sample proportion of $10/12$, or 0.83333, is observed is the same as the chance of exactly 10 successes, namely, 0.2960, as shown in Exhibit 11.4C. The full distribution for p can then be obtained by editing Exhibit 11.4C. Exhibit 11.4E shows the results and Exhibit 11.4F plots the resulting distribution.

E X H I B I T **11.4E**

Distribution of p for
$n = 12$ and $\pi = 0.83$

$p = k/12$	$Pr(p = k/12)$
0/12	0.000001
1/12	0.000001
2/12	0.000001
3/12	0.000015
4/12	0.000164
5/12	0.001280
6/12	0.007292
7/12	0.030515
8/12	0.093116
9/12	0.202056
10/12	0.295953
11/12	0.262718
12/12	0.106890

The binomial distribution can also arise in situations involving continuous variables, where you might not at first expect it. That is, you can measure one or more continuous variables but count only whether or not the results fall into a specified

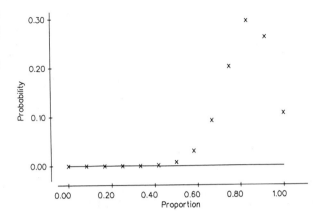

EXHIBIT 11.4F
A Plot of the Distribution of
Proportions when
$n = 12$ and $\pi = 0.83$

range. This makes the results a yes-no problem. The number of results falling into the specified range will then have a binomial distribution.

For example, suppose a process measures a variable x such as length, time, or weight. The distribution of x is not binomial—it might be normal, for instance. But suppose further that the product is considered acceptable only if x falls in the range a to b. Now the situation is yes-no. Assume that when the process is in control, the probability is 0.99 that x will fall in that range. If n independent values of x are observed in each sample and the total number y of unacceptable products is studied, y has a binomial distribution with n trials and "success" rate $\pi = 0.01$.

SECTION

11.5 Exercises

11.5A   In five Bernoulli trials with success rate 0.5,
  a   what is the chance of observing exactly two successes?
  b   what is the chance of observing no successes?
  c   what number of successes is most likely?

11.5B   If $n = 5$ and $\pi = 0.3$,
  a   what is the chance of observing exactly two successes?
  b   what is the chance of observing no successes?
  c   what number of successes is most likely?

11.5C   If $n = 5$ and $\pi = 0.3$, compare $Pr(1 \leq y \leq 3)$ with $Pr(1 < y < 3)$.

11.5D   A firm maintains 22 cars for business purposes. From past experience, it is known that approximately 10% will require major engine service during a one-year period.
  a   What is the probability that exactly one car will require major engine repair next year?
  b   Are the Bernoulli trial assumptions reasonable here?

11.5E   Use a statistical computer package to create a graph of the binomial probability function for a variety of values of n and π. Comment on the different shapes obtained.

11.5F **a** For $n = 7$, compare the binomial probability functions when $\pi = 0.2$ and when $\pi = 0.8$. Do you see any similarities? You may make the comparison either numerically or algebraically.

b Can you generalize this to other n and other pairs of values for π?

11.5G If a balanced coin is tossed five times, what is the chance that the proportion of heads observed is 0.4? Is 0.5? Is less than 0.1?

SECTION

11.6 Runs (Optional)

This section shows how to calculate the probability that a series of Bernoulli trials will have a "run" of successes or failures. The section also shows how information about such runs can help in monitoring processes.

The word *run* is used here in the sense of "a run of good luck," to extend in time, or to continue. Within the context of Bernoulli trials, a *success run* of length k is a sequence of k consecutive successes preceded and followed by at least one failure. The chance of k successes in a row is just π^k. For example, for a fair coin with $\pi = 0.5$, the probability of four heads in a row is $(0.5)^4 = 1/16 = 0.0625$, and the chance of eight consecutive heads is just $(0.5)^8 = 1/256 \simeq 0.004$.

The theory of runs may be applied to control charts to provide useful supplementary rules that indicate an out-of-control situation. In process analysis, where a sequence of means is considered, it is common to look for runs above or below the center line. Since when the process is in control the means are distributed approximately symmetrically about that center line, a value of $\pi = 0.5$ may be used to evaluate the chance of occurrence of various run lengths. Unusually long runs above or below the center line are strong indicators of an out-of-control process. Since runs all along the sequence are being searched for, probability calculations associated with runs are more difficult than those for the binomial distribution. In particular, the chance of observing runs of a given length will also depend on the length of the sequence searched. For sequence lengths in common use for control charts, Mosteller[†] has shown that the following rule provides good protection against tampering with a process that is in control while still offering evidence that the process mean has changed:

- A run of eight consecutive subgroup means above or below the center line indicates an out-of-control process.

EXAMPLE **11.6A**

Exercise 10.9A introduced a Procter & Gamble process for packaging a hair conditioner. The tightness of the cap was of concern. The original process was deemed to be in control but not up to specifications. The most likely source of variation was suspected to be the gripper pads that hold the cap

---

[†]Fredrick Mosteller, "Note on an Application of Runs to Quality Control Charts," *Annals of Mathematical Statistics*, 12 (1941), 228–232.

during the tightening. The pads were then redesigned to better conform to the grippable surface. The pad material was also changed to a material that had worked well in a similar application. After these changes, the process was again run. The control chart data obtained are given in Exhibit 11.6A.

The standard deviation chart (not shown) gives no indication of an out-of-control situation. However, the mean chart in Exhibit 11.6B does show some unusual behavior. For the first half of the sequence, the means are nearly always above the center line; in the last half, they are nearly all below the center line. Could this be caused by a downward shift in the process mean halfway through? Although such a suspicion is warranted, the data do not provide conclusive evidence that the mean has changed. The initial long run above the center line is of length 6, while the long run below the center line is of length 7. There are no runs of length 8, so the chart does not indicate that special causes of variation are at work. In addition, the process improvements have been effective. The fraction of product not meeting specifications has been reduced considerably compared with the situation shown in Exercise 10.9A. The company continued to investigate the causes of variation in the capping process with the goal of further stability and reduced variation. Control charts continued to alert them to potential problems and to document process improvements. ∎

EXHIBIT **11.6A**
Cap Tightness from Procter & Gamble Hair Conditioner Line

```
filename: P&G2.DAT
P&G second data set
(Source: Jeffrey Enck, Procter & Gamble,
Iowa City, Iowa)
Torque on hair conditioner caps after process improvement
24 14 18 27
17 32 31 27
21 27 24 21
24 26 31 34
28 32 24 16
22 37 36 21
16 17 22 34
20 19 16 16
18 30 21 16
14 15 14 14
25 15 16 15
19 15 15 19
19 30 24 10
15 17 17 21
34 22 17 15
17 20 17 20
15 17 24 20
```

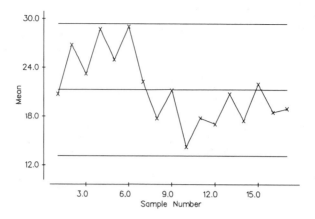

SECTION

11.7 The Mean and Standard Deviation

This section shows how to determine the mean and standard deviation of the binomial distribution and related sample proportion. How you use these statistics is explained in Section 11.9.

In Chapter 9, μ was called the mean of the normal curve, and it was interpreted as a measure of the middle of a distribution. How should the mean of the binomial distribution be defined?

Mean of a Binomial Distribution

Consider a particular binomial situation with n trials and success probability π. Repeat this same binomial experiment a large number of times, say m times. Each time the experiment is performed, a certain number of successes is observed. Let y_i denote the number of successes in the ith experiment. The data can be laid out as follows:

Experiment Number	Number of Successes Observed
1	y_1
2	y_2
3	y_3
$\vdots$	$\vdots$
m	y_m

Suppose the results of the m experiments are tallied. Each of the y's is either a 0, a 1, a 2, ..., or an n. Let #(y) denote the number of times that the particular value y was observed in the m experiments. Then by grouping the 0's, 1's, 2's, ..., together, the mean number of successes can be written as

$$\text{Mean} = \frac{y_1 + y_2 + \cdots + y_m}{m}$$

$$= \frac{[0 \times \#(0)] + [1 \times \#(1)] + \cdots + [n \times \#(n)]}{m}$$

$$= \left[0 \times \frac{\#(0)}{m} \right] + \left[1 \times \frac{\#(1)}{m} \right] + \cdots + \left[n \times \frac{\#(n)}{m} \right]$$

But if m is large, the fractions $\#(y)/m$ will be close to the long-run fraction or probability of observing exactly y successes. Thus, after repeating the binomial experiment a large number of times, the mean number of successes should be close to

$$0 \times Pr(0 \text{ successes}) + 1 \times Pr(1 \text{ success})$$
$$+2 \times Pr(2 \text{ successes}) + \cdots + n \times Pr(n \text{ successes})$$

This defines μ_y, the (theoretical) mean of the binomial distribution. This is also called the mean of y.

Obviously this could amount to a lot of computation! Let the computer calculate the mean in a few cases. Exhibit 11.7A shows the results for the cases ($n = 6$, $\pi = 0.5$), ($n = 12$, $\pi = 0.25$), and ($n = 15$, $\pi = 0.5$). Notice that in each case the mean is numerically equal to $n\pi$ (apart from rounding). This is not just a coincidence. It may be established using mathematical statistics that for a binomial distribution with n trials and success probability π, the mean of the distribution is always equal to

binomial mean

$$\mu_y = n\pi$$

Standard Deviation of a Binomial Distribution

Using similar reasoning, the (theoretical) standard deviation of the binomial distribution can be defined as

$$\text{Standard deviation} = [(0 - n\pi)^2 \times Pr(0 \text{ successes}) + (1 - n\pi)^2 \times Pr(1 \text{ success})$$
$$+ (2 - n\pi)^2 \times Pr(2 \text{ successes}) + \cdots + (n - n\pi)^2$$
$$\times Pr(n \text{ successes})]^{1/2}$$

or

$$\text{Standard deviation} = \sigma_y = \sqrt{\sum_{k=0}^{n} [(k - n\pi)^2 \times Pr(k \text{ successes})]}$$

Again theory can be used to show that for a binomial distribution, the standard deviation is given by

binomial standard deviation

$$\sigma_y = \sqrt{n\pi(1 - \pi)}$$

	$n = 6, \pi = .5$		$n = 12, \pi = .25$		$n = 15, \pi = .5$	
k	Probability	Product	Probability	Product	Probability	Product
0	0.015625	0.00000	0.031676	0.000000	0.000031	0.00000
1	0.093750	0.09375	0.126705	0.126705	0.000458	0.00046
2	0.234375	0.46875	0.232293	0.464586	0.003204	0.00641
3	0.312500	0.93750	0.258104	0.774311	0.013885	0.04166
4	0.234375	0.93750	0.193578	0.774311	0.041656	0.16663
5	0.093750	0.46875	0.103241	0.516207	0.091644	0.45822
6	0.015625	0.09375	0.040149	0.240897	0.152740	0.91644
7			0.011471	0.080299	0.196381	1.37466
8			0.002390	0.019119	0.196381	1.57104
9			0.000354	0.003186	0.152740	1.37466
10			0.000035	0.000354	0.091644	0.91644
11			0.000002	0.000024	0.041656	0.45822
12			0.000001	0.000012	0.013885	0.16663
13					0.003204	0.04166
14					0.000458	0.00641
15					0.000031	0.00046
Total		3.00000		3.000001		7.50000

k = Number of successes
Probability = $Pr(k$ successes)
Product = $k \times Pr(k$ successes)

For example, for a binomial distribution with $n = 12$ and $\pi = 0.83$, the standard deviation is

$$\sigma_y = \sqrt{12 \times 0.83 \times (1 - 0.83)} = \sqrt{1.6932} = 1.30$$

and the mean is $\mu_y = 12 \times 0.83 = 9.96$.

Exhibit 11.7B shows a plot of $\sqrt{\pi(1 - \pi)}$ as a function of π over the range zero to one. Notice that the curve is symmetric around $\pi = 0.5$. Also notice that the curve has its largest value of 0.5 for $\pi = 0.5$ and decreases as π moves away from 0.5 in either direction. Thus a binomial distribution has its largest variability when $\pi = 0.5$. The variability decreases as π moves away from 0.5 in either direction. These facts help explain the standard deviations observed in Exhibits 11.2A, D, and E for several values of π.

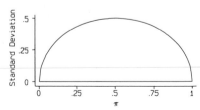

Proportions

The sample proportion $p = y/n$ is also of interest in analyzing Bernoulli trials. We have already seen how to find its distribution from the binomial distribution. Using facts about linear transformations analogous to those discussed in Section 4.6, the mean of the distribution of p is

mean of the binomial proportion

$$\mu_p = \pi$$

and the standard deviation of that distribution is

standard deviation of the binomial proportion

$$\sigma_p = \sqrt{\frac{\pi(1-\pi)}{n}}$$

With $n = 12$ and $\pi = 0.83$, the mean of p is $\mu_p = 0.83$ and the standard deviation of p is

$$\sigma_p = \sqrt{\frac{0.83(1-0.83)}{12}} = \sqrt{0.01175833} = 0.1084$$

SECTION

11.8 Exercises

11.8A   Use a statistical package as in Exhibit 11.7A to compute the probabilities for various binomial distributions. Evaluate the standard deviation of the distributions numerically from the definition and show that the theoretical formula $\sigma_y = \sqrt{n\pi(1-\pi)}$ gives the correct answer in these cases.

11.8B   Repeat Exercise 11.8A but use the distribution for p and verify numerically that $\sigma_p = \sqrt{\pi(1-\pi)/n}$.

11.8C   If five items are observed at random on a production line where about 5% of the items on average are defective, what are the mean and standard deviation of the proportion of defective items observed? For the number of defectives observed?

11.8D   Use a statistical package to simulate a large number (maybe 1000) of binomial variables with $n = 12$ and $\pi = 0.4$. Store the simulated values for use in parts (a) and (b).

   a   Plot a histogram of the simulated values and compare it to the corresponding exact binomial distribution.

   b   Calculate the mean and standard deviation of the simulated values and compare them to the known theoretical values.

11.8E   (Calculus required) Show that for π between 0 and 1, $\sqrt{\pi(1-\pi)}$ increases to a maximum value of 0.5 at $\pi = 0.5$ and then decreases. (*Hint:* Consider $[\sqrt{\pi(1-\pi)}]^2 = \pi(1-\pi) = \pi - \pi^2$, differentiate with respect to π, set equal to zero, and solve.)

SECTION

11.9 The Normal Approximation (Optional)

This section explains that with fairly large sample sizes, the numbers of successes in Bernoulli trials are normally distributed. It then shows how to use this fact to approximate the probability of observing a given number of successes in a particular sample of trials.

Exhibits 11.9A–C display a variety of binomial distributions in density histogram form. To facilitate comparison with a normal curve, only the outer contours of the density histogram are shown. The rectangles in the histogram are centered on the values for the number of successes, 0, 1, ..., n, and each rectangle has width one and height equal to the corresponding binomial probability given in Section 11.4. Since the rectangles have width one, their *areas* are the probabilities associated with each of the values 0, 1, ..., n. These areas can be compared to areas under a normal curve with the same mean and standard deviation. According to the plots, these areas are very nearly the same. As the next paragraph argues, this is no fluke. Rather, it is a consequence of the central limit effect.

EXHIBIT 11.9A
Binomial Distribution with
$n = 20$ and $\pi = 0.5$
(normal distribution overlaid)

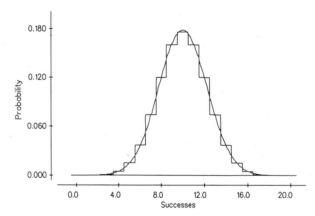

Consider n Bernoulli trials with success rate π. The total number of successes y can be thought of as the sum $y_1 + y_2 + \cdots + y_n$, where y_i is a binary variable equal to 1 if the ith trial results in a success and $y_i = 0$ otherwise. In other words, y_i is the number of successes on the ith trial. Furthermore, the sample proportion of successes can be expressed as

$$p = \frac{y}{n} = \frac{y_1 + y_2 + \cdots + y_n}{n} = \bar{y}$$

For example, if $n = 5$ and the sequence SFFSF is observed, then $y_1 = 1$, $y_2 = 0$, $y_3 = 0$, $y_4 = 1$, $y_5 = 0$, and $p = \bar{y} = (1 + 0 + 0 + 1 + 0)/5 = 2/5 = 0.4$. The point here is that p is in fact an average, and as such the central limit effect for means of process values, explained in Section 9.5, applies if n is reasonably large. In this case,

E X H I B I T   **11.9B**
Binomial Distribution with
$n = 50$ and $\pi = 0.1$
(normal distribution overlaid)

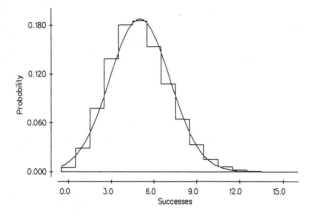

E X H I B I T   **11.9C**
Binomial Distribution with
$n = 60$ and $\pi = 0.7$
(normal distribution overlaid)

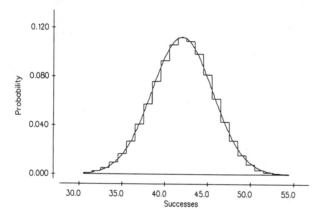

the process being sampled is the process of the 1's and 0's, which has mean π and standard deviation $\sigma = \sqrt{\pi(1-\pi)}$. Thus

$$\sigma_p = \frac{\sigma}{\sqrt{n}} = \frac{\sqrt{\pi(1-\pi)}}{\sqrt{n}} = \sqrt{\frac{\pi(1-\pi)}{n}}$$

and the following rule can be stated:

normal approximation

Normal approximation to the distribution of the proportion p: For large n, the distribution of p is approximately a normal distribution with mean $\mu_p = \pi$ and standard deviation

$$\sigma_p = \sqrt{\frac{\pi(1-\pi)}{n}}$$

E X A M P L E   **11.9A**

Consider a bank loan officer who is investigating missing information on loan applications. From past experience, the loan officer knows that about 30%

of all applications have information missing. Suppose that a random set of 25 loan applications is examined for missing information. A "success" here means that the loan application in question has missing information. Under these circumstances, what is the chance that the sample contains at most 20% successes—that is, $Pr(p \leq 0.2)$? To do the approximation, the mean $\mu_p = 0.3$ and the standard deviation $\sigma_p = \sqrt{0.3(1 - 0.3)/25} = 0.09165$ are needed. The corresponding standardized or z-value is $(0.2 - 0.3)/0.09165 = -1.09111$. From the normal distribution table, Exhibit 9.3G, the area below -1.09 is found to be 0.1379. Thus, the chance is about 14%.

With computer software, this probability can be obtained exactly. Since $n = 25$, $p \leq 0.2$ is equivalent to $y \leq 25 \times 0.2 = 5$. The probabilities of 0, 1, 2, 3, 4, or 5 successes are added. Exhibit 11.9D gives the probabilities. Adding them yields the exact result $0.0001 + 0.0014 + \cdots + 0.1030 = 0.1934$, or about 19% compared to the normal approximation value of 14%. The normal approximation can actually be improved a bit, as will be shown in the next subsection, "The Continuity Correction."

The computer can add the binomial probabilities. This is precisely what the *cumulative distribution function (CDF)* does. The CDF is the probability of k or fewer successes.[†] Exhibit 11.9E displays the answer needed in the loan application problem. (This answer of 0.1935 differs slightly from the

EXHIBIT **11.9D**
The Binomial Probability
Function for $n = 25$ and
$\pi = 0.3$

k	$Pr(y = k)$
0	0.0001
1	0.0014
2	0.0074
3	0.0243
4	0.0572
5	0.1030
6	0.1472
7	0.1712
8	0.1651
9	0.1336
10	0.0916
11	0.0536
12	0.0268
13	0.0115
14	0.0042
15	0.0013
16	0.0004
17	0.0001
18	0.0000

[†]See Appendix 2 for more details.

previous one of 0.1934 because rounded probabilities from Exhibit 11.9D were added, while the computer keeps many more digits in its internal calculations.) ∎

The Continuity Correction

Since $p = y/n$, the normal approximation may alternatively be stated in terms of y: For large n, the binomial distribution is approximately a normal distribution with mean $= n\pi$ and standard deviation $= \sqrt{n\pi(1-\pi)}$.

For the case $n = 25$ and $\pi = 0.3$, Exhibit 11.9F shows the complete normal curve and the outline of a bar chart for the binomial probabilities. Since the width of the bars is 1.0, the binomial probabilities are displayed as areas under the bars so that they can be compared directly to the areas under the approximating normal curve.

Once we think in terms of areas as probabilities, it is natural to approximate the probability of five or fewer successes by the area under the normal curve below 5.5 (rather than 5). This is called the *correction for continuity*.

Using the correction for continuity, the new approximation can be obtained using either statistical software or the normal distribution table in Exhibit 9.3G with the z-value $(5.5 - 7.5)/2.2913 = -0.873$. Either way, the probability is about 19% when rounded. This agrees with the correct result.

Suppose we need to approximate the chance of getting at least 7 successes but no more than 10, again with $n = 25$ and $\pi = 0.3$. Using the continuity correction, the area under the appropriate normal curve from 6.5 to 10.5 is found. With z-values of $(6.5 - 7.5)/2.2913 = -0.44$ and $(10.5 - 7.5)/2.2913 = 1.31$, respectively, the probability $0.9049 - 0.3300 = 0.5749$ is obtained from the normal distribution table.

EXHIBIT 11.9E
The CDF for the Binomial Distribution with $n = 25$, $\pi = 0.3$, and $k = 5$

k	$Pr(y$ **less or** $= k)$
5	0.1935 ← **Already accumulated.**

EXHIBIT 11.9F
Normal Approximation to the Binomial with $n = 25, \pi = 0.3$

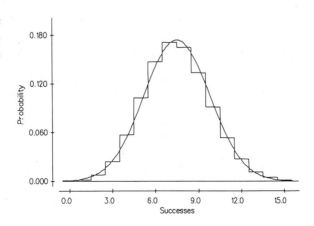

Ignoring the continuity correction would lead to the approximation $Pr(7 \leq y \leq 10) \simeq Pr(-0.22 \leq z \leq 1.09) = 0.4492$. The exact value obtained by adding the values at 7, 8, 9, and 10 from Exhibit 11.9D is 0.5615, and we again see the usefulness of the continuity correction in the normal approximation.

As a final calculation in this example, we approximate the probability of exactly nine successes. Notice that without the continuity correction the approximation would give zero as the answer and would be worthless! With the correction, $Pr(y = 9) = Pr(8.5 \leq y \leq 9.5) \simeq Pr(0.44 \leq z \leq 0.87) = 0.8078 - 0.6700 = 0.1378$, compared with the exact value from Exhibit 11.9D of 0.1336.

E X A M P L E   **11.9B**

Suppose that a marketing process measures the dollar amount of weekly sales of razor blades in the Midwest. For this stable, nonseasonal product, experience has shown that weekly sales are well approximated by a normal distribution with mean $1500 and standard deviation $350. If in any week sales drop below $1000, the company has a policy of looking carefully at market conditions to assess its competitive position. Otherwise the process continues to run without any special intervention or unusual inspection. Suppose weekly sales amounts are determined independently of each other. What can be said about the number of times the company will go looking for problems when none in fact exist? That is, if the process continues to operate without substantial change, how many "false alarms" might be observed in n weeks using this policy?

Consider a 26-week period. For each week, sales either exceed $1000 or they dip below $1000. If y denotes the total number of weeks in which sales go below $1000, then under our assumptions, y will have a binomial distribution with $n = 26$ trials. The "success" rate will be determined as the chance that a normal variable with mean $1500 and standard deviation $350 falls below $1000. The corresponding z-score is $(1000 - 1500)/350 = -1.43$, and from the normal distribution table in Exhibit 9.3G, $\pi = (1 - 0.9236) = 0.0764$. The mean number of false alarms is then $26 \times 0.0764 = 1.9864$ or about two, and the standard deviation of the number of false alarms is

$$\sqrt{26 \times 0.0764 \times (1 - 0.0764)} = \sqrt{1.8346} = 1.35$$

What is the chance of having two or *more* false alarms in the 26-week period? This is most easily obtained by calculating the chance of 0 or 1 false alarms and subtracting the result from 1. Using the binomial distribution,

$$Pr(0 \text{ successes}) + Pr(1 \text{ success}) = \frac{26!}{0!26!}(0.0764)^0(1 - 0.0764)^{26}$$
$$+ \frac{26!}{1!25!}(0.0764)^1(1 - 0.0764)^{25}$$
$$= 0.1266 + 0.2724 = 0.3990$$

Thus the chance of two or more false alarms in 26 weeks is $1 - 0.399 = 0.601$, or about 60%.

Now approximate the probability with the normal approximation. Using the continuity correction, $Pr(2 \leq y) = Pr(1.5 \leq y) \simeq Pr[(1.5 - 1.9864)/1.35 \leq z] = Pr(-0.36 \leq z) = 0.6406$. It is generally agreed that the normal approximation to the binomial distribution will be reasonably accurate if both $n\pi \geq 5$ and $n(1 - \pi) \geq 5$ are satisfied. These inequalities are *not* both satisfied in this example, so the approximation's accuracy should be doubted.

Of course, the normal approximation and the continuity correction are both of interest only if a statistical computing package is not readily available to do the exact binomial calculations. ▪

SECTION

11.10 Exercises

11.10A Consider 25 Bernoulli trials with $\pi = .3$, as in Exhibits 11.9D, E, and F.

    a   Find the exact probability of between 5 and 11 successes, inclusive.

    b   Use the normal approximation without the continuity correction to approximate the probability found in part (a).

    c   Use the normal approximation *with* the continuity correction to approximate the probability found in part (a) and compare your result to those found in parts (a) and (b).

11.10B If a balanced coin is tossed 50 times, approximate the chance that it comes up heads exactly 25 times. Compare this to the correct binomial value.

11.10C If a production line produces 10% nonconforming items on average and a random set of 100 items is inspected, estimate the chance that more than 20 of the items are nonconforming. Use statistical software to compare the approximation with the correct binomial value.

SECTION

11.11 Testing Hypotheses About π (Optional)

This section introduces the ways in which probabilities in Bernoulli processes can lead to useful statements about whether claims are true or false. These ideas are explored more fully in Chapter 17.

Statistical Hypotheses

We are frequently faced with a process that is reasonably modeled as a Bernoulli process. But the success probability, π, is rarely known. The π can be estimated using the process proportion p and the accuracy of this estimate can be assessed through the distribution of p, subjects that have been thoroughly discussed earlier in the chapter. However, in some settings a "theory" or perhaps past experience suggests a value for π. For example, a *fair* coin should have $\pi = 1/2$ for heads (or tails) and a *well-balanced* die should have $\pi = 1/6$ for any particular face. In other situations, a range of values may be claimed for the true value of π. For instance, a politician may claim that a certain position is held by a majority of her constituents ($\pi > 0.5$) or a company may claim that adults aged 18 to 25 prefer its product to its competitors' ($\pi > 0.5$). Or, for example, the long-run market share for a particular product has been 20% ($\pi = 0.20$). Once a new advertising program is initiated the firm hopes the data will show that $\pi > 0.20$.

statistical hypothesis

In a general Bernoulli setting, a **statistical hypothesis** is a statement about the value of π. The goal of *testing* statistical hypotheses is to determine whether the data from the Bernoulli process support the statistical hypothesis postulated.

The Null and Alternative Hypotheses

Any discussion of hypothesis testing involves introducing many new concepts. Instead of presenting the ideas in general terms, we introduce them using a specific example. This quote is from an article in the April 1978 issue of *Consumer Reports*, "Let it be Lowenbrau—American Style":

> What do you get when you pay a premium for a beer with a grand old European name? We got wind of the controversy involving *Lowenbrau*, a beer that originated in Germany but is now also brewed in the United States under license by Miller Brewing Co.
>
> One element of the controversy surfaced when Anheuser-Busch Inc.—brewers of an admittedly domestic premium beer, *Michelob*—asked the Federal Trade Commission to investigate Miller for possible "consumer deception." Anheuser-Busch claims, among other things, that *Lowenbrau* made by Miller in the United States is brewed with different ingredients and under a different process than the German beer.
>
> Whether that's true or not, there's another interesting comparison to be made. Miller also brews *Miller High Life* beer. An evident difference between Miller's *Lowenbrau* and *Miller High Life* is price. Miller beer with the German name sells for $2.50 a six-pack; Miller beer with the Miller name sells for $1.80. Miller must believe there's a difference between the two to merit the big price difference.
>
> To determine whether there is a difference between domestic *Lowenbrau* and *Miller High Life* that would be discernible to the average beer drinker, we assembled a taste-test panel of 24 staffers. Panelists were given three glasses of beer to taste, two of which were from the same bottle, and asked to identify which glass contained the beer that was different.[†]

In this example, the taste tests to be modeled are considered as 24 Bernoulli trials. "Success" corresponds to a correct identification of the different beer. The symbol π denotes the true but unknown proportion of "average beer drinkers" who, under the conditions of the taste test, would correctly choose the different beer. Again quoting from the article:

[†]Copyright 1978 by Consumers Union of United States, Inc., Mount Vernon, NY 10553. Reprinted by permission from CONSUMER REPORTS, April 1978.

If the panelists were only guessing which of the three glasses of beer was the correct one, they would be expected to get the right answer about one-third of the time, or 8 of the 24.

Skeptics, such as the writers at *Consumers Reports*, might hypothesize that $\pi = 1/3$, which corresponds to random guessing. Miller Brewing Company, on the other hand, might claim that $\pi > 1/3$, corresponding to various degrees of discrimination between the two beers. There are two competing claims here: $\pi = 1/3$ versus $\pi > 1/3$. The hypothesis of "no difference" between the two beers, here $\pi = 1/3$, is called the **null hypothesis**. A null hypothesis is usually denoted H_0 and is frequently read as "H-zero" or "H-nought." The hypothesis that competes with the null hypothesis, here $\pi > 1/3$, is called the **alternative hypothesis** and is denoted H_1. A test of a statistical hypothesis is designed to use the observed data to assess the strength of the evidence against the null hypothesis. In a research setting, the null hypothesis of no difference or no effect is frequently set up as a "straw person" with the hope that the empirical evidence will be sufficient to refute the null hypothesis and establish that a real effect does exist.

Before claiming that any statement is established, supporting evidence from the data must be produced. If $\pi = 1/3$, the mean number of correct identifications is $(1/3)24 = 8$. Again quoting from *Consumer Reports*, "Only 11 of the total of 24 judgments were correct." Is this evidence sufficient to conclude that the tasters are doing better than random guessing? To address this issue further, the errors that decision makers face must be discussed.

The Two Types of Errors

Intuition suggests that the null hypothesis, H_0: $\pi = 1/3$, should be rejected if the number of correct identifications, y, is large enough. A reasonable *decision rule* is to select a critical number of successes y_0 and decide to reject H_0 if and only if $y \geq y_0$. However, whatever the value of π, we know that y will have a binomial distribution over all the values $0, 1, \ldots, 24$ and that any of these values *may* occur. When selecting the value for y_0, the errors displayed in the following table must be considered:

	Truth	
Decision	H_0 true ($\pi = 1/3$)	H_0 false ($\pi > 1/3$)
Do not reject H_0	Correct decision	Type II error
Reject H_0	Type I error	Correct decision

The table displays four possible situations. If $\pi = 1/3$, we may still observe y_0 or more correct identifications. Our decision then is to reject H_0. This is an incorrect decision and is called a **Type I error**. It is also possible that $\pi > 1/3$ but we observe $y < y_0$ and erroneously declare H_0 to be valid. This is called a **Type II error**. A decision reached using any statistical test may be wrong in either of these two ways.[†]

[†]Some statisticians have recently defined a **Type III error** as the error committed when the wrong problem is solved!

Type I Errors

Standard practice is to select the critical value y_0 so that the probability of a Type I error is "sufficiently small." Sufficiently small is frequently interpreted to mean 0.05 or even 0.01 or smaller. This is the chance of falsely rejecting a true null hypothesis. With such probabilities, we protect ourselves against making a Type I error very often.

In the beer-tasting example, there are $n = 24$ trials and the null hypothesis says that $\pi = 1/3$. We would choose y_0 so that the total probability in a binomial distribution (with $n = 24$ and $\pi = 1/3$) at y_0 and larger values (the right-hand tail probability) is about 0.05. Exhibit 11.11A shows the required individual binomial probabilities and the sums that need to be considered. To keep the probability of a Type I error at or below 0.05, $y_0 = 13$ must be chosen. That is, the decision rule is to reject H_0 and declare that the beers have tastable differences if and only if 13 or more correct identifications are observed in the 24 taste tests. With this choice of critical value, Exhibit 11.11A shows that the exact probability of a Type I error is 0.02844. In general, the maximum Type I error probability is called the **significance level** of the test. The significance level is usually denoted by the Greek letter α (alpha).

significance level

Binomial Probabilities with
$n = 24$ and $\pi = 1/3$

y_0	$Pr(y = y_0)$	$Pr(y \geq y_0)$	
0	0.000059	1.00000	
1	0.000713	0.99994	
2	0.004099	0.99923	
3	0.015029	0.99513	
4	0.039451	0.98010	
5	0.078903	0.94065	
6	0.124929	0.86175	
7	0.160623	0.73682	
8	0.170661	0.57619	
9	0.151699	0.40553	
10	0.113774	0.25383	
11	0.072401	0.14006	
12	0.039217	0.06766	← Larger than 0.05
13	0.018100	0.02844	← First y_0 at which tail probability is ≤ 0.05
14	0.007111	0.01034	
15	0.002370	0.00323	
16	0.000667	0.00086	
17	0.000157	0.00019	
18	0.000030	0.00004	
19	0.000005	0.00001	
20	0.000001	0.00000	
21	0.000001	0.00000	
22	0.000001	0.00000	
23	0.000001	0.00000	
24	0.000001	0.00000	

Source: Minitab's PDF and CDF commands with the binomial subcommand.

In the beer-tasting example, remember that only 11 of the total of 24 taste-test judgments were correct. *Consumer Reports* interpreted this as follows: "Although the 11 correct choices were an improvement over pure guesswork, we don't consider that to be statistically significant evidence that a beer drinker can tell domestic Lowenbrau from Miller High Life." That is, since 11 is less than the critical value of 13, the evidence is considered insufficient to refute the null hypothesis of random guessing.

Type II Errors

Since the alternative hypothesis H_1: $\pi > 1/3$ specifies a range of values for π, the probability of a Type II error must be calculated for each value of π of interest in that range. Suppose that in fact $\pi = 0.9$, meaning that beer drinkers are very discriminating. The probability of a Type II error saying that the beers are not distinguishable when they are is the chance that 12 or fewer successes are observed in a binomial distribution with $n = 24$ and $\pi = 0.90$. Using computer software, this probability is found to be 0.0000. If drinkers are a little less discriminating, say $\pi = 0.80$, then the chance of a Type II error is 0.0010. Exhibit 11.11B shows a small table of Type II error probabilities.

π	0.40	0.50	0.60	0.70	0.80	0.90
Pr(Type II Error)	0.8857	0.5806	0.2130	0.0314	0.0010	0.0000

Notice that if there is a 50-50 chance of discriminating between the beers, the probability of a Type II error is 0.5806—quite large. In general, the closer the particular value of π ($> 1/3$) is to the null value of $1/3$, the more difficult it is to detect from the data that the null hypothesis is false. However, a value of π just a little larger than $1/3$ does not indicate substantial discrimination among beer drinkers, and a Type II error would have little practical significance.

On the other hand, since the probabilities when $\pi \geq .70$ are very small, we are quite confident that in making our decision to retain H_0 we have not committed a serious Type II error. It is not likely that we have failed to detect the fact that beer drinkers can discriminate quite well.

p-Values

Some statisticians prefer a related but alternative framework for deciding whether or not the evidence provided by the data is sufficient to refute the null hypothesis. If the observed data are unlikely to have occurred under the supposition that the null hypothesis is true and are more likely to have occurred if the alternative hypothesis is true, the data represent evidence against the null hypothesis and in favor of the alternative hypothesis. In our example, the more successes obtained, the more the evidence points toward discriminating beer drinkers rather than the null hypothesis of random guessing.

p-value

In general, the **p-value** of a test is the probability of getting an outcome at least as extreme as the outcome actually observed. The *p*-value is computed under the assumption that the null hypothesis is true. The question is, if the null hypothesis is true, what are the chances that we would observe this value or one more extreme? *Extreme* is determined according to the alternative hypothesis. In the beer-drinking example, 11 successes were observed. The alternative hypothesis suggests that more successes would be observed than under the null hypothesis. The smaller the *p*-value, the stronger the evidence against the null hypothesis. Note, however, that the *p*-value is *not* the probability that the null hypothesis is correct.

In our example, an outcome at least as extreme as the one observed means 11 *or more* successes. This is called a *one-sided p*-value. The *p*-value is computed from a binomial distribution with $n = 24$ and $\pi = 1/3$ and we have (from the computer)

$$p\text{-value} = Pr(11 \text{ or more successes when } \pi = 1/3) = 0.1401$$

or about 14%. As in our earlier test, we usually do not feel that the evidence is sufficient to reject the null hypothesis unless the *p*-value is smaller than 5%, or even less. As quoted earlier, "Although the 11 correct choices were an improvement over pure guesswork, we don't consider that to be statistically significant evidence that a beer drinker can tell domestic Lowenbrau from Miller High Life."

If the *p*-value is smaller than the specified significance level α, the evidence is said to be *statistically significant* at level α. Significance testing is presented in Chapter 17 in more general settings and more detail.

SECTION

11.12 Exercises

11.12A   A taste test was designed to compare preferences for Coke versus Pepsi. Twenty tasters were assembled and each was presented with two glasses, labeled A and B, one of which contained Coke and the other Pepsi. The glasses were not otherwise identified, but their correct identity was known to the people conducting the test. After sipping from each glass, the tasters were asked to identify which glass contained the Pepsi. Let π denote the probability that a person correctly chooses the glass of Pepsi.

a   A common null hypothesis in such a situation is that the choice is made at random. State this hypothesis in terms of π.

b   In words, the alternative hypothesis is that the tasters can choose the glass of Pepsi better than expected with random guessing. Express this alternative hypothesis in terms of π.

c   Would you consider it convincing evidence that people can discriminate between Coke and Pepsi if 15 of the 20 tasters correctly identify the Pepsi?

d   Based on the data given in part (c), what is the *p*-value of the test?

11.12B   Last season an otherwise star basketball player made only 60% of his foul shots. This season he has made 16 of his first 21 foul shot attempts. Do you find this to be statistically significant evidence that his foul shooting has improved over last year?

a   What is the null hypothesis?

b   With significance level of about 5%, would you reject the null hypothesis on the basis of these data?

c What is the *p*-value for these data?

d If in fact his true long-run foul shooting probability this year is 80%, what is the chance that a rule that rejects the old value of 60% when 17 or more successes out of 21 tries are made will detect the new, improved percentage? That is, what is the chance of *not* making a Type II error using this decision rule when the percentage has improved from 60% to 80%?

11.12C A coin is suspected of being biased toward heads. It is tossed 11 times. The null hypothesis is that the coin is fair. Find the critical value y_0 for the number of heads at or above which fairness should be rejected. Assume a desired significance level of about 5%.

Chapter Summary

Many two-outcome processes may be adequately modeled as sequences of Bernoulli trials. Recall that the assumptions of constant success rate, π, and independence of the trials must be satisfied, at least approximately, to use the theory described in this chapter. Usually we are interested in either the number of successes y or, equivalently, the proportion of successes p in a fixed number of trials n. The distribution of the number of successes is called the binomial distribution; its formula is given in Section 11.4. However, statistical software allows easy calculation of any binomial probabilities required.

The mean and standard deviation of the binomial distribution were developed in Section 11.7. The mean is

$$\mu_y = n\pi$$

and the standard deviation is

$$\sigma_y = \sqrt{n\pi(1-\pi)}$$

For the variable p, the sample proportion, the mean is

$$\mu_p = \pi$$

and the standard deviation is

$$\sigma_p = \sqrt{\frac{\pi(1-\pi)}{n}}$$

For the Bernoulli distribution, the mean is π and the standard deviation is $\sqrt{\pi(1-\pi)}$.

Recall that the sample proportion of successful trials p can be thought of as a sample mean from the 0–1 process. Thus the mean of the distribution of p is the same as the mean of the process, and the standard deviation of the distribution of p is the standard deviation of the process divided by the square root of the number of observations n. If n is reasonably large, the binomial distribution may be meaningfully approximated by a normal distribution with the same mean and standard deviation. Better approximations are obtained if the continuity correction is used. The normal approximation loses some of its traditional value when a statistical computer package is used because exact calculations are easily made in many cases.

Supplementary Exercises for Chapter 11

11A   The American College Testing Program in Iowa City, Iowa, designs and produces many tests, including the college entrance exam commonly known as the ACT exam. The scores on the ACT exam for incoming freshmen at the University of Iowa are approximately normally distributed with mean 23.2 and standard deviation 3.1.

a   What is the chance that a randomly selected freshman has a score exceeding 26?

b   If five freshmen are selected randomly, what is the chance that all have ACT scores exceeding 26?

c   If five freshmen are selected randomly, what is the chance that exactly one of them has an ACT score exceeding 26?

d   If five freshmen are selected randomly, what is the mean number of them whose ACT scores exceed 26?

11B   According to empirical evidence, a polygraph lie-detector test will falsely accuse a person of lying about 20% of the time.

a   A firm tests four employees using the polygraph. If in fact they all answer truthfully, what is the probability that at least one of them will be declared a liar?

b   Repeat part (a) with the firm testing 50 employees.

11C   Compare the standard deviation of a binomial distribution with $n = 100$ and $\pi = 0.01$ with the standard deviation of a binomial distribution with $n = 200$ and $\pi = 0.005$. Can you generalize this comparison?

11D   Random testing for illegal drugs is a controversial idea, especially since no drug test is perfect. Suppose a test that produces false positives at a rate of 2% is used. That is, the test will declare about 2% of the people in a large drug-free group to be drug users.

a   If 6 drug-free people are tested, what is the chance that there is at least one false positive?

b   If 60 drug-free people are tested, what is the chance that there is at least one false positive?

11E   Compare the binomial and approximating normal distributions as in Exhibit 11.9A for the cases

a $n = 20, \pi = 0.4$ **b** $n = 10, \pi = 0.5$ **c** $n = 15, \pi = 0.1$ **d** $n = 15, \pi = 0.9$

Glossary for Chapter 11

alternative hypothesis   A statement about how the null hypothesis can be false.

Bernoulli process (or Bernoulli trials)   A sequence of independent binary variable trials with constant success rate.

binomial distribution   The theoretical distribution of the number of successes in n Bernoulli trials with success rate π.

binomial mean $n\pi$

binomial probability function   The probability of k successes in n Bernoulli trials with success rate π.

binomial standard deviation $\sqrt{n\pi(1 - \pi)}$

mean of the binomial proportion	$\mu_p = \pi$
null hypothesis	The hypothesis of "no difference."
p-value	The probability of getting an outcome at least as extreme as the outcome observed.
significance level	The maximum probability of a Type I error.
standard deviation of the binomial proportion	$\sigma_p = \sqrt{\frac{\pi(1-\pi)}{n}}$
statistical hypothesis	A statement about a model parameter.
Type I error	Deciding a true hypothesis is false.
Type II error	Deciding a false hypothesis is true.
Type III error	Solving the wrong problem.

Control Charts for Binary Variables

Chapter Objectives

After mastering this chapter, you will be able to:

- Construct p charts for equal and unequal sample sizes

- Interpret control charts for binary variables

12.1 Introduction

As discussed in Chapter 11, in every business there are many situations in which binary variables are of interest—a loan is approved or rejected, a bank check is input correctly or not, a service is acceptable or not, a dimension on a part is acceptable or not, several dimensions on a product are jointly acceptable or not, and so forth. Can control charts be adapted to monitor binary variables as was done with continuous variables? In fact the adaptation is quite straightforward.

In Chapter 11 *success* was used as a generic term for many different specific outcomes in 0–1 processes. In this chapter successes are called *defectives*, and π denotes the long-run proportion of defectives in a constant-cause process. Chapter 11 showed that for a constant-cause binary process, the distribution of the sample fraction p in a sample of size n is completely determined by π and n. Thus, control can be monitored by checking the constancy of π over time. Controlling dispersion and mean level do not have to be considered separately, as they were with continuous variables.

SECTION

12.2 *p* Charts

p chart

A **p chart** is based on a sequence plot of the fraction of defectives in successive subgroups, or samples, collected from the process over time. We let p_i denote the fraction of defectives in the ith subgroup. Similarly, y_i and n_i denote the number of defectives and sample size, respectively, of the ith subgroup. Then $p_i = y_i/n_i$, for $i = 1, 2, \ldots, k$.

From Chapter 11, recall that the distribution of a sample fraction p has mean $\mu_p = \pi$ and standard deviation $\sigma_p = \sqrt{\pi(1-\pi)/n}$. Furthermore, if the sample size n is not too small, the distribution of p can be adequately approximated by a normal distribution. Thus, a three-sigma control chart on the fraction of defectives can be constructed by plotting p_i versus i for $i = 1, 2, \ldots, k$. To estimate π, we use the grand average

CL for *p* charts

$$\bar{p} = \frac{\text{Total number of defectives}}{\text{Total number of trials}} = \frac{\sum_{i=1}^{k} y_i}{\sum_{i=1}^{k} n_i} = \frac{\sum_{i=1}^{k} n_i p_i}{\sum_{i=1}^{k} n_i}$$

The center line, CL, is at $\bar{p}$. The control limits for the ith sample are at

UCL for *p* charts

$$UCL_i = \bar{p} + 3\sqrt{\frac{\bar{p}(1-\bar{p})}{n_i}}$$

LCL for *p* charts

$$LCL_i = \bar{p} - 3\sqrt{\frac{\bar{p}(1-\bar{p})}{n_i}}$$

Notice that sample sizes can be unequal. This is common in applications. Notice also that, depending on the values of $\bar{p}$ and n_i, the lower control limit can be negative. (The distribution of p is only *approximately* normal.) If LCL is negative, it is set equal to zero.

EXAMPLE   12.2A

As a first example, consider the data in Exhibit 12.2A. The exhibit shows the results of 25 samples, each of size 50, from a binary process. The value p_i for each sample is also given. The overall fraction defective is $\bar{p} = (7 + 9 + 1 + \ldots + 7 + 3)/(25 \times 50) = 129/1250 = 0.1032$. So

$$\sqrt{\frac{\bar{p}(1-\bar{p})}{n_i}} = \sqrt{\frac{0.1032(1 - 0.1032)}{50}} = 0.043023$$

and the control limits are given by

$$UCL = 0.1032 + (3 \times 0.043023) = 0.232$$
$$LCL = 0.1032 - (3 \times 0.043023) = -0.0259$$

We increase the LCL to zero.

Sample	Number of Defectives	p	Sample	Number of Defectives	p
1	7	0.14	14	6	0.12
2	9	0.18	15	4	0.08
3	1	0.02	16	6	0.12
4	5	0.10	17	5	0.10
5	7	0.14	18	5	0.10
6	2	0.04	19	3	0.06
7	6	0.12	20	6	0.12
8	9	0.18	21	3	0.06
9	3	0.06	22	10	0.20
10	4	0.08	23	5	0.10
11	5	0.10	24	7	0.14
12	5	0.10	25	3	0.06
13	3	0.06			

The p chart for these data is in Exhibit 12.2B. It shows there is no reason to doubt that the process is driven by a constant-cause system.

In contrast, suppose that the 25th sample had produced 13 defects. Then the overall $\bar{p}$ increases to 0.1112. The (trial) control limits become $UCL = 0.1112 + (3 \times 0.04446) = 0.24458$ and $LCL = 0.1112 - (3 \times 0.04446) = -0.02218$ (which is again replaced by zero). The control chart shown in Exhibit 12.2C clearly indicates the out-of-control situation in sample 25. ■

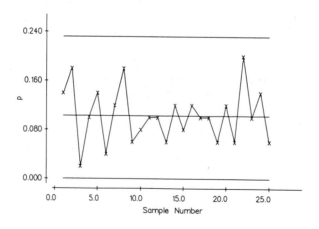

EXHIBIT 12.2C
Fraction Defective Control Chart:
Process Out of Control at Sample
25

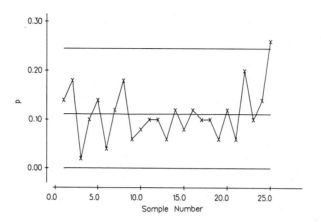

SECTION

12.3 Exercises

12.3A   In 20 samples each of size 60, a total of 36 defectives was observed.

a   What is the value of $\bar{p}$?

b   What are the control limits for the p chart based on samples of size 60?

c   If five defectives are observed in one sample, would the process be considered out of control?

12.3B   Twenty samples of various sizes produced a total of 36 defectives out of 1200 total observations.

a   What is the value of $\bar{p}$?

b   What are the control limits for the p chart for a sample of size 60?

c   What are the control limits for the p chart for a sample of size 40?

d   If five defectives are observed in a sample of size 40, would the process be considered out of control at that point?

SECTION

12.4 Applications of the p Chart

The two brief case histories in this section show the use of p charts in different industries.

Banking—Check Processing

Nearly all North American banks have automated check processing using magnetic ink character recognition (MICR) technology. Although almost all MICR characters printed on checks can be read automatically, a few are misread because of defects in the characters. When this happens, the automatic reader rejects the check and it must be processed by hand. Needless to say, the rejects are much more costly to handle. Statistical process control has been very effective in monitoring the process and minimizing such costs.[†]

Exhibit 12.4A presents data on defective checks for four five-day weeks. Notice that the sample sizes vary over the four-week period from a low of 930 to a high of 1080. Exhibit 12.4B is the control chart for proportion defective. Notice that the control limits vary because they are based on the differing sample sizes. For sample

E X H I B I T **12.4A**
Number of Defective Checks
Per Day

```
filename: BADCHEKS.DAT
Number of defective checks
(Source: W.J.Latzko, Quality and Productivity for
Bankers and Financial Managers, Marcel Dekker,
New York, 1986)
Four weeks of daily data
Sample size, Defects
 930    8
1080   12
1050   16
1020    4
1050    8
1040   14
 920   11
1000   16
 990    4
 950    8
 970   13
 950    4
1030    6
 980   13
1050    4
1070   12
 980   11
 940   19
1050   11
 950    6
```

E X H I B I T **12.4B**
Control Chart for Defective
Checks

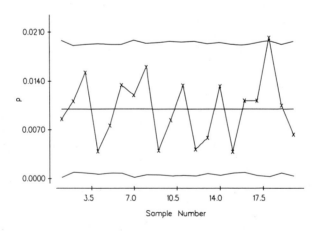

†More details may be found in William J. Latzko, *Quality and Productivity for Bankers and Financial Managers* (New York: Dekker, 1986).

18, the proportion defective exceeds the upper control limit, so the process would be declared out of control at that time.

Manufacturing

The Winegard Company uses an automated process to manufacture printed circuit boards used in pay telephones. Each board contains 236 positions, each of which must be properly soldered for the board to work correctly. Exhibit 12.4C gives data on the number of defective solder joints per board for a trial production run of 26 boards in December 1986. The defective joints must be resoldered by hand—a costly process. Exhibit 12.4D displays the p chart for the 26 boards. Here $\bar{p} = 0.060$ and two points lie above the upper control limit. More important, most of the first 13 values of p_i are below the center line, while most of the last 13 values are above the center line.

EXHIBIT 12.4C
Defective Solder Joint Data

Board Number	Number of Defects	p (no. defects/236)	Board Number	Number of Defects	p (no. defects/236)
1	14	0.059	14	22	0.093
2	5	0.021	15	12	0.051
3	7	0.030	16	19	0.081
4	10	0.042	17	38	0.161
5	10	0.042	18	14	0.059
6	6	0.025	19	23	0.097
7	10	0.042	20	15	0.064
8	6	0.025	21	10	0.042
9	18	0.076	22	29	0.123
10	9	0.038	23	13	0.055
11	9	0.038	24	14	0.059
12	9	0.038	25	18	0.076
13	6	0.025	26	20	0.085

EXHIBIT 12.4D
Control Chart for Defective Solder Joints

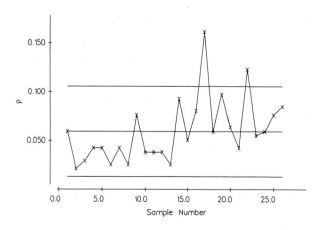

A review of the process with the research and development department revealed that the belt speed through the automatic soldering machine was 12 feet per minute for the first 13 runs but 16 feet per minute for the last 13. Exhibit 12.4E, a control chart for just the first 13 values, shows that the initial portion of the process appears to be in control, with $\bar{p} = 0.039$.

EXHIBIT 12.4E
Control Chart for Defective
Solder Joints: First 13 Samples
Only

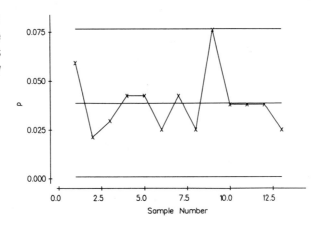

Finally, Exhibit 12.4F displays a control chart for the full sequence but with control limits based only on samples 1 through 13. The change in the last half of the series is more evident than before. Clearly, the lower belt speed produced substantially fewer bad solder joints.

EXHIBIT 12.4F
Control Chart for Defective
Solder Joints: Limits Based on
Samples 1–13 Only

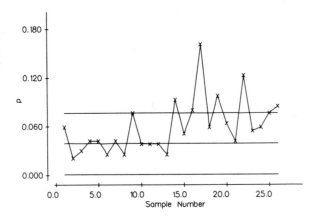

SECTION

12.5 Exercises

12.5A The following data give the number of new car loan applications that contained missing information at a large bank. The data were collected for 20 weeks, with each week's data based on a sample of 30 applications.

```
filename: LOANS.DAT
Number of new car loans with missing information
20 weeks of data, samples of size 30 each week
 9 7 6 7 5 7 3 5 4 9 6 7 4 7 5 7 4 7 6 2
```

a What percentage (overall) of the applications contain missing information?

b Does the application system seem to be in control with respect to missing information?

12.5B The data set below gives the number of defectives in 30 samples each of size 100. The defectives refer to plating defects of assembled parts in a manufacturing process.

```
filename: PLATING.DAT
Plating defects on assembled parts
(Source: K.Ishakawa, Guide to Quality Control,
 2nd rev. ed., Asian Productivity Organization
 White Plains, New York: UNIPUB 1986)
 30 samples of size 100 each
1 6 5 5 4 3 2 2 4 6 2 1 3 1 4 5 4 1 6 15 12 6 3 4 3 3 2 5 7 4
```

a Display a p chart for the data and note whether the process is or is not in control.

b Redo the chart, basing the control limits only on data that are deemed in control. What value of $\bar{p}$ should be used to compute the control limits for future use?

SECTION

12.6 Other Control Charts

Control charts for defectives are sometimes based on the percentage of defectives or the total number of defectives instead of on the fraction, or proportion, of defectives.

Charts plotting the percentage of defectives are easily made. The center line is at $100\bar{p}$, the overall percentage of defectives. The control limits are

$$UCL_i = 100\bar{p} + 3\sqrt{\frac{100\bar{p}(100 - 100\bar{p})}{n_i}}$$

$$LCL_i = 100\bar{p} - 3\sqrt{\frac{100\bar{p}(100 - 100\bar{p})}{n_i}}$$

If total defectives are used, the y_i are plotted with control limits given by $\bar{y} \pm 3\sqrt{n\bar{p}(1 - \bar{p})}$ where $\bar{y} = (y_1 + y_2 + \cdots + y_k)/k$. The disadvantage of this approach is that it cannot be used with unequal sample sizes, since $\bar{y}$ then makes no sense as a center line.

Both these alternative charts, however, will lead to the same decisions as p charts do about whether the process is or is not in control.

Chapter Summary

Sequence plots of the fractions of defectives in successive subgroups, together with the appropriate control limits, help us find special causes of variation in processes of binary variables. The charts also help prevent unnecessary tampering with a stable process. Basic facts from the binomial distribution permit an easy development of the required control limits.

Supplementary Exercises for Chapter 12

12A In 15 samples each of size 40, a total of 29 defectives was observed.

    a What is the value of $\bar{p}$?

    b What is the value of the lower control limit?

    c If one of the samples contains only one defective, would that sample be declared out of control?

12B The data below give the number of customers served (sample sizes) and number of customer complaints (defectives) about service over a 25-week period. From week 21 on a new service procedure was implemented with the hope of reducing customer complaints.

    a What was the mean number of complaints during the first 20 weeks?

    b Was the process in control during the first 20 weeks?

    c Do the data support the claim that the new procedures reduce customer complaints?

    d Write a one-to-two-page report to management documenting the improvement. Use graphs and descriptive statistics where appropriate but as little technical jargon as possible.

```
filename: IMPROVE.DAT
Process improvement data
Starting with sample 21 a new procedure was implemented
Variables: sample size, number of defects
48   14                   50   15
46   15                   44   21
45   19                   44   14
47   17                   51   12
44   14                   54   11
43   14                   55   18
43   16                   50   13
42   12                   55   14
55   17                   45    4
46   12                   44    5
51   17                   57    5
60   13                   56    4
                          48    3
```

12C Manufacturing television picture tubes is a complex process. The data file below gives information on defective tubes and sample sizes produced daily by General Electric over the period January 2 to 31. Construct a p chart for these data and interpret its meaning.

```
filename: TVTUBES.DAT
Defective picture tubes at General Electric
(Source: E.R.Ott, Process Quality Control,
 New York: McGraw Hill, 1975)
sample size, number of defectives
2145  202                3052  226
2876  104                2874  122
2607  178                2850  219
2424  102                2051  205
2786  170                2379   94
2239   83                1955   98
2449  488                1971  125
2745   97                2120   80
3268    8                2476  173
2885   56                2630   59
2681   46                2948  165
1414  158                2966   89
2829  239                2560  117
```

12D   The value of $3\sqrt{n\bar{p}(1-\bar{p})}$ enters into the calculation of upper and lower control limits when plotting the numbers of defectives instead of the proportions of defectives.(See Section 12.6.)

a   Compare the value of $3\sqrt{n\bar{p}(1-\bar{p})}$ when $\bar{p}=0.01$ and $n=100$ with the value when $\bar{p}=0.005$ and $n=200$.

b   Can you make any generalizations from part (a)?

Glossary for Chapter 12

CL for p charts $CL = \bar{p} = \dfrac{\text{Total number of defectives}}{\text{Total number of trials}} = \dfrac{\sum_{i=1}^{k} y_i}{\sum_{i=1}^{k} n_i} = \dfrac{\sum_{i=1}^{k} n_i p_i}{\sum_{i=1}^{k} n_i}$

LCL for p charts $LCL_i = \bar{p} - 3\sqrt{\dfrac{\bar{p}(1-\bar{p})}{n_i}}$

p charts   Control charts based on sequence plots of sample proportions.

UCL for p charts $UCL_i = \bar{p} + 3\sqrt{\dfrac{\bar{p}(1-\bar{p})}{n_i}}$

Randomized Data Collection and Inference

13

Data Collection

Chapter Objectives

After mastering this chapter, you will be able to:

- State the differences among simple observation, designed experiments, and surveys

- Give examples of simple observation, designed experiments, and surveys

- Discuss the importance of making comparisons in data analysis

- Explain the meaning of stratification

- Outline the six basic steps in data collection

Chapter 1 introduced three ways to collect data: simple observation, experiments, and surveys. This chapter discusses each of these tools in more detail, though still in a conceptual, nonmathematical way. The chapter explains the importance of making sure that data can be used to make comparisons and outlines a process for collecting data efficiently and effectively. The chapter closes with a case study that illustrates some basics of data collection and analysis. These ideas are developed in more detail in the chapters that follow. Chapters 14 to 16 will focus on surveys and will show how to analyze the data they gather. Chapters 17 to 19 will say more about experiments.

SECTION

13.1 Simple Observation

Simple observation, as defined in Chapter 1, means just observing outcomes of a process as they become available, or systematically observing outcomes at predetermined times. But the fact that this data-collection tool is called "simple" does not mean that analyzing the data collected is a simple matter. Our computer culture has made it easy to capture vast amounts of data electronically. For example, much of the data that A. C. Nielsen uses to make television program ratings is collected through "people meters," hand-held devices that viewers activate when they watch television and deactivate when they stop watching. Computers are also used to collect data from manufacturing processes, from supermarket checkout stations, from securities markets, and from peoples' brains as they watch advertisements. Computers give us such extensive ability to collect data that the resulting databases can be overwhelming. One of the challenges of the information age is to learn how to extract relevant information efficiently from huge databases.

EXAMPLE   13.1A

Large databases are not necessarily informative. W. Edwards Deming cites the following example.[†] In a manufacturing plant, a vast amount of data on plant operations was collected and put into a computer. The computer printed the data in a thick stack of paper, which was laid on a manager's desk each morning. Because the printout was cumbersome and because of the press of the day's activities, the manager never looked at the data. How different it would have been if the computer had been programmed to provide sequence plots that showed the manager at a glance the status of his operations! Even more to the point, since the computer was available, it could and should have been programmed to make the plots in real time, not to give only a report on yesterday. Modern manufacturing depends on keeping processes in control moment by moment, not day by day or month by month.   ▪

EXAMPLE   13.1B

Cohen, LuValle, Mitchell, and Sproles report on methods for "accelerated life testing" of the reliability of electronic connectors.[‡] Accelerated tests measure how components perform at high stress levels because the components rarely fail under "normal" conditions. From performance in the accelerated tests, engineers try to infer the performance characteristics of the components under normal conditions. Cohen and his colleagues report the need to use computer-controlled data acquisition systems to collect as much as hundreds of thousands of measurements during a life test.

To use the enormous databases that result, analysts must be able to summarize the data using graphic displays and mathematical models that succinctly present the information lurking in millions of bits of data. In this case, the collection and analysis of vast amounts of data were justified by the study's clearly focused objectives and its potential contributions to cost savings and consumer satisfaction.   ▪

[†]W. Edwards Deming, *Quality, Productivity, and Competitive Position* (Cambridge, Mass.: MIT Center for Advanced Engineering Study, 1982), pp. 75–76.

[‡]Howard M. Cohen, Michael J. LuValle, J. Peter Mitchell, and Edward S. Sproles, Jr., "Reliability Evaluations of Interconnection Products," *AT&T Technical Journal*, 66(4), (1987), 70–80.

13.2 Surveys

Surveys differ from simple observation in that they are "frozen" in time—a sample of elements is selected for measurement during a specified, brief interval. Surveys come in many shapes and sizes. In general, though, they have the following characteristics:

- A survey is done during a brief interval of time, called the *observation period*. A survey is cross-sectional—that is, the data from a survey are basically intended to be informative about the characteristics of a population during this observation period.

- A relatively large number of elements, or a large sample, is observed. Often, many different measurements or data items are gathered from each element in the sample, usually through filling out a questionnaire or checklist.

- Conducting a survey is a complicated process that must be carefully managed to get high-quality results. Surveys often generate large databases that must be carefully analyzed and then summarized using charts and tables.

The most advanced kind of survey is the *probability sample survey*. Probability sample surveys have the following additional characteristics:

- The elements are selected according to a probability sampling design whose construction usually requires advanced training in statistics.

- Successful probability sampling supports rigorous, objective inferences about the characteristics of a population.

E X A M P L E   **13.2A**

The December 1, 1987, issue of the *New York Times* reported the results of a *New York Times*/CBS News poll. A probability sample of 1553 adults in the United States were interviewed and asked whether they approved or disapproved of the way then–President Reagan was handling his job. The sample was contacted by telephone, using a random digit dialing selection technique, between November 20 and 24, 1987. On the basis of this sample, the poll estimated that about 45% of adults in the United States approved of Reagan's handling of his job, with a "margin of sampling error" of about three percentage points. Roughly speaking, this means that if all the adults in the United States had been contacted by telephone and interviewed, between 42% and 48% of them would have approved of Reagan's performance.[†]

[†]"Roughly speaking" means that there was about a 5% probability that the margin of sampling error was bigger than three percentage points and that a variety of nonsampling errors could have been at work to cause some degree of bias in the estimates. See Chapters 14 and 15 for a thorough discussion of these more technical points.

The data were collected to answer a specific question: What percentage of adult Americans approve of Reagan's handling of his job? The answer was subject to the following limitations:

- It applied only to adults who could be reached by telephone through random digit dialing.
- It applied only to opinion held between November 20 and 24, 1987.
- It was accurate only to about plus or minus three percentage points.
- It was subject to an unspecified amount of bias not due to probability sampling.

The poll is an example of a *cross-sectional study*. It applies to a fixed period of time and does not convey variation in opinion over time. Because polls are taken weekly, it would be possible to study variation over time if data from previous polls were tracked down. A thorough study of these data would try to account for the sampling variation in each poll (cross-sectional variation) and the longitudinal variation (variation across time). If such a study were done, one might feel able to predict the evolution of opinion about the president's performance of his job. Even with the benefit of a long series of measurements, however, we would probably be unwilling to make any but the most tentative predictions because we know how quickly reality, and resulting opinion, can change. Thus, while a sequence plot of poll results may provide a useful context for any particular poll result, it may have little value as a predictive tool. ▪

EXAMPLE 13.2B   Contrast the poll in Example 13.2A with the count and sequence plot of daily numbers of photocopies introduced in Chapters 1 and 2. In the photocopy study, complete counts of the number of copies made each day could be plotted and their longitudinal variations searched for clues about future behavior. If the machine had not counted all copies automatically, a sampling scheme could have been devised to collect counts of copies at several fixed times during the day. This also would have yielded quite precise estimates of daily totals, which could be plotted over time and used for predictions.

Some surveys are useful in this way, to give information about changes over time. For example, regular surveys of housing starts have yielded information on predictable seasonal variation—more houses will be started in spring than fall, for example. This information is used as a "correction" to determine the real trend in home building. And it is used by suppliers, realtors, and lenders to anticipate fluctuations in their business. ▪

SECTION

13.3 Exercises

13.3A   As part of a market-research effort, an employee conducts a random digit dialing telephone survey during the third week of June. She makes 1500 contacts, but only 1125 of the people answer her questions, so she has 375 nonrespondents. She finds that 720 of the 1125 respondents say they have purchased a certain product in the last three months, so she can say that 64%[= 100(720/1125)%] of the respondents claim to have purchased the product. She has no evidence concerning the purchase behavior of the nonrespondents, but she can compute the percentage of purchasers out of the 1500 contacts using various assumptions about the nonresponders.

a Compute the percentage of purchasers out of the 1500 contacts assuming each of the following conditions:

- None of the 375 nonresponders was a purchaser.
- All 375 nonresponders were purchasers.
- Of the nonresponders, 64% were purchasers.

b Comment on the ambiguity in the percentages created by nonresponse to surveys in light of the calculations you made in part (a).

c Redo this exercise assuming there is only a 10% nonresponse rate—that is, that 150 people refused to answer the questions. Continue to assume that 64% of the respondents were purchasers. How does the nonresponse rate affect the ambiguity in the percentages?

13.3B The following table reports monthly unemployment rates for the United States from August 1979 through July 1982.

					Month							
Year	1	2	3	4	5	6	7	8	9	10	11	12
1979								6.9	6.6	6.3	6.4	6.0
1980	7.0	6.8	6.6	5.7	5.4	6.2	6.2	5.8	5.6	5.4	5.5	5.6
1981	6.3	6.4	6.1	5.5	5.1	5.9	5.8	5.8	5.6	5.6	5.6	5.6
1982	6.8	6.8	6.6	6.5	6.9	7.8	7.9					

As a guideline, assume that because of sampling error any of these figures could be off by ±0.3. Sampling errors arise because a sample of about 60,000 households provides the information on unemployment each month. For example, the actual August 1979 figure might be anywhere from 6.6 to 7.2, and the actual September 1979 figure might be anywhere from 6.3 to 6.9. Thus the possibility that actual unemployment rates are the same in the two months cannot be ruled out. Now compare December 1979 with January 1980. The December 1979 figure might be anywhere between 5.7 and 6.3, while the January 1980 figure might be anywhere between 6.7 and 7.3. Even taking sampling error into account, the actual figures are substantially different; that is, they are almost certainly too far apart to be due to sampling error.

a Compute the month-to-month changes in the table above. How many of them evidence a substantial change in unemployment rate, after taking sampling error into account? What percentage of the changes provide such evidence?

b Sampling theory suggests that if sampling error alone accounted for the month-to-month changes, at most one or two of them would appear substantial, because sampling error is expected occasionally to generate changes that appear substantial. Given this fact, what do you conclude about the process that generates unemployment rates? Specifically, does it appear that the month-to-month changes are due to sampling error alone?

13.3C Give some examples from your own experience in which sampling was used. Explain why sampling was necessary. Explain the implications of trying to observe the entire population instead of using sampling.

13.4 Experiments

Simple observation and surveying emphasize discovering characteristics of a process or a population. They can be thought of as "passive listening devices." Experiments, on the other hand, are active because with them we attempt to discern what would be true of a process or population if it were changed. An experiment is the study of the effects of change in a limited environment that is to some degree under the experimenter's control. This section uses an extended example to explain the basics of designing efficient experiments that yield accurate results.

Designing an Experiment

Baking conditions, such as time and temperature, are important concerns in developing a cake mix that will perform well for a wide variety of users. Consider a mix whose instructions say, "Bake at 325°F for 60 minutes." Because oven and timer settings vary, the mix must bake satisfactorily at *ranges* of temperatures and times.

A typical experimental design is to choose various *combinations* of temperature and time settings, prepare cakes at each of these combinations, submit the cakes to a taste test that yields numerical scores, and analyze the scores for evidence that the mix performs well, or fails to perform well, over the combinations of settings.

To illustrate, assume that the range of temperatures to be studied is 300°F to 350°F and the range of times is 55 minutes to 65 minutes. A possible experimental strategy is to study the recommended times and temperatures and the extremes of the ranges. With this strategy, the three temperature levels to be studied are 300°F, 325°F, and 350°F, and the three time levels are 55 minutes, 60 minutes, and 65 minutes. In the two-way table in Exhibit 13.4A, the dots mark the nine possible combinations.

E X H I B I T **13.4A**
Two-Way Layout of
Combinations of Three
Temperatures and Three Times in
Cake-Baking Experiment

		Times		
		55 minutes	60 minutes	65 minutes
	300°F	.	.	.
Temperatures	325°F	.	.	.
	350°F	.	.	.

replication

In the terminology of experimental design, a **replication** is a single run of an experiment in which all the planned treatments are run at all the planned levels. In this case, a replication consists of baking cakes at each of the nine combinations and then obtaining taste-test scores for each of the nine cakes. Careful implementation of the design would involve at least the following elements:

- Use an oven and a timer that provide extremely precise and accurate settings. In the experiment, do not try to mimic what actual users do in their kitchens;

try to guarantee that the information is collected at the temperatures and times required by the experimenter. Substantial error in the experimental equipment compromises the precision of the experimental findings.

- Develop a protocol (that is, a detailed list of instructions) for preparing the cake mix and the oven so that the cakes are prepared under essentially identical conditions.

- Prepare the cakes at combinations chosen in a random order. This is done for two reasons. First, if there are effects that carry over systematically from one baking to the next, moving systematically through the table of combinations introduces these carryover effects into the data. Second, the random selection of combinations creates a sound theoretical basis for the use of statistical inference methods in analyzing the data. Tables of random digits are available for making random choices.[†]

blinding

- Make sure that the people who taste the cakes do not know the experimental conditions under which the cakes were prepared. This is called **blinding** the tasters and eliminates bias stemming from the tasters' prior opinions about "ideal" baking conditions.

double blinding

- Make sure that the people who conduct the taste tests do not know the experimental conditions under which the cakes were prepared. A person who knows the experimental conditions can transmit clues to the taste tester that can seriously affect the results. The blinding of the conductor as well as the tester is called **double blinding**. Double blinding is one of the most important tools in designing experiments involving human subjects, because the opportunities for introducing personal bias are so subtle and so numerous that they defy the most strenuous good-faith efforts of experimenters to avoid them.

- Offer cakes to the taste testers in a random order to avoid carryover effects from test to test.

- Recruit taste testers who can truly discriminate differences between cakes. Some people are much better tasters than others. The difficulties in choosing reliable tasters and strategies for choosing good tasters are ably discussed by Buchanan, Given, and Goldman.[‡]

Factorial Experiments

factorial experiment

Because experimentation must often be done on a limited scale and because it can be expensive and time consuming, the ability to extract a maximum of information from a minimum of data is important. One of the most useful types of experiments for this purpose is the **factorial experiment**, an experiment in which all possible combinations of the treatment levels are run in a replication. It is based on the principle that if the effects of several factors are to be studied, the most efficient procedure is to vary several factors at once instead of one at a time. The cake-baking

[†] See the discussion of randomization in Chapter 1.

[‡] Bruce Buchanan, Moshe Given, and Arich Goldman, "Measurement of Discrimination Ability in Taste Tests: An Empirical Investigation," *Journal of Marketing Research*, 24 (1987), 154–163.

example describes an experiment with two *factors:* time and temperature. Three *levels* of each factor are studied, so the experiment involves $3 \times 3 = 9$ combinations in each replication.

A single replication of the experiment yields information about the performance of the cake mix at the different temperature/time combinations. But it yields no information about possible *variation* induced by the materials, equipment, or tasters. To assess this sort of variation, experimenters conduct a number of replications. Specifically, suppose the experimenter has decided that 12 cakes are to be prepared at each level of each factor. In the context of the factorial experiment, this requires four replications. Exhibit 13.4B shows the number of observations obtained for each combination of levels and for each factor. Notice that a total of 36 cakes are baked to conduct the four replications.

E X H I B I T 13.4B
Number of Observations in Four Replications of a Factorial Experiment Involving Two Factors Each at Three Levels

		Times			
		55 minutes	60 minutes	65 minutes	**Total**
	300°F	4	4	4	12
Temperatures	325°F	4	4	4	12
	350°F	4	4	4	12
	Total	12	12	12	36

Now consider the number of cakes required if the experimenter decides to vary the factors one at a time. This means that for each level of temperature, 12 cakes would be baked at each level of time. This would also yield, for each level of time interval, 12 cakes baked at each level of temperature. This yields a total of $3 \times 3 \times 12 = 108$ cakes to be baked and tested—three times the number of cakes needed in the factorial experiment. Given that the experimenter requires only 12 cakes per level to be baked in order to discriminate between the levels, the use of the one-at-a-time design is clearly wasteful of time and resources.

Another weakness of the one-at-a-time design is that the combinations of factors cannot be applied in a random order, thus denying the experimenter the opportunity to efficiently control a potential source of bias. This weakness would be present even if the experimenter baked only four cakes at each level of each factor, thus baking the same number of cakes as in the factorial experiment.

The point we are making may seem obvious, but the use of one-at-a-time designs is surprisingly common. The factorial design is usually the much superior design.

Factorial designs also provide a useful framework in which to add and delete factors as a study progresses. For instance, an experimenter may wish to learn the effect of humidity on the cakes. If the humidity of the room can be controlled, this third factor might be studied at two or three levels. The experimental design is then displayed in a three-way table. If the experimenter notices that the quality of the cakes is not much affected by realistic variations in baking time, the time factor could be eliminated and a two-factor study involving temperature and humidity pursued.

The collection of relatively small amounts of data over a series of experiments is an economical way to study certain processes, particularly if each small experiment yields information efficiently, as is the case with factorial experiments.

See Chapter 19 for details on factorial experiments.

SECTION

13.5 Exercises

13.5A   Identify the two most important factors affecting the shooting of basketball free throws. Design an experiment involving different levels of these factors that could be used to help someone improve his or her free-throwing ability. How would you carry out the experiment you designed?

13.5B   Let the process of interest be studying for a class of your choice. Identify the two most important factors affecting the quality of your studying. Design an experiment involving different levels of these factors that could be used to improve this quality. How would you carry out the experiment you designed?

SECTION

13.6 Comparisons

Most analyses based on data are comparative because we judge new knowledge or understanding by comparing it to what we already know or understand. Efficient data collection takes this basic fact of human learning explicitly into account. This section introduces a basic technique needed for comparing data: stratification, or separating data into categories. It discusses two important kinds of stratification: grouping data by source of variation, and using experimental and control groups.

EXAMPLE   **13.6A**

Before-and-after studies play a major role in a variety of applications. If you take a pretest before you start some training and then take a posttest after the training, the difference in the two test scores is a measure of the value of the training. If you maintain data on a quality measure of a process (percent defectives, for example), you may compare the sequence plot of that measure before a quality-improvement program is instituted with the sequence plot that evolves after the program is underway. Comparing measurements taken before and after an intervention is one of the most common methods of analysis. ▪

Stratification

stratification

Stratification is the classification of observations into categories in order to make comparisons. Stratification is a process you use all the time. You may classify restaurants as expensive, moderately priced, or inexpensive. Or you may classify them as fast food, haute cuisine, or other. You classify people by the clubs or organizations they belong to, their professions, their ages, their job descriptions, their hair color, and so on. You may classify companies by the quality of the goods and services they offer or by their sales or assets.

Stratification is such a natural and useful activity that calling it a statistical tool may seem pretentious. We do not mean to imply that statistical uses lay a special claim to stratification. Rather, no approach to problem formulation and analysis can ignore the idea of stratification. It is fundamental. Our emphasis on stratification serves to make explicit and purposeful a process that is used naturally all the time.

EXAMPLE 13.6B

Exhibit 13.6A displays percent of households reporting access to a motor vehicle in 1989, by characteristic of householder. Identification of four subgroups of the population—urban owner, rural owner, urban renter, and rural renter—is an example of stratification. ■

EXHIBIT 13.6A

Percent of Households Reporting Access to a Motor Vehicle, by Characteristic of Householder, 1989

| | Urban vs. Rural | |
Owner vs. Renter	Urban	Rural
Homeowner	95	96
Renter	77	89

Source: Bureau of the Census Statistical Brief, SB/92-2, U.S. Department of Commerce, April 1992, based on the 1989 American Housing Survey.

EXAMPLE 13.6C

Geographic region is a popular stratifier. The states in the United States are frequently grouped as shown in Exhibit 13.6B. ■

EXAMPLE 13.6D

Gender and age of people are other characteristics often used in practice. Exhibit 13.6C displays percent of adults who reported voting in 1966 and in 1990, by gender and age categories. Declines in percentage of voters are apparent in all strata. ■

Comparison in Experiments

control group

Control group and experimental group are important stratifiers in scientific studies. The experimental group receives a new treatment, whereas the **control group** receives no treatment or a standard treatment. Measurements on the two groups are compared to see if the new treatment makes a difference. In science, the control group is the frame of reference against which comparisons are made; studies lacking a control group are rarely considered "scientific." In some before-and-after studies, like the

EXHIBIT 13.6B
Geographic Regions in the
United States

Region	States Included
Northeast	Connecticut, Maine, Massachusetts, New Hampshire, New Jersey, New York, Pennsylvania, Rhode Island, Vermont
North Central	Illinois, Indiana, Iowa, Kansas, Michigan, Minnesota, Missouri, Nebraska, North Dakota, Ohio, South Dakota, Wisconsin
South	Alabama, Arkansas, Delaware, District of Columbia, Florida, Georgia, Kentucky, Louisiana, Maryland, Mississippi, North Carolina, Oklahoma, South Carolina, Tennessee, Texas, Virginia, West Virginia
West	Alaska, Arizona, California, Colorado, Hawaii, Idaho, Montana, Nevada, New Mexico, Oregon, Utah, Washington, Wyoming

EXHIBIT 13.6C
Percent of Voters by Gender,
Age, and Year

Gender	Year	Age 18–44	Age 45 and Over	Ages Combined
Male	1966	50	66	58
	1990	35	60	45
Female	1966	48	58	53
	1990	37	56	45

Source: Bureau of the Census Statistical Brief, SB/91-23, U.S. Department of Commerce, Nov. 1991.

pretest and posttest described in Example 13.6A, the "before" part is the control group and the "after" part is the experimental group.

EXAMPLE 13.6E

Lack of adequate control groups has led many experimenters into error. For example, in 1958, a new procedure was introduced for treating ulcers, called gastric freezing, which was widely adopted. A later paper reported the results of the treatment on 24 patients, but the results were not compared with those of a control group.[†]

[†]Owen H. Wangensteen and others, "Achieving Physiological Gastrectomy by Gastric Freezing," *Journal of the American Medical Association*, 180 (6) (1962), 439–444.

placebo

In 1963, an experiment was performed in which ulcer patients were divided into two groups.[†] The experimental group, containing 82 patients, received the gastric freezing treatment, while the control group, containing 78 patients, received a **placebo**, a nontreatment disguised so the patients thought it was real. Patients were assigned to the groups at random. The patients were observed for two years after treatment by doctors who did not know which groups the patients were in (so there was double blinding).

The experimenter reported that during the first six weeks of follow-up, 47% of the experimental group and 39% of the control group showed improvement, and 29% of the patients in both groups were symptom-free. However, as time passed most patients in both groups became worse. For practical purposes, the two groups behaved the same, casting serious doubt on the value of gastric freezing. This and other experiments served to show that gastric freezing was of no use in treating ulcers.[‡]

The initial experiment had no control group. Later experiments showed that gastric freezing had a *placebo effect*. Even though it was of no use, the patients initially responded favorably to the treatment. Even patients who *thought* they had been treated by gastric freezing responded about as well as those who really had! ■

The examples you have seen, from cake-baking to ulcer treatments, illustrate three basic principles of designed experiments:

- Control
- Randomization
- Replication

Control of experimental factors is needed to make explicit what factors are allowed to have an effect on the response. Randomization is needed to protect against biases due to the effects of unsuspected or uncontrollable factors. Replication is needed to reduce the effects of natural variation to a degree that allows the effects of the experimental factors to be detected.

Lack of control over factors, especially lack of a control group, usually means that desired comparisons cannot be made. Lack of randomization or lack of blinding means that a lurking variable may be the true cause of the variation or relationships observed in the data.[§] Lack of sufficient replication means that natural variation in the experimental units or measuring devices may mask the effect of one or more experimental factors.

[†]Julian M. Ruffin, Julian and others, "A Cooperative Double-Blind Evaluation of Gastric 'Freezing' in the Treatment of Duodenal Ulcer," *New England Journal of Medicine*, 281 (1969), 16–19.

[‡]See L. I. Miao, "Gastric Freezing: An Example of the Evaluation of Medical Therapy by Randomized Clinical Trials," in J. P. Bunker, B. A. Barnes, and F. Mosteller, eds., *Costs, Risks, and Benefits of Surgery* (New York: Oxford University Press, 1977), pp. 198–211.

[§]See the discussion of lurking variables in Chapter 6.

The subject of designed experiments is a large and fascinating one. Some business applications appear in Chapters 18 and 19.

S E C T I O N

13.7 Exercises

13.7A The August 4, 1988, issue of *U.S.A. Today* reports results from the Department of Transportation's (DOT) monthly study of on-time takeoffs and landings of the 13 largest commercial airlines. On time is defined as within 15 minutes of scheduled time, and the report does not include flights that are delayed because of mechanical failure.

The June 1988 percentage of on-time flights was 84.3%, the highest percentage since the DOT started reporting the figures in September 1987. The previous high was April 1988, with 82.6%. The three top and three bottom airlines, with their percentages of on-time flights, were America West Airlines (92.8), Southwest Airlines (90.8), American (88.2), Pan American (72.2), USAir (76.6), and Trans World Airlines (79).

What might be the value to the individual customer of the stratification by airline? What impact do you think this kind of report might have on the individual airlines? Compare the impacts of the DOT policy with the alternative one of releasing figures for the airline industry as a whole but not for individual airlines.

A potential problem with the DOT report is that in an effort to "look good" in the report, an airline will shortcut procedures that are hard to observe, such as maintenance and preflight preparation. Do you think the DOT's policy of not including flights delayed by mechanical failure adequately addresses this issue? If not, what other procedures would you recommend? Try to anticipate the impacts of implementing your recommendations, including costs.

13.7B Choose two grocery stores and keep weekly records of the prices the stores charge for a pound of a certain brand of coffee, a gallon of milk, or some other commodity of your choice. Compare the data from the two stores. A variation on this exercise is to keep track of prices on a "market basket" of commodities—that is, a list of items. This sort of exercise lies behind the construction of the Consumer Price Index, which in turn is used to compute inflation rate.

13.7C If you work in an office or factory, identify a quality measure (such as error rate, failure rate, or service time) for an important process and identify as many sources of variation in this measure as you can. Suggest how data on these items could be collected.

13.7D Consider the sequence plot in Exhibit 2.4A, which displays numbers of copies made daily on a copy machine. The copy machine is available to any member of the department during the workday, and the department members are asked to limit jobs to 25 copies. An honor system is used. Now suppose that on November 23, a metering system is installed on the machine, and each user must pay for the copies he or she makes. What do you think is the likely appearance of the continuation of the sequence plot? This is an example of a *change in policy*. Describe it in the language of experiments developed in Section 13.6. Cite other examples in which data are or could be used to document the effects of a change in policy.

13.7E In Jesse's business he issues a large number of checks, but some of these checks are never cashed. He plans to follow up on a sample of uncashed checks to try to determine why they are not cashed. He decides to divide the checks into those written for less than $100 and those written for $100 or more. He plans to draw a random sample of size 40 from the first group and a random sample of size 80 from the second group. He has consulted a statistician who assures him that the data so collected can be used to obtain the information he is interested in, as long as he carefully follows up all the checks in his sample. What sources of variation have been eliminated with this sampling design? What sources of variation remain?

13.7F Rita has been commissioned to estimate the number of municipal water towers in Wisconsin. She designs the following sampling survey procedure. She divides the state into three geographic regions called upper, middle, and lower. These regions consist of collections of counties. She selects ten counties from each region using a table of random digits. Next she selects three municipalities from each selected county, using a table of random digits. She calls each selected municipality's government office and asks how many water towers are located in the municipality. What sources of variation have been eliminated with this sampling design? What sources of variation remain?

S E C T I O N

13.8 Steps in Data Collection

Data form a basis for action, but the extent to which a given set of data can be relied on depends on its quality. If we perform or supervise the data collection ourselves, we can judge directly whether they satisfy our quality requirements. If, however, we use data collected by an outside supplier, we must use indirect means for judging the quality of the data. We may have to rely on a brief technical appendix to a research report or perhaps a telephone conversation with the supplier. Regardless of the situation, two questions about the data collection must be answered satisfactorily:

data design quality

- **Data design quality**: Are the data relevant to the problem we wish to solve?

data production quality

- **Data production quality**: Were the data collected with sufficient skill and care?

When we do our own data collection we have control over the relevance of the data, so design quality tends to be high. Such data are called *primary source* or simply **primary data**.

primary data (primary source)

Outside sources typically supply general-purpose data. The Census Bureau, for example, collects millions of bits of data each year and publishes them in a variety of formats. The surveys the bureau conducts are so large that they are unlikely to be done by smaller organizations, and they yield data that are national in scope. While valuable for many purposes, such data tend to leave many "microlevel" questions unanswered. The same remarks apply to general-purpose market-research surveys, which tend to emphasize industrywide findings or findings about broad consumer groups. Thus, while the production quality achieved by a large organization like the Census Bureau is high, the design quality of the resulting data can range from high to low, depending on the specific needs of the user. Data collected by a person or organization not the user of the data are called **secondary source** or simply **secondary data**.

secondary data (secondary source)

Although each attempt at data collection must be tailored to the specific problem being attacked, the following sequence of six steps provides good guidelines to follow in your planning. If you are not collecting data but are using a secondary source, you may compare your source's procedures against these guidelines.

Step 1: State the Purpose for Collecting the Data

If you collect the data yourself, you can be specific about the purpose. A secondary source, such as the Census Bureau or a market-research firm, often has a general purpose because it has many users with many different specific purposes. In general, the more specific the purpose, the better. Statements that start out with "To provide information about . . ." or "To serve the needs of . . ." are often not much use. A statement of purpose should include the universe of elements from which a sample is drawn, define the time period over which the data are collected, state the method of data collection, and indicate how the data will be used.

Step 2: Determine Sources

If the source is primary, record the names of the people in your organization who are responsible for collecting the data. If the source is secondary, record the specific publications or electronic databases used. Also cite the name, address, and telephone number of the data-collection organization. The source actually used may be chosen only after a search of many possible sources. For future reference, keep a list of sources considered.

Step 3: Determine Data Capture and Presentation Methods

We have consulted with analysts who collected data and then set out to find an appropriate program with which to do the data manipulation and analysis. Because they lacked a proper appreciation of what data analysis entails, they did not leave sufficient time to do a careful and thorough job, nor did they collect the data to make their entry into the computer as simple as possible. These analysts suffered from wasted time and frustration that could have been avoided with a little anticipation.

A group of students was asked to analyze a case study that reported a regression analysis of variables used to predict energy consumption in large commercial buildings in the Midwest. The students discovered that heating degree days, a measure of how cold a day is, was negatively correlated with energy consumption, a decidedly counterintuitive result. They discovered that this nonsense correlation was caused by bias in the selection of the buildings: the larger buildings were concentrated in warmer parts of the Midwest, while smaller buildings were concentrated in colder parts of the Midwest. This example illustrates the intimate relationship between data collection and data analysis. Generally speaking, even a skillful analysis will not salvage much information from carelessly collected data.

Data may be collected on sheets of paper and then transferred to worksheets or computer files for analysis. If you use this method, design the data sheets to ensure the speed and accuracy of each operation. For example, a questionnaire should be easy to read and fill out, and it should make the responses stand out for easy transfer to the computer if this is to be done. Long, disorganized questionnaires discourage respondents and lower the quality of their answers. They also promote errors in data transfer.

Elimination of intermediate steps saves time and increases accuracy.

EXAMPLE   13.8A   A bank asked credit applicants to fill out a form from which the data were input to a computer file. Many customers complained of errors in documents subsequently received from the bank. Investigation found that the credit application was the culprit. Its design made data transfer difficult. Redesign of the form led to a huge decrease in input errors. Even more errors were eliminated when the application form was done away with altogether.

> Credit officers began inputting the data on terminals at their desks as they interviewed applicants. Applicants were able to preview the information on the screen and verify its accuracy. ∎

Often the data sheet can combine the steps of data collection and data presentation. If, for example, a sequence plot is to be made, it can be constructed on the data sheet as the data are recorded. This saves an intermediate data-transfer step and makes the graph immediately available to support decision making.

Plan data sheets or computer files used for entering and storing data so that (1) data can be easily collected and, if necessary, transferred and (2) there are as few steps as possible between data collection and presentation. This kind of planning will save time and reduce errors. For example, a questionnaire should be easy to read and fill out. Responses should stand out and be formatted for easy transfer to computer, if this is to be done. If clerks must enter dd/mm/yy, do not design your form so that people write February 17, 1994.

When you collect data, record the date and the person or machine who collected it. Failure to do this renders the data useless if they are examined later and no one can determine the circumstances surrounding their collection. The more data collection you supervise, the harder it is to remember when they were collected and who collected them. The data sheet or file should always ask for this basic information, and recording the information should be part of every data collector's job description.

Step 4: Train Personnel

Training the people who collect the data is essential in ensuring the quality of the data. Training includes not only the mechanics of filling out a data sheet or interviewing a respondent but also the importance of the data. Why is it being collected? What decisions will be made and what difference will they make to the organization? What will go wrong if the data contain errors?

Training should also include practice with the data-collection procedures and tools. Trainees must be encouraged to point out problems and make suggestions for improvement. Suggestions that lead to simplification of procedures and improved accuracy of the data should be rewarded concretely. Training should also include what to do if a difficulty (such as an uncooperative interviewee) is encountered.

The more you foster teamwork, the more closely the data collectors will follow the prescribed procedures and hence collect the data as intended. An important part of teamwork is an agreement not to pass problems on to other members of the team. If a problem is encountered, it is either solved on the spot or brought to the attention of the team so that countermeasures may be developed.

If data are collected over a long period of time, training should be an ongoing activity. As difficulties are met, procedures for solving the problems must be worked out and shared with the team. Improvements in procedures may be suggested at any time. As these are adopted, they need to be shared with the team. At all times a manager must make sure that all the data collectors know their responsibilities, are following current procedures, and are communicating effectively with other members of the team.

Step 5: Collect the Data Accurately

Once procedures are established and personnel trained, collect the data accurately. Data collection is a process involving a series of steps. Each step must be conducted correctly if the finished product, the data, are to be of the highest quality. Hence, each step of the process must be controlled. When problems are met in a particular step, they must be solved there and not passed on to the next step. The most effective means of error control is for every worker to be trained to spot and eliminate problems.

If you supervise a long-term data-collection project, you need to do some auditing. This allows you to spot problems that the workers are missing, and it will also allow you to see if your workers need more training. Auditing is usually done by sampling some of the work done at each step. Chapters 14 to 16 explain how to design and carry out sampling plans. We do not go into details here but simply note the importance of auditing work in progress. It is not sufficient to audit finished product, because then it is too late to counter the problems that led to inferior work.

Step 6: Document the Work

Minimal documentation is a data sheet describing the data along with dates of collection and names of data collectors. More elaborate documentation, such as a covering memorandum that states the problem addressed and some background on how the data-collection procedures were arrived at, or a full research report, will often be required. Data displays should be thoroughly labeled so that a user can glean the essential facts needed to make decisions. Fuller explanations may be given in supporting text, but the basic facts about the data should be included in the display itself.

SECTION

13.9 Exercises

13.9A Identify as many secondary sources of data as you can by searching a library, talking to a librarian, interviewing an information manager in a company, or any other means you can think of.

13.9B Choose one of the secondary sources of data you found in completing Exercise 13.9A. Identify the way the source reports the process by which it gathers and reports data. Does the source adequately address the limitations of the data? Justify your conclusions.

13.9C The accounting department is entering data sets for the marketing department. The marketing department frequently sends over cases that have missing information, and the accounting department keys them in as is. As the missing information is supplied, the data set is updated. Explain why this is a wasteful, inefficient way to process the data. Suggest an appropriate data-collection process that not only eliminates wasted steps but ensures a high probability of few or no errors in the final results. (The procedure outlined above was observed by one of the authors during a consultation with a company!)

13.9D   When Jeff audited the data he collected last week, he found that the measurement for one of the items was missed. In order to have the data ready for analysis the next day, Jeff decided to use a measurement collected three weeks ago. Under what circumstances do you think Jeff would be justified in taking the action he did? What could be wrong with what he did? How could Jeff tell if his action was justified?

SECTION

13.10 A Case Study

Data are frequently presented as counts, but counting is not as easy as it may seem. Even producers of high-quality surveys, such as the Census Bureau, must confess to having no sure way to guarantee 100% accuracy. A simple game—counting *e*'s—can be used as a basis for collecting data, both informally and experimentally, and as a cautionary tale about counting. Classes that have tried this exercise report substantial learning about the challenges of data collection.

The task is to count the number of *e*'s in a sentence. Subjects are shown the sentence and given only a short time (roughly 30 seconds) to perform the task. Usually a subject is asked to count the *e*'s in several sentences. A group of subjects invariably comes up with different counts, thus illustrating the difficulty of a seemingly simple task. The average count for a group is almost always less than the actual number of *e*'s in a sentence, thus documenting a bias in the counting process: a systematic tendency to undercount.

Recently one of our colleagues suggested that subjects would produce higher-quality counts if the sentences were held upside down. This case study reports two experiments designed to test our colleague's theory.

The First Experiment—A Classroom Trial

A class of 67 students was shown four sentences, one at a time, projected on a screen at the front of the room. Two of the sentences were shown right-side up (Rsu), and two were upside down (Usd). The students recorded their counts on index cards. The cards were collected and the data keyed into an electronic database. The top part of Exhibit 13.10A shows tallies of the differences between the reported counts and the actual numbers of *e*'s in the four sentences. These differences are called "errors," with the understanding that a 0 error means a correct count. In the exhibit, S1 Error stands for the error committed for sentence 1, S2 Error the error for sentence 2, and so on. Sentences 1 and 2 were shown right-side up and sentences 3 and 4 were shown upside down. The actual numbers of *e*'s in the sentences were 8, 14, 11, and 10.

The bottom part of Exhibit 13.10A shows tallies for the totals of the errors for the two right-side-up sentences and the total of the errors for the two upside-down sentences. The exhibit also shows means and standard deviations of all the distributions. A mean error not equal to zero suggests bias, while the standard deviation of the errors is a measure of variation, as usual. We see that the right-side-up sentences yielded larger biases *and* larger standard deviations than the upside-down sentences!

While suggestive, these results are hardly conclusive. To be convincing, the findings on the orientation of sentences needs to be documented much more extensively.

EXHIBIT 13.10A

Tallies, Means, and Standard Deviations of Error Distributions in an Experiment in Which Subjects Counted *e*'s in Four Sentences

S1 Error	Count	S2 Error	Count	S3 Error	Count	S4 Error	Count
−2	3	−4	1	−4	1	−2	2
−1	17	−3	9	−2	1	−1	8
0	46	−2	15	−1	12	0	57
3	1	−1	15	0	48	Total	$\overline{67}$
Total	$\overline{67}$	0	27	1	5		
		Total	$\overline{67}$	Total	$\overline{67}$		
Mean	−0.3		−1.1		−0.2		−0.2
Standard deviation	0.7		1.1		0.7		0.5

Rsu Error	Count	Usd Error	Count
−5	1	−6	1
−4	8	−2	5
−3	6	−1	13
−2	15	0	44
−1	12	1	4
0	24	Total	$\overline{67}$
1	1		
Total	$\overline{67}$		
Mean	−1.4		−0.3
Standard deviation	1.5		1.0

The Second Experiment—A Field Trial

A class of 38 students was asked to perform the following field trial. Each student chose five sentences and wrote them on index cards. The correct number of *e*'s in each sentence was determined. Each student found six subjects, three of whom were assigned by the flip of a coin to the experimental group. The other three made up the control group. The control group counted the *e*'s in the five sentences held right-side up, while the experimental group counted the *e*'s in the five sentences held upside down. For each group, the correct total number of *e*'s in the five sentences was subtracted from the number of *e*'s counted to produce an aggregate counting error figure for the group.

The 38 aggregate error figures for each group are the basic data for our analysis. The errors are shown in dotplots, and descriptive statistics are given in Exhibit 13.10B. Not only distributions of the errors for the control (Rsu) and experimental (Usd) groups but also distributions of the differences between the errors for the groups that counted the same sentences (Rsu − Usd) are shown.

The average errors for the control and experimental groups are −10.13 and −8.18, suggesting substantial undercounting on the average. On the other hand, there appears to be little practical difference between the Rsu and Usd procedures. The average difference between them is −1.95 with a standard deviation of 7.50. The data suggest that both methods produce substantial undercounting and provide little support for

E X H I B I T **13.10B**
Tallies, Means, and Standard
Deviations of Error Distributions
in an Experiment in Which
Subjects Counted *e*'s in Five
Sentences

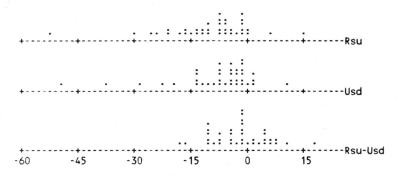

	n	Mean	Median	Standard Deviation
Rsu	38	−10.13	−8.00	11.26
Usd	38	−8.18	−5.00	11.26
Rsu − Usd	38	−1.95	−2.00	7.50

$n = 38$ cases in control group (Rsu); $n = 38$ cases in
experimental group (Usd). Rsu means right-side up; Usd
means upside down

the theory that the Usd procedure is superior to the Rsu procedure. The data are
analyzed by more formal methods in Chapter 17.

The field trial is implemented quite differently from the classroom exercise reported earlier. For one thing, more sentences were involved, which should provide
a better test of the theory that Usd is better than Rsu. On the other hand, different
sentences were used for each control and experimental group. This undoubtedly contributed some variation to the error distributions. On the other hand,[†] we do not want
to base our conclusions on a very limited number of sentences. In other words, we
would like our conclusions to hold up regardless of the type of sentences analyzed.
Another difference is the use of randomization in the field trial, a step not taken in
the classroom exercise. On the whole, the field trial is a sterner test of the theory, and
the data do not support the notion of a major difference between Rsu and Usd. We
do not find the conclusion conclusive, however. Further experimentation would be
required before we would consider the case closed.

Here are some suggested questions and activities to help you follow up on this
case.

- How might the conclusions have been affected by the fact that the Rsu and Usd
  sentences were different?

- The field trial was not blinded. How might this have affected the results?

- Design an experiment that improves on the ones described in the case.

[†]There are at least three hands in this presentation. Some practitioners insist that statisticians consult with
one hand tied behind their backs to avoid all the caveats preceded by the phrase "on the other hand." We
naturally do not favor this practice!

- Conduct your experiment and compare your results with those reported in the case.

Chapter Summary

Numerical facts are either irrelevant or relevant, either inaccurate or accurate. One part of the art of data analysis is distinguishing the irrelevant from the relevant. Another part is establishing the degree of accuracy of the relevant facts. In other words, a data analyst needs to pay attention to data quality so conclusions have a basis whose strengths and weaknesses are known.

Data stem from simple observation, from designed experiments, and from surveys. Regardless of the method used to collect data, the process used is a sequence of steps that should, ideally, allow objective assessment of the relevance and reliability of the data.

Supplementary Exercises for Chapter 13

13A   A colleague of ours once spent a week in a motel with his family. Everyone in his family noticed at breakfast that the motel staff threw away a great deal of food. They began to think of ways that this waste could be reduced. Subsequently, our colleague asked a team of students to consult with the manager of the food operation in the motel to try to reduce waste and at the same time make the service more efficient. Find a food-service establishment whose manager agrees to let you (preferably along with some colleagues) act as a research team whose objective is to eliminate waste and increase efficiency. Identify basic processes and develop data-collection schemes that will provide insight into how the processes work and how they can be improved. (You will find some helpful suggestions on how to do this in Chapter 25.)

13B   Repeat Exercise 13A using a different set of processes. Some suggestions include check processing in a bank, the receptionist area in a company, and document examination for certification.

13C   An experiment is conducted to measure the impact of three different diets on the growth rate of young rats. Diet A is the "standard" diet and is treated as the control or basis for comparison. Diets B and C are experimental. Fifteen newborn rats are to be assigned to each diet. The rats are to be weighed at birth and at age 1 month. Difference between birth weight and weight at 1 month will be analyzed for evidence that the diets have different impacts. Explain in detail how randomization and double blinding can be incorporated into the experiment. Devise a graphic scheme for displaying the data the experiment will produce that will make it possible to compare the diets at a glance.

13D   A consortium of eight business schools agrees to conduct an experiment to measure student satisfaction with microcomputers. The two factors are type of operating system and method of delivery. Type of operating system has two levels, corresponding to the two most popular operating systems. The brand of hardware used was not considered critical, so this was not used as a factor. Method of delivery also has two levels: micro lab funded by the school and student required to purchase own computer and software. The experimental design is a 2×2 factorial, and there are two business schools at each combination of levels of the two factors. To standardize the evaluation process, 50 MBA students are selected at random from each school and asked to fill out a questionnaire. In return for filling out the questionnaire, each student is given a gift certificate from the local bookstore. One item on the questionnaire asks the students to rate their satisfaction with the computer facilities on a five-point scale, with 1 representing extreme dissatisfaction and 5 representing extreme satisfaction. The average of the 50 responses to this item is the datum provided by a given school. (Other items on the questionnaire can be handled similarly.)

a How many replications of the 2×2 factorial design are used in the experiment?

b What sort of generalization is justified by the randomization used in the experiment?

c Comment on the applicability of the results of this experiment to business schools not included in the experiment.

Glossary for Chapter 13

blinding	Not allowing subjects in an experiment to know which treatment they receive.
control group	A group of subjects that does not receive an experimental treatment, or receives a placebo, to give a base of comparison for treatments in an experiment.
data design quality	The plan for collecting the data is relevant to the problem to be solved.
data production quality	Data are collected with sufficient skill and care to be useful.
double blinding	Not allowing subjects or those who test them or evaluate responses to know what treatments the subjects receive.
factorial experiment	An experiment in which all possible combinations of the treatment levels are run in a replication.
placebo	A nontreatment disguised so that subjects think it is real.
primary data (primary source)	Data collected by the person or organization that also analyzes the data.
replication	A single run of an experiment in which all the planned treatments are run at all the planned levels.
secondary data (secondary source)	Data collected by one person or organization and analyzed by another person or organization.
stratification	Separating observations into groups or categories in order to make comparisons.

14

Fundamental Concepts of Surveying

Chapter Objectives

After mastering this chapter, you will be able to:

- Define survey, element, universe, and census

- Distinguish between probability and nonprobability surveys

- List problems common to all surveys

- Explain and give a detailed numerical example of simple random sampling

SECTION

14.1 Introduction

Much of our information comes from surveys, and although it would be impossible to list all the decisions informed by survey data, a few examples are suggestive. A politician tailors an election campaign to appeal to the preferences of constituents revealed in an opinion poll. A government entitlement program uses population data collected by the Census Bureau to determine a county's eligibility for funds. From a survey conducted in a shopping mall, a mall operator determines the types of tenants most likely to appeal to customers. A company learns from a survey of employees that 16% of the employees spend time caring for elderly friends or relatives and that such employees spend an average of about six hours per week giving care. A service organization learns from a survey of financial contributors that over half of the contributors have made repeated donations. Many other examples could be cited to illustrate the pervasive use of surveys.

Surveys are conducted by government agencies, private survey or polling organizations, survey research groups, and private firms and organizations. Demand for information is supported by dollars. For example, the 1990 Census of the Population of the United States is estimated to have cost $2.6 billion. A. C. Nielsen, the largest marketing research firm in the world, reported gross revenues in 1986 of $615 million.

Despite the widespread use of surveying, misconceptions, misunderstandings, and ignorance of the fundamentals of surveying are also widespread. As a consequence,

370

opportunities for collecting high-quality data are frequently missed, and data of poor quality receive more credence, not to mention remuneration, than they deserve.

This and the next two chapters present the fundamentals of surveying. This chapter begins with expanded definitions of survey-related terms introduced in the previous chapter. Sources of error common to all surveys are discussed. Basic characteristics of probability surveys are introduced—characteristics that are treated in a more rigorous way in the next chapter. The chapter ends with a long appendix that reprints an informative brochure on surveying published by the American Statistical Association.

SECTION

14.2 Definitions

To prevent confusion and misunderstanding, we begin with some carefully worded definitions. A detailed definition of the word *survey* is needed first.

Survey

survey

A **survey** is a process of systematically obtaining information on a universe of elements. Almost every word in this definition justifies comment. Remember that surveying is a process. It consists of a sequence of steps. The quality of the final product of the survey is a result of the care that goes into planning and executing each step.

The word *systematically* implies that a survey is conducted to achieve a goal according to a plan that reflects careful and thorough thinking. The word *systematically* is used to distinguish this approach from haphazard or informal methods of obtaining information. The latter methods are the most common ways of obtaining information, but they are not always sufficient. Surveys provide information that is difficult or impossible to obtain by less formal methods.

Information is data collected with a purpose and often summarized in useful tables, charts, or equations. To be informative, data must answer a question or help solve a problem; in other words, informative data are used as a basis for action. This presupposes a need on the part of the investigator to answer a question or solve a problem, and this presupposes the formulation of the question or problem before the data are collected. Before conducting a survey, it is important to formulate the purpose for doing the survey. Otherwise, opportunities for collecting useful data may be missed.

The word *universe* means the collection of elements about which we wish to be informed. This definition is expanded in turn in the next subsections.

Elements

elements

The **elements** of a survey are the basic units or individuals about which information is sought. Elements may be people, trees, companies, entries in a book or computer file, and so on. What an element is depends on the study being performed.

Universe

universe

The **universe** is the collection of all the elements of interest. It is essential that elements be sufficiently well defined so that they can be determined to be in or not in the universe at the time the survey is conducted. If this can be done, we say that we have an *operational definition* of the elements. Obtaining operational definitions is often surprisingly difficult, and compromises frequently need to be made. Moreover, two investigators may legitimately decide on different operational definitions. This, in turn, may mean that they will get different universes and draw different conclusions, even though they supposedly are studying the same problem. For example, suppose you want information about retired people. Do you include people drawing a pension but holding a full-time job? A part-time job? People "retired" involuntarily but seeking a job? Are permanently disabled people "retired"? What about people in nursing homes, too ill to respond to your survey? Thus, in employing the results of a survey, you must be clear about the operational definitions used. Inattention to this point leads to unfortunate misunderstandings.

Census

census

A **census** is a survey conducted with the intention of obtaining information from every element in the universe. The census of a universe of appreciable size or complexity is both time consuming and costly, and detecting and correcting errors sometimes creates intractable difficulties. The main advantage of a census, assuming the errors can be satisfactorily controlled, is the great detail it yields. As discussed below, a well-conducted probability sample survey can be expected to yield higher-quality though less detailed data than a census. A census should be conducted only if such detail is really needed.

Nonprobability Sample Survey

Sample surveys are conducted with the intention of obtaining information from only a portion of the universe. There are two types of sample surveys: those that use probability methods to select the elements to be measured and those that do not. The nonprobability surveys latter are called **nonprobability surveys**.

A common nonprobability survey is one in which a questionnaire is sent to a large number of elements, possibly the whole universe, and only those questionnaires that are voluntarily returned are analyzed. Such surveys can be quite informative, because the elements that return the questionnaire may be of intrinsic interest. The danger with nonprobability surveys is that an investigator will draw unwarranted conclusions about the whole universe from the data in the sample.

To illustrate, suppose that people who have one opinion about an issue, say those opposed to restrictions on owning handguns, are more likely to return a questionnaire than those favoring restrictions or lacking strong opinions. The overrepresentation in the sample of those opposing restrictions would give a biased picture of the general population's opinions about handgun ownership.

As a second illustration, consider a long, detailed survey sent to business establishments. Larger establishments with more resources may be more likely to respond than smaller establishments where everyone works overtime just to keep up.

If a probability mechanism is not used to draw the sample, inferences from the sample about the universe must be made on the basis of judgment, and different judges may legitimately render different verdicts.

Despite some of the dangers of nonprobability surveys, such surveys, as well as casual or fortuitous observation, are the source of quite a bit of data, even in the scientific world. For example, scientists seriously study fortuitously discovered dinosaur bones and outcroppings of rocks. No scientist would refuse to study a chemical element or an atomic particle discovered by accident. Examples of useful volunteer surveys in the business world include suggestion boards hung in factories or offices and customer suggestion boxes set out in hotel rooms and bank lobbies.

It is unfortunate that data from nonprobability surveys are so often mishandled, usually by treating them as if they were data from probability surveys. On the other hand, do not equate being scientific with using probability surveys. Both probability and nonprobability surveys may be used scientifically; they can equally well be used for trivial or sinister purposes.

Probability Sample Surveys

probability surveys

In **probability surveys**, each element of the universe has a known probability of entering the sample. Because of this, a sample drawn by probability methods may be used to make inferences about the whole universe, within probabilistically specified limits.

equal complete coverage

Another subtlety is that a probability sample allows us to make inferences about the equal complete coverage of the universe. The **equal complete coverage** is the set of measurements that would be obtained if the survey procedures were used on every element in the universe. Survey procedures include the operational definitions, the measurement methods, the methods of error detection and control, and so forth. A survey using one set of procedures will not necessarily yield the same information about traits of the universe that would be obtained using another set of procedures, a dilemma analogous to Heisenberg's uncertainty principle in physics—what you observe depends on how you look for it. Understanding the procedures used is essential to understanding the results of a survey.

EXAMPLE 14.2A

Consider two survey organizations seeking information about purchase behavior of households. One organization selects households at random and uses personal interviews to obtain the information. During the interviews, respondents are asked to recall their last two purchases of certain products. The other organization uses diaries to obtain the information. Selected households are asked to maintain diaries of their purchases of certain products over a period of time. The diaries are then collected and the data extracted from them.

> The equal complete coverage for the first organization would be personal interviews conducted at all households in the universe and the information from all these households based on the recall of the respondents. The equal complete coverage for the second organization would be diaries collected from all the households in the universe. Even assuming exactly the same households in both universes, the equal complete coverages are different because the data-collection methods are different. Data based on recall are subject to different types of error than data based on diaries. Any procedures the organizations use to correct the data become part of the equal complete coverage. Neither organization can be said to have a superior procedure, but they are demonstrably different and would yield different equal complete coverages. ▪

For any given set of procedures, the equal complete coverage of the universe yields a set of numerical characteristics, such as mean age, mean income, mean number of visits to a shopping mall, or proportion of heads of households who are female. Any sample drawn from the universe will also yield a set of numerical characteristics, but in general these will differ from those of the equal complete coverage. They will also be different in different samples. This variation in the numerical characteristics from sample to sample is called **sampling variation**.

sampling variation

SECTION

14.3 Exercises

14.3A   Go through several issues of your favorite newspaper and clip all the reports of survey results you can find. For each example, answer the following questions.

a   What organization conducted the survey?

b   Who wrote the newspaper report? What organization did the author represent?

c   Was the survey a census, nonprobability, or probability survey?

d   If it was a probability survey, were the limits of sampling variation reported?

e   Were the survey procedures reported in any detail? If so, which ones? Which ones were not reported?

Develop other pertinent questions that might be asked and answer them. On the basis of your study, what recommendations would you make to the newspaper on the reporting of surveys?

14.3B   In a sample-survey class, one of the authors asked the class members to use a probability-survey design to draw a sample of lines from a novel and to count the number of words in each line. On the basis of the sample, each class member was to estimate the number of words in the novel. One problem the class had to solve was to formulate an operational definition of the word *word*. Your job is to attack this operational definition problem. If more than one legitimate definition of *word* emerges, as it did in the class project described, try to anticipate the effects of using the different definitions on the final estimate of the number of words in the novel.

14.3C   **a**   Suppose you manage a fast food restaurant. Develop a customer questionnaire that you believe would provide useful information for the improvement of your service.

b   Collect such questionnaires from a number of fast food restaurants in your area and compare them on any set of quality criteria you choose. What types of information do the restaurants seem to be most interested in?

c   What groups of people are not likely to fill out such questionnaires? Would the opinions of any such groups be especially valuable to the manager of a fast food restaurant? How might a manager obtain information from such groups?

14.3D   The following sentences briefly describe a design commonly used to survey the nation: Divide the country into compact geographic regions, usually large urban/suburban areas and groups of less populated counties. Further subdivide these geographic regions into blocks, usually the size of several city blocks. Select a sample of large geographic regions. From these select a sample of blocks. Finally, from the blocks select a sample of housing units to be visited. When the household is visited, the interviewer may have instructions to obtain information about everyone in the household or to obtain information about a person with certain characteristics, such as a female head of household.

a   If the interviewer obtains information about every resident of the household, what is the element? What is the universe?

b   If the interviewer is to obtain information only about female heads of households, what is the element? What is the universe?

14.3E   A large industrial firm in Madison, Wisconsin, surveyed its employees to discover the amount of time the employees spent caring for elderly relatives and friends. One problem that arose was how to develop an operational definition of *employee*. The sample was drawn from a recent payroll list. For each person on the list, it could be seen whether the person was full- or part-time, whether the person was laid off or working, and the age of the person, among other things. On the basis of the information given, suggest several operational definitions of *employee*. How might the different definitions affect estimates of proportion of employees giving care to elderly persons and of amount of time spent giving care?

SECTION

14.4 Problems Common to All Surveys

Some difficulties and problems are common to all surveys, whether they are done by census or by sampling. These problems would arise even if the study did not involve sampling. Probability surveys add one more source of error, namely, sampling error, which is discussed in Chapter 15. Here the focus is on **nonsampling error**, which is the difference between the value of a sample estimate and corresponding equal complete coverage value that is due to some cause other than the sampling process.

nonsampling error

Coverage Problems

Almost every survey suffers to some degree from coverage error, which means that not all the intended elements contribute data to the survey. This problem may be caused by a defective design that excludes part of the universe from consideration, or by defective lists of elements, or by inability to get responses from some listed elements.

For example, because of inadequate preliminary fieldwork, a newly developed residential area may not be identified. Or procedures may not be adequate to search out residents of older inner-city areas, where residences are not easy to spot from streets or hallways and residents may lack phones or settled addresses. In another example, shoppers in a mall, asked what stores they would like to see added, may give answers quite different from those of people who do not visit the mall. And these nonvisitors are the potential source of new customers!

Error from being unable to reach respondents is common if a survey tries to contact respondents at home. Since people who are seldom at home are likely to have characteristics different from those who are easier to reach, this error can be serious if it is not recognized and dealt with.

Yet another problem is refusal of respondents to answer even when they are reached. People may refuse to answer because of hostility, ignorance, or lack of time, among other reasons. A related problem is that respondents who do not know an answer or who are not willing to answer truthfully sometimes make something up. A well-known example is that after elections, far more people say they voted for the winner than actually did. Unfortunately, this form of error is usually hard to detect, making it especially insidious.

Finally, there is interviewer error. Instructions may be poorly worded, or interviewers may not follow them. Interviewers may be reluctant to visit a residence for fear of crime or watchdogs. Such error may result in a blank questionnaire—or one in which the interviewer makes up the responses.

bias   Data that are subject to coverage errors are said to **biased**. To go back to our first example, a survey on age of dwellings would be biased if either new developments were missed or older households were undercounted. The average would be biased.

Coverage errors are hard to detect even with hard work. Unfortunately, the bias resulting from coverage errors can be quite severe, greatly weakening the value of the survey. In a good survey, therefore, substantial resources are devoted to preventing, detecting, and correcting coverage errors.

Problems with Survey Instruments

survey instruments   **Survey instruments** are the devices used to gather data. The most obvious example is a questionnaire that is filled out either by the respondent or by an interviewer as the respondent is interviewed. Other examples are diaries, data sheets, and computers that have been programmed to ask questions and receive answers.

The type of instrument used and especially the wording of the questions asked can have a major effect on the responses. Clarity, ease of use, and length are important. Subtle differences such as whether a question is phrased positively or negatively or its location on a questionnaire can have an effect. Although the design of survey instruments is a matter of social science, it is important for relevant statistical results. Because the survey instrument can have such a profound effect, it needs to be field tested carefully. See the discussion under the subheading "Designing a Survey" in the appendix to this chapter.[†]

[†]For further discussion of this critical topic, also see Howard Schuman and Stanley Presser, *Questions and Answers in Attitude Surveys* (San Diego, Calif.: Academic Press, 1981).

Personnel Problems

A telephone survey may use only a few people to make the calls and enter data into a computer file. An extensive survey that uses personal interviews requires a large field staff and typically a large office staff as well. As discussed in Chapter 13, careful training and supervision of surveyors is essential to the success of a survey. This is just as important in the clerical processes as in the data-gathering processes. Clerical work can be a major source of errors, unless it is carefully planned and managed.

For example, imagine that clerks must enter into a computer answers coded A, B, C, D, and E. Errors in entering A or B will generally be obvious. But because C, D, and E are close together on the keyboard, one clerk's tendency to confuse any pair of such letters could inject significant error unless the work is carefully checked.

interviewer bias

Interviewers also can introduce bias into surveys. What is called **interviewer bias** can result when an interviewer asks questions in a way that signals what answer is wanted. Or it can enter less directly, through respondents' reactions to the person asking the questions. In a personal interview, the gender, mannerisms, race, and age of the two people involved can affect the outcome of the interview. In a telephone interview, the gender and voice quality of the interviewer may affect the results. The interviewer effect can be subtle. Research shows that interviewers with different characteristics may elicit quite different responses from the same or similar respondents. It is difficult, if not impossible, to say which response is more nearly correct. Probably the best action is to have each interviewer talk to as representative a group of respondents as possible. Trying to match interviewers and respondents by their personal characteristics seems to invite biases that would be hard to document.

The fact that different interviewers affect respondents differently is the greatest danger in a survey that relies on personal interviews. Research suggests that these dangers are so prevalent that to ignore them is to risk the very credibility of the survey, if not the surveyor. See Exercises 14.5C and D for documentation.

Lack of Audit and Error Control

Errors creep into the best surveys. The best defense against errors is rigorous quality-control measures at all stages of the survey process. These measures include commitment to surveywide quality by everyone, careful training and supervision of workers, adoption of procedures that make the work easy and instill pride in the workers, and the use of statistical methods to monitor the quality of the work.

In surveys that require a large work force, a certain amount of auditing is necessary. Usually a sample survey of the work is inspected by supervisors, and if the work is unsatisfactory, retraining or transfer of workers is called for. In surveys in which interviewers visit respondents in their homes, supervisors may revisit a sample of the homes and conduct a second interview to check the quality of the interviewer's work. Likewise, in telephone surveys a sample of numbers can be redialed and the respondents reinterviewed.

The audit and error control aspects of surveying are all too often neglected in practice because they are time consuming and costly, yet they are absolutely necessary to guarantee high-quality data. The need for these measures is one of the main reasons sample surveying is more prevalent than censusing. It is less costly to conduct audits and error controls in a sample of 1000 elements than in a census of 200 million elements. In fact, more stringent quality measures can be imposed on a small study than on a large study, and at less cost. This means that data from a carefully conducted sample survey can actually be of much higher quality than data from a census, while costing less to collect.

Another reason why it is better to opt for a small sample and stringent error control is found in the brochure *What Is a Survey?*, reprinted in the appendix to this chapter. This brochure, published by the American Statistical Association and prepared by some of the leading exponents of modern sample surveying, rewards careful study. In the section "Shortcuts to Avoid," note the following sentence: "A low response rate does more damage in rendering a survey's results questionable than a small sample, since there is no valid way of scientifically inferring the characteristics of the [universe] represented by the nonrespondents."

The practical implication is that it is better to opt for a small survey and stringent error-control measures, including follow-up of nonrespondents, than to have such a large sample that error controls must be relaxed to stay within budget. This implication can be hard to accept because intuitively it seems that a larger sample must be more informative. In this instance, intuition fails.

Risky Shortcuts

In the "Shortcuts to Avoid" section of the appendix to this chapter, the authors cite the four most common failings in survey practice. These are failure to use proper sampling procedures (especially using a sample that is convenient rather than properly designed), failure to pretest field procedures, failure to follow up on nonrespondents, and failure to exercise quality control throughout the survey process. Avoid these failings when you conduct surveys and watch for them in surveys that you are invited to use as a basis for action.

The Error Triangle

To summarize the discussion of errors in surveys, a figure called the *error triangle* is presented in Exhibit 14.4A. The total error present in the data, represented by the hypotenuse of the right triangle, is made up of two parts: sampling error, or error due to the sampling process, and nonsampling error. These errors are shown in triangular form because in statistical terms

$$(\text{Total error})^2 = (\text{Sampling error})^2 + (\text{Nonsampling error})^2$$

which is literally a Pythagorean theorem for errors. Thus, if one source of error is reduced, the other becomes proportionally more important. You will see this triangle again in Chapter 16, dealing with the standard error of the sum or difference of two estimates.

The error triangle shows that the effort that goes into a survey must be appropriately allocated to the two types of error. Perhaps the greatest danger in using probability surveys is that too much effort will be expended on reducing sampling

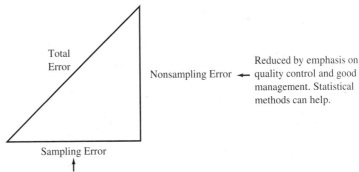

EXHIBIT **14.4A**
The Error Triangle

Total
Error

Nonsampling Error ← Reduced by emphasis on quality control and good management. Statistical methods can help.

Sampling Error
↑
Reduced by the use of technical devices such as increasing sample size and stratification.

error, because this is relatively easy to do. Of course, failing to adopt a valid probability sampling design would have equally disastrous consequences. Proper attention must be paid to all aspects of the survey process.

Generally speaking, sampling error is easier to deal with than nonsampling error because there are a number of technical tools for controlling sampling error at minimum cost. Nonsampling error must be controlled through good management and process control. For example, a survey with a high nonresponse rate (say 50% or more) can be subject to so much bias that no reliable inference can be drawn about the universe.

SECTION

14.5 Exercises

14.5A Suppose you work for an organization that is planning to survey the adult population of the United States, and you are a member of the coverage task force. List some groups that you believe are likely to be hard to reach. Develop strategies for reaching these groups.

14.5B Suppose 800 questionnaires are sent to business establishments in Wisconsin. Suppose further that 150 of the establishments return the questionnaire, and 113 of these say they favor building a business school on Rib Mountain. Which of the following are valid inferences from these data?

    a   81.25% of the establishments did not return the questionnaire.

    b   75.33% of those returning the questionnaire favor the Rib Mountain site.

    c   If all 650 of the nonresponding establishments do not favor the Rib Mountain site, then only 14.125% of the 800 surveyed establishments favor the Rib Mountain site.

    d   The survey data as reported contain no information about the 650 nonresponding establishments other than that they did not respond.

14.5C Locate and read Harper W. Boyd, Jr., and Ralph Westfall, "Interviewer Bias Once More Revisited," *Journal of Marketing Research*, 7 (1970), 249–253. Write a brief memo explaining the problem of interviewer bias and what researchers knew about it, according to Boyd and Westfall, at the time the article was written.

14.5D Locate and read Charles F. Cannell, Lois Oksenberg, and Jean M. Converse, "Striving for Response Accuracy: Experiments in New Interviewing Techniques," *Journal of Marketing*

Research, 14 (1977), 306–315. Write a brief memo explaining the investigated sources of response error and the authors' recommendations for improving response accuracy.

14.5E Suppose you wish to interview a sample of residents of your home town by telephone. What sorts of coverage errors would you encounter if you drew your sample of telephone numbers from the white pages of the telephone book?

SECTION

14.6 Characteristics of Probability Surveys

Probability sample surveys have several distinguishing characteristics. This section fleshes out the bare-bones definitions given earlier.

Using Probability—Uniform Random Digits

Probability methods make it possible to use portions of a universe to draw conclusions about the whole universe. In the chapters on process analysis, you saw that when a process is in statistical control, data from the process can be used to make predictions about the future behavior of the process. Analogously, in surveying, the use of probability methods for sample selection imposes a state of statistical control on the data that allows "predictions" about the universe. In surveying, however, the universe is fixed in time, and the prediction is an inference about the state of the universe at that fixed time. In other words, the predictions from control charts are longitudinal, whereas the predictions from a probability sample are cross-sectional.

In its simplest form, probability sampling uses a table of random digits like that given in Exhibit 1.7C as a tool to select a sample.[†] Every element in the universe from which the sample is drawn must have an equal chance of being selected. Chapter 15 explains in more detail how to draw such a sample.

The Product of a Probability Survey

The result of a probability survey is not a detailed accounting of all the elements in the universe. That is the product of a census. The probability survey instead yields a *profile* of the universe. Usually this profile is a list of estimates of certain numerical characteristics of the elements of the universe. For example, estimates may include average age of employees, average age of inventory of certain parts, or proportion of employees who have taken an adult education course in the last 12 months.

The survey would not allow us to identify *which* employees had taken an adult education course. It would only allow us to infer what *proportion* of the employees had taken a course. A census would provide the more detailed information. Which level of information is needed depends on the decision to be informed or the question to be answered by the survey. If the proportion is all that is needed, then doing a census is a waste of time and money.

[†]If you wish to pursue the question "What is random?" refer to Kevin McKean, "The Orderly Pursuit of Pure Disorder," *Discover*, Jan. 1987, pp. 73–81. A popular table of random digits is *A Million Random Digits with 100,000 Normal Deviates*, published by the RAND Corporation in 1955.

Determining Sample Design and Sample Size

In a census, the size of the study is determined by the size of the universe because all elements are examined. In sampling, the analyst chooses the size of the study and the design by which the data are collected. The sample design and the sample size are chosen to achieve some level of precision in the inferences about the universe. *Precision* means the width of the limits within which predictions about the universe are made. The narrower the limits the more precise the prediction.

E X A M P L E   **14.6A**   You are likely to find that the typical opinion poll reported in your newspaper is based on a sample of between 1000 and 1500 people. The limits on the sampling error in such polls are typically reported to be three percentage points. (Find reports of several polls and verify these statements. Can you find any major deviations from the figures reported?) Contrast these figures with the Current Population Survey, which is conducted each month by the Census Bureau for the Bureau of Labor Statistics, and which yields the employment and unemployment figures for the nation. The sample size for the Current Population Survey is roughly 60,000 people. It yields very small limits on sampling error in the overall national estimates. The sample is large so that it can be broken down by such categories as age, race, gender, and geographic region. The estimate of the unemployment rate for black males in the upper Midwest is subject to much larger sampling error than the estimate of the unemployment rate for all workers in the United States. Example 14.6B demonstrates the effect of varying the sample size.   ▪

Precision is not the only consideration in choosing sample size. Because sampling is done to achieve some economy of time and resources, the goal is to achieve either the best precision subject to limits on cost and time expended, or a needed level of precision for the least cost. Several approaches to a particular sampling problem are often available. Determining the most efficient approach is not always easy, and compromises are common.

An Illustration of Simple Random Sampling

The fundamental design of probability surveying is called *simple random sampling*. The principles behind this design are explained here by working through an example based on an artificially small universe. In realistic problems, the universe is much larger, but the basic principles are the same.

E X A M P L E   **14.6B**   Exhibit 14.6A gives us information on all nine residential parcels of land in the small village of Toy, New York. The information shown was obtained from a file kept by the local assessor. A vacant parcel is one that consists of land only. An improved parcel is one on which a residential structure has been erected. Also shown in the exhibit are some numerical characteristics of the universe. Verify these figures.

Now we will create an artificial situation that illustrates probability sampling. Pretend that the last two columns in Exhibit 14.6A are missing. You may select only two parcels at random, and for only those two will the information in the last two columns be revealed. Using that information, you are to make a guess at the figures at the bottom of the exhibit. Before we define "at random," we write down all the samples of two parcels it is possible to get. This is done in Exhibit 14.6B. Each sample also lists the data to be revealed if that sample is chosen.

There are 36 distinct pairs of parcels that can constitute samples. If each one of these pairs has the same probability of being chosen, a simple random sampling design is being used. (In Chapter 15, you will see how to implement a simple random sampling design using a table of random digits.)

The simplest characteristic of the universe to estimate is the mean of some variable, such as the mean assessed value. The mean assessed value in the universe is $59,111.11, or roughly 59.111 in $1000 units. Suppose by chance we draw the first sample in Exhibit 14.6B. The mean of the assessed values in this sample is $32,000, or just 32 in $1000 units. This is below the universe mean value by 27.111, a rather large margin of sampling error. The last sample in Exhibit 14.6B has a mean assessed value of $88,500, or 88.5 in $1000 units. The margin of sampling error in this sample is 29.389. Since the parcels were listed in ascending order of value, these first and last samples are the extremes. All the other samples have means closer to the universe mean.

Parcel Number	Address	Vacant or Improved	Assessed Value ($1000s)
1	30 Muir Dr.	Vacant	30
2	12 Dairy La.	Improved	34
3	14 Dairy La.	Vacant	47
4	10 Dairy La.	Improved	50
5	5 Badger St.	Improved	57
6	8 Dairy La.	Improved	67
7	13 Badger St.	Improved	70
8	3 Muir Dr.	Improved	72
9	10 La Follette Blvd.	Improved	105

Proportion Vacant = 2/9 = .2222 . . .
Median assessed value = $57,000
Total assessed value = $532,000
Mean assessed value = $59,111.11 = $532,000/9

E X H I B I T **14.6B**
All Possible Samples of Two
Parcels from Troy, New York
(assessed values in $1000s)

Parcels in Sample	Number Vacant	Assessed Values	Total Assessed Values	Mean Assessed Values
1 and 2	1	30, 34	64	32
1 and 3	2	30, 47	77	38.5
1 and 4	1	30, 50	80	40
1 and 5	1	30, 57	87	43.5
1 and 6	1	30, 67	97	48.5
1 and 7	1	30, 70	100	50
1 and 8	1	30, 72	102	51
1 and 9	1	30, 105	135	67.5
2 and 3	1	34, 47	81	40.5
2 and 4	0	34, 50	84	42
2 and 5	0	34, 57	91	45.5
2 and 6	0	34, 67	101	50.5
2 and 7	0	34, 70	104	52
2 and 8	0	34, 72	106	53
2 and 9	0	34, 105	139	69.5
3 and 4	1	47, 50	97	48.5
3 and 5	1	47, 57	104	52
3 and 6	1	47, 67	114	57
3 and 7	1	47, 70	117	58.5
3 and 8	1	47, 72	119	59.5
3 and 9	1	47, 105	152	76
4 and 5	0	50, 57	107	53.5
4 and 6	0	50, 67	117	58.5
4 and 7	0	50, 70	120	60
4 and 8	0	50, 72	122	61
4 and 9	0	50, 105	155	77.5
5 and 6	0	57, 67	124	62
5 and 7	0	57, 70	127	63.5
5 and 8	0	57, 72	129	64.5
5 and 9	0	57, 105	162	81
6 and 7	0	67, 70	137	68.5
6 and 8	0	67, 72	139	69.5
6 and 9	0	67, 105	172	86
7 and 8	0	70, 72	142	71
7 and 9	0	70, 105	175	87.5
8 and 9	0	72, 105	177	88.5

Another way to look at the data is to display a dotplot of the nine assessed values in the universe of parcels and of the 36 sample mean assessed values in Exhibit 14.6B. This is done in Exhibit 14.6C. The population mean assessed value, 59.111, is shown as an asterisk (*). The diagram shows the variation in the sample means, which is the sampling variation of the means. Such a

E X H I B I T **14.6C**
Dotplot of Population of
Assessed Values and Sample
Mean Assessed Values for
Samples of Size 2 and Size 3

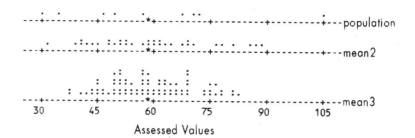

Assessed Values

		Characteristics of	
		Sample Means	
	Universe	Size 2	Size 3
Number	9	36	84
Sum	532	2128	4965.333
Average	59.111	59.111	59.111
Minimum	30	32	37
Maximum	105	88.5	82.333
Median	57	58.5	58
Standard Deviation	22.817	14.229	10.756

sampling distribution

diagram of the means of all possible samples of a given size displays the **sampling distribution** of the sample mean.

The descriptive statistics under the diagrams show that the sampling variation in the sample means is less than the variation in the universe assessed values. Whereas the universe values range from 30 to 105 with a standard deviation of 22.82, the sample means range from 32 to 88.5 with a standard deviation of 14.229.

A general property of random sampling designs is that the standard deviation of the collection of sample means is less than the standard deviation of the values in the universe. A mathematical formula explained in Chapter 15 gives the relationship between these two standard deviations.

The assessed values in the universe and the sample means have the same average values, namely 59.111. This illustrates another general property. The average of all the sample means that can be generated from a simple random sampling design is equal to the average of universe values from which the samples are drawn.

Exhibit 14.6C also shows the sampling distribution of the mean of samples of size 3. The detailed calculations are left as Exercise 14.7A, but the results reinforce the remarks just made. Note that the average value of the means of all the 84 possible means of samples of size 3 is 59.111. For samples of size 3, the sample means range from a low of 37 to a high of 82.333, with a standard deviation of 10.756, which is lower than the universe standard deviation and the standard deviation of the means of samples of size 2.

If you estimate from samples of size 3 rather than size 2, you have a better chance of coming closer to the actual values of the nine parcels. But you still can have a large error, whose size will depend on which sample of three parcels you use.   ■

Sampling Error

sampling error

Sampling error is the difference between the value of a sample estimate and a corresponding equal complete coverage value that is due only to the sampling process. The following analogy should help you understand simple random sampling and the errors that can result. Imagine that the elements possible in a random sample are like the cards possible if you are dealt a hand from a deck of cards. The cards you get are subject to chance, beyond your control. But once the cards are dealt, you use your skill and cunning to reap the greatest gain from the cards you have been dealt. How well you do depends on the cards dealt to the other players in the game and how well they play their hands. If all players play skillfully, some hands are more favorable than others, so there need be no dishonor in defeat if you play your hand in the best way possible.

Likewise, from some random samples it is possible to make estimates that are very close to the equal complete coverage values, whereas with others large sampling errors occur no matter how skillfully estimates are formed. Statistical theory suggests the best way to obtain estimates given a sampling design and a characteristic of interest. It also provides a way to place a bound on the magnitude of the sampling error of the estimate. If you follow the prescribed procedures, you are playing your hand the best way possible, even though by chance you may commit a rather large error. Of course, researchers have some control over the sizes of the errors, because they can choose the design and the sample size. But regardless of the choices, some sampling error will be present, and the card-playing analogy will apply.

SECTION

14.7 Exercises

14.7A Construct the sampling distribution pictured in the third dotplot in Exhibit 14.6C. It is the distribution of sample mean assessed values of all possible samples of size 3 from the universe in Exhibit 14.6A. You need to write down the 84 possible samples of size 3, list the assessed values of the three parcels in each sample, and average these values. Finally, make a dotplot of the 84 mean values.

14.7B Repeat the analysis for both $n = 2$ and $n = 3$ in Example 14.6B but analyze the variable "Vacant or Improved." Do this by assigning a 0 to vacant parcels and a 1 to improved parcels. Analyze these numerical values just as the assessed values were analyzed in the example. Note that the mean values are just the proportions of parcels that are improved. This example shows that proportions are just means of a binary variable. As part of this exercise, identify the universe, the elements, and the sampling distribution of the sample means. What would be the behavior of samples of size 4? Make a qualitative statement but do not carry out all the calculations for $n = 4$.

Chapter Summary

A survey is a process of systematically obtaining information from a universe of elements. In contrast to nonprobability surveys, probability surveys allow inferences about the whole universe within probabilistically defined limits. Regardless of the type of survey, effort and resources must be spent to combat coverage problems, problems with the survey instrument, personnel problems, failure to pretest field procedures, failure to follow up on nonrespondents, and failure to exercise quality control throughout the survey process. A probability survey uses random sampling to yield a profile of the universe through a list of estimates of certain numerical characteristics of the elements. The basic requirement of the probability survey is that each element have a known probability of being part of the sample. From this requirement, the distribution of a sample quantity—such as the sample mean—can be constructed by considering the results of all possible samples that could come from the universe.

Supplementary Exercises for Chapter 14

14A From a deck of bridge cards take the 2 through the 10 of hearts (a total of nine cards). Let the cards be the elements of your universe, and let the numbers on the cards be the measurements associated with the elements.

a Determine the mean and standard deviation of the whole set of measurements. [*Answer:* mean = 6, standard deviation = $\sqrt{15}/\sqrt{2} = \sqrt{7.5} \simeq 2.739$.]

b List all 36 possible samples of size $n = 2$ from the universe and list the measurements associated with the elements in the samples.

c For each sample listed in part (b), compute the mean and standard deviation. Make dotplots of the 36 means and the 36 standard deviations. Compute the mean of the 36 means. [*Answer* = 6.] Note that this is equal to the mean of the measurements in the universe. Compute the mean of the 36 standard deviations. [*Answer* = $(10/3)/\sqrt{2} \simeq 2.357$.] Note that this is not equal to the standard deviation of the measurements in the universe.

d Describe in general terms the result of repeating parts (b) and (c) for the 84 possible samples of size $n = 3$ from the universe. Do not carry out the computations.

e Carry out the computations in parts (b) and (c) for the 84 samples of size $n = 3$ from the universe. Compare your findings with the predictions you made in part (d).

14B Refer to Exercise 14A, parts (b) and (c).

a Suppose that circumstances prevent you from obtaining the 10 of hearts in your sample, an example of coverage error. Write down the 28 possible samples of size $n = 2$ under these circumstances, and write down the corresponding measurements. Repeat part (c) of Exercise 14A for these samples. Note that the mean of the sample means is not equal to the mean of all the measurements in the universe, namely, 6. Comment on how the coverage error affects the distributions of the sample means and sample standard deviations.

b Repeat part (a) assuming that circumstances prevent you from obtaining the 6 of hearts. Compare the impact of this coverage error with the one you studied in part (a).

14C Come up with some examples of coverage errors and describe the circumstances that caused them. How can a low response rate to a questionnaire have the same effect as coverage error?

14D Coming up with an operational definition of *resident* can be difficult. To illustrate, find out the requirements your state imposes to determine if a person or family is eligible for state welfare benefits. Is there a residency requirement? Now find out the requirements imposed to determine if a student pays in-state tuition at the state university. Come up with other concepts for which operational definitions are difficult. Some suggestions are learning, strong, timely, and cost-effective.

14E Why is the question "Were you robbed in the last six months?" ambiguous?

14F It is a well-established principle of science that the very act of subjecting an element to measurement alters the element. A common but often unstated assumption in surveying is that this fundamental dilemma can be ignored for practical purposes. The following references argue to the contrary. They raise the possibility that surveys, especially opinion polls, are part of a system of opinion and action control imposed by the political elite. Read and comment on these references. In particular, comment on the impact on public opinion of marketing surveys. Take as one example the Nielsen television ratings.

- Edward Walsh, "Polls Are Telling Us More, But Are They Telling It Like It Is?" *Washington Post*, Apr. 13, 1987, weekly edition, p. 37.

- Benjamin Ginsberg, *The Captive Public: How Mass Opinion Promotes State Power* (New York: Basic Books, 1987). (For a review of this book, see Ralph Braccio, "History of Mass Public Opinion and the Political Process," *Christian Science Monitor*, Apr. 16, 1987, p. 28.)

14G Drawing on your reading, your personal experience, or both, make a list of examples in which the results of a survey were used as a basis for action. In each instance state whether the survey was a census, nonprobability, or probability survey.

14H Find a recent issue of *Employment and Earnings*, a publication of the Bureau of Labor Statistics. Read the description of the Current Population Survey and the Establishment Survey. Compare and contrast these two surveys in terms of who carries them out, the universes, the types of surveys they are, the data obtained from them, and the way the results are reported.

14I Find and read Lester R. Frankel, "Statistics and People—The Statistician's Responsibilities," *Journal of the American Statistical Association*, 71 (353) (1976), 9–16. According to Frankel, what are a statistician's responsibilities toward the users of the product of a survey? Toward those who supply the raw data? How does Frankel suggest these responsibilities be met?

. . . .

Glossary for Chapter 14

bias	Systematic difference between an estimate from survey data and the value that would be obtained by equal complete coverage.
census	A survey conducted with the intention of obtaining information from every element in the universe.
elements	The basic units or individuals about which information is sought in a survey.
equal complete coverage	The set of measurements obtained if the survey procedures were used on every element in the universe.
interviewer bias	Distortions in responses caused by inappropriate cues from the interviewer or respondents' reactions to the interviewer.
nonprobability survey	Survey in which probability methods are *not* used to select the elements to be measured.
nonsampling error	The difference between the value of a sample estimate and a corresponding equal complete coverage value that is due to some cause other than the sampling process.
probability survey	Survey in which each element of the universe has a known probability of entering the sample.
sampling distribution	Distribution of values of a sample statistic formed from all possible samples.
sampling error	The difference between the value of a sample estimate and a corresponding equal complete coverage value that is due only to the sampling process.
sampling variation	The variation of numerical characteristics from sample to sample.
survey	A process of systematically obtaining information on a universe of individuals.
survey instrument	Device used to capture data, such as a questionnaire or diary.
universe	The collection of all the elements of interest.

APPENDIX

What Is a Survey?[†]

Introduction

The growing popularity of surveys for throwing light on different problems has led to a tendency to overlook the fact that surveys involve many technical problems. Too many surveys seem to be conducted

more or less on an ad hoc basis, with the result that the GIGO (garbage in, garbage out) principle is brought into play. This brochure seeks to help the nonstatistician to avoid this danger by providing a nontechnical introduction to sample surveys of human populations and the many different ways in which surveys are used.

   The principal focus is on the design of a survey and on the collection of survey data—two areas in which the many intricacies involved are frequently overlooked. However, attention is also given to the

[†]By Robert Ferber (Chair), Paul Sheatsley, Anthony Turner, and Joseph Waksberg, the Subcommittee of the Section on Survey Research Methods of the American Statistical Association. Reprinted with the permission of the American Statistical Association.

need for proper evaluation of survey data, an essential prerequisite for assessing the value of a survey as well as a basis for proper analysis of the data. (Analysis of survey data is a major topic in itself and is not covered here.)

This brochure can be used in a variety of ways, such as:

- By statisticians and survey agencies, to give prospective clients some appreciation of what is involved in a sample survey.

- By research executives, to help their nonresearch counterparts understand how surveys are conducted.

- By instructors in introductory social science and other courses, to give students a brief introduction to sample surveys.

- By international agencies and others advising in other countries, to give government officials in these other countries an understanding of the various steps of a sample survey.

It should be stressed that this brochure is *not* intended to provide students of statistics or prospective specialists in the field with a comprehensive understanding of survey methods. For this purpose, the books listed at the end of the brochure need to be used, plus many of the specialized sources dealing with the techniques of survey design and data collection. This brochure is meant for nonspecialists, for the users of survey data. If it leads them to have a better appreciation of what is involved in a sample survey, its purpose will have been served.

Characteristics of Surveys

The Need

Any observation or investigation of the facts about a situation may be called a survey. But today the word is most often used to describe a method of gathering information from a number of individuals, a "sample," in order to learn something about the larger population from which the sample has been drawn. Thus, a sample of voters is surveyed in advance of an election to determine how the public perceives the candidates and the issues. A manufacturer makes a survey of the potential market before introducing a new product. A government agency commissions a survey to gather the factual information it needs in order to draft new legislation. For example, what medical care do people receive, and how is it paid for? Who uses food stamps? How many people are unemployed?

It has been said that the United States is no longer an industrial society but an "information society." That is, our major problems and tasks no longer focus merely on the production of goods and services necessary to our survival and comfort. Rather, our major problems and tasks today are those of organizing and managing the incredibly complex efforts required to meet the needs and wishes of nearly 220 million Americans. To do this requires a prompt and accurate flow of information on preferences, needs, and behavior. It is in response to this critical need for information on the part of the government, business, and social institutions that so much reliance is placed upon surveys.

Surveys come in many different forms and have a wide variety of purposes, but they do have certain characteristics in common. Unlike a census, they gather information from only a small sample of people (or farms, businesses, or other units, depending on the purpose of the study). In a bona fide survey, the sample is not selected haphazardly or only from persons who volunteer to participate. It is scientifically chosen so that each individual in the population has a known chance of selection. In this way, the results can be reliably projected to the larger public.

Information is collected by means of standardized questions so that every individual surveyed responds to exactly the same question. The survey's intent is not to describe the particular individuals who by chance are part of the sample but to obtain a statistical profile of the population. Individual respondents are never identified and the survey's results are presented in the form of summaries, such as statistical tables and charts.

The sample size required for a survey will depend on the reliability needed which, in turn, depends on how the results will be used. Consequently, there is no simple rule for sample size that can be used for all surveys. However, analysts usually find that a moderate sample size is sufficient for most needs. For example, the well-known national polls generally use samples of about 1500 persons to reflect national attitudes and opinions. A sample of this size produces accurate estimates even for a country as large as the United States with a population of over 200 million.

When it is realized that a properly selected sample of only 1500 individuals can reflect various characteristics of the total population within a very small margin of error, it is easy to understand the value of surveys in a complex society such as ours. They provide a speedy and economical means of determining facts about our economy and people's knowledge, attitudes, beliefs, expectations, and behavior.

Who Does Surveys?

We all know of the public opinion polls that are reported in the press and broadcast media. The Gallup Poll and the Harris Survey issue reports periodically, describing national public opinion on a wide range of current issues. State polls and metropolitan area polls, often supported by a local newspaper or TV station, are reported regularly in many localities. The major broadcasting networks and national news magazines also conduct polls and report their findings.

But the great majority of surveys are not exposed to public view. The reason is that, unlike the public opinion polls, most surveys are directed to a specific administrative or commercial purpose. The wide variety of issues with which surveys deal is illustrated by the following listing of actual uses:

1   The U.S. Department of Agriculture conducted a survey to find out how poor people use food stamps.

2   Major TV networks rely on surveys to tell them how many and what types of people are watching their programs.

3   Auto manufacturers use surveys to find out how satisfied people are with their cars.

4   The U.S. Bureau of the Census compiles a survey every month to obtain information on employment and unemployment in the nation.

5   The National Center for Health Statistics sponsors a survey every year to determine how much money people are spending for different types of medical care.

6   Local housing authorities make surveys to ascertain satisfaction of people in public housing with their living accommodations.

7   The Illinois Board of Higher Education surveys the interest of Illinois residents in adult education.

8   Local transportation authorities conduct surveys to acquire information on people's commuting and travel habits.

9   Magazine and trade journals utilize surveys to find out what their subscribers are reading.

10 Surveys are used to ascertain what sort of people use our national parks and other recreational facilities.

Surveys of human populations also provide an important source of basic social science knowledge. Economists, psychologists, political scientists, and sociologists obtain foundation or government grants to study such matters as income and expenditure patterns among households, the roots of ethnic or racial prejudices, comparative voting behavior, or the effects of employment of women on family life. (Surveys are also made of nonhuman populations, such as of animals, soils, and housing; they are not discussed here, although many of the principles are the same.)

Moreover, once collected, survey data can be analyzed and reanalyzed in many different ways. Data tapes with identification of individuals removed can be made available for analysis by community groups, scientific researchers, and others.

Types of Surveys

Surveys can be classified in a number of ways. One dimension is by size and type of sample. Many surveys study the total adult population, but others might focus on special population groups: physicians, community leaders, the unemployed, or users of a particular product or service. Surveys may be conducted on a national, state, or local basis and may seek to obtain data from a few hundred or many thousand people.

Surveys can also be classified by their method of data collection. Thus, there are mail surveys, telephone surveys, and personal interview surveys.

There are also newer methods of data collection by which information is recorded directly into computers. This includes measurement of TV audiences carried out by devices attached to a sample of TV sets that automatically record in a computer the channels being watched. Mail surveys are seldom used to collect information from the general public because names and addresses are not often available and the response rate tends to be low, but the method may be highly effective with members of particular groups; for example, subscribers to a specialized magazine or members of a professional association. Telephone interviewing is an efficient method of collecting some types of data and is being increasingly used. A personal interview in a respondent's home or office is much more expensive than a telephone survey but is necessary when complex information is to be collected.

Some surveys combine various methods. Survey workers may use the telephone to "screen" for eligible respondents (say, women of a particular age group) and then make appointments for a personal interview. Some information, such as the characteristics of the respondent's home, may be obtained by observation rather than questioning. Survey data are also sometimes obtained by self-administered questionnaires filled out by respondents in groups, e.g., a class of school children or a group of shoppers in a central location.

One can further classify surveys by their content. Some surveys focus on opinions and attitudes (such as a pre-election survey of voters), while others are concerned with factual characteristics or behavior (such as a survey of people's health, housing, or transportation habits). Many surveys combine questions of both types. Thus, a respondent will be asked if s(he) has heard or read about an issue, what s(he) knows about it, his (her) opinion, how strongly s(he) feels and why, interest in the issue, past experience with it, and also certain factual information that will help the survey analyst classify the responses (such as age, sex, marital status, occupation, and place of residence).

The questions may be open-ended ("Why do you feel that way?") or closed ("Do you approve or disapprove?"); they may ask the respondent to rate a political candidate or a product on some kind of scale;

they may ask for a ranking of various alternatives. The questionnaire may be very brief—a few questions taking five minutes or less; or it can be quite long—requiring an hour or more of the respondent's time. Since it is inefficient to identify and approach a large national sample for only a few items of information, there are "omnibus" surveys that combine the interests of several clients in a single interview. In such surveys, the respondent will be asked a dozen questions on one subject, half a dozen more on another subject, and so on.

Because changes in attitude or behavior cannot be reliably ascertained from a single interview, some surveys employ a "panel design," in which the same respondents are interviewed two or more times. Such surveys are often used during election campaigns, or to chart a family's health or purchasing pattern over a period of time. They are also used to trace changes in behavior over time, as with the social experiments that study changes by low-income families in work behavior in response to an income maintenance plan.

What Sort of People Work on Surveys?

The survey worker best known to the public is the interviewer who calls on the phone, appears at the door, or stops people at a shopping center. Contrary to the cartoons that typically portray the survey interviewer as a man wearing a hat and carrying a briefcase, the interviewer will usually be a woman between the ages of 30 and 60 who is skilled at approaching strangers, explaining the survey, and conducting the interview. Women interviewers arouse less fear and suspicion than men, and the part-time flexible nature of the work makes the job an attractive form of employment for many women.

Behind the interviewers are the in-house research staff who design the survey, determine the sample design, develop the questionnaire, supervise the data collection, carry out the clerical and computer operations necessary to process the completed interviews, analyze the data, and write the reports. In most survey research agencies, the senior people will have taken courses in survey methods at the graduate level and will hold advanced degrees in sociology, statistics, marketing, or psychology, or they will have the equivalent in business experience. Middle-level supervisors and research associates frequently have similar academic backgrounds, or they have advanced out of the ranks of clerks, interviewers, or coders on the basis of their competence and experience.

Are Responses Confidential?

The privacy of the information supplied by survey respondents is of prime concern to all reputable survey organizations. At the U.S. Bureau of the Census, for example, the confidentiality of much of the data collected is protected by law (Title 13 of the U.S. Code). In Canada, the Statistics Act guarantees the confidentiality of data collected by Statistics Canada. Other countries have similar safeguards. Also, a number of professional organizations that rely on survey methods have codes of ethics that prescribe rules for keeping survey responses confidential. The recommended policy for survey organizations to safeguard such confidentiality includes:

1   Using only code numbers for the identity of a respondent on a questionnaire, and keeping the code separate from that of the questionnaires.

2   Refusing to give names and addresses of survey respondents to anybody outside of the survey organization, including clients.

3   Destroying questionnaires and identifying information about respondents after the responses have been put onto computer tape.

4   Omitting the names and addresses of survey respondents from computer tapes used for analysis.

5   Presenting statistical tabulations by broad enough categories that individual respondents cannot be singled out.

How a Survey Is Carried Out

As noted earlier, a survey usually has its beginnings when an individual or institution is confronted with an information need and there are no existing data that suffice. A politician may wish to tap prevailing voter opinions in his district about a proposal to build a superhighway through the county. A government agency may wish to assess the impact on the primary recipients and their families of one of its social welfare programs. A university researcher may wish to examine the relationship between actual voting behavior and expressed opinion on some political issue or social concern.

Designing a Survey

Once the information need has been identified and a determination made that existing data are inadequate, the first step in planning a survey is to lay out the objectives of the investigation. This is generally the function of the sponsor of the inquiry. The objectives should be as specific, clear-cut, and unambiguous as possible. The required accuracy level of the data has a direct bearing on the overall survey design. For example, in a sample survey whose main purpose is to estimate the unemployment rate for a city, the approximate number of persons to be sampled can be estimated mathematically when one knows the amount of sampling error that can be tolerated in the survey results.

Given the objectives, the methodology for carrying out the survey is developed. A number of interrelated activities are involved. Rules must be formulated for defining and locating eligible respondents, the method of collecting the data must be decided upon, a questionnaire must be designed and pretested, procedures must be developed for minimizing or controlling response errors, appropriate samples must be designed and selected, interviewers must be hired and trained (except for surveys involving self-administered questionnaires), plans must be made for handling nonresponse cases, and tabulation and analysis must be performed.

Designing the questionnaire represents one of the most critical stages in the survey development process, and social scientists have given a great deal of thought to issues involved in questionnaire design. The questionnaire links the information need to the realized measurement.

Unless the concepts are clearly defined and the questions unambiguously phrased, the resulting data are apt to contain serious biases. In a survey to estimate the incidence of robbery victimization, for example, one might want to ask, "Were you robbed during the last six months?" Though apparently straightforward and clear-cut, the question does present an ambiguous stimulus. Many respondents are unaware of the legal distinction between robbery (involving personal confrontation of the victim by the offender) and burglary (involving breaking and entering but no confrontation), and confuse the two in a survey. In the National Crime Survey, conducted by the Bureau of the Census, the questions on robbery victimization do not mention "robbery." Instead, several questions are used that, together, seek to capture the desired responses by using more universally understood phrases that are consistent with the operational definition of robbery.

Designing a suitable questionnaire entails more than well-defined concepts and distinct phraseology. Attention must also be given to its length, for unduly long questionnaires are burdensome to the respondent, are apt to induce respondent fatigue and hence response errors, refusals, and incomplete questionnaires, and may contribute to higher nonresponse rates in subsequent surveys involving the same respondents. Several other factors must be taken into account when designing a questionnaire to minimize or prevent biasing the results and to facilitate its use both in the field and in the processing center. They include such diverse considerations as the sequencing of sections or individual questions in the document, the inclusion of check boxes or precoded answer categories versus open-ended questions, the questionnaire's physical size and format, and instructions to the respondent or to the interviewer on whether certain questions are to be skipped depending on response patterns to prior questions.

Selecting the proper respondent in a sample unit is a key element in survey planning. For surveys where the inquiry is basically factual in nature, any knowledgeable person associated with the sample unit may be asked to supply the needed information. This procedure is used in the Current Population Survey, where the sample units are households and any responsible adult in a household is expected to be able to provide accurate answers on the employment-unemployment status of the eligible household members.

In other surveys, a so-called household respondent will produce erroneous and/or invalid information. For example, in attitude surveys it is generally accepted that a randomly chosen respondent from among the eligible household members produces a more valid cross section of opinion than does the nonrandomly selected household respondent. This is because a nonrandomly selected individual acting as household respondent is more likely to be someone who is at home during the day, and the working public and their attitudes would be underrepresented.

Another important feature of the survey planning process is devising ways to keep response errors and biases to a minimum. These considerations depend heavily on the subject matter of the survey. For example, memory plays an important role in surveys dealing with past events that the respondent is expected to report accurately, such as in a consumer expenditure survey. In such retrospective surveys, therefore, an appropriate choice of reference period must be made so that the respondent is not forced to report events that may have happened too long ago to remember accurately. In general, attention must be given to whether the questions are too sensitive, whether they may prejudice the respondent, whether they unduly invade the respondent's privacy, and whether the information sought is too difficult even for a willing respondent to provide. Each of these concerns has an important bearing on the overall validity of the survey results.

Sampling Aspects

Virtually all surveys that are taken seriously by social scientists and policy makers use some form of scientific sampling. Even the decennial Censuses of Population and Housing use sampling techniques for gathering the bulk of the data items, although 100 percent enumeration is used for the basic population counts. Methods of sampling are well-grounded in statistical theory and in the theory of probability. Hence, reliable and efficient estimates of a needed statistic can be made by surveying a carefully constructed sample of a population, as opposed to the entire population, provided of course that a large proportion of the sample members give the requested information.

The particular type of sample used depends on the objectives and scope of the survey, including the overall survey budget, the method of data collection, the subject matter, and the kind of respondent needed. A first step, however, in deciding on an appropriate sampling method is to define the relevant population. This target population can be all the people in the entire nation or all the people in a certain city, or it can be a subset such as all teenagers in a given location. The population of interest need not be people; it may be wholesale businesses or institutions for the handicapped or government agencies, and so on.

The types of samples range from simple random selection of the population units to highly complex samples involving multiple stages or levels of selection with stratification and/or clustering of the units into various groupings. Whether simple or complex, the distinguishing characteristic of a properly designed sample is that all the units in the target population have a known, nonzero chance of being included in the sample. It is this feature that makes it scientifically valid to draw inferences from the sample results about the entire population that the sample represents.

Ideally, the sample size chosen for a survey should be based on how reliable the final estimates must be. In practice, usually a trade-off is made between the ideal sample size and the expected cost of the survey. The complexity of a sample plan often depends on the availability of auxiliary information that can be used to introduce efficiencies into the overall design. For example, in a recent federal government survey on characteristics of health-care institutions, existing information about the type of care provided and the number of beds in each institution was useful in sorting the institutions into "strata," or groups by type and size, in advance of selecting the sample. The procedure permitted more reliable survey estimates than would have been possible if a simple random selection of institutions had been made without regard to size or type.

A critical element in sample design and selection is defining the source of materials from which a sample can be chosen. This source, termed the sampling frame, generally is a list of some kind, such as a list of housing units in a city, a list of retail establishments in a county, or a list of students in a university. The sampling frame can also consist of geographic areas with well-defined natural or artificial boundaries, when no suitable list of the target population exists. In the latter instance, a sample of geographic areas (referred to as segments) is selected and an interviewer canvasses the sample "area segments" and lists the appropriate units—households, retail stores, or whatever—so that some or all of them can be designated for inclusion in the final sample.

The sampling frame can also consist of less concrete things, such as all possible permutations of integers that make up banks of telephone numbers, in the case of telephone surveys that seek to include unlisted numbers. The quality of the sampling frame—whether it is up to date and how complete—is probably the dominant feature for ensuring adequate coverage of the desired population.

Conducting a Survey

Though a survey design may be well conceived, the preparatory work would be futile if the survey were executed improperly. For personal or telephone interview surveys, interviewers must be carefully trained in the survey's concepts, definitions, and procedures. This may take the form of classroom training, self-study, or both. The training stresses good interviewer techniques on such points as how to make initial contacts, how to conduct interviews in a professional manner, and how to avoid influencing or biasing responses. The training generally involves practice interviews to familiarize the interviewers with the variety of situations they are likely to encounter. Survey materials must be prepared and issued to each interviewer, including ample copies of the questionnaire, a reference manual, information about the identification and location of the sample units, and any cards or pictures to be shown to the respondent.

Before conducting the interview, survey organizations frequently send an advance letter to the sample member explaining the survey's purpose and the fact that an interviewer will be calling soon. In many surveys, especially those sponsored by the federal government, information must be given to the respondent regarding the voluntary or mandatory nature of the survey, and how the answers are to be used.

Visits to sample units are scheduled with attention to such considerations as the best time of day to call or visit and the number of allowable callbacks for no-one-at-home situations. Controlling the quality of the field work is an essential aspect of good survey practice. This is done in a number of ways, most often through observation or rechecking of a subsample of interviews by supervisory or senior personnel, and through office editing procedures to check for omissions or obvious mistakes in the data.

When the interviews have been completed and the questionnaires filled out, they must be processed in a form so that aggregated totals, averages, or other statistics can be computed. This will involve clerical coding of questionnaire items that are not already precoded. Occupation and industry categorizations are typical examples of fairly complex questionnaire coding that is usually done clerically. Also procedures must be developed for coding open-ended questions and for handling items that must be transcribed from one part of the questionnaire to another.

Coded questionnaires are keypunched, entered directly onto a tape so that a computer file can be created, or entered directly into the computer. Decisions may then be needed on how to treat missing data and "not answered" items.

Coding, keypunching, and transcription operations are subject to human error and must be rigorously controlled through verification processes, either on a sample basis or 100 percent basis. Once a computer file has been generated, additional computer editing, as distinct from clerical editing of the data, can be accomplished to alter inconsistent or impossible entries, e.g., a six-year-old grandfather.

When a "clean" file has been produced, the survey data are in a form where analysts can specify to a computer programmer the frequency counts, cross-tabulations, or more sophisticated methods of data presentation or computation that are needed to help answer the concerns outlined when the survey was initially conceived.

The results of the survey are usually communicated in publications and in verbal presentations at staff briefings or more formal meetings. Secondary analysis is also often possible to those other than the survey staff by making available computer data files at nominal cost.

Shortcuts to Avoid

As we have seen, conducting a creditable survey entails scores of activities, each of which must be carefully planned and controlled. Taking shortcuts can invalidate the results and badly mislead the user.

Four types of shortcuts that crop up often are failure to use a proper sampling procedure, no pretest of the field procedures, failure to follow up nonrespondents, and inadequate quality control.

One way to ruin an otherwise well-conceived survey is to use a convenience sample rather than one that is based on a probability design. It may be simple and cheap, for example, to select a sample of names from a telephone directory to find out which candidate people intend to vote for. However, this sampling procedure could give incorrect results since persons without telephones or with unlisted numbers would have no chance to be reflected in the sample, and their voting preferences could be quite different from persons who have listed telephones. This is what happened with the *Literary Digest* presidential poll of 1936 when use of lists of telephone owners, magazine subscribers, and car owners led to a prediction that President Roosevelt would lose the election.

A pretest of the questionnaire and field procedures is the only way of finding out if everything "works," especially if a survey employs a new procedure or a new set of questions. Since it is rarely possible to foresee all the possible misunderstandings or biasing effects of different questions and procedures, it is vital for a well-designed survey plan to include provision for a pretest. This is usually a small-scale pilot study to test the feasibility of the intended techniques or to perfect the questionnaire concepts and wording.

Failure to follow up nonrespondents can ruin an otherwise well-designed surveys, for it is not uncommon for the initial response rate to most surveys to be under 50 percent. Plans must include returning to sample households where no one was home, attempting to persuade persons who are inclined to refuse, and, in the case of mail surveys, contacting all or a subsample of the nonrespondents by telephone or personal visit to obtain a completed questionnaire. A low response rate does more damage in rendering a survey's results questionable than a small sample, since there is no valid way of scientifically inferring the characteristics of the population represented by the nonrespondents.

Quality control, in the sense of checking the different facets of a survey, enters in at all stages—checking sample selection, verifying interviews, and checking the editing and coding of the responses, among other things. In particular, sloppy execution of the survey in the field can seriously damage the results. Without proper quality control, errors can occur with disastrous results, such as selecting or visiting the wrong household, failing to ask questions properly, or recording the incorrect answer. Insisting on proper standards in recruitment and training of interviewers helps a great deal, but equally important is proper review, verification, and other quality control measures to ensure that the execution of a survey corresponds to its design.

Using the Results of a Survey

How Good Is the Survey?

The statistics derived from a survey will rarely correspond exactly with the unknown truth. (Whether "true" values always exist is not important in the present context. For fairly simple measurements—the average age of the population, the amount of livestock on farms, etc.—the concept of a true value is fairly straightforward. Whether true values exist for measurements of such items as attitudes toward political candidates, I.Q.'s, etc., is a more complex matter.)

Fortunately, the value of a statistic does not depend on its being exactly true. To be useful, a statistic need not be exact, but it does need to be sufficiently reliable to serve the particular needs. No overall criterion of reliability applies to all surveys since the margin of error that can be tolerated in a study depends on the actions or recommendations that will be influenced by the data. For example, economists examining unemployment rates consider a change of 0.2 percent as having an important bearing on the U.S. economy. Consequently, in the official U.S. surveys used to estimate unemployment, an attempt is made to keep the margin of error below 0.2 percent. Conversely, there are occasions when a high error rate is acceptable. Sometimes a city will conduct a survey to measure housing vacancies to determine if there is a tight housing supply. If the true vacancy rate is very low, say 1 percent, survey results that show double this percentage will not do any harm; any results in the range of 0 to 2 or 3 percent will lead to the same conclusion—a tight housing market.

In many situations the tolerable error will depend on the kind of result expected. For example, during presidential elections the major television networks obtain data on election night from a sample of election precincts, in order to predict the election results early in the evening. In a state in which a large difference is expected (pre-election polls may indicate that one candidate leads by a substantial majority and is likely to receive 60 percent of the vote), even with an error of 5 or 6 percent it would still be possible to predict the winner with a high degree of accuracy. A relatively small sample size may be adequate in such a state. However, much more precise estimates are required in states where the two candidates are fairly evenly matched and where, say, a 52–48 percent vote is expected.

Thus, no general rule can be laid down to determine the reliability that would apply to all surveys. It is necessary to consider the purpose of the particular study, how the data will be used, and the effect of errors of various sizes on the action taken based on the survey results. These factors will affect the sample size, the design of the questionnaire, the effort put into training and supervising the interview staff, and so on. Estimates of error also need to be considered in analyzing and interpreting the results of the survey.

Sources of Errors

In evaluating the accuracy of a survey, it is convenient to distinguish two sources of errors: (1) sampling errors and (2) nonsampling errors, including the effect of refusals and not-at-homes, respondents providing incorrect information, coding or other processing errors, and clerical errors in sampling.

Sampling Errors   Good survey practice includes calculation of sampling errors, which is possible if probability methods are used in selecting the sample. Furthermore, information on sampling errors should be made readily available to all users of the statistics. If the survey results are published, data on sampling errors should be included in the publication. If information is disseminated in other ways, other means of informing the public are necessary. Thus, it is not uncommon to hear television newscasters report on the size of sampling errors as part of the results of some polling activity.

There are a number of ways of describing and presenting data on sampling errors so that users can take them into account. For example, in a survey designed to produce only a few statistics (such as the votes that the candidates for a particular office are expected to get), the results could be stated that Candidate A's votes are estimated at 57 percent with the error unlikely to be more than 3 percent, so that this candidate's votes are expected to fall in the range of 54–60 percent. Other examples can be found in most publications of the principal statistical agencies of the U.S. government, such as the Bureau of the Census.

Nonsampling Errors   Unfortunately, unlike sampling errors, there is no simple and direct method of estimating the size of nonsampling errors. In most surveys, it is not practical to measure the possible effect on the statistics of the various potential sources of error. However, in the past 30 or 40 years, there has been a considerable amount of research on the kinds of errors that are likely to arise in different kinds of surveys. By examining the procedures and operations of a specific survey, experienced survey statisticians will frequently be able to assess its quality. Rarely will this produce actual error ranges, as for sampling errors. In most cases, the analyst can only state that, for example, the errors are probably relatively small and will not affect most conclusions drawn from the survey, or that the errors may be fairly large and inferences are to be made with caution.

Nonsampling errors can be classified into two groups—random types or errors whose effects approximately cancel out if fairly large samples are used, and biases that tend to create errors in the same direction and thus cumulate over the entire sample. With large samples, the possible biases are the principal causes for concern about the quality of a survey.

Biases can arise from any aspect of the survey operation. Some of the main contributing causes of bias are:

1 *Sampling operations*. There may be errors in sample selection, or part of the population may be omitted from the sampling frame, or weights to compensate for disproportionate sampling rates may be omitted.

2 *Noninterviews*. Information is generally obtained for only part of the sample. Frequently there are differences between the noninterview population and those interviewed.

3 *Adequacy of respondent*. Sometimes respondents cannot be interviewed and information is obtained about them from others, but the "proxy" respondent is not always as knowledgeable about the facts.

4 *Understanding the concepts*. Some respondents may not understand what is wanted.

5 *Lack of knowledge*. Respondents in some cases do not know the information requested, or do not try to obtain the correct information.

6 *Concealment of the truth*. Out of fear or suspicion of the survey, respondents may conceal the truth. In some instances, this concealment may reflect a respondent's desire to answer in a way that is socially acceptable, such as indicating that s(he) is carrying out an energy conservation program when this is not actually so.

7 *Loaded questions*. The question may be worded to influence the respondents to answer in a specific (not necessarily correct) way.

8 *Processing errors*. These can include coding errors, data keying, computer programming errors, etc.

9 *Conceptual problems*. There may be differences between what is desired and what the survey actually covers. For example, the population or the time period may not be the one for which information is needed, but had to be used to meet a deadline.

10 *Interviewer errors*. Interviewers may misread the question or twist the answers in their own words and thereby introduce bias.

Obviously, each survey is not necessarily subject to all these sources of error. However, a good survey statistician will explore all of these possibilities. It is considered good practice to report on the percent of the sample that could not be interviewed and as many of the other factors listed as practicable.

Budgeting a Survey

We have seen from the preceding sections that many different stages are involved in a survey. These include tasks such as planning, sample design, sample selection, questionnaire preparation, pretesting, interviewer hiring and training, data collection, data reduction, data processing, and report preparation. From a time point of view, these different stages are not necessarily additive since many of them overlap. This is illustrated in the diagram on page 400 which portrays the sequence of steps involved in a typical personal interview survey. Some steps, such as sample design and listing housing units in the areas to be covered in the survey, can be carried out at the same time a questionnaire is being revised and put into final form. Although they are not additive, all of these steps are time consuming, and one of the most common errors is to underestimate the time needed by making a global estimate without considering these individual stages.

How much time is needed for a survey? This varies with the type of survey and the particular situation. Sometimes a survey can be done in two or three weeks, if it involves a brief questionnaire and if the data are to be collected by telephone from a list already available. More usually, however, a survey of several hundred or a few thousand individuals will take anywhere from a few months to more than a year, from initial planning to having results ready for analysis.

A flow diagram for a particular survey is very useful in estimating the cost of such a survey. Such a diagram ensures that allowance is made for the expense involved in the different tasks, as well as for quality checks at all stages of the work. Thus, among the factors that enter into an expense budget are the following:

1 Staff time for planning the study and steering it through the various stages.

2 Labor and material costs for pretesting the questionnaire and field procedures.

3 Supervisory costs for interviewer hiring, training, and supervision.

4 Interviewer labor costs and travel expense (and meals and lodging, if out of town).

5 Labor and expense costs of checking a certain percentage of the interviews (by reinterviews).

6 Cost of preparing codes for transferring information from the questionnaire.

7 Labor and material costs for editing, coding, and keypunching the information from the questionnaire onto computer tape.

8 Cost of spot-checking to assure the quality of the editing, coding, and keypunching.

9 Cost of "cleaning" the final data tapes, that is, checking the tapes for inconsistent or impossible answers.

10 Programming costs for preparing tabulations and special analyses of the data.

11 Computer time for the various tabulations and analyses.

12 Labor time and material costs for analysis of the data and report preparation.

13 Telephone charges, postage, reproduction, and printing costs.

An integral part of a well-designed survey, both in terms of time and of costs, is allowance for quality checks all along the way. For example, checks have to be made that the sample was selected according to specifications, that the interviewers did their work properly, that the information from the questionnaires was coded accurately, that the keypunching was done correctly, and that the computer programs used for data analysis work properly. For these reasons, a good survey does not come cheap, although some are more economical than others. As a rule, surveys made by personal interview are more expensive than by mail or by telephone; and costs will increase with the complexity of the questionnaire and the amount of analysis to be carried out. Also, surveys that involve more interviews tend to be cheaper on a per interview basis than surveys with fewer interviews. This is particularly so where the sampling size is less than about a thousand because "tooling up" is involved for just about any survey, except one that is to be repeated on the same group.

Where to Get More Information

Several professional organizations have memberships heavily involved in survey research. They also frequently have workshops or sessions on surveys as parts of their regional and annual meetings. The principal organizations are the following:

1   The American Statistical Association is concerned with survey techniques and with general application of survey data. It has a separate Section on Survey Research Methods that sponsors sessions on surveys at the annual meetings of the association. The many chapters of the association in the various parts of the country also periodically have meetings and workshops on survey methods, and its publications, the *Journal of the American Statistical Association* and the *American Statistician*, carry numerous articles about surveys.

2   The American Marketing Association is concerned, among other things, with the application of survey methods to marketing problems. Like the American Statistical Association, it sponsors sessions on survey methods at its annual meetings, and still other sessions are sponsored by its local chapters. Its publications, the *Journal of Marketing* and the *Journal of Marketing Research*, frequently contain articles on surveys.

3   The American Association for Public Opinion Research focuses on survey methods as applied to social and media problems. Its journal, the *Public Opinion Quarterly*, regularly carries articles on survey techniques and on the application of survey methods to political and social problems.

A number of other professional associations such as the American Sociological Association, the American Political Science Association, the Association for Consumer Research, the American Public Health Association, the American Psychological Association, the Canadian Psychological Association, and the Statistical Society of Canada, place emphasis periodically on survey methods. There are also various business-oriented associations such as the Advertising Research Foundation and the American Association of Advertising Agencies, that give attention to survey methods as applied to business. These and other associations publish a number of journals that carry a great deal of material on survey methods.

There are many good books on survey methods written for nontechnical readers. A few of these are:

1   Judith Tanur et al., *Statistics: A Guide to the Unknown* (San Francisco: Holden-Day, 1972).

2   Philip Hauser, *Social Statistics in Use* (New York: Russell Sage Foundation, 1975).

3   William H. Williams, *A Sampler on Sampling* (New York: Wiley, 1978).

Stages of a Survey

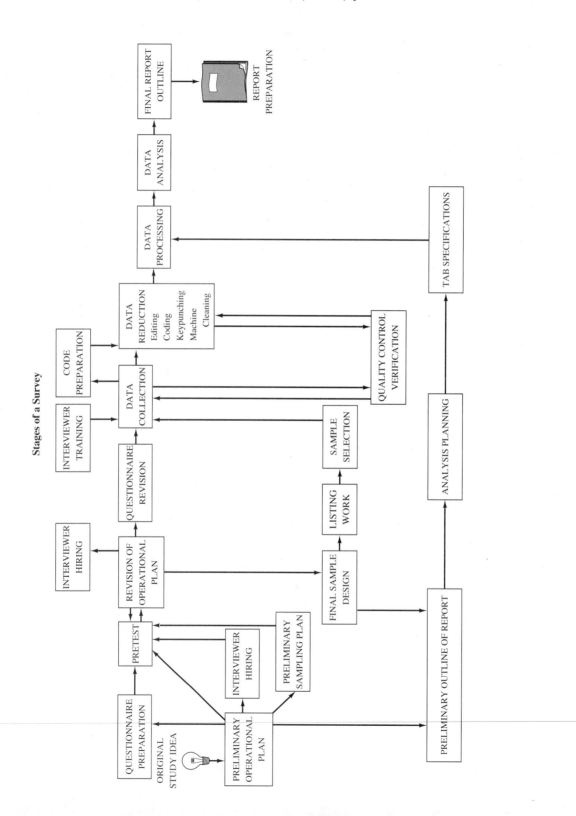

15

Survey Designs

Chapter Objectives

After mastering this chapter, you will be able to:

- Explain how to draw a simple random sample

- Compute a confidence interval for a population mean or proportion based on a simple random sample

- Explain how a confidence interval depends on sample size

- Explain stratified, cluster, and systematic sampling

15.1 Introduction

Chapter 15 begins the technical study of probability sampling, building on the concepts presented in the previous chapter. This chapter shows how to do simple random sampling. It explains the notation and display of data used with such sampling. It shows how to draw inferences from the data obtained and compute how closely those inferences are likely to match the actual universe from which the sample was drawn. It also cautions against common misuses and misunderstandings of random-sampling theory and methods. The chapter also introduces stratification and clustering—two additional probability sampling designs that build on simple random sampling.

The next chapter shows how to interpret a complex survey, including some important calculations useful in evaluating survey data. As you work on the technical steps of survey design and estimation, though, do not forget the basic surveying tasks outlined in the last chapter, such as field testing, ensuring adequate coverage, training, and auditing for errors.

15.2   Simple Random Sampling: Methods, Results, Notation

As mentioned in Chapter 14, the most elementary sampling design is simple random sampling. This section explains how to take a simple random sample. It also defines the terms and notation used for the data collected and their characteristics.

Random sampling is mainly used in conjunction with other techniques, like stratification and clustering, discussed later in this chapter.

But in small studies, random sampling can be the sole method of sampling. Surveying is by no means the exclusive property of big surveying outfits, nor is it a tool useful only for large studies. Consider a project done by the word processing department of a large government agency.[†] As the quality-improvement team began to meet to identify the problems they felt were important, they surveyed employees in other departments that used word processing heavily. They were surprised to find that their work was perceived to be of rather high quality in terms of error rate but that their turnaround time was too long. This finding prompted them to determine the causes of slow turnaround and to work on ways to speed up their service without increasing the error rate. Their work ultimately led to a reduction of average turnaround from two weeks to eight hours *and* a reduction in error rate! Thus, a simple survey of customers helped the team quickly identify the most important needs for improvement.

The Sampling Plan

simple random sample

A **simple random sample** is a sample taken so that each possible sample of size n has the same chance of being selected. To implement simple random sampling, you need a list of the elements of the universe from which the sample will be drawn.

frame

The list is called a **frame**. Ideally, each element is shown on the list once and only once. In practice, constructing a frame can be quite difficult, and the frame may have errors. Some elements may be left off the list; others may appear more than once. Although the probabilities of drawing elements from the frame are known, these probabilities cannot be attributed to the elements of the universe unless there is an exact correspondence between the universe and the frame. Thus frame construction is a critical step in simple random sampling.

Part of frame construction is the numbering of the elements. Each element must be assigned a unique number. The numbering starts with 0 and is consecutive. This makes it easy to use random digits to draw the sample.

The way to draw elements at random from the frame is described in the next subsection. Once the drawing is done, the elements must be contacted and measured—that is, surveyed. This could mean contacting a household in person or by phone and interviewing a designated member of the household, or it could mean driving to a

---

[†]William Hunter, Jan O'Neill, and Carol Wallen, *Doing More with Less in the Public Sector: A Progress Report from Madison, Wisconsin*, Report No. 13, Center for Quality and Productivity Improvement, University of Wisconsin–Madison, June 1986.

telephone pole and measuring a number of its physical characteristics. The way the data are collected depends on the plan developed for the particular survey.

How to Draw a Simple Random Sample

E X A M P L E   15.2A

Suppose a frame lists 2164 elements, and a sample of 50 elements is desired. Fifty numbers between 0000 and 2163 need to be selected at random. The elements associated with these numbers are drawn into the sample. The first element is associated with the number 0000, the second element with 0001, and so on. The last element is associated with 2163.

How are the 50 numbers selected at random? A table of uniform random digits such as the one in Exhibit 1.7C or 15.2A is used. The simplest way to use the table is to pick an arbitrary starting point in the table, then work across the rows of the table, grouping the digits in groups of four to make four-digit numbers. Any such four-digit number that falls between 0000 and 2163 draws an element into the sample. Elements are allowed to appear only once in a given sample, so if a random number is repeated, the number is ignored and the corresponding element is not entered into the sample a second time. This is called *sampling without replacement*. Likewise, numbers that do not fall between 0000 and 2163 are ignored.

The table of random digits in Exhibit 15.2A has 50 rows and 20 columns. To pick the arbitrary starting point, we asked a colleague to pick any number between 1 and 50. He picked 23. We asked another colleague to pick a number between 1 and 20. He picked 5. We started our list of random digits in row 23 and column 5 of Exhibit 15.2A. Reading across the row, the first four-digit number is 0320, which is between 0000 and 2163. This number brings element 321 into the sample. The next four-digit number is 4125. This is greater than 2163, so it does not draw an element into the sample. The next few four-digit random numbers are 3535, 5852, 9645, 4460, 9798, 5525, 2614, 3415, and 1302. The process continues until 50 elements have been drawn from the frame. A larger table than the one shown in Exhibit 15.2A may be needed to complete the sample.

The procedure outlined above assigns the same probability of being drawn to each possible sample of 50 elements from the frame, approximately 9×10^{-103}. Even though such a probability is unfathomably small, it applies to each possible sample of size 50. Of course, one such sample is certainly selected by the random sampling procedure. Each element has 50 chances out of 2164 of being included in the sample. This probability, $50/2164 = .0231$, about 23 chances out of 1000, is not beyond comprehension and is intuitively reasonable, since 50 elements are drawn from 2164.   ▪

This example illustrates the approach to use in drawing a simple random sample from any frame. The number of digits that need to be grouped into random numbers is determined by the number of elements in the frame. If there are 100 elements,

EXHIBIT **15.2A**
Table of Random Digits

Row	1	2	3	4	5	6	7	8	9	10	11	12	13	14	15	16	17	18	19	20
1	2	1	9	4	6	3	9	5	5	7	1	7	2	4	4	6	7	1	7	8
2	9	5	5	6	6	0	3	0	7	3	5	5	7	0	8	4	2	8	9	6
3	2	5	2	3	2	0	0	4	5	3	1	4	8	1	3	7	7	6	4	0
4	3	9	4	4	3	8	5	4	3	9	0	2	8	4	6	4	9	7	7	6
5	6	4	0	9	4	6	8	0	5	5	7	6	1	1	9	8	1	5	4	1
6	1	3	7	3	8	1	9	9	8	7	5	8	0	3	7	0	1	4	2	1
7	0	3	0	9	9	6	9	1	2	1	4	7	4	7	5	5	2	3	1	9
8	9	7	8	2	2	1	1	6	7	6	0	9	7	8	0	1	2	5	2	1
9	9	9	3	6	1	3	3	9	7	6	8	5	9	1	2	4	9	7	0	1
10	7	5	0	3	6	8	9	5	4	9	9	4	6	5	0	4	9	7	4	9
11	7	8	5	7	1	7	9	3	7	1	1	7	1	9	1	5	7	8	1	1
12	4	2	6	8	1	1	8	7	6	0	5	6	7	1	2	1	9	8	3	4
13	0	0	7	5	9	4	1	8	6	4	4	0	6	6	8	4	0	9	7	8
14	0	4	6	0	5	3	8	7	9	0	7	1	0	2	4	7	4	7	5	7
15	0	4	0	1	8	0	6	8	8	7	5	5	1	2	1	5	8	7	7	4
16	5	4	8	5	3	4	1	9	1	5	0	1	9	5	3	0	3	3	9	1
17	0	5	4	8	7	9	0	4	9	9	0	0	5	0	8	8	1	4	0	3
18	6	2	4	8	9	9	0	2	2	5	0	1	6	0	8	7	7	6	4	0
19	0	1	8	4	2	2	3	5	9	2	5	7	8	0	6	1	9	4	9	0
20	8	9	8	2	4	1	0	0	9	6	8	9	5	4	3	9	1	4	9	6
21	4	9	8	1	1	9	0	6	0	6	9	9	7	3	7	0	4	2	7	2
22	2	9	4	1	8	2	9	9	3	3	8	2	8	3	5	0	3	5	4	3
23	5	3	4	1	0	3	2	0	4	1	2	5	3	5	3	5	5	8	5	2
24	9	6	4	5	4	4	6	0	9	7	9	8	5	5	2	5	2	6	1	4
25	3	4	1	5	1	3	0	2	1	3	3	1	2	9	4	8	9	8	2	8
26	7	7	2	9	6	2	4	6	3	2	1	3	6	7	3	9	4	1	6	7
27	5	3	9	2	7	8	2	6	7	6	6	9	1	5	9	2	5	4	4	3
28	6	7	7	8	7	7	8	1	0	4	1	7	0	6	4	3	6	8	0	6
29	6	4	6	0	6	0	2	3	3	0	6	7	3	5	0	7	3	9	8	7
30	0	7	2	6	5	9	1	7	4	2	2	7	9	2	9	5	2	9	5	0
31	1	3	7	8	4	5	2	4	2	6	7	3	2	9	9	3	5	1	6	4
32	1	8	5	6	6	3	7	7	0	0	1	9	2	6	1	4	2	1	0	9
33	0	7	6	5	0	3	8	2	6	0	1	0	4	4	0	1	1	4	9	7
34	7	1	7	3	2	6	6	4	5	0	6	2	6	6	9	3	6	8	8	4
35	1	0	5	9	9	6	7	7	6	3	5	1	3	3	7	4	4	0	6	1
36	9	9	6	7	7	2	8	3	9	8	8	0	1	8	8	8	0	2	1	2
37	5	3	4	9	7	9	2	9	2	9	9	1	1	1	5	3	5	0	6	5
38	0	4	6	6	8	5	2	9	3	5	2	9	2	0	0	7	3	1	3	6
39	6	9	8	4	0	3	4	2	8	2	8	0	9	1	7	3	0	8	9	6
40	3	0	3	0	5	0	7	8	0	9	1	3	0	7	8	6	8	6	0	8
41	9	5	1	2	8	1	8	2	6	3	9	9	0	1	0	7	7	2	3	3
42	5	3	2	2	2	4	0	0	3	9	6	8	9	1	7	4	2	7	6	8
43	2	1	6	1	3	3	1	6	5	7	7	3	5	1	7	4	5	7	3	8
44	5	7	1	4	4	7	1	2	9	1	8	5	9	9	7	7	9	8	7	9
45	9	0	0	5	4	6	3	6	1	5	0	0	4	8	3	5	9	5	3	2
46	0	5	0	0	0	2	1	9	2	3	0	1	0	2	8	6	6	3	6	7
47	0	2	4	1	1	5	0	2	5	5	7	7	8	2	2	9	0	4	0	9
48	4	0	1	7	9	7	7	3	0	2	0	7	0	0	1	2	3	2	2	6
49	1	6	0	8	0	7	8	6	6	6	6	5	2	7	1	1	8	2	1	7
50	5	9	9	5	0	7	4	7	1	1	5	4	6	3	5	9	7	5	6	4

digits need to be grouped two at a time: 00, 01, ..., 99. If there are 10,000 elements, digits need to be grouped four at a time: 0000, 0001, ..., 9999.

Certain notation is used frequently in simple random sampling. The number of elements in the frame is denoted by N, the size of the sample by n. The proportion n/N is called the **sampling fraction** and is denoted by f—that is, $f = n/N$. This is the probability of including any given element in the sample. It is also the proportion of the frame elements included in the sample.

sampling fraction

Data from a Sample

Suppose we want to draw a sample of size 50 from a group of employees. A recent payroll list that can be used as a frame is available, and it has 2164 names on it. After the sample is drawn, the selected employees will be contacted and asked 20 questions. If all goes well, 20 responses from each of the 50 employees, a total of 1000 responses, will constitute the data set. Now consider 2 of the 20 questions:

- Question 1: Are you male or female?
- Question 2: How many hours per week do you spend caring for elderly parents or friends?

Males are numerically coded with a 0 and females with a 1. The data set, in skeleton form, would then look like this:

Employee Number	Gender	Hours	xxxx	xxxx
1	1	5	xxxx	xxxx
2	0	0	xxxx	xxxx
3	1	0	xxxx	xxxx
⋮	⋮	⋮	⋮	⋮
50	1	10	xxxx	xxxx

The symbol xxxx stands for other variables and values not explicitly considered in this example. The vertical ellipsis points indicate items left out of the display to save space. Our job is to use the data to estimate characteristics of the universe. For instance, what proportion of all employees are female? This information is on hand for a sample of 50 employees. But what about the whole group? We would also like to know the average of reported hours per week the whole group spent on caring. The information gathered from the 50 employees allows us to estimate the group average within limits. How is this done? These questions are answered in Section 15.4. Before turning to them, though, some additional notation and definitions must be introduced.

Populations and Parameters

To distinguish between the universe and the samples drawn from it, notation that refers to the universe and notation that refers to the sample must be used. Exhibit 15.2B shows the structure of a universe of individual elements, denoted by $I_1, I_2, \ldots, I_N$, from which two measurements are obtained: gender and number of hours. The responses to the question of gender are assumed to be coded 0 for male and 1 for female. The notation for these responses is $Y_1, Y_2, \ldots, Y_N$. In other words, Y_1 stands for the numerical code attached to the response of the first individual, Y_2 for the second individual, and so on. The responses to the question of number of hours are denoted by $X_1, X_2, \ldots, X_N$. The numerical values are simply those that would be reported by the employees. The measurements in Exhibit 15.2B are hypothetical because they stand for what the employees would report if responses were elicited from them in the manner in which responses are elicited in the survey. In other words, they are equal complete coverage measurements.

EXHIBIT 15.2B
Structure of a Universe Showing Two Populations and No Stratification

Elements (employees)	y measurements (0 = male, 1 = female)	x measurements (number of hours)
I_1	Y_1	X_1
I_2	Y_2	X_2
$\vdots$	$\vdots$	$\vdots$
I_N	Y_N	X_N
Total	τ_y	τ_x
Mean (average)	μ_y	μ_x
Standard deviation	S_y	S_x

$$\tau_x = \sum_{i=1}^{N} X_i \qquad \mu_x = \frac{\tau_x}{N} \qquad S_x = \sqrt{\frac{1}{N-1} \sum_{i=1}^{N} (X_i - \mu_x)^2}$$

$$\tau_y = \sum_{i=1}^{N} Y_i \qquad \mu_y = \frac{\tau_y}{N} \qquad S_y = \sqrt{\frac{1}{N-1} \sum_{i=1}^{N} (Y_i - \mu_y)^2}$$

At the bottom of the columns of measurements, the sums, averages, and standard deviations of the measurements are shown. These are called parameters because they are characteristics of the equal complete coverage of the universe. The measured characteristics are called **variables**. In Exhibit 15.2B there are two variables: gender and number of hours. The set of all equal complete coverage measurements on a variable is called a **population**. Exhibit 15.2B displays two populations: the male/female population and the hours-of-caring population.

Populations also have parameters. For example, the sum and average under the male/female measurements are two of the parameters of this population. The usual statistical notation for a total is the Greek letter t, which is called tau. The symbol is τ. The statistical symbol for an average, or mean, is the Greek m, called mu. The symbol is μ, as noted earlier (Chapter 9, for instance). Any numerical characteristic of a population is called a **parameter**. Statistical notation for parameters tends to use Greek letters. In survey literature, the standard deviation is an exception to this rule, as is shown in Exhibit 15.2B and emphasized further below.

variables

population

parameter

The numerical values in the male/female population are denoted by Y's, and the values in the hours-of-caring population by X's. As shorthand, these populations are sometimes referred to as the y population and the x population. Such terminology enables us to speak abstractly about populations. For example, think of an arbitrary universe for which x, y, u, v, and w populations have been defined. Numerical characteristics of the x population are parameters of that population; numerical characteristics of the u population are parameters of that population; and so on. The symbols denoting the parameters of a population may be subscripted with the letter denoting the population. For example, the mean of the y population may be denoted by μ_y.

Characteristics may be shared by two or more of the populations. For example, suppose the correlation coefficient between the values of the x population and the u population were computed. The correlation coefficient would be called a parameter of the joint x, u population. Statistical notation for the correlation coefficient of a joint population is the Greek r, called rho. The symbol is ρ.

Suppose y is the variable indicating gender. We might compute the correlation coefficient for all x, u values associated with females and then compute the correlation coefficient for all x, u values associated with males. Technically speaking, these correlation coefficients are parameters of the joint u, x, y population.

Statisticians commonly use the standard deviation as a measure of variation. For any population the standard deviation may be computed by the formula given in Chapter 4. For example, for the y population the standard deviation is, in symbols,

$$S_y = \sqrt{\frac{1}{N-1} \sum_{i=1}^{N} (Y_i - \mu_y)^2} \qquad \textbf{(15.1)}$$

where the index of summation runs from 1 to N, the number of numbers in the population.[†]

population proportion   One more parameter needs to be defined: a **population proportion**. Interpret the y population in Exhibit 15.2B as measurements on the male/female variable. Then each Y_i is equal to either 0 or 1, depending on whether the employee is male or female. The sum of this column of Y_i values is just the number of females in the frame, and the average of the column is just the proportion of females. For finite populations, counts and proportions are simply totals and means. Nevertheless, it is traditional to denote proportions by π.

It can be shown (see Exercise 15.3F) that the standard deviation of a population of 0's and 1's is

$$\sqrt{\pi(1-\pi)\frac{N}{N-1}} \qquad \textbf{(15.2)}$$

For large values of N, the ratio $N/(N-1)$ is close to 1, so the standard deviation is close to $\sqrt{\pi(1-\pi)}$, which is the standard deviation of the Bernoulli distribution introduced in Chapter 11. The Bernoulli distribution is a mathematical model for

---

[†]In some discussions, authors use another definition of the standard deviation. They divide the sum of squares by N instead of $N-1$ and denote the resulting quantity by σ.

a process, whereas the expression in Equation (15.2) is the standard deviation of a finite binary population. That is why the Bernoulli formula is not exactly equal to the finite population formula.

Notation for Data and Statistics

Exhibit 15.2C shows a format for the data collected by simple random sampling. Remember that a simple random sample of size n means that each possible sample of size n has the same probability of being selected. Once a sample is drawn and the data collected, the data may be displayed as in Exhibit 15.2C. The first column shows the elements drawn into the sample. These are denoted by $i_1, i_2, \ldots, i_n$. In the exhibit two measurements were taken from each element, a y measurement and an x measurement. For concreteness, you can think of the y variable as gender, coding males as 0 and females as 1, and the x variable as number of hours. Notice that sample measurements are denoted by lowercase letters, whereas population measurements are denoted by uppercase letters (see Exhibit 15.2B). Below the columns of data a number of numerical characteristics are shown: totals, means, standard deviations, and standard errors. Only the standard errors are unfamiliar at this point; they are discussed in Section 15.4.

EXHIBIT 15.2C
Data Format for Simple Random Sampling

Elements (employees)	y measurements (0 = male, 1 = female)	x measurements (number of hours)
i_1	y_1	x_1
i_2	y_2	x_2
$\vdots$	$\vdots$	$\vdots$
i_n	y_n	x_n
Total	$\displaystyle\sum_{i=1}^{n} y_i$	$\displaystyle\sum_{i=1}^{n} x_i$
Mean (average)	$\bar{y} = p$	$\bar{x}$
Standard deviation	$s_y = \sqrt{p(1-p)\dfrac{n}{n-1}}$	$s_x = \sqrt{\dfrac{1}{n-1}\displaystyle\sum_{i=1}^{n}(x_i - \bar{x})^2}$
Standard error	$se_p = \dfrac{s_y}{\sqrt{n}} fpc$	$se_{\bar{x}} = \dfrac{s_x}{\sqrt{n}} fpc$

where fpc = finite population correction = $\sqrt{\dfrac{N-n}{N}} = \sqrt{1-f}$ and $f = \dfrac{n}{N}$

SECTION

15.3 Exercises

15.3A Suppose you wish to survey private residences in your city or town. Comment on the use of the telephone directory as a sampling frame. What items in the directory do not correspond to elements in your universe? What elements of your universe are not included in the frame? Suggest another possible frame for this study.

15.3B   You wish to survey the employees over the age of 30 in your organization by sampling, and you decide to use a payroll list as your frame. What sorts of problems might this choice of frame entail? Suggest another possible frame for this study.

15.3C   Your building manager wishes to study uses of various parts of the building, which is very large. The manager has detailed floor plans for all parts of the building. Suggest how she might draw a sample of locations from her plans. Discuss how to design the study so that building use may be studied by time of day and day of the week.

15.3D   Your firm has 6273 employees, and you wish to draw a simple random sample of 400 employees from a payroll file. Set up a scheme to use a table of random digits to draw the sample.

15.3E   Exhibit 14.6A displayed a small universe with two populations: Vacant or Improved and Assessed Value. For the Vacant or Improved population, code vacant as 0 and improved as 1. Attach to each item in Exhibit 14.6A an appropriate piece of notation as defined in Exhibit 15.2B. For example, $N = 9$. If Y_i is defined as 0 if parcel i is vacant and 1 if parcel i is improved, then $Y_1 = 0$ would be written in place of the word vacant for the parcel at 30 Muir Dr. Once all the notation has been assigned, compute the population parameters defined at the bottom of Exhibit 15.2B and record them.

15.3F   A certain population consists of 22 0's and 29 1's. Verify that Equations (15.1) and (15.2) both yield the same numerical value for the standard deviation of this population. Now do the calculation assuming there are M 0's and $N - M$ 1's.

15.3G   The data below are actual responses to a student survey done in a statistics class of about 250 students. For this exercise the first 20 responses were chosen from the data base. The rows correspond to students (elements); the columns correspond to questions on the questionnaire (variables). Responses are shown for these five items:

1   What is your gender? (0 = male, 1 = female)

2   I won't have much use for statistics beyond this course.

3   I am worried about how well I will do in this course.

4   I think statistics is a boring subject to learn.

5   Large lecture courses offer little opportunity for individual attention.

For the last four questions, students responded with one of the numbers from 1 to 5. Response 1 meant "strongly agree" with the statement, 2 meant "agree," 3 meant "neutral," 4 meant "disagree," and 5 meant "strongly disagree."

0	4	1	2	2	0	4	2	2	1
1	3	4	2	2	0	4	4	2	3
0	4	1	2	2	1	2	1	3	1
1	2	2	1	1	0	3	2	1	3
1	5	4	3	2	0	5	1	1	1
0	5	4	3	3	0	4	5	1	3
0	4	1	4	1	1	3	2	1	1
0	3	4	1	1	0	4	5	4	3
0	2	2	2	2	1	1	3	1	1
0	4	5	4	4	0	3	1	1	1

For this exercise, treat these data as a universe with 20 elements, for which five variables have been measured. Referring to Exhibit 15.2B, calculate the totals, means, and standard deviations for all five variables.

15.3H   Consider a universe consisting of $N = 5$ elements with associated X and Y values as defined below.

Case	Element	X_i	Y_i
1	I_1	8	1
2	I_2	9	1
3	I_3	10	0
4	I_4	10	1
5	I_5	13	0

a   Verify that $\mu_x = 10$, $S_x = \sqrt{3.5}$, and $\mu_y = \pi = 0.6$.

b   List the 10 possible samples of size $n = 2$, along with the associated values for X and Y. Compute the sample means $\bar{x}$ and $\bar{y} = p$ for each sample. Verify that the average of the 10 $\bar{x}$'s is 10 ($= \mu_x$) and of the 10 $\bar{y}$'s is 0.6 ($= \pi$). Construct dotplots of the $\bar{x}$'s and $\bar{y}$'s. These are the sampling distributions of the sample means. Compare the variability of these sampling distributions with the variability in the X and Y populations.

c   Repeat part (b) for samples of size $n = 3$.

d   Suppose a third variable (Z) may be measured, and its population values are $Z_1 = 8$, $Z_2 = 9$, $Z_3 = 9$, $Z_4 = 10$, and $Z_5 = 12$. Compute ρ_{xz}, the population correlation coefficient between X and Z. For each possible sample of size $n = 3$, compute the sample correlation coefficient r_{xz}. Construct a dotplot of the sampling distribution of this statistic. Compute the mean of this distribution. Is it equal to ρ_{xz}?

S E C T I O N

15.4   Interval Estimation

statistics

Numerical characteristics of samples, such as totals, means, and standard deviations, are called **statistics**. The statistics of random samples allow us to make probabilistic inferences about the parameters of populations. Inference means the statistics are used to predict, or infer, within limits, the values of population parameters. This section explains how those inferences are made. An example illustrates how to do the necessary computation.

Means and Confidence Intervals

The sample mean may be treated as an estimate of the population mean. But different samples have different means because of sampling variation. Thus, any sample mean is unlikely to be equal to the population mean. How different can the sample mean and the population mean be? Using statistical theory, limits to the difference can be established provided the sample is drawn by a probability method such as simple random sampling.

To illustrate, we estimate the population mean of the x sample in Exhibit 15.2C. Statistical theory holds that the difference between the sample mean and the population mean is almost certainly less (in absolute value) than three standard errors. A

standard error

standard error is the standard deviation of the sampling distribution of a statistic. The formula for the standard error of $\bar{x}$ is given in Exhibit 15.2C. In symbols,

$$|\mu_x - \bar{x}| \leq 3se_{\bar{x}}$$

or

$$\bar{x} - 3se_{\bar{x}} \leq \mu_x \leq \bar{x} + 3se_{\bar{x}}$$

Thus if an interval whose endpoints are the sample mean minus 3 standard errors and the sample mean plus 3 standard errors is computed, this interval almost certainly contains the population mean. Because of this property, the interval is called a

confidence interval

confidence interval for μ_x.

Think of constructing all possible samples of size n from the universe, taking the x measurements and computing the sample means for all these samples. This program was carried out for a small universe in Exhibit 14.6B. The focus of attention is now the sampling distribution: the distribution of all the sample means. In practice, this distribution is not constructed, but in theory it exists and its properties can be studied. For moderately large sample sizes, n, and small to moderate sampling fractions, f, the distribution is well approximated by a normal curve with mean μ_x and standard deviation

$$SE_{\bar{x}} = \frac{S_x}{\sqrt{n}} fpc \tag{15.3}$$

The normal approximation is the result of a central limit effect like those you saw in Chapter 9 for means of samples of process values. Those values were approximately normally distributed, with their mean equal to the mean of all the process values. Central limit effects can be derived theoretically and demonstrated empirically. Even the small samples in Exhibits 14.6B and 14.6C, dealing with only nine pieces of real estate, show some evidence of a central limit effect, tending to mound around the middle values. For larger, and more practical, sample sizes, the effect is even more pronounced.

Because of the normal approximation, practically all the sample means obtained by simple random sampling differ from the population mean by no more than 3 of the standard errors given in Equation (15.3). This is a property of the normal curve. Other properties of the normal curve may also be used. For example, roughly 95% of the sample means differ from the population mean by no more than 2 of the standard errors given in Equation (15.3).

As noted, the standard error of the sample means is nothing more than the standard deviation of the distribution of all possible sample means. The standard error of sample means is a function of S_x, N, and n—that is, the standard deviation of the population, the population size, and the sample size. The standard error decreases as the sample size increases. In the example in Exhibit 14.6C, the distribution of means with $n = 3$ was less spread out than the distribution of means with $n = 2$. This makes intuitive sense: more information should decrease uncertainty.

In practice, only one of the many possible samples is obtained. The information in that sample must be used to make estimates of population parameters. As noted above, the sample mean is used to estimate the population mean. The standard error in Equation (15.3) must also be estimated because it depends on the parameter S_x, which is typically unknown. As with means, the sample standard deviation is used to estimate the population standard deviation. Thus in practice,

$$se_{\bar{x}} = \frac{s_x}{\sqrt{n}} fpc \tag{15.4}$$

This is the formula for the standard error of the x sample mean given in Exhibit 15.2C.

A confidence interval is computed as follows:

[Sample mean $- z \times$ Standard error,   Sample mean $+ z \times$ Standard error]

The sample mean and standard error are computed from the sample. The value of z is chosen to achieve the level of confidence required. For example, $z = 3$ is associated with a 99.7% level of confidence because 0.997 is the area under a normal curve over the interval that runs from the mean minus 3 standard deviations to the mean plus 3 standard deviations. The value $z = 2$ (or 1.96) is associated with a 95% level of confidence, and so on. As the value of z increases, the level of confidence increases, but so does the length of the interval. On the other hand, the length of the interval decreases as the value of n increases.

In practice, the length of the interval is interpreted as a measure of precision in the estimate. The narrower the interval, the more precisely the population mean has been estimated. Many practitioners use half the length of the interval as a measure of precision, since this is a bound on the absolute value of the difference between the sample and population means. We also follow this practice.

Once a sample is obtained and the data are collected, a confidence interval is computed using the value of z believed to be appropriate. The interval is interpreted as an estimate of the population mean. Half the length of the interval measures the precision with which the population mean has been estimated. This procedure involves estimating the population standard deviation with the sample standard deviation.

Proportions

It is traditional to distinguish samples of 0's and 1's from samples of measurements, even though the procedures for analyzing the two types of samples are the same. Only the notation changes to reflect the two types of data. Assume the y sample is from a population of 0's and 1's. Then $\bar{y} = p$, which is just the proportion of 1's in the sample.

In Exercise 15.5I, you are asked to show that in this binary case the general formula for a standard deviation reduces to $\sqrt{p(1-p)n/(n-1)}$. Thus in this binary case, it follows that the sample standard error of p is

$$se_p = \frac{s_y}{\sqrt{n}} fpc = fpc \frac{\sqrt{p(1-p)\dfrac{n}{n-1}}}{\sqrt{n}} = \sqrt{\frac{p(1-p)}{n-1}} fpc \tag{15.5}$$

where $fpc = \sqrt{1-f} = \sqrt{1-n/N}$. This form of the standard error is used in Exhibit 15.2C, where it is assumed that the y population is a 0–1 population.

Effect of Sample Size and Universe (Population) Size

**finite population
correction factor**

In all the standard error formulas, the factor fpc appears. This is the **finite population correction factor**. It is the proportion of the universe elements *not* sampled: $1 - f = (N - n)/N$. This correction factor is needed as a consequence of drawing a simple random sample from a finite population of numbers. If N is very much larger than n—for example, where a sample of 1500 consumers is drawn from all those in the United States—the finite population correction factor is virtually equal to one and can be dropped from the formulas for practical purposes. But if n is a substantial fraction of N, say $f = 0.10$ or more, the finite population correction makes a difference. It serves to decrease the standard error and hence to decrease the length of the confidence interval and to increase the measure of precision of the estimate.

Although the universe size, N, sometimes affects the standard error of estimates, it plays a relatively minor role. The sample size and the population standard deviation are the main determinants of precision. Once the population is targeted and simple random sampling is chosen as the sampling design, only the sample size may be manipulated to achieve a desired level of precision. Section 15.6 discusses choosing sample sizes.

E X A M P L E   **15.4A**

This example illustrates how to compute sample statistics, using the example survey that asked employees their gender and how much time they spend caring for the elderly. (A sample-survey class actually carried out this study, asking many more questions.) For this illustration, assume that a simple random sample of size $n = 30$ was drawn from the group of 2164 employees, that each employee in the sample was mailed a questionnaire, and that they all mailed back the completed form. The data and some statistics are in Exhibit 15.4A.

The totals, means, and standard deviations may be calculated by hand or by computer. Here are the computations needed to obtain the standard errors. For the x sample (hours), $n = 30$, $s_x = 17.96$, and $N = 2164$. So

$$se_{\bar{x}} = \frac{17.96}{\sqrt{30}} \sqrt{\frac{2164 - 30}{2164}} = 3.26$$

For the y sample (gender), $n = 30$, $p = 0.2$, and $N = 2164$. So

$$s_y = \sqrt{\frac{p(1 - p)n}{n - 1}} = \sqrt{\frac{0.2(0.8)(30)}{29}} = 0.4068$$

and

$$se_p = \sqrt{\frac{p(1 - p)}{n - 1}} \, fpc = \sqrt{\frac{0.16}{29}} \sqrt{\frac{2134}{2164}} = (0.0743)(0.9930) = 0.0738$$

E X H I B I T **15.4A**
Data from a Survey of
Employees at a Madison,
Wisconsin, Company

Element	Gender	Hours	Element	Gender	Hours
1	0	0	16	0	14
2	1	98	17	0	0
3	0	0	18	0	0
4	0	0	19	1	0
5	0	0	20	0	0
6	0	0	21	0	0
7	1	0	22	1	1.5
8	0	0	23	0	0
9	0	0	24	0	0
10	0	7	25	0	0
11	1	0	26	0	0
12	0	0	27	0	0
13	0	0	28	0	0
14	1	4	29	0	0
15	0	0	30	0	0
Total				6	124.5
Average				0.2	4.15
Standard deviation				0.4068	17.96
Standard error				0.0738	3.26

Note: Respondents reported giving care to elderly relatives or friends
in the spring of 1987. The sampling design was simple random; the frame size was 2164;
and the sample size was 30.

The computation of confidence intervals is now quite straightforward.
The 99.7% confidence interval for the x population mean—that is, the mean
of the population of reported number of hours per week spent giving care—is

$$\bar{x} \pm 3se_{\bar{x}} = 4.15 \text{ hours } \pm 3(3.26 \text{ hours}) = 4.15 \text{ hours } \pm 9.78 \text{ hours}$$

We interpret the interval as follows: If we had surveyed the whole
universe of employees using the same mail out/mail back procedure, the
same questionnaire, and the same data processing techniques that were used
to obtain data from the sample, the average of the reported hours spent for
the whole group would almost certainly have been between −5.6 hours and
13.9 hours.

In this illustration, the lower endpoint of the interval is negative, which is
impossible. A 0 should certainly be an absolute lower bound on the number of
hours. The negative endpoint is a consequence of a relatively large standard
error, indicating very little precision in the estimate of average number of
hours. This lack of precision is due to the large standard deviation (17.96)
and the small sample size (30).

In the study conducted by the sample-survey class, a sample of size 350
was drawn and interviewed, which naturally led to much greater precision in

the estimates. Actual surveys commonly involve hundreds or even thousands of participants. This example is small scale to illustrate computations.

The 99.7% confidence interval for the proportion of female employees is

$$p \pm 3se_p = 0.2 \pm 3(0.0738) = 0.2 \pm 0.2214$$

Again a negative left endpoint is obtained, which would be reported as zero in practice. The interval shows that the proportion of female employees in the company is almost certainly less than 0.42 (that is, 42%). A larger sample would have allowed for more precision about the proportion of female employees. For example, the actual sample of size 350 gave the proportion of female employees as 0.27 with a standard error of 0.038, so the 99.7% confidence interval for the proportion of female workers was 0.27 ± 0.11. Thus, we were almost certain that between 16% and 38% of the universe of employees were females. ▪

SECTION

15.5 Exercises

15.5A Draw a simple random sample of size $n = 4$ from the universe in Exercise 15.3G. Use the sample to estimate the mean response for each of the five variables; construct 90% confidence intervals. Do any of your confidence intervals fail to contain the actual population mean? There are 4845 possible samples of size 4 from this universe. Approximately how many of them produce 90% confidence intervals that do not contain the population mean of a specified variable?

15.5B A questionnaire was sent to a simple random sample of 50 customers, who filled it out and returned it. Thirty-eight of the customers responded that your delivery times were too slow. Estimate the proportion of all your customers who feel your delivery times are too slow, using a 99.7% confidence interval. (Assume the frame size is very large so that the finite population correction may be ignored.) Give a precise statement of the meaning of the interval. What interval would you get if the sample size were 100 (assuming $p = 0.76$)? What is the percentage reduction in interval length resulting from the doubling of the sample size?

15.5C Example 15.4A is based on an actual survey of 350 employees. The frame, which was a payroll list, contained 2164 entries. In the sample, 27% of the employees said they were females.

 a Compute the standard error and the 99.7% confidence interval for $N = 2164$, $n = 350$, and $p = 0.27$, assuming a simple random sampling design. (*Answer:* 0.022, [0.20, 0.34].)

 b The results reported from the survey are proportion of females = 0.27 with a standard error of 0.038. The standard error is higher than the standard error you got in part (a). This is due to the necessary correction for nonresponse in the actual survey. How much precision was lost because some of the employees did not respond?

15.5D For simple random sampling, the standard error of a sample proportion is

$$se_p = \sqrt{[p(1-p)/(n-1)][(N-n)/N]}$$

For given N and n, what value of p maximizes this standard error? [*Answer:* $\frac{1}{2}$.] In designing a survey, you often place a bound on the sampling error, which is usually measured by half the width of some confidence interval.

a   Let B denote the specified upper bound on the sampling error in a 95% confidence interval, so $B = 2se_p$. Let $semax$ denote the standard error with $\frac{1}{2}$ substituted for p. If we set $B = 2semax$ and solve for n, then we have a "safe" value for n. It is safe because it corresponds to a bound on the worst possible value of the standard error. Your job in this part is to solve the resulting equation

$$B = 2\sqrt{[(\tfrac{1}{2})(\tfrac{1}{2})/(n-1)][(N-n)/N]}$$

for n. [*Answer:* $N(1 + B^2)/(NB^2 + 1)$.]

b   In this part, you are to solve for a safe value of n for an arbitrary level of confidence. Let z denote the number of standard errors required to achieve the desired level of confidence. Then set $B = zsemax$ and solve for n. [*Answer:* $N(z^2/4 + B^2)/(NB^2 + z^2/4)$.]

15.5E   You plan to draw a sample of employees from an agency that is divided into a number of departments as follows:

Department	Number of Employees
A	349
B	278
C	181
D	82
E	42
F	12
G	4
Total	948

Each department manager wants to have at least one member of his or her department in the sample, and two of the managers (of departments F and G) insist that all their employees be surveyed. Your study group has set a target to estimate proportions in each department to within eight percentage points. You have the resources to include about 10% of all employees in the sample. How would you try to satisfy the constraints? (This is based on an actual experience.)

15.5F   In Exercise 15.5E, suppose the sample sizes finally decided on were, by department, 30, 25, 18, 8, 4, 12, and 4.

a   Compute the finite correction factors for each department.

b   Suppose the sampled employees are asked a 0–1 type question, and in every department the proportion of 1's is .8, rounded to one decimal place. Compute the standard errors of the estimated proportions for each department. Comment on the relative impacts of department size and sample size on these standard errors.

c   On the basis of your analysis so far, do you feel that the proposed sample sizes are reasonable? If not, what would you recommend?

15.5G   Suppose you have sampled from a frame with N elements and obtained an estimated proportion of p with a standard error of se_p. You have been asked to estimate the total number of elements responding with a 1 (to the 0–1 question).

a   Develop an appropriate estimate, standard error, and confidence interval. [*Answer:* Np, Nse_p, and $Np \pm zNse_p$.]

b   For the data in Exercise 15.5B, estimate the number of customers who feel your delivery times are too slow if the frame has $N = 3000$ elements.

15.5H   Suppose you have sampled from a frame with N elements and obtained an estimated mean of $\bar{x}$ with a standard error of $se_{\bar{x}}$. You have been asked to estimate the population total value of x. Develop an appropriate estimate, standard error, and confidence interval. [*Answer:* $N\bar{x}$, $Nse_{\bar{x}}$, $N\bar{x} \pm zNse_{\bar{x}}$.]

15.51   Suppose a sample of size n from a 0–1 population yields m 1's and $n - m$ 0's. Let $p = m/n$ denote the sample proportion. Show that the sample mean is equal to p and the sample standard deviation is equal to $\sqrt{p(1 - p)n/(n - 1)}$.

SECTION

15.6   Choosing Sample Sizes

As discussed earlier in the chapter, sample size is important in reducing sampling variation. In simple random sampling, the standard error of a sample mean is $(fpc)s/\sqrt{n}$, where $fpc = \sqrt{(N - n)/N}$. The fpc varies somewhat with sample size n, but the main impact of the sample size is revealed in the term $s/\sqrt{n}$. Three observations need to be made here:

1   The standard error decreases as sample size increases because $\sqrt{n}$ divides s.

2   As sample size increases, the standard error decreases as the square root of the sample size, so the rate of decrease in the standard error is much slower than the rate of increase in the sample size. But since the cost of sampling typically increases in proportion to the sample size, there is a rather severe decreasing marginal return to investment in sample size.

3   Decreases in s result in direct decreases in the standard error. Thus strategies that reduce s pay off better than increases in sample size. One such strategy is stratification, which is discussed in Section 15.10. Stratification is the separation of the elements into groups on the basis of characteristics that can be identified at the design stage. For example, if the gender of individuals is shown in the frame, it may pay to draw separate samples from the males and females. This will reduce overall variation if males and females respond very differently to the questions in the survey.

There are cogent arguments in sampling theory to keep sample sizes to a minimum. There are also good arguments based on minimizing total survey costs. As noted in Chapter 14, preventing and detecting nonsampling error consume resources. The larger the sample size, the more effort is required to manage nonsampling errors, not to mention recruiting and training workers. A survey must be judged not only on precision but also on quality and cost. If an acceptable level of precision cannot be delivered without sacrificing quality, then all the resources devoted to the survey are wasted. Thus one of the most important factors in deciding to do a survey is whether the survey will produce sufficient precision and quality to justify doing the survey at all.

One aspect of planning is to compute the sample size needed to achieve a given level of precision. In Exercise 15.5D, you were asked to develop such a sample-size formula for the estimation of a proportion, using simple random sampling, namely

$$n = \frac{N(z^2/4 + B^2)}{NB^2 + z^2/4}$$

This formula gives a sample size appropriate where sampling error is the only source of error. In practice, where surveys suffer from nonresponse, interviewer error, clerical error, and other defects, the nominal level of precision in the formula is rarely achieved.

Planning a survey involves guesswork. Sample-size formulas are helpful guidelines, but they need to be used in conjunction with other knowledge to come up with a final plan. One way to use them is to propose a sample size and then work out the standard error and bound on the sampling error implied by that sample size. Testing several sample-size choices gives you an appreciation for the sensitivity of the precision of the estimates to sample size. Finally, remember that there is never a "correct" survey design for a given problem. Different investigators may develop different plans, all of which are reasonable. The important thing is to execute the plan as faithfully as possible. Then, provided that nonsampling errors are not overwhelming, the survey's results will be valid, even if the standard errors are bigger than desired. Validity is important, even when desired levels of precision are not achieved, because a survey can be a valuable source of information that will help in planning the next survey. It also may become part of a collection of high-quality surveys that all point to a very important conclusion, even though no one of them is conclusive by itself.

SECTION

15.7 Exercises

15.7A   In simple random sampling, the theoretical standard deviation of the mean is $(fpc)S/\sqrt{n}$, and the theoretical bound on the sampling error between the population and sample means is $B = z(fpc)S/\sqrt{n}$, where z is chosen to achieve a given level of confidence. Assuming B, z, and S are given, solve this equation for n. [*Answer:* $z^2 N S^2/(N B^2 + z^2 S^2)$.]

Notice that to use this formula we need a guess at S, the population standard deviation. Guessing at S must be part of the survey design process. Various methods for doing this are discussed in books on surveying. Here we simply ask you to develop a feel for the implications of the formula by doing some numerical calculations. To keep things simple, assume $fpc = 1$ and take $B = 1$. Set up a two-way table with rows corresponding to $z = 1.645$, 2, and 3, and columns corresponding to $S = 0.5$, 1.0, 2.0, and 10.0. Now fill in the table with the values of n corresponding to these choices of z and S. Comment on the behavior of n as the two factors z and S vary. Compute rates of change. Which factor z or S has the greater impact?

15.7B   A service organization has a list of members and a list of contributors who are not members. The membership list has 3000 names; the contributor list has 10,000 names. The organization plans to draw a simple random sample from each list. A sample of size 300 is planned for the membership list. One of the planners argues that a sample between 3 and 3.5 times this size from the contributors list is needed to achieve the same level of precision as planned for the membership list. What do you recommend? Why?

15.7C   A simple random sample of $n = 49$ observations from a large universe yields a sample mean of 1556 and a standard deviation of 91. Compute the standard error of the mean. [*Answer:* 13.]

15.8 Misunderstanding and Misuse of Random Sampling

In this section, we make an important distinction.

Random Versus Representative Samples

Some people use the word *representative* when referring to samples. For example, a lawyer trying to discredit evidence collected by probability sampling may say a sample cannot be representative of a population. Presumably the lawyer means that the sample is not a mirror image of the universe. This is certainly factual. The sample may have 20% females, whereas the universe may have 25% females. If a case turns on knowing precisely the number of females in a universe, then there is no choice but to census the universe! The probability sample only predicts characteristics of the universe within limits.

What is fundamental is not the representativeness of the probability sample but the type of information required. If only a census will answer the question, then using a sample is inappropriate. On the other hand, if the information needed can be obtained by sampling, then to census is to engage in waste.

Base arguments on important issues! The validity of a probability sample is a legitimate issue, but if the sample is obtained by a correct process, then it is both superficial and a waste of time to argue about its representativeness.

Another unfortunate use of representativeness is quota sampling. This involves constructing a sample whose characteristics match some demographic targets. For example, interviewers might be sent into a shopping mall and told to interview 100 people who satisfy the following quotas:

Women	Totals
	60
Teenagers	15
With young children	20
Wearing business suits	15
Over 50	10

Men	
	40
Teenagers	15
With young children	10
Wearing business suits	10
Wearing Hawaiian shorts	5

The quotas may make the sample representative of some universe, but they fail to satisfy more constraints than they satisfy, so the sample will be unrepresentative in some way. In the example above, no attempt was made to satisfy constraints on income, place of residence, and so on. Samples cannot completely mirror a universe. Quota sampling has led to some dramatically bad results, including the famous preelection polls of 1948, which predicted so certainly that Dewey would be elected president that newspapers headlined Dewey's victory even as Truman beat him resoundingly.

Another misuse of representativeness arises in nonprobability surveys and the treatment of nonresponse. Suppose, for example, that a nonprobability sample is selected, or that 40% of the people to whom questionnaires are sent do not return them. A favorite pastime of people who conduct such surveys is to compute demographic characteristics (such as age, income, and geographic location) of the respondents. They compare these characteristics to those in published censuses or other surveys. If there is a close correspondence, these practitioners say that their sample is representative. That is their operational definition, which they have a right to.

But then they take a fatal misstep. They use the sample as if it were a probability sample. They compute estimates, standard errors, and confidence intervals and publish them as if they had the same meaning they would have had if the sample had been drawn by a probability method. There is no logical foundation in sampling theory for doing this.

Surveys and Forecasting

The successful forecasting of winners on election nights is a familiar phenomenon. These predictions are based on surveys of "key precincts" that have successfully helped to predict elections in the past. More speculative forecasts made on the basis of polls taken before election day asking people how they plan to vote are also familiar. The more sophisticated of such polls also try to forecast the probability with which a respondent will actually vote.

The more time that elapses between when a survey is done and when a forecasted event will occur, the more speculative the forecast is. If a particular survey is part of a series of surveys, then the whole series of results is needed to assess the relevance of the particular survey to some future event.

The reason for this is somewhat subtle but absolutely crucial for a correct use of survey information. Sampling variation and measures of it, such as standard errors, refer only to errors due to observing only part of the universe during the sampling period. The difference between an estimate and the equal complete coverage value is a sampling error, and the standard error of the estimate gives us an idea of the likely magnitude of the difference. However, this standard error gives no information about the difference between an estimate from one survey and an estimate that will occur in some future survey. Analyzing a single cross section does not yield information about forecasting errors. To develop such longitudinal information, longitudinal data must be analyzed. Thus, a time series analysis of a series of survey results may give some information on likely future results.

One implication of this fact is that a long-term perspective is needed to do sensible forecasting. Data collected in a standardized fashion over a long period of time are needed to get good insights into the longitudinal behavior of a process. A hodgepodge of surveys collected by different methods and with varying degrees of quality is a poor basis for forecasting or any other decision making.

Another implication is that we need to be realistic about what can be learned from a survey. For example, a market researcher once studied powdered instant fruit-flavored drinks for a large U.S. foods corporation. The market researcher did a large number of studies to determine the marketability of the new product. An advanced analysis of these studies suggested to the research team that the new product was a winner, but after a brief initial success the product's sales decreased quickly and it was removed from the market. The researcher concluded, "If we had only studied the question of repeat sales!" The researchers learned of the initial attractiveness of their product but not of the second thoughts of people who actually tried it. A longitudinal study might have produced the warning signals that could have led to better product development.

SECTION

15.9 Exercises

15.9A State U has about 40,000 students. One of the student newspapers interviews a sample of 100 students. They set up a booth on the library mall and tell a reporter to start interviewing people at 10:00 A.M. on Wednesday morning and to gather interviews until 100 interviews are conducted. The newspaper prepares an article reporting the results of the survey. They claim that the sample was random and quote standard errors of the estimates. What does statistical theory say about these results?

15.9B Quota sampling has surface appeal but can give badly biased results. See Frederick Mosteller and others, *The Pre-election Polls of 1948* (New York: Social Research Council, 1949); and David Freedman, Robert Pisani, and Roger Purvis, *Statistics* (New York: Norton, 1978), chap. 19, section 3, pp. 305ff. F. F. Stephan and P. J. McCarthy, *Sampling Opinions* (New York: Wiley, 1958), gives an excellent comparison of quota and random sampling methods. See also Alan Stuart, "Nonprobability Sampling," in William H. Kruskal and Judith M. Tanur, eds., *International Encyclopedia of Statistics*, vol. 2 (New York: Free Press, 1978), pp. 885–889. Read these references, plus any others you can find, and prepare a memo on the dangers of quota sampling. Why is it that a sample can satisfy a large number of constraints and still yield badly biased results?

15.9C Recommend a design for a longitudinal study that might have helped the market researcher whose story appears at the end of Section 15.8.

15.9D An exit survey of shoppers in a mall results in a 99.7% confidence interval for the average expenditure at the mall of [$2.74, $10.95]. An analyst concludes that a randomly encountered shopper at the mall will almost certainly spend between $2.74 and $10.95 at the mall.

a What is wrong with the analyst's argument?

b What is wrong with the statement that the average shopper spends between $2.74 and $10.95 at the mall?

c Use your intuition to construct a typical distribution of expenditures at the mall. Think of a group of 10,000 shoppers. What fraction of them spend nothing? What fraction spend something but less than $5. Continue in this fashion. Try to construct a distribution you think is reasonable and has a mean between $2.74 and $10.95.

d This problem describes an attempt by an analyst to use a survey estimate of a mean to make a prediction about individual behavior, a fallacious use of the estimate. It is possible to use survey data to make predictions about individuals, but a measure of variation that applies to individuals must be used to do this. For example, let y denote the reported expenditure variable. The survey yields a standard deviation of the individual expenditures, denoted by s_y. Let the standard error of the mean expenditure be denoted by $se_{\bar{y}}$. To estimate the expenditure of an individual shopper, use the sample mean, $\bar{y}$. When the mean is used as a predictor of individual behavior, the standard error of the prediction error is $\sqrt{s_y^2 + se_{\bar{y}}^2}$. Denote the latter standard error by the symbol ise_y, for *individual standard error*. If the population of the expenditure values is approximately normally distributed, a 99.7% confidence interval for an individual expenditure is $\bar{y} \pm 3ise_y$. Other multiples of the standard error yield other levels of probability, in the usual way.

15.9E   This is a numerical illustration of the theory outlined in part (d) of Exercise 15.9D. Suppose the survey yields a standard deviation of expenditures of $27.40 and a standard error of mean expenditure of $2.70. The mean reported expenditure is $6.80. If the population of expenditure values is approximately normally distributed, compute a 99.7% confidence interval for the expenditure of a randomly encountered shopper. To what universe of individuals does this interval apply? Now compute the 99.7% confidence interval for the mean expenditure. Explain why the two intervals are different.

SECTION

15.10   Stratification, Clustering, and Systematic Sampling

In practice, populations are usually quite complex and hard to sample, and the methods used to extract information from them must be correspondingly advanced. Although not all the complexities of sampling designs are considered in this section, three fundamental tools of sampling are presented: stratification, clustering, and systematic sampling. Acquaintance with these tools will give you a better appreciation of sampling in practice.

What Is Stratification?

stratification
stratified sampling

Stratification is the grouping of elements in a frame according to some common characteristic or characteristics. **Stratified sampling** is a design in which random samples are drawn from strata in the frame.

EXAMPLE   15.10A

A supplier of paper that is made into corrugated board uses three different production lines to produce the paper. Although the three lines are considered identical, a study shows that paper produced by one of the lines is consistently stronger than that produced by the other two lines. The study of output by production line is an example of stratification.[†]   ■

EXAMPLE   15.10B

One of the fundamental tenets of marketing is market segmentation, which is the formation of groups of potential customers according to such characteristics as age, geographic location, psychological traits, and so on. The grouping of customers is an example of stratification.   ■

[†]This example is adapted from P. G. Moore, *Statistics and the Manager* (London: MacDonald, 1966), pp. 5–7.

E X A M P L E   **15.10C**   In the hospital study in Chapter 16, hospitals are grouped by geographic region and size, another illustration of stratification.   ▪

In each of the examples, stratification was chosen to help solve a problem: finding sources of variation in a paper product, identifying a target market, and studying the feasibility of a uniform reimbursement plan for hospitals. Statistically speaking, an important result of stratification is a reduction in the sampling variability of estimates of important parameters. The intuitive explanation for this is that grouping elements by a common characteristic removes some variation from the population that would otherwise show up in the estimates. Reducing variability is not always the primary objective of stratification, however. If the comparison of certain groups is an objective of the survey, these groups may be used as strata even though the stratification may do little to further the reduction of sampling variability. Thus stratification is both a natural strategy in the study of groups and a helpful statistical device for controlling variation.

How Is Stratified Sampling Performed?

To introduce stratification into a sampling design, there must be a frame that shows the stratum to which each element belongs. For example, the sample may come from a list of names of people who are either members of an organization or nonmembers who have made a financial contribution. A sample of members and a sample of nonmembers are drawn, which gives stratification by membership status. In Example 15.10A, it is natural to stratify because output is obtained from each production line. In Example 15.10C, the job of compiling lists of hospitals and attaching geographic and bed-size codes is clearly a massive one. Yet it is necessary to carry out the stratification done in the study.

Once the frame is constructed, a separate probability sample is drawn from each stratum. Using a fresh set of random numbers in sampling each stratum guarantees the independence of the samples. After the samples are drawn, the measurement of the selected elements takes place and the data are ready for analysis.

How Are Estimates Formed from Stratified Samples?

A sample from a single stratum is analogous to a sample from a single population. If a simple random sample is drawn from a stratum, then that sample is used just as in simple random sampling to estimate the stratum mean, total, or proportion. No new theory is required for this.

To estimate the difference between two strata means, totals, or proportions, the Pythagorean rule for computing the standard errors of differences between estimates, discussed in Chapter 16, is used.

In this section, the theory is presented for the case when a stratified random sample is drawn from a population and we wish to estimate the overall population mean, total, or proportion.

Notation for Two Strata

In this section the notation for two strata is developed. Once you master the problem with two strata, you will find it easy to deal with any number of strata. Independent simple random samples are taken from the strata.

The existence of a frame of elements designated as belonging to stratum 1 or stratum 2 is taken for granted. Let N_1 denote the number of stratum 1 elements in the frame and N_2 the number of stratum 2 elements in the frame. Denote by $N = N_1 + N_2$ the total number of elements in the frame. Let n_1 denote the number of elements drawn into the sample from stratum 1, and n_2 the number of elements from stratum 2. The total number of elements in the two samples is $n = n_1 + n_2$. Let $f_1 = n_1/N_1$ and $f_2 = n_2/N_2$ denote the sampling fractions for the two strata. The total sampling fraction is

$$f = \frac{n}{N} = \frac{(n_1 + n_2)}{N} = \left(\frac{N_1}{N}\right)\left(\frac{n_1}{N_1}\right) + \left(\frac{N_2}{N}\right)\left(\frac{n_2}{N_2}\right) = \left(\frac{N_1}{N}\right)f_1 + \left(\frac{N_2}{N}\right)f_2$$

The quantities $\sqrt{1 - f_1}$, $\sqrt{1 - f_2}$, and $\sqrt{1 - f}$ are the finite population corrections.

Equal complete coverage of stratum 1 would yield a set of N_1 measurements whose mean and standard deviation are denoted by μ_1 and S_1. Similarly, equal complete coverage of stratum 2 would yield a set of N_2 measurements whose mean and standard deviation are denoted by μ_2 and S_2.

The simple random sample from stratum 1 yields data from which any statistics may be computed. To keep the presentation concrete, assume that the objective is to estimate means. Thus from the data from stratum 1, the mean, standard deviation, and standard error of the mean, which are denoted by $\bar{y}_1$, s_1, and

$$\sqrt{\frac{(1 - f_1)s_1^2}{n_1}} = \frac{(fpc_1)s_1}{\sqrt{n_1}}$$

would be computed.

Similarly, the mean, standard deviation, and standard error of the mean from the data from stratum 2 are denoted by $\bar{y}_2$, s_2, and

$$\sqrt{\frac{(1 - f_2)s_2^2}{n_2}} = \frac{(fpc_2)s_2}{\sqrt{n_2}}$$

The goal is to estimate the population mean, which is denoted by μ. First observe that the relationship between μ, μ_1, and μ_2 is

$$\mu = \left(\frac{N_1}{N}\right)\mu_1 + \left(\frac{N_2}{N}\right)\mu_2 \tag{15.6}$$

which is analogous to the relationship between the overall sampling fraction and the stratum sampling fractions. The overall mean is a weighted average of the stratum means, where the weights are the proportions of stratum 1 and stratum 2 elements in the frame. See Exercise 15.11A for a sketch of the proof of Equation (15.6).

Because $\bar{y}_1$ and $\bar{y}_2$ are estimates of μ_1 and μ_2, it is natural to estimate μ with

$$\bar{y}_{st} = \left(\frac{N_1}{N}\right)\bar{y}_1 + \left(\frac{N_2}{N}\right)\bar{y}_2 \tag{15.7}$$

The mean estimate based on the stratified sample is denoted by $\bar{y}_{st}$. The theoretical standard error of this estimate is

$$S_{\bar{y}.st} = \sqrt{\left(\frac{N_1}{N}\right)^2 (1-f_1)\frac{S_1^2}{n_1} + \left(\frac{N_2}{N}\right)^2 (1-f_2)\frac{S_2^2}{n_2}} \tag{15.8}$$

The derivation of this expression will be studied later. For now we complete the outline of the estimation procedure that would be used in practice. The theoretical standard error in Equation (15.8) could not be computed in practice because the stratum standard errors would not be known. As is usual in such cases, sample standard errors are substituted to produce an estimated standard error. This yields

$$s_{\bar{y}.st} = \sqrt{\left(\frac{N_1}{N}\right)^2 (1-f_1)\frac{s_1^2}{n_1} + \left(\frac{N_2}{N}\right)^2 (1-f_2)\frac{s_2^2}{n_2}} \tag{15.9}$$

An approximate 99.7% confidence interval for the population mean is then

$$\bar{y}_{st} \pm 3s_{\bar{y}.st} \tag{15.10}$$

provided n_1 and n_2 are large enough.

E X A M P L E   15.10D

A frame consists of elements divided into two strata, stratum 1 having $N_1 = 700$ elements and stratum 2 having $N_2 = 2100$ elements. Simple random samples of size $n_1 = 42$ and $n_2 = 63$ are drawn from the two strata, yielding means and standard deviations of $\bar{y}_1 = 117$, $s_1 = 9$, $\bar{y}_2 = 109$, and $s_2 = 10$. Construct a 99.7% confidence interval for the population mean.

To construct the confidence interval for the population mean, the quantities in Equations (15.7) and (15.9) must be computed. Note that $f_1 = 42/700 = 0.06$, and $f_2 = 63/2100 = 0.03$. The mean estimate in Equation (15.7) is

$$\bar{y}_{st} = \left[\frac{700}{2800} \times 117\right] + \left[\frac{2100}{2800} \times 109\right] = (.25)(117) + (.75)(109) = 111$$

The standard error estimate in Equation (15.9) is

$$s_{\bar{y}.st} = \sqrt{\frac{(.25)^2(1-.06)(9)^2}{42} + \frac{(.75)^2(1-.03)(10)^2}{63}}$$

$$= \sqrt{0.11330 + 0.86607} = 0.99$$

approximately. These quantities are now substituted into Equation (15.10) to get

$$111 \pm 3(0.99) = 111 \pm 3.0 = [108, 114]$$

as the 99.7% confidence interval for the population mean. The confidence interval tells us we may know the population mean to within about 3.0 units of measurement.   ∎

Formulas for Any Number of Strata

Let I denote the number of strata, let $N_1, N_2, \ldots, N_I$ denote the number of elements in the strata, and let $n_1, n_2, \ldots, n_I$ denote the number of elements drawn into the samples from each stratum. Let $W_i = N_i/N$ and $f_i = n_i/N_i$, $i = 1, 2, \ldots, I$, denote the proportion of elements and the sampling fraction from stratum i. Let $\bar{y}_1, \bar{y}_2, \ldots, \bar{y}_I$ and $s_1, s_2, \ldots, s_I$ denote the sample means and standard deviations of the data from the various strata. Then the estimate of the population mean is

$$\bar{y}_{st} = W_1\bar{y}_1 + W_2\bar{y}_2 + \cdots + W_I\bar{y}_I \tag{15.11}$$

and the estimated standard error of this mean is

$$s_{\bar{y}.st} = \sqrt{W_1^2(1 - f_1)\frac{s_1^2}{n_1} + W_2^2(1 - f_2)\frac{s_2^2}{n_2} + \cdots + W_I^2(1 - f_I)\frac{s_I^2}{n_I}} \tag{15.12}$$

Equation (15.11) is a generalization of Equation (15.7), and Equation (15.12) is a generalization of Equation (15.9).

A 99.7% confidence interval for the population mean is

$$\bar{y}_{st} \pm 3s_{\bar{y}.st} \tag{15.13}$$

What Is Clustering?

clustering

Clustering is a type of grouping that groups elements according to their "nearness" to each other. In contrast to stratification, clustering tends to increase the variability of estimates based on probability samples. As compensation, clustering tends to reduce the costs of sampling because clusters of elements tend to be near one another.

E X A M P L E   **15.10E**

You wish to give a test to children in a school. To minimize disruption, you agree to choose five classes of children and to give the test to every child in those five classes. The classes are clusters. The students in a class have much in common that may be quite different from the other students in the school—the teacher, for example. A stratified design could have been constructed using classes as strata. This would have required you to draw a sample of children from each class, which would have been too disruptive.   ∎

E X A M P L E   **15.10F**

If personal interviews are to be conducted in a large geographic region, a cluster design is often used to cut down on the travel time of the interviewers. The region is divided into small subregions, the clusters. A sample of clusters is selected and households from these subregions are selected for interview. The households are also clusters, so this example illustrates multistage clustering. Multistage clustering is very common in large-scale surveys.   ▪

EXAMPLE   15.10G

A fast food company sells franchises to local entrepreneurs. Part of the franchise agreement is that the parent company may inspect a local establishment without warning. The parent may choose local establishments at random for inspection. The establishments are clusters.   ▪

EXAMPLE   15.10H

In random digit dialing surveys, blocks of telephone numbers are chosen at random and all the numbers in a block are called. This is done because telephone companies typically issue numbers in blocks and will make the block information available to researchers.   ▪

Clustering may be combined with stratification.

EXAMPLE   15.10I

As a continuation of Example 15.10F, the clusters may be formed into strata and a sample of clusters taken from each stratum. This is typically done in large-scale surveys.   ▪

cluster sampling

These examples show that **cluster sampling**, a design in which a random sample of clusters is selected, is quite different from simple random sampling of elements. Because the elements within a cluster have similar characteristics, they do not provide independent bits of information as do the elements in a simple random sample. Thus, an estimate based on a cluster sample is usually less precise than an estimate based on a simple random sample with the same number of elements. On the other hand, a simple random sample may be very expensive to obtain because of the costs of frame construction, travel time, or both. Thus for many surveys, clustering is the only affordable course of action. Sometimes, as in Example 15.10E, it can be the only course of action.

Notation for a Simple Cluster Sampling Design

The formulas for general cluster sampling are too complicated to present in this elementary introduction. A very simple case that has some practical applications is presented instead. Consult a book on sample surveys for a complete treatment of cluster sampling.[†]

Assume that the population elements have been arranged into N clusters of equal size; the clusters are assumed to have equal numbers of elements. A simple random sample of n clusters is selected, and all the elements in the selected clusters are

[†]William G. Cochran, *Sampling Techniques*, 2nd ed. (New York: Wiley, 1953).

measured. Let $\bar{y}_1, \bar{y}_2, \ldots, \bar{y}_n$ denote the means of the observations from the sampled clusters. The estimate of the population mean is the average of these sample means:

$$\bar{y}_{cl} = (\bar{y}_1 + \bar{y}_2 + \cdots + \bar{y}_n)/n \qquad (15.14)$$

which is just the mean of the cluster means.

The estimated standard error of the estimate is

$$s_{\bar{y}_{cl}} = \sqrt{\frac{(N-n)\sum_{i=1}^{n}(\bar{y}_i - \bar{y}_{cl})^2}{Nn(n-1)}} \qquad (15.15)$$

which is just the standard error of the sample mean displayed in Equation (15.14).

The results in Equations (15.14) and (15.15) are simple only because very restrictive assumptions are made. In practice the clusters are rarely of equal size, and the cluster sizes show up in the general formulas. The formulas above also assume every element in a cluster is measured, but in practice elements are often sampled from clusters, which greatly complicates the formulas. These important complications are not discussed in this text.

What Is Systematic Sampling?

systematic sampling

Systematic sampling, a design in which elements are chosen systematically from the frame after a random start (or starts) has been chosen, often replaces simple random sampling in practice. It can be much easier to implement than simple random sampling, and it can produce more precise estimates under certain conditions. Systematic sampling is ideally suited to the sampling of lists.

Suppose the frame consists of a list of items stored in a book, card file, or electronically stored file. Let M denote the number of items in the file, and suppose a 10% sample is desired, that is, $m = 0.1M$, where sample size is denoted by m. For simplicity, assume m is an integer. A systematic sample is drawn using these steps:

1   Select a starting digit between 1 and 10 at random.

2   Choose the item in the file corresponding to the randomly chosen starting digit.

3   Choose every tenth item thereafter in the file.

To illustrate, suppose the file has 3000 items, and a 10% sample, that is, a sample of size 300, is desired. Choose an integer between 1 and 10 at random; suppose it turns out to be 2. The sample would then consist of items 2, 12, 22, 32, ..., 2992 from the file.

The systematic sample is easy to draw because it is a simple matter for a clerk or computer to step through the file and select the sample items.

More generally, let f denote a number between 0 and 1 such that $m = fM$ and $1/f$ are integers. Then a $100f\%$ systematic sample is drawn using these steps:

1   Select a starting digit between 1 and $1/f$ at random.

2   Choose the item in the file corresponding to the randomly chosen starting digit.

3   Choose every $1/f$th item thereafter in the file.

Characteristics of a Systematic Sample

The systematic sampling design described above makes limited use of randomization. The design assigns equal probabilities of $f = m/M$ to each element in the frame because the number of possible samples is $1/f$, and each element appears in one and only one sample. In systematic sampling, most combinations of m elements cannot be drawn as samples, whereas with simple random sampling all possible combinations of m elements are possible. On the other hand, if the elements are placed in the frame in random order, systematic sampling is equivalent to simple random sampling. In the latter case, the estimation formulas of simple random sampling may be used for a systematic sample.

In general, though, the simple random sample formulas cannot be reliably used with a systematic sample. One way to see this is to note that the systematic sampling design is a form of cluster sampling in which only one cluster is drawn at random. Equations (15.14) and (15.15) apply to this case with $N = M/m$ and $n = 1$. Equation (15.15) for the estimated standard error is undefined for $n = 1$ because of the resulting division by zero.

Statistical theory shows that the theoretical standard error of the systematic sample mean is

$$SE(\bar{y}_{sys}) = \sqrt{\frac{S^2}{m}[1 + (m-1)\rho]} \qquad \textbf{(15.16)}$$

where ρ is the correlation coefficient between all possible pairs of elements from the frame. If the elements in the frame are randomly shuffled, $\rho = 0$, and the standard formulas apply; otherwise we may have $\rho > 0$ or $\rho < 0$, depending on the arrangement of the elements in the frame. If the value of ρ is not known a priori, the standard error in Equation (15.16) is difficult to estimate. Yates suggests the estimate

$$\sqrt{\frac{\sum_{i=1}^{m-1}(y_{i+1} - y_i)^2}{2m(m-1)}} \qquad \textbf{(15.17)}$$

which is a sensible practical approximation.[†]

SECTION

15.11 Exercises

15.11A   Prove Equation (15.6). [*Hint:* The total y-value in stratum i is $N_i\mu_i$, $i = 1, 2$, so the total y-value in the population is $N_1\mu_1 + N_2\mu_2$. The population mean is the total y-value in the population divided by the number of elements in the population, which is N. In other words, $\mu = (N_1\mu_1 + N_2\mu_2)/N$, from which Equation (15.6) follows immediately.]

15.11B   You are given the following data concerning a stratified sampling problem with two strata.

[†]Frank Yates, *Sampling Methods for Censuses and Surveys*, 3rd ed. (New York: Hafner, 1953), pp. 229–230.

Stratum (i)	1	2
N_i	2,000	3,000
n_i	50	50
$\bar{y}_i$	10,000	7,000
s_i	2,000	1,500

Construct a 99.7% confidence interval for the population mean μ.

15.11C   Redo Exercise 15.11B with the following choices of n_1 and n_2, and with all other values the same.

Case	n_1	n_2
1	25	75
2	10	90
3	90	10
4	75	25
5	20	180
6	50	150
7	100	100
8	150	50
9	180	20

Comment on the effects of changing the allocation of sample sizes and on the effect of doubling the total sample size. Try to give intuitive explanations of these effects. (*Hint:* You will probably want to computerize your solution to this problem to avoid tedious calculations.)

15.11D   You are given the following data for a stratified sampling problem involving three strata, that is, $I = 3$.

Stratum (i)	1	2	3
N_i	500	700	800
n_i	50	70	80
$\bar{y}_i$	89	50	43
s_i	200	210	180

Find a 99.7% confidence interval for the population mean. Use several different choices of n_1, n_2, and n_3, and comment on the effects of these choices.

15.11E   Refer to Exhibit 6.2A. Let each successive group of five parcels displayed there be a cluster. Select two clusters at random and use the resulting sample to estimate the average market value of the whole set of cases with a 99.7% confidence interval. Does the interval contain the average market value of the whole set of cases?

15.11F   Refer to Exercise 15.11E. How many possible cluster samples of size 2 are there? Display each one and compute the 90% confidence interval for average market value for each one. How many of the intervals do not contain the actual average market value for all the cases?

15.11G   Select a systematic sample of size 10 from the list of cases in Exhibit 6.2A. Use the sample to estimate the average market value for the whole set of cases, using a 99.7% confidence interval. Does the confidence interval contain the average market value for all the cases?

15.11H Refer to Exercise 15.11G. How many possible systematic samples of size 10 are there? Display each one and estimate average market value for each one, using 90% confidence intervals. How many of the intervals fail to contain the average market value of all the cases?

Chapter Summary

Simple random sampling gives each possible sample of a given size the same chance of being drawn. The purpose of drawing a probability sample is to estimate a population parameter, which is a numerical characteristic of a variable measured on each element in the universe. The numerical characteristic of a variable measured on each element in a sample differs from the parameter, but probability theory can be used to derive its sampling distribution. From the sampling distribution, bounds on the errors in the sample characteristics can be derived. The bounds are usually expressed as confidence intervals. The degree of sampling error—and hence the width of the confidence interval—can be controlled by choosing the sample size, but if samples are expensive, the cost of achieving a high degree of precision may be prohibitive. An approach to controlling sampling error for lower cost is to use different sampling designs. Two common alternatives to simple random sampling are stratified sampling and cluster sampling. A sampling design that often yields results comparable to simple random sampling but is easier to implement is systematic sampling.

Supplementary Exercises for Chapter 15

15A Use the restaurant section of the yellow pages of your local telephone book as a frame. Draw a simple random sample of 30 entries. Determine whether or not the entry corresponds to a chain of restaurants. To do this you must form an operational definition of "chain." Estimate the proportion of chain restaurants in your area using a 99.7% confidence interval. What sort of biases may be present in your estimate? Why does the confidence interval not account for the biases? What does it account for? What could you do to reduce the biases if you did this study again?

15B A marketing department draws a simple random sample of 1000 households from a city and attempts to conduct personal interviews with the heads of these households. After much effort, the department finds that they have found only 815 heads to interview, the others having never been home at the time of the call. They decide to draw a random sample of 500 additional households and to interview heads of these households until 185 interviews have been completed. The resulting sample of 1000 interviews is then to be analyzed. What biases are introduced by this procedure? What types of households are likely to be overrepresented in the sample? Underrepresented?

15C A very large organization of analysts has asked each analyst to draw an independent random sample of size 30 from a gigantic population of numbers that has mean 100 and standard deviation 10. The analysts are to compute the means of their samples and bring them to their annual meeting. At the meeting the analysts plan to construct a histogram of their sample means and compute the mean and standard deviation of their sample means. Describe in as much detail as you can what the analysts will observe.

15D An agricultural organization wishes to survey a sample of farms in Texas. One proposed method of sampling farms is to select points at random on a state map. The three farms closest to each point will be surveyed. What sort of bias might this sampling design cause?

15E Which of the following five statements does *not* describe a consequence of using probability methods in surveying?

1 Probability methods mean that each individual in the universe has a specified probability of entering the sample.

2 Probability selection of samples imposes a state of statistical control that allows prediction within limits.

3 Probability methods allow prediction within limits of the equal complete coverage.

4 The intent of a probability survey is to obtain a statistical profile of a population rather than detailed information on individuals.

5 With probability methods, one does not have to worry about coverage errors because these are incorporated into the standard errors of the estimates.

15F A simple random sample of $n = 25$ observations yields a sample mean of 26.23 and a standard deviation of 13.91. Compute the standard error of the mean.

15G An analyst has received a survey of households from a certain city that reports a 99.7% confidence interval for the average household income of [$15,372, $31,928]. The analyst writes in her report to management that if a household were drawn at random from the city and its income determined, it would almost certainly be between $15,372 and $31,928. What is wrong with her argument? How would you help her formulate a correct statement?

15H Choose a building near you that experiences a lot of traffic. If you attend a college or university, the student union is a good choice. Design a sampling plan to estimate the number of occupants of the building at 10:00 A.M. on a specified day. (This exercise will help you appreciate the task of the Census Bureau, which must estimate the number of "occupants" of the United States on April 1 of a census year!)

15I If you attend a college or university, design a stratified sampling scheme using faculty as one stratum and students as the other stratum. What will you use as a frame? Decide on a question of interest, for example, degree of satisfaction with computer facilities or athletic facilities. Carry out the sampling scheme. Compare faculty and student responses to the question. Estimate the average response of faculty and students combined.

Glossary for Chapter 15

clustering	Grouping elements according to their "nearness" to each other.
cluster sampling	A design in which a random sample of clusters is selected.
confidence interval	An interval computed from a sample such that the collection of such intervals from all possible samples has a specified probability of containing a parameter.
finite population correction factor (fpc)	$fpc = \sqrt{(N-n)/N}$
frame	The list of elements of the universe from which a sample is drawn.
N	Number of elements in a frame.
n	Size of the sample.
parameter	Numerical characteristic of a population—for example, the mean, denoted by μ.

population The set of measurements on a variable that the whole universe would yield were a census taken.

sampling fraction (f) $f = n/N$

simple random sample A sample taken so that each possible sample of size n has the same chance of being selected.

standard error The standard deviation of the sampling distribution of a statistic.

statistics Numerical characteristics of a sample, usually thought of as estimates of population parameters.

stratification Grouping elements in a frame according to some common characteristic or characteristics.

stratified sampling A design in which random samples are drawn from strata in the frame.

systematic sampling A design in which elements are chosen systematically from the frame after a random start (or starts) has been chosen.

variable A measured characteristic of elements.

Interpreting the Results of a Survey

Chapter Objectives

After mastering this chapter, you will be able to:

- Explore tables looking for interesting comparisons

- Calculate standard errors of sums and differences

- Assess the risks associated with multiple confidence intervals using the Bonferroni approach

16.1 Introduction to the Report

This chapter uses a published report to show how to interpret the results of a survey. First you look for interesting patterns and variations in the survey result. Then you learn how to calculate standard errors and confidence intervals for sums and differences of estimates. These calculations help you judge whether patterns you see in survey results are likely to reflect the actual universe or to result from chance. The report is *Diagnosis-Related Groups Using Data from the National Hospital Discharge Survey: United States, 1982,* by Robert Pokras and Kurt K. Kubishke. It was published January 18, 1985, by the National Center for Health Statistics (NCHS) as part of the series *advancedata* from Vital and Health Statistics.[†] The whole publication appears in the appendix to this chapter.

The report is relatively brief because it presents only a portion of the information gathered in a large survey called the National Hospital Discharge Survey (NHDS), which is conducted annually by the NCHS. The data in the report are taken from the 1982 NHDS.

Take a few minutes to look through the appendix to this chapter to develop a feel for the report's contents. The body consists of only two parts: Introduction and Highlights. Four tables, numbered 1 through 4, make up more than 50% of its contents.

[†]The National Center for Health Statistics is part of the Public Health Service, which is located at 3700 East-West Highway, Hyattsville, MD 20782.

The References section, which follows the body, is followed by the Technical Notes section, which consists of almost two pages of text and two tables numbered I and II.

Our focus will be on the tables and the technical notes. But first, we outline the problem the report addresses: estimating characteristics of diagnosis-related groups (DRGs). As noted in the Introduction of the report, DRGs were formed to help set uniform reimbursement rates for care of Medicare inpatients. Such patients compose about 30% of all discharges from short-stay nonfederal hospitals.

Two behavioral characteristics are studied in this report:

1   Number of discharges

2   Average length of stay in the hospital

Understanding these characteristics is important not only for the administration of Medicare but also for the administration of organizations that compete for health care dollars. For example, one thing you learn from this report is that the average length of stay in hospital is different in different parts of the country and in hospitals of different size. Yet the purpose of DRGs is to support a uniform reimbursement schedule for Medicare. What are the causes of the variation in length of stay? Are they related to quality of care, costs of materials, or ways of doing business that could be changed? Do they appear simply because the data were collected during a period when hospitals were just learning to deal with the reimbursement system based on DRGs? The report raises these and other important questions for further study and thought.

If you were working in a hospital that tended to keep patients longer than average, your hospital would be allocating more of its Medicare reimbursement to patient care than a hospital with shorter lengths of stay. You would want to look at the differences in the hospitals and to make sure the differences in lengths of stay had sound medical causes. On the basis of your study you might decide to lobby for changes in the Medicare reimbursement system. Or you might want to use some of the differences you find in a marketing effort to highlight the quality characteristics of your hospital.

SECTION

16.2   Initial Exploration of Tables

Before getting into the technical details, it is usually a good idea to form some initial impressions by treating the data in the tables as purely descriptive and looking for interesting patterns or variations. This creates a useful context for the inferential statistical analysis to follow

Look at Table 1 first. It displays numbers of discharges and average lengths of stay of patients under the age of 65, overall and by four geographic regions. These figures are given for all discharges and for discharges in 20 DRGs. The DRGs are listed down the page according to decreasing numbers of discharges for all regions combined. The major source of discharges for people under the age of 65 is "Vaginal delivery without complicating diagnoses"—that is, normal childbirth. The number of discharges reported is 2784 thousand, which we call about 2.8 million for convenience and clarity. The second largest source of discharges is "Medical back problems," with

790,000 discharges, and so on. Total discharges in 1982 are estimated at almost 28 million.

The four geographic regions are Northeast, North Central, South, and West. The states belonging to each region are given in the Technical Notes section under the heading "Definition of Terms." The regions are listed across the page according to decreasing average lengths of stay for all DRGs combined. The lengths of stay in the South and West appear to be substantially less than those in the Northeast and North Central. The national average length of stay is estimated at 5.9 days.

It is useful to compare the rankings within subgroups to overall rankings. For example, Exhibit 16.2A compares numbers of discharges and average lengths of stay for total discharges and vaginal delivery without complicating diagnoses. Notice that the orders of the average lengths of stay are the same for both All Discharges and Vaginal Delivery but that there is a reversal between the Northeast and West in the Number of Discharges. A reversal occurs when regions change places in the two rankings.

EXHIBIT 16.2A
Comparison of All Discharges and Vaginal Delivery Without Complicating Diagnoses for Four Regions of the United States, 1982

Number of Discharges		Average Length of Stay	
All Discharges (100s)	Vaginal Delivery (1000s)	All Discharges (days)	Vaginal Delivery (days)

	Number of Discharges		Average Length of Stay	
	All Discharges (100s)	Vaginal Delivery (1000s)	All Discharges (days)	Vaginal Delivery (days)
1000	S		6.5	NE
		S		NC
900			6.0	
800	NC		5.5	S
		NC		
700			5.0	W
600			4.5	
	NE	W		
500		NE	4.0	
400	W		3.5	NE
			3.0	NC
			2.5	S
			2.0	W

Note: NE = Northeast; NC = North Central; S = South; W = West

Source: National Hospital Discharge Survey, National Center for Health Statistics.

What other reversals do you find in Table 1 of the report? Look down the column of DRGs for a given geographic region and notice that the numbers of discharges are not always ordered the same way they are for national figures. There is some variation by geographic region.

The data could be ordered in other ways. For example, DRGs could be listed in decreasing order of average length of stay. Exhibit 16.2B shows the top five DRGs by this criterion, along with the averages for all regions and individual regions.

	Average Length of Stay				
Diagnosis-Related Group	All Regions	Northeast	North Central	South	West
Psychoses	16.5	19.1	19.7	13.8	11.6
Unrelated operating room procedures	11.2	13.8	12.0	9.7	10.1
Alcohol- and substance-induced organic mental syndrome	10.6	9.8	11.9	10.7	10.9
Diabetes, age greater than 35 years	8.2	9.9	8.7	7.4	6.4
Total cholecystectomy with common bile duct exploration, age less than 70 years without substantial comorbidity and/or complication	7.8	8.1	7.9	8.1	6.7

Source: National Hospital Discharge Survey, National Center for Health Statistics.

Within a given geographic region, the top five DRGs may not correspond to those given in Exhibit 16.2B. Our examination reveals variation among regions of the country in terms of both numbers of discharges and average lengths of stay.

Age is another source of variation. Table 2 of the report shows the same information as Table 1 except that it applies to people 65 years of age and over. It is no surprise that vaginal deliveries fail to make the list of important DRGs! Lens procedures account for the largest number of discharges nationwide, though they are not the greatest source of discharges in every region of the country.

Now compare average lengths of stay for "Unrelated operating room procedures" for the two age groups by region. This is done in Exhibit 16.2C.

For a given region, the average length of stay for the two age groups can be compared. The simplest way to compare is to subtract the length of stay for one group from the length of stay for the other group. The last column in Exhibit 16.2C shows these subtractions. The average lengths of stay are greater for the older age group, but the differences vary by geographic region. The smallest difference is in the West (4.9 days), the largest in the Northeast (6.2 days).

Similarly, for a given age group, average lengths of stay for different regions can be compared. Again this is done by subtracting. Take the group aged under 65 years. The average length of stay for the Northeast region is 13.8 days; for the North

E X H I B I T   **16.2C**
Comparison of Lengths of Stay
(in days) Due to Unrelated
Operating Room Procedures in
Short-Stay Nonfederal Hospitals,
by Age Grouping and by
Geographic Region, United
States, 1982

| | Age | | | | |
| | Under 65 Years | | 65 Years or More | | |
Region	Length of Stay	Difference	Length of Stay	Difference	**Difference**
All	11.2	—	17.3	—	6.1
Northeast	13.8		20.0		6.2
North Central	12.0	1.8	17.5	2.5	5.5
West	10.1	1.9	15.0	2.5	4.9
South	9.7	0.4	15.8	−0.8	6.1

Source: National Hospital Discharge Survey, National Center for Health Statistics.

Central region it is 12.0 days. The difference is 1.8 days, and this is recorded in the first Difference column in the exhibit. The second entry in that same column is $1.9 = 12.0 − 10.1$, the difference between the average lengths of stay in the North Central region and the West region. The other differences are calculated likewise. Comparing the differences between regions for the two age groups shows that the regional differences are somewhat larger for the older age group.

In this section, we have studied two of the tables in the report looking for interesting patterns of variation, and we have not been disappointed. The most striking finding is in the regional differences in average length of stay. It is also interesting that the South, which is far from the most densely populated region of the country, produces the largest numbers of discharges in both age groups.

Findings of similar magnitude and interest can be found in Tables 3 and 4; this search is left to you as an exercise. We also invite you to more fully explore Tables 1 and 2.

Our enthusiasm for our findings must be tempered by the realization that the numbers in the tables we have examined are estimates based on probability samples and so are subject to sampling error. They may also suffer from biases caused by nonsampling errors. How much impact do these sources of error have on the tentative conclusions we have drawn from the numbers treated strictly descriptively? That question is answered in the next section.

SECTION

16.3 Some Simple Interval Estimates

This section shows how to interpolate standard errors and determine confidence levels for survey findings in the survey report. These figures give you an idea of possible sampling errors affecting the findings.

Structure of Technical Notes

Before computing some simple interval estimates, we examine the Technical Notes of the report. We need to learn from these notes how to compute the standard errors of the estimates in the tables so we can compute confidence intervals.

The standard errors of the estimates in this report are computed by a much more complicated process than the one you have learned for simple random sampling, because the design used to collect the data is much more complicated than simple random sampling.

In the report of a complicated survey, we have to depend on the competence of the surveyor to produce proper standard errors as well as to indicate to what extent the data have or have not been adjusted for nonsampling error biases. In this case, the NCHS is quite a reliable source of information, and we have faith in their work. We nevertheless have some concerns that subtle problems with the data may not be presented in a brief report. We are prepared to question findings that do not correspond to our common sense. If such findings emerge, we would call NCHS to get our questions answered.

The Technical Notes are in two sections: Survey Methodology and Definition of Terms. The methodology section gives a brief sketch of the survey design and the estimation results, especially standard errors. Notice that the design involved stratification, the subject of Section 15.10, and probability sampling techniques much more subtle than simple random sampling. Such techniques are vital in conducting a large-scale survey of national scope. In the Data Collection and Estimation section we read that the estimates have been adjusted for nonresponse, so we know not all the chosen hospitals participated in the survey. The definition section sets forth the operational definitions used in the survey. For example, read the definitions of *Hospitals* and *Bed size of hospital.* Think about how the definitions might have been formulated differently, but still plausibly. Think about how these definitions would have been employed in the survey. What sorts of problems might have arisen? Definitions are crucial, especially if you compare the results of this survey with another survey that uses different definitions.

The techniques required to compute standard errors for such a survey have not yet been presented. Fortunately, the Sampling Errors and Rounding of Numbers section tells us how to get standard errors from Tables I and II. Table I is used for estimates of number of discharges, Table II for estimates of average lengths of stay.

Standard Errors

relative standard error

Look at Table I first. The table reports **relative standard errors**—that is, standard errors divided by the estimate. To convert a relative standard error to a standard error, the relative standard error must be multiplied by the estimate. That is why the table gives a range of sizes of the estimate. Note carefully that the relative standard errors are reported as percents. Thus they have the form $rse = 100(se/\text{Estimate})$, where rse is the relative standard error and se is the standard error. We see that

$$se = (rse)(\text{Estimate})/100 \qquad \textbf{(16.1)}$$

To illustrate, consider the number of discharges in the Northeast region due to vaginal deliveries without complicating diagnoses. This is reported in Table 1 as 524,000. How much sampling variation is present in this number? Table I is used to get the standard error. The estimate is approximately 500,000, so that line in the table is used. The corresponding relative standard error is 5.9. Formula (16.1) says the standard error is, therefore,

$$se = (5.9)(524,000)/100 = 30,916 \qquad \textbf{(16.2)}$$

The actual reported estimate was used in this calculation, not the approximate one of 500,000. A confidence interval will be computed and interpreted below.

If the size of the estimate is not close to any of the values in Table I, interpolation can be used to get relative standard errors. If the estimate is larger than 4 million, it is safe to treat the number as essentially exact, having no sampling error.

Now try your hand at a calculation. In Table 2, the number of discharges for lens procedures in the North Central region is reported as 127,000. Find the standard error of this estimate. You'll get slightly different answers depending on whether or not you decide to interpolate in Table I. If you interpolate, you get a standard error of about 10,414. If you do not interpolate but instead use the size of estimate = 100,000 in Table I, you get a standard error of about 10,795. The difference in the two standard errors is of little practical importance.

Now look at Table II. This table gives standard errors of estimates of average lengths of stay measured in days. The standard errors depend on the number of discharges reported and the average length of stay reported. To illustrate, look at the average length of stay for medical back problems in the North Central region. This is reported in Table 1 as 7.3 days. The number of discharges, also reported in Table 1, is 245,000. The crudest way to use Table II is to find the values nearest the reported values and use the standard error given in the table. To do this you would use number of discharges = 100,000 (the value nearest to 245,000) and average length of stay in days = 6 (the value nearest to 7.3). The corresponding standard error is 0.6 day.

A more precise way to use the table is to interpolate. Here is a format for interpolating in a two-way table:

	Average Length of Stay		
Number of Discharges	6	7.3	10
100,000	0.6		0.9
245,000		?	
500,000	0.5		0.8

The question mark shows the standard error we are after. Numerical analysts have developed many two-way interpolation schemes, but the rather small adjustments that we require do not warrant learning a sophisticated approach. Informally, we see that we need to go about 60% of the way between 100,000 and 500,000 in the Number of Discharges column and 33% of the way between 6 and 10 in the Average Length of Stay row. We enter 0.54 in the slot corresponding to number of discharges = 245,000 and average length of stay = 6. We enter 0.84 in the slot corresponding to number of discharges = 245,000 and average length of stay = 10. The value 33% of the way between these two numbers is about 0.64, and this will be used as our standard error. Notice that it is only slightly different from our crude value of 0.6.

Now you try a calculation. In Table 2, the average length of stay for unrelated operating room procedures in the North Central region is reported as 17.5 days, and the number of discharges is reported as 65,000. Use Table II to find a standard error for the estimated average length of stay. You will find the interpolated value is very little different from the crude value of 1.4.

Confidence Intervals

Many confidence intervals have the form

$$\text{Estimate} \pm (\text{Factor})(\text{Standard error})$$

where the factor used determines the level of confidence. As a rule, a factor of 3, which corresponds to a 99.7% confidence level, is preferred. A 0.3% risk of misestimating a parameter is acceptable, as a guideline, in an environment in which many estimations are made. Each estimation is made with a 0.997 probability of being correct, but this probability does not apply to a set of estimations.

If the estimations are made on independent samples, then the binomial distribution presented in Chapter 11 can be used to compute characteristics of sets of estimates. Let n denote the number of confidence intervals in the set, and assume for simplicity that all the confidence coefficients are 0.997. Then the probability that all n of the intervals contains the corresponding parameters of interest is the probability of n successes, namely, $(0.997)^n$. The probability that at least one of the intervals does not contain the parameter of interest is $1 - (0.997)^n$. The probability that exactly one of the intervals does not contain the parameter of interest is $n(0.997)^{n-1}(0.003)$. Values of these probabilities for selected values of n are given in Exhibit 16.3A.

E X A M P L E   16.3A

Look at the $n = 18$ line in Exhibit 16.3A. The figures say that if 18 independent 99.7% confidence intervals are made, there is a 94.7% chance that all the intervals are correct, a 5.1% chance that exactly one interval is incorrect, and a 5.3% chance that at least one interval is incorrect.

People who engage in scientific studies tend to use a factor of 2 in the confidence interval formula, which corresponds to about a 95% level of confidence. This is scientific tradition, but it is not without its critics. For example, if 18 independent 95% confidence intervals are made, there is a 39.7% chance that all the intervals are correct, a 37.6% chance that exactly one interval is incorrect, and a 60.3% chance that at least one interval is incorrect. These probabilities are distinctly inferior to the ones for $n = 18$ in Exhibit 16.3A. ■

In practical applications, intervals are often constructed for parameters of many variables for which the same sample provides data. In such situations, the confidence intervals are not independent. The characteristics of dependent intervals are more difficult to calculate than those for independent intervals because a simple model

EXHIBIT **16.3A**
Probabilistic Behavior of Sets of
n Independent Confidence
Intervals

Number of Intervals n	Probability All Intervals Correct $(0.997)^n$	Probability One Interval Incorrect $n(0.997)^{n-1}(0.003)$	Probability at Least One Interval Incorrect $1 - (0.997)^n$
1	.997000	.0030000	.0030000
2	.994009	.0059820	.0059910
3	.991027	.0089461	.0089731
4	.988054	.0118924	.0119462
5	.985090	.0148209	.0149104
6	.982134	.0177317	.0178657
7	.979188	.0206250	.0208121
8	.976250	.0235007	.0237496
9	.973322	.0263589	.0266784
10	.970402	.0291999	.0295984
11	.967490	.0320235	.0325096
12	.964588	.0348299	.0354121
13	.961694	.0376192	.0383059
14	.958809	.0403914	.0411910
15	.955932	.0431467	.0440675
16	.953065	.0458848	.0469350
17	.950206	.0486063	.0497940
18	.947355	.0513110	.0526450

like the binomial cannot be used. We therefore simply state the most useful practical result: if n $100(1 - \alpha)\%$ confidence intervals are computed, then the probability that they are all correct is at least $1 - n\alpha$, and the probability that at least one is incorrect is no more than $n\alpha$.[†]

EXAMPLE   **16.3B**

To illustrate the result stated in the previous paragraph, consider two decision makers who have made 18 dependent confidence interval estimates, one using 3-standard-error intervals, the other 2-standard-error intervals. The probability that the former has constructed 18 correct intervals is at least $1 - 18(0.003) = 1 - 0.054 = 0.946$. This is very close to the probability that would have applied if the intervals had been independent, which is reported as 0.947 in Exhibit 16.3A. The probability that the decision maker who uses 2-standard-error intervals makes 18 correct ones is at least $1 - 18(0.05) = 1 - 0.9 = 0.1$, not a very reassuring guarantee.   ∎

[†]This result is based on Bonferroni's inequality. It can be generalized to say that if n confidence intervals with confidence coefficients $1 - \alpha_1, 1 - \alpha_2, \ldots, 1 - \alpha_n$ are made, the chance that they are all correct is at least $1 - \alpha_1 - \alpha_2 - \cdots - \alpha_n$, and the chance that at least one is incorrect is at most $\alpha_1 + \alpha_2 + \cdots + \alpha_n$. See Appendix 2.

Even 3-standard-error confidence intervals can prove inadequate in the face of a large number of applications. In practice, we recommend using 3-standard-error intervals as a guideline, but you need to keep track of the number of intervals you compute and make sure that $1 - n\alpha$ does not get too small. As n increases, you need to decrease α to control the risk of making too many incorrect intervals.

Numerically, the computation of a confidence interval is quite simple once the value of the estimate and the value of the standard error are known. For example, in the Northeast region the number of discharges due to vaginal deliveries without complicating diagnoses was estimated as 524,000 with a standard error of 30,916. A 99.7% confidence interval for the number of discharges is thus

$$524,000 \pm 3(30,916) = 524,000 \pm 92,748$$

Because the original estimate was given to only three significant figures (524), the confidence limits should also be rounded to three significant figures. Thus our final report is that the number of discharges is (almost certainly)

$$524,000 \pm 93,000$$

We are quite confident that if sampling error were the only source of error, then the equal complete coverage number of discharges would be somewhere between 431,000 and 617,000.

Because we are told that the estimates have been adjusted for nonresponse, we feel that at least one source of bias has been minimized. We do not know what other sources of bias may be present in the data, so we do not want to make an unqualified statement about the total number of discharges. That is why we said *if sampling error were the only source of error.* Since the report mentions no major source of nonsampling bias, we feel that the confidence interval in fact deserves roughly the 99.7% level of confidence.

Keep in mind that we are estimating the equal complete coverage number of discharges, that is, the number we would have gotten if we had applied the survey methods to the whole universe of hospitals.

Confidence intervals for average length of stay are handled in exactly the same way, so a detailed example is not given. Instead we turn to making comparisons, a more interesting, but slightly more complicated, process.

SECTION

16.4 Comparison of Groups: Estimates, Standard Errors, and Confidence Intervals

In exploring Tables 1 and 2 in Section 16.2, most of our time was spent making comparisons. In Exhibit 16.2A, regional frequency and length of stay for a DRG were compared with the frequency and stays for all DRGs combined. A number of DRGs that did not behave exactly like the combined category were noted in Table 1. This showed variation among DRGs with respect to regions. In Exhibit 16.2B, DRGs were compared and ranked with respect to average length of stay. Again regional differences were found, this time in the rankings. In Exhibit 16.2C, average lengths of stay for unrelated operating room procedures were compared across four geographic regions and two age groups. The geographic differences appeared to be more pronounced for the older age group than for the younger.

Every number in the three exhibits is an estimate, so each one is subject to sampling and nonsampling errors. This means that a part of every difference computed is error. Our job is to discover what part of any difference we have calculated is error and what part points to a genuine difference in the equal complete coverage values associated with the universe.

This is done by computing standard errors of the numbers obtained when estimates are subtracted. Some of the rules for computing standard errors of functions of estimates are quite simple. Fortunately, these simple rules often suffice, and they will be the focus here. Formulas for standard errors of more complicated functions can be found in more advanced books on statistics.

Sums and Differences of Two Estimates

The easiest and most useful rule is the **Pythagorean rule** for sums and differences of independent estimates.[†]

Pythagorean rule

> Whether two independent estimates are added or subtracted, the standard error of the result is computed by taking the square root of the sum of the squares of the standard errors of the estimates.

The rule can also be stated symbolically. Let E_1 and E_2 be two estimates whose standard errors are se_1 and se_2. Then the standard error of either $E_1 + E_2$ or $E_1 - E_2$ is

standard error of a sum or difference

$$se = \sqrt{se_1^2 + se_2^2}$$

You see why this is called the Pythagorean rule: The same formula is used to find the length of the hypotenuse of a right triangle. Exhibit 16.4A shows the result geometrically. You saw this triangle before, showing the interaction of sampling and nonsampling error in Chapter 14.

[†]Estimates are independent if different random numbers are used to select the data used to form the estimates. This will typically be the case when, as in the NHDS, the universe is stratified—that is, broken into several distinct groups. Fresh random numbers are used to draw data from each group. Technically speaking, the DRGs are poststratification groups and so are only conditionally independent. For practical purposes, their standard errors may be computed as if they were completely independent.

E X H I B I T **16.4A**
The Pythagorean Rule for
Computing the Standard Error of
a Sum or Difference

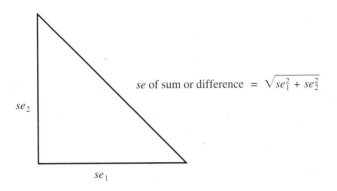

$$se \text{ of sum or difference } = \sqrt{se_1^2 + se_2^2}$$

Examples

To illustrate the result numerically, some standard errors are attached to the differences shown in Exhibit 16.2C. The difference between the Northeast and North Central regions for people under the age of 65 is

$$1.8 = 13.8 - 12.0 \tag{16.3}$$

To compute the standard error for the difference, we first find standard errors of the estimates that are subtracted. Table II provides a standard error of 1.0 for the estimate 13.8 and a standard error of 0.9 for the estimate 12.0. The standard errors have been computed crudely and rounded to one significant decimal place. Equation (16.3) is repeated, with standard errors placed in parentheses under the estimates:

$$
\begin{aligned}
1.8 &= 13.8 - 12.0 \\
(\ \ ) &\quad (1.0)\ \ (0.9)
\end{aligned}
\tag{16.4}
$$

We must now compute the standard error of the difference 1.8 and insert it under the estimate. Using the Pythagorean rule,

$$se = \sqrt{(1.0)^2 + (0.9)^2} = \sqrt{1.81} = 1.3 \tag{16.5}$$

We can now state that we estimate the difference in the equal complete coverage lengths of stay in the Northeast and North Central regions to be 1.8 days with a standard error of 1.3 days. A 99.7% confidence interval for the difference in days is

$$1.8 \pm 3(1.3) = 1.8 \pm 3.9 = [-2.1, 5.7] \tag{16.6}$$

The confidence interval says the equal complete coverage difference could be positive or negative. A positive difference indicates a longer average length of stay in the Northeast than in the North Central. A negative difference indicates a longer average length of stay in the North Central than in the Northeast. The sampling error in the estimate does not allow us to rule out either possibility conclusively. The average length of stay in the Northeast may be as much as 5.7 days longer than the average length of stay in the North Central, or the average length of stay in the North Central may be as much as 2.1 days longer than the average length of stay in the

Northeast. Larger samples from these regions would have been needed to get more conclusive information.

Now try your hand at a calculation. The difference between the Northeast and North Central for patients over the age of 65 is

$$2.5 = 20.0 - 17.5$$

Compute the confidence interval for the difference in the equal complete coverage values. Do the data allow you to conclude that one region almost certainly has a longer average length of stay than the other?

As another example, compute the standard error of the difference between average lengths of stay for the two age groups in the North Central region. The desired difference is

$$5.5 = 17.5 - 12.0$$
$$(\quad)\quad(1.4)\quad(0.9) \tag{16.7}$$

The standard errors of the estimates have been found in the usual way from Table II. The computation of the standard error of the difference is

$$se = \sqrt{(1.4)^2 + (0.9)^2} = \sqrt{2.77} = 1.7 \tag{16.8}$$

Thus a 99.7% confidence interval for the difference in the equal complete coverage values in days is

$$5.5 \pm 3(1.7) = 5.5 \pm 5.1 = [0.4, 10.6] \tag{16.9}$$

The evidence is fairly conclusive that in the North Central region, the average length of stay for people over age 65 is greater than the average length of stay for people under the age of 65. The difference could be as small as 0.4 day and as large as 10.6 days.

Exhibit 16.4B is a repeat of Exhibit 16.2C with the standard errors of all the numbers shown in parentheses. You may wish to verify a few of the calculations just to internalize the process. Try to compute a confidence interval or two and give interpretations. Remember, it is the confidence interval that conveys the information. The calculations are simply an intermediate step.

EXHIBIT 16.4B
Repeat of Exhibit 16.2C with
Standard Errors (in
parentheses); Comparison of
Lengths of Hospital Stay (in
days) by Age Grouping and
Region

| | Age | | | | |
| | Under 65 Years | | 65 Years or More | | |
Region	Length of Stay	Difference	Length of Stay	Difference	**Difference**
All	11.2		17.3		6.1
	(0.8)		(1.0)		(1.3)
Northeast	13.8		20.0		6.2
	(1.0)		(1.4)		(1.7)
		1.8		2.5	
		(1.3)		(2.0)	
North Central	12.0		17.5		5.5
	(0.9)		(1.4)		(1.7)
		1.9		2.5	
		(1.3)		(2.1)	
West	10.1		15.0		4.9
	(1.0)		(1.6)		(1.9)
		0.4		−0.8	
		(1.3)		(1.9)	
South	9.7		15.8		6.1
	(0.9)		(1.1)		(1.4)

SECTION

16.5 Exercises

16.5A   Refer to Exhibit 16.4B. Verify each of the estimates and standard errors for the West region. For the West region compute the 99.7% confidence interval for the difference between the average length of stay for persons over age 65 and for persons under age 65. Give a precise verbal interpretation of the interval. Now compute the 95% confidence interval for the same difference and give a precise verbal interpretation of that interval. One interval contains zero while the other does not. How do you explain this apparent contradiction?

16.5B   Refer to Exhibit 16.4B. For patients under age 65, compute the 99.7% confidence interval for the difference between the average length of stay in the Northeast region and in the West region. Does there appear to be a conclusive difference in the two regions? Repeat the exercise for patients 65 years of age and older.

16.5C   Independent simple random samples are selected from two large groups of people and measurements on a variable y collected. These are the descriptive statistics:

Group	Sample Size	Mean ($\bar{y}$)	Standard Deviation
A	75	110	8.7
B	120	107	10.2

Compute the standard error of the difference between the group means. Compute a 99.7% confidence interval for the difference in the equal complete coverage means. An analyst claims the data conclusively show that group A has a larger mean than group B. What is your response?

16.5D In a large company, a simple random sample of managers is selected and the managers are asked if they favor a certain change in the company's pension plan. An independent simple random sample of hourly workers is also selected and asked the same question. The results are displayed below.

Group	Sample Size	Number in Favor of Change	Proportion in Favor of Change
Managers	50	32	0.64
Hourly workers	100	51	0.51

An analyst claims the data show that a substantially higher proportion of managers than hourly workers favor the change. Compute the 99.7% confidence interval for the difference in the equal complete coverage proportions and comment on the analyst's claim in the light of the confidence interval. Do the data provide conclusive evidence that a majority of all managers favor the change? A majority of all hourly workers?

16.5E Locate a published report of a probability survey. Examine the report for discussion of sampling design, standard errors, treatment of nonsampling errors, and operational definitions. How fully and clearly are these issues discussed? On the basis of your study, formulate a judgment on the credibility and usefulness of the report. Formulate at least one comparison for which the report provides sufficient information to compute a confidence interval. Formulate at least one comparison for which the report does *not* provide sufficient information to compute a confidence interval.

Chapter Summary

Many organizations collect important data and give summaries of their findings in reports. When a probability survey is used to collect the data, the report should give standard errors of the estimates, allowing a more sophisticated interpretation of the findings. For example, one can assess the probable difference between two parameters by computing a confidence interval. Doing so requires the calculation of the standard error of the difference between the estimates, which is done with the Pythagorean rule. The Pythagorean rule, $se = \sqrt{se_1^2 + se_2^2}$, applies to both the sum and difference of independent estimates. If several confidence intervals are computed at the same confidence level, the probability of all of them being correct is less than the probability associated with the individual intervals. To reduce the risk of computing many incorrect intervals, it is a good idea to keep the confidence levels of the individual intervals high, say at 99.7%.

Supplementary Exercises for Chapter 16

16A An auditor must examine two sets of accounts and determine the dollar amount of the difference between the amount recorded in the account and the amount the auditor considers correct. She does not have time to examine every account and so examines simple random samples from each set of accounts. Here are the results of her work. The data are reported in $1000 units.

Set	Number[†]	Sample Size	Mean	Standard Deviation
A	4,000	75	110	8.7
B	10,000	120	107	10.2

[†]This is the total number of accounts in the set.

a   Compute a 99.7% confidence interval for the total amount of difference between recorded and correct values in set A.

b   Compute a 99.7% confidence interval for the total amount of difference between recorded and correct values in set B.

c   Compute a 99.7% confidence interval for the total amount of difference between recorded and correct values in the two sets.

16B   An instructor teaches two sections of the same class. At the end of the class each student is asked to rate the instructor on her overall performance on a five-point scale, with 1 indicating poor performance and 5 indicating outstanding performance. Here is a summary of the responses from the two classes:

Section	Section Size	Mean	Standard Deviation
A	75	3.9	0.9
B	120	4.1	1.2

The instructor believes that student ratings are subject to a certain amount of subjectivity that can be approximated by assuming that they behave *as if* they were obtained by simple random sampling from a population of ratings. She therefore feels justified in computing confidence intervals using the data. The confidence intervals display the range of average ratings possible provided her assumption is valid.

a   Accepting the instructor's assumption, compute the 99.7% confidence interval for the average rating from section A.

b   Accepting the instructor's assumption, compute the 99.7% confidence interval for the average rating from section B.

c   Accepting the instructor's assumption, compute the 99.7% confidence interval for the average rating from the two sections combined.

d   Accepting the instructor's assumption, compute the 99.7% confidence interval for the difference between the average ratings from the two sections. Do the sections seem to have rated her differently?

16C   A random digit dialing survey of city residents was conducted to estimate use of natural and artificial Christmas trees. A survey of 800 residences produced 693 residences that set up Christmas trees in their homes last year. These residences were asked if the tree was natural or artificial. There were 245 artificial trees and 448 natural trees. Using a sample size of $n = 693$, compute the 99.7% confidence interval for the difference between the proportion of the city population that uses artificial trees and the proportion of the city population that uses natural trees. Also compute the 99.7% confidence interval for the proportion of city residents who display no tree at all.

Glossary for Chapter 16

Pythagorean rule   Formula for the standard error of a sum or difference of two independent estimates.

relative standard error   Standard errors divided by the estimate, often expressed as a percent.

standard error of a sum or difference $se = \sqrt{se_1^2 + se_2^2}$

APPENDIX

Diagnosis-Related Groups Using Data from the National Hospital Discharge Survey: United States, 1982[†]

Introduction

This report presents selected estimates for 1982 of diagnosis-related groups (DRGs) based on data from the National Hospital Discharge Survey (NHDS). A similar report has been published for 1981.[1] The current plan is to publish reports on DRGs regularly because they determine the reimbursement rates of Medicare inpatients, about 30 percent of all discharges from short-stay nonfederal hospitals.[2]

Developed at the Yale School of Organization and Management, DRGs are being used by the Health Care Financing Administration, some states, and some third-party payers to reimburse hospitals for inpatient care on a prospective basis.[3] This approach to health care reimbursement operates on the principle that patients with similar medical conditions should receive similar care and use approximately the same amount of resources; therefore, in general a hospital should be reimbursed the same amount for each patient in a DRG. While there is

variation in resource consumption among individuals within a DRG, these are expected to balance across all patients.

DRGs were developed under the guiding principle that "The primary objective in the construction of DRGs was a definition of case type, each of which could be expected to receive similar outputs or services from a hospital."[4] Their formulation was accomplished using clinical judgment and statistical procedures that classify patients by measuring resource utilization. The first step in this process was to cluster the universe of medical diagnoses into broad, mutually exclusive categories. These groups were formed to be consistent in their anatomical or physio-pathological classification, or in a manner in which they are clinically managed. Once these major diagnostic groups were formed, an interactive statistical program (AUTOGROUP[4]) was used to further classify each major group into discrete DRGs. This process incorporated patient information regarding diagnoses (primary and secondary), procedures, sex, and age to explain maximally a patient's length of stay. In all, there currently are 470 DRGs.

Prospective reimbursement was authorized under the Tax Equity and Fiscal Responsibility Act of 1983. Under this act hospitals participating in the Medicare program were brought into this system beginning with their fiscal year as of October 1, 1983.

[†]By Robert Pokras and Kurt K. Kubishke, Division of Health Care Statistics. From *Vital and Health Statistics of the National Center for Health Statistics*, Number 105, January 18, 1985. Used with permission.

The Health Care Financing Administration, which operates the Medicare program, is allowing several years for hospitals to make a transition to prospective reimbursement by adjusting DRG payments based on certain hospital characteristics and geographic location. At the end of this phase-in period, care provided to a Medicare inpatient will translate into a preestablished payment based solely on the patient's DRG.

There is an important issue related to the NHDS and the implementation of this prospective reimbursement system: how this system may affect the selection of a patient's principal diagnosis and/or comorbidities. Because the NHDS is designed to collect data on the morbidity of the hospital inpatient population, any external influence on diagnostic practices may affect NHDS data. For example, two patients admitted to a hospital for treatment of chest pain—one diagnosed as having chest pain and the other diagnosed as having angina—will be placed into different DRGs and have different reimbursement rates. There is speculation that in cases such as this prospective reimbursement may influence the selection of a diagnosis,[3] which in turn may affect estimates produced from the NHDS. After prospective payment has been in place for a few years, it may be possible to examine trends in NHDS data and determine the magnitude, if any, of this type of effect.

The statistics in this report are based on data collected by means of the NHDS, a continuous survey conducted by the National Center for Health Statistics since 1965. Data for this survey are sampled from short-stay nonfederal general and specialty hospitals in the 50 states and the District of Columbia. The sample for 1982 contained approximately 214,000 medical records from 426 hospitals. The relevant variables required to produce DRGs (diagnoses, procedures, sex, age, and other variables) were abstracted from the face sheet of each sampled medical record, and NHDS data thereby could be used to produce national estimates of DRGs. These estimates may be of value for hospitals to compare their experience with that of other hospitals. For this reason, statistics in this report are frequency estimates and associated average length of stay for DRGs by hospital bed size and region of the country.

Highlights

The frequency and average length of stay for the most common DRGs are presented by age, region of the country, and hospital bed size (Tables 1–4). Age is dichotomized as under 65 years of age and 65 years of age and older. This allows a comparison with the Medicare population because Medicare covers most hospital costs for approximately 94 percent of discharges 65 years of age and over. Tables 1 and 2 provide regional data, while Tables 3 and 4 provide bed-size data for these DRGs. Within each of these sets of tables, the first (Tables 1 and 3) are for patients under 65 years of age, and the second (Tables 2 and 4) are for patients 65 years of age and over.

By definition, some DRGs are only for patients in a specific age range. In such a case the DRG title and the table title (Tables 1–4) together define the age group of the estimate. That is, the most restrictive case of either the table or DRG title determines the age group of the estimate. For example, "Diabetes, age greater than 35 years" in Table 2 only refers to patients 65 years of age and over because of the table title; whereas "Simple pneumonia and pleurisy, age greater than 69 years and/or substantial comorbidity and complication" in Table 2 would not include a patient under 70 years of age because of the restriction in the DRG title.

The most common DRG for patients under 65 years of age was "Vaginal delivery without complicating diagnoses" (Table 1), with an estimated 2.8 million discharges in 1982. "Cesarean section without substantial comorbidity and/or complication," with 649,000 discharges, also was among the most frequent DRGs in this age group. For patients 65 years of age and older (Table 2), "Lens procedures" was the most common DRG, 429,000, and "Atherosclerosis, age greater than 69 years and/or substantial comorbidity and complication," 427,000, was the second most common DRG for the elderly.

The average length of stay for specific DRGs in the four regions of the country generally reflects the pattern found for all patients: the Northeast and North Central have the longest average length of stay and the West has the shortest. Regional length-of-stay differences were greater for patients 65 years of age or more than for younger patients. The West

T A B L E **1**   Number of Discharges and Average Length of Stay of Patients under 65 Years of Age Discharged from Short-Stay Hospitals, by Selected Diagnosis-Related Groups and Geographic Regions: United States, 1982 (Discharges from nonfederal short-stay hospitals. Excludes newborn infants.)

Diagnosis-Related Group	All Regions	Northeast	North Central	South	West	All Regions	Northeast	North Central	South	West
	Number in Thousands					Average Length of Stay in Days				
All discharges	27,896	5,564	7,929	9,804	4,598	5.9	6.5	6.3	5.6	5.0
Vaginal delivery without complicating diagnoses	2,784	524	765	937	559	2.9	3.4	3.3	2.7	2.2
Medical back problems	790	121	245	298	125	7.2	9.0	7.3	6.8	6.2
Esophagitis, gastroenteritis, and miscellaneous digestive disorders, age 18–69 years without substantial comorbidity and/or complication	673	97	178	320	78	4.1	4.5	4.2	4.2	3.3
Cesarean section without substantial comorbidity and/or complication	649	125	145	258	121	5.7	6.7	6.2	5.3	4.8
Nonradical hysterectomy, age less than 70 years without substantial comorbidity and/or complication	495	70	128	212	85	7.2	7.9	7.6	7.1	6.2
Unrelated operating room procedures	401	75	116	145	65	11.2	13.8	12.0	9.7	10.1
Esophagitis, gastroenteritis, and miscellaneous digestive disorders, age 0–17 years	392	69	111	173	39	3.8	3.9	3.8	3.8	3.3
Psychoses	388	95	118	108	68	16.5	19.1	19.7	13.8	11.6
Alcohol- and substance-induced organic mental syndrome	360	157	90	68	45	10.6	9.8	11.9	10.7	10.9
Dilation and curettage of uterus: conization except for malignancy	345	111	85	118	32	1.8	1.7	1.9	2.0	1.2
Abortion with dilation and curettage of uterus	325	136	65	86	39	1.3	1.0	1.7	1.5	1.1
Bronchitis and asthma, age 0–17 years	313	65	96	118	34	3.9	4.6	3.8	3.8	3.3
Simple pneumonia and pleurisy, age 0–17 years	279	36	86	131	28	4.7	5.3	5.0	4.6	4.1
Tonsillectomy and/or adenoidectomy, age 0–17 years	279	43	106	83	48	1.8	1.7	1.9	2.1	1.2
Inguinal and femoral hernia procedures, age 18–69 years without substantial comorbidity and/or complication	271	76	74	80	42	4.2	4.0	4.4	4.7	3.0
Diabetes, age greater than 35 years	259	52	72	104	30	8.2	9.9	8.7	7.4	6.4

T A B L E **1**   (Continued)

Diagnosis-Related Group	All Regions	Northeast	North Central	South	West	All Regions	Northeast	North Central	South	West
	Number in Thousands					Average Length of Stay in Days				
Vaginal delivery with sterilization and/or dilation and curettage of uterus	247	44	57	110	37	3.6	4.2	4.1	3.3	2.8
Other factors influencing health status	242	53	68	75	46	3.5	3.6	3.8	3.2	3.4
Total cholecystectomy with common bile duct exploration, age less than 70 years without substantial comorbidity and/or complication	233	48	63	83	39	7.8	8.1	7.9	8.1	6.7
Bronchitis and asthma, age 18–69 years without substantial comorbidity and/or complication	227	45	62	81	38	5.3	5.9	5.8	4.9	4.6

T A B L E **2**   Number of Discharges and Average Length of Stay of Patients 65 Years of Age and Over Discharged from Short-Stay Hospitals, by Selected Diagnosis-Related Groups and Geographic Regions: United States, 1982 (Discharges from nonfederal short-stay hospitals. Excludes newborn infants.)

Diagnosis-Related Group	All Regions	Northeast	North Central	South	West	All Regions	Northeast	North Central	South	West
	Number in Thousands					Average Length of Stay in Days				
All discharges	10, 697	2, 283	3, 008	3, 631	1, 774	10.1	12.3	10.3	9.4	8.2
Lens procedures	429	81	127	119	102	2.9	3.0	3.3	3.0	2.4
Atherosclerosis, age greater than 69 years and/or substantial comorbidity and complication	427	99	109	157	62	8.7	10.9	9.0	8.2	6.3
Heartfailure and shock	387	88	108	132	59	9.7	11.8	10.3	8.8	7.7
Esophagitis, gastroenteritis, and miscellaneous digestive disorders, age greater than 69 years and/or substantial comorbidity and complication	376	63	102	169	42	6.7	8.3	6.9	6.3	5.8
Chronic obstructive pulmonary disease	300	54	76	117	54	9.8	11.9	10.2	8.8	9.2
Specific cerebrovascular disorders except transient ischemic attack	295	64	76	103	52	15.4	20.4	16.2	13.2	12.2

T A B L E 2 (Continued)

Diagnosis-Related Group	All Regions	Northeast	North Central	South	West	All Regions	Northeast	North Central	South	West
	Number in Thousands					Average Length of Stay in Days				
Simple pneumonia and pleurisy, age greater than 69 years and/or substantial comorbidity and complication	276	51	80	106	38	10.7	11.8	10.6	10.7	9.5
Unrelated operating room procedures	226	59	65	72	29	17.3	20.0	17.5	15.8	15.0
Diabetes, age greater than 35 years	208	49	56	77	24	10.0	13.9	9.7	8.4	8.1
Angina pectoris	195	49	47	67	32	6.6	8.0	6.4	6.6	4.9
Medical back problems	186	38	58	63	27	9.3	11.5	9.7	7.7	8.8
Cardiac arrhythmia and conduction disorders, age greater than 69 years and/or substantial comorbidity and complication	181	35	51	65	30	7.1	9.1	7.2	7.1	4.8
Circulatory disorders with acute myocardial infarction without cardiovascular complications, discharged alive	174	44	44	62	24	12.2	13.6	12.9	11.8	9.4
Hypertension	158	28	43	70	17	7.9	8.8	7.7	7.6	8.4
Transient ischemic attacks	155	39	42	52	22	7.6	9.6	7.8	7.3	4.3
Bronchitis and asthma age greater than 69 years and/or substantial comorbidity and complication	148	22	38	59	29	8.3	9.2	8.0	8.3	8.0
Transurethral prostatectomy, age greater than 69 years and/or substantial comorbidity and complication	144	29	42	45	28	9.3	11.1	9.5	9.4	6.8
Kidney and urinary tract infections age greater than 69 years and/or substantial comorbidity and complication	142	23	34	67	17	8.5	9.9	8.8	8.1	7.1
Respiratory neoplasms	137	36	34	43	24	10.9	11.0	11.9	11.2	9.0
Hip and femur procedures except major joint, age greater than 69 years and/or substantial comorbidity and complication	135	27	45	38	25	19.5	25.1	19.9	18.5	14.3

T A B L E **3**   Number of Discharges and Average Length of Stay of Patients under 65 Years of Age Discharged from Short-Stay Hospitals by Selected Diagnosis-Related Groups and Hospital Bed Size: United States, 1982 (Discharges from nonfederal short-stay hospitals. Excludes newborn infants.)

Diagnosis-Related Group	All Hospitals	6-99 Beds	100-199 Beds	200-299 Beds	300-399 Beds	500 or More Beds	All Hospitals	6-99 Beds	100-199 Beds	200-299 Beds	300-399 Beds	500 or More Beds
	Number in Thousands						Average Length of Stay in Days					
All discharges	27, 896	4, 664	4, 906	4, 459	6, 909	6, 958	5.9	4.5	5.3	5.7	6.2	6.8
Vaginal delivery without complicating diagnoses	2, 784	425	466	433	700	759	2.9	2.4	2.8	2.8	3.1	3.2
Medical back problems	790	170	137	150	185	149	7.2	6.3	7.0	7.5	7.6	7.6
Esophagitis gastroenteritis and miscellaneous digestive disorders age 18-69 years without substantial comorbidity and/or complication	673	191	116	115	143	108	4.1	3.3	4.3	4.6	4.2	4.8
Cesarean section without substantial comorbidity and/or complication	649	75	123	93	175	183	5.7	5.4	5.2	5.5	5.8	6.1
Nonradical hysterectomy, age less than 70 years without substantial comorbidity and/or complication	495	51	111	80	126	125	7.2	7.1	6.5	7.4	7.3	7.5
Unrelated operating room procedures	401	50	65	65	98	123	11.2	6.9	7.7	12.8	13.0	12.5
Esophagitis, gastroenteritis, and miscellaneous digestive disorders, age 0–17	392	82	97	60	78	75	3.8	2.7	3.7	3.8	4.0	4.8
Psychoses	388	34	74	40	137	103	16.5	12.0	14.5	15.1	15.8	20.9
Alcohol- and substance-induced organic mental syndrome	360	105	59	39	97	60	10.6	9.6	13.5	12.9	9.9	9.4
Dilation and curettage of uterus; conization except for malignancy	345	56	78	43	81	87	1.8	1.8	1.7	2.1	1.9	1.6
Abortion with dilation and curettage of uterus	325	36	68	41	78	102	1.3	1.6	1.4	1.5	1.2	1.1
Bronchitis and asthma, age 0–17 years	313	59	79	50	70	56	3.9	3.4	3.8	4.5	4.1	3.8
Simple pneumonia and pleurisy, age 0–17 years	279	85	63	48	49	35	4.7	4.1	4.9	5.0	5.2	4.9
Tonsillectomy and/or adenoidectomy, age 0–17 years	279	52	55	63	68	41	1.8	1.6	1.8	1.9	1.7	1.9
Inguinal and femoral hernia procedures, age 18–69 years without substantial comorbidity and/or complication	271	40	50	45	72	64	4.2	4.2	3.9	4.4	4.2	4.2
Diabetes, age greater than 35 years	259	57	43	53	56	50	8.24	6.2	7.2	8.2	9.4	9.7

T A B L E **3** (Continued)

Diagnosis-Related Group	All Hospitals	6-99 Beds	100-199 Beds	200-299 Beds	300-399 Beds	500 or More Beds	All Hospitals	6-99 Beds	100-199 Beds	200-299 Beds	300-399 Beds	500 or More Beds
	Number in Thousands						Average Length of Stay in Days					
Vaginal delivery with sterilization and/or dilation and curettage of uterus	247	47	47	41	47	65	3.6	3.4	3.3	3.5	3.7	3.8
Other factors influencing health status	242	35	38	39	58	73	3.5	3.1	4.0	3.5	3.6	3.4
Total cholecystectomy with common bile duct exploration, age less than 70 years without substantial comorbidity and/or complication	233	44	41	34	65	48	7.8	7.2	7.5	8.4	8.4	7.4
Bronchitis and asthma, age 18–69 years without substantial comorbidity and/or complication	227	60	37	38	45	46	5.3	4.8	5.3	5.0	5.7	5.8

T A B L E **4** Number of Discharges and Average Length of Stay of Patients 65 Years of Age or Over Discharged from Short-Stay Hospitals by Selected Diagnosis-Related Groups and Hospital Bed Size: United States, 1982 (Discharges from nonfederal short-stay hospitals. Excludes newborn infants.)

Diagnosis-Related Group	All Hospitals	6-99 Beds	100-199 Beds	200-299 Beds	300-399 Beds	500 or More Beds	All Hospitals	6-99 Beds	100-199 Beds	200-299 Beds	300-399 Beds	500 or More Beds
	Number in Thousands						Average Length of Stay in Days					
All discharges	10,697	2,172	1,832	1,907	2,638	2,148	10.1	8.1	9.6	10.2	10.8	11.5
Lens procedures	429	32	94	85	118	99	2.9	2.9	3.0	2.6	3.0	3.1
Atherosclerosis, age greater than 69 years and/or substantial comorbidity and complication	427	90	87	80	107	63	8.7	7.3	8.1	8.8	9.6	10.2
Heart failure and shock	387	113	70	68	82	54	9.7	8.1	9.3	10.5	10.8	11.0
Esophagitis, gastroenteritis, and miscellaneous digestive disorders, age greater than 69 years and/or substantial comorbidity and complication	376	123	60	64	78	51	6.7	5.6	7.2	6.9	8.3	6.5
Chronic obstructive pulmonary disease	300	76	48	58	71	48	9.8	8.1	9.5	10.7	10.6	10.5

T A B L E **4**   (Continued)

Diagnosis-Related Group	All Hospitals	6-99 Beds	100-199 Beds	200-299 Beds	300-399 Beds	500 or More Beds	All Hospitals	6-99 Beds	100-199 Beds	200-299 Beds	300-399 Beds	500 or More Beds
	Number in Thousands						Average Length of Stay in Days					
Specific cerebrovascular disorders except transient ischemic attack	294	66	54	60	63	50	15.4	11.2	15.8	16.1	14.9	20.1
Simple pneumonia and pleurisy, age greater than 69 years and/or substantial comorbidity and complication	276	98	45	42	56	36	10.7	9.3	10.9	11.7	11.8	11.6
Unrelated operating room procedures	226	29	42	45	58	52	17.3	14.1	17.3	16.0	17.5	19.9
Diabetes, age greater than 35 years	208	50	37	44	44	33	10.0	8.2	9.2	10.3	10.9	12.1
Angina pectoris	195	54	34	40	44	23	6.6	5.9	6.3	6.3	7.6	7.4
Medical back problems	186	45	33	36	41	31	9.3	7.8	8.3	8.5	11.6	10.2
Cardiac arrhythmia and conduction disorders, age greater than 69 years and/or substantial comorbidity and complication	181	49	31	33	37	30	71	5.7	6.6	7.8	7.8	8.5
Circulatory disorders with acute myocardial infarction without cardiovascular complications, discharged alive	174	35	27	31	46	35	12.2	11.2	11.6	12.1	12.9	12.9
Hypertension	158	39	31	29	27	32	7.9	6.2	7.3	9.3	7.7	9.6
Transient ischemic attacks	155	36	34	30	32	24	7.6	5.5	7.5	7.6	9.7	8.2
Bronchitis and asthma age greater than 69 years and/or substantial comorbidity and complication	148	7	31	25	28	17	8.3	6.9	9.6	8.7	8.8	8.2
Transurethral prostatectomy, age greater than 69 years and/or substantial comorbidity and complication	144	14	31	27	38	33	9.3	9.2	8.3	10.2	9.2	9.5
Kidney and urinary tract infections, age greater than 69 years and/or substantial comorbidity and complication	142	48	26	20	31	18	8.5	7.2	9.2	8.5	9.2	9.4
Respiratory neoplasms	137	22	19	19	40	37.	10.9	7.7	10.8	10.0	11.8	12.4
Hip and femur procedures except major joint, age greater than 69 years and/or substantial comorbidity and complication	135	16	23	24	40	32	19.5	18.3	18.1	17.9	20.3	21.3

had an average length of stay of 5.0 days for patients under 65 years of age, and the Northeast had an average length of stay of 6.5 days, a difference of 1.5 days, or 30 percent greater. For older patients, however, the Northeast had an average length of stay 4.1 days greater than the elderly patients in the West (12.3 versus 8.2 days), a difference of 50 percent.

Overall there was a tendency for length of stay to increase with hospital bed size (Tables 3 and 4) for patients under 65 years of age as well as for older patients, but this pattern is not consistent for some of the individual DRGs for which average length of stay in small and medium-size hospitals is equal to or greater than the average length of stay in large hospitals (500 or more beds).

The average length of stay associated with a DRG (Tables 1–4) allows hospitals to compare their experience with that of other hospitals. While comparison is tenuous on a case-by-case basis, a hospital with an average length of stay 2, 3, or more days longer than the national average for a specific DRG may need to examine why it is so far from the norm. This kind of comparison may be worthwhile as a starting point, but even within a DRG, average length of stay is not an exact measure of resource consumption.

The change to prospective payment for Medicare in patient reimbursement is likely to affect areas such as cost savings, quality of care, medical records keeping, and certain areas of medical practice. However, for at least two reasons data currently available on DRGs from the NHDS (this report and a similar report using 1971 data[1]) should not be used to evaluate the success of prospective payment. First, the prospective payment program was not implemented until October 1983, and, second, historical trends must be studied to shed light on short-term changes in hospital utilization.

For example, from 1981 to 1982 average length of stay decreased 0.4 day for patients 65 years of age and over, and some specific DRGs also showed a reduction in average length of stay. However, length of stay in short-stay nonfederal hospitals has been decreasing for over a decade (the average length of stay for patients 65 years of age and over was 12.2 days in 1972[5] compared with 10.1 days in 1982), and it will take more time to understand the effects

prospective payment will have, if any, on hospital utilization.

References

1   National Center for Health Statistics, R. Pokras: Diagnosis-related groups using data from the National Hospital Discharge Survey, United States, 1982. *Advance Data from Vital and Health Statistics.* No. 98. DHHS Pub. No. (PHS) 84–1250. Public Health Service, Hyattsville, Md., July 20, 1984.

2   National Center for Health Statistics, E. J. Graves: Utilization of short-stay hospitals, United States, 1982 Annual Summary. *Vital and Health Statistics.* Series 13, No. 78. DHHS Pub. No. (PHS) 84–1739. Public Health Service. Washington. U.S. Government Printing Office, Aug. 1984.

3   J. Alsofrom: Playing the numbers. *Medical World News,* Oct. 24, 1983, pp. 38–55.

4   R. B. Fetter, S. Youngsoo, J. L. Freeman, and others: Case mix definition by diagnostic related groups. *Medical Care* 18(2), Supplement. (Copyright 1980: Used with the permission of *Medical Care.*)

5   National Center for Health Statistics. W. F. Lewis: Utilization of short-stay hospitals, summary of nonmedical statistics, United States, 1972. *Vital and Health Statistics.* Series 13, No. 19. DHEW Pub. No. (HRA) 75–1770. Health Resources Administration. Washington. U.S. Government Printing Office, June 1975.

6   National Center for Health Statistics, M. G. Sirken: Utilization of short-stay hospitals, summary of nonmedical statistics, United States, 1965. *Vital and Health Statistics.* Series 13, No. 2. PHS Pub. No. 1000. Public Health Service. Washington. U.S. Government Printing Office, Aug. 1967.

7   National Center for Health Statistics, M. J. Witkin: Utilization of short-stay hospitals by characteristics of discharged patients, United States, 1965. *Vital and Health Statistics.* Series 13, No. 3. PHS Pub. No. 1000. Public Health Service. Washington. U.S. Government Printing Office, Dec. 1967.

8   National Center for Health Statistics, R. Pokras: Surgical and non-surgical procedures in short-stay hospitals, United States, 1979. *Vital and Health Statistics.* Series 13, No. 70. DHHS Pub. No. (PHS) 83–1731. Public Health Service. Washington. U.S. Government Printing Office, Feb. 1983.

9   U.S. Public Health Service and Health Care Financing Administration: *International Classification of Diseases, 9th Revision, Clinical Modification.* DHHS Pub. No. (PHS) 80–1260. Public Health Service. Washington. U.S. Government Printing Office, Sept. 1980.

10   *Federal Register,* Vol. 48, No. 171, Part II, Rules and Regulations, Sept. 1, 1983.

Technical Notes

Survey Methodology

Source of Data   The National Hospital Discharge Survey (NHDS) encompasses patients discharged from short-stay hospitals, exclusive of military and Veterans Administration hospitals, located in the 50 states and the District of Columbia. Only hospitals with six or more beds and an average length of stay of less than 30 days for all patients are included in the survey. Discharges of newborn infants are excluded from this report.

The universe of the survey consisted of 6965 short-stay hospitals contained in the 1963 Master Facility Inventory of Hospitals and Institutions. New hospitals were sampled for inclusion in the survey in 1972, 1975, 1977, and 1981. The sample for 1982 consisted of 550 hospitals. Of these, 71 refused to participate and 53 were out of scope either because the hospital had gone out of business or because it failed to meet the definition of a short-stay hospital. Thus 426 hospitals participated in the survey during 1982 and provided approximately 214,000 abstracts of medical records.

Sample Design   All hospitals with 1000 or more beds in the universe of short-stay hospitals were selected with certainty in the sample. All hospitals with fewer than 1000 beds were stratified, the primary strata being 24 size-by-region classes. Within each of these

24 primary strata, the allocation of the hospitals was made through a controlled selection technique so that hospitals in the sample would be properly distributed with regard to type of ownership and geographic division. Sample hospitals were drawn with probabilities ranging from certainty for the largest hospitals to 1 in 40 for the smallest hospitals.

Sample discharges were selected within the hospitals using the daily listing sheet of discharges as the sampling frame. These discharges were selected by a random technique, usually on the basis of the terminal digit or digits of the patient's medical record number, a number assigned when the patient was admitted to the hospital. The within-hospital sampling ratio for selecting sample discharges varied inversely with the probability of selection of the hospital.

Data Collection and Estimation   The sample selection and the transcription of information from the hospital records for abstract forms were performed by the hospital staff or by representatives of the National Center for Health Statistics or by both. The data were abstracted from the face sheets of the medical records. All discharge diagnoses were listed on the abstract in the order of the principal one, or the first-listed one if the principal one was not identified, followed by the order in which all other diagnoses were entered on the face sheet of the medical record.

Statistics produced by NHDS are derived by a complex estimating procedure. The basic unit of estimation is the sample inpatient discharge abstract. The estimating procedure used to produce essentially unbiased national estimates in NHDS has three principal components: inflation by reciprocals of the probabilities of sample selection, adjustment for nonresponse, and ratio adjustment to fixed totals. These components of estimation are described in appendix I of two earlier publications.[6,7]

Diagnosis-Related Groups   The diagnosis-related groups (DRGs) used in this report were produced using the most current DRG program available at the time (summer of 1983). This is a computer program that groups patients into DRGs based on diagnostic, surgical, and patient information. The program is maintained and is commercially available at Health Systems International (DRG Support Group, 100 Broadway, New Haven, Conn. 06511). However, the actual program used to produce estimates in this report was obtained from the Health Care Financing Administration.

To help interpret the data in this report, two points are worth mentioning. First, the entire NHDS file was used to produce estimates, including outliers. None of the data was excluded, or trimmed, because of an abnormally long length of stay. Second, the NHDS only codes three ICD-9-CM Class 4 procedures[8,9]: circumcision, code 64.0; episiotomy, code 73.6; and removal of intrauterine contraceptive device, code 97.71. In certain instances Class 4 procedures can alter the DRG designation for a patient. The effect of not coding these procedures in the NHDS on determining DRGs is unknown but probably quite small. In all other respects, the DRGs presented in this report are consistent with those in the *Federal Register* of Thursday, September 1, 1983.[10]

In publications from the National Center for Health Statistics using NHDS data, several schemes have been used to group patients into categories based on either their diagnoses or the procedures performed. These groups were developed to report general purpose statistics to the many users of NHDS data, and any similarity between the titles of those categories and DRG titles is coincidental.

Sampling Errors and Rounding of Numbers

The standard error is a measure of the sampling variability that occurs by chance because only a sample, rather than an entire universe, is surveyed. The relative standard error of the estimate is obtained by dividing the standard error by the estimate itself and is expressed as a percent of the estimate. Table I shows relative standard errors for discharges and first-listed diagnoses for 1982. The standard errors for average lengths of stay are shown in Table II. Estimates have been rounded to the nearest thousand. For this reason detailed figures within tables do not always add to the totals.

T A B L E I   Approximate Relative Standard Errors of Estimated Number of Discharges and First-Listed Diagnoses: United States, 1982

Size of Estimate	Relative Standard Error (%)
10,000	16.3
50,000	10.2
100,000	8.5
300,000	6.6
500,000	5.9
1,000,000	5.1
4,000,000	4.0

T A B L E II   Approximate Standard Errors of Average Lengths of Stay by Number of Discharges: United States, 1982

Number of Discharges	Average Length of Stay in Days			
	2	6	10	20
	Standard error in days			
10,000	0.7	1.2	1.7	2.2
50,000	0.3	0.7	1.0	1.4
100,000	0.3	0.6	0.9	1.2
500,000	0.2	0.5	0.8	0.9
1,000,000	0.2	0.5	0.8	0.7
5,000,000	0.2	0.5	0.8	—

Tests of Significance   In this report, the determination of statistical inference is based on the two-tailed Bonferroni test for multiple comparisons. Terms relating to differences, such as "higher" and "less," indicate that the differences are statistically significant. Terms such as "similar" or "no difference" mean that no statistically significant difference exists between the estimates being compared. A lack of comment on the difference between any two estimates does not mean that the difference was tested and found to be not significant.

Definition of Terms

Patient—A person who is formally admitted to the inpatient service of a short-stay hospital for observation, care, diagnosis, or treatment. In this report the number of patients refers to the number of discharges during the year, including any multiple discharges of the same individual from one or more short-stay hospitals.

Average length of stay—The total number of patient days accumulated at time of discharge by patients discharged during the year divided by the number of patients discharged.

Age—Patient's age refers to age at birthday prior to admission to the hospital inpatient service.

Discharge—Discharge is the formal release of a patient by a hospital; that is, the termination of a period of hospitalization by death or by disposition to place of residence, nursing home, or another hospital. The terms "discharges" and "patients discharged" are used synonymously.

Geographic region—Hospitals are classified by location in one of the four geographic regions of the United States that correspond to those used by the U.S. Bureau of the Census (see below).

Hospitals—Short-stay special and general hospitals have six beds or more for inpatient use and an average length of stay of less than 30 days. Federal hospitals and hospital units of institutions are not included.

Bed size of hospital—Size is measured by the number of beds, cribs, and pediatric bassinets regularly maintained (set up and staffed for use) for patients; bassinets for new-born infants are not included. In this report the classification of hospitals by bed size is based on the number of beds at or near midyear reported by the hospitals.

Region	States Included
Northeast	Maine, New Hampshire, Vermont, Massachusetts, Rhode Island, Connecticut, New York, New Jersey, and Pennsylvania
North Central	Michigan, Ohio, Illinois, Indiana, Wisconsin, Minnesota, Iowa, Missouri, North Dakota, South Dakota, Nebraska, and Kansas
South	Delaware, Maryland, District of Columbia, Virginia, West Virginia, North Carolina, South Carolina, Georgia, Florida, Kentucky, Tennessee, Alabama, Mississippi, Arkansas, Louisiana, Oklahoma, and Texas
West	Montana, Idaho, Wyoming, Colorado, New Mexico, Arizona, Utah, Nevada, Washington, Oregon, California, Hawaii, and Alaska

Significance Tests, Confidence Intervals, and Prediction Intervals

Chapter Objectives

After mastering this chapter, you will be able to:

- Explain the meaning of probabilistic inference

- Perform a t test for a process mean

- Construct a confidence interval for a process mean using a t statistic

- Perform a two-sample t test to compare two process means

- Construct a confidence interval for the difference in two process means

- Explain the use of F statistics and look up percentiles in an F distribution table

- Compute a chi-square statistic for a contingency table and look up percentiles in a chi-square distribution table

17.1 Introduction: Probabilistic Inference

Data analysis is guided by models that predict responses from processes. A model embodies assumptions, some of which are taken for granted, some of which are subject to adjustments that bring the model and the data into as close agreement as possible. The adjustable parts of a model are **parameters**. **Probabilistic inference** is drawing conclusions about model parameters from process data, using the methods of probability.

parameters
probabilistic inference

Let us think of each process response as partly predictable and partly unpredictable. A model attempts to identify the predictable part of response and quantify the magnitude of the unpredictable part. In general terms we write

$$\text{Response} = \text{Model Prediction} + \text{Prediction Error}$$

If the model prediction captures what is truly predictable about the process response, the prediction error should be random. A random sequence of errors exhibits the characteristics of a "constant-cause system," namely that a predictable proportion of the errors will fall between any given pair of limits, as described by W. E. Deming in the quotation near the beginning of Section 10.2. Another important characteristic of a random sequence is lack of correlation among the responses in the sequence. If the responses are correlated, then they can be further modeled, which implies that they are predictable in a way that random responses are not. By modeling, we attempt to separate the predictable from the unpredictable parts of process responses.

Randomness arises in statistical modeling in three ways: naturally, through imposition by the analyst, and as a by-product of model fitting. Some processes are just naturally random, such as the responses of coin tosses, dice rolls, card deals, or childbirths. In Chapters 14 and 15, we showed that random digits can be used to impose randomness on a universe of elements so that measurements on a random sample of elements yield predictions about the whole universe within specified limits with specified probabilities. This is the foundation of probability surveys. In Chapters 18 and 19, we will show how randomness can be imposed in the context of experiments to yield information about processes. If randomness can be imposed on the process, the assumption of randomness has strong justification, and conclusions drawn using the methods of probability are likely to be valid. In practice, we are not always able to impose randomness, but we may still be able to make predictions such that the prediction errors behave as if they were random, to a satisfactory degree of approximation. In any case, if randomness is a reasonable assumption, then the methods of probability can be used. On the other hand, if randomness is not a reasonable assumption, then the methods of probability have little justification and conclusions based on them have doubtful validity. Thus the assessment of random behavior is a critical part of any modeling effort that uses the methods of probability.

Naturally occurring randomness is illustrated by coin tossing in Example 1.7A. Two further examples illustrate imposed randomness and randomness resulting from modeling.

EXAMPLE 17.1A

The field trial described in the case study in Section 13.10 demonstrates imposed randomness. Each student who conducted the experiment described there randomly allocated three subjects to one treatment and three subjects to another treatment by flipping a coin. ▪

EXAMPLE 17.1B

The sequence of monthly flour price indices in Exhibit 2.10B is clearly not in statistical control because it meanders, but the sequence of changes in Exhibit 2.10C is stable. In fact, a control chart analysis and an autocorrelation analysis of the sequence of changes confirms that it can be treated as a random sequence. This suggests that an appropriate prediction model for the monthly flour price index is to predict next month's index with the value of the current month's index. If the price index continues to perform as it has in the past, this prediction model will yield prediction errors that behave as if they were random. ▪

In statistical practice, a collection of observed responses from a process guides the building of a model, which is then used to make predictions of the response variable. Next, prediction errors, which are the differences between the observed responses and the predictions from the model, are calculated. Finally, the resulting sequence of prediction errors is examined to see if they behave as if they were random, at least to some satisfactory degree of approximation. When observed data are used to adjust the parameters of a model so the model "fits" the data, we write

$$\text{Observed Response} = \text{Fitted Value} + \text{Residual}$$

where the term *residual* refers to the difference between the prediction made by the fitted model and the actual process response, which is the observation. One use of probabilistic inference is the fitting of models to data.

We fit models to process data to help make predictions about future responses of the process, not just those already observed. Assessing what a fitted model implies about future responses is another use of probabilistic inference. One major assumption of such analysis is that the process will continue its past behavior into the future, which is another way of saying that the process has a stable component, or a component that is in statistical control. Thus predictions from a fitted model are conditional on the assumption of stability. If a process deviates from the assumption of stability, then its responses will not conform to the predictions of the model, an argument we gave when we introduced control charts as tools for monitoring processes in Chapters 10 and 12. By this and many other examples, we show that modeling is a systematic way to try to discern the future from the past and to detect in future behavior substantial deviations from past behavior.

When a random component can be found in a process, the methods of probability can be used to form a link between process responses and model parameters, and this link can be exploited powerfully to draw valid conclusions about the process, from even very small samples of data. In this chapter we illustrate this idea through the estimation of long-run process means. The probabilistic inference tools introduced are significance tests, confidence intervals, and prediction intervals. This chapter deals with only one and two process means to keep the exposition simple. Chapters 14 to 16 and 18 to 24 show how to use probabilistic methods in more complex situations.

SECTION

17.2 The t Statistic for a Single Sample Mean

This section discusses the standardization of the sample mean. Introducing notation, let $y_1, y_2, \ldots, y_n$ denote a sample of n numbers, let $\bar{y}$ denote the mean of the sample, and let s denote the sample standard deviation. Assume the sample is from a process or from a very large population so that in either case the question of a finite population correction factor can be ignored. The long-run process or population mean is denoted by μ, which is the theoretical mean. Then the sample standard error of the sample mean is $s/\sqrt{n}$, and the standardized mean is

t statistic for the process mean

$$t = \frac{\bar{y} - \mu}{s/\sqrt{n}} = \frac{\sqrt{n}(\bar{y} - \mu)}{s} \qquad (17.1)$$

This is the difference between the sample and theoretical means divided by the sample standard error. Usual statistical notation for this quantity is the letter t, and the quantity is called a t statistic. Many statistics are referred to as t statistics because the idea of dividing the difference between a sample and theoretical quantity by a sample standard error is pervasive in statistical applications. This type of calculation is also called *Studentizing*. The important thing to notice is that the t statistic in Equation (17.1) links the sample mean, the data, with the theoretical mean, the parameter, together in the same equation. The British statistician who discovered the t statistic, W. S. Gossett, wrote a paper about his discovery under the pseudonym Student because the management of the brewery he worked for did not want their competitors to know they possessed the discovery or how they used it.

How does randomness impact the t statistic defined in Equation (17.1)? We use simulation to demonstrate the answer. A sample size $n = 5$ is used and 500 samples of size 5 from a normal distribution with mean $\mu = 0$ and standard deviation $\sigma = 1$ are simulated. For each of the 500 samples, a new mean $\bar{y}$, a new standard deviation s, and a new t statistic t are computed. Suppose the first sample consisted of the following five values:

$$-1.20873 \quad -0.11594 \quad -2.14575 \quad 0.78050 \quad -0.38638 \qquad \textbf{(17.2)}$$

You may verify that $\bar{y} = -0.615$, $s = 1.112$, $s/\sqrt{n} = 1.112/\sqrt{5} = 0.497$, and the value of the t statistic is

$$t = (-0.615 - 0)/0.497 \simeq -1.24$$

The process above was simulated 500 times using software. Exhibit 17.2A shows a dotplot of the 500 t statistics generated by the simulation. Notice that the distribution appears quite symmetric and mound shaped, which suggests that it may be normal. But that is not the case. To show the lack of normality, Exhibit 17.2B displays the normal probability plot of the 500 t statistics. The deviation from the straight line that should have been obtained if the distribution had been normal is clear. The theoretical distribution of the t statistics has more area in the tails than a normal distribution, and it is less peaked at the center.

In comparison, Exhibit 17.2A shows the 500 simulated sample means standardized by the actual process standard deviation of 1—that is, it shows a dotplot of quantities computed by the formula

$$z = \frac{\sqrt{5}(\bar{y} - 0)}{1} = \sqrt{5}\bar{y} \qquad \textbf{(17.3)}$$

The theoretical distribution of the t statistic is called the t distribution with 4 degrees of freedom. The name suggests that the distribution depends on a parameter that is one less than the sample size $n = 5$, and this is correct. If a different sample size n had been used, a t distribution would have been simulated, but it would have had a degrees of freedom parameter equal to $n - 1$.

E X H I B I T **17.2A**
Dotplot of 500 Simulated t
Statistics from 500 Random
Samples of Size $n = 5$ from a
Standard Normal Distribution.
Also shown is a dotplot of the
500 sample means
standardized by the process
standard deviation of $\sigma = 1$.

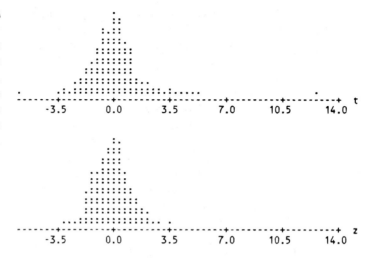

E X H I B I T **17.2B**
Normal Probability Plot of 500
Simulated t statistics with 4
Degrees of Freedom

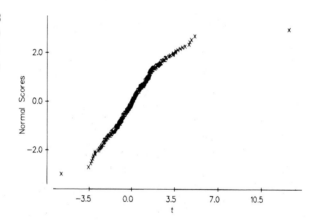

t **distribution**

Let $y_1, y_2, \ldots, y_n$ denote a sample of size n drawn randomly from a normal process with mean μ and standard deviation σ. Let $\bar{y}$ and s denote the sample mean and standard deviation. Then the distribution of the t statistic defined in Equation (17.1) is the t distribution with $n - 1$ degrees of freedom.

The following result can be derived mathematically.

t **distribution with** $n-1$
degrees of freedom

Mathematical Result.   A t **distribution with** $n-1$ **degrees of freedom** is symmetric and mound shaped. Provided $n - 1 \geq 2$, the mean of the t distribution is 0. Provided $n - 1 \geq 3$, the standard deviation of the t distribution is $\sqrt{(n - 1)/(n - 3)}$. When $n - 1 = 1$, the mean and standard deviation of the t distribution do not exist. When $n - 1 = 2$, the mean exists but the standard deviation does not. As n grows large without bound, the t distribution converges to the standard normal distribution.

To illustrate the computation of the standard deviation, consider a t distribution with 4 degrees of freedom—that is, $n - 1 = 4$. The standard deviation is

$$\sqrt{\frac{n-1}{n-3}} = \sqrt{\frac{4}{5-3}} = \sqrt{\frac{4}{2}} \simeq 1.414$$

For a t distribution with $n - 1 = 20$,

$$\sqrt{\frac{n-1}{n-3}} = \sqrt{\frac{20}{21-3}} = \sqrt{\frac{20}{18}} \simeq 1.054$$

Exhibit 17.2C shows plots of t distributions with 4 and 20 degrees of freedom. Also shown are the means, standard deviations, and 95th percentiles of t distributions with 4, 20, and 60 degrees of freedom, and the mean, standard deviation, and 95th percentile of the standard normal distribution. All of these distributions have mean 0, which is also the median because of symmetry. The t distribution with 4 degrees of freedom has standard deviation 1.414, and the distribution with 20 degrees of freedom has standard deviation 1.054, indicating a decrease in variability with increase in degrees of freedom. Because the distribution with 4 degrees of freedom is more spread out, its 95th percentile is larger than that of the distribution with 20 degrees of freedom.

E X H I B I T 17.2C
Graphs of Two t Distributions and a Table of Means, Standard Deviations, and 95th Percentiles

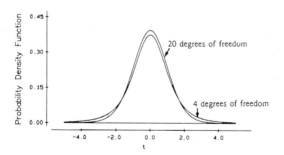

	t Distribution with Degrees of Freedom			Standard Normal Distribution
	4	20	60	
Mean	0	0	0	0
Standard deviation	1.414	1.054	1.017	1
95th percentile	2.132	1.725	1.671	1.645

One implication of the mathematical result above is that as degrees of freedom are increased, the listed characteristics of the t distribution get closer and closer to those of the standard normal distribution. Exhibit 17.2D gives a table of selected percentiles of t distributions for selected degrees of freedom. Notice that for degrees

E X H I B I T **17.2D**   Percentiles of Selected t Distributions with ν Degrees of Freedom. (The body of the table contains values of t corresponding to areas a. The parameter a is the area bounded by the horizontal axis, a vertical line through t, and the pdf of the t distribution with ν degrees of freedom.)

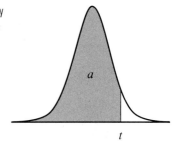

| | | | | | | | a = area | | | | | | | | |
ν	0.550	0.600	0.650	0.700	0.750	0.800	0.850	0.900	0.950	0.975	0.990	0.995	0.997	0.998	0.999
1	0.158	0.325	0.510	0.727	1.000	1.376	1.963	3.078	6.314	12.706	31.821	63.657	106.100	159.156	318.317
2	0.142	0.289	0.445	0.617	0.816	1.061	1.386	1.886	2.920	4.303	6.965	9.925	12.852	15.764	22.327
3	0.137	0.277	0.424	0.584	0.765	0.978	1.250	1.638	2.353	3.182	4.541	5.841	6.994	8.053	10.215
4	0.134	0.271	0.414	0.569	0.741	0.941	1.190	1.533	2.132	2.776	3.747	4.604	5.321	5.951	7.173
5	0.132	0.267	0.408	0.559	0.727	0.920	1.156	1.476	2.015	2.571	3.365	4.032	4.570	5.030	5.893
6	0.131	0.265	0.404	0.553	0.718	0.906	1.134	1.440	1.943	2.447	3.143	3.707	4.152	4.524	5.208
7	0.130	0.263	0.402	0.549	0.711	0.896	1.119	1.415	1.895	2.365	2.998	3.499	3.887	4.207	4.785
8	0.130	0.262	0.399	0.546	0.706	0.889	1.108	1.397	1.860	2.306	2.896	3.355	3.705	3.991	4.501
9	0.129	0.261	0.398	0.543	0.703	0.883	1.100	1.383	1.833	2.262	2.821	3.250	3.573	3.835	4.297
10	0.129	0.260	0.397	0.542	0.700	0.879	1.093	1.372	1.812	2.228	2.764	3.169	3.472	3.716	4.144
11	0.129	0.260	0.396	0.540	0.697	0.876	1.088	1.363	1.796	2.201	2.718	3.106	3.393	3.624	4.025
12	0.128	0.259	0.395	0.539	0.695	0.873	1.083	1.356	1.782	2.179	2.681	3.055	3.330	3.550	3.930
13	0.128	0.259	0.394	0.538	0.694	0.870	1.079	1.350	1.771	2.160	2.650	3.012	3.278	3.489	3.852
14	0.128	0.258	0.393	0.537	0.692	0.868	1.076	1.345	1.761	2.145	2.624	2.977	3.234	3.438	3.787
15	0.128	0.258	0.393	0.536	0.691	0.866	1.074	1.341	1.753	2.131	2.602	2.947	3.197	3.395	3.733
16	0.128	0.258	0.392	0.535	0.690	0.865	1.071	1.337	1.746	2.120	2.583	2.921	3.165	3.358	3.686
17	0.128	0.257	0.392	0.534	0.689	0.863	1.069	1.333	1.740	2.110	2.567	2.898	3.138	3.326	3.646
18	0.127	0.257	0.392	0.534	0.688	0.862	1.067	1.330	1.734	2.101	2.552	2.878	3.113	3.298	3.611
19	0.127	0.257	0.391	0.533	0.688	0.861	1.066	1.328	1.729	2.093	2.539	2.861	3.092	3.273	3.579
20	0.127	0.257	0.391	0.533	0.687	0.860	1.064	1.325	1.725	2.086	2.528	2.845	3.073	3.251	3.552
21	0.127	0.257	0.391	0.532	0.686	0.859	1.063	1.323	1.721	2.080	2.518	2.831	3.056	3.231	3.527
22	0.127	0.256	0.390	0.532	0.686	0.858	1.061	1.321	1.717	2.074	2.508	2.819	3.041	3.214	3.505
23	0.127	0.256	0.390	0.532	0.685	0.858	1.060	1.319	1.714	2.069	2.500	2.807	3.027	3.198	3.485
24	0.127	0.256	0.390	0.531	0.685	0.857	1.059	1.318	1.711	2.064	2.492	2.797	3.014	3.183	3.467
25	0.127	0.256	0.390	0.531	0.684	0.856	1.058	1.316	1.708	2.060	2.485	2.787	3.003	3.170	3.450
26	0.127	0.256	0.390	0.531	0.684	0.856	1.058	1.315	1.706	2.056	2.479	2.779	2.992	3.158	3.435
27	0.127	0.256	0.389	0.531	0.684	0.855	1.057	1.314	1.703	2.052	2.473	2.771	2.982	3.147	3.421
28	0.127	0.256	0.389	0.530	0.683	0.855	1.056	1.313	1.701	2.048	2.467	2.763	2.973	3.136	3.408
29	0.127	0.256	0.389	0.530	0.683	0.854	1.055	1.311	1.699	2.045	2.462	2.756	2.965	3.127	3.396
30	0.127	0.256	0.389	0.530	0.683	0.854	1.055	1.310	1.697	2.042	2.457	2.750	2.957	3.118	3.385
31	0.127	0.256	0.389	0.530	0.682	0.853	1.054	1.309	1.696	2.040	2.453	2.744	2.950	3.109	3.375
32	0.127	0.255	0.389	0.530	0.682	0.853	1.054	1.309	1.694	2.037	2.449	2.738	2.943	3.102	3.365
33	0.127	0.255	0.389	0.530	0.682	0.853	1.053	1.308	1.692	2.035	2.445	2.733	2.937	3.094	3.356
34	0.127	0.255	0.389	0.529	0.682	0.852	1.052	1.307	1.691	2.032	2.441	2.728	2.931	3.088	3.348
35	0.127	0.255	0.388	0.529	0.682	0.852	1.052	1.306	1.690	2.030	2.438	2.724	2.926	3.081	3.340
40	0.126	0.255	0.388	0.529	0.681	0.851	1.050	1.303	1.684	2.021	2.423	2.704	2.902	3.055	3.307
50	0.126	0.255	0.388	0.528	0.679	0.849	1.047	1.299	1.676	2.009	2.403	2.678	2.870	3.018	3.261
60	0.126	0.254	0.387	0.527	0.679	0.848	1.045	1.296	1.671	2.000	2.390	2.660	2.849	2.994	3.232
120	0.126	0.254	0.386	0.526	0.677	0.845	1.041	1.289	1.658	1.980	2.358	2.617	2.798	2.935	3.160
inf	0.126	0.253	0.385	0.524	0.674	0.842	1.036	1.282	1.645	1.960	2.326	2.576	2.748	2.878	3.090

of freedom greater than 30, the percentiles of the t distributions are little different from those of the standard normal.

In Exhibit 17.2D the degrees of freedom parameter is denoted by ν, so $\nu = n - 1$. This is standard statistical notation for degrees of freedom. It is convenient because in other applications of the t distribution, the degrees of freedom parameter is not equal to $n - 1$ but some other function of n. Using the general notation ν for degrees of freedom allows the table in Exhibit 17.2D to be used for a large number of applications.

SECTION

17.3 Exercises

17.3A   Simulate a random sample of size $n = 7$ from a standard normal distribution and compute the value of the sample mean, the sample standard deviation, the t statistic in Equation (17.1), and the z statistic, $z = \sqrt{7} \cdot \bar{y}$. Repeat the simulation 100 times, storing the 100 values of $\bar{y}$, s, t, and z. Make dotplots and compute descriptive statistics of each of these variables. Relate your findings to those discussed in the text.

17.3B   Suppose $n = 25$, $\mu = 0$, $\bar{y} = -4.27$, and $t = -2.1$. What is the value of s?

17.3C   Suppose $\bar{y} = 4.27$, $\mu = 3$, $s = 0.79$, and $t = 8.04$. What is the value of n?

17.3D   Suppose $n = 18$, $\bar{y} = 97.6$, $\mu = 100$, and $s = 5.3$. What is the value of t?

17.3E   For each case below, find the requested percentile of the t distribution with the indicated degrees of freedom ν.

Case	ν	Percentile
a	10	90th
b	10	40th
c	15	95th
d	15	97.5th
e	15	20th
f	30	99.9th
g	30	99.5th
h	30	0.5th

17.3F   You plan to draw a random sample of size $n = 20$ from a process in statistical control and with a normal cross-sectional distribution whose mean is $\mu = 100$.

a   For what percentage of such samples will the value of the t statistic $t = \sqrt{n}(\bar{y} - 100)/s$ be greater than 2.093?

b   For what percentage of such samples will the value of the t statistic be between -2.861 and 2.861?

17.3G   Find a value b such that with probability 0.99 the values of the t statistic with 7 degrees of freedom are between $-b$ and b.

17.3H   Write a one-to-two page essay on the differences between $z = \sqrt{n}(\bar{y} - \mu)/\sigma$ and $t = \sqrt{n}(\bar{y} - \mu)/s$. Use simulations to illustrate your points.

SECTION

17.4 Application to Significance Testing

We approach the topic of significance testing first informally, then formally.

Informal Introduction

significance testing

Significance testing is a process of probabilistic inference that uses sampling distributions to compare behavior in data with theories about the process that generated the data. Consider a situation in which data from a process in statistical control whose cross-sectional distribution is normal are drawn, the value of the long-run process mean, denoted by μ, is in doubt, and the value of the long-run process standard deviation σ is not known. One way to approach inference about μ is to venture a guess, called a theory or hypothesis, about the value of μ. After the data are collected, the value of the guess is compared with the value of the sample mean.

Because sample means vary from sample to sample, a criterion for determining whether a specific sample mean deviates from the guess by more than an amount that can be attributed to natural sampling variation is needed. The t statistic in Equation (17.1) and its associated t distribution with $n - 1$ degrees of freedom provide such a criterion.

EXAMPLE   17.4A

Suppose you plan to take a sample of size $n = 5$ from the process. Also assume that you have formulated a hypothesis that $\mu = 1$. This is the guess at μ. From the theory presented above, you know that if the guess coincides with the actual long-run process mean, then the statistic

$$t = \frac{\bar{y} - 1}{s/\sqrt{5}} = \frac{\sqrt{5}(\bar{y} - 1)}{s} \tag{17.4}$$

has a t distribution with 4 degrees of freedom. This distribution describes the variation inherent in the random sampling of the process. The table in Exhibit 17.2D shows that the 99.5th percentile of this distribution is 4.604. This means that if the long-run process mean is indeed 1, then 99% of the values of the t statistics in Equation (17.4) that could be obtained by random sampling of the process are between -4.604 and 4.604.

How might this result be used? One form of significance testing uses it as follows:

1   Draw a random sample of five items from the process.

2   Compute the sample mean $\bar{y}$, standard deviation s, and t statistic t.

3   If $|t| \leq 4.604$, declare the difference between the sample mean and the hypothesized mean of 1 to be due to random variation.

4 If $|t| > 4.604$, declare the difference between the sample mean and the hypothesized mean of 1 to be *statistically significant* at the 1% significance level.

Step 4 requires elaboration. The reference to a 1% significance level comes from the fact that 4.604 is the 99.5th percentile of the t distribution with 4 degrees of freedom. As noted above, if the hypothesized value of 1 and the actual long-run value of the process mean coincide, then there is only a 1% chance that the t statistic value falls outside the interval defined by $|t| \leq 4.604$. If a value outside this interval is observed, it is tempting to conclude that there is a discrepancy between the hypothesized value and the actual long-run process mean. This is the reasoning behind the phrase *statistically significant*.

In more informal terms, an outcome $|t| > 4.604$ in this case is not likely to be due to chance alone; there is likely a "cause" other than pure chance of the result. The cause that most readily comes to mind is that the hypothesis is defective. ∎

The reasoning introduced in Example 17.4A assumes certain things that may not stand up under scrutiny. For example, the process sampled from may not be in statistical control. Or the sampling process may be defective, so that the data do not really satisfy the assumption of randomness. Or the data may contain measurement errors that bias the value of $\bar{y}$. Finally, the cross-sectional distribution of the process may seriously deviate from the normal form assumed. The reasoning behind significance testing presupposes that none of these problems is present. Before a conclusion based on significance testing can be reached, the experimenter must be satisfied that none of the problems mentioned seriously affect the data. Otherwise, completely unwarranted conclusions could be drawn with significance testing.

The point in the preceding paragraph is profoundly important for practical applications. The mechanics and interpretation of significance testing are so appealing that practitioners are tempted to apply them without thinking deeply about the assumptions that must be satisfied to obtain valid inferences. There are many slippery curves to negotiate when performing inference!

For the moment, think about inferential situations in which a significance test would be appropriate, that is, situations in which none of the serious problems mentioned above are present. Consider two variations on the significance test outlined above. One variation is to use a different sample size. The sample size $n = 5$ was chosen for illustration. In practice, the sample size is one of the important design choices available to the investigator.

Your intuition probably suggests, and rightly so, that the choice of n affects the performance of a significance test. In particular, tests based on larger values of n ought to be better able than those based on smaller values of n to detect a given amount of discrepancy between the hypothesized and actual values of the process mean, a conclusion that statistical theory confirms.

This result should not lead you to conclude that large sample sizes are necessarily better than small ones. Remember that collecting data is costly, and the larger the sample the greater the chance that nonsampling errors will creep undetected into the data.

Another caution is that statistical significance does not automatically imply *practical* importance. A significance test based on a large sample will signal statistical significance for a small deviation from a hypothesized mean. If such a small deviation from a hypothesized mean has no useful practical implication, then the temptation to celebrate the statistically significant finding must be resisted. The researcher must understand the process under study well enough to know the magnitude of a practically important deviation. Estimating the magnitude of the deviation from a hypothesized mean, using confidence intervals, then yields the most directly useful information from the data. More than the concept of statistical significance is needed as a guide to practical action.

Another variation on the significance test introduced above is to change the level of significance. A 1% level of significance was obtained by choosing a 99.5th percentile of the t distribution as the dividing line between sampling variation and special-cause variation. In theory, there is no single dividing line that is better than any other. The 95th percentile, which is 2.132 for a t distribution with 4 degrees of freedom, could have been chosen just as easily. Had this been done, the significance level would have been 10%. This means that if the hypothesized value and the long-run process mean coincide, then 10% of all t statistics that can possibly be obtained by random sampling of the process are outside the interval $|t| \leq 2.132$. If this criterion is chosen, 10% of the time statistically significant results will be obtained even though the hypothesis coincides with the long-run process mean.

E X A M P L E   **17.4B**   We established in Example 17.1B that the observed month-to-month changes in the Buffalo flour price index behave as if they were random. Moreover, to a good approximation they behave as if they were random drawings from a normal distribution, as is seen by the approximate straight-line behavior of their normal probability plot in Exhibit 17.4A. Thus the use of the t statistic to draw inferences about the long-run mean change in the Buffalo flour price index appears justified. Could the long-run mean change be 0? Let us test this hypothesis at the 1% significance level. We note that there are 99 changes computed from the 100 original observations, so $n = 99$, and this implies that the degrees of freedom equal $n - 1 = 98$. The 99.5th percentile of the t distribution with 98 degrees of freedom is not given in the table in Exhibit 17.2D, but rough approximation suggests it is about 2.6. We will use $[-2.6, 2.6]$ as the interval of plausible values of the t statistic when randomness is the only cause of variation.

Now we use statistical software to find that the sample mean and standard deviation of the $n = 99$ changes in the price index are $\bar{y} = 8.67$ and $s = 77.03$, so the value of the standard deviation divided by the square root of the sample size is 7.74. We therefore calculate the value of the t statistic as

$$\frac{8.67 - 0}{7.74} = \frac{8.67}{7.74} = 1.12$$

E X H I B I T **17.4A**
Normal Probability Plot of
Changes in Buffalo Flour Price
Index

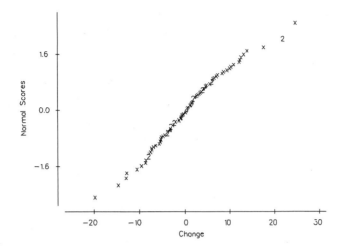

which falls within the interval of plausible values. We conclude that the data are not inconsistent with the hypothesis that the long-run mean value of the price index changes is zero. Such a finding lends additional support to the notion that the price index value in the next month is adequately predicted by the values of the index in the current month. If the data had suggested that the mean change were not zero, a nonzero constant added to the current price index would provide a more credible prediction than just the current price index alone. As we stated, the data analysis does not support the adding of a constant. ∎

Formal Introduction

In this subsection, some of the formal terminology and notation of the theory of significance testing is introduced. A brief introduction in the context of the binomial distribution appears in Section 11.11, which you may wish to reread. Here a normal process in statistical control is sampled to test the validity of a guess at the long-run process mean μ.

null hypothesis

The numerical value of the guess is called the **null hypothesis** and is denoted by H_0. If μ_0 denotes the numerical guess at μ, then H_0: $\mu = \mu_0$ defines the null hypothesis. Once a null hypothesis is defined, the notation H_0 is used to refer to it. A null hypothesis is false whenever the actual value of μ is not equal to μ_0. In practice, the direction of any difference can be important. For example, in the beer-tasting test described in Section 11.11 interest focused on whether consumer's ability to discriminate between two kinds of beer was *superior* to purely random discrimination. If interest centers only on whether a process mean is greater than the null hypothesis value or only on whether a process mean is less than the value, we

one-sided alternative hypothesis

say we are testing a **one-sided alternative hypothesis**—that is, a hypothesis that is an alternative to the null hypothesis. If, as in our informal introduction above, we

**two-sided alternative
hypothesis
alternative hypothesis**

focus only on whether the process mean is different from the null hypothesis value, we say we have a **two-sided alternative hypothesis**.

In significance testing, the **alternative hypothesis** is denoted by H_1. If the alternative is two-sided, we write $H_1: \mu \neq \mu_0$. If the alternative hypothesis is that the process mean is greater than the null hypothesis value, we write $H_1: \mu > \mu_0$, and if the alternative is that the process mean is less than the null hypothesis value, we write $H_1: \mu < \mu_0$.

test statistic

To conduct a test of significance, a **test statistic** that forms a comparative link between some function of the data and the long-run process mean μ is defined. The researcher must be able to state the sampling distribution of the test statistic when the null hypothesis is assumed to be true. Saying that the null hypothesis is true means that a "good guess" has been made—that is, that μ_0 and the actual long-run value of μ coincide.

The test statistic must be constructed so that if a good guess is not made, the statistic sends an appropriate signal, which is exactly what the t statistic does. Here is the logic. Because the sampling distribution of the t statistic is known when H_0 is true, an interval of values expected to be observed, called the *interval of plausible values,* can be constructed. Now if after the data are collected and the value of the t statistic

**t-statistic for the process
mean**

$$t = \frac{\bar{y} - \mu_0}{s/\sqrt{n}} = \frac{\sqrt{n}(\bar{y} - \mu_0)}{s} \tag{17.5}$$

is computed, and the t statistic falls outside the interval of plausible values, then there is reason to suspect that the hypothesis was not really a good guess. Notice that the value of t is obtained by dividing the difference between the sample mean obtained from the data and the null hypothesis value μ_0 by the sample standard error of the mean.

critical region

When the value of the t statistic computed for actual data falls outside the interval of plausible values, it has fallen into the **critical region** of the test and the value is statistically significant. If the researcher believes the signal the test gives and concludes that the hypothesis is not a goodx guess, then *the null hypothesis is rejected.* The implication of this language is that if the actual value of the t statistic falls in the interval of plausible values, then *the null hypothesis is not rejected.* The form of the critical region is adapted to the form of the alternative hypothesis. For example, if the alternative hypothesis is one-sided such that $H_1: \mu > \mu_0$, the critical region is a set of t-values *greater than* a value determined from the t table. The value is chosen from the table so that a t distribution, with the appropriate degrees of freedom, assigns an area equal to the significance level to the region. If the alternative hypothesis is one-sided such that $H_1: \mu < \mu_0$, the critical region is a set of t-values *less than* a value determined from the t table. The value is chosen from the table so that a t distribution, with the appropriate degrees of freedom, assigns an area equal to the significance level to the critical region. As demonstrated in our informal introduction, if the alternative hypothesis is such that $H_1: \mu \neq \mu_0$, the critical region consists of two extreme intervals chosen so that the appropriate t distribution assigns area equal to half the significance level to each of the intervals.

The interval of plausible values plays a fundamental role. Values of the t statistic not in this interval are deemed to be "critical" and to signal rejection of the null hypothesis. The interval of plausible values is chosen to make it unlikely that the test statistic rejects the null hypothesis when it is true. More formally, the interval of plausible values is chosen so that when the null hypothesis is true, an acceptably small proportion of possible t statistics falls outside the interval, according to the sampling t distribution with $n - 1$ degrees of freedom.

In Exhibit 17.2A, when the null hypothesis was assumed to be true, the t statistics had a t distribution with 4 degrees of freedom. This implied that when the null hypothesis was assumed to be true, 99% of the possible t statistic values were between -4.604 and 4.604, and the interval between these values was used as the interval of plausible values. The probability of rejecting a true null hypothesis was therefore only 0.01 (or 1%). Since only one out of a hundred possible t statistic values would lead to rejecting a true null hypothesis, the researcher would feel confident that the test of significance is not misleading. Put another way, if a t statistic value outside the interval of plausible values (and therefore inside the critical region) is observed, this justifies doubts about the truth of the null hypothesis. The 1% probability that

significance level

the t statistic falls into the critical region is called the **significance level** of the test. It is a measure of the risk of incorrectly concluding that the null hypothesis is false.

There is no purely objective way to choose the interval of plausible values. In Example 17.4A it would have been just as valid to have chosen the interval between -2.776 and 2.776 as the interval of plausible values. From the table in Exhibit 17.2D, you learn that when the null hypothesis is true, 95% of the possible t statistics fall in this interval. This means that when the null hypothesis is true, the probability that a t statistic falls in the critical region is 0.05 (or 5%). The significance level of this test is 5%. This test is riskier than the test with the 1% significance level because there is a higher probability of rejecting a true null hypothesis.

So should the test with the smallest possible significance level always be used? If this were the whole story, the best test would never reject a null hypothesis, yielding a significance level of 0. But this is clearly ridiculous. There is more to the story.

The risk of rejecting a true null hypothesis is only one kind of risk. Another is the risk of not rejecting a false null hypothesis. It is the trade-off between these two risks that forces researchers to use nonzero significance levels. A test that never rejects a null hypothesis cannot signal that the guess at μ is no good. Researchers run some risk of rejecting a true null hypothesis to discover a false one. Such is the trade-off inherent in trying to discover new knowledge from imperfect or incomplete data.

As stated before, there is no completely objective method for choosing the significance level of a significance test. A thorough analysis of approaches to the choice leads into a long and arduous theoretical discussion that is beyond the scope of this book. The prevailing practice is to choose significance levels more or less by convention, the most common choices being 10%, 5%, and 1%. The smaller the significance level, the larger the interval of plausible values, and the larger the t statistic has to be, in absolute value, to fall in the critical region and signal rejection of the null hypothesis.

In practice, the analysis of data leads to formulating and testing many hypotheses. If 10 true null hypotheses are independently tested at the 5% significance level, then the probability that all 10 tests correctly fail to reject the null hypotheses is only $(0.95)^{10} \simeq 0.60$. On the other hand, if the hypotheses are tested at the 0.3% significance level, the probability that all 10 tests correctly fail to reject the null hypotheses is $(0.997)^{10} \simeq 0.97$. The risk of making errors is much lower for the smaller significance level.

Type I error
Type II error

Type III error

Three types of errors are possible in significance testing: Type I, Type II, and Type III. **Type I error** is rejecting a true null hypothesis. This means that the significance level is the probability of committing a Type I error. **Type II error** is not rejecting a false null hypothesis. In some problems it is possible to compute probabilities of Type II errors, but their calculation is usually a formidable technical exercise.[†]

Type III error refers to answering an irrelevant question. In formulating problems researchers usually try to define the problem in terms that make it easy to solve. Doing this creates the risk of "defining away" the real problem, that is, setting up a problem that can be solved but whose salient features do not match the real problem. The resulting solution may be quite impressive in its technical detail and in the slickness of its presentation, but it does not help improve the process that needs improving. There is a double cost to Type III errors: the cost of the resources spent in deriving a "solution," and the cost of still having to deal with the fundamental problem that has not been solved.

t test for the process mean

A test of significance based on the t statistic defined in Equation (17.5) is called a *t* **test for the process mean**. There are many other t tests, one of which is introduced in Section 17.10.

E X A M P L E   **17.4C**

Example 17.4A showed that for a test of significance based on the t distribution with 4 degrees of freedom, a 1% significance level test consists of rejecting the null hypothesis if the value of the t statistic falls outside the interval $[-4.604, 4.604]$. Using the sample in display (17.2) and assuming the null hypothesis H_0: $\mu = 0$, the value of the t statistic was found to be $t \simeq -1.24$, so for this sample the t test says not to reject the null hypothesis that the underlying process mean is 0, at the 1% significance level.

What if H_0: $\mu = 1$ had been used as the null hypothesis? Then the t statistic would have been

$$t = \frac{-0.615 - 1}{0.497} \simeq -3.25$$

which is also in the interval of plausible values. This t test says not to reject the null hypothesis that the underlying process mean is 1, at the 1% significance level. On the basis of the data in display (17.2) and a t test at the 1% significance level, neither 0 nor 1 can be rejected as plausible values of the underlying process mean.

[†]The null hypothesis is false whenever the actual value of μ is not equal to μ_0. The probability of a Type II error is different for different values of the actual process mean μ. Rather than report probabilities of Type II errors, most investigators prefer to report probabilities of rejecting the null hypothesis for different values of μ. The resulting function is called the *power function* of the significance test. A value of μ that is not equal to μ_0 is called an alternative hypothesis to the null hypothesis. The probability of rejecting the null hypothesis when the actual process mean has alternative value μ is called the power of the test at that alternative. Power refers to the test's ability to reject a false null hypothesis. The higher the power, the better the test is able to detect that the corresponding alternative, rather than the null, hypothesis is true.

What if H_0: $\mu = 1.7$ had been used as the null hypothesis? Then the t statistic would have been

$$t = \frac{-0.615 - 1.7}{0.497} \simeq -4.66$$

which is outside the interval of plausible values and is therefore statistically significant at the 1% significance level. The t test says to reject the hypothesis that the underlying process mean is 1.7.   ▪

E X A M P L E   17.4D

The field trial described in Section 13.10 yielded, among other things, $n = 38$ outcomes that were aggregate counting errors subjects made when counting e's in sentences held right side up. According to Exhibit 13.10B, the sample mean of the outcomes is $\bar{y} = -10.13$ and the standard deviation is $s = 11.26$. Thus the standard deviation divided by the square root of the sample size is $11.26/6.1644 = 1.827$.

We illustrate testing the null hypothesis that the mean error is 0 versus the one-sided alternative that it is negative—that is, that on average subjects tend to undercount e's. This alternative is consistent with the notion that counting is harder than it seems at first sight. In symbols, we have H_0: $\mu = 0$ and H_1: $\mu < 0$. We choose a significance level of 1%, so we must look up the first percentile of the t distribution with 37 degrees of freedom, which is about -2.4. The critical region of the test is therefore $(-\infty, -2.4]$, because the t distribution assigns an area of 0.01 to the interval. In other words, we will reject the null hypothesis in favor of the one-sided alternative if the value of the t statistic is less than -2.4.

The value of the t statistic is $(-10.13 - 0)/1.827 = -5.5$, which is less than -2.4. We therefore reject the hypothesis that subjects do not undercount e's. The evidence in favor of the alternative hypothesis is statistically significant at the 1% significance level.   ▪

p-Values

Because investigators choose different significance levels to reflect different levels of risk they are willing to run of making a Type I error, they can draw differing conclusions from the value of the t statistic. For example, it is possible for an investigator with a 5% significance level to reject a null hypothesis while at the same time another investigator looking at the same data with a 1% significance level does not reject the null hypothesis. This simply means that the value of the t statistic falls in the critical region of the former investigator but not in the critical region of the latter. It follows that a result cannot be declared universally statistically significant.

On the other hand, it is desirable to report results as compactly as possible, either to keep a report short or to ensure speedy assimilation of the information. The scientific community has developed a style of reporting that conveys the essential findings of significance tests while allowing people with differing attitudes toward

p-values

risk to apply their own significance levels to the findings. The reporting style uses ***p*-values**, empirical significance levels.

The essential ingredients of a significance test include:

- A model for the underlying process
- A sampling plan that takes account of or imposes a state of statistical control on the data
- A null hypothesis to be tested
- An alternative hypothesis
- A test statistic
- The sampling distribution of the test statistic when the null hypothesis is true
- A criterion for deciding when to reject the null hypothesis
- Ability to compute the significance level, which is the probability that the test rejects a true null hypothesis.

The last two ingredients are the ones that are modified to produce *p*-values. Rather than begin with an abstract discussion, we begin with an example.

EXAMPLE 17.4E

Consider the *t* test introduced in Examples 17.4A and C, which used the sample of size $n = 5$ in display (17.2). If the null hypothesis is H_0: $\mu = 0$, the value of the *t* statistic is -1.24. Working with the two-sided alternative, we saw that the result is not significant at either the 1% or the 5% significance levels.

To obtain the *p*-value associated with this outcome, the observed value of $t = -1.24$ is treated as if it were on the boundary of the plausible values. In other words, we act as if the interval of plausible values of *t* were $[-1.24, 1.24]$. The *p*-value is the significance level associated with this interval, namely, the probability that a *t* statistic value outside of this interval would be observed when the null hypothesis is true. The table of *t* distribution percentiles is not extensive enough to show the required probability. Statistical software is used to do the calculations. Statistical software was used to obtain the *p*-value of 0.2827.

The interpretation of the *p*-value is as follows. If a significance level greater than 28.27% had been chosen, then the *t* statistic actually obtained, $t = -1.24$, would have been declared statistically significant. Any investigator whose significance level is less than 28.27% will not find the actual *t* statistic value statistically significant. This style of reporting leaves it up to the person receiving the report to draw a conclusion from the test. The conclusion drawn will depend on the receiver's attitude toward risk. Few people who have given significance testing any thought will have significance levels as high as 28.27%, so it would be fairly safe to assume that there will be general agreement about the meaning of the test in this case. On the other hand, if a test yields a *p*-value between 0.05 and 0.01, there is considerable potential for investigators to disagree. Current practice suggests that *p*-values less than 0.01 command general agreement that the result is statistically significant.   ▪

A general procedure for computing p-values consists of the following steps:

- Compute the value of the test statistic.
- Make the value of test statistic obtained from the data a boundary between significant and nonsignificant values of the test statistic—that is, act as if the obtained value had been used to set up the critical region of the test in the first place.
- Compute the significance level associated with the "empirical" critical region obtained in the previous step; this is the p-value.

Reporting the p-value along with other essential information about the test allows investigators to draw conclusions in light of their own attitudes toward risk.

The next example demonstrates how to compute a p-value for a one-sided alternative.

EXAMPLE   17.4F

In Example 17.4C, we found a t statistic value of -5.5 in the context of testing a null hypothesis of $\mu = 0$ against the one-sided alternative $\mu < 0$. The p-value is the area a t distribution with 37 degrees of freedom assigns to the interval $(-\infty, -5.5]$, a probability that cannot be looked up in the printed t table. Statistical software can be used to find that the p-value is 0.000001431. Thus an investigator would reject the null hypothesis unless his or her significance level is less than 0.000001431.   ▪

SECTION

17.5 Exercises

17.5A Assume you have drawn a random sample of size $n = 15$ observations from a normal process with unknown mean μ and unknown standard deviation σ. The sample mean and standard deviation are $\bar{y} = 105.6$ and $s = 8.7$. You have been asked to comment on the null hypothesis $H_0: \mu = 100$ in light of the two-sided alternative hypothesis.

a Perform the t test at the 5% significance level.

b Perform the t test at the 1% significance level.

c Compare the conclusions of the two tests in parts (a) and (b).

17.5B Compute the p-value for the test in Exercise 17.5A.

17.5C Repeat Exercise 17.5A using the one-sided alternative hypothesis $H_1: \mu > 100$.

17.5D Compute the p-value for the test in Exercise 17.5C. Why is it different from the p-value computed in Exercise 17.5B?

17.5E Assume you have drawn a random sample of size $n = 15$ observations from a normal process with unknown mean μ and unknown standard deviation σ. The sample mean and standard deviation are $\bar{y} = 33.6$ and $s = 5.2$. You have been asked to comment on the null hypothesis H_0: $\mu = 36.5$ in light of the two-sided alternative hypothesis.

a Perform the t test at the 5% significance level.

b Perform the t test at the 1% significance level.

c Compare the conclusions of the two tests in parts (a) and (b).

17.5F Compute the p-value for the test in Exercise 17.5E.

17.5G Repeat Exercise 17.5E using the one-sided alternative hypothesis H_1: $\mu < 36.5$.

17.5H Compute the p-value for the test in Exercise 17.5G. Why is it different from the p-value computed in Exercise 17.5F?

17.5I Explain why a result that is statistically significant at the 1% level is also significant at the 5% level.

17.5J Repeat Exercise 17.5A with $n = 9$, $\bar{y} = 102.4$, $s = 9.8$, and H_0: $\mu = 100$.

17.5K Repeat Exercise 17.5A with $n = 900$, $\bar{y} = 102.4$, $s = 9.8$, and H_0: $\mu = 100$.

17.5L Compare the results of Exercises 17.5J and K. What is the impact of sample size on a test's ability to reject the null hypothesis?

17.5M Explain why different analysts can draw opposite conclusions from the same data using significance tests. What are some of the considerations that go into choosing a significance level? Can there be a completely objective way of choosing a significance level?

17.5N Exhibit 13.10B reports statistics on 38 total counting errors committed by subjects who were asked to count e's in sentences held upside down. Use these statistics to test the null hypothesis H_0: $\mu = 0$ versus the alternative hypothesis H_1: $\mu < 0$. Use a 1% significance level. What does the result imply about the subjects' ability to count e's? Compute the p-value of the test.

17.5O Write a three-to-five page essay interpreting mean control charts as applications of the t test for a process mean. What role does statistical control play in this application? What impact does lack of statistical control have on the validity of the significance test?

17.5P Write a three-to-five page essay that outlines the rationale of significance testing using the t test for a process mean. Use simulations to illustrate your points. Why must researchers risk drawing wrong conclusions?

17.5Q Find an article in a publication in your field in which a t test is reported. Write a brief essay on the problem addressed by the article. Does the article discuss clearly the process used to collect data? Was it in statistical control? Are you convinced that the conclusions drawn from the test are valid? Why or why not? What significance level was used? Why?

SECTION

17.6 Confidence Intervals for One Process Mean

Example 17.4C demonstrates that a t statistic is a function of both the data and the null hypothesis; it is a vehicle for comparing a hypothesized value of the process mean with data drawn from the process. For a given sample of data, some hypotheses yield significant t statistics and some do not. The set of null hypothesis mean values that **confidence interval** cannot be rejected by a set of data is called a **confidence interval** for the underlying process mean. A confidence interval is interpreted as the set of plausible guesses at the long-run process mean.

EXAMPLE   **17.6A**

Use the data in display (17.2), the t statistic in display (17.4) and a 1% significance level, for which the interval of plausible values of t is $[-4.604, 4.604]$. Then the set of null hypotheses μ_0 not rejected by the t test at the 1% significance level is the set that yields t statistics in the interval of plausible values, namely those for which

$$-4.604 \leq \frac{(-0.615 - \mu_0)}{0.497} \leq 4.604$$

or those for which

$$(-4.604)(0.497) \leq -0.615 - \mu_0 \leq (4.604)(0.497)$$

or for which

$$-2.90 \leq \mu_0 \leq 1.673 \quad \blacksquare$$

Example 17.6A demonstrates that a confidence interval calculation involving the one-sample t statistic requires as inputs the sample size, the sample mean, the sample standard deviation and a significance level. While the sample size, mean and standard deviation are fixed characteristics of a given sample, the significance level is a subjectively chosen percentage reflecting an experimenter's attitude toward risk. Different choices of significance levels produce different confidence intervals because they change the intervals of plausible values. Thus a confidence interval must be accompanied by a statement of the significance level on which it is based. In practice,

confidence coefficient

this is usually reported as a **confidence coefficient**, which is just 100% minus the significance level, reported as a percent. Thus in Example 17.6A, the confidence coefficient is 99% = 100% − 1%, because of the chosen 1% significance level. If a 5% significance level had been chosen, the interval of plausible values would have been $[-2.776, 2.776]$, and the 95% confidence interval would have been $[-1.99, 0.76]$. The effect of lowering the confidence coefficient is to shorten the confidence interval and to increase the risk that the interval does not contain the value of the underlying process mean.

EXAMPLE   **17.6B**

In Example 17.4B, we tested the null hypothesis that the long-run mean of changes in the Buffalo flour price index was 0. The t test was not significant at the 1% significance level, and this was interpreted to say that a lag 1 prediction rule was a reasonable one for the price index. Even when a specific null hypothesis value is not rejected, compute a confidence interval to show the whole range of values that could not be rejected by the test. If this range is wide, the justification for focusing narrowly on the specific null hypothesis tested is weak.

The mean and standard deviation of the $n = 99$ changes in the Buffalo price index are $\bar{y} = 8.67$ and $s = 77.03$, so the value of the standard deviation divided by the square root of the sample size is 7.74. Using a 1%

significance level, or equivalently a 99% confidence coefficient, we calculate the confidence interval to be those values of μ_0 for which

$$-2.6 \leq \frac{(8.67 - \mu_0)}{7.74} \leq 2.6$$

or

$$-11.5 \leq \mu_0 \leq 28.8$$

Thus, while 0 is a plausible value for the process mean, so is any number between -11.5 and 28.8. If the process mean were really 20, we would like to know it, because we would make better predictions of the monthly index in the long run by using the previous month's value plus 20. The data do not tell us whether this is a better strategy than using the previous month's value only. The confidence interval documents a considerable range of uncertainty.   ∎

A formula for a confidence interval can be obtained by following the general form of the calculations given in Examples 17.6A and B. For an appropriately specified number of degrees of freedom, let $t_{1-\alpha/2}$ stand for the number from the t table for which the t distribution assigns area $1 - \alpha/2$ to the interval $(-\infty, t_{1-\alpha/2}]$. This means that it assigns area $\alpha/2$ to each of the intervals $(-\infty, -t_{1-\alpha/2})$ and $(t_{1-\alpha/2}, \infty)$. Then the interval $[-t_{1-\alpha/2}, t_{1-\alpha/2}]$ is the interval of plausible values for the t test with significance level α. The confidence interval is found by determining the values of the null hypothesis values μ_0 such that the t statistic falls in the interval of plausible values—that is

$$-t_{1-\alpha/2} \leq \frac{(\bar{y} - \mu_0)}{s/\sqrt{n}} \leq t_{1-\alpha/2}$$

or

$$\bar{y} - t_{1-\alpha/2} \times \frac{s}{\sqrt{n}} \leq \mu_o \leq \bar{y} + t_{1-\alpha/2} \times \frac{s}{\sqrt{n}}$$

The confidence interval is often expressed as

$$\bar{y} \pm t_{1-\alpha/2} \times \frac{s}{\sqrt{n}} \tag{17.6}$$

which shows that the confidence interval has $\bar{y}$ as a midpoint, lower endpoint formed by subtracting $t_{1-\alpha/2}s/\sqrt{n}$ from $\bar{y}$, and upper endpoint formed by adding $t_{1-\alpha/2}s/\sqrt{n}$ to $\bar{y}$.

We see from the discussion in the previous paragraphs that the length of the confidence interval is 2 times $t_{1-\alpha/2}s/\sqrt{n}$. As noted in Example 17.6B, if the confidence interval is wide, it demonstrates considerable uncertainty about the value of the process mean. If an investigator has control over the size of the sample, n, the width of the interval can be controlled by making n large. We see this by noting that the width tends to decrease as n increases. In many problems, the sample size is limited either because the process can be observed over only a limited period of time or because the expense of collecting the data prohibits taking a large sample. In such cases, the width of the confidence interval cannot be controlled, and the confidence interval may be so wide that it merely quantifies our ignorance about the process mean.

SECTION

17.7 Exercises

17.7A Assume you have drawn a random sample of size $n = 15$ observations from a normal process with unknown mean μ and unknown standard deviation σ. The sample mean and standard deviation are $\bar{y} = 105.6$ and $s = 8.7$.

    a Compute the 99% confidence interval for μ.

    b Compute the 95% confidence interval for μ.

17.7B Assume you have drawn a random sample of size $n = 15$ observations from a normal process with unknown mean μ and unknown standard deviation σ. The sample mean and standard deviation are $\bar{y} = 33.6$ and $s = 5.2$.

    a Compute the 99% confidence interval for μ.

    b Compute the 95% confidence interval for μ.

17.7C Repeat Exercise 17.7A with $n = 9$, $\bar{y} = 102.4$, $s = 9.8$.

17.7D Repeat Exercise 17.7A with $n = 900$, $\bar{y} = 102.4$, $s = 9.8$.

17.7E Compare the results of Exercises 17.7C and D. What is the impact of sample size on a confidence interval?

SECTION

17.8 Prediction Intervals

Prediction is a necessary part of decision making. When a budget is prepared, a vital element of it is a prediction of future revenue. When a hiring plan is made, a vital part of it is a prediction of staff needs in new areas of activity, and old. When a plan for purchase of materials is made, a vital part of it is a prediction of the number of items that must be made to meet demand. And when the decision is made to continue operation of a process as is, a prediction has been made that the process is in control and is performing satisfactorily.

For a process with an identifiable random component, the methods of probability yield calculations of intervals that contain future outcomes of the process with specified probabilities, provided the process remains in statistical control. We exhibit such intervals in this section for the case of a process that yields normally distributed outcomes.

Let $y_1, y_2, \ldots, y_n$ denote outcomes from a process that is random and has a normal distribution with mean μ and standard deviation σ. We construct a prediction interval for the next outcome of the process y_{n+1}, assuming that $y_1, y_2, \ldots, y_n$ will have been observed and are available to help with the prediction of y_{n+1}. We specify that the prediction interval should have probability $1 - \alpha$ of capturing y_{n+1}. Then the required prediction interval is

$$\bar{y} \pm t_{1-\alpha/2} \times s\sqrt{1 + \frac{1}{n}} \qquad\qquad \textbf{(17.7)}$$

The formula is similar to the formula for the confidence interval for the mean of the process; the difference is in the factor $\sqrt{1 + 1/n}$, which is larger than the factor $\sqrt{1/n}$ that appears in the confidence interval formula. The prediction interval is larger than the confidence interval because it must account for the randomness in the next outcome y_{n+1} as well as the uncertainty about μ contained in the observed data $y_1, y_2, \ldots, y_n$.

EXAMPLE   **17.8A**

The last flour price index given in Exhibit 2.10A, 1929, is for November 1980. How would we predict the index for December 1980, with 95% probability? We have established that the sequence of monthly changes behaves randomly and approximately normally with estimated mean 0.867 and standard deviation 7.703. These statistics are based on 99 changes, so there are 98 degrees of freedom. The 97.5th percentile of the t distribution with 98 degrees of freedom is approximately 1.99, from interpolation in the t table. Thus the 95% prediction interval of the next change in the Buffalo price index is

$$0.867 \pm 1.99 \times 7.703\sqrt{1 + 1/99} = 0.867 \pm (1.99)(7.7418) = 0.867 \pm 15.406$$

or, expressing the interval in the same number of significant figures given in the data, 0.87 ± 15.41, which yields the interval $[-14.5, 16.3]$. If we believe with 95% probability that the index will change between November 1980 and December 1980 by an amount between -14.5 and 16.3, then we believe the index in December 1980 will be between $192.9 - 14.5$ and $192.9 + 16.3$— that is, between 178.4 and 209.2. The interval $[178.4, 209.2]$ is our 95% prediction interval for the Buffalo price index in December 1980. ▪

SECTION

17.9 Exercises

17.9A   A sequence of 25 outcomes from a random normal process yields sample mean and standard deviation 103 and 9. Compute the 99% prediction interval for the next outcome from the process.

17.9B   A sequence of 18 outcomes from a random normal process yields sample mean and standard deviation 60 and 15. Compute the 95% prediction interval for the next outcome from the process.

17.9C   A sequence of 9 outcomes from a random normal process yields sample mean and standard deviation 25 and 7. Compute the 95% prediction interval for the next outcome from the process.

17.9D   Exhibit 10.8I shows data on number of days to collection of accounts receivable from Company XYZ, grouped in groups of 5 observations. Analysis in Section 10.8 suggests that the sample means of the first 13 groups are in statistical control.

   a   Compute the means of the first 13 groups of 5 observations.

   b   Calculate the sample mean and standard deviation of the 13 means computed in part (a).

   c   Use the statistics you computed in part (b) to prepare the 99% prediction interval for the mean of the 14th group of observations.

d   Compare the endpoints of the prediction interval in part (c) with the upper and lower control limits displayed in Exhibit 10.8M.

S E C T I O N

17.10   Two-Sample t Statistics for the Difference Between Two Means

As the next two examples demonstrate, a typical application of inferential statistics is to use two sample means to infer differences in process means.

E X A M P L E   17.10A

A process in statistical control is to be improved. A control chart of some quality characteristics has been kept during the period prior to improvement efforts. A new method of operating is now standardized and the process is brought into statistical control. The control chart kept after standardizing the improvement is compared to the control chart kept before improvement in hopes of documenting a measurable effect. If the new mean level of the characteristic is significantly different from the old mean level, then a measurable effect can be claimed. Two-sample t significance tests can be used to document the effect.   ▪

E X A M P L E   17.10B

An insurance company wishes to measure the impact of two advertising documents on potential buyers of insurance. A mailing list of prospects is divided into two groups at random. One group receives one advertising document, the other group receives the other document. The prospects are followed up in the company's usual way by telephone and personal visit, if appropriate. After one year the amounts of insurance sold to members of the two groups are recorded. Among other comparisons, the means of the two sets of amounts are compared. Because the groups were formed at random, a state of statistical control that justifies the procedure discussed in this section is imposed on the experiment.   ▪

Both examples have the following elements in common:

- Continuous data
- Two processes to be compared
- Data generated independently from two processes
- The processes generating the data in statistical control

If these elements are present, then the two-sample t procedure usually works quite well for practical purposes. The details of the testing procedure are presented below.

Two-Sample t Test of No Difference Between Process Means

Let n_1 denote the number of items of data from the first process, and let $\bar{y}_1$ and s_1 denote the sample mean and standard deviation of the data. Let n_2, $\bar{y}_2$, and s_2 denote the same quantities for the second process. A **two-sample t statistic** is formed by computing

two-sample t statistic

$$t = \frac{\bar{y}_1 - \bar{y}_2}{\sqrt{\dfrac{s_1^2}{n_1} + \dfrac{s_2^2}{n_2}}}$$

(17.8)

E X A M P L E   **17.10C**

As a numerical illustration, suppose the data yield the following statistics:

i	$\bar{y}_i$	s_i	n_i
1	21.0	2.2	32
2	22.5	1.9	13

The numerator of the t statistic is

$$\bar{y}_1 - \bar{y}_2 = 21.0 - 22.5 = -1.5$$

The denominator of the t statistic is

$$\sqrt{\frac{s_1^2}{n_1} + \frac{s_2^2}{n_2}} = \sqrt{\frac{2.2^2}{32} + \frac{1.9^2}{13}} = \sqrt{0.15125 + 0.27769} \simeq 0.655$$

Finally, the value of the t statistic is

$$t = \frac{-1.5}{0.655} = -2.29 \quad \blacksquare$$

The theory in the next paragraph underlies the use of the t statistic as a significance test statistic for comparing two means. The theory assumes the cross-sectional distributions of the underlying processes are normal.

Let μ_1 and μ_2 denote the long-run means of the two underlying processes. Adopt a null hypothesis of equality of these two means—that is, H_0: $\mu_1 = \mu_2$. If this hypothesis cannot be rejected, the evidence for a difference between the process means is very weak. Given the assumptions outlined above, the following statement can be asserted:

If the null hypothesis H_0: $\mu_1 = \mu_2$ is true, then the sampling distribution of the t statistic in Equation (17.8) is approximated by a t distribution with degrees of freedom ν computed by the formula

$$\frac{1}{\nu} = \frac{a^2}{n_1 - 1} + \frac{(1 - a)^2}{n_2 - 1}$$

(17.9)

where the parameter a is computed from the formula

$$a = \frac{\dfrac{s_1^2}{n_1}}{\dfrac{s_1^2}{n_1} + \dfrac{s_2^2}{n_2}}$$

(17.10)

This result allows the following significance test to be conducted:

1 Compute the t statistic in Equation (17.8).

2 Compute the degrees of freedom ν in Equation (17.9).

3 Choose a significance level α.

4 Determine $t_{1-\alpha/2}$.

5 Reject H_0 at the $100\alpha\%$ significance level if $|t| > t_{1-\alpha/2}$; otherwise, do not reject H_0.

In implementing this test, you will find that the degrees of freedom parameter ν is seldom an integer, but tables of the t distribution report only integer values of the degrees of freedom. For practical applications, simply use the smallest integer degrees of freedom that is greater than ν. As an alternative, computer software that gives percentiles of the t distribution can compute the exact percentile for degrees of freedom that are not integers.

E X A M P L E   **17.10D**   Continuing Example 17.10C, compute the degrees of freedom and perform the significance test. The value of the parameter a is

$$a = \frac{\dfrac{2.2^2}{32}}{\dfrac{2.2^2}{32} + \dfrac{1.9^2}{13}} = \frac{0.15125}{0.15125 + 0.27769} = 0.352612$$

Thus

$$\frac{1}{\nu} = \left[\frac{0.352612^2}{31}\right] + \frac{(1 - 0.352612)^2}{12} = 0.004011 + 0.034926 = 0.038937$$

and $\nu = 1/0.038937 \simeq 25.68 \simeq 26$. Using the t-table row corresponding to 26 degrees of freedom, the 97.5th percentile is 2.056 and the 99.5th percentile is 2.779. These are the tabled values needed to perform significance tests at the 5% and 1% significance levels.

Using the data in Example 17.10C, the value of the t statistic is -2.29. Because $|t| = 2.29 > 2.056$, the null hypothesis would be rejected at the 5% significance level. Because $|t| = 2.29 < 2.779$, the null hypothesis would not be rejected at the 1% significance level. This example underlines the importance of having some idea of the desired level of risk when doing the significance test. The t statistic signals different actions depending on the level of significance, which is a parameter chosen by the experimenter. It is impossible to use the test as a basis for action if you have no idea what significance level is appropriate.

This example also shows how different analysts can reach different conclusions after looking at the same data. Two analysts with different significance levels can actually come to opposite conclusions about the implications of a statistic. When this happens, the analysts may

1 Negotiate a significance level they can both agree on

2 Agree to seek more data and perform the test again to see if the conclusion is clear-cut

3 Simply agree to disagree ∎

Two-Sample t Test for Arbitrary Difference of Group Means

Occasionally, researchers need to test whether the difference between two group means is equal to a nonzero quantity. Then the null hypothesis is

$$H_0: \mu_1 - \mu_2 = \delta$$

where δ denotes the specified difference between the theoretical means. The significance testing procedure exactly parallels that outlined in the preceding subsection except that the t statistic is computed from the formula

$$t = \frac{\bar{y}_1 - \bar{y}_2 - \delta}{\sqrt{\dfrac{s_1^2}{n_1} + \dfrac{s_2^2}{n_2}}} \qquad (17.11)$$

instead of the formula in Equation (17.8).

Pooled Two-Sample t Statistic

In some applications, particularly those associated with randomized experiments, as described in Chapters 18 and 19, it is reasonable to assume that the two long-run process standard deviations are equal. Then the two-sample t statistic is modified to reflect this assumption. The formula (17.11) becomes

$$t = \frac{\bar{y}_1 - \bar{y}_2 - \delta}{s_p \sqrt{\dfrac{1}{n_1} + \dfrac{1}{n_2}}} \qquad (17.12)$$

where

$$s_p = \sqrt{\frac{(n_1 - 1)s_1^2 + (n_2 - 1)s_2^2}{n_1 + n_2 - 2}} \qquad (17.13)$$

is known as the *pooled standard deviation*. The pooled standard deviation is formed by creating a term under the square root sign that is the ratio of two sums. The sum in the numerator adds the sums of squared deviations from the means of the two samples, while the sum in the denominator adds the degrees of freedom from the two samples. This is the sense in which the two samples are pooled. The justification for the pooling is the assumption that the two process standard deviations are equal, so both samples have information about the common standard deviation.

The degrees of freedom associated with the t statistic in Equation (17.12) equals $n_1 + n_2 - 2$.

E X A M P L E   **17.10E**

Using the data in Example 17.10C and display (17.13), the pooled standard deviation is

$$s_p = \sqrt{\frac{(32-1)2.2^2 + (13-1)1.9^2}{32 + 13 - 2}} = \sqrt{\frac{193.36}{43}} = 2.12$$

and, using display (17.12), the pooled two-sample t statistic for testing the null hypothesis that $\delta = 0$ is

$$t = \frac{21.0 - 22.5}{2.12\sqrt{\frac{1}{32} + \frac{1}{13}}} = \frac{-1.5}{2.12(0.328897)} = \frac{-1.5}{0.697} = -2.15$$

which differs little from the more general two-sample t statistic computed in Example 17.10C. ▪

Unless one of the process standard deviations is more than twice the other one, it is probably safe to use the pooled t statistic. A virtue of using the pooled statistic is that the formula for degrees of freedom is very simple, namely $n_1 + n_2 - 2$. In the example above the degrees of freedom equal $32 + 13 - 2 = 43$.

SECTION

17.11 Exercises

17.11A   For each case below, use the two-sample t test to test the null hypothesis that the two process means are equal, at both the 5% and 1% significance levels.

   a $n_1 = 20, n_2 = 20, \bar{y}_1 = 30.4, \bar{y}_2 = 18.9, s_1 = 25.1, s_2 = 27.8$
   b $n_1 = 20, n_2 = 20, \bar{y}_1 = 30.4, \bar{y}_2 = 18.9, s_1 = 40.6, s_2 = 27.8$
   c $n_1 = 200, n_2 = 200, \bar{y}_1 = 30.4, \bar{y}_2 = 18.9, s_1 = 25.1, s_2 = 27.8$
   d $n_1 = 20, n_2 = 10, \bar{y}_1 = 30.4, \bar{y}_2 = 18.9, s_1 = 25.1, s_2 = 27.8$
   e $n_1 = 10, n_2 = 20, \bar{y}_1 = 30.4, \bar{y}_2 = 18.9, s_1 = 40.6, s_2 = 27.8$

17.11B   For each case in Exercise 17.11A, use the two-sample t test at both the 5% and the 1% significance levels to test $H_0: \mu_1 - \mu_2 = 10$.

17.11C   Exhibit 13.10B reports statistics on 38 total counting errors committed by subjects who were asked to count e's in sentences held right-side up and 38 total counting errors committed by subjects who were asked to count e's in sentences held upside down. Use the pooled two-sample t statistic to test the null hypothesis $H_0: \delta = 0$ versus the alternative hypothesis $H_1: \delta \neq 0$—that is, that on average the number of e's counted is the same whether the sentences are held right-side up or upside down. Use a 5% significance level. Compute the p-value of the test.

17.11D   A consumer advocacy group wishes to assess the ability of tax preparers to prepare complex tax returns correctly. The group designs a tax case for a family with an annual gross income of $150,000 that involves several thorny tax issues. The group selects a random sample of 10 preparers in City A and an independent random sample of preparers in City B. The tax case is sent to the preparers. After the preparers' returns are collected, the advocacy group computes the differences between the tax computed by the preparers and the actual tax that should have been computed. The data therefore consist of two sets of errors, one for preparers in City A and one for the preparers in City B. Here are the data (errors stated in dollars):

City A	City B	City A	City B
100.45	2008.12	649.32	1037.20
56.45	1987.09	425.99	2439.94
102.13	857.52	820.13	1390.51
290.29	1943.27	2500.00	1594.38
811.41	1820.29	1091.29	2083.41

a Compute the sample means and standard deviations for the two groups of preparers.

b Compute the general two-sample t statistic for testing the null hypothesis that the theoretical mean errors of preparers in the two cities are the same.

c Compute the p-value of the test.

d Is the result statistically significant at the 1% significance level? Discuss the implications of the result.

17.11E Find an article in a publication in your field in which a two-sample t test is reported. Write a brief essay on the problem addressed by the article. Does the article discuss clearly the processes used to collect data? Were they in statistical control? Are you convinced that the conclusions drawn from the test are valid? Why or why not? What significance level was used? Why?

17.11F Using the notation of Section 17.10, show that if $a = 1/2$, then $\nu = 4(n_1 - 1)(n_2 - 1)/(n_1 + n_2 - 1)$. Show further that if $n_1 = n_2 = n/2$, then $\nu = n - 2$. Under what conditions does $a = 1/2$?

SECTION

17.12 Confidence Intervals for a Difference in Means

The t statistic in Equation (17.11) can be used as a basis for an approximate confidence interval for the difference in the theoretical means of the two groups. Theory says that under appropriate conditions, to a good approximation, the statistic in Equation (17.11) has a t distribution with ν degrees of freedom, where ν is given by Equation (17.9). Thus, solving the inequality

$$|t| < t_{1-\alpha/2} \tag{17.14}$$

for δ provides an interval of differences that cannot be rejected by the significance test at the $100\alpha\%$ significance level. This interval of values is a $100(1 - \alpha)\%$ confidence interval for the difference between the theoretical means of the two groups. The interval can be shown to be

$$\bar{y}_1 - \bar{y}_2 - t_{1-\alpha/2}\sqrt{\frac{s_1^2}{n_1} + \frac{s_2^2}{n_2}} < \delta < \bar{y}_1 - \bar{y}_2 + t_{1-\alpha/2}\sqrt{\frac{s_1^2}{n_1} + \frac{s_2^2}{n_2}} \tag{17.15}$$

EXAMPLE   17.12A

Example 17.10C displayed data for which

$$\bar{y}_1 - \bar{y}_2 = -1.5 \quad \text{and} \quad \sqrt{\frac{s_1^2}{n_1} + \frac{s_2^2}{n_2}} = 0.655$$

To get a 99% confidence interval for the difference in the theoretical means of the two groups, use $t_{0.005} = 2.779$ and compute the interval

$$-1.5 - 2.779(0.655) < \delta < -1.5 + 2.779(0.655)$$

or

$$-1.5 - 1.8 < \delta < -1.5 + 1.8$$

or

$$-3.3 < \delta < 0.3$$

In this instance, we have 99% confidence that the difference between the first and second group mean is between -3.3 and 0.3, indicating that we cannot conclude, with this level of confidence, that one mean is larger than the other.   ▪

If the pooled version of the t statistic is used, the formula for the confidence interval changes to

$$\bar{y}_1 - \bar{y}_2 - t_{1-\alpha/2}s_p\sqrt{\frac{1}{n_1} + \frac{1}{n_2}} < \delta < \bar{y}_1 - \bar{y}_2 + t_{1-\alpha/2}s_p\sqrt{\frac{1}{n_1} + \frac{1}{n_2}} \qquad \textbf{(17.16)}$$

EXAMPLE   17.12B

For the data in Example 17.10C, the difference in the sample means is -1.5, the pooled standard deviation is 2.12, and

$$s_p\sqrt{\frac{1}{n_1} + \frac{1}{n_2}} = 2.12\sqrt{\frac{1}{32} + \frac{1}{13}} = 0.697$$

and degrees of freedom are $32 + 13 - 2 = 43$, so the 99% confidence interval for δ is

$$[-1.5 - 2.69(0.697), -1.5 + 2.69(0.697)] = [-3.4, 0.4] \quad ▪$$

SECTION

17.13 Exercises

17.13A   For each case in Exercise 17.11A, use the two-sample t statistic to construct 95% and 99% confidence intervals for $\mu_1 - \mu_2$. Which of the intervals contain 0? Which of the intervals contain 10?

17.13B For each case in Exercise 17.11A, use the pooled two-sample t statistic to construct 95% and 99% confidence intervals for $\mu_1 - \mu_2$. Which of the intervals contain 0? Which of the intervals contain 10? Compare your results to those in Exercise 17.13A.

17.13C Exhibit 13.10B reports statistics on 38 total counting errors committed by subjects who were asked to count e's in sentences held right-side up and 38 total counting errors committed by subjects who were asked to count e's in sentences held upside down. Use the pooled two-sample t statistic to construct a 95% confidence interval for δ, the average number of e's counted held right-side up minus the average number of e's counted upside down. Does the interval contain 0? Explain the implication of your result.

17.13D Use your calculations from Exercise 17.11D to compute a 99% confidence interval for the difference in average errors for tax preparers in the two cities. Discuss the implications of your result.

S E C T I O N

17.14 F Statistics and F Distributions

We saw in Section 17.10 that the pooled two-sample t statistic could be used to test the null hypothesis that two process means are equal. When the alternative hypothesis is that the two process means are not equal—that is, when the alternative is two-sided—the *square* of the two-sample t statistic can be used as the test statistic. The reason is very simple. Letting t denote the value of the statistic computed from the samples and $t_{1-\alpha/2}$ denote the critical value of the t distribution with the appropriate degrees of freedom, the null hypothesis is rejected at the $100\alpha\%$ significance level if $|t| > t_{1-\alpha/2}$, which is equivalent to rejecting the null hypothesis if $t^2 > t_{1-\alpha/2}^2$.

The square of the pooled two-sample t statistic is an example of what statisticians call an F statistic. F statistics are very important in statistical problems known as Analysis of Variance problems. We discuss such problems at length in Chapters 18 and 19. Here we simply introduce F statistics and the associated F distributions, leaving a discussion of applications to the later chapters.

F Statistics for Testing the Equality of Two Process Means Versus the Two-Sided Alternative Hypothesis

We consider two cases: equal sample sizes from the two processes and unequal sample sizes from the two processes.

When $n_1 = n_2 = n$, say, the square of the pooled two-sample t statistic, which is the F statistic, may be written as follows:

$$F = t^2 = \left[\frac{\bar{y}_1 - \bar{y}_2}{s_p\sqrt{\dfrac{1}{n_1} + \dfrac{1}{n_2}}} \right]^2 = \left[\frac{(\bar{y}_1 - \bar{y}_2)/\sqrt{\dfrac{1}{n_1} + \dfrac{1}{n_2}}}{s_p} \right]^2 = \frac{(n/2)(\bar{y}_1 - \bar{y}_2)^2}{s_p^2}$$

which we may finally write as

$$F = \frac{(n/2)(\bar{y}_1 - \bar{y}_2)^2}{(n-1)((s_1^2 + s_2^2)/(2(n-1)))}$$

The numerator of the F statistic is just the square of the difference in the sample means multiplied by $n/2$. The denominator is just the average of the squares of the sample standard deviations of the samples taken from the two processes.

Both the numerator and the denominator of the F statistic have associated degrees of freedom. For the F statistic displayed above, the numerator degrees of freedom is 1 and the denominator degrees of freedom is $n + n - 2 = 2(n - 1)$. The numerator degrees of freedom is one less than the number of means compared. The denominator degrees of freedom equals the degrees of freedom associated with the pooled standard deviation.

Recall that the general pooled two-sample t statistic, Equation (17.12), is

$$t = \frac{\bar{y}_1 - \bar{y}_2}{s_p \sqrt{\dfrac{1}{n_1} + \dfrac{1}{n_2}}}$$

where the squared pooled standard deviation is

$$s_p^2 = [(n_1 - 1)s_1^2 + (n_2 - 1)s_2^2]/(n_1 + n_2 - 2)$$

The expression for the square of the general t statistic has the essential features of the expression given above. The numerator is a function of the square of the difference in the sample means and the denominator is a function of the squares of the sample standard deviations. The numerator degrees of freedom equals 1 and the denominator degrees of freedom equals $n_1 + n_2 - 2$.

The General F Statistic and F Distribution

The essential idea behind Analysis of Variance problems is to compare the means of any number of processes. The null hypothesis is that the process means are all equal; the alternative is that at least one of the process means is different from the others. A key assumption is that the process standard deviations are equal, so that a pooled estimate of these standard deviations can be computed from the sample data. The general F statistic is the ratio of positive quantities. The numerator is a function of the sample means of the data from the processes, and the denominator is a function of the standard deviations. The numerator has degrees of freedom that is a function of the number of process means being compared. The general symbol for numerator degrees of freedom is ν_1. The denominator has degrees of freedom that is a complicated function of sample sizes. It's general symbol is ν_2.

F distribution

An **F distribution** is the sampling distribution of an F statistic showing the variation in the statistic that results from the randomness of the samples when the null hypothesis is true. The theoretical derivation of F distributions assumes that all process data have normal distributions.

The next example shows a simulation of a particular F distribution.

E X A M P L E   **17.14A**

We used a computer to simulate 500 random drawings from an F distribution with degrees of freedom $\nu_1 = 10$ and $\nu_2 = 5$. Exhibit 17.14A shows a dotplot and some descriptive statistics of the 500 values of F. Notice that the F

distribution is skewed to the right. Its mean is 1.6656, and its standard deviation is 2.2231. These are close to the theoretical mean and standard deviation of an F distribution with 10 and 5 degrees of freedom, which are $5/3 \simeq 1.67$ and $\sqrt{65/9} \simeq 2.69$.

A printout of the 500 F values (not shown here) shows that the 476th largest value is 4.5701. This is the sample estimate of the 95th percentile of the F distribution with 10 and 5 degrees of freedom. The actual 95th percentile of the theoretical distribution is 4.74, so the sample estimate is too low by about 0.17. The 496th largest value in the sample, which is an estimate of the 99th percentile of the F distribution with 10 and 5 degrees of freedom, is 12.4746. The actual 99th percentile of the F distribution is 10.05, so the estimate is too high by about 2.42. Had more values been simulated, more reliable estimates of the percentiles would have been obtained.   ∎

E X H I B I T **17.14A**
Dotplot and Descriptive Statistics for 500 Simulated Values from the F Distribution with 10 and 5 Degrees of Freedom

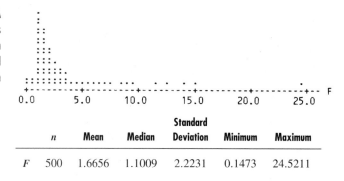

	n	Mean	Median	Standard Deviation	Minimum	Maximum
F	500	1.6656	1.1009	2.2231	0.1473	24.5211

Mathematical statistics shows that the theoretical mean and standard deviation of the F distribution with v_1 and v_2 degrees of freedom are

$$\mu = \frac{v_2}{v_2 - 2} \quad \text{and} \quad \sigma = \sqrt{\frac{2v_2^2(v_1 + v_2 - 2)}{v_1(v_2 - 2)^2(v_2 - 4)}} \qquad \textbf{(17.17)}$$

Note that the mean does not exist if v_2 is less than or equal to 2, and the standard deviation does not exist if v_2 is less than or equal to 4.

Tables of F distributions are complicated because they must display distributions for each possible combination of the numerator and denominator degrees of freedom. Exhibit 17.14B shows a limited F distribution table, which gives only the 95th and 99th percentiles for selected distributions. Access to computer software is essential for practical uses of the F distribution. There is no use limiting yourself to the percentiles shown in the typical tables.

SECTION

17.15 Exercises

17.15A   For an F distribution with 7 and 13 degrees of freedom, find the 95th and 99th percentiles.

17.15B   For each case below, find the mean, standard deviation, 95th percentile and 99th percentile of the indicated F distribution.

a $v_1 = 2, v_2 = 5$

b $v_1 = 2, v_2 = 10$

c $v_1 = 4, v_2 = 20$

d $v_1 = 8, v_2 = 12$

e $v_1 = 8, v_2 = 8$

SECTION

17.16 Comparison of Means When Data Are Binary—Chi-Square

Even though the sampling distributions of the F statistics discussed in Section 17.14 are derived assuming the data are normally distributed, the statistics can be applied when the data are binary, provided the sample sizes are large. In this type of application the F distributions are approximations to the true sampling distributions, and they in turn are usually approximated by a distribution called chi-square. In this section we briefly indicate how some of these applications are carried out in practice.

Recalling the discussion in Chapter 11, let $y_{11}, y_{12}, \ldots, y_{1n_1}$ denote a random sample of data from a Bernoulli process with long-run proportion of successes equal to π_1. Let $y_{21}, y_{22}, \ldots, y_{2n_2}$ denote an independent random sample of data from another Bernoulli process with long-run proportion of successes equal to π_2. The sample mean for the first sample is just the proportion of the sample items that are successes, so we denote the sample mean by the symbol p_1. Similarly, the sample mean for the second sample is the proportion of sample items that are successes, so we denote the sample mean by the symbol p_2.

Recall that the theoretical mean and standard deviation of a Bernoulli process are both functions of the long-run proportion of successes. For the first Bernoulli process introduced above, the theoretical mean and standard deviation are $\mu_1 = \pi_1$ and $\sigma_1 = \sqrt{\pi_1(1 - \pi_1)}$, and for the second Bernoulli process introduced above, the theoretical mean and standard deviation are $\mu_2 = \pi_2$ and $\sigma_2 = \sqrt{\pi_2(1 - \pi_2)}$.

Now we wish to test the null hypothesis that the two Bernoulli processes have equal means, but the formulas in the previous paragraphs show that this also implies that the processes have equal standard deviations. In other words, the null hypothesis of equal means literally implies that the two processes are identical. This was not an implication of the null hypothesis in the more general case considered in Sections 17.10 and 17.14, but it is an implication that must be taken into account when computing an F statistic for binary data. This is done by computing the pooled sample standard deviations in the following special way: treat the two samples as one sample from a single Bernoulli process and compute the estimated standard deviation from this combined sample. In other words, if y_1 denotes the number of successes in the sample from the first process, and y_2 denotes the number of successes in the

E X H I B I T **17.14B** Table of 95th and 99th Percentiles of Selected F Distributions (Rows are numerator degrees of freedom; columns are denominator degrees of freedom. Entries in a cell are the 95th on top of the 99th percentile.)

Area .95 or .99

v_1	1	2	3	4	v_2 5	6	7	8	9	10
1	161.45	18.51	10.13	7.71	6.61	5.99	5.59	5.32	5.12	4.97
	4052.18	98.51	34.12	21.20	16.26	13.75	12.25	11.26	10.56	10.04
2	199.50	19.00	9.55	6.94	5.79	5.14	4.74	4.46	4.26	4.10
	4999.50	99.00	30.82	18.00	13.27	10.93	9.55	8.65	8.02	7.56
3	215.71	19.16	9.28	6.59	5.41	4.76	4.35	4.07	3.86	3.71
	5403.35	99.17	29.46	16.69	12.06	9.78	8.45	7.59	6.99	6.55
4	224.58	19.25	9.12	6.39	5.19	4.53	4.12	3.84	3.63	3.48
	5624.57	99.25	28.71	15.98	11.39	9.15	7.85	7.01	6.42	5.99
5	230.16	19.30	9.01	6.26	5.05	4.39	3.97	3.69	3.48	3.33
	5763.63	99.30	28.24	15.52	10.97	8.75	7.46	6.63	6.06	5.64
6	233.99	19.33	8.94	6.16	4.95	4.28	3.87	3.58	3.37	3.22
	5858.97	99.33	27.91	15.21	10.67	8.47	7.19	6.37	5.80	5.39
7	236.77	19.35	8.89	6.09	4.88	4.21	3.79	3.50	3.29	3.14
	5928.34	99.36	27.67	14.98	10.46	8.26	6.99	6.18	5.61	5.20
8	238.88	19.37	8.85	6.04	4.82	4.15	3.73	3.44	3.23	3.07
	5981.05	99.37	27.49	14.80	10.29	8.10	6.84	6.03	5.47	5.06
9	240.54	19.39	8.81	6.00	4.77	4.10	3.68	3.39	3.18	3.02
	6022.45	99.39	27.35	14.66	10.16	7.98	6.72	5.91	5.35	4.94
10	241.88	19.40	8.79	5.96	4.74	4.06	3.64	3.35	3.14	2.98
	6055.82	99.40	27.23	14.55	10.05	7.87	6.62	5.81	5.26	4.85
11	242.98	19.41	8.76	5.94	4.70	4.03	3.60	3.31	3.10	2.94
	6083.29	99.41	27.13	14.45	9.96	7.79	6.54	5.73	5.18	4.77
12	243.91	19.41	8.75	5.91	4.68	4.00	3.58	3.28	3.07	2.91
	6106.29	99.42	27.05	14.37	9.89	7.72	6.47	5.67	5.11	4.71
13	244.69	19.42	8.73	5.89	4.66	3.98	3.55	3.26	3.05	2.89
	6125.84	99.42	26.98	14.31	9.83	7.66	6.41	5.61	5.05	4.65
14	245.36	19.42	8.72	5.87	4.64	3.96	3.53	3.24	3.03	2.87
	6142.64	99.43	26.92	14.25	9.77	7.61	6.36	5.56	5.01	4.60
15	245.95	19.43	8.70	5.86	4.62	3.94	3.51	3.22	3.01	2.85
	6157.26	99.43	26.87	14.20	9.72	7.56	6.31	5.52	4.96	4.56

EXHIBIT **17.14B**
(Continued)

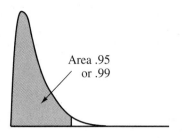

Area .95
or .99

v_1	11	12	13	14	v_2 15	16	17	18	19	20
1	4.84	4.75	4.67	4.60	4.54	4.49	4.45	4.41	4.38	4.35
	9.65	9.33	9.07	8.86	8.68	8.53	8.40	8.29	8.19	8.10
2	3.98	3.89	3.81	3.74	3.68	3.63	3.59	3.56	3.52	3.49
	7.21	6.93	6.70	6.52	6.36	6.23	6.11	6.01	5.93	5.85
3	3.59	3.49	3.41	3.34	3.29	3.24	3.20	3.16	3.13	3.10
	6.22	5.95	5.74	5.56	5.42	5.29	5.19	5.09	5.01	4.94
4	3.36	3.26	3.18	3.11	3.06	3.01	2.97	2.93	2.90	2.87
	5.67	5.41	5.21	5.04	4.89	4.77	4.67	4.58	4.50	4.43
5	3.20	3.11	3.03	2.96	2.90	2.85	2.81	2.77	2.74	2.71
	5.32	5.06	4.86	4.70	4.56	4.44	4.34	4.25	4.17	4.10
6	3.10	3.00	2.92	2.85	2.79	2.74	2.70	2.66	2.63	2.60
	5.07	4.82	4.62	4.46	4.32	4.20	4.10	4.02	3.94	3.87
7	3.01	2.91	2.83	2.76	2.71	2.66	2.61	2.58	2.54	2.51
	4.89	4.64	4.44	4.28	4.14	4.03	3.93	3.84	3.77	3.70
8	2.95	2.85	2.77	2.70	2.64	2.59	2.55	2.51	2.48	2.45
	4.74	4.50	4.30	4.14	4.00	3.89	3.79	3.71	3.63	3.56
9	2.90	2.80	2.71	2.65	2.59	2.54	2.49	2.46	2.42	2.39
	4.63	4.39	4.19	4.03	3.90	3.78	3.68	3.60	3.52	3.46
10	2.85	2.75	2.67	2.60	2.54	2.49	2.45	2.41	2.38	2.35
	4.54	4.30	4.10	3.94	3.81	3.69	3.59	3.51	3.43	3.37
11	2.82	2.72	2.64	2.57	2.51	2.46	2.41	2.37	2.34	2.31
	4.46	4.22	4.03	3.86	3.73	3.62	3.52	3.43	3.36	3.29
12	2.79	2.69	2.60	2.53	2.47	2.43	2.38	2.34	2.31	2.28
	4.40	4.16	3.96	3.80	3.67	3.55	3.46	3.37	3.30	3.23
13	2.76	2.66	2.58	2.51	2.45	2.40	2.35	2.31	2.28	2.25
	4.34	4.10	3.91	3.75	3.61	3.50	3.40	3.32	3.24	3.18
14	2.74	2.64	2.55	2.48	2.42	2.37	2.33	2.29	2.26	2.22
	4.29	4.05	3.86	3.70	3.56	3.45	3.35	3.27	3.20	3.13
15	2.72	2.62	2.53	2.46	2.40	2.35	2.31	2.27	2.23	2.20
	4.25	4.01	3.82	3.66	3.52	3.41	3.31	3.23	3.15	3.09

sample from the second process, the number of successes in the combined sample is $y_1 + y_2$, and the number of failures is $n_1 + n_2 - (y_1 + y_2)$. The pooled estimate of the standard deviation, which we denote s_c, then becomes simply

$$s_c = \sqrt{\frac{y_1 + y_2}{n_1 + n_2} \cdot \left(1 - \frac{y_1 + y_2}{n_1 + n_2}\right)} \tag{17.18}$$

the pooled two-sample t statistic becomes

$$t = \frac{p_1 - p_2}{s_c\sqrt{\dfrac{1}{n_1} + \dfrac{1}{n_2}}} \tag{17.19}$$

and the F statistic is just the square of this t statistic. The null hypothesis of equal process means is rejected at the $100\alpha\%$ significance level if the value of the F statistic is larger than the $100(1 - \alpha)$th percentile of the F distribution with 1 and $n_1 + n_2 - 2$ degrees of freedom.

The test based on the F distribution is theoretically justified only for large samples. When the samples are small, the F statistic has a distribution that is cumbersome to compute. As a safe guideline for practice, use the F distribution as we have suggested only if each of the following quantities is greater than 5: $(n_1 + n_2)p_1$, $(n_1 + n_2)(1 - p_1)$, $(n_1 + n_2)p_2$, $(n_1 + n_2)(1 - p_2)$. These guidelines make sure that the total sample size $n_1 + n_2$ is sufficiently large enough that the F distribution produces a reliable test of significance.

Two-Way Table Display

When the data are binary, they can be summarized in two-way tables, as discussed in Chapter 5. The table in Exhibit 17.16A shows the format.

E X H I B I T 17.16A
Two-Way Table of Data Collected
from Two Bernoulli Processes

Source of Data	Number of Successes	Number of Failures	Total
Process 1	y_1	$n_1 - y_1$	n_1
Process 2	y_2	$n_2 - y_2$	n_2
Total	$y_1 + y_2$	$n_1 + n_2 - y_1 - y_2$	$n_1 + n_2$

The table displays all of the quantities needed to compute the F statistic. By dint of considerable algebra, it can be shown that an alternative formula for the statistic is

$$F = \frac{(n_1 + n_2 - 2)[y_1(n_2 - y_2) - y_2(n_1 - y_1)]^2}{n_1 n_2 (y_1 + y_2)(n_1 + n_2 - y_1 - y_2)} \tag{17.20}$$

Because $n_1 + n_2$ must be large in practice, there is no practical difference between $n_1 + n_2 - 2$ and $n_1 + n_2$, so the latter factor is used as the leading term in the numerator. When this is done, the statistic is denoted by X^2 and called *Pearson's chi-square statistic:*[†]

$$X^2 = \frac{(n_1 + n_2)[y_1(n_2 - y_2) - y_2(n_1 - y_1)]^2}{n_1 n_2 (y_1 + y_2)(n_1 + n_2 - y_1 - y_2)} \qquad \text{(17.21)}$$

chi-square distribution

The chi-square approximation is based on the mathematical fact that when the denominator degrees of freedom is large, the F distribution depends only on its numerator degrees of freedom and is the distribution known as chi-square. Thus there is a **chi-square distribution** for each possible value of numerator degrees of freedom, which is denoted by the symbol v. The table in Exhibit 17.16B shows selected percentiles of chi-square distributions for degrees of freedom 1 through 30.

The row that is relevant for testing the equality of means of two Bernoulli processes is $v = 1$. The following example shows how to implement the test using the X^2 statistic and the chi-square distribution with 1 degree of freedom.

EXAMPLE   17.16A

Nonresponse, which means that respondents fail to fill out questionnaires or refuse to answer questions over the phone, is common in surveys. Nonresponse can bias the results of a survey to the point that they become meaningless. One way to estimate the potential magnitude of nonresponse is to conduct a pilot study. If the pilot study suggests that nonresponse will be substantial, the size of the final survey must be scaled down so more resources can be targeted to follow up on the nonrespondents.

Here is the result of a pilot study on a sample of 100 insurance companies. The companies were divided into two groups: Large and Other. Size was measured by reported assets in the annual statements of the companies. Random samples of 30 Large and 70 Other companies were chosen and questionnaires sent. The table below shows the numbers of respondents and nonrespondents in each group.

Company Size	Responded? Yes	No	Total
Other	25	45	70
Large	20	10	30
Total	45	55	100

We wish to test the null hypothesis that the two types of companies have the same rates of nonresponse. We use a 5% significance level.

[†]See K. Pearson, "On a Criterion That a Given System of Deviations from the Probable in the Case of a Correlated System of Variables Is Such That It Can Be Reasonably Supposed to Have Arisen from Random Sampling," *Philosophical Magazine,* 50(5) (1900), 157–175.

E X H I B I T **17.16B** Selected Percentiles of Chi-Square Distributions with ν Degrees of Freedom (The body of the table shows values of c such that $1 - \alpha$ is the area bounded by the horizontal axis, a vertical line located at c, and the chi-square curve.)

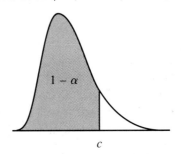

ν	$1 - \alpha$											
	0.01	**0.05**	**0.10**	**0.30**	**0.50**	**0.70**	**0.90**	**0.95**	**0.975**	**0.99**	**0.995**	**0.999**
1	0.00	0.00	0.02	0.15	0.46	1.07	2.71	3.84	5.02	6.64	7.88	10.83
2	0.02	0.10	0.21	0.71	1.39	2.41	4.61	5.99	7.38	9.21	10.60	13.82
3	0.12	0.35	0.58	1.42	2.37	3.67	6.25	7.82	9.35	11.35	12.84	16.27
4	0.30	0.71	1.06	2.20	3.36	4.88	7.78	9.49	11.14	13.28	14.86	18.47
5	0.55	1.15	1.61	3.00	4.35	6.06	9.24	11.07	12.83	15.09	16.75	20.52
6	0.87	1.64	2.20	3.83	5.35	7.23	10.65	12.59	14.45	16.81	18.55	22.46
7	1.24	2.17	2.83	4.67	6.35	8.38	12.02	14.07	16.01	18.48	20.28	24.32
8	1.65	2.73	3.49	5.53	7.34	9.52	13.36	15.51	17.54	20.09	21.96	26.13
9	2.09	3.33	4.17	6.39	8.34	10.66	14.68	16.92	19.02	21.67	23.59	27.88
10	2.56	3.94	4.86	7.27	9.34	11.78	15.99	18.31	20.48	23.21	25.19	29.59
11	3.05	4.57	5.58	8.15	10.34	12.90	17.28	19.67	21.92	24.73	26.76	31.26
12	3.57	5.23	6.30	9.03	11.34	14.01	18.55	21.03	23.34	26.22	28.30	32.91
13	4.11	5.89	7.04	9.93	12.34	15.12	19.81	22.36	24.74	27.69	29.82	34.53
14	4.66	6.57	7.79	10.82	13.34	16.22	21.06	23.69	26.12	29.14	31.32	36.12
15	5.23	7.26	8.55	11.72	14.34	17.32	22.31	25.00	27.49	30.58	32.80	37.70
16	5.81	7.96	9.31	12.62	15.34	18.42	23.54	26.30	28.85	32.00	34.27	39.25
17	6.41	8.67	10.09	13.53	16.34	19.51	24.77	27.59	30.19	33.41	35.72	40.79
18	7.02	9.39	10.87	14.44	17.34	20.60	25.99	28.87	31.53	34.81	37.16	42.31
19	7.63	10.12	11.65	15.35	18.34	21.69	27.20	30.14	32.85	36.19	38.58	43.82
20	8.26	10.85	12.44	16.27	19.34	22.78	28.41	31.41	34.17	37.57	40.00	45.32
21	8.90	11.59	13.24	17.18	20.34	23.86	29.62	32.67	35.48	38.93	41.40	46.80
22	9.54	12.34	14.04	18.10	21.34	24.94	30.81	33.92	36.78	40.29	42.80	48.27
23	10.20	13.09	14.85	19.02	22.34	26.02	32.01	35.17	38.08	41.64	44.18	49.73
24	10.86	13.85	15.66	19.94	23.34	27.10	33.20	36.42	39.36	42.98	45.56	51.18
25	11.52	14.61	16.47	20.87	24.34	28.17	34.38	37.65	40.65	44.31	46.93	52.62
26	12.20	15.38	17.29	21.79	25.34	29.25	35.56	38.88	41.92	45.64	48.29	54.05
27	12.88	16.15	18.11	22.72	26.34	30.32	36.74	40.11	43.20	46.96	49.65	55.48
28	13.57	16.93	18.94	23.65	27.34	31.39	37.92	41.34	44.46	48.28	50.99	56.89
29	14.26	17.71	19.77	24.58	28.34	32.46	39.09	42.56	45.72	49.59	52.34	58.30
30	14.95	18.49	20.60	25.51	29.34	33.53	40.26	43.77	46.98	50.89	53.67	59.70

Pearson's X^2 is calculated as follows:

$$X^2 = \frac{100[(25)10 - 20(45)]^2}{(70)(30)(40)(55)} = 8.129$$

We must compare this value to the 95th percentile of the chi-square distribution with 1 degree of freedom, which is shown in Exhibit 17.16B to be 3.84. Because 8.129 is larger than this percentile, we reject the hypothesis that the two types of companies fail to respond at the same rate. From the data table we see that the estimated response rate for Large companies is $0.67 = 20/30$, whereas the estimated response rate for Other companies is $0.36 = 25/70$. Perhaps the questionnaire is complicated and appears too formidable to a small company that is short of staff; or perhaps the subject matter of the questionnaire appears less relevant to a small company than to a large one.

Clearly nonresponse is a large potential problem. More testing of the viability of the survey is definitely in order. ∎

An Alternative Sampling Design

Pearson's X^2 statistics can be used to analyze data that arise from a sampling design that is different from the one discussed above, namely independent samples from two Bernoulli processes. The alternative design consists of selecting a random sample of subjects and measuring two binary variables on each subject. When a two-way table displays data from such a design, it is called a contingency table. Here is an example.

EXAMPLE 17.16B

A marketing research study consists of showing an ad for a new product on television stations in a limited, pilot market for four weeks. A random sample of households is then contacted and the head of the household is asked if he or she has heard of the new product. The respondent is also asked to state if his or her age falls in one of two ranges: under 30 or 30 or above. Here are the numbers of respondents categorized by age and "recall"—that is, whether they say they have heard of the product.

Age of Respondent	Heard of Product? Yes	No	Total
Under 30	50	50	100
30 or Above	170	480	650
Total	220	530	750

The null hypothesis is that the percentage of recalls in the two age groups is the same. The testing procedure is exactly the same as before. You may verify that the value of the X^2 statistic is 23.8, which is well beyond even the 99.9th percentile of the chi-square distribution with 1 degree of freedom. The two groups do not have the same percentage of recalls. Examination of the data table shows that the estimated percentage of recalls for the under 30 group is 50%, while the percentage for the 30 or above group is 26%. ∎

SECTION

17.17 Exercises

17.17A For each of the 2 × 2 tables below compute the value of X^2 and perform the chi-square test of the null hypothesis of no difference at the 5% and 1% significance levels.

a $a = 5, b = 50, c = 175, d = 1750$

b $a = 25, b = 50, c = 175, d = 350$

c $a = 5, b = 50, c = 175, d = 350$

d $a = 25, b = 50, c = 175, d = 1750$

e $a = 50, b = 50, c = 175, d = 350$

a	c
b	d

17.17B Consider these two tables:

Row	Table I	Table II
First	50, 100	100, 50
Second	100, 50	50, 100

a Compute the value of X^2 for each table.

b Do the statistics computed in part (a) reject the null hypothesis of no difference at the 5% significance level? At the 1% level?

17.17C Consider 2 × 2 tables with the following counts in their bodies:

a First row: 250, 300   Second row: 0, 450

b First row: 550, 0   Second row: 0, 450

c First row: 165, 385   Second row: 135, 315

Compute the value of X^2 for each table. What do these values imply about the null hypothesis of no difference?

17.17D The 2 × 2 table below is taken from J. I. Mann, M. P. Vessey, M. Thorogood, and R. Doll, "Myocardial Infarction in Young Women with Special Reference to Oral Contraceptive Practice," *British Medical Journal*, 2 (1975), 241–245. (*Myocardial infarction* means heart attack.)

Heart Attack

		Yes	No	**Total**
	Yes	45	83	128
Smoker	No	14	74	88
	Total	59	157	216

a   Compute the row percents and assess informally whether knowledge of smoking habits makes much difference in predicting heart attacks.

b   Compute X^2 for the table above. What does it imply?

c   The relationship between smoking and heart attacks has been controversial, frequently pitting the tobacco industry against a variety of claimants in expensive court battles. Even though data such as those in the table above often support a direct relationship, it is technically inappropriate to infer causality because people choose to smoke, and the propensity to smoke and the propensity to have heart attacks could be caused by some other factor, although such a factor has not yet been identified scientifically. If you are interested in this question, you may wish to track down newspaper articles, court testimony, papers in medical journals, and reports by the U.S. Surgeon General that deal with the controversy. It is an education in the widespread use of data and statistical methods on a problem with massive commercial and public health implications.

17.17E   Consider a 2×2 table with

First row: a, $400 - a$
Second row: $500 - a$, $a + 100$

a   The parameter a may assume any integer value between 0 and 400. Display the tables for $a = 0, 50, 100, 150, 200, 250, 300, 350$, and 400. Include counts and row percents in the tables.

b   Verify that for the general table,

$$X^2 = 1000[a(a + 100) - (500 - a)(400 - a)]^2/(500)^2(400)(600)$$

Compute X^2 for $a = 0, 50, 100, 150, 200, 250, 300, 350$, and 400. Comment on the degree of statistical significance the statistics reflect.

17.17F   The law school and the business school admissions committees provide the following summary of their activities for the previous academic year.

Law School

Gender of Applicant	Number Admitted	Number Not Admitted	**Total**
Male	120	120	240
Female	180	180	360
Total	300	300	600

Business School

Gender of Applicant	Number Admitted	Number Not Admitted	Total
Male	400	800	1200
Female	200	400	600
Total	600	1200	1800

a Compute the row percents for each table. Are the two schools consistent in their treatment of men and women in terms of admission rates?

b Compute the values of Pearson's X^2 for each table. What do the values of these statistics imply about the treatment of men and women by the two admissions committees?

c Aggregate the two tables, that is, add the figures in the corresponding cells of the tables to produce a table that reports the combined activity of the two schools. Compute the row percents and the value of Pearson's X^2 for the new table. What do these statistics imply about the treatment of men and women by the two schools combined? What causes the paradox?

Chapter Summary

Probabilistic inference is drawing conclusions about model parameters from process data, using the methods of probability. Parameters are those parts of a mathematical model that can be adjusted to bring the model and the data in as close conformance as possible. For probabilistic methods to be effective, the process must have a random component. Sometimes randomness occurs naturally, as in coin flips; sometimes randomness can be imposed on a process, as in probability surveys and randomized controlled experiments; and sometimes randomness occurs as a by-product of modeling. When a random component can be found in a process, the methods of probability can be used to form a link between process outcomes and model parameters that can be exploited powerfully to draw valid conclusions about the process, from even very small samples.

This chapter explains three probability distributions that pervade statistical practice: the t distribution, the F distribution and the chi-square distribution. All of these distributions can be used to test hypotheses about process means. Significance testing is a process of probabilistic inference that uses sampling distributions to compare behavior in data with theories about the process that generated the data. The essential ingredients of a significance test include:

- A model for the underlying process
- A sampling plan that takes account of or imposes a state of statistical control on the data
- A null hypothesis to be tested
- An alternative hypothesis
- A test statistic

- The distribution of the test statistic when the null hypothesis is true
- A criterion for deciding when to reject the null hypothesis
- Ability to compute the significance level, which is the probability that the test rejects a true null hypothesis.

Perhaps even more important than significance tests are confidence intervals, sets of null hypotheses that cannot be rejected by a set of data. A confidence interval for a parameter is interpreted as the set of plausible guesses at the parameter. A large confidence interval documents the inability to make a precise probabilistic inference about the parameter with the data at hand. If more precise inference is required, then more data must be collected.

In this chapter, we show how t statistics and the t distribution can be used to make probabilistic inferences about a long-run process mean, about the next outcome of the process, and about the difference between two process means. We also show that F statistics and the F distribution can be applied to the problem of comparing two means. The F distribution is important because it can be used in problems that require comparison of more than two means, problems discussed in Chapters 18 and 19.

When the data are binary and samples are large, the F statistic is modified and becomes Pearson's chi-square statistic, and the F distribution is approximated with the chi-square distribution.

Supplementary Exercises for Chapter 17

17A For each of the 2 × 2 tables below calculate the value of Pearson's X^2 and assess significance.

a
14	37
8	23

b
14	46
8	23

c
28	37
78	16

17B For each case below use the two-sample t test to test the null hypothesis that the two process means are equal, at both the 5% and the 1% significance levels. Also compute the p-value for each test and interpret its meaning.

a $n_1 = 15, n_2 = 15, \bar{y}_1 = 29, s_1 = 3, \bar{y}_2 = 27, s_2 = 2.8$
b $n_1 = 25, n_2 = 15, \bar{y}_1 = 29, s_1 = 3, \bar{y}_2 = 27, s_2 = 2.8$

17C For each case in Exercise 17B compute the 99% confidence interval for $\mu_1 - \mu_2$. Interpret the meaning of the intervals.

17D Use the data in Exercise 16A. Use the two-sample t test to test the null hypothesis H_0: $\mu_1 - \mu_2 = 0$, where μ_1 is the population mean of Set A and μ_2 is the population mean of Set B.

17E Use the data in Exercise 16B. Use the two-sample t test to test the null hypothesis H_0: $\mu_1 - \mu_2 = 0$, where μ_1 is the theoretical mean response of Section A and μ_2 is the theoretical mean response of Section B.

17F   The theoretical standard deviation of the difference between two sample means, when two independent simple random samples are drawn, is

$$\sigma_{\bar{y}_1 - \bar{y}_2} = \sqrt{\frac{\sigma_1^2}{n_1} + \frac{\sigma_2^2}{n_2}}$$

Thus $3\sigma_{\bar{y}_1 - \bar{y}_2}$ is the theoretical bound on the error in a 99.7% confidence interval for $\mu_1 - \mu_2$. In practice, knowledge of the process of interest can be used to determine a difference of practical significance. In other words, knowledge of the process places a bound on $\mu_1 - \mu_2$ without the expense of taking any more data from the process. To justify data collection and analysis, therefore, we must have assurance that the statistical bound, $3\sigma_{\bar{y}_1 - \bar{y}_2}$, will probably yield more precise information than we already possess. Let B denote an error bound that would be an improvement over current knowledge. If we knew σ_1 and σ_2, we could set

$$B = 3\sigma_{\bar{y}_1 - \bar{y}_2} \tag{17.22}$$

and solve for values of n_1 and n_2 that would yield this bound. In practice, we again appeal to knowledge of the process of interest to obtain rough estimates of σ_1 and σ_2 and then solve the equation. Solve Equation (17.22) under the following circumstances:

a $\sigma_1 = \sigma_2 = \sigma$ and $n_1 = n_2 = n$

b $\sigma_1 = 2\sigma_2$ and $n_1 = n_2 = n$

c $\sigma_1 = 2\sigma_2$ and $n_1 = 2n_2$

d $\sigma_1 = k\sigma_2$ and $n_1 = n_2 = n$, for some $k > 0$

e $\sigma_1 = k\sigma_2$ and $n_1 = kn_2$, for some $k > 0$

f $\sigma_1 = k_1\sigma_2$ and $n_1 = k_2n_2$, for some $k_1 > 0$ and $k_2 > 0$

Glossary for Chapter 17

alternative hypothesis	A hypothesis other than the null hypothesis.
chi-square distribution	The approximate sampling distribution of Pearson's X^2 statistic when the null hypothesis is true.
confidence coefficient	One minus the significance level of the test on which a confidence interval is based.
confidence interval	The set of parameter values that a significance test does not reject in response to a given set of data.
critical region	Those values of a test statistic that cause rejection of the null hypothesis
F distribution	Sampling distribution of the F statistic showing the variation in the statistic that results from randomness of samples.
null hypothesis	The hypothesis assumed to be true when deriving the sampling distribution of a test statistic used to compute the significance level.
one-sided alternative hypothesis	$\mu > \mu_0$ (or $\mu < \mu_0$)
parameters	The adjustable parts of a model.
power	Probability of rejecting the null hypothesis when an alternative hypothesis is true.
probabilistic inference	Drawing conclusions about model parameters from process data, using the methods of probability.

p-values	Empirical significance levels.
significance level	The probability that the test statistic falls outside the critical region when the null hypothesis is true.
significance testing	A process of probabilistic inference that uses sampling distributions to compare behavior in data with theories about the process that generated the data.
t distribution with $n-1$ degrees of freedom	The sampling distribution of the *t* statistic for the sample mean when the data come from a normal distribution.
test statistic	A statistic used in a significance test.
t statistic for the process mean	$t = \dfrac{\bar{y} - \mu_0}{s/\sqrt{n}} = \dfrac{\sqrt{n}(\bar{y} - \mu_0)}{s}$
two-sample *t* statistic	$t = \dfrac{\bar{y}_1 - \bar{y}_2}{\sqrt{\dfrac{s_1^2}{n_1} + \dfrac{s_2^2}{n_2}}}$
two-sided alternative hypothesis	$\mu \neq \mu_0$
Type I error	Rejecting a true null hypothesis.
Type II error	Failing to reject a false null hypothesis.
Type III error	Giving a sophisticated answer to an irrelevant question.

Completely Randomized Experimental Designs and the Analysis of Variance

Chapter Objectives

After mastering this chapter, you will be able to:

- Conduct an experiment using a completely randomized design

- Analyze the data from a completely randomized design

- Explain the entries in an analysis-of-variance table

- Construct confidence intervals for the difference between the effects of two treatments

We noted in Chapters 1 and 13 that experiments are basic tools for collecting data. In this chapter and the next, we show how randomization can be used to determine which experimental units receive the experimental treatments. Randomization makes it possible to derive objective estimates of the magnitudes of the different impacts that the treatments have on the responses of the experimental units.

Because randomized experiments lead to readily understood inferences, they are viewed as ideal tools for data collection. Consequently, researchers have developed plans for experiments in a wide variety of settings. This chapter and the following one are only a brief introduction to a vast subject.[†] In this chapter we use the word *experiment* to mean a randomized experiment. An **experimental unit** is a unit to which a treatment is applied and from which a measured response is taken. The data consist of a record of the treatments applied to experimental units and the measured responses of the units.

The purpose of a randomized experiment is to estimate the average amount of difference in the responses caused by different treatments. Of course, the responses

experimental unit

[†]An accessible reference that stresses the whole process of planning and managing experiments in industry and business is R. D. Moen, T. W. Nolan, and L. P. Provost, *Improving Quality Through Planned Experimentation* (New York: McGraw-Hill, 1991). A book that stresses more of the technical details is G. E. P. Box, W. G. Hunter, and J. S. Hunter, *Statistics for Experimenters* (New York: Wiley, 1978).

vary somewhat even when different treatments cause no difference at all, so one of the challenges in analyzing experimental data is to distinguish variation due to the treatments from variation inherent in the process under study.

Think of each response as made up of a portion that is due to treatment and a portion that is due to random variation. Such a model is especially appropriate for randomized studies because the experimenter explicitly uses randomization to force the responses to have the stated structure. Nevertheless, the model must be made more explicit before it can be used for data analysis, for as it stands it does not suggest how to calculate the portion due to treatment and the portion due to random variation. Traditionally, the model for experimental data is written $y = \theta + e$, where y stands for the response, θ stands for the *long-run average* response, and e stands for the random variation. The form of θ is determined by the **experimental design**, the plan used to collect the data. In this chapter, we consider only completely randomized designs.

experimental design

The model outlined in the previous paragraph leads to data analysis whose fundamental step is to write each response in the form

$$\text{Observed Response} = \text{Fitted Value} + \text{Residual}$$

or $y = \hat{\theta} + \hat{e}$, where $\hat{\theta}$ stands for the estimated value of θ and $\hat{e}$ stands for the difference between the response and the estimated treatment effect. Once this is done, the randomization used in assigning units to treatments forms the basis of inferential statements about the treatment effects. In particular, we seek to estimate the magnitude and sign of the difference between the impact of one treatment and another.

These general remarks are now made concrete by considering specific examples.

SECTION

18.1   Completely Randomized Design with Two Treatments

The simplest experimental design involves just two treatments. Using a marketing experiment as an example, this section shows how to randomize the experimental units in a two-treatment design and how to analyze the resultant data. Building on material presented in Chapter 17, the section shows how to analyze the data using a randomization test or one of two approximations.

EXAMPLE   18.1A

Test marketing examines the effectiveness of different aspects of marketing a product in a realistic setting. As an illustration, consider a cereal that is already established in the market. Eight urban grocery stores of comparable size and sales volume are chosen to be the experimental units. None of them has used end-of-aisle displays for the cereal under study in the past, and the store managers have agreed to participate in the experiment.

One of the treatments is to be shelf display only, while the other treatment is to be shelf *and* end-of-aisle display. Comparison of the sales in the stores that use only shelf display with the sales of the stores that use both methods of display should yield a measure of the effect on sales caused by the end-of-aisle displays. For the comparison to be reliable, however, all the other causes of variation in sales should be kept under control. Some control is exercised in the choice of stores. They are all urban, about the same size, have about the same sales volume, and have never used end-of-aisle displays for the cereal under study.

Because the cereal is an established one, another control is possible, namely, comparison of sales during the experimental period with sales before the experimental period. Take sales in the three months before the study period as the basis of comparison, leading to the following scheme:

Treatment	Base Period	Experimental Intervention	Study Period
Shelf display only	3-month sales	None	3-month sales
Shelf and end-of-aisle display	3-month sales	End-of-aisle display	3-month sales

The study period is taken to be the same length as the base period—three months. This scheme allows us to compute the response simply as the difference between sales of the cereal in the study period and sales of the cereal in the base period.

The experimental scheme used above can be displayed schematically as follows:

Group 1 O_1 X_1 O_2
Group 2 O_3 X_2 O_4

where O stands for observation and X stands for experimental intervention. The observations are the amounts of sales of the cereal in the designated three-month periods. In the cereal study, because all the stores use shelf display, the experimental intervention distinguishing the two groups of stores is the end-of-aisle display. Hence, X_1 is designated as "none" and X_2 as "end-of-aisle display." When a group is designated to receive no treatment, that group is called the **control group**, while the treated group is called the **experimental group**.

Finally, the natural variation in cereal sales from store to store must be controlled for in some fashion. In the **completely randomized design**, this is done by assigning stores to the two groups *at random*. For simplicity, we assign four of the stores to each group. Thus, during the three-month study period, the four stores assigned to the control group make no end-of-aisle display of the cereal. The other four stores use both shelf and end-of-aisle displays. All the causes of different sales performance, other than end-of-aisle display, should thus be distributed roughly equally between the two groups by the randomization. ▪

control group
experimental group

completely randomized design

How to Randomize

Here is one way to assign the stores to treatments at random. Let the eight stores be designated by the symbols A, B, C, D, E, F, G, and H. Take four red cards and four black cards from an ordinary bridge deck and shuffle them thoroughly. Lay the cards out in a row next to the letters A through H. A letter associated with a red card assigns the corresponding store to the control group, while a letter associated with a black card assigns the corresponding store to the experimental group. One possible result of this process is shown in Exhibit 18.1A. Stores A, C, G, and H are in the control group; stores B, D, E, and F are in the experimental group. There are 70 different ways that stores could have been assigned to the two groups.[†] Because the cards are shuffled thoroughly, the assignment given above had 1 chance out of 70 of being selected.

E X H I B I T 18.1A
Random Assignment of Stores to Groups Using Cards—Cereal Experiment

Store	Card Color
A	Red
B	Black
C	Red
D	Black
E	Black
F	Black
G	Red
H	Red

In place of cards, random digits could have been used to assign stores to treatments. A sequence of random digits taken from a table or from computer output might look like this: 8, 4, 9, 8, 0, 8, 1, 1, 3, 3, 8, 8, 3, 5, 8, 3, 8, 2,. Eliminating repeated digits, we obtain the sequence 8, 4, 9, 0, 1, 3, 5, 2. Match this sequence up with the stores A, B, C, D, E, F, G, H. Let the stores with the smallest four digits be control-group stores. This puts stores D, E, F, and H in the control group and stores A, B, C, and G in the experimental group. Again, this is just one of the 70 possible random assignments. For small problems, cards are convenient randomization devices. For problems with a large number of units, random digits are more convenient because they can be used in conjunction with computers to help with the data processing.

To summarize, Example 18.1A introduces a completely randomized design with two treatments (end-of-aisle and no end-of-aisle display) and eight experimental units (stores). The response of a store is the difference in cereal sales in two time periods, one before and one after the introduction of the experimental intervention, end-of-aisle display.

[†]Counting theory shows that if $2n$ experimental units are to be assigned to two groups of size n, the number of ways this can be done is $(2n)!/(n!)^2$. In the cereal experiment, $n = 4$, so the number of assignments is $8!/(4!)^2 = (8)(7)(6)(5)/(4)(3)(2)(1) = 70$.

A Model for the Completely Randomized Design

General notation for a completely randomized design with two treatments is the following. A total of $n_1 + n_2$ experimental units is assigned at random to the treatments, n_1 to treatment 1 and n_2 to treatment 2. The responses of the n_1 units assigned to treatment 1 are denoted by $y_{11}, y_{12}, \ldots, y_{1n_1}$ while the responses of the n_2 units assigned to treatment 2 are denoted by $y_{21}, y_{22}, \ldots, y_{2n_2}$. The theoretical model for these responses is

$$y_{1j} = \mu_1 + e_{1j} \text{ for } j = 1, 2, \ldots, n_1 \qquad \text{(treatment 1)}$$

and

$$y_{2j} = \mu_2 + e_{2j} \text{ for } j = 1, 2, \ldots, n_2 \qquad \text{(treatment 2)}$$

The responses from treatment 1 have long-run mean μ_1, while those from treatment 2 have long-run mean μ_2. The primary goal of data analysis is to estimate $\mu_1 - \mu_2$. The e's stand for the random variation in the response.

Data Analysis

We now continue the cereal study introduced in Example 18.1A, showing how to analyze data from the completely randomized design introduced there.

EXAMPLE 18.1B

When the study outlined in Example 18.1A is carried out, data, which are differences in sales before and after the experimental intervention, become available for analysis. Exhibit 18.1B displays one such set of data. The numbers in the Before and After columns are measures of volume of sales during the period before the study period and during the study period, respectively. The numbers in the Difference columns are values of the quantity (After − Before) for each store. For the control group, these are $O_2 - O_1$ in the schematic diagram on page 510; for the experimental group, they are $O_4 - O_3$. Notice that the volume of sales increased for each control-group store as well as for each experimental-group store—the study period was an "up" period for the cereal in all the stores. The average increase in sales for the control-group stores is

EXHIBIT 18.1B
Data from Cereal Experiment

Control Group				Experimental Group			
Store	Before	After	Difference	Store	Before	After	Difference
A	800	820	20	B	730	770	40
C	760	770	10	D	825	855	30
G	840	855	15	E	640	670	30
H	695	720	25	F	825	850	25

$(20 + 10 + 15 + 25)/4 = 17.5$, while the average increase in sales for the experimental-group stores is $(40 + 30 + 30 + 25)/4 = 31.25$. This yields a difference of $31.25 - 17.5 = 13.75$ that might be attributable to the end-of-aisle display, but one must be careful not to jump to a conclusion. Sales are subject to natural variation, and the stores were divided into groups at random. Some, if not all, the observed difference in average sales could be due to these sources of variation.

Exhibit 18.1C displays the situation graphically. The A's show sales increases for the control-group stores, while the B's show sales increases for the experimental-group stores. (The 2 indicates the two stores with sales increases of 30 units.) The M's are the sample means of the two groups, namely 17.5 and 31.25, plotted in the context of the actual outcomes. The sample means are clearly different. Is the difference due to chance alone, or is part of the difference due to the use of end-of-aisle displays?

Thus, the question is: Do the data point to a substantially greater increase, on average, in stores that use the end-of-aisle displays than in stores that do not—that is, to an increase that is not due just to chance? Notice that if a control group had not been used, *all* the average increase in the experimental stores might have been attributed to the end-of-aisle displays, but this would have been an error, because some of the increase is due to other factors that also affect sales in the control-group stores.

Notice also that the randomized assignment of stores to groups ensures that subjective judgment does not enter into this process. If judgment had been used to assign the stores to groups, it might have systematically assigned stores with one characteristic (on size or geographic location, for example) to the control group and with another characteristic to the experimental group.

E X H I B I T   **18.1C**
Graph of Grocery Store Sales with and Without End-of-Aisle Displays for Cereal

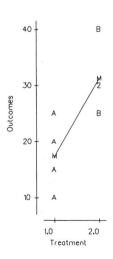

If this systematic difference were connected to the sales performance, the difference in sales would not be attributable to the end-of-aisle display. In other words, without randomization, there would be no basis for deciding whether a difference could be attributed to the display or to some other cause lurking in the assignment of stores to groups. Finally, randomization gives a clear-cut and simple way to analyze the data, as discussed next.

The first step in the analysis is to set up the null hypothesis that the end-of-aisle display really makes no difference in sales. If this is the case, the observed data could in principle have come from any assignment of stores to control and experimental groups. To create a context for analyzing the observed data, look at the data that might have resulted from each possible assignment of stores to groups. The table in Exhibit 18.1D lists all 70 such assignments. For each assignment, the data from a given store are used to form a difference in mean sales increases for the two groups. For example, in assignment 1, stores ABCD are in the control group, and stores EFGH are in the experimental group. Using the data associated with these stores, the control group has mean $(20 + 40 + 10 + 30)/4 = 25$, and the experimental group has mean $(30 + 25 + 15 + 25)/4 = 23.75$. The difference in mean sales is $23.75 - 25 = -1.25$, which appears in the last column of the table. The 70 differences in the table are the data that might have been observed in the experiment if in fact the end-of-aisle display made no difference in sales, or as statisticians say, if the null hypothesis were true.

A dotplot of the 70 differences in the means is shown in Exhibit 18.1E. The distribution is symmetric about zero. Only two of the possible allocations of stores to groups yields a difference as large as the one observed in the data, namely, 13.75. From this perspective, the observed difference is unlikely—only 2 chances out of 70 or 2.86% probability—when the null hypothesis is true.

The next step is to set up an alternative hypothesis. The effect of interest is that the end-of-aisle dislay *increases* sales. This is a one-sided alternative hypothesis. Concentrating on this hypothesis means that the possibility that end-of-aisle displays might *decrease* sales is really of no interest.

Finally, the strength of the evidence in favor of the alternative hypothesis is assessed. This is done by computing a *p*-value. Evidence in favor of the alternative hypothesis, and therefore against the null hypothesis, takes the form of a large *positive* difference in the mean increases of the two groups. In other words, if the alternative hypothesis is true, we expect the average increase in sales for the experimental-group stores to be greater than the average increase for the control-group stores. The greater the positive mean difference, the greater the evidence in favor of the alternative hypothesis. For the one-sided alternative hypothesis in this example, the *p*-value is simply the probability that a difference as great or greater than the one actually observed could have been observed, assuming the null hypothesis is true. Because the observed difference is the largest that could have been observed when the

EXHIBIT 18.1D Calculation of Mean Differences for All 70 Possible Assignments of Stores to Groups—Cereal Experiment

Assignment	Control Group	Sales	Mean	Experimental Group	Sales	Mean	Differences in Means
1	ABCD	20,40,10,30	25	EFGH	30,25,15,25	23.75	−1.25
2	EBCD	30,40,10,30	27.5	AFGH	20,25,15,25	21.25	−6.25
3	FBCD	25,40,10,30	26.25	AEGH	20,30,15,25	22.5	−3.75
4	GBCD	15,40,10,30	23.75	AEFH	20,30,25,25	25	1.25
5	HBCD	25,40,10,30	26.25	AEFG	20,30,25,15	22.5	−3.75
6	AECD	20,30,10,30	22.5	BFGH	40,25,15,25	26.25	3.75
7	AFCD	20,25,10,30	21.25	BEGH	40,30,15,25	27.5	6.25
8	AGCD	20,15,10,30	18.75	BEFH	40,30,25,25	30	11.25
9	AHCD	20,25,10,30	21.25	BEFG	40,30,25,15	27.5	6.25
10	ABED	20,40,30,30	30	CFGH	10,25,15,25	18.75	−11.25
11	ABFD	20,40,25,30	28.75	CEGH	10,30,15,25	20	−8.75
12	ABGD	20,40,15,30	26.25	CEFH	10,30,25,25	22.5	−3.75
13	ABHD	20,40,25,30	28.75	CEFG	10,30,25,15	20	−8.75
14	ABCE	20,40,10,30	25	DFGH	30,25,15,25	23.75	−1.25
15	ABCF	20,40,10,25	23.75	DEGH	30,30,15,25	25	1.25
16	ABCG	20,40,10,15	21.25	DEFH	30,30,25,25	27.5	6.25
17	ABCH	20,40,10,25	23.75	DEFG	30,30,25,15	25	1.25
18	EFCD	30,25,10,30	23.75	ABGH	20,40,15,25	25	1.25
19	EGCD	30,15,10,30	21.25	ABFH	20,40,25,25	27.5	6.25
20	EHCD	30,25,10,30	23.75	ABFG	20,40,25,15	25	1.25
21	FGCD	25,15,10,30	20	ABEH	20,40,30,25	28.75	8.75
22	FHCD	25,25,10,30	22.5	ABEG	20,40,30,15	26.25	3.75
23	GHCD	15,25,10,30	20	ABEF	20,40,30,25	28.75	8.75
24	EBFD	30,40,25,30	31.25	ACGH	20,10,15,25	17.5	−13.75
25	EBGD	30,40,15,30	28.75	ACFH	20,10,25,25	20	−8.75
26	EBHD	30,40,25,30	31.25	ACFG	20,10,25,15	17.5	−13.75
27	FBGD	25,40,15,30	27.5	ACEH	20,10,30,25	21.25	−6.25
28	FBHD	25,40,25,30	30	ACEG	20,10,30,15	18.75	−11.25
29	GBHD	15,40,25,30	27.5	ACEF	20,10,30,25	21.25	−6.25
30	EBCF	30,40,10,25	26.25	ADGH	20,30,15,25	22.5	−3.75
31	EBCG	30,40,10,15	23.75	ADFH	20,30,25,25	25	1.25
32	EBCH	30,40,10,25	26.25	ADFG	20,30,25,15	22.5	−3.75
33	FBCG	25,40,10,15	22.5	ADEH	20,30,30,25	26.25	3.75
34	FBCH	25,40,10,25	25	ADEG	20,30,30,15	23.75	−1.25
35	GBCH	15,40,10,25	22.5	ADEF	20,30,30,25	26.25	3.75
36	AEFD	20,30,25,30	26.25	BCGH	40,10,15,25	22.5	−3.75
37	AEGD	20,30,15,30	23.75	BCFH	40,10,25,25	25	1.25
38	AEHD	20,30,25,30	26.25	BCFG	40,10,25,15	22.5	−3.75
39	AFGD	20,25,15,30	22.5	BCEH	40,10,30,25	26.25	3.75
40	AFHD	20,25,25,30	25	BCEG	40,10,30,15	23.75	−1.25
41	AGHD	20,15,25,30	22.5	BCEF	40,10,30,25	26.25	3.75
42	AECF	20,30,10,25	21.25	BDGH	40,30,15,25	27.5	6.25
43	AECG	20,30,10,15	18.75	BDFH	40,30,25,25	30	11.25
44	AECH	20,30,10,25	21.25	BDFG	40,30,25,15	27.5	6.25
45	AFCG	20,25,10,15	17.5	BDEH	40,30,30,25	31.25	13.75

EXHIBIT **18.1D** (continued)

Assignment	Control Group	Sales	Mean	Experimental Group	Sales	Mean	Differences in Means
46	AFCH	20,25,10,25	20	BDEG	40,30,30,15	28.75	8.75
47	AGCH	20,15,10,25	17.5	BDEF	40,30,30,25	31.25	13.75
48	ABEF	20,40,30,25	28.75	CDGH	10,30,15,25	20	−8.75
49	ABEG	20,40,30,15	26.25	CDFH	10,30,25,25	22.5	−3.75
50	ABEH	20,40,30,25	28.75	CDFG	10,30,25,15	20	−8.75
51	ABFG	20,40,25,15	25	CDEH	10,30,30,25	23.75	−1.25
52	ABFH	20,40,25,25	27.5	CDEG	10,30,30,15	21.25	−6.25
53	ABGH	20,40,15,25	25	CDEF	10,30,30,25	23.75	−1.25
54	EFGD	30,25,15,30	25	ABCH	20,40,10,25	23.75	−1.25
55	EFHD	30,25,25,30	27.5	ABCG	20,40,10,15	21.25	−6.25
56	EGHD	30,15,25,30	25	ABCF	20,40,10,25	23.75	−1.25
57	FGHD	25,15,25,30	23.75	ABCE	20,40,10,30	25	1.25
58	EFCG	30,25,10,15	20	ABDH	20,40,30,25	28.75	8.75
59	EFCH	30,25,10,25	22.5	ABDG	20,40,30,15	26.25	3.75
60	EGCH	30,15,10,25	20	ABDF	20,40,30,25	28.75	8.75
61	FGCH	25,15,10,25	18.75	ABDE	20,40,30,30	30	11.25
62	EBFG	30,40,25,15	27.5	ACDH	20,10,30,25	21.25	−6.25
63	EBFH	30,40,25,25	30	ACDG	20,10,30,15	18.75	−11.25
64	EBGH	30,40,15,25	27.5	ACDF	20,10,30,25	21.25	−6.25
65	FBGH	25,40,15,25	26.25	ACDE	20,10,30,30	22.5	−3.75
66	AEFG	20,30,25,15	22.5	BCDH	40,10,30,25	26.25	3.75
67	AEFH	20,30,25,25	25	BCDG	40,10,30,15	23.75	−1.25
68	AEGH	20,30,15,25	22.5	BCDF	40,10,30,25	26.25	3.75
69	AFGH	20,25,15,25	21.25	BCDE	40,10,30,30	27.5	6.25
70	EFGH	30,25,15,25	23.75	ABCD	20,40,10,30	25	1.25

EXHIBIT **18.1E** Dotplot of 70 Mean Differences—Cereal Experiment

```
                        •          •        •         •
                 •      :     :        :        :        •
           •     :      :     :        :        :        :       •
     •     :     :      :     :        :        :        :       :      •
     :     :     :      :     :        :        :        :       :      :       :
  ─────────────────────────────────────────────────────────────────────────────
-13.75       -8.75        -3.75          1.25          6.25          11.25
     -11.25        -6.25        -1.25         3.75          8.75  ·      13.75
```

null hypothesis is true, and because there are only 2 assignments out of 70 that yield this difference, the p-value is $2/70 = 0.0286$.

In this chapter, we call an experimental outcome statistically significant when its p-value is less than 0.05. This is the most commonly used criterion for statistical significance. Statistically significant evidence against the null hypothesis is interpreted as justification for rejecting it. The argument goes that when a p-value is smaller than 0.05, a result has been observed that is relatively unlikely to have occurred if the null hypothesis is true, suggesting that an alternative hypothesis is very likely to be operating on the outcome. By this interpretation the cereal experiment has found credible evidence in support of the alternative hypothesis that end-of-shelf displays increase sales. ▪

randomization test

The significance test illustrated in Example 18.1B is called a **randomization test** because it uses the random allocation of experimental units (stores) to treatments (presence or absence of end-of-aisle display) as a basis for the inference about the differential effect of the treatments. Strictly speaking, the randomization test documents the effects of the treatments only on the experimental units used. Thus, any inference that the same effects would be observed if other units had been used is based on judgment. Of course, if the experimental units are chosen to be typical of other units, this more global inference may be quite appropriate. In the example, the stores were urban and of a certain size, so the assertion that end-of-aisle displays tend to make a difference in all urban stores of this size is credible. If the stores had been randomly selected from a population of urban stores of similar size, the inference would be even more objectively justified. Whether end-of-aisle displays would have comparable effects in nonurban or different-sized stores cannot be determined from the experiment, but if similar experiments were run on other types of stores and end-of-aisle displays produced statistically significant results in these experiments, a much broader conclusion would be quite rigorously justified. On the other hand, such experiments would be costly, and the decision may be made that the effect of end-of-aisle displays is sufficiently documented with the experiment already performed. If so, end-of-aisle displays may be used in types of stores not studied in the experiment, even though no experiment had been run on them.

An observational study would consist of comparing sales in a sample of stores that already used end-of-aisle displays to sales in a sample of stores that do not use end-of-aisle displays. Higher average sales in the stores that use end-of-aisle displays might lend credence to the effectiveness of the displays, but one could object to the observational study on the grounds that other factors that are highly correlated with use of end-of-aisle displays are the true cause of the superior sales. For example, larger stores are more likely to use the displays and to have higher sales than smaller stores. One might adjust for this phenomenon by measuring sales of the cereal as a percentage of total sales in the stores, thus "controlling" for size of store. Another possibility is that end-of-aisle displays are used by stores that do more aggressive advertising, and the advertising is the true cause of greater sales. *Randomization tends to spread the effects of such factors evenly between the control and experimental groups, so that differences between groups can more readily be attributed to the factor under study.*

The randomization test, while easy to grasp in principle, is tedious to implement in practice because the listing of all possible allocations is cumbersome. Either of two approximations can be used in practice to ease the burden of implementation. If one of these approximations is used, the calculation of the exact randomization distribution is unnecessary.

The t Distribution Approximation

The first approximation, which is the simplest, is to replace the randomization distribution with a t distribution. In Example 18.1B, this would entail computing a two-sample t statistic. The two-sample t statistic was introduced in Section 17.10. The formulas introduced there allowed the sample variances of the two groups to be different or to be pooled. In the application to data from a completely randomized design, we impose the restriction that the two groups have a common variance, which is natural because the stores are assigned to groups at random, so the variation within groups should be about the same. As indicated in Section 17.10, the formula for the two-sample t statistic with *common group standard deviations and equal sample sizes* in each group is

$$t = \frac{\bar{y}_1 - \bar{y}_2}{s_p\sqrt{\dfrac{1}{n} + \dfrac{1}{n}}}$$

where n denotes the number of experimental units in each group, $\bar{y}_1$ and $\bar{y}_2$ are the means of the observations from each group, and $s_p^2 = (s_1^2 + s_2^2)/2$ denotes the average of the squares of the standard deviations of the data in each group. When the null hypothesis is true, this statistic is taken to have a t distribution with $2n - 2 = 2(n - 1)$ degrees of freedom, which is the distribution used to compute the p-value.

Notice that the numerator of the t statistic is the difference of the group means, which is the statistic whose randomization distribution was used to assess the p-value in Example 18.1B. The t statistic simply scales the difference in the means by an estimated standard deviation and approximates the distribution of this scaled statistic with a t distribution. This avoids the calculation of the randomization distribution. The next example applies the t statistic to the cereal study.

E X A M P L E   **18.1C**

The calculations based on the data in Exhibit 18.1B are as follows. The difference between the means of the two groups has already been determined to be 13.75. The squared standard deviations for the control group and experimental group are

$$s_1^2 = \frac{(20 - 17.5)^2 + (10 - 17.5)^2 + (15 - 17.5)^2 + (25 - 17.5)^2}{4 - 1}$$

$$= 41.66667$$

and

$$s_2^2 = \frac{(40 - 31.25)^2 + (30 - 31.25)^2 + (30 - 31.25)^2 + (25 - 31.25)^2}{4 - 1}$$

$$= 39.58333$$

so that the average is $s_p^2 = (41.66667 + 39.58333)/2 = 40.625$ and $s_p = \sqrt{40.625} = 6.37377$. The value of the t statistic is therefore

$$t = \frac{\bar{y}_1 - \bar{y}_2}{s_p\sqrt{\dfrac{1}{n} + \dfrac{1}{n}}} = \frac{13.75}{6.37377\sqrt{\dfrac{1}{4} + \dfrac{1}{4}}} = \frac{13.75}{4.51} = 3.05$$

The degrees of freedom for this statistic equals $2(4 - 1) = 6$, and the p-value is the area above 3.05 in the right-hand tail of this distribution. Using statistical software, we find the p-value to be 0.0113. Compare this value with the exact value computed from the randomization distribution above, namely, 0.0286. The p-value approximation provided by the t distribution is quite a bit smaller than the exact value, but both values are statistically significant—that is, smaller than 0.05.

According to theory, if there had been more stores in each group, say 10 or more, the t distribution would have yielded a better approximation to the exact p-value. In practice, the t distribution approximation is often used with confidence when the groups are sufficiently large, but this example warns that the approximation can be crude if the groups are small.   ∎

The Simulation Approximation

The second approximation uses simulation. Statistical software is used to make repeated random assignments of stores to groups and to compute the differences between the means of the two groups for each simulated assignment. The distribution of the simulated mean differences is an approximation to the randomization distribution. This approximation is straightforward, and the tedious work is done by the computer.

EXAMPLE   **18.1D**

To illustrate an implementation for the data in Exhibit 18.1B, the computer was programmed to make 1000 assignments. A table of the resulting 1000 mean differences is given in Exhibit 18.1F. Note that 23 of the 1000 simulated mean differences equal 13.75, yielding an estimated p-value of $23/1000 = 0.023$, which compares favorably with the exact value of $2/70 = 0.0286$—much more favorably than the approximation from the t distribution, which is 0.0113. If a computer is available and readily programmed, the simulation approximation is a strong contender for practical use.   ∎

Mean Difference	Count
−13.75	30
−11.25	54
−8.75	68
−6.25	93
−3.75	118
−1.25	134
1.25	141
3.75	121
6.25	96
8.75	83
11.25	39
13.75	23
Total	1000

Other Alternative Hypotheses

In the cereal experiment, a one-sided alternative hypothesis was tested against the null hypothesis that the end-of-aisle display made no difference in sales. Another option is to use a two-sided alternative, which means that the end-of-aisle display makes a difference in sales, but the difference could be positive or negative. Experiments in which there is ambiguity about the direction of the difference that a treatment might have employ two-sided alternatives. The evidence in favor of the two-sided alternative is then taken to be the values of the mean differences that are as extreme as the one actually observed *in both positive and negative directions*. In the cereal experiment with a two-sided alternative, therefore, mean differences equal to or greater than 13.75 *and* mean differences equal to or less than −13.75 are taken to be evidence in favor of the alternative. Referring to the dotplot in Exhibit 18.1E, we see that the p-value must be $4/70 = 0.0571$ because four assignments out of 70 yield these extreme values. Notice that this p-value is not statistically significant. In fact, the data from this particular experiment cannot yield statistically significant evidence in support of the two-sided hypothesis. Different data, however, might have done so.

Examination of the two approximations reveals some interesting possibilities. If we use the t distribution approximation, we simply double the p-value obtained for the one-sided alternative, because the t distribution is symmetric. This approximation thus yields an approximate p-value of $2(0.0113) = 0.0226$, which is statistically significant. Thus, the inference based on the t distribution approximation is at odds with the inference from the exact distribution.

The simulation approximation yields a p-value of $(23 + 30)/1000 = 0.053$, which is not statistically significant and is in agreement with the inference from the exact distribution. This need not always be the case with the simulation approximation. The simulation replications can yield a contradictory inference, though the chance of doing so is small if a large number of replications are performed.

Finally, in some experiments, use of a one-sided alternative hypothesis in the negative direction is appropriate. This would not have been appropriate in the cereal experiment because the statistic used was the difference (After − Before). If the statistic (Before − After) had been used, the one-sided alternative of interest would have been in the negative direction because that would have implied the effectiveness of end-of-aisle displays.

S E C T I O N

18.2 Exercises

18.2A   Sixty of the 300 students signed up for a finance course have cumulative grade-point averages of 3.5 or greater (out of a possible 4.0). Six of these students are selected at random to be experimental units. Cards are used to pick three of the students at random to attend a section of the course that consists of lectures with no class participation. The other three attend a section of the course that consists of intense class discussion of case studies. The reading assignments and examinations in the two sections are exactly the same. After the course is over, the total examination scores for all 300 students are computed and percentiles in the distribution of total scores determined for each student. Here are the data for the six students chosen as experimental units.

Section	Student	Percentile
I: Lectures	Claire	80
	Bill	85
	Matt	79
II: Cases	Gene	85
	Jill	94
	Pat	88

a   Prepare the exact randomization distribution of the difference in mean percentiles of the two groups assuming the null hypothesis of no difference in mean response due to delivery style is true.

b   Compute the exact *p*-value associated with the one-sided hypothesis that Section II yields higher test scores on the average. Assess the statistical significance of the result.

c   Interpret the result in part (b).

18.2B   Use simulation (with 1000 replications) to estimate the exact *p*-value in Exercise 18.2A. Compare the approximation to the one obtained from the exact distribution.

18.2C   Ten subjects are to be assigned at random to two treatments, five subjects to each group. How many possible different assignments are there?

18.2D   Twelve subjects are to be assigned at random to two treatments, six subjects to each group. How many possible different assignments are there?

18.2E   Randomization tests can be used on categorical data. Here is an example. Six tasters are assigned randomly to two brands of cola, three to each brand. Each taster is allowed to drink a small amount of the cola and asked to identify the brand. A "success" is correct identification of the brand. Here are the data.

Taster	Brand	Outcome (1 = success, 0 = failure)
Ann	B	0
Pete	B	0
Jeff	A	1
Heather	A	0
Bob	B	0
Lynette	A	1

The proportion of successes on brand A is 2/3, while the proportion of successes on brand B is 0. Let the test statistic be the difference between these proportions—that is, $2/3 - 0 = 2/3$. The randomization distribution of this statistic is derived by assuming the truth of the null hypothesis that tasters have the same long-run success rate on both brands, forming all possible assignments of tasters to brands, and computing the value of the test statistic for each assignment.

a   Derive the randomization distribution for the data above.

b   Let the alternative hypothesis be that the success rate for brand A is greater than the success rate for brand B. Compute the p-value for this alternative and assess statistical significance.

c   Notice that the randomization distribution is the same for any data set that has outcomes equivalent to those given above. For example, if Jeff had failed and Heather succeeded, the analysis would not have changed. Compare the analysis of categorical data to the analysis of continuous data, in light of this remark.

18.2F   The completely randomized design can be used to analyze a sequence of trials. Here is an example. Don wished to compare his efficiency in hitting the bull's-eye on a dart board at two distances from the board: 6 feet and 9 feet. His experiment consisted of 25 throws at the board at each of the distances. To introduce randomization, he prepared a deck of 50 cards, 25 red and 25 black, and shuffled the cards thoroughly. A red card told Don to throw at 6 feet, a black card at 9 feet. Turning the cards over one at a time, he made the throws dictated by the cards. Below are Don's data. Treatment 1 is the 6-foot distance, treatment 2 the 9-foot distance. A success is a dart in the bull's-eye. The response is 0 if the bull's-eye is missed, 1 if the bull's-eye is hit. The treatments occur in random order determined by the cards.

Throw	Treatment	Response	Throw	Treatment	Response
1	2	0	16	2	0
2	2	0	17	2	0
3	1	0	18	2	0
4	2	0	19	2	0
5	2	0	20	2	0
6	1	0	21	1	0
7	1	0	22	1	0
8	1	0	23	2	0
9	1	0	24	1	0
10	1	0	25	1	1
11	2	0	26	2	1
12	1	1	27	1	0
13	2	0	28	2	0
14	2	0	29	1	0
15	1	1	30	1	0

Throw	Treatment	Response	Throw	Treatment	Response
31	2	0	41	1	0
32	2	0	42	1	0
33	2	0	43	2	0
34	2	0	44	2	0
35	1	0	45	1	1
36	1	0	46	2	0
37	1	1	47	1	0
38	1	0	48	1	1
39	2	0	49	2	1
40	2	0	50	1	1

Here are two frequency histograms showing the numbers of failures and successes for each treatment:

Outcome	Count		
0	18	******************	Treatment 1
1	7	*******	(6-foot distance)

Outcome	Count		
0	23	***********************	Treatment 2
1	2	**	(9-foot distance)

The data can be displayed in a 2 × 2 table, as shown below:

Treatment	Response 1	0	Total
1	7	18	25
2	2	23	25
Total	9	41	50

a Compute the proportion of the 6-foot throws that were successes and the proportion of the 9-foot throws that were successes.

b The null hypothesis is that the distances make no difference in the long-run proportion of successful throws. An appropriate statistic for testing this against a two-sided alternative hypothesis is Pearson's X^2. Compute the value of X^2 for these data. [Answer: 3.4.]

c Assess the statistical significance of your result in part (b) using a chi-square distribution with 1 degree of freedom.

SECTION

18.3 Introduction to the Analysis of Variance

When a two-sided alternative hypothesis is used, the calculation of the t statistic in a completely randomized design with two groups can be set forth in a format called the *analysis of variance* (ANOVA). This section shows how to use analysis of variance to compare results from two groups, whether or not the groups are of equal size.

Instead of looking at extreme positive and negative values of the statistic, the analysis of variance looks at the square of the t statistic, which is called the F *statistic*, which was discussed in Section 17.14. For a completely randomized design with two treatments and equal numbers of subjects in each treatment group, the formula that yields the analysis-of-variance F statistic is

$$t^2 = \left[\frac{\bar{y}_1 - \bar{y}_2}{s_p \sqrt{\frac{1}{n} + \frac{1}{n}}} \right]^2 = \left[\frac{(\bar{y}_1 - \bar{y}_2)/\sqrt{\frac{1}{n} + \frac{1}{n}}}{s_p} \right]^2 = \frac{(n/2)(\bar{y}_1 - \bar{y}_2)^2}{s_p^2}$$

$$= \frac{(n/2)(\bar{y}_1 - \bar{y}_2)^2}{(n-1)((s_1^2 + s_2^2)/(2(n-1)))} = F$$

The calculations are usually presented in a table, called an *ANOVA table*. Exhibit 18.3A shows a typical ANOVA table with both the formulas used to fill the table and the numerical results derived from them for the cereal experiment.

E X H I B I T **18.3A**
Analysis-of-Variance Table for
Completely Randomized Design
with Two Groups of Equal Size,
from the Cereal Experiment

Source of Variation	Sum of Squares	Degrees of Freedom	Mean Squares	F Statistic
Between groups	$\frac{n}{2}(\bar{y}_1 - \bar{y}_2)^2$	1	$\frac{n}{2}(\bar{y}_1 - \bar{y}_2)^2$	F
Within groups	$(n-1)(s_1^2 + s_2^2)$	$2(n-1)$	$\frac{(n-1)(s_1^2 + s_2^2)}{2(n-1)} = s_p^2$	
Total	$(2n-1)s^2$	$2n-1$		

Source of Variation	Sum of Squares	Degrees of Freedom	Mean Squares	F Statistic
Between groups	378.1	1	378.1	9.31
Within groups	243.8	6	40.6	
Total	621.9	7		

The quantity denoted by s^2 is the square of the standard deviation of the data from the two groups merged into a single sample of size $2n$. The ANOVA table displays two sources of variation: between groups and within groups. The within-groups sum of squares is the total of the sum of squared deviations from the mean in the control-group sample and squared deviations from the mean in the experimental-group sample. There are $2(n-1) = 6$ degrees of freedom associated with this sum of squares in the cereal experiment. The sum of squares divided by degrees of freedom, which is called the within-groups mean square in the table, yields the square of the pooled standard deviation—that is, 40.6 in the cereal experiment. The between-groups sum of squares is proportional to the square of the difference between the means of the groups. In the cereal experiment, the between-groups sum of squares is $2(31.25 - 17.5)^2 = 2(13.75)^2 = 378.1$. This sum of squares has 1 degree of freedom, so the between-group mean square is $378.1/1 = 378.1$. The value of the F statistic is (between-group mean square)/(within-group mean square) $= 378.1/40.6 = 9.31$.

To round out the ANOVA table, the total sum of squares is the sum of squares obtained by treating all the data, from both control group and experimental group, as a single sample. For the cereal data, the observations have mean $\bar{y} = 195/8 = 24.375$, sum of squared deviations from the mean $(20 - 24.375)^2 + (10 - 24.375)^2 + \cdots + (25 - 24.375)^2 = 621.9$, and degrees of freedom $8 - 1 = 7$, so $s^2 = 621.9/7 = 88.843$, and $s = \sqrt{88.843} = 9.43$. This standard deviation, which comes from treating the data as one homogeneous sample, is quite a bit larger than the standard deviation $s_p = \sqrt{40.6} = 6.37$ that comes from taking the groups into account. Notice that for sums of squares and degrees of freedom, the sum of the within-groups and between-groups quantities adds up to the total quantity. These summations can be proved algebraically; they are mathematical identities. (See the appendix to this chapter.)

Because extreme values of the test statistic provide evidence in favor of the two-sided alternative hypothesis, and because the F statistic is the square of the t statistic, large values of F provide evidence in favor of the two-sided alternative. The data from the cereal experiment yield a t statistic of 3.05, so the F statistic is $(3.05)^2 = 9.31$, as displayed in the ANOVA table.

How is the p-value of the statistic computed? The exact calculation of the p-value comes from the randomization distribution. In other words, for each of the 70 possible assignments in Exhibit 18.1C, compute the value of the statistic and examine the resulting distribution of statistics. Statistical software has been used to do this; Exhibit 18.3B shows the dot diagram of the distribution. Four of the assignments yield $F = 9.31$, which is the most extreme value possible, so the p-value is $4/70 = 0.0571$, which agrees with the previous calculation based on the difference of means. This is no accident. Theory can be used to show that the two statistics must yield the same p-value when the exact randomization distribution is used.

EXHIBIT **18.3B**   Dotplot of F Statistics of the 70 Random Assignments in Exhibit 18.1C—Cereal Experiment

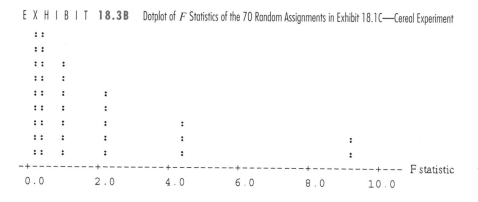

The F distribution with 1 and $2(n-1)$ degrees of freedom can be used to approximate the exact randomization distribution. To do this in the cereal experiment, use the F distribution with 1 and 6 degrees of freedom, and compute the area in the right-hand tail of the distribution above 9.31. The p-value is found, using computer software, to be 0.0226, which is 2(0.0113), consistent with the approximation based on the t distribution presented in Example 18.1C. Likewise, the approximate p-value based on simulation is the same as before, but one would hardly program the computer to simulate assignments of stores to groups and to compute the F statistic. This would unnecessarily use up computer time, as the computation of the mean differences is simpler and yields the same approximate p-value.

Unequal Group Sizes

Assignment of experimental units to control and experimental groups in equal numbers is not necessary. The ANOVA methodology works when the groups are not the same size. If n_1 and n_2 denote the numbers of experimental units in control and experimental groups, there is no change in the procedure for obtaining the randomization distribution, though the number of possible assignments does depend on n_1 and n_2. For example, if in the cereal experiment 5 stores had been used for the control group and 3 for the experimental group, there would have been only 56 possible assignments.[†] The formula for the t statistic reflects the different group sizes as follows:

$$t = \frac{\bar{y}_1 - \bar{y}_2}{s_p\sqrt{\dfrac{1}{n_1} + \dfrac{1}{n_2}}}$$

where $s_p^2 = \left[(n_1 - 1)s_1^2 + (n_2 - 1)s_2^2\right]/[n_1 + n_2 - 2]$. The ANOVA table is in Exhibit 18.3C. The quantity denoted by s^2 is the square of the standard deviation of the data from the two groups merged into a single sample of size $n_1 + n_2$. The F statistic is the ratio of the between-groups mean square to the within-groups mean square.

E X H I B I T 18.3C
Analysis-of-Variance Table in Symbols for Complete Randomized Design with Two Groups of Unequal Size

Source of Variation	Sum of Squares	Degrees of Freedom	Mean Squares	F Statistic
Between groups	$\left(\dfrac{n_1 n_2}{n_1 + n_2}\right)(\bar{y}_1 - \bar{y}_2)^2$	1	$\left(\dfrac{n_1 n_2}{n_1 + n_2}\right)(\bar{y}_1 - \bar{y}_2)^2$	F
Within groups	$(n_1 - 1)s_1^2 + (n_2 - 1)s_2^2$	$n_1 + n_2 - 2$	s_p^2	
Total	$(n_1 + n_2 - 1)s^2$	$n_1 + n_2 - 1$		

[†]If $n_1 + n_2$ experimental units are to be assigned to groups of size n_1 and n_2, the number of ways this can be done is $(n_1 + n_2)!/(n_1!n_2!)$, so if $n_1 = 5$ and $n_2 = 3$, there are $8!/(5!3!) = (8)(7)(6)/((3)(2)(1)) = 56$ ways to make the assignments.

Comparison of Two Treatments

The completely randomized design can be used to compare an experimental group with a control group, as illustrated in the cereal experiment. It can also be used to compare two treatments. In this case, there is no untreated control group. All of the procedures discussed above are unchanged; only terminology changes. The two groups are referred to as treatment 1 and treatment 2. As an example, consider comparing shelf placement of cereal. Treatment 1 could be display of cereal on a shelf that is "eye-level" for most shoppers, while treatment 2 could be display on the bottom shelf. As another example, consider comparing two sizes of cereal boxes. Treatment 1 could be large box and treatment 2 small box.

Another variation on the experimental design introduced in Example 18.1A is important in practice. In many situations, the "before" observations denoted by O_1 and O_3 are not available. For example, the cereal could be a new product, so no previous sales figures exist. Then the design would be displayed as

Control group O_2
Experimental group X O_4

The mean difference would be (average O_4) − (average O_2). The analysis of this design is the same as given above, but the conclusions refer only to the experimental period. There is no comparison to previous history.

SECTION

18.4   Exercises

18.4A This exercise refers back to Exercise 18.2A.

    a Prepare an ANOVA table for the data in Exercise 18.2A.

    b Use the appropriate F distribution to compute an approximate p-value.

    c State the alternative hypothesis tested by the test in part (b).

    d Compare the p-value you computed in part (b) with the exact p-value obtained in part (b) of Exercise 18.2A. Are the qualitative conclusions the same? Compute the magnitude of the difference between the approximate and exact p-values as a percentage of the exact p-value.

18.4B Verify all the numerical values given in Exhibit 18.3A.

18.4C You are given $n_1 = 10, n_2 = 10, \bar{y}_1 = 50, \bar{y}_2 = 60, s_1^2 = 81,$ and $s_2^2 = 100$. Complete the ANOVA table.

18.4D You are given $n_1 = 12, n_2 = 8, \bar{y}_1 = 50, \bar{y}_2 = 60, s_1^2 = 81,$ and $s_2^2 = 100$. Complete the ANOVA table.

18.4E Loose labels on cans waste time and product. A manufacturer producing high percentages of cans with loose labels conducted an experiment to see if different rates of application of glue made a difference in the percentage of cans with loose labels. The two treatments were two application rates: 8 ounces per hour and 12 ounces per hour. An experimental unit was an 8-hour shift, and the response was the percentage of cans with loose labels produced during the shift. Sixteen experimental units were assigned to treatments at random, 8 to each treatment. The responses were as follows.

Application Rate	Percent Loose Labels
8 ounces/hour	8, 1, 2, 5, 6, 8, 5, 7
12 ounces/hour	7, 4, 2, 1, 5, 3, 1, 2

a   Compute the means and standard deviations of the data from each treatment group.

b   Prepare the ANOVA table.

c   Use the F distribution approximation to compute the p-value.

d   State the null and alternative hypotheses that are tested by the statistics computed above.

e   Interpret the results of the test.

18.4F   A group of 25 genetically similar mice is randomly assigned to cages, one mouse per cage. Cards are used to assign the cages to control and treatment groups, 10 to the control, 15 to the treatment. The control is a placebo, while the treatment is a drug. In random order, the mice are infected with tuberculosis. The response is the number of days until a mouse dies. Here are the data.

Control group: 5, 6, 7, 7, 7, 8, 8, 8, 9, 12
Experimental group: 7, 8, 8, 8, 8, 9, 9 12, 13, 13, 14, 14, 17, 17, 18

a   Prepare the ANOVA table and use the appropriate distribution to obtain an approximate p-value.

b   What null and alternative hypotheses are tested by the procedure you implemented in part (a)?

c   Use the appropriate distribution to test the alternative hypothesis that the drug results in *longer* average survival times than the placebo. Compute the approximate p-value and use it to assess statistical significance. Interpret your result.

18.4G   Redo the analysis of the data in Example 18.1B assuming that store F was assigned to the control group, so that $n_1 = 5$ and $n_2 = 3$. Use the numerical outcomes given in Example 18.1B.

18.4H   This exercise refers back to Exercise 18.4F.

a   Redo Exercise 18.4F assuming that 10 mice are assigned to each of the two groups. Use the first 10 observations listed under "Experimental group" as data from that group.

b   Redo part (a) replacing one of the values 13 by the value 18 in the experimental-group data. Compare the results with those obtained in part (a).

18.4I   As Exercise 18.4H illustrates, a change in the data results in a new randomization distribution. This means that a new randomization distribution must be derived for each new data set obtained. One way to avoid this is to replace the data with ranks. For the data in Example 18.1B, the replacement can be displayed as follows (with rank 1 given to the largest difference, rank 2 to the second largest difference, and so forth).

Store	C	G	A	H	F	D	E	B
Difference	10	15	20	25	25	30	30	40
Rank	8	7	6	4.5	4.5	2.5	2.5	1

Notice that "ties" in the data are broken by simply averaging the ranks that would have been assigned if there had been no ties. For example, stores D and E would have had ranks 2 and 3 if their differences had been 29 and 30. Because they both had differences equal to 30 (a tie), they are assigned the average rank 2.5 = (2 + 3)/2. The analysis goes forward as before with the ranks treated as the data. The simplest statistic to use is the difference between the total ranks achieved by the control and experimental groups. For the data above, this statistic has value

$$(8 + 7 + 6 + 4.5) - (4.5 + 2.5 + 2.5 + 1) = 25.5 - 10.5 = 15$$

If there had been no ties, the ranks would have simply been an arrangement of the numbers $1, 2, \ldots, 8$. The randomization distribution would be the same for any sample of size 8. In this sense, the use of ranks avoids the need to derive the randomization distribution afresh for each data set. When ties occur, though, the randomization distribution needs to be derived because the pattern of ties affects the distribution. Some data come naturally as ranks, rather than measurements. This exercise shows that such data can be analyzed using the idea of randomization tests.

a   Derive the randomization distribution for the ranked data in Exercise 18.2A. Use the difference in total ranks achieved by the two groups as the test statistic. Compare the analysis with that given in the text.

b   Consider analyzing the data referred to in Exercise 18.4H using ranks. Compare the analyses in parts (a) and (b) of that exercise. Discuss generally the potential loss of information implied by replacing data with ranks. Notice that no such loss occurs if the original data are ranks. Also, when the original data are ranks, the likelihood of ties is much less than it is when data are replaced with ranks.

SECTION

18.5 Completely Randomized Design with More Than Two Groups

The first four sections of this chapter have introduced the completely randomized design for two treatments, but the design can accommodate any number of treatments. This and the next three sections present the design in its generality. This section shows how to use analysis of variance when the experiment involves more than two groups.

Let k denote the number of treatments to be compared, and let $n_1, n_2, \ldots, n_k$ denote the numbers of subjects assigned to the treatments. The null hypothesis is that the treatments are not different on average, while the alternative hypothesis is that at least one of the treatments is different, on average, from the others (of course, they could all be different from each other). If subjects are assigned at random to treatments, in principle a randomization distribution can be formed by making all possible assignments of subjects to treatments and computing the F statistic for each assignment. Formulas for the sums of squares needed to compute the F statistic are in the appendix at the end of this chapter.

In principle, the distribution of all possible F statistics is used to determine whether the F statistic computed from the observed data is sufficiently extreme to constitute evidence in favor of the alternative hypothesis. In practice, the exact randomization distribution is usually approximated by an F distribution with appropriate degrees of freedom. The numerator degrees of freedom equals $k - 1$, one less than the number of treatments or groups, which is also referred to as the between-groups degrees of freedom. The denominator degrees of freedom equals $n - k$, the number of subjects minus the number of groups, which is also referred to as the within-groups degrees of freedom. The approximate p-value is simply the area in the right-hand tail of the F distribution determined by values greater than the value of the F statistic computed from the observed data.

A p-value less than 0.05 is interpreted as statistically significant evidence that the alternative hypothesis is true. A p-value greater than 0.05 is interpreted to mean that the data do not provide sufficient evidence to reject the null hypothesis. These interpretations must be taken in context, as the next section shows.

EXAMPLE   18.5A

An automobile manufacturer employs sales representatives who make calls on dealers. The manufacturer wishes to compare the effectiveness of four different call frequency plans for the sales representatives. Thirty-two representatives are chosen at random from the sales force and assigned randomly to the four call plans, eight per plan. This is done by making a deck of 32 cards with 8 cards from each suit. The cards should be shuffled thoroughly and one card assigned to each sales representative. The suit determines which call plan the representative uses. (Alternatively, random digits may be used.) The representatives follow their plans for six months, and their sales for the six-month study period are recorded. Exhibit 18.5A displays the data.

Exhibit 18.5B displays the outcomes from the different call plans, and the mean outcomes, which are labeled M. The means vary, but the variation in the individual outcomes is more striking than the variation in the means. Do the data support the idea that one of the call plans helps produce a higher average level of sales in the long run?

The null hypothesis is that the four plans are equally effective in terms of sales. The alternative hypothesis is that they are not all equally effective. The ANOVA table is shown in Exhibit 18.5C. In the table, SS stands for sum of squares, DF for degrees of freedom, MS for mean square, and F for the F statistic. The p-value based on the F distribution with 3 and 28 degrees of freedom is also displayed. The between-groups degrees of freedom is 3, which is one less than the number of groups. The total degrees of freedom is 31, which is one less than the number of sales representatives. The within-groups degrees of freedom is the difference: $31 - 3 = 28$. Formulas for the sums of squares are displayed in the appendix to this chapter. When

EXHIBIT 18.5A
Data from Call Plan
Experiment—Completely
Randomized Design with Four
Groups (data are coded
six-month sales figures)

Plan			
A	B	C	D
36	39	44	31
40	45	43	43
32	54	38	46
44	53	40	43
35	46	41	36
41	42	35	49
44	35	37	46
42	39	37	48

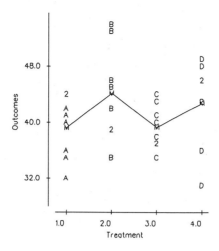

Source	SS	DF	MS	F	p
Between	143.8	3	47.9	1.68	0.194
Within	799.7	28	$28.6 = s_p^2$		
Total	943.5	31			

statistical software is used, detailed knowledge of the formulas is not needed. The mean squares are the sums of squares divided by their degrees of freedom. Thus, $47.9 = 143.8/3$, and $28.6 = 799.7/28$. The F statistic is the between-groups mean square divided by the within-groups mean square, or $1.68 = 47.9/28.6$. The p-value is computed by the statistical software. It is the F distribution approximation of the exact p-value that comes from the randomization distribution. In practice, this approximation is almost always used. The interpretation of this p-value is that, on the basis of the data collected, any differences among the four call plans are not statistically significant, because the p-value is greater than 0.05.

One other statistic of interest is the square root of the within-groups mean square, which is $\sqrt{28.6} \approx 5.3$ from Exhibit 18.5C. This statistic is denoted by s_p and is an estimate of the standard deviation of the observations in any given group. The assumption is made that the data in each group display about the same amount of variation because the subjects have been assigned randomly to the groups.   ■

SECTION

18.6 Exercises

18.6A A total of 300 students is signed up to take a finance class, which is to be taught in three lecture sections of 100 students each. Each section has a different lecturer, but the students all have the same reading assignments and exams. Thirty students are selected at random to be experimental units and are then assigned randomly to the three sections, 10 per section. The response is the sum of a student's exam scores. There are 200 points possible. The lectures are denoted A, B, and C. Here are the data.

Lecture		
A	B	C
79	120	200
55	89	121
125	145	177
30	34	170
111	90	113
146	140	200
95	160	109
160	114	145
112	140	89
86	58	116

Here are dotplots of the data from the three lectures.

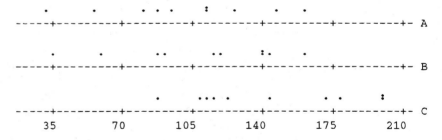

Here are the means and standard deviations for the data.

Lecture	n	Mean	Standard Deviation
A	10	99.90	39.71
B	10	109.00	40.76
C	10	144.00	40.22

Here is the ANOVA table.

Source	SS	DF	MS	F	p
Between	10842	2	5421	3.35	0.050
Within	43707	27	1619		
Total	54549	29			

a   Explain the null and alternative hypotheses in mathematical symbols and in words.

b   Assess the statistical significance of the result.

c   Interpret the result in part (b).

18.6B   A total of 300 students signed up to take a statistics class, which is to be taught in three lecture sections of 100 students each. Each section has a different lecturer, but the students all have the same reading assignments and exams. Thirty students are selected at random to be experimental units and are then assigned randomly to the three sections, 10 per section. The response is the sum of the student's exam scores. There are 200 points possible. The lectures are denoted A, B, and C. Here are the data.

Lecture		
A	B	C
160	193	99
175	101	46
161	71	117
128	122	91
80	144	103
43	111	123
86	96	97
125	73	89
90	169	106
83	92	92

Here are dotplots of the data from the three lectures.

Here are the means and standard deviations for the data.

Lecture	n	Mean	Standard Deviation
A	10	113.10	43.30
B	10	117.20	40.34
C	10	96.30	20.86

Here is the ANOVA table.

Source	SS	DF	MS	F	p
Between	2453	2	1226	0.93	0.405
Within	35435	27	1312		
Total	37887	29			

a   Explain the null and alternative hypotheses in mathematical symbols and in words.

b   Assess the statistical significance of the result.

c   Interpret the result in part (b).

SECTION

18.7 Confidence Intervals for Average Differences Among Treatments

If the null hypothesis is not rejected, it is not advisable to assume that the null hypothesis is true. It may be that not enough data were collected to bring about rejection, but a larger experiment would detect a difference among the treatments.

On the other hand, if the null hypothesis is rejected, it is possible that the experiment has detected a statistically significant difference among the treatments that is of no practical importance. This sort of finding is possible when a very large experiment is run. Large sample sizes are capable of detecting very small differences that are not of much practical importance. Thus, when a statistically significant result is obtained, it is advisable to estimate the magnitudes of the differences among the average impacts of the treatments using the method of confidence intervals, as discussed in this section. Even when the null hypothesis is not rejected, confidence intervals can be used to estimate the magnitudes of differences between treatments. If some of the estimated differences seem to be of sufficient magnitude to be of practical importance, the next step is to run a new experiment large enough to estimate the differences conclusively.

This section explains how to calculate and interpret the relevant confidence intervals for experiments with more than two groups. We explain here just one of several ways to compare all possible combinations of responses in an experiment with more than two groups. Making all possible comparisons is referred to as making *multiple comparisons*. Let $\mu_1, \mu_2, \ldots, \mu_k$ denote the underlying long-run means of the responses to the treatments, and let $\bar{y}_1, \bar{y}_2, \ldots, \bar{y}_k$ denote the means of the data in the k groups corresponding to the treatments. Let $n = n_1 + n_2 + \cdots + n_k$ denote the total number of observations. If all possible confidence intervals, considered as a group, are to be correct with 95% probability, say, each of the individual confidence intervals must be correct with probability greater than 95%. The reasoning is analogous to that needed to compare many flips of a coin with one flip. The probability that a single flip results in a head is 0.5, but the probability that six consecutive flips result in heads is $(0.5)^6 = 0.015625$.

Tukey[†] showed that a set of simultaneous confidence intervals for *all possible* differences of the form $\mu_i - \mu_j$ is formed by computing

$$\bar{y}_i - \bar{y}_j \pm \frac{q_{k,n-k}}{\sqrt{2}} s_p \sqrt{\frac{1}{n_i} + \frac{1}{n_j}}$$

for each $i < j$. The factor $q_{k,n-k}$ is a factor that must be looked up in a published table.[‡] Tables typically give factors that yield 95% and 99% levels of confidence in the set of intervals. The parameter $n - k$ is referred to as degrees of freedom.

E X A M P L E   18.7A

To illustrate, consider the data on sales calls in Example 18.5A. There are $k = 4$ groups and $n - k = 32 - 4 = 28$ degrees of freedom. The means of the sales for plans A, B, C, and D are 39.25, 44.125, 39.375, and 42.75, respectively. Also $s_p = \sqrt{28.6} = 5.34$, and each group has 8 observations. From the table in Pearson and Hartley (see footnote), the factor $q_{4,28} = 3.86$ produces a set of 95% intervals. The set of intervals is shown in Exhibit 18.7A.

The calculation for plan A − plan B runs as follows. The mean of the data from group 1 (plan A) is 39.250, while the mean from group 2 (plan B) is 44.125, so $\bar{y}_1 - \bar{y}_2 = 39.250 - 44.125 = -4.875$. The rest of the calculation is

$$\frac{q_{4,28}}{\sqrt{2}} s_p \sqrt{\frac{1}{n_1} + \frac{1}{n_2}} = \frac{3.86}{\sqrt{2}} (5.34) \sqrt{\frac{1}{8} + \frac{1}{8}} = 7.288$$

The other calculations follow the same pattern.

All the confidence intervals contain 0, so none of the differences is statistically significantly different from 0. Plainly, if 0 belongs to the confidence interval, 0 is a plausible value for the difference in the treatment effects—that is, $\mu_1 - \mu_2$, which means that a significance test would not

E X H I B I T 18.7A
The Set of Simultaneous 95% Confidence Intervals for the Differences in the Theoretical Means for the Data in Exhibit 18.5A

Difference	Confidence Interval
Plan A − Plan B	$-4.875 \pm 7.288 = [-12.1, 2.4]$
Plan A − Plan C	$-0.125 \pm 7.288 = [-7.4, 7.2]$
Plan A − Plan D	$-3.5 \pm 7.288 = [-10.8, 3.8]$
Plan B − Plan C	$4.75 \pm 7.288 = [-2.5, 12.0]$
Plan B − Plan D	$1.375 \pm 7.288 = [-5.9, 8.7]$
Plan C − Plan D	$-3.375 \pm 7.288 = [-10.7, 3.9]$

[†]J. W. Tukey, "Comparing Individual Means in the Analysis of Variance," *Biometrics*, 5 (1949), 99–114. The formula in the text produces exact confidence levels provided the data are random samples from normal distributions and the numbers of observations in the groups are equal. Under other circumstances, the confidence level is an approximation.

[‡]One source of the factors is E. S. Pearson and H. O. Hartley, *Biometrika Tables for Statisticians*, vol. 1, 3rd ed. (Cambridge, England: Cambridge University Press for Biometrika trustees, 1966), Table 29.

find the difference statistically significant. On the other hand, the difference between plan A and plan B could be as much as 12 units of sales (in favor of plan B). Similarly, the difference between plan B and plan C (again in favor of plan B) could be as much as 12 units of sales. More data might substantiate a statistically significant advantage for plan B. If 12 units of sales is a practically important difference, it would be wise to perform a follow-up experiment with more observations, or perhaps excluding plan D, to investigate plan B's effectiveness.   ■

EXAMPLE   18.7B

To illustrate, suppose that a new experiment involving plan A, plan B, and plan C is run with 15 sales representatives assigned to each plan, and suppose that part of the experimental design is the intention to compare plan B with plan A and plan C. Then in the analysis it would be legitimate to construct confidence intervals for $\mu_2 - \mu_1$ and $\mu_2 - \mu_3$ only. These two intervals are narrower than the simultaneous intervals because the focus is on the two comparisons of interest instead of on all possible comparisons. The intervals, which are based on the two-sample t statistic, would take the form

$$\bar{y}_2 - \bar{y}_1 \pm t_* s_p \sqrt{\frac{1}{15} + \frac{1}{15}}$$

$$\bar{y}_2 - \bar{y}_3 \pm t_* s_p \sqrt{\frac{1}{15} + \frac{1}{15}}$$

where t_* is an appropriate percentile from the t distribution with $42 = 44 - 2$ degrees of freedom. If the goal is to make the two intervals correct with at least 95% probability, the factor is chosen as the 98.75th percentile of the t distribution. This choice is based on Bonferroni's inequality.

Recall from Appendix 2 that Bonferroni's inequality says that if n confidence intervals with confidence coefficients $1 - \alpha_1, 1 - \alpha_2, \ldots, 1 - \alpha_n$, are made, the chance that they are all correct is at least $1 - \alpha_1 - \alpha_2 - \cdots - \alpha_n$. For example, if c preselected pairs of means are to be compared and an overall 95% probability of all intervals being correct is desired, each comparison could be based on an interval with a $(1 - 0.05/c)$ level of confidence. This would assure the 95% overall confidence level, subject to the approximate validity of the assumptions made in using the t distribution, of course.

Suppose, hypothetically, for the sake of illustration, that the experiment is performed, and the means and the pooled standard deviation come out the same as in the experiment reported in Example 18.5A. Using statistical software, the appropriate t factor is found to be 2.3246. Thus the two simultaneous confidence intervals for $\mu_2 - \mu_1$ and $\mu_2 - \mu_3$ are

$$(44.125 - 39.250) \pm (2.3246)(5.34)(0.3651) = 4.875 \pm 4.533 = [0.3, 9.4]$$

and

$$(44.125 - 39.375) \pm (2.3246)(5.34)(0.3651) = 4.75 \pm 4.533 = [0.2, 9.3]$$

> These intervals point to the superiority of plan B to both plan A and plan C, but notice that the amount of difference, on average, could be as small as 0.2 or 0.3, or as large as 9.3 or 9.4. The conclusions are not very precise because of the great amount of variation in the sales within the groups.   ∎

The illustration above shows that even with a sample size of 45 sales representatives, the conclusion that can be drawn from the experiment is rather imprecise. This leads to the question of whether a more efficient design might be available that would allow more definitive conclusions without increasing the cost of the experiment. A design with this potential—the randomized block design—is presented in Chapter 19.

SECTION

18.8 Exercises

18.8A   This exercise refers to Exercise 18.6A.

  a   Compute the Tukey 95% simultaneous confidence intervals for differences in means, given that $q_{3,27} = 3.5$. Interpret your result.

  b   Use the appropriate t distribution and Bonferroni's inequality to compute simultaneous 95% confidence intervals for $\mu_1 - \mu_2$ and $\mu_2 - \mu_3$. Interpret your result.

18.8B   This exercise refers to Exercise 18.6B.

  a   Compute the Tukey 95% simultaneous confidence intervals for differences in means, given that $q_{3,27} = 3.5$. Interpret your result.

  b   Use the appropriate distribution and Bonferroni's inequality to compute simultaneous 95% confidence intervals for $\mu_1 - \mu_2$ and $\mu_2 - \mu_3$. Interpret your result.

18.8C   Refer to the experiment described in Exercise 18.2A. Let μ_1 denote the long-run average percentile for students taking section I of the course, and let μ_2 denote the long-run average percentile for students taking section II.

  a   Use the data in Exercise 18.2A to determine the 95% confidence interval for $\mu_1 - \mu_2$.

  b   Interpret the result in part (a).

  c   Why is a multiple comparison not needed here?

18.8D   The data for the cereal experiment are reported in Exhibit 18.1B. Let μ_1 denote the long-run average gain in sales for the control group, and let μ_2 denote the long-run average gain in sales for the experimental group.

  a   Use the data in Exhibit 18.1B to determine the 95% confidence interval for $\mu_1 - \mu_2$.

  b   Interpret the result in part (b).

  c   Why is a multiple comparison not needed here?

18.8E   Refer to the loose-label experiment described in Exercise 18.4E. Let μ_1 denote the long-run average percentage of cans with loose labels when the application rate of the glue is 8 ounces per hour, and let μ_2 denote the long-run average percentage of cans with loose labels when the application rate of the glue is 12 ounces per hour.

  a   Use the data in Exercise 18.4E to determine the 95% confidence interval for $\mu_1 - \mu_2$.

  b   Interpret the result in part (b).

  c   Why is a multiple comparison not needed here?

Chapter Summary

In an experiment, the experimenter may use randomization to determine which experimental units receive the experimental treatments. The purpose of such an experiment is to estimate the average amount of difference various treatments cause in the responses. An experimental design is a plan to collect the data. In a completely randomized design with two treatment groups, experimental units are assigned to the two treatments at random. If one of the groups receives no treatment, it is a control group, and the other group is the experimental group. Randomization can be done using physical devices such as cards or using random digits.

Analysis of data from a completely randomized design is done in principle by conducting a randomization test. The null hypothesis of the test is that the two treatments have no differential effect. The alternative hypothesis can be one-sided or two-sided. A one-sided alternative is that the average effect of a specified treatment is expected to be greater than (or less than) the average effect of the other treatment. A two-sided alternative simply states that the two treatments have different average effect; the direction of the difference is not stated. A test statistic, which is the difference between the sample means of the data from the two groups, is used to perform the test. The distribution of all possible values of the statistic, assuming the null hypothesis is true, is constructed, and the p-value is computed as the probability that a value is at least as extreme as the one obtained in the experiment. If the p-value is *less* than 0.05, the result of the experiment is statistically significant, which is interpreted to mean that the experimental outcomes support the alternative hypothesis.

The randomization test is difficult to implement because construction of the distribution of the test statistic in all possible samples is cumbersome. Thus, one of two approximations is usually used in practice: the two-sample t distribution or simulation. These approximations make calculation of the distribution from all possible samples unnecessary. If a computer is available, simulation is an attractive practical method.

Analysis of variance is a format for displaying statistical calculations needed in the analysis of data from randomized controlled experiments. For the completely randomized design, total variation is broken down into two components: between groups and within groups. The ANOVA table shows sums of squares, degrees of freedom, mean squares, and the F statistic. The F statistic is used to test the null hypothesis that the treatments do not have different effects. The format of the ANOVA table is the same regardless of whether the groups are of equal or unequal size, even though the formulas needed to compute the entries in the table are different for the two cases.

The completely randomized design can be adapted to any number of groups and any number of subjects per group. The null hypothesis is that the long-run average response in each group is the same—that is, that the treatments have no effect on the long-run *average* responses of the groups. The alternative hypothesis is that the long-run average response of at least one of the groups is different from the others. The hypotheses are tested by computing the F statistic, usually by constructing an ANOVA table and referring its value to an F distribution with appropriate degrees of freedom. This process yields a p-value. If the p-value is less than 0.05, the outcome of the experiment is statistically significant. In practice, the computations are done by computer.

For the completely randomized design, a comparison of the theoretical mean responses in the groups can take two forms: simultaneous intervals for all possible comparisons and simultaneous intervals for selected comparisons of particular interest. In the latter case, the comparisons should be made part of the planning of the experiment. Making all possible comparisons is called multiple comparisons. Several multiple comparisons techniques exist. The text describes the method developed by Tukey. In the case of a few preselected comparisons of interest, confidence intervals may be based on the two-sample statistic, and Bonferroni's inequality may be used to construct simultaneous intervals.

Supplementary Exercises for Chapter 18

18A Four expert tasters, Jill, Judy, Todd, and Lee, were randomly assigned to two brands of cola and asked to rate their colas on a seven-point scale: 1, 2, 3, 4, 5, 6, 7. Here are the results.

Cola A		Cola B	
Taster	Rating	Taster	Rating
Jill	7	Todd	3
Judy	5	Lee	5

Determine the randomization distribution of $\bar{y}_1 - \bar{y}_2$ for this experiment and display the distribution in a dot diagram.

18B A completely randomized design with two groups and 15 subjects in each group yields a pooled two-sample t statistic value of 1.9. If the alternative hypothesis is $H_1 : \mu_1 \neq \mu_2$, is the p-value greater or less than 0.05? Draw a picture to demonstrate why your answer is true.

18C In a completely randomized design with three groups, if n_1 subjects are to be assigned to treatment 1, n_2 subjects to treatment 2, and n_3 subjects to treatment 3, the total number of different assignments that can be made is $(n_1 + n_2 + n_3)!/(n_1!)(n_2!)(n_3!)$. If 12 subjects are to be assigned, 4 to each treatment, how many different assignments are possible?

18D An oil company is developing a new unleaded gasoline. It screens three proposed formulas, labeled X, Y, and Z, to see if any one of them shows exceptional promise. Twelve test automobiles, all mid-sized and the same brand, are assigned at random to the formulas, four automobiles to each. The automobiles are test driven for three months using their assigned formulas. The data shown below are the miles per gallon (MPG) chalked up by the automobiles.

Formula		
X	Y	Z
25	26	24
26	27	25
25	27	25
26	28	27

a   Prepare dotplots of the MPG outcomes for the three formulas and locate the means on the dotplots. Do the plots suggest substantial differences in performance?

b   Do an ANOVA on the data and assess statistical significance. Is the conclusion consistent with the visual impression you formed in part (a)?

18E   To test the effect of shelf height on sales of cakes, a manufacturer conducts an experiment using nine cooperating supermarkets. The treatments are bottom shelf (B), eye-level shelf (E), and top shelf (T). Three stores are assigned randomly to each treatment, and numbers of units sold in the study period of one month are recorded. Here are the data.

	Shelf	
B	E	T
582	781	524
558	604	499
525	584	521

a   Prepare dotplots of the units sold for the three shelf heights and locate the means on the dotplots. Do the plots suggest substantial differences in performance?

b   Do an ANOVA on the data and assess statistical significance. Is the conclusion consistent with the visual impression you formed in part (a)?

18F   A sports lab tests golf balls for durability. The balls are put into a machine that simulates drives with a driver club. The outcome is the number of drives needed to crack or chip the ball. An experiment to test four brands of balls, denoted A, B, C, and D, was conducted as follows. Four balls of each brand were purchased at a sporting goods store. The *order* in which the balls were tested by the machine was determined *at random* to avoid any biases that might be caused by machine performance. The data are given below.

	Brand		
A	B	C	D
355	364	290	270
273	244	273	325
307	307	337	374
281	242	331	220

a   Prepare dotplots of the numbers of drives for the four brands and locate the means on the dotplots. Do the plots suggest substantial differences in performance?

b   Do an ANOVA on the data and assess statistical significance. Is the conclusion consistent with the visual impression you formed in part (a)?

18G   For the problem outlined in Exercise 18D, compute simultaneous 95% confidence intervals for all possible differences in treatment means using Tukey's method. The appropriate q factor is 3.95. Give a verbal interpretation of the intervals.

18H   For the problem outlined in Exercise 18E, compute simultaneous 95% confidence intervals for all possible differences in treatment means using Tukey's method. The appropriate q factor is 4.34. Give a verbal interpretation of the intervals.

18I   For the problem outlined in Exercise 18F, compute simultaneous 95% confidence intervals for all possible differences in treatment means using Tukey's method. The appropriate q factor is 4.20. Give a verbal interpretation of the intervals.

18J A Department of Transportation analyst conducted a study to compare the degree of support for fast rail train service between Madison and Milwaukee, Wisconsin. A questionnaire was designed that yielded an index of support for the service. Random samples of size 8 were selected from three groups of people: University of Wisconsin faculty (group A); members of the Rotary Club, excluding university faculty members (group B); and state government employees, excluding university faculty members (group C). The resulting indices of support are reported below.

Group		
A	B	C
74	47	80
86	78	52
75	72	72
60	50	49
59	53	61
66	62	57
81	80	70
62	65	66

   a Prepare dotplots of the indices from the three groups, all on the same scale. Locate the sample mean of each group on its dotplot.

   b Prepare the ANOVA table for these data.

   c State the null hypothesis that is tested by the F statistic in the ANOVA table.

   d Determine the p-value associated with the F statistic in part (c).

   e Determine the statistical significance of the F statistic and interpret this result.

   f Using Tukey's method, determine the simultaneous 95% confidence intervals for all possible differences in group means and interpret the results of your calculations. The q factor for this problem is $q = 3.55$.

18K Supermarket chains offer house brands of many products that compete with nationally distributed products. Many people wonder if the house brands measure up in quality to the national brands. The experiment in this exercise compares different brands of 16-ounce cans of fruit cocktail. The observed response for a can is obtained by draining the contents of liquid and weighing the resulting net contents. For your study, choose three national brands and two house brands distributed by chains located in your town or city. Select five cans of each brand at random from the shelves of local grocery stores and determine the net weights for each can.

   a Prepare dotplots of the weights from the five brands, all on the same scale. Locate the sample mean of each brand on its dotplot.

   b Prepare the ANOVA table for these data.

   c State the null hypothesis that is tested by the F statistic in the ANOVA table.

   d Determine the p-value associated with the F statistic in part (c).

   e Determine the statistical significance of the F statistic and interpret this result.

   f Using Tukey's method, determine the simultaneous 95% confidence intervals for all possible differences in group means and interpret the results of your calculations. The q factor for this problem is $q = 4.20$.

18L Use a completely randomized design to conduct an experiment of your choosing. Write a brief report, not more than five pages, about your experiment. Here are two possible outlines for the report. Each was used by students who did this exercise.

Suggested Outline I

> Objective of the study
> Hypotheses
> Method of analysis
> Design of the experiment
> Results

Suggested Outline II

> Design of the experiment
>
>> Description of the experiment
>> Randomization
>> Data collection
>
> Data presentation
>
>> Hypothesis testing (ANOVA)
>> Confidence intervals
>
> Conclusion

18M   For the problem outlined in Exercise 18F, the experimental design required comparison of brand A with the other brands because the sponsor of the experiment was the manufacturer of brand A. Use the Bonferroni method to compute simultaneous 95% confidence intervals for the required differences in the means. Give a verbal interpretation of the intervals. Compare the intervals with those obtained in Exercise 18I.

. . . .

Glossary for Chapter 18

completely randomized design	An experimental plan that assigns a specified number of subjects to a specified number of treatments at random.
control group	A group of subjects to which no treatment is applied. A control group is often used to provide a baseline for comparing the effects of the treatment or treatments.
experimental design	A plan used to collect data in a controlled randomized experiment.
experimental group	A group to which a treatment is applied in an experiment in which there is also a control group.
experimental unit	A unit (or subject) to which a treatment is applied and from which a measured response is taken.
randomization test	A test that uses the random allocation of experimental units to treatments by computing the value of a test statistic for each possible allocation and assessing the significance of the actual experimental outcomes in the context of all the possible outcomes.

APPENDIX

Analysis-of-Variance Formulas for Completely Randomized Designs

All ANOVA formulas are based on the paradigm Observed Response = Fitted Value + Residual.

Completely Randomized Design

In the completely randomized design, let y_{ij} denote the observation on the jth subject assigned to the ith treatment, $\bar{y}_{i.}$ denote the mean of the n_i observations on the ith treatment, and $\bar{y}_{..}$ denote the mean of all the data. Recall that k denotes the number of treatments. Then for each $j = 1, 2, \ldots, n_i$ and $i = 1, 2, \ldots, k$,

$$y_{ij} = \bar{y}_{..} + (\bar{y}_{i.} - \bar{y}_{..}) + (y_{ij} - \bar{y}_{i.})$$

The quantity $\bar{y}_{..} + (\bar{y}_{i.} - \bar{y}_{..})$ is the Fitted Value and the quantity $(y_{ij} - \bar{y}_{i.})$ is the Residual. The Fitted Value Response is the overall mean of the data plus an adjustment that is the difference between the ith treatment mean and the overall mean. The quantity $\bar{y}_{i.} - \bar{y}_{..}$ is called the *effect* of treatment i. If the adjustment is large, the response to the ith treatment differs substantially on average from the overall level of response. The ANOVA table is based on the algebraic identity

Total Sum of Squares $=$

$$\sum_{i=1}^{k}\sum_{j=1}^{n_i}(y_{ij} - \bar{y}_{..})^2 = \sum_{i=1}^{k}\sum_{j=1}^{n_i}[(\bar{y}_{i.} - \bar{y}_{..}) + (y_{ij} - \bar{y}_{i.})]^2$$

$$= \sum_{i=1}^{k}\sum_{j=1}^{n_i}(\bar{y}_{i.} - \bar{y}_{..})^2 + \sum_{i=1}^{k}\sum_{j=1}^{n_i}(y_{ij} - \bar{y}_{i.})^2 + 2\sum_{i=1}^{k}\sum_{j=1}^{n_i}[(\bar{y}_{i.} - \bar{y}_{..})(y_{ij} - \bar{y}_{i.})]$$

$$= \sum_{i=1}^{k}n_i(\bar{y}_{i.} - \bar{y}_{..})^2 + \sum_{i=1}^{k}\sum_{j=1}^{n_i}(y_{ij} - \bar{y}_{i.})^2$$

$=$ Between-groups Sum of Squares $+$ Within-groups Sum of Squares

The identity follows immediately from the fact that

$$\sum_{j=1}^{n_i}(y_{ij} - \bar{y}_{i.}) = 0$$

which states nothing more than that the sum of the deviations from the mean of a sample is equal to zero. The algebraic identity for degrees of freedom is

$$\underbrace{n_1 + n_2 + \cdots + n_k - 1}_{} = \underbrace{(k - 1)}_{} + \underbrace{(n_1 - 1) + (n_2 - 1) + \cdots + (n_k - 1)}_{}$$

or

Total Degrees of Freedom $=$ Between-group Degrees of Freedom
$+$ Within-group Degrees of Freedom

Randomized Block and Factorial Designs

Chapter Objectives

After mastering this chapter, you will be able to:

- Conduct an experiment using a randomized block design

- Analyze the data from a randomized block design

- Conduct an experiment using a factorial design

- Analyze the data from a factorial design

SECTION

19.1 Randomized Block Designs

The completely randomized design discussed in Example 18.5A yielded imprecise inferences because the great variation among sales representatives was randomly distributed across the plans. The design discussed in this section restricts the impact of variation among subjects by first grouping the subjects into relatively homogeneous groups, called *blocks*, and then assigning subjects from each block to treatments. In the call plan experiment, this idea is readily carried out by using past sales data on the representatives to compute the average monthly sales for each one of them. The four representatives with the lowest four averages are put in the first block. The four representatives with the next highest averages are put in the second block, and so on. Cards or random digits are used to assign the representatives in the first block to the four plans, one per plan. This process is repeated for each block, so that eight representatives are assigned to each plan. The analysis of this *randomized block design* permits the separation of the variation among the blocks and the variation among the treatments (plans).

EXAMPLE **19.1A**

The data in Exhibit 19.1A are from the randomized block design described above. The sales representatives have been ordered from lowest to highest average previous sales. Within each block of four, cards of different suits were shuffled and drawn to assign representatives to plans. Plan A is treatment 1, plan B treatment 2, and so forth. The last column in Exhibit 19.1A shows the sales resulting from the experiment.

Exhibit 19.1B shows an *incorrect* analysis of variance of the new sales data as if they were from a completely randomized design—in other words, ignoring the blocks. This analysis is quite similar to the analysis given in

E X H I B I T **19.1A**
Data from a Randomized Block
Design—Call Plan Experiment

Sales Rep	Previous Average Sales	Assigned Treatment	New Sales
1	29	1	27
2	31	4	27
3	32	2	31
4	33	3	24
5	33	1	38
6	33	2	40
7	35	4	37
8	36	3	32
9	36	2	39
10	37	3	34
11	37	1	35
12	37	4	39
13	38	2	41
14	38	3	34
15	39	4	36
16	39	1	39
17	40	2	43
18	40	4	39
19	40	3	37
20	40	1	36
21	40	4	42
22	41	3	36
23	41	1	38
24	41	2	42
25	41	2	46
26	42	1	41
27	42	3	42
28	43	4	42
29	44	4	45
30	46	1	44
31	47	2	50
32	50	3	42

EXHIBIT **19.1B**
Analysis of Variance of Data in
Exhibit 19.1A Assuming a
Completely Randomized Design

Source	SS	DF	MS	F	p
Between	169.6	3	56.5	1.90	0.152
Within	832.3	28	29.7		
Total	1001.9	31			

Section 18.5; the differences among the plans appear not to be statistically significant.

In contrast, Exhibit 19.1C displays the *correct* analysis of variance taking the blocks into account, showing both treatments and blocks as sources of variation. The line labeled "Within blocks" yields an estimate of the variation that cannot be assigned to the other two sources: between treatments and between blocks. The null hypothesis of interest is that treatments (plans) do not differ on the average. The appropriate F statistic is the ratio of the between-treatments mean square to the within-blocks mean square, namely, $26.4 = 56.54/2.14$. The degrees of freedom associated with this statistic are 3 and 21, the between-treatments degrees of freedom and the within-blocks degrees of freedom. The p-value is essentially zero, much less than 0.05, which means that the evidence in favor of the alternative hypothesis is very strong.

The randomized block experiment thus finds decisive evidence that the plans differ in their average effect. The secret to this finding is blocking sales representatives according to their past performance and making sure that one representative from each performance block was assigned to one of the plans. This design prevents the chance assignment of a large number of representatives with less successful sales histories, say, to a particular plan. Such an assignment is not ruled out by the completely randomized design, but such an assignment would make the plan seem relatively ineffective just because of the representatives assigned to it.

To summarize, the randomized block experiment has produced statistically significant evidence that not all the call plans have the same long-run average effect on sales. This finding was masked by variation among sales representatives when a completely randomized experiment was used.   ■

EXHIBIT **19.1C**
Analysis of Variance of the Data
from a Randomized Block
Design in Exhibit 19.1A

Source	SS	DF	MS	F	p
Between treatments	169.6	3	56.54	26.4	0.000
Between blocks	787.4	7	112.48		
Within blocks	44.9	21	2.14		
Total	1001.9	31			

The formulas that lead to the analysis of variance in Exhibit 19.1C are displayed in the appendix to this chapter. In practice, statistical software is invariably used to carry out the calculations, so mastery of the formulas is not important. What is important is understanding how to conduct the experiment, how to tell the program to analyze the data using the appropriate design, and how to interpret the output from the program.

Some interesting relationships are illustrated by comparing the tables in Exhibits 19.1B and C. First, the total sum of squares is the same in both tables because this quantity is always computed by treating the data as one homogeneous sample. Next, the within sum of squares in Exhibit 19.1B is equal to the sum of the between-blocks and within-blocks sums of squares in Exhibit 19.1C—that is, $832.3 = 787.4 + 44.9$. The randomized block design yields a decomposition of the variation associated with blocks into the between and within components. The between-blocks component is not used in assessing the significance of the null hypothesis of common treatment effects. This is the benefit achieved by exercising control through blocking the variation among sales representatives.

Another observation is that the between treatments degrees of freedom is equal to 3, which is one less than the number of treatments, just the same as in the completely randomized design. The degrees of freedom associated with between-blocks variation is 7, which is one less than the number of blocks. The within-blocks degrees of freedom equals $21 = 31 - 3 - 7$. In all ANOVA tables, the sums of squares and the degrees of freedom add up to the column totals.

The randomized block design turned out to be much more precise than the completely randomized design in Example 18.5A because the variation among sales representatives was substantial. If the sales representatives had been more-or-less comparable, the randomized block design would have been an inefficient choice because 7 degrees of freedom would have been used in controlling unimportant variation. See Exercise 19.2B for a numerical example in which the randomized block design is less efficient than the completely randomized block design. In practice, the choice between the completely randomized design and the randomized block design hinges on whether or not the chosen blocking variable is related to the measured responses.

To the extent that a completely randomized design does not distribute representatives of comparable ability evenly over the plans, it is less efficient than the randomized block design. A quantitative measure of the efficiency of the randomized block design in the call plan application is a comparison of the within-groups mean square in Exhibit 19.1B to the within-blocks mean square in Exhibit 19.1C. These two mean squares are the denominators of the F statistics in the analyses. A smaller denominator makes it easier to obtain a large F, which leads to the rejection of the null hypothesis. The ratio of the one to the other is $29.7/2.14 \cong 14$, which is interpreted to say that the randomized block design is about 14 times as efficient as the completely randomized design. No wonder the p-value in Exhibit 19.1B is 0.152, while the p-value in Exhibit 19.1C is 0.000.

Confidence Intervals

Confidence interval analysis in the randomized block design parallels that in the completely randomized design. For the Tukey simultaneous intervals for all possible comparisons, use the square root of the within-block mean square for s_p. Exhibit 19.1D shows the data in Exhibit 19.1A arranged in a two-way table, the marginal means, and the Tukey intervals.

Block	Treatment 1	2	3	4	Mean
1	27	31	24	27	27.25
2	38	40	32	37	36.75
3	35	39	34	39	36.75
4	39	41	34	36	37.5
5	36	43	37	39	38.75
6	38	42	36	42	39.5
7	41	46	42	42	42.75
8	44	50	42	45	45.25
Mean	37.25	41.5	35.125	38.375	38.063

Difference	Confidence Interval
Plan A − Plan B	$-4.250 \pm 2.04 \cong [-6.3, -2.2]$
Plan A − Plan C	$2.125 \pm 2.04 \cong [0.1, 4.2]$
Plan A − Plan D	$-1.125 \pm 2.04 \cong [-3.2, 0.9]$
Plan B − Plan C	$6.375 \pm 2.04 \cong [4.3, 8.4]$
Plan B − Plan D	$3.125 \pm 2.04 \cong [1.1, 5.2]$
Plan C − Plan D	$-3.250 \pm 2.04 \cong [-5.3, -1.2]$

The tabled factor for a set of 95% Tukey intervals is $q_{4,21} = 3.95$, and $s_p = \sqrt{2.14} = 1.463$. To obtain the interval for plan A − plan B, compute[†]

$$(37.25 - 41.5) \pm \frac{3.95}{\sqrt{2}}(1.463)\sqrt{\frac{1}{8} + \frac{1}{8}} = -4.25 \pm (2.793)(1.463)(0.5)$$

$$= -4.25 \pm 2.04$$

The other intervals are computed similarly. According to the intervals in Exhibit 19.1D, plans A and D are not statistically significantly different, plan A is superior to plan C, and plan B is superior to plans A and C. A 95% confidence level is associated with these statements.

[†]Recall that the formula is $\bar{y}_i - \bar{y}_j \pm \dfrac{q_{k,n-k}}{\sqrt{2}} s_p \sqrt{\dfrac{1}{n_i} + \dfrac{1}{n_j}}$.

Analysis of the table in Exhibit 19.1D reveals a substantial increase in block means as block number increases. The trend in these means is accounted for by the blocking, so it does not interfere with the comparison of the call plans, which documents the value of blocking in the experiment. Note also that the sales for plan B (treatment 2) are always the largest within the block. The evidence clearly points to the superiority of plan B.

If a limited number of important comparisons are identified as part of the experimental plan, those comparisons can be made using intervals based on the *t* distribution, as illustrated in Section 18.7.

S E C T I O N

19.2 Exercises

19.2A A total of 300 students signed up to take a finance class, which is to be taught in three lecture sections of 100 students each. Each section has a different lecturer, but the students all have the same reading assignments and exams. Thirty students are selected at random to be experimental units and are then assigned using a randomized block design to the three sections, 10 per section. The blocking variable is cumulative grade-point average (GPA). Ten blocks are formed by putting the students in increasing order by GPA and then grouping them in blocks of three. Within each block, students are randomly assigned to lectures.

The response is the sum of a student's three exam scores. There are 200 points possible. The lectures are denoted 1, 2, and 3. Here are the data. (Filename: EX19_2A.DAT.)

GPA	Section	Block	Test Score	GPA	Section	Block	Test Score
1.54	1	1	12	2.81	1	6	97
1.67	2	1	46	2.81	3	6	129
1.86	3	1	72	2.83	2	6	118
1.99	1	2	47	3.02	1	7	106
2.06	3	2	85	3.10	3	7	141
2.09	2	2	74	3.12	2	7	129
2.17	1	3	63	3.13	2	8	133
2.27	2	3	83	3.26	1	8	121
2.41	3	3	103	3.53	3	8	143
2.55	2	4	91	3.53	2	9	159
2.56	3	4	111	3.62	1	9	135
2.60	1	4	82	3.82	3	9	173
2.62	2	5	102	3.85	3	10	180
2.75	3	5	121	3.86	2	10	174
2.78	1	5	92	4.00	1	10	176

Here are the data arranged by block and lecture, with means in the margins of the table.

| | | Lecture | | |
Block	1	2	3	Block Mean
1	12	46	72	43.33
2	47	74	85	68.67
3	63	83	103	83.00
4	82	91	111	94.67
5	92	102	121	105.00
6	97	118	129	114.67
7	106	129	141	125.33
8	121	133	143	132.33
9	135	159	173	155.67
10	176	174	180	176.67
Lecture Mean	93.10	110.90	125.80	109.93 = overall mean

Here is the ANOVA table.

Source	SS	DF	MS	F	p
Lectures	5360	2	2680	45.91	0.000
Between blocks	43283	9	4809		
Within blocks	1051	18	58		
Total	49694	29			

a Interpret the ANOVA table. State the null and alternative hypotheses and assess statistical significance. Show how the "Lectures" F value of 45.91 was computed from entries in the MS column. How is the corresponding p-value computed?

b Here is the ANOVA table treating the data as coming from a completely randomized design.

Source	SS	DF	MS	F	p
Between lectures	5360	2	2680	1.63	0.214
Within lectures	44333	27	1642		
Total	49694	29			

Compare this table with the one that correctly treats the data as coming from a randomized block design. How much more efficient is the randomized block design than the completely randomized design?

c Compute the Tukey 95% simultaneous confidence intervals for all possible differences in pairs of means and interpret your results. You are given that $q_{3,18} = 3.61$.

19.2B This exercise uses simulated data to illustrate that a randomized block design can be less efficient than a completely randomized design. The data that follow were simulated so that the analysis of variance for a completely randomized design with three treatments shows a statistically significant difference in the treatment means. The information in the "Block" column is added arbitrarily, so the blocking has no relation to the response. (Filename: EX19_2B.DAT.)

Block	Treatment	Response	Block	Treatment	Response
1	1	9	6	1	19
1	2	−14	6	2	−9
1	3	29	6	3	26
2	1	23	7	1	−21
2	2	−7	7	2	13
2	3	19	7	3	32
3	1	20	8	1	22
3	2	5	8	2	−8
3	3	−1	8	3	22
4	1	−18	9	1	−11
4	2	25	9	2	30
4	3	29	9	3	5
5	1	19	10	1	7
5	2	−11	10	2	−8
5	3	16	10	3	37

Here are the ANOVA tables for the completely randomized and randomized block designs.

Analysis of Variance for Completely Randomized Design

Source	SS	DF	MS	F	p
Between treatments	2101.3	2	1050.6	4.54	0.020
Within treatments	6241.7	27	231.2		
Total	8343.0	29			

Analysis of Variance for Randomized Block Design

Source	SS	DF	MS	F	p
Between treatments	2101.3	2	1050.6	3.09	0.070
Between blocks	116.3	9	12.9	0.04	1.000
Within blocks	6125.4	18	340.3		
Total	8343.0	29			

a Compare the information in the two ANOVA tables.

b Prepare a table of data by block and treatment and show the means in the margins. What light does this shed on the ineffectiveness of the randomized block design for these data?

c Discuss the practical implications of this example. Under what circumstances is a randomized block design ill-advised?

19.2C The randomized block design can be applied to sequences of binary data. A particularly simple form of application is the *randomized pair* design, which is illustrated in this exercise. Don wishes to compare his success rate at two distances from a dart board: 6 feet and 9 feet. Success is hitting the bull's-eye. He plans to make 100 throws from each distance. Over such a long series of throws, he is very likely not to remain a "constant" source of variation, so to make sure that throws from each distance occur close together in the sequence of throws, he uses the randomized pair design. The 200 throws consist of 100 blocks of two. For each pair of adjacent throws, one will be from 6 feet and one from 9 feet. Which one comes first in the pair is determined by the flip of a coin: heads means 6 feet, tails means 9 feet. The pairs of throws are blocks, and randomization occurs within each block. The actual data record is 200 lines long and is not displayed here. Instead, the data are summarized in the accompanying table.

		9-Foot Throw		
		Failure	Success	Total
6-Foot Throw	Failure	62	11	73
	Success	25	2	27
	Total	87	13	100

The number 62 is the number of times both the 6-foot and the 9-foot throw within a block resulted in failure. The number 11 is the number of times, within a block, the 6-foot throw resulted in failure and the 9-foot throw in success. The numbers 25 and 2 have similar interpretations. The number 73 is the number of 6-foot throws that resulted in failure, while 27 is the number of 6-foot throws that resulted in success. The proportion of successes from 6 feet is $27/100 = 0.27$, and the proportion of successes from 9 feet is $13/100 = 0.13$. The difference in proportions is $(27 - 13)/100 = 14/100 = 0.14$. Note that $27 = 25 + 2$, and $13 = 11 + 2$, so $27 - 13 = 25 - 11 = 14$. The blocks in which both throws are a success "cancel" out in the subtraction, and the blocks in which both throws are a failure do not enter the calculation at all. Another way of saying this is that the blocks in which both responses are the same do not provide any information about the difference in the treatments. The number of blocks that provide useful information is $25 + 11 = 36$.

If the null hypothesis of no treatment difference is true, the 36 relevant blocks can be thought of as 36 independent Bernoulli trials with long-run probability of success $\pi = 0.5$. The one-sided p-value is the probability that such a sequence produces 11 or fewer successes. The two-sided p-value is just twice the one-sided p-value because the binomial distribution is symmetric when $\pi = 0.5$.

a   Compute the one-sided p-value and assess the statistical significance of the result. State the alternative hypothesis being tested.

b   An approximation to the p-value for the two-sided alternative is simply to produce the ANOVA table for data assuming a randomized block design. There are 100 blocks and two treatments. This approximation is crude because the ANOVA table assumes continuous data, whereas the actual data are binary. Here is the ANOVA table.

Source	SS	DF	MS	F	p
Treatments	0.9800	1	0.9800	5.70	0.019
Between blocks	14.0000	99	0.1414		
Within blocks	17.0200	99	0.1719		
Total	32.0000	199			

c   Compare the approximate p-value in the ANOVA table with the exact two-sided p-value, which can be computed from the result in part (a).

SECTION

19.3   General Factorial Designs

So far we have introduced designs that allowed us to study the impact of one factor on a response variable, the completely randomized and randomized block designs.

The completely randomized design depended on randomization to control the effects of all but the one factor of interest, while the randomized block design used grouping to control the effects of important factors and randomization to control the effects of other factors.

This section deals with more complex designs needed when interest focuses on the simultaneous impact of several factors on the response. Factorial designs were introduced in Chapter 13. Later sections demonstrate special techniques to use when factors have only two levels.

Besides making it possible to study the *simultaneous* impact of several factors on a response, factorial designs allow you to assess the interactive effects of variables. **interaction** **Interaction** refers to situations in which the level of the response variable is not a linear function of the combinations of the levels of the factors. Such situations are important but impossible to discover if factors are varied one at a time.

This section introduces some of the notation and terminology used in factorial design. General notation and formulas are in the appendix to this chapter. The section then uses a simple design with two factors to show how to assess the impact of different combinations of factors on the response variable.

Let k denote the number of factors whose impact is to be studied, and let y denote the response variable. Let m_1 denote the number of levels of factor 1, m_2 the number of levels of factor 2, $\ldots$, m_k the number of levels of factor k. For example, consider an experiment with a machine setup. Suppose two setup procedures are possible, and these are the two levels of the first factor. The second factor is work shift, and because there are three shifts, there are three levels of this factor. Finally, let the third factor be day of the week, a factor with 6 levels because the workers work Monday through Saturday. In this example, $m_1 = 2$, $m_2 = 3$, and $m_3 = 6$, and there are $2 \times 3 \times 6 = 36$ possible combinations of levels, so it takes 6 weeks to run the study so that every combination of setup and shift is observed with each possible day of the week. Such a study would be one replication of the factorial experiment. To produce a second replication requires another 6 weeks. Performing a second replication means that there are two observations of the response variable for each possible combination of the factor levels, and it is the replications that permit the study of interactions. We use the notation n to denote the number of replications. As this example illustrates, the factorial experiment can be a rather large one, so in practice we strive to keep the number of levels and/or the number of factors small.

The impact of a single factor, holding all the impacts of the other factors fixed, **main effect** is called a **main effect**. If interaction is present, the interpretation of main effects is problematic because the impact a factor has on the response variable depends on the levels of other factors.

E X A M P L E   **19.3A**

Consider the experiment to study the impact of baking time and temperature on the taste of a cake made from a mix, introduced in Example 13.4A. The variables baking time and baking temperature are the factors. The responses are ratings of the taste of the cakes given by expert tasters. In this experiment, three times and three temperatures are used, so it is called a 3×3 factorial, meaning two factors at three levels each. The three levels of the Time are

−1: 10% below the time stated on the cake mix package

0: time stated on the cake mix package

+1: 10% above the time stated on the cake mix package

The three levels of Temperature are

−1: 10% below the temperature stated on the cake mix package

0: temperature stated on the cake mix package

+1: 10% above the temperature stated on the cake mix package

The numbers −1, 0, and +1 are standard notation for the low, center, and high levels of the factors, respectively. The numbers −1, 0, and +1 have no other meaning.

There are nine combinations of the levels of the factors, and because three taste testers evaluate cakes baked at a given combination, there are three replications. This implies that $9 \times 3 = 27$ tasters and cakes are involved in the experiment. To avoid bias, the 27 cakes are baked according to a random allocation of combinations. This randomization is done by creating a deck of 27 cards, three for each of the nine combinations, and laying the well-shuffled cards down in a row. The baked cakes are assigned to tasters at random by arranging the tasters' names in random order and giving one cake to each taster in that order. The tasters score the cakes on a seven-point scale, with 0 meaning well below average, 1 below average, 2 somewhat below average, 3 average, 4 somewhat above average, 5 above average, and 6 well above average. Exhibit 19.3A shows the data.

Notice that for each level of time, nine observations have been made, and likewise for each level of temperature. Also, for each of the nine combinations of levels of the two factors, three observations have been

EXHIBIT 19.3A
Data from Cake Baking Experiment—3 × 3 Factorial Design

Taster	Time	Temperature	Rating	Taster	Time	Temperature	Rating
1	−1	−1	0	15	0	0	6
2	−1	−1	0	16	0	1	1
3	−1	−1	3	17	0	1	2
4	−1	0	0	18	0	1	3
5	−1	0	2	19	1	−1	4
6	−1	0	4	20	1	−1	5
7	−1	1	4	21	1	−1	6
8	−1	1	5	22	1	0	1
9	−1	1	6	23	1	0	3
10	0	−1	2	24	1	0	5
11	0	−1	3	25	1	1	0
12	0	−1	4	26	1	1	1
13	0	0	3	27	1	1	2
14	0	0	6				

made. Despite the small number of observations (27), a large number of comparisons can be made. For example, the low level of time (-1) can be compared to the high level of time ($+1$), and the comparison is based on two means of nine observations. As another example, with time fixed at the center level (0), the low level of temperature (-1) can be compared to the high level of temperature ($+1$), and the comparison is based on two means of three observations. Factorial designs allow a rich menu of comparisons, so that one is not limited to the estimation of the effects of variables in "splendid isolation."

Exhibit 19.3B shows the ANOVA table for the experiment. The sources of variation are identified as Time, Temperature, Interaction, and Within-groups. The Total degrees of freedom is $26 = 27 - 1$, which is one less than the number of cakes tested. Two degrees of freedom are associated with time, which is one less than the number of levels of this factor, and similarly for temperature. The Interaction degrees of freedom equals $4 = (2)(2) = (3 - 1)(3 - 1)$, the product of the degrees of freedom associated with the two factors. Interaction can be thought of as the multiplicative (joint) effect of the two factors. The within-groups (residual) degrees of freedom is found by subtracting each of Time, Temperature and Interaction degrees of freedom from the Total degrees of freedom. Thus, $18 = 26 - 2 - 2 - 4$.

Formulas for the sums of squares are given in the appendix to this chapter. The mean squares are the sums of squares divided by their corresponding degrees of freedom. The F statistics are the Time, Temperature, and Interaction mean squares divided by the within-groups mean square.

The p-values are obtained from F distributions. For the Time and Temperature effects, the F distribution with 2 and 18 degrees of freedom is used. The p-value for time, and for temperature, is the area to the right of 0.47 under the F distribution with 2 and 18 degrees of freedom. The p-value for Interaction is the area to the right of 7.34 under the F distribution with 4 and 18 degrees of freedom. As usual, statistical software handles the calculation. Hand calculation and table lookups are not needed in practice.

The p-values in Exhibit 19.3B say that Time and Temperature do not have statistically significant effects, but Interaction is strongly statistically significant. How is such information interpreted? It is helpful to look at a

EXHIBIT **19.3B**
Analysis of Variance for Cake Baking Experiment, 3×3 Factorial Design (data in Exhibit 19.3A)

Source	SS	DF	MS	F	p
Time	2	2	1.000	0.47	0.630
Temperature	2	2	1.000	0.47	0.630
Interaction	62	4	15.500	7.34	0.001
Within groups	38	18	2.111		
Total	104	26			

table of means, as shown in Exhibit 19.3C. The body of the table shows the means of the three ratings for each combination of levels of the factors. The margins show the means of the nine ratings given to each level of each factor. The overall mean, 3, is the average of all 27 ratings. The marginal means differ very little from the overall mean of 3, which is why the Time and Temperature main effects are not statistically significant. On the other hand, the means in the body of the table vary from a low of 1 to a high of 5. One way to appreciate the implications of this variation is to plot the means in an interaction plot, as shown in Exhibit 19.3D.

The three levels of temperature appear on the horizontal axis. The three means associated with the +1 level (or high level) of time and the three levels of temperature are 5, 3, and 1. These are plotted with the symbol H in Exhibit 19.3D. The other levels of time are plotted similarly, with M denoting the 0 (medium) level of time and L denoting the −1 (low) level of time. The plotting symbols are connected by lines. Because the lines so constructed cross each other, there is interaction between time and temperature. *A diagram associated with no interaction has parallel lines.*

The plot in Exhibit 19.3D shows that the highest mean rating is achieved with the following combinations of time and temperature: (+1, −1), (0, 0), and (−1, +1). Thus, it is possible to compensate for a lower time by using

E X H I B I T **19.3C**
Mean Ratings from Cake Baking Experiment (data are in Exhibit 19.3A)

		Temperature Levels			Marginal Means
		−1	0	+1	
	−1	1.0000	2.0000	5.0000	2.6667
Time Levels	0	3.0000	5.0000	2.0000	3.3333
	+1	5.0000	3.0000	1.0000	3.0000
Marginal Means		3.0000	3.3333	2.6667	3.0000

E X H I B I T **19.3D**
Interaction Plot of Means in Exhibit 19.3C (H denotes high level of Time, M denotes medium level of Time, and L denotes low level of Time)

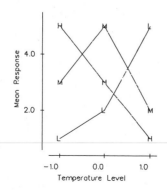

a higher temperature and vice versa. The lowest average rating is achieved with the following combinations of time and temperature: $(-1, -1)$ and $(+1, +1)$. In other words, a combination of low time and temperature or high time and temperature produces an unsatisfactory cake.

The fact that the time and temperature effects were not statistically significant should not be interpreted to mean these factors are unimportant. The effects are small for the amount of deviation from suggested levels studied (10%). Certainly it is possible to think of deviations that would produce strong effects, but these were not part of the study. Moreover, when an experiment demonstrates significant interaction, interpretation of main effects is problematic because the effects of an interacting variable are not the same for every level of the other interacting variable. ▪

SECTION

19.4 Exercises

19.4A A 2×3 factorial experiment with replication yields the following table of means.

		Levels of Factor B		
		−1	0	1
Levels of	−1	5	8	15
Factor A	+1	8	11	18

  a Compute the marginal means.
  b Prepare an interaction plot.
  c Assess the presence or absence of interaction from the plot in part (b).

19.4B A 2×3 factorial experiment with replication yields the following table of means.

		Levels of Factor B		
		−1	0	1
Levels of	−1	15	8	5
Factor A	+1	8	18	11

  a Compute the marginal means.
  b Prepare an interaction plot.
  c Assess the presence or absence of interaction from the plot in part (b).

19.4C Here are data from a $2 \times 3 \times 3$ experiment (factors denoted by **A**, **B**, and **C**).

Case	A	B	C	y	Case	A	B	C	y
1	−1	−1	−1	3.4	28	1	−1	−1	4.9
2	−1	−1	0	3.7	29	1	−1	0	3.8
3	−1	−1	1	2.8	30	1	−1	1	4.4
4	−1	0	−1	2.3	31	1	0	−1	6.3
5	−1	0	0	2.6	32	1	0	0	5.5
6	−1	0	1	3.5	33	1	0	1	6.7
7	−1	1	−1	4.8	34	1	1	−1	6.2
8	−1	1	0	4.3	35	1	1	0	6.0
9	−1	1	1	5.9	36	1	1	1	7.7
10	1	−1	−1	4.4	37	−1	−1	−1	0.4
11	1	−1	0	4.4	38	−1	−1	0	4.6
12	1	−1	1	5.0	39	−1	−1	1	4.4
13	1	0	−1	4.5	40	−1	0	−1	5.9
14	1	0	0	5.0	41	−1	0	0	2.8
15	1	0	1	5.8	42	−1	0	1	5.9
16	1	1	−1	6.5	43	−1	1	−1	3.3
17	1	1	0	6.7	44	−1	1	0	4.3
18	1	1	1	9.0	45	−1	1	1	5.5
19	−1	−1	−1	3.5	46	1	−1	−1	5.6
20	−1	−1	0	6.9	47	1	−1	0	2.7
21	−1	−1	1	6.9	48	1	−1	1	9.1
22	−1	0	−1	5.4	49	1	0	−1	6.7
23	−1	0	0	3.4	50	1	0	0	6.4
24	−1	0	1	5.4	51	1	0	1	4.5
25	−1	1	−1	4.4	52	1	1	−1	2.7
26	−1	1	0	3.7	53	1	1	0	7.4
27	−1	1	1	9.0	54	1	1	1	7.5

a   For each level of **A**, prepare interaction diagrams for the other two factors **B** and **C**. Interpret the diagrams.

b   Use statistical software to produce an ANOVA table for the full factorial model and interpret it. Compare the conclusions with those you drew in part (a).

c   Use statistical software to produce an ANOVA table for the model that includes only main effects. Obtain fitted values and residuals. Plot residuals versus fitted values and produce the normal probability plot of the residuals. Interpret the results. (Filename: EX19_4C.DAT.)

19.4D   Find a journal article in your field that uses a factorial experiment. After reading the article, identify the factors, the levels of the factors, the response variable, and the number of replications. What conclusions are drawn in the article?

SECTION

19.5 Special Case of Factors at Two Levels

An experiment with k factors at two levels each is a 2^k factorial design. Such factorial designs, in which each factor has only two levels, have proven to be especially powerful in practice. This is partly because such designs are easy to implement and partly because special computational and graphic techniques make the results easy to interpret. This section shows how to analyze 2^k designs, discussing two of the special techniques you can use with such experiments.

E X A M P L E   19.5A

Gotlieb and Dubinsky[†] studied the impact of three factors—target product price, rival product price, and credibility of information source—on level of consumer involvement. A combination of factors that increases involvement is more likely to capture a consumer's attention than a combination that does not.

Subjects were university juniors and seniors who had previous experience using a VCR. A subject read four print advertisements: an advertisement for a brand of VCR that had appeared in national magazines, an advertisement for a boat that had appeared in national magazines, a bogus advertisement for a Toshiba VCR that contained price information, and a bogus advertisement for a bogus VCR (called *Chaing*) that contained price information. The Chaing VCR was the target product and the Toshiba VCR the rival product. The two levels of price for the Chaing VCR were $289 and $429. The two levels of price for the Toshiba were $199 and $599. For each combination of Chaing price and Toshiba price, two levels of credibility were introduced into the Chaing advertisements. The low level was identification of a car salesperson who was a satisfied buyer of a Chaing as the source of the information in the advertisement. The high level was identification of an electrical engineer who was a satisfied buyer of a Chaing as the source of the information in the advertisement. The ads for the boat and the unnamed third brand of VCR were presented to the subjects only for orientation purposes.

After reading the advertisements, a subject answered a battery of 20 test items on seven-point scales. The test items were constructed to yield a measure of the subject's involvement with the choice between Chaing and Toshiba. A subject's response was the total of the points on the test.

Gotlieb and Dubinsky set forth a theory that suggested that the "third-order" interaction—that is, interaction among all three factors—should be statistically significant, but main effects and the three "second-order" interactions should not be statistically significant. Refer to their paper for the theoretical discussion and also for more details about methodology and measurement scales.

Although Gotlieb and Dubinsky do not report raw data, they report results in enough detail to permit a realistic simulation of their data. The data in Exhibit 19.5A are the result of a simulation. Fourteen subjects are assigned to each of the eight combinations of levels of factors, yielding a total of 112 subjects.[‡] **T** denotes target product price, **R** denotes rival product price, **C**

[†]J. B. Gotlieb and A. J. Dubinsky, "Influence of Price on Aspects of Consumers' Cognitive Process," *Journal of Applied Psychology*, 76(4) (1991), 541–549. A follow-up study is reported in J. B. Gotlieb and D. Sard, "Effects of Price Advertisements on Perceived Quality and Purchase Intentions," *Journal of Business Research*, 22 (1991), 195–210.

[‡]Gotlieb and Dubinsky deviated slightly from this allocation, but we use it in the simulation to avoid discussion of the complications that result from unequal allocations.

EXHIBIT **19.5A**
Data from a 2^3 Factorial
Experiment—Consumer
Cognitive Process Study

Subject	T	R	C	y	Subject	T	R	C	y	Subject	T	R	C	y
1	0	0	0	90	39	0	1	0	87	77	1	0	1	81
2	0	0	0	87	40	0	1	0	91	78	1	0	1	100
3	0	0	0	92	41	0	1	0	91	79	1	0	1	93
4	0	0	0	85	42	0	1	0	87	80	1	0	1	84
5	0	0	0	81	43	1	1	0	86	81	1	0	1	106
6	0	0	0	88	44	1	1	0	102	82	1	0	1	54
7	0	0	0	79	45	1	1	0	67	83	1	0	1	73
8	0	0	0	50	46	1	1	0	70	84	1	0	1	67
9	0	0	0	45	47	1	1	0	128	85	0	1	1	44
10	0	0	0	66	48	1	1	0	92	86	0	1	1	96
11	0	0	0	88	49	1	1	0	68	87	0	1	1	76
12	0	0	0	82	50	1	1	0	101	88	0	1	1	113
13	0	0	0	105	51	1	1	0	45	89	0	1	1	103
14	0	0	0	60	52	1	1	0	96	90	0	1	1	90
15	1	0	0	116	53	1	1	0	101	91	0	1	1	94
16	1	0	0	73	54	1	1	0	65	92	0	1	1	98
17	1	0	0	80	55	1	1	0	47	93	0	1	1	100
18	1	0	0	96	56	1	1	0	109	94	0	1	1	94
19	1	0	0	52	57	0	0	1	75	95	0	1	1	71
20	1	0	0	98	58	0	0	1	108	96	0	1	1	99
21	1	0	0	94	59	0	0	1	61	97	0	1	1	111
22	1	0	0	94	60	0	0	1	60	98	0	1	1	102
23	1	0	0	91	61	0	0	1	96	99	1	1	1	71
24	1	0	0	36	62	0	0	1	64	100	1	1	1	83
25	1	0	0	43	63	0	0	1	108	101	1	1	1	58
26	1	0	0	98	64	0	0	1	103	102	1	1	1	94
27	1	0	0	102	65	0	0	1	69	103	1	1	1	58
28	1	0	0	37	66	0	0	1	79	104	1	1	1	70
29	0	1	0	52	67	0	0	1	78	105	1	1	1	41
30	0	1	0	105	68	0	0	1	81	106	1	1	1	67
31	0	1	0	74	69	0	0	1	68	107	1	1	1	116
32	0	1	0	53	70	0	0	1	45	108	1	1	1	77
33	0	1	0	48	71	1	0	1	92	109	1	1	1	31
34	0	1	0	59	72	1	0	1	91	110	1	1	1	53
35	0	1	0	58	73	1	0	1	97	111	1	1	1	89
36	0	1	0	74	74	1	0	1	93	112	1	1	1	64
37	0	1	0	98	75	1	0	1	71					
38	0	1	0	85	76	1	0	1	54					

denotes information source credibility, and y denotes response, which is a measure of involvement. A 0 denotes low level of a factor; a 1 denotes high level of a factor.

Exhibit 19.5B shows the ANOVA table. Effects associated with single factors, such as **T**, **R**, and **C**, are called "main effects." Effects that involve two factors, such as **RT**, are called second-order interactions. The effect denoted by **CRT** is called a third-order interaction. The table is consistent with the predictions of the theory—that is, only the third-order interaction is statistically significant.

To appreciate the nature of the third-order interaction, **CRT**, consider the interaction graph in Exhibit 19.5C. It shows the interaction between **T** and **R** for the low level of **C** and the interaction between **T** and **R** for the high level of **C**. Most of the interaction effect occurs when **C** is high. The highest involvement occurs when Target Product Price is low, Rival Product Price is high, and Information Source Credibility is high. The lowest involvement occurs when Target Product Price is high, Rival Product Price is high, and Information Source Credibility is high. The second highest value of involvement occurs when Target Product Price is high, Rival Product Price is low, and Information Source Credibility is low. It seems clear that a price differential increases involvement, and that Information Source Credibility interacts in a complicated way with price differential.   ▪

Calculation of Effects

An ingenious scheme permits the computation of the effects in a 2^k experiment using only the means of the observations in each combination of levels of the factors. The scheme is based on denoting the low level of a factor by -1 and the high level by

Source	SS	DF	MS	F	p
C	40.1	1	40.1	0.09	0.759
R	16.5	1	16.5	0.04	0.844
T	153.2	1	153.2	0.36	0.549
CR	3.2	1	3.2	0.01	0.931
CT	1323.4	1	1323.4	3.12	0.080
RT	685.1	1	685.1	1.62	0.206
CRT	2082.9	1	2082.9	4.92	0.029[†]
Within	44056.5	104	423.6		
Total	48361.0	111			

[†]Statistically significant at the 5% significance level.

EXHIBIT 19.5C
Table of Means and Interaction
Graph for Consumer Involvement
Data

Low Level of C		Levels of R		High Level of C		Levels of R	
		0	**1**			**0**	**1**
Levels	**0**	78.43	75.86	**Levels**	**0**	78.21	92.21
of T	**1**	79.29	84.07	**of T**	**1**	82.57	69.43

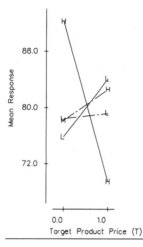

Plotting symbols connected by dotted lines are for low levels of Rival Product Price (**R**). Plotting symbols connected by solid lines are for high levels of (**R**). Plotting symbol H denotes high level of information source credibility (**C**); L denotes low level of **C**.

+1. To illustrate, Exhibit 19.5D gives the standard layout for the data provided in Exhibit 19.5A.

The column labeled **Mean** is simply a column of eight 1's, one for each possible combination of factors. The column labeled **T** is an alternating series of −1's and +1's, the column labeled **R** is a series of two −1's followed by two +1's, and the column labeled **C** is four −1's followed by four +1's. This is called the **standard form** of the 2^3 design. The column labeled **TR** is formed by multiplying the column labeled **T** by the column labeled **R** row by row, and similarly for the columns labeled

standard form

EXHIBIT 19.5D
Computational Scheme for
Computing Effects
for a 2^3 Factorial
Experiment—Consumer
Involvement Study (Means
taken from Exhibit 19.5C)

Mean	T	R	C	TR	TC	RC	TRC	Mean y
+1	−1	−1	−1	+1	+1	+1	−1	78.43
+1	+1	−1	−1	−1	−1	+1	+1	79.29
+1	−1	+1	−1	−1	+1	−1	+1	75.86
+1	+1	+1	−1	+1	−1	−1	−1	84.07
+1	−1	−1	+1	+1	−1	−1	+1	78.21
+1	+1	−1	+1	−1	+1	−1	−1	82.57
+1	−1	+1	+1	−1	−1	+1	−1	92.21
+1	+1	+1	+1	+1	+1	+1	+1	69.43
8	4	4	4	4	4	4	4	**Divisor**

TC and **RC**. The column labeled **TRC** is formed by multiplying the three indicated columns together row by row. The row labeled **Divisor** puts 8, the number of possible combinations of levels, at the bottom of the first column and puts $4 = 8/2$ at the bottom of all the other columns.

To compute an effect, multiply the column under that effect by the column of *Mean y* values row by row, sum the products, and divide by the indicated **Divisor**. For example, the computation of the main effect **T** is

$$\frac{(-1)(78.43) + (+1)(79.29) + (-1)(75.86) + \cdots + (-1)(92.21) + (+1)(69.43)}{4}$$

$$= -2.3375$$

The computation of the three-way interaction effect **TRC** is

$$\frac{(-1)(78.43) + (+1)(79.29) + (-1)(75.86) + \cdots + (-1)(92.21) + (+1)(69.43)}{4}$$

$$= -8.6225$$

Exhibit 19.5E displays all the computed effects.

E X H I B I T   19.5E
Computed Effects for Consumer Involvement Data

Effect	Computed Value
Mean	80.00875
T	−2.3375
R	0.7675
C	1.1925
TR	−4.9475
TC	−6.8725
RC	−0.3375
TRC	−8.6225

The overall mean is 80.00875. The other effects are interpreted as deviations from this mean, so the **TRC** three-way interaction produces the largest deviation. It is the only effect that tests statistically significant in the ANOVA table. Statistical theory shows that the estimated standard error of the effects (except for the **Mean** effect)[†] is $s_p/\sqrt{2n}$, where s_p denotes the square root of the within-group mean square and n denotes the number of observations in each combination of levels of the factors. From the ANOVA table in Exhibit 19.5B, $s_p = \sqrt{423.6} = 20.582$, so the estimated standard error of the effects is $20.582/\sqrt{2(14)} \cong 3.89$, and 2 standard errors is about 7.8. The effect **TRC**, the third-order interaction among target price, rival price, and information credibility, is the only one (other than the **Mean**) that is larger in absolute value than 7.8. The calculations in this paragraph illustrate another way of determining statistically significant effects.

[†]The estimated standard deviation of the **Mean** effect is $s_p/\sqrt{abn}$. See the appendix to this chapter for notation.

A Note on Standard Form

The standard form of a 2^k factorial design is usually written as a table with 2^k rows, representing the experimental runs, and k columns, representing the factors. The Mean column—a column of $+1$'s—is usually not included in the display, so the first column consists of alternating -1's and $+1$'s. The second column consists of repetitions of the pattern of two -1's followed by two $+1$'s. The third column consists of repetitions of the pattern of four -1's followed by four $+1$'s, and so on. The Divisor of the Mean column, which is usually not displayed, is 2^k, while the Divisor of each of the remaining columns is 2^{k-1}.

An Example with Four Factors

Running a large factorial experiment with replications can be time consuming and expensive. Experimenters try to counteract these consequences by imposing restrictions on the factors. These restrictions imply that fewer runs are needed to extract the most important information from the experiment. One of the most common restrictions is to treat high-order interactions as if they were zero, a restriction that often **high-order interactions** makes good practical and theoretical sense. **High-order interactions** are interactions among a large number of factors, usually three or more.

EXAMPLE   19.5B

Wagner, Strong, and Elvehjem[†] studied the effects of four preparation factors on the retention of niacin in peas. The first factor, **P**, was whether the peas were blanched (-1) or processed ($+1$). The second factor, **C**, was cooking temperature, with -1 denoting $175°$ F and $+1$ denoting $200°$ F. The third factor, **T**, was cooking time, with -1 denoting 2.5 minutes and $+1$ denoting 8 minutes. The fourth factor, **S**, was size of pea, with -1 denoting small and $+1$ denoting large.[‡] Interest centered on whether the blanching or processing of the peas affected the response. One batch of peas was prepared at each of the $2^4 = 16$ combinations of the levels of the factors. The data are reported in Exhibit 19.5F. The Batch column shows one of the possible randomizations of the order in which the batches could have been prepared, which was determined by a set of cards shuffled and laid down by the 16 different combinations. The factors have been arranged in standard form for convenience of calculation and discussion. The response variable y is a measure of niacin content of the peas after cooking.

   The computational scheme outlined in the previous subsection is used to compute the estimated effects. Exhibit 19.5G shows the necessary additional columns created by multiplying together the appropriate combination of columns in Exhibit 19.5F. The Divisor for the Mean column (which is not

[†]R. Wagner, F. M. Strong, and C. A. Elvehjem, "Effects of Blanching on the Retention of Ascorbic Acid, Thiamine, and Niacin in Vegetables," *Industrial and Engineering Chemistry*, 39 (1947), 990–993.

[‡]In the article, three sizes of peas were studied. For purposes of illustration here, only two sizes are used.

EXHIBIT 19.5F
Data From a 2^4 Factorial
Experiment—Niacin-in-Peas
Experiment

Batch	P	C	T	S	y
8	−1	−1	−1	−1	91
16	1	−1	−1	−1	86
6	−1	1	−1	−1	84
15	1	1	−1	−1	83
14	−1	−1	1	−1	72
13	1	−1	1	−1	68
7	−1	1	1	−1	78
2	1	1	1	−1	76
1	−1	−1	−1	1	112
10	1	−1	−1	1	101
12	−1	1	−1	1	98
11	1	1	−1	1	94
5	−1	−1	1	1	73
4	1	−1	1	1	73
3	−1	1	1	1	73
9	1	1	1	1	76

displayed) is 16, the number of possible combinations. For each of the columns in Exhibits 19.5F and G, the Divisor is $8 = 16/2$. Exhibit 19.5H displays the estimated effects.

Because the experiment is not replicated, there are only 16 observations, and therefore 16 degrees of freedom in the sample. There are no degrees of freedom left for estimating the within-group standard deviation. All is not lost, however, if it is sensible to act as if many of the interaction effects are

EXHIBIT 19.5G
Additional Columns Needed for
Computation of Effects—
Niacin-in-Peas Experiment

PT	PS	CT	CS	TS	PCT	PCS	PTS	CTS	PCTS
1	1	1	1	1	−1	−1	−1	−1	1
−1	−1	1	1	1	1	1	1	−1	−1
1	1	−1	−1	1	1	1	−1	1	−1
−1	−1	−1	−1	1	−1	−1	1	1	1
−1	1	−1	1	−1	1	−1	1	1	−1
1	−1	−1	1	−1	−1	1	−1	1	1
−1	1	1	−1	−1	−1	1	1	−1	1
1	−1	1	−1	−1	1	−1	−1	−1	−1
1	−1	1	−1	−1	−1	1	1	1	−1
−1	1	1	−1	−1	1	−1	−1	1	1
1	−1	−1	1	−1	1	−1	1	−1	1
−1	1	−1	1	−1	−1	1	−1	−1	−1
−1	−1	−1	−1	1	1	1	−1	−1	1
1	1	−1	−1	1	−1	−1	1	−1	−1
−1	−1	1	1	1	−1	−1	−1	1	−1
1	1	1	1	1	1	1	1	1	1

zero. This is usually done by treating interactions of order three and higher as zero. In Exhibit 19.5H, this assumption "recovers" 5 degrees of freedom, those associated with **PCT**, **PCS**, **PTS**, **CTS**, and **PCTS**. The estimated standard deviation of an effect is simply the square root of the average of the squares of these zero effects—that is

$$\sqrt{\frac{(-0.75)^2 + (0.5)^2 + (2.25)^2 + (0)^2 + (-0.25)^2}{5}} = 1.089725$$

Assuming a null hypothesis that the other effects come from a normal distribution with mean 0 and standard deviation estimated by 1.089725, you can use the t distribution with 5 degrees of freedom to assess the magnitude of the other effects. There are 10 effects, apart from the **Mean**, to assess, so using Bonferroni's inequality and shooting for a 5% overall error rate, the estimated standard deviation should be multiplied by the 99.75th percentile of the t distribution with 5 degrees of freedom, which is 4.7734. Thus any effect larger in absolute value than $(4.7734)(1.089725) \cong 5.2$ is judged statistically significant. This singles out the effects **T** (time), **S** (size), **CT** (cooking temperature $\times$ time), and **TS** (time $\times$ size) as statistically significant. ∎

EXHIBIT 19.5H
Estimated Effects for
Niacin-in-Peas Experiment

Effect	Estimate
Mean	83.625
P	−3.000
C	−1.750
T	−20.000
S	7.750
PC	2.000
PT	2.250
PS	0.000
CT	6.000
CS	−2.750
TS	−7.500
PCT	−0.750
PCS	0.500
PTS	2.250
CTS	0.000
PCTS	−0.250

Daniel's Approach to Analyzing Data from a 2^k Design

Another approach, due to Daniel[†], is both graphic and less restrictive than the approach in the previous example. You treat the effects (apart from the **Mean**) as a sample from a normal distribution and prepare a normal probability plot of these effects. Effects that deviate substantially from a straight line through the plot are treated as statistically significant.

E X A M P L E 19.5C

Exhibit 19.5I shows the estimated effects from the peas experiment in Example 19.5B, their normal scores, and the normal probability plot. Again **T, S, CT,** and **TS** are highlighted. None of the interactions involving **P** (type of processing) is statistically significant. This suggests using a model that includes the main effects of **P, C, T,** and **S** and only the two-way interactions among **C, T,** and **S**. The analysis of variance for such a model is given in Exhibit 19.5J. In this analysis of variance, the within-groups SS has 8 degrees of freedom because 8 interactions are assumed to be zero.

The factor **P** does not have a statistically significant effect on the niacin content. A 95% confidence interval for the **P** main effect is[‡]

$$-3 \pm t_{0.975} s_p \sqrt{\frac{1}{8} + \frac{1}{8}}$$

where $t_{0.975}$ is the 97.5th percentile of a t distribution with 8 degrees of freedom. Thus, $t_{0.975} \cong 2.5$ and $s_p = \sqrt{7.50} \cong 2.74$, so the confidence interval is

$$-3 \pm (2.5)(2.74)\left(\frac{1}{2}\right) \cong -3 \pm 3.4$$

The evidence suggests that if **P** has an effect it is negative, but the experiment as run does not yield a statistically significant effect. A second replication of the experiment would almost certainly be enough to settle the issue.

When inferences are made using assumptions that some interactions equal zero, it is a good idea to examine residuals for signs that the assumptions may be suspect. Perhaps the most useful diagnostic is the normal probability plot of the residuals. Recall that the residuals are computed by subtracting fitted values from observed responses. Exhibit 19.5K shows the observations, the fitted values, the normal scores of the residuals, and a normal probability plot.[§] The two smallest and two largest residuals deviate somewhat from a straight line. They are a signal that the assumptions behind the analysis of

[†]Cuthbert Daniel, "Use of Half-Normal Plot in Interpreting Factorial Two-Level Experiments," *Technometrics*, 1 (1959), 311–341.

[‡]The estimate of the **P** effect is the difference between two means of 8 observations.

[§]These quantities were obtained from statistical software.

E X H I B I T **19.5I**
Normal Probability Plot of Effects
in Exhibit 19.5H (Mean
excluded, **T** = time, **S** = size,
C = cooking time)

Estimate	Normal Score
−3.00	−0.94388
−1.75	−0.51308
−20.00	−1.74192
7.75	1.74192
2.00	0.51308
2.25	0.82207
0.00	0.08191
6.00	1.24441
−2.75	−0.71154
−7.50	−1.24441
−0.75	−0.33350
0.50	0.33350
2.25	0.82207
0.00	0.08191
−0.25	−0.16438

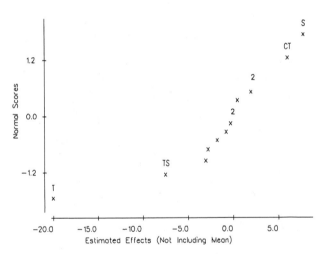

E X H I B I T **19.5J**
Analysis of Variance for Reduced
Model Explained in
Text—Niacin in Peas

Source	SS	DF	MS	F	p
P	36.00	1	36.00	4.80	0.060
C	12.25	1	12.25	1.63	0.237
T	1600.00	1	1600.00	213.33	0.000
S	240.25	1	240.25	32.03	0.000
CT	144.00	1	144.00	19.20	0.002
CS	30.25	1	30.25	4.03	0.079
TS	225.00	1	225.00	30.00	0.000
Within groups	60.00	8	7.50		
Total	2347.75	15			

Batch	y	fits	resids	nsco.res
1	91	90.0	1.0	0.66030
2	86	87.0	−1.0	−0.66030
3	84	85.0	−1.0	−0.66030
4	83	82.0	1.0	0.66030
5	72	71.5	0.5	0.23247
6	68	68.5	−0.5	−0.23247
7	78	78.5	−0.5	−0.23247
8	76	75.5	0.5	0.23247
9	112	108.0	4.0	1.77150
10	101	105.0	−4.0	−1.77150
11	98	97.5	0.5	0.23247
12	94	94.5	−0.5	−0.23247
13	73	74.5	−1.5	−0.98637
14	73	71.5	1.5	0.98637
15	73	76.0	−3.0	−1.28113
16	76	73.0	3.0	1.28113

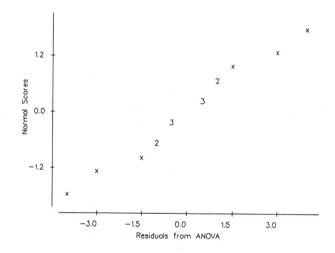

variance in Exhibit 19.5J are only approximate. Probably the best strategy is to replicate the experiment so that more confidence can be placed in the analysis. ▪

SECTION

19.6 Exercises

19.6A Write a 2^4 design in standard form.

19.6B This exercise is adapted from a design problem suggested by Green.[†] A subject is asked to rank 16 descriptions of a transatlantic flight. The 16 descriptions are determined by a 2^4 design in which the factors and levels are as follows:

	Levels	
Factor	Low	High
Aircraft type (**A**)	B-707	B-747
Departure time relative to time most preferred (**D**)	Within 4 hours	Within 1 hour
Anticipated plane load (**L**)	90% full	50% full
Price (**P**)	Full economy fare	15% discount off full fare

Data for a subject are listed below. (Filename: EX19_6B.DAT.)

Row	A	D	L	P	y	Row	A	D	L	P	y
1	−1	−1	−1	−1	2	9	−1	−1	−1	1	1
2	1	−1	−1	−1	9	10	1	−1	−1	1	13
3	−1	1	−1	−1	3	11	−1	1	−1	1	6
4	1	1	−1	−1	10	12	1	1	−1	1	14
5	−1	−1	1	−1	8	13	−1	−1	1	1	5
6	1	−1	1	−1	11	14	1	−1	1	1	15
7	−1	1	1	−1	7	15	−1	1	1	1	4
8	1	1	1	−1	12	16	1	1	1	1	16

a Calculate the estimated effects.

b Produce the normal probability plot of the effects and determine which of the effects appear to be significant.

c Produce the ANOVA table that results from assuming three- and four-factor interactions are negligible (statistical software required). Interpret the table.

d Compare the conclusions drawn in parts (b) and (c).

19.6C Prepare the 16 descriptions of transatlantic flights on 16 different index cards.

a Present the cards to a subject with instructions to rank the cards from least attractive to most attractive descriptions.

b Analyze the data as you did in Exercise 19.6B.

19.6D Write a 2^5 design in standard form.

[†]P. E. Green, "On the Design of Choice Experiments Involving Multifactor Alternatives," *Journal of Consumer Research*, 1 (1974), 61–68.

19.6E The data below are responses in an experiment that used a 2^5 design. The data are reported with the design in standard form. (Filename: EX19_6E.DAT.)

Values of Response y (read across rows)

53	51	68	74	44	42	71	69	59	59	81	80	60	61	82	80
55	52	66	69	50	43	71	66	63	65	82	83	66	66	83	87

  a Calculate the estimated effects for these data.

  b Produce the normal probability plot of the effects and determine which of the effects appear to be significant.

  c Use statistical software to produce the ANOVA table based on assuming three-, four-, and five-factor interactions are negligible. Interpret the table.

  d Compare the results obtained in parts (b) and (c).

19.6F A second replication of the experiment in Exercise 19.6E produces the following 32 responses. (Filename: EX19_6F.DAT.)

Values of Response y (read across rows)

49	46	63	71	48	44	69	67	60	62	81	86	64	62	81	79
47	52	72	72	45	53	64	70	58	58	83	81	61	61	81	82

  a Use these data combined with the data in Exercise 19.6E and statistical software to produce the ANOVA table for the full factorial model. Interpret the output.

  b Suggest an appropriate reduced model, fit it, and do a residual analysis. Interpret the results.

Chapter Summary

The randomized block design counteracts the effects of variability among the experimental units by forming the units into relatively homogeneous groups, called blocks. The number of units placed in a block equals the number of treatments. Units in each block are assigned at random to the treatments, which means that a completely randomized design is applied to each group, with one unit assigned to each treatment. The null hypothesis for the randomized block design is exactly the same as it is for the completely randomized design—that is, there is no difference in long-run average effect of the treatments. The ANOVA table for the randomized block design breaks total variation into three sources: treatments, between blocks, and within blocks. An F statistic is used to test the hypothesis. Confidence intervals are computed to assess the magnitudes of the differences in the long-run average effects. If the units are relatively homogeneous, or equivalently if the blocks are not homogeneous, the randomized block design can be less efficient than the completely randomized design, but blocking is usually effective in practice.

A factorial experiment consists of k factors, which are set at different levels, and a response variable. The purpose of the experiment is to assess the impact of different combinations of the levels of the factors on the response variable. Analysis of variance allows us to test the null hypothesis that a factor or combination of factors has no impact on the response variable. If the experiment involved replications, so that responses are available from more than one subject at each combination of levels of the factors, the presence of interaction can be assessed. If there is no interaction, the factors impact the response independently. In this case, the main effects are the important ones. If interaction is present, the relationship between the factors and the response is complicated, and interpretation of main effects is problematic. The interaction plot is the most effective way to appreciate the nature of the interaction.

Restricting each of the factors in a factorial experiment to two levels opens up the possibility of some clever analysis devices. One of the most important is Daniel's approach, which is graphic. When the factors have two levels, a fairly large number of factors can be included without making the experiment excessively large. When experimental runs are expensive and/or time consuming, the factorial experiment may be run without replication and the impact of main and low-order interaction effects assessed by treating higher-order interaction effects as zero.

Supplementary Exercises for Chapter 19

19A A manufacturer of deli meats uses a randomized block design to test three new packaging machines that have been loaned to the manufacturer by three different vendors. The blocks are three employees of the packaging department. Each employee is trained on each machine. Then the employees are randomly assigned to the machines, which are the treatments, and asked to use them for exactly one hour. The data are the numbers of defective packages produced in the hour. Notice that each employee uses each machine. The data are given below.

Operator	Machine A	B	C
1	9	8	7
2	10	12	3
3	11	10	9

a Do an ANOVA and assess statistical significance.

b Use the Tukey method to construct simultaneous 95% confidence intervals for the differences in the treatment means and give a verbal interpretation of the intervals. The appropriate q factor is 5.91.

c Describe how a completely randomized design for this experiment would have been conducted. What source of variation is controlled by the blocking? Does this source of variation appear to be substantial?

19B Ten golfers are used to test four brands of golf ball for driving distance. Each golfer hits each brand of ball, with the order in which the balls are presented to the golfers determined at random. The outcome is the distance of the drive, in yards. Here are the data. (Filename: EX19B.DAT.)

		Brand					Brand		
Golfer	A	B	C	D	Golfer	A	B	C	D
1	218	217	236	206	6	250	252	272	243
2	242	237	263	229	7	205	215	230	207
3	226	231	248	226	8	231	234	243	229
4	232	243	250	225	9	255	256	279	252
5	223	229	235	213	10	190	197	212	198

a   Do an ANOVA and assess statistical significance.

b   Use the Tukey method to construct simultaneous 95% confidence intervals for the differences in the treatment means and give a verbal interpretation of the intervals. The appropriate q factor is 3.85.

c   Describe how a completely randomized design for this experiment would have been conducted. What source of variation is controlled by the blocking? Does this source of variation appear to be substantial?

19C   A contractor uses three people to estimate the costs of jobs. Consistency of estimates is important but hard to achieve. The estimators are engaged in an improvement project to develop strategies for making their estimates as consistent as possible. The estimators have conducted an experiment to assess their progress. Six pending projects are selected at random, and each estimator does a complete analysis and cost estimate for each project. The order in which they do the project analyses is determined at random. The outcomes are the cost estimates (in thousands of dollars). Here are the data.

	Estimator		
Project	A	B	C
1	23	37	29
2	61	73	62
3	97	121	103
4	81	102	89
5	49	84	54
6	55	82	60

a   Do an ANOVA and assess statistical significance.

b   Use the Tukey method to construct simultaneous 95% confidence intervals for the differences in the treatment means and give a verbal interpretation of the intervals. The appropriate q factor is 3.88.

19D   A $3 \times 3 \times 3$ factorial design is given below in standard form along with data from two replications of the experiment. (Filename: EX19D.DAT.)

Case	Factor A	B	C	Replication 1	2	Case	Factor A	B	C	Replication 1	2
1	−1	−1	−1	7	11	15	0	0	1	4	4
2	−1	−1	0	4	4	16	0	1	−1	4	3
3	−1	−1	1	3	3	17	0	1	0	3	2
4	−1	0	−1	3	7	18	0	1	1	2	1
5	−1	0	0	3	8	19	1	−1	−1	36	36
6	−1	0	1	2	10	20	1	−1	0	32	28
7	−1	1	−1	2	10	21	1	−1	1	20	21
8	−1	1	0	1	6	22	1	0	−1	16	17
9	−1	1	1	0	1	23	1	0	0	11	8
10	0	−1	−1	14	24	24	1	0	1	6	14
11	0	−1	0	12	17	25	1	1	−1	11	6
12	0	−1	1	6	4	26	1	1	0	9	14
13	0	0	−1	10	13	27	1	1	1	4	1
14	0	0	0	6	5						

a Do an ANOVA and assess the statistical significance of main effects and interactions.

b Prepare an interaction diagram and interpret it.

Glossary for Chapter 19

high-order interaction   Interaction among a large number of factors, usually three or more.

interaction   Refers to situations in which the mean of the response variable is not a linear function of the combinations of the levels of the factors.

main effect   The impact of a single factor, holding all the impacts of the other factors fixed.

standard form   The arrangement of a case in a factorial experiment in a way that makes calculation of effects easy.

APPENDIX

Formulas for Analysis of Variance

We briefly present the ANOVA formulas for the randomized block design and the factorial design with two factors.

Randomized Block Design

Let k denote the number of treatments, B the number of blocks, and y_{ij} the observation on the subject from block j who is given treatment i, $i = 1, 2, \ldots, k$ and $j = 1, 2, \ldots, B$. Also let $\bar{y}_{i.}$ denote the mean of the observations on the ith treatment,

$\bar{y}_{.j}$ the mean of the observations in the jth block, and $\bar{y}_{..}$ the mean of all the data. The equation Observed Response = Fitted Value + Residual takes the form

$$y_{ij} = \underbrace{\bar{y}_{..} + (\bar{y}_{i.} - \bar{y}_{..}) + (\bar{y}_{.j} - \bar{y}_{..})}_{\text{Fitted Value}} + \underbrace{(y_{ij} - \bar{y}_{i.} - \bar{y}_{.j} + \bar{y}_{..})}_{\text{Residual}}$$

The Fitted Value is a two-part adjustment to the overall mean, one part being a deviation of the ith treatment mean from the overall mean, the other part being a deviation of the jth block mean from the overall mean. Some algebra leads to the ANOVA equation

$$\text{Total Sum of Squares} = \sum_{i=1}^{k}\sum_{j=1}^{B}(y_{ij} - \bar{y}_{..})^2$$

$$= \sum_{i=1}^{k}\sum_{j=1}^{B}\left[(\bar{y}_{i.} - \bar{y}_{..}) + (\bar{y}_{.j} - \bar{y}_{..}) + (y_{ij} - \bar{y}_{i.} - \bar{y}_{.j} + \bar{y}_{..})\right]^2$$

$$= \sum_{i=1}^{k}\sum_{j=1}^{B}(\bar{y}_{i.} - \bar{y}_{..})^2 + \sum_{i=1}^{k}\sum_{j=1}^{B}(\bar{y}_{.j} - \bar{y}_{..})^2 + \sum_{i=1}^{k}\sum_{j=1}^{B}(y_{ij} - \bar{y}_{i.} - \bar{y}_{.j} + \bar{y}_{..})^2$$

$$= \sum_{i=1}^{k}B(\bar{y}_{i.} - \bar{y}_{..})^2 + \sum_{j=1}^{B}k(\bar{y}_{.j} - \bar{y}_{..})^2 + \sum_{i=1}^{k}\sum_{j=1}^{B}(y_{ij} - \bar{y}_{i.} - \bar{y}_{.j} + \bar{y}_{..})^2$$

or Total SS = Between-treatment SS + Between-block SS + Within-block SS. The degrees-of-freedom decomposition is

$$kB - 1 = (k - 1) + (B - 1) + kB - k - B + 1$$
$$= (k - 1) + (B - 1) + (k - 1)(B - 1)$$

Factorial Designs with Replication

The formulas for the case with two factors **A** and **B** are given. Factor **A** has a levels and Factor **B** has b levels. There are n subjects assigned to each combination of levels of the two factors. This is a simple design, but generalization of the formulas to more complicated cases is a technical issue beyond the scope of this presentation.

Let y_{ijk} denote the observation on the kth subject assigned to the combination that results from using level i of factor **A** and level j of factor **B**. Let $\bar{y}_{ij.}$ denote the mean of the observations obtained for combination i, j, $\bar{y}_{i..}$ denote the mean of all the observations obtained on level i of factor **A**, $\bar{y}_{.j.}$ denote the mean of all the observations obtained on level j of factor **B**, and $\bar{y}_{...}$ denote the mean of all the observations. Because there are n observations on ab combinations, there is a total of abn observations. From the principles developed in the appendix to the previous chapter, it is immediately apparent that the breakdown of degrees of freedom is

$$abn - 1 = (a - 1) + (b - 1) + (a - 1)(b - 1) + ab(n - 1)$$

The equation Observed Response = Fitted Value + Residual takes the form

$$y_{ijk} = \bar{y}_{...} + (\bar{y}_{i..} - \bar{y}_{...}) + (\bar{y}_{.j.} - \bar{y}_{...}) + (\bar{y}_{ij.} - \bar{y}_{i..} - \bar{y}_{.j.} + \bar{y}_{...}) + (y_{ijk} - \bar{y}_{ij.})$$

The last term on the right-hand side of this equation is the Residual. Some terminology is given below:

Term	Formula for Effect
Overall Mean	$\bar{y}_{...}$
Level i of A	$\bar{y}_{i..} - \bar{y}_{...}$
Level j of B	$\bar{y}_{.j.} - \bar{y}_{...}$
Level ij of interaction	$\bar{y}_{ij.} - \bar{y}_{i..} - \bar{y}_{.j.} + \bar{y}_{...}$

Here is a table of numerical values of the effects of the levels for the data in Example 19.1A. The body of the table contains the interaction effects; the main effects are given in the margins.

		Temperature Levels (B)			
		−1	0	1	Time Main Effects
Time Levels	−1	−1.6667	−1.0000	2.6667	−0.3333
(A)	0	−0.3333	1.3333	−1.0000	0.3333
	1	2.0000	−0.3333	−1.6667	0.0000
Temperature Main Effects		0.0000	0.3333	−0.3333	

Note that the **A** main effects sum to 0, the **B** main effects sum to 0, and the **Interaction** effects sum to 0. These sums are 0 by construction; they are algebraic identities. These identities may be used to demonstrate the breakdown of the sums of squares displayed below.

$$
\text{Total Sum of Squares} = \sum_{i=1}^{a}\sum_{j=1}^{b}\sum_{k=1}^{n}(y_{ijk} - \bar{y}_{...})^2
$$

$$
= \sum_{i=1}^{a}\sum_{j=1}^{b}\sum_{k=1}^{n}(\bar{y}_{i..} - \bar{y}_{...})^2 + \sum_{i=1}^{a}\sum_{j=1}^{b}\sum_{k=1}^{n}(\bar{y}_{.j.} - \bar{y}_{...})^2
$$

$$
+ \sum_{i=1}^{a}\sum_{j=1}^{b}\sum_{k=1}^{n}(\bar{y}_{ij.} - \bar{y}_{i..} - \bar{y}_{.j.} + \bar{y}_{...})^2 + \sum_{i=1}^{a}\sum_{j=1}^{b}\sum_{k=1}^{n}(y_{ijk} - \bar{y}_{ij.})^2
$$

$$
= \sum_{i=1}^{a} bn(\bar{y}_{i..} - \bar{y}_{...})^2 + \sum_{j=1}^{b} an(\bar{y}_{.j.} - \bar{y}_{...})^2
$$

$$
+ \sum_{i=1}^{a}\sum_{j=1}^{b} n(\bar{y}_{ij.} - \bar{y}_{i..} - \bar{y}_{.j.} + \bar{y}_{...})^2 + \sum_{i=1}^{a}\sum_{j=1}^{b}\sum_{k=1}^{n}(y_{ijk} - \bar{y}_{ij.})^2
$$

or

Total SS = **A** main effect SS + **B** main effect SS + **Interaction** SS + **Residual** SS

Statistical software implements these formulas and formulas for much more complicated models, making mastery of the formulas of little practical value.

4

Modeling and Inference

Inference in Regression Models

Chapter Objectives

After mastering this chapter, you will be able to:

- State the theoretical assumptions of the multiple regression model

- Interpret multiple regression model parameters

- Test hypotheses and construct confidence intervals for β coefficients

- Construct prediction intervals for new responses

- Explain the regression fallacy

- Explain why the R^2 statistic may be misleading

- Explain how to do discriminant analysis with regression

20.1 A Statistical Model for Regression Analysis

Chapters 7 and 8 presented the basics of straight-line and multiple regression models and illustrated many concepts about them with specific examples and data sets. This chapter and the next two cover regression models in more detail, exploring their more advanced aspects. This chapter concentrates on means of assessing a model's utility, given that the basic assumptions behind regression models are reasonably well satisfied. Chapter 21 considers important techniques for assessing whether those assumptions are satisfied and transforming the data to better satisfy them. Chapter 22 covers the problem of selecting the best set of predictor variables.

This chapter begins by discussing the meaning and estimation of the parameters in a regression model. We then examine simple models with only one predictor variable. Simulation is used to verify the results of statistical theory for these simple models. You see how to use significance tests and intervals to assess the models' utility. These techniques are then extended to models with several predictors. You are introduced to discriminant analysis, which uses regression techniques to study problems with binary or categorical response values. Some cautions about use of regression are presented, and an appendix gives alternative notation and equations normally found in software dealing with regression analysis.

Basics of Regression Analysis

predictor variables
response variable

In the terminology of regression, the **predictor variables** are the variables used to predict or explain the **response variable**, which is the variable to be predicted or explained. Recall that regression models involve both a mathematical curve that describes the behavior of the response variable y under a range of settings of the k predictor variables $x_1, x_2, \ldots, x_k$, and a notion of the variability in the response expected for particular settings of the predictor values. As in Chapter 8, some predictor variables may be squares or cross products of other variables, logarithms of other variables, or binary indicator variables.

Regression analysis has several general objectives:

- To determine whether relationships exist between variables
- To describe the relationships if they exist
- To assess the accuracy in the descriptions of the relationships
- To assess the importance of each of the predictors in a relationship

Formally, the **multiple regression model** assumes that the relationship may be expressed as

multiple regression model

$$y = \beta_0 + \beta_1 x_1 + \beta_2 x_2 + \cdots + \beta_k x_k + e \qquad \textbf{(20.1)}$$

regression parameters
error term

where $\beta_0, \beta_1, \beta_2, \ldots, \beta_k$ are unknown **regression parameters** and e is the **error term**. Error is not used here in the sense of mistake. Rather, the error term encompasses all the variation in the response that is not modeled by the linear function of the predictor variables. The error term is not observed.

The data set consists of n cases (or observations) with values for the predictor variables for the ith cases denoted $x_{i1}, x_{i2}, \ldots, x_{ik}$ and the corresponding response denoted y_i. The multiple regression model for the full data set may then be expressed through the n equations

$$y_i = \beta_0 + \beta_1 x_{i1} + \beta_2 x_{i2} + \cdots + \beta_k x_{ik} + e_i \qquad \text{for } i = 1, 2, \ldots, n \qquad \textbf{(20.2)}$$

To support the inference procedures developed in this chapter, several assumptions about the statistical nature of the error terms must be made. The following formal assumptions will be needed in various stages of inference:

basic assumptions of
regression analysis

- The errors are independent of one another—that is, the size of any one error has no influence on the size of any other error.
- The errors have a normal distribution with 0 mean and standard deviation σ.

These assumptions are equivalent to assuming that the y's arise independently with y_i coming from a normal distribution with mean $\beta_0 + \beta_1 x_{i1} + \beta_2 x_{i2} + \cdots + \beta_k x_{ik}$ and standard deviation σ. The parameter σ will be unknown and will be estimated from the observed data.

For the case of a single predictor x, Exhibit 20.1A depicts some of the model assumptions in a graphic display.

E X H I B I T **20.1A** The Simple Linear Regression Model

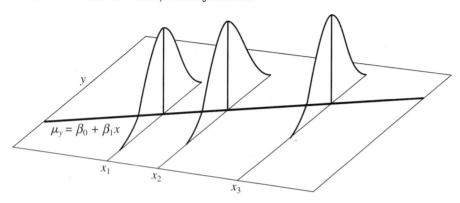

SECTION

20.2 Interpreting the Regression Parameters

The parameter β_0 is the *intercept* or *constant term* that represents the value of y expected when all the predictors are zero. However, in many examples, zero values for all the predictors would be meaningless, as the observed ranges of the predictors are all far from zero. In those cases, the intercept parameter does not have a useful literal interpretation. The regression parameters $\beta_1, \ldots, \beta_k$ are most easily interpreted when there are no squared or cross-product terms in the model. The parameters $\beta_1, \ldots,$ β_k are sometimes called *partial slopes* in the sense that β_i is the change in the mean of y with respect to a unit change in the predictor variable x_i with all other predictors, $x_1, x_2, \ldots, x_{i-1}, x_{i+1}, \ldots, x_k$ held constant. Of course, if one of the other predictors is x_i^2, this interpretation fails. Also, in many applications the predictor variables are themselves related, so again it is unrealistic to consider changing one predictor without changing another one. The problem of related predictors is introduced later in this chapter and covered more completely in the Chapter 22 discussion of collinearity.

In most applications of regression, the model represents only a convenient approximation of the "truth." Data collected on the same predictor variables over a different range of values may be modeled by a somewhat different mathematical function, so that the parameters $\beta_0, \beta_1, \ldots, \beta_k$ would have different meanings. Every regression model must be interpreted within its own context, which includes the range of values for the predictors and response.

Again excluding models with squared and cross-product predictors, the sign of β_i indicates the *direction* of the relationship between the mean of the response y and the predictor x_i, all other predictors being held constant. A positive value for β_i implies a positive relationship; a negative value implies a negative relationship.

The units of each coefficient β_i will depend on the units of the response y and the predictor x_i. For example, if the response is measured as market value of a house in thousands of dollars and the predictor is square footage of the house, the corresponding regression coefficient has units of thousands of dollars per square foot. For the 60 residential parcels reported in Exhibit 6.2A, a regression of market values on square footage produces the regression coefficient estimate of 0.018362. Thus, for each additional square foot of living area, the market value is predicted to increase by about $18. If the assessed value of the house (in thousands of dollars) is used as an additional predictor, then its regression coefficient has units of thousand dollars in market value per thousand dollars of assessed value. The more complicated model in Example 8.7B gave

$$\text{Predicted market value} = 1.111 + 0.0448883 \text{ Sq.ft} - 0.000015064 \,(\text{Sq.ft})^2$$
$$+ 4.15 \text{ Med} + 5.216 \text{ Hi} + 0.22337 \text{ Assessed} \quad \textbf{(20.3)}$$

where Med and Hi are binary indicator variables for the grade of the house. Here the coefficient 4.15 indicates that a medium-grade house has a predicted market value of $4150 *above* a low-grade house, while the 5.216 coefficient translates to an increase of about $5216 in predicted market value for a high-grade house above that for a low-grade house with the Sq.ft (and hence Sq.ft.sq) and Assessed variables held constant. Also, each dollar in assessed value is reflected in about a $0.22 increase in predicted market value (all other variables being held constant). The regression coefficients associated with square footage cannot be interpreted separately since square feet and square feet squared *must* change together.

SECTION

20.3 Exercises

20.3A Use Equation (20.3) to find the predicted market value for a house with 1100 square feet of living space, medium grade, and assessed value of $40,000. (Remember that assessed value is measured in thousands of dollars.)

20.3B Use Equation (20.3) to find the predicted market value for a high-grade house with assessed value of $42,100 and with 1300 square feet of living space.

20.3C Use Equation (20.3) to find the predicted market value for a house with 900 square feet of living space, low grade, and assessed value of $31,000.

20.3D According to Equation (20.3), is the relationship between market value and assessed value positive or negative?

20.3E The following model was used by a chain of audio-video retail stores to predict profits:

$$y = \beta_0 + \beta_1 x_1 + \beta_2 x_2 + \beta_3 x_3 + e$$

where y is profit, x_1 is dollar sales of audio items, x_2 is dollar sales of video items, and x_3 is the store size in hundreds of square feet. Interpret each of the coefficients β_0, β_1, β_2, and β_3.

20.3F The following regression model was investigated to predict a building's energy consumption:

$$y = \beta_0 + \beta_1 x_1 + \beta_2 x_2 + \beta_3 x_3 + \beta_4 x_4 + e$$

where y represents energy consumption (in thousands of BTUs), x_1 is the total outside wall area (in hundreds of square feet), x_2 is the total outside window area (in hundreds of square feet), x_3

is the total roof area (in hundreds of square feet), and x_4 is a binary variable indicating whether the building is fully insulated ($x_4 = 1$) or not ($x_4 = 0$). Interpret each of the coefficients β_0, β_1, β_2, β_3, and β_4.

20.3G   A telemarketing firm is experimenting with two different training programs (I and II) for its current sales employees. They propose testing the effectiveness of the program by measuring each employee's sales production for the three months following the training and using the model

$$\widehat{\text{Sales}} = \beta_0 + \beta_1 \, \text{Training}$$

where Training $= 0$ for training program I and Training $= 1$ for training program II.

a   Interpret the model in the special case where $\beta_1 = 0$.

b   Interpret the parameters β_0 and $\beta_0 + \beta_1$.

c   Sketch a scatterplot of sales versus training that would support the contention that the two training programs led to different sales results.

d   Sketch a scatterplot of sales versus training that would support the contention that there was no discernible difference between the training programs.

20.3H   The telemarketing firm in Exercise 20.3G decides to use a more realistic model since they believe that the length of time (in months) that the employee has been with their firm will also affect sales performance. So they formulate the two-predictor model

$$\widehat{\text{Sales}} = \beta_0 + \beta_1 \, \text{Time} + \beta_2 \, \text{Training}$$

where again Training $= 0$ for training program I and Training $= 1$ for training program II.

a   Interpret the model in the special case where $\beta_2 = 0$.

b   Interpret the parameters β_0 and $\beta_0 + \beta_2$.

c   Sketch a scatterplot of sales versus time that would support the contention that there was a discernible difference between the two training programs. Indicate on the plot by different plotting symbols which points correspond to which training program.

d   Sketch a scatterplot of sales versus training that would support the contention that there was no discernible difference between the two training programs. Indicate on the plot by different plotting symbols which points correspond to which training program.

SECTION

20.4   Estimating Parameters Using Least Squares

Chapter 7 introduced the basic ideas of least squares. Within the formal regression model framework just outlined, the least-squares method is an intuitive and reasonable method for producing estimates for the unknown regression parameters $\beta_0, \beta_1, \ldots, \beta_k$.

least-squares estimates   The **least-squares estimates** b_0, b_1, $\ldots$, b_k are the values for the parameters $\beta_0, \beta_1, \ldots, \beta_k$ that minimize the sum of squares

$$\sum_{i=1}^{n} [y_i - \beta_0 - \beta_1 x_{i1} - \beta_2 x_{i2} - \cdots - \beta_k x_{ik}]^2 \tag{20.4}$$

The appendix to this chapter shows that b_0, b_1, $\ldots$, b_k may be found by solving a system of linear equations called the *normal equations.* As noted in Chapters 7 and 8, computer software is readily available for solving these equations and thus obtaining the estimates.

Once estimates for the regression parameters are available, the **residuals** are obtained as

residuals

$$\text{Residual} = \text{Observed Response} - \text{Fitted Value}$$

or

$$\hat{e}_i = y_i - \hat{y}_i \tag{20.5}$$

where the ith **fitted value**, $\hat{y}_i$, is

fitted value

$$\hat{y}_i = b_0 + b_1 x_{i1} + b_2 x_{i2} + \cdots + b_k x_{ik} \tag{20.6}$$

Notice that the residual $\hat{e}_i$ is not the same as the error term e_i, since the regression parameters are replaced by their *estimated* values to obtain fitted values. Residuals are estimated error terms.

Finally, the **residual standard deviation**, s, where

residual standard deviation

$$s = \sqrt{\frac{1}{n-k-1} \sum_{i=1}^{n} \hat{e}_i^2} \tag{20.7}$$

with $n - k - 1$ degrees of freedom, is interpreted as an estimate of the standard deviation σ of the error terms.

To summarize, the regression model $y = \beta_0 + \beta_1 x_1 + \cdots + \beta_k x_k + e$ expresses how the data are generated. Once data are available, we use the method of least squares to obtain estimates $b_0, b_1, \ldots, b_k$ of the regression parameters, $\beta_0, \beta_1, \ldots, \beta_k$.

SECTION

20.5 Exercises

20.5A   Use Equation (20.3) to find the residual for the house with 890 square feet of living space, medium grade, $20,200 assessed value, and market value of $35,000.

20.5B   Interpret, geometrically, the process of finding least squares estimates of β_0 and β_1 when the model contains only one predictor. A stylized scatterplot should be used in the description.

20.5C   Consider the three (x, y) pairs $(0, 5)$, $(1, 3)$, and $(2, 1)$. Argue *without calculation* that the least squares estimate of the slope parameter is -2.

20.5D   Use the following small data set:

x	y
1	1
2	1
3	2
4	2

a   Verify that the least squares line of y versus x is

$$y = 0.5 + 0.4x$$

b   Verify that the least squares line when the roles of x and y are reversed is

$$x = -0.5 + 2y$$

c   Plot the scatterplot of the data and graph both lines on the plot. Why are these different lines?

SECTION

20.6   Inference for Models with One Predictor

This section illustrates inferences appropriate in regression models. First, using the property data from Chapter 7, we show two ways of testing significance of regression coefficients. Then we use simulations to illustrate and confirm several theoretical properties. Using both the market and simulated data to illustrate, we show how to calculate and use confidence intervals for the regression coefficients. Finally, we use similar techniques to establish prediction intervals, which predict the range within which new response values are likely to fall.

Significance Tests on Regression Coefficients

To show how to test the significance of regression coefficients, we first use the straight-line model, introduced in Chapter 7.

$$y = \beta_0 + \beta_1 x + e \qquad \textbf{(20.8)}$$

In such a model it is important to assess whether or not the parameter β_1 is zero. If $\beta_1 = 0$, the model becomes $y = \beta_0 + e$, which says that the response varies randomly around the fixed level β_0 that is *not* different for different values of x. In the terminology of significance tests, we need to assess whether the estimate b_1 of β_1 is significantly different from zero.

t ratio for b_1

In the one-predictor model, the test may equally well be based on either the *t* **ratio for b_1**—that is, $b_1/se(b_1)$—or on the F ratio of regression mean square to residual mean square introduced in Section 8.10. Exhibit 20.6A shows typical regression output from fitting the straight-line model to the 60 parcels in Exhibit 6.2A, using Market as the response variable and Sq.ft as the predictor. The display gives many useful statistics, including the parameter estimates (under Coef), the standard errors of those estimates (under Stdev), and the ratios of these two quantities (under *t*- ratio). The *t* ratio is

$$t \text{ ratio for } b_1 = \frac{b_1}{se(b_1)} = \frac{0.018362}{0.002134} = 8.60 \qquad \textbf{(20.9)}$$

EXHIBIT 20.6A

Regression Output for Market
Regressed on Sq.ft

```
The regression equation is

Market = 20.5 + 0.0184 Sq.ft

Predictor          Coef        Stdev       t-ratio           p
Constant         20.508        2.075          9.88       0.000
Sq.ft          0.018362     0.002134          8.60       0.000

s = 3.981        R-sq = 56.1%      R-sq(adj) = 55.3%

Analysis of Variance

SOURCE           DF           SS           MS          F          p
Regression        1       1173.1       1173.1      74.01      0.000
Error            58        919.3         15.8
Total            59       2092.4
```

For the one-predictor model the standard error, $se(b_1)$, has a reasonably simple formula.[†] However, the specific formula is of little interest. Software is used for all computations, including standard errors.

Statistical theory establishes that, under the regression assumptions, the sampling distribution of $(b_1 - \beta_1)/se(b_1)$ is a t distribution with $n - 2$ degrees of freedom. Hence, under the hypothesis that $\beta_1 = 0$, the t ratio $b_1/se(b_1)$ may be used to test $\beta_1 = 0$. The hypothesis $\beta_1 = 0$ is rejected if the corresponding t ratio is too large in magnitude. In this example the t ratio of 8.60 with $60 - 2 = 58$ degrees of freedom indicates clear statistical significance. The output also shows a p-value of 0.000, meaning the p value is less than 0.0005, which further signals the clear significance of b_1.

Statistical theory, again under the standard regression assumptions, shows that the sampling distribution of the F ratio of regression mean square to residual mean square is an F distribution with 1 and $n - 2$ degrees of freedom if $\beta_1 = 0$ is true. Otherwise, the F ratio tends to be inflated and the hypothesis $\beta_1 = 0$ should be rejected for large values of F. The observed F ratio of 74.01 with 1 and 24 degrees of freedom, and p-value of 0.000 indicates the strong statistical significance of the predictor Sq.ft in predicting Market value.

Different software packages label some output items somewhat differently. In the analysis of variance table in Exhibit 20.6A, the line labeled "Error" gives the degrees of freedom (DF), sum of squares (SS), and mean square (MS) of the residuals. In many packages, this line is labeled "Residual." See the appendix to Chapter 8 for a comparison of different outputs.

Note also that, to within rounding error,

$$F \text{ ratio} = 74.01 \simeq \left(\frac{0.018362}{0.002134}\right)^2 = (t \text{ ratio for } b_1)^2$$

[†]For the one-predictor model, it may be shown that the standard error of the slope coefficient estimate is given by

$$se(b_1) = \frac{s}{\sqrt{\sum_{i=1}^{n}(x_i - \bar{x})^2}}$$

With a one-predictor model, it may be shown that the F ratio will always equal the square of this t ratio, so that either significance test may be used to assess the usefulness of the predictor.

Regression Theory Illustrated Through Simulation

As noted in Appendix 3, simulation is a valuable technique for learning (and sometimes discovering) complex statistical theory. Regression theory is no exception.

Standard regression theory will be illustrated using 25 cases from the following regression model:

$$y = 10 + 3x + e \qquad \text{(20.10)}$$

with $\sigma = 2$. Exhibit 20.6B displays the 25 x values used for all the simulations. The x's range from a minimum of 6.1 to a maximum of 13.9, with a mean of 10.000 and a standard deviation of 1.914. The full dotplot of the x's is also shown in the display. In the simulation we know the true model that generates the data, namely the straight-line model with $\beta_0 = 10$, $\beta_1 = 3$, $\sigma = 2$, and the x-values given in Exhibit 20.6B.

E X H I B I T 20.6B
Data for One Regression
Simulation of
$y = 10 + 3x + e$
with $n = 25$

Case	x	y	$e/2$	Case	x	y	$e/2$
1	6.1	27.1550	−0.57250	14	10.2	40.5016	−0.04919
2	7.0	30.6433	−0.17837	15	10.4	36.7930	−2.20347
3	7.5	31.9737	−0.26315	16	10.7	42.8571	0.37857
4	7.9	35.2806	0.79029	17	10.7	41.2343	−0.43284
5	8.2	34.5976	−0.00122	18	11.1	42.4704	−0.41479
6	8.5	38.8857	1.69283	19	11.1	44.8549	0.77746
7	8.9	36.2589	−0.22055	20	11.5	47.0112	1.25562
8	8.9	34.8010	−0.94948	21	11.8	46.0120	0.30599
9	9.2	38.8264	0.61318	22	12.1	44.6774	−0.81130
10	9.4	38.8036	0.30181	23	12.5	47.2986	−0.10070
11	9.6	39.6669	0.43345	24	13.0	48.1982	−0.40091
12	9.8	41.0976	0.84881	25	13.9	50.1098	−0.79508
13	10.0	37.5849	−1.20753				

Variable	n	Mean	Standard Deviation
x	25	10.000	1.914

```
Dotplot of x

          .         .  .    .  . .  :  ... ...  :  :  . . . .      .      .
  -+---------+---------+---------+---------+---------+---------+----- x
  6.0       7.5       9.0      10.5      12.0      13.5
```

The exhibit also shows the result of *one* simulation. The e's were created as independent normally distributed variables with 0 mean and standard deviation of

2. (Actually, standard normal variables were first created and then each was multiplied by 2.) Then the y's were obtained as indicated in Equation (20.10). Finally, for this one data set a regression of y on x was carried out, with the results shown in Exhibit 20.6C. Notice that the slope estimate is 2.89 compared with the known value of 3 and the intercept estimate of 11.0 compared with the true model value of 10. According to the p-values shown, both of these estimates are significantly different from zero. The t statistics $(b_1 - 3)/se(b_1) = (2.8896 - 3)/0.1805 = -0.61$ and $(b_0 - 10)/se(b_0) = (11.008 - 10)/1.836 = 0.55$ may also be computed. These statistics assess the difference between the parameter estimates and the true values of the parameters. They show that these estimated values are not significantly different from the values 3 and 10 used in the simulation, so statistically speaking, they are "good" estimates of the parameters. In a practical problem, we do not know the true parameter values; we can only calculate estimates from the data. The simulations suggest that if the model assumptions are valid, the estimates are close, in a statistical sense, to the true values.

E X H I B I T 20.6C
Regression on Simulated Data

```
The regression equation is

y = 11.0 + 2.89 x

Predictor        Coef        Stdev     t-ratio          p
Constant       11.008        1.836        5.99      0.000
x              2.8896       0.1805       16.01      0.000

s = 1.693      R-sq = 91.8%      R-sq(adj) = 91.4%

Analysis of Variance

SOURCE       DF          SS          MS         F         p
Regression    1      734.29      734.29    256.30     0.000
Error        23       65.89        2.86
Total        24      800.18
```

Exhibit 20.6D gives the scatterplot of the data, the estimated regression line shown as a solid line, and (since this is a simulation) the true regression line shown as a dashed line. Notice that the underestimation of the slope is partially compensated for by the overestimation of the intercept term.

Using these same 25 predictor values for x and the model in Equation (20.10), the regression simulation was repeated 500 times, each time obtaining a new set of errors and hence responses y. For each of the 500 data sets, the regression calculations were performed and the results such as b_0, b_1, s, and R^2 saved for further analysis. In particular, Exhibit 20.6E shows the histogram of the 500 values of b_1 obtained. Notice that there were a few simulated data sets where the estimated slope was as small as 2.3 or 2.4 and others where the slope estimates were as large as 3.5 or 3.6. However, the majority of the simulations gave slopes in the range of about 2.8 to 3.2. Furthermore, the distribution is nicely symmetric with a mean of 3.0047 compared to the true value of 3.

According to statistical theory the sampling distribution of b_1 is a normal distribution with mean 3 and certain known standard deviation depending on σ and the values for x. To illustrate the correctness of this theory, the histogram of the

EXHIBIT **20.6D**

Estimated Regression Line with
True Line (dashed) Overlaid

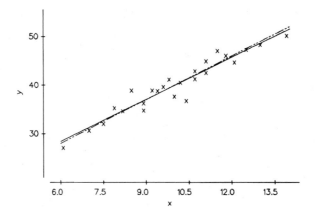

EXHIBIT **20.6E**

Distribution of b_1 from 500
Simulations with $\beta_1 = 3$

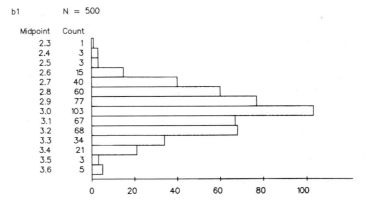

standardized b_1 values has been plotted in Exhibit 20.6F, which should be compared to a standard normal distribution. Finally, in Exhibit 20.6G the distribution of the t statistic $(b_1 - 3)/se(b_1)$ is shown. Theory says that this distribution is a t distribution with $25 - 2 = 23$ degrees of freedom. Such a distribution is difficult to distinguish from a standard normal distribution, but it should contain a few more extreme values. These can be seen if Exhibits 20.6F and 20.6G are compared. Calculation shows that the standard deviations of these two distributions are 1.0184 and 1.0476, respectively, again indicating the slightly wider spread in the t distribution. From the mathematical result in Section 17.2, the corresponding theoretical values are 1 for a standard normal distribution and 1.0465 for a t distribution with 23 degrees of freedom. Exhibits 20.6H and I show the normal scores plots for the standardized b_1 values and for the t statistic $(b_1 - 3)/se(b_1)$ values. Again, the graph in Exhibit 20.6H is a fairly straight line, but the one in Exhibit 20.6I shows more deviation from a straight line, especially in the extremes or tails. The t distribution with 23 degrees of freedom

E X H I B I T **20.6F**
Distribution of b_1 Standardized
by Its Theoretical Mean and
Standard Deviation

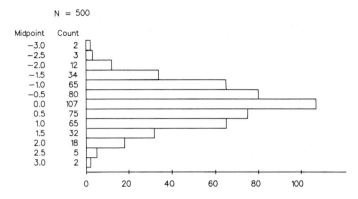

E X H I B I T **20.6G**
Distribution of t statistic
$(b_1 - 3)/se(b_1)$

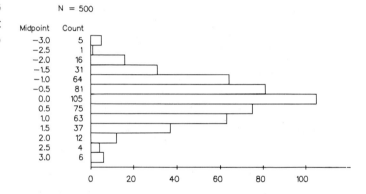

E X H I B I T **20.6H**
Normal Scores Plot of b_1
Standardized by Its Theoretical
Mean and Standard Deviation

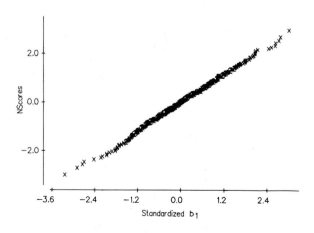

E X H I B I T **20.6I**
Normal Scores Plot of the
t statistic $(b_1 - 3)/se(b_1)$

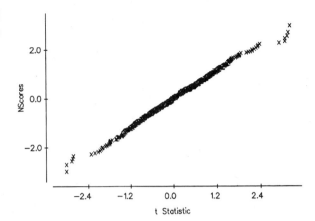

is nearly normal but not quite. Similar plots could be done for the estimates of the intercept parameter, but the slope parameter is of much more practical interest.

In Exhibits 20.6C and 20.6D, the underestimated slope was compensated for somewhat by an overestimated intercept. This was not a fluke of that particular simulation. The pairs of estimates of slope and intercept are strongly negatively correlated over the 500 simulations. Exhibit 20.6J displays the scatterplot of the 500 pairs of b_0 and b_1. Notice that when the slope is overestimated, the intercept usually is underestimated to compensate, and vice versa.

E X H I B I T **20.6J**
Scatterplot of b_0 versus b_1
from 500 Simulations Showing
Negative Relationship Between
These Estimates

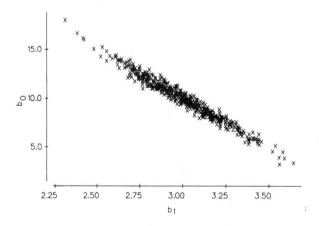

Once the 500 simulations have been carried out and the results saved, a great many distributions and relationships can be investigated. Exhibit 20.6K gives the distribution of s. Theory predicts that s will be nearly normally distributed for large degrees of freedom, but that the distribution will be skewed to the right for smaller sample sizes. In our example the degrees of freedom are 23, but Exhibit 20.6K still shows some of this skewness. Notice that even though the true value of σ is 2, one sample produced a value for s as large as about 3.4.

EXHIBIT **20.6K**
Distribution of s from the 500
Simulations with $\sigma = 2$
(notice the skewness toward
high values)

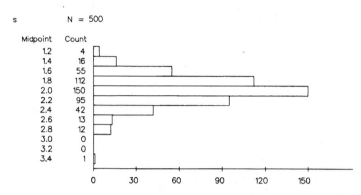

Exhibit 20.6L displays the scatterplot of slope estimates and corresponding estimates of σ. The lack of correlation between these two quantities, which may be established by statistical theory, is seen clearly in this plot. An under-, over-, or accurate estimate of the slope has no effect whatsoever on the estimate of σ.

EXHIBIT **20.6L**
Scatterplot of b_1 Versus s from
the 500 Simulations (notice the
lack of relationship)

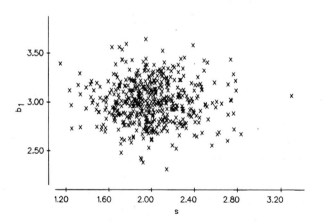

Confidence Intervals for the Regression Coefficients

Rather than testing for significance, estimates of unknown parameters are frequently given together with appropriate error bounds. In general, confidence intervals for individual regression parameters β_i are calculated as

$$b_i \pm t \cdot se(b_i)$$

where the multiplier t is either a convenient predetermined value like 3, which balances the confidence level and sample size n, or else is determined from the t distribution with $n - 2$ degrees of freedom to achieve a prescribed confidence level.

The information given in Exhibit 20.6A allows a confidence interval for the true but unknown slope in regressing Market value on Sq.ft to be obtained quickly. Using a multiplier of 3,

$$0.018362 \pm 3(0.002134)$$

or

$$0.018362 \pm 0.006402$$

or, rounding,

$$0.0184 \pm 0.0064$$

Stated otherwise, we can be confident that the true slope lies somewhere in the interval from 0.012 to 0.025 or that the true change in predicted market value per square foot of living area is in the range from \$12 to \$25. Notice that this interval does *not* include the value of zero. Thus the confidence interval is consistent with rejecting the hypothesis $\beta_1 = 0$.

For the regression in Exhibit 20.6C on the simulated data, the 3-standard-error confidence interval for the slope is

$$2.8896 \pm 3(0.1805)$$

or

$$2.8896 \pm 0.5415$$

or

$$2.89 \pm 0.54$$

In interval form, this is 2.35 to 3.43, which nicely surrounds the true value of 3 in this simulation. For a given t multiplier or prescribed confidence level, each of the 500 replications from this model produces its own confidence interval for the slope. In fact, 22, or 4.4%, of the 95% confidence intervals so produced failed to include the true value of 3. Only 7 out of the 500, or 1.4%, did not cover the true slope value when the intervals were based on plus or minus 3 standard errors. The t distribution with 23 degrees of freedom predicts that 0.6% will miss, so that theory is substantiated reasonably well in this simulation.

Prediction Intervals

In prediction, the future value of the response is "guessed" when the predictor variable is set at a particular value x^*. For example, suppose you are considering selling a house that has 1000 square feet of living space. What is the predicted market value of this house and how precise is the prediction? Let the value of the future response be denoted y^*. The prediction $\hat{y}^*$ is given by $\hat{y}^* = b_0 + b_1 x^*$.

prediction interval

prediction error

prediction standard error

A **prediction interval** is an interval that has a prescribed probability of containing a new response y^* corresponding to x^*. The precision of the prediction is assessed by looking at the properties of the **prediction error** $y^* - \hat{y}^* = y^* - b_0 - b_1 x^*$. Under the regression assumptions it may be shown that the prediction error has a normal distribution with mean 0 and a standard deviation that has a complicated formula. The estimate of this standard deviation is called the **prediction standard error** (*predse*).[†] For our purposes, only the following facts concerning conditions of the prediction standard error are important:

- It is proportional to s.
- It is alway larger than s.
- It is close to s if n is large and x^* is not too far from $\bar{x}$.
- It is smallest when $x^* = \bar{x}$ and increases as x^* moves away from $\bar{x}$ in either direction.

Prediction intervals are calculated by the formula

$$\text{Prediction} \pm t \cdot predse$$

or

$$b_0 + b_1 x^* \pm t \cdot predse$$

where t is selected either as a convenient multiplier such as 3 or else to achieve a prescribed confidence level using the t distribution with $n - 2$ degrees of freedom.

Exhibit 20.6M gives a plot of the 60 market values versus square footage values with the 95% prediction limits also displayed. The prediction limits were obtained by computing the limits at each observed x value and then connecting the limits with straight lines. The prediction limits displayed are not themselves straight lines, as you may verify by measuring the vertical distance between the curves. The limits widen out a little as x^* moves away from $\bar{x}$ in either direction. This is caused by the increase in *predse*. The effect is most prominent on the extreme right-hand side of the plot.

The simulation of the model in Equation (20.10) may also be used to illustrate the theoretical properties of the predictions from regression models. Recall that 500 replications of the model were obtained, each with a sample size of 25, $\bar{x} = 10.0$, and largest x-value of 13.9. For prediction purposes, both a middle value for x^*, namely 10, and an extreme value of $x^* = 14$, where prediction is somewhat more difficult, will be considered. For each of the 500 replications, additional values for the response y were obtained according to the model $y = 10 + 3x + e$ for both $x = 10$ and $x = 14$. Once the regression parameters are estimated for a given sample

[†]For the simple one-predictor model, it may be shown that under the basic assumptions of regression analysis, the prediction standard error is given by

$$predse = s \sqrt{1 + \frac{1}{n} + \frac{(x^* - \bar{x})^2}{\sum_{i=1}^{n}(x_i - \bar{x})^2}}$$

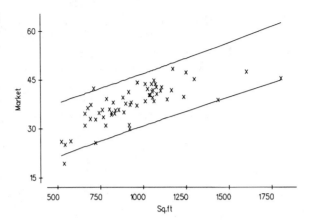

of 25 observations, the predictions and prediction limits for these two x-values are produced. There are then, for each of these two x-values, 500 actual values, predicted values, and upper and lower prediction limits. The predictions may then be compared to the actual values obtained for y in several ways.

In the first analysis, simply count the number of replications where the prediction limits failed to surround the actual value. Since 95% prediction intervals are being computed, we should miss about 5% of the time, or 25 out of 500. With $x = 10$, the simulation process actually missed 27 times, and with $x = 14$, 26 failures were observed, both of which agree well with the theory. Exhibits 20.6N and O display the actual values and 95% prediction limits for the first 80 replications. Here replications 30, 53, and 59 correspond to misses for the middle x case, and replications 29, 35, and 50 are misses for the extreme x case. In addition, the prediction-limit widths vary with replication, because these widths are determined by the varying estimates of σ. Also, generally speaking, the prediction-interval widths are wider when attempting to predict at the extreme x-value.

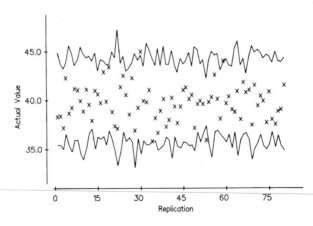

E X H I B I T **20.60**
95% Prediction Limits and
Simulated Actual
Values—Extreme x Case

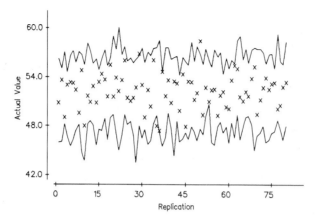

Rather than just counting the number of misses, the distribution of the actual prediction error could also be considered in both prediction situations. This error has a normal distribution with mean 0 and a theoretical standard deviation. Exhibit 20.6P shows this distribution for the 500 replications with $x = 10$. Exhibit 20.6Q gives a similar display with $x = 14$. Both distributions are quite symmetric and centered around zero, but the second distribution is slightly more spread out, as theory predicts. The standard deviations of the two distributions are, in fact, 2.0131 and 2.2062, respectively, which compare well with the corresponding theoretical values of 2.0396 and 2.2108.

Inference in straight-line regression involves:

- Testing hypotheses and constructing confidence intervals for the β parameters

- Constructing prediction intervals for new responses corresponding to a chosen value of the predictor

E X H I B I T **20.6P**
Distribution of Prediction Error
from Simulation—
Middle x Case

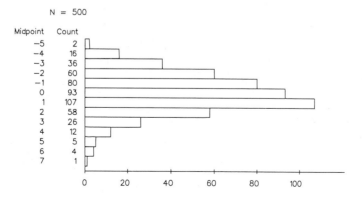

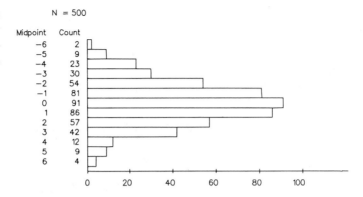

E X H I B I T **20.6Q**
Distribution of Prediction Error
from Simulation—
Extreme x Case

The inferences are valid if the theoretical assumptions of the model are satisfied by the process that generates the data. These assumptions include the form of the mathematical curve—that is, the straight line—and the behavior of the errors, namely, independent, normal with mean 0 and constant standard deviation.

SECTION

20.7 Exercises

20.7A Use the information provided in Exhibit 20.6A to obtain a confidence interval on the intercept parameter β_0 for Market regressed on Sq.ft. Use a multiplier of 3.

20.7B Use the computer output shown in Exhibit 20.6C.

a Find a confidence interval for the slope parameter β_1 (which is known to be 3). Use a multiplier of 2 so that the interval has a confidence level of about 95%.

b Does the interval include the true value of 3?

c If simulations were repeated 1000 times, approximately what percentage of the confidence intervals constructed as in part (a) would *not* include the number 3?

20.7C Use Exhibit 20.6C to verify that in simple linear regression the F ratio for regression is the same as the square of the t ratio for the slope coefficient.

20.7D Based on Exhibit 20.6J, if you were told that the intercept estimate was 5.0, what would you predict for the corresponding slope estimate?

20.7E Based on Exhibit 20.6L, if you were told that the slope estimate was 3.50, what would you predict for the corresponding estimate of σ?

20.7F Consider a regression situation such as reported in Exhibit 20.6B. Two predictions are to be made: one with $x = 6.9$ and the other with $x = 10.1$. Which of these two predictions will have *wider* 95% prediction intervals?

20.7G The data set in Exercise 7.7D gave the average height of girls by age.

a Use age to predict height in a straight-line regression model.

b Test whether age is significant as a predictor of girls' average height.

c The response in this data set is the *average* height for girls at each age. Would it be reasonable to use the regression equation developed in part (a) to predict an *individual* girl's height? Would s be useful as a measure of the precision of that prediction? Why or why not? (Filename: AGEHGT_G.DAT.)

20.7H The data set in Exercise 7.7E gave boys' average heights by age. Use age to predict height in a straight-line regression model. (Filename: AGEHGT_B.DAT.)

  a Test whether age is significant as a predictor of boys' height.

  b Compare the prediction equation for boys' height with the prediction equation for girls' height found in Exercise 20.7G.

20.7I The data file below lists the capacities of a collection of ice chests and coolers as stated by the manufacturers versus the actual size as measured by the staff at Consumers Union and reported in *Consumer Reports,* June 1989.

  a Using the stated size as the predictor variable, fit a simple linear regression to the actual size.

  b Test the significance of the estimated regression coefficient.

  c Predict the actual size of a cooler that claims to be 12 cubic feet. Find a 2-standard-error prediction interval for the actual size.

```
filename: COOLERS.DAT
Capacity of ice chests and coolers
(Source: Consumer Reports, June 1989)
Stated capacity, actual capacity (cubic feet)
17     15.5
18     15.5
15     16.75
15     15.5
12     13.5
15     13.5
 8      8.25
12     10.75
 8      7.5
 6      6.75
 6      6.5
 6      6.75
13.5   13.5
12     12.5
12     12.25
12     12.25
12     12
```

20.7J Hardwood trees are harvested in a selective manner for the manufacture of fine furniture. The volume of lumber in a selected tree is critical in determining the worth of the tree to the buyer and determines the price paid to the grower. However, volume is not easily measured before the tree is harvested. Two common measurements made before cutting down the tree are DBH (the diameter of the tree at breast height, 4.5 feet off the ground) and the height of the tree measured with sighting instruments. After the tree is harvested, the volume of lumber may be measured. A regression model relating volume to diameter and/or height will be helpful to the lumber buyers. The data file that follows gives the diameters, heights, and volumes of 31 trees harvested in the Allegheny National Forest in Pennsylvania. (This data set is used in several later exercises.)

  a Fit a regression model that predicts volume from diameter.

  b Fit a regression model that predicts volume from height.

  c Compare the models fit in parts (a) and (b).

```
filename: TREES.DAT
Data on black cherry trees
Allegheny National Forest, Pennsylvania
(Source: B.F.Ryan, B.L.Joiner and T.A.Ryan, Minitab Handbook,
2d ed., PWS-KENT, Boston, 1986)
Diameter in inches at 4.5 feet above ground level
Height of tree in feet
Volume of tree in cubic feet
Diameter, Height, Volume
    8.3      70      10.3
    8.6      65      10.3
    8.8      63      10.2
   10.5      72      16.4
   10.7      81      18.8
   10.8      83      19.7
   11.0      66      15.6
   11.0      75      18.2
   11.1      80      22.6
   11.2      75      19.9
   11.3      79      24.2
   11.4      76      21.0
   11.4      76      21.4
   11.7      69      21.3
   12.0      75      19.1
   12.9      74      22.2
   12.9      85      33.8
   13.3      86      27.4
   13.7      71      25.7
   13.8      64      24.9
   14.0      78      34.5
   14.2      80      31.7
   14.5      74      36.3
   16.0      72      38.3
   16.3      77      42.6
   17.3      81      55.4
   17.5      82      55.7
   17.9      80      58.3
   18.0      80      51.5
   18.0      80      51.0
   20.6      87      77.0
```

20.7K The lack of relationship between price and quality rating of 24 compact disc players was discussed in Examples 6.2D and 7.4B and is displayed in Exhibit 7.4E. Use an F test to confirm the lack of relationship. (Filename: CDPLAYER.DAT.)

SECTION

20.8 Inference for Models with Many Predictors

This section shows how to adapt the tools used for making inferences from simple models to use with more complex models with many predictors.

Significance Tests on Regression Coefficients

Consider the real-property data set once more. In Chapter 8, several models involving many predictor variables were developed. How is the usefulness of the predictors assessed in these more complex situations? The F test based on the ratio of the regression mean square to the residual mean square is a place to start. This ratio is appropriate for testing the hypothesis $H_0: \beta_1 = \beta_2 = \cdots = \beta_k = 0$. If true, this of course would say that the variation in the response y is simply chance variation. Statistical theory says that if H_0 is true, the sampling distribution of the F ratio is an F distribution with k and $n - k - 1$ degrees of freedom. If H_0 is not true, the F ratio tends to be larger than it is under H_0. Thus large values for the F ratio argue against

H_0. Notice that "H_0 *not* true" only means that *some* of the coefficients $\beta_1, \beta_2, \ldots, \beta_k$ are not zero—not necessarily that *all* of them are nonzero.

Exhibit 20.8A shows the regression results for predicting Market value using both Sq.ft and Sq.ft.sq. The analysis-of-variance table gives the F ratio as 58.26 with 2 and 57 degrees of freedom. The p-value of 0.000 indicates that this is indeed a large F ratio, and we can confidently conclude that at least one of the coefficients on Sq.ft or Sq.ft.sq is not zero.

E X H I B I T   20.8A

Regression of Market on Sq.ft and Sq.ft.sq

```
The regression equation is

Market = 0.07 + 0.0597 Sq.ft - 0.000020 Sq.ft.sq

Predictor         Coef        Stdev     t-ratio        p
Constant         0.073        4.998        0.01     0.988
Sq.ft         0.059729     0.009614        6.21     0.000
Sq.ft.sq    -0.00001960   0.00000447       -4.39     0.000

s = 3.473       R-sq = 67.2%      R-sq(adj) = 66.0%

Analysis of Variance

SOURCE      DF          SS         MS        F        p
Regression   2     1405.07     702.54    58.26    0.000
Error       57      687.33      12.06
Total       59     2092.40
```

However, is the inclusion of the extra predictor Sq.ft.sq really important in the model? Does $\beta_2 = 0$? Notice here that nothing at all is being said about β_1. The question is not whether Sq.ft.sq is an important predictor, but rather whether or not it is an important predictor *in addition* to the Sq.ft variable. The hypothesis $\beta_2 = 0$ (with β_1 arbitrary) may be tested by looking at the t ratio, $b_2/se(b_2)$, associated with the x_2 variable. If indeed $\beta_2 = 0$ is true, it may be shown that the sampling distribution of this t ratio is a t distribution with $n - k - 1 = 57$ degrees of freedom. Exhibit 20.8A shows that the t ratio for Sq.ft.sq is -4.39, which leads to a p-value of 0.000. Thus Sq.ft.sq is a useful predictor even when Sq.ft is already included in the prediction model.

A formula for computing the standard error of an estimated regression coefficient for models with more than one predictor is given in the appendix to this chapter [Equation (A10)], but such detail is not needed here. As usual, statistical software supplies the necessary standard errors.

In general, the significance of an individual regression coefficient b_i in a multiple regression model with k predictors can be tested by looking at the magnitude of the corresponding t ratio, $b_i/se(b_i)$. If indeed $\beta_i = 0$ is true, the sampling distribution of this t ratio is a t distribution with $n - k - 1$ degrees of freedom. Otherwise, the t ratio will tend to be larger and the null hypothesis $\beta_i = 0$ should be rejected for values of the t ratio that are far enough from zero.

Exhibit 20.8B gives the multiple regression results of Market on Sq.ft, Sq.ft.sq, Grade (through the binary indicator variables Med and Hi), and Assessed. The F ratio of 45.80 with 5 and 54 degrees of freedom is very large with a p-value of 0.000. At least some of these predictors are of value in predicting Market. The t ratios for the

```
The regression equation is

Market = 1.11 + 0.0449 Sq.ft - 0.000015 Sq.ft.sq + 4.15 Med
                              + 5.22 Hi + 0.223 Assessed

Predictor         Coef        Stdev      t-ratio         p
Constant         1.111        4.242        0.26       0.794
Sq.ft         0.044883     0.008073        5.56       0.000
Sq.ft.sq    -0.00001506   0.00000366       -4.12       0.000
Med              4.150        1.081        3.84       0.000
Hi               5.216        1.926        2.71       0.009
Assessed       0.22337      0.06940        3.22       0.002

s = 2.719        R-sq = 80.9%      R-sq(adj) = 79.2%

Analysis of Variance

SOURCE          DF           SS          MS          F          p
Regression       5       1693.16      338.63      45.80      0.000
Error           54        399.24        7.39
Total           59       2092.40
```

individual coefficients all indicate significance of the predictors even when the other variables are in the model. Assuming that the model assumptions are reasonably well satisfied, this multiple regression model looks very useful for predicting market value.

Confidence Intervals for Regression Coefficients

Confidence intervals for an individual regression coefficient β_i in models with several predictors can be constructed just as they were for simpler models. We use $b_i \pm t \cdot se(b_i)$, the only added complication being the computation of $se(b_i)$. Since statistical software provides this computation, no new difficulties are encountered. As examples, consider the model results presented in Exhibit 20.8B. We can be quite confident that the partial slope coefficient associated with the Assessed predictor lies in the interval

$$0.22337 \pm 3(0.06940)$$

or

$$0.22337 \pm 0.2082$$

Rounding gives the final interval of $(0.015, 0.432)$. Notice that this interval does *not* include zero, again indicating that Assessed is a useful predictor in addition to the other predictors in this model.

The 3-standard-error confidence interval for the binary predictor 11 variable Med, indicating the effect of a medium-grade property compared with a low-grade one, is

$$4.150 \pm 3(1.081)$$

or

$$4.150 \pm 3.243$$

which rounds to the interval $(0.91, 7.39)$. We are confident that, on average, a medium-grade house will have a market value above a low-grade house of between about $900 and $7400, all other predictor variables being equal.

Prediction Intervals

The facts about prediction intervals for a future response y^* in regression models with one predictor generalize quite easily to the more complicated models. The predictions are obtained from $b_0 + b_1 x_1^* + b_2 x_2^* + \cdots + b_k x_k^*$ and the prediction error is $y^* - (b_0 + b_1 x_1^* + b_2 x_2^* + \cdots + b_k x_k^*)$. The corresponding prediction intervals are formed as

$$\text{Prediction} \pm t \cdot predse$$

or

$$b_0 + b_1 x_1^* + b_2 x_2^* + \cdots + b_k x_k^* \pm t \cdot predse$$

where t is selected either as a convenient multiplier such as 3 or else to achieve a prescribed confidence level using the t distribution with $n - k - 1$ degrees of freedom. As mentioned earlier, the specific formula for the prediction standard error is not necessary here but can be found in the appendix to this chapter [Equation (A12)]. The following basic properties of the prediction standard error are important:

- It is proportional to s.
- It is always larger than s.
- It is close to s if n is large and all of the predictor variables are near their respective means.
- It is smallest when all the predictor variables are set to their respective means.

Exhibit 20.8C shows 95% prediction intervals for the market value response based on the two-variable quadratic curve model using Sq.ft and Sq.ft.sq. (The estimates for this model may be reviewed in Exhibit 20.8A.) In this display, the widening of the prediction limits for more extreme values of the predictors is noticeable. Compare the predictions and prediction limits here to those in Exhibit 20.6M, where the simpler straight-line model was considered. Such a comparison is facilitated by overlaying the two sets of prediction limits as in Exhibit 20.8D. In this display, it is clear that the quadratic model produces prediction limits that are narrower and better follow the shape of the scatterplot.

Now consider predictions based on the full set of predictors, Sq.ft, Sq.ft.sq., Med, Hi, and Assessed. Since two of the predictors are binary, a considerable amount of information can be displayed in a single plot. Exhibit 20.8E shows the scatterplot of the market values versus square feet with the grade variable coded as L = low grade, M = medium grade, and H = high grade. Exhibit 20.8E also displays the 95% prediction limits for this full model. The effect of every variable but assessed value can be seen in this plot.

Analogous with inference for the straight-line model, inference for the multiple linear regression model involves:

- Hypothesis tests and confidence intervals for the β coefficients
- Prediction intervals for new responses

EXHIBIT **20.8C**
95% Prediction Limits for Market
Using the Quadratic Model

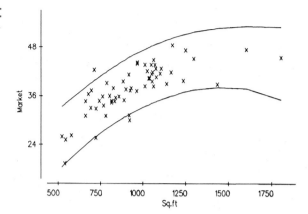

EXHIBIT **20.8D**
95% Prediction Limits for Market
Using Both Linear and Quadratic
Models

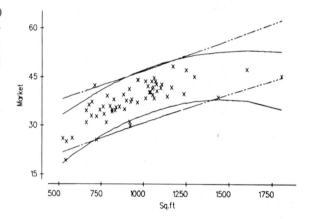

EXHIBIT **20.8E**
95% Prediction Limits for Market
Using All Predictors

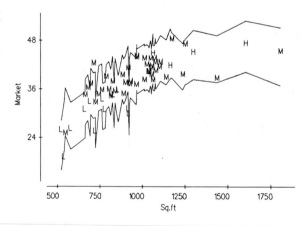

The meaning of the β coefficients in the multiple model is somewhat subtle. The coefficient β_j of x_j, for example, is the change in the mean response when x_j changes by one unit and all other predictors are held fixed. The assumptions on the error terms are the same for all regression models.

SECTION

20.9 Exercises

20.9A   Use the regression results presented in Exhibit 20.8B to test whether or not Sq.ft.sq is an important predictor variable even after Sq.ft, Med, Hi, and Assessed are included in the model for Market.

20.9B   The data file that follows gives 28 cases on 11 potential predictor variables for predicting the selling price of houses in Erie, Pennsylvania, in the early 1970s. (This data set is used in later exercises.)

```
filename: HOUSEPRI.DAT
Sale price of homes with 11 predictors
(Source: Narula and Wellington, Technometrics (1977): 185-190.)
Variables: price ($100), taxes ($), number of baths,lot size,
square feet living space, number of garages, number of rooms,
number of bedrooms, age in years,
type(1=brick, 2=brick and frame, 3=aluminum and frame, 4=frame)
style (1=two story, 2=one and one-half story, 3=ranch)
number of fireplaces
259   492 1.0   3472   998 1.0   7 4 42 3 1 0
295   502 1.0   3531 1500 2.0   7 4 62 1 1 0
279   454 1.0   2275 1175 1.0   6 3 40 2 1 0
259   456 1.0   4050 1232 1.0   6 3 54 4 1 0
299   506 1.0   4455 1121 1.0   6 3 42 3 1 0
299   389 1.0   4455  988 1.0   6 3 56 2 1 0
309   590 1.0   5850 1240 1.0   7 3 51 2 1 1
289   560 1.0   9520 1501 0.0   6 3 32 1 1 0
849  1542 2.5   9800 3420 2.0  10 5 42 2 1 1
829  1446 2.5  12800 3000 2.0   9 5 14 4 1 1
359   583 1.0   6435 1225 2.0   6 3 32 1 1 0
315   530 1.0   4988 1552 1.0   6 3 30 1 2 0
310   627 1.0   5520  975 1.0   5 2 30 1 2 0
309   596 1.0   6666 1121 2.0   6 3 32 2 1 0
300   505 1.0   5000 1020 0.0   5 2 46 4 1 1
289   560 1.0   9520 1501 0.0   6 3 32 1 1 0
369   825 1.5   5150 1664 2.0   8 4 50 4 1 0
419   670 1.5   6902 1488 1.5   7 3 22 1 1 1
405   778 1.5   7102 1376 1.0   6 3 17 2 1 0
439   904 1.0   7800 1500 1.5   7 3 23 3 3 0
375   599 1.0   5520 1256 2.0   6 3 40 4 1 1
379   754 1.5   4000 1690 1.0   6 3 22 1 1 0
445   880 1.5   9890 1820 2.0   8 4 50 1 1 1
379   609 1.5   6726 1652 1.0   6 3 44 4 1 0
389   836 1.5   9150 1777 2.0   8 4 48 1 1 1
369   814 1.0   8000 1504 2.0   7 3  3 1 3 0
458   914 1.5   7326 1831 1.5   8 4 31 4 1 0
410  1200 1.5   5000 1200 2.0   6 3 30 3 1 1
```

a   Use taxes, number of baths, and square feet as predictors and test the overall model using the F ratio statistic.

b   Using the same model as in part (a), test whether the number-of-baths variable is an important predictor in addition to the other two predictors, taxes and square feet.

c   Using the model of part (a), find a 3-standard-error confidence interval for the regression coefficient associated with square feet.

d   Predict the sales price of a house that has 1.5 baths, taxes of $850, and 1500 square feet of living space. What are the 2-standard-error prediction limits for this prediction?

20.9C Consider the house-price data in Exercise 20.9B. Regression analysis may also be used to investigate relationships among various predictor variables. (Filename: HOUSEPRI.DAT.)

   a Fit a model that uses lot size and number of rooms to predict the square feet in the house.

   b What percentage of the variation in house square footage values is explained by these two variables?

   c Are both of these predictors important once the other is in the model?

20.9D The data file that follows lists sales and advertising data for Crest toothpaste over the years 1967 through 1980. Crest sales are to be related to Crest advertising dollars, the ratio of Crest advertising to Colgate advertising (the major Crest competitor), and U.S. disposable family income for those years.

   a Estimate a regression model that predicts Crest sales using a linear combination of Crest advertising dollars, advertising ratio, and disposable income.

   b Test the overall worth of the model using the F ratio.

   c Procter & Gamble, the manufacturer of Crest toothpaste, is especially interested in the effect of its advertising on Crest sales. Test whether or not the Crest advertising dollars contribute substantially to the prediction equation given that the other variables are in the model.

```
filename: CREST.DAT
Crest toothpaste sales and advertising data
(Source: C.I.Allmon, Business Economics (1982))
Variables: year, Crest sales ($1000s),
advertising ($1000s), advertsing ratio (Crest to Colgate),
personal disposable income ($billion)
1967   105000   16300   1.25    547.9
1968   105000   15800   1.34    593.4
1969   121600   16000   1.22    638.9
1970   113750   14200   1.00    695.3
1971   113750   15000   1.15    751.8
1972   128925   14000   1.13    810.3
1973   142500   15400   1.05    914.5
1974   126000   18250   1.27    998.3
1975   162000   17300   1.07   1096.1
1976   191625   23000   1.17   1194.4
1977   189000   19300   1.07   1311.5
1978   210000   23056   1.54   1462.9
1979   224250   26000   1.59   1641.7
1980   245000   28000   1.56   1821.7
```

20.9E Consider the tree data from Exercise 20.7J.

   a Fit a model that predicts volume with a linear combination of diameter and height.

   b Evaluate the worth in the model of the height predictor after diameter is in the model.

   c Compare the model in part (a) to models that use diameter and height separately.

   d Predict the volume of a tree that has a diameter of 14 inches and a height of 80 feet.

   e Predict the volume of a tree with diameter 9 inches and height 76 feet.

   f Is 9 inches an unusual diameter? Is 75 feet an unusual height? Is this combination of diameter and height unusual in this data set?

   g Compare the widths of the prediction intervals associated with the predictions found in parts (d) and (e).

(Other multiple regression models for these data are considered in Chapters 21 and 22.) (Filename: TREES.DAT.)

20.9F Exhibit 8.5A lists data on the gasoline consumption, weight, and origin of several cars. Exhibit 8.5B shows the results of fitting the parallel lines model

$$\text{CityGas} = \beta_0 + \beta_1 \text{Weight} + \beta_2 \text{Foreign}$$

where Foreign is an indicator variable indicating origin of manufacture. The null hypothesis $H_0: \beta_2 = 0$ conjectures that, once Weight is taken into account, there is no difference between Foreign and Domestic makes. (Filename: AUTOSPEC.DAT.)

a   Find the t ratio associated with β_2.

b   Test the hypothesis $H_0: \beta_2 = 0$.

c   Based on part (b), do you recommend continued use of the parallel lines model or would a single line for both Foreign and Domestic makes suffice?

20.9G   Exercise 7.7D introduced data on the relationship between girls' heights and ages. The straight-line model considered there was extended to the quadratic model

$$\text{Height} = \beta_0 + \beta_1 \text{Age} + \beta_2 (\text{Age})^2$$

in Exercise 8.4D. (Filename: AGEHGT_G.DAT.)

a   Find the t ratio associated with β_2.

b   Test the hypothesis $H_0: \beta_2 = 0$.

c   In the light of the results of part (b), do you recommend retaining the quadratic model or reverting to the simpler straight-line model?

S E C T I O N

20.10   Pitfalls in Regression Interpretation

Although regression models are probably the most frequently used of all statistical models, they are subject to substantial misinterpretation. In this section, we discuss the regression fallacy and the interpretation of R^2.

The Regression Fallacy

Exhibit 20.10A gives a scatterplot of first and second exam scores for 39 students in a statistics class.[†] As is typical, there is quite a lot of scatter in these data. Some students who did poorly on the first exam managed to score better on the second, and some who scored well on the first exam did less well on the second one. The mean score on the first exam for the 10 lowest students is 44.8; these same students averaged 50.1 on the second exam. Similarly, the 10 best students on the first test had a mean score of 94.4 on that exam and only 82.4 on the second. The word *regression* was introduced by Sir Francis Galton because he perceived this effect as a *regression toward the mean* or even regression toward mediocrity.[‡]

Actually, the students have not regressed at all. There will always be differences between the two scores due at least to measurement error. The *regression fallacy* occurs if these differences are interpreted as an important effect—not simply due to the spread of data points around the regression line. Exhibit 20.10B shows the same scatterplot of exam scores along with the solid regression line and dashed 45° line.

[†] Both sets of exam scores were standardized and then relocated and scaled so that they have the same mean and standard deviation. These data first appeared in Exhibit 3.4C.

[‡] Galton's *Natural Inheritance* was published in London in 1889 by Macmillan. A modern critique of Galton's work may be found in Stephen M. Stigler, *The History of Statistics* (Boston: Harvard University Press, 1986).

EXHIBIT **20.10A**
First and Second Exam Scores
for 39 Students

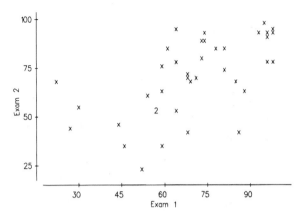

EXHIBIT **20.10B**
First and Second Exam Scores
with Solid Regression and
Dashed 45° Line

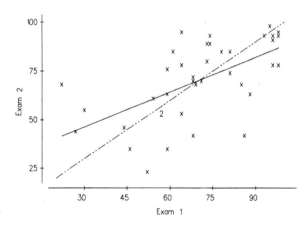

The 45° line represents the naive prediction that a student will score the same on the second exam as she did on the first. The regression line has a slope of about 0.6 compared to the slope of 1 for the 45° line.

Although regression analysis is one of the most useful statistical techniques, it must be interpreted and used carefully.

As a second example of this fallacy, consider introducing a new product into 10 different regions of the country. Sales may differ in the regions due to real factors such as different age or income distributions in the regions. But there will also be chance variation of sales not explained by these factors. Suppose that after one year, regions 2 and 5 have outstanding sales while regions 8 and 9 have the lowest sales. Should the sales managers in regions 2 and 5 be praised and those in regions 8 and 9 be reprimanded? If the chance component of sales is susbstantial, then there is every reason to believe that next year's sales will be lower in regions 2 and 5 and higher in 8 and 9 regardless of the skill of the sales managers. Without statistical reasoning, including the understanding of chance variation, the regression fallacy can be very misleading. To avoid the regression fallacy, use *data* to fit a regression curve. This gives a concrete basis for interpreting the process under study.

Interpreting R^2

Regression analysis may be carried out on data that have been obtained from a designed experiment where the values of the predictor variables are under the researcher's control, or on data that are observational or happenstance. The exam scores on the first exam used in the preceding section were not determined in advance by the analyst. In any case, all the formal inferences assume that the values for the predictor variables are fixed. What are the implications of selecting different values for the predictors?

The Population

A collection of 200 pairs of data whose scatterplot is shown in Exhibit 20.10C is used to illustrate. These data will be treated as a population from which various kinds of samples of size 30 are selected. Here are some relevant facts about this population: the regression line $\hat{y} = -75.7 + 0.857x$, $s = 0.6435$, and $R^2 = 62.4\%$.

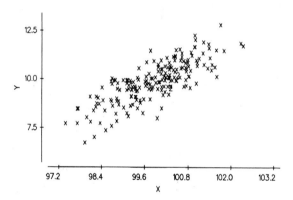

EXHIBIT 20.10C
Population of Regression Data

A Random Sample

Now suppose that a random sample of 30 cases is selected from the 200 predictor values. These cases, of course, carry along the corresponding 30 response values. Exhibit 20.10D displays the scatterplot of the 30 selected cases and Exhibit 20.10E gives the regression results for this sample. The parameter estimates based on this sample reproduce the corresponding values in the population quite well:

$$\hat{Y}\text{sample} = -72.4 + 0.825\,X\text{sample},\ s = 0.5616,\ \text{and}\ R^2 = 60.1\%$$

EXHIBIT **20.10D**

A Random Sample of the Regression Data in Exhibit 20.10C

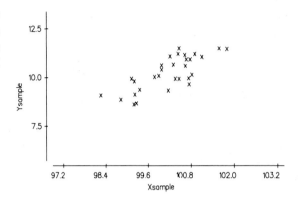

EXHIBIT **20.10E**

Regression Results for the Random Sample in Exhibit 20.10D

```
The regression equation is

Ysample = -72.4 + 0.825 Xsample

Predictor        Coef        Stdev      t-ratio          p
Constant       -72.42        12.72        -5.69      0.000
Xsample        0.8251       0.1270         6.50      0.000

s = 0.5616      R-sq = 60.1%      R-sq(adj) = 58.7%
```

An Outer Sample

Suppose now that the population is "sampled" by selecting the 15 cases with the smallest values for the predictor and the 15 cases with the largest values for the predictor—an "outer" sample. Exhibit 20.10F gives the scatterplot of the 30 pairs and Exhibit 20.10G the regression results. Here the estimated regression line and estimate of σ are quite reasonable ($\hat{Y}\text{outer} = -75.2 + 0.851 X\text{outer}$, and $s = 0.6717$) but the $R^2 = 84.8\%$ value is substantially inflated compared to the population value of 62.4%. By omitting all the middle-sized x-values, we have also omitted all the middle-sized y-values and thus increased the spread of the y-values relative to their spread in the population. But the spread around the regression line has been kept nearly the same as in the population. Since R^2 is 100 times one minus the ratio of the spread around the regression line to the spread in the response values, the effect is the inflated R^2 value.

E X H I B I T **20.10F**
An Outer Sample of the
Regression Data in
Exhibit 20.10C

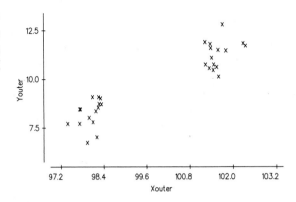

E X H I B I T **20.10G**
Regression Results for the Outer
Sample in Exhibit 20.10F

```
The regression equation is

Youter = - 75.2 + 0.851 Xouter

Predictor        Coef       Stdev     t-ratio         p
Constant      -75.227       6.797      -11.07     0.000
Xouter        0.85147     0.06809       12.51     0.000

s = 0.6717      R-sq = 84.8%     R-sq(adj) = 84.3%
```

A Middle Sample

In this illustration, 30 cases whose x-values are in the middle range of the 200 x-values are selected. When the cases are ordered according to the value of the x-values, cases 85 through 115 are used. A scatterplot in which the scales were chosen to fill the plot in both the vertical and horizontal directions is shown in Exhibit 20.10H. Our initial reaction is that the plot is quite boring, showing very little if any relationship between x and y. To keep this plot in perspective, the same data are replotted in Exhibit 20.10I but using the same scales on the axes as in the original scatterplot of Exhibit 20.10C.

E X H I B I T **20.10H**
A Middle Sample of the
Regression Data in
Exhibit 20.10C

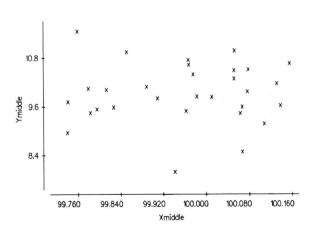

E X H I B I T 20.10I
A Middle Sample Plotted on the
Same Scale as Exhibit 20.10H

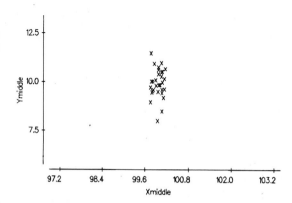

From this exhibit it is apparent that it will be difficult to estimate the true regression line! Exhibit 20.10J gives the results of the regression calculations. Although the results look disastrous (nothing is "significant" and the R^2 value is 0.1%), the fitted line does give good predictions for x-values very near the mean of the x's ($\simeq 100$). For example, the fitted value at $x = 100$ is $\hat{y} = -6.3 + 0.162(100) = 9.9$, which compares well with the population y-values for x's near 100 (see Exhibit 20.10C). In addition, the estimate of σ given as $s = 0.7523$ is not too bad when compared to the population value of 0.6435.

E X H I B I T 20.10J
Regression Using the Middle
Sample of Exhibit 20.10H

```
* NOTE *  Xmiddle is nearly constant    A warning given by Minitab

The regression equation is

Ymiddle = - 6 + 0.16 Xmiddle

Predictor       Coef       Stdev      t-ratio        p
Constant        -6.3       106.7        -0.06      0.954
Xmiddle        0.162       1.067         0.15      0.880

s = 0.7523      R-sq = 0.1%     R-sq(adj) = 0.0%
```

These special nonrandom samples of predictor values should be kept in mind when interpreting R^2 values. This example has important implications for interpretation. If we have no control over the distribution of the predictors, we may by chance get a sample that artificially reports a high or low value of R^2. In other words, we run the risk of a biased estimate of R^2. This suggests using extreme caution in using R^2 as a measure of quality of the predictions from the model.

SECTION

20.11 Exercise

20.11A The population of x, y values whose scatterplot is shown in Exhibit 20.10C is listed in Appendix 4 and is available in the file RSQUARE.DAT.

a Select a new random sample of 30 of the x, y pairs and scatterplot the pairs selected. Compare your plot to Exhibit 20.10D.

b Perform a simple linear regression using your sample and compare your results to those reported in Exhibit 20.10E.

c Using the ordered x-values, select a systematic sample by selecting every sixth pair until 30 pairs have been selected.

d Scatterplot the pairs selected in part (c) and compare this to the results in part (a) and to Exhibit 20.10D.

e For the systematic sample, perform a linear regression and compare the results to those in part (b) and Exhibit 20.10E.

SECTION

20.12 Binary Response Variables and Discriminant Analysis

discriminant analysis

This section introduces regression-like problems with a binary-valued response variable. This type of problem is usually discussed under the topic of **discriminant analysis**, which means analysis of a model whose response is categorical for the purpose of discriminating among response values on the basis of the predictor variables. To give a binary example, banks have large databases of people who have applied for loans and have either been given the loans or not. The banks would like to build a model that would predict the creditworthiness of a customer on the basis of variables such as family income, current indebtedness, amount of savings, home ownership status, and marital status. The binary response here is either to make the loan (success) or not (failure). Or a human resources manager would like to predict whether a job candidate will be successful at a job, using variables such as MBA grade-point average, a measure of computer skills, and so forth. Graduate schools of business attempt to predict a student's potential for success in an MBA program using GMAT scores, undergraduate GPA, and grades in specified courses as predictors.

The Internal Revenue Service receives millions of tax returns each year and they audit a select few of them.[†] Some of these audits yield a lot of return in additional taxes; some yield very little. Based on past data, the IRS uses discriminant analysis to predict whether or not an audit of an individual's tax return would be likely to find errors large enough to make the audit cost-effective. The predictor variables in this example include quantities such as the amounts claimed as charitable giving and as medical and business expenses. This section shows how regression techniques can be applied to produce this special type of prediction.

The data set in Exhibit 20.12A is used to illustrate. These data were gleaned from *Moody's Industrial Manuals* from 1968 to 1972 and contain annual financial data on

---

[†]Rick Wartzman, "Don't Wave a Red Flag at the IRS," *Wall Street Journal,* Feb. 24, 1993, p. C1.

21 firms that went bankrupt approximately two years later and 25 firms that were financially sound at the end of the same period. The goal is to obtain predictions of bankruptcy "worthiness" that may be applied to firms in the future. Good predictions allow us to avoid investing in businesses whose future looks bleak. Based on financial theory, four variables were selected as potentially useful predictor variables. They are four ratios: cash flow to total debt (CF/TD), net income to total assets (NI/TA), current assets to current liabilities (CA/CL), and current assets to net sales (CA/NS). The objective is to determine the linear combination of these predictors that best discriminates between the bankrupt firms and the sound firms. However, the simpler problem of discrimination based on a single predictor is first considered.

EXHIBIT **20.12A**

Financial Data on Bankrupt and Financially Sound Firms

```
filename: BANKRUPT.DAT
Bankrupcy financial data
21 bankrupt firms and 25 sound firms
(Source: R.A.Johnson and D.W.Wichern, Applied Multivariate Analysis,
2d ed., Englewood Cliffs, N.J.: Prentice-Hall, 1988
Their source: Moody's Industrial Manuals, 1968-1972)
Variables: 1=bankrupt,0=not;CF/TD;NI/TA;CA/CL;CA/NS
CF=cash flow, TD=total debt, NI=net income, TA=total assets
CA=current assets, CL=current liabilities, NS=net sales,
1  -.4485  -.4106  1.0865  .4526    |  0  .3776   .1075   3.2651  .3548
1  -.5633  -.3114  1.5134  .1642    |  0  .1933   .0473   2.2506  .3309
1   .0643   .0156  1.0077  .3978    |  0  .3248   .0718   4.2401  .6279
1  -.0721  -.0930  1.4544  .2589    |  0  .3132   .0511   4.4500  .6852
1  -.1002  -.0917  1.5644  .6683    |  0  .1184   .0499   2.5210  .6925
1  -.1421  -.0651   .7066  .2794    |  0 -.0173   .0233   2.0538  .3484
1   .0351   .0147  1.5046  .7080    |  0  .2169   .0779   2.3489  .3970
1  -.0653  -.0566  1.3737  .4032    |  0  .1703   .0695   1.7973  .5174
1   .0724  -.0076  1.3723  .3361    |  0  .1460   .0518   2.1692  .5500
1  -.1353  -.1433  1.4196  .4347    |  0 -.0985  -.0123   2.5029  .5778
1  -.2298  -.2961   .3310  .1824    |  0  .1398  -.0312    .4611  .2643
1   .0713   .0205  1.3124  .2497    |  0  .1379   .0728   2.6123  .5151
1   .0109   .0011  2.1495  .6969    |  0  .1486   .0564   2.2347  .5563
1  -.2777  -.2316  1.1918  .6601    |  0  .1633   .0486   2.3080  .1978
1   .1454   .0500  1.8762  .2723    |  0  .2907   .0597   1.8381  .3786
1   .3703   .1098  1.9941  .3828    |  0  .5383   .1064   2.3293  .4835
1  -.0757  -.0821  1.5077  .4215    |  0 -.3330  -.0854   3.0124  .4730
1   .0451   .0263  1.6756  .9494    |  0  .4785   .0910   1.2444  .1847
1   .0115  -.0032  1.2602  .6038    |  0  .5603   .1112   4.2918  .4443
1   .1227   .1055  1.1434  .1655    |  0  .2029   .0792   1.9936  .3018
1  -.2843  -.2703  1.2722  .5128    |  0  .4746   .1380   2.9166  .4487
0   .5135   .1001  2.4871  .5368    |  0  .1661   .0351   2.4527  .1370
0   .0769   .0195  2.0069  .5304    |  0  .5808   .0371   5.0594  .1268
```

Exhibit 20.12B displays the dotplots of each of the four potential predictor variables broken down by bankrupt firms and financially sound firms. A good predictor of bankruptcy would be such that its distribution for bankrupt firms would be quite separated from its distribution for financially sound firms—the distributions would not overlap at all. Of course in the real world, predictors are not perfect. The dotplots show that CA/CL (cash assets to cash liabilities) seems to best separate the bankrupt firms from the nonbankrupt firms. Thus the problem of predicting bankruptcy is considered based on this single predictor.

Although a binary response variable does *not* meet the standard regression assumptions (since it is not even approximately normally distributed, for example), it is still reasonable to consider predicting the binary response with a linear

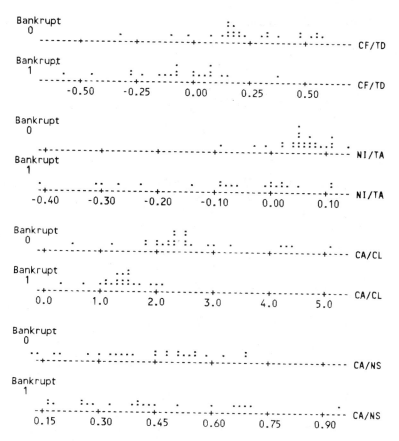

function of the predictor(s) and choosing the linear combination using the principle of least squares. If this regression is carried out, the regression equation is Bankrupt $= 1.08 - 0.307$ CA/CL. Exhibit 20.12C gives the fitted values from this model. The fitted values from bankrupt firms are attempting to predict the value 1, while the fitted values from the sound firms are predicting the value 0. A simple discrimination rule is to predict that a firm will go bankrupt if its fitted value is closer to 1 than to 0, that is, if its fitted value is greater than 0.5. Similarly, a firm is predicted to be sound if its fitted value is less than 0.5. (In the unlikely event that a fitted value is exactly 0.5, the decision must be made arbitrarily, say by flipping a coin.)

Using this decision rule, Exhibit 20.12C shows that among the 21 bankrupt firms, firms 13 and 16 are misclassified. Similarly, among the 25 sound firms, firms 31, 34, 38, and 41 are misclassified. Exhibit 20.12D gives the dotplots of the fitted values for both the bankrupt and sound firms. Again, notice the separation between the two distributions.

For future use, we will calculate the value of CA/CL for a firm, plug it into the expression $1.08 - 0.307$ CA/CL, and predict that the firm will go bankrupt if the resulting value is greater than 0.5; otherwise, we will predict that the firm is financially sound.

EXHIBIT **20.12C**

Fitted Values from Regressing Bankrupt on CA/CL

ROW	Bankrupt	CA/CL	Fitted	
1	1	1.0865	0.747617	
2	1	1.5134	0.616465	
3	1	1.0077	0.771826	
4	1	1.4544	0.634591	
5	1	1.5644	0.600797	
6	1	0.7066	0.864330	
7	1	1.5046	0.619168	
8	1	1.3737	0.659383	
9	1	1.3723	0.659814	
10	1	1.4196	0.645282	
11	1	0.3310	0.979722	
12	1	1.3124	0.678216	
13	1	2.1495	0.421042	← misclassified
14	1	1.1918	0.715267	
15	1	1.8762	0.505005	
16	1	1.9941	0.468784	← misclassified
17	1	1.5077	0.618216	
18	1	1.6756	0.566634	
19	1	1.2602	0.694253	
20	1	1.1434	0.730136	
21	1	1.2722	0.690566	
22	0	2.4871	0.317324	
23	0	2.0069	0.464851	
24	0	3.2651	0.078306	
25	0	2.2506	0.389982	
26	0	4.2401	-0.221234	
27	0	4.4500	-0.285719	
28	0	2.5210	0.306909	
29	0	2.0538	0.450443	
30	0	2.3489	0.359782	
31	0	1.7973	0.529245	← misclassified
32	0	2.1692	0.414990	
33	0	2.5029	0.312470	
34	0	0.4611	0.939753	← misclassified
35	0	2.6123	0.278860	
36	0	2.2347	0.394867	
37	0	2.3080	0.372347	
38	0	1.8381	0.516710	← misclassified
39	0	2.3293	0.365804	
40	0	3.0124	0.155941	
41	0	1.2444	0.699107	← misclassified
42	0	4.2918	-0.237117	
43	0	1.9936	0.468937	
44	0	2.9166	0.185373	
45	0	2.4527	0.327893	
46	0	5.0594	-0.472939	

EXHIBIT **20.12D**

Distribution of Fitted Values Using a Single Predictor CA/CL

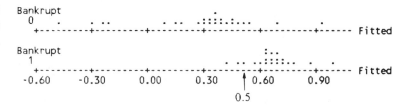

Discriminant analysis can also be used when several predictors are available. With four predictors it is, of course, an impossible task to separate the joint distributions of those predictors as to bankrupt and sound firms. However, using regression, the four variables can be reduced to one manageable variable through the fitted values. The binary response is regressed on all the predictors and the resulting fitted values are used to provide the discrimination values. Using all four financial variables in Exhibit 20.12A as predictors produces the regression equation

$$\widehat{\text{Bankrupt}} = 0.793 - 0.160\text{CF/TD} - 1.14\text{NI/TA} - 0.226\text{CA/CL} + 0.300\text{CA/NS}$$

The fitted values are listed in Exhibit 20.12E. Among the 21 bankrupt firms, firms 15, 16, and 20 are misclassified. Similarly, among the 25 sound firms, one firm (34) is misclassified. Exhibit 20.12F gives the dotplots of the fitted values for both the bankrupt and sound firms. Once more, notice the good separation between the two distributions.

For future use, we evaluate

$$0.793 - 0.160\text{CF/TD} - 1.14\text{NI/TA} - 0.226\text{CA/CL} + 0.300\text{CA/NS}$$

for a firm and predict that it will go bankrupt only if this value is greater than 0.5.

E X H I B I T 20.12E

Fitted Values from Regression of Bankrupt on Four Predictors

ROW	Bankrupt	CF/TD	NI/TA	CA/CL	CA/NS	Fitted	
1	1	-0.4485	-0.4106	1.0865	0.4526	1.22269	
2	1	-0.5633	-0.3114	1.5134	0.1642	0.94515	
3	1	0.0643	0.0156	1.0077	0.3978	0.65694	
4	1	-0.0721	-0.0930	1.4544	0.2589	0.65979	
5	1	-0.1002	-0.0917	1.5644	0.6683	0.76093	
6	1	-0.1421	-0.0651	0.7066	0.2794	0.81422	
7	1	0.0351	0.0147	1.5046	0.7080	0.64362	
8	1	-0.0653	-0.0566	1.3737	0.4032	0.67883	
9	1	0.0724	-0.0076	1.3723	0.3361	0.58120	
10	1	-0.1353	-0.1433	1.4196	0.4347	0.78780	
11	1	-0.2298	-0.2961	0.3310	0.1824	1.14681	
12	1	0.0713	0.0205	1.3124	0.2497	0.53697	
13	1	0.0109	0.0011	2.1495	0.6969	0.51404	
14	1	-0.2777	-0.2316	1.1918	0.6601	1.03020	
15	1	0.1454	0.0500	1.8762	0.2723	0.37104	← misclassified
16	1	0.3703	0.1098	1.9941	0.3828	0.27358	← misclassified
17	1	-0.0757	-0.0821	1.5077	0.4215	0.68476	
18	1	0.0451	0.0263	1.6756	0.9494	0.66272	
19	1	0.0115	-0.0032	1.2602	0.6038	0.69165	
20	1	0.1227	0.1055	1.1434	0.1655	0.44488	← misclassified
21	1	-0.2843	-0.2703	1.2722	0.5128	1.01291	
22	0	0.5135	0.1001	2.4871	0.5368	0.19667	
23	0	0.0769	0.0195	2.0069	0.5304	0.46473	
24	0	0.3776	0.1075	3.2651	0.3548	-0.02033	
25	0	0.1933	0.0473	2.2506	0.3309	0.29953	
26	0	0.3248	0.0718	4.2401	0.6279	-0.10935	
27	0	0.3132	0.0511	4.4500	0.6852	-0.11411	
28	0	0.1184	0.0499	2.5210	0.6925	0.35611	
29	0	-0.0173	0.0233	2.0538	0.3484	0.41022	
30	0	0.2169	0.0779	2.3489	0.3970	0.25859	
31	0	0.1703	0.0695	1.7973	0.5174	0.43630	
32	0	0.1460	0.0518	2.1692	0.5500	0.38616	
33	0	-0.0985	-0.0123	2.5029	0.5778	0.43123	
34	0	0.1398	-0.0312	0.4611	0.2643	0.78143	← misclassified
35	0	0.1379	0.0728	2.6123	0.5151	0.25303	
36	0	0.1486	0.0564	2.2347	0.5563	0.36761	
37	0	0.1633	0.0486	2.3080	0.1978	0.24991	
38	0	0.2907	0.0597	1.8381	0.3786	0.37729	
39	0	0.5383	0.1064	2.3293	0.4835	0.20515	
40	0	-0.3330	-0.0854	3.0124	0.4730	0.40543	
41	0	0.4785	0.0910	1.2444	0.1847	0.38743	
42	0	0.5603	0.1112	4.2918	0.4443	-0.25867	
43	0	0.2029	0.0792	1.9936	0.3018	0.31097	
44	0	0.4746	0.1380	2.9166	0.4487	0.03633	
45	0	0.1661	0.0351	2.4527	0.1370	0.21390	
46	0	0.5808	0.0371	5.0594	0.1268	-0.44628	

EXHIBIT **20.12F**
Distributions of Fitted Values
Using Four Predictors

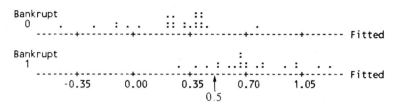

EXHIBIT **20.12F**
Distributions of Fitted Values
Using Four Predictors

This material has introduced you to discriminant analysis. To do a high-quality discriminant analysis, additional topics must be considered. For example, the accuracy of the discrimination must be evaluated. Procedures for selecting good predictors and assessing the worth of each predictor are also needed.

Generalizations of discriminant analysis as discussed here are also important. For example, the response variable may be categorical but with more than two values to be discriminated among. In addition the costs of making various kinds of errors and the probabilities, prior to looking at the predictors, of an observation belonging to a particular group may be brought into the problem.

SECTION

20.13 Exercises

20.13A Using the house-selling price data of Exercise 20.9B, consider discriminating among houses with and without fireplaces.

a Use the variables taxes, rooms, bedrooms, and style to predict the number of fireplaces.

b Use the fitted values from the regression in part (a) to check each case for misclassification. (Filename: HOUSEPRI.DAT.)

20.13B Exploration for natural resources such as oil, gas, or mineral deposits is expensive and time consuming. It is important to be able to discriminate between productive and nonproductive areas on the basis of measurements that can be made at reasonable expense. The data below give the values of 13 variables believed to help predict whether or not a particular region will be productive for mining a certain heavy metal in heavily forested areas in Sweden. The measurements are made in stream sediments from areas known to be either productive or nonproductive. A set of six measurements are also available for areas whose productivity is unknown.

a Using a binary response variable, which is 1 for productive areas and 0 for nonproductive areas, fit a multiple regression using all 13 of the listed predictors.

b Use the fitted values from the regression results of part (a) to classify each of the observations where the productivity of the area is known. Which observations are misclassified?

c Use the regression results of part (a) to classify each of the observations whose productivity is unknown. (Filename: DISCRIM.DAT.)

```
filename: DISCRIM.DAT
Trace element analysis of stream sediment in Sweden
(Source: J.C.Davis, Statistics and Data Analysis in Geology
Wiley, New York, 1973)
Variables:group (0=productive, 1=nonproductive, 2=productivity unknown)
     Ti  Mn   Ag   Ba  Co  Cr  Cu  Ni  Pb   Sr   V  Zn  Au
0   728  13 30.0  720  30  15  73   5   7    6   7  19   2
0  1030  12  0.7 1280  20  16  25   5   7    9   5   5   2
0   650   7  1.0 1070  20  20  48  70  10   21   5  17   1
0   700  15  0.7  760  30  16  70  40  11   24   4  25   1
0   510  10  0.5  740  20  14  39   5   8    5   6  13   2
0  1060  21  0.3  980  30   5  25   3   7   15  16  11   1
0  1420  20  0.2  690  30   7  25   5   6   16   7  18   1
0   970   9  0.2  680  35   7  38   3   7    8  11  25   1
0   230  15  0.2  710   5  11  50   2   7    8   3  12   1
0  1210  63  0.1 1520  30   3  24   3   8   32  16  19   2
0   300  11  0.2  510   5   3  15   3   3   24   3   5   2
0   750  24  0.7  690  30   3  31   1  10   21   4  28   3
0   780  18  4.0  730  55   4  24   3   2    9  32   9   1
0   690  15  1.0  326  30   5  25   1   9    7  20   7   4
0  1120  31  1.5  660  50   4  20   4   5   14  28   9   1
0   520  14  0.8  680  35   5  42   2   5    3  15  15   1
0   510  15  0.9  700  25   6  67   4   8    4  19   9   1
0  1060  29  0.4 1640  25   2  21   3   3   32   9  20   1
0  1150  32  0.7  710  30   3  15   2   2   26  27  18   1
0   710  18  0.9  490  75   5   8   1   3    8  18  10   2
1   482   5  0.1  160  20   7  30   1   0   72  14  20   1
1   304   5  0.2  150  20   3  82   1   2  158  16   7   1
1    89   6  0.1   50  10   1  61   1   0   34   4   5   2
1   210   5  0.1  100  15   3  77   1   0   65   9   8   2
1   506   7  0.3  140  20   5 154   2   0  124  14   8   1
1   198   7  0.1   80  15   2  63   2   0   72   8  11   0
1   322   6  0.2  160  20   3  45   2   1  110  12   6   1
1   328   8  0.2   90  15   1  40   3   2  148   7   4   0
1   202   7  0.1    8  15   2 104   2   0   42   8   7   0
1   460   7  0.3  160  20   6  48   1   2   78  15   5   2
1   310   5  0.2  100  15   3  65   1   2   71  10   4   1
1   302   6  0.2    9  15   1  69   0   3  131  11   3   2
1   186   5  0.1   70  10   2  63   0   1   48   8   5   0
1   280   7  0.1  110  15   2  58   1   2   73  12   8   1
1   104  16  0.1   20   5   1  37   0   1   14   3   8   1
1   464   8  0.3  220  15   2 121   2   2  120  21  16   0
1   499   9  0.3  190  20   4  59   2   3   48  23  12   2
1   283   8  0.2  120  15   2   4   1   2   69  14   6   0
1   450   7  0.2  140  20   3  82   2   1   71  17   7   0
1   290   6  0.1   80  15   1  99   0   0   76   8   9   1
2   426   8  0.3  180  20   6 128   3   3   46  11   8   2
2   650  12  0.5  380  30   4  72   5   2   32   9  16   1
2  1220  52  1.5  630  25   8  39   4   9   21  20  18   1
2   108  16  0.2   80   5   1 120   0   1   16   3   8   0
2   382   5  0.2  170  25   4  60   2   1  110  16   4   2
2   102  24  0.1   20   0   1  28   0   0  132   2   6   0
```

Chapter Summary

Once the predictor variables and the response variable are chosen, the multiple linear regression model is usually fitted to the data by the method of least squares. The method produces reliable inferences about the parameters provided model assumptions about the error term reasonably mirror the behavior of the data. Even when these assumptions apply, the parameter estimates are subject to variation from sample to sample of data. The precision of an estimate can be expressed through significance tests and confidence intervals. Regression models also yield prediction intervals for new responses that correspond to a set of chosen values of the predictors. Prediction intervals reflect the uncertainty in the parameter estimates and the inherent variation in the process. Sampling also affects the behavior of R^2, making its interpretation delicate.

Supplementary Exercises for Chapter 20

20A Exercise 8.9H dealt with the time it took to assemble an electronic printed circuit board in terms of seven predictor variables.

a Carry out the regression of completion time on the seven predictors.

b Interpret each of the estimated regression coefficients obtained.

c Use the F ratio to test the overall worth of the model.

d What is the value of the t ratio for the variable Total Number of Components? (Filename: BOARDS.DAT.)

20B Supplementary Exercise 7F gave the average starting salaries for men and women graduates of several MBA programs. Consider using men's salaries to predict women's salaries in a straight-line model. (Filename: MBASALRY.DAT.)

a Assess the overall significance of the regression.

b Find a 95% confidence interval for the regression coefficient associated with men's salaries.

c A new school has an average starting salary of $55,000 for men. Construct a 95% prediction interval for the average starting salary for women from this school.

20C Supplementary Exercise 7G gave rankings of various MBA programs based on *Business Week,* Corporate, and Graduates assessments. Consider the model that uses Corporate and Graduates rankings to predict *Business Week* rankings. (Filename: MBARANK.DAT.)

a Assess the overall significance of the model using the F ratio.

b Assess the significance of the Corporate ranking after the Graduate ranking is in the model.

c Assess the significance of the Graduate ranking after the Corporate ranking is in the model.

20D Use the Expressway gasoline consumption reported in Supplementary Exercise 6B and consider the predictor variables Weight and the indicator variable Foreign—that is, a parallel-lines model. (Filename:AUTOSPEC.DAT.)

a Assess the significance of the indicator variable.

b Do you recommend the use of the parallel-lines model, or would a single-line model be adequate?

20E Section 4.10 presented actual Los Angeles traffic data for freeways, minor arterial streets, and major arterial streets (including Ventura Boulevard). In an attempt to predict traffic volumes at a particular location, traffic planners build complicated models that incorporate demographic information such as housing density, income levels, and employment levels near that location. Barton-Aschman Associates of Pasadena, California, constructed such a model and are interested in comparing their model predictions with actuality. A small portion of the large data set that contains 396 observations is shown below. The full data set is in Appendix 4 and is available in the file named TRAFFIC.DAT.

a If the model were perfect, then the actual volume would equal the estimated volume, and a 45° line through the origin would describe the relationship between actual and estimated traffic volumes. Display the scatterplot of actual volume versus estimated volume. Does a 45° line seem to fit the plot?

b Perform the regression of actual volume on estimated volume and interpret the output.

c Plot the residuals versus fitted values for the regression model fit in part (a). Interpret.

d Now consider a model that allows different intercepts for different road types. That is,

$$\widehat{\text{Actual}} = \beta_0 + \beta_1 \text{ Freeway} + \beta_2 \text{ Major} + \beta_3 \text{ Estimated}$$

where Freeway = 1 for freeways and 0 otherwise and Major = 1 for major arterials (including Ventura Boulevard) and 0 otherwise. Estimate this model and interpret the coefficients.

e Plot the residuals versus fitted values for the regression model fit in part (d) and interpret.

f Now consider each of the road types separately. Display scatterplots of actual volumes against estimated volumes for each of the three road types.

g Estimate separate regression models for the three road types and interpret the scatterplots of residuals versus fitted values in each case.

h What can be concluded from the preceding analyses? Does the traffic planner's model seem to predict actual volumes well? Separately by road types?

```
Los Angeles traffic data: 396 observations
(Source: Lee Cryer, Barton-Aschman Associates
Pasadena, CA)
Variables: road type (1=freeway,2=minor arterial
3=major arterial,4=Ventura Boulevard)
estimated traffic volume, actual traffic volume
1   106848   126000
1   121121   126000
1   109751   126000
1   129345   126000
:      :        :

3    22920    14942
3    16712    13232
2     5220     7097
2     9664     4925
2     7531     5204
2     5853     8174
4    12967    11727
2     7657     5677
4    16242    21622
4    16135    20071
```

Glossary for Chapter 20

discriminant analysis	Analysis of a model whose response is categorical for the purpose of discriminating among response values on the basis of the predictor variables.
error term	The part of the response that is not modeled by the linear function of the predictor variables.
fitted value	The value predicted by the model $\hat{y}_i = b_0 + b_1 x_{i1} + \cdots + b_k x_{ik}$.
least-squares estimates	The estimates $b_0, b_1, \ldots, b_k$ of the unknown parameters $\beta_0, \beta_1, \ldots, \beta_k$.
multiple regression model	$y = \beta_0 + \beta_1 x_1 + \beta_2 x_2 + \cdots + \beta_k x_k + e$
prediction error	The new response value minus the prediction based on the model.
prediction interval	An interval that has a prescribed probability of containing a new response.
prediction standard error	The estimated standard deviation of the difference between a new response value and the predicted value.

predictor variables   The variables used to predict or explain the response variable.

regression parameters   The coefficients $\beta_0, \beta_1, \ldots, \beta_k$.

residual   The actual response value minus the value predicted by the model.

residual standard deviation $s = \sqrt{\dfrac{1}{n-k-1} \sum_{i=1}^{n} \hat{e}_i^2}$

response variable   The variable to be predicted or explained.

t ratio for b_i   The ratio $b_i/se(b_i)$.

APPENDIX

The Matrix Approach to Multiple Regression

The multiple regression model that has been written as the n equations

$$y_i = \beta_0 + \beta_1 x_{i1} + \beta_2 x_{i2} + \cdots + \beta_k x_{ik} + e_i \qquad \text{for } i = 1, 2, \ldots, n \qquad \textbf{(A1)}$$

may also be expressed very economically in vector-matrix notation. First define the column vectors

$$\underset{(n \times 1)}{\mathbf{y}} = \begin{bmatrix} y_1 \\ y_2 \\ \vdots \\ y_n \end{bmatrix}, \quad \underset{[(k+1) \times 1]}{\boldsymbol{\beta}} = \begin{bmatrix} \beta_0 \\ \beta_1 \\ \vdots \\ \beta_k \end{bmatrix}, \quad \underset{(n \times 1)}{\mathbf{e}} = \begin{bmatrix} e_1 \\ e_2 \\ \vdots \\ e_n \end{bmatrix}$$

and the matrix

$$\underset{[n \times (k+1)]}{X} = \begin{bmatrix} 1 & x_{11} & x_{12} & \cdots & x_{1k} \\ 1 & x_{21} & x_{22} & \cdots & x_{2k} \\ \vdots & \vdots & \vdots & & \vdots \\ 1 & x_{n1} & x_{n2} & \cdots & x_{nk} \end{bmatrix}$$

Then, recalling the definition of matrix multiplication, Equations (A1) may be written compactly as

$$\mathbf{y} = X\boldsymbol{\beta} + \mathbf{e} \qquad \textbf{(A2)}$$

The principle of ordinary least squares says to estimate the components of β by minimizing the quantity

$$S(\beta) = \sum_{i=1}^{n} [y_i - \beta_0 - \beta_1 x_{i1} - \beta_2 x_{i2} - \cdots - \beta_k x_{ik}]^2 = (\mathbf{y} - X\boldsymbol{\beta})'(\mathbf{y} - X\boldsymbol{\beta}) \quad \textbf{(A3)}$$

This may be accomplished by solving the system of $k+1$ linear equations obtained from computing the partial derivatives and setting

$$\frac{\partial}{\partial \beta} S(\beta) = 0$$

This in turn yields the so-called *normal equations:*

$$X'X\beta = X'y \tag{A4}$$

Here X' denotes the transpose of the matrix X.

A proof using algebra (but not calculus) that a solution of the normal equations provides the least squares estimates may be obtained as follows: Let b be any solution of the normal equations (A4). Then

$$
\begin{aligned}
S(\beta) &= (y - X\beta)'(y - X\beta) \\
&= [(y - Xb) - X(\beta - b)]'\,[(y - Xb) - X(\beta - b)] \\
&= (y - Xb)'(y - Xb) + [X(\beta - b)]'\,[X\beta - b] \\
&\quad + (y - Xb)'X(\beta - b) + [X(\beta - b)]'\,(y - Xb)
\end{aligned}
$$

But since b satisfies the normal equations (A4), it is easy to see that the final two "cross-product" terms are each zero. Thus we have the identity

$$S(\beta) = (y - Xb)'(y - Xb) + [X(\beta - b)]'\,[X(\beta - b)] \tag{A5}$$

The first term on the right-hand side of Equation (A5) does not involve β; the second term is the sum of squares of the elements of the vector $X(\beta - b)$. This sum of squares can never be negative and is clearly smallest (namely, zero) when $\beta = b$. Thus a solution to the normal equations will provide ordinary least-squares estimates of the components of β.

If the $(k + 1) \times (k + 1)$ dimensional matrix $X'X$ is invertible, Equation (A4) has a unique solution, which may be written as

$$b = (X'X)^{-1}X'y \tag{A6}$$

The column vector of *fitted values* is then

$$\hat{y} = Xb = X(X'X)^{-1}X'y \tag{A7}$$

and the column vector of *residuals* is

$$\hat{e} = y - \hat{y} = \left[I - X(X'X)^{-1}X'\right]y \tag{A8}$$

By direct calculation, it is easy to see that the matrix $H = X(X'X)^{-1}X'$ has the special property $H'H = H$ so that H is an *idempotent* matrix. It may also be argued that H is a symmetric matrix so that $H' = H$. The matrix H is sometimes called the *hat matrix* since the observation vector y is premultiplied by H to produce $\hat{y}$ (y hat). It is easy to show that $I - H$ is also symmetric and idempotent.

The estimate of σ is then

$$s = \sqrt{\frac{\hat{e}'\hat{e}}{n - k - 1}} = \sqrt{\frac{(y - \hat{y})'(y - \hat{y})}{n - k - 1}} = \sqrt{\frac{y'(I - H)y}{n - k - 1}} \tag{A9}$$

with $n - k - 1$ degrees of freedom.

Under the usual regression assumptions, it may be shown that the individual regression coefficient, b_i, has a normal distribution with mean β_i. The standard deviation of the distribution of b_i is given by σ times the square root of the ith diagonal element of the matrix $(X'X)^{-1}$. The standard error of b_i is obtained similarly by replacing σ by s. That is,

$$se(b_i) = s\sqrt{\left[(X'X)^{-1}\right]_{ii}}$$ (A10)

Let $x^* = (1, x_1^*, x_2^*, \ldots, x_k^*)$ be a row vector containing specific values for the k predictor variables for which we want to predict a future value for the response, y^*. The prediction is given by x^*b and the *prediction error* is $y^* - x^*b$. The standard deviation of the prediction error can be shown to be

$$\sigma_{y^*-x^*b} = \sigma\sqrt{1 + x^*(X'X)^{-1}x^{*\prime}}$$ (A11)

The *prediction standard error,* denoted *predse,* is obtained by replacing σ by s in Equation (A11). That is,

$$predse = s\sqrt{1 + x^*(X'X)^{-1}x^{*\prime}}$$ (A12)

Finally, the breakdown of the total sum of squares may be expressed as

$$(y - \bar{y})'(y - \bar{y}) = (\hat{y} - \bar{y})'(\hat{y} - \bar{y}) + (y - \hat{y})'(y - \hat{y})$$ (A13)
$$\left[\text{Total SS} = \text{Regression SS} + \text{Residual SS}\right]$$

with degrees of freedom $n - 1$, k, and $n - k - 1$, respectively. Here $\bar{y}$ is a column vector with the mean $\bar{y}$ in all positions.

Regression Diagnostics and Transformations

Chapter Objectives

After mastering this chapter, you will be able to:

- Define standardized residuals and use them to detect violations of the assumptions of the multiple linear regression model

- Detect outliers and explain their effects on a fitted regression model

- Use leverage and Cook's distance to diagnose influential observations

- Explain the purposes and effects of logarithmic and reciprocal transformations

21.1 Introduction

All the regression theory and methods presented in Chapter 20 and earlier rely to a certain extent on the standard regression assumptions. In particular, it was assumed that the data were generated by a process that could be modeled according to

$$y_i = \beta_0 + \beta_1 x_{i1} + \beta_2 x_{i2} + \cdots + \beta_k x_{ik} + e_i \quad \text{for } i = 1, 2, \ldots, n \qquad \textbf{(21.1)}$$

model diagnostics

where the error terms $e_1, e_2, \ldots, e_n$ are independent of one another and are each normally distributed with mean 0 and common standard deviation σ. But in any practical situation, assumptions are always in doubt and hold only approximately at best. The second part of any statistical analysis is to stand back and criticize the model and its assumptions. This phase is frequently called **model diagnostics**. If under close scrutiny the assumptions seem to be approximately satisfied, the model can be used to predict and to understand the relationship between the response and the predictors. Otherwise, ways to improve the model are sought, once more checking the assumptions of the new model. This process is continued until either a satisfactory model is found or it is determined that none of the models are completely satisfactory. Sometimes answers are required immediately and a model with known deficiencies must suffice. Ideally, the adequacy of the model is assessed by checking it with a new set of data. However, that is a rare luxury; most often diagnostics based on the original data set must suffice.

This chapter first outlines diagnostics that detect departures from the standard assumptions of regression models. It begins with the important topic of residuals, showing how to standardize and plot them to detect such departures. It then deals with outliers, unusual observations that may unduly affect the regression. Next, we explain methods of transformation that bring regression models closer to the standard assumptions, improving constancy of standard deviations, simplification of relationships, and normality of error terms. The chapter ends with a case study showing the practical use of regression analysis, transformations, and diagnostics in a gender discrimination lawsuit.

21.2 Residuals

This section shows how to standardize residuals and use those standardized values to detect departures from the usual regression assumptions. In particular, you see how standardization can be used to detect whether the error terms are normally distributed, whether the chosen regression model captures all the curvature in the relationship, and whether error terms have common standard deviations.

Standardized Residuals

Most of the regression assumptions apply to the error terms $e_1, e_2, \ldots, e_n$. However, the error terms cannot be obtained, and the assessment of the errors must be based on the *residuals* obtained as actual value minus the fitted value that the model predicts with all unknown parameters estimated from the data. Recall that in symbols, the ith residual is

$$\hat{e}_i = y_i - b_0 - b_1 x_{i1} - b_2 x_{i2} - \cdots - b_k x_{ik} \quad \text{for } i = 1, 2, \ldots, n \qquad \textbf{(21.2)}$$

To analyze residuals (or any other diagnostic statistic), their behavior when the model assumptions *do* hold and, if possible, when at least some of the assumptions *do not* hold must be understood. If the regression assumptions all hold, it may be shown that the residuals have normal distributions with 0 means. It may also be shown that the distribution of the ith residual has the standard deviation $\sigma \sqrt{1 - h_{ii}}$ where h_{ii} is the ith diagonal element of the "hat matrix" determined by the values of the set of predictor variables. This matrix may be found in the appendix to Chapter 20, but the particular formula given there is not needed here. In the simple case of a single predictor model it may be shown that

$$h_{ii} = \frac{1}{n} + \frac{(x_i - \bar{x})^2}{\sum_{j=1}^{n}(x_j - \bar{x})^2} \qquad \textbf{(21.3)}$$

Note in particular that the standard deviation of the distribution of the ith residual is *not* σ, the standard deviation of the distribution of the ith error term e_i. It may be shown that, in general,

$$\frac{1}{n} \le h_{ii} \le 1 \tag{21.4}$$

so that

$$0 \le \sigma\sqrt{1 - h_{ii}} \le \sigma\sqrt{1 - \frac{1}{n}} < \sigma \tag{21.5}$$

It may be seen from Equation 21.3 and also argued in the general case that h_{ii} is at its minimum value, $1/n$, when the predictors are all equal to their mean values. On the other hand, h_{ii} approaches its maximum value, 1, when the predictors are very far from their mean values. Thus residuals obtained from data points that are far from the center of the data set tend to be smaller than the corresponding error terms. Curves fit by least squares usually fit better at extreme values for the predictors than in the central part of the data. Exhibit 21.2A displays the h_{ii} values (along with many other diagnostic statistics that will be discussed) for the regression of Market values on the single predictor of Sq.ft. Notice that h_{ii} is equal to $1/60 \simeq 0.017$ for middle values of Sq.ft. The largest value for h_{ii}, 0.230, occurs at the largest value of the predictor. These values of h_{ii} lead to multipliers $\sqrt{1 - 0.017} = 0.992$ and $\sqrt{1 - 0.230} = 0.8775$, respectively, for the standard deviations of the corresponding residuals.

standardized residuals

To compensate for the differences in variability among the distributions of the different residuals, it is usually better to consider the **standardized residuals**. These are defined by[†]

$$i\text{th standardized residual} = \frac{\hat{e}_i}{s\sqrt{1 - h_{ii}}} \quad \text{for } i = 1, 2, \ldots, n \tag{21.6}$$

Notice that the unknown σ has been estimated by s. If n is large and if the regression assumptions are all approximately satisfied, the standardized residuals should behave about like standard normal variables. Exhibit 21.2A also lists the residuals and standardized residuals for all 60 cases.

Even if all the regression assumptions are met, the residuals (and standardized residuals) are not independent. For example, the residuals for a model that includes an intercept term always add to zero. This alone implies they are negatively correlated. It may be shown that, in fact, the theoretical correlation coefficient between the ith and jth residuals (or standardized residuals) is

$$\frac{-h_{ij}}{\sqrt{(1 - h_{ii})(1 - h_{jj})}} \tag{21.7}$$

[†]Unfortunately, the terminology used here has not been standardized. The term *studentized* residual is used by some authors. Others call $\hat{e}_i/s$ standardized residuals. We reserve the term *studentized* residual for another form given in Section 21.4.

E X H I B I T **21.2A**

Diagnostic Statistics for the
Regression of Market on Sq.ft.

ROW	Sq.ft	Market	Resids	Std Res	t-Resid	hii	CookD
1	521	26.0	-4.07	-1.06	-1.06	0.068	0.041
2	538	19.4	-10.99	-2.85	-3.05	0.064	0.276
3	544	25.2	-5.30	-1.37	-1.38	0.062	0.063
4	577	26.2	-4.90	-1.27	-1.27	0.055	0.047
5	661	31.0	-1.65	-0.42	-0.42	0.039	0.004
6	662	34.6	1.94	0.50	0.49	0.039	0.005
7	677	36.4	3.46	0.89	0.88	0.037	0.015
8	691	33.0	-0.20	-0.05	-0.05	0.035	0.000
9	694	37.4	4.15	1.06	1.06	0.034	0.020
10	712	42.4	8.82	2.25	2.34	0.032	0.083
11	721	32.8	-0.95	-0.24	-0.24	0.031	0.001
12	722	25.6	-8.17	-2.08	-2.15	0.031	0.068
13	743	34.8	0.65	0.17	0.16	0.028	0.000
14	760	35.8	1.34	0.34	0.34	0.026	0.002
15	767	33.6	-0.99	-0.25	-0.25	0.025	0.001
16	780	31.0	-3.83	-0.97	-0.97	0.024	0.012
17	787	39.2	4.24	1.08	1.08	0.024	0.014
18	802	36.0	0.77	0.19	0.19	0.022	0.000
19	814	34.8	-0.65	-0.17	-0.16	0.021	0.000
20	815	34.4	-1.07	-0.27	-0.27	0.021	0.001
21	825	38.0	2.34	0.59	0.59	0.021	0.004
22	834	34.6	-1.22	-0.31	-0.31	0.020	0.001
23	838	35.6	-0.30	-0.07	-0.07	0.020	0.000
24	858	35.8	-0.46	-0.12	-0.12	0.019	0.000
25	883	39.6	2.88	0.73	0.73	0.018	0.005
26	890	35.0	-1.85	-0.47	-0.47	0.017	0.002
27	899	37.6	0.58	0.15	0.15	0.017	0.000
28	918	41.2	3.84	0.97	0.97	0.017	0.008
29	920	31.2	-6.20	-1.57	-1.59	0.017	0.021
30	923	30.0	-7.46	-1.89	-1.93	0.017	0.030
31	926	37.4	-0.11	-0.03	-0.03	0.017	0.000
32	931	38.0	0.40	0.10	0.10	0.017	0.000
33	965	37.2	-1.03	-0.26	-0.26	0.017	0.001
34	966	44.0	5.75	1.46	1.47	0.017	0.018
35	967	44.2	5.94	1.50	1.52	0.017	0.019
36	1011	43.6	4.53	1.15	1.15	0.018	0.012
37	1011	38.4	-0.67	-0.17	-0.17	0.018	0.000
38	1024	42.2	2.89	0.73	0.73	0.019	0.005
39	1033	40.4	0.92	0.23	0.23	0.019	0.001
40	1040	40.4	0.80	0.20	0.20	0.019	0.000
41	1047	43.6	3.87	0.98	0.98	0.020	0.010
42	1051	41.4	1.59	0.40	0.40	0.020	0.002
43	1052	39.6	-0.22	-0.06	-0.06	0.020	0.000
44	1056	41.8	1.90	0.48	0.48	0.020	0.002
45	1060	44.8	4.83	1.23	1.23	0.021	0.016
46	1060	38.4	-1.57	-0.40	-0.40	0.021	0.002
47	1070	43.6	3.44	0.87	0.87	0.021	0.008
48	1075	42.8	2.55	0.65	0.65	0.022	0.005
49	1079	40.6	0.28	0.07	0.07	0.022	0.000
50	1100	41.6	0.89	0.23	0.23	0.024	0.001
51	1106	42.8	1.98	0.50	0.50	0.024	0.003
52	1138	39.0	-2.40	-0.61	-0.61	0.028	0.005
53	1164	41.8	-0.08	-0.02	-0.02	0.031	0.000
54	1171	48.4	6.39	1.63	1.66	0.032	0.044
55	1237	39.8	-3.42	-0.88	-0.88	0.042	0.017
56	1249	47.2	3.76	0.97	0.96	0.044	0.021
57	1298	45.2	0.86	0.22	0.22	0.053	0.001
58	1435	38.8	-8.06	-2.12	-2.19	0.087	0.213
59	1602	47.4	-2.52	-0.68	-0.68	0.142	0.039
60	1804	45.4	-8.23	-2.36	-2.46	0.230	0.832

where h_{ij} is the ijth element of the hat matrix. Again, the general formula for these elements is not needed here. For the simple single-predictor case, it may be shown that

$$h_{ij} = \frac{1}{n} + \frac{(x_i - \bar{x})(x_j - \bar{x})}{\sum_{i=1}^{n}(x_i - \bar{x})^2}$$

(21.8)

From Equations (21.3), (21.7), and (21.8) (and in general) we see that the correlations will be small except for small data sets and/or for residuals associated with data points very far from the central part of the predictor values. From a practical point of view, this small correlation is ignored, and the assumptions on the error terms are assessed by comparing the properties of the standardized residuals to those of independent, standard normal variables.

Residual Plots

Plots of the standardized residuals against other variables are very useful in detecting departures from the standard regression assumptions. Exhibit 21.2B shows an ideal residual plot in which standardized residuals versus case number have been plotted for 25 cases. If the regression assumptions are met, the distributions of all the standardized residuals are approximately standard normal distributions, and the residuals are approximately uncorrelated. Thus, a random pattern should be apparent in such a plot.

E X H I B I T 21.2B
Plot of Ideal Standardized
Residuals Versus Case Number

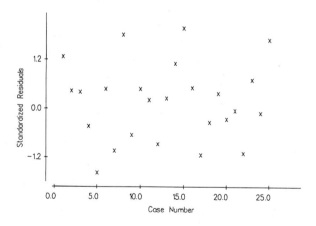

Departures from the standard regression assumptions can occur in infinitely many ways. What is needed are diagnostic procedures that will detect the most common of those departures. Useful diagnostic plots include plotting residuals against fitted values, against individual predictors, or against time.

Many of the most common problems may be seen by plotting standardized residuals against the corresponding fitted values. In this plot, it is relatively easy to see if mostly negative (or mostly positive) residuals are associated with the largest and smallest fitted values. Such a plot would indicate curvature that the chosen regression curve did not capture. Exhibit 21.2C gives an example of such a residual plot. Here the residuals for the four smallest and three largest fitted values are all negative, indicating the curvature that is lacking in the model. Exhibit 21.2D displays the corresponding residual plot when the quadratic model is used for the same data set. Now the residuals for extreme values of fitted values are a mixture of positives and negatives and show no general model inadequacies.

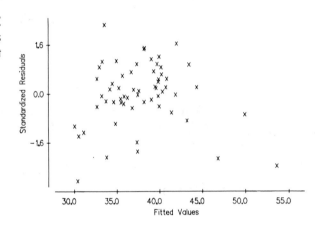

E X H I B I T **21.2D**
Standardized Residuals Versus
Fitted Values—Market on Sq.ft
and Sq.ft.sq

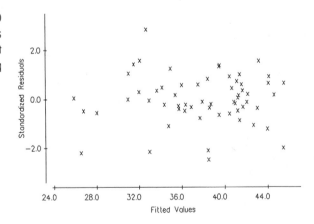

Another important use for the plot of residuals versus fitted values is to detect lack of a common standard deviation among different error terms. Contrary to the assumption of common standard deviation, it is not uncommon for variability to increase as the values for the response variable increase. Exhibit 21.2E gives an example of the residual plot in such a situation. Here the city miles per gallon values for 45 cars have been regressed on their weight and a binary variable giving their type of transmission—automatic or manual. For this type of data, the variability of city gas mileage is larger for the more efficient cars. This is reflected in the residual plot as greater variability in the residuals as the fitted values increase. This example is used again in Section 21.8 in a discussion of transformations that will correct this problem of lack of common standard deviation. Autocorrelation in residuals, another problem that may be detected with various residual plots, is discussed in Chapter 23.

EXHIBIT 21.2E
Standardized Residuals Versus
Fitted Values—City MPG on
Weight and Transmission Type

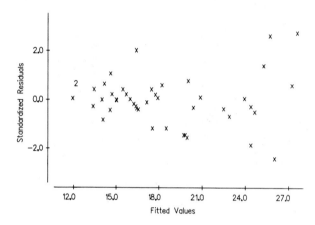

To summarize:

- Residuals are differences between observed responses and fitted values.
- Residual plots are examined for clues that one or more of the model assumptions is violated by the data.
- The most common residual plots are standardized residuals versus fitted values, standardized residuals versus predictors, and a sequence plot of the standardized residuals.

SECTION

21.3 Exercises

21.3A   Consider the data of Exercise 7.7D giving the average height of girls at various ages and the regression of height in terms of age.

   a   Plot the residuals versus the fitted values. Comment on the shape of the plot.

   b   Plot the residuals versus the age variable. Comment on the shape of this plot compared to the one in part (a).

   c   Plot the standardized residuals versus the fitted values and comment on the display.

   d   Fit a new model that includes age and age squared as predictors of height.

   e   Plot the residuals versus the fitted values for the model estimated in part (d). Comment on this plot. (Filename: AGEHGT_G.DAT.)

21.3B   Use the tree data of Exercise 20.7J to predict volume using a linear combination of diameter and height. Plot the standardized residuals versus the fitted values and comment on the information about the quality of the model conveyed in this plot. (Filename: TREES.DAT.)

21.3C   Consider the house selling price data in Exercise 20.9B. In that exercise, you fit the model that predicts selling price using taxes, number of baths, and square feet as predictors.

   a   Plot the standardized residuals versus the fitted values and comment on the plot.

   b   Plot the standardized residuals versus taxes and comment on the plot.

   c   Plot the standardized residuals versus bedrooms and comment on the plot.

   d   Plot the standardized residuals versus square feet and comment on the plot. (Filename: HOUSEPRI.DAT.)

21.3D   Consider the regression model that related Crest toothpaste sales to Crest advertising, advertising ratio (Crest to Colgate), and family disposable income. The data are reported in Exercise 20.9D.

   a   Plot the standardized residuals versus the fitted values and comment on the plot.

   b   Plot the standardized residuals versus advertising and comment on the plot.

   c   Plot the standardized residuals versus advertising ratio and comment on the plot.

   d   Plot the standardized residuals versus disposable income and comment on the plot.

   e   Plot the standardized residuals versus year and comment on the plot. (Filename: CREST.DAT.)

SECTION

21.4   Outliers

In regression analysis, the model is assumed to be appropriate for all the observations. It is not unusual, however, for one or two cases to be inconsistent with the general pattern of the data in one way or another. When a single predictor is used, such cases are easily spotted in the scatterplot of data. When several predictors are employed, such cases are much more difficult to detect. The nonconforming data points are usually called **outliers**. For example, it could be the result of a correctable recording error. Other outliers may be due to responses obtained when unmeasured variables were quite different from those affecting the rest of the data. Regardless of the reason for the outlier, it can substantially affect the regression analysis.

outliers

     This section explains how to detect outliers with unusual response values. Section 21.6 deals with detecting outliers with unusual predictor values, and what to do when outliers are detected. Unusual responses should be detectable by looking for unusual residuals, preferably by checking for unusually large standardized residuals. If the normality of the error terms is not in question (see Section 21.8), a standardized residual larger than 3 is unusual and the corresponding case should be investigated for a special cause for this value. Some statistical software warns you by flagging all cases with standardized residuals outside of ± 2. This warning must be considered with care since with data sets of, say, 60 observations, standardized residuals this large are not that unusual even if the regression assumptions are all met.

Studentized Residuals

studentized residuals

A difficulty with looking at standardized residuals is that an outlier, if present, will also affect the estimate of σ that enters into the denominator of the standardized residual. Typically, an outlier will inflate s and thus deflate the standardized residuals, masking the outlier. One way to circumvent this problem is to estimate the value of σ used in calculating the ith standardized residual using all the data *except* the ith case. Let $s_{(i)}$ denote such an estimate where the subscript (i) indicates that the ith case has been deleted. This leads to the **studentized residuals** defined by

$$i\text{th studentized residual} = \frac{\hat{e}_i}{s_{(i)}\sqrt{1 - h_{ii}}} \qquad \text{for } i = 1, 2, \ldots, n \qquad \textbf{(21.9)}$$

These are sometimes called externally studentized residuals, externally standardized residuals, studentized deleted residuals, or t residuals. Obtaining the many required residuals is not as tedious as it might appear, since clever methods have been discovered for doing so without extensive calculation. Most statistical software packages calculate them routinely.

Effect of Outliers

A small artificial data set is used to illustrate the detection of outliers and their effect on analysis. Exhibit 21.4A shows a scatterplot that will be considered the "correct" data against which results will be compared when an outlier is introduced. Exhibit 21.4B shows the standard regression results for these data. Then $\hat{y} = 31.114 + 1.66781x$ and $s = 1.001$ are considered the "correct" values for the regression line and residual standard deviation. The exhibit also lists the standardized and studentized residuals; no anomalies are observed.

Now suppose that case 7 with $x = 25$ and $y = 73.8$ is misrecorded as $y = 80.1$. With a single predictor variable, the outlier in Exhibit 21.4C is easy to see. However, with several predictors this would not be true. Suppose y is regressed on x with the outlier present. Exhibit 21.4D shows the results, with $\hat{y} = 30.667 + 1.7133x$ and $s = 2.638$. The outlier has pulled the regression equation slope up and grossly inflated

EXHIBIT 21.4A
A Scatterplot with
"Correct" Data

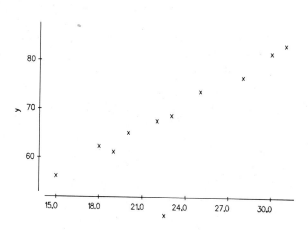

EXHIBIT **21.4B**

Regression and Diagnostic
Statistics for "Correct" Data

```
The regression equation is

y = 31.1 + 1.67 x

Predictor        Coef      Stdev     t-ratio         p
Constant       31.114      1.477       21.07     0.000
x             1.66781    0.06245       26.71     0.000

s = 1.001       R-sq = 98.9%      R-sq(adj) = 98.8%


ROW     x      y   std res   t-resid    hii    CookD
 1     15   56.2      0.09      0.08    0.36    0.002
 2     18   62.4      1.42      1.53    0.20    0.252
 3     19   61.2     -1.75     -2.09    0.17    0.304
 4     20   65.1      0.68      0.65    0.14    0.037
 5     22   67.6     -0.22     -0.20    0.10    0.003
 6     23   68.7     -0.81     -0.80    0.10    0.037
 7     25   73.8      1.05      1.06    0.11    0.071
 8     28   76.6     -1.35     -1.44    0.19    0.218
 9     30   81.6      0.53      0.51    0.29    0.057
10     31   83.2      0.47      0.45    0.34    0.059
```

EXHIBIT **21.4C**

Scatterplot with Outlier at
$x = 25$

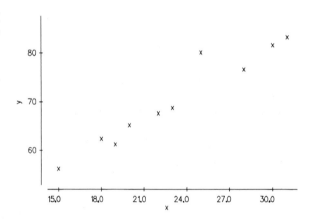

the value of s. The large value for s is especially disturbing, since the standard errors of the regression coefficients and prediction standard errors are all proportional to s. The widths of all confidence intervals and prediction intervals will be greatly increased and the precision of the inferences will be misleading. Notice that the software warns you when it finds a standardized residual exceeding 2. The corresponding studentized residual (t residual) is equal to 7.03, more clearly indicating the outlier problem. Looking for large studentized residuals is an effective method for spotting individual outlying response values.

Once we are convinced that case 7 is unusual, we may, if possible, go back to the data-collection process and correct the data point. Otherwise, we may have to be content with deleting that case from the data set and proceeding from there. The regression results with case 7 deleted are shown in Exhibit 21.4E. Now the regression line and value of s are nearly equal to the corresponding values for the "correct" data, and the diagnostic statistics indicate no further difficulties.

EXHIBIT 21.4D
Regression with Outlier at
$x = 25$

```
The regression equation is

y = 30.7 + 1.71 x

Predictor      Coef       Stdev    t-ratio       p
Constant     30.667      3.892       7.88    0.000
x            1.7144      0.1646     10.42    0.000

s = 2.638      R-sq = 93.1%     R-sq(adj) = 92.3%


Unusual Observations
Obs.     x       y      Fit Stdev.Fit  Residual  St.Resid
  7    25.0   80.100  73.527    0.891     6.573     2.65R

R denotes an observation with a large St. Resid.   (← Minitab warning)


ROW    x      y    std res   t-resid    hii    CookD

  1   15    56.2    -0.09     -0.08    0.36    0.002
  2   18    62.4     0.37      0.35    0.20    0.017
  3   19    61.2    -0.85     -0.83    0.17    0.071
  4   20    65.1     0.06      0.06    0.14    0.000
  5   22    67.6    -0.31     -0.30    0.10    0.006
  6   23    68.7    -0.56     -0.53    0.10    0.017
  7   25    80.1     2.65      7.03    0.11    0.451
  8   28    76.6    -0.87     -0.86    0.19    0.092
  9   30    81.6    -0.22     -0.21    0.29    0.010
 10   31    83.2    -0.29     -0.27    0.34    0.022
```

EXHIBIT 21.4E
Regression After Deleting Case 7

```
The regression equation is

y = 31.2 + 1.66 x

Predictor      Coef       Stdev    t-ratio       p
Constant     31.193      1.467      21.26    0.000
x            1.65953     0.06246    26.57    0.000

s = 0.9933     R-sq = 99.0%     R-sq(adj) = 98.9%


ROW    x      y    std res   t-resid    hii    CookD

  1   15    56.2     0.14      0.13    0.36    0.006
  2   18    62.4     1.51      1.70    0.21    0.295
  3   19    61.2    -1.69     -2.02    0.17    0.293
  4   20    65.1     0.78      0.76    0.14    0.051
  5   22    67.6    -0.11     -0.10    0.11    0.001
  6   23    68.7    -0.71     -0.68    0.11    0.031
  7    *     *        *         *       *       *
  8   28    76.6    -1.20     -1.25    0.21    0.198
  9   30    81.6     0.75      0.73    0.31    0.128
 10   31    83.2     0.71      0.69    0.37    0.150
```

EXAMPLE 21.4A

How do these diagnostic methods work with real data? The property data example is used to illustrate. Exhibit 21.4F lists diagnostic statistics for the quadratic regression of Market value on Sq.ft and Sq.ft.sq. Notice that for most cases the standardized and studentized residuals differ by very little. However, in row 10 the standardized residual is 2.86, whereas the studentized residual is 3.06, giving a clear signal that the 10th case is unusual. In fact, the

EXHIBIT **21.4F**

Diagnostic Statistics—Quadratic
Model of Market on Sq.ft and
Sq.ft.sq

ROW	Sq.ft	Market	Resids	Std Res	t-Resid	hii	CookD
1	521	26.0	0.13	0.04	0.04	0.144	0.000
2	538	19.4	-7.13	-2.20	-2.28	0.128	0.236
3	544	25.2	-1.56	-0.48	-0.48	0.122	0.011
4	577	26.2	-1.81	-0.55	-0.55	0.096	0.011
5	661	31.0	0.01	0.00	0.00	0.051	0.000
6	662	34.6	3.58	1.06	1.06	0.051	0.020
7	677	36.4	4.87	1.44	1.45	0.045	0.033
8	691	33.0	1.01	0.30	0.30	0.041	0.001
9	694	37.4	5.32	1.56	1.58	0.040	0.034
10	712	42.4	9.74	2.86	3.06	0.035	0.100
11	721	32.8	-0.15	-0.04	-0.04	0.033	0.000
12	722	25.6	-7.38	-2.16	-2.24	0.033	0.053
13	743	34.8	1.17	0.34	0.34	0.029	0.001
14	760	35.8	1.66	0.48	0.48	0.027	0.002
15	767	33.6	-0.75	-0.22	-0.22	0.026	0.000
16	780	31.0	-3.74	-1.09	-1.09	0.024	0.010
17	787	39.2	4.26	1.24	1.25	0.024	0.012
18	802	36.0	0.63	0.18	0.18	0.022	0.000
19	814	34.8	-0.90	-0.26	-0.26	0.022	0.001
20	815	34.4	-1.33	-0.39	-0.38	0.022	0.001
21	825	38.0	1.99	0.58	0.58	0.021	0.002
22	834	34.6	-1.65	-0.48	-0.48	0.021	0.002
23	838	35.6	-0.76	-0.22	-0.22	0.021	0.000
24	858	35.8	-1.09	-0.32	-0.31	0.020	0.001
25	883	39.6	2.07	0.60	0.60	0.020	0.003
26	890	35.0	-2.70	-0.79	-0.78	0.021	0.004
27	899	37.6	-0.33	-0.09	-0.09	0.021	0.000
28	918	41.2	2.82	0.82	0.82	0.021	0.005
29	920	31.2	-7.23	-2.11	-2.17	0.021	0.032
30	923	30.0	-8.50	-2.48	-2.60	0.021	0.045
31	926	37.4	-1.17	-0.34	-0.34	0.022	0.001
32	931	38.0	-0.69	-0.20	-0.20	0.022	0.000
33	965	37.2	-2.26	-0.66	-0.65	0.023	0.003
34	966	44.0	4.52	1.32	1.33	0.023	0.014
35	967	44.2	4.70	1.37	1.38	0.023	0.015
36	1011	43.6	3.18	0.93	0.93	0.026	0.008
37	1011	38.4	-2.02	-0.59	-0.59	0.026	0.003
38	1024	42.2	1.52	0.44	0.44	0.027	0.002
39	1033	40.4	-0.45	-0.13	-0.13	0.027	0.000
40	1040	40.4	-0.59	-0.17	-0.17	0.028	0.000
41	1047	43.6	2.48	0.72	0.72	0.028	0.005
42	1051	41.4	0.21	0.06	0.06	0.028	0.000
43	1052	39.6	-1.61	-0.47	-0.47	0.028	0.002
44	1056	41.8	0.51	0.15	0.15	0.029	0.000
45	1060	44.8	3.44	1.01	1.01	0.029	0.010
46	1060	38.4	-2.96	-0.86	-0.86	0.029	0.007
47	1070	43.6	2.06	0.60	0.60	0.030	0.004
48	1075	42.8	1.17	0.34	0.34	0.030	0.001
49	1079	40.6	-1.10	-0.32	-0.32	0.030	0.001
50	1100	41.6	-0.46	-0.13	-0.13	0.032	0.000
51	1106	42.8	0.65	0.19	0.19	0.032	0.000
52	1138	39.0	-3.66	-1.07	-1.07	0.035	0.014
53	1164	41.8	-1.24	-0.36	-0.36	0.037	0.002
54	1171	48.4	5.26	1.55	1.56	0.037	0.031
55	1237	39.8	-4.16	-1.23	-1.23	0.044	0.023
56	1249	47.2	3.11	0.92	0.91	0.046	0.013
57	1298	45.2	0.63	0.19	0.18	0.053	0.001
58	1435	38.8	-6.62	-2.00	-2.06	0.096	0 141
59	1602	47.4	1.95	0.64	0.64	0.228	0.040
60	1804	45.4	1.37	0.65	0.65	0.628	0.237

response of 42.4 is exceptionally large for a square footage of 712. Perhaps a predictor other than square footage will help explain the market value for this case. Also note that case 10 lies above the 95% upper prediction limit for this model (see Exhibit 20.8C). No other cases have studentized residuals larger than 3 in magnitude.   ▪

S E C T I O N

21.5 Exercises

21.5A   Calculate and examine the studentized residuals for the regression of average girls' heights in terms of age. The data are given in Exercise 7.7D. Are any outliers apparent? (Filename: AGEHGT_G.DAT.)

21.5B   Calculate and examine the studentized residuals for the regression of actual capacity of ice chests in terms of stated capacity. The data appear in Exercise 20.7I. Are any outliers indicated from the studentized residuals? (Filename: COOLERS.DAT.)

21.5C   The data in Exercise 20.9B gave house prices and several predictor variables. Consider the regression of house price in terms of taxes, number of baths, and square feet. Find the studentized residuals for this model. Are any outliers apparent in this regression? (Filename: HOUSEPRI.DAT.)

21.5D   Exercise 20.9D gave data on Crest toothpaste sales and several potential predictors. For the model that uses advertising dollars, advertising ratio, and personal disposable income to predict sales, calculate the studentized residuals. Are any of these residuals exceptionally large? (Filename: CREST.DAT.)

S E C T I O N

21.6 Influential Observations

influence

The principle of ordinary least squares gives equal weight to each case. On the other hand, each case does not have the same effect on the fitted regression curve. For example, observations with extreme predictor values can substantially affect the slope of a fitted value. Such data are said to have great **influence** on the regression analysis. On the other hand, some observations with extreme predictor values actually have little effect on the regression analysis. This section outlines some of the diagnostic statistics that have been developed to quantify the amount of influence or lack of influence that individual cases have in a regression analysis. The first measure of influence is provided by the diagonal elements of the hat matrix.

Leverage

leverage

When considering the influence of individual cases on regression analysis, the ith diagonal element of the hat matrix, h_{ii}, is often called the **leverage** for the ith case, which means a measure of the ith data point's influence in a regression with respect to the predictor variables. In what sense does h_{ii} measure influence? It may be shown that $\hat{y}_i = h_{ii} y_i + \sum_{j \neq i} h_{ij} y_j$ so that $\partial \hat{y}_i / \partial y_i = h_{ii}$, that is, h_{ii} is the rate of change of the ith fitted value with respect to the ith response value. If h_{ii} is small, then a small change in the ith response results in a small change in the corresponding fitted value. However, if h_{ii} is large, then a small change in the ith response produces a large change in the corresponding $\hat{y}_i$.

Further interpretation of h_{ii} as leverage is based on the material in Section 21.2. There it was shown that the standard deviation of the sampling distribution of the ith residual is not σ but $\sigma \sqrt{1 - h_{ii}}$. Furthermore, h_{ii} is equal to its smallest value, $1/n$, when all the predictors are equal to their mean values. These are the values for the predictors that have the least influence on the regression curve and imply, in general, the largest residuals. On the other hand, if the predictors are far from their means, then h_{ii} approaches its largest value of 1 and the standard deviation of such residuals is quite small. In turn, this implies a tendency toward small residuals, and the regression curve is pulled toward these influential observations.

Exhibit 21.6A shows a scatterplot and fitted regression line for which the observation at $x = 6$ has a great deal of influence on the resulting line. The numerical regression results and diagnostic statistics for these data are given in Exhibit 21.6B. Notice that all the values of h_{ii} are about 0.1 *except* for the influential case 10, where $h_{10,10} = 0.93$. The influence of this case is dramatically revealed by omitting it from the data and refitting the regression line. Exhibit 21.6C displays both the original line and the substantially different dashed line obtained from the reduced data set. The numerical regression results corresponding to the nine cases are shown in Exhibit 21.6D. Once case 10 is removed, everything in the analysis changes completely, emphasizing the influence of that one case.

EXHIBIT **21.6A**
Scatterplot and Regression Line
to Illustrate Influence of Case
with $x = 6$ and $y = 6$

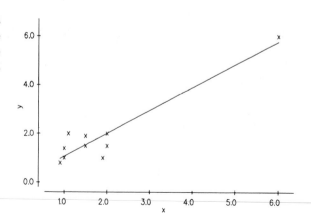

EXHIBIT **21.6B**
Regression Results for Data in
Exhibit 21.6A

```
The regression equation is

y = 0.130 + 0.942 x

Predictor       Coef      Stdev    t-ratio       p
Constant      0.1300     0.2704       0.48   0.644
x             0.9418     0.1141       8.25   0.000

s = 0.5156      R-sq = 89.5%      R-sq(adj) = 88.2%

Unusual Observations
Obs.    x       y    Fit  Stdev.Fit  Residual  St.Resid
10   6.00   6.000  5.781      0.497     0.219     1.58 X   (← Minitab warning)

X denotes an observation whose X value gives it large influence.


ROW     x      y   std res  t-resid    hii    CookD

  1    0.9    0.8   -0.37    -0.35    0.15    0.012
  2    1.0    1.0   -0.15    -0.14    0.14    0.002
  3    1.0    1.4    0.69     0.66    0.14    0.038
  4    1.1    2.0    1.73     2.05    0.13    0.226
  5    1.5    1.5   -0.09    -0.08    0.11    0.000
  6    1.5    1.9    0.73     0.71    0.11    0.032
  7    1.9    1.0   -1.88    -2.35    0.10    0.196
  8    2.0    1.5   -1.05    -1.06    0.10    0.062
  9    2.0    2.0   -0.03    -0.03    0.10    0.000
 10    6.0    6.0    1.58     1.78    0.93   16.034
```

EXHIBIT **21.6C**
Scatterplot, Regression Line with
Case $(x = 6, y = 6)$
Removed and Original
Regression Line (solid line)

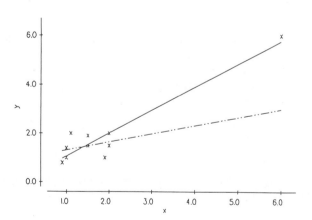

EXHIBIT **21.6D**
Regression Results for Data in
Exhibit 21.6C

```
The regression equation is

y = 0.981 + 0.331 x

Predictor       Coef      Stdev    t-ratio       p
Constant      0.9807     0.5337       1.84   0.109
x             0.3313     0.3569       0.93   0.384

s = 0.4570      R-sq = 11.0%      R-sq(adj) = 0.0%
```

How large might a leverage value be before a case is considered to have large influence? It may be shown algebraically that the average leverage over all cases is $(k + 1)/n$—that is,

$$\frac{1}{n} \sum_{i=1}^{n} h_{ii} = \frac{k + 1}{n} \qquad \textbf{(21.10)}$$

where k is the number of predictors in the model. On the basis of this result, many authors suggest marking cases as influential if their leverage exceeds two or three times $(k + 1)/n$. In Exhibit 21.6B, $k = 1$ and $n = 10$ so that $(k + 1)/n = 2/10 = 0.2$. Thus case 10 with $h_{10,10} = 0.93$ is quite influential according to this criterion.

E X A M P L E   **21.6A**

Returning to the property data, Exhibit 21.2A lists the leverage values for the simple straight-line regression of Market on Sq.ft. Here $k = 1, n = 60$, and $(k + 1)/n = 2/60 = 0.033$. Using $2(0.033) = 0.066$ and $3(0.033) = 0.099$ as guides, cases 1 and 58 should be considered influential and cases 59 and 60 very influential. When the quadratic model is used, the criteria are based on $(2 + 1)/60 = 0.05$. According to Exhibit 21.4F, cases 1, 2, and 3 exceed twice that amount and cases 59 and 60 exceed three times that amount.   ∎

Cook's Distance

As good as large leverage values are in detecting cases influential on the regression analysis, this criterion is not without its faults. Leverage values are completely determined by the values of the predictor variables and do not involve the response values at all. A data point that possesses large leverage but also lies close to the trend of the other data will not have undue influence on the regression results. Exhibits 21.6E and 21.6F give an example in which high leverage does *not* imply that an observation is truly influential in a regression analysis. Exhibit 21.6F shows a leverage value of 0.78 for case 10 with $x = 10$. However, as shown in Exhibit 21.6G and 21.6H, when the case with $x = 10$ is omitted from the data set, the regression results change very little. The fitted regression lines and the values of s are nearly the same with or without case 10. A better criterion for measuring influence would involve both the response and predictor values.

E X H I B I T 21.6E
Scatterplot and Regression Line:
Potential Influence of Case with
$x = 10$

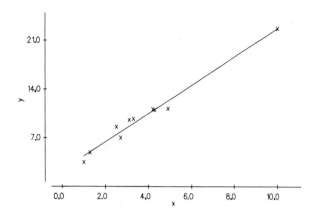

E X H I B I T 21.6F
Regression Results for the Data
in Exhibit 21.6E

The regression equation is

y = 2.33 + 2.04 x

Predictor	Coef	Stdev	t-ratio	p
Constant	2.3287	0.4740	4.91	0.000
x	2.0352	0.1068	19.05	0.000

s = 0.8118   R-sq = 97.8%   R-sq(adj) = 97.6%

Analysis of Variance

SOURCE	DF	SS	MS	F	p
Regression	1	239.16	239.16	362.88	0.000
Error	8	5.27	0.66		
Total	9	244.44			

Unusual Observations

Obs.	x	y	Fit	Stdev.Fit	Residual	St.Resid
10	10.0	22.700	22.681	0.717	0.019	0.05 X

X denotes an observation whose X value gives it large influence.

ROW	x	y	std res	t-resid	hii	CookD
1	1.0	3.5	-1.21	-1.25	0.23	0.218
2	1.3	4.9	-0.10	-0.10	0.20	0.001
3	2.5	8.6	1.56	1.75	0.13	0.176
4	2.7	7.0	-1.08	-1.09	0.12	0.078
5	3.1	9.5	1.12	1.15	0.11	0.076
6	3.3	9.7	0.85	0.84	0.10	0.042
7	4.2	11.1	0.29	0.27	0.10	0.005
8	4.3	11.0	-0.10	-0.10	0.11	0.001
9	4.9	11.2	-1.45	-1.58	0.12	0.148
10	10.0	22.7	0.05	0.05	0.78	0.005

Cook's distance

Several statistics have been proposed to better measure the influence of individual cases. One of the most popular is called **Cook's distance**, which is a measure of a data point's influence on regression results that considers both the predictor variables

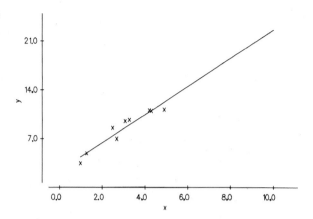

E X H I B I T   **21.6H**
Regression Results for Data in
Exhibit 21.6E with Case at
$x = 10$ Omitted

```
The regression equation is

y = 2.36 + 2.03 x

9 cases used: 1 case contained missing values

Predictor       Coef      Stdev     t-ratio        p
Constant      2.3557     0.7592        3.10    0.017
x             2.0256     0.2314        8.75    0.000

s = 0.8677      R-sq = 91.6%      R-sq(adj) = 90.4%
```

and the response variable.[†] The basic idea is to compare the predictions of the model when the ith case is and is not included in the calculations. In particular, Cook's distance, D_i, for the ith case is defined to be

$$D_i = \frac{\sum_{j=1}^{n}(\hat{y}_j - \hat{y}_{j(i)})^2}{(k+1)s^2} \tag{21.11}$$

where $\hat{y}_{j(i)}$ is the predicted or fitted value for case j using the regression curve obtained when case i is omitted.[‡] Large values of D_i indicate that case i has a great influence on the regression results, since then $\hat{y}_j$ and $\hat{y}_{j(i)}$ differ substantially for many cases. The deletion of a case with a large value of D_i will alter conclusions substantially. If D_i is not large, regression results will not change dramatically even if the leverage of the ith case is large.

[†]The statistic that later became known as Cook's distance was first proposed by R. D. Cook in "Detection of Influential Observations in Linear Regression." *Technometrics*, 19 (1977):15–18.

[‡]There are many relationships among the various diagnostic statistics that are useful for motivation or computation. An alternative form useful for computational purposes is

$$D_i = \frac{1}{(k+1)}\frac{\hat{e}_i^2}{s^2}\frac{h_{ii}}{(1-h_{ii})^2}$$

The data and analyses given in Exhibits 21.6E–H provide an example. Case 10 has already shown high leverage even though the results do not change much when that case is deleted. Exhibit 21.6F displays the values of Cook's distance for all cases. Case 10 should not be singled out as having a large value for D_{10}.

In contrast, return to the earlier data and analysis given in Exhibits 21.6A–D. Here case 10 had a substantial impact on the regression results and, indeed, the values of D_i listed in Exhibit 21.6B show a very large value for that influential case.

How do you decide when to consider D_i large? One interpretation of Cook's distance suggests using the F distribution. Some authors have suggested that cases with D_i larger than the median of an F distribution with $k + 1$ and $n - k - 1$ degrees of freedom should be investigated further with regard to their true influence on the regression analysis. With one predictor (and 2 numerator degrees of freedom), the median of the relevant F distribution ranges from 0.76 with 10 cases to 0.70 with 102 cases. With five predictors, the medians are 0.9 for typical sample sizes. In general, if the largest value of D_i is substantially less than 1, no cases are especially influential. On the other hand, cases with D_i greater than 1 should certainly be investigated further to more carefully assess their influence on the regression analysis results.

Several other alternative influence statistics have been studied recently, but most behave quite similarly to Cook's distance. They are discussed in more specialized books on regression analysis.

E X A M P L E   **21.6B**   Exhibit 21.6I gives the diagnostic statistics for the full model of the property data. Here Market was regressed on Sq.ft, Sq.ft.sq., Grade based on the indicator variables Med and Hi, and Assessed value. With respect to influence, cases 2 and 60 have the largest values of Cook's distance: 0.448 and 0.326, respectively. Neither value indicates excessive influence despite the high leverage value of 0.70 for case 60. However, the data should be investigated for possible outliers in cases 2 and 10 with studentized residuals (t-resids) of −3.55 and 3.35, respectively. Contrary to the conclusions with earlier simpler models, cases 59 and 60 do not appear to have unusual response values in this final model.   ▪

What is next once influential observations have been detected? If the influential observation is due to incorrect recording of the data point, an attempt to correct that observation should be made and the regression analysis rerun. If the data point is known to be faulty but cannot be corrected, that observation should be excluded from the data set. If it is determined that the influential data point is indeed accurate, it is likely that the proposed regression model is not appropriate for the problem at hand. Perhaps an important predictor variable has been neglected or the form of the regression curve is not adequate. The problem of selecting appropriate predictors is discussed in Chapter 22. Section 21.8 discusses transformations as a method to obtain better regression curves in some situations.

E X H I B I T **21.61** Diagnostic Statistics for the Full Regression Model of Market on Sq.ft, Sq.ft.sq, Med, Hi, and Assessed

ROW	Sq.ft	Market	Std Res	t-Resids	hii	CookD	ROW	Sq.ft	Market	Std Res	t-Resids	hii	CookD
1	521	26.0	1.61	1.64	0.23	0.127	31	926	37.4	-0.22	-0.22	0.05	0.000
2	538	19.4	-3.22	-3.55	0.21	0.448	32	931	38.0	-0.55	-0.55	0.03	0.001
3	544	25.2	-2.12	-2.20	0.19	0.174	33	965	37.2	-0.23	-0.23	0.09	0.001
4	577	26.2	-0.30	-0.29	0.13	0.002	34	966	44.0	1.02	1.02	0.05	0.009
5	661	31.0	0.58	0.57	0.11	0.007	35	967	44.2	1.42	1.44	0.03	0.010
6	662	34.6	0.72	0.71	0.10	0.009	36	1011	43.6	0.79	0.79	0.04	0.004
7	677	36.4	0.98	0.98	0.08	0.013	37	1011	38.4	-0.99	-0.99	0.03	0.005
8	691	33.0	1.17	1.17	0.10	0.024	38	1024	42.2	0.28	0.28	0.03	0.000
9	694	37.4	0.76	0.76	0.08	0.008	39	1033	40.4	-0.29	-0.29	0.03	0.000
10	712	42.4	3.07	3.35	0.06	0.107	40	1040	40.4	-0.09	-0.09	0.03	0.000
11	721	32.8	-0.69	-0.69	0.06	0.005	41	1047	43.6	0.44	0.43	0.05	0.002
12	722	25.6	-0.69	-0.69	0.16	0.016	42	1051	41.4	-0.11	-0.11	0.03	0.000
13	743	34.8	-0.51	-0.50	0.05	0.002	43	1052	39.6	-0.27	-0.27	0.04	0.001
14	760	35.8	-0.31	-0.30	0.05	0.001	44	1056	41.8	0.07	0.07	0.03	0.000
15	767	33.6	0.76	0.76	0.10	0.010	45	1060	44.8	0.57	0.56	0.28	0.021
16	780	31.0	-0.39	-0.39	0.10	0.003	46	1060	38.4	-1.07	-1.08	0.03	0.007
17	787	39.2	1.10	1.11	0.04	0.008	47	1070	43.6	0.92	0.92	0.04	0.005
18	802	36.0	-0.47	-0.46	0.04	0.001	48	1075	42.8	-0.04	-0.03	0.05	0.000
19	814	34.8	-0.12	-0.12	0.09	0.000	49	1079	40.6	-0.36	-0.36	0.03	0.001
20	815	34.4	-0.25	-0.25	0.09	0.001	50	1100	41.6	-0.57	-0.57	0.05	0.003
21	825	38.0	-0.13	-0.13	0.04	0.000	51	1106	42.8	-0.28	-0.28	0.07	0.001
22	834	34.6	0.97	0.97	0.10	0.017	52	1138	39.0	-1.33	-1.34	0.04	0.012
23	838	35.6	-0.90	-0.90	0.03	0.004	53	1164	41.8	-1.26	-1.27	0.27	0.096
24	858	35.8	0.88	0.88	0.11	0.017	54	1171	48.4	1.55	1.57	0.08	0.033
25	883	39.6	0.26	0.25	0.03	0.000	55	1237	39.8	-0.67	-0.67	0.10	0.008
26	890	35.0	-1.04	-1.05	0.04	0.007	56	1249	47.2	1.70	1.73	0.06	0.033
27	899	37.6	-0.38	-0.38	0.03	0.001	57	1298	45.2	0.31	0.31	0.27	0.006
28	918	41.2	0.09	0.09	0.07	0.000	58	1435	38.8	-1.83	-1.87	0.14	0.088
29	920	31.2	-1.22	-1.22	0.12	0.035	59	1602	47.4	0.42	0.41	0.36	0.016
30	923	30.0	-0.31	-0.31	0.25	0.006	60	1804	45.4	0.91	0.91	0.70	0.326

S E C T I O N

21.7 Exercises

21.7A Calculate and examine the leverage values and Cook's distances for the regression of average girl's height in terms of age. The data are given in Exercise 7.7D. Are any outliers apparent from either of these diagnostic statistics? If so, what do they suggest about the model? (Filename: AGEHGT_G.DAT.)

21.7B Calculate and examine the leverage values and Cook's distances for the regression of actual capacity of ice chests in terms of stated capacity. The data appear in Exercise 20.7I. Are any outliers indicated from these statistics? (Filename: COOLERS.DAT.)

21.7C The data in Exercise 20.9B gave house prices and several predictor variables. Consider the regression of house price in terms of taxes, number of baths, and square feet. Find the leverage values and Cook's distances for this model. Do these statistics indicate any outliers in this regression? (Filename: HOUSEPRI.DAT.)

21.7D Exercise 20.9D gave data on Crest toothpaste sales and several potential predictors. For the model that uses advertising dollars, advertising ratio, and personal disposable income to predict sales, calculate the leverage values and Cook's distances. Are any of these leverage values or Cook's distance values exceptionally large? (Filename: CREST.DAT.)

21.8   Transformations

So far, we have discussed a variety of methods for detecting the failure of some of the underlying assumptions of regression analysis. Transformations of the response and/or the predictor variables provide a powerful method of turning marginally useful regression models into valuable ones, with more credible assumptions and therefore more reliable predictions. Some of the most common and useful transformations are logarithms, square roots, and reciprocals. Careful consideration of these and other possible transformations for data can clarify and simplify the structure of relationships among variables. This section shows how transformations can lessen problems of varying standard deviations, curved relationships, and nonnormal error terms.

Sometimes transformations occur "naturally" in the ordinary reporting of data. As an example, consider a bicycle computer that displays, among other things, the current speed of the bicycle in miles per hour. What is really measured is the time it takes for each revolution of the wheel. Since the exact circumference of the tire is stored in the computer, the reported speed is calculated as a constant divided by the measured time per revolution of the wheel. The speed reported is basically a reciprocal transformation of the measured variable.

As a second example, consider gasoline consumption in a car. Usually these values are reported in miles per gallon. However, they are obtained by measuring the fuel consumption on a test drive of fixed distance. Miles per gallon are then calculated by computing the reciprocal of the gallons per mile figure. *Consumer Reports* specifically states,

> We take each group of vehicles on a 195-mile "open-road" trip. . . . The trip consists of circuits on a 33-mile loop of road. . . . A precision gauge monitors fuel consumption during the 195-mile trip, again at a steady 55 mph on an interstate highway, and finally on a one-mile circuit that simulates city driving.[†]

Many more commonplace uses of transformations are described by David Hoaglin.[‡]

Nonconstant Standard Deviation

In Exhibit 21.2E, the plot of residuals versus fitted values suggested that the variability in the response was not constant over different values of the predictor variables. This plot is based on the multiple regression of city miles per gallon values for 45 cars on weight and transmission type (automatic = 1, manual = 0) of the car. The data, listed in Exhibit 21.8A, are part of a much larger set of variables considered in Chapter 22.

Exhibit 21.8B gives the scatterplot of city miles per gallon versus weight. The binary predictor variable transmission type is indicated by using A as the plotting

---

[†]Copyright 1989 by Consumers Union of United States, Inc., Mount Vernon, NY 10533. Reprinted by permission from CONSUMER REPORTS, April 1989.

[‡]David C. Hoaglin, "Transformations in Everyday Experience," *Chance*, 1 (1988), 40–45.

```
filename: CARS1.DAT
Car data from Consumer Reports, 1987-1988
Variables: city MPG, weight and
transmission type (1=automatic, 0=manual)
22  2365  0  Acura Integra RS        21  2695  0  Ford Probe
22  2430  0  Toyota Corolla FX16     18  2885  0  Dodge Daytona
29  1895  0  Honda Civic 2dr         13  3310  1  Ford Mustang LX
21  2320  1  Chevrolet Nova          13  3430  1  Chevy Camaro RS
18  2330  1  Mercury Tracer          18  2670  1  Plymouth Sundance
20  2255  1  Plymouth Colt           19  2925  1  Toyota Camry LE
18  2350  1  Pontiac Le Mans         16  2735  1  Pontiac Grand AM LE
28  1635  0  Ford Festiva            15  3155  1  Ford Taurus
24  2070  0  Mazda 323               16  2995  1  Eagle Premier
22  2115  0  Mitsubishi Precis       15  3150  1  Dodge Dynasty
23  1840  0  Yugo GVS                16  2950  1  Buick Century
27  1970  0  Toyota Tercel           15  3295  1  Mercury Cougar
31  1575  0  Chevrolet Sprint        16  2915  1  Chrysler Le Baron Coupe
24  2185  0  Hyundai Excel           16  3220  1  Buick Regal Coupe
24  2115  0  VW Fox                  16  2900  1  Chrysler New Yorker Turbo
16  3040  1  Mazda 626 4ws turbo     15  3205  1  Toyota Camry wagon
19  2620  1  Audi 80                 16  2930  1  Eagle Medallion wagon
14  3230  1  Mitsubishi Galant Sigma 14  3320  1  Nissan Maxima wagon
18  2745  1  Mitsubishi Galant       16  3080  1  Volvo 240 wagon
17  2573  1  Peugeot 405 DL          13  3625  1  Plymouth Gran Voyager
17  2802  1  Ford Tempo GLS          12  3665  1  Ford Aerostar
18  2699  1  Chevrolet Corsica LT    13  3625  1  Nissan GXE van
                                     14  3415  1  Mitsubishi van
```

symbol for the cars with automatic transmissions and M for those with manual transmissions. The lack of a constant standard deviation for different levels of predictors is only barely perceptible in this plot. The residual plot of Exhibit 21.2E is much clearer in this regard.

E X H I B I T **21.8B**
Scatterplot of City MPG Versus
Weight and Transmission Type

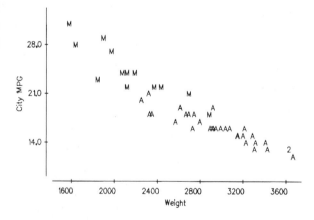

As noted above, miles per gallon is not necessarily the most natural way to measure gasoline consumption. It would be just as easy to go back to the original data of gallons per mile by taking reciprocals of the reported miles per gallon (MPG) figures. Exhibit 21.8C shows the scatterplot of gallons per mile (GPM) versus the

E X H I B I T **21.8C**
Scatterplot of City GPM Versus
Weight and Transmission Type

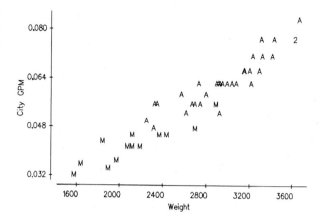

weight of the cars, with transmission type again indicated by the plotting symbols A and M. Comparing this display to that given in Exhibit 21.8B shows that the situation of nonconstant standard deviation is improved. The residual plot for this regression, shown in Exhibit 21.8D, presents the situation quite clearly. Here there are no striking difficulties with the assumption of constant variability over the full range of cases. This residual plot should be compared to the corresponding plot in Exhibit 21.2E, which uses the original response of miles per gallon.

E X H I B I T **21.8D**
Residual Plot of City GPM
Regressed on Weight and
Transmission Type

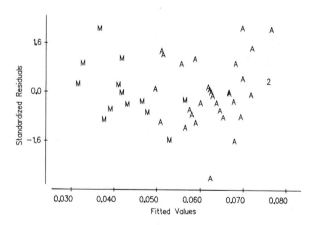

logarithm transformation

Another common transformation is the **logarithm transformation**. It may be shown that a logarithm transformation will tend to correct the common problem of nonconstant standard deviation if the standard deviation of e_i is proportional to the mean of y_i. If the mean of y doubles, so does the standard deviation of e, and so forth. Exhibit 21.8E gives an example where a log transformation is warranted.

E X H I B I T **21.8E**

Monthly Sales of Winnebago
Recreational
Vehicles—November
1966–February 1972

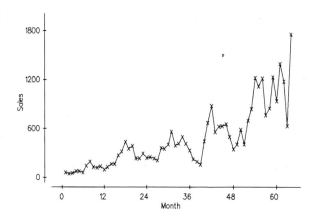

E X A M P L E **21.8A**

Winnebago Industries, Inc., of Forest City, Iowa, is a widely known maker of recreational vehicles. From 1966 to 1972, Winnebago experienced a tremendous growth in sales. The data are listed in Exercise 23B and are available in data file WINNEBAG.DAT. Exhibit 21.8E displays a sequence plot of the monthly sales from November 1966 through February 1972. The sequence plot also clearly shows the greater monthly variation in sales values as the general level of the series increases. However, the sequence plot of the logarithm of sales shown in Exhibit 21.8F shows a much more equal monthly variability for high and low levels of log sales. This example and many others where logarithms are helpful will be referred to in the discussion of time series models in Chapters 23 and 24. ∎

E X H I B I T **21.8F**

Sequence Plot of Logarithm of
Monthly Winnebago
Sales—November
1966–February 1972

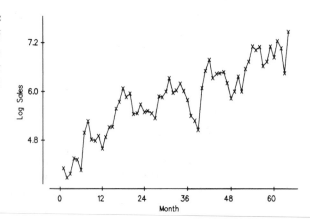

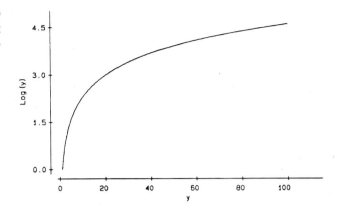

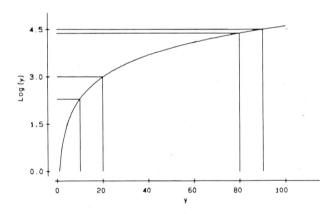

The natural logarithm curve for values of y from 1 to 100 is displayed in Exhibit 21.8G. Notice how the rate of increase in the curve gets less and less as y gets larger and larger. This effect is what allows the log transformation to correct the problem of increasing standard deviation with increasing mean y. Exhibit 21.8H shows the same log curve with lines indicating the effect of certain changes in y. Note that when y changes 10 units from 10 to 20, the change in $\log(y)$ is much larger than when y changes 10 units from 80 to 90. This is a clear demonstration of why the log transformation works so well to equalize variability that increases with the mean of y.

In general, the power (or **Box-Cox transformation** defined as

power (Box-Cox) transformation

$$y = x^{\lambda} \tag{21.12}$$

for some choice of constant power λ, is quite useful in statistical practice. It is known as the Box-Cox transformation because of the important work of George Box and David Cox.[†] Notice that $\lambda = -1$ corresponds to the reciprocal transformation, $\lambda = 0.5$ is the square root transformation, and $\lambda = 2$ provides the square transformation. Putting Equation (21.12) into a slightly different but equivalent form, one can argue that the logarithm transformation is obtained as the limiting transformation when λ tends to zero. Usually it suffices to proceed by trial and error and consider the effects of each of the transformations defined by powers of $-1, -0.5, -0.25, 0, 0.25, 0.5, 1,$ and 2 where $\lambda = 0$ is interpreted as the log transformation. As already seen, sometimes these power transformations have intuitive appeal in addition to their empirical justification.

Nonlinearity

Transformations are also quite useful in turning curved relationships into simple straight-line relationships.

One example is exponential growth or exponential decay models, where a response y is related to a predictor x by the equation

$$y = c_1 e^{c_2 x} \qquad (21.13)$$

exponential growth
exponential decay

where c_1 and c_2 are constants and e is the base for the natural logarithms. Equation (21.13) describes **exponential growth** when c_2 is positive, and **exponential decay** when it is negative. As an example of exponential growth, this equation describes the growth of a savings account with initial value c_1, rate of interest c_2 per time unit, continuous compounding for x time units, and no additional deposits to the account over the time period considered. Exhibit 21.8I shows graphs of both exponential growth and exponential decay using as examples the curves $y = 10e^{0.2x}$ and $y = 50e^{-0.5x}$.

In statistical applications, Equation (21.13) represents the mean of response y for a predictor with value x, and the constants c_1 and c_2 are unknown parameters to be estimated from observed data. If the statistical errors are added to Equation (21.13), the resulting model is *not* linear in the parameters. However, taking natural logarithms of both sides of the equation and recalling the laws for logarithms and exponents yields

$$\log(y) = \log(c_1) + c_2 x \qquad (21.14)$$

[†] George E. P. Box and David R. Cox, "An Analysis of Transformations," *Journal of the Royal Statistical Society*, B(26)(1964), 211–243. The form

$$y = \frac{x^\lambda - 1}{\lambda}$$

produces $\log(y)$ as $\lambda \to 0$.

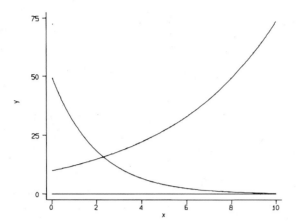

Exhibit 21.8J shows the graph of $\log(y)$ versus x for the curves displayed in Exhibit 21.8I. This is the same as plotting the functions used in Exhibit 21.8I on a log scale. The log transformation straightens out the exponential curves perfectly.

Assuming that for the relationship defined by Equation (21.14) the errors are additive, and reverting to the standard notation for parameters, the result is the model

$$\log(y_i) = \beta_0 + \beta_1 x_i + e_i \tag{21.15}$$

The parameters β_0 and β_1 could then be estimated by regressing $\log(y)$ on x. Note that additive errors in the $\log(y)$ model translate back to *multiplicative* errors in the original relationship.

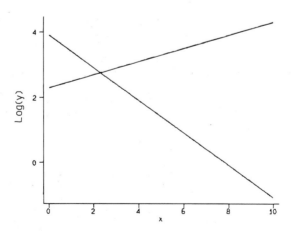

EXAMPLE 21.8B

In economic analysis, a common model relating quantity produced, Q, to capital, C, and labor, L, input to a system is the *Cobb-Douglas production function*

$$Q = \alpha C^{\beta_1} L^{\beta_2} \tag{21.16}$$

where α, β_1, and β_2 are parameters. Again, this is nonlinear in the parameters, but taking logs and then assuming an additive error term produces the multiple linear regression model

$$\log(Q) = \beta_0 + \beta_1 \log(C) + \beta_2 \log(L) + e \tag{21.17}$$

with response $\log(Q)$ regressed on the predictors $\log(C)$ and $\log(L)$.[†] ∎

EXAMPLE 21.8C

Some other applications suggest "diminishing returns" such as depicted in Exhibit 21.8K. Here the curve $y = x/(1 + 0.5x)$ has been plotted.

Exhibit 21.8L shows, however, that a straight line is obtained if for the same function displayed in Exhibit 21.8K, $1/y$ versus $1/x$ is graphed. In general, the curve $y = x/(c_1 + c_2 x)$ may be straightened by taking reciprocals of both sides of the equation to obtain

$$\frac{1}{y} = \frac{c_1 + c_2 x}{x} = c_2 + c_1 \left(\frac{1}{x}\right) \tag{21.18}$$

That is, in the reciprocals of y and x there is a straight line with slope c_1 and intercept c_2. Again assuming that additive errors apply to the relationship defined by Equation (21.18), the reciprocal of y would be regressed on the

EXHIBIT **21.8K**
A Hyperbolic Curve:
$y = x/(1 + 0.5x)$

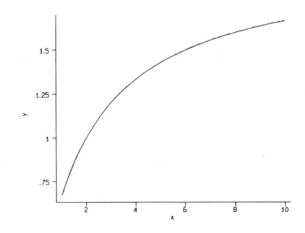

[†]In economics, β_1 is called the *capital elasticity* and β_2 is the *labor elasticity*.

E X H I B I T   **21.8L**
1/y Versus 1/x from
Exhibit 21.8K

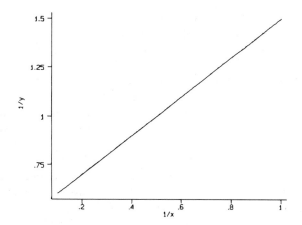

reciprocal of x to obtain estimates of the unknown parameters. The regression assumptions in the transformed variables would then be further assessed.   ▪

Exhibit 21.8M summarizes some of the common transformations that simplify a variety of curved relationships found in practice. Be aware that not all relationships can be made even approximately linear by transformation. For example, if β_0, β_1, and β_2 are unknown, the function $y = \beta_0 + \beta_1 e^{\beta_2 x}$ cannot be transformed so that it is linear in the parameters. If such a curve must be fit to data, more advanced techniques in nonlinear regression analysis are used. Also keep in mind that the error terms are always assumed to be additive in the final transformed model—not in the original model. In the case study in Section 21.10, and in Chapter 22, several transformations are illustrated.

E X H I B I T   **21.8M**
Linearizing Transformations

Transformation	Original Relationship	Transformed Relationship	
$\log(y),\ x$	$y = c_1 e^{c_2 x}$	$\log(y) = \beta_0 + \beta_1 x$	$(\beta_0 = \log c_1, \beta_1 = c_2)$
$\log(y),\ \log x$	$y = c_1 x^{c_2}$	$\log(y) = \beta_0 + \beta_1 \log(x)$	$(\beta_0 = \log c_1, \beta_1 = c_2)$
$\dfrac{1}{y}, \dfrac{1}{x}$	$y = \dfrac{x}{c_1 + c_2 x}$	$\dfrac{1}{y} = \beta_0 + \beta_1 \left(\dfrac{1}{x}\right)$	$(\beta_0 = c_2, \qquad \beta_1 = c_1)$

Nonnormality of Error Terms

In the regression context, the assumption of normal distributions for the error terms justifies the use of t and F distributions for the significance tests and confidence intervals that were discussed in Chapter 20. Normality of the errors is also required for the proper interpretation of prediction intervals. However, the ordinary least-squares estimates of the regression parameters, $\beta_0, \beta_1, \ldots, \beta_k$, are usually quite reasonable regardless of normality *as long as there are no outliers in the data set.* As mentioned earlier in this chapter, outliers must be detected and dealt with if the regression analysis is to be meaningful.

Normality of the error terms is studied by looking at the distribution of the residuals or standardized residuals using any or all of the following tools: histograms, dotplots, stem-and-leaf diagrams, or normal scores plots. Recall from Chapter 9 that normal scores or normal probability plots are the easiest to consider, since we then need only to compare the plot to a straight line to "test" for normality. Also, specific departures from a straight line depict certain specific characteristics in the error distribution. Exhibit 21.8N shows several possible departures and their implications. A heavy-tailed error distribution means that more extreme values (both large and small) than would be expected in a normal distribution are present. This can be especially bothersome because it may indicate outliers in the data set. Light-tailed distributions, on the other hand, have fewer extreme values than a normal distribution.

Fortunately, in many practical analyses a transformation can be found that will improve many, if not all, of the problems of nonlinearity of the relationship, lack of constant standard deviation, and lack of normality of the error terms simultaneously! The case study in Section 21.10 illustrates the value of transformation in regression modeling.

E X H I B I T **21.8N** Normal Scores Plots and Their Interpretation

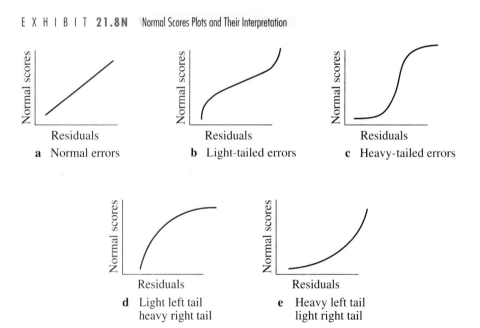

a Normal errors

b Light-tailed errors

c Heavy-tailed errors

d Light left tail
heavy right tail

e Heavy left tail
light right tail

SECTION

21.9 Exercises

21.9A Review the regression of actual ice chest values in terms of their stated values. The data are given in Exercise 20.7I. The scatterplot of standardized residuals versus fitted values indicated that somewhat larger variability appears with residuals that correspond to larger fitted values.

a Transform both the actual and stated values using their reciprocals. Display the scatterplot of these transformed values and interpret.

b Perform the regression of 1/actual in terms of 1/stated. Compare the results to those obtained in Exercise 20.7I where the model was actual in terms of stated. In particular, consider the plot of standardized residuals versus fitted values. (Filename: COOLERS.DAT.)

21.9B Consider the real estate data that first appeared in Exhibit 6.2A. Curvature was noticed in the scatterplot of market versus square feet in Exhibit 6.2C. The curvature was modeled earlier using square feet squared as an additional predictor. Consider some alternative methods based on transformations.

a Plot market against the logarithm of square feet. Does this transformation of the predictor help straighten the relationship?

b Plot market against the reciprocal of square feet. Does this transformation of the predictor improve the linearity of the relationship?

c Compare four models: market versus square feet, market versus square feet and square feet squared, market versus log(Sq.ft), and market versus 1/Sq.ft. Compare residual standard deviations, R-squared values, residual versus fitted plots, leverage values, and Cook's distance.

d Now consider a multiple regression model that models Market in terms of 1/Sq.ft, Med, Hi, and Assessed. Compare the results of this model to those shown in Exhibit 20.8B. (Filename: REALPROP.DAT.)

21.9C The data below report three variables: Expressway MPG, Weight, and Number of transmission gears for the same 45 cars reported in Exhibit 21.8A.

a Prepare a scatterplot of Expressway MPG against weight. Does the plot suggest a linear model or should a transformation be considered?

b Plot Expressway GPM against Weight. Does a straight-line model seem more tenable in these terms?

c Fit a model that predicts Expressway GPM in terms of Weight and Number of transmission gears. Are the regression coefficients significantly different from zero for both predictors?

d Plot the residuals versus the fitted values for the model in part (c). Would the plot be best described as random scatter?

e Plot the residuals versus each of the predictor variables Weight and Number of transmission gears. Would each of these plots be best described as random scatter?

f Display a normal scores plot for the residuals from the model in part (c). Does the plot support the normality assumption for the error terms?

EXHIBIT **21.9A**

```
filename: CARS2.DAT
Car data from Consumer Reports, 1987-1988
Variables: expressway MPG, weight, and
number of transmission gears
36  2365  5  Acura Integra RS
38  2430  5  Toyota Corolla FX16
51  1895  4  Honda Civic 2dr
38  2320  3  Chevrolet Nova
35  2330  3  Mercury Tracer
36  2255  3  Plymouth Colt
43  2350  3  Pontiac Le Mans
47  1635  4  Ford Festiva
38  2070  4  Mazda 323
39  2115  4  Mitsubishi Precis
39  1840  4  Yugo GVS
49  1970  4  Toyota Tercel
58  1575  5  Chevrolet Sprint
41  2185  4  Hundai Excel
41  2115  4  VW Fox
35  3040  4  Mazda 626 4ws turbo
35  2620  3  Audi 80
29  3230  4  Mitsubishi Galant Sigma
35  2745  4  Mitsubishi Galant
32  2573  4  Peugeot 405 DL
32  2802  3  Ford Tempo GLS
39  2699  3  Chevrolet Corsica LT
43  2695  5  Ford Probe
43  2885  5  Dodge Daytona
28  3310  4  Ford Mustang LX
32  3430  4  Chevy Camaro RS
34  2670  3  Plymouth Sundance
44  2925  4  Toyota Camry LE
36  2735  3  Pontiac Grand AM LE
37  3155  4  Ford Taurus
36  2995  4  Eagle Premier
34  3150  3  Dodge Dynasty
33  2950  3  Buick Century
33  3295  4  Mercury Cougar
34  2915  3  Chrysler Le Baron Coupe
37  3220  4  Buick Regal Coupe
31  2900  3  Chrysler New Yorker Turbo
33  3205  4  Toyota Camry wagon
30  2930  3  Eagle Medallion wagon
31  3320  4  Nissan Maxima wagon
31  3080  4  Volvo 240 wagon
28  3625  3  Plymouth Gran Voyager
28  3665  4  Ford Aerostar
27  3625  4  Nissan GXE van
27  3415  4  Mitsubishi van
```

21.9D Consider the data set of average girls' height by age given in Exercise 7.7D.

a Transform both height and age using logarithms. Plot log(height) versus log(age) and describe the plot. Would a straight-line model seem appropriate in these terms?

b Fit a linear model that predicts log(height) with log(age) and test the significance of the model using the F ratio.

c For the model estimated in part (b), plot the residuals against the fitted values and comment on the plot. (Filename: AGEHGT_G.DAT.)

21.9E Example 7.6C introduced data on the aluminum concentration of the forest floor at various distances from an aluminum reduction plant. Neither the straight-line model (Exhibit 7.6E) nor the quadratic model (Exhibit 8.2E) were acceptable for these data. Let y be the aluminum concentration and let x be the distance from the plant. (Filename: LITTER.DAT.)

a Construct the scatterplot of y versus $1/x^2$.

b Based on the plot in part (a), would you recommend trying the model $y = \beta_0 + \beta_1(1/x^2)$?

c Display the scatterplot of y versus $1/\log(x)$.

  d   Comment on the plot in part (c).

  e   Use least squares to fit the model $y = \beta_0 + \beta_1(1/\log(x))$.

  f   Interpret the estimate of β_1 from part (e).

  g   Assess the significance of the estimate of β_1 from part (e).

  h   Which of the two models considered in (b) and (e) do you prefer? Why?

SECTION

21.10   A Case Study—Gender Discrimination in the Workplace?

Salary discrimination on the basis of gender, whether overt or otherwise, is a serious problem in our society. It is also illegal. However, detecting and measuring it are not easy. Even in entry-level jobs, many valid factors other than gender may and should be considered in setting salaries. In 1978, a discrimination lawsuit was brought against the Harris Bank of Chicago. As a result of this suit the data in Exhibit 21.10A were made public by the defense statisticians.[†] The data give beginning salaries together with several valid measures of job qualifications, such as education level and previous

EXHIBIT **21.10A**   Salary Data from the Harris Bank of Chicago—1970

Salary data from J. Bus. & Econ. Stats, Oct. 1987
Variables: beginning salary, years of education
previous experience (in months)
time of hire (months after Jan. 1, 1969)
gender (1=female, 0=male)

Salary	Educ	Exper	Hire	Gen		Salary	Educ	Exper	Hire	Gen		Salary	Educ	Exper	Hire	Gen
3900	12	0.0	1	1		5220	12	127.0	29	1		5040	15	14.0	3	0
4020	10	44.0	7	1		5280	8	90.0	11	1		5100	12	180.0	15	0
4290	12	5.0	30	1		5280	8	190.0	1	1		5100	12	315.0	2	0
4380	8	6.2	7	1		5280	12	107.0	11	1		5220	12	29.0	14	0
4380	8	7.5	6	1		5400	8	173.0	34	1		5400	12	7.0	21	0
4380	12	0.0	7	1		5400	8	228.0	33	1		5400	12	38.0	11	0
4380	12	0.0	10	1		5400	12	26.0	11	1		5400	12	113.0	3	0
4380	12	4.5	6	1		5400	12	26.0	33	1		5400	15	17.5	8	0
4440	15	75.0	2	1		5400	12	38.0	22	1		5400	15	359.0	11	0
4500	8	52.0	3	1		5400	12	82.0	29	1		5700	15	36.0	5	0
4500	12	8.0	19	1		5400	12	169.0	27	1		6000	8	320.0	21	0
4620	12	52.0	3	1		5400	12	244.0	1	1		6000	12	24.0	2	0
4800	8	70.0	20	1		5400	15	24.0	13	1		6000	12	32.0	17	0
4800	12	6.0	23	1		5400	15	49.0	27	1		6000	12	49.0	8	0
4800	12	11.0	12	1		5400	15	51.0	21	1		6000	12	56.0	33	0
4800	12	11.0	17	1		5400	15	122.0	33	1		6000	12	252.0	11	0
4800	12	63.0	22	1		5520	12	97.0	17	1		6000	12	272.0	19	0
4800	12	144.0	24	1		5520	12	196.0	32	1		6000	15	25.0	13	0
4800	12	163.0	12	1		5580	12	132.5	30	1		6000	15	35.5	32	0
4800	12	228.0	26	1		5640	12	55.0	9	1		6000	15	56.0	12	0
4800	12	381.0	1	1		5700	12	90.0	23	1		6000	15	64.0	33	0
4800	16	214.0	15	1		5700	12	116.5	25	1		6000	15	108.0	16	0
4980	8	318.0	25	1		5700	15	51.0	17	1		6300	16	45.5	3	0
5100	8	96.0	33	1		5700	15	61.0	11	1		6300	15	72.0	17	0
5100	12	36.0	15	1		5700	15	241.0	34	1		6600	15	64.0	16	0
5100	12	29.0	14	1		6000	12	121.0	30	1		6600	15	84.0	33	0
5100	15	115.0	1	1		6000	15	78.5	13	1		6600	15	215.5	16	0
5100	15	165.0	4	1		6120	12	208.5	21	1		6840	15	41.5	7	0
5100	16	123.0	12	1		6300	12	86.5	33	1		6900	12	175.0	10	0
5160	12	18.0	12	1		6300	15	231.0	15	1		6900	15	132.0	24	0
5220	8	102.0	29	1		4620	12	11.5	22	0		8100	16	54.5	33	0

[†] H. V. Roberts, *Harris Trust and Savings Bank: An Analysis of Employee Compensation.* Report 7946, CMSBE, Graduate School of Business. University of Chicago, 1979. A discussion of the relevant issues can be found in A. P. Dempster, "Employment Discrimination and Statistical Science," *Statistical Science,* 3(2)(1988), 149–195.

experience, for 61 female and 32 male "skilled entry-level" clerical employees. In this case study, the beginning salaries for males and females will be compared after taking individual qualifications into account. If after adjusting for these valid qualifications there is still a real difference between the beginning salaries for males and females, gender discrimination may justifiably be claimed.[†]

Transformations of Response and Predictor Variables

Variables available as predictors of beginning salaries were years of education at the time of hiring, years of previous work experience, and time of hire. All of these employees were hired between 1969 and 1971. To account for the general effect of beginning salaries increasing over this two-year period (inflation), a time variable measured as month of hire since January 1, 1969, was also included as a predictor. Exhibit 21.10B gives some basic descriptive statistics of the various variables. Notice that mean beginning salaries for women were lower than those for men, but that the men had higher mean years of education and months of experience. Also, most of the employees' education had spanned either 8, 12, or 15 years.

E X H I B I T **21.10B**
Descriptive Statistics of Salary Variables by Gender (1 = female, 0 = male)

	Gender	N	Mean	Median	Standard Deviation
Salary	0	32	5957	6000	691
	1	61	5139	5220	540
Education (years)	0	32	13.5	15	1.9
	1	61	12.0	12	2.3
Experience (months)	0	32	103	56	102
	1	61	99	82	86
Time of hire	0	32	15	14.5	9.7
	1	61	17	17.0	10.5

Education	Count
8	12
10	1
12	49
15	27
16	4
(N=93)	

How should salaries depend on variables such as amount of education, experience, and time of hire? Most would agree that an additional year of education might be reflected in a percentage increase in beginning salary. Similarly, an additional year of experience would lead, up to a point, to another percentage increase. For these reasons, it is quite natural to use a log transformation on salary before beginning the regression analysis. Thus the response is log(salary).

[†] Daniel W. Schafer, "Measurement-Error Diagnostic and the Sex Discrimination Problem," *Journal of Business and Economic Statistics*, 5(4) (1987), 529–537.

Exhibit 21.10C shows the scatterplot of log(salary) versus education. There is a slight upward trend, and no compelling reason to rule out a linear trend is observed. Similarly, Exhibit 21.10D displays the relationship between log(salary) and time of hire. A slow upward drift of salaries over the 35-month study period is discernible in the plot.

EXHIBIT **21.10C**
Scatterplot of Log(Salary)
Versus Education

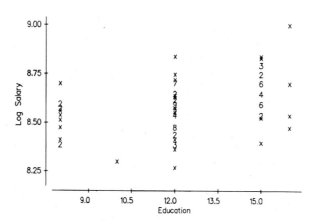

EXHIBIT **21.10D**
Scatterplot of Log(Salary)
Versus Time of Hire

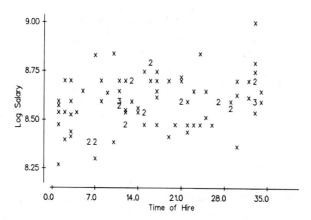

Finally, Exhibit 21.10E gives the scatterplot of log(salary) against experience. Males and females are distinguished with appropriate plotting symbols. Notice that at all experience levels the males generally have the higher log salaries and thus higher salaries. This plot does not reveal the effect of the other predictors, however, so the full regression analysis must be done.

Since only entry-level jobs are being considered, there is an effect of diminishing returns in the relationship of experience on beginning salary. From Exhibit 21.10E,

E X H I B I T   **21.10E**
Scatterplot of Log(Salary)
Versus Experience with Gender
Indicated

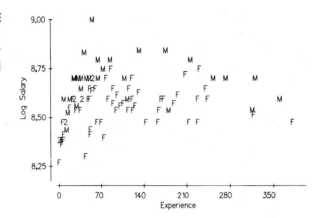

there is an evident increase of beginning (log) salaries up to about 70 or 80 months of prior experience. But then the relationship seems to level off. For an entry-level position, very large amounts of experience do not correspond to large beginning salaries. One approach to modeling this relationship would be to use a quadratic curve in the experience variable, as was done in Chapter 8 with the square footage variable. However, other viable possibilities include using logs or reciprocals of the experience variable.

Trying to take logs of the experience variable results in an immediate problem. It is not possible to take the logarithm of zero! A similar difficulty arises when trying to calculate the reciprocal of zero. When zero occurs as a predictor value it is customary to add a small constant to all of the values before taking logs or reciprocals. What value should be added? The goal is to produce a relationship between log(salary) and a transformed experience variable that is reasonably modeled by a straight line. With a computer, it is easy to try several different transformations and compare the results. For this data set, 1, 6, and 12 months were added before taking both logs and reciprocals. A quadratic function of experience was also tried. In each case, the resulting regression equation and the significance of the regression coefficients were considered. The adequacy of the model with respect to model assumptions through diagnostics was also considered. Although the regression results were not very different, the reciprocal of (experience + 12 months) was finally chosen because it produced the best model with respect to nearly all criteria. Exhibit 21.10F gives the scatterplot of log(salary) versus this transformed predictor. Now the relationship is approximately linear but with plenty of scatter. Note that since 75 months of experience transforms into a value of $1/(75 + 12) = 1/87 = 0.0115$, all the people with 75 or more months of experience are grouped together with transformed predictors between 0 and 0.0115. Thus this transformation achieves the desired effect.

Regression Calculations

The regression of log(salary) can now be done using the predictor variables: education, time, 1/(experience + 12), and gender. If the model explains a large portion of the

E X H I B I T **21.10F**
Scatterplot of Log(Salary)
Versus 1/(Experience + 12)
with Gender Indicated

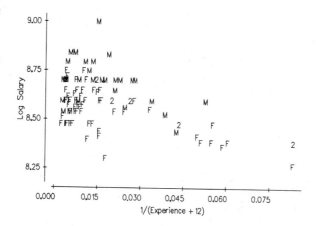

variation in beginning salaries and if gender discrimination has not taken place, it would be expected that the regression coefficient associated with gender would not be significantly different from zero. On the other hand, if that coefficient is significant (and if subsequent analysis reveals a good model), the model suggests that gender discrimination has occurred in setting beginning salaries. Exhibit 21.10G displays the initial regression results for this data set. All the regression coefficients are significantly different from zero with t statistics (t ratios) greater than 3 and p-values 0.001 or smaller. An R^2 of 62.5% indicates that a substantial portion of the variation in beginning salaries is explained by these predictors. The regression coefficient associated with gender is -0.123 with a corresponding t ratio of -6.54, indicating a real effect of gender on beginning salaries even after allowing for the

E X H I B I T **21.10G**
Regression of Log(Salary) on
Education, Time, 1/(Experience
+ 12) and Gender

```
The regression equation is

Log(Salary)=8.49+0.0138Educa.+0.00336Time-2.70(1/(Exp+12))-0.123Gender

Predictor        Coef        Stdev      t-ratio         p
Constant      8.49315      0.05840      145.44      0.000
Educa.        0.013757     0.003922       3.51      0.001
Time          0.0033629    0.0008507      3.95      0.000
1/(Exp+12)   -2.7045       0.4661        -5.80      0.000
Gender       -0.12318      0.01883       -6.54      0.000

s = 0.08093      R-sq = 62.5%      R-sq(adj) = 60.8%

Analysis of Variance

SOURCE        DF         SS          MS         F          p
Regression     4      0.95966     0.23991     36.63      0.000
Error         88      0.57638     0.00655
Total         92      1.53604

Unusual Observations
Obs.   Educa.  Log(Salary)    Fit  Stdev.Fit  Residual   St.Resid
  2     10.0     8.29904    8.48278   0.01606   -0.18374    -2.32R
 62     12.0     8.43815    8.61712   0.02095   -0.17897    -2.29R
 91     12.0     8.83928    8.67739   0.01750    0.16189     2.05R
 93     16.0     8.99962    8.78356   0.02305    0.21606     2.79R

R denotes an observation with a large St. Resid.
```

effect of education, experience, and time of hire (inflation). Since the coding of the binary gender variable is female $= 1$ and male $= 0$, the regression coefficient of -0.123 corresponds to reduced log(salary) for females of -0.123, all other qualifications (as measured by education, experience, and time of hire) being equal. In original salary terms, this corresponds to a factor of $e^{-0.123} = 0.88$. Thus salaries for females are generally only 88% of the salaries of males with comparable qualifications.

Diagnostics

The discussion in the preceding paragraph assumes that the model assumptions are satisfied at least approximately. Model diagnostics are used to check this out. Exhibit 21.10H shows the scatterplot of standardized residuals against fitted values. No obvious difficulties are revealed in this display. With the exception of the smallest fitted values, the variability appears to be quite similar across all levels of fitted values. Exhibit 21.10I gives a similar display of standardized residuals plotted against the time-of-hire predictor variable. Here again, constant variability across all values for the time-of-hire predictor is supported.

EXHIBIT **21.10H**
Standardized Residuals Versus
Fitted Values—Salary
Discrimination Data

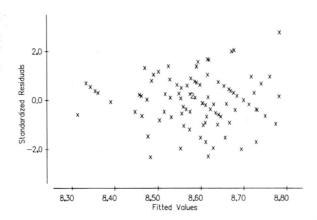

Exhibit 21.10J gives a similar plot for the experience predictor. Again this plot does not suggest any weakness of the model with respect to nonconstant variability. Exhibit 21.10K shows residuals versus education level. There appear to be some differences of variability in residuals for different levels of education, but the effect is not severe. Checks of normality are the next step.

The histogram of the standardized residuals is presented in Exhibit 21.10L. The distribution is quite symmetric and generally mound shaped. However, to better assess the normality, a normal scores plot is done. Exhibit 21.10M gives the normal scores plot of the standardized residuals for this model. Recall that normality is supported by a straight-line plot. Here the results are quite good, and the correlation coefficient between normal scores and the standardized residuals is .996.

EXHIBIT **21.10I**
Standardized Residuals Versus
Time of Hire—Salary
Discrimination Data

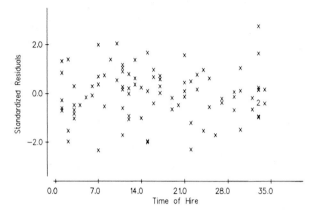

EXHIBIT **21.10J**
Standardized Residuals Versus
Experience—Salary
Discrimination Data

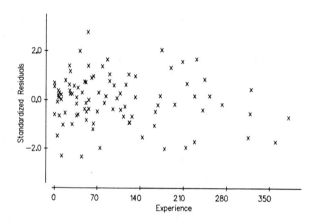

EXHIBIT **21.10K**
Standardized Residuals Versus
Education—Salary
Discrimination Data

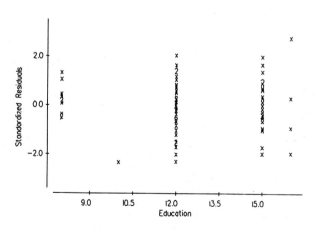

EXHIBIT **21.10L**

Histogram of Standardized
Residuals—Salary
Discrimination Data

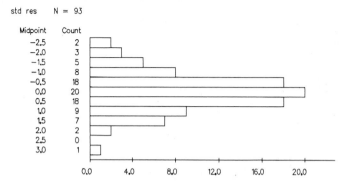

EXHIBIT **21.10M**

Normal Scores Plot of
Standardized
Residuals—Salary
Discrimination Data

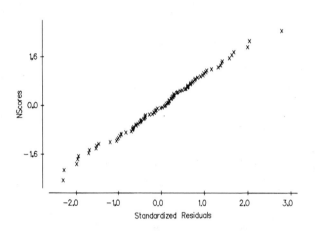

Finally, diagnostics for outliers and influential cases are considered. Among other things, Exhibit 21.10G lists the largest standardized residuals. Recall that there are 93 cases, so that the largest standardized residual, 2.79, should not be considered as too unusual. As a further check on outliers, the studentized residuals are calculated. After deleting case 93, the corresponding studentized residual increases only to 2.9, so again there is no indication of an outlier for this case. Exhibit 21.10N displays a dotplot of all the studentized residuals. No case presents a serious outlier problem.

Exhibit 21.10N also displays the dotplot of Cook's distances for the 93 cases. Again case 93 corresponds to the most extreme value for Cook's distance. However, it is only equal to 0.137, which is considerably smaller than 1. Thus no difficulty with influential cases occurs in this regression model.

In summary, the assumptions of constant variability and normality of the error terms seem very reasonable for this choice of regression model. Exercise 22.9E provides additional practice in evaluating the reasonableness of the assumptions when alternative transformations of the response and predictor variables are used.

EXHIBIT 21.10N
Studentized Residuals and
Cook's Distance—Salary
Discrimination Data

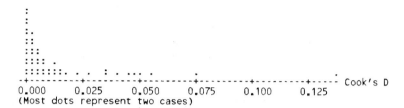

(Most dots represent two cases)

Chapter Summary

Mathematical models require us to make assumptions that may or may not mirror the behavior of real processes. An important task, therefore, is to assess the extent to which model assumptions and process behavior correspond. Examination of residuals from the model fitting process is the primary tool for making this assessment. If the data exhibit a serious violation of model assumptions, remedial action is needed. This may be revision of the model, through addition or deletion of predictors, or it may be transformation of some or all of the variables to bring the data in line with the model.

Supplementary Exercises for Chapter 21

21A Exercise 8.9H and Exercise 20A dealt with the time it takes to assemble an electronic printed circuitboard in terms of seven predictor variables.

   a Plot the residuals of the model against the fitted values and interpret the plot.

   b Plot the residuals of the model against each of the predictor variables and interpret each plot.

   c Display the normal scores for the residuals of the model. Interpret this plot.

   d Plot the standardized residuals of the model against each of the predictor variables. Interpret the plots.

   e Calculate leverage values for each case and interpret their magnitudes.

   f Calculate Cook's distance statistics for each case and interpret their magnitudes. (Filename: BOARDS.DAT.)

21B Consider the Los Angeles traffic data that first appeared in Section 4.10 and was further analyzed in Exercise 20B. Using the full data set (ignoring road type), consider transforming both actual and estimated traffic volumes using a square root transformation.

   a Display the scatterplot of the transformed variables. Does a 45° line seem appropriate here?

b Estimate the simple regression of square root actual volume on square root estimated volume.

c Display the scatterplot of residuals versus fitted values and interpret.

d Calculate leverage values for each case and interpret their magnitudes. A dotplot of the leverage values would be helpful.

e Calculate Cook's distance statistics for each case and interpret their magnitudes. (Again a dotplot of the distance statistics would be helpful.)

f Check the residuals with respect to normality. (Filename: TRAFFIC.DAT.)

21C Example 7.8A discussed the relationship between two methods for measuring battery life for portable computers, Rundown and ZDigit. Consider the straight-line model that uses Rundown to predict ZDigit. (Filename: COMPUTER.DAT.)

a Assess the presence of outliers using studentized residuals.

b Assess the influence of observations using leverage.

c Assess the influence of observations using Cook's distance.

d Assess normality in the model by displaying a normal scores plot of the standardized residuals.

21D Supplementary Exercise 7A gave data relating estimates and actual costs of 26 construction projects. Consider constructing a model that uses estimated costs to predict actual costs. (Filename: ESTIMATE.DAT.)

a Display the scatterplot of y versus x.

b Comment on the plot in part (a). Do you think the errors could be assumed to have the same variability at all levels of estimated costs?

c Plot $\log(y)$ versus $\log(x)$.

d Comment on the plot of part (c).

e Use least-squares to fit the model $\log(y) = \beta_0 + \beta_1 \log(x)$.

f Display the plot of standardized residuals versus fitted values for the model of part (e). Comment on the plot with respect to variability in residuals.

21E Exercise 21.9E develops the model $y = \beta_0 + \beta_1(1/\log(x))$ for relating aluminum concentration (y) to distance (x) from a plant. (Filename: LITTER.DAT.)

a Plot standardized residuals versus fitted values to assess the model fit.

b Analyze the data for outliers.

c Analyze the data for influential observations.

21F The four Anscombe data sets were introduced in Exercise 6.3H. Recall that the fitted straight lines are identical in all of the four data sets. (Filename: ANSCOMBE.DAT.)

a Plot standardized residuals versus fitted values to assess the model fit for each of the four straight-line models.

b Analyze each of the four data sets for outliers.

c Analyze each of the four data sets for influential observations.

21G In a student project by Anita Iwanski, Steven Hansen, and Lori Thornton, data on new car sales in the 72 counties of Wisconsin were collected for 1990. The average age, average income, and unemployment rates were also obtained by county. The data appear in Appendix 4. (Filename: AUTOSALE.DAT.)

a Produce scatterplots (or a scatterplot matrix) of Sales versus each of Age, Income, and Unemployment rate. Comment on the relationship seen in the plots.

b Fit simple straight-line models of Sales regressed on each of the predictors Age, Income, and Unemployment rate.

c Comment on the strength of relationship shown in each of the three models considered in part (b).

d Now fit a multiple regression model using Age, Income, and Unemployment rate together as predictors. Comment on the value of the variable Age after Income and Unemployment rate are already in the model.

e Assess the influence of observations from individual counties by looking at leverage and Cook's distance. (The whole of Menominee county is a Native American Indian reservation. Note the low average age and high unemployment rate.)

f Redo the regression analysis with Menominee county sales excluded. Comment on the differences between this fit and the one obtained in part (d).

Glossary for Chapter 21

Box-Cox transformation	A transformation from the power family $y = x^\lambda$ for some choice of constant power λ.
Cook's distance	A measure of a data point's influence on regression results that considers both the predictor variables and the response variable.
exponential decay	Described by the curve $y = c_1 e^{c_2 x}$ with c_2 negative.
exponential growth	Described by the curve $y = c_1 e^{c_2 x}$ with c_2 positive.
influence	A measure of the effect each data point has on the regression results.
leverage	A measure of a data point's influence in a regression with respect to the predictor variables.
logarithm transformation	A transformation useful for simplifying certain curved relationships and for stabilizing variability when the standard deviation of a response is proportional to the mean of the response.
model diagnostics	Testing the assumptions of a model.
outliers	Data that are inconsistent with the general pattern of the other data.
standardized residuals	Residuals that have been corrected to have a standard deviation of 1.
studentized residuals	Residuals that have been standardized using data that exclude the ith case.

22

Regression Model Selection

Chapter Objectives

After mastering this chapter, you will be able to:

- Construct and interpret added variable plots

- Define and explain the implications of collinearity

- Explain the effects of model under- and overspecification

- Use best subset regression to select a model

- Implement F tests for subsets of coefficients

- Use stepwise regression to select a model

22.1 Introduction

In the regression work in previous chapters, it has been assumed that the "correct" predictor variables are available. If this is so, the analyst merely carries out the regression calculations after discovering appropriate transformations of the response and/or predictor variables and dealing with outliers and influential data points. In practice, though, many potentially useful predictor variables are available, some that are actually useful and others of dubious value. This chapter deals with how to choose the best predictor variables and the best model. The choice is made difficult by the desire to satisfy sometimes contradictory criteria. As we will see, we can be faced with various pros and cons for adding variables to or deleting variables from a model. Moreover, finding a model that fits the data well need not guarantee that the model predicts yet-to-be observed cases. Thus, selecting a model should always be viewed as a tentative action, subject to revision as new information comes to light.

First, we discuss ways to determine the utility of adding a given predictor to a model, using mainly added variable plots. Next, we study problems that arise when one predictor is related to another, learning to detect and handle collinearity. Third, we study effects of leaving out important predictors or including too many predictors.

We outline a number of techniques designed to select sets of predictors: s, Mallows' C_p criterion, the F test for subsets of coefficients, and types of stepwise regression.

Exhibit 22.1A displays data from *Consumer Reports* on the gas mileage of 45 cars tested and reported on over the period of January 1987 through February 1989. The goal is to construct a regression model that will predict gasoline efficiency in terms of other easily measured variables. Three different gas mileage ratings—city, trip, and expressway—are given, together with eight potential predictor variables: weight, engine displacement, number of cylinders, horsepower, a binary transmission variable (0 = manual or 1 = automatic), number of gears in the transmission (3, 4, or 5), a size categorical variable (1, 2, 3, 4, or 5), and a binary variable for foreign or U.S.

E X H I B I T **22.1A**
Car Mileage Data

```
filename: CARS.DAT
Car data from Consumer Reports
January 1987 through February 1989 issues
11 variables and 45 cases
MPG: city, trip and expressway; weight; displacement
number of cylinders; horsepower
transmission:1=auto,0=manual; number of transmission gears
size/type: 1=small, 2=compact, 3=medium, 4=wagon, 5=minivan
foreign/domestic: 1=foreign, 0=domestic
22 32 36 2365 1.6 4 113 0 5 1 1  Acura Integra RS
22 33 38 2430 1.6 4 108 0 5 1 1  Toyota Corolla FX16
29 42 51 1895 1.3 4  60 0 4 1 1  Honda Civic 2dr
21 36 38 2320 1.6 4  74 1 3 1 0  Chevrolet Nova
18 32 35 2330 1.6 4  82 1 3 1 1  Mercury Tracer
20 34 36 2255 1.5 4  68 1 3 1 1  Plymouth Colt
18 36 43 2350 1.6 4  74 1 3 1 1  Pontiac Le Mans
28 41 47 1635 1.3 4  58 0 4 1 1  Ford Festiva
24 36 38 2070 1.6 4  82 0 4 1 1  Mazda 323
22 34 39 2115 1.5 4  68 0 4 1 1  Mitsubishi Precis
23 35 39 1840 1.1 4  52 0 4 1 1  Yugo GVS
27 43 49 1970 1.5 4  78 0 4 1 1  Toyota Tercel
31 51 58 1575 1.0 3  48 0 5 1 1  Chevrolet Sprint
24 37 41 2185 1.5 4  68 0 4 1 1  Hyundai Excel
24 36 41 2115 1.8 4  81 0 4 1 1  VW Fox
16 28 35 3040 2.2 4 145 1 4 2 1  Mazda 626 4ws turbo
19 34 35 2620 2.0 4 108 1 3 2 1  Audi 80
14 25 29 3230 3.0 6 142 1 4 2 1  Mitsubishi Galant Sigma
18 29 35 2745 2.0 4 102 1 4 2 1  Mitsubishi Galant
17 28 32 2573 1.9 4 110 1 4 2 1  Peugeot 405 DL
17 27 32 2802 2.3 4 100 1 3 2 0  Ford Tempo GLS
18 31 39 2699 2.0 4  90 1 3 2 0  Chevrolet Corsica LT
21 36 43 2695 2.2 4 110 0 5 2 0  Ford Probe
18 31 43 2885 2.5 4 100 0 5 2 0  Dodge Daytona
13 23 28 3310 5.0 8 225 1 4 2 0  Ford Mustang LX
13 23 32 3430 5.0 8 170 1 4 2 0  Chevy Camaro RS
18 29 34 2670 2.2 4  97 1 3 2 0  Plymouth Sundance
19 35 44 2925 2.0 4 115 1 4 2 1  Toyota Camry LE
16 28 36 2735 2.5 4  98 1 3 2 0  Pontiac Grand AM LE
15 29 37 3155 3.0 6 140 1 4 3 0  Ford Taurus
16 30 36 2995 3.0 6 150 1 4 3 0  Eagle Premier
15 27 34 3150 3.0 6 136 1 3 3 0  Dodge Dynasty
16 29 33 2950 2.8 6 125 1 3 3 0  Buick Century
15 26 33 3295 3.8 6 140 1 4 3 0  Mercury Cougar
16 28 34 2925 2.5 4 100 1 3 3 0  Chrysler Le Baron Coupe
16 29 37 3220 2.8 6 125 1 4 3 0  Buick Regal Coupe
16 26 31 2900 2.2 4 146 1 3 3 0  Chrysler New Yorker Turbo
15 27 33 3205 2.5 4 153 1 4 4 1  Toyota Camry wagon
16 26 30 2930 2.2 4 103 1 4 4 0  Eagle Medallion wagon
14 25 31 3320 3.0 6 157 1 4 4 1  Nissan Maxima wagon
16 26 31 3080 2.3 4 114 1 4 4 1  Volvo 240 wagon
13 24 28 3625 3.0 6 136 1 3 5 0  Plymouth Gran Voyager
12 23 28 3665 3.0 6 145 1 4 5 0  Ford Aerostar
13 22 27 3625 2.4 4 106 1 4 5 1  Nissan GXE van
14 23 27 3415 2.4 4 107 1 4 5 1  Mitsubishi van
```

domestic manufacture (1 = foreign, 0 = domestic). A small portion of these data were reported in Chapter 21, along with the way in which the gas mileage figures were obtained.

For the reasons discussed in Chapter 21, all of the miles-per-gallon figures are transformed to their reciprocals, gallons per mile (GPM), before further analysis. Thus the gallons-per-mile variables will be modeled as functions of the weight of the car, displacement of the engine, and other available predictor variables. Here the city gallons per mile are modeled; you are asked to model both trip and expressway gallons per mile in the exercises.

Exhibits 22.1B and C display the scatterplots of city GPM versus weight and versus horsepower. Because there is a direct relationship between city GPM and each of these predictors, a regression of city GPM in terms of either predictor is potentially useful. However, our interest is in the one multiple regression model that includes the best set of predictors. What is needed is a measure and graphic display of the *additional* effect of a predictor, such as horsepower, to a model that already includes other predictors, such as weight.

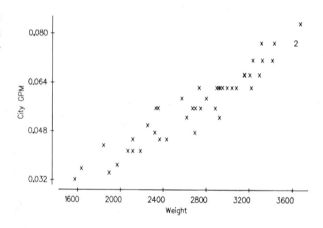

E X H I B I T 22.1B
Scatterplot of City GPM Versus Weight

Exhibit 22.1D shows the results of three regressions: city GPM on weight, city GPM on horsepower, and city GPM on both weight and horsepower. The exhibit shows that weight alone explains 90.9% of the variation in GPM, and horsepower alone explains 63.1% of that same variation. The best linear combination of these two predictors explains 91.0% of the variation—a very small increase from the 90.9% explained by weight alone. As noted in Section 20.8, in the two-predictor case, the *t* ratio for horsepower provides a measure of the additional usefulness of that predictor after weight is already in the model. In Exhibit 22.1D, the *t* ratio for horsepower *when weight is in the model* is only 0.83, showing that horsepower is of little additional use. A graphic display of the added variable effect is provided by the added variable plot, discussed in the next section.

E X H I B I T **22.1C**
Scatterplot of City GPM Versus
Horsepower

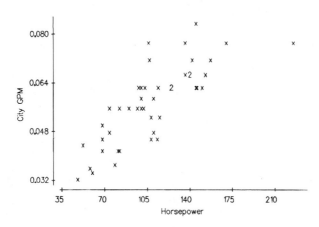

E X H I B I T **22.1D**
Regression of City GPM on
Weight, on Horsepower, and on
Weight and Horsepower

```
The regression equation is

city GPM = -0.00346 + 0.000022 weight

Predictor        Coef        Stdev      t-ratio         p
Constant     -0.003462     0.002996      -1.16      0.254
weight      0.00002220    0.00000107      20.68      0.000

s = 0.003881     R-sq = 90.9%     R-sq(adj) = 90.7%
```

```
The regression equation is

city GPM = 0.0264 + 0.000283 HP

Predictor        Coef        Stdev      t-ratio         p
Constant      0.026447     0.003787       6.98      0.000
HP          0.00028319    0.00003303       8.57      0.000

s = 0.007800     R-sq = 63.1%     R-sq(adj) = 62.2%
```

```
The regression equation is

city GPM = -0.00263 + 0.000021 weight + 0.000023 HP

Predictor        Coef        Stdev      t-ratio         p
Constant     -0.002627     0.003171      -0.83      0.412
weight      0.00002096    0.00000184      11.42      0.000
HP          0.00002334    0.00002810       0.83      0.411

s = 0.003895     R-sq = 91.0%     R-sq(adj) = 90.6%
```

S E C T I O N

22.2   Added Variable Plots

Exhibits 22.1B and C show that city GPM is directly related to both weight and horsepower. However, Exhibit 22.2A shows that weight and horsepower are themselves closely related—the heavier the car, the higher its engine horsepower. How can we determine what added effect a predictor will have after we have taken into account one or more other predictor variables? One way to do this is with the added variable plot, discussed in this section.

E X H I B I T **22.2A**
Scatterplot of Horsepower
Versus Weight

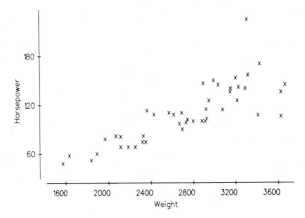

E X H I B I T **22.2A**
Scatterplot of Horsepower
Versus Weight

If the regression calculations for a response variable y with predictor variables $x_1, x_2, \ldots, x_k$ are carried out, we say that y has been regressed on $x_1, x_2, \ldots, x_k$. Using this terminology, suppose city GPM is regressed on weight and the residuals are saved. These residuals may be interpreted as the part of city GPM that is *not* explained by the predictor weight. Now perform the regression with horsepower as response and weight as predictor—that is, regress horsepower on weight. Save these residuals also. These residuals are the portion of the horsepower variable *not* explained by weight. Now plot the first set of residuals against the second set. This **added variable plot** is the **added variable plot** and shows the relationship, if any, between city GPM and horsepower *after adjusting for the effect of weight*. If the plot shows a trend of some sort, horsepower should be included in the model to account for this. If, on the other hand, the relationship shown in the added variable plot is very weak, adding horsepower to the model that already includes weight will be fruitless. The added variable plot shown in Exhibit 22.2B shows no useful relationship between the two

E X H I B I T **22.2B**
Added Variable Plot for
Horsepower After Regressing
City GPM on Weight

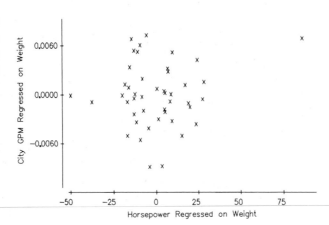

sets of residuals ($r = 0.13$) and confirms the conclusions based on Exhibit 22.1D. The correlation coefficient in an added variable plot is called the *partial correlation coefficient*. The partial correlation coefficient between city GPM and horsepower after adjusting for the effect of weight is 0.13.

The roles of the predictors weight and horsepower may be reversed and the added variable plot for weight considered after using horsepower in the model. Exhibit 22.2C displays the plot. Here there is a strong relationship (partial $r = 0.87$), indicating that weight is indeed a useful predictor in addition to horsepower. At this point, weight appears to be a clear winner as a predictor of city GPM, but since horsepower has little additional predictive power, another predictor to use with weight is sought. Exhibit 22.2D displays the added variable plot for transmission type after including weight in the model. The (partial) correlation coefficient in this plot is 0.44, which supports the visual perception of a weak upward trend. On the basis of this plot a model with two predictors, weight and transmission type, is considered, and more predictors are sought.

EXHIBIT **22.2C**
Added Variable Plot for Weight After Regressing City GPM on Horsepower

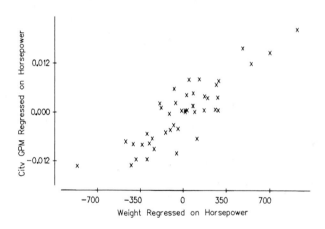

With more variables involved, how is the added variable plot defined? An example will illustrate. Consider adding the predictor displacement after weight and transmission type are in the model. City GPM is first regressed on weight and transmission type and the residuals are saved. Then displacement is regressed on weight and transmission type, obtaining a second set of residuals. As expected, the added variable plot for displacement is the plot of the first set of residuals against the second. As before, any trend indicates the usefulness of displacement in addition to weight and transmission type. The absence of trend shows the futility of using displacement in addition to the other two variables. For our data set, the added variable plot given in Exhibit 22.2E indicates that displacement has little additional predictive power (partial $r = 0.34$) in a model already containing weight and transmission type. This correlation is called the partial correlation coefficient between city GPM and displacement after adjusting for the effects of both weight and transmission type. This plot also displays two possible outliers with residual values at about 1.8 and 2.0 on

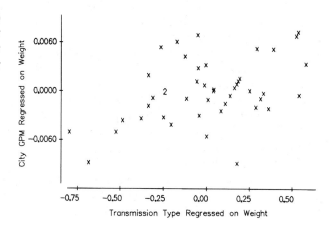

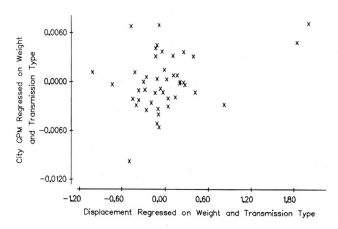

the horizontal axis. These two residuals correspond to the Camaro and Mustang, each with a large engine displacement of 5.0 liters in the original data. If these two cases are omitted from the correlation calculation, the value of (partial) r drops to 0.065, reinforcing the perception of no real relationship in Exhibit 22.2E.

Suppressor Variables

In a multiple regression setting, the combined effect of several predictors may be difficult to discern. Scatterplots of the response versus each of the predictors may not be very helpful. Frequently, the added effect of another predictor improves the regression only marginally, in the sense that the R^2 value for the multiple regression is less than the sum of the R^2 values for the regressions of y on each predictor individually. Exhibit 22.1D provides an example. Here weight alone produces an R^2 of 90.7% and horsepower produces R^2 of 63.1%, but the multiple regression including both variables has an R^2 of 91.0%.

However, in some situations it is possible that the R^2 value for the multiple regression is *larger* than the sum of the R^2 values from each of the simple regressions. An example is based on the data given in Exhibit 22.2F.

E X H I B I T 22.2F
Suppressor Variable Example

```
filename: SUPPRESS.DAT
Data for supressor variable example
   Y      x1     x2
197.4   20.8   29.3
194.2   18.9   29.8
199.8   20.5   30.3
199.9   19.7   30.9
195.7   19.8   29.7
198.4   19.9   30.0
197.1   19.0   30.9
197.9   19.8   30.2
198.5   19.1   31.2
198.1   21.8   28.2
196.5   20.6   28.6
198.8   19.3   31.3
200.0   21.8   28.7
195.5   19.3   30.0
199.0   19.1   31.9
200.7   20.4   30.7
196.8   19.8   29.4
197.5   21.3   27.6
197.1   19.2   30.6
201.1   21.1   30.5
196.5   19.3   30.0
199.3   19.6   31.0
198.4   19.8   29.8
196.0   19.9   28.7
197.3   18.6   31.1
```

Scatterplots of the response y versus each of the predictor variables are provided in Exhibits 22.2G and 22.2H. Neither plot shows a strong relationship between the response and the predictor when the predictors are considered separately. This

E X H I B I T 22.2G
Scatterplot of y Versus x_1

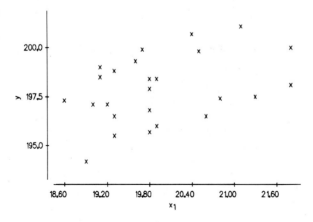

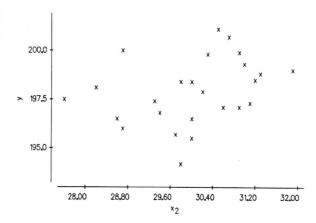

impression is confirmed by the simple regression results shown in Exhibit 22.2I. The individual R^2 values are 15.5% and 10.4%, respectively. The t ratios for the coefficients of x_1 and x_2 in the simple regressions are quite small: 2.05 and 1.63, respectively.

```
The regression equation is

y = 183 + 0.755 x1

Predictor        Coef        Stdev      t-ratio          p
Constant      182.847        7.342        24.90      0.000
x1             0.7551       0.3679         2.05      0.052

s = 1.605       R-sq = 15.5%      R-sq(adj) = 11.8%

Analysis of Variance

SOURCE        DF           SS          MS          F        p
Regression     1       10.843      10.843       4.21    0.052
Error         23       59.217       2.575
Total         24       70.060


The regression equation is

y = 182 + 0.518 x2

Predictor        Coef        Stdev      t-ratio          p
Constant      182.358        9.522        19.15      0.000
x2             0.5178       0.3171         1.63      0.116

s = 1.652       R-sq = 10.4%      R-sq(adj) = 6.5%

Analysis of Variance

SOURCE        DF           SS          MS          F        p
Regression     1        7.280       7.280       2.67    0.116
Error         23       62.780       2.730
Total         24       70.060
```

However, a model that contains both predictors changes the results dramatically. Exhibit 22.2J shows the results. Here the value of R^2 has jumped to 84.9%—considerably larger than the sum of the individual R^2s. The t ratios for each predictor are now large, 10.41 and 10.05, respectively. The added variable plot in Exhibit 22.2K clearly shows the usefulness of the x_2 variable after x_1 is in the model.

EXHIBIT 22.2J
Multiple Regression of y on x_1 and x_2

```
The regression equation is

y = 95.7 + 2.31 x1 + 1.87 x2

Predictor        Coef        Stdev      t-ratio          p
Constant       95.735        9.232        10.37      0.000
x1             2.3123        0.2221       10.41      0.000
x2             1.8679        0.1859       10.05      0.000

s = 0.6939       R-sq = 84.9%      R-sq(adj) = 83.5%

Analysis of Variance

SOURCE         DF           SS          MS          F          p
Regression      2       59.467      29.734      61.75      0.000
Error          22       10.593       0.481
Total          24       70.060
```

EXHIBIT 22.2K
Added Variable Plot for x_2 After Regressing y on x_1

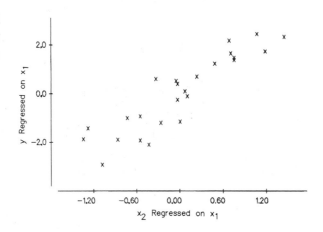

In situations such as this, one predictor is said to *suppress* or *mask* the effect of the other predictor.[†]

Although added variable plots are useful tools for assessing the additional usefulness of predictor variables, a large number of regression calculations must be carried out and a large number of plots considered to discover the important predictors.

[†]Further details and examples of suppressor variables may be found in David Hamilton, "Sometimes $R^2 > r^2_{yx_1} + r^2_{yx_2}$," *American Statistician*, 41 (2) (1987), 129–132.

Added variable plots help us assess the additional effect of a predictor variable in explaining the variation in the response variable once other predictor variables are in the model. Why not just consider a large regression model that includes any and all possible predictors? Are there any difficulties with such an approach? Section 22.4 considers these questions in detail.

SECTION

22.3 Exercises

22.3A Consider the car mileage data in Exhibit 22.1A. Display and interpret the added variable plot for displacement after regressing city GPM on weight. (Filename: CARS.DAT.)

22.3B Use the car mileage data in Exhibit 22.1A again but consider expressway GPM as the response variable.

    a Plot the scatterplot of expressway GPM versus weight.

    b Plot the scatterplot of expressway GPM versus gears.

    c Display and interpret the added variable plot for the number of gears after weight is in the regression model.

    d Display and interpret the added variable plot for weight after number of gears is in the regression model. (Filename: CARS.DAT.)

22.3C For the suppressor variable example in Exhibit 22.2F, display the added variable plot of y on x_1 given x_2. (Filename: SUPPRESS.DAT.)

22.3D Use the house price data listed in Exercise 20.9B.

    a Construct and interpret the added variable plot for square feet after taxes are used to predict house price.

    b Construct and interpret the added variable plot for number of rooms after taxes, number of baths, and square feet are used to predict house price. (Filename: HOUSEPRI.DAT.)

22.3E Reconsider the real estate data from Exhibit 6.2A. (Filename: REALPROP.DAT.)

    a Construct the added variable plot for the Sq.ft variable after the Assessed variable is in the model.

    b Interpret the plot of part (a). In particular, does the plot suggest that Sq.ft should also be in the model?

    c Does the plot of part (a) suggest that $(Sq.ft)^2$ should also be added to the model?

SECTION

22.4 Collinearity

This section discusses the effects on regression models of predictor variables that are themselves related. It shows how to detect and deal with problems of collinearity, predictors that are linearly related.

Detection

Suppose that in the car data, the car weight in kilograms in addition to the car weight in pounds is used as a predictor variable. Let x_1 denote the weight in pounds and let

x_2 denote the weight in kilograms. Now since one kilogram is the same as 2.2046 pounds,

$$\beta_1 x_1 + \beta_2 x_2 = \beta_1(2.2046 x_2) + \beta_2 x_2 = (2.2046\beta_1 + \beta_2)x_2 = \gamma x_2$$

with $\gamma = 2.2046\beta_1 + \beta_2$. Here γ represents the "true" regression coefficient associated with the predictor weight when measured in kilograms. Regardless of the value of γ, there are infinitely many different values for β_1 and β_2 that produce the same value for γ. If both x_1 and x_2 are included in the model, then β_1 and β_2 cannot be uniquely defined and cannot be estimated from the data.

The same difficulty occurs if there is a linear relationship among any of the predictor variables. If for some set of predictor variables $x_1, x_2, \ldots, x_m$ and some set of constants $c_1, c_2, \ldots, c_{m+1}$ not all zero,

$$c_1 x_1 + c_2 x_2 + \cdots + c_m x_m = c_{m+1} \tag{22.1}$$

collinear

for all values of $x_1, x_2, \ldots, x_m$ in the data set, the predictors $x_1, x_2, \ldots, x_m$ are said to be **collinear**. Exact collinearity rarely occurs with actual data, but approximate collinearity occurs when predictors are nearly linearly related. As discussed later, approximate collinearity also causes substantial difficulties in regression analysis. Variables are said to be collinear even if Equation (22.1) holds only approximately. Setting aside for the moment the assessment of the effect of collinearity, how is it detected?

The search for collinearity begins by displaying scatterplots of one predictor against another, as was done in Exhibit 22.2A. That exhibit showed that horsepower and weight were related quite substantially. With many potential predictors, a large number of scatterplots must be considered. The scatterplot matrix introduced in Section 8.7 is the basic graphic tool for detecting collinearity. Exhibit 22.4A gives the scatterplot matrix for nine variables in the car data set. In this display each of the nine variables (including the response) is plotted against each of the other variables. For example, the first row of scatterplots plots city GPM against each of the potential predictors. In the second row, weight is plotted against each other variable. Note that the first plot in the second row is weight versus city GPM—the inverse of the plot of city GPM versus weight.

With categorical variables, many points usually pile up on top of one another and disappear in the plot. A technique called *jittering*, which adds a small random amount to these variables in a random direction so they will be slightly separated and all points will appear on the plot distinctly, can be used to circumvent this difficulty. The scatterplots of the response and of the continuous predictors versus the categorical predictors are useful, but very little information is obtained when one categorical variable is plotted against another categorical variable. Relationships among categorical variables are best seen in tables.

Many such relationships are also assessed by calculating the correlation coefficients between all pairs of predictor variables and displaying them in a table, as in Exhibit 22.4B. Here, for example, horsepower and weight have a correlation of 0.810, and number of cylinders and displacement have correlation of 0.889. The missing upper values of the table need not be filled in because they are repeated. For example,

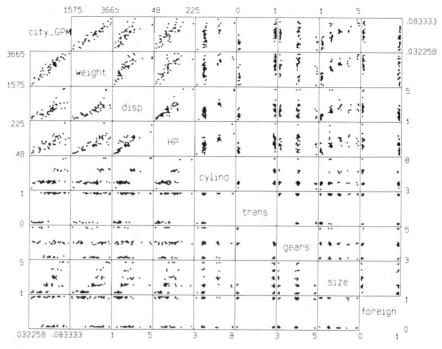

E X H I B I T **22.4A**
Scatterplot Matrix for Car Data

Note: Plot produced with the Stata statistical package.

E X H I B I T **22.4B**
Correlation Table for Predictor
Variables

	weight	disp	cylind	HP	trans	size	gears
disp	0.791						
cylind	0.611	0.889					
HP	0.810	0.880	0.775				
trans	0.713	0.532	0.384	0.546			
size	0.838	0.493	0.333	0.535	0.575		
gears	-0.125	-0.052	-0.031	0.033	-0.615	-0.144	
foreign	-0.462	-0.575	-0.478	-0.417	-0.373	-0.328	0.324

the correlation between weight and number of cylinders is the same as the correlation between number of cylinders and weight.

However, these scatterplots and correlations are only between pairs of predictors. They cannot assess more complicated (near) linear relationships among several predictors as expressed in Equation (22.1). To do so, you must calculate the multiple coefficient of determination, R_j^2, obtained from regressing the jth predictor variable on all the other predictor variables. That is, x_j is temporarily treated as the response in this regression, as was done in added variable plots. The closer this R_j^2 is to 1 (or 100%), the more serious the collinearity problem is with respect to the jth predictor. As an example, if weight is regressed on the other seven predictors, an R^2 value of 93% is obtained, indicating a collinearity problem that needs to be considered further.

Effect on Parameter Estimates

The effect of collinearity on the estimates of the regression coefficients may be best seen from the expression giving the standard errors of those coefficients. Standard errors give a measure of expected variability for the coefficient estimates—the smaller the standard error, the better the coefficient tends to be estimated. It may be shown that the standard error of the jth coefficient, b_j, is given by

$$se(b_j) = s \sqrt{\frac{1}{1 - R_j^2} \cdot \frac{1}{\sum\limits_{i=1}^{n}(x_{ij} - \overline{x}_j)^2}} \qquad \textbf{(22.2)}$$

where, as before, R_j^2 is the R^2 value obtained from regressing the jth predictor variable on all other predictors. Equation (22.2) shows that, with respect to collinearity, the standard error will be smallest when R_j^2 is zero—that is, the jth predictor is not linearly related to the other predictors. Conversely, if R_j^2 is near 1, the standard error of b_j is large and the estimate is much more likely to be far from the true value of β_j. The quantity

$$\text{VIF}_j = \frac{1}{1 - R_j^2} \qquad \textbf{(22.3)}$$

variance inflation factor (VIF)

is called the **variance inflation factor (VIF)**. The larger the value of VIF for a predictor x_j, the more severe the collinearity problem. As a guideline, many authors recommend that a VIF greater than 10 suggests a collinearity difficulty worthy of further study. This is equivalent to flagging predictors with R_j^2 greater than 90%.

Exhibits 22.4C and D display regression results for two models: city GPM on weight and transmission type, and city GPM on all eight predictors. Each printout also gives the corresponding VIF value for each predictor. As we shall see, the simpler model is excellent. With the simpler model, the regression coefficient for weight is estimated as 0.00001903 with standard error 0.00000139. In the more complicated model, the corresponding estimate is 0.00001445 with standard error 0.00000341. The latter standard error is about three times larger. Looking further, the estimate of the regression coefficient for transmission type and its standard error are 0.005286 and 0.001650, respectively, for the simple model, while they change to 0.003541 and 0.002529 in the large model. Again, these changes are substantial and lead to confusion about the true effect of an automatic versus manual transmission on gas mileage.

Effect on Inference

If collinearity affects parameter estimates and their standard errors, it follows that t ratios will also be affected. Exhibits 22.4C and D show that the t ratios associated with weight in the two models are 13.71 and 4.23, respectively, both of which indicate that weight is an important variable. However, the t ratios for transmission type change from 3.20 to 1.40, apparently showing in the model with eight predictors that transmission type is *not* important. The collinearity has confused the effects of the

EXHIBIT 22.4C
City GPM Regressed on Weight
and Transmission Type

```
The regression equation is

city GPM = 0.00146 + 0.000019 weight + 0.00529 trans

Predictor         Coef        Stdev      t-ratio        p     VIF
Constant      0.001455     0.003121         0.47    0.644
weight       0.00001903   0.00000139        13.71    0.000     2.0
trans         0.005286     0.001650         3.20    0.003     2.0

s = 0.003520     R-sq = 92.7%     R-sq(adj) = 92.3%

Analysis of Variance

SOURCE        DF          SS           MS         F        p
Regression     2     0.0065673    0.0032837   265.02    0.000
Error         42     0.0005204    0.0000124
Total         44     0.0070877
```

EXHIBIT 22.4D
City GPM Regressed on All Eight
Predictors, Showing the Effect of
Collinearity—Variance Inflation

```
The regression equation is

city GPM = 0.00845 + 0.000014 weight + 0.00265 disp
           + 0.00102 cylind - 0.000010 HP + 0.00354 trans
           - 0.00179 gears + 0.00115 size + 0.00224 foreign

Predictor         Coef        Stdev      t-ratio        p     VIF
Constant      0.008454     0.006493         1.30    0.201
weight       0.00001445   0.00000341        4.23    0.000    14.4
disp          0.002650     0.002053         1.29    0.205    12.9
cylind        0.001024     0.001019         1.00    0.322     5.6
HP           -0.00001006   0.00003423       -0.29    0.770     6.2
trans         0.003541     0.002529         1.40    0.170     5.6
gears        -0.001786     0.001386        -1.29    0.206     3.2
size          0.0011498    0.0008478        1.36    0.183     4.8
foreign       0.002241     0.001349         1.66    0.105     1.9

s = 0.003250     R-sq = 94.6%     R-sq(adj) = 93.4%

Analysis of Variance

SOURCE        DF          SS           MS         F        p
Regression     8     0.00670755   0.00083844   79.39    0.000
Error         36     0.00038018   0.00001056
Total         44     0.00708774
```

various predictors. Note that the estimated regression coefficient for horsepower is negative, seemingly indicating that an increase in horsepower leads to *lower* gallons per mile and better fuel economy!

Effect on Prediction

The effect of collinearity on prediction depends on the values specified for the predictors. If the relationships among the predictors used in fitting the model are preserved in the predictor values used for prediction, the predictions will be little affected by collinearity. On the other hand, if the specific predictor values differ markedly from the relationships among the predictors in the model, then the predictions will be poor.

For example, in June 1989, *Consumer Reports* tested a Mazda 929 that weighed 3480 pounds and had a 3.0 liter V6 engine with 158 horsepower. In addition, the tested car had an automatic transmission with four gears, was size 3, and was of foreign manufacture. The city MPG tested out at 14 MPG. Using the small model with only weight and transmission type as predictors, the predicted city GPM is 0.07335 GPM, which translates to 13.6 MPG. Using the full model with eight predictors yields a similar prediction of 13.7 MPG. Both of these predictions are quite reasonable and both produce 3-standard-error prediction intervals that contain the true value of 14 MPG.

In contrast, consider a fictitious car that weighs 2800 pounds and has a 5.0-liter engine that generates 100 horsepower. The car has an automatic transmission with three gears, is size 4, and is of foreign manufacture. The predictor values for weight and transmission type are similar to the actual data and lead to a prediction of 16.7 MPG. However, the other predictor values are unlike those in the data set. In particular, the large engine (5.0 liters) has only four cylinders and 100 horsepower. The full eight-predictor model predicts a city MPG of 14.9, markedly different from the prediction of 16.7 based on the smaller model. Collinearity places restrictions on the predictor variables that may be hidden from the user of the regression model. As a result, values well within the ranges of the individual predictors may, when considered jointly, form a pattern that goes against those restrictions, because it is so different from the pattern in predictors used to build the model. For example, for the fictitious car each of the individual predictor values, weight = 2800, cylinders = 4, displacement = 5.0, HP = 100, automatic transmission with three gears, size = 3, and foreign = 0, is within the range of the predictors in the data set. However, this *combination* of values is far from any combination in the data set.

What to Do About Collinearity

The best defense against the problems associated with collinear predictors is to keep models as simple as possible. Variables that add little to the usefulness of a regression model should be deleted from the model. Sections 22.6 and 22.8 present methods for selecting the better predictor variables. When collinearity is detected among variables that cannot reasonably be deleted from a regression model, avoid extrapolation and beware of inferences based on individual regression coefficients.

SECTION

22.5 Exercises

22.5A Consider the car mileage data of Exhibit 22.1A and let expressway GPM be the response of interest.

a Compare a model that uses weight and number of gears as predictors with a model that uses all of the predictors in the data set. In particular, look at t ratios for the predictors and VIF values.

b Compare the models considered in part (a) in terms of predicting the expressway GPM of the Ford Probe. (Filename: CARS.DAT.)

22.5B Look once more at the house price data given in Exercise 20.9B.

a Compare a model that uses taxes, number of baths, and square feet to predict house price with a model that uses all the predictors available. Interpret the t ratios for the predictors in both models. Also compare VIF values.

b Use both models in part (a) to predict the price of the first house in the data set. (Filename: HOUSEPRI.DAT.)

SECTION

22.6 Effects of Model Misspecification

Analysts making a regression model usually face a pool of potential predictors, developed through empirical analysis based on scatterplots and careful consideration of potential relationships in the application. Thus, most regression problems require decisions on which of many potential predictors to include in a model. In addition to the initial predictors, possible cross products of initial predictors, and transformed predictors such as logarithms, reciprocals, and squares must be considered. A model that does not include the best predictor variables is called a **misspecified model**. The challenge is to avoid misspecification by choosing the right predictors from the pool. This section discusses the effects of misspecification.

misspecified model

Effect of Underspecification

Suppose you want to estimate the effect on city GPM of having a car with an automatic transmission. A first approach might be to fit a regression model that uses only the binary transmission-type variable. Exhibit 22.6A displays the results from this fit and gives the estimate of about 0.021 gallon per mile as the price for having an automatic transmission. The standard error of this estimate is about 0.0027, which leads to a 3-standard-error confidence interval for the automatic transmission effect of $[0.021 - 3(0.0027), 0.021 + 3(0.0027)] = [0.0129, 0.0291]$ gallons per mile.

EXHIBIT **22.6A**
An Underspecified Model

```
The regression equation is

city GPM = 0.0421 + 0.0214 trans

Predictor        Coef       Stdev      t-ratio         p
Constant      0.042116    0.002258      18.65      0.000
trans         0.021408    0.002678       7.99      0.000

s = 0.008142    R-sq = 59.8%    R-sq(adj) = 58.8%
```

However, there is substantial empirical and theoretical evidence that weight is an important variable in determining city GPM. Exhibit 22.4C showed that in a model that contains both weight and transmission type as predictors, the estimated effect of transmission type is 0.005286 gallon per mile with a standard error of 0.001650. This standard error is nearly half of the previous value of 0.002678. The 3-standard-error confidence interval for the automatic transmission effect in this more complete model is

$$[0.0053 - 3(0.0016), 0.0053 + 3(0.0016)] = [0.0005, 0.0101]$$

gallons per mile. This interval does not even overlap the corresponding interval based on the model that uses only transmission type. Leaving out the important predictor of weight has the effect of overestimating the effect of having an automatic transmission.

underspecified model
An **underspecified model** is a model that fails to include important predictor variables. In general, omitting important predictor variables will

- Produce inaccurate estimates of the regression coefficients
- Produce inaccurate predictions of new response values
- Overestimate σ with s
- Overestimate the standard errors of the regression coefficients since s is too large
- Overestimate the prediction standard error since s is too large

An important exception to the first two statements occurs when all the predictor variables are uncorrelated among themselves. However, even in that case, s tends to overestimate σ, which leads to overestimation of standard errors of regression coefficients and standard errors of prediction.

Effect of Overspecification

When extra predictors are included in a model, the most important effect, beyond the difficulty with possible collinearity, is that the standard errors of the regression coefficients and the standard errors of prediction are larger than they need be. An
overspecified model
overspecified model is a model that includes extra predictor variables. This effect may be seen by again comparing the results given in Exhibits 22.4C and D. In the two-predictor model, the estimated regression coefficient for weight is 0.00001903 with a standard error of 0.00000139. In the eight predictor model, the regression coefficient changes only a little, to 0.00001445, but the standard error nearly triples to 0.00000341. Similarly, the regression coefficient for the transmission-type variable and its standard error change from 0.005286 and 0.001650 in the two-predictor model to 0.00341. Similarly, the regression coefficient for the transmission-type variable and its standard error change from 0.005286 and 0.001650 in the two-predictor model to 0.003541 and 0.002529 in the overspecified model. Here again the standard error is substantially larger in the latter case.

For a variety of reasons, then, it is important to find the "best" predictor variables in a multiple regression model.

SECTION
22.7 Exercise

22.7A Consider again the expressway MPG data given in Exercise 21.9C. First transform the response to GPM using the reciprocal transformation. Consider using three different models to predict expressway GPM: weight alone, number of gears alone, and using a linear combination of weight and gears.

   a Compare the residual standard deviations of three models. Which is the smallest?

   b Compare the coefficient on weight in the simple linear regression model with the corresponding coefficient in the multiple regression model. Are they similar or different?

   c Compare the coefficient on number of gears in the simple linear regression model with the corresponding coefficient in the multiple regression model. Are they similar or different?

d Interpret the regression coefficient associated with number of transmission gears in the simple linear regression model and then in the multiple regression model. (Filename: CARS2.DAT.)

22.8 Best Subset Methods

In this section, we consider model-selection criteria.

Criteria for Selecting Predictor Variables

Several statistics already discussed form the basis for criteria for selecting predictor variables. Generally speaking, models with smaller values of the residual standard deviation, s, are preferred over models with larger values of s. Similarly, larger values of R^2 correspond to preferable models. However, R^2 *always increases* as more variables are added to a model. The adjusted R^2, $R^2(\text{adj}) = 100[1 - (s^2/s_y^2)]\%$, can be used to compare models with different numbers of predictors but, since s_y is fixed, large values for $R^2(\text{adj})$ correspond exactly to small values of s. You may just as well choose a model on the basis of values of s. **Best subset regression** is a method for choosing the best predictor variables by considering all possible subsets of predictors and one or more criteria. A statistic based on selecting variables that improve the predictive power of the model is Mallows' C_p criterion.

best subset regression

Mallows' C_p Criterion

Suppose k variables are in the pool of potential predictors. Let s be the residual standard deviation obtained from the regression model that includes all k predictors—the full model. Now consider a model that includes only a particular subset of predictors and let p be the number of regression coefficients (including β_0, if present) in the subset model. For this subset model, let RSS_p denote the sum of squares of the residuals. Then the C_p statistic for this subset model is defined as[†]

Mallows' C_p criterion

$$C_p = \frac{RSS_p}{s^2} + 2p - n \tag{22.4}$$

If the subset model contains all the important predictors, it may be shown that, on average, $C_p = p$. On the other hand, if the subset model is missing important predictors, C_p will tend to be larger than p. Two subset models may be compared by comparing their values of C_p. Mallows suggested that good models have $C_p \simeq p$.

A plot of C_p versus p can be used to look for the models that satisfy this criterion. Note that there will be k different one-variable models and thus k values of C_p for one-variable models. There are $k(k-1)/2$ different choices of predictors for models with two predictors, plus an intercept, and each of these will have its own value for C_p. The better of these models will have C_p near p, which is 3 in this case. In

[†]C. L. Mallows, "Some Comments on C_p," *Technometrics*, 15 (1973), 661–676.

general, models with fewer predictors and with C_p near p will be the better models. Once a small number of models has been singled out, they are studied carefully with respect to outliers, influential observations, normality of the errors, and constancy of the standard deviation of the errors before choosing a final model for use.

To illustrate these selection methods, the car data with eight potential predictors are again used. Exhibit 22.8A gives the Minitab output from the command BREGRESS (best regression). Here the summary results for each of the five "best" models of each possible size are displayed. "Best" is in the sense of smallest value of s^2. The values of R^2, R^2(adj), and C_p are also given for each model reported. The X's under the predictor variable names indicate that those predictors are included in the corresponding model. For example, the best model with three predictors uses weight, transmission type, and number of cylinders as predictors. For this model, $s = 0.0032797$, $C_p = 4.8$, and $p = 3 + 1 = 4$. Exhibit 22.8B displays the plot of C_p versus p with the p versus p 45° line overlayed.

Since models with C_p small, near p, and with the least number of predictors are preferred, this plot confirms the superiority of this three-predictor model.

EXHIBIT 22.8A
Best Subset Regression of City GPM

Vars	R-sq	Adj. R-sq	Cp	s	Weight	Disp	Cylind	HP	Trans	Gears	Size	Foreign
1	90.9	90.7	20.3	0.0038806	X							
1	64.8	64.0	195.1	0.0076156		X						
1	63.4	62.6	204.3	0.0077619						X		
1	63.1	62.2	206.7	0.0078001				X				
1	59.8	58.8	228.9	0.0081423					X			
2	92.7	92.3	10.3	0.0035200	X		X					
2	92.5	92.2	11.3	0.0035546	X				X			
2	91.7	91.3	16.5	0.0037359	X		X					
2	91.6	91.2	17.7	0.0037746	X	X						
2	91.0	90.6	21.3	0.0038947	X					X		
3	93.8	93.3	4.8	0.0032797	X		X		X			
3	93.5	93.1	6.4	0.0033437	X	X			X			
3	93.5	93.1	6.5	0.0033459	X		X			X		
3	93.4	92.9	7.4	0.0033814	X	X				X		
3	93.0	92.5	10.0	0.0034780	X			X		X		
4	94.1	93.5	4.9	0.0032457	X		X		X	X		
4	94.0	93.4	5.0	0.0032504	X	X				X	X	
4	94.0	93.4	5.4	0.0032678	X		X			X	X	
4	93.9	93.3	5.7	0.0032785	X		X		X	X		
4	93.9	93.3	6.0	0.0032901	X	X			X		X	
5	94.2	93.5	5.6	0.0032336	X	X				X	X	X
5	94.2	93.5	5.8	0.0032423	X		X		X	X		X
5	94.2	93.4	6.0	0.0032509	X	X			X	X		X
5	94.2	93.4	6.2	0.0032562	X		X		X		X	X
5	94.1	93.4	6.3	0.0032621	X	X	X			X		X
6	94.5	93.6	6.0	0.0032083	X	X			X	X	X	X
6	94.4	93.5	6.7	0.0032364	X		X		X	X	X	X
6	94.3	93.5	7.0	0.0032481	X	X	X			X	X	X
6	94.3	93.4	7.1	0.0032520	X	X	X		X	X		X
6	94.3	93.4	7.1	0.0032525	X	X	X		X		X	X
7	94.6	93.6	7.1	0.0032093	X	X	X		X	X	X	X
7	94.5	93.4	8.0	0.0032501	X	X		X	X	X	X	X
7	94.4	93.3	8.7	0.0032786	X	X	X	X	X		X	X
7	94.4	93.3	8.7	0.0032789	X	X	X	X	X	X		X
7	94.4	93.3	8.8	0.0032864	X	X	X	X	X	X	X	
8	94.6	93.4	9.0	0.0032497	X	X	X	X	X	X	X	X

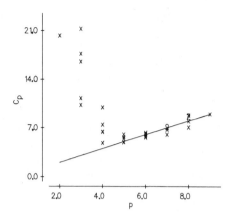

All criteria for selecting good predictor variables require judgment. Small values of s and C_p near p could conflict. However, any reasonable criterion will help eliminate many poor models and allow us to concentrate on a small number of potentially useful models.

SECTION

22.9 Exercises

22.9A Use the car mileage data of Exhibit 22.1A with expressway GPM as the response. Use a best subsets regression package to compare different possible sets of predictors.

    a Which model produces the smallest value for residual standard deviation?

    b Which model gives the largest value for adjusted R^2?

    c Which model gives the smallest value for C_p? (Filename: CARS.DAT.)

22.9B Use the car mileage data of Exhibit 22.1A with trip GPM as the response. Use a best subsets regression package to compare different possible sets of predictors.

    a Which model produces the smallest value for residual standard deviation?

    b Which model gives the largest value for adjusted R^2?

    c Which model gives the smallest value for C_p? (Filename: CARS.DAT.)

22.9C Return to the house price data of Exercise 20.9B. Use a best subsets regression package to compare different possible sets of predictors.

    a Which model produces the smallest value for residual standard deviation?

    b Which model gives the largest value for adjusted R^2?

    c Which model gives the smallest value for C_p? (Filename: HOUSEPRI.DAT.)

22.9D Consider the tree data listed in Exercise 20.7J. Two predictors are given: diameter and height. Create three more predictors: diameter^2, height^2, and diameter $\times$ height.

    a Use a best subsets regression program to select among models that may include any linear combination of the five predictors: diameter, diameter^2, height, height^2, and diameter $\times$ height.

    b Trees are roughly cylindrical in shape. The volume of a cylinder is given by the area of the base times the height. Since the area of a circle is proportional to its diameter squared, our simple geometrical argument suggests that diameter^2 $\times$ height might be a useful predictor of a tree's volume. Fit the one-predictor model volume $= \beta_0 + \beta_1$

(diameter^2 × height) + e and compare it to all of the possible models based on subsets of the predictors: diameter, diameter^2, height, height^2, and diameter × height considered in part (a). (Filename: TREES.DAT.)

22.9E   Consider the Harris Bank salary data presented in Section 21.10. The model presented there contains four predictors: educational level, time of hire, 1/(experience + 12), and gender. Create additional predictors: log(experience + 1), log(experience + 6), log(experience + 12), 1/(experience + 1), and 1/(experience + 6)

a   Plot log(salary) against each of these transformed experience predictors and interpret the plots.

b   Use a best subsets regression package to compare all possible subsets among the predictors: educational level, time of hire, gender, log(experience + 1), log(experience + 6), log(experience + 12), 1/(experience + 1), 1/(experience + 6), and 1/(experience + 12). (Filename: SALARY.DAT.)

SECTION

22.10   The F Test for Subsets of Coefficients (Optional)

In some settings, researchers want to test whether certain groups of regression parameters are zero. If they are, the corresponding predictors may be safely omitted from the model. For example, we may ask if the grade (med and hi) variables and assessed value variables as a group are important in modeling market value once square feet and square feet squared are in the regression model we have been considering throughout this book. In general, the model

$$y = \beta_0 + \beta_1 x_1 + \cdots + \beta_k x_k + e \qquad \text{(22.5)}$$

is considered to be reasonable on the basis of theory or earlier regression work. But the question centers on whether or not the p additional predictor variables x_{k+1}, x_{k+2}, ..., x_{k+p} should also be included in the model. That is, the expanded model

$$y = \beta_0 + \beta_1 x_1 + \cdots + \beta_k x_k + \beta_{k+1} x_{k+1} + \cdots + \beta_{k+p} x_{k+p} + e \qquad \text{(22.6)}$$

is being considered, but statistical confirmation of the added complication is needed. Formally, the hypothesis $H_0: \beta_{k+1} = \beta_{k+2} = \cdots = \beta_{k+p} = 0$ needs to be tested. The model of Equation (22.6) must yield a smaller residual sum of squares, and a statistical test may be based on the reduction in the sum of squares of residuals obtained when going from the reduced model of Equation (22.5), $SSE_{reduced}$, to the full model of Equation (22.6), SSE_{full}. A large reduction goes against the null hypothesis, while a more moderate reduction supports the null hypothesis. Under the usual regression assumptions it may be established that, when H_0 is true, the F ratio

$$F = \frac{(SSE_{reduced} - SSE_{full})/p}{SSE_{full}/(n - k - p - 1)} \qquad \text{(22.7)}$$

will follow an F distribution with p and $n - k - p - 1$ degrees of freedom for the numerator and the denominator, respectively. The null hypothesis $H_0: \beta_{k+1} = \beta_{k+2} = \cdots = \beta_{k+p} = 0$ is rejected if the observed F ratio is *larger* than an appropriate cut-off value obtained from the F distribution or if the p-value obtained from the upper tail of the F distribution is small enough.

EXAMPLE   **22.10A**   Exhibit 20.8A displays the regression results when fitting market value using square feet and square feet squared as predictors. The exhibit shows that $SSE_{reduced} = 687.33$. Exhibit 20.8B gives the regression results for the full model, which includes, in addition, the grade variables (med and hi) and the assessed variable. Here $SSE_{full} = 399.24$ with 54 degrees of freedom, and the current question may be phrased as, Is the reduction from an SSE of 687.33 to 399.24 *significant*? The F ratio of Equation (22.7) is given as

$$F = \frac{(687.33 - 399.24)/3}{399.24/(60 - 2 - 3 - 1)} = 12.99$$

with 3 and 54 degrees of freedom. Using a statistical package, the p-value is 0.0000 and we conclude that the additional predictors are indeed useful additions to the model.   ∎

SECTION

22.11 Exercises

22.11A   Consider the simple real estate model that relates market value linearly to square feet of living space. The regression results are in Exhibit 20.6A. Use the method of this section to assess the value of adding the set of variables square feet squared, grade variables med and hi, and assessed value to the model. The required regression results for the full model appear in Exhibit 20.8B.

22.11B   Use the F ratio described in Section 22.10 to test whether square feet squared should be included in the market value model in addition to square feet. The SSE for the reduced model is given in Exhibit 20.6A and the SSE for the full model is in Exhibit 20.8A. In addition, show that the F ratio obtained is the square of the t ratio for testing $H_0: \beta_2 = 0$ in the full model. This t ratio is shown in Exhibit 20.8A. When only *one* additional predictor is considered, that is, $p = 1$, it may be shown that the square of the t ratio for this parameter in the full model will always equal the F ratio of Equation (22.7). Thus a one-sided test based on the F ratio will be equivalent to a two-sided test based on the t ratio.

22.11C   Consider the Harris Bank salary data presented in Section 21.10. The model presented there contains four predictors: educational level, time of hire, 1/(experience + 12), and gender. Use the F test of Section 22.10 to evaluate the worth of adding the variables 1/(experience + 12) and gender to a simpler model that uses just educational level and time of hire to predict log(salary). (Filename: SALARY.DAT.)

SECTION

22.12 Stepwise Regression

Methods broadly classified as stepwise regression were developed to find good subsets of predictors with less computation than best subset methods. These methods are useful when a very large number of potential predictors makes calculating the best subset regression prohibitively time-consuming or expensive. The modeling proceeds sequentially by adding or deleting variables from the current model according to one of the criteria discussed previously. First, all one-predictor models are examined and the best one selected. Then the next model is obtained from the preceding one either by adding or deleting variables. Three somewhat different variations of the required steps are commonly considered: forward selection, backward elimination, and true stepwise regression.

forward selection

Starting with the best one-predictor model, **forward selection** selects additional predictor variables by adding variables one at a time to the model. At each step of the selection process the variable in the collection of predictors not already in the model that most reduces the residual sum of squares is added to the model. A rule based on one of the criteria for good models is chosen to decide when to stop adding variables.

backward elimination

Backward elimination begins with a model that contains all the predictors. Variables are then eliminated one by one on the basis of their t ratios. The variable with the *smallest* t ratio is dropped first. The multiple regression model is then reestimated and again the variable with the smallest t ratio is dropped. This process is continued until some predetermined criterion is met.

stepwise regression

Stepwise regression combines the previous two ideas. In forward selection a variable that enters the model can never be dropped later in the process. In backward elimination, once a variable is dropped it can never reenter the model. Neither method takes into account the fact that the addition or deletion of a variable affects the contributions of the other variables in the model. A variable dropped in backward elimination may become important later after other variables are dropped, and a variable added in forward selection may become unimportant later after other variables have entered the model. Stepwise regression begins with the best one-predictor model and proceeds with forward selection, but rechecks at each stage to see if variables should be dropped from the model once other variables have entered. Criteria for keeping or deleting variables are based on the F test of Section 22.10.

Exhibit 22.12A shows the output from Minitab's STEPWISE command, slightly edited and with subcommands to force forward selection only. Weight is the best single predictor. Transmission type was added second and number of cylinders third. According to the criteria used by Minitab, no further predictors should be added. Note that this final model agrees with our earlier choice of model based on looking at all subsets of predictors and using the C_p plot.

EXHIBIT 22.12A
Forward Selection of Predictors
with City GPM

```
Forward selection of city GPM on eight predictors, with N=45
 Step            1         2         3
 Constant -3.46E-03 0.0014551 0.0001472

 weight     0.00002   0.00002   0.00002
 t-ratio      20.68     13.71     11.15

 trans                 0.0053    0.0057
 t-ratio                 3.20      3.67

 cylind                          0.00150
 t-ratio                            2.72

 s          0.00388   0.00352   0.00328
 R-sq         90.86     92.66     93.78
```

Exhibit 22.12B gives the regression results when backward elimination is used. Horsepower is the first variable to be deleted. In the third step the number of cylinders is eliminated. The final model presented includes weight, displacement, gears, and foreign. Unfortunately, this is far from the best model, which contains weight, transmission type, and number of cylinders. None of the stepwise procedures is guaranteed to find the best models.

Finally, Exhibit 22.12C presents the results of the full stepwise regression method. For this data set, stepwise regression leads to the same model as forward selection in Exhibit 22.12A. Such agreement is not guaranteed in general. All "automatic" selection procedures must be used with caution. Automatic procedures can never replace the skill and subject-matter knowledge that the analyst brings to any given regression problem.

E X H I B I T 22.12B

Backward Elimination for Predictors of City GPM

Backward elimination for city GPM on eight predictors, with N=45

Step	1	2	3	4	5
Constant	0.008454	0.009095	0.012001	0.013141	0.009591
weight	0.00001	0.00001	0.00001	0.00002	0.00002
t-ratio	4.23	4.34	4.26	5.92	12.69
disp	0.0027	0.0024	0.0039	0.0039	0.0032
t-ratio	1.29	1.28	3.33	3.28	3.09
cylind	0.0010	0.0010			
t-ratio	1.00	0.99			
HP	-0.00001				
t-ratio	-0.29				
trans	0.0035	0.0034	0.0031		
t-ratio	1.40	1.39	1.27		
gears	-0.00179	-0.00189	-0.00206	-0.00336	-0.00336
t-ratio	-1.29	-1.42	-1.57	-4.04	-4.02
size	0.00115	0.00118	0.00119	0.00098	
t-ratio	1.36	1.42	1.43	1.19	
foreign	0.0022	0.0022	0.0024	0.0028	0.0027
t-ratio	1.66	1.66	1.81	2.20	2.09
S	0.00325	0.00321	0.00321	0.00323	0.00325
R-sq	94.64	94.62	94.48	94.25	94.04

E X H I B I T 22.12C

Stepwise Regression of City GPM on Eight Potential Predictors

Stepwise regression of city GPM on eight predictors, with N=45

Step	1	2	3
Constant	-3.46E-03	0.0014551	0.0001472
weight	0.00002	0.00002	0.00002
t-ratio	20.68	13.71	11.15
trans		0.0053	0.0057
t-ratio		3.20	3.67
cylind			0.00150
t-ratio			2.72
S	0.00388	0.00352	0.00328
R-sq	90.86	92.66	93.78

SECTION

22.13 Exercises

22.13A   Use the car mileage data of Exhibit 22.1A with expressway GPM as the response. Use a stepwise regression package to compare different possible sets of predictors. Compare the results to those obtained in Exercise 22.9A. (Filename: CARS.DAT.)

22.13B   Use the car mileage data of Exhibit 22.1A with trip GPM as the response. Use a stepwise regression package to compare different possible sets of predictors. Compare the results to those obtained in Exercise 22.9B. (Filename: CARS.DAT.)

22.13C   Return to the house price data of Exercise 20.9B. Use a stepwise regression package to compare different possible sets of predictors. Compare the results to those obtained in Exercise 22.9C. (Filename: HOUSEPRI.DAT.)

22.13D   Consider the tree data listed in Exercise 20.7J. Use a stepwise regression program to select among models, which may include any linear combination of these predictors: diameter, $diameter^2$, height, $height^2$, diameter $\times$ height, and $diameter^2 \times$ height. Compare the results to those obtained in Exercise 22.9D. (Filename: TREES.DAT.)

Chapter Summary

While many variables may be candidates for predictors, not all of them necessarily prove effective. In selecting the variables to be included as predictors in a regression model, one must guard against two dangers:

- Failing to include critical variables (model underspecification)
- Including so many variables that they interfere with each other (model overspecification and perhaps collinearity)

Techniques for selecting variables include added variable plots, best subset regression, F tests for subsets of coefficients, and stepwise regression. All of these techniques must be used with caution and good sense, and the model finally selected should always be viewed as a tentative one, subject to revision in light of new information and model diagnostics.

Supplementary Exercises for Chapter 22

22A   Exercise 8.9H, Exercise 20A, and Exercise 21A dealt with the time it takes to assemble an electronic printed circuit board in terms of seven predictor variables.

a   Calculate the correlation coefficients between all the predictor variables and interpret.

b   Calculate the variance inflation factors for each predictor variable in the full regression model and interpret their magnitudes.

c   Display the added variable plot for assessing the added effect of the variable Number of Transistors after adjusting for the effect of the variable Number of Components. Interpret this plot.

d Use a best subsets regression program to select the best regression models with one, two, ..., seven predictor variables. Use the C_p criterion to select the best model. (Filename: BOARDS.DAT.)

22B The Chevrolet Lumina APV was a new domestic model in 1990, a rather radical, plastic bodied, ultrastreamlined all-purpose vehicle (minivan). It weighs 3630 pounds, has a 3.1 liter V6, 120 horsepower engine, and transmits its power to the front wheels through an automatic, three-gear transmission.

a Use the results displayed in Exhibit 22.4C to predict the city GPM for this vehicle.

b Use the results displayed in Exhibit 22.4D to predict the city GPM for this vehicle and compare your answer to the one in part (a).

c In the January 1990 issue of *Consumer Reports* the Lumina APV test results gave a city MPG of 12. Compare this to the predictions found in parts (a) and (b).

22C The data file below gives additional car data that was not available when the data set in Exhibit 22.1A was constructed.

```
filename CARS3.DAT
More car data from Consumer Reports
March 1989 through June 1989
Variables: MPG (city, trip, expressway), weight, displacement,
number of cylinders, horsepower,
transmission type (1=automatic, 0=manual)
number of transmission gears
size, foreign/domestic
   14 26 35 3300 3.0 6 141 1 4 3 0  Dodge Dynasty
   15 27 38 3325 3.8 6 165 1 4 3 0  Oldsmobile 88 Royale Brougham
   13 24 30 3790 5.0 8 150 1 4 5 0  Ford LTD Crown Victoria
   12 21 29 3855 5.0 8 170 1 4 5 0  Chevrolet Caprice Classic
   25 37 43 2340 1.5 4  81 0 5 1 1  Eagle Summit LX
   24 37 44 2275 1.6 4  90 0 5 1 1  Nissan Sentra XE
   26 38 46 2075 1.5 4  78 0 5 1 1  Toyota Tercel Deluxe
   23 38 47 2345 1.9 4  90 0 5 1 0  Ford Escort LX
   13 25 29 3265 2.7 6 160 1 4 3 1  Acura Legend L
   14 24 30 3480 3.0 6 158 1 4 3 1  Mazda 929
   15 26 33 3200 3.0 6 160 1 4 3 1  Nissan Maxima GXE
   16 26 32 3480 3.0 6 190 1 4 3 1  Toyota Cressida
```

a Using the models displayed in Exhibits 22.4C and D, predict the city GPM for each of these new cases.

b Compare the external predictive power of the two models by computing the mean of the squared prediction errors based on these additional data only.

22D The data below give values for a variety of characteristics that may affect the speeds of automated guideway transit systems used at amusement parks or airports to transport people over relatively short distances. The goal is to explain the speeds of the systems in terms of the other variables. The variables are:

Speed (km/hr)

DCTM (Indicator of direct current traction motor, 1 = yes, 0 = no)

SLIM (Indicator of single-sided linear induction motor, 1 = yes, 0 = no)

Vehicles (number in system)

Length (of a vehicle in meters)

Width (of a vehicle in meters)

Height (of a vehicle in meters)

Weight (of a vehicle in pounds)

Seats (number)

Standing room (number)

Capacity (seated plus standing)

Crush load (number of people per lane per hour)

Path length (total length of track in system)

Headway (minimum time between trains)

Stations (number in system)

System (name)

Use these data to build a regression model to explain how Speed is related to the other variables. Be sure to consider transformations of variables such as log(Speed), $\sqrt{\text{Vehicles}}$, and $\sqrt{\text{Headway}}$. Do a complete analysis including selecting variables, checking significance, looking for outliers and influential observations, and investigating normality.

```
Filename: TRANSIT.DAT
Data on guideway transit systems from a student project by Danelle Harringa
Source: Transportation and Traffic Engineering Handbook, 2ed, Prentice-Hall, 1982
Variables: Speed (km/hr), DCTM (direct current traction motor), SLIM (single sided linear
induction motor), Vehicles (number), Length, Width, Height, Weight, Capacity (seated or standing),
Crush load (people per lane per hour), Path length, Headway (minimum time between trains),
Stations, System
```

Speed	DCTM	SLIM	Vehicles	Length	Width	Height	Weight	Capacity	Crush	Path	Headway	Stations	System
32	1	0	2	3.66	1.68	1.59	21350	6	0	6	6	8	0.55	1	Aerial Transit System
48	1	0	2	7.53	2.04	2.65	63600	10	14	24	30	20	1.29	3	Bradley Field
48	1	0	2	11.06	2.99	3.35	117880	8	92	100	150	100	2.25	2	Busch Gardens
19	1	0	32	4.27	1.83	2.25	10670	12	0	12	12	120	2.09	2	California Expo
22	1	0	32	4.27	1.83	2.25	10670	12	0	12	12	132	3.21	1	Carowinds
80	1	0	2	7.01	2.04	3.29	80000	12	20	32	50	15	0.15	1	Dashaveyor
64	0	1	3	6.10	3.29	2.99	53350	12	0	12	12	2	0.80	3	Duke University
48	1	0	2	7.53	2.04	2.65	63600	10	14	24	30	20	0.80	2	Fairlane Shopping Center
16	1	0	24	4.27	1.83	2.25	10670	12	0	12	12	75	1.29	2	Hershey Park
19	1	0	18	12.20	1.52	2.29	32000	6	4	10	14	60	1.93	8	Houston International Airport
24	0	0	10	3.66	2.23	2.23	39600	6	4	10	14	20	2.57	3	PRT
10	1	0	54	4.27	1.83	2.25	10670	12	0	12	12	210	3.38	1	King's Dominion
10	1	0	63	4.27	1.83	2.25	10670	12	0	12	12	180	3.22	1	King's Island
13	1	0	36	4.27	1.83	2.25	10670	12	0	12	12	60	1.29	3	Magic Mountain
45	1	0	4	11.06	2.97	3.35	117880	0	100	100	150	85	0.80	2	Miami Airport
48	1	0	2	2.93	1.67	2.04	17790	6	0	6	6	5	0.30	1	Monocab
48	1	0	45	4.72	2.04	2.68	38250	8	7	15	21	15	8.53	3	Morgantown
13	1	0	4	12.19	1.83	2.74	32000	8	8	16	24	240	0.37	2	Pearl Ridge
72	0	1	2	4.36	2.65	2.50	32000	6	0	6	6	6	0.30	1	PRT
48	1	0	12	11.28	2.83	3.35	113430	12	90	102	125	100	2.74	8	Sea-Tac
45	0	0	2	3.81	2.04	2.74	33440	6	4	10	12	5	2.25	8	StaRRcar
45	1	0	8	11.06	2.83	3.35	95640	0	100	100	125	70	0.11	1	Tampa Airport
56	0	0	2	5.64	1.16	1.98	9340	8	0	8	8	3	1.00	3	Uniflo
22	0	1	150	2.43	1.46	1.16	4180	4	0	4	4	14	1.40	1	Walt Disney

· · · · ■ ■ ■ ■ ■ ■

Glossary for Chapter 22

added variable plot	Plot for assessing the effect of a predictor variable after adjusting for the effect of one or more predictor variables.
backward elimination	A special stepwise regression method that eliminates more and more predictors to find the "best" model.
best subset regression	A method for choosing the best predictor variables by considering all possible subsets of predictors.
collinear	Predictor variables that are approximately linearly related.

forward selection	A special stepwise regression method that selects more and more predictors to find the "best" model.
Mallows' C_p criterion	A criterion for choosing the better predictor variables.
misspecified model	A model that does not include the "correct" predictor variables.
overspecified model	A model that includes extra predictor variables.
stepwise regression	A sequential method for choosing the best predictor variables.
underspecified model	A model that fails to include important predictor variables.
variance inflation factor (VIF)	A measure of an individual predictor's collinearity with the other predictors.

Time Series Data

Chapter Objectives

After mastering this chapter, you will be able to:

- Diagnose residuals from a time series regression for evidence of autocorrelation

- Model first differences of a series when appropriate

- Fit and interpret distributed lag models

- Fit and interpret autoregressive models

- Do simple and double exponential smoothing on a time series

- Give models that yield simple and double exponential smoothing as optimal forecast techniques

23.1 Introduction

Data are often measurements of a variable taken at regular intervals, such as weekly, monthly, quarterly, or yearly. Stock prices are reported daily, interest rates are posted weekly, and sales figures are given monthly, quarterly, and annually. Inventory and production levels are also recorded at regular time periods. The list goes on and on. The sequence plots of Chapter 2 and the notion of autocorrelation introduced in Section 6.8 are important aspects of the longitudinal analysis of time series data that will be expanded on in this chapter.

Data collected from a process over time provide a unique opportunity for predicting future values of the series. If an adequate statistical model for past series behavior can be found and if the process continues to operate similarly in the future, then predictions can be made on the basis of the model. But predictions alone are not enough. If the model adequately describes the series behavior, a measure of accuracy can be attached to the predictions. Prediction intervals that are likely to contain future values are an important aspect of the prediction process. This chapter extends regression modeling ideas to data collected at regular intervals over time. First, you examine simple models of the relationship between a response variable and functions of the time variable. You learn to use additional tools for diagnosing autocorrelation in residuals, a common problem in modeling time series data. Next, you learn methods to use when correlations are between changes in levels rather than between the predictors' actual values. You learn the basics of handling series where the correlation involves past as well as present values of a variable, and of correlating the values of a series with past values in that same series. Finally, you learn methods for smoothing variation in a series to make it easier to see any general trend. The next chapter concludes the study of time series by extending these methods to analyze seasonal time series, those where a trend or phenomenon recurs over regular periods.

SECTION

23.2 Time Series Regression

For time series that exhibit a strong upward or downward trend, a regression model with time as a predictor may be considered.

Time as a Predictor

linear time trend

The simplest such model is a **linear time trend**, which is a trend modeled as a straight line. Here it is assumed that the series y_t at time t can be expressed as

$$y_t = \beta_0 + \beta_1 t + e_t \qquad \textbf{(23.1)}$$

This method is illustrated using the data on hourly wages in Exhibit 23.2A. Six years of monthly data are available, but the last year's data are held out to check the prediction accuracy of the model. That is, the 60 observations from July 1981 through June 1986 are used to fit the model and predict values for the 12 months following. The predictions can then be compared with the actual values to assess the forecasting performance of the model. A linear time trend model seems plausible based on the sequence plot in Exhibit 23.2B.

The regression results are shown in Exhibit 23.2C. Notice that wages tend to increase by about 0.0146 dollars per month. Also notice that the regression coefficient on the time predictor has a t ratio of 49.62, which most would deem highly significant. The R^2 value of 97.7% is also extremely large. Exhibit 23.2D displays the sequence plot with the straight-line fit overlayed. Surely this is a "good model," and it is used to forecast the 12 values for the coming year.

EXHIBIT **23.2A**

Hourly Wages in the Apparel and Textile Industry by Month—1981–1987

```
filename: APAWAGES.DAT
Hourly wages - apparel and other textile products
(Source: Survey of Current Business, September issues, 1981-1987)
July 1981 through June 1987
 Jul  Aug  Sep  Oct  Nov  Dec  Jan  Feb  Mar  Apr  May  Jun
4.92 4.96 5.04 5.05 5.04 5.04 5.18 5.13 5.15 5.18 5.16 5.18
5.19 5.20 5.23 5.21 5.24 5.28 5.33 5.33 5.33 5.35 5.33 5.36
5.35 5.35 5.39 5.40 5.43 5.44 5.50 5.46 5.48 5.49 5.48 5.50
5.53 5.55 5.63 5.61 5.61 5.68 5.73 5.70 5.73 5.74 5.69 5.70
5.70 5.69 5.75 5.74 5.75 5.80 5.82 5.79 5.80 5.81 5.78 5.79
5.79 5.83 5.91 5.87 5.87 5.90 5.94 5.93 5.93 5.94 5.89 5.91
```

EXHIBIT 23.2B
Sequence Plot of Hourly Wages
in the Apparel and Textile
Industry—1981–1987

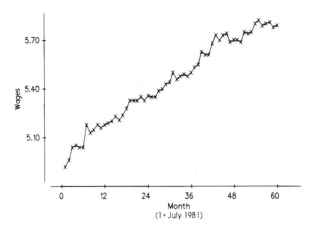

EXHIBIT 23.2C
Wages Regressed on Time

```
The regression equation is

Wages = 5.00 + 0.0146time

Predictor        Coef        Stdev      t-ratio          p
Constant      5.00218      0.01030      485.58      0.000
time        0.0145735    0.0002937       49.62      0.000

s = 0.03940      R-sq = 97.7%      R-sq(adj) = 97.7%
```

EXHIBIT 23.2D
Sequence Plot of Wages with
Straight-Line Fit

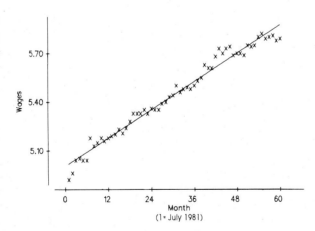

Exhibit 23.2E lists the actual values along with predictions and the 95% prediction intervals obtained from standard regression calculations. More digits are displayed here than would be appropriate for a final report. These should be considered as working values obtained from standard computer results.

A better perspective on the predictions may be seen through various graphs. Exhibit 23.2F shows the original sequence plot with the wage data plotted as A's, the fitted straight line as a solid line, the future-wage data plotted as B's, and the future predictions shown as a dashed line. This exhibit shows that the predictions

EXHIBIT **23.2E**

Predictions, Prediction Intervals, and Actual Wages Based on Straight-Line Model

Month	Prediction	Prediction Interval	Actual Value
61	5.89116	[5.80962, 5.97269]	5.79
62	5.90573	[5.82406, 5.98740]	5.83
63	5.92031	[5.83850, 6.00211]	5.91
64	5.93488	[5.85294, 6.01682]	5.87
65	5.94945	[5.86737, 6.03154]	5.87
66	5.96403	[5.88179, 6.04626]	5.90
67	5.97860	[5.89621, 6.06098]	5.94
68	5.99317	[5.91063, 6.07571]	5.93
69	6.00775	[5.92505, 6.09045]	5.93
70	6.02232	[5.93946, 6.10518]	5.94
71	6.03689	[5.95387, 6.11992]	5.89
72	6.05147	[5.96827, 6.13467]	5.91

EXHIBIT **23.2F**

Wages—Predictions and Actual Values from Straight-Line Model

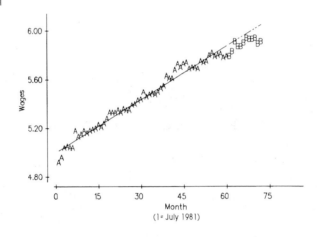

are uniformly too high. But how wide are the prediction intervals and how are they placed relative to the actual values? Perhaps the intervals include all or most of the future data. Again, graphic displays readily show the facts.

Exhibit 23.2G displays the actual wage values for the year preceding the forecasts (A's), the year of the forecasts (also A's), the forecasts (B's), and the upper and lower 95% prediction limits. Three of the 12 actual values are outside the intervals. In particular, the first month's prediction interval missed the actual value. This model is clearly inadequate for forecasting the wage rate series.

One approach to improving the forecasts is to use a model that allows for curvature in the trend, similar to what was done with regression models for cross-sectional data. The simplest such model includes an additional term with time squared as a predictor. This defines a model with **quadratic time trend**:

quadratic time trend

$$y_t = \beta_0 + \beta_1 t + \beta_2 t^2 + e_t \qquad (23.2)$$

The quadratic trend regression results for the wages time series are given in Exhibit 23.2H. They show that both the linear and quadratic terms are highly significant and the R^2 value is 98.2%. The adjusted R^2 has increased to 98.1%, and the value

E X H I B I T **23.2G**
Actual Values, Predictions, and
Prediction Limits from
Straight-Line Model

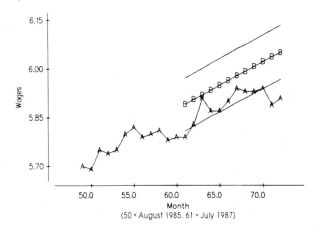

Month
(50 = August 1985, 61 = July 1987)

E X H I B I T **23.2H**
Wages Regressed on Time and
Time Squared

```
The regression equation is

Wages = 4.96 + 0.0187time -0.000068time^2

Predictor        Coef        Stdev      t-ratio        p
Constant      4.95919      0.01404      353.34      0.000
time          0.018733     0.001062      17.65      0.000
time^2       -0.00006819  0.00001687    -4.04      0.000

s = 0.03504      R-sq = 98.2%      R-sq(adj) = 98.1%
```

of s has decreased to 0.03504 (compare the results for the straight-line model in Exhibit 23.2C). Exhibit 23.2I shows the 60 actual series values, the fitted quadratic trend, the prediction curve based on the quadratic trend, and the actual future year's values. The last year's values used in model fitting, the predictions and prediction limits, and the future year's values are displayed in Exhibit 23.2J.

E X H I B I T **23.2I**
Predictions and Actual Values
from Quadratic Trend Model

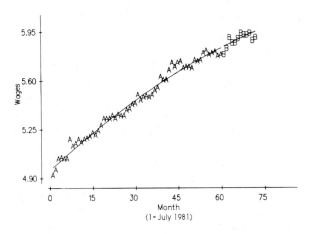

Month
(1 = July 1981)

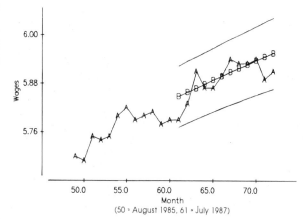

(50 = August 1985, 61 = July 1987)

Compared to results in Exhibits 23.2F and G, in which the straight-line model was used, the quadratic model does a much better job of following the trend in the series. However, as we will soon see, the regression assumption of independent error terms is seriously violated with both models. Although these models are extremely simple, there are few applications of them where the standard regression assumptions are reasonably well satisfied as revealed by residual analysis. Other models that take account of the autocorrelation in the data are usually much more appropriate. This series is used again in Exercise 24.6G, where a considerably better model is illustrated.

Diagnostics: Autocorrelation Revisited

Autocorrelation, introduced in Chapter 6, is present in nearly all time series data. Even after modeling the general trend with a line, a quadratic curve, or other curve, the errors around that curve are generally autocorrelated. When modeling time series data, an important diagnostic tool is a sequence plot of the residuals. As always, we hope to see no patterns in this plot. Any trends here indicate the inadequacy of the model. In particular, autocorrelation indicates that relationships among variables that have not been captured by the model are present. By accounting for the autocorrelation in the model, we should be able to better predict future values of the series.

Exhibit 23.2K shows the sequence plot of residuals when fitting the wages series with a straight-line trend model. Two things are apparent from this plot. The residuals at both ends of the series are all negative. This indicates the curvature in the general trend that was not captured in the straight-line model. As important, however, is the fact that residuals that are close together in time are nearly always of the same sign, either both positive or both negative. That is, they lie on the same side of the mean residual of zero. The residuals are at least moderately autocorrelated at the first lag, or lag 1. This autocorrelation may be more easily seen in the scatterplot of residuals versus residuals lagged one month shown in Exhibit 23.2L. The correlation in this plot is 0.597, documenting the relationship seen in the plot. Of course, it is possible

EXHIBIT **23.2K**
Sequence Plot of Residuals for
Wages with Straight-Line Trend
Model

EXHIBIT **23.2K**
Sequence Plot of Residuals for
Wages with Straight-Line Trend
Model

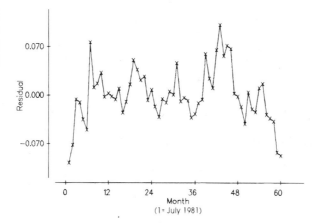

EXHIBIT **23.2L**
Residuals Versus Lagged
Residuals for Wages with
Straight-Line Trend Model

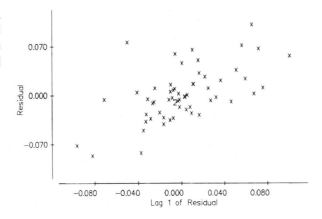

that the perceived autocorrelation is not real but only an artifact of using the wrong trend model for this data set.

Similar plots for the quadratic trend model are considered next. Exhibit 23.2M gives the sequence plot of residuals for the wage series when modeled with the quadratic trend. The problem of numerous negative residuals at both ends of the series has now been addressed. However, the residuals are still autocorrelated. This can be seen more readily in the scatterplot of residuals versus lagged residuals in

E X H I B I T **23.2M**
Sequence Plot of Residuals for
Wages with Quadratic Trend
Model

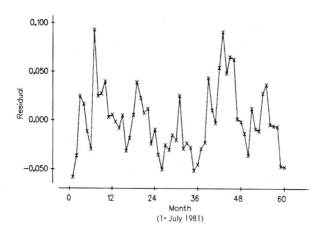

E X H I B I T **23.2N**
Residuals Versus Lagged
Residuals for Wages with
Quadratic Trend Model

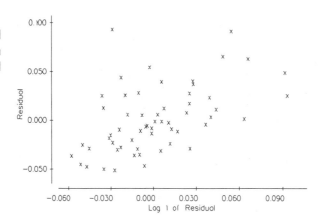

Exhibit 23.2N. The correlation in this display is 0.520, again showing moderate autocorrelation in the residuals at lag 1.

To better assess the magnitude of autocorrelations in residuals, the theoretical results obtained by Bartlett are used.[†] He showed that for independent data and large n, the sampling distribution of an autocorrelation coefficient is approximately normal with mean zero and standard deviation $1/\sqrt{n}$. Thus an autocorrelation larger than $2/\sqrt{n}$ or $3/\sqrt{n}$ in magnitude would be considered statistically significant and independence would be strongly questioned. In the present example, $n = 60$. The observed autocorrelation 0.520 is larger than $3/\sqrt{60}$, or 0.387. Thus the autocorrelation is excessive for independent data.

[†]M. S. Bartlett, "On the Theoretical Specification of Sampling Properties of Autocorrelated Time Series," *Journal of the Royal Statistical Society*, B, 8 (1946), 27–41.

The Durbin-Watson Statistic[†]

Another statistic frequently used to detect autocorrelation in regression residuals is the **Durbin-Watson statistic**, which is calculated as

Durbin-Watson statistic (DW)

$$DW = \frac{\sum_{t=2}^{n}(\hat{e}_t - \hat{e}_{t-1})^2}{\sum_{t=1}^{n}\hat{e}_t^2}$$

By straightforward algebra it can be shown that, to a good first approximation, $DW \simeq 2(1 - r_1)$ where r_1 is the lag 1 autocorrelation in the residuals. Thus if the residuals are not autocorrelated so that $r_1 \simeq 0$, DW is expected to be about 2. If the residuals are strongly positively autocorrelated with $r_1 \simeq 1$, then $DW \simeq 0$; if the residuals are strongly negatively autocorrelated with $r_1 \simeq -1$, then $DW \simeq 4$. Thus, values of DW near 2 support independence of the error terms; values of DW nearer the extremes of 0 or 4 support a hypothesis of autocorrelated errors. Nearly all statistical software calculates the Durbin-Watson statistic automatically.

Consider the linear time trend model for wages reported in Exhibit 23.2C and with residuals plotted in Exhibit 23.2K. For these residuals, $DW = 0.73$, which is reasonably close to $2(1 - r_1) = 2(1 - 0.597) = 0.81$. This value, closer to 0 than to 2, signals the problem with positively autocorrelated residuals. Similarly, the quadratic trend model with regression results in Exhibit 23.2H and residuals sequence plotted in Exhibit 23.2M has a DW of 0.93. Although 0.93 is slightly closer to 2 than 0.73, this still indicates important positive autocorrelation in the errors.

The Durbin-Watson statistic has a serious limitation, namely it checks for autocorrelation in the errors only at lag 1. Autocorrelation should also be checked at several other lags, especially those at which it may be suspected. You can do this most effectively using scatterplots.

Formal tests of significance of lag 1 autocorrelation in the errors may be based on DW. However, the sampling distribution of DW, even when the errors are independent, depends on the specific values for the predictor variables in the regression problem being considered. It is not feasible to tabulate or even computerize the percentiles of all these distributions. It is possible to tabulate upper and lower bounds on the critical percentiles so that unambiguous conclusions may be reached in many cases. However, the test may be inconclusive. In the quadratic trend model for wages with 60 cases and two predictors (time and time squared) and under the hypothesis of independent errors, the first percentile of the distribution of DW is between 1.35 and 1.48.[‡] Thus the observed value of $DW = 0.93$, which is below 1.35, provides

---

[†]This statistic was proposed in a series of three papers by J. Durbin and G. S. Watson, "Testing for Serial Correlation in Least Squares Regression, I, II and III," *Biometrika*, 37 (1950), 409–428; 38 (1951), 159–178; and 58 (1971), 1–19.

[‡]Further discussion of these tests and tables of the bounds on the critical percentiles may be found, for example, in R. B. Miller and D. W. Wichern, *Intermediate Business Statistics* (New York: Holt, Rinehart and Winston, 1977).

conclusive evidence of positive autocorrelation at lag 1 in the errors of the quadratic trend model.

Differences

In some applications, two or more time series have been collected over the same time period and interest centers on the relationship between the series. The example used here introduces some subtle issues in longitudinal data analysis.

Exhibit 23.2O shows annual figures on the index of industrial production (IIP) and the unemployment rate (Unemployment) for the United States from 1973 to 1982. A scatterplot of Unemployment versus IIP is shown in Exhibit 23.2P. The IIP is a measure of output from the manufacturing sector of the economy. Consequently, it is expected to be strongly negatively correlated with Unemployment. In other words, when industrial production is high, the demand for workers is expected to keep the unemployment rate low, and vice versa. The scatterplot shows a disappointingly weak negative correlation. On the basis of the scatterplot, it would be reasonable to conclude that Unemployment is virtually unrelated to IIP. Because this flies in the face of intuition and economic theory, we may be tempted to conclude that at least one of the two measures does not accurately reflect reality. This conclusion, however, is faulty. The difficulty with the analysis put forward so far is an inappropriate interpretation of the scatterplot and a mishandling of the time dimension.

E X H I B I T **23.2O**
Annual Index of Industrial
Production and the
Unemployment Rate

Year	IIP	Unemployment
1973	130	4.8
1974	129	5.5
1975	118	8.3
1976	131	7.6
1977	138	6.9
1978	146	6.0
1979	153	5.8
1980	147	7.0
1981	151	7.5
1982	139	9.5

Source: U.S. Bureau of the Census, *Statistical Abstract of the United States: 1984*, 104th ed. (Washington, D.C.: U.S. Government Printing Office, 1983).

The plotting symbols A, B, ..., J in Exhibit 23.2P show time order—that is, A denotes 1973, B denotes 1974, and so on. Connecting these symbols in alphabetical order yields the scatterplot in Exhibit 23.2Q. The line segment running from A to B shows that there was a decrease in IIP and an increase in Unemployment between

EXHIBIT 23.2P
Scatterplot of Unemployment
Versus IIP for 1973–1982

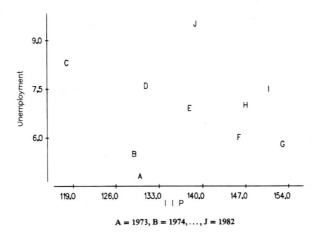

A = 1973, B = 1974,..., J = 1982

EXHIBIT 23.2Q
Scatterplot as in Exhibit 23.2P
but with Lines Showing Time
Order

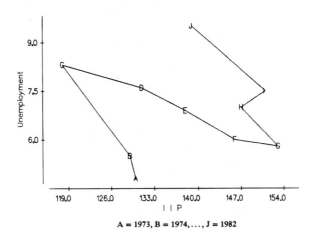

A = 1973, B = 1974,..., J = 1982

1973 and 1974. Similar changes occurred between 1974 and 1975. The line running from C to D shows that there was an increase in IIP and a decrease in Unemployment.

These changes correspond to our intuitive understanding of the relationship between IIP and Unemployment. The table in Exhibit 23.2R shows the annual changes in the two variables. The change variables (differences) are labeled DIIP and DUnemployment because the annual changes are called *first differences* of the original series (see Section 2.10). Notice that except for 1981, the changes in IIP and Unemployment are of opposite sign.

Exhibit 23.2S shows the scatterplot of DUnemployment versus DIIP. The correlation of $r = -0.95$ shows a very strong negative linear relationship between the two variables, suggesting that *changes* in the index of industrial production should be useful in predicting *changes* in unemployment rate.

The analysis of the first differences suggests that IIP and Unemployment do a good job of documenting changes. If changes can be predicted accurately, then the

Year	IIP	Unemployment	DIIP	DUnemployment
1973	130	4.8	*	*
1974	129	5.5	−1	0.7
1975	118	8.3	−11	2.8
1976	131	7.6	13	−0.7
1977	138	6.9	7	−0.7
1978	146	6.0	8	−0.9
1979	153	5.8	7	−0.2
1980	147	7.0	−6	1.2
1981	151	7.5	4	0.5
1982	139	9.5	−12	2.0

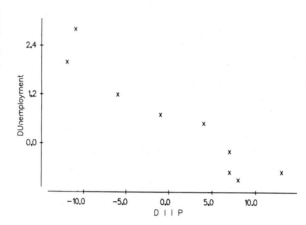

level of a series can be tracked; the predicted change could be added to the current level of the series to get a prediction of the next level of the series.

To examine the predictiveness of the relationship in Exhibit 23.2S, a straight line was fitted by least squares. The following results were obtained:

$$\text{DUnêmployment} = 0.660 - 0.138\text{DIIP} \qquad \textbf{(23.3)}$$

with $s = 0.4302$ and $R^2 = 90.3\%$. Residual analysis is tenuous here, since there are only nine data points after differencing. However, the sequence plot in Exhibit 23.2T and the plot of residuals versus lagged residuals in Exhibit 23.2U do not indicate any difficulties with the assumption of independent error terms.

Since the standard deviation of DUnemployment is 1.29, the regression model should produce substantially better predictions than the observed differences in unemployment rate. This statement is subject to a major condition, however. To achieve the promised accuracy in the prediction of DUnemployment, the estimate of the value of DIIP for the next year (1983) must be accurate.

Inspection of the differenced data in Exhibit 23.2R shows that DIIP is much more variable than DUnemployment. You may verify that DIIP has a mean of 1 and a standard deviation of 9, whereas the mean and standard deviation of DUnemployment

EXHIBIT **23.2T**
Sequence Plot of Residuals for
DUnemployment Regressed on
DIIP

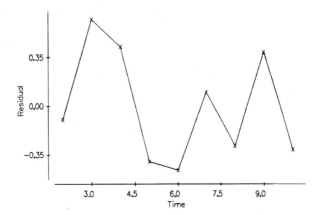

EXHIBIT **23.2U**
Residuals Versus Lagged
Residuals for DUnemployment
Regressed on DIIP

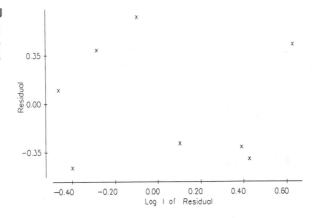

are 0.522 and 1.294, respectively. Thus, using the past data on DIIP gives very little accuracy in predicting future values of DIIP. The choice of the value for DIIP to use in the regression prediction must come from other considerations. If there is a great deal of uncertainty in the changes in industrial production, then this will increase the uncertainty in the prediction of future changes. One way to convey this notion is to list several values of DIIP and the corresponding 2-standard-deviation prediction intervals for DUnemployment, as in the table below.

Predicted Range of
Unemployment Rates Depending
on Industrial Production

$x =$ **DIIP**	$\hat{y} = 0.66 - 0.138x$	**2-Standard-Deviation Prediction Interval for $y =$ DUnemployment**	
−11	2.178	[1.2	3.2]
−5	1.350	[0.5	2.3]
1	0.522	[−0.4	1.4]
7	−0.306	[−1.2	0.6]
13	−1.134	[−2.1	−0.0]

You see that the value of DIIP chosen has a substantial impact on the prediction of DUnêmployment and a modest impact on the size of the prediction interval. Because the past history of the DIIP gives little information about the future, knowledge of other aspects of the economy would have to be analyzed in trying to come up with the best choice of DIIP. If a reliable choice of DIIP remains elusive, one may fall back on the prediction interval based on the unemployment series alone, namely,

$$\bar{y} \pm 2s_y = [0.522 - 2(1.294), 0.522 + 2(1.294)]$$
$$= [-2.1, 3.1]$$

which virtually contains the union of the intervals produced by the regression model displayed above. Since the interval predicts that the unemployment rate may record anything between a decrease of 2.1 percentage points to an increase of 3.1 percentage points, it conveys little if any definitive information.

In this section examples have illustrated the use of the relationship between two times series to create a prediction model. The time series that were analyzed showed that even though the series of *levels* may be only weakly correlated, the series of *changes* may well be highly correlated. Be on the lookout for this phenomenon when analyzing time series, because when it occurs the changes allow a good predictive model to be built, whereas the levels are not a reliable basis for a predictive model.

The model in this section relates values of two variables *in the same year*. This means that to predict a future value of y, a good estimate of a future value of x must be chosen—a task that may prove difficult in practice. In some time series applications, current values of y can be related to past values of x. If so, current values of x can be used to predict future values of y. Such models are of great practical value and will be discussed in Section 23.4

SECTION

23.3 Exercises

23.3A Calculate the autocorrelation coefficients at lags 1 and 2 for the time series 4, 5, 7, 5, 6, 8, 7.

23.3B Consider the flour price index for Buffalo, New York, listed in Exhibit 2.10A and plotted in Exhibit 2.10B and the flour price index for Kansas City given in Exercise 2.11A. These monthly series were obtained for the same period of time but at different geographic locations.

a Investigate a model that predicts the Buffalo value using the Kansas City value for the same month. Are the residuals autocorrelated?

b Comment on the applicability of the model obtained in part (a) for predicting the Buffalo value from the Kansas City value. (Filenames: BUFLOUR.DAT and KCFLOUR.DAT.)

23.3C You are given that the current level of a time series is 600 and you are given the following 2-standard-deviation prediction interval for the next *change* in the series: $[-25, 31]$. What is the prediction interval for the next *level* of the series?

23.4 Lagged Variables

The previous section related values of two variables measured at the same time. Under these conditions, a good estimate of a future value of x must be chosen to predict a future value of y. This task often proves difficult in practice. Sometimes, though, *past* values of x can be related to current values of y. Such *lagged* models, often of great practical value, are the subject of this section.

Distributed Lags

Market researchers have long been interested in the longitudinal relationship between advertising and sales. However, in the absence of controlled experimentation, causal relationships are difficult, if not impossible, to establish. Data often arise haphazardly in the normal course of business. Correlation between two variables *could* reflect causation from one to the other but could also be due to causation in the reverse direction or to a relationship with a third variable. The goal, then, is not to establish causative relationships but simply to build models that help *predict* one variable from another.

The data set in Exhibit 23.4A is used to illustrate the ideas in this section. Sales for a weight control product were measured monthly in multiples of equivalent serving units (to account for the different sizes of packages sold). Advertising for this product was measured in monthly dollars of advertising. Advertising dollars were attributed to the actual month in which the advertising appeared rather than to the month in which

EXHIBIT 23.4A
Monthly Sales and Advertising Expenditures for 36 Months

```
filename: SALESADS.DAT
Sales and advertising for 36 months
(Source: F.M.Bass and D.G.Clarke, "Testing Distributed Lag Models
of Advertising Effect," J. Marketing Research (1972) 298-308.)
Variables: sales, advertising
12.0  15        30.5  33
20.5  16        28.0  62
21.0  18        26.0  22
15.5  27        21.5  12
15.3  21        19.7  24
23.5  49        19.0   3
24.5  21        16.0   5
21.3  22        20.7  14
23.5  28        26.5  36
28.0  36        30.6  40
24.0  40        32.3  49
15.5   3        29.5   7
17.3  21        28.3  52
25.3  29        31.3  65
25.0  62        32.2  17
36.5  65        26.4   5
36.5  46        23.4  17
29.6  44        16.4   1
```

E X H I B I T **23.4B**

Sequence Plot of Advertising
Expenditures for a Weight
Control Product

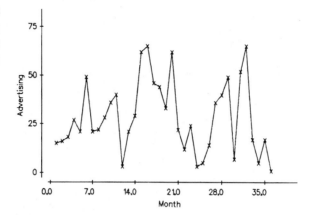

E X H I B I T **23.4C**

Sequence Plot of Sales of a
Weight Control Product

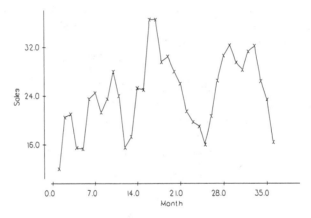

the advertising bills were sent or paid. Considerable variability over time in both sales and advertising is shown in the sequence plots given in Exhibits 23.4B and 23.4C.

To begin to understand the relationships between Sales and Advertising, consider the combined sequence plot shown in Exhibit 23.4D. Here standardized versions of both sequences have been plotted on the same graph, but 3 has been added to each standardized Advertising value so that the sequences will not plot on top of each other. In this plot the series generally go up and down together, although this pattern is not completely regular. There are periods in which Sales increase despite no increase in Advertising, and there are other periods in which Sales do not increase even when Advertising dollars increase. The drop in Advertising at month 30 is not reflected in a corresponding drop in Sales.

To further investigate the relationships, Sales versus Advertising is scatterplotted in Exhibit 23.4E. The relationship shown here is roughly linear but somewhat disappointing, in that the correlation coefficient is only 0.631. If Sales is regressed on Advertising, the prediction equation

$$\widehat{\text{Sales}} = 18.3 + 0.208 \text{ Advertising} \tag{23.4}$$

EXHIBIT **23.4D**

Overlaid Sequence Plots of
Standardized Sales and
Standardized Advertising $+3$
for a Weight Control Product

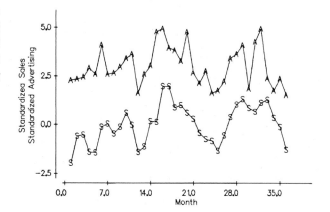

with $s = 4.863$ and $R^2 = 39.9\%$ is obtained. However, the residuals are far from random. Exhibit 23.4F shows the sequence plot of the residuals based on Equation (23.4). The autocorrelation at lag one month is 0.317, which indicates lack of independence. We proceed to models that account for the relationship between Sales and Advertising in a more complicated way.

EXHIBIT **23.4E**

Scatterplot of Sales versus
Advertising for a Weight Control
Product

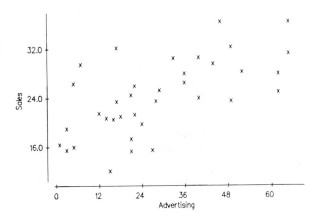

Market researchers have postulated that the effects of advertising may carry over beyond the month in which the ad is viewed or heard. That is, advertising seen in March may affect March, April, and May sales to some extent. The scatterplot shown in Exhibit 23.4G displays the approximate linear relationship between Sales and Advertising lagged one month. Here the correlation in 0.674, so it is reasonable to consider a model that includes lagged Advertising as a predictor variable.

In general, a model of the form

distributed lag model

$$y_t = \beta_0 + \beta_1 x_t + \beta_2 x_{t-1} + \cdots + \beta_k x_{t-k} + e_t \qquad \textbf{(23.5)}$$

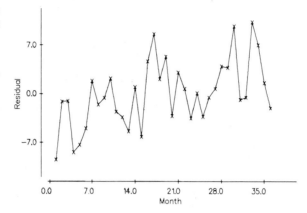

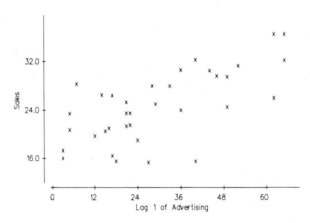

involving k lags on the predictor variable x_t might be considered. Such models are called **distributed lag models**. However, this model may involve many regression coefficients, each of which must be estimated from the data. Because typical series lengths will not permit accurate estimation of a large number of parameters, a simplification of the model is necessary.

Koyck Model

Frequently the general distributed lag model may be simplified by assuming that β_1, $\beta_2, \ldots, \beta_k$ are of the special form $\beta_1 = \alpha_0$, $\beta_2 = \alpha_0\lambda$, $\beta_3 = \alpha_0\lambda^2$, $\beta_4 = \alpha_0\lambda^3, \ldots,$ $\beta_k = \alpha_0\lambda^{k-1}$. This particular distributed lag model is called the **Koyck** or **geometric distributed lag model**:

Koyck (or geometric) model

$$y_t = \beta_0 + \alpha_0 x_t + \alpha_0\lambda x_{t-1} + \alpha_0\lambda^2 x_{t-2} + \cdots + \alpha_0\lambda^k x_{t-k} + e_t \qquad \textbf{(23.6)}$$

Only three parameters, β_0, α_0, and λ, need to be estimated in this model. In most cases the parameter λ is restricted to lie between 0 and 1 so that the coefficients on lagged x_t decay in magnitude geometrically as the lag increases. In our example, this corresponds to advertising in March having an effect on March sales but a diminished effect on April sales, a further diminished effect on May sales, and so on.

If k is large enough that λ^{k+1} can be considered negligibly small, then Equation (23.6) can be rewritten as

$$y_t = \beta_0^* + \lambda y_{t-1} + \alpha_0 x_t + e_t^* \tag{23.7}$$

where $\beta_0^* = \beta_0(1 - \lambda)$ and $e_t^* = e_t - \lambda e_{t-1}$.

To estimate the parameters in the model defined by Equation (23.7), y_t is regressed on two predictors: y_{t-1} and x_t. The results of such a regression for the Sales and Advertising series are shown in Exhibit 23.4H. The estimated model uses $\hat{\lambda} = 0.528$ and $\hat{\alpha}_0 = 0.146$, both of which would be deemed highly significant by the usual t ratio tests. In addition, the estimated (transformed) intercept term is 7.45 and the residual standard deviation is 3.480 with an R^2 of 67.2%. Exhibit 23.4I displays overlaid sequence plots of the actual Sales series (plotted as S's) and the series of fitted values (plotted as F's). Notice how well the fitted values track the actual values.

E X H I B I T **23.4H**
Estimation of Koyck Distributed Lag Model of Sales on Advertising for a Weight Control Product

```
The regression equation is

Sales = 7.45 + 0.528 Lag1Sales + 0.146 Advertising

35 cases used; one case contained missing values

Predictor        Coef       Stdev    t-ratio        p
Constant         7.453       2.467       3.02    0.005
Lag1Sales       0.5276      0.1021       5.17    0.000
Advertising    0.14650     0.03305       4.43    0.000

s = 3.480       R-sq = 67.2%      R-sq(adj) = 65.2%
```

E X H I B I T **23.4I**
Sequence Plot of Actual and Fitted Values for Sales of a Weight Control Product

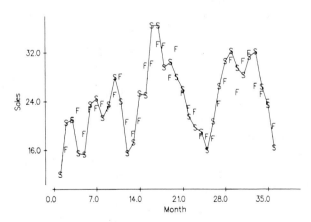

Assuming for now that the diagnostics support the postulated model, notice how easy it is to forecast with this model. Suppose that n denotes the time of the last available data: x_n and y_n. According to Equation (23.7), the next value of y satisfies

$$y_{n+1} = \beta_0^* + \lambda y_n + \alpha_0 x_{n+1} + e_{n+1}^* \qquad \text{(23.8)}$$

Since e_{n+1}^* is a future error, the best prediction for its value is its mean of zero. In our example, Advertising is under our control so that x_{n+1} may be chosen for next month according to our budget and sales goals. The forecast of next month's sales is then given by

$$\hat{y}_{n+1} = \beta_0^* + \lambda y_n + \alpha_0 x_{n+1} \qquad \text{(23.9)}$$

where the parameters are replaced by their estimates based on the data.

In our example the value for Sales at month 36 is 16.4, and Advertising ranges from a low of 1 to a high of about 60. For illustration, suppose 30 is budgeted for next month's advertising. Then the predicted sales are Sales $= 7.45 + 0.528(16.4) + 0.146(30) = 20.4892$, or 20.5. For planning, a variety of trial values may be considered for next month's advertising and the predicted sales consequences investigated. As always, the associated prediction intervals should also be presented so that the precision of the predictions may be assessed. Three scenarios are given below:

Advertising	Predicted Sales	95% Prediction Interval	Interval Length
10	17.57	[10.16, 24.98]	14.82
30	20.50	[13.11, 27.89]	14.78
60	24.90	[17.09, 32.70]	15.61

Notice that the prediction interval is least precise—that is, widest—when we attempt to predict using an extreme value for the Advertising variable.

To forecast two months ahead, Equation (23.8) is used but n is increased by 1. The error term in this equation is forecast as zero, and x_{n+2} must be specified, but what should be done with y_{n+1}? Simply use the forecast given in Equation (23.9). Thus, the two-month-ahead forecast is obtained from

$$\hat{y}_{n+2} = \beta_0^* + \lambda \hat{y}_{n+1} + \alpha_0 x_{n+2} \qquad \text{(23.10)}$$

Similarly, forecasts for l time units into the future are produced using

$$\hat{y}_{n+l} = \beta_0^* + \lambda \hat{y}_{n+l-1} + \alpha_0 x_{n+l} \qquad \text{(23.11)}$$

To complete this example, diagnostic analysis of the fitted model is done. Exhibit 23.4J gives the sequence plot of the residuals and Exhibit 23.4K displays the scatterplot of residuals versus fitted values. No special patterns are apparent in these plots, and this perception is reinforced by the small lag 1 autocorrelation of -0.05.

Finally, we look at the normality of the error terms. The histogram of standardized residuals is shown in Exhibit 23.4L. The mound shape of the histogram is further substantiated in the straightness of the normal scores plot given in Exhibit 23.4M. The correlation coefficient in the normal scores plot is a strong 0.993. On all accounts, the Koyck distributed lag model is excellent for the Sales-Advertising time series data.

E X H I B I T **23.4J**
Sequence Plot of Residuals from
Distributed Lag Model of Sales
on Advertising for a Weight
Control Product

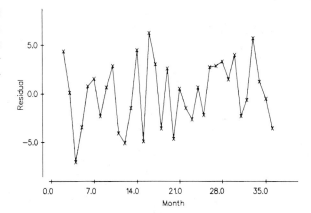

E X H I B I T **23.4K**
Residuals Versus Fitted Values
for Distributed Lag Model of
Sales on Advertising

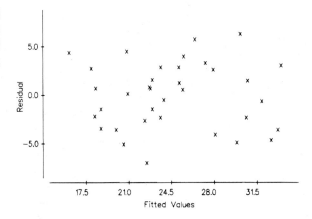

E X H I B I T **23.4L**
Histogram of Standardized
Residuals from Distributed Lag
Model of Sales on Advertising

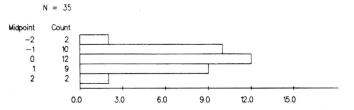

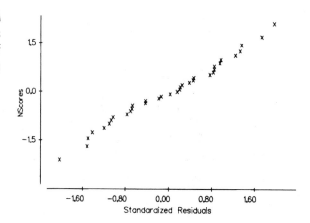

EXHIBIT **23.4M**
Normal Scores Plot for Residuals
from Distributed Lag Model of
Sales on Advertising

23.5 Exercise

23.5A   Consider the flour price index for Buffalo, New York, listed in Exhibit 2.10A and plotted in Exhibit 2.10B and the flour price index for Kansas City given in Exercise 2.11A. These monthly series were obtained for the same months but at different geographic locations.

a   Fit the Koyck model using the Buffalo series as the response and Kansas City series as the predictor. Check the residuals for autocorrelation.

b   Comment on the usefulness of the model considered in part (a) for prediction purposes.

c   Consider a Koyck distributed lag model that uses the Kansas City flour price index *lagged one month* as the predictor and the Buffalo index as the response. That is, replace x_t by x_{t-1} in Equation (23.7). Estimate this model and test the significance of the regression coefficients.

d   Comment on the practicality of the model considered in part (c) for prediction purposes. (Filenames: BUFLOUR.DAT and KCFLOUR.DAT.)

23.6 Autoregression

autoregressive model

With many time series, no accompanying predictor time series is available and no distinctive time trend is evident in the data. In such cases, the single available series may be modeled in terms of its own past behavior, using an **autoregressive model**. This section introduces simple lag 1 and lag 2 models of time series and their changes.[†]

[†]For more details the reader may consult G. E. P. Box and G. M. Jenkins, *Time Series Analysis*, rev. ed. (San Francisco: Holden-Day, 1976). More accessible accounts are given in B. L. Bowerman and R. T. O'Connell, *Times Series Forecasting*, 2d ed. (Boston: Duxbury Press, 1987); and J. D. Cryer, *Times Series Analysis* (Boston: Duxbury Press, 1986).

A series y_t is said to follow an autoregressive model of order p if for each time point t

AR (p) model

$$y_t = \beta_0 + \beta_1 y_{t-1} + \beta_2 y_{t-2} + \cdots + \beta_p y_{t-p} + e_t \qquad \text{(23.12)}$$

where e_t is an error term that is independent of past series values $y_{t-1}, y_{t-2}, \ldots$. The terminology *autoregression* is self-evident: y has been regressed on itself at lagged time values. For short, y_t is said to satisfy an **AR (p) model**. Here the focus is on the simpler AR(1) and AR(2) cases.

Exhibit 23.6A lists the 57 values for a certain industrial time series. The values given are deviations from a desired target value of a dimension of a product produced by a complex machine tool. The process employs a control mechanism to reset some of the parameters of the machine tool depending on the magnitude of the deviation of the dimension from the target value on the last item produced. Exhibit 23.6B shows the sequence plot of the series. The series wanders about the desired target deviation of zero but tends to stay on the same side of zero for deviations that are close together in time. Such behavior reflects positive autocorrelation for small time lags.

EXHIBIT 23.6A

Data from an Industrial Machining Process— Deere & Co.

```
filename: DEERE3.DAT
Machining data from Deere & Co.
(Source: Jerri Matchinsky, M.S. thesis,
University of Iowa, 1988)
Deviations from target value in ten millionths of an inch
(Read across, row by row)
-500 -1250  -500 -3000 -2375 2000 2375  1500  -625  250
   0   625  3125  2125  2250 3875 1000   250   750  750
-375  -625  -875 -1125   250 -250 -125 -1750   625  125
 625  -375   875  -500   250  625 -250  2375 -2000  125
 125 -1000   375 -1250   500 1625 1875  1875  3000 3625
 750 -1125 -2875 -5750 -1750 -750 -750
```

EXHIBIT 23.6B

Sequence Plot of Deviations from Target—Deere & Co. Machining Process

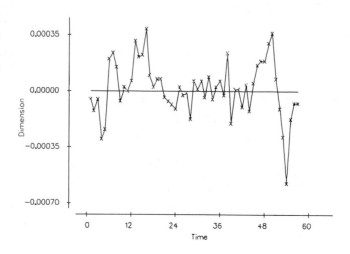

The scatterplot of deviations versus lag 1 deviations shown in Exhibit 23.6C confirms the autocorrelation graphically. Here the correlation is 0.533.

E X H I B I T **23.6C**
Plot of Deviations from Target
Versus Lag 1 Deviations from
Target—Deere & Co. Machining
Process

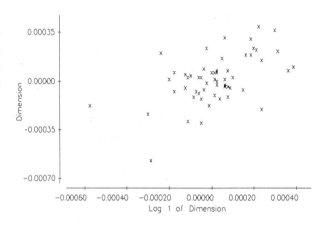

AR(1) Models

An **AR(1) model** is an autoregressive model in which the predictor variable is the response variable at the previous time point. Consider the AR(1) model

AR(1) model

$$y_t = \beta_0 + \beta_1 y_{t-1} + e_t \qquad\qquad (23.13)$$

Exhibit 23.6D gives the regression results of fitting this model to our series. The t ratio associated with β_1 is 4.62, so the regression coefficient on the lagged deviation is statistically different from zero and the lag 1 deviation should help in the prediction of the next deviation. Notice that the intercept term is not significantly different from zero. This should not be surprising since deviations from a desired target value are being measured and the machine is constantly readjusted in an attempt to achieve the target value. Also note that the value of R^2 is only 28.4%. Initially this may seem disappointing, but to what should the predictions produced by this model be compared? What alternative model might be used for prediction?

E X H I B I T **23.6D**
Regression Results for the AR(1)
Model of the Deere & Co.
Machining Process

```
The regression equation is

Dimension = 0.000007 + 0.533 Lag1Dimension

56 cases used; 1 case contained missing values

Predictor         Coef        Stdev      t-ratio       p
Constant     0.00000747   0.00001982      0.38     0.708
Lag1Dimension    0.5332       0.1153      4.62     0.000

s = 0.0001476   R-sq = 28.4%    R-sq(adj) = 27.0%
```

For a series that behaves like this one, an alternative model would be that of a purely random process with a mean of 0.00002 inch and standard deviation of 0.00017 inch. These correspond to the mean and standard deviation of the series values. Based on a purely random process, predictions for all future deviations are the mean deviation of 0.00002 inch. The precision of these predictions is measured by the standard deviation of the process, 0.00017 inch.

On the other hand, the AR(1) model bases its predictions on the equation

$$\hat{y}_{n+l} = 0.000007 + 0.533 y_n \tag{23.14}$$

and, more generally, for l periods ahead,

$$\hat{y}_{n+l} = 0.000007 + 0.533 \hat{y}_{n+l-1} \qquad \text{for } l \geq 1 \tag{23.15}$$

The prediction standard error here is proportional to 0.0001476, which should be compared to the standard deviation of 0.00017 of the deviations series. This amounts to a very worthwhile improvement over the alternative simpler model.

To complete the analysis, the sequence plot of the residuals from the AR(1) model is given in Exhibit 23.6E. No trends are evident, and this perception is confirmed by the lag 1 autocorrelation in the residuals of only -0.009. Further analysis of the residuals confirms their approximate normality.

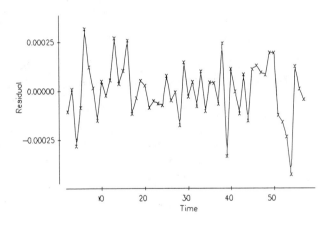

E X H I B I T   **23.6E**
Sequence Plot of Residuals from the AR(1) Model for the Deere & Co. Machining Process

Exhibit 23.6F displays the series values (plotted with A's) with the sequence of fitted values (F's) from the AR(1) model overlaid. Notice how, to a large extent, the fitted values trace the path of the actual values.

As a final check on the AR(1) model, suppose that an additional lagged term, y_{t-2}, is added to the model. Exhibit 23.6G displays the regression results. First note that the regression coefficient for lag 2 is not statistically significant: the t ratio is only 0.06. Furthermore, the estimate of the regression coefficient for lag 1 is essentially unchanged from the AR(1) model and is still highly significant. Clearly, adding an additional lagged value to the model is not helpful, and the AR(1) model is supported by this further check.

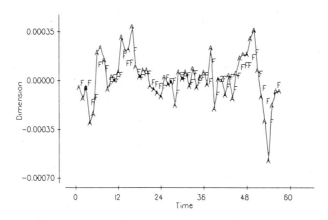

EXHIBIT 23.6G
Regression Results for an AR(2)
Model for the Deere & Co.
Machining Process

```
The regression equation is

Dimension = 0.000009 + 0.525 Lag1Dimension + 0.008 Lag2Dimension

55 cases used; 2 cases contained missing values

Predictor          Coef        Stdev     t-ratio        p
Constant     0.00000941   0.00002033      0.46      0.646
Lag1Dimension   0.5246        0.1381      3.80      0.000
Lag2Dimension   0.0079        0.1383      0.06      0.954

s = 0.0001497    R-sq = 28.2%    R-sq(adj) = 25.4%
```

In other cases, adding additional lagged y-values can be very helpful, as you will see in the next subsection, on the AR(2) model.

AR(2) Models

An **AR(2) model** is an autoregressive model in which the two predictor variables are the response variable at the previous two time points. An autoregressive model of order two satisfies the relationship

AR(2) model

$$y_t = \beta_0 + \beta_1 y_{t-1} + \beta_2 y_{t-2} + e_t \qquad (23.16)$$

where the error term e_t at time t is independent of earlier series values $y_{t-1}, y_{t-2}, \ldots$. An example of a series that is well modeled by an AR(2) model is the sequence of quarterly U.S. unemployment rates for the period first quarter 1948 through first quarter 1978. The series values are given in Exhibit 23.6H and the sequence plot is shown in Exhibit 23.6I.

Neighboring unemployment rates are quite similar. Large changes do not occur over short periods of time. However, larger changes do take place over longer periods. How can this autocorrelation be modeled? Exhibits 23.6J and 23.6K display the scatterplots of the unemployment rates versus lag 1 and versus lag 2 unemployment

EXHIBIT **23.6H**

U.S. Quarterly Unemployment
Rates: First Quarter 1948
Through First Quarter 1978

```
filename: UNEMP.DAT
U.S. quarterly unemployment rates (seasonally adjusted)
(Source: J.D.Cryer, Time Series Analysis,
Boston: PWS-Kent, 1986)
First quarter 1948 through first quarter 1978, n=121
(Read across, row by row)
3.73 3.67 3.77 3.83 4.67 5.87 6.70 6.97 6.40 5.57 4.63 4.23
3.50 3.10 3.17 3.37 3.07 2.97 3.23 2.83 2.70 2.57 2.73 3.70
5.27 5.80 5.97 5.33 4.73 4.40 4.10 4.23 4.03 4.20 4.13 4.13
3.93 4.10 4.23 4.93 6.30 7.37 7.33 6.37 5.83 5.10 5.27 5.60
5.13 5.23 5.53 6.27 6.80 7.00 6.77 6.20 5.63 5.53 5.57 5.53
5.77 5.73 5.50 5.57 5.47 5.20 5.00 5.00 4.90 4.67 4.37 4.10
3.87 3.80 3.77 3.70 3.77 3.83 3.83 3.93 3.73 3.57 3.53 3.43
3.37 3.43 3.60 3.60 4.17 4.80 5.17 5.87 5.93 5.97 5.97 5.97
5.83 5.77 5.53 5.27 5.03 4.93 4.77 4.67 5.17 5.13 5.50 6.57
8.37 8.90 8.37 8.40 7.63 7.43 7.83 7.93 7.37 7.07 6.90 6.63
6.20
```

EXHIBIT **23.6I**

Sequence Plot of Quarterly U.S.
Unemployment Rates:
1948–1978

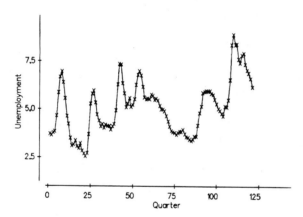

EXHIBIT **23.6J**

Scatterplot of Unemployment
Rate Versus Lag 1
Unemployment Rate

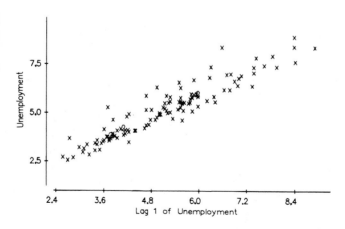

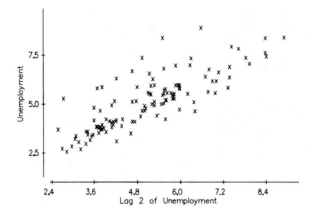

rates, respectively. The autocorrelation at lag 1 is 0.943 and at lag 2 is 0.815. Perhaps, an AR(2) will account for this autocorrelation structure.

The regression results of fitting an AR(2) model to this series are given in Exhibit 23.6L. Notice that both the lag 1 and lag 2 predictors are shown to have coefficients that differ significantly from zero. You are asked to do the residual analysis of this model in the exercises in Section 23.7. Assuming that the analysis indicates that the model is adequate, the model can be used for prediction purposes.

E X H I B I T **23.6L**
Regression Results for the AR(2)
Model of Unemployment Rates

```
The regression equation is

Unemployment = 0.505 + 1.55 Lag1Unemployment - 0.651 Lag2Unemployment

119 cases used; 2 cases contained missing values

Predictor              Coef      Stdev    t-ratio       p
Constant             0.5051     0.1267       3.99   0.000
Lag1Unemployment    1.55368    0.07074      21.96   0.000
Lag2Unemployment   -0.65148    0.07081      -9.20   0.000

s = 0.3632     R-sq = 93.5%     R-sq(adj) = 93.4%
```

Forecasts from this model for one time unit ahead are obtained from

$$\hat{y}_{n+1} = \beta_0 + \beta_1 y_n + \beta_2 y_{n-1} \tag{23.17}$$

To forecast two steps ahead, use

$$\hat{y}_{n+2} = \beta_0 + \beta_1 \hat{y}_{n+1} + \beta_2 y_n \tag{23.18}$$

where $\hat{y}_{n+1}$ is the one-step-ahead forecast obtained in Equation (23.17). Finally, for l steps ahead, you can calculate the forecasts with

AR(2) forecast

$$\hat{y}_{n+l} = \beta_0 + \beta_1 \hat{y}_{n+l-1} + \beta_2 \hat{y}_{n+l-2} \qquad \text{for } l > 2 \tag{23.19}$$

In our series, the last two values are 6.63 for the fourth quarter of 1977 and 6.20 for the first quarter of 1978. The unemployment rate for the second quarter of 1978 is then forecast as

$$\widehat{\text{Unemployment}}_{n+1} = 0.505 + 1.55(6.20) - 0.651(6.63) = 5.80$$

The forecast for the third quarter of 1978 is then

$$\widehat{\text{Unemployment}}_{n+2} = 0.505 + 1.55(5.80) - 0.651(6.20) = 5.4588$$

and the forecast for the next quarter is

$$\widehat{\text{Unemployment}}_{n+3} = 0.505 + 1.55(5.4588) - 0.651(5.80) = 5.19034$$

In this way, as many forecasts as desired may be calculated one after the other.

Autoregression of Changes

A final example considers autoregression of changes in the variable's values, rather than of the values themselves. Consider the series of monthly AA railroad bond yields given in Exhibit 23.6M. The sequence plot in Exhibit 23.6N again shows a strong

E X H I B I T **23.6M**
Monthly Bond Yields on Railroad
Bonds—January 1968 through
June 1976

```
filename: RRBONDS.DAT
Monthly AA railroad bond yields (%X100)
(Source: J.D.Cryer, Time Series Analysis,
Boston: PWS-Kent, 1986)
January 1968 through June 1976, n=102
(Read across, row by row)
639 643 640 653 667 667 663 654 649 651 659 672
670 675 692 702 706 710 722 729 740 755 763 788
818 826 821 819 827 848 881 879 878 878 868 856
844 824 820 819 813 815 822 818 815 792 769 775
771 773 780 779 774 772 775 770 766 771 773 772
767 775 777 777 776 779 787 790 791 792 802 799
792 780 790 799 810 814 828 862 874 892 872 869
870 859 857 870 867 856 854 862 861 855 846 847
845 838 828 823 814 812
```

E X H I B I T **23.6N**
Sequence Plot of Monthly
Railroad Bond Yields

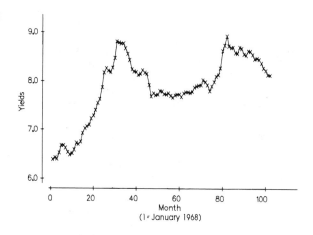

tendency for neighboring values to be quite similar. There is strong autocorrelation in this series. The lag 1 autocorrelation coefficient is 0.96 and at lag 2 it is 0.92. By lag 3 it is still 0.86. These high autocorrelations at several lags are a sign that models for the *changes* in the series should be considered. Exhibit 23.6O displays the sequence plot of the monthly changes.

EXHIBIT **23.6O**
Monthly Changes in Bond Yields

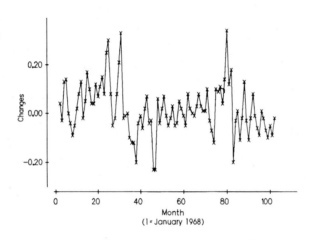

EXHIBIT **23.6P**
Regression Results for AR(1)
Model Changes in Bond Yields

```
The regression equation is

Changes = 0.00871 + 0.468 Lag1Changes

100 cases used; 2 cases contained missing values

Predictor        Coef       Stdev     t-ratio        p
Constant      0.008707    0.009413       0.93    0.357
Lag1Changes   0.46814     0.08931        5.24    0.000

s = 0.09282     R-sq = 21.9%      R-sq(adj) = 21.1%
```

Now consider the changes as a time series and evaluate the autocorrelation in this transformed series. The autocorrelation at lag 1 is 0.468, but at other higher lags the autocorrelations are negligible. Perhaps an AR(1) model *for the series of changes* will produce a reasonable model for the behavior of this series. Exhibit 23.6P shows the results of the estimation of parameters in the model. You are asked to do a residual analysis in the exercise in Section 23.7.

If y_t represents the bond yield at time t, the AR(1) model for changes says that

$$y_t - y_{t-1} = \beta_0 + \beta_1(y_{t-1} - y_{t-2}) + e_t \qquad \textbf{(23.20)}$$

or

$$y_t = \beta_0 + (\beta_1 + 1)y_{t-1} - \beta_1 y_{t-2} + e_t \qquad \textbf{(23.21)}$$

which looks like an AR(2) model. However, here the two regression coefficients on the response lagged one and two time units are not two separate parameters. Rather, they are related to the *same* parameter, β_1. In Section 23.7, you are asked to estimate a general AR(2) model for the bond yields and verify that the AR(2) results confirm the simpler analysis of the changes in the yields. As suggested by Equation (23.21), forecasting with this AR(1) model for the changes will proceed just as it did for the AR(2) model in Equations (23.17–23.19).

SECTION

23.7 Exercises

23.7A   Consider the flour price index for Buffalo, New York, listed in Exhibit 2.10A and plotted in Exhibit 2.10B.

   a   Fit an AR(1) model to this series and investigate the autocorrelation in the residuals.

   b   Fit an AR(1) model to the logarithm of this series. Investigate the autocorrelation in the residuals from this model.

   c   Which of these two models fits the series better? (Filename: BUFLOUR.DAT.)

23.7B   Refer to the metal exports data given in Exercise 6.8A. Fit an AR(1) model. What prediction rule does your fitted model suggest? What predictive performance do you expect it to have in future years, assuming the process remains stable? (Filename: STEELEXP.DAT.)

23.7C   Fit an AR(2) model to the Buffalo flour price index series. The data are in Exhibit 2.10A. Compare this model to the AR(1) model obtained in Exercise 23.7A. (Filename: BUFLOUR.DAT.)

23.7D   Consider the time series of hourly wages shown in Exhibit 23.2A. Models for this series with fixed linear or quadratic trend contain substantial residual autocorrelation. Fit an AR(1) model to this series and compare the results to those obtained earlier. In particular, look at the autocorrelation in the residuals and especially at lags 1, 2, 12, 24, and 36. This series is considered again in Exercise 24.6G. (Filename: APAWAGES.DAT.)

23.7E   The time series given below gives the final position in the "x direction" after an industrial robot is finished with a planned set of movements. The measurements are expressed as deviations from a desired position. The robot is put through this planned set of exercises many times with the hope that its behavior will be repeatable and thus predictable.

```
filename: ROBOT.DAT
Robot data: x position after "exercising"
(Source: William Fulkerson, Deere & Co.
 Technical Center, Moline, Illinois.)
(Read across, row by row)
 -1  42   4  35  -4   0  14  34    2  24 -12
 25  24  -9  40   1 -13  49  -6   -3  -9   3
-13  10  33  12  31  20  -6 -17   28   0  12
 12  38  10   4   1  17  -4  20    0  22   3
 37  58  28   0  -8  -4  -4  27  -24 -20 -35
-15 -14 -31  11 -39 -43 -37  -4  -31 -47 -12
-28 -72 -75 -21 -35 -41 -32 -24  -49 -69 -60
-64 -78 -64 -81 -54 -90 -80 -92 -103 -70 -91
-62 -90 -74 -52 -70 -79 -39 -54  -69 -71 -77
-75 -37 -69 -90 -75 -64 -76 -65  -54 -73 -90
-87 -47 -52 -46 -48 -67 -22 -63  -64 -58
```

   a   Construct a sequence plot of the data. Describe the plot. Are there any evident patterns? Would a model that says that the successive positions arise independently from some common distribution seem appropriate?

   b   Find the autocorrelation at lag 1 and at lag 2.

   c   Fit an AR(1) model to this series and comment on the results.

      d   Check the residuals from the AR(1) fit with respect to autocorrelation and normality.

23.7F   Consider the AR(2) model that was suggested for the quarterly U.S. unemployment rates in Exhibit 23.6H. The estimation results appear in Exhibit 23.6L.

      a   Analyze the scatterplot of residuals versus fitted values for model inadequacies.

      b   Check the residuals for autocorrelation at lags 1, 2, and 3. Compare their magnitudes to $3/\sqrt{n}$.

      c   Check the residuals for normality by inspecting their histogram and normal scores plot.

      d   Fit an AR(3) model to this series and compare the resulting coefficients to those of the AR(2) model. Do the results confirm the AR(2) model? (Filename: UNEMP.DAT.)

23.7G   Return to the AA railroad bond yields given in Exhibit 23.6M. An AR(1) model was fit to the changes of this series and the results reported in Exhibit 23.6L.

      a   Analyze the scatterplot of residuals versus fitted values for model inadequacies.

      b   Check the residuals for autocorrelation at lags 1, 2, and 3. Compare their magnitudes to $3/\sqrt{n}$.

      c   Check the residuals for normality by inspecting their histogram and normal scores plot.

      d   Fit an AR(2) model to the changes in this series and compare the resulting coefficients to those of the AR(1) model. Do the results confirm the AR(1) model? (Filename: RRBONDS.DAT.)

S E C T I O N

23.8 Exponential Smoothing

Sometimes it is necessary to mask short-term, irregular variation in a time series in order to see any general trend. A technique for doing this is exponential smoothing.[†]

    We first explain the basics of simple exponential smoothing, useful when the mean does not change much in the short run, and discuss how to choose the smoothing constant. We then introduce double exponential smoothing, appropriate when there are important short-term as well as long-term changes in the mean. We again discuss choosing the appropriate constant.

Simple Exponential Smoothing

Simple exponential smoothing, in which the series is smoothed once, is appropriate when the series mean is relatively constant in the short run but changes over longer periods. It is illustrated here using quarterly percent changes in Iowa nonfarm income per capita, shown in Exhibit 23.8A. The original data and the percent changes shown extend from the first quarter of 1948 through the third quarter of 1975. (If the percent changes were being reported, they would be rounded off to around the nearest tenth of a percent. For calculations in this analysis, however, several more decimal places are retained, as shown in the exhibit.) Exhibit 23.8B, the sequence plot of the percent changes, shows a great deal of variation over the time period displayed. The series shows no seasonality or consistent trends toward wage increases or decreases.

[†]E. S. Gardner, "Exponential Smoothing: The State of the Art," *Journal of Forecasting*, 4 (1985), 1–28, provides a review of these techniques, which originated with R. G. Brown for the U.S. Navy during World War II.

EXHIBIT **23.8A**   Iowa Nonfarm Income per Capita and Growth Rates—1948–1975

Income	Percent Change	Quarter	Year	Income	Percent Change	Quarter	Year	Income	Percent Change	Quarter	Year
601	*	1	1948	1013	1.19880	2	1957	1760	2.62391	3	1966
604	0.49917	2	1948	1021	0.78973	3	1957	1812	2.95455	4	1966
620	2.64901	3	1948	1028	0.68560	4	1957	1809	-0.16556	1	1967
626	0.96774	4	1948	1027	-0.09728	1	1958	1828	1.05030	2	1967
641	2.39617	1	1949	1048	2.04479	2	1958	1871	2.35230	3	1967
642	0.15601	2	1949	1070	2.09924	3	1958	1892	1.12239	4	1967
645	0.46729	3	1949	1095	2.33645	4	1958	1946	2.85412	1	1968
655	1.55039	4	1949	1113	1.64384	1	1959	1983	1.90134	2	1968
682	4.12214	1	1950	1143	2.69542	2	1959	2013	1.51286	3	1968
678	-0.58651	2	1950	1154	0.96238	3	1959	2045	1.58967	4	1968
692	2.06490	3	1950	1173	1.64645	4	1959	2069	1.17359	1	1969
707	2.16763	4	1950	1178	0.42626	1	1960	2107	1.83664	2	1969
736	4.10184	1	1951	1183	0.42445	2	1960	2144	1.75605	3	1969
753	2.30978	2	1951	1205	1.85968	3	1960	2183	1.81903	4	1969
763	1.32802	3	1951	1208	0.24896	4	1960	2231	2.19881	1	1970
775	1.57274	4	1951	1209	0.08278	1	1961	2304	3.27208	2	1970
775	0.00000	1	1952	1223	1.15798	2	1961	2343	1.69271	3	1970
783	1.03226	2	1952	1238	1.22649	3	1961	2377	1.45113	4	1970
794	1.40485	3	1952	1245	0.56543	4	1961	2393	0.67312	1	1971
813	2.39295	4	1952	1258	1.04418	1	1962	2461	2.84162	2	1971
823	1.23001	1	1953	1278	1.58983	2	1962	2494	1.34092	3	1971
826	0.36452	2	1953	1294	1.25196	3	1962	2532	1.52366	4	1971
829	0.36320	3	1953	1314	1.54560	4	1962	2565	1.30332	1	1972
831	0.24125	4	1953	1323	0.68493	1	1963	2631	2.57310	2	1972
830	-0.12034	1	1954	1336	0.98262	2	1963	2682	1.93843	3	1972
838	0.96386	2	1954	1355	1.42216	3	1963	2782	3.72856	4	1972
854	1.90931	3	1954	1377	1.62362	4	1963	2849	2.40834	1	1973
872	2.10773	4	1954	1416	2.83224	1	1964	2930	2.84310	2	1973
882	1.14679	1	1955	1430	0.98870	2	1964	3029	3.37884	3	1973
903	2.38095	2	1955	1455	1.74825	3	1964	3102	2.41004	4	1973
919	1.77187	3	1955	1480	1.71821	4	1964	3181	2.54674	1	1974
937	1.95865	4	1955	1514	2.29730	1	1965	3282	3.17510	2	1974
927	-1.06724	1	1956	1545	2.04756	2	1965	3391	3.32115	3	1974
962	3.77562	2	1956	1589	2.84790	3	1965	3488	2.86051	4	1974
975	1.35135	3	1956	1634	2.83197	4	1965	3568	2.29358	1	1975
995	2.05128	4	1956	1669	2.14198	1	1966	3657	2.49439	2	1975
1001	0.60302	1	1957	1715	2.75614	2	1966	3705	1.31255	3	1975

EXHIBIT **23.8B**
Sequence Plot of Percent Change in Iowa Nonfarm Income

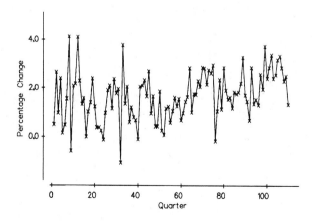

However, wages appear to become more volatile. That is, the mean level of the series appears to change over time, being higher at the end of the series than at the beginning. The objective of smoothing is to estimate the current mean level of the series in situations where the mean is suspected of changing over time.

exponential smoothing

The equation governing the **exponential smoothing** method may be expressed many different equivalent ways. The smoothed series at time t is

$$\hat{\beta}_t = \alpha y_t + \alpha(1-\alpha)y_{t-1} + \alpha(1-\alpha)^2 y_{t-2} + \cdots + \alpha(1-\alpha)^{t-1} y_1 \quad \textbf{(23.22)}$$

smoothing constant

where α is a **smoothing constant** that is selected in the range $0 < \alpha < 1$. Since $0 < \alpha < 1$, the weights that are applied to the current and past observations, $\alpha, \alpha(1-\alpha), \alpha(1-\alpha)^2, \ldots$, decrease *exponentially* (or geometrically) with increasing time lag and at a rate determined by the discount factor $1 - \alpha$. For example, if $\alpha = 0.1$, then the weights are $\alpha = 0.1, \alpha(1-\alpha) = 0.09, \alpha(1-\alpha)^2 = 0.081, \alpha(1-\alpha)^3 = 0.0729$, and so on. If the weight on the current observation is increased to $\alpha = 0.4$, then the sequence of weights $0.4, 0.24, 0.144, 0.0864, \ldots$ decreases more rapidly and relatively more weight is given to the most recent observations. It may be shown that the weights nearly add to 1, so that the smoothed value at time t is an *exponentially weighted average* of current and past observations. The smoothed value at time t, $\hat{\beta}_t$, is the forecast of the value for the series for time $t + 1$.

The smooth curve given in Exhibit 23.8C was obtained using a smoothing constant of $\alpha = 0.1$. Exhibit 23.8D shows the same series smoothed with $\alpha = 0.5$. Here the current observation is given much more weight than the others and the smoothed curve follows the variation in the series to a much greater extent, rather than smoothing it out. To better see the effect of the larger smoothing constant, just the last portion of the sequence plot is plotted in Exhibit 23.8E. Here it is easier to see that the smoothed series (plotted as S's) is attempting to follow the individual variations in the actual series (A's) too closely. If the series has a large swing upward, then the smoothed series is frequently pulled up too much at the next time point when the series of percent change tends to revert to a lower value.

EXHIBIT **23.8C**
Percent Change in Iowa
Nonfarm Income: Sequence Plot
of Series and Smoothed
Sequence Plot ($\alpha = 0.1$)

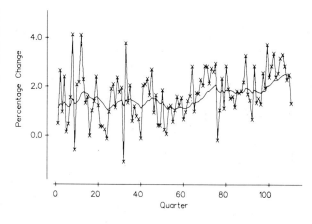

E X H I B I T **23.8D**
Percent Change in Iowa
Nonfarm Income: Sequence Plot
of Series and Smoothed
Sequence Plot ($\alpha = 0.5$)

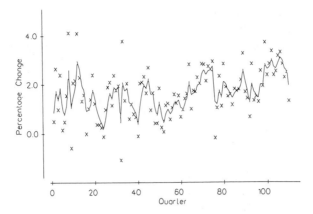

E X H I B I T **23.8E**
Percent Change in Iowa
Nonfarm Income: Expanded
Sequence Plot of Series and
Smoothed Sequence Plot
($\alpha = 0.5$, A=actual values,
S=smoothed values)

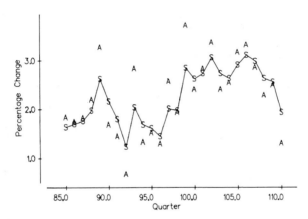

The smoothed series is not usually calculated using Equation (23.22). Rather, rewriting the right-hand side of Equation (23.22) as

$$\hat{\beta}_t = \alpha y_t + (1 - \alpha)[\alpha y_{t-1} + \alpha(1 - \alpha)y_{t-2} + \cdots + \alpha(1 - \alpha)^{t-2}y_1]$$

it can be seen that

updating equation

$$\hat{\beta}_t = \alpha y_t + (1 - \alpha)\hat{\beta}_{t-1} \qquad \text{(23.23)}$$

which provides a convenient recursive expression for calculation. Equation (23.23), known as the updating equation, shows that the smoothed series at time t can be expressed as a weighted average of the current observation, y_t with weight α, and the previous smoothed series value with weight $1 - \alpha$.

To use Equation (23.23), an initial value $\hat{\beta}_0$ is needed. A variety of choices have been advocated. Some authors use $\hat{\beta}_0 = y_1$, while others use $\hat{\beta}_0 = \bar{y}$ or more complicated calculations. A simple compromise is to set $\hat{\beta}_0$ equal to the *average of the first six series values.* Once the value of $\hat{\beta}_0$ is determined, the next smoothed value is obtained from

$$\hat{\beta}_1 = \alpha y_1 + (1 - \alpha)\hat{\beta}_0$$

In turn, the smoothed value at $t = 2$ is

$$\hat{\beta}_2 = \alpha y_2 + (1 - \alpha)\hat{\beta}_1$$

and so forth.

For our illustration series, the average of the first six data points is 1.18923, so that with $\alpha = 0.1$,

$$\hat{\beta}_1 = 0.1(0.49917) + 0.9(1.18923) = 1.120224$$

and

$$\hat{\beta}_2 = 0.1(2.64901) + 0.9(1.120224) = 1.2731026$$

and so forth. Several of the smoothed values for both $\alpha = 0.1$ and $\alpha = 0.5$ are given in Exhibit 23.8F. (They were obtained with computer software.)

EXHIBIT **23.8F**
Percent Change in Iowa Nonfarm Income: Exponential Smoothing Results with $\alpha = 0.1$ and $\alpha = 0.5$

t	Percent Change y_t	Smoothed $\alpha = 0.1$	Smoothed $\alpha = 0.5$
0		1.18923	1.18923
1	0.49917	1.12022	0.84420
2	2.64901	1.27310	1.74660
3	0.96774	1.24257	1.35717
4	2.39617	1.35793	1.87667
5	0.15601	1.23773	1.01634
6	0.46729	1.16069	0.74181
7	1.55039	1.19966	1.14610
8	4.12214	1.49191	2.63412
9	-0.58651	1.28407	1.02380
10	2.06490	1.36215	1.54435
11	2.16763	1.44270	1.85599
$\vdots$	$\vdots$	$\vdots$	$\vdots$
106	3.32115	2.48498	3.11443
107	2.86051	2.52253	2.98747
108	2.29358	2.49964	2.64052
109	2.49439	2.49911	2.56746
110	1.31255	2.38046	1.94001

A Model for Simple Exponential Smoothing (Optional)

A statistical model that leads to exponential smoothing as an optimal forecasting method may be defined as follows. Assume that the observed time series can be expressed as the "regression"

$$y_t = \beta_t + e_t \qquad (23.24)$$

where the unobserved and slowly changing "mean" component, β_t, follows a random walk model:

$$\beta_t = \beta_{t-1} + a_t \qquad (23.25)$$

As explained in Section 6.8 and Appendix 3, a random walk is nothing more than a process whose first differences behave as if they were random outcomes. Here a_t is another sequence of error terms independent of the e_t error terms. Then the changes or differences in y_t may be written as

$$y_t - y_{t-1} = e_t - e_{t-1} + a_t = e_t^* \qquad (23.26)$$

where the sequence e_t^* contains negative autocorrelation at lag 1 but no autocorrelation at any other lags. A series y_t that satisfies Equation (23.26) is called an *integrated moving average (IMA)* series. More specifically, this is an IMA (1,1) series. The first 1 refers to the first differencing and the second 1 refers to the fact that the differenced series has nonzero autocorrelation only at lag 1.

The IMA model described here is a special case of a much more general class of models called ARIMA (AutoRegressive-Integrated-Moving Average) models. A general discussion of these models is beyond the scope of this book. They are explored extensively in the specialized time series books cited earlier.

Choice of Smoothing Constant

Some authors have suggested that the smoothing constant be selected rather arbitrarily, say, as $\alpha = 0.1$. Others have suggested choosing α based on a subjective assessment of the variation in the series being smoothed. If the perceived changes in the level of the series seem to dominate the short-term variations, a large value of α should be used. However, if the short-term variation is more prominent than the level changes, then a small value for the smoothing constant is advised.

A more objective approach is to select a smoothing constant that leads to good "forecasts" of the observed series. That is, use $\hat{\beta}_t$ to forecast y_{t+1} for a range of values of t and choose α to minimize the root mean square prediction error, RMSPE, defined as

$$\text{RMSPE} = \sqrt{(\text{Mean prediction error})^2 + (\text{Standard deviation of prediction error})^2}$$

Since the forecasts involve powers of α, this minimization cannot be accomplished directly. Rather, the smoothed series and the corresponding RMSPE are computed for a range of α values and the α chosen for the final smoothing is the one that produces the smallest value for RMSPE.

Since we recommend using the average of the first six series values to initialize the smoothing, and the smoothing procedure needs several values to stabilize, we skip over the first six observations and begin calculating the one-step-ahead forecasts at the seventh observation. Prediction errors are then obtained from the seventh series value through the end of the series, and the RMSPE is based on these errors. Exhibit 23.8G displays some of these calculations for $\alpha = 0.1$ and for $\alpha = 0.5$. For example, the prediction error when using $\alpha = 0.1$ at time $t = 7$ is $1.55039 - 1.16069 = 0.38970$. At the next time point the prediction error is $4.12214 - 1.19966 = 2.92248$, and so on. After obtaining all of the prediction errors, the mean and standard deviation of the prediction errors and finally the RMSPE are calculated. In our example with $\alpha = 0.1$, the mean prediction error is 0.11729 and the standard deviation is 0.96177, which leads to RMSPE $= \sqrt{(0.11729)^2 + (0.96177)^2} = 0.9689$. Similar calculations using $\alpha = 0.5$ produce a smaller mean prediction error of 0.023042, but a larger standard deviation of prediction errors of 1.0417. These combine to give a larger RMSPE, 1.0419.

E X H I B I T 23.8G
Percent Change in Iowa
Nonfarm Income: Calculations of
Prediction Errors and RMSPE

		$\alpha = 0.1$		$\alpha = 0.5$	
t	**Percentage Change** y_t	**Smoothed** (at $t - 1$)	**Prediction** Error	**Smoothed** (at $t - 1$)	**Prediction** Error
1	0.49917	1.18923	(−0.69006)	1.18923	(−0.69006)
2	2.64901	1.12022	(1.52878)	0.84420	(1.80481)
3	0.96774	1.27310	(−0.30536)	1.74660	(−0.77886)
4	2.39617	1.24257	(1.15360)	1.35717	(1.03899)
5	0.15601	1.35793	(−1.20192)	1.87667	(−1.72066)
6	0.46729	1.23773	(−0.77044)	1.01634	(−0.54905)
7	1.55039	1.16069	0.38970	0.74181	0.80857
8	4.12214	1.19966	2.92248	1.14610	2.97604
9	−0.58651	1.49191	−2.07842	2.63412	−3.22063
10	2.06490	1.28407	0.78083	1.02380	1.04109
11	2.16763	1.36215	0.80548	1.54435	0.62328
⋮	⋮	⋮	⋮	⋮	⋮
106	3.32115	2.39207	0.92907	2.90772	0.41343
107	2.86051	2.48498	0.37553	3.11443	−0.25392
108	2.29358	2.52253	−0.22896	2.98747	−0.69389
109	2.49439	2.49964	−0.00524	2.64052	−0.14613
110	1.31255	2.49911	−1.18656	2.56746	−1.25491

Exhibit 23.8H lists the RMSPE corresponding to a variety of values of α for the percent changes of the Iowa income series. Exhibit 23.8I plots these values, showing that the best choice for α is 0.10 or 0.11. Notice, however, that the value for RMSPE is nearly constant over the range from $\alpha = 0.07$ to $\alpha = 0.15$, so that any value in this range would provide about the same amount of smoothing.

E X H I B I T **23.8H**
Percent Change in Iowa
Nonfarm Income: RMSPE for
Various Smoothing Constants

α	RMSPE	α	RMSPE
0.01	1.05039	0.12	0.96915
0.02	1.01453	0.13	0.96960
0.03	0.99561	0.14	0.97021
0.04	0.98473	0.15	0.97096
0.05	0.97814	0.20	0.97620
0.06	0.97406	0.25	0.98342
0.07	0.97155	0.30	0.99228
0.08	0.97005	0.35	1.00264
0.09	0.96924	0.40	1.01440
0.10	0.96890	0.45	1.02750
0.11	0.96890	0.50	1.04193

E X H I B I T **23.8I**
Percent Change in Iowa
Nonfarm Income: Plot of RMSPE
Versus Smoothing Constant

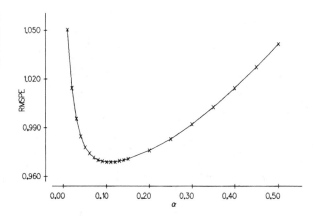

Double Exponential Smoothing

Simple exponential smoothing provides good forecasts for series that in the short run vary around a reasonably constant mean but for which the mean level changes over longer periods. Equations (23.24) and (23.25) present a specific statistical model for such behavior. Other series may be better modeled by a process that assumes that the short-term behavior is approximated by a linear time trend but with the slope and intercept changing over a longer time horizon. Double exponential smoothing leads to better estimates in this case. The model is written as

$$y_t = \beta_{0,t} + \beta_{1,t}t + e_t \tag{23.27}$$

where the intercept $\beta_{0,t}$ and slope $\beta_{1,t}$ vary over time. Estimates of the intercept and slope are obtained by smoothing the time series twice, hence the name **double exponential smoothing**.

For double exponential smoothing, S_t' denotes the smoothed value at time t for the series y_t:

$$S_t' = \alpha y_t + (1 - \alpha)S_{t-1}' \tag{23.28}$$

Then the smoothed values are smoothed a second time to obtain S_t'' where

$$S_t'' = \alpha S_t' + (1 - \alpha)S_{t-1}'' \tag{23.29}$$

Finally, based on algebra not given here, the estimates of the changing intercept and slope are obtained from

$$\hat{\beta}_{0,t} = 2S_t' - S_t'' \tag{23.30}$$

and

$$\hat{\beta}_{1,t} = \frac{\alpha}{1 - \alpha}(S_t' - S_t'') \tag{23.31}$$

If n denotes the time of the last available series value, the forecast l time units into the future is given by extrapolating the linear trend using the current estimates of the intercept and slope:

$$\hat{y}_{n+l} = \hat{\beta}_{0,n} + \hat{\beta}_{1,n}l \qquad \textbf{for } l = 1, 2, \ldots \tag{23.32}$$

For illustration we use one year's data on weekly thermostat sales, plotted in Exhibit 23.8J and with data reported in Exhibit 23.8K.

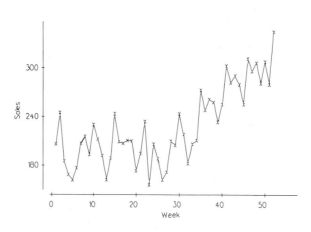

EXHIBIT 23.8J
Sequence Plot of Weekly Thermostat Sales

E X H I B I T **23.8K**
Weekly Thermostat Sales Data

```
filename: THERMOST.DAT
Weekly thermostat sales
(Source: R.G.Brown, Smoothing, Forecasting and Prediction of
Discrete Time Series, Engelwood Cliffs, NJ: Prentice-Hall, 1962)
(Read across, row by row)
206 245 185 169 162 177 207 216 193 230 212 192 162
189 244 209 207 211 210 173 194 234 156 206 188 162
172 210 205 244 218 182 206 211 273 248 262 258 233
255 303 282 291 280 255 312 296 307 281 308 280 345
```

Initializing Double Exponential Smoothing

As with single exponential smoothing, the recursive calculations of Equations (23.28) and (23.29) must be started with initial values S_0' and S_0''. Although several different initializations are advocated in the smoothing literature, we recommend fitting a straight-line trend to the first six series values. Solving Equations (23.30) and (23.31) for S_0' and S_0'' in terms of $\hat{\beta}_0$ and $\hat{\beta}_1$ leads to the expressions

$$S_0' = \hat{\beta}_{0,0} - \frac{1-\alpha}{\alpha}\hat{\beta}_{1,0} \tag{23.33}$$

and

$$S_0'' = \hat{\beta}_{0,0} - 2\frac{1-\alpha}{\alpha}\hat{\beta}_{1,0} \tag{23.34}$$

Here $\hat{\beta}_{0,0}$ and $\hat{\beta}_{1,0}$ are the intercept and slope of the linear time trend fitted to the first six values of the series by regressing $y_1, y_2, \ldots, y_6$ on $1, 2, \ldots, 6$.

For illustration, consider smoothing the thermostat sales series. Exhibit 23.8L gives the time trend fit to the first six series values. Using a smoothing constant of $\alpha = 0.24$, Equations (23.33) and (23.34) yield

$$S_0' = 231.67 - \frac{.76}{.24}(-11.714) = 268.764$$

$$S_0'' = 231.67 - 2\left[\frac{.76}{.24}\right](-11.714) = 305.859$$

E X H I B I T **23.8L**
Thermostat Sales Series Initial
Value Calculations—Linear Time
Trend Fitted to First Six Values

```
The regression equation is

Sales = 232 - 11.7 week

Predictor        Coef        Stdev     t-ratio        p
Constant        231.67       22.30       10.39      0.000
week            -11.714       5.727       -2.05      0.110
```

Exhibit 23.8M shows the results of double exponential smoothing for the weekly sales series using these initial values and $\alpha = 0.24$. Here the fitted value at time t is the one-step-ahead forecast considering y_t as the last series value.[†]

E X H I B I T **23.8M**
Double Exponential Smoothing
of Thermostat Sales Series

Week	Sales	S'	S''	Fitted
0	*	268.762	305.857	*
1	206	253.699	293.339	219.952
2	245	251.611	283.324	201.541
3	185	235.625	271.877	209.883
4	169	219.635	259.338	187.925
5	162	205.802	246.490	167.393
6	177	198.890	235.066	152.266
7	207	200.836	226.851	151.290
8	216	204.476	221.481	166.607
9	193	201.721	216.738	182.100
10	230	208.508	214.763	181.962
11	212	209.346	213.463	200.278
12	192	205.183	211.476	203.929
⋮	⋮	⋮	⋮	⋮
42	282	263.329	243.481	284.038
43	291	269.970	249.838	289.445
44	280	272.377	255.248	296.459
45	255	268.207	258.358	294.916
46	312	278.717	263.244	281.166
47	296	282.865	267.953	299.076
48	307	288.657	272.922	302.486
49	281	286.820	276.257	309.362
50	308	291.903	280.012	300.717
51	280	289.046	282.180	307.548
52	345	302.475	287.051	298.080

The choice of the smoothing constant can again be based on minimizing the RMSPE for the observed series values. Exhibits 23.8N and 23.8O give the calculated values and a plot showing that $\alpha = 0.24$ provides the best fit. As with other data sets, a range of values of the smoothing constant provide nearly equivalent values for the RMSPE.

In the exercises in Section 23.9, you are asked to examine the residuals from the double exponential smoothing with regard to their autocorrelation, normality, and so

[†]The minor differences between the initial values here and those calculated earlier are due to round-off error. The smoothing was done with computer software that uses many more digits internally.

α	RMSPE	α	RMSPE
0.10	42.6330	0.22	30.2193
0.11	39.2751	0.23	30.1682
0.12	36.8230	0.24	30.1530
0.13	35.0195	0.25	30.1676
0.14	33.6841	0.26	30.2072
0.15	32.6899	0.27	30.2678
0.16	31.9476	0.28	30.3464
0.17	31.3934	0.29	30.4403
0.18	30.9819	0.30	30.5475
0.19	30.6799	0.35	31.2316
0.20	30.4633	0.40	32.0816
0.21	30.3143	0.50	34.0968

E X H I B I T **23.8O**
RMSPE Values for Double
Exponential Smoothing of
Thermostat Sales Series

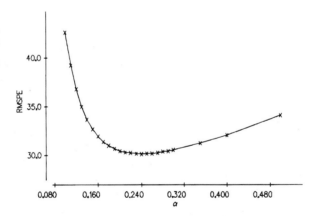

forth. For now, it is assumed that the diagnostic checks have been performed and that the model appears to be acceptable.

After the double smoothing is complete, forecasts are obtained using Equations (23.30), (23.31), and (23.32) for a set of lead values $l = 1, 2, \ldots$ into the future. For example, with the sales data, $S'_{52} = 302.475$ and $S''_{52} = 287.051$ that yield intercept and slope coefficients of

$$\hat{\beta}_{0,52} = 2S'_{52} - S''_{52} = (2 \times 302.475) - 287.051 = 317.899$$

and

$$\hat{\beta}_{1,52} = \frac{\alpha}{1 - \alpha}(S'_{52} - S''_{52}) = \frac{.24}{.76}(302.475 - 287.051) = 4.8707$$

For these data, forecasts l weeks ahead are given by

$$\hat{y}_{52+l} = 317.899 + 4.8707l$$

E X H I B I T **23.8P**

Forecasts for the Next Six Weeks' Thermostat Sales

t	l	$\hat{y}_{52+l}$
53	1	322.770
54	2	327.640
55	3	332.511
56	4	337.382
57	5	342.253
58	6	347.123

The forecasts are listed in Exhibit 23.8P for leads $l = 1, 2, \ldots, 6$.

Exhibit 23.8Q displays a sequence plot of the actual sales series (plotting symbol A), the fitted values (symbol F) based on double exponential smoothing, and the predictions (symbol P) for six weeks into the future.

E X H I B I T **23.8Q**

Thermostat Sales Series: Sequence Plot of Actual Sales Values, Fitted Values, and Forecasts for Six Weeks

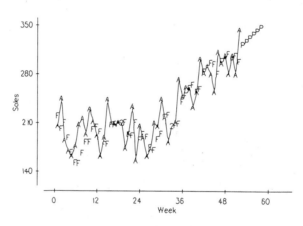

A Model for Double Exponential Smoothing (Optional)

In direct analogy with the model described by Equations (23.25) and (23.26), a time series model for which double exponential smoothing produces optimal forecasts can be described as

$$y_t = \beta_t + e_t \tag{23.35}$$

where

$$\beta_t = \beta_{t-1} + \alpha_t \tag{23.36}$$

and

$$\alpha_t = \alpha_{t-1} + u_t \tag{23.37}$$

Here u_t is a sequence of independent errors that are also independent of the e_t errors. Notice that α_t is the *rate of change* or slope of the β_t sequence at time t so that the slope of the "trend" β_t is changing according to a random walk model.[†] This is another example of an integrated moving-average process, specifically, an IMA(2, 2) process: the second difference of the y_t series has nonzero autocorrelation only at lags 1 and 2. A general study of these types of models is beyond the scope of this text. Refer to books specializing in time series models for more information.

SECTION

23.9 Exercises

23.9A A time series begins with values 5, 7, 6, 9, 6, 5, 6, and 7.

   a Using an initial value of $\hat{\beta}_0 = 6$ and a smoothing constant of $\alpha = 0.1$, find the smoothed series values.

   b Plot the series and overlay the series of smoothed values.

23.9B The time series given in Exercise 23.7E gave the final position in the "x direction" after an industrial robot finished a planned set of movements. The measurements are expressed as deviations from a desired position.

   a Use simple exponential smoothing with $\alpha = 0.1$ to smooth the series. Compare the fit of this model to that of the AR(1) model considered in Exercise 23.7E.

   b Use simple exponential smoothing with $\alpha = 0.05, 0.15$, and 0.2 in addition to $\alpha = 0.1$ in part (a) on the series. Which smoothing constant provides the smallest RMSPE? (Filename: ROBOT.DAT.)

23.9C Use the Deere & Co. machining data of Exhibit 23.6A.

   a Exponentially smooth the series using $\alpha = 0.1$.

   b Plot the sequence plot of the series and overlay the smoothed series. Comment on the plot.

   c Exponentially smooth the series using $\alpha = 0.7$.

   d Plot the sequence plot of the series and overlay the smoothed series obtained in part (c). Comment on the plot. (Filename: DEERE3.DAT.)

23.9D Use double exponential smoothing on the AA railroad bond yields of Exhibit 23.6M.

   a Use a smoothing constant of $\alpha = 0.1$.

   b Overlay the smoothed series on the sequence plot of the bond yields. Comment on the appearance of the plot.

   c Now use a smoothing constant $\alpha = 0.6$.

   d Again overlay the smoothed series from part (c) on the sequence plot of the bond yields. Comment on the appearance of this plot. (Filename: RRBONDS.DAT.)

Chapter Summary

Data collected at regular intervals over time from a time series. A distinguishing feature of times series is autocorrelation, which is correlation between lagged values

[†]See Appendix 3 for more details on random walks.

of a series. In particular, if the residuals from a time series regression exhibit auto-correlation, an important assumption of the regression model—independence of the errors—is violated. The model needs to be enriched to account for the autocorrelation. Distributed lag and autoregressive models attempt to account for autocorrelation. Exponential smoothing, on the other hand, attempts to smooth out the fluctuations in a series so as to enhance whatever trend may exist. Nevertheless, models can be produced that yield exponential smoothing as an optimal forecast procedure. It follows that when the assumptions of these models are violated, application of exponential smoothing fails to be optimal.

Supplementary Exercises for Chapter 23

23A Sequence data from an industrial process at Deere & Co. were first encountered in Exercise 2A. Using those data

a Compute the autocorrelations at lags 1, 2, and 3 and comment on their magnitudes.

b Construct scatterplots of the series versus the series lagged one time unit. Does the plot suggest that the lag 1 autocorrelation is a useful measure of the dependence in the series?

c Fit an AR(1) model to this series. Check the residuals for any lack of fit or lack of normality.

d Fit an AR(2) model to the series. Does this model confirm the AR(1) model estimated and checked in part (c)?

e Perform simple exponential smoothing on this series. Use smoothing coefficients of 0.1, 0.4, and 0.8. Plot the resulting smoothed series and compare them to the original series. (Filename: DEERE2.DAT.)

23B Monthly unit sales of motor homes by Winnebago Industries are listed below. A sequence plot of the logarithms of these data was presented in Exhibit 21.8F.

a Display a sequence plot of the month-to-month changes in log(sales). Are any patterns apparent?

b Now construct the sequence plot using plotting symbols that indicate the months as in Exhibit 21.12B. Are any patterns apparent now?

c Calculate the autocorrelation of log(sales) at lag 12 and interpret its magnitude. (These data are used again in Exercise 24C.)

```
filename: WINNEBAG.DAT
Monthly unit sales of motor homes
Winnebago Industries, Forest City, Iowa
November 1966 through February 1972
(Source: H.V.Roberts, Data Analysis for Managers,
Redwood City, CA: The Scientific Press, 1988)
Jan  Feb  Mar  Apr  May  Jun  Jul  Aug  Sep  Oct  Nov  Dec
                                                      61   48
 53   78   75   58  146  193  124  120  134   99  130  166
168  267  314  432  355  384  232  235  293  242  248  236
209  358  352  406  562  389  416  493  409  328  222  195
156  439  671  874  558  621  628  652  495  344  405  586
403  700  837 1224 1117 1214  762  846 1228  937 1396 1174
628 1753
```

23C The data file below gives the number of new passenger cars registered in the United States annually for the years 1950 through 1988.

a Display the sequence plot of these data.

b Fit a quadratic time trend model to these data and check the residuals for autocorrelation at lag 1.

c   Now display the sequence plot of the percent changes from year to year.

d   Show that the mean rate of growth per year is 3.01% and the standard deviation of growth rates is 14.75%.

e   Show that the percent changes have roughly a normal-shaped distribution.

f   Calculate the autocorrelation in the percent changes at lags 1, 2, and 3 and argue that these are small correlations. Combining the results of parts (c), (d), (e), and (f), the percent changes are said to behave as if they were drawn randomly and independently from a normal distribution with mean 3.01% and standard deviation 14.75%.

```
filename: NEWCARS.DAT
Annual new passenger car registrations in the U.S.
1951-1988, in 100,000s
(Source: Survey of Current Business, various issues)
(Read across, row by row)
 5061  4158  5739  5535  7170  5955  5982  4655  6041
 6577  5855  6939  7557  8065  9314  9009  8357  9404
 9447  8388  9831 10409 11351  8701  8262  9752 10826
11946 10357  8761  8444  7754  8924 10129 10889 11140
10122 10480
```

Glossary for Chapter 23

AR(1) model   An autoregressive model in which the predictor variable is the response variable at the previous time point.

AR(2) model   An autoregressive model in which the two predictor variables are the response variable at the previous two time points.

AR(p) model $y_t = \beta_0 + \beta_1 y_{t-1} + \beta_2 y_{t-2} + \cdots + \beta_p y_{t-p} + e_t$

autoregressive model   A time series model using lagged values of the response variable as predictor variables.

distributed lag model   A model relating a response variable to the lagged values of a predictor variable.

double exponential smoothing   Performing exponential smoothing on a series twice.

Durbin-Watson statistic $DW = \dfrac{\sum\limits_{t=2}^{n}(\hat{e}_t - \hat{e}_{t-1})^2}{\sum\limits_{t=1}^{n}\hat{e}_t^2}$

exponential smoothing   An ad hoc technique for smoothing out the random variation in a series.

Koyck (or geometric) model   A particular distributed lag model in which a response is related to an exponentially weighted combination of the predictor variable at many lags.

linear time trend   Trend modeled as a straight line.

quadratic time trend   Trend modeled as a quadratic curve in time.

smoothing constant   The constant in exponential smoothing that determines the extent of the smoothing.

24

Seasonal Time Series

Chapter Objectives

After mastering this chapter, you will be able to:

- Recognize seasonal time series

- Fit and interpret seasonal indicator variables

- Fit and interpret seasonal autoregression models

- Do seasonal exponential smoothing

- Model seasonal differences when appropriate

24.1 Seasonality

Sections 2.6 and 2.12 introduced sequence plots of seasonal data. This chapter outlines four techniques for modeling seasonal data: seasonal indicators, seasonal autoregression, seasonal exponential smoothing, and seasonal differencing. It is difficult to predict which will forecast most accurately; seasonal forecasting models must be tested in the real world. A final brief discussion gives basics of seasonal adjustment.

A *seasonal* phenomenon is one that occurs with a more-or-less regular period, such as every 12 months. Some seasonal phenomena are directly related to the seasons of the year. For example, in the northern parts of the United States, the level of building construction is generally higher during the summer months when temperatures are more favorable to outdoor work. Other seasonal phenomena, such as the Christmas holidays, dramatically influence economic series such as retail sales and levels of employment in certain industries. Employment levels are also affected by the seasonal influx of students into the summer job market. Since the seasonal phenomenon is frequently predictable, models that reflect seasonality should help analysts forecast the behavior of processes affected by seasonality.

A time series of average monthly temperatures in Dubuque, Iowa, over the years 1964 through 1975 is used to illustrate. The last year, 1975, is held out from all model building so that the model forecasts can be compared with the actual series values for that year. The data are listed in Exhibit 24.1A and the sequence plot is shown in Exhibit 24.1B. The seasonal pattern for this series is very regular, and no other patterns are apparent in the plot.

EXHIBIT 24.1A
Average Monthly Temperatures
for Dubuque,
Iowa—1964–1975

```
filename: TEMPDUB.DAT
Average monthly temperatures in Dubuque, Iowa
(Source: J.D.Cryer, Time Series Analysis,
Boston: Duxbury, 1986)
January 1964 through December 1975, n=144
Jan  Feb  Mar  Apr  May  Jun  Jul  Aug  Sep  Oct  Nov  Dec
24.7 25.7 30.6 47.5 62.9 68.5 73.7 67.9 61.1 48.5 39.6 20.0
16.1 19.1 24.2 45.4 61.3 66.5 72.1 68.4 60.2 50.9 37.4 31.1
10.4 21.6 37.4 44.7 53.2 68.0 73.7 68.2 60.7 50.2 37.2 24.6
21.5 14.7 35.0 48.3 54.0 68.2 69.6 65.7 60.8 49.1 33.2 26.0
19.1 20.6 40.2 50.0 55.3 67.7 70.7 70.3 60.6 50.7 35.8 20.7
14.0 24.1 29.4 46.6 58.6 62.2 72.1 71.7 61.9 47.6 34.2 20.4
 8.4 19.0 31.4 48.7 61.6 68.1 72.2 70.6 62.5 52.7 36.7 23.8
11.2 20.0 29.6 47.7 55.8 73.2 68.0 67.1 64.9 57.1 37.6 27.7
13.4 17.2 30.8 43.7 62.3 66.4 70.2 71.6 62.1 46.0 32.7 17.3
22.5 25.7 42.3 45.2 55.5 68.9 72.3 72.3 62.5 55.6 38.0 20.4
17.6 20.5 34.2 49.2 54.8 63.8 74.0 67.1 57.7 50.8 36.8 25.5
20.4 19.6 24.6 41.3 61.8 68.5 72.0 71.1 57.3 52.5 40.6 26.2
```

EXHIBIT 24.1B
Sequence Plot of Average
Monthly
Temperatures—1964–1974:
January–December Indicated by
A–L, Respectively

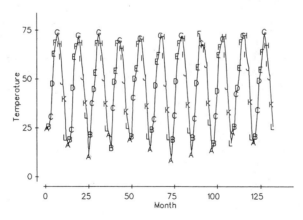

SECTION

24.2 Exercises

24.2A The data file below gives the monthly production of milk in pounds per cow for the period January 1962 through December 1975. Plot and interpret the sequence plot of this time series. Use appropriate plotting symbols so that seasonality may be looked for. Is there a general trend of any sort beyond seasonality?

```
filename: MILKPROD.DAT
Milk production in pounds per cow per month
(Source: J.D.CRYER, Time Series Analysis,
Boston: Duxbury, 1986)
January 1962 through December 1975, n=168
589  561  640  656  727  697  640  599  568  577  553  582
600  566  653  673  742  716  660  617  583  587  565  598
628  618  688  705  770  736  678  639  604  611  594  634
658  622  709  722  782  756  702  653  615  621  602  635
677  635  736  755  811  798  735  697  661  667  645  688
713  667  762  784  837  817  767  722  681  687  660  698
717  696  775  796  858  826  783  740  701  706  677  711
734  690  785  805  871  845  801  764  725  723  690  734
750  707  807  824  886  859  819  783  740  747  711  751
804  756  860  878  942  913  869  834  790  800  763  800
826  799  890  900  961  935  894  855  809  810  766  805
821  773  883  898  957  924  881  837  784  791  760  802
828  778  889  902  969  947  908  867  815  812  773  813
834  782  892  903  966  937  896  858  817  827  797  843
```

24.2B   The data set below gives the monthly bus ridership values for Portland, Oregon, during the period January 1973 through 1982.

```
filename: PORTBUS.DAT
Portland, Oregon, average monthly bus ridership (/100)
(Source: J.D.Cryer, Time Series Analysis,
Boston: Duxbury, 1986.)
January 1973 through June 1982, n=114
Jan  Feb  Mar  Apr  May  Jun  Jul  Aug  Sep   Oct   Nov   Dec
648  646  639  654  630  622  617  613  661   695   690   707
817  839  810  789  760  724  704  691  745   803   780   761
857  907  873  910  900  880  867  854  928  1064  1103  1026
1102 1080 1034 1083 1078 1020  984  952 1033  1114  1160  1058
1209 1200 1130 1182 1152 1116 1098 1044 1142  1222  1234  1155
1286 1281 1224 1280 1228 1181 1156 1124 1152  1205  1260  1188
1212 1269 1246 1299 1284 1345 1341 1308 1448  1454  1467  1431
1510 1558 1536 1523 1492 1437 1365 1310 1441  1450  1424  1360
1429 1440 1414 1424 1408 1337 1258 1214 1326  1417  1417  1329
1461 1425 1419 1432 1394 1327
```

a   Plot the sequence plot. Does there appear to be seasonality in the series? Are there any general trends upward or downward?

b   Plot the sequence plot for the logarithms of the ridership values. Comment on the seasonality and other patterns shown in this plot.

24.2C   The data below are the total U.S. air passenger miles for the period January 1960 through December 1977.

```
filename: AIRMILES.DAT
Monthly U.S. air passenger miles (millions)
(Source: J.D.Cryer, Time Series Analysis,
Boston, Duxbury, 1986)
January 1960 through December 1977, n=216
(Read across, row by row)
2.42   2.14   2.28   2.50   2.44   2.72   2.71   2.74   2.55   2.49   2.13   2.28
2.35   1.82   2.40   2.46   2.38   2.83   2.68   2.81   2.54   2.54   2.37   2.54
2.62   2.34   2.68   2.75   2.66   2.96   2.93   2.70   2.65   2.46   2.59
2.75   2.45   2.85   2.99   2.89   3.43   3.25   3.59   3.12   3.16   2.86   3.22
3.24   2.95   3.32   3.29   3.32   3.91   3.80   4.02   3.53   3.61   3.22   3.67
3.75   3.25   3.70   3.98   3.88   4.47   4.60   4.90   4.20   4.20   3.80   4.50
4.40   4.00   4.70   5.10   4.90   5.70   3.90   4.20   5.10   5.00   4.70   5.50
5.30   4.60   5.90   5.50   5.40   6.70   6.80   7.40   6.00   5.80   5.50   6.40
6.20   5.70   6.40   6.70   6.30   7.80   7.60   8.60   6.60   6.50   6.00   7.60
7.00   6.00   7.10   7.40   7.20   8.40   8.50   9.40   7.10   7.00   6.60   8.00
10.45   8.81  10.61   9.97  10.69  12.40  13.38  14.31  10.90   9.98   9.20  10.94
10.53   9.06  10.17  11.17  10.84  12.09  13.66  14.06  11.14  11.10  10.00  11.98
11.74  10.27  12.05  12.27  12.03  13.95  15.10  15.65  12.47  12.29  11.52  13.08
12.50  11.05  12.94  13.24  13.16  14.95  16.00  16.98  13.15  12.88  11.99  13.13
12.99  11.69  13.78  13.70  13.57  15.12  15.55  16.73  12.68  12.65  11.18  13.27
12.64  11.01  13.30  12.19  12.91  14.90  16.10  17.30  12.90  13.36  12.26  13.93
13.94  12.75  14.19  14.67  14.66  16.21  17.72  18.15  14.19  14.33  12.99  15.19
15.09  12.94  15.46  15.39  15.34  17.02  18.85  19.49  15.61  16.16  14.84  17.04
```

a   Display the sequence plot for this time series. Comment on any apparent seasonality. Are there any other general trends or patterns?

b   Display the sequence plot of the logarithms of the series. Comment on the patterns seen here.

SECTION

24.3   Seasonal Indicators

seasonal indicators

A common method for incorporating seasonal effects into time series models is to use a regression model with **seasonal indicators**, which are binary (or indicator) predictor variables for the various months of the year. Such models are generally useful where the seasonality is regular and unchanging, since the model will make exactly the same adjustment each year. Other predictors, such as linear time trends, may be used in combination with the seasonal indicators if appropriate.

For the temperature series, consider the model

$$y_t = \beta_0 + \gamma_1 \text{Jan}_t + \gamma_2 \text{Feb}_t + \gamma_3 \text{Mar}_t + \cdots + \gamma_{11} \text{Nov}_t + e_t \qquad \textbf{(24.1)}$$

where the binary seasonal indicators are defined as

$$\text{Jan}_t = \begin{cases} 1 \text{ if } t = \text{January} \\ 0 \text{ if } t \neq \text{January} \end{cases}$$

$$\text{Feb}_t = \begin{cases} 1 \text{ if } t = \text{February} \\ 0 \text{ if } t \neq \text{February} \end{cases}$$

$$\vdots$$

and

$$\text{Nov}_t = \begin{cases} 1 \text{ if } t = \text{November} \\ 0 \text{ if } t \neq \text{November} \end{cases}$$

Here $t = \text{January}$ means that time t corresponds to a January in some year. Similarly, $t = \text{February}$, and so forth. Notice that no binary variable for December is included. The intercept term, β_0, provides the estimate of the December effect in the model, so that December serves as a base month. Then γ_1 is the adjustment to β_0 to be made for all Januarys. Similarly, γ_2 is the differential effect, either positive or negative, for all Februarys relative to the December level of β_0.

The basic results from fitting the model of Equation (24.1) to the temperature series are shown in Exhibit 24.3A. Here the intercept is estimated as 23.4°, which is interpreted as the predicted value for all Decembers. Januarys are predicted to be 7.15° colder than Decembers; Julys are predicted to be 48.3° warmer than Decembers; and so on. This seasonal indicators model accounts for 97.2% of the variation in the observed temperature series.

A sequence plot of the residuals from this model is shown in Exhibit 24.3B. No seasonal patterns or other patterns are detected here. This conclusion is reinforced by the absence of autocorrelation in the residual series, which you may verify.

Forecasting is the next step. Forecasts for any month are easily obtained from the estimated regression coefficients as described above. The predictions, 2-standard-deviation prediction intervals, and the actual 1975 values are listed in Exhibit 24.3C.

EXHIBIT **24.3A**

Regression on Seasonal Indicator Variables—Monthly Temperature Series

The regression equation is

temperature = 23.4 − 7.15 Jan − 2.66 Feb + 9.78 Mar + 23.6 Apr
              + 34.3 May + 44.0 Jun + 48.3 Jul + 45.8 Aug
              + 38.0 Sep + 27.4 Oct + 12.9 Nov

Predictor	Coef	Stdev	t-ratio	p
Constant	23.409	1.018	23.00	0.000
Jan	-7.145	1.439	-4.96	0.000
Feb	-2.664	1.439	-1.85	0.067
Mar	9.782	1.439	6.80	0.000
Apr	23.591	1.439	16.39	0.000
May	34.345	1.439	23.86	0.000
Jun	44.000	1.439	30.57	0.000
Jul	48.282	1.439	33.55	0.000
Aug	45.764	1.439	31.80	0.000
Sep	37.955	1.439	26.37	0.000
Oct	27.427	1.439	19.06	0.000
Nov	12.882	1.439	8.95	0.000

s = 3.375   R-sq = 97.2%   R-sq(adj) = 97.0%

EXHIBIT **24.3B**

Sequence Plot of Residuals from Seasonal Indicators Model for Temperature Series

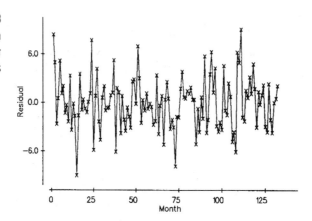

EXHIBIT **24.3C**

Predictions and Prediction Intervals for Temperature Series

		Prediction Interval		1975
Month	Prediction	Lower	Upper	Actual Value
Jan	16.264	9.282	23.245	20.4
Feb	20.745	13.764	27.727	19.6
Mar	33.191	26.209	40.173	24.6 ←——— miss
Apr	47.000	40.018	53.982	41.3
May	57.755	50.773	64.736	61.8
Jun	67.409	60.427	74.391	68.5
Jul	71.691	64.709	78.673	72.0
Aug	69.173	62.191	76.155	71.1
Sep	61.364	54.382	68.345	57.3
Oct	50.836	43.855	57.818	52.5
Nov	36.291	29.309	43.273	40.6
Dec	23.409	16.427	30.391	26.2

Only one actual value, an unusually cold March, misses being covered by the 12 prediction intervals. Exhibit 24.3D shows the prediction intervals graphically.

E X H I B I T **24.3D**

Actual Values, Predictions, and Prediction Intervals for the Temperature Series: A=Actual, U=Upper Limit, L=Lower Limit

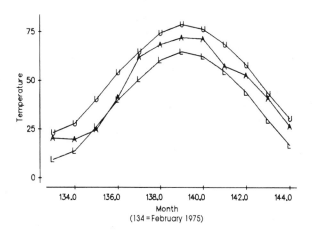

The seasonal indicators model implies a very regular and unchanging seasonality for a time series. Most series are less regular. Consider the time series of bus ridership in Iowa City, Iowa. The monthly averages of weekday ridership over the period September 1971 through December 1982 are listed in Exhibit 24.3E, and the corresponding sequence plot is shown in Exhibit 24.3F. Weather is an important seasonal factor affecting bus ridership. During warmer months potential bus riders have the option of walking or bicycling, but in winter their transportation options are reduced. Lower ridership in summer months is also due, in part, to the lower summer enrollment at the University of Iowa. Again, the last year of data, 1982, is held out from all of the model fitting so that the actual series values can be compared with the forecasts.

E X H I B I T **24.3E**

Weekday Bus Ridership in Iowa City, Iowa—September 1971–December 1982

```
filename: ICBUS.DAT
Weekday bus ridership, Iowa City, Iowa (monthly averages)
(Source: J.D.Cryer, Time Series Analysis,
Boston: Duxbury, 1986)
September 1971 through December 1982, n=136
(Read across, row by row)
3603  4448  4734  4353  5438  5954  4838  4532  3599  3248  3230  2790
4738  5043  5367  5262  5065  5824  4612  4823  3564  3651  3625  3170
5022  5018  5326  5412  6345  6698  5605  5260  3789  4023  3775  3384
5303  5506  5645  5168  6173  6776  5957  5777  3833  4200  3891  3595
5862  5719  5957  5226  6467  6383  5589  5296  3943  4188  3673  3475
5392  5583  5738  4944  6552  6451  5354  5081  3874  3973  3751  3621
5328  5427  5419  5983  6568  8346  6800  6308  4857  4663  4499  3878
6031  6325  6764  6929  7557  8182  6892  6860  5181  5462  5328  4331
7279  7772  8262  7499  8081 10121  8745  8045  5906  5274  5283  4956
7879  8289  8422  7832  7857 10008  8057  7791  6147  5438  5494  5253
8154  8604  8832  7815 10179 11460  9641  9243  6824  6149  6161  5962
9068  9538  9988  7916
```

E X H I B I T **24.3F**
Sequence Plot of Weekday Bus
Ridership in Iowa City, Iowa:
January–December Indicated by
A–L, Respectively

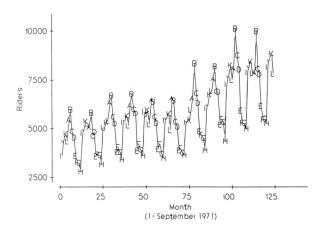

E X H I B I T **24.3F**
Sequence Plot of Weekday Bus
Ridership in Iowa City, Iowa:
January–December Indicated by
A–L, Respectively

The sequence plot in Exhibit 24.3F displays several important features. First, notice the upward trend in the general level of ridership over this time period. Second, notice that the variation in ridership levels over the later portion of the time period is much greater than in the earlier part of the series. This signals that a logarithm transformation should be used to try to equalize the variability around the general upward trend. Finally, a careful reading of the plot reveals that ridership values 12 months apart are quite similar relative to the general upward trend. Summer months are generally associated with lower ridership, and winter months are nearly always high ridership periods.

Exhibit 24.3G gives the sequence plot of the logarithms of ridership values. Now the variation is quite similar in magnitude over the whole time period, but the upward linear trend and the seasonality are still apparent. To better isolate the seasonality,

E X H I B I T **24.3G**
Sequence Plot of the Logarithm
of Weekday Bus Ridership in
Iowa City, Iowa:
January–December Indicated by
A–L, Respectively

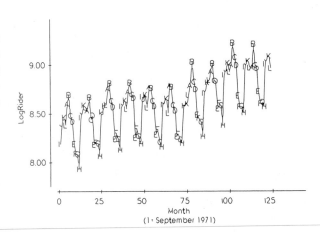

a linear time trend is fit to log(ridership) and the nature of the residual series is considered.

The sequence plot of residuals shown in Exhibit 24.3H shows that the seasonality accounts for a substantial portion of the variation in the series after the linear time trend has been fit to the series. It may be verified that for these residuals the autocorrelation is 0.829 at lag 12, 0.720 at lag 24, and 0.601 at lag 36. Models that account for this seasonality should substantially improve forecasting and, more generally, explain considerably more of the variation in such time series.

E X H I B I T **24.3H**
Sequence Plot of Residuals from
Linear Time Trend of Log
Ridership

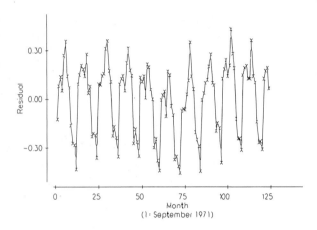

Exhibit 24.3I gives the regression results for the linear time trend, seasonal indicators model applied to the Log Ridership series. This exhibit also gives the predicted values and 2-standard-deviation prediction intervals for the next year corresponding to $t = 125, 126, \ldots, 136$. (Many more digits are shown here than would be reported in a summary of the results.) In Exhibit 24.3J the sequence of fitted values is plotted to graphically demonstrate how the seasonality is superimposed on the upward linear trend.

Forecasts and actual series values for the held-out year are plotted in Exhibit 24.3K. As expected, the forecasts mimic the seasonality plus upward drift of the series. Unfortunately, the residuals from this model behave rather badly. The sequence plot of residuals appears in Exhibit 24.3L. The autocorrelation is 0.7 at lag 1, 0.6 at lag 2, 0.5 at lag 3, and so on. Given this behavior of the residuals, prediction intervals are not presented, since their justification rests partly on the assumption of independent error terms. The seasonality and trend in this series are not regular enough to be adequately modeled by the seasonal indicators plus trend model. Other models for this series must be considered.

```
The regression equation is

LogRider = 8.37 + 0.00499 time + 0.125 Jan  + 0.233 Feb
             + 0.0475 Mar   + 0.0007 Apr  - 0.297 May
             - 0.308 Jun    - 0.352 Jul   - 0.460 Aug
             - 0.0194 Sep   + 0.0262 Oct + 0.0618 Nov

Predictor        Coef        Stdev    t-ratio        p
Constant      8.36736      0.02634     317.72    0.000
time        0.0049891    0.0001936      25.76    0.000
Jan           0.12461      0.03369       3.70    0.000
Feb           0.23313      0.03368       6.92    0.000
Mar           0.04749      0.03368       1.41    0.161
Apr           0.00073      0.03368       0.02    0.983
May          -0.29683      0.03367      -8.81    0.000
Jun          -0.30835      0.03367      -9.16    0.000
Jul          -0.35235      0.03367     -10.46    0.000
Aug          -0.45976      0.03368     -13.65    0.000
Sep          -0.01935      0.03287      -0.59    0.557
Oct           0.02620      0.03286       0.80    0.427
Nov           0.06177      0.03286       1.88    0.063

s = 0.07707      R-sq = 93.0%     R-sq(adj) = 92.3%

Time      Fit    Stdev.Fit    95% Prediction Interval
125    9.11560    0.02752      (8.95341,9.27780)
126    9.22912    0.02752      (9.06692,9.39132)
127    9.04847    0.02752      (8.88627,9.21067)
128    9.00669    0.02752      (8.84449,9.16889)
129    8.71412    0.02752      (8.55192,8.87632)
130    8.70759    0.02752      (8.54539,8.86979)
131    8.66858    0.02752      (8.50638,8.83077)
132    8.56616    0.02752      (8.40396,8.72836)
133    9.01156    0.02710      (8.84964,9.17348)
134    9.06210    0.02710      (8.90018,9.22402)
135    9.10265    0.02710      (8.94073,9.26457)
136    9.04587    0.02710      (8.88395,9.20780)
```

E X H I B I T **24.3J**
Sequence Plot of the Fitted
Values for Linear Trend plus
Seasonal Indicators Model

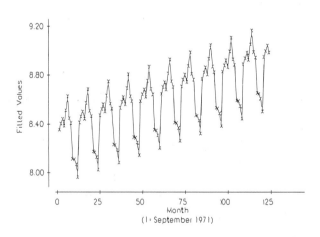

EXHIBIT 24.3K
Forecasts and Actual Values for
Last Year of Log Ridership
Series, January–December,
1982: A=Actual, F=Forecast

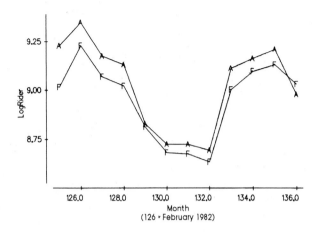

EXHIBIT 24.3L
Sequence Plot of Residuals from
Seasonal Indicators Model of
Log Ridership Series

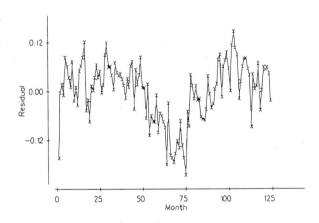

SECTION

24.4 Exercises

24.4A Refer to the milk production data set of Exercise 24.2A.

a Fit a model to these data consisting of seasonal indicator variables. Plot a sequence plot of the residuals. Does this model capture most of the features of this time series?

b Consider a model with seasonal indicators plus a linear time trend. Display the sequence plot of the residuals from this model. Of the models in parts (a) and (b), which captures the features of the data better?

c Calculate the autocorrelations at lags 1 and 2 of the residuals from the model considered in part (b). Does the model considered in part (b) seem to adequately describe the series? (Filename: MILKPROD.DAT.)

24.4B Use the logarithms of the Portland, Oregon, bus ridership data given in Exercise 24.2B.

a Fit a model that includes seasonal indicators and a linear time trend. Plot a sequence plot that overlays the log (series) and the fitted values. Do the fitted values follow the observed series?

b Plot the sequence plot of the residuals. Do they appear random or are there patterns in them over time?

c Evaluate the autocorrelations in the residuals at lags 1 and 2 and comment on their magnitude. (Filename: PORTBUS.DAT.)

24.4C Consider the U.S. air passenger miles data set in Exercise 24.2C. Use the logarithms of the data throughout this exercise.

a Fit a model that includes seasonal indicators plus a linear time trend. Plot a sequence plot that overlays the log (series) and the fitted values. Do the fitted values follow the observed series?

b Comment on the sequence plot of the residuals. Do they appear random or are there patterns in them over time?

c Calculate the autocorrelations in the residuals at lags 1 and 2 and comment on their size. (Filename: AIRMILES.DAT.)

SECTION

24.5 Seasonal Autoregression

Seasonal autoregressive models allow for seasonality differently than seasonal indicator models do. As in the earlier autoregressive models, the series y_t is regressed on itself at various lags, but now the seasonal lags 12, 24, ... play a special role. In **seasonal autoregression**, the predictor variable is lagged at multiples of the seasonal period. A purely seasonal autoregressive model of order 1 (season) is expressed as

seasonal autoregression

$$y_t = \beta_0 + \beta_{12} y_{t-12} + e_t \tag{24.2}$$

This model relates the behavior of y_t to the behavior of the series 12 months ago but only indirectly to the values 24, 36, ... months ago.

In addition to seasonality, the Log Ridership series also drifts upward over time. To account for this type of nonseasonal behavior, the model given in Equation (24.2) is extended to include both a seasonal relationship at lag 12 and a short-term relationship at lag 1:

$$y_t = \beta_0 + \beta_1 y_{t-1} + \beta_{12} y_{t-12} + e_t \tag{24.3}$$

Exhibit 24.5A displays the results of fitting such a model to the Log Ridership series. Because y_{13} is the first response for which both predictors y_{12} and y_1 are available, the first 12 values of the series cannot be used as responses. The seasonal autoregressive model estimated here says that the current value of Log Ridership is explained (predicted) by taking about 85% of the ridership of one year ago plus 13% of last month's value plus a constant term of 0.239. This simple three-parameter model (including the intercept term) accounts for 89.8% (adjusted) of the variation in the series. This should be compared to the 13-parameter seasonal indicators model, which had an R^2 (adjusted) of 92.3%.

Forecasts from the seasonal autoregressive model are obtained in a manner similar to those for earlier autoregressive models. Equation (24.3) is updated to time $t + 1$ as

$$y_{t+1} = \beta_0 + \beta_1 y_t + \beta_{12} y_{t-11} + e_{t+1} \tag{24.4}$$

E X H I B I T **24.5A**
Seasonal Autoregression for Log
Ridership Series

```
The regression equation is

LogRider = 0.239 + 0.127Lag1LogRider + 0.852Lag12LogRider

112 cases used; 12 cases contained missing values

Predictor            Coef      Stdev    t-ratio        p
Constant           0.2392     0.2779       0.86    0.391
Lag1LogRider       0.12693    0.04344      2.92    0.004
Lag12LogRider      0.85152    0.04456     19.11    0.000

s = 0.08507     R-sq = 90.0%     R-sq(adj) = 89.8%
```

Then, since e_{t+1} is independent of all observations up to time t, it is forecast by its mean of zero. At time t both y_t and y_{t-11} are available and the forecast one step ahead from time t is given by

$$\hat{y}_{t+1} = \beta_0 + \beta_1 y_t + \beta_{12} y_{t-11} \qquad \textbf{(24.5)}$$

Replacing $t + 1$ by $t + 2$ in Equation (24.4) yields

$$y_{t+2} = \beta_0 + \beta_1 y_{t+1} + \beta_{12} y_{t-10} + e_{t+2} \qquad \textbf{(24.6)}$$

However, at time t, y_{t+1} has not been observed. Two steps ahead is thus forecast using

$$\hat{y}_{t+2} = \beta_0 + \beta_1 \hat{y}_{t+1} + \beta_{12} y_{t-10} \qquad \textbf{(24.7)}$$

In a similar fashion, forecasts any number of steps into the future may be produced one at a time.

Consider forecasting the bus ridership series:

$$\hat{y}_{124+1} = 0.2392 + 0.12693 y_{124} + 0.85152 y_{113}$$
$$= 0.2392 + 0.12693(8.96380) + 0.85152(8.96916)$$
$$= 9.01439$$

and

$$\hat{y}_{124+2} = 0.2392 + 0.12693 \hat{y}_{124+1} + 0.85152 y_{114}$$
$$= 0.2392 + 0.12693(9.01439) + 0.85152(9.21114)$$
$$= 9.22687$$

and so forth. Exhibit 24.5B lists the forecasts and actual values for a full year; the sequence plot is shown in Exhibit 24.5C. These results should be compared to those obtained with the seasonal indicators model, which were displayed in Exhibit 24.3K.

E X H I B I T **24.5B**

Forecasts and Actual Values for

Log Ridership in 1982

Month	Forecast	1982 Actual Value
Jan	9.01439	9.22808
Feb	9.22687	9.34662
Mar	9.06919	9.17378
Apr	9.02058	9.13162
May	8.81260	8.82820
Jun	8.68185	8.72404
Jul	8.67398	8.72599
Aug	8.63478	8.69316
Sep	9.00422	9.11251
Oct	9.09686	9.16304
Nov	9.13089	9.20914
Dec	9.03104	8.97664

E X H I B I T **24.5C**

Sequence Plot of Forecasts and
Actual Values for Log Ridership
in 1982: A=Actual, F=Forecast

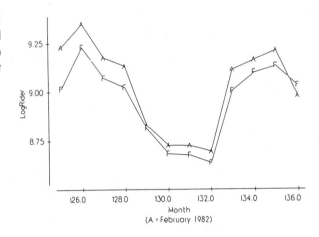

E X H I B I T **24.5D**

Sequence Plot of Residuals from
Seasonal Autoregression of Log
Ridership

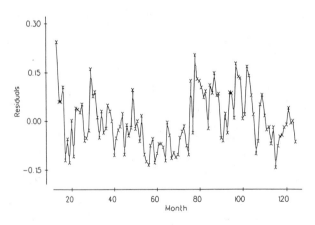

Exhibit 24.5D gives the sequence plot of the residuals from the fitted seasonal autoregressive model. Unfortunately, they are unacceptably autocorrelated. The autocorrelation is 0.51 at lag 1, 0.45 at lag 2, and 0.26 at lag 3. In the autoregression there are 112 cases after lagging, and these estimated autocorrelations of the residuals may be compared to their approximate standard error of $1/\sqrt{112} = 0.09$. Although

the seasonal autoregression is an improvement over the seasonal indicators model, the search for a better model continues.

S E C T I O N

24.6 Exercises

24.6A Use the data for Deere & Co. monthly sales of oil filters given in Exhibits 2.6A and 6.8A. Consider the seasonal AR model $\hat{y}_t = \beta_0 + \beta_1 y_{t-12}$.

    a Fit the seasonal autoregressive model, obtaining the fitted values, residuals, and standard deviation of the residuals.

    b Prepare a sequence plot of the residuals and comment on any patterns you detect.

    c Compute the autocorrelation coefficients of the residuals for lags 1 through 12. Comment on their magnitudes. (Filename: OILFILT.DAT.)

24.6B Refer to the Deere & Co. oil-filter sales data of Exhibits 2.6A and 6.8A. Consider the AR model $\hat{y}_t = \beta_0 + \beta_1 y_{t-1} + \beta_2 y_{t-12}$

    a Fit the seasonal autoregressive model, obtaining the fitted values, residuals, and standard deviation of the residuals.

    b Prepare a sequence plot of the residuals and comment on any patterns you detect.

    c Compute the autocorrelation coefficients of the residuals for lags 1 through 12. Comment on their magnitudes.

    d Compare your results to those in Exercise 24.6A. (Filename: OILFILT.DAT.)

24.6C Use the milk production time series listed in Exercise 24.2A.

    a Fit the model $y_t = \beta_0 + \beta_2 y_{t-1} + \beta_{12} y_{t-12} + e_t$.

    b Check the sequence plot of the residuals from the model for lack of randomness.

    c Calculate the autocorrelations of the residuals at lags 1 through 12 and comment on their magnitude. (Filename: MILKPROD.DAT.)

    d Compare the model of this exercise to the one considered in Exercise 24.4A. Which does a better job of capturing the structure in the observed time series?

24.6D Use the logarithms of the Portland, Oregon, bus ridership series given in Exercise 24.2B.

    a Fit the seasonal autoregressive model $y_t = \beta_0 + \beta_1 y_{t-1} + \beta_{12} y_{t-12} + e_t$.

    b Check the sequence plot of the residuals for patterns indicating lack of randomness.

    c Calculate the autocorrelations of the residuals at lags 1 through 12 and comment on their size.

    d Compare the autoregressive model of this exercise to the seasonal indicators model of Exercise 24.4B. Which does a better job of capturing the structure in the observed time series? (Filename: PORTBUS.DAT.)

24.6E Use the logarithms of the U.S. air passenger miles time series given in Exercise 24.2C.

    a Fit the model $y_t = \beta_0 + \beta_1 y_{t-1} + \beta_{12} y_{t-12} + e_t$.

    b Check the sequence plot of the residuals for patterns indicating lack of randomness.

    c Calculate the autocorrelations of the residuals at lags 1 through 12 and comment on their size.

    d Compare the autoregressive model of this exercise to the seasonal indicators model of Exercise 24.4C. Which does a better job of capturing the structure in the observed time series? (Filename: AIRMILES.DAT.)

24.6F Consider the monthly Dubuque temperature series listed in Exhibit 24.1A.

a   Fit a seasonal autoregression of the form $y_t = \beta_0 + \beta_1 y_{t-1} + \beta_{12} y_{t-12} + e_t$. Compare the results to those given in Exhibit 24.3A, where a seasonal indicators model is used.

b   Now fit the model $y_t = \beta_0 + \beta_{12} y_{t-12} + \beta_{24} y_{t-24} + e_t$ [a seasonal AR(2) model]. Compare this model to the one obtained in part (a) and to the model reported in Exhibit 24.3A. (Filename: TEMPDUB.DAT.)

24.6G   Consider the hourly wages time series shown in Exhibit 23.2A. In Exercise 23.7D, you saw that an AR(1) model fit the series better than a model with a fixed linear or quadratic trend but that the residuals showed signs of seasonality. Now fit the seasonal autoregressive model: $y_t = \beta_0 + \beta_1 y_{t-1} + \beta_{12} y_{t-12} + e_t$. Compare this model to earlier models. In particular, check the autocorrelation in the residuals at the seasonal lags 12 and 24. (Filename: APAWAGES.DAT.)

24.6H   Fit a simple AR(1) model, $y_t = \beta_0 + \beta_1 y_{t-1} + e_t$, to the logarithms of the bus ridership series given in Exhibit 24.3E.

a   Plot the sequence of residuals. Are any patterns evident?

b   Calculate the autocorrelation in the residuals obtained in part (a) at lags 12 and 24. Comment. (Filename: ICBUS.DAT.)

SECTION

24.7 Seasonal Exponential Smoothing

The ideas of exponential smoothing can be extended to seasonal time series without difficulty. **Winters' additive model** for seasonal exponential smoothing assumes that the series may be written as

Winters' additive model

$$y_t = \beta_{0,t} + \beta_{1,t} t + S_t + e_t \tag{24.8}$$

where $\beta_{0,t}$ is a slowly changing intercept term, $\beta_{1,t}$ is a slowly changing slope, S_t is a seasonal term that changes slowly from year to year, and e_t is the error term. The seasonal terms are assumed to add to zero over any given consecutive 12 months, so that they measure the seasonal effect around the overall level of $\beta_{0,t}$.

As in our previous encounter with exponential smoothing, initial estimates for the parameters are obtained based on the initial behavior of the series. These estimates are then smoothed according to equations that put some weight on old estimates of the parameters and complementary weight on the current information. In **seasonal exponential smoothing** there are three smoothing equations:

seasonal exponential smoothing

$$\hat{\beta}_{0,t+1} = \alpha_1 (y_{t+1} - \hat{S}_{t-11}) + (1 - \alpha_1)(\hat{\beta}_{0,t} + \hat{\beta}_{1,t}) \tag{24.9}$$
$$\hat{\beta}_{1,t+1} = \alpha_2 (\hat{\beta}_{0,t+1} - \hat{\beta}_{0,t}) + (1 - \alpha_2)\hat{\beta}_{1,t} \tag{24.10}$$

and

$$\hat{S}_{t+1} = \alpha_3 (y_{t+1} - \hat{\beta}_{0,t+1}) + (1 - \alpha_3)\hat{S}_{t-11} \tag{24.11}$$

where α_1, α_2, and α_3 are three smoothing constants, each chosen in the interval $(0,1)$. Each of these equations has an intuitive meaning. The intercept at time $t + 1$, $\hat{\beta}_{0,t+1}$, is updated by smoothing the current, deseasonalized observation, $y_{t+1} - \hat{S}_{t-11}$, with what would have been the new "intercept," $\hat{\beta}_{0,t} + \hat{\beta}_{1,t}$, at time $t + 1$. The new slope at time $t + 1$, $\hat{\beta}_{1,t+1}$, is updated by smoothing the old slope, $\hat{\beta}_{1,t}$, with a new estimate of slope, $\hat{\beta}_{0,t+1} - \hat{\beta}_{0,t}$. Finally, the seasonal effect at time $t + 1$ is updated by combining the old seasonal effect of one year ago, $\hat{S}_{t-11}$, with a current estimate of the seasonal effect $y_{t+1} - \hat{\beta}_{0,t+1}$.

Forecasts of future values from time t using this model are obtained from the equations

$$\hat{y}_{t+l} = \hat{\beta}_{0,t} + \hat{\beta}_{1,t}l + \hat{S}_{t+l-12} \qquad \text{for } l = 1, 2, \ldots, 12 \qquad \textbf{(24.12)}$$

$$\hat{y}_{t+l} = \hat{\beta}_{0,t} + \hat{\beta}_{1,t}l + \hat{S}_{t+l-24} \qquad \text{for } l = 12, 13, \ldots, 24 \qquad \textbf{(24.13)}$$

and so forth. In words, the current linear time trend is projected and then adjusted according to the appropriate seasonal effect corresponding to the month being forecast.

Initialization of Seasonal Exponential Smoothing

Seasonal exponential smoothing, exponential smoothing that accounts for seasonality, may be initialized by several different methods. We recommend fitting a seasonal indicators plus linear trend model to the first 24 observations. The seasonal indicator variables are modified by subtracting the binary variable Dec_t from each of the binary variables Jan_t, Feb_t, ..., Nov_t and regressing on the modified indicators $Jan(mod)_t = Jan_t - Dec_t$, $Feb(mod)_t = Feb_t - Dec_t$, ..., $Nov(mod)_t = Nov_t - Dec_t$ in addition to the time variable $1, 2, \ldots, 24$. With this modification, the initial December seasonal $\hat{S}_{12,0}$ is the negative of the sum of the other initial seasonals—that is,

$$\hat{S}_{12,0} = -(\hat{S}_{1,0} + \hat{S}_{2,0} + \cdots + \hat{S}_{11,0})$$

This ensures that the seasonals add to zero and have the proper interpretation as seasonal effects above or below the general level of β_0. The initial values $\hat{\beta}_{0,0}$ and $\hat{\beta}_{1,0}$ are taken as the intercept and slope estimates from the initial regression.

Exhibit 24.7A displays the regression results needed to initialize seasonal exponential smoothing of the Log Ridership series. The values $\hat{\beta}_{0,0} = 8.28176$, $\hat{\beta}_{1,0} = 0.006848$, $\hat{S}_{1,0} = -0.00325$, $\hat{S}_{2,0} = 0.12644$, ..., $\hat{S}_{11,0} = -0.26025$ are in the left-hand column. Then $\hat{S}_{12,0} = -(-0.00325 + 0.12644 + \cdots - 0.26025) = -0.40738$ is obtained. Since this process can be computer automated, little thought or hand calculation is needed in the end.

E X H I B I T **24.7A**

Initialization of Seasonal
Exponential Smoothing for Log
Ridership

```
The regression equation is

LogRider = 8.28 + 0.00685 time - 0.0033 Jan(mod)
        + 0.126 Feb(mod)  + 0.182 Mar(mod) + 0.123 Apr(mod)
        + 0.209 May(mod)  + 0.317 Jun(mod) + 0.0896 Jul(mod)
        + 0.0724 Aug(mod) - 0.201 Sep(mod) - 0.247 Oct(mod)
        - 0.260 Nov(mod)
```

Predictor	Coef	Stdev	t-ratio	p
Constant	8.28176	0.03433	241.23	0.000
time	0.006848	0.002476	2.77	0.018
Jan(mod)	-0.00325	0.05112	-0.06	0.950
Feb(mod)	0.12644	0.05052	2.50	0.029
Mar(mod)	0.18188	0.05003	3.64	0.004
Apr(mod)	0.12320	0.04966	2.48	0.031
May(mod)	0.20855	0.04941	4.22	0.001
Jun(mod)	0.31685	0.04929	6.43	0.000
Jul(mod)	0.08955	0.04929	1.82	0.097
Aug(mod)	0.07241	0.04941	1.47	0.171
Sep(mod)	-0.20095	0.04966	-4.05	0.002
Oct(mod)	-0.24705	0.05003	-4.94	0.000
Nov(mod)	-0.26025	0.05052	-5.15	0.000

```
s = 0.07278    R-sq = 94.4%    R-sq(adj) = 88.3%
```

Choice of Smoothing Constants

Values for three smoothing constants, constants that control the degree of smoothing in exponential smoothing procedures, need to be selected to carry out Winters' seasonal exponential smoothing procedure. Even with modern computers, calculating the RMSPE for a large number of values of *all three* smoothing constants can be prohibitive. Recall that in nonseasonal situations the RMSPE is usually quite flat over a broad range of values of the smoothing constant. (Review Exhibits 23.8I and 23.8O.) The choice of value of the smoothing constant is not extremely critical to the smoothing procedure. However, since the seasonal effects are smoothed over several years rather than over several months, past information on seasonal effects should not be discounted too quickly—that is, a larger smoothing constant is suggested for seasonal effects than for nonseasonal effects. As a compromise, we recommend simply using $\alpha_1 = \alpha_2 = 0.1$ and $\alpha_3 = 0.4$.

Exhibit 24.7B shows the Log Ridership series smoothed with this choice. The calculations proceed according to Equations (24.9–24.11) with the initial values obtained earlier. From Equation (24.9),

$$\hat{\beta}_{0,1} = 0.1(y_1 - \hat{S}_{-11}) + 0.9(\hat{\beta}_{0,0} + \hat{\beta}_{1,0})$$
$$= 0.1[8.18952 - (-0.003251)] + 0.9(8.28176 + 0.0068476) = 8.27902$$

Similarly, for the slope update,

$$\hat{\beta}_{1,1} = 0.1(\hat{\beta}_{0,1} - \hat{\beta}_{0,0}) + 0.9\hat{\beta}_{1,0}$$
$$= 0.1(8.27902 - 8.28176) + 0.9(0.0068476) = 0.0058888.$$

Finally, the first seasonal update is

$$\hat{S}_1 = 0.4(y_1 - \hat{\beta}_{0,1}) + 0.6\hat{S}_{-11}$$
$$= 0.4(8.18952 - 8.27902) + 0.6(-0.003251) = -0.037751$$

At each time point, the updating is continued until the end of the series is reached.

The *fitted value at time t* is given by the one-step-ahead forecast using data only through time $t - 1$. From Equation (24.12) the fitted value is

$$\hat{y}_t = \hat{\beta}_{0,t-1} + \hat{\beta}_{1,t-1} + \hat{S}_{t-12} \tag{24.14}$$

Once seasonal exponential smoothing is complete, a forecast may be made using Equation (24.12):

$$\hat{y}_{124+1} = \hat{\beta}_{0,124} + 1\hat{\beta}_{1,124} + \hat{S}_{124-11}$$
$$= 8.94102 + 0.0034900 + 0.138557 = 9.083067$$

and

$$\hat{y}_{124+2} = \hat{\beta}_{0,124} + 2\hat{\beta}_{1,124} + \hat{S}_{124-10}$$
$$= 8.94102 + 2(0.0034900) + 0.317979 = 9.265979$$

and so on. Forecasts and actual value for 1982 are listed in Exhibit 24.7C and plotted in Exhibit 24.7D.

EXHIBIT 24.7B
Seasonal Exponential Smoothing with $\alpha_1 = 0.1$, $\alpha_2 = 0.1$, and $\alpha_3 = 0.4$

t	LogRider	Intercept	Slope	Seasonal	Fitted
-11	*	*	*	-0.003251	*
-10	*	*	*	0.126439	*
-9	*	*	*	0.181883	*
-8	*	*	*	0.123204	*
-7	*	*	*	0.208551	*
-6	*	*	*	0.316846	*
-5	*	*	*	0.089554	*
-4	*	*	*	0.072405	*
-3	*	*	*	-0.200952	*
-2	*	*	*	-0.247050	*
-1	*	*	*	-0.260249	*
0	*	8.28176	0.0068476	-0.407378	*
1	8.18952	8.27903	0.0058892	-0.037753	8.28536
2	8.40021	8.28380	0.0057777	0.122426	8.41136
3	8.46253	8.28869	0.0056883	0.178665	8.47146
4	8.37862	8.29048	0.0052988	0.109179	8.41758
5	8.60117	8.30546	0.0062671	0.243413	8.50433
6	8.69182	8.31805	0.0068995	0.339614	8.62857
7	8.48426	8.33193	0.0075971	0.114664	8.41451
8	8.41892	8.34022	0.0076670	0.074921	8.41193
9	8.18841	8.35204	0.0080817	-0.186022	8.14694
10	8.08579	8.35739	0.0078089	-0.256869	8.11307
11	8.08024	8.36273	0.0075617	-0.269146	8.10495
12	7.93380	8.36738	0.0072705	-0.417860	7.96291
13	8.46337	8.38730	0.0085352	0.007778	8.33690
14	8.52576	8.39658	0.0086102	0.125126	8.51826
15	8.58802	8.40561	0.0086518	0.180166	8.58386
16	8.56827	8.41874	0.0091002	0.125317	8.52344
17	8.53011	8.41373	0.0076887	0.192600	8.67126
18	8.66974	8.41229	0.0067758	0.306750	8.76103
19	8.43642	8.40933	0.0058027	0.079632	8.53373
20	8.48115	8.41424	0.0057137	0.071715	8.49006
21	8.17864	8.41443	0.0051606	-0.205929	8.23394
22	8.20276	8.42359	0.0055609	-0.242456	8.16272
23	8.19561	8.43271	0.0059169	-0.256329	8.16001
24	8.06149	8.44270	0.0063240	-0.403201	8.02077
⋮	⋮	⋮	⋮	⋮	⋮
115	8.99430	8.91975	0.0049058	0.126249	9.09004
116	8.96072	8.91868	0.0043082	0.074322	9.02050
117	8.72372	8.92384	0.0043932	-0.204710	8.71522
118	8.60117	8.91974	0.0035443	-0.272733	8.68606
119	8.61141	8.91960	0.0031756	-0.288288	8.64827
120	8.56656	8.92645	0.0035432	-0.379744	8.52980
121	9.00626	8.93119	0.0036625	0.068632	8.99433
122	9.05998	8.93700	0.0038773	0.111383	9.03850
123	9.08614	8.94230	0.0040193	0.136170	9.07193
124	8.96380	8.94102	0.0034900	0.051367	9.01674

EXHIBIT 24.7C
Actual Values and Forecasts from Seasonal Exponential Smoothing

Month	Forecast	1982 Actual Value
Jan	9.08307	9.22808
Feb	9.26598	9.34662
Mar	9.07774	9.17378
Apr	9.02930	9.13162
May	8.75376	8.82820
Jun	8.68923	8.72404
Jul	8.67716	8.72599
Aug	8.58920	8.69316
Sep	9.04106	9.11251
Oct	9.08731	9.16304
Nov	9.11558	9.20914
Dec	9.03427	8.97664

E X H I B I T **24.7D**
Sequence Plot of Actual Values
and Forecasts from Seasonal
Exponential Smoothing

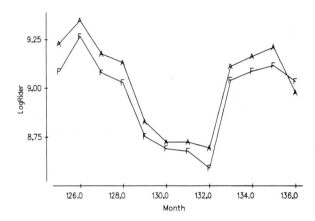

Again, the forecasts nicely follow the seasonal pattern and upward trend in the historic data. The residual standard deviation here is 0.0738, which is marginally smaller than the corresponding quantity for the time trend, seasonal indicators model of Exhibit 24.3I. The residual standard deviation for the seasonal autoregressive model of Exhibit 24.5A was a little larger, at 0.08507. However, the residuals here still contain significant autocorrelation. The sequence plot of the residuals is shown in Exhibit 24.7E. The autocorrelation is 0.42 at lag 1 and 0.33 at lag 2.

E X H I B I T **24.7E**
Sequence Plot of Residuals from
Seasonal Exponential Smoothing

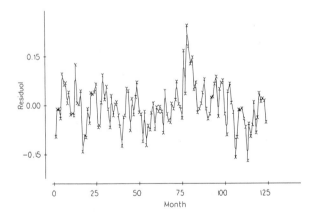

External RMSPE

To compare the forecasting ability of the three models considered for the Log Ridership series, the external RMSPE for each of them must be evaluated. Since data are reasonably plentiful, the 12 months of 1982 have been held out from the model-building process. The true test of a forecasting model is its ability to generate accurate forecasts on new data. The RMSPE applied to new data is called the external RM-SPE. Using December 1981 as the last available observation, each of the 12 months of 1982 is forecast. The prediction errors are the actual values for 1982 minus the values that the model forecasts. RMSPE is then obtained as always for these external prediction errors. Exhibit 24.7F lists the external RMSPE for each method considered in this chapter: regression with seasonal indicator predictor variables, seasonal autoregression, and seasonal exponential smoothing. On the basis of external RMSPE, the seasonal autoregression is slightly better than regression with seasonal indicators, and the seasonal exponential smoothing is better than either of the other methods by a worthwhile margin. Recall, however, that all three of these methods have substantial autocorrelation in their residuals. A model incorporating seasonal differencing that produces acceptable residuals for these data is discussed in Section 24.9.

EXHIBIT 24.7F
External RMSPE for Three
Methods

Method	Mean PE	Standard Deviation PE	RMSPE
Seasonal indicators	0.086193	0.058651	0.104376
Seasonal autoregression	0.076298	0.065186	0.100352
Seasonal exponential smoothing	0.072430	0.049662	0.087820

SECTION

24.8 Exercises

24.8A Consider the milk production series of Exercise 24.2A.

a Using the smoothing constants $\alpha_1 = \alpha_2 = 0.1$ and $\alpha_3 = 0.4$, find the exponentially smoothed series.

b Plot the smoothed series and the original on the same sequence plot. Comment on the appearance.

c Plot the sequence of residuals from the smoothed series. Do they appear random? (Filename: MILKPROD.DAT.)

24.8B Use the series of logarithms of bus ridership values for Portland, Oregon. The data are in Exercise 24.2B.

a Using the smoothing constants $\alpha_1 = \alpha_2 = 0.1$ and $\alpha_3 = 0.4$, find the exponentially smoothed series.

b Plot the smoothed series and the original on the same sequence plot. Comment on the appearance.

c Plot the sequence plot of residuals from the smoothed series. Do they appear random? (Filename: PORTBUS.DAT.)

24.8C The series of monthly U.S. air passenger miles is given in Exercise 24.2C. Use the logarithms of these values.

a Find the exponentially smoothed series using smoothing constants $\alpha_1 = \alpha_2 = 0.1$ and $\alpha_3 = 0.4$.

b Overlay the smoothed series and the original on the same sequence plot. Comment on the appearance.

    c   Display the sequence plot of residuals from the smoothed series. Do they appear random? (Filename: AIRMILES.DAT.)

24.9 Seasonal Differencing

Chapter 23 showed that period-to-period changes in some series are more easily modeled than the original series values. These changes are commonly called *differences*. Series with moderate to strong seasonality, but not as regular as the seasonality shown in the temperature series of Exhibit 24.1B, may frequently be better modeled by considering season-to-season changes called **seasonal differences**. That is, the changes from one January to the next, one February to the next, and so forth are considered. In symbols, the seasonally differenced series is

seasonal differences

$$z_t = y_t - y_{t-12} \tag{24.15}$$

The seasonally differenced series may then be modeled using any of the previous models, such as autoregression on lagged variables or seasonal indicators and trends.

    Usually such series also exhibit some slow drift or nonseasonal trend. In those cases a nonseasonal, month-to-month difference will also be necessary to obtain a series that may be adequately modeled. Calculating a nonseasonal difference of the series z_t, the doubly differenced series w_t is obtained:

$$w_t = z_t - z_{t-1} = (y_t - y_{t-12}) - (y_{t-1} - y_{t-13}) \tag{24.16}$$

A model that works well for a large variety of seasonal series and captures any short-term and seasonal variation remaining after differencing is given by

$$w_t = \beta_0 + \beta_1 w_{t-1} + \beta_{12} w_{t-12} + e_t \tag{24.17}$$

After taking seasonal and nonseasonal differences, the series satisfies a mixed nonseasonal, seasonal AR model as in Equation (24.3).

    Exhibit 24.9A displays the autoregression results when Equation (24.17) is estimated for the Log Ridership series. Both the lag 1 and lag 12 predictors are statistically significant with large t ratios. The residual standard deviation of $s = 0.06641$ is smaller than that obtained for the seasonal autoregressive model ($s = 0.08507$), for the time trend plus seasonal indicators model of Exhibit 24.3I ($s = 0.07707$), or for exponential smoothing ($s = 0.0738$).

    In addition, the residuals are well behaved with regard to autocorrelation. Exhibit 24.9B shows the sequence plot of residuals. No patterns are indicated there. Calculation shows that the autocorrelation in the residuals is only -0.087 at lag 1 and only -0.088 at lag 12. Further investigation, which is left for the exercises, shows that no important autocorrelation exists at any lags and that the assumption of normal errors is quite plausible.

The regression equation is

DDLogRider = - 0.00151 - 0.308 Lag1 - 0.281 Lag12

99 cases used; 25 cases contained missing values

```
Predictor       Coef        Stdev     t-ratio         p
Constant    -0.001513     0.006678      -0.23     0.821
Lag1        -0.30788      0.09116       -3.38     0.001
Lag12       -0.28111      0.08293       -3.39     0.001

s = 0.06641     R-sq = 20.1%     R-sq(adj) = 18.4%
```

Analysis of Variance

```
SOURCE        DF          SS          MS         F        p
Regression     2      0.106281    0.053141     12.05    0.000
Error         96      0.423443    0.004411
Total         98      0.529724
```

Note: DDLogRider is the seasonal and nonseasonal difference of the Log Ridership series.

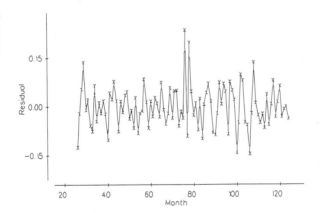

Forecasting using the model in Equation (24.17) proceeds as with earlier autoregressive models. Using Equations (24.16) and (24.17) with t replaced by $t + 1$ yields

$$(y_{t+1} - y_t) - (y_{t-11} - y_{t-12}) = \beta_0 + \beta_1[(y_t - y_{t-1}) - (y_{t-12} - y_{t-13})]$$
$$+ \beta_{12}[(y_{t-11} - y_{t-12}) - (y_{t-23} - y_{t-24})] + e_t$$

$$(24.18)$$

Then rewriting in forecast terms,

$$\hat{y}_{t+1} = \beta_0 + (1 + \beta_1)y_t - \beta_1 y_{t-1} + (1 + \beta_{12})y_{t-11} - (1 + \beta_1 + \beta_{12})y_{t-12}$$
$$+ \beta_1 y_{t-13} - \beta_{12} y_{t-23} + \beta_{12} y_{t-24}$$

$$(24.19)$$

This expression is long but easily implemented for forecasting purposes. Once $\hat{y}_{t+1}$ is available, forecasting two steps ahead uses a new version of Equation (24.19) with $t + 1$ replacing t throughout.

Exhibit 24.9C shows the forecasts and actual values for the 12 months of 1982 for the Log Ridership series. This should be compared to Exhibits 24.3K, 24.5C, and 24.7D for the earlier models. The mean prediction error for these 12 predictions is 0.12067, while the standard deviation of the prediction errors is 0.05006, leading to an RMSPE of 0.1306, somewhat larger than the values given in Exhibit 24.7F for the earlier models.

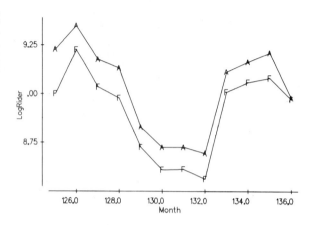

SECTION
24.10 Exercises

24.10A Consider the seasonal differences model for the Log Ridership series of Exhibit 24.3E.

 a Carry out the regression calculations shown in Exhibit 24.9A. Check the autocorrelations in the residuals at lags 2, 3, 24, and 36.

 b Evaluate the normality of the error terms by looking at the residuals. In particular, display a histogram of the standardized residuals and a normal scores plot of the residuals. Comment on the plots.

 c Display the scatterplot of residuals versus fitted values and comment. (Filename: ICBUS.DAT.)

24.10B Use the logarithms of Portland, Oregon, bus ridership given in Exercise 24.2B.

 a Fit a seasonal differences model as in Equation (24.17).

 b Evaluate the autocorrelations in the residuals at lags 1, 2, 12, and 24. Comment.

 c Evaluate the normality of the error terms by looking at the residuals. In particular, display a histogram of the standardized residuals and a normal scores plot of the residuals. Comment on the plots.

 d Display the scatterplot of residuals versus fitted values and comment. (Filename: PORTBUS.DAT.)

24.10C Use the milk production series given in Exercise 24.2A.

 a Fit a seasonal differences model as in Equation (24.17).

 b Evaluate the autocorrelations in the residuals at lags 1, 2, 12, and 24. Comment.

c Evaluate the normality of the error terms by looking at the residuals. In particular, display a histogram of the standardized residuals and a normal scores plot of the residuals. Comment on the plots.

d Display the scatterplot of residuals versus fitted values and comment. (Filename: MILKPROD.DAT.)

24.10D Use the logarithms of the U.S. air passenger miles series as given in Exercise 24.2C.

a Fit a seasonal differences model as in Equation (24.17).

b Evaluate the autocorrelations in the residuals at lags 1, 2, 12, and 24. Comment.

c Evaluate the normality of the error terms by looking at the residuals. In particular, display a histogram of the standardized residuals and a normal scores plot of the residuals. Comment on the plots.

d Display the scatterplot of residuals versus fitted values and comment. (Filename: AIRMILES.DAT.)

SECTION

24.11 Seasonal Adjustment

In April 1982, then–President Ronald Reagan announced that unemployment had just fallen by 88,000 workers in the preceding month. However, the Bureau of Labor Statistics (BLS) had reported an increase of 98,000 in the unemployment ranks. The president had reported actual numbers while the BLS was using so-called seasonally adjusted figures in an attempt to take into account the fact that unemployment typically decreases from February to March. Seasonal adjustment is a somewhat controversial procedure.

seasonal adjustment

A rise in weekly hours worked in December does not necessarily indicate an upturn in the economy, since increased hours are almost always worked in December. To avoid this misinterpretation, the BLS reports **seasonally adjusted** values, which attempt to compensate for this known seasonal variation. Exhibit 2.12B gave the sequence plot of *unadjusted* monthly hours worked per week in the manufacturing sector from 1982 to 1987. Exhibit 24.11A lists the corresponding seasonally adjusted values and Exhibit 24.11B displays the series values after seasonal adjustment. The 1982 recession is still apparent, but notice how the December values have been brought more into line with other monthly values.

The actual adjustment procedures used by the BLS are complicated and a considerable current research effort is devoted to discovering better adjustment procedures. An idea of the size and direction of the adjustment may be seen by computing the ratios of unadjusted to adjusted values. Exhibit 24.11C gives the sequence plot of these

EXHIBIT **24.11A**
Seasonally Adjusted Average Hours Worked per Week in Manufacturing

```
filename: MANHRSSA.DAT
Seasonally adjusted average hours worked per week (X10)
Manufacturing, July 1982 through June 1987
(Source: Survey of Current Business, September issues, 1982-1987.)
Jul Aug Sep Oct Nov Dec Jan Feb Mar Apr May Jun
391 390 388 389 390 390 397 392 395 401 400 401
402 403 407 406 406 406 409 409 407 411 406 406
405 405 406 405 405 406 406 401 404 402 404 404
404 406 407 407 407 409 408 407 407 407 407 406
406 408 408 407 408 408 409 411 409 406 410 410
```

E X H I B I T **24.11B**

Seasonally Adjusted Average
Hours Worked per Week in
Manufacturing, July 1982–
June 1987

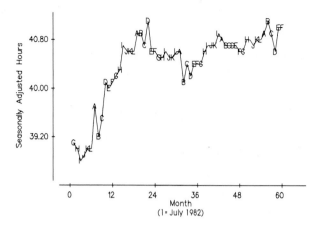

E X H I B I T **24.11C**

Seasonal Adjustment Factors,
Weekly Hours Worked:
January–December Indicated by
A–L, Respectively

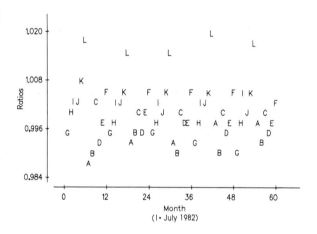

ratios for the weekly hours data. December figures, which are typically higher than values for other months, are adjusted downward by 1.5% to 2%, whereas January, February, and July figures, typically low, are adjusted upward by up to 1%. August, September, and October values are changed very little since their adjustment factors are about 1.

Chapter Summary

Since seasonal patterns are frequently predictable, models that reflect seasonality help forecast the behavior of seasonal processes. In this chapter, we have presented four techniques for modeling seasonal time series: seasonal indicators, seasonal autoregression, seasonal differencing, and seasonal exponential smoothing.

Seasonal indicators are binary predictors that model an extremely regular and unchanging seasonal pattern. Seasonal autoregressions model less regular seasonal patterns by including predictors that are lagged by the seasonal period. Seasonal differencing is sometimes needed to stabilize a series before an autoregression is fitted to it. Seasonal exponential smoothing extends the ideas in Chapter 23 to the seasonal case.

All the techniques are complicated and require statistical software for their implementation.

Supplementary Exercises for Chapter 24

24A   Use the monthly total U.S. retail sales (in billions of dollars) for 1983 through 1987 first considered in Exercise 2C.

a   Fit a model to these data using 12 seasonal indicators plus a linear time trend and save the residuals from the model for further analysis.

b   Consider the autocorrelation in the residuals at lags 1, 2, and 12 and comment on their magnitude.

c   Construct a sequence plot of the residuals and comment on its appearance.

d   Does a normal scores plot of the residuals suggest a normal distribution for the errors in the model? (Filename: RETAIL.DAT.)

24B   Consider the monthly retail sales data in Exercise 2C and Exercise 24A.

a   Fit a seasonal autoregressive model of the form $y_t = \beta_0 + \beta_1 y_{t-1} + \beta_{12} y_{t-12} + e_t$ to these data. Save the residuals from the model for further analysis.

b   Consider the autocorrelation in the residuals at lags, 1, 2, and 12 and comment on their magnitude.

c   Construct a sequence plot of the residuals and comment on its appearance.

d   Does a normal scores plot of the residuals support the assumption of a normal distribution for the errors in the model?

e   Compare this model to the one discussed in Exercise 24A. (Filename: RETAIL.DAT.)

24C   In Exercise 23B seasonality in the monthly unit sales of Winnebago motor homes was discovered. Consider a model based on ordinary and seasonal differences of the log(sales) data as in Equations (24.16) and (24.17).

a   Use regression to fit such a model to the sales data.

b   Assess the significance of both of the predictor variables.

c   On the basis of your results in part (b), drop one of the predictors and reestimate the simpler model, saving the residuals for further analysis.

d   Assess the adequacy of this model by looking at the scatterplot of residuals versus fitted values, checking the normality assumption, and calculating the autocorrelations of the residuals at lags 1 and 12. (Filename: WINNEBAG.DAT.)

24D   The data file below gives monthly electric power usage in the United States over the period January 1983 through July 1989.

a   Compare the sequence plots of power usage and logarithms of power usage. Which should be used for further modeling?

b   Fit a model that predicts log(power) with lag 12 log(power). Interpret the output.

c   Check the residuals by plotting them against fitted values and by looking at their normality.

```
filename: POWER.DAT
Monthly electric power usage in the U.S.
billions of kilowatt-hours, January 1983 to July 1989
(Source: Survey of Current Business, various issues)
(Read across, row by row)
 Jan   Feb   Mar   Apr   May   Jun   Jul   Aug   Sep   Oct   Nov   Dec
166.3 144.5 152.2 140.4 143.2 160.4 192.0 203.6 173.7 161.4 158.2 180.5
186.9 161.7 169.7 151.1 160.4 180.9 193.8 204.2 174.3 170.1 168.1 174.2
200.2 172.3 170.3 160.5 170.4 181.5 205.4 206.1 183.7 174.7 169.5 193.9
195.9 169.1 168.4 159.6 171.1 188.8 218.6 204.0 185.5 176.3 173.3 213.6
222.7 194.0 201.8 189.5 206.1 225.6 247.9 247.6 213.0 203.0 200.3 220.5
237.6 216.8 213.8 195.8 208.2 232.5 257.2 267.4 220.0 210.4 209.4 232.6
231.3 219.1 226.4 207.7 219.8 235.4 256.7
```

Glossary for Chapter 24

seasonal adjustment A procedure applied to a time series in an attempt to account for known seasonality.

seasonal autoregression An autoregressive model with the predictor variable lagged at multiples of the seasonal period.

seasonal differences The series of season-to-season changes.

seasonal exponential smoothing Exponential smoothing that accounts for seasonality.

seasonal indicator model A time series model with a parameter for each month of the year.

seasonal indicators Binary variables indicating the various seasons.

Winters' additive model A model that leads to seasonal exponential smoothing.

5

Statistics in Organizations

A Perspective on Statistics in Organizations

Chapter Objectives

After mastering this chapter, you will be able to:

- Explain Deming's process diagram for a firm

- Define and show how to use basic statistical tools for problem formulation

- Explain why scientific language and statistical tools are important for making operations in a firm efficient

SECTION

25.1 Introduction

People form organizations to achieve objectives. As time passes an organization's objectives are likely to increase in number and complexity.

EXAMPLE 25.1A

A local chess club may start as a group of chess enthusiasts who meet once a week in someone's living room. As the group grows, it seeks a larger meeting place. In time it may decide to join a national association, promote chess education in schools, sponsor tournaments, and invite chess masters to give lectures and exhibitions. Achieving these objectives requires increasing levels of organizational, fund-raising, and promotional activity. ■

Businesses also grow in this fashion. Examples are computer hardware and software companies that started with inventions created in someone's basement. The discussion in this chapter is in terms of business firms. And it is a working assumption that employees want to help the firm achieve its objectives, at least because the employee may lose his or her job should the firm falter.

Effective management encourages never-ending improvement in the organization by helping employees find pride in their work and by valuing their participation in improvement efforts. From this point of view there is mutual reinforcement in the objectives of the firm and the objectives of its members.

SECTION

25.2 Organizational Structure

Even though business firms vary widely in size, complexity, and organizational details, a few general terms apply to most firms. For example, a firm often has four levels of employees: top management, middle management, supervisors, and hourly workers. Not all firms have employees in these four categories, and some firms may find it necessary to define other levels. Such details are not pertinent here. Abstract theories invariably require modification when they are applied to specific cases. The concern here is to develop connections between management and science that will serve as useful guides to action.

top management

Top management primarily seeks to find ways and means of ensuring the long-term survival and growth of the firm. This means finding new markets for existing products and services and finding new products and services that the firm can successfully offer for sale. It also means supporting the never-ending improvement of quality of all aspects of the firm's business. Top management creates, communicates, and supports the implementation of policy. Ideally, this means being in constant dialogue with all levels of the organization concerning the improvement of performance.

middle management

Middle management oversees the implementation of policy, including its communication throughout the firm. Middle managers make short-term decisions in the light of the long-term objectives set forth by top management. Middle management also plays a critical role in fostering communication throughout the organization. This includes identifying needs for training and authorizing the training that enables members of the firm to perform effectively and efficiently.

supervisors

Supervisors oversee the daily activities of hourly workers. They help workers adhere to established procedures, at the same time encouraging workers to make suggestions for improvement. They also see that workers have proper training and materials to do their jobs. This includes clear instruction on what people's jobs are and what is considered acceptable performance in the job. In many cases, they are given responsibility for implementing policy as communicated by middle management.

hourly workers

Hourly workers primarily follow established work procedures. If given the opportunity, they may form groups to identify and work on solutions to problems (quality-control circles, for example). They may also be encouraged to make individual suggestions for improvement.

Large firms are divided into departments. For example, a manufacturer has, in addition to a production department, departments of design, marketing, accounting, finance, service, personnel, purchasing, and so on. Each department consists of specialists and a variety of supporting staff. A large department can take on a life of its own, that is, it can operate as an autonomous organization with it own set of specialized objectives. It may even look upon the parent firm as a "client," whose existence may be threatened if the department's expert advice is not followed. This sort of situation is difficult to avoid in large firms, but the energies of the departments can be channeled constructively through forceful policy deployment by top management.

It is important to identify the productive activities of a firm and to see how the firm's departments contribute to the efficient conduct of these activities. The concept of a process helps do this. Exhibit 25.2A is a process diagram introduced by W. Edwards Deming in his teaching in Japan in the 1950s. It helps us visualize the productive activity of a manufacturing firm. Notice that the components of the diagram are not confined to agents within the firm. Suppliers of raw materials and tools, as well as paying customers (purchasers of final product) are part of the process. Deming asserts that paying customers are the most important part of the process, because the firm's success depends on not only supplying a product customers will buy today but also persuading the customer to buy the product again and discovering new products that customers will buy in the future.

EXHIBIT 25.2A

Deming's Process Diagram

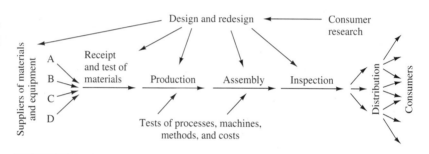

Source: W. Edwards Deming, *Out of the Crisis* (Cambridge, Mass.: MIT Center for Advanced Engineering Study, 1986), p. 4. Used with permission.

Deming's diagram suggests many crucial interactions among the firm's departments and between the firm and agents outside the firm. For example, people involved in sales, distribution, and service often learn from personal contact with customers what they like or do not like about their dealings with the firm. This knowledge is valuable if it is brought back to the firm and treated as data that can be used for improvement. Yet many firms do not encourage people to share such information, or, if it is shared, it is treated as evidence that the customer is too demanding.

Another critical interaction is that between the design and engineering departments and the production department. It is easy to fall into the situation in which a design presented to the production department is either difficult or impossible to make. It is much more time- and cost-effective to require cooperation between the departments from the beginning.

Finally, the firm and its suppliers interact. A firm can substantially reduce its costs by insisting on the practice of good quality control by its suppliers. This may even require setting up training courses for the suppliers and giving "report cards" to the suppliers, informing them on how the quality, cost, and scheduling of their products meet the expectations of the firm. Such practices have become common in the automobile industry.

Deming's diagram is emphasized to show the importance of identifying processes that matter. This almost invariably cuts across departmental lines and demonstrates the importance of communication between components in a process and among processes in systems.

The need for communication implies the need for a common language. This language must be precise and suitable for the discussion of problems that arise in making business processes work. Experience suggests that statistics is an indispensable part of such a language.

SECTION

25.3   Science in Organizations

Ideally, the primary objective of a business firm is to provide goods and services of such quality, affordability, and timeliness as to exceed the expectations of paying customers. A business is a network of processes, where a process is viewed as a sequence of steps taken to achieve a goal. To pursue its primary objective, a business firm engages in a never-ending effort to improve its processes, because no process works perfectly. Because science helps us think formally about processes, it is a natural tool to use to attack business problems.

Scientific methods taken together constitute a systematic approach to learning, using theory and observation. In business and industry, the motivation for learning is the solution of problems that arise from a firm's attempts to offer desirable products and services as economically as possible.

In Chapter 1, Deming's wheel—planning (P), doing (D), checking (C), and acting (A)—was suggested as a model for "practical science," that is, science with decision making and action as the goal. This chapter discusses questions of implementation and organization to put that model into effect. In the complex organizations of our "information society," implementation is a constant struggle against barriers to achievement and communication.

Mistakes are inevitable, and the good decision of today may appear as the short-sighted blunder of tomorrow. Every mistake, and every problem, represents an opportunity to seek improvements in the processes that produced the mistake or problem. Yet no organization has the resources to launch major improvement projects for every process. The key to successful management is seeking the *fundamental* processes, whose improvement has a sizable impact on the goals of the organization, and making their control the priority of the organization. In this sense, the goals of effective management and science are the same, because science also searches for fundamental, unifying processes.

A number of authors recommend that quality improvement be the guide in seeking the fundamental processes of an organization. This attitude is accessibly presented by Imai.[†] He asserts that the secret to world-class performance is unflagging commitment to quality improvement (Q), cost control (C), and timely scheduling (S). Actions taken to enhance QCS add value to the organization; other actions constitute waste. If cost

---

[†]Masaaki Imai, *Kaizen: The Key to Japan's Competitive Success* (New York: Random House, 1986).

control and timely scheduling are considered part of the quality of the organization's performance, then quality improvement can be seen as the driving principle behind world-class performance.

Another part of success is producing goods and services that can be sold! Holding the patent on a high-quality product with no perceived value is not an attractive prospect. Thus, achieving a profitable share of the market must be at the heart of an organization's activities.

These two principles, quality improvement and market share, are affirmed by a report from PIMS (Profit Impact of Market Strategy).[†] The report is the result of a worldwide study of factors that make business firms competitive. Here are two of its most significant conclusions:

> In the long run, the most important single factor affecting a Business Unit's performance is the Quality of its products and services relative to those of competitors.

and

> [M]arket share is key to a company's growth and profitability. . . one factor above all others, quality, drives market share. And when superior quality and large market share are both present, profitability is virtually guaranteed.

The PIMS report suggests that quality is the key to market share and profitability as well. From this and other writing it is obvious that a rigorous focus on quality improvement promises tangible rewards.

S E C T I O N

25.4 Statistical Tools in Problem Formulation

Complex organizations, faced with complex problems, inevitably form task forces, committees, or teams to attack the problems. Because teamwork is so valuable, this discussion assumes that a team has been formed to find ways to improve some step in a process.[‡] How might the team proceed? An approach that has proven successful in practice is presented here. In the course of the presentation some useful tools are introduced and some tools that were discussed earlier come into play. Do not think of this presentation as a recipe that must be followed in every problem. The approach can, and indeed should, be modified as circumstances warrant.

The approach recommended is based on the experience of companies that are recognized as leaders in quality improvement. An interesting piece of documentation is the record of quality-improvement tools used by Yokogawa Hewlett-Packard (HP)

[†]PIMS is a system of study housed in the Strategic Planning Institute, a nonprofit corporation governed by its member companies. It originated in the planning department of General Electric in the 1960s and was developed in the 1970s by the Marketing Science Institute. The report quoted from is Robert D. Buzzell and Bradley T. Gale, *The PIMS Principles* (New York: Free Press, 1987).

[‡]For a modern treatment of teamwork in organizations, see Peter Scholtes, *The Team Handbook*, 1988, Joiner Associates, Inc., P.O. Box 5445, Madison, WI 53705-0445.

in its drive to win the Deming Prize in Japan.[†] Yokogawa HP was the first subsidiary of a U.S. firm to win the Deming Prize. Exhibit 25.4A shows a list of statistical quality-improvement tools and the number of users of these tools in Yokogawa HP.

A number of statistical tools are listed in Exhibit 25.4A. The late Kaoru Ishikawa, one of the early leaders of the quality-improvement thrust in Japan, has stated that in more than 90% of the problems attacked with statistical tools only the following seven tools need be used: cause-and-effect diagrams, Pareto diagrams, graphs, checksheets, histograms, scatter diagrams (scatterplots), and stratification.[‡] Some of these tools have been presented elsewhere in the text. The presentation here covers the rest plus some others that are especially useful.

EXHIBIT **25.4A**
Numbers of Users of Selected Statistical Tools at Yokogawa Hewlett-Packard

Statistical Tool	Number of Users
Cause-and-effect diagram	996
Pareto diagram	885
Brainstorming	807
Graph	672
Checksheet	628
Flow diagram	586
Histogram	424
Affinity diagram	326
Control chart	216
Scatter diagram	117
Analysis of variance	75
Binomial probability analysis	42
Weibull analysis	37
Industrial engineering	32
Other	250

Step 1: Flow Diagrams

flow diagram

Flow diagrams rank sixth in Exhibit 25.4A. A **flow diagram** is simply a series of boxes connected by arrows that show the flow of work in the step. If several activities take place in a step, a flow diagram for each activity may be constructed and then the way in which the activities relate to each other can be shown. Exhibit 25.4B shows a flow diagram for the construction of a density histogram. Exhibit 25.4C shows

---

[†]The Deming Prize, developed in Japan, is given to companies in recognition of high achievement in quality improvement. The competition for the prize is stiff. In 1989, Florida Power and Light became the first company on U.S. soil to win this coveted prize.

[‡]Kaoru Ishikawa, ed., "Special Issue: Seven Management Tools for QC," *Statistical Application Research, Union of Japanese Scientists and Engineers,* 33(2)(June 1986). See K. Ishikawa, *Guide to Quality Control* (Ann Arbor, Mich.: UNIPUB, 1986) for an elementary presentation of the seven tools in a manufacturing setting.

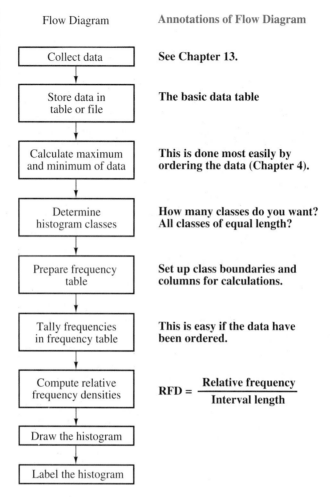

EXHIBIT **25.4B**
Flow Diagram of the
Construction of a Density
Histogram (see Section 3.6 for
an explanation of the process)

Flow Diagram

Annotations of Flow Diagram

| Collect data |

See Chapter 13.

| Store data in table or file |

The basic data table

| Calculate maximum and minimum of data |

This is done most easily by ordering the data (Chapter 4).

| Determine histogram classes |

How many classes do you want? All classes of equal length?

| Prepare frequency table |

Set up class boundaries and columns for calculations.

| Tally frequencies in frequency table |

This is easy if the data have been ordered.

| Compute relative frequency densities |

$$\mathbf{RFD} = \frac{\textbf{Relative frequency}}{\textbf{Interval length}}$$

| Draw the histogram |

| Label the histogram |

a flow diagram for a student moving through a registration station in a university department.

Exhibit 25.4B illustrates the technique of annotating a flow diagram. The annotation space can also be used to make note of problems that arise in implementing the process. Suppose a flow diagram that shows how the process should work ideally is drawn. In practice, the flow diagram of the actual process may contain many more steps than shown in the ideal diagram. Are the extra steps necessary? If so, they must be shown in the "ideal" flow diagram. If not, then eliminating them eliminates waste and results in increased quality. In this application, the ideal diagram is a theory that is tested against the data coming from the actual process. By expanding the ideal diagram where necessary and eliminating unnecessary steps in the actual process, theory and practice are brought together and tighter control is exerted over the process.

Exhibit 25.4C illustrates the technique of using different shaped boxes to display types of steps. The diamond-shaped boxes indicate decision steps, or branches,

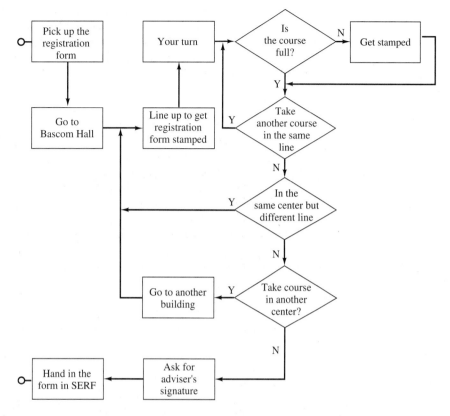

in which the direction taken depends on the answer to a yes-or-no question. The rectangles indicate steps that must be taken to get through the process.

Construction of the flow diagram yields valuable insights. Steps that are taken almost unconsciously in practice are documented and exposed to scrutiny. It is not unusual to discover unnecessary steps in the process that can be eliminated, resulting in immediate gains in quality. Discussion of the flow diagram in a team meeting often yields consensus on which step in the flow diagram should be improved first.

Step 2: Operational Definitions

For each activity in the flow diagram, what takes place must be defined operationally. A detailed discussion of operational definitions appears in Chapter 9 of Deming's *Out of the Crisis.*[†] Deming notes that creating operational definitions improves the efficiency of operations because workers who understand their jobs work confidently toward common goals and tend to exhibit less variation in their work. What constitutes satisfactory work? Exactly how is the work done? What constitutes unsatisfactory

---

[†]W. Edwards Deming, *Out of the Crisis* (Cambridge, Mass.: MIT Center for Advanced Engineering Study, 1986).

operational definition

work? Who is the customer for the work? Are the customers's needs clear? Are there deadlines or quotas to meet? Are they essential? How does the work add value to the final product or service? The **operational definition** answers who, what, when, where, why, and how. If any of these questions cannot be answered, an activity is not well defined and is therefore not in control.

EXAMPLE   25.4A

Suppose the job is to count the number of words on this page. How do you operationally define "word"? Is a numeral a word? The page number? What about hyphenated words? What about abbreviations?

Select an operational definition of "word." Give the definition to three people and ask them to perform the job, that is, to count the words on this page. Usually, when this is done, the people get different numbers of words because the job is complex and requires a great deal of concentration. Given that different people get different answers, how do you come to a conclusion about the number of words on this page? Can you suggest a counting process that would tend to eliminate the differences?   ■

This example illustrates variation in a process. Even a job that has a theoretically correct outcome, such as the number of words on this page, will exhibit variation in practice.

EXAMPLE   25.4B

What does it mean for a commercial airline flight to be "on time"? Does it mean that the plane always arrives at the gate on or before the stated time of arrival? Does it mean that over a series of, say, 30 arrivals its average time of arrival is equal to the stated time of arrival?   ■

EXAMPLE   25.4C

What does it mean for a commercial airline to be "safe"?   ■

Concepts such as safety, timeliness, color, roundness, and so on, are difficult to define operationally. Doing so requires statistical analysis, because of variation.

Step 3: Conformance Analysis

conformance analysis

Operational definitions are a basis for deciding whether output conforms to standards. Sometimes lack of conformance is obvious to casual observation. In most cases, it is necessary to collect data over a period of time to determine lack of conformance. In the latter case, statistical methods come into play. **Conformance analysis** is the collection of data to determine whether standards for a process are met. For example, a commercial airline flight may be considered *on time* if its average arrival time in 30 flights is within five minutes of its stated arrival time. To operationalize this definition, *arrival* must be specifically defined. Does it mean touchdown time on the runway, time of parking at the gate, or time when the first passenger deplanes? The proposed definition of *on time* leaves plenty of room for *variation* in the arrival times because only the mean is required to conform. A definition that also involves limits on the amount of deviation from stated arrival time on each flight is more stringent.

If several activities show lack of conformance, the team must decide which activity or activities to improve first—activities with implications for worker saftey receive top priority. Activities with important economic implications also receive high priority. The priorities are set with reference to policies deployed by top management.

Step 4: Cause-and-Effect Analysis

Suppose one activity has been chosen for study and a measure of performance, such as being on time, has been chosen. To improve performance, the factors that influence (or cause) performance must be understood. To do this involves intense study of the activity. One stage of cause-and-effect analysis is a brainstorming session in which team members' ideas about causes are recorded. Brainstorming sessions can be free-wheeling or structured. The nominal group technique is a structured format designed to give all members of the team equal opportunity to share ideas.[†] Brainstorming is tool number 3 in Exhibit 25.4A.

Another stage of cause-and-effect analysis is intensive observation of workers performing the activity, with an eye to spotting unsuspected causes of variation in the performance measure. The measurement process itself can be a source of variation. For example, if inspectors examine parts for defects, different inspectors might use different criteria unless the question of standardization is carefully addressed.

A useful guideline in cause-and-effect analysis is to keep asking "Why?" or as is sometimes said, "Ask why five times," because fundamental causes are not obvious. A tool that can help in this effort is the **cause-and-effect diagram**, or **(CE diagram)**, an example of which appears in Exhibit 25.4D. The diagram is also known as an Ishikawa diagram, after its inventor Kaoru Ishikawa, and as a fishbone chart, because the diagram reminds some observers of the skeleton of a fish. It is tool number 1 in Exhibit 25.4A.

cause-and-effect diagram (CE diagram)

The CE diagram in Exhibit 25.4D was constructed in a brainstorming session with some students who were asked, "What factors contribute to variation in your final grade in a course?" The characteristic of interest, in this case "final grade," is placed in a box at the right-hand side of the chart, and a horizontal line, emanating from the center of the box, is drawn across the chart. The major direct factors are displayed in boxes around the border of the diagram: Exams, Other Students' Performance, Lecture Attendance, Professor's Attitude, and Homework or Projects.

For each major direct factor, the question "Why does this factor cause variation?" was asked. In response to this question about exams, the most important factors were Exam questions, State of student, Preparation, Location, Time, and Exam center environment. These are shown as branches (or fish bones!) coming off of the line connecting the Exams box with the central line. For each of these factors, the question "Why does this factor contribute to variation in the exam score?" is asked. The

[†]This is especially important if the team has introverted and extroverted members. See Andre L. Delbecq, Andrew H. Van de Ven, and David H. Gustafson, *Group Techniques for Program Planning: A Guide to Nominal Group and Delphi Processes* (Glenview, Ill: Scott Foresman, 1975).

E X H I B I T **25.4D**
Cause-and-Effect Diagram

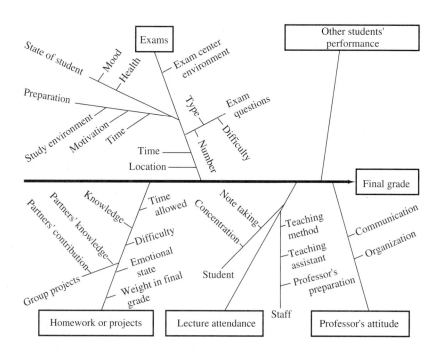

answers to this question for Exam questions yielded: Difficulty, Type, and Number of questions. This questioning process is continued until all the causes of variation the group can think of are displayed on the chart.

Because cause-and-effect diagrams are used in brainstorming sessions, they are typically written on flip charts, blackboards, or overhead projector transparencies. They are typically modified at successive meetings or by people who are assigned the job of "cleaning them up." The presentation of a diagram in printed form, as in Exhibit 25.4D, does not convey the dynamic way the diagram is used in practice. The best way to appreciate the value of cause-and-effect diagrams is to create them in real problem-solving environments.[†]

Step 5: Pareto Analysis

Pareto principle

The cause-and-effect analysis typically produces a large list of causes, some of which have an important bearing on performance, many of which do not. The **Pareto principle** states that only a few causes are responsible for most of the variation.

The next step is therefore to select the important causes and to set aside the less important ones, possibly for future study. The important causes are not always obvious. Sometimes they can be selected through further brainstorming or by collecting

---

[†]For a more detailed presentation of cause-and-effect diagrams, see K. Ishikawa, *Guide to Quality Control,* chapter 3 and sec. 13.3.

votes from team members. At other times, it is necessary to collect data on the **causes** and the performance measure to discover which causes are really important.

E X A M P L E **25.4D**

Exhibit 25.4E shows part of a checksheet that might be used to collect data on a commercial airline flight.[†] The performance measures are time of touchdown in destination airport and time of arrival at gate in destination airport. Among the causes, not all of which are listed in the exhibit, are time of departure from gate at originating airport, time of takeoff at originating airport, pilot, copilot, aircraft, windspeed, and condition of sky. An important step in analyzing these data is the construction of scatterplots with a performance measure on the vertical axis and a cause on the horizontal axis.[‡]

Causes showing the greatest degree of correlation with the performance measure are of special interest. If these causes can be brought under control, that is, made predictable, and if the amount of variation in them can be reduced, then the variation in the performance measure will also be made predictable and reduced.

Here is an actual case. It was discovered that the time between departure from gate and takeoff at the originating airport was quite variable, so this time became the focus of a cause-and-effect study. Why was the time so variable? What steps might be taken to reduce the variation? A study of traffic patterns at the originating airport turned up a lull in departures near the established departure time of the flight under study. A slight schedule change resulted in a substantial reduction in variation. This translated into a decrease in the variation of arrival times, making life easier for employees and making customers happier. A survey of customers showed the number of repeat trips up, and customers said they were recommending the flight to friends. ■

E X H I B I T **25.4E**
Excerpt from a Checksheet Used to Monitor Airline Flight Arrivals

Flight Number	Date	Recorder	Aircraft	Gate Departure Time	Takeoff
4407	3/18	JBR	47083219	8:00 A.M.	8:30 A.M.
4321	3/18	JBR	47083219	12:20 P.M.	1:00 P.M.

[†]Checksheets are tool number 5 in Exhibit 25.4A

[‡]Scatter diagrams (or scatterplots) are tool number 10 in Exhibit 25.4A

This case shows how the study of one process leads naturally to the study of another process. Study of arrival at one airport led to the study of takeoff at another airport. Looking from one step in a process to an earlier step for sources of improvement is called *moving upstream*. Solving problems *upstream* means that those problems will not be transmitted *downstream*, which means that they will not reach any of the customers in the process, including the all-important paying customer.

The point of Pareto analysis is that the most important problems should be tackled first because solving them will yield the largest return. A typical step in Pareto analysis is the construction of a Pareto diagram.[†] A **Pareto diagram** displays the important causes of variation, as reflected in data collected on the causes. Diagrams constructed before and after process improvement efforts take place document the effects of improvements and suggest causes of variation that need attention next. This application fits into step 4 of the Shewhart cycle introduced in Chapter 1, namely, deciding what to do next.

Pareto diagram

EXAMPLE   25.4E

Fuller describes a study of a marketing department that was filling telephone orders.[‡] A study of their activities revealed that they were spending a great deal of time on nonproductive work. The data were collected by having employees record their activities at randomly chosen times during the workday. Exhibit 25.4F displays a table and a Pareto diagram showing the number of times an employee engaged in one of four nonproductive activities during a three-day study period.[§] These activities were processing returns (PR), converting backlog (CB), expediting shipments (ES), and checking order status (COS). All these activities were undertaken because of orders not filled correctly or not shipped on time.

Constructing a Pareto diagram is quite simple. The first step is to prepare a table that shows the activities recorded, the numbers of times the activities were observed, and the percentage of the total number of times represented by each count. In Exhibit 25.4F, the total number of times is 41, and the number of times processing returns were observed is 20. Thus $100(20/41) = 49\%$. Similar calculations complete the table.

The Pareto diagram has two vertical axes, the left one corresponding to the Number column in the table, the right one corresponding to the Percent column in the table. On the horizontal axis, the activities are listed, creating bases of equal length for the rectangles shown in the diagram. The activities are listed in decreasing order of occurrence. Doing this means that the most frequently observed activity lies on the left extreme of the diagram, and the least frequently observed activity lies on the right extreme. The heights of

---

[†] Pareto diagrams are tool number 2 in Exhibit 25.4A.

[‡] The data for this example are from F. Timothy Fuller, "Eliminating Complexity from Work: Improving Productivity by Enhancing Quality," *National Productivity Review* (Autumn 1985), 327–344.

[§] Employees were reassured that they were not at fault for engaging in unproductive activities; they were part of the process. The purpose of the study was to find and eliminate unproductive work so that the employees could contribute more effectively to the marketing effort.

EXHIBIT 25.4F
Pareto Analysis of Fuller's
Marketing Group Data
(three-day study period)

Activity	Number	Percent
PR	20	49
CB	8	19
ES	7	17
COS	6	15
	41	100

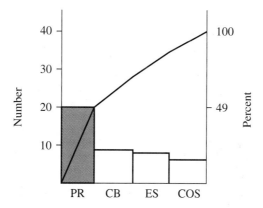

the rectangles are drawn to show the frequencies of the activities, and then the sides of the rectangles are drawn.

The next step is to locate the *cumulative percents* of the activities using the right-hand axis. The cumulative percent for the first rectangle is, of course, 49; for the second it is $49 + 20 = 69$. The 69 is plotted over the right-hand side of the rectangle labelled CB. The next cumulative percent is $49 + 20 + 16 = 69 + 16 = 85$, which is plotted over the right-hand side of the rectangle labelled ES. The last cumulative percent is, of course, 100, and it is plotted over the right-hand side of the last rectangle. Now draw straight lines between the plotted cumulative percents as shown in the exhibit. The last step is to label the axes and add a title to the diagram. In Exhibit 25.4F the tallest rectangle is lightly shaded to highlight the most frequent activity, suggesting the one that may deserve first priority in problem solving.

As a hypothetical continuation of Fuller's study, suppose that efforts to reduce unnecessary activities are made. During a later three-day period, Fuller's study is repeated with the results shown in Exhibit 25.4G. The new Pareto diagram is also displayed next to the old one in Exhibit 25.4G. Comparison of the "arms" showing the cumulative percentages of unnecessary work clearly shows the beneficial results of the improvement efforts. Comparison of the activities ranked on the horizontal axis shows that old sources of unnecessary work have been brought under better control (PR and CB), and a new one (ES) now deserves priority. ▪

EXHIBIT **25.4G**
Pareto Analysis of Hypothetical
Before and After Analysis Based
on Fuller's Marketing Group
Data (three-day study period)

	Before		After	
Activity	Number	Percent	Number	Percent
PR	20	49	7	24
CB	8	19	5	17
ES	7	17	10	35
COS	6	15	7	24
	41	100	29	100

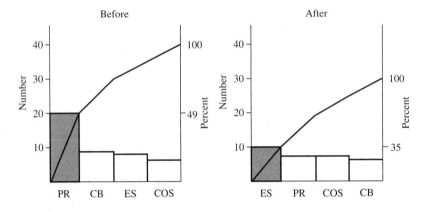

The example from Fuller's article reinforces the idea behind Pareto analysis: the majority of problems are due to a small number of identifiable causes. The Pareto diagram in Exhibit 25.4F shows the four major sources of unproductive activity found in Fuller's study and also shows that the single source "processing returns" accounted for almost half of the instances recorded. Such a finding helps to channel improvement efforts where they will do the most good. As Exhibit 25.4G demonstrates, the Pareto diagrams from a series of studies help to document the effects of improvement efforts and point to the most productive direction for the next round of efforts.

When Pareto diagrams are to be compared, you must be sure that the data were collected on comparable bases. In our example, this was done by suggesting that Fuller's study be replicated literally—that is, that three-day study periods be used in both the Before and After studies. It was also assumed that the two three-day periods were comparable in terms of overall level of activity. Comparisons across studies that have different time periods or different data-collection methods are difficult at best, though sometimes sophisticated adjustments can be performed to obtain rough comparability. For routine practical work, however, it is best to stick to comparing the obviously comparable and avoid comparing data from studies with obvious substantive differences.

Many authorities recommend that Pareto analysis take the *costs* of the activities into account. The concern is that a very frequent problem may nevertheless imply less overall cost than a relatively rare but disastrous problem. For example, you are probably willing to put up with a little static in your telephone line in return for being able to count on the line's availability. If the telephone company spent its resources trying to eliminate the last bit of static from the line but failed to keep the lines in good repair, it would not be acting rationally.

As another example, consider the problem of round-off error in calculations on an electronic computer. Theoretically, most calculations involve some error because of the finiteness of the machine, but reliable methods of controlling this error are available. Although it might be useful for someone to develop even better methods for controlling round-off error, it is much more important for most people to learn to write programs accurately. A "bug" in a program, while rare, spoils the whole program, whereas round-off error, while common, is a relatively harmless threat.

Before basing a Pareto analysis on frequencies, as we did in our example, we need to decide that the seriousness of the problems is roughly proportional to the frequencies. If seriousness fails to satisfy this criterion, activities should be measured in some other way. A possible modification of the Fuller study is to keep track of *how much time* employees spend on each activity. Then time spent would replace the frequencies in the table in Exhibit 25.4F. Notice that measuring time spent is more difficult and costly than simply counting instances, so using time spent would have to be justified on economic grounds. Our example underlines the importance of judging the *relevance* of the measurements used in a Pareto analysis.

SECTION

25.5   Exercises

25.5A   Sit in a diner or fast food restaurant and write down all the processes you observe. Draw flow diagrams of some of the processes. At what points do the processes seem to have problems? List some of the causes of the problems you see. If possible, persuade the manager of the establishment to discuss some problems he or she perceives. Again, if possible, try to obtain permission to ask some of the employees about barriers to achievement and communication in the establishment. (You often find that employees know about problems that have not been shared with the manager!)

25.5B   Repeat Exercise 25.5A for any business establishment of your choice.

25.5C   Choose a process that interests you and that you can observe. Draw a flow diagram of how you think the process should work. Then draw a flow diagram of how the process actually works. Suggest improvements in the process. How would you go about collecting data from the process? How would these data help you find the fundamental steps in the process?

25.5D   If possible collect data on problems that occur in the process you studied in Exercises 25.5A, B, and C. Make a Pareto diagram of the problems and identify the most frequent problem. How would you try to counteract this problem?

25.5E   In your place of work, or in your classroom, organize a quality team. Have the team brainstorm on the problems they face. Decide on the most important problem and work on countermeasures to the problem. This exercise will be most successful if the manager or classroom instructor supports the effort.

25.6 Organizing for Quality Improvement

Quality improvement does not just happen; it takes commitment, effort, and organizational skill. A scientific approach to quality improvement requires the timely flow of precisely formulated information—that is, high-quality *communication*. A scientific approach also requires that, so far as possible, communication be based on the collection, analysis, and presentation of data; in other words, the use of statistics. Two organizational principles follow from these remarks:

1   Barriers to communication must be identified and eliminated.

2   Statistics must be part of the everyday vocabulary of the organization.

At this point, some key points made earlier are reiterated and a model for the effective introduction of statistics into a firm is offered.

Barriers to communication are so numerous that they defy any attempt to list them. Common ones are departmentalization, fear, mistrust, laziness, failure to appreciate the importance of communication, and lack of commitment to the concept of never-ending improvement. Imai cites a number of organizational countermeasures to the barriers, among them cross-functional management, quality function deployment, management by policy, and the firmwide training of employees in statistical methods.[†] The point we stress here is that knowledge of statistical methods is fundamental to organizing for quality. This does not mean knowledge by a few specialists, but by *all* members of the firm. Naturally, statistical specialists are responsible for learning, and creating, new methodology to solve new problems, but they also need to be involved in training nonspecialists and in helping them to apply statistical methods to the solution of their everyday problems.

Adopting the methods of science to help solve business problems means adopting statistical tools. Firmwide training in statistical tools is important, but whose job is it to see that the training is done so that the following conditions are met:

1   The training is understandable.

2   The use of statistical tools is taught as part of a scientific approach to problem formulation and solution.

3   The training is put to use to solve important problems in the firm.

These objectives cannot be left to chance. Someone who is answerable to top management and is well trained in statistics must have responsibility for coordinating all the statistical activities of the firm. Otherwise the use of statistics will be sporadic.

Even very skillful applications of statistics have less than full impact if they are not fitted into a strategic plan within the firm. The gains from the applications need to be communicated to the rest of the firm. If the techniques that have worked in one part of the firm can be applied successfully in another part, the second application may go much more quickly than the first, provided the appropriate information

---

[†] Imai, *Kaizen.*

is communicated. In addition, new procedures need to be standardized to achieve maximum gain. Finally, a statistical coordinator with support from top management must have authority to seek out problems that can be attacked scientifically and whose solution will result in important improvements. This type of activity is not possible for a statistician who is assigned to a department, for he or she then faces the familiar barriers to communication. The organizational step of creating a person, or office, in charge of statistical coordination helps to break down the barriers to communication while at the same time encouraging maximum use of statistical methods for process improvement and hence increased productivity of the firm.

Exhibit 25.6A shows a model presented by W. Edwards Deming in *Out of the Crisis* and based on a model originated by Morris Hansen at the Census Bureau. Here the statistical coordinator answers to top management and oversees the statistical activities in all areas of the firm. One of the most important of these activities is training, so that all members of the firm can work effectively to improve the processes for which they are responsible. Only in this way can firmwide, never-ending improvement take place. It is too big a job for any one person or small group of people. It must involve everyone!

EXHIBIT 25.6A
Deming's Model for Location of Statistical Coordinator in an Organization

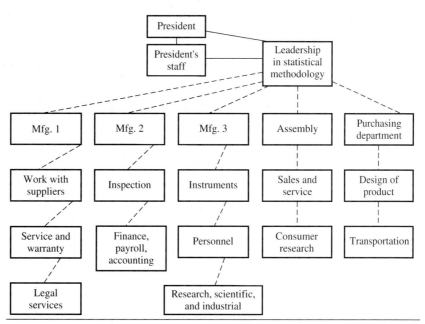

Source: W. Edwards Deming, *Out of the Crisis* (Cambridge, Mass.: MIT Center for Advanced Engineering Study, 1986), p. 467. Used with permission.

S E C T I O N

25.7 Exercises

25.7A   Read Vernon R. Alden, "Who Says You Can't Crack Japanese Markets?" *Harvard Business Review,* 87(1)(1987), 52–56.

    a   State the four myths about Japan that Alden cites.

    b   State Alden's three suggestions for breaking the legal barriers to the Japanese market.

    c   State Alden's three suggestions for breaking the social and cultural barriers to the Japanese market.

    d   Make a list of all the Western companies that Alden uses as examples of firms that have overcome trade barriers with Japan.

25.7B   Locate a business in your community that engages in international trade. Make an appointment with one of the top managers of the company and discuss the difficulties and rewards of foreign trade.

25.7C   This exercise emphasizes the value of new technology in furthering the development of the discipline of statistics. It also illustrates the role of competition. The reading shows the torturous path required to get the technology "accepted." The improvement and acceptance of the technology grew in parallel.

    Find a copy of Joel Shurkin, *Engines of the Mind: A History of the Computer* (New York: Norton, 1984). Read Chapter 3, pages 86–92. It is the story of Herman Hollerith, who was able to adapt the idea of machines driven by punch cards to the processing of data from the U.S. Census. Hollerith created the Tabulating Machine Company, but ill health forced him to allow the company to be merged with some others by Charles Ranlett Flint in 1911. The new company was called Computing-Tabulating-Recording Company (CTR). The new company also increased Hollerith's ability to compete with Powers' company, which got started because the Census Bureau did not believe in a sole supplier. Powers' company eventually merged with Remington Rand, which later became Sperry Rand, maker of the UNIVAC. In May 1914, CTR hired Thomas Watson as general manager. Watson soon took control of the company and in 1924 changed its name to International Business Machines (IBM). Hollerith died in 1929.

    Comment on how each of the following ideas is touched on in this story: never-ending improvement, management of technology, Hollerith as an employer, and basing decisions on data.

25.7D   Collect at least three articles from newspapers, magazines, or journals concerning quality and productivity improvement in business. Find articles that explicitly mention management techniques or philosophies. Articles that simply say that quality is a good thing are not acceptable! Write a two-page essay summarizing these articles. Try to highlight a common theme that runs through the articles, or, if the articles contain conflicting ideas, compare and contrast them. Conclude your essay with a recommendation of a specific quality issue that warrants further study, on the basis of the material in the articles.

Chapter Summary

An organization is a complex of processes. Any process can be improved through systematic study and by focusing on the fundamental causes of inefficiencies. A scientific approach to problem solving and process improvement leads naturally to the use of statistical tools. Fortunately, most processes can be improved by applying relatively simple tools that can be used by any member of the firm, even top management. To make the most effective use of statistical training, a "master statistician" needs to be able to work across all the functions of the firm and to be answerable to top management. The master statistician will also be responsible for the sophisticated use of advanced statistical tools. Organizing for process improvement is crucial in today's competitive environment.

Supplementary Exercises for Chapter 25

25A Develop, preferably in the context of a study team, operational definitions of the concepts of quality, cost control, and scheduling in one or more of the following areas:

    a Providing care in a nursing home

    b Running a purchasing department

    c Designing a research project

    d Forming a study team

    e Developing an action plan for introducing new hardware and software into a clerical office

    f Developing a pilot quality improvement project

    g Writing a paper

25B Read and summarize Chapter 6 of Robert D. Buzzell and Bradley T. Gale, *The PIMS Principles* (New York: Free Press, 1987).

25C What are the Deming Prize and the Baldridge Prize? How do companies win them? Which companies have won them?

25D Do a study to find out why the accounting profession treats capital equipment, such as desks and chairs, as assets and treats people, in terms of their salaries and fringe benefits, as liabilities. A quality perspective treats people, and their ability to improve processes, as assets. Think about how to bring this perspective into the accounting profession.

25E Read F. Timothy Fuller, "Eliminating Complexity from Work: Improving Productivity by Enhancing Quality," *National Productivity Review* (Autumn 1985), 327–334. Apply the ideas in this article to a process of interest to you. This could be your own schedule of daily activities or a process at work.

25F Explain why quality improvement is a never-ending process of PDCA.

Glossary for Chapter 25

cause-and-effect diagram	A "fishbone" diagram that shows causes of causes of causes, and so on, so that truly fundamental causes of variation are documented. Also called an Ishikawa diagram.
conformance analysis	Collection of data to determine if standards for a process are met; part of the check step in the PDCA cycle.
flow diagram	A series of boxes connected by arrows that show the flow of work in a step in a process.
operational definition	The result of answering who, what, when, where, why, and how.
Pareto diagram	A diagram that displays causes of variation ranked by importance.
Pareto principle	Only a few causes are responsible for most of the variation in a process.

Tables

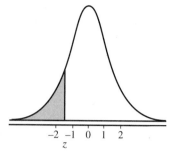

Each entry is the total area under the standard normal curve to the left of z. Values were obtained by rounding the results from Minitab's CDF command.

z	0.00	0.01	0.02	0.03	0.04	0.05	0.06	0.07	0.08	0.09
−3.9	0.0000	0.0000	0.0000	0.0000	0.0000	0.0000	0.0000	0.0000	0.0000	0.0000
−3.8	0.0001	0.0001	0.0001	0.0001	0.0001	0.0001	0.0001	0.0001	0.0001	0.0001
−3.7	0.0001	0.0001	0.0001	0.0001	0.0001	0.0001	0.0001	0.0001	0.0001	0.0001
−3.6	0.0002	0.0002	0.0001	0.0001	0.0001	0.0001	0.0001	0.0001	0.0001	0.0001
−3.5	0.0002	0.0002	0.0002	0.0002	0.0002	0.0002	0.0002	0.0002	0.0002	0.0002
−3.4	0.0003	0.0003	0.0003	0.0003	0.0003	0.0003	0.0003	0.0003	0.0003	0.0002
−3.3	0.0005	0.0005	0.0005	0.0004	0.0004	0.0004	0.0004	0.0004	0.0004	0.0003
−3.2	0.0007	0.0007	0.0006	0.0006	0.0006	0.0006	0.0006	0.0005	0.0005	0.0005
−3.1	0.0010	0.0009	0.0009	0.0009	0.0008	0.0008	0.0008	0.0008	0.0007	0.0007
−3.0	0.0013	0.0013	0.0013	0.0012	0.0012	0.0011	0.0011	0.0011	0.0010	0.0010
−2.9	0.0019	0.0018	0.0018	0.0017	0.0016	0.0016	0.0015	0.0015	0.0014	0.0014
−2.8	0.0026	0.0025	0.0024	0.0023	0.0023	0.0022	0.0021	0.0021	0.0020	0.0019
−2.7	0.0035	0.0034	0.0033	0.0032	0.0031	0.0030	0.0029	0.0028	0.0027	0.0026
−2.6	0.0047	0.0045	0.0044	0.0043	0.0041	0.0040	0.0039	0.0038	0.0037	0.0036
−2.5	0.0062	0.0060	0.0059	0.0057	0.0055	0.0054	0.0052	0.0051	0.0049	0.0048
−2.4	0.0082	0.0080	0.0078	0.0075	0.0073	0.0071	0.0069	0.0068	0.0066	0.0064
−2.3	0.0107	0.0104	0.0102	0.0099	0.0096	0.0094	0.0091	0.0089	0.0087	0.0084
−2.2	0.0139	0.0136	0.0132	0.0129	0.0125	0.0122	0.0119	0.0116	0.0113	0.0110
−2.1	0.0179	0.0174	0.0170	0.0166	0.0162	0.0158	0.0154	0.0150	0.0146	0.0143
−2.0	0.0228	0.0222	0.0217	0.0212	0.0207	0.0202	0.0197	0.0192	0.0188	0.0183
−1.9	0.0287	0.0281	0.0274	0.0268	0.0262	0.0256	0.0250	0.0244	0.0239	0.0233
−1.8	0.0359	0.0351	0.0344	0.0336	0.0329	0.0322	0.0314	0.0307	0.0301	0.0294
−1.7	0.0446	0.0436	0.0427	0.0418	0.0409	0.0401	0.0392	0.0384	0.0375	0.0367
−1.6	0.0548	0.0537	0.0526	0.0516	0.0505	0.0495	0.0485	0.0475	0.0465	0.0455
−1.5	0.0668	0.0655	0.0643	0.0630	0.0618	0.0606	0.0594	0.0582	0.0571	0.0559
−1.4	0.0808	0.0793	0.0778	0.0764	0.0749	0.0735	0.0721	0.0708	0.0694	0.0681
−1.3	0.0968	0.0951	0.0934	0.0918	0.0901	0.0885	0.0869	0.0853	0.0838	0.0823
−1.2	0.1151	0.1131	0.1112	0.1093	0.1075	0.1056	0.1038	0.1020	0.1003	0.0985
−1.1	0.1357	0.1335	0.1314	0.1292	0.1271	0.1251	0.1230	0.1210	0.1190	0.1170
−1.0	0.1587	0.1562	0.1539	0.1515	0.1492	0.1469	0.1446	0.1423	0.1401	0.1379
−0.9	0.1841	0.1814	0.1788	0.1762	0.1736	0.1711	0.1685	0.1660	0.1635	0.1611
−0.8	0.2119	0.2090	0.2061	0.2033	0.2005	0.1977	0.1949	0.1922	0.1894	0.1867
−0.7	0.2420	0.2389	0.2358	0.2327	0.2296	0.2266	0.2236	0.2206	0.2177	0.2148
−0.6	0.2743	0.2709	0.2676	0.2643	0.2611	0.2578	0.2546	0.2514	0.2483	0.2451
−0.5	0.3085	0.3050	0.3015	0.2981	0.2946	0.2912	0.2877	0.2843	0.2810	0.2776
−0.4	0.3446	0.3409	0.3372	0.3336	0.3300	0.3264	0.3228	0.3192	0.3156	0.3121
−0.3	0.3821	0.3783	0.3745	0.3707	0.3669	0.3632	0.3594	0.3557	0.3520	0.3483
−0.2	0.4207	0.4168	0.4129	0.4090	0.4052	0.4013	0.3974	0.3936	0.3897	0.3859
−0.1	0.4602	0.4562	0.4522	0.4483	0.4443	0.4404	0.4364	0.4325	0.4286	0.4247
−0.0	0.5000	0.4960	0.4920	0.4880	0.4840	0.4801	0.4761	0.4721	0.4681	0.4641

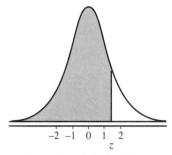

Each entry is the total area under the standard normal curve to the left of z. Values were obtained by rounding the results from Minitab's CDF command.

z	0.00	0.01	0.02	0.03	0.04	0.05	0.06	0.07	0.08	0.09
0.0	0.5000	0.5040	0.5080	0.5120	0.5160	0.5199	0.5239	0.5279	0.5319	0.5359
0.1	0.5398	0.5438	0.5478	0.5517	0.5557	0.5596	0.5636	0.5675	0.5714	0.5753
0.2	0.5793	0.5832	0.5871	0.5910	0.5948	0.5987	0.6026	0.6064	0.6103	0.6141
0.3	0.6179	0.6217	0.6255	0.6293	0.6331	0.6368	0.6406	0.6443	0.6480	0.6517
0.4	0.6554	0.6591	0.6628	0.6664	0.6700	0.6736	0.6772	0.6808	0.6844	0.6879
0.5	0.6915	0.6950	0.6985	0.7019	0.7054	0.7088	0.7123	0.7157	0.7190	0.7224
0.6	0.7257	0.7291	0.7324	0.7357	0.7389	0.7422	0.7454	0.7486	0.7517	0.7549
0.7	0.7580	0.7611	0.7642	0.7673	0.7704	0.7734	0.7764	0.7794	0.7823	0.7852
0.8	0.7881	0.7910	0.7939	0.7967	0.7995	0.8023	0.8051	0.8078	0.8106	0.8133
0.9	0.8159	0.8186	0.8212	0.8238	0.8264	0.8289	0.8315	0.8340	0.8365	0.8389
1.0	0.8413	0.8438	0.8461	0.8485	0.8508	0.8531	0.8554	0.8577	0.8599	0.8621
1.1	0.8643	0.8665	0.8686	0.8708	0.8729	0.8749	0.8770	0.8790	0.8810	0.8830
1.2	0.8849	0.8869	0.8888	0.8907	0.8925	0.8944	0.8962	0.8980	0.8997	0.9015
1.3	0.9032	0.9049	0.9066	0.9082	0.9099	0.9115	0.9131	0.9147	0.9162	0.9177
1.4	0.9192	0.9207	0.9222	0.9236	0.9251	0.9265	0.9279	0.9292	0.9306	0.9319
1.5	0.9332	0.9345	0.9357	0.9370	0.9382	0.9394	0.9406	0.9418	0.9429	0.9441
1.6	0.9452	0.9463	0.9474	0.9484	0.9495	0.9505	0.9515	0.9525	0.9535	0.9545
1.7	0.9554	0.9564	0.9573	0.9582	0.9591	0.9599	0.9608	0.9616	0.9625	0.9633
1.8	0.9641	0.9649	0.9656	0.9664	0.9671	0.9678	0.9686	0.9693	0.9699	0.9706
1.9	0.9713	0.9719	0.9726	0.9732	0.9738	0.9744	0.9750	0.9756	0.9761	0.9767
2.0	0.9772	0.9778	0.9783	0.9788	0.9793	0.9798	0.9803	0.9808	0.9812	0.9817
2.1	0.9821	0.9826	0.9830	0.9834	0.9838	0.9842	0.9846	0.9850	0.9854	0.9857
2.2	0.9861	0.9864	0.9868	0.9871	0.9875	0.9878	0.9881	0.9884	0.9887	0.9890
2.3	0.9893	0.9896	0.9898	0.9901	0.9904	0.9906	0.9909	0.9911	0.9913	0.9916
2.4	0.9918	0.9920	0.9922	0.9925	0.9927	0.9929	0.9931	0.9932	0.9934	0.9936
2.5	0.9938	0.9940	0.9941	0.9943	0.9945	0.9946	0.9948	0.9949	0.9951	0.9952
2.6	0.9953	0.9955	0.9956	0.9957	0.9959	0.9960	0.9961	0.9962	0.9963	0.9964
2.7	0.9965	0.9966	0.9967	0.9968	0.9969	0.9970	0.9971	0.9972	0.9973	0.9974
2.8	0.9974	0.9975	0.9976	0.9977	0.9977	0.9978	0.9979	0.9979	0.9980	0.9981
2.9	0.9981	0.9982	0.9982	0.9983	0.9984	0.9984	0.9985	0.9985	0.9986	0.9986
3.0	0.9987	0.9987	0.9987	0.9988	0.9988	0.9989	0.9989	0.9989	0.9990	0.9990
3.1	0.9990	0.9991	0.9991	0.9991	0.9992	0.9992	0.9992	0.9992	0.9993	0.9993
3.2	0.9993	0.9993	0.9994	0.9994	0.9994	0.9994	0.9994	0.9995	0.9995	0.9995
3.3	0.9995	0.9995	0.9995	0.9996	0.9996	0.9996	0.9996	0.9996	0.9996	0.9997
3.4	0.9997	0.9997	0.9997	0.9997	0.9997	0.9997	0.9997	0.9997	0.9997	0.9998
3.5	0.9998	0.9998	0.9998	0.9998	0.9998	0.9998	0.9998	0.9998	0.9998	0.9998
3.6	0.9998	0.9998	0.9999	0.9999	0.9999	0.9999	0.9999	0.9999	0.9999	0.9999
3.7	0.9999	0.9999	0.9999	0.9999	0.9999	0.9999	0.9999	0.9999	0.9999	0.9999
3.8	0.9999	0.9999	0.9999	0.9999	0.9999	0.9999	0.9999	0.9999	0.9999	0.9999
3.9	1.0000	1.0000	1.0000	1.0000	1.0000	1.0000	1.0000	1.0000	1.0000	1.0000

T A B L E   **2**   Table of 95th and 99th Percentiles of Selected *F* Distributions

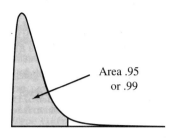

Area .95
or .99

Rows are numerator degrees of freedom; columns are denominator degrees of freedom. Entries in a cell are the 95th on top of the 99th percentile.

ν_1	1	2	3	4	ν_2 5	6	7	8	9	10
1	161.45	18.51	10.13	7.71	6.61	5.99	5.59	5.32	5.12	4.97
	4052.18	98.51	34.12	21.20	16.26	13.75	12.25	11.26	10.56	10.04
2	199.50	19.00	9.55	6.94	5.79	5.14	4.74	4.46	4.26	4.10
	4999.50	99.00	30.82	18.00	13.27	10.93	9.55	8.65	8.02	7.56
3	215.71	19.16	9.28	6.59	5.41	4.76	4.35	4.07	3.86	3.71
	5403.35	99.17	29.46	16.69	12.06	9.78	8.45	7.59	6.99	6.55
4	224.58	19.25	9.12	6.39	5.19	4.53	4.12	3.84	3.63	3.48
	5624.57	99.25	28.71	15.98	11.39	9.15	7.85	7.01	6.42	5.99
5	230.16	19.30	9.01	6.26	5.05	4.39	3.97	3.69	3.48	3.33
	5763.63	99.30	28.24	15.52	10.97	8.75	7.46	6.63	6.06	5.64
6	233.99	19.33	8.94	6.16	4.95	4.28	3.87	3.58	3.37	3.22
	5858.97	99.33	27.91	15.21	10.67	8.47	7.19	6.37	5.80	5.39
7	236.77	19.35	8.89	6.09	4.88	4.21	3.79	3.50	3.29	3.14
	5928.34	99.36	27.67	14.98	10.46	8.26	6.99	6.18	5.61	5.20
8	238.88	19.37	8.85	6.04	4.82	4.15	3.73	3.44	3.23	3.07
	5981.05	99.37	27.49	14.80	10.29	8.10	6.84	6.03	5.47	5.06
9	240.54	19.39	8.81	6.00	4.77	4.10	3.68	3.39	3.18	3.02
	6022.45	99.39	27.35	14.66	10.16	7.98	6.72	5.91	5.35	4.94
10	241.88	19.40	8.79	5.96	4.74	4.06	3.64	3.35	3.14	2.98
	6055.82	99.40	27.23	14.55	10.05	7.87	6.62	5.81	5.26	4.85
11	242.98	19.41	8.76	5.94	4.70	4.03	3.60	3.31	3.10	2.94
	6083.29	99.41	27.13	14.45	9.96	7.79	6.54	5.73	5.18	4.77
12	243.91	19.41	8.75	5.91	4.68	4.00	3.58	3.28	3.07	2.91
	6106.29	99.42	27.05	14.37	9.89	7.72	6.47	5.67	5.11	4.71
13	244.69	19.42	8.73	5.89	4.66	3.98	3.55	3.26	3.05	2.89
	6125.84	99.42	26.98	14.31	9.83	7.66	6.41	5.61	5.05	4.65
14	245.36	19.42	8.72	5.87	4.64	3.96	3.53	3.24	3.03	2.87
	6142.64	99.43	26.92	14.25	9.77	7.61	6.36	5.56	5.01	4.60
15	245.95	19.43	8.70	5.86	4.62	3.94	3.51	3.22	3.01	2.85
	6157.26	99.43	26.87	14.20	9.72	7.56	6.31	5.52	4.96	4.56

T A B L E   **2**   (Continued)

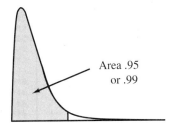

Area .95
or .99

Rows are numerator degrees of freedom; columns are denominator degrees of freedom. Entries in a cell are the 95th on top of the 99th percentile.

ν_1	11	12	13	14	ν_2 15	16	17	18	19	20
1	4.84	4.75	4.67	4.60	4.54	4.49	4.45	4.41	4.38	4.35
	9.65	9.33	9.07	8.86	8.68	8.53	8.40	8.29	8.19	8.10
2	3.98	3.89	3.81	3.74	3.68	3.63	3.59	3.56	3.52	3.49
	7.21	6.93	6.70	6.52	6.36	6.23	6.11	6.01	5.93	5.85
3	3.59	3.49	3.41	3.34	3.29	3.24	3.20	3.16	3.13	3.10
	6.22	5.95	5.74	5.56	5.42	5.29	5.19	5.09	5.01	4.94
4	3.36	3.26	3.18	3.11	3.06	3.01	2.97	2.93	2.90	2.87
	5.67	5.41	5.21	5.04	4.89	4.77	4.67	4.58	4.50	4.43
5	3.20	3.11	3.03	2.96	2.90	2.85	2.81	2.77	2.74	2.71
	5.32	5.06	4.86	4.70	4.56	4.44	4.34	4.25	4.17	4.10
6	3.10	3.00	2.92	2.85	2.79	2.74	2.70	2.66	2.63	2.60
	5.07	4.82	4.62	4.46	4.32	4.20	4.10	4.02	3.94	3.87
7	3.01	2.91	2.83	2.76	2.71	2.66	2.61	2.58	2.54	2.51
	4.89	4.64	4.44	4.28	4.14	4.03	3.93	3.84	3.77	3.70
8	2.95	2.85	2.77	2.70	2.64	2.59	2.55	2.51	2.48	2.45
	4.74	4.50	4.30	4.14	4.00	3.89	3.79	3.71	3.63	3.56
9	2.90	2.80	2.71	2.65	2.59	2.54	2.49	2.46	2.42	2.39
	4.63	4.39	4.19	4.03	3.90	3.78	3.68	3.60	3.52	3.46
10	2.85	2.75	2.67	2.60	2.54	2.49	2.45	2.41	2.38	2.35
	4.54	4.30	4.10	3.94	3.81	3.69	3.59	3.51	3.43	3.37
11	2.82	2.72	2.64	2.57	2.51	2.46	2.41	2.37	2.34	2.31
	4.46	4.22	4.03	3.86	3.73	3.62	3.52	3.43	3.36	3.29
12	2.79	2.69	2.60	2.53	2.47	2.43	2.38	2.34	2.31	2.28
	4.40	4.16	3.96	3.80	3.67	3.55	3.46	3.37	3.30	3.23
13	2.76	2.66	2.58	2.51	2.45	2.40	2.35	2.31	2.28	2.25
	4.34	4.10	3.91	3.75	3.61	3.50	3.40	3.32	3.24	3.18
14	2.74	2.64	2.55	2.48	2.42	2.37	2.33	2.29	2.26	2.22
	4.29	4.05	3.86	3.70	3.56	3.45	3.35	3.27	3.20	3.13
15	2.72	2.62	2.53	2.46	2.40	2.35	2.31	2.27	2.23	2.20
	4.25	4.01	3.82	3.66	3.52	3.41	3.31	3.23	3.15	3.09

TABLE 3   Percentiles of Selected t and ν Degrees of Freedom

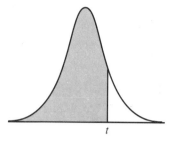

The body of the table contains values of t corresponding to areas a. The parameter a is the area bounded by the horizontal axis, a vertical line through t, and the pdf of the t distribution with ν degrees of freedom.

							a = area								
ν	0.550	0.600	0.650	0.700	0.750	0.800	0.850	0.900	0.950	0.975	0.990	0.995	0.997	0.998	0.999
1	0.158	0.325	0.510	0.727	1.000	1.376	1.963	3.078	6.314	12.706	31.821	63.657	106.100	159.156	318.317
2	0.142	0.289	0.445	0.617	0.816	1.061	1.386	1.886	2.920	4.303	6.965	9.925	12.852	15.764	22.327
3	0.137	0.277	0.424	0.584	0.765	0.978	1.250	1.638	2.353	3.182	4.541	5.841	6.994	8.053	10.215
4	0.134	0.271	0.414	0.569	0.741	0.941	1.190	1.533	2.132	2.776	3.747	4.604	5.321	5.951	7.173
5	0.132	0.267	0.408	0.559	0.727	0.920	1.156	1.476	2.015	2.571	3.365	4.032	4.570	5.030	5.893
6	0.131	0.265	0.404	0.553	0.718	0.906	1.134	1.440	1.943	2.447	3.143	3.707	4.152	4.524	5.208
7	0.130	0.263	0.402	0.549	0.711	0.896	1.119	1.415	1.895	2.365	2.998	3.499	3.887	4.207	4.785
8	0.130	0.262	0.399	0.546	0.706	0.889	1.108	1.397	1.860	2.306	2.896	3.355	3.705	3.991	4.501
9	0.129	0.261	0.398	0.543	0.703	0.883	1.100	1.383	1.833	2.262	2.821	3.250	3.573	3.835	4.297
10	0.129	0.260	0.397	0.542	0.700	0.879	1.093	1.372	1.812	2.228	2.764	3.169	3.472	3.716	4.144
11	0.129	0.260	0.396	0.540	0.697	0.876	1.088	1.363	1.796	2.201	2.718	3.106	3.393	3.624	4.025
12	0.128	0.259	0.395	0.539	0.695	0.873	1.083	1.356	1.782	2.179	2.681	3.055	3.330	3.550	3.930
13	0.128	0.259	0.394	0.538	0.694	0.870	1.079	1.350	1.771	2.160	2.650	3.012	3.278	3.489	3.852
14	0.128	0.258	0.393	0.537	0.692	0.868	1.076	1.345	1.761	2.145	2.624	2.977	3.234	3.438	3.787
15	0.128	0.258	0.393	0.536	0.691	0.866	1.074	1.341	1.753	2.131	2.602	2.947	3.197	3.395	3.733
16	0.128	0.258	0.392	0.535	0.690	0.865	1.071	1.337	1.746	2.120	2.583	2.921	3.165	3.358	3.686
17	0.128	0.257	0.392	0.534	0.689	0.863	1.069	1.333	1.740	2.110	2.567	2.898	3.138	3.326	3.646
18	0.127	0.257	0.392	0.534	0.688	0.862	1.067	1.330	1.734	2.101	2.552	2.878	3.113	3.298	3.611
19	0.127	0.257	0.391	0.533	0.688	0.861	1.066	1.328	1.729	2.093	2.539	2.861	3.092	3.273	3.579
20	0.127	0.257	0.391	0.533	0.687	0.860	1.064	1.325	1.725	2.086	2.528	2.845	3.073	3.251	3.552
21	0.127	0.257	0.391	0.532	0.686	0.859	1.063	1.323	1.721	2.080	2.518	2.831	3.056	3.231	3.527
22	0.127	0.256	0.390	0.532	0.686	0.858	1.061	1.321	1.717	2.074	2.508	2.819	3.041	3.214	3.505
23	0.127	0.256	0.390	0.532	0.685	0.858	1.060	1.319	1.714	2.069	2.500	2.807	3.027	3.198	3.485
24	0.127	0.256	0.390	0.531	0.685	0.857	1.059	1.318	1.711	2.064	2.492	2.797	3.014	3.183	3.467
25	0.127	0.256	0.390	0.531	0.684	0.856	1.058	1.316	1.708	2.060	2.485	2.787	3.003	3.170	3.450
26	0.127	0.256	0.390	0.531	0.684	0.856	1.058	1.315	1.706	2.056	2.479	2.779	2.992	3.158	3.435
27	0.127	0.256	0.389	0.531	0.684	0.855	1.057	1.314	1.703	2.052	2.473	2.771	2.982	3.147	3.421
28	0.127	0.256	0.389	0.530	0.683	0.855	1.056	1.313	1.701	2.048	2.467	2.763	2.973	3.136	3.408
29	0.127	0.256	0.389	0.530	0.683	0.854	1.055	1.311	1.699	2.045	2.462	2.756	2.965	3.127	3.396
30	0.127	0.256	0.389	0.530	0.683	0.854	1.055	1.310	1.697	2.042	2.457	2.750	2.957	3.118	3.385
31	0.127	0.256	0.389	0.530	0.682	0.853	1.054	1.309	1.696	2.040	2.453	2.744	2.950	3.109	3.375
32	0.127	0.255	0.389	0.530	0.682	0.853	1.054	1.309	1.694	2.037	2.449	2.738	2.943	3.102	3.365
33	0.127	0.255	0.389	0.530	0.682	0.853	1.053	1.308	1.692	2.035	2.445	2.733	2.937	3.094	3.356
34	0.127	0.255	0.389	0.529	0.682	0.852	1.052	1.307	1.691	2.032	2.441	2.728	2.931	3.088	3.348
35	0.127	0.255	0.388	0.529	0.682	0.852	1.052	1.306	1.690	2.030	2.438	2.724	2.926	3.081	3.340
40	0.126	0.255	0.388	0.529	0.681	0.851	1.050	1.303	1.684	2.021	2.423	2.704	2.902	3.055	3.307
50	0.126	0.255	0.388	0.528	0.679	0.849	1.047	1.299	1.676	2.009	2.403	2.678	2.870	3.018	3.261
60	0.126	0.254	0.387	0.527	0.679	0.848	1.045	1.296	1.671	2.000	2.390	2.660	2.849	2.994	3.232
120	0.126	0.254	0.386	0.526	0.677	0.845	1.041	1.289	1.658	1.980	2.358	2.617	2.798	2.935	3.160
inf	0.126	0.253	0.385	0.524	0.674	0.842	1.036	1.282	1.645	1.960	2.326	2.576	2.748	2.878	3.090

T A B L E   4   Selected Percentiles of Chi-Square Distributions with ν Degrees of Freedom

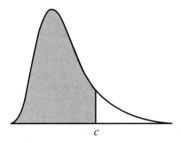

The body of the table shows values of c such that $1 - \alpha$ is the area bounded by the horizontal axis, a vertical line located at c, and the chi-square curve.

						$1 - \alpha$						
ν	0.01	0.05	0.10	0.30	0.50	0.70	0.90	0.95	0.975	0.99	0.995	0.999
1	0.00	0.00	0.02	0.15	0.46	1.07	2.71	3.84	5.02	6.64	7.88	10.83
2	0.02	0.10	0.21	0.71	1.39	2.41	4.61	5.99	7.38	9.21	10.60	13.82
3	0.12	0.35	0.58	1.42	2.37	3.67	6.25	7.82	9.35	11.35	12.84	16.27
4	0.30	0.71	1.06	2.20	3.36	4.88	7.78	9.49	11.14	13.28	14.86	18.47
5	0.55	1.15	1.61	3.00	4.35	6.06	9.24	11.07	12.83	15.09	16.75	20.52
6	0.87	1.64	2.20	3.83	5.35	7.23	10.65	12.59	14.45	16.81	18.55	22.46
7	1.24	2.17	2.83	4.67	6.35	8.38	12.02	14.07	16.01	18.48	20.28	24.32
8	1.65	2.73	3.49	5.53	7.34	9.52	13.36	15.51	17.54	20.09	21.96	26.13
9	2.09	3.33	4.17	6.39	8.34	10.66	14.68	16.92	19.02	21.67	23.59	27.88
10	2.56	3.94	4.86	7.27	9.34	11.78	15.99	18.31	20.48	23.21	25.19	29.59
11	3.05	4.57	5.58	8.15	10.34	12.90	17.28	19.67	21.92	24.73	26.76	31.26
12	3.57	5.23	6.30	9.03	11.34	14.01	18.55	21.03	23.34	26.22	28.30	32.91
13	4.11	5.89	7.04	9.93	12.34	15.12	19.81	22.36	24.74	27.69	29.82	34.53
14	4.66	6.57	7.79	10.82	13.34	16.22	21.06	23.69	26.12	29.14	31.32	36.12
15	5.23	7.26	8.55	11.72	14.34	17.32	22.31	25.00	27.49	30.58	32.80	37.70
16	5.81	7.96	9.31	12.62	15.34	18.42	23.54	26.30	28.85	32.00	34.27	39.25
17	6.41	8.67	10.09	13.53	16.34	19.51	24.77	27.59	30.19	33.41	35.72	40.79
18	7.02	9.39	10.87	14.44	17.34	20.60	25.99	28.87	31.53	34.81	37.16	42.31
19	7.63	10.12	11.65	15.35	18.34	21.69	27.20	30.14	32.85	36.19	38.58	43.82
20	8.26	10.85	12.44	16.27	19.34	22.78	28.41	31.41	34.17	37.57	40.00	45.32
21	8.90	11.59	13.24	17.18	20.34	23.86	29.62	32.67	35.48	38.93	41.40	46.80
22	9.54	12.34	14.04	18.10	21.34	24.94	30.81	33.92	36.78	40.29	42.80	48.27
23	10.20	13.09	14.85	19.02	22.34	26.02	32.01	35.17	38.08	41.64	44.18	49.73
24	10.86	13.85	15.66	19.94	23.34	27.10	33.20	36.42	39.36	42.98	45.56	51.18
25	11.52	14.61	16.47	20.87	24.34	28.17	34.38	37.65	40.65	44.31	46.93	52.62
26	12.20	15.38	17.29	21.79	25.34	29.25	35.56	38.88	41.92	45.64	48.29	54.05
27	12.88	16.15	18.11	22.72	26.34	30.32	36.74	40.11	43.20	46.96	49.65	55.48
28	13.57	16.93	18.94	23.65	27.34	31.39	37.92	41.34	44.46	48.28	50.99	56.89
29	14.26	17.71	19.77	24.58	28.34	32.46	39.09	42.56	45.72	49.59	52.34	58.30
30	14.95	18.49	20.60	25.51	29.34	33.53	40.26	43.77	46.98	50.89	53.67	59.70

Theoretical Distributions and Properties

Uncertainty pervades everyday experience. Whether we engage in casual observation, formal surveying, or experimentation, we must allow for the vagaries of chance. Probability and probability distributions are the mathematical tools for the formal study of chance outcomes.

In this appendix we give a brief survey of probability theory, theoretical distributions and variables, and moments of transformed variables. All these topics play an important role in the development of sound statistical approaches to data analysis and modeling.

Probability Theory

Probability theory is a mathematical model for randomness and its consequences. The simplest model contemplates an event that can happen when any one of several outcomes happens. For example, the roll of an ordinary die can result in one of six outcomes: 1, 2, 3, 4, 5, 6. Probabilities are numbers attached to the outcomes so as to measure their relative likelihood. For example, an assignment of 1/6 probability to each of the six faces of the die says we believe the faces to be equally likely, whereas an assignment of probabilities 1/4, 1/12, 1/6, 1/6, 1/12, 1/4 says we believe the die favors some of the outcomes over the others.

In mathematical language, an **event** is a set of outcomes. The event that contains all the outcomes that can happen is the **universe**, denoted by $\mathcal{U}$. As in the die illustration, **probabilities** are assigned to the outcomes so that they are positive fractions that total 1. We then say that the probability that the universe can happen is 1 and write $Pr(\mathcal{U}) = 1$. The symbol Pr stands for probability.

Every event is a subset of the universe. For example, when we roll the die we might focus on outcomes that are even—that is, 2, 4, 6. We denote such an event by a capital Roman letter such as A. For example, we could write A = {2, 4, 6}. The probability that A happens is the sum of the probabilities of the outcomes contained in A. For the die with equally likely outcomes, this means the probability of A is $1/6 + 1/6 + 1/6 = 1/2$, or $Pr(A) = 1/2$. For the die with outcome probabilities 1/4, 1/12, 1/6, 1/6, 1/12, 1/4, we have $Pr(A) = 1/12 + 1/6 + 1/4 = 18/36 = 1/2$. Notice that the two dice are equally likely to yield even outcomes, even though they are not equally likely to yield the individual outcomes 2, 4, 6.

Events, being sets, satisfy all the mathematical properties of sets. Thus, we can talk about union and intersection of events. For example, if two events A and B have no outcomes in common, their intersection is empty, and we say they are disjoint. Letting $\emptyset$ denote the "empty set," we may write $A \cap B = \emptyset$, if A and B are disjoint. The empty set is assigned probability 0, so if $A \cap B = \emptyset$, we may write $Pr(A \cap B) = 0$.

The addition rule of probability says

$$Pr(A \cup B) = Pr(A) + Pr(B) - Pr(A \cap B)$$

Notice that this implies

$$Pr(A \cup B) \leq Pr(A) + Pr(B)$$

If $A \cap B = \emptyset$, then

$$Pr(A \cup B) = Pr(A) + Pr(B)$$

and in general if $A_1, A_2, \ldots$, etc. is a sequence of events such that no two of the events has an outcome in common—that is, if $A_i \cap A_j = \emptyset$ for all $i \neq j$, then

$$Pr(A_1 \cup A_2 \cup \ldots \text{ etc.}) = Pr(A_1) + Pr(A_2) + \cdots \text{ etc.}$$

Another general result is that

$$Pr(A_1 \cup A_2 \cup \ldots \text{ etc.}) \leq Pr(A_1) + Pr(A_2) + \cdots \text{ etc.}$$

The complement of an event A is just the set of outcomes not in A. Letting A^c denote the complement of A, we have $A \cup A^c = \mathcal{U}$, and it follows that

$$Pr(A^c) = 1 - Pr(A)$$

It can also be shown that

$$(A_1 \cup A_2 \cup \ldots \cup A_k)^c = A_1^c \cap A_2^c \cap \ldots \cap A_k^c$$

This result can be used to derive **Bonferroni's inequality**:

$$Pr(A_1^c \cap A_2^c \cap \ldots \cap A_k^c) \geq 1 - Pr(A_1) - Pr(A_2) - \cdots - Pr(A_k)$$

This result has far-reaching statistical implications. Let A_i, $i = 1, 2, \ldots, k$, denote the event that statistical inference procedure i, such as a confidence interval or a hypothesis test or a prediction interval, is in error. Then the probability that all k of the procedures are not in error is

$$Pr(A_1^c \cap A_2^c \cap \ldots \cap A_k^c) \geq 1 - Pr(A_1) - Pr(A_2) - \cdots - Pr(A_k)$$

For example, if we construct ten 95% confidence intervals, the probability that they are all correct is equal to at least $1 - .05 - \cdots - .05 = 1 - 10(.05) = .5$. On the other hand, if we construct ten 99% confidence intervals, the probability that they are all correct is equal to at least $1 - .01 - \cdots - .01 = 1 - 10(.01) = .9$. A guarantee that the system of intervals is correct with probability at least .9 is more comforting than a guarantee that the system is correct with probability at least .5.

Two events A and B are independent if $Pr(A \cap B) = Pr(A)Pr(B)$. The concept of independence is important in model building. For example, the outcomes in a sequence of coin tosses are usually assumed to be independent, and this assumption underlies the derivation of the binomial distribution in Chapter 11. Error terms in regression models, as discussed in Chapter 20, are also usually assumed to be independent for purposes of deriving probabilistic inferences.

From the elementary principles outlined above, an impressive volume of mathematics has developed, and probability theory continues to be a fruitful area for new discoveries. The most important parts of the mathematics of probability for statistical practice are those dealing with distributions. This appendix outlines some of the more important results underlying statistical practice.

Theoretical Cumulative Distribution Functions

Cumulative distribution functions are like fingerprints. Each distribution has a unique cumulative distribution, so distributions can be compared and distinguished by comparing and distinguishing their cumulative distribution functions.

Theoretically, any function that assigns values to the set of real numbers such that the smallest value is 0, the largest value is 1, and the function is nondecreasing is a *cumulative distribution function (cdf)* of some distribution.

E X A M P L E   **A2A**   The function F defined by

$$F(y) = 0, \quad \text{for } y < 0$$
$$= y^2, \quad \text{for } 0 \leq y < 1$$
$$= 1, \quad \text{for } y \geq 1$$

satisfies the conditions of a cdf. Verify this statement and sketch a graph of the function.   ∎

The link between cumulative distribution functions and probability is as follows. For any number y, let I_y denote the set of numbers less than or equal to y, and suppose that a probability is assigned to I_y. Then I_y is an event with probability $Pr(I_y)$. The cumulative distribution function is simply $F(y) = Pr(I_y)$. In theory, once we know the function $F(y)$, we can derive from it probabilities for any other set of numbers of interest.

E X A M P L E   **A2B**   Let $f(z)$ be the function whose graph is the standard normal curve, as defined in Chapter 9, and define the function F by

$$F(y) = \int_{-\infty}^{y} f(z) \, dz$$

Then, using a standard interpretation of definite integrals from calculus, $F(y)$ is the *area* bounded by the horizontal axis, a vertical line between y and $f(y)$, and the curve defined by the set of points $\{f(z): -\infty < z < y\}$. You can easily verify that $0 \leq F(y) \leq 1$ for all values of y, and F is nondecreasing. You can also see that

$$\lim_{y \to -\infty} F(y) = 0 \quad \text{and} \quad \lim_{y \to \infty} F(y) = 1,$$

so at least in the limit, F satisfies the conditions of making 0 and 1 the minimum and maximum values of the function.   ∎

Example A2B illustrates a general technique for constructing cdf's. Start with a function f such that

- $f(z) \geq 0$ for all values of z.
- The integral of f exists.
- The integral of f over the real line is 1.

Then $F(y) = \int_{-\infty}^{y} f(z)\, dz$ is a cdf. The corresponding distribution is said to be a *continuous distribution,* a distribution in which the variable y assumes an infinite number of values in a continuous manner. By the fundamental theorem of calculus, the derivative of F exists for all but at most a finite number of values in any finite subinterval of the real line, and when its derivative F' does exist, $F'(y) = f(y)$. For distributions of the continuous type, the function f is called the *probability density function (pdf)* of the distribution.

The distribution in Example A2A is of the continuous type. You can show that F is differentiable except at $y = 0$ and $y = 1$, and that the pdf is

$$f(y) = F'(y) = 2y, \text{ for } 0 < y < 1 \quad \text{and} \quad f(y) = 0, \text{ for } y < 0 \text{ and } y > 1$$

The definitions of $f(0)$ and $f(1)$ are immaterial because they do not enter into the calculation of F. It is conventional to define $f(0) = f(1) = 0$ in such cases.

EXAMPLE **A2C**

Consider a binomial distribution with $n = 4$ and $\pi = 0.6$, as introduced in Chapter 11. Define $f(y) = Pr(\text{number of successes} = y)$. Then unless $y = 0, 1, 2, 3,$ or $4, f(y) = 0$. The following table of probabilities is obtained from the formula for the binomial distribution.

y	$f(y)$
0	0.0256
1	0.1536
2	0.3456
3	0.3456
4	0.1296

The cdf for this probability distribution is defined by

$$
\begin{aligned}
F(y) &= 0, & \text{for } y < 0 \\
&= 0.0256, & \text{for } 0 \le y < 1 \\
&= 0.1792, & \text{for } 1 \le y < 2 \\
&= 0.5248, & \text{for } 2 \le y < 3 \\
&= 0.8704, & \text{for } 3 \le y < 4 \\
&= 1.0000, & \text{for } 4 \le y
\end{aligned}
$$

You can verify that $F(y)$ is the probability that four Bernoulli trials, with $\pi = 0.6$, yield y or fewer successes. You can also verify that $f(y) = F(y) - F(y^-)$, where

$$
F(y^-) = \lim_{x \uparrow y} F(x),
$$

the limit of F from the left of y. ■

Example A2C illustrates a *discrete distribution*. This type of distribution arises if the cdf is a step function with at most a countable number of jumps. The typical cases are distributions with jumps at the nonnegative integers (called *count distributions*) and jumps at only a finite number of values. The corresponding *mass function* defined by

$$
f(y) = F(y) - F(y^-)
$$

assigns positive masses (interpreted as probabilities) to the set of jump points. The symbol J is used to denote the set of points where the mass function has positive values. This is also the set of points where the cdf jumps. The mass function has value 0 for all real numbers not in J.

Distributions constructed from data from real-world processes are of the discrete type. Distributions of the continuous type allow us to work with somewhat idealized distributions using the methods of calculus.

Different distributions have different cumulative distribution functions, so the cdf's act like fingerprints for distributions. Some useful characteristics of the corresponding distribution can be extracted from a cdf. Perhaps the most commonly studied characteristics are the moments.

Moments of Theoretical Distributions

If F is of the continuous type, we work with the corresponding pdf f. If F is of the discrete type, we work with the corresponding mass function f. For a discrete distribution, J is the set of jump points of F—that is, the set of y-values at which F takes a step up.

DEFINITION ■   The mean of a theoretical distribution is denoted by μ and defined by

$$\mu = \int_{-\infty}^{+\infty} yf(y)\,dy \qquad \text{in the continuous case}$$

$$\mu = \sum_{y \in J} yf(y) \qquad \text{in the discrete case}$$

If either the integral or the sum above does not exist, we say that the mean does not exist.[†]   ■

The mean of a distribution is also called the *first moment about zero*. This terminology comes from the following general definition.

DEFINITION ■   The pth moment about zero of a theoretical distribution is denoted by μ_p' and defined by

$$\mu_p' = \int_{-\infty}^{+\infty} y^p f(y)\,dy \qquad \text{in the continuous case}$$

$$\mu_p' = \sum_{y \in J} y^p f(y) \qquad \text{in the discrete case}$$

provided the integral or sum is finite. If either is not finite, the corresponding moment does not exist.[††]   ■

From these definitions it follows that $\mu = \mu_1'$, that is, that the mean is the first moment about zero. The phrase *moment about zero* is mysterious until the next definition of a moment about an arbitrary value is introduced.

DEFINITION ■   For a theoretical distribution the pth moment about an arbitrary point a is denoted by $\mu_p'(a)$ and defined by

$$\mu_p'(a) = \int_{-\infty}^{+\infty} (y - a)^p f(y)\,dy \qquad \text{in the continuous case}$$

$$\mu_p'(a) = \sum_{y \in J} (y - a)^p f(y) \qquad \text{in the discrete case}$$

provided the integral or sum is finite. If either is not finite, the corresponding moment does not exist.   ■

[†] Technically, for the mean to exist the sum or integral has to be absolutely convergent.
[††] Technically, the definition requires the integral or sum of the pth power of the absolute value of y times $f(y)$ to be finite.

From this definition, we see that $\mu_p' = \mu_p'(0)$—that is, the notation for the pth moment about zero has been simplified by dropping the "(0)." The moments about zero have special importance in statistical theory and so have acquired this special notation. Other moments of special importance are the moments about the mean.

D E F I N I T I O N ■   The pth moment about the mean is denoted by $\overline{\mu}_p$ and defined by

$$\overline{\mu}_p = \mu_p(\mu) = \int_{-\infty}^{+\infty} (y - \mu)^p f(y) \, dy \qquad \text{in the continuous case}$$

$$\overline{\mu}_p = \mu_p(\mu) = \sum_{y \in J} (y - \mu)^p f(y) \qquad \text{in the discrete case}$$

provided the mean is finite and the sum or integral exists.   ■

D E F I N I T I O N ■   The variance of a distribution is the second moment about the mean, provided the mean is finite. The variance is denoted by σ^2, that is, $\sigma^2 = \overline{\mu}_2$. The standard deviation is the positive square root of the variance, provided the variance exists. The standard deviation is denoted by σ.   ■

T H E O R E M   1 $$\sigma^2 = \mu_2' - (\mu_1')^2 = \mu_2' - \mu^2 \quad ■$$

E X A M P L E   **A2D**   Consider the pdf of the distribution introduced in Example A2A. The pth moment about 0 is

$$\mu_p' = \int_{-\infty}^{+\infty} y^p f(y) \, dy = \int_0^1 y^p 2y \, dy = 2 \int_0^1 y^{p+1} \, dy = \frac{2}{p + 2}$$

Setting $p = 1$ gives the mean $\mu = \frac{2}{3}$. Using Theorem 2 gives the variance $\sigma^2 = \mu_2' - \mu^2 = \frac{2}{4} - \left(\frac{2}{3}\right)^2 = \frac{1}{18}$. This yields a standard deviation of $\sqrt{\frac{1}{18}} \approx 0.2357$.

The pth moment about the arbitrary value a is

$$\mu_p'(a) = \int_{-\infty}^{+\infty} (y - a)^p f(y) \, dy$$

$$= \int_0^1 (y - a)^p 2y \, dy$$

$$= 2 \int_0^1 (y - a)^p (y - a + a) \, dy$$

$$= 2 \int_0^1 (y - a)^{p+1} \, dy + 2 \int_0^1 (y - a)^p (a) \, dy$$

Setting $a = \mu$ and $p = 3$,

$$\overline{\mu}_3 = 2 \int_0^1 \left(y - \frac{2}{3} \right)^4 \, dy + 2 \int_0^1 \left(y - \frac{2}{3} \right)^3 \left(\frac{2}{3} \right) \, dy = -\frac{1}{135} \quad \blacksquare$$

Mathematical Expectation

The calculations presented in this section can be summarized by defining *mathematical expectation*. Consider the continuous case first.

D E F I N I T I O N ▪   Let y be a variable with cdf F and pdf f, of the continuous type. Let $g(y)$ denote a function of y. Then the integral

$$\int_{-\infty}^{+\infty} [g(y)] f(y) \, dy$$

provided the integral exists, is called the mathematical expectation of $g(y)$ and is denoted by the symbol $E[g(y)]$.   ▪

Now consider the discrete case.

D E F I N I T I O N ▪   Let y be a variable with cdf F and mass function f, of the discrete type. Let $g(y)$ denote a function of y. Then the sum

$$\sum_{y \in J} [g(y)] f(y)$$

provided the sum exists, is called the mathematical expectation of $g(y)$ and is denoted by the symbol $E[g(y)]$.   ▪

Except for the distinction between continuous and discrete cases, these two definitions are identical. The notation $E[g(y)]$ applies to both cases. The *concept* of expectation is the same regardless of whether the *implementation* is with the continuous or discrete case. In more advanced treatments the notation $E[g(y)]$ can apply to cases more general than continuous or discrete. Thus it has great unifying power.

The moments just defined are obtained with different specifications of g:

Specification of g	Moment
$g(y) = y$	mean μ
$g(y) = y^p$	pth moment about 0
$g(y) = (y - a)^p$	pth moment about a
$g(y) = (y - \mu)^2$	variance σ^2

Theorem 1 can be expressed as $\sigma^2 = E[y^2] - \mu^2$, which can also be written $E[y^2] = \sigma^2 + \mu^2$, that is, the second moment about zero is the variance plus the square of the mean. This is a general principle of mathematical statistics. The notation of mathematical expectation allows us to express it succinctly without referring to specific implementations like the continuous or discrete cases.

Moments of Transformed Variables

Moments are fundamental to statistical applications of probability theory. In this section, we outline important results for both empirical and theoretical distributions.

Empirical Distributions

Let $y_1, y_2, \ldots, y_n$ denote a data set with mean $\bar{y}$, variance s_y^2, and standard deviation $s_y = +\sqrt{s_y^2}$. We first investigate the effect of making the same linear transformation of each item in the data set. Specifically, define a new data set $x_1, x_2, \ldots, x_n$ by $x_i = a + by_i$ for each $i = 1, 2, \ldots, n$. Assume that $b \neq 0$. Let the mean, variance, and standard deviation of the x data set be denoted by $\bar{x}$, s_x^2, and $s_x = +\sqrt{s_x^2}$. The relationship between the means, variances, and standard deviations of the two data sets are given in Theorem 2.

THEOREM   2

$$\bar{x} = a + b\bar{y}$$
$$s_x^2 = b^2 s_y^2$$
$$s_x = |b| s_y, \text{ where } |b| \text{ denotes the absolute value of } b \quad \blacksquare$$

EXAMPLE   A2E

Standardization is a linear transformation—that is,

$$x_i = \frac{y_i - \bar{y}}{s_y} = -\left(\frac{\bar{y}}{s_y}\right) + \left(\frac{1}{s_y}\right) \cdot y_i \quad \text{for } i = 1, 2, \ldots, n$$

In our general notation, $a = -(\bar{y}/s_y)$ and $b = (1/s_y)$. Applying Theorem 2, we find that $\bar{x} = 0$ and $s_x^2 = 1 = s_x$. Standardization is a transformation that yields a data set with mean 0 and standard deviation 1. $\blacksquare$

Now consider a data structure with n cases and observations on two variables for each case, as indicated below.

Case (i)	x_i	y_i	$w_i = x_i + y_i$	$v_i = x_i - y_i$
1	x_1	y_1	$w_1 = x_1 + y_1$	$v_1 = x_1 - y_1$
2	x_2	y_2	$w_2 = x_2 + y_2$	$v_2 = x_2 - y_2$
:	:	:	:	:
n	x_n	y_n	$w_n = x_n + y_n$	$v_n = x_n - y_n$

Also shown in the table are columns of case-by-case sums and differences of the x and y observations. The sums are denoted by w's, the differences by v's. How are the means and variances of the w's and the v's related to the means and variances of the x's and y's? Theorem 3 explains.

T H E O R E M   **3**

$$\bar{w} = \bar{x} + \bar{y}$$
$$\bar{v} = \bar{x} - \bar{y}$$
$$s_w^2 = s_x^2 + s_y^2 + 2s_{xy}$$
$$s_v^2 = s_x^2 + s_y^2 - 2s_{xy}$$

where $(n - 1)s_{xy} = \sum_{i=1}^{n}(x_i - \bar{x})(y_i - \bar{y}) = \sum_{i=1}^{n} x_i y_i - n\bar{x}\bar{y}$ ∎

The quantity denoted by s_{xy} is called the covariance between the x observations and the y observations. As its name implies, it is a measure of covariation between the two data sets. To bring this idea home, refer to the definition of the correlation coefficient in Chapter 6. It can now be seen that r, the correlation coefficient, may be expressed as

$$r = \frac{s_{xy}}{s_x s_y}$$

that is, the covariance divided by the product of the standard deviations of the x observations and the y observations. From this, the correlation coefficient is 0 whenever the covariance is equal to 0. When $r = 0$, the x and y variables are said to be uncorrelated.

Theoretical Distributions

Consider a theoretical distribution that is either continuous with pdf $f(y)$ or discrete with mass function $f(y)$. Let $g(y)$ denote a function that maps the values of the y variable into some set of real numbers. The transformation creates a new variable, say, $x = g(y)$, which has a distribution. Let $h(y)$ denote the pdf or mass function of the new x distribution. Then there is a natural relationship between the moments of the x distribution and a certain function of the y distribution, which is spelled out in Theorem 4.

THEOREM   4

Given the definitions above, and subject to some mild restrictions on the function g, the following conditions exist:

If the y and x distributions are both continuous, then

$$\int_{-\infty}^{+\infty} x^p h(x)dx = \int_{-\infty}^{+\infty} [g(y)]^p f(y)dy$$

provided the second integral exists.

If the y distribution is discrete, then the x distribution is necessarily discrete, and the pth moment of the x distribution is

$$\sum_{x \in J_x} x^p h(x) = \sum_{y \in J_y} [g(y)]^p f(y)$$

provided the second sum exists. The symbols J_x and J_y denote the sets for which $h(x)$ and $f(y)$ are positive.   ■

Theorem 4 may be expressed in the notation of mathematical expectation as $E[x^p] = E[g(y)^p]$, where $x = g(y)$. This notation succinctly states a general principle of mathematical statistics.

EXAMPLE   A2F

Let μ_y and σ_y denote the mean and standard deviation of the y variable, and let $x = g(y) = (y - \mu_y)/\sigma_y$, the standardizing transformation. Theorem 4 can be used to show that the mean and standard deviation of the x variable are $\mu_x = 0$ and $\sigma_x = 1$.   ■

Theorem 4 can be applied to derive the following result: the mathematical expectation of a linear function of y is that linear function of the mathematical expectation. Simply use $x = g(y) = a + by$. In the notation of mathematical expectation, $E[a + by] = a + bE[y]$.

The last case covered is computing the sum or difference of two variables and asking for the mean and variance of the sum or difference. Let x and y be two variables that are either both of the continuous type or both of the discrete type. (Although the theory also covers the case where the variables are not both of the same type, that case is not discussed here.) Define new variables $w = x + y$ and $v = x - y$.

THEOREM   5

$$\mu_w = \mu_x + \mu_y$$
$$\mu_v = \mu_x - \mu_y$$
$$\sigma_w^2 = \sigma_x^2 + \sigma_y^2 + 2\sigma_{xy}$$
$$\sigma_v^2 = \sigma_x^2 + \sigma_y^2 - 2\sigma_{xy}$$

where σ_{xy} denotes the covariance between the x and y variables. The technical definition of the covariance of a theoretical joint distribution of two variables is beyond the scope of this text. The theoretical quantity is analogous to the sample quantity defined in Theorem 3. ∎

The theoretical *correlation coefficient* between two variables, x and y, is denoted by ρ and defined by $\rho = \sigma_{xy}/\sigma_x\sigma_y$, which is the covariance divided by the product of the standard deviations of the two variables. When the covariance is 0, the correlation coefficient is 0, and the variables are said to be uncorrelated.

Theorem 5 is a special case of the following general result.

THEOREM 6

Let x and y be variables with theoretical distributions having means μ_x and μ_y, variances σ_x^2 and σ_y^2, and covariance σ_{xy}. Define the new variable $w = ax + by$. Then the mean and variance of the theoretical distribution of w are

$$\mu_w = a\mu_x + b\mu_y$$

and
$$\sigma_w^2 = a^2\sigma_x^2 + b^2\sigma_x^2 + 2ab\sigma_{xy} \quad ∎$$

3

Simulation

Because statistical methods deal with variation, they are always applied in an environment of uncertainty. Rude surprises can stymie the cleverest attempts to overcome the undesirable effects of uncertainty because the degree of reliability or the relevance of the data can never be completely known. One way to prepare for some of these surprises is to study statistical calculations in environments where uncertainty is deliberately and artificially introduced. This is done by generating randomness, a property of uncertain outcomes that can be modeled using the mathematics of probability. In such experiments the researcher has more knowledge and control of the process creating the uncertainty than in practice. Thus, the consequences of randomness can be isolated and the insights gained can be applied to the analysis of data from real processes.

In Chapter 1, the notion of randomization was introduced. The distinction between surveys and experiments that employed randomization and those that did not was emphasized. In Chapters 9 and 11, two important models for random variation were presented: normal distributions and binomial distributions. Chapters 13 to 19 showed how to make probabilistic inferences from data collected with the aid of randomization. All these instances illustrate the practical utility of the concept of random variation.

The theory and practical implementation of randomness in this text are based on the random drawing of numbers from the unit interval $[0, 1)$, the set of real numbers between 0 and 1, 0 included, 1 excluded. A physical model for such drawings is the "spinner" pictured in Exhibit A3A. Ideally, imagine that all the

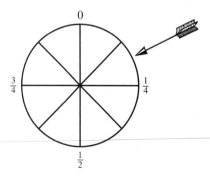

E X H I B I T   **A3A**   An Ideal Spinner That Chooses Numbers at Random from $[0, 1)$

numbers between 0 and 1 are represented on the circle. When the circle is spun, it finally comes to rest and the pointer points at a number that can be read off the circle. This is an idealization because in reality there is no infinitely thin pointer, and an infinitely fine scale cannot be read off the circle.

Theorists have developed computer algorithms that approximate the implementation of the ideal spinner to sufficient accuracy for practical use. Some algorithms programmed in statistical software are used here to illustrate important practical facts about randomness.

Exhibit A3B shows a frequency histogram of 500 drawings generated by an algorithm designed to produce random drawings from the numbers in the interval [0, 1). The histogram groups the 500 numbers into 10 subintervals of length 0.1. Intuition about randomness suggests that each of the subintervals should contain about $\frac{1}{10}$, or 50, of the numbers drawn. The frequencies of the subintervals are close to 50, though only two subintervals contain exactly 50 numbers. The deviations of the frequencies from the expected, or "ideal," number of 50 are one of the effects of randomness.

The ideal distribution of the random drawings from [0, 1) is called the *uniform distribution*. Exhibit A3B also shows this distribution.

Although the frequencies based on a set of random drawings are expected to deviate from the ideal frequencies, not all deviations would conform to our intuition about randomness. For example, if the frequencies in the 10 subintervals

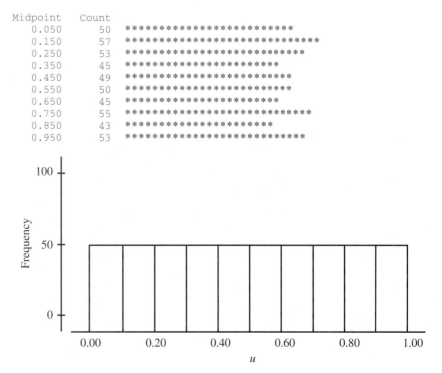

E X H I B I T   **A3B**   Histogram of 500 Random Drawings from [0, 1) and Histogram of the Ideal Uniform Distribution

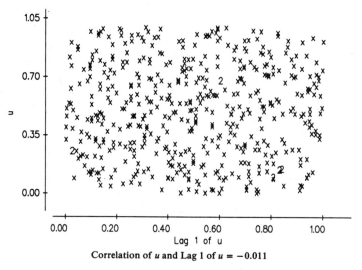

Correlation of *u* and Lag 1 of *u* = −0.011

E X H I B I T   **A3C**   First Lag Autocorrelation Analysis of Sequence of 500 Random Drawings from [0, 1) Made by Minitab

were 90, 80, 70, 60, 50, 50, 30, 30, 20, 20, we would conclude the drawings were not made randomly because there would be a clear bias in favor of the first four subintervals and against the last four.

Not all deviations from randomness are this blatant. Statistical tools are needed to help evaluate the hypothesis of randomness in less clear-cut practical cases.

Exhibit A3B shows a cross-sectional analysis of the 500 random drawings. But randomness also has longitudinal impact. Think of the *sequence* of drawings: the first, followed by the second, followed by the third, and so on. Intuition suggests that at a given stage in the sequence, knowledge of the outcomes of the drawings up to that stage should provide no help in predicting the outcome of the next drawing. This intuitive hypothesis may be tested by looking at the scatterplot of the adjacent values in the sequence and by computing the first lag autocorrelation coefficient of the sequence, as discussed in Section 6.8. Exhibit A3C displays these items. There is essentially no first lag autocorrelation in the sequence, a finding consistent with the hypothesis of randomness. Further analysis of the sequence not presented here shows there is no autocorrelation at any lag.

For practical purposes, software packages produce an adequate approximation to random drawings from [0, 1). From such a set of drawings, random drawings may be constructed from virtually any other distribution.

E X A M P L E   **A3A**   The following transformation was applied to each of the 500 random drawings reported in Exhibit A3B: $v = 2u - 1$, where *u* stands for one of the outcomes from [0, 1). This results in a new set of 500 numbers

```
Midpoint    Count
 -0.900       50   **************************
 -0.700       57   ******************************
 -0.500       53   ****************************
 -0.300       45   ************************
 -0.100       49   **************************
  0.100       50   **************************
  0.300       45   ************************
  0.500       55   *****************************
  0.700       43   ***********************
  0.900       53   ****************************
```

	n	Mean	Standard Deviation
u	500	0.4939	0.2903
$v = 2u - 1$	500	-0.0121	0.5807

E X H I B I T   **A3D**   Histogram and Descriptive Statistics of 500 Numbers Created by the Transformation $v = 2u - 1$, where u is Randomly Drawn from [0, 1)

(the v's) that range from -1 to 1 because the u's range from 0 to 1. Exhibit A3D shows a histogram of the 500 new numbers. Notice that the new numbers behave randomly. All the transformation did was to change the range of the numbers from [0, 1) to [-1, 1).

The transformation has an effect on the descriptive statistics of the numbers. Exhibit A3D shows the means and standard deviations for the two sets of numbers. The mean of the original set of numbers is 0.494, while the mean of the transformed set is -0.012. The standard deviation of the original set is 0.29, while the standard deviation of the transformed set is 0.58.[†]

If the ideal uniform distribution with 50 observations in each of the 10 classes had been used, the original set of numbers would have had a mean of 0.5 and a standard deviation of $\sqrt{1/12} = 0.29$. The mean and standard deviation of the new set of numbers formed by the transformation $v = 2u - 1$ would then be 0 and $2\sqrt{1/12} = 0.58$, using the rule in the footnote at the bottom of the page. You see that these "ideal" results are close to those obtained with the 500 numbers randomly drawn from [0, 1). This is another indication that the random number algorithm in the software produces plausible results.

Theory justifies treating the new set of numbers as random drawings from the interval [-1, 1). If such a set of drawings is needed for problem solving, a set of random drawings from [0, 1) may be chosen and transformed. ■

[†]The standard deviation of the new set is twice the standard deviation of the original set of numbers. This conforms to a mathematical property of linear transformations of random quantities. If a set of numbers, denoted by u, has standard deviation denoted by σ, the set of numbers denoted by $v = a + bu$ has standard deviation $|b|\sigma$, where $|b|$ denotes the absolute value of b. Also, if the mean of the original set of numbers is denoted by μ, the mean of the transformed set is $a + b\mu$. In this illustration, $\mu = 0.494$, $\sigma = 0.29$, $a = -1$, and $b = 2$. See Appendix 2 for a more complete discussion.

E X A M P L E   **A3B**   In Example A3A, the effects of a linear transformation on numbers drawn at random from [0, 1) were illustrated. This example shows the effects of a nonlinear transformation, the natural logarithm, which is denoted by log. Because all the values of u are fractions, their natural logarithms are negative. To make the new numbers positive, they are defined by the transformation $w = -\log(u)$, where u stands for one of the numbers drawn at random from [0, 1). The histogram of the new set of numbers in Exhibit A3E shows that their distribution is not uniform. The nonlinear logarithmic transformation has changed uniformly distributed numbers into numbers that have an *exponential distribution*, a probability distribution on [0, ∞) such that the probability assigned to the intervals of the form [0, w) is $1 - e^{-w}$. Exhibit A3E also shows a plot of the function $g(w) = e^{-w}$ for positive values of w. Notice the resemblance of this curve to the shape of the histogram.

Theory justifies treating the new numbers, denoted by w's, as random drawings from a population of numbers with the exponential dis-

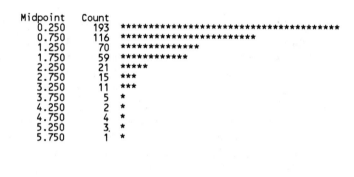

```
Midpoint   Count
  0.250     193   ****************************************
  0.750     116   ************************
  1.250      70   **************
  1.750      59   *************
  2.250      21   *****
  2.750      15   ***
  3.250      11   ***
  3.750       5   *
  4.250       2   *
  4.750       4   *
  5.250       3   *
  5.750       1   *
```

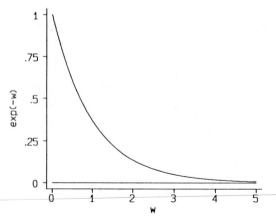

E X H I B I T   **A3E**   Histogram of 500 Random Drawings from an Exponential Distribution and a Graph of the Exponential Curve

tribution pictured in Exhibit A3E. Generally speaking, numbers drawn randomly from [0, 1)—that is, numbers with a uniform distribution—can be transformed into numbers with other distributions by making suitable transformations of them.   ■

In practice, transformations of numerical data that are subject to variation are constantly performed. The theory presented in this appendix provides insight into the consequences of these transformations and therefore helps us draw prudent conclusions from the data.

Simulating Random Walks

A pure *random walk* is the running totals of independent outcomes from a stable process with mean 0 and standard deviation σ.

To introduce the topic of random walks, consider a simple gambling game: matching pennies. You and a friend each toss a penny into the air and let the pennies fall. If the pennies match—that is, they both show heads or both show tails—you win your friend's penny. If they do not match, your friend wins your penny. You keep playing until one of you runs out of pennies or you tire of the game. The following table shows the possible outcomes of the game and the probabilities of the outcomes:

		Your Penny	
		Head	Tail
Your Friend's Penny	Head	1/4	1/4
	Tail	1/4	1/4

The chance of both pennies showing heads is 1/4, as is the chance of both pennies showing tails. Thus, the chance of a match is 1/2. This means that the chance of the pennies not matching is also 1/2. Each of you has a 50-50 chance of winning a penny.

Consider a sequence of plays of the game, keeping track not only of the result of each play but also of your net gain over the sequence. Exhibit A3F shows the result of 19 plays. In the Outcome column, a -1 means you lost a penny, whereas a 1 means you won a penny. The numbers in the Net Gain column are the running totals of the numbers in the Outcome column. For example, for play number 5, you won a penny, and your net gain after play number 5 is 3, meaning that in the first 5 plays you won three more pennies than you lost. At the end of the sequence of 19 plays, you are ahead by 5 pennies.

Play	Outcome	Net Gain
1	−1	−1
2	1	0
3	1	1
4	1	2
5	1	3
6	−1	2
7	−1	1
8	−1	0
9	−1	−1
10	1	0
11	1	1
12	−1	0
13	−1	−1
14	1	0
15	1	1
16	1	2
17	1	3
18	1	4
19	1	5

E X H I B I T   **A3F**   Results of 19 Plays of the Matching-Pennies Game

The game is essentially a sequence of Bernoulli trials. If your winning a penny is called a "success," and your friend's winning a penny a "failure," the probability of success is $\pi = 1/2$. If success is coded as $u = 1$ and failure as $u = 0$, the outcome of a play is

$$y = 2u - 1$$

And if $y_1, y_2, \ldots, y_n$ is a sequence of n outcomes, your net gain over the sequence is

$$y_1 + y_2 + \cdots + y_n = \sum_{i=1}^{n} y_i$$

These formulas make it easy to simulate the matching-pennies game on a computer, which can play much faster than you and your friend can with real pennies. A good understanding of the properties of the game can be gained by studying the data from simulations.

To illustrate, 360 Bernoulli (0–1) trials were generated with $\pi = 1/2$. The result of each trial, u, was transformed by $2u - 1$ to obtain the outcome of that play of the game. This yielded a sequence of −1's and +1's. The latter sequence was cumulated to obtain the sequence of net gains, which is plotted in a sequence plot in Exhibit A3G.

The process plotted in Exhibit A3G meanders. Between trials 1 and 50 it hovers about 0; in the next 120 trials it stays mostly below 0; and in the remaining trials it stays strictly above 0. There are long stretches where one player is ahead.

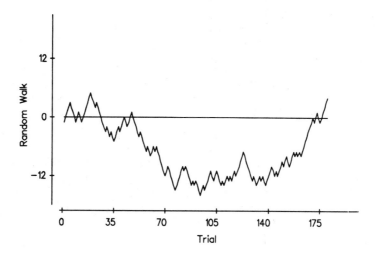

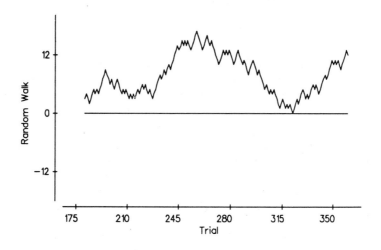

	n	Mean	Standard Deviation	Minimum	Maximum
Gambles	360	0.0333	1.001	− 1	1
Random walk	360	0.494	8.859	−16	17

E X H I B I T   **A3G**   Sequence Plot of Net Gains from 360 Plays of Matching Pennies

This is rather surprising behavior for a process that is generated by a stable Bernoulli process. The *cumulation* of stable Bernoulli outcomes produces a wildly unstable process!

Now in the 360 plays represented in Exhibit A3G, you win 186 times, and your friend wins 174 times; almost an even split, as is expected from a Bernoulli process with $\pi = 1/2$. The average of your winnings is $\bar{y} = [186(1) + 174(-1)]/360 = 0.03 \approx 0$, the long-run average of the Bernoulli-like winnings process. A game with 0 long-run average winnings for each player is called "fair" in mathematical literature.

The average of the cumulative winnings, or your net gain, is 0.494, which is also close to 0. The mathematical theory of random walks says that, for a fair game, the long-run average of the net gains is 0. In other words, in the long run the swings above and below 0 tend to cancel each other out in such a way that the average net gain is zero. Neither player should expect to gain much in a very long sequence of plays.

However, the sequence plot in Exhibit A3G shows that both players can expect to win or lose substantial amounts at some point during the long sequence of plays. If the game had stopped at the "right time," you would have had a net gain of 17 pennies. Your friend could have won 16 pennies if the game has stopped at a "right time" for her. Moreover, the theory says that the longer you play, the larger the excursions away from 0 will be! In theory, the only limit to your winnings, provided you stop at the "right time," is your friend's total assets, and vice versa.

You can confirm this result by thinking of your net gain as a total of n independent observations from a stable Bernoulli-like process with mean $\mu = 0$ and standard deviation $\sigma = 1$.[†] From the discussion of the central limit effect in Chapter 9, we know that the mean of the total is $n\mu = n(0) = 0$ and the standard deviation of the total is $\sqrt{n}\sigma = \sqrt{n}(1) = \sqrt{n}$, which gets larger as the number of plays, n, gets larger. This is why, in principle, there is no limit to the sizes of the excursions away from the mean of 0 in very long sequences of plays.

The general definition of random walk shows that any stable process with mean 0 and standard deviation σ can be substituted for the Bernoulli-like process used to illustrate the matching-pennies game. Different distributions are appropriate for different applications.

An important generalization of the random walk is the *random walk with drift*. This process is obtained by assuming that the y variables have nonzero mean δ (the lowercase Greek d, called delta). The parameter δ is called the *drift parameter*. If δ is positive and very small, the random walk will appear to drift gradually upward over a long period of time. This is the case for many stock prices, so the random walk with drift rather than the pure random walk is often used as a model for stock prices.

[†]The underlying Bernoulli process variable u has $\pi = 0.5$, mean $1 \cdot \pi = 0.5$, and standard deviation $\sqrt{1 \cdot \pi(1 - \pi)} = 0.5$. The winnings variable is $y = 2u - 1 = a + b \cdot u$, where $a = -1$ and $b = 2$. From Appendix 2, the mean of the winnings variable is $2(0.5) - 1 = 0$, and the standard deviation of the winnings variable is $2(0.5) = 1$.

4

Selected Data Set Listings

These six large data sets are not listed in the text chapters:

Amana Microwave Oven Assembly-Line Data (AMANA.DAT), used in Chapter 2.

Car Sales Data by County in Wisconsin (AUTOSALE.DAT), used in Chapter 21.

Computer Battery Life Data (COMPUTER.DAT), used in Chapters 7 and 21.

Population of 200 Regression Data (RSQUARE.DAT), used in Chapter 20.

Restaurant Survey Data (RESTRNT.DAT), used in Chapters 5 and 6.

Los Angeles Traffic Data (TRAFFIC.DAT), used in Chapters 4 and 20.

Amana Microwave Oven Assembly-Line Data

Left and Right distances between the oven wrapper edge and the waveguide measured on microwave ovens produced by Amana Refrigeration, Inc. There are observations on 120 ovens. Further description of the data is given in Chapter 2 in Exhibit 2.8A.

```
filename: AMANA.DAT
Microwave oven assembly data, 1986
(Source: Robert Cech, Amana Refrigeration, Amana, Iowa)
Left and Right measurements on waveguide position
56  54    50  62    58   62    66   78    50  39    44  50
70  58    56  66    72   42    50   56    56  47    50  39
71  74    51  58    44   44    84   71    48  35    51  44
58  58    44  50    55   68    89   86    58  50    54  48
52  32    56  58    40   50    71   80    60  39    44  47
58  54    50  50    74   78    69   78    60  48    50  48
38  32    48  58    50   58    73   79    51  61    48  56
60  60    40  46    80   85    80   66    64  60    44  50
60  54    50  56    70   83    79   81    59  60    47  54
70  82    48  58    92   67    64   70    51  46    41  50
48  42    44  54    90   59    45   59    50  59    50  44
52  40    50  58    81   74    22   27    60  64    45  39
68  68    54  55    60   48    42   44    54  59    48  51
48  52    32  56    68   78    66   56    58  45    47  64
50  51    58  56    80   72    56   71    41  47    50  49
48  46    60  52    73   90    69   69    40  49    46  51
52  62    56  64    64   73    34   35    51  54    55  57
56  66    70  72    80  121    36   40    56  58    56  51
65  80    80  94    78   96    36   44    28  39    48  46
45  54    74  68    81   78    45   40    55  41    51  48
```

Car Sales Data by County in Wisconsin

Filename: AUTOSALE.DAT
Data on car sales, average age, income, and
unemployment rate for the 72 counties of Wisconsin.
Based on a student project
Variables: Sales, Age, Income, Umemp, County

Sales	Age	Income	Umemp	County	Sales	Age	Income	Umemp	County
18.4288	40.2	21.548	10.6	ADAMS	23.8821	32.7	30.143	3.9	MARATHON
18.5810	33.7	19.012	9.7	ASHLAND	20.2229	35.6	22.396	7.4	MARINETT
17.1288	34.5	22.570	6.5	BARROW	25.8096	39.1	22.234	5.9	MARQUETTE
18.0611	37.2	20.666	9.0	BAYFIELD	18.2519	24.5	14.122	20.7	MENOMINEE
32.7400	31.4	31.303	4.6	BROWN	22.1459	32.3	27.867	6.8	MILWAUKEE
15.6802	34.9	23.573	4.0	BUFFALO	17.9892	33.7	24.799	4.7	MONROE
14.8273	39.2	20.153	8.5	BURNETT	20.8099	35.0	22.927	7.3	OCONTO
21.1134	31.3	34.050	3.6	CALUMET	29.4833	38.7	23.901	6.4	ONEIDA
16.1765	33.4	25.858	6.2	CHIPPEWA	35.2715	31.4	33.770	4.0	OUTAGAMIE
13.0818	33.9	22.177	5.2	CLARK	43.3607	34.6	42.695	2.5	OZAUKEE
26.7699	35.3	28.360	4.3	COLUMBIA	19.4175	35.1	22.992	4.8	PEPIN
17.3777	34.9	21.436	5.6	CRAWFORD	19.8688	29.3	30.520	5.3	PIERCE
38.3862	30.7	32.703	3.2	DANE	17.9450	34.6	24.267	6.7	POLK
23.3284	33.8	29.166	4.3	DODGE	22.9786	29.3	28.686	5.0	PORTAGE
23.1218	36.5	26.259	6.3	DOOR	19.7436	36.8	22.662	5.6	PRICE
21.8401	34.8	22.122	9.5	DOUGLAS	29.7542	32.9	32.751	5.9	RACINE
14.5089	28.5	24.452	6.3	DUNN	16.6657	35.3	21.946	5.4	RICHLAND
21.5301	30.3	25.886	6.3	EAU CLAIRE	31.3526	33.0	30.362	6.2	ROCK
15.2505	36.2	22.416	7.5	FLORENCE	13.3298	35.2	19.617	9.7	RUSK
25.5431	33.4	29.441	4.1	FOND DU LAC	24.9547	31.6	36.716	4.1	ST.CROIX
21.1942	35.7	16.907	11.0	FOREST	26.8015	34.2	26.217	6.0	SAUK
20.9281	31.5	24.505	4.9	GRANT	20.4499	38.2	18.094	11.7	SAWYER
27.0938	34.4	28.435	4.0	GREEN	18.3815	35.3	23.841	6.0	SHAWANO
23.3768	36.8	25.708	6.1	GREEN LAKE	26.0115	33.8	31.603	4.1	SHEBOYGAN
20.7444	33.2	25.914	3.9	IOWA	12.2216	32.3	24.304	6.5	TAYLOR
21.9405	42.1	17.537	7.1	IRON	15.0022	35.7	23.864	4.6	TREMPEALEAU
17.2414	35.5	21.409	7.7	JACKSON	16.4344	36.2	21.548	5.0	VERNON
22.5868	32.8	20.749	3.8	JEFFERSON	26.9385	42.9	20.352	7.7	VILAS
17.9677	35.5	22.073	6.6	JUNEAU	30.6800	33.1	30.345	3.9	WALWORTH
31.4633	32.5	30.638	6.8	KENOSHA	18.6611	38.0	19.962	7.9	WASHBURN
22.2481	33.9	26.927	3.4	KEWAUNEE	32.7920	32.5	28.431	3.1	WASHINGTON
24.2687	31.2	26.857	4.8	LACROSSE	44.2282	34.0	44.565	2.9	WAUKESHA
19.2212	33.6	24.479	3.6	LAFAYETTE	19.8681	35.0	26.083	5.5	WAUPACA
17.0213	36.6	20.703	6.4	LANGLADE	18.8806	30.6	21.888	7.2	WAUSHARA
19.0420	34.9	25.175	6.6	LINCOLN	22.6462	32.5	30.007	4.4	WINNEBAGO
22.6185	34.6	27.467	5.0	MANITOWOC	19.4416	33.3	29.735	6.1	WOOD

Computer Battery Life Data

Battery life is measured in two ways: ZDigit and Rundown. The weight of the battery and make and model of the computer are also given. The data is further described in Example 7.8A.

```
filename: COMPUTER.DAT
Battery Life for portable computers
Source: PC Magazine, August, 1992
Variables: ZDigit(hours), Rundown (hours), Battery weight (lbs.), Make & model
```

ZDigit	Rundown	Weight	Make & model	ZDigit	Rundown	Weight	Make & model
4.78	2.88	1.1	Altec 386/25	4.33	3.33	1.0	Micro Express NB913
1.85	1.62	2.2	Aquiline NT33	4.10	2.93	1.0	Micro Express NB925
2.30	1.78	1.2	AST Prem Exec 386SX/20	2.52	2.47	1.3	Micro Express NB2500
6.20	3.92	1.2	AST Prem Exec 386SX/25	4.12	2.03	1.4	Mitsuba Ninja 386SX/20
4.80	2.93	1.1	Austin 386SX-25	2.73	2.03	0.6	NBCC 386SL/20
2.75	1.98	1.8	BCC Avanti 025	5.25	4.10	0.8	NCR Safari NSX/20
1.62	1.82	1.2	BCC SL007	1.83	1.63	0.8	NCR System 3170
2.98	1.75	1.1	Blackship NB 320S	3.75	2.08	1.0	NEC UltraLite SL/20
2.98	2.20	1.3	Blue Star 386DX/25	2.75	1.63	1.0	NEC UltraLite SL/20P
4.35	3.05	1.0	Blue Star 386SX/25	1.83	1.75	0.7	NEC UltraLite III
2.05	1.62	0.8	Bondwell 386SL/F	4.57	3.57	1.0	MicroStar NP-913 386SX/20
3.43	2.28	1.3	Compaq LTE Lite/25	4.80	3.15	1.0	MicroStar NP-925 386SX/25
3.43	2.27	1.3	Compaq LTE Lite/20	2.75	2.57	1.7	Olivetti S20
4.12	2.98	1.8	Compaq LTE 386s/20	3.67	2.57	1.4	Packard Bell 386SX/20
5.47	1.52	0.5	CompuAdd Express 325NXL	2.75	2.47	1.4	PC Brand 386SX/25
3.43	2.73	1.3	Compudyne 386SXL/25	3.87	3.12	1.4	Poly 320T
2.08	2.20	1.3	Compudyne 486DX/33	2.53	2.03	1.4	Positive PC320ND
2.30	1.60	1.4	Cumulus Express 386SX/20	1.40	1.23	0.7	Proteus 386/20NB
2.27	1.70	1.2	Dauphin 1050	3.65	2.25	1.1	Sanyo MBC-18NB6H
3.43	2.15	0.8	DECpc 320P	2.07	1.78	0.8	Sharp PC-6781
3.43	2.43	1.3	Dell System NL25	3.87	2.65	1.4	Swan 386SX/20
5.20	3.03	1.6	Dell System 325N	2.07	1.60	0.8	Swan 386SX/25
3.48	2.55	0.7	Epson NB-SL/20	2.50	2.65	0.9	Tandy 3830 SL
3.65	2.28	0.7	Epson NB-SL/25	2.38	2.25	1.3	Tandy 4860 HD
2.52	1.77	0.7	Everex Tempo Carrier 386SX/20	4.33	3.80	1.0	Tartan NP-925
5.68	3.57	1.3	Gateway Nomad 325SXL	5.25	3.42	1.1	Tenex NB25SX
4.57	3.68	1.3	Gateway Nomad 420SXL	3.20	2.48	1.2	TI TravelMate 3000 WinSX
5.50	4.08	1.3	Gateway Nomad 425DXL	4.10	3.37	1.5	Toshiba T2200SX
2.30	1.75	1.1	Identity 386SX/20	3.67	3.62	1.4	Toshiba T3300SX
2.30	1.75	0.7	Insight 386-25SXL	4.32	3.67	2.3	Toshiba T4400SX (LCD)
2.50	1.88	1.3	Intelec Haikan 386SX/20	3.92	3.20	2.3	Toshiba T4400SX (Plasma)
3.20	2.68	1.4	KRIS Master 386SX/25	2.57	2.57	0.7	Transource Verxion 386SX/20
4.33	3.10	1.4	Matrix 386SX/20				

Population of 200 Regression Data

These data are used in Section 20.11 to illustrate difficulties in interpreting R^2

```
filename: RSQUARE.DAT
Population of 200 Y and X values
```

Y	X	Y	X	Y	X
7.7216	97.390	9.4082	99.398	10.5848	100.342
8.4778	97.719	10.0677	99.404	9.9352	100.364
7.7187	97.724	9.9640	99.424	10.4771	100.383
8.4557	97.740	10.5509	99.434	11.1437	100.384
6.7515	97.935	9.5574	99.456	10.0875	100.411
8.0277	97.981	8.9212	99.470	10.9831	100.428
9.0801	98.086	8.7668	99.473	11.2113	100.440
7.8140	98.099	8.2434	99.547	10.3640	100.442
8.3641	98.179	8.9679	99.574	11.1437	100.443
7.0371	98.206	9.8732	99.615	9.9331	100.462
8.5759	98.240	9.6428	99.626	11.4849	100.466
9.1042	98.256	10.1303	99.639	9.8936	100.466
8.7486	98.262	9.9066	99.651	10.5048	100.483
9.0460	98.305	10.8610	99.653	9.9248	100.485
8.7265	98.335	9.7618	99.656	10.1802	100.520
7.7648	98.366	9.7667	99.712	10.1911	100.524
9.5704	98.413	10.2679	99.719	11.5284	100.570
8.9114	98.439	9.5005	99.722	10.1004	100.573
8.3608	98.489	8.9544	99.740	10.9566	100.586
7.3781	98.515	9.7174	99.742	10.5631	100.599
8.9414	98.656	11.4663	99.759	11.1717	100.623
9.8830	98.670	10.0461	99.779	11.3292	100.630
8.8700	98.675	9.4557	99.783	10.6046	100.635
7.6031	98.677	9.5380	99.795	10.9252	100.667
10.0445	98.691	10.0226	99.813	9.6129	100.683
9.7655	98.693	9.5913	99.827	10.5870	100.729
8.6292	98.700	10.9460	99.852	9.9740	100.735
9.9338	98.751	10.0910	99.889	10.8506	100.739
9.9384	98.785	9.8073	99.909	9.6707	100.750
8.2317	98.803	8.0018	99.941	10.5250	100.753
9.0142	98.827	9.4913	99.962	10.4211	100.753
8.8822	98.828	10.7485	99.967	10.9387	100.772
7.8507	98.832	10.6406	99.968	10.8419	100.786
9.4946	98.838	10.3909	99.976	11.0124	100.801
9.7688	98.856	9.8486	99.983	10.6489	100.813
8.6732	98.878	9.8353	100.010	10.1225	100.816
8.8615	98.879	10.5057	100.051	10.1457	100.825
9.4466	98.910	10.2935	100.052	9.5475	100.849
9.9286	99.002	10.9814	100.052	10.4423	100.865
8.5382	99.009	9.4287	100.063	11.3707	100.881
9.9369	99.104	9.6036	100.067	11.2337	100.912
9.9029	99.108	8.4918	100.067	11.6613	100.973
8.2602	99.109	9.9808	100.076	12.2551	100.984
9.4517	99.110	10.5207	100.079	11.6505	100.986
9.7667	99.111	9.1734	100.107	12.0307	100.996
9.9274	99.139	10.1677	100.131	9.7924	101.022
8.1069	99.147	9.6243	100.138	10.9549	101.024
9.7023	99.157	10.6597	100.156	10.6963	101.047
9.5023	99.166	9.3408	100.162	10.8563	101.049
8.6325	99.196	9.9286	100.163	11.0482	101.107
9.9136	99.199	10.2979	100.168	11.3591	101.213
9.7994	99.208	10.0891	100.184	11.8929	101.226
9.0986	99.222	11.0848	100.214	10.7626	101.238
9.1281	99.224	10.6025	100.235	10.5514	101.341
9.4777	99.237	9.6156	100.244	11.8054	101.379
9.4478	99.242	9.2066	101.261	11.5956	101.391
9.5831	99.255	10.1315	100.269	11.1049	101.412
8.6809	99.271	10.0666	100.269	10.4703	101.453
9.8395	99.284	10.5068	100.281	10.7383	101.467
9.6125	99.317	10.8306	100.284	10.6276	101.542
9.5515	99.327	10.0337	100.286	11.5006	101.583
9.0917	99.332	10.2038	100.291	10.1321	101.599
9.4938	99.342	9.9186	100.308	12.8224	101.712
9.3727	99.359	10.6547	101.309	11.4666	101.793
9.0947	99.363	9.5292	100.317	11.8573	102.278
8.9342	99.375	9.6373	100.319	11.7150	102.341
8.4906	99.395	9.5195	100.324		

Restaurant Survey Data

These data are from a 1980 survey conducted by the University of Wisconsin Small Business Development Center. The data are used extensively in Chapters 5 and 6.

```
filename: RESTRNT.DAT
Wisconsin restaurant survey data
Variable: Description
ID number
Business Outlook categorized as
        1 = very unfavorable . . . 6 = very favorable
Sales: Gross 1979 sales in $1000's
New capital: New capital invested in 1979
Value: Estimated market value of business ($1000's)
Cost of goods: Cost of goods sold as % of sales
Wages: Wages as % of sales
Advertising: $ as % of sales
Type: 1=fast food, 2=supper club, 3=other
Seats: number of dining seats
Owner: 1=sole proprietorship, 2=partnership, 3=corp.
Full Time: # of full time employees
Part Time: # of part time employees
Size: Size of restaurant categorized as
        1 = 1 to 9.5 full time equivalent employees
        2 = 10 to 20 full time equivalent employees
        3 = more than 20 full time equivalent employees
        (Full time equivalent=full time + 1/2part time)
```

1	2	480	0	600	35	25	2	2	200	3	8	30	3
2	4	507	22	375	59	20	5	2	150	1	6	25	2
3	5	210	25	275	40	24	3	1	46	1	0	17	1
4	5	246	*	80	43	30	1	1	28	3	2	13	1
5	2	148	*	85	45	35	1	3	44	1	*	*	*
6	3	50	*	135	40	30	10	2	50	3	2	*	*
7	2	72	0	125	85	10	5	2	50	1	0	5	1
8	3	99	7	150	43	25	1	2	130	1	1	8	1
9	4	160	5	85	*	*	*	*	*	2	2	10	1
10	4	243	7	150	38	15	2	2	50	2	2	19	2
11	4	200	3	225	42	22	2	1	64	1	3	12	1
12	4	1000	20	1500	20	20	10	1	240	3	30	40	3
13	4	350	*	*	31	35	*	1	111	3	10	19	2
14	3	550	0	410	50	26	2	2	125	3	6	16	2
15	3	500	10	1000	50	40	10	2	120	1	4	28	2
16	4	1100	8	900	*	*	*	*	*	3	13	47	3
17	3	416	0	400	40	21	4	1	92	3	7	15	2
18	2	650	*	*	63	32	5	1	90	3	20	25	3
19	5	292	0	425	42	13	1	2	150	3	1	16	1
20	3	400	10	350	30	25	5	2	90	1	15	10	2
21	3	42	0	15	64	35	1	3	15	2	0	0	1
22	2	100	15	185	50	15	1	2	80	3	0	7	1
23	4	75	0	160	*	*	*	2	76	1	0	10	1
24	3	180	0	180	50	20	2	2	65	1	1	14	1
25	4	201	0	250	70	27	3	2	178	1	0	20	2
26	6	273	60	300	32	28	10	3	110	3	7	13	2
27	4	150	0	150	*	*	*	2	60	*	51	80	3
28	5	60	4	100	*	*	*	1	0	1	0	0	1
29	4	1200	50	800	35	32	3	3	150	3	35	45	3
30	3	247	4	*	38	*	2	1	60	3	4	8	1
31	2	290	3	200	39	29	1	1	85	3	16	14	3
32	2	58	*	75	45	28	5	2	25	3	2	2	1
33	4	400	0	100	40	35	1	3	85	3	18	15	3
34	3	75	*	26	40	40	5	3	20	2	4	4	1
35	5	*	*	*	32	40	4	2	200	*	*	*	*
36	4	144	0	25	45	25	0	3	0	1	6	3	1
37	4	65	0	25	48	20	1	1	0	1	2	2	1
38	3	*	*	*	*	*	*	1	210	*	*	*	*
39	4	465	0	75	38	28	7	1	111	3	6	32	3
40	5	*	*	*	50	40	10	3	0	3	10	5	2
41	5	510	3	750	35	29	4	1	152	3	30	25	3

```
 42 3   440    0      *  38 20   5 1   62 3    9  16 2
 43 4   608   30    395  31 28   2 3  165 3   30  12 3
 44 3   200    3    350  43 21   4 1   68 2    3  18 2
 45 1    90    5     40  60 30  10 1   60 1    3   3 1
 46 5    45    3     40  40 20   3 3    0 1    0   7 1
 47 6    36    1      *  65 25   5 1    0 2    3   0 1
 48 4   249    6    275  65 30   5 1   52 1    8  10 2
 49 5   200    5     60  35 20   2 3   24 3    4  20 2
 50 2    80    0    150  60 30   5 2   70 1    1   4 1
 51 1   500    5    350  40 30   3 1   72 3   20   6 3
 52 2   125   10    140  50 20   5 2   68 3    0   8 1
 53 2   101    0    140  54 13   1 2   58 1    2   3 1
 54 4   110    2    160  60 20   1 2   60 1    0   6 1
 55 3  1200    0   2500  37 29   3 1  200 3   80  45 3
 56 1     *    *      *  33 25  25 3  120 3   25   5 3
 57 4  4700   20   1500  50 20   4 1  200 3   15  50 3
 58 3    48    0     45  45 25   2 3   10 3    0  12 1
 59 2   150   20    150  45 25   5 3    0 3   10  20 2
 60 1   185   40      *  40 40   4 1   62 3    2  18 2
 61 4   157    2    250   *  *   * 1   99 1    3   8 1
 62 6   621    9      0  36 23   3 1  120 3    5  45 3
 63 2   257   10    365  40 22   0 1  100 1   14   3 2
 64 2   137    0     75  55 30   3 1    0 3    1   3 1
 65 1   190    0    400  60 40   0 1  125 1    2  11 1
 66 1     *    *      *   *  *   * *    0 *    *   * *
 67 2   320    6    350  50 20   3 2   96 1   10  10 2
 68 5   650    *      *  50 30   1 2  140 3   20  15 3
 69 5  6110   61      *  38 19   5 1  100 3   10  30 3
 70 2   385    4    150  36 29   4 3   48 3   20  28 3
 71 5   360   75    325  29 23   3 1  120 3    4  15 2
 72 1   276    *    200  65 30   5 1    0 3   20   3 3
 73 6   600   20    500  38 22   2 2  125 3   28   5 3
 74 2   330    0    100  45 25   2 1    0 1    2  14 1
 75 3   215   10    125  45 30   2 1   15 1   11   0 2
 76 3   425   15   1750  39 27  12 3  250 1    2  70 3
 77 4   250   10     10  40 40  10 2   80 3   10   4 2
 78 2   120    0     80   *  *   * 3   30 1    1   2 1
 79 3    60   30     45  60 30  10 1   16 2    0   4 1
 80 3   141    6     80  85 10   5 1   34 2    0   4 1
 81 5   800   50    500  50 25   5 3  120 2   35  13 3
 82 3   207    4    200  48 20   1 1    0 *    *   * *
 83 5  1016   16   1000  40 36   1 3  200 3   20  40 3
 84 3    60    0     40  50 20   3     80 3    2   4 1
 85 3   309   10    500  52 18   2 2   80 1    6  14 2
 86 2   960   20    400  54 22   2 3    0 3    7  40 3
 87 3   150    *    650  70 20  10 2  220 3    3  18 2
 88 4    56    5    125  40 20  10 2   44 1    0   2 1
 89 6   250    5    100  33 30   2 1   55 3   10  15 2
 90 4   275   10    295  50 25   5 2   85 3   10   3 2
 91 5   150   50    300  30 30   0 1   77 3    4  13 2
 92 4   325    2    175  45 25   5 3  125 3   20   6 3
 93 5   110    5    235  50 30  20 2   65 2    2  10 1
 94 3   250    5    230  50 30   4 2   90 3    4  12 2
 95 3   550    0    500  48 22   2 2  100 3   13   6 2
 96 1   100    3    200  35 25   0 1   50 3    0   6 1
 97 3    32    1     42  35 10   2 1   30 1    3   0 1
 98 7   366   10    300  42 25   1 2  150 3   12  40 3
 99 5    70    3    150  50  7   2 2   50 3    3   2 1
100 3   531    2    450  46 30   1 3   72 3    1  39 3
101 4   225    0    300  50 40   0 1   43 1   10   4 2
102 3   108    5    110   *  *   * *    * 2    0   8 1
103 3   100    *      *  86 14   0 3    0 1    3   2 1
104 4    40    4     75  30  1   1 3   20 1    *   2 *
105 4   750    0   1000  40 22   5 2  140 2   15  25 3
106 2   312    *    250  40 34   2 3  110 3    6  20 2
107 2    50    5     75  40 20   5 3   56 1    0   5 1
108 5   163    3    115  50 28   5 2   75 3    5   4 1
109 1    75    1     55   *  *   * 3   32 1    0   0 1
110 6   550    6    600  48 24   1 2   76 2    3  30 2
111 1  3450    8    100   *  *   * 2   80 3    3   9 1
112 3    50    4    305  45  9   4 2   60 1    4   6 1
113 5    80    0     50  43 18   2 3    0 1    0   6 1
114 3   435   10    250  30 14   5 3   36 1    1  11 1
115 1    70    2     75  30 35   0 1    0 1    1   2 1
116 1    78    0    125  90  0  10 3   62 1    5   0 1
117 5   210   20    225  80 18   2 1   28 1    0   5 1
118 4   280    *    300  40 16   8 1   50 3    2  18 2
119 4   192    *    300  35 85   5 2   82 3    8   4 2
120 4   116   15    135  50  *   * 1   28 1    2   7 1
121 5   245    0    450  36 24   2 2  100 3    7  20 2
122 1   110    *    160   *  *   * 2   80 1    0   0 1
123 2   229    *    150  35 25   5 1   72 3    7   8 2
124 4   275    *   1100  60 40   0 1   96 3    4   7 1
125 1   100    *     75  50 20   2 3   46 1    4   4 1
126 4   647   10    350  50 30   5 1   90 3    5  12 2
127 4   300    1    100   *  *   * 3    * 3    *   * *
128 7    54    0      *  35 20  15 3   70 *    0   0 1
129 5   400    *    300   *  *   * 3   78 3    3  25 2
130 2   120    2    100  84 15   1 2   55 1    1   5 1
131 5     *    *      *  30 15   9 1   40 3   10  15 2
132 1   179    6     70  43 23   2 1   27 1    1  15 1
133 4   300    3    175  35 30   1 1   30 3    7   8 2
134 3   500  125    300  45 78   5 1  125 3   10  22 3
135 2   150   12    210  45 15   2 2   60 1    0  10 1
136 3   135    2     90  60 18   2 1   42 1    3   4 1
137 5   400    4    250  42 35   1 1   36 3   13   3 2
138 1   480    *    450  57 38   0 2  200 2   30   8 3
139 3   530   40    200  40 30   8 2  180 3   25  12 3
140 5     *    *      *   *  *   * 3   20 1    0   2 1
141 5   600   12     90  35 30   5 1   30 3   36   4 3
142 4     *    4    150  42  0   2 3   50 1    7   3 1
143 2   125    1      *  55 20   2 1   35 3    3   8 1
144 2   382    0    190   *  *   * 1   51 3    4   0 1
145 5     *    *    400  30 13   4 1  100 3    2   7 1
146 3   200   10    200  30 30   5 3   50 3    4  12 2
147 5   800   21    750  38 25   3 3  144 3   20  21 3
148 4   144    *    200  40 20   1 2   50 1    2   5 1
149 4   130    1    150   0 40   1 2   60 3    3   9 1
150 2  1010   50      *  50 25   3 2  127 3   25  35 3
151 5    60    5    150   *  *   * 3   25 1    0   2 1
152 4   292   20    100  49 30   8 2   75 2    6  24 2
153 3   100   56      *  45 25   5 2   75 3    6  14 2
154 3    98    0     70  70 28   2 1   32 1    0   7 1
155 2   250    6    250  50 25   1 2   90 3    7   7 2
156 4   172    1    200  35 14   3 1    0 1    0  20 2
157 3   145   12    155   *  *   * 2   74 1    1   9 1
158 4     *    *      *   *  *   * 2    0 3    *   0 *
159 1     *    *      *   *  *   * *    * *    *   * *
160 4     *    *      *   *  *   * 1    0 3    3   1 1
161 3    37    1     20  45 10   1 3   12 1    1   1 1
162 3     *    *      *   *  *   3 1   82 2    5  22 2
163 4    77    0    150   *  *   * 1   35 2    4   1 1
164 3   400    *    400   *  *   * 1   44 3    6   8 2
165 4  1000   20      *  40 34   2 2    * 2    *   * *
166 2   250   15    750  40 20   5 2   95 3   26  13 3
167 4    50    *     90   *  *   * 3   24 1    0   0 1
168 1   120    6      *  80 15   5 1   70 1    1   6 1
169 4   750   78      0  30 32   3 3   94 2   40   6 3
170 5   190    8     75  42 31   1 3   60 3    6   3 1
171 1   140    5    180  40  5   5 2   87 1    3   3 1
172 4    80   52     60  36 23   1 2  100 1    0   8 1
173 5    55    0     50  50 20  10 3   40 3    0   6 1
174 5   690    0    250  45 21   3 3  196 3    8  35 3
175 4   200    1    175  49 19   2 1  100 1    0  18 1
176 4    28    2     55  33  0   1 3   34 3    0   0 1
177 5    40    1      0   *  *   * 3   24 3    1   3 1
```

```
178 4    2   0     2 30  5  0 1  10 3    0   2 1       229 3  250  50 1000 35 35  0 3 150 3  25  30 3
179 2  217   0   750 51 29  4 2  95 3    3  25 2       230 2   30   5   40 30 30  3 3  55 1   1   4 1
180 4  250   0   300 40 30 10 1  20 3   10  10 2       231 2   20   1    0 45 20  2 3   0 3   0   3 1
181 3  990   * 1500 40 29  5 1 175 3   12  43 3        232 *    *   *    * 40 10  5 1   0 *   *   * *
182 4    2   2     * 90 10  0 1   0 2    0   4 1       233 2  125   5  125 50 30 10 1  65 1   0   6 1
183 3   50  20   325 50 30 20 2  75 3    2   3 1       234 4  720  13  650 37 24  6 1 150 3   6  25 2
184 7  290 150   450 51 59  3 2 110 1    5  14 2       235 4    *   *    * 40 30  5 3 150 3  25 100 3
185 1   75  10   140  *  *  * 1   0 1    0   0 1       236 1  240   3  225 50 20  2 2  30 1   5   6 1
186 1    *   *     *  *  *  * * *  1 0 1    0   0 1     237 4   10   *   10 50 38  2 3  35 2   3  10 1
187 5  400  10   300 20 25  5 2  85 3   10  10 2       239 6   59   *    *  *  *  * 3   0 2   2   4 1
188 3   30   3    60 49 30  1 1   0 2    2   4 1       240 3 1080  20 1000 32 30  5 3 170 3  40  50 3
189 2   70   0    32 40 30  1 3  65 1    2   3 1       241 1  225   1  150 34 22  4 3 120 3  18   5 3
190 2  250   0     0 37 14  4 1  16 3    3  13 1       242 3    *   *    *  *  *  * * 3   4  20 2
191 5 1600  20  1000 34 32  4 1  52 3   20  55 3       243 2   70   7  225 25 35 10 3  43 1   4   2 1
192 2  290   0   125 60 35  5 1  70 3    6   2 1       244 1  430  35  500 42 26  2 2   0 3   6  30 3
193 4  203   2    40 39 31  4 1   0 1    8   4 2       245 4  198   *  130 45 21  1 1  62 1   5   8 1
194 5    *   *     * 60 30  0 1  16 1    0   3 1       246 5   65  12  150 35 30  2 1  35 1  10   4 2
195 2  100   5   300 60  0  1 2  50 2    0   0 1       247 2   69   3   18 44 26  1 3  43 1   0   9 1
196 3  551   0  1500  *  *  * 1 100 3   10  25 3       248 4  230   0    0 35 36  3 3 150 3  20  12 3
197 3  220  10    70 42 40  4 1  85 3    6   7 1       249 4  250  25  850 40 15  1 1  40 3   0   * *
198 3  225  10   550 50 15  5 1 200 3    1  15 1       250 5  140  80  140  *  *  * * *  1   2  12 1
199 3  140  14   175 33 10  5 1   0 4    1  10 1       251 5  180   5  150 40 25  5 1 130 3   2   6 1
200 1  154   0    20 45 28  0 *  80 3    6   5 1       252 3   60   7    * 40 10  2 1  18 1   1   0 1
201 4   39   0    65 42 42  0 1  75 1    0  30 2       253 1   80   0  150 51 18  0 1   0 1   1   2 1
202 4  565   0   500  *  *  * 2  85 3   15  35 3       254 1   42   0   75 65 25 10 1  36 1   0   3 1
203 3    0   2     0 43 15  2 2  75 1    1   4 1       255 4    8   0   14 25 15  0 3   0 1   *   2 *
204 2 1096  73  2000 34 29  1 1 142 3   42  30 3       256 3  210   *  350  *  *  * 2 100 1   0  16 1
205 4   35   1     0 90 10  0 1  60 1    4   0 1       257 3   95   0   70 45 25  2 3  42 1   4   1 1
206 5   53  20   125 40 20  5 1  30 3    5   7 1       258 4   55  50   89 65 30  5 3  32 3   0   2 1
207 2  390   8   450  *  *  * 3  30 16 3               259 5  121   1  160 55 30  5 1  30 1   3   2 1
208 3    *   *     * 32 34  2 1 104 3    2  16 2       260 3   75  10   80 40 26  5 3  26 1   2   2 1
209 4    *   *    80  *  *  * 3  45 1    1   9 1        261 1    *   *    * 45 21  4 3 205 3   8  32 3
210 5  500  25   450 45 35  1 2 132 3   18  20 3       262 6  250  10  300 38 29  4 1  50 3   5  20 2
211 4  180   5   300 58 40  2 3  30 3    8   3 1       263 4  220  10  350 55 25 10 2  70 1   0  15 1
212 6   89   4   120 45 15  2 1   0 1    1   2 1       264 4  120  10   80 35 60  2 1  80 1   2  22 2
213 1   77  10   175 35 10  1 3   0 1    0   5 1       265 2   25   1   40 40 10  6 1   0 *   *   * *
214 1  460   3    75 40 23  6 1  94 3    2  35 2       266 1  500   0  175 75 20  5 2 200 3  32   1 3
215 3  440  35  1000 38 39  3 3 110 3   40  30 3       267 3    *   *  475 45 20 10 2  80 1   2  15 1
216 5   56   8   125 40 33  2 3   0 1   12   0 2       268 3  200  10   70 45 20 25 1  70 3   0  10 1
217 4   15  23    30 52 46  2 1   0 1    0   0 2       269 4  250   3    5 35 50  0 3  15 2   1   3 1
218 5  150   *   150  *  *  * * *  2    0   7 1        270 5  215   1  100 36 33  2 3  98 3   5  17 2
219 5 8064 300 12000 37 31  3 1 550 3  250  60 3       271 4    *   *    *  *  *  * 2  36 2   7   6 2
220 3  200   *     * 20 20  * 1  20 3    1   8 1       272 3  733  35  500 53 21  0 1   0 1   6  40 3
221 3   30   *   350 50 20  5 1  80 3    0   4 1       273 1    *   *    *  *  *  * 3   0 1   0   0 1
222 5   71   0   185 40  8  0 3   0 1    0   3 1       274 1  200   1  210 50 20  5 2  70 *   *   * *
223 4   11   0     0 99  0  0 1   4 1    0   0 1       275 5  305   0  450 58 27  2 2  85 3   3  25 2
224 1  267   2   125 40 25  5 1  44 3    2  13 1       276 1  110   5  175  *  *  * 2  99 1   0   7 1
225 7  325  10   400 46 25  3 2  70 1    3   9 1       277 2    *   *  100  *  *  * 3  45 1   3   6 1
226 1  155   0    85 35 35  5 3  70 1   10   3 2       278 3  100  20  250 24 30 10 3 100 3   0   7 1
227 4 1000 100  5000 35 20  7 1 180 3   30  20 3       279 4  355   *   95 40 20  5 1 130 3   8  12 2
228 3   85  30    45 45 25  2 1  54 1    1   6 1
```

Los Angeles Traffic Data

Only the roadtype and actual volume variables are used in Chapter 4. All variables in this data set are used in the Chapter 20 exercises. There are 396 observations.

```
filename: TRAFFIC.DAT
Los Angeles traffic data: 396 observations
(Source: Lee Cryer, Barton-Aschman Associates, Pasadena, CA)
Variables: roadtype (1=freeway, 2=minor arterial 3=major arterial, 4=Ventura
Boulevard)
actual traffic volume, estimated traffic volume
```

1	126000	106848	4	15130	13651	1	60000	70425	1	119000	115522
1	126000	121121	4	14785	13310	1	60000	71140	1	119000	115599
1	126000	109751	2	6164	12953	1	49000	62060	1	126000	131159
1	126000	129345	4	19482	13195	1	49000	62809	1	126000	132824
1	137000	136049	4	14481	12211	1	42000	57395	1	127000	131829
1	137000	143882	4	14245	12779	1	36000	52376	1	127000	131578
1	137000	134221	4	15963	12016	1	42000	56657	1	137000	133549
1	126000	93397	4	11860	11906	1	56000	60523	1	137000	142886
1	126000	105125	4	16259	12219	1	56000	60593	1	137000	134546
1	126000	103249	4	16971	13474	3	7773	16333	1	92000	72623
1	92000	97804	4	18252	13183	3	17124	22100	1	126000	89910
1	113000	118250	4	17714	12831	3	6993	12333	1	126000	120187
1	92000	76863	4	20819	11915	3	3522	1052	1	125000	112790
1	92000	86452	4	19001	13186	3	10671	12140	1	125000	113059
1	66000	90369	4	24525	14664	3	13376	13258	1	124000	111572
1	114000	113392	4	20151	16947	4	5957	16455	1	124000	110727
1	110000	108444	2	3676	9858	4	12721	9332	1	116000	110103
4	13186	11789	4	21074	14776	4	16915	15245	1	116000	110067
4	11623	13566	4	21775	16272	4	14782	10053	1	116000	110103
4	11628	11241	4	15162	10960	4	13447	11982	1	112000	110466
1	110000	111046	4	14843	11028	4	12624	11883	1	116000	110067
1	110000	99858	4	14530	13285	4	21918	15386	1	112000	107666
1	102000	96531	2	8007	5947	4	9489	11789	1	99000	89273
1	102000	92448	1	99000	105257	4	10604	6907	1	66000	75046
1	66000	83263	1	104000	108749	3	11302	13691	4	21506	17036
1	66000	93756	1	112000	110769	3	10188	12420	3	14829	15955
4	2970	2018	1	112000	107599	2	2322	9656	3	18746	12346
1	52000	68028	1	92000	94674	3	13253	11313	3	10572	14018
1	55000	65378	1	92000	98295	3	12560	14170	2	7128	3738
1	86000	98437	1	92000	96779	3	16147	14641	2	10010	9918
1	82000	978375	1	90000	93243	2	8238	3559	4	24719	9432
1	52000	68326	1	90000	92994	2	1671	6228	3	22254	19463
1	55000	65972	1	88000	88755	3	15549	17968	3	29230	16436
1	55000	59788	1	88000	88303	3	16807	13174	4	15995	9442
1	55000	60150	1	88000	88755	3	10026	12988	3	17317	23548
1	56000	60593	1	88000	88303	3	12143	14888	2	12904	7892
1	57000	55432	1	80000	85058	2	7135	2639	2	4038	1050
1	56000	60523	1	80000	81959	3	18515	11974	2	9113	4766
1	57000	55259	1	80000	83251	3	14218	15198	3	12603	12244
1	84000	107808	1	110000	122229	3	14525	11642	2	12814	19933
1	36000	52664	1	110000	112271	3	12781	11602	3	15993	17664
1	86000	98117	1	110000	105969	3	8025	10798	3	16658	16887
1	84000	107923	1	102000	88226	3	13271	16717	4	14425	10840
1	82000	97731	1	102000	96531	3	19267	14430	2	9564	3045
1	77000	97022	1	99000	87493	3	17481	16247	3	13453	19106
1	77000	97259	1	72000	79312	3	15762	16838	3	16535	14482
1	77000	94923	1	66000	76186	3	9077	1749	3	18456	17075
1	77000	95199	1	72000	79303	2	1405	1669	3	14714	14507
1	80000	80506	1	72000	77541	2	16555	2263	2	9275	3056
1	113000	122218	1	72000	77659	2	5337	9183	2	15274	11414
1	92000	101705	1	71000	74996	3	14437	18769	2	2971	7639
1	92000	108603	1	71000	75182	3	12908	17581	3	8355	7441
1	92000	97227	1	69000	73461	3	6189	5481	2	16233	7928
1	92000	91056	1	69000	74287	3	16453	15482	2	7316	5501

3	14960	14277	2	8236	9493	4	6552	2520	4	15237	12473
3	14783	17624	2	10615	14381	4	15880	10401	3	16195	14673
3	11804	8017	3	12074	12363	2	1514	642	3	13397	14530
2	5891	1345	2	11914	4071	2	6568	8845	2	5038	8505
3	7434	13402	2	4426	4447	3	16441	17594	2	12511	9873
1	66000	85274	3	13290	14224	2	2387	3548	2	12403	11355
1	76000	87077	2	4218	6386	2	2831	2622	3	17458	13861
1	76000	88032	3	9799	14296	2	5923	1845	2	15262	11320
1	86000	101423	3	4000	1064	2	8483	1818	2	7087	11137
1	99000	104076	3	11548	12494	2	8986	5160	2	8896	8100
1	86000	102346	2	8353	4805	2	7236	3811	3	12899	15672
1	104000	109166	2	4815	9585	2	5883	6994	2	9846	8048
1	110000	111935	3	28777	19910	3	20446	19538	4	14564	14660
1	114000	107083	2	20446	20088	2	1263	1787	4	13821	11435
1	110000	112307	3	12058	13581	3	18710	13122	2	3041	3811
1	114000	113386	3	12614	14635	2	8783	5973	3	4940	13114
1	114000	113315	2	8319	8841	2	9715	10917	2	5433	4645
1	114000	113309	2	5361	6416	2	14516	10564	2	3521	6625
3	16872	16844	2	4084	1309	2	10579	11763	3	15488	16514
3	17432	15558	3	7247	8301	2	6258	9328	2	11663	10421
2	6147	7335	2	5365	2062	3	15284	11367	2	9422	10158
3	14398	14766	2	4147	3103	3	8527	5158	2	15238	10709
3	16451	15841	3	11731	9574	2	7494	7459	2	9449	11523
2	8351	7756	2	5237	4900	2	3289	2845	2	8796	7900
2	6115	9795	2	1158	3667	2	3717	2533	2	9807	14105
3	13502	10874	2	4043	5025	2	3198	2351	3	15204	18214
2	8512	6688	3	18961	13640	3	11743	9526	3	15670	20317
2	7789	3644	2	12699	4629	2	9549	4256	2	7095	10225
3	4671	9958	2	5212	9723	2	5277	2344	2	8570	9181
3	7228	9178	3	15278	15360	2	11258	1696	2	11156	18525
3	7287	13605	2	3098	3200	3	12189	13576	3	7875	14109
3	15813	16201	2	9417	7610	3	17440	16570	2	11771	8945
3	10034	4455	3	15475	18756	3	17208	19671	3	18989	13914
4	29370	15569	2	2646	2479	3	24300	21643	3	12203	15842
2	4371	6900	2	5428	6922	2	9416	10525	3	15256	24588
4	16502	13352	3	8950	11600	2	6003	4169	3	14942	22920
1	14836	14495	2	9339	9472	2	10100	10509	3	13232	16712
4	15667	14474	3	13121	10932	2	7397	3566	2	7097	5220
3	6453	7841	3	7494	16452	2	5153	750	2	4925	9664
3	5975	4170	3	23179	33268	2	8259	8109	2	5204	7531
3	9494	7776	3	19141	15736	2	15481	4696	2	8174	5853
1	11017	8450	2	954	1679	3	18530	27195	4	11727	12967
3	7077	2402	2	17500	21588	2	10099	6849	2	5677	7657
3	8308	16020	3	13324	14762	3	17616	17932	4	21622	16242
2	3672	3872	4	12739	13309	3	16106	14997	4	20071	16135

References

Alden, Vernon R. "Who Says You Can't Crack Japanese Markets?" *Harvard Business Review,* 87(1) (1987), 52–56.

Allmon, Carolyn I. "Advertising and Sales Relationships for Toothpaste: Another Look." *Business Economics* 17(4) (1982), 55–61.

Anscombe, Frank, "Graphs in Statistical Analysis." *American Statistician,* 27 (1973), 17–21.

Assael, H. *Consumer Behavior and Marketing Action.* 3rd ed. Boston: PWS-KENT, 1987.

Barabba, Vincent P., Richard O. Mason, and Ian I. Mitroff. "Federal Statistics in a Complex Environment: The Case of the 1980 Census." *American Statistician,* 37(3) (1983), 203–212.

Bartlett, M. S. "On the Theoretical Specification of Sampling Properties of Autocorrelated Time Series." *Journal of the Royal Statistical Society,* B, 8 (1946), 27–41.

Bass, Frank M., and Darral G. Clarke. "Testing Distributed Lag Models of Advertising Effect." *Journal of Marketing Research,* 9(3) (1972), 298–308.

Beyer, W., W. J. Fleming, and D. Swineford. "Changes in Litter Near an Aluminum Reduction Plant." *Journal of Environmental Quality,* 16(3) (1987), 246–250.

Blattberg, Robert C., and Abel P. Jeuland. "Micromodeling Approach to Investigate the Advertising-Sales Relationship." *Management Science,* 27(9) (1981), 988–1005.

Bowerman, Bruce L., and R. T. O'Connell. *Time Series Forecasting.* 2nd ed. Boston: PWS-KENT, 1987.

Box, G. E. P. "Robustness in the Strategy of Scientific Model Building." In R. L. Lanner and G. N. Wilkerson, eds., *Robustness in Statistics.* New York: Academic Press, 1979, pp. 201–236.

Box, G. E. P., and David R. Cox. "An Analysis of Transformations." *Journal of the Royal Statistical Society,* B, 26 (1964), 211–243.

Box, G. E. P., W. G. Hunter, and J. S. Hunter. *Statistics for Experimenters.* New York: Wiley, 1978.

Box, G. E. P., and G. M. Jenkins. *Time Series Analysis.* Rev. ed. San Francisco: Holden-Day, 1976.

Boyd, Harper W., Jr., and Ralph Westfall. "Interviewer Bias Once More Revisited." *Journal of Marketing Research,* 7 (1970), 249–253.

Braccio, Ralph. "History of Mass Public Opinion and the Political Process." *Christian Science Monitor,* Apr. 16, 1987, p. 28.

Brown, R. G. *Smoothing, Forecasting, and Prediction of Discrete Time Series.* Englewood Cliffs, N.J.: Prentice Hall, 1962.

Buchanan, Bruce, Moshe Given, and Arich Goldman. "Measurement of Discrimination Ability in Taste Tests: An Empirical Investigation." *Journal of Marketing Research,* 24 (1987), 154–163.

Buzzell, Robert D., and Bradley T. Gale. *The PIMS Principles*. New York: Free Press, 1987.

Cannell, Charles F., Lois Oksenberg, and Jean M. Converse. "Striving for Response Accuracy: Experiments in New Interviewing Techniques." *Journal of Marketing Research*, 14 (1977), 306–315.

Cochran, William G. *Sampling Techniques*. 2nd ed. New York: Wiley, 1953.

Cohen, Howard M., Michael J. LuValle, J. Peter Mitchell, and Edward S. Sproles, Jr. "Reliability Evaluations of Interconnection Products." *AT&T Technical Journal*, 66(4) (1987), 70–80.

Cook, R. Dennis. "Detection of Influential Observations in Linear Regression." *Technometrics*, 19(2) (1977), 15–18.

Cryer, Jonathan D. *Time Series Analysis*. Boston: PWS-KENT, 1986.

Daniel, Cuthbert. "Use of Half-Normal Plot in Interpreting Factorial Two-Level Experiments." *Technometrics*, 1 (1959), 311–341.

Davis, John C. *Statistics and Geology*. New York: Wiley, 1973.

Delbecq, André L., Andrew H. Van de Ven, and David H. Gustafson. *Group Techniques for Program Planning: A Guide to Nominal Group and Delphi Processes*. Glenview, Ill.: Scott Foresman, 1975.

Deming, W. Edwards. "Some Principles of the Shewhart Methods of Quality Control." *Mechanical Engineering*, 66 (1944), 173–177.

Deming, W. Edwards. *Sample Design in Business Research*. New York: Wiley, 1960.

Deming, W. Edwards. "Sample Surveys." In William H. Kruskal and Judith M. Tanur, eds., *International Encyclopedia of Statistics*. vol. 2. New York: Free Press, 1978, pp. 867–885.

Deming, W. Edwards. *Quality, Productivity, and Competitive Position*. Cambridge, Mass.: MIT Center for Advanced Engineering Study, 1982.

Deming, W. Edwards. *Out of the Crisis*. Cambridge, Mass.: MIT Center for Advanced Engineering Study, 1986.

Dempster, Arthur P. "Employment Discrimination and Statistical Science." *Statistical Science*, 3(2) (1988), 149–195.

Draper N. R., and H. Smith. *Applied Regression Analysis*. 2nd ed. New York: Wiley, 1981.

Drucker, Peter F. "The Coming of the New Organization." *Harvard Business Review*, 88(1), 45–53.

Durbin, J., and G. S. Watson. "Testing for Serial Correlation in Least Squares Regression. I." *Biometrika*, 37 (1950), 409–428.

Durbin, J., and G. S. Watson. "Testing for Serial Correlation in Least Squares Regression. II." *Biometrika*, 38 (1951), 159–178.

Durbin, J., and G. S. Watson. "Testing for Serial Correlation in Least Squares Regression. III." *Biometrika*, 58 (1971), 1–19.

Ehrenberg, A. S. C. *Primer in Data Reduction*. New York: Wiley, 1982.

Frankel, Lester R. "Statistics and People—The Statistician's Responsibilities." *Journal of the American Statistical Association*, 71(353) (1976), 9–16.

Freedman, David, Robert Pisani, and Roger Purvis. *Statistics*. New York: Norton, 1978.

Fuller, F. Timothy. "Eliminating Complexity from Work: Improving Productivity by Enhancing Quality." *National Productivity Review*, (Autumn 1985), 327–344.

Galton, Francis. *Natural Inheritance*. London: Macmillan, 1889.

Gardner, E. S. "Exponential Smoothing: The State of the Art." *Journal of Forecasting*, 4 (1985), 1–28.

Ginsberg, Benjamin. *The Captive Public: How Mass Opinion Promotes State Power*. New York: Basic Books, 1987.

Goodman, Leo A., and William H. Kruskal. "Measures of Association for Cross-classifications." *Journal of the American Statistical Association*, 49 (1954), 732–764.

Gotlieb, J. B., and A. J. Dubinsky. "Influence of Price on Aspects of Consumers' Cognitive Process." *Journal of Applied Psychology*. 76(4), (1991), 541–549.

Gotlieb, J. B., and D. Sard. "Effects of Price Advertisements on Perceived Quality and Purchase Intentions." *Journal of Business Research*, 22 (1991), 195–210.

Green, P. E. "On the Design of Choice Experiments Involving Multifactor Alternatives." *Journal of Consumer Research,* 1 (1974), 61–68.

Gundaker, Bruce F., David E. Martinich, and Michael J. Tortorella. "Quality Technology in Product Realization Systems." *AT&T Technical Journal,* 66(5) (Sept./Oct. 1987), 5–20.

Hamilton, David. "Sometimes $R^2 > r_{yx_1}^2 + r_{yx_2}^2$." *American Statistician,* 41(2) (1987), 129–132.

Hellevik, Ottar. *Introduction to Causal Analysis: Exploring Survey Data by Crosstabulation.* London: Allen & Unwin, 1984.

Hoaglin, David C. "Transformations in Everyday Experience." *Chance,* 1 (1988), 40–45.

Homans, George C. *Social Behavior: Its Elementary Forms.* New York: Harcourt Brace Jovanovich, 1961.

Hunter, William, Jan O'Neill, and Carol Wallen. *Doing More with Less in the Public Sector: A Progress Report from Madison, Wisconsin.* Report No. 13, Center for Quality and Productivity Improvement, University of Wisconsin–Madison, June 1986.

Imai, Masaaki. *Kaizen: The Key to Japan's Competitive Success.* New York: Random House, 1986.

Ishikawa, Kaoru. *Guide to Quality Control.* 2nd ed. White Plains, N.Y.: Kraus, 1986.

Ishikawa, Kaoru, ed. *Statistical Application Research, Union of Japanese Scientists and Engineers (Special Issue: Seven Management Tools for QC)* 33(2) (1986).

Jaffe, A. J., and Spirer, H. F. *Misused Statistics: Straight Talk for Twisted Numbers.* New York: Dekker, 1987.

Johnson, H. Webster, Anthony J. Faria, and Ernest L. Maier. *How to Use the Business Library: With Sources of Business Information.* 5th ed. Cincinnati: South-Western Publishing, 1984.

Johnson, Richard A., and Dean W. Wichern. *Applied Multivariate Analysis.* 2nd ed. New York: Wiley, 1988.

Juran, J. M., and F. M. Gryna, eds. *Juran's Quality Control Handbook.* 4th ed. New York: McGraw-Hill / ASQC Quality Press, 1988.

Kruzas, Anthony, and Linda Varekamp Sullivan, eds. *Encyclopedia of Information Systems and Services.* 6th ed. Detroit: Gale Research, 1985.

Latzko, William J. *Quality and Productivity for Bankers and Financial Managers.* New York: Dekker, 1986.

Mallows, Colin L. "Some Comments on C_p." *Technometrics,* 15 (1973), 661–676.

Mann, J. I., M. P. Vessey, M. Thorogood, and R. Doll. "Myocardial Infarction in Young Women with Special Reference to Oral Contraceptive Practice." *British Medical Journal,* 2 (1975), 241–245.

Martiz/Rogers. "Early Model New Car Buyers' Study." As quoted in *PC Week,* June 28, 1988, p. 1.

Matchinsky, Jerri Marie. "Methods in Simultaneous Comparison Charts: Means and Standard Deviations." Master of Science thesis, University of Iowa, 1988.

May, Eleanor G. *A Handbook for Business on the Use of Federal and State Statistical Data.* Washington, D.C.: Department of Commerce, 1979.

McKean, Kevin. "The Orderly Pursuit of Pure Disorder." *Discover,* Jan. 1987, pp. 73–81.

Miao, L. I. "Gastric Freezing: An Example of the Evaluation of Medical Therapy by Randomized Clinical Trials." In J. P. Bunker, B. A. Barnes, and F. Mosteller, eds., *Costs, Risks, and Benefits of Surgery.* New York: Oxford University Press, 1977, pp. 198–211.

Miller, Robert B. *Minitab Handbook for Business and Economics.* Boston: PWS-KENT, 1988.

Miller, Robert B., and Dean W. Wichern. *Intermediate Business Statistics.* New York: Holt, Rinehart and Winston, 1977.

A Million Random Digits with 100,000 Normal Deviates. Santa Monica, Calif.: RAND Corporation, 1955.

Moen, R. D., T. W. Nolan, and L. P. Provost. *Improving Quality Through Planned Experimentation.* New York: McGraw-Hill, 1991.

Moore, P. G. *Statistics and the Manager.* London: MacDonald, 1966.

Mosteller, Frederick. "Note on an Application of Runs to Quality Control Charts." *Annals of Mathematical Statistics,* 12 (1941), 228–232.

Mosteller, Frederick. "Nonsampling Errors." In William H. Kruskal and Judith M. Tanur, eds., *International Encyclopedia of Statistics.* Vol. 1. New York: Free Press, 1978, pp. 208–229.

Mosteller, Frederick, and John W. Tukey. *Data Analysis and Regression: A Second Course in Statistics.* Reading, Mass.: Addison-Wesley, 1977.

Mosteller, Frederick, and others. *The Pre-election Polls of Nineteen Forty-Eight.* New York: Social Research Council, 1949.

Muller, Mervin E. "Random Numbers." In William H. Kruskal and Judith M. Tanur, eds., *International Encyclopedia of Statistics.* Vol. 2. New York: Free Press, 1978, pp. 839–897.

Myers, Raymond H. *Classical and Modern Regression Analysis.* 2nd ed. Boston: PWS-KENT, 1990.

Narula, Subash C., and John F. Wellington. "Prediction, Linear Regression and the Minimum Sum of Relative Errors." *Technometrics,* 19(2) (1977), 185–190.

Ott, Ellis R. *Process Quality Control.* New York: McGraw-Hill, 1975.

Pearson, Karl. "Mathematical Contributions to the Theory of Evolution, III. Regression, Heredity, and Panmixia." *Philosophical Transcriptions of the Royal Society,* A, 187 (1896), 253–318.

Pearson, E. S., and H. O. Hartley. *Biometrika Tables for Statisticians.* Vol. 1. 3rd ed. Cambridge, England: Cambridge University Press for Biometrika Trustees, 1966.

Pearson, Karl. "On a Criterion That a Given System of Deviations from the Probable in the Case of a Correlated System of Variables is Such That It Can be Reasonably Supposed to Have Arisen from Random Sampling." *Philosophical Magazine,* 50(5) (1990), 157–175.

Pokras, Robert, and Kurt K. Kubishke, *Diagnosis-Related Groups Using Data for the National Hospital Discharge Survey: United States, 1982.* Washington, D.C.: National Center for Health Statistics, Jan. 18, 1985.

Ramsay, James O. "Monotone Regression Splines in Action." *Statistical Science,* 3(4) (1988), 425–441.

Roberts, Harry V. *Harris Trust and Savings Bank: An Analysis of Employee Compensation.* Report 7946, CMSBE, Graduate School of Business, University of Chicago, 1979.

Roberts, Harry V. *Data Analysis for Managers.* Redwood City, Calif.: Scientific Press, 1988.

Rogers, R. Mark. "Tracking the Economy: Fundamentals for Understanding Data." *Economic Review,* Federal Reserve Bank of Atlanta (Mar./Apr. 1989), 30–48.

Ruffin, Julian M., and others. "A Cooperative Double-Blind Evaluation of Gastric 'Freezing' in the Treatment of Duodenal Ulcer." *New England Journal of Medicine,* 281 (1969), 16–19.

Ryan, Barbara F., Brian L. Joiner, and Thomas A. Ryan, Jr. *Minitab Handbook.* 2nd ed. Boston: PWS-KENT, 1988.

Schafer, Daniel W. "Measurement-Error Diagnostics and the Sex Discrimination Problem." *Journal of Business and Economic Statistics,* 5(4) (1987), 529–537.

Scheaffer, Richard L., William Mendenhall, and Lyman Ott. *Elementary Survey Sampling.* 4th ed. Boston: PWS-KENT, 1990.

Schmoyer, R. K. "Asymptotically Valid Prediction Intervals for Linear Models." *Technometrics,* 34(4), (1992), 399–408.

Scholtes, Peter. *The Team Handbook.* Madison, Wis.: Joiner Associates, 1987.

Schuman, Howard, and Stanley Presser. *Questions and Answers in Attitude Surveys.* San Diego, Calif.: Academic Press, 1981.

Shewhart, Walter A. *Economic Control of Quality of Manufactured Product.* New York: Van Nostrand, 1931.

Shurkin, Joel. *Engines of the Mind: A History of the Computer.* New York: Norton, 1984.

Snee, Ronald D. "Graphical Analysis of Process Variation." *Journal of Quality Technology,* 15 (1983), 76–88.

Stephan, F. F., and P. J. McCarthy. *Sampling Opinions.* New York: Wiley, 1958.

Stigler, Stephen M. *The History of Statistics.* Cambridge, Mass.: Harvard University Press, 1986.

Stuart, Alan. "Nonprobability Sampling." In William H. Kruskal and Judith M. Tanur, eds., *International Encyclopedia of Statistics.* Vol. 2. New York: Free Press, 1978, pp. 885–889.

Sugiman, Toshio, and Jyuji Misumi. "Development of a New Evacuation Method for Emergencies: Control of Collective Behavior by Emergent Small Groups." *Journal of Applied Psychology,* 73(1) (1988), 3–10.

Tiao, George C., and Ruey S. Tsay. *Model Specification in Multivariate Time Series.* Technical Report No. 61, Graduate School of Business, University of Chicago, Aug. 14, 1987.

Tufte, E. R. *The Visual Display of Quantitative Information.* Cheshire, Conn.: Graphics Press, 1983.

Tukey, John W. "Comparing Individual Means in the Analysis of Variance." *Biometrics,* 5 (1949), 99–114.

U.S. Bureau of the Census. *Statistical Abstract of the United States: 1984.* 104th ed. Washington, D.C.: Government Printing Office, 1984.

U.S. Bureau of the Census. *Statistical Abstract of the United States: 1989.* 109th ed. Washington, D.C.: Government Printing Office, 1988.

Wagner, Clifford H. "Simpson's Paradox in Real Life." *American Statistician,* 36 (1982), 46–48.

Wagner, R., F. M. Strong, and C. A. Elvehjem. "Effects of Blanching on the Retention of Ascorbic Acid, Thiamine, and Niacin in Vegetables." *Industrial and Engineering Chemistry,* 39, (1947), 990–993.

Walsh, Edward. "Polls Are Telling Us More, But Are They Telling It Like It Is?" *Washington Post,* weekly edition, Apr. 13, 1987, p. 37.

Wangensteen, Owen H., and others. "Achieving 'Physiological Gastrectomy' by Gastric Freezing." *Journal of the American Medical Association,* 180(6) (1962), 439–444.

Wartzman, Rick. "Don't Wave a Red Flag at the IRS." *Wall Street Journal,* Feb. 24, 1993, p. C1.

Wasserman, Paul, Charlotte Georgi, and James Way. *Encyclopedia of Business Information Sources.* 5th ed. Copyright © 1980, 1983 by Paul Wasserman.

Weisberg, Sanford. *Applied Linear Regression Analysis.* 2nd ed. New York: Wiley, 1985.

Yates, Frank. *Sampling Methods for Censuses and Surveys.* 3rd ed. New York: Hafner, 1953.

Glossary

Added variable plot	Plot for assessing the effect of a predictor variable after adjusting the effect of another predictor variable.
Alternative hypothesis	A hypothesis other than the null hypothesis.
AR(1) model	An autoregressive model in which the predictor variable is the response variable at the previous time point.
AR(2) model	An autoregressive model in which the two predictor variables are the response variable at the previous two time points.
Autocorrelation	Correlation between a time series and its lagged values.
Autoregressive model	A time series model using lagged values of the response variable as predictor variables.
b_i	Regression coefficient associated with the ith predictor variable.
Backward elimination	A special stepwise regression method that eliminates more and more predictors to find the "best" model.
Bernoulli process (Bernoulli trials)	A sequence of independent binary variable trials with constant success rate.
Best subset regression	A method for choosing the best predictor variables by considering all possible subsets of predictors.
Bias	Systematic difference between an estimate from survey data and the value that would be obtained by equal complete coverage.
Binomial distribution	The theoretical distribution of the number of successes in n Bernoulli trials with success rate π.
Binomial mean	$n\pi$
Binomial probability function	The probability of k successes in n Bernoulli trials with success rate π.
Binomial standard deviation	$\sqrt{n\pi(1 - \pi)}$
Blinding	Not allowing subjects in an experiment to know which treatment they receive.
Body of a table	The cells defined by all the combinations of categories of the variables in a table of categorical data.
Box-Cox transformation	A transformation from the power family $y = x^\lambda$ for some choice of constant power λ.
Cases	Rows in a data table.
Categorical data	Data that are arranged in classes or categories.
Cause-and-effect diagram (CE diagram)	A "fishbone" diagram that shows causes of causes of causes, and so on, so that truly fundamental causes of variation are documented. Also called an Ishikawa diagram.

Cell	Location in a table defined by the intersection of a category of one variable with a category of another variable.
Census	A survey conducted with the intention of obtaining information from every element in a universe.
Central limit effect	The distribution of a mean or total is approximately normal under many circumstances.
Chi-square distribution	The approximate sampling distribution of Pearson's X^2 statistic when the null hypothesis of no association is true.
CL	Center line on a control chart.
Class frequencies	The frequencies of counts of data values within the class intervals.
Class intervals	Intervals dividing up the values of a variable.
Clustering	Grouping elements according to their "nearness" to each other.
Cluster sampling	A design in which a random sample of clusters is selected.
Coded data	Replacing data by a code for simplicity.
Collapsing	Combining categories of a categorical variable to create a variable with fewer categories.
Collinearity	Approximate linear relationships among predictor variables.
Common causes (chance causes)	Causes of variation in a measured variable that are due to chance and remain in a system unless the process is fundamentally altered.
Conditions	Fixed levels of predictor variables.
Confidence coefficient	One minus the significance level of the test on which a confidence interval is based.
Confidence interval	An interval computed from a sample such that the collection of such intervals from all possible samples has a specified probability of containing a parameter.
Conformance analysis	Collection of data to determine if standards for a process are met. Part of the check step in the PDCA cycle.
Consequences	Responses to a set of conditions in a model.
Constant term	An alternative name for the y-intercept in the equation of a straight line.
Control group	A group of subjects that does not receive an experimental treatment, or that receives a placebo, to give a base of comparison.
Control limits	Limits within which the plotted process characteristic (subgroup mean or standard deviation) is expected to vary when the process is in control.
Cook's distance	A measure of a data point's influence on regression results that considers both the predictor variables and the response variable.
Correlation coefficient	$$r = \frac{1}{n-1} \sum_{i=1}^{n} \left[\left(\frac{x_i - \bar{x}}{s_x} \right) \left(\frac{y_i - \bar{y}}{s_y} \right) \right]$$
Critical region	Those values of a test statistic that cause rejection of the null hypothesis.
Cross-sectional data	Data where the time dimension is either absent or ignored.
Data design quality	The plan for collecting the data is relevant to the problem to be solved.
Data production quality	Data are collected with sufficient skill and care to be useful.
Degrees of freedom for residuals	The number of observations minus the number of fitted coefficients in the regression model.
Density histogram	A graphic display of a distribution especially useful with unequal width class intervals.
Designed experiment	A designed study in which a randomization device is used to determine which treatment is applied to which elements.
Designed study	A study in which the elements are chosen or assigned by a randomization device.
Differences	The series of changes from one time period to the next.
Discriminant analysis	Analysis of a model whose response is categorical for the purpose of discriminating among response values on the basis of the predictor variables.
Distributed lag model	A model relating a response variable to the lagged values of a predictor variable.

Dotplot	The display of a distribution on a number line with no grouping.
Double blinding	Not allowing subjects or those who test them or evaluate responses to know what treatments the subjects receive.
Ecological correlation	Correlation computed from data that are aggregates of smaller units of study.
Elements	The basic units or individuals about which information is sought in a survey.
Equal complete coverage	The set of measurements obtained if the survey procedures are used on every element in a universe.
Error term	The part of the response that is not modeled by the linear function of the predictor variables in a regression model.
Experiment	The study of the effects of change in an environment that is, to some degree, under the control of the experimenter.
Exponential smoothing	An ad hoc technique for smoothing out the random variation in series.
Extrapolation	Using a fitted curve to predict responses with predictor values that are far outside the range of the predictor variables used in fitting the relationship
f	Sampling fraction, $f = n/N$.
Factorial experiment	An experiment in which all combinations of the treatment levels are run in a replication.
Finite population correction factor	$fpc = \sqrt{(N - n)/N}$
First differences	The sequence of changes from one data value to the next.
First quartile	The data value one-quarter from the bottom of an ordered list.
Fitted value	The value on the fitted curve corresponding to particular values of the predictor variables.
Flow diagram	A series of boxes connected by arrows that show the flow of work in a step in a process.
Forward selection	A special stepwise regression method that selects more and more predictors to find the "best" model.
Frame	The list of elements of the universe from which a sample is actually drawn.
Frequency histogram	A graphic display of a frequency distribution.
General linear model (GLM)	$\hat{y} = b_0 + b_1 x_1 + b_2 x_2 + \cdots + b_k x_k$
Influence	A measure of the effect each data point has on the regression results.
Interaction	Where the mean response is not a linear function of the combinations of the levels of the factors.
Interquartile range	The difference between the third quartile and the first quartile.
Interviewer bias	Differences in responses caused by inappropriate cues from the interviewer or respondents' reactions to the interviewer.
Koyck (or geometric) model	A particular distributed lag model in which a response is related to an exponentially (or geometrically) weighted combination of the predictor variable at many lags.
Lag	An interval of time between observations in a time series.
Lagged variable	A variable given by the value at a previous time point.
LCL	Lower control limit on a control chart.
Least squares	A method that fits a curve to data pairs (x_1, y_1), (x_2, y_2), . . . ,(x_n, y_n) by minimizing the sum of squared vertical distances between the y-values and the curve.
Least-squares regression line	The line with equation $y = b_0 + b_1 x$ where the regression coefficients b_0 and b_1 are selected to minimize the sum of squared vertical differences from the observed responses to the line.
Levels	The actual values of a sequence where the first differences or changes may be of primary interest.
Leverage	A measure of a data point's influence in a regression with respect to the predictor variables.

Linear time trend	Trend modeled as a striaght line over time.
Linear transformation	Replacing a variable y by $a + by$ for some choice of constants a and b.
Logarithm transformation	A transformation useful for simplifying certain curved relationships and for stabilizing variability when the standard deviation of a response is proportional to the mean of the response.
Longitudinal study	A study of the evolution of a process over time.
Lurking variable	A third variable whose influence plausibly explains the correlation between two other variables.
Main effects	The impact of a single factor, holding the impacts of the other factors fixed.
Mallows' C_p criterion	A criterion for choosing the better predictor variables in a regression model.
Mean	The arithmetic average of the data values.
Mean chart	Statistical process control chart designed to detect changes in the mean of a process.
Meandering series	A series whose observations close in time are also close in value but whose observations far apart in time may be quite different.
Median	The middle value for a data set ordered in magnitude.
Misspecified model	A model that does not include the "correct" predictor variables.
Model diagnostics	The testing of a model with respect to assumptions.
Multiway table	A table in which the cells are defined by the categories of several categorical variables.
N	Number of elements in a frame.
n	Sample size, number of cases in a regression data set, or number of trials considered to obtain a total number of successes in Bernoulli trials.
Nonprobability survey	Survey in which probability methods are not used to select the elements to be measured.
Nonsampling error	The difference between the value of a sample estimate and a corresponding equal complete coverage value that is due to some other cause than the sampling process.
Normal curve	The mathematical curve that describes the normal distribution. See Equation (9.1).
Normal distribution table	A table of areas under the standard normal curve.
Normal probability plot	A plot of normal scores versus values used to support normality of a distribution and to detect lack of normality.
Normal scores	A set of "ideal" values from a normal distribution.
Null hypothesis	The hypothesis assumed to be true when deriving the sampling distribution of a test statistic used to compute the significance level.
Observational study	A study in which randomization is not used to select elements for observation.
Operational definition	The result of answering who, what, when, where, why, and how.
Ordered categories	Those categories that cannot be displayed in an arbitrary order without losing some information.
Ordinary least squares (OLS)	A method that fits a curve to data pairs (x_1, y_1), (x_2, y_2), . . . ,(x_n, y_n) by minimizing the sum of squared vertical distances between the y-values and the curve.
Outlier	An observation that is separated from the main body of the data.
Overspecified model	A model that includes unnecessary predictor variables.
p	The proportion of successes in n trials.
π	The success probability on each trial.
Parameter	Numerical characteristic of a population, for example, the mean, denoted by μ.
Pareto diagram	A diagram that displays causes of variation ranked by importance.
Pareto principle	Only a few causes are responsible for most of the variation in a process.
p-chart	A control chart based on sequence plots of sample proportions.

p-value	The probability of getting an outcome at least as extreme as the outcome observed.
PDCA	Plan, Do, Check, Act. The steps in Deming's wheel taken over and over again to bring about improvements in processes.
Percentage changes	The relative changes from one data value to the next data value on a percentage basis and relative to the previous data value.
Percentile	A number below which a specified percent of a distribution's values lie.
Period	Time span at which a sequence *may* tend to repeat its general behavior—12 for monthly data, 4 for quarterly data, and so on.
Placebo	A nontreatment disguised so that subjects think it is real.
Population	The set of all measurements on a variable that a whole universe would yield were a census taken.
Prediction	Using a fitted relationship to estimate the value of a response not observed.
Prediction error	The new response value minus the prediction based on the model.
Prediction interval	An interval that has a prescribed probability of containing a new response.
Prediction standard error	The estimated standard deviation of the difference between a new response value and the predicted value.
Predictor variables	The variables used to predict or explain the response variable.
predsd	Notation for the estimated standard deviation of a prediction error in a regression model.
Primary data	Data collected by the person or organization that also analyzes the data.
Probabilistic inference	Drawing conclusions about model parameters from process data using the methods of probability.
Probability	The hypothesized limiting value of the porportion of occurrrences of an event in a large number of repetitions of a process that may yield the event.
Probability survey	Survey in which each element of a universe has a known probability of entering the sample.
Process	A sequence of steps taken to achieve a goal or outcome.
Process analysis	Activities undertaken to understand and model the steps in a process and the relationships among the steps or analysis of past process data to find appropriate limits for future control.
Process control	Activities undertaken to keep process outcomes as close as possible to a predetermined target or to effect an improvement in the performance of the process.
Quadratic time trend	Trend modeled as a quadratic curve in time.
Quantile plot	A plot used to assess the shape of a distribution.
Quantile-quantile plot	Scatterplot of the quantiles of two distributions, one versus the other, used to assess the similarity of the two distributions.
Quota sample	A sample drawn so that some of its characteristics match predetermined targets; for example, percentage female is 50.
r	Symbol for the correlation coefficient. Also used for the number of rows in a two-way table.
R^2	Notation for the multiple coefficient of determination.
R^2(adj)	Notation for the adjusted coefficient of determination.
Randomness	A property of uncertain outcomes that can be modeled using the mathematics of probability.
Random walk	The sequence of running totals of independent outcomes from a stable process.
Range	The difference between the largest and smallest data value.
Regression line	The line fitted to the scatterplot of response variable versus the predictor variable by least squares.
Regression model	A mathematical curve summarizing a relationship among variables together with measures of variation from the curve.

Relative frequency histogram	A graphical display of a relative frequency distribution especially useful for comparing distributions of different-sized data sets.
Replication	A single run of an experiment in which all the planned treatments are run at all the planned levels.
Residual	The observed response minus the value predicted by the model.
Residual plot	A plot of residuals versus the corresponding fitted values.
Residual standard deviation, s	The square root of the sum of squared residuals divided by their degrees of freedom.
Response variable	The variable to be predicted or explained.
s	Notation for standard deviation.
Sample	A collection of elements from a universe or process.
Sampling distribution	Distribution of values of a statistic in repeated drawings from a stable process or random samples from a fixed universe.
Sampling error	The difference between the value of a sample estimate and a corresponding equal complete coverage value that is due only to the sampling process.
Sampling variation	The variation of numerical characteristics from sample to sample.
Scatterplot	An (x, y) plot that displays the statistical relationship between two variables.
Seasonal adjustment	A procedure applied to a time series in an attempt to account for known seasonality.
Seasonal autoregression	An autoregressive model with the predictor variable lagged at multiples of the seasonal period.
Seasonal differences	The series of season to season changes.
Seasonal exponential smoothing	Exponential smoothing that accounts for seasonality.
Seasonal indicators	Binary variables indicating the various seasons.
Seasonality	The tendency of a sequence to repeat its general behavior at regular time periods.
Secondary data	Data collected by one person or organization and analyzed by another person or organization.
Sequence plot	A graph of a time series with time displayed on the horizontal axis and values of the variable of interest on the vertical axis.
Significance level	Probability of rejecting a true null hypothesis.
Significance testing	A process of probabilistic inference that uses sampling distributions to compare behavior in data with theories about the process that generated the data.
Simple observation	Observation of outcomes from a process.
Simple random sample	A sample taken so that each possible sample of size n has the same chance of being selected.
Simpson's paradox	A paradox in which an overall average changes in a way opposite to the changes in the averages for component parts.
Skewed distribution	An asymmetric distribution with values stretched out on either the high or low end.
Slope	The coefficient b_1 in the equation $y = b_0 + b_1 x$.
Smoothing constants	The constants in exponential smoothing that determine the extent of the smoothing.
Special causes (assignable causes)	Causes of variation in a measured variable that are individually important and affect process results only some of the time.
Standard deviation	A measure of variability obtained as the square root of the number obtained from the sum of squared deviations of the observations from their mean divided by $n - 1$.
Standard deviation chart	Statistical process control chart designed to detect changes in the variability of a process.
Standard error	The standard deviation of the sampling distribution of a statistic.

Standard form   An arrangement of cases in a factorial experiment in a way that makes calculation easy.

Standard normal curve   A normal curve with mean 0 and standard deviation 1.

Standardization   Replacing a variable y by $(y - \bar{y})/s$, case by case.

Standardized least-squares regression line   The equation $y_* = rx_*$ where y_* and x_* are standardized values of y and x.

Standardized residuals   Residuals that have been corrected to have a standard deviation of 1.

Standardized value   See z-value.

Statistical process control   Statistical methods used to detect changes in processes.

Statistically significant   A phrase used when the value of a test statistic is an extreme value in the appropriate sampling distribution that assumes the null hypothesis to be true.

Statistics   Numerical characteristics of a sample, usually thought of as estimates of population parameters.

Stem-and-leaf display   A display of a distribution using the digits of the data to form the groupings and graphical display of frequencies.

Stepwise regression   A sequential method for choosing the best predictor variables.

Stratification   Separating observations into groups or categories in order to make comparisons or grouping elements in a frame according to some common characteristic or characteristics.

Stratified sampling   A design in which random samples are drawn from strata in the frame.

Studentized residuals   Residuals that have been standardized using data that excludes the ith case.

Subgroups   Samples of a process variable used to measure the current mean and standard deviation for process analysis.

Survey   A data collection tool in which a sample of elements is selected from a universe of elements for measurement.

Survey instrument   Device—such as a questionnaire or diary—used to record data.

Symmetric distribution   A distribution whose left and right sides are mirror images of one another.

Systematic sampling   A design in which elements are chosen systematically from the frame after a random start (or starts) has been chosen.

Table of random digits   A table of the digits $0, 1, \ldots, 9$ constructed so that each of the digits has an equal chance of occurring at any location in the table.

Tally   A count of the number of cases in each category of a variable.

t distribution with $n - 1$ degrees of freedom   The sampling distribution of the t statistic for the sample mean when the data come from a normal distribution.

Test statistic   A statistic used in a significance test.

Third quartile   The data value one-quarter from the top of an ordered list.

Time series   A sequence of observations collected from a process at fixed epochs of time.

Treatment   A set of conditions set up by an experimenter and applied to an element.

t statistic for the process mean $t = \dfrac{\bar{y} - \mu}{s/\sqrt{n}} = \dfrac{\sqrt{n}(\bar{y} - \mu)}{s}$

Two-sample t statistic $t = \dfrac{\bar{y}_1 - \bar{y}_2}{\sqrt{\dfrac{s_1^2}{n_1} + \dfrac{s_2^2}{n_2}}}$

Two-way table   A breakdown of the number of respondents (or counts) in each category formed by intersecting the categories of two variables.

Type I error	Rejecting a true null hypothesis.
Type II error	Failing to reject a false null hypothesis.
Type III error	Solving the wrong problem.
UCL	Upper control limit on a control chart.
Underspecified model	A model that fails to include important predictor variables.
Universe	The collection of all elements that might be drawn into a sample for a survey.
Variable	A measured characteristic of elements.
Variance inflation factors (VIF)	A measure of an individual predictor's collinearity with the other predictors.
y-**intercept**	The coefficient b_0 in the equation of a straight line: $y = b_0 + b_1 x$
z-**scores** (z-**values**)	Standardized values or units: $z = (y - \mu)/\sigma$

Answers to Selected Exercises

4.3A

	Q_1	Median	Q_3	Interquartile Range	Range
a	5	7	11	6	11
b	5	7	11	6	38
c	4	7	13	9	11

4.3B $28,000 **4.3C** No

4.5A

	Mean	Standard Deviation
a	7.9	3.8
b	11.7	13.2
c	8.0	4.2

4.5B $28,060 **4.5C** Yes

4.5H

	n	Mean	Standard Deviation
	30	512.1	189.3
	29	488.4	140.3
Percent reduction		5	26

4.5I $576.45 **4.5J** $563.57

4.7A b

	Mean	Standard Deviation
Coded	1.415	4.366
Inches	0.0000354	0.00010915

4.7C Median = 1,462,240 yen, $Q_3 - Q_1$ = 323,380 yen

4.7D Mean = $1004.80, standard deviation = $251.20

4.9B Standard deviation$_{before}$ = 0.0011 inches, standard deviation$_{after}$ = 0.0009 inches

4.9D

	Mean	Standard Deviation
Left	56.51	13.54
Right	57.87	15.20

CHAPTER 5

5.3B

Outlook	Size	Cases
2	1	7
2	3	1
3	1	8
4	1	9
4	2	2, 10
5	1	3, 4

5.3C a

	Grade	
	−1	0
Sq.ft	597.6	657.8
Assess	20.92	22.96
Market	27.12	35.20
A/M	0.811	0.672

5.5A

Size	Count	Percent
1	5	62.5
2	2	25.0
3	1	12.5
N=	8	100
*=	2	

This is *not* the presentation-quality version of the table.

5.7B a

Future Use Counts

	1	2	3	4	5
Male	0	1	3	8	2
Female	1	2	2	0	1

Future Use Percents

	1	2	3	4	5
Male	0	7	22	57	14
Female	17	33	33	0	17

b

Anxiety

		1	2	3	4	5
Future Use	1	0	0	1	0	0
	2	1	2	0	0	0
	3	1	2	0	2	0
	4	3	1	0	1	3
	5	1	0	0	2	0

c

Anxiety

		1–3	4–5
Future Use	1–3	7	2
	4–5	5	6

A slight tendency for anxiety to be associated with low future use.

5.7D Percent responding favorably to question concerning economic outlook for the coming year, by type of ownership

Outlook	Sole Proprietorship	Partnership	Corporation	Overall
% favorable	43	63	51	49

Source: 1980 Wisconsin Restaurant Survey conducted by the University of Wisconsin Small Business Development Center. A mail survey of a random sample of 1000 restaurants in 19 Wisconsin counties yielded 269 responses to the table. There were 106 sole proprietorships, 27 partnerships, and 136 corporations.

5.11C **a** Table of counts:

```
Control: Gender = Male            Control: Gender = Female
Rows: Age    Columns: Classification    Rows: Age    Columns: Classification

         1      2      3      4    All            1      2      3      4    All

  1      0      0      0      0      0      1      2      0      0      0      2
  2     10      2      0      0     12      2     17      0      0      0     17
  3      2      1      0      1      4      3      1      1      0      1      3
  4      1      0      1      0      2      4      0      0      1      2      3
  5      0      0      0      1      1      5      0      0      0      1      1
All     13      3      1      2     19    All     20      1      1      4     26
```

b Table of row percents:

```
Control: Gender = Male
Rows: Age    Columns: Classification

          1       2       3       4     All

  1      --      --      --      --      --
  2    83.33   16.67     --      --   100.00
  3    50.00   25.00     --    25.00  100.00
  4    50.00     --    50.00     --   100.00
  5      --      --      --   100.00  100.00
All    68.42   15.79    5.26   10.53  100.00
```

```
Control: Gender = Female
Rows: Age    Columns: Classification

          1       2       3       4     All

  1   100.00     --      --      --   100.00
  2   100.00     --      --      --   100.00
  3    33.33   33.33     --    33.33  100.00
  4      --      --    33.33   66.67  100.00
  5      --      --      --   100.00  100.00
All    76.92    3.85    3.85   15.38  100.00
```

c Table of column percents:

```
Control: Gender = Male
Rows: Age    Columns: Classification

          1       2       3       4      All

  1      --      --      --      --       --
  2    76.92   66.67     --      --     63.16
  3    15.38   33.33     --    50.00    21.05
  4     7.69     --    100.00     --    10.53
  5      --      --      --    50.00     5.26
All   100.00  100.00  100.00  100.00   100.00
```

```
Control: Gender = Female
Rows: Age    Columns: Classification

          1       2       3       4      All

  1    10.00     --      --      --      7.69
  2    85.00     --      --      --     65.38
  3     5.00   100.00     --    25.00    11.54
  4      --      --    100.00   50.00    11.54
  5      --      --      --    25.00     3.85
All   100.00  100.00  100.00  100.00   100.00
```

CHAPTER 6

6.3E   The cross-sectional distribution of sales is roughly the same from year to year. If there had been a strong upward trend over years, then the cross-sectional distributions would also show an upward trend. The converse would be true for a downward trend.

6.3F   A roughly linear relationship; quite similar to the first plot suggested; a slight linear tendency with much more scatter than observed in the first two plots.

6.5D

	N	Mean	Median	Standard Deviation
Sq.ft	5	1478	1435	228
Assessed	5	25.72	23.60	4.71
Market	5	44.80	45.40	3.50

The correlations between the various variables are given in the following table:

	Sq.ft	Assessed
Assessed	.853	
Market	.048	.497

6.5G   Each data set has the same descriptive statistics.

	Mean	Standard Deviation	Correlation Between x and y
x	9	3.32	0.82
y	7.5	2.03	0.82

Because the scatterplots are very different and the descriptive statistics are the same, just looking at descriptive statistics is not sufficient for data analysis. Graphical techniques must be used to learn about processes.

6.5H $r = -0.765$. The plot below uses letters A, B, C, and D to denote sales in the four years, so that some of the longitudinal behavior is displayed. In a raw scatterplot the longitudinal effects are usually masked.

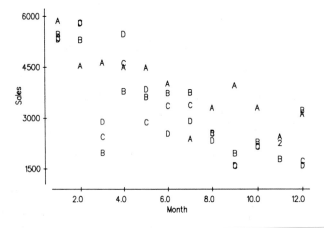

6.5K   All standardization does is change the scales of the x- and y-axes. It does not affect the relationship between the variables.

6.9G   a

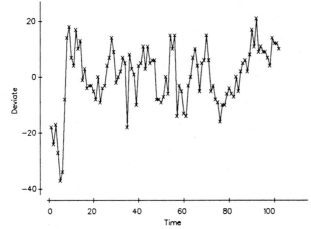

b

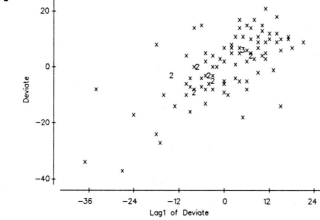

c

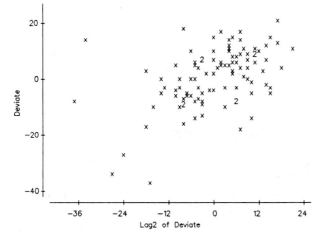

d   0.662491   0.458035   0.234878   0.173877   0.009692
   −0.139303   −0.210566   −0.172548   −0.111801   −0.081636
   −0.122458   −0.064257

e   The autocorrelations start at 0.66 and decay slowly to 0.009 at lag 5; then they become negative but stay relatively small. The sequence is autocorrelated and may be slightly meandering.

6.9H   **b**

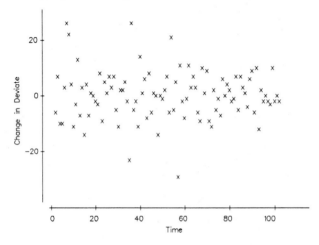

c

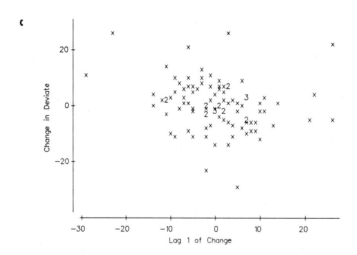

e   −0.226772   0.045118   −0.282222   0.148595   −0.021883
   −0.062226

f   The autocorrelations are all relatively close to zero, indicating no strong pattern in the sequence of changes.

g   The slight meandering in the original sequence has been eliminated by the computation of the changes. The original sequence could be treated as a random walk.

CHAPTER 7

7.3D   **a**

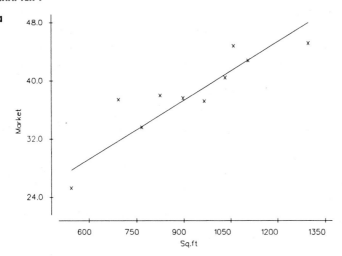

b and c

```
ROW   Sq.ft   Market  trialfit   trialres    sq.res

 1     544    25.2     27.688     -2.488      6.1901
 2     694    37.4     31.738      5.662     32.0583
 3     767    33.6     33.709     -0.109      0.0119
 4     825    38.0     35.275      2.725      7.4256
 5     899    37.6     37.273      0.327      0.1069
 6     965    37.2     39.055     -1.855      3.4410
 7    1033    40.4     40.891     -0.491      0.2411
 8    1060    44.8     41.620      3.180     10.1124
 9    1106    42.8     42.862     -0.062      0.0038
10    1298    45.2     48.046     -2.846      8.0997
```

d   The sum of the squared residuals is 67.691.

7.5A   **a** $(y - 20)/3 = 0.7\,[(x - 50)/2]$
   b   1.05
   c -32.5
   d   17.9

7.5E   **a**   The same output occurs for *each* data set:

```
The regression equation is

y1 = 3.00 + 0.500 x1

Predictor      Coef       Stdev     t-ratio        p
Constant      3.000       1.125        2.67     0.026
x1           0.5001      0.1179        4.24     0.002

s = 1.237        R-sq = 66.7%     R-sq(adj) = 62.9%

Analysis of Variance

SOURCE       DF         SS        MS        F        p
Regression    1     27.510    27.510    17.99    0.002
Error         9     13.763     1.529
Total        10     41.273
```

7.5G   **a**   Rating $= 80.1 + 0.0077$ Price

7.5J   **a**   Market $= 20.5 + 0.0184$ Sq.ft

      b   The equation for the 10-case line is Market $= 16.3 + 0.0239$ Sq.ft, so the intercept is smaller and slope larger for the 10-case line than for the 60-case line.

7.7B $\hat{y} = 3.76 + 0.688x$, with $s = 1.73$. The residual plot shows that Illinois is an outlier that casts doubt on the adequacy of the straight-line model.

7.7D   **a**   Height $= 27.6 + 2.58$ Age

      b

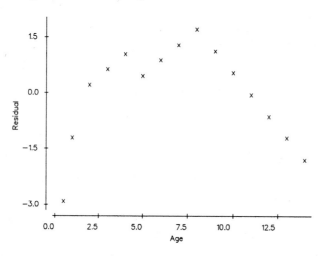

      c   The curvature in the residual plot is severe and indicates decisively that the straight-line model is not a good description of the relationship between Age and Height.

7.7F   **a**   Market $= 24.7 + 0.557$ Assessed

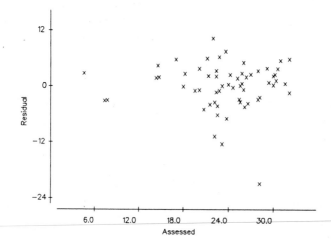

b   The straight-line model appears to be adequate for most cases, but the case with the large negative residual shows substantial deviation from the model.

7.9A **a**   Copies = 385 + 8.21 Time

b   The unusual value at time period 26, which is November 16, produces the largest positive residual, which distances itself substantially from the other points in the plot.

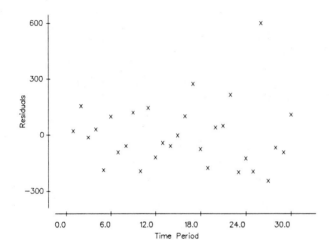

c   Copies = 410 + 5.15 Time

d   The y-intercept increases and the slope decreases after the removal of the outlier. The main suggestion is that the rate of increase in copies over the time has been less than would be predicted by the model fitted to the data that included the outlier. The slope of the model fitted without the outlier, 5.15, is probably a better estimate of the rate of increase than the original estimate of 8.21.

CHAPTER 8

8.4D **a**   Height = 25.2 + 3.64 Age − 0.0741 (Age)^2

b   Height = 25.2 + 3.64(12) − 0.0741(144) = 58.212 inches

c   The model gives Height = 25.2 + 3.64(20) − 0.0741(400) = 68.346 inches, which is about $5\frac{2}{3}$ feet, which is plausible.

d   For the straight-line model, $s = 1.349$; for the quadratic model, $s = 0.509$, which is a substantial reduction from the straight-line model.

8.6C **a**   Height = 27.7 + 2.58 Age + 0.133 Sex, where Sex is 0 for females and 1 for males.

b   The slope coefficient is about the same in this model and in the model that fitted females alone.

c   The s for the above model is 1.384, which is about the same as for the model fitted to females alone.

d   Height = 25.1 + 3.69 Age − 0.0782 (Age)^2 + 0.133 Sex

8.6E   **a**   Market = 20.1 + 0.0132 Sq.ft + 6.47 Medium + 7.79 High, with s = 3.249.

   b   This implies that a Low-grade property has a predicted market value 7.79 thousand dollars below a High-grade one, and a Medium-grade property has a predicted market value 1.32 thousand dollars below a High-grade one. This is exactly what the model in the text implied, and the residual standard deviations are equal as well. In other words the two models are entirely equivalent.

8.9A   **a**   Data Set 1: y = 0.1 + 1.3x, with s = 1.017. Data Set 2: y = 7.9 − 1.3x, with s = 1.017.

   b   For Data Set 1, the fitted values are 1.4, 2.7, 4.0, 5.3, and 6.6, while the residuals are −0.4, 1.3, −1.0, −0.3, and 0.4. For Data Set 2, the fitted values are 6.6, 5.3, 4.0, 2.7, and 1.4, while the residuals are 0.4, −0.3, −1.0, 1.3 and −0.4.

   c   The plots are the same for both data sets.

   d   The plot of residuals versus x is the same as the plot of residuals versus fitted values for Data Set 1; the plots are reversed for Data Set 2.

   e   The sign of the slope affects the plot versus x but not versus the fitted values.

8.9C   **b**   Sales = b_0 + b_1 Capital + b_2 Wages + b_3 Full Time + b_4 Sole + b_5 Partnership, where Sole is 1 if the restaurant is a sole proprietorship and 0 otherwise, and Partnership is 1 if the restaurant is a partnership and 0 otherwise. Note that we do not include a variable for restaurants that are corporations. Such restaurants are accounted for when Sole = 0 and Partnership = 0.

8.9E

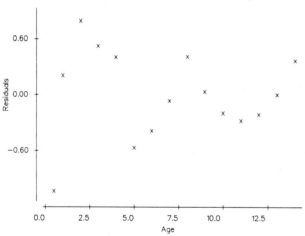

The residual plot does not present a random pattern. It appears to have three "cycles" defined by three peaks and two troughs. We should seek a more satisfactory model.

8.11C   The Total SS = 638.23, the Regression MS = 170.3, the Error MS = 21.2217, and the F statistic = 8.02.

CHAPTER 9

9.4A	**a**	0.8413	**9.4B**	**a**	0	**9.4D**	**a**	1.5
	b	0.9904		**b**	2.3		**b**	−1
	c	0.3085		**c**	1.96		**c**	2.4
	d	0.1359		**d**	1			
	e	0.1587						
	f	0.0107						

9.4G **a**   0.2417
        b   0.1587
        c   0.2743
        d   0.4013
        e   0.1915
        f   0.5914

9.4H **a**   137.2
        b   100
        c   110.3
        d   89.2

9.4I $15,000 is 3 standard deviations above the mean. Such an extreme value should not be expected for quite a long time. $8,000 is really an implausible value. It is hard to imagine that the stated normal distribution applies to the process.

9.6A 0.13%   **9.6C** 0.11%   **9.8D** −0.84, −0.253, 0.253, 0.84

CHAPTER 10

10.4A [39.6, 48.0]

10.4B **a** $LCL = 8.2, CL = 10.1, UCL = 11.9$
        b   0.06, 0.43
        c   0.05, 0.17

10.6A $LCL = 0.95, UCL = 7.26$

10.6B $LCL = 0.1, CL = 1.1, UCL = 2.9$

CHAPTER 11

11.5A **a**   0.3125
        b   0.03125
        c   2 and 3 have the same probability of 0.3125.

11.5B **a**   0.3087
        b   0.16807
        c   1 is most likely.

11.5C $Pr(1 \leq y \leq 3) = 0.80115$ and $Pr(1 < y < 3) = Pr(y = 2) = 0.3087$

11.5D **a**   0.24072

11.5F $Pr(\text{proportion} = 0.4) = 0.3125, Pr(\text{proportion} = 0.5) = 0,$
        $Pr(\text{proportion} < 0.1) = 0.03125$

11.8C

	Mean	Standard Deviation
Proportion	0.05	0.09747
Number	0.25	0.48734

11.10A **a**   0.8653
        b   0.7991 (% error = 7.7% too low)
        c   0.8648 (% error = 0.06% too low). The continuity correction makes a whale of a difference.

11.12A **a** $H_0: \pi = \frac{1}{2}$

        b $H_0: \pi > \frac{1}{2}$

        c $Pr(y \geq 15 \mid \pi = 0.5) = 0.02069$

        d same as part **c**

11.12B **a** $H_0: \pi = .6$

        b No

        c 0.0967

        d $Pr(y \geq 17 \mid \pi = 0.8) = 0.586$

11.12C 9

CHAPTER 12

12.3A **a** $CL = 0.03$

        b $LCL = 0, UCL = 0.096$

        c No

12.3B **a** 0.03

        b $[0, 0.096]$ **c** $[0, 0.111]$ **d** Yes

CHAPTER 13

13.3A **a** 48%, 73%, 64%

        c 57.6%, 67.6%, 64%. There is less variation between extremes when the nonresponse rate is lower.

CHAPTER 14

14.3D **a** A person in a household; all people living in a household.

        b A female head of household; all female heads of households.

14.5B A, B, C, and D are all true.

CHAPTER 15

15.5B Doubling the sample size reduces the length of the interval by a factor of $\sqrt{2}$. This is a 41% reduction in interval length.

15.5F **a**

Department	N	n	fpc	se_p	$3se_p$
A	349	30	0.956	0.07	0.21
B	278	25	0.954	0.08	0.24
C	181	18	0.949	0.09	0.27
D	82	8	0.950	0.14	0.42
E	42	4	0.951	0.22	0.66
F	12	12	0	0	0
G	4	4	0	0	0
Total	948	101	—	—	—

        The sample size is much more important than the department size.

        c The group will fall woefully short of its goal of estimating within 8 percentage points in each department. If the agency as a whole is sampled, using simple random sampling, then the goal of an 8% error margin is attainable because the standard error will be approximately $\sqrt{0.9} \times \sqrt{(0.8)(0.2)/100} \simeq 0.04$ and $2\,se_p = 0.08$.

15.7A $n = z^2 S^2 / B^2$. For reference take $B = 1$. Then the table of sample sizes is

z	S	n
1.645	0.5	1
	1.0	3
	2.0	11
	10.0	271
2	0.5	1
	1.0	4
	2.0	16
	10.0	400
3	0.5	3
	1.0	9
	2.0	36
	10.0	900

For a value of B not equal to 1, just divide the n values in the table by the value of B^2 to get the sample size required for the given value of B.

15.9E For an individual, the prediction interval is [$0, $89.40], while for the average, the confidence interval is [$0, $14.90].

CHAPTER 16

16.5B For ages less than or equal to 65, the confidence interval is $[-0.5, 7.9]$. For ages greater than 65, the confidence interval is $[-1.4, 11.4]$. In neither case is there a conclusive difference. The data do not support a claim that the average length of stay is longer in the Northeast than in the West or vice versa.

16.5C $[-1.11, 7.11]$

16.5D Confidence interval for difference $= [-0.12, 0.38]$. Confidence interval for proportion of managers $= [0.44, 0.84]$. Confidence interval for proportion of hourly workers $= [0.36, 0.66]$. Neither group is decisively in favor.

CHAPTER 17

17.3B 10.167   **17.3C** 25   **17.3D** -1.921

17.3E
a 1.372
b -0.260
c 1.753
d 2.131
e -0.866
f 3.385
g 2.750
h -2.750

17.3F
a 2.5%   **17.3G** 3.499
b 99%

17.5E $t = -2.16$
a Reject the null hypothesis at the 5% significance level.
b Do not reject the null hypothesis at the 1% significance level.
c They yield opposite inferences.

17.5F   0.0486   **17.5G** $t = -2.16$, so the result is significant at the 5% level but not at the 1% level.

17.5H   0.0243. Because we use only one tail area corresponding to the one-sided alternative hypothesis.

17.7A   **a**   [98.9, 112.3]
             b   [100.8, 110.4]

17.7B   **a**   [29.6, 37.6]   **17.7C**   **a**   [91.4, 113.4]
             b   [30.7, 36.5]   **b**   [94.9, 109.9]

17.9A   [77.3, 128.7]   **17.9B**   [27.5, 92.5]

17.11A   **a** $t = 1.4$, $df = 38$, do not reject the null hypothesis
              c $t = 4.34$, df large implies use of normal distribution, reject the null hypothesis
              d $t = 1.1$, $df = 28$, do not reject the null hypothesis
              e $t = 0.81$, $df = 28$, do not reject the null hypothesis

17.11B   **a** $t = 0.18$, not significant
              c $t = 0.56$, not significant
              d $t = 0.14$
              e $t = 0.105$

17.11D   **a** $\bar{y}_A = 685$, $\bar{y}_B = 1716$, $s_A = 730$, $s_B = 494$
              b $t = -3.7$
              c   0.0021
              d   Yes. Find a preparer in the city where you have the best chance of getting the job done right, or, better yet, find the best preparer. The results of the experiment show that it pays to shop around because not all preparers achieve comparable levels of performance.

17.17A   **a** $X^2 = 0$, not significant
              b $X^2 = 0$
              c $X^2 = 13.67$, significant at both levels
              d $X^2 = 47.138$
              e $X^2 = 10.127$

17.17B   **a** $X^2 = 33.33$ for both tables.
              b   yes, yes

17.17D   **a**   Row percents: Yes: 35, 65
                                    No: 16, 84
                                    Total: 27, 73

              Smokers seem to have about twice the chance of having heart attacks as non-smokers.

              b $X^2 = 9.73$. The p value is between 0.01 and 0.001. If the sampling assumptions are valid, this is a statistically significant result, showing that smokers and nonsmokers have heart attacks at different rates.

CHAPTER 18

18.2A   **a**   In the randomization distribution, each of the values $-5/3$ and $5/3$ occurs three times, each of the values $-23/3$, $-7/3$, $7/3$, and $23/3$ occurs twice, and each of the values $-17/3$, $-13/3$, $-11/3$, $11/3$, $13/3$, and $17/3$ occurs once.

b The difference that actually occurs in the experiment is $-23/3$, so the p value is $2/20 = 0.1$. The p value is larger than 0.05, so the outcome is not statistically significant in the usual sense.

c The experiment in fact cannot yield a statistically significant result, as can be seen from the randomization distribution. This is due to the students' all being good ones, so their grades are not very different. A larger group of good students is needed to assess the difference, if any, between the two sections. Of course, the size of the experiment was kept small so it could be analyzed by hand.

18.2C   252   **18.2D**   924

18.4A   **a and b**

Source	Sum of Squares	Degrees of Freedom	Mean Squares	F	p
Between	88.2	1	88.2	5.63	0.077
Within	62.7	4	15.7		
Total	150.9	5			

c The F statistic tests for the two-sided alternative hypothesis that the lectures do not have the same effect. Note that this is *not* the alternative tested in Exercise 18.2A, which was one-sided.

d The exact p value for the two-sided alternative is twice the p value computed in Exercise 18.2A, so it is 0.2. The qualitative conclusion is the same, that is, do not reject the null hypothesis, but the approximate p value computed from the F distribution, 0.077, is not accurate. The percentage difference between the actual and approximate p values is $100(0.2 - 0.077)/0.077 = 160\%$. This is not surprising. The F distribution approximation is not reliable when the sample sizes are so small.

18.4C

Source	Sum of Squares	Degrees of Freedom	Mean Squares	F
Between	500	1	500	5.52
Within	1629	18	90.5	
Total	2129	19		

18.4E   **a** For 8-ounce rate, mean $= 5.25$ and standard deviation $= 2.605$; for 12-ounce rate, mean $= 3.125$ and standard deviation $= 2.1$.

b

Source	Sum of Squares	Degrees of Freedom	Mean Squares	F
Between	18.0625	1	18.0625	3.23
Within	78.375	14	5.598	
Total	96.4375	15		

c 0.094

d The null hypothesis is that the two application rates make no difference in the long-run average percentage of loose labels. The alternative hypothesis is that the two application rates do make a difference in the long-run average percentage of loose labels. Rejection of the null hypothesis would lead to a study to determine the best application rate to minimize the percentage of loose labels, thus improving the quality of the production process.

18.8A   **a** $\dfrac{q}{\sqrt{2}} s_P \sqrt{\dfrac{1}{n_i} + \dfrac{1}{n_j}} = 2.47 \times 40.23368 \times 0.4472 = 44.5$,   C $-$ A: 44.1 ± 44.5, C $-$ B: 35 ± 44.5, B $-$ A: 9.1 ± 44.5. None of the differences is statistically significant.

b Each of the two confidence intervals should have confidence level $1 - 0.05/2 = 0.975$. Thus the t factor should be the 98.75th percentile of the t distribution with 27 degrees of freedom, namely 2.373. The factor added and subtracted to form the confidence interval is therefore $(2.373)(40.23368)(0.4472) = 42.7$. For the comparison $A - B$, the interval is -9.1 ± 42.7. For the comparison $B - C$, the interval is -35 ± 42.7. Neither difference tested is statistically significant because each interval contains zero.

CHAPTER 19

19.2A **a** The null hypothesis is that the students score the same, on average, regardless of the lecture attended. The alternative hypothesis is that the lectures have different long-run effects on the students' performance. The F statistic is simply $2680/58 = 45.91$. The p value is the area under the F curve to the right of 45.91. Because the p value is less than 0.05, we say the result of the experiment is statistically significant. The evidence from the experiment favors the conclusion that the lectures make a difference in student performance.

b The bulk of the variation in the data comes from student-to-student variation *within* the lectures, and the completely randomized design handles this variation inefficiently compared to the randomized block design. If the data are analyzed as data from a completely randomized design, the evidence does not favor rejection of the null hypothesis of no lecture effect on student performance (p value = 0.214). This conclusion is contradicted by the results of the randomized block experiment.

c $\dfrac{3.61}{\sqrt{2}} \, 7.616 \sqrt{\dfrac{1}{10} + \dfrac{1}{10}} = 8.7$ The comparison between lecture 3 and lecture 2 is 14.9 ± 8.7, the comparison between lecture 3 and lecture 1 is 32.7 ± 8.7, and the comparison between lecture 2 and lecture 1 is 17.8 ± 8.7. *All* the differences are statistically significant.

19.4C **a** The mean values needed to construct the interaction graph are given below.

```
CONTROL: A = -1
ROWS: B      COLUMNS: C

             -1       0       1

-1     2.4333  5.0667  4.7000
 0     4.5333  2.9333  4.9333
 1     4.1667  4.1000  6.8000


CONTROL: A =  1
ROWS: B      COLUMNS: C

             -1       0       1

-1     4.9667  3.6333  6.1667
 0     5.8333  5.6333  5.6667
 1     5.1333  6.7000  8.0667
```

(b)
Analysis of Variance for y

Source	DF	SS	MS	F	P
A	1	24.536	24.536	12.12	0.001
B	2	16.685	8.342	4.12	0.024
C	2	25.868	12.934	6.39	0.004
A*B	2	1.640	0.820	0.41	0.670
A*C	2	0.468	0.234	0.12	0.891
B*C	4	11.935	2.984	1.47	0.230
A*B*C	4	17.515	4.379	2.16	0.093
Error	36	72.873	2.024		
Total	53	171.521			

(c)
Analysis of Variance for y

```
Source      DF        SS        MS       F      P
A            1    24.536    24.536   11.28  0.002
B            2    16.685     8.342    3.83  0.029
C            2    25.868    12.934    5.94  0.005
Error       48   104.432     2.176
Total       53   171.521

ROW     y      fits    residual    nsc.res

  1    3.4   3.25000    0.15000    0.11525
  2    3.7   3.41667    0.28333    0.40180
  3    2.8   4.79444   -1.99444   -1.37071
  4    2.3   3.67778   -1.37778   -1.07637
  5    2.6   3.84444   -1.24444   -0.92330
  .
  .
  .
 50    6.4   5.19259    1.20741    0.85446
 51    4.5   6.57037   -2.07037   -1.66278
 52    2.7   5.93148   -3.23148   -2.27366
 53    7.4   6.09815    1.30185    0.99689
 54    7.5   7.47593    0.02407    0.02300
```

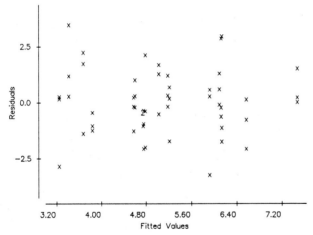

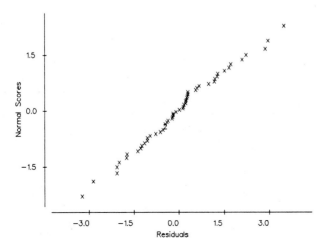

19.4B **a**

```
MEAN      8.5
A         8.0
D         1.0
L         2.5
P         1.5
AD        0
AL       -0.5
AP        2.5
DL       -1.0
DP        0.5
LP       -1.0
ADL       1.0
ADP      -0.5
ALP       1.0
DLP      -0.5
ADLP      0.5
```

b

```
ROW Effects nsc.eff (Mean not included)

A       8.0    1.74192
D       1.0    0.33350
P       2.5    1.08183
L       1.5    0.71154
AD      0.0   -0.33350
AP     -0.5   -0.71154
AL      2.5    1.08183
DP     -1.0   -1.44893
DL      0.5   -0.08191
PL     -1.0   -1.44893
ADP     1.0    0.33350
ADL    -0.5   -0.71154
APL     1.0    0.33350
DPL    -0.5   -0.71154
ADPL    0.5   -0.08190
```

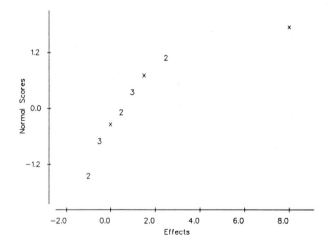

The **A** main effect clearly stands out in the plot.

c

```
Analysis of Variance for y

Source     DF         SS         MS        F       P
A           1    256.000    256.000    116.36  0.000
D           1      4.000      4.000      1.82  0.235
L           1     25.000     25.000     11.36  0.020
P           1      9.000      9.000      4.09  0.099
A*D         1      0.000      0.000      0.00  1.000
A*L         1      1.000      1.000      0.45  0.530
A*P         1     25.000     25.000     11.36  0.020
D*L         1      4.000      4.000      1.82  0.235
D*P         1      1.000      1.000      0.45  0.530
L*P         1      4.000      4.000      1.82  0.235
Error       5     11.000      2.200
Total      15    340.000
```

The p values pick out the **A** and **L** main effects, and the **AP** interaction as statistically significant.

d   The small amount of data collected from one person makes it difficult to decide if the statistically significant effects are real. Using many subjects for replication would give more definitive results for the group, but the results would no longer necessarily apply to individuals. The analysis for the individual above clearly points to the importance of airplane type. It is plausible that this effect interacts with price. Since we are making multiple tests, it might be wise to use 1% significance levels for the individual tests, in which case only the **A** effect would be considered statistically significant, and this certainly agrees with the graphical analysis in part **b**.

CHAPTER 20

20.3A $45,350   **20.3B** $48,628   **20.3D**   Positive   **20.5A**   −$2791   **20.7A**   20.5 ± 6.2

20.7B   **a**   [2.53, 3.25]

    b   Yes

    c   5%

20.7C $t^2 = (16.01)^2 = 256.3 = F$

20.7F   The prediction for $x = 6.9$ because it is farther from the mean of the x values than is 10.1.

20.7G   **a**   Height $= 27.6 + 2.58$ age, $s = 1.35$, $R^2 = 98.7\%$

    b   The standard error of the slope estimate is 0.08163, yielding a t statistic of 31.66 and a p value of 0.000. The relationship is statistically significant.

    c   The regression of average ages vastly understates the variability in individual heights, even though the regression based on averages might be useful in predicting individual heights.

20.7H   Height $= 27.8 + 2.57$ age, $s = 1.468$, $R^2 = 98.5\%$

    a   The standard error of the slope estimate is 0.08881, yielding a t statistic of 28.97 and a p value of 0.000.

20.9A   The t ratio is -4.12 with a p value of 0.000. The contribution of square feet squared is statistically significant.

20.9D   **a**   Sales $= 34,105 + 3.75$ advert $- 30,046$ ratio $+ 85.9$ pdi
        t ratios   1.90 -1.31 4.80
        $s = 9574$, $R^2 = 96.9\%$
    Only the coefficient on pdi is statistically significant.

    b $F = 104.51$ with p value 0.000. The overall relationship is statistically significant.

    c $t = 1.90$ with p value 0.087. The contribution of advertising is not statistically significant at the 5% level in the presence of the other variables.

CHAPTER 21

21.7A The regression equation is

Height = 27.6 + 2.58 Age

Predictor	Coef	Stdev	t-ratio	p
Constant	27.6242	0.6716	41.13	0.000
Age	2.58424	0.08163	31.66	0.000

s = 1.349   R-sq = 98.7%   R-sq(adj) = 98.6%

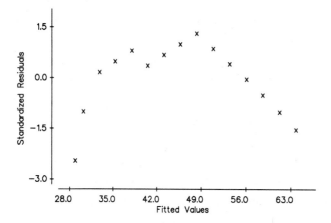

The residual plot demonstrates the inadequacy of the model. The diagnostic statistics below only hint at the inadequacy.

Row	Age	Height	Std Res	Fitted	Leverage	Cook's D
1	0.5	26	-2.45171	28.9163	0.222886	0.862001
2	1.0	29	-1.00121	30.2084	0.199890	0.125216
3	2.0	33	0.16759	32.7927	0.159388	0.002663
4	3.0	36	0.49400	35.3769	0.126205	0.017623
5	4.0	39	0.81170	37.9611	0.100342	0.036742
6	5.0	41	0.35160	40.5454	0.081798	0.005507
7	6.0	44	0.66908	43.1296	0.070575	0.016997
8	7.0	47	0.98662	45.7139	0.066671	0.034767
9	8.0	50	1.30795	48.2981	0.070087	0.064468
10	9.0	52	0.86395	50.8823	0.080822	0.032816
11	10.0	54	0.41645	53.4666	0.098878	0.009515
12	11.0	56	-0.04024	56.0508	0.124253	0.000115
13	12.0	58	-0.51257	58.6350	0.156948	0.024456
14	13.0	60	-1.00836	61.2193	0.196962	0.124695
15	14.0	62	-1.53753	63.8035	0.244297	0.382106

21.9D   **a**

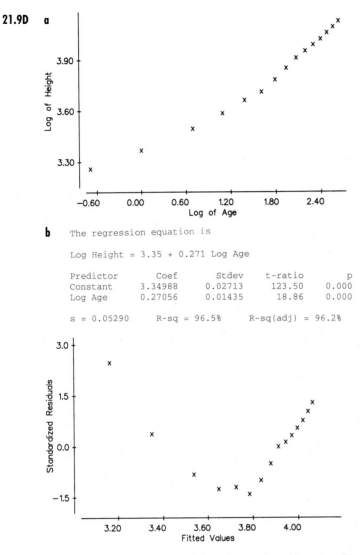

b   The regression equation is

Log Height = 3.35 + 0.271 Log Age

Predictor	Coef	Stdev	t-ratio	p
Constant	3.34988	0.02713	123.50	0.000
Log Age	0.27056	0.01435	18.86	0.000

s = 0.05290   R-sq = 96.5%   R-sq(adj) = 96.2%

The plot demonstrates the inadequacy of the transformation. The statistics reported below only hint at the problem.

ROW	Log Height	Log Age	Std Res	Fitted	Leverage	Cook's D
1	3.25810	-0.69315	2.47479	3.16234	0.464936	2.66094
2	3.36730	0.00000	0.38353	3.34988	0.262961	0.02624
3	3.49651	0.69315	-0.82998	3.53742	0.131700	0.05224
4	3.58352	1.09861	-1.25885	3.64712	0.087698	0.07617
5	3.66356	1.38629	-1.20430	3.72496	0.071153	0.05555
6	3.71357	1.60944	-1.40423	3.78533	0.066708	0.07047
7	3.78419	1.79176	-0.98860	3.83466	0.068517	0.03594
8	3.85015	1.94591	-0.51506	3.87637	0.073863	0.01058
9	3.91202	2.07944	-0.00932	3.91250	0.081321	0.00000
10	3.95124	2.19722	0.13637	3.94436	0.090077	0.00092
11	3.98898	2.30259	0.32107	3.97287	0.099641	0.00570
12	4.02535	2.39790	0.53485	3.99866	0.109699	0.01762
13	4.06044	2.48491	0.77076	4.02220	0.120049	0.04052
14	4.09434	2.56495	1.02366	4.04385	0.130555	0.07867
15	4.12713	2.63906	1.28980	4.06391	0.141122	0.13667

CHAPTER 22

22.3D **b** price $= -10.7 + 0.19$ taxes $+ 81.9$ baths $+ 0.101$ sqft, while rooms $= 4.01 + 0.000798$ taxes $- 0.288$ baths $+ 0.00163$ sqft. The added variable plot of the residuals from these two regressions is

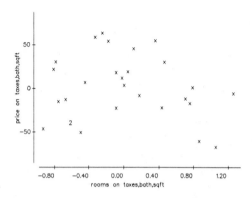

The plot gives no justification for adding the rooms variable to the model that already contains taxes, baths and sqft.

22.5B **a** The model using all of the predictors and indicators for type and style yields a significant overall F statistic but no significant individual t statistics except for sqft. The collinearity is severe. The VIFs of the variables taxes, baths, sqft, rooms, and bedrooms are roughly 14, 17, 17, 19, and 20, all of which signal trouble. Some extraneous variables need to be removed from the model.

22.9C **a** and **b**

Indicator variables T1, T2, T3, S1, and S2 were created to handle the categorical variables type and style. These indicators were included in the list of potential predictors, and consequently the variables type and style were not included in the list. The model that produced the smallest s and the largest adjusted R^2 had predictors baths, sqft, garages, age, T1, S1, and number of fireplaces.

c The model that yielded the smallest C_p had predictors taxes, sqft, age, T1, and number of fireplaces. Both models seem plausible. The one with the small C_p promises to have more predictive power, but this would have to be checked with data external to that used to construct the model.

22.13C A stepwise regression program was run with default settings. The model produced had predictors taxes, baths, and sqft, but the baths variable did not have a statistically significant coefficient. Notice that the model chosen in Exercise 22.9C part **c** did not include baths as a predictor.

CHAPTER 23

23.3A 0.167 and -0.250 **23.3C** [575, 631]

23.7B

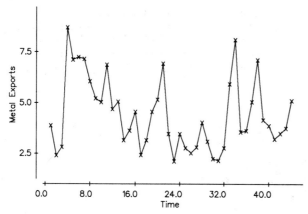

```
The regression equation is

MetalExp = 2.34 + 0.474 Lag1

43 cases used; 1 case contained missing values

Predictor        Coef        Stdev     t-ratio         p
Constant       2.3437       0.6521        3.59     0.001
Lag1           0.4740       0.1377        3.44     0.001

s = 1.580      R-sq = 22.4%     R-sq(adj) = 20.5%
```

The prediction for the next observation is 0.474 times the current observation plus 2.34. The residual autocorrelations suggest no model inadequacy.

	Lag1	Lag2	Lag3
Residual autocorrelations	0.064	−0.155	−0.051

The standard deviation of future prediction errors should be about 1.58. Compare this to the standard deviation of future predictions based on the sample mean, namely, 1.754.

	n	Mean	Median	Standard Deviation
Metalexp	44	4.418	3.875	1.754

23.9A **a** 5.90, 6.01, 6.01, 6.31, 6.28, 6.15, 6.13, 6.22

CHAPTER 24

24.2B **a** First plot the sequence plot without using special plotting symbols as below.

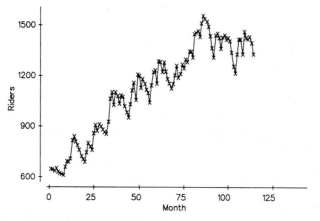

There is a general upward trend with variation along the way. The variation around the overall trend is somewhat larger where the series values are larger. This suggests considering the logarithm of the series for further analysis. Near the end of the series there seems to be a downturn or at least a leveling off of the series values. Without special plotting symbols seasonal patterns are difficult to spot. The plot is repeated using plotting symbols A = January, B = February, . . . , L = December.

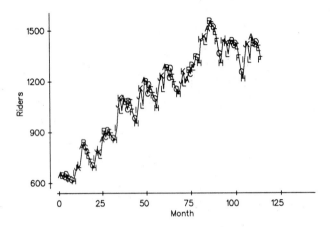

In this plot the seasonal pattern becomes more apparent. Ridership is generally low in August (symbol H) and higher during the winter months (December = L, January = A). The logarithms of the series are then considered. The sequence plot follows.

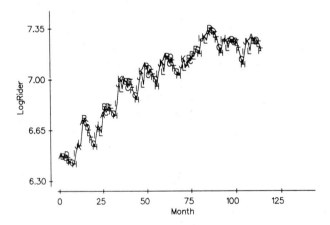

Here the seasonal pattern is still apparent but the unequal variation at different series levels has been corrected. The logarithm of the series will be used for all further analysis.

24.4B   **a**   After setting up the required time variable and binary seasonal indicator variables the regression results are as follows:

```
The regression equation is

LogRider = 6.54 + 0.00743 Time + 0.0651 Jan + 0.0685 Feb + 0.0322 Mar
              + 0.0472 Apr   + 0.0169 May - 0.0207 Jun - 0.0349 Jul
              - 0.0705 Aug   + 0.0015 Sep - 0.0526 Oct + 0.0546 Nov

Predictor        Coef       Stdev      t-ratio        p
Constant      6.54267     0.03694      177.13      0.000
Time        0.0074345   0.0002810       26.46      0.000
Jan           0.06505     0.04532        1.44      0.154
Feb           0.06848     0.04532        1.51      0.134
Mar           0.03221     0.04531        0.71      0.479
Apr           0.04715     0.04530        1.04      0.300
May           0.01691     0.04530        0.37      0.710
Jun          -0.02072     0.04530       -0.46      0.648
Jul          -0.03494     0.04650       -0.75      0.454
Aug          -0.07054     0.04649       -1.52      0.132
Sep           0.00147     0.04649        0.03      0.975
Oct           0.05257     0.04648        1.13      0.261
Nov           0.05462     0.04648        1.18      0.243

s = 0.09859     R-sq = 87.7%     R-sq(adj) = 86.3%

Analysis of Variance

SOURCE          DF           SS          MS          F         p
Regression      12      7.01846     0.58487      60.17     0.000
Error          101      0.98182     0.00972
Total          113      8.00027
```

Only the time variable appears to be significant in the regression equation. The sequence plot of fitted values traces out the linear time trend with the small seasonal effect added on top. The fitted values are consistently too high in the early and later parts of the series. This model completely misses the changing nature of the last part of the series.

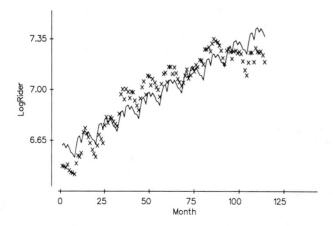

The connected line shows the fitted values. Xs mark the actual series values.

b   Sequence plot of the residuals from the fitted model.

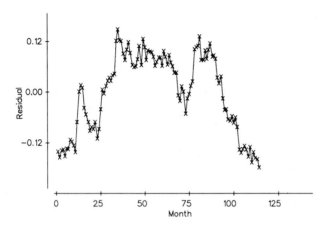

This residual plot does not appear to be close to random.

c   The autocorrelation in the residuals is 0.932 at lag 1 and 0.863 at lag 2. These are very large correlations and give further indications of the nonrandom nature of the residuals.

24.6D **a**   Using the model of Equation (24.3) yields the following regression results:

```
The regression equation is

LogRider = 0.676 + 0.651 Lag1 + 0.256 Lag12

102 cases used; 12 cases contained missing values

Predictor        Coef        Stdev      t-ratio         p
Constant       0.6760       0.1567         4.31     0.000
Lag1          0.65149      0.05663        11.50     0.000
Lag12         0.25635      0.04561         5.62     0.000

s = 0.04538     R-sq = 95.5%      R-sq(adj) = 95.4%

Analysis of Variance

SOURCE        DF          SS          MS          F         p
Regression     2      4.2833      2.1416    1039.92     0.000
Error         99      0.2039      0.0021
Total        101      4.4871
```

In this regression both the lag 1 and lag 12 predictors are quite important (*t* ratios of 4.31 and 5.62, respectively).

b   The sequence plot of the residuals shows no indication of model inadequacy.

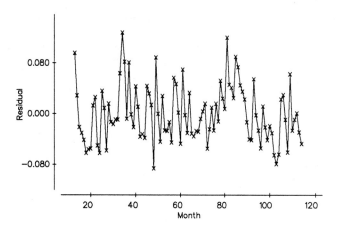

c   The autocorrelations in the residuals are as follows:

Lag	1	2	3	4	5	6
Autocorrelation	0.258	0.084	0.244	0.169	0.040	0.017
Lag	7	8	9	10	11	12
Autocorrelation	0.006	0.023	−0.002	−0.198	−0.146	0.319

These are much smaller than the corresponding autocorrelations for the model considered in Exercise 24.4B.

d   This model contains only three regression parameters, the constant or intercept term, the lag 1 term, and the lag 12 term. In contrast, the model in Exercise 24.4B used 13 regression coefficients. In the present model all of the predictors are statistically significant. The residual standard deviation for the present model is 0.04538, which is smaller than the value of 0.09859 obtained with the previous model.

In addition, the present model is less rigid than the time trend plus seasonal indicators model. This can be seen graphically by plotting the fitted and actual series values.

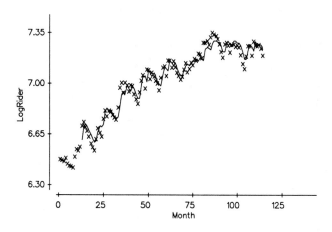

The connected lines trace out the fitted values, with Xs denoting actual values. Notice how the values fitted from the seasonal autoregressive model follow the actual values better than those with the previous model. (Note that no fitted values are available for the first 12 months due to the nature of the lagged regression model.) All in all, this simpler model does a much better job of explaining the behavior of the time series.

24.8B   **b**   Sequence plot of actual series values (Xs) and exponentially smoothed values (connected lines). The smoothed series follows the actual series quite well most of the time but seems to have difficulty near the end of the series where the series nature appears to be changing.

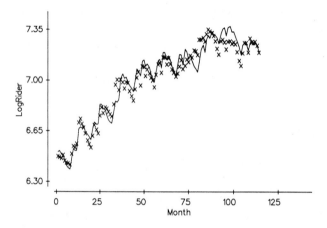

c   The sequence plot of the residuals from exponential smoothing does not support randomness in the residuals.

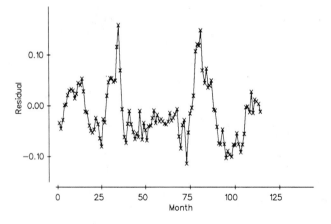

24.10B **a** After computing the required differences, the regression calculations give the following results:

```
The regression equation is

W(t) = 0.00153 + 0.021 W(t-1) - 0.273 W(t-12)

89 cases used; 25 cases contained missing values

Predictor        Coef      Stdev     t-ratio        p
Constant    -0.001533   0.003503      -0.44    0.663
W(t-1)        0.0212     0.1073        0.20    0.844
W(t-12)      -0.2727     0.1072       -2.54    0.013

s = 0.03282     R-sq = 7.9%     R-sq(adj) = 5.7%

Analysis of Variance

SOURCE         DF        SS          MS        F        p
Regression      2   0.007910    0.003955     3.67    0.030
Error          86   0.092650    0.001077
Total          88   0.100560
```

In this regression the lag 12 predictor is marginally significant but the lag 1 predictor is not significant at all.

b Very little autocorrelation is present in the residuals, as shown in the following table:

	Lag1	**Lag2**	**Lag12**	**Lag24**
Autocorrelation	0.015	−0.053	−0.084	−0.194

c The histogram and normal scores plot for the standardized residuals give good support for normality of the error terms in the model.

```
Std Res    N = 89    N* = 25
```

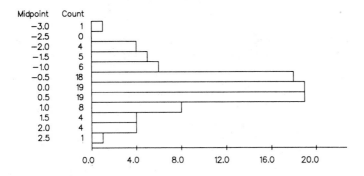

```
Midpoint   Count
   -3.0      1
   -2.5      0
   -2.0      4
   -1.5      5
   -1.0      6
   -0.5     18
    0.0     19
    0.5     19
    1.0      8
    1.5      4
    2.0      4
    2.5      1

         0.0    4.0    8.0   12.0   16.0   20.0
```

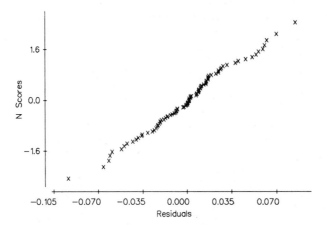

d The scatterplot of residuals versus the corresponding fitted values gives no indications that the model assumptions are violated.

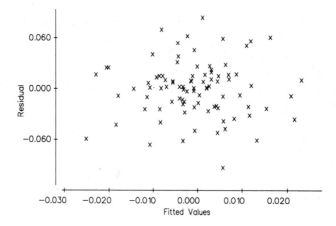

If a data set is listed in the text, then it is simply indexed by page number here. If the data set is not listed in the text, then it is indexed here and listed in Appendix 4: Selected Data Set Listings. All the data sets are available on the disk included with the book.